영단기
TOEFL
LISTENING

커넥츠 영단기

영단기 **TOEFL LISTENING**

저자	신화식
기획 총괄	김도훈
기획·편집	이현지
마케팅·영업	손지한, 김정현, 양윤화, 김보경
디자인	안다혜
홈페이지	eng.conects.com

영단기 영어 전문 온라인 학습 및 어학원 eng.conects.com

저자의 한마디

　TOEFL(Test of English as a Foreign Language)을 준비하시는 분들께 꼭 전하고 싶은 말이 있습니다. TOEFL Listening에서 가장 중요한 것은 test point(출제포인트)입니다. 또한 TOEIC, TEPS 등 각 영어 시험마다 출제포인트가 매우 다르기 때문에 준비하는 시험에 맞게 대비를 해야 합니다. 하지만 많은 분들이 TOEFL Listening 출제포인트에 대해 알지 못하고 막연한 듣기 연습으로 소중한 시간을 허비하는 것을 현장에서 지켜보면서 안타까운 마음을 감출 수 없었습니다.

　예를 들어 보겠습니다. TOEFL Listening의 동물학 분야에서는 다양한 동물에 관한 지문이 출제됩니다. 그런데, 출제되는 동물이 매번 바뀌어도 주요 출제포인트, 즉 동물이 환경에 적응하는 방법을 문제로 출제하는 것은 바뀌지 않습니다. 따라서 단기간 점수향상 비법은 이와 같은 주제별 출제논리를 이해하고 학습해서 실제시험에 잘 적용할 수 있는 능력이라고 해도 과언이 아닙니다. 또한 주제별 출제포인트를 알아내려면 주제별로 많은 지문을 묶어서 학습하는 것이 효과적입니다. 주제별로 단어도 겹치고 화자의 화법이나 설명방식도 비슷하므로 신속한 듣기 능력 향상에 매우 도움이 된다는 사실을 10년 이상의 현장 강의를 통해 확인했습니다. 주제별로 묶어 들으며 듣기 능력을 향상시키고, 해당 주제 문제들의 출제포인트를 학생들과 같이 탐구하고 분석한 것이, 제가 지금까지 단기간에 Listening 점수가 급상승한 다수의 고득점자를 배출할 수 있었던 이유입니다.

　이제 〈영단기 TOEFL Listening〉의 출간을 통해 가장 효과적인 TOEFL Listening 학습 방법을 많은 분들과 나누고자 합니다. Listening에 약하신 분들도 쉽게 공부할 수 있도록, 지문을 주제별로 묶어 이에 대한 배경지식과 출제포인트를 상세하게 짚어 드렸습니다. 부디 좀 더 많은 학생들이 이 학습방법을 통해 실제 시험에서 노력한 만큼 점수로 보상을 받았으면 하는 간절한 마음뿐입니다. 우리 학생들이, 저 거대한 태평양을 넘어 문화가 완전히 다른 나라에서 힘겨운 전공 공부를 시작하기도 전에 TOEFL이라는 장벽에 막혀 미리 힘을 빼고 가는 일이 없도록, 이 책이 조금이나마 도움이 되길 바랍니다.

　이 책을 통해 감사의 마음을 전하고 싶은 분들이 많이 있습니다. 먼저, 밤낮으로 고생하시면서 이 책을 공동집필해 주신 조다난 김 선생님께 무한한 감사의 말씀을 전하고 싶습니다. 저에게 강의를 하고 책을 쓸 수 있는 모든 지식과 기반을 마련해 주신 아버님과 삶의 든든한 버팀목이셨던 지금은 고인이 되신 어머님, 책 기획부터 감수까지 언제나 아낌없는 지원을 해 주었던 제 아내에게 이 책을 바칩니다.

　〈영단기 TOEFL Listening〉은 많은 분들의 도움을 통해 완성되었습니다. 이 책을 쓸 수 있게 기회를 주신 ST&Company 윤성혁 대표님을 비롯해 도움을 주신 직원 분들께 감사 드립니다. 이 책을 출판해 주신 ST&Books 김병기 이사님, 책의 방향을 잡아 주신 장혜정 부장님, 그리고 책을 완벽하게 만들어 주신 이현지 님께도 감사를 드립니다.

저자 신화식

목차

Diagnostic Test   018

Chapter 1. Conversation Question Types

01 Main Idea	028
02 Topic of the Paper	030
03 Problem	032
04 Solution (Suggestion)	034
05 Example	036
06 Cause	038
Practice Questions I	040
07 Similarity / Difference	042
08 Advantage / Disadvantage	044
09 Future Action	046
10 Requirement	048
11 Opinion / Attitude	050
12 Replay Question (Headset)	052
Practice Questions II	054

Chapter 2. Conversation Topics

Unit 1. Instructor's Office Hours

01 Class	060
02 Course Grade / Exam	068
03 Field Trip	076
04 Paper	084
05 Project / Research	092
06 Major	100

Unit 2. Service Encounters

01	Class / Credit / Transcript / Financial Aid	110
02	Housing (Dorm)	118
03	Library / Bookstore	126
04	Part-time Job / Job Fair / Internship	134
05	School Facility	142
06	기타 (Miscellaneous)	150

Chapter 3. Lecture Question Types

01	Main Idea	160
02	Function / Purpose	162
03	Problem	164
04	Solution (Suggestion)	166
05	Example	168
06	Cause & Effect	170
07	Similarity / Difference	172
08	Advantage / Disadvantage	174
09	Misunderstanding / Correction	176
Practice Questions I		178
10	Definition (Term) / Origin	182
11	Two Click / Three Click	184
12	Ordering	186
13	Matching	188
14	Opinion / Attitude	190
15	Replay Question (Headset)	192
16	Requirement (Condition)	194
17	Character	196
18	Imply / Infer	198
Practice Questions II		200

Chapter 4. Lecture Topics

Unit 3. Arts
01 Architecture — 208
02 Art & Science — 218
03 Painting — 228
04 Literature — 238
05 Film & Theater History — 248
06 Photography — 258

Unit 4. Life Science
01 Animal Communication — 270
02 Animal Adaptation — 280
03 Botany — 290
04 Ecology — 300
05 Physiology — 310
06 Paleontology — 320

Unit 5. Physical Science
01 Astronomy — 332
02 Chemistry — 342
03 Earth Science — 352
04 Environmental Science — 362
05 Geology — 372
06 Engineering — 382

Unit 6. Social Science
01 Anthropology — 394
02 Archaeology — 404
03 Business — 414
04 Education — 424
05 Psychology — 434
06 Sociology — 444

Actual Test 1 — 456
Actual Test 2 — 468

이 책의 구성 및 학습법

Chapter 1 & 3. Question Types

Main Idea

1 문제의 핵심
지문 전체를 포괄하는 하나의 주제를 찾는 문제 유형으로, 지문에 어울리는 제목을 붙인다는 생각으로 답을 고르면 된다. 대개 첫 번째 문제로 출제되며, Conversation의 경우 학생의 방문 목적을, Lecture의 경우 강의의 주제를 주로 묻는다. 영미권의 글에서는 논리 구조상 핵심을 첫 부분에서 짚고 가므로, 주제나 토픽이 지문의 도입부에 제시되는 경우가 많다.

2 문제의 예시
· Why does the man visit[go to see] the professor?
· Why does the student go to the university office?
· What is the conversation mainly about?

3 100% 문제 공략법
01 도입부에 주목한다. Main Idea 문제는 거의 도입부에 정답의 단서가 나온다. 뿐만 아니라 도입부에서 대화의 목적

문제 유형 소개

대화문과 강의에 나오는 각 문제 유형을 소개하고, 그에 맞는 문제 공략법과 단서 표현을 제시한다. 또한, 수험자의 이해를 돕기 위한 Example Question이 각 유형마다 제시된다.

❷ 100% 문제 공략법과 단서 표현을 미리 숙지한 후 본격적인 Chapter 2 & 4 학습을 준비하도록 한다. 수험자가 취약한 문제 유형에 더 큰 초점을 두고 학습하는 것이 좋다.

Practice Questions I

[01 ~ 06] Listen to part of a lecture in a business class. Then answer the questions.
◁ MP3 30

문제 유형에 익숙해지기

문제 유형 학습에서 배운 내용을 바로 적용해 볼 수 있는 Practice Questions가 각 2회분씩 제공된다. 본 학습에 들어가기 전 문제 유형에 대한 감을 잡아가는 warm-up test라고 생각하면 된다.

❷ 앞서 학습한 유형별 문제 공략법과 단서 표현을 이용해 출제 문제를 예측해서 푸는 습관을 들이도록 한다.

005

Chapter 2. Conversation Topics

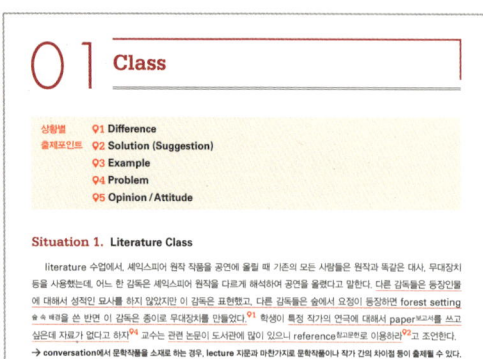

상황별 출제포인트

지금까지 출제된 문제를 분석해 출제 가능성이 높은 대화 상황과 관련 문제들을 엄선한 '상황별 출제포인트'를 제시하였다. 대화문의 흐름에 따라 어떤 문제가 출제될지 한 눈에 볼 수 있도록 한글로 정리해 놓은 것이 특징이다.

- 상황별로 자주 출제되는 문제 유형을 익혀 놓으면, 실제 시험에서 출제될 문제를 어느 정도 예측할 수 있으므로 상황별 설명 글을 그냥 넘기지 말고 꼭 읽어 보도록 한다.

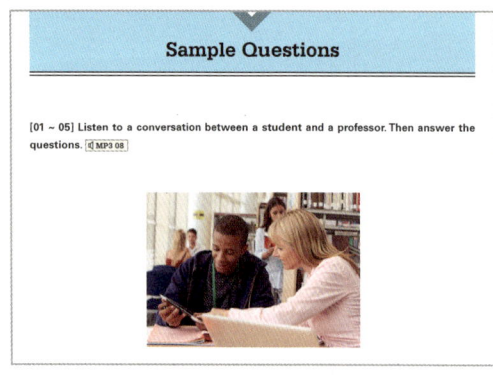

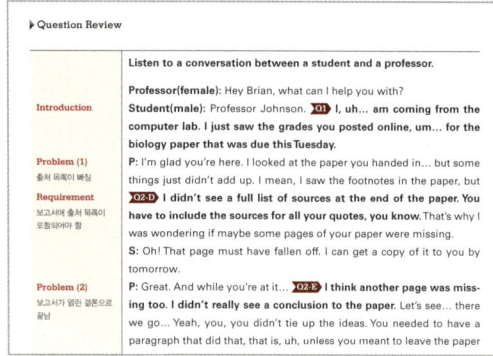

Sample Questions & Question Review

실전 문제와 거의 동일한 수준으로 구성된 연습 문제를 풀어보는 코너이다. 문제를 푼 후 바로 뒤 장에서 상황별 출제포인트와 정답의 단서를 확인할 수 있다.

- 상황별 출제포인트와 정답 단서와의 관계를 알아보고, 글의 흐름과 맥락을 포함한 전체적인 글의 구성을 이해하는 데 집중해서 학습하도록 한다.

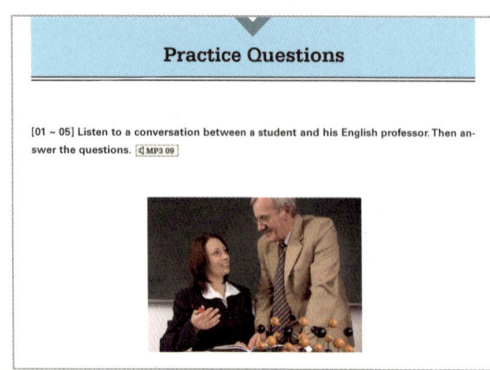

Practice Questions

기출 문제를 정밀 분석하여 출제 가능성이 매우 높은 대화 상황과 문제를 엄선해 출제한 실전 문제이다.

- 시간을 재 최대한 실제 시험과 비슷한 상황에서 문제를 풀어 보도록 한다.

Chapter 4. Lecture Topics

주제별 출제포인트

실제 시험 대비 적중률 높은 강의 '주제별 출제포인트'를 제시하였다. 또한, 과목별 배경지식과 자주 출제되는 소주제도 소개한다.

❯ 주제별 출제포인트를 미리 숙지해 지문을 들으면서 출제될 문제를 예측하는 습관을 들이는 것이 좋다. 문제를 예측하는 감이 키워지면 지문을 들으며 동시에 필요한 정보만을 note-taking 하는 능력도 키울 수 있다. 자신만의 요약 필기법을 만드는 것도 좋은 전략이다.

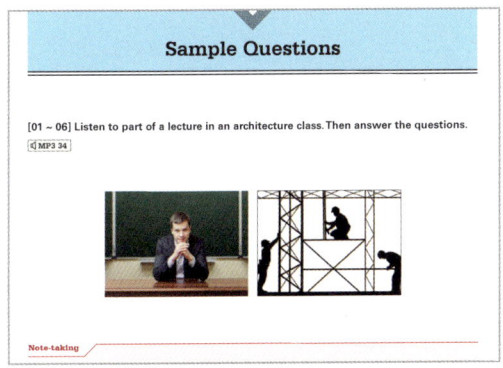

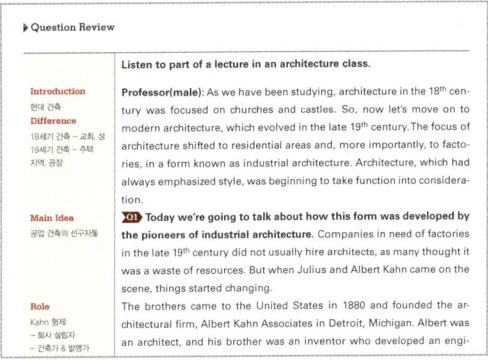

Sample Questions & Question Review

실전 문제와 거의 동일한 수준으로 구성된 연습 문제를 풀어보는 코너이다. 문제를 푼 후 바로 뒤 장에서 주제별 출제포인트와 정답의 단서를 확인할 수 있다.

❯ 시험 직전 공부할 시간이 많지 않다면, flow chart 위주로 학습하도록 한다. 비교적 짧은 시간 내에 효율적으로 여러 다른 주제의 배경지식과 출제포인트를 학습할 수 있다.

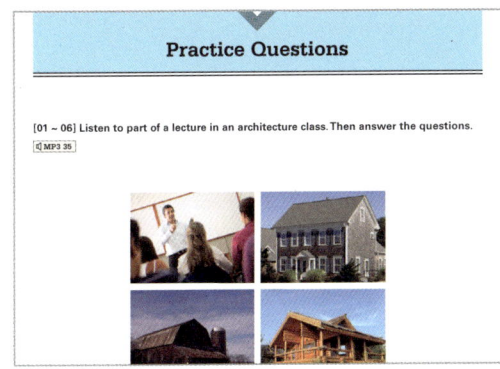

Practice Questions

기출 문제를 정밀 분석하여 출제 가능성이 매우 높은 강의 주제와 문제를 엄선해 출제한 실전 문제이다.

❯ 시간을 재 최대한 실제 시험과 비슷한 상황에서 문제를 풀어 보도록 한다.

이 책의 특장점

1

**반복적으로 나오는
지문별 출제포인트
완전 정복**

출제포인트는 특정 상황별/주제별 지문의 논리 전개가 어떻게 문제와 연결되는지를 보여주는 것으로 **TOEFL Listening** 학습의 핵심이다. 따라서 출제포인트를 숙지하면 상황별/주제별 지문의 흐름뿐만 아니라 문제 예측이 가능해지고 정답을 찾기가 수월해진다. 본서는 출제포인트 학습 효과를 극대화하기 위해 **Conversation**과 **Lecture** 지문을 상황별/주제별로 분류하여 교재를 구성하였다. 유사 상황/주제의 지문을 묶어서 학습함으로써 상황/주제에 대한 이해가 높아지고 출제포인트 정복이 가능해진다.

2

**실전 길이와
난이도를 반영한
지문 최다 수록**

TOEFL에서 고득점을 목표로 한다면 무엇보다 실전 환경과 같은 연습이 필수이다. 짧은 지문에서 좀 더 긴 지문으로 단계적으로 적응해가면서 학습하는 것도 좋지만, 실전 수준의 난이도와 길이를 가진 지문을 더 많이 접한다면, 힘들더라도 같은 시간을 투자해 더 큰 성취를 이룰 수 있다. 또한, 실제로 출제가능성이 높은 지문을 더 많이 접해 볼 수 있으므로 실전 대비 효과도 더 크다. 본서는 **90**개 이상의 실전 수준의 지문을 수록하여 경쟁서들 대비 최다 실전 지문을 연습할 수 있게 하였다.

3

**문제가 예측되는
세분화된 문제 유형 분류와
유형별 단서 표현**

상황별/주제별 지문이 문제로 연결되는 출제포인트는 각 문제 유형을 통해 나타난다. 따라서 문제 유형이 정교할수록 지문을 통한 문제 예측 역시 정확해지는 것은 당연한 일이다. 본서는 Conversation 과 Lecture에서 각각 12개 유형과 18개 유형으로 문제를 분류하였다. 각 문제 유형마다 지문에서 문제와 연결시킬 수 있는 단서 표현이 제시되기 때문에 더욱 정교하고 정확한 예측이 가능하다. 이를 바탕으로 note-taking을 해 두면 오답으로 빠질 확률은 현저하게 낮아질 것이다.

4

**강의 전개와 출제포인트를
한 눈에 보여주는
flow chart**

강의의 전개방식과 주제별 출제포인트를 동시에 학습할 수 있는 flow chart가 〈영단기 TOEFL Listening〉의 마지막 특징이다. 아무리 많은 배경지식을 공부한다 할지라도, 어디서 문제가 출제될지 모르고 학습하는 것은 무의미하다. 본서에서는 flow chart를 통해 주제별로 자주 출제되는 문제 유형을 강의의 흐름과 함께 시각적으로 보여줌으로써 학습자가 출제포인트에 대한 감을 익힐 수 있게 한다. 지문을 들으면서 출제될 문제를 예측하는 능력을 키우면, 필요한 정보만 note-taking 해 정확하게 문제를 풀 수 있게 된다.

iBT TOEFL 소개

❯ iBT TOEFL의 특징

iBT(Internet-based Test) TOEFL(Test of English as a Foreign Language)은 인터넷을 기반으로 한 시험으로, 수험자의 영어 능력을 (미국) 대학 수업 수준을 기준으로 평가하는 시험이다. TOEFL은 Reading, Listening, Speaking, Writing의 총 네 가지의 영역으로 이루어져 있으며, Speaking과 Writing은 Listening이나 Reading 능력을 결합해 평가하는 통합형(Integrated) 문제 유형을 포함한다.

❯ iBT TOEFL의 구성

Section	문항 수	시험 소요시간	배점 점수 범위	배점 수준
Reading	3-4개 지문 각 지문 당 10문항	54~72분	0-30	상 22-30 중 15-21 하 0-14
Listening	Lecture: 3-4개 강의 　　　각 강의 당 6문항 Conversation: 2-3개 대화 　　　각 대화 당 5문항	41~57분	0-30	상 22-30 중 15-21 하 0-14
	Break: 10분			
Speaking	Integrated: 1문항 Independent: 3문항	17분	0-30	우수 26-30 양호 18-25 부족 10-17 취약 0-9
Writing	Integrated: 1문항 Independent: 1문항	50분	0-30	우수 24-30 양호 17-23 부족 1-16
		총 소요 시간 약 3시간	총점 0-120	

01_ 시험 응시 정보

TOEFL 시험은 연 50회 이상 실시되며 시험 장소도 다양하므로, ETS 온라인 홈페이지를 통해 시험 날짜와 수험자와 가장 가까운 곳에 있는 시험장을 확인한다.

- ◆ 접수 방법 : www.ets.org 또는 www.toeflkorea.or.kr에서 온라인 등록 시험
- ◆ 비용 : US$ 210 (2021년 3월 기준)
  추가 등록 : US$ 40   시험 날짜 변경 : US$ 60
- ◆ 지불 방법
  - 신용/직불카드로 결제 가능
  - 미국 또는 미국령 내에 본인의 은행 계좌가 있는 경우 PayPal이나 전자 수표도 사용 가능

    시험 등록 및 취소 규정 : 등록은 시험 날짜 7일 전에 마감되며, 추가 등록은 시험 날짜 3일 전에 마감된다.
    날짜 변경이나 등록 취소는 시험 날짜 3일 전까지 해야 하며, 날짜 변경은 ETS 온라인 홈페이지에서 가능하다.
    - 시험 등록 후 0~7일 내 ~ 시험일 3일 전 : 응시료 전액 환불
    - 시험일 3일 전 ~ 시험 당일이나 이후 : 환불되지 않음

02_ 성적 확인 및 성적표 발송

- ◆ 성적표 확인 : 시험 응시일로부터 대략 10일 후에 온라인상에서 성적 확인 가능
- ◆ 성적표 발송 : 시험 응시일 전에 선택한 최대 4개 기관까지 무료로 성적표 발송 가능
  추가 성적표를 요청할 경우 각 기관당 US$ 19씩 추가비용 발생
- ◆ 성적표의 유효기간 : 2년

03_ 시험 당일 준비물

- ◆ 공인된 신분증 (여권, 주민등록증, 운전면허증 중 택 1)
- ◆ 등록 번호

04_ 시험 당일 주의사항

시험 시작 30분 전까지 시험장에 도착하도록 한다. 시험장 안에는 신분증만 들고 들어갈 수 있게 허용된다. 따로 물품 보관 장소가 없는 시험장의 경우 수험자의 의자 아래에 준비된 비닐 가방에 개인용품을 보관하도록 한다.

- ◆ 입실절차
  - 체크인: 해당 고사실 입실 전 사진 촬영과 신분 확인 후 기밀 서약서 작성
  - 노트 필기를 위한 용지와 필기구 제공. 시험 종료 후 반환

iBT TOEFL Listening 소개

iBT TOEFL Listening Section은 크게 Conversation(대화)과 Lecture(강의) 지문으로 이루어져 있다. 대화는 주로 학교 내에서 흔히 발생하는 상황에 대해 학생이 교수나 담당 직원과 나누는 대화 내용을 다룬다. 강의는 주로 대학 강의에서 다루는 학문 분야에 대한 내용이 나온다. TOEFL Listening Test는 정답을 맞추는 데 기억력에 의존해 모든 내용을 암기하기 보다는 전체적인 내용을 이해하고 정리하는 능력을 더 요하며, Test 동안 note-taking을 자유롭게 할 수 있다.

iBT TOEFL Listening 시험 구성

지문 구성	문제 유형	문항 수
• **1set 구성**: 3분 내외의 대화문 1개 +4~6분 내외의 강의 2개 • 시험은 기본 2set로 구성되며 더미가 있을 경우 총 3set가 나옴	총 18개의 유형	대화문당 5문항, 강의당 6문항, 총 34문항(2set)

*더미는 ETS에서 응시자와 문제의 수준을 테스트하기 위해 만든 문제 set이며, 3set 중 어떤 것이 더미인지 알 수는 없으나 대개 마지막 세트인 경우가 많다. 대체적인 의견으로는 더미 set의 문제는 점수에 포함되지 않는다고 한다.

iBT TOEFL Listening 문제 유형

문제 유형	해당 문제 유형
Listening for Basic Comprehension 들은 내용에 대한 기본적인 이해능력을 요하는 문제	Main Idea Function / Purpose Problem Solution (Suggestion) Example Cause & Effect Similarity / Difference Advantage / Disadvantage Misunderstanding / Correction Definition (Term) / Origin Requirement (Condition) Character
Listening for Pragmatic Understanding 들은 내용에 대한 실질적인 의미를 파악하는 문제	Replay Question (Headset) Imply / Infer Opinion / Attitude
Listening for Connecting Information 들은 내용을 종합해서 푸는 문제	Two Click / Three Click Matching Ordering

▷ Note-taking Golden Rule 3

문제로 출제되는 부분만 적는 것은 가능한가?

결론부터 말하면 가능하다. 지문의 어느 부분이 어떤 문제로 연결될지 예측할 수만 있다면 불가능한 일이 아니다. 그러기 위해서 우선 지문과 문제의 관계를 분석하고, 많은 지문을 읽고 문제를 풀어보면서 부단한 연습과 훈련을 해야 한다.

Rule 1. 지문을 들으면서 문제를 예측하라!
Conversation은 상황별, Lecture는 주제별로 특정한 글의 전개 방식을 가지며 이것은 반드시 문제와 연결된다. 예를 들어, 실험과 관련된 Lecture에서는 '실험 목적 → 실험 방법 → 실험 결과'의 순서로 지문이 전개되며 이와 관련된 문제가 나올 가능성이 매우 높다. 병(disease)이 주제인 경우에는 '병의 원인 → 치료법' 등이 소개될 것이며 역시 이를 묻는 문제가 출제될 것이다. 따라서 도입부에서 지문의 주제를 파악한다면 앞으로 이어질 지문의 흐름과 나올 문제를 예측할 수 있으며, 이런 예측을 토대로 note-taking할 부분을 선별할 수 있다.

Rule 2. 단서 표현을 중심으로 note-taking하라!
Listening에서 문제 예측의 정확도를 높여주는 것이 바로 지문에 나오는 문제 유형별 '단서 표현'이다. 단서 표현은 앞으로 나올 문제와의 연관성이 매우 높아서 지문에서 특정 단서 표현을 듣는다면 어떤 문제로 연결될지 예측할 수 있다. 예를 들어, TOEFL Listening에서 사람의 역할에 대해 물어본 문제들과 그 지문을 분석해 보면, 지문에서 그 사람을 언급할 때 'invent(발명하다)', 'create(만들다)', 또는 'first found(최초로 발견했다)' 등의 어휘를 자주 사용한 것을 알 수 있다. 지문에 "John Smith invented A"란 문장이 나온다면, 이는 앞으로 John Smith의 역할을 묻는 문제가 출제될 수 있다는 것을 의미한다. 따라서, 지문을 들을 때 역할 문제 유형이 나올 것을 대비하여 단서 표현인 'invented'와 정답이 될 수 있는 핵심 내용인 'John Smith'와 'A'를 함께 note-taking해 두면 된다.

Rule 3. 자신만의 약자 체계를 만들어라!
note-taking 시간을 단축하기 위해서 약자를 많이 외워야 한다는 부담감을 가질 수 있지만, 그럴 필요가 없다. note-taking의 목적은 문제를 풀 때 활용하는 데 있으므로 자신이 알아볼 수 있는 약자 체계와 note-taking rule 만들어서 사용하면 된다. 예를 들어, 이름은 first name과 last name의 initial만 쓰고(John Smith = JS), invent는 I라고(invent = I) 쓸 수 있다. 약자 체계의 정답은 없지만, 듣기에 방해가 되지 않을 정도로 최대한 간단하게 적어야 한다.

iBT TOEFL Listening 화면 구성

01_ 디렉션 화면

Listening Section Directions

Please check to make sure your headset is on.
To change the volume level, click the icon in the upper right-hand corner of the screen.
Adjust the volume by moving the arrow on the volume indicator.
Click the volume icon again to close it.

This section uses conversations and lectures to test your listening skills.
It is divided into two parts that are timed separately. Each part contains a conversation and two lectures. You will listen to each one only once.

Each conversation or lecture will be followed by questions asking about the main idea and supporting details. Some may be related to a speaker's purpose or attitude. Be sure to answer the questions based on what you've heard.

02_ 지문이 나올 때의 화면

1 지문 내용의 진행 정도를 보여준다.

03_문제 제시 화면

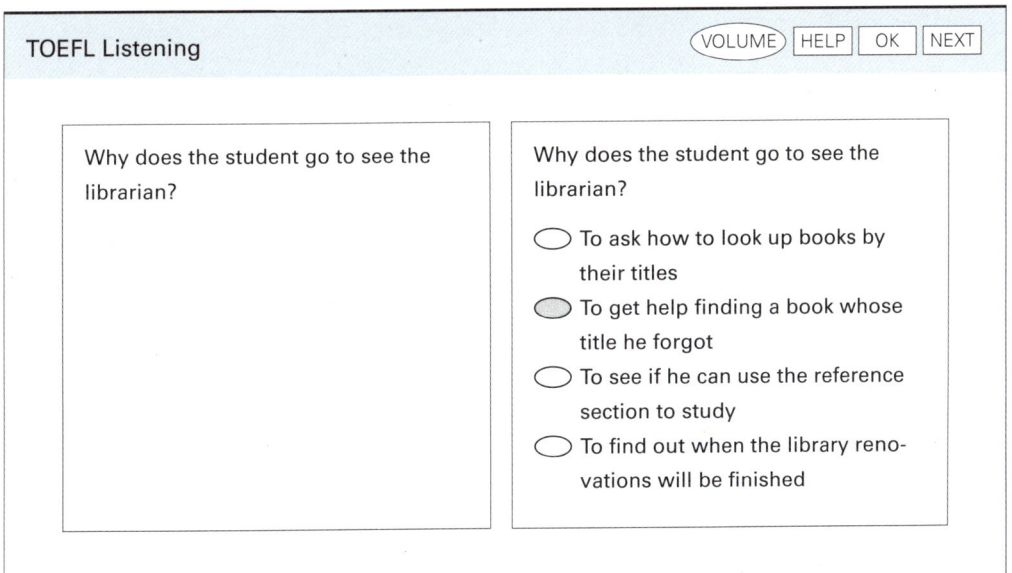

04_이미지 제시 화면

학습 계획표

20일 완성 시험을 앞두고 집중적인 학습이 필요한 학습자

	Day 1	Day 2	Day 3	Day 4	Day 5
Conv.	Diagnostic Test 현 위치 파악	Chap. 1 1/2	Chap. 1 1/2	Chap. 3 1/2	Chap. 3 1/2
Lecture					
	Day 6	**Day 7**	**Day 8**	**Day 9**	**Day 10**
Conv.	U1_Class	U1_Grade / Exam	U1_Field Trip	U1_Paper	U1_Project
Lecture	U3_Architecture, Art & Science	U3_Painting, Literature	U3_Film, Photography	U4_Animal Communication, Animal Adaptation	U4_Botany, Ecology
	Day 11	**Day 12**	**Day 13**	**Day 14**	**Day 15**
Conv.	U1_Major	U2_Class / Credit	U2_Housing	U2_Library	U2_Part-time Job
Lecture	U4_Physiology, Paleontology	U5_Astronomy, Chemistry	U5_Earth Science, Environmental Science	U5_Geology, Engineering	U6_Anthropology, Archaeology
	Day 16	**Day 17**	**Day 18**	**Day 19**	**Day 20**
Conv.	U2_School Facility	U2_기타	Actual Test 1	Actual Test 2	Actual Test 오답 복습
Lecture	U6_Business, Education	U6_Psychology, Sociology			

* 토플 대표 강사 온라인 강의(유료)는 영단기 Web site에서!

www.engdangi.com

45일 완성 차근차근 순서별 학습을 원하는 학습자

Day 1	Day 2	Day 3	Day 4	Day 5
Diagnostic Test 현 위치 파악	Chap. 1 01 ~ 06	Chap. 1 07 ~ 12	Practice Questions I, II	U1_Class
Day 6	**Day 7**	**Day 8**	**Day 9**	**Day 10**
U1_Grade / Exam	U1_Field Trip	U1_Paper	U1_Project	U1_Major
Day 11	**Day 12**	**Day 13**	**Day 14**	**Day 15**
U2_Class / Credit	U2_Housing	U2_Library	U2_Part-time Job	U2_School Facility
Day 16	**Day 17**	**Day 18**	**Day 19**	**Day 20**
U2_기타	Chap. 3 01 ~ 09	Chap. 3 10 ~ 18	Practice Questions I, II	U3_Architecture
Day 21	**Day 22**	**Day 23**	**Day 24**	**Day 25**
U3_Art & Science	U3_Painting	U3_Literature	U3_Film & Theater History	U3_Photography
Day 26	**Day 27**	**Day 28**	**Day 29**	**Day 30**
U4_Animal Communication	U4_Animal Adaptation	U4_Botany	U4_Ecology	U4_Physiology
Day 31	**Day 32**	**Day 33**	**Day 34**	**Day 35**
U4_Paleontology	U5_Astronomy	U5_Chemistry	U5_Earth Science	U5_Environmental Science
Day 36	**Day 37**	**Day 38**	**Day 39**	**Day 40**
U5_Geology	U5_Engineering	U6_Anthropology	U6_Archaeology	U6_Business
Day 41	**Day 42**	**Day 43**	**Day 44**	**Day 45**
U6_Education	U6_Psychology	U6_Sociology	**Actual Test 1**	**Actual Test 2**

TOEFL Listening

Diagnostic Test

TOEFL Listening	VOLUME HELP OK NEXT

Listening Section Directions

Please check to make sure your headset is on.
To change the volume level, click the icon in the upper right-hand corner of the screen.
Adjust the volume by moving the arrow on the volume indicator.
Click the volume icon again to close it.

This section uses conversations and lectures to test your listening skills.
It is divided into two parts that are timed separately. Each part contains a conversation and two lectures. You will listen to each one only once.
Each conversation or lecture will be followed by questions asking about the main idea and supporting details. Some may be related to a speaker's purpose or attitude. Be sure to answer the questions based on what you've heard.

Each question must be answered. After each answer, click "next". Then confirm your answer by clicking "ok". This will take you to the next question. Once you click "ok", you cannot go back and change your answer.
When taking an actual test, you will see the time remaining on a clock at the top of the screen.

Part 1 정답 및 해석 p. 002

TOEFL Listening

VOLUME HELP OK NEXT
PAUSE TEST SECTION EXIT

[01 ~ 05] Listen to a conversation between a student and a librarian. Then answer the questions. MP3 01

TOEFL Listening

01 Why does the student go to see the librarian?
    Ⓐ To ask how to look up books by their titles
    Ⓑ To get help finding a book whose title he forgot
    Ⓒ To see if he can use the reference section to study
    Ⓓ To find out when the library renovations will be finished

02 What does the librarian say about the books in the reference section?
    Ⓐ They have been moved to a new location.
    Ⓑ They can only be checked out by professors.
    Ⓒ Undergraduates cannot take them home.
    Ⓓ None of them are currently available.

03 Why does the student mention that the library is getting renovated?
    Ⓐ He feels the university policy is unfair.
    Ⓑ He is worried it will delay his project.
    Ⓒ He is having trouble hearing the librarian.
    Ⓓ He thinks the noise would be distracting.

04 What does the librarian suggest the student do?
    Ⓐ Borrow the book on behalf of his professor
    Ⓑ Ask his professor to file a complaint about the policy
    Ⓒ Find a research assistant who will check out the book
    Ⓓ Have his professor borrow the book for him

Listen again to part of the conversation. Then answer the question. 🔊 MP3 01_1

05 Why does the student say this?
    Ⓐ He is annoyed that he needs to get additional permission.
    Ⓑ He thinks that his professor has checked out too many books.
    Ⓒ He does not think he should ask his professor to do another task.
    Ⓓ He is worried that he will forget some of the things he needs to do.

Part 1 정답 및 해석 p. 004

```
TOEFL Listening                                VOLUME  HELP  OK  NEXT
PAUSE TEST   SECTION EXIT                              HIDE TIME  03:30
```

[06 ~ 11] Listen to part of a lecture in a psychology class. Then answer the questions.

🔊 MP3 02

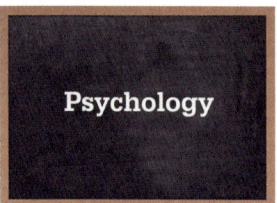  

06   What is the main purpose of the lecture?
     Ⓐ To explain the symptoms of insomnia
     Ⓑ To describe excessive sleep disorders
     Ⓒ To give an alternative definition of sleep
     Ⓓ To discuss why people have trouble sleeping

07   According to the professor, why is hypersomnia considered a more serious problem than insomnia?
     Ⓐ It tends to occur more commonly in very young children.
     Ⓑ It is a mental condition rather than a physical illness.
     Ⓒ It causes people to have a harder time functioning normally.
     Ⓓ It stops people from maintaining their health with extended sleep.

08   What are mentioned as common symptoms of people suffering from narcolepsy? Choose two answers.
     Ⓐ They are not able to achieve a deep level of sleep.
     Ⓑ They are unable to stay awake during the daytime.
     Ⓒ They can only sleep for short periods of time.
     Ⓓ They lose control of their muscles while awake.

09 According to the professor, why is it difficult to diagnose children with narcolepsy?

　Ⓐ Children normally take naps during the day.
　Ⓑ Children rarely experience sleep disorders.
　Ⓒ Children do not suffer from muscle paralysis.
　Ⓓ Children do not reach the REM stage of sleep.

10 What does the professor say about treating narcolepsy?

　Ⓐ The best cure is simply going to bed earlier.
　Ⓑ It can usually be done without a doctor's help.
　Ⓒ Different symptoms must be treated separately.
　Ⓓ There is no way to help people with narcolepsy.

11 According to the professor, what can narcoleptics do to prevent sleep attacks?

　Ⓐ Avoid stressful social situations
　Ⓑ Take several naps during the daytime
　Ⓒ Make sure they sleep eight hours a night
　Ⓓ Start taking a drug that keeps them alert

Part 1 정답 및 해석 p. 006

```
TOEFL Listening                          VOLUME  HELP  OK  NEXT
PAUSE TEST   SECTION EXIT                        HIDE TIME  03:30
```

[12 ~ 17] Listen to part of a lecture in a US history class. Then answer the questions.

🔊 MP3 03

12 What is the lecture mainly about?
   Ⓐ The reasons Americans moved west
   Ⓑ The history of mail service in the United States
   Ⓒ The development of transportation technologies
   Ⓓ The fastest way to carry people across the United States

13 According to the professor, why was there a need for a nationwide mail system?
   Ⓐ People needed to send gold from California.
   Ⓑ The majority of the local mail systems had failed.
   Ⓒ The population in California increased greatly.
   Ⓓ California officially became part of the United States.

14 What does the professor say about the initial mail service to California?
   Ⓐ It made California a bad place to live.
   Ⓑ It was very similar to today's mail system.
   Ⓒ It did not need many people to deliver the mail.
   Ⓓ It took a long time to reach its destination.

15 According to the professor, what problems did people face when delivering mail by stagecoach? Choose two answers.

Ⓐ There were no bridges across some rivers.
Ⓑ It was too expensive to build the stagecoaches.
Ⓒ Stagecoaches could not use some of the roads.
Ⓓ Stagecoaches couldn't carry both passengers and mail.

16 Why does the professor mention Lincoln's inaugural address?

Ⓐ To illustrate the importance of presidential speeches
Ⓑ To give an example of how the new telegraph system was used
Ⓒ To demonstrate the speed at which the Pony Express delivered mail
Ⓓ To identify what type of mail could not be carried by the Pony Express

17 What does the student mean when she says this?

Ⓐ She believes the professor accidentally contradicted himself.
Ⓑ She is not familiar with the type of ship the professor mentioned.
Ⓒ She is surprised that ships were used to deliver mail within the U.S.
Ⓓ She disagrees with the government's decision to deliver mail by steamship.

Conversation

Conversation Question Types

Conversation Question Types

01. Main Idea
02. Topic of the Paper
03. Problem
04. Solution (Suggestion)
05. Example
06. Cause
07. Similarity / Difference
08. Advantage / Disadvantage
09. Future Action
10. Requirement
11. Opinion / Attitude
12. Replay Question (Headset)

Chapter I

Conversation Question Types

01 Main Idea

1 문제의 핵심

지문 전체를 포괄하는 하나의 주제를 찾는 문제 유형으로, 지문에 어울리는 제목을 붙인다는 생각으로 답을 고르면 된다. 대개 첫 번째 문제로 출제되며, Conversation의 경우 학생의 방문 목적을, Lecture의 경우 강의의 주제를 주로 묻는다. 영미권의 글에서는 논리 구조상 핵심을 첫 부분에서 짚고 가므로, 주제나 토픽이 지문의 도입부에 제시되는 경우가 많다.

2 문제의 예시

- **Why does the man visit[go to see]** the professor?
- **Why does the student go to** the university office?
- What is the conversation **mainly about**?

3 100% 문제 공략법

01 도입부에 주목한다. Main Idea 문제는 거의 도입부에 정답의 단서가 나온다. 뿐만 아니라 도입부에서 대화의 목적이나 앞으로 대화가 흘러갈 방향에 대한 정보도 들을 수 있으므로 대화의 첫 부분을 집중해서 들어야 한다.
02 Conversation의 storyline은 주로 학생에게 문제가 발생하여 교수 또는 학교 직원을 찾아가서 해결하는 내용으로 전개된다.
03 도입부와 본론의 화제가 달라지는 storyline의 경우 학생이 찾아온 이유를 놓치기 쉬우므로 주의해야 한다.
04 처음에 언급되는 학생의 방문 이유와 뒤에 주로 논의되는 내용이 다르면 방문 목적과 대화의 주제를 구별해야 한다. 예를 들어, 학생이 교수를 찾아와 paper에 대한 얘기를 잠깐하고 바로 이어서 우연히 교수의 은퇴 소식을 들었다면서 그 이야기를 주로 한다면, Why does the student visit the professor?(방문 목적)에 대한 답은 'paper'이고, What is the conversation mainly about?(대화의 주제)에 대한 답은 '교수의 은퇴'가 될 수 있다.

4 대화 속 단서 표현

주로 학생이 먼저 도움을 요청하거나 상대방이 도움이 필요한지를 묻는 표현 뒤에 학생의 방문 이유나 목적이 나온다.
- What can I do for you?
- How may I help you?
- I am having a problem ~ / I couldn't
- I hope you can help me ~
- But anyway, what I wanted to ask was ~ *도입부에서 다른 이야기를 하다가 본론으로 들어가는 경우

▶ **Example Question**

Script

Employee: May I help you?
Student: Yeah, um, I need to talk to you about my tuition.
E: Okay, what seems to be the problem?
S: Well, I tried to register for my classes, but I couldn't access the registration page. I got a notice saying that I owed tuition. But, the thing is, I'm on a scholarship, so the tuition should have already been paid.

Question

Why does the student go to the registrar's office?
Ⓐ To confirm that she wants to accept a scholarship
Ⓑ To find out why she can't register for classes
Ⓒ To register for her general requirement classes
Ⓓ To ask why her scholarship is smaller than her tuition

> 이것을 듣고 답을 찾아라!
> 'I couldn't ~'으로 시작하는 문장을 들으면 학생이 수업 등록 페이지에 접속할 수 없어서 도움을 요청하러 찾아왔다는 것을 알 수 있다. 이렇게 대화 초반에 등장하는 학생의 방문 이유를 놓치지 않고 들어야 한다.

지문 해석
직원: 무엇을 도와드릴까요?
학생: 네, 음, 제 학비에 대해 이야기를 좀 하고 싶어서요.
직원: 네, 무슨 문제인가요?
학생: 음, 수업 등록을 하려고 했는데, 등록 페이지에 접속할 수가 없어요. 학비가 미납되었다는 공지를 받았고요. 그런데, 실은, 저는 장학금을 받고 있어서 학비가 이미 지불되었어야 하는데요.

문제 해석 및 정답
학생이 교무처를 찾아간 이유는?
Ⓐ 장학금을 수락하고 싶다는 것을 확인시켜 주려고
Ⓑ 수업 등록을 할 수 없는 이유를 알아보려고
Ⓒ 일반 필수 과목들을 등록하려고
Ⓓ 장학금이 학비보다 더 적은 이유를 문의하려고

어휘
tuition 등록금   registration 등록   access (컴퓨터에) 접속하다   owe (돈을) 빚지고 있다   scholarship 장학금

02 Topic of the Paper

1 문제의 핵심

수업이 대화의 토픽일 때, 수업 내용, paper의 주제, presentation의 내용, 시험 내용 등을 묻는 문제 유형이다. 자주 출제되는 편은 아니지만, 가끔씩 출제되기 때문에 더 놓치기 쉬운 문제이므로 주의가 필요하다.

2 문제의 예시

수업 내용	• What did the student learn **from this course**?
paper 주제	• What is **the topic of** the biology paper?
	• What is **the topic of** the student's report?
	• What is **the subject of** the student's paper?
project 주제	• What did the student study **in her laboratory project**?
기타(학교 신문)	• What will the student write about in his first article **for the newspaper**?

3 100% 문제 공략법

수업 관련 내용을 문제화하여 출제하므로, 대화의 도입부에 paper, research, exam과 관련된 상황이 등장하면 이 유형의 문제가 출제될 가능성이 높다. paper나 research에 대해 상세한 내용을 묻기보다는 전체적인 주제를 묻는 문제가 나온다.

> Tip paper의 내용을 너무 세부적인 것까지 note-taking을 하다 보면 전체 주제를 놓치기 쉬우므로 주의해야 한다. 또한 교수가 학생에게 "전에 OO교수와 A 주제로 연구했지? 나와는 B 주제로 research 해보지 않을래?"처럼 제안하는 내용이 나오면, 이전 교수와 연구한 주제가 오답 보기로 제시될 수 있다.

4 대화 속 단서 표현

topic, about 등 주제를 나타낼 때 함께 쓰이는 표현이 대표적인 단서 표현이다.

- the topic of my paper / research is ~
- I am writing a paper about ~
- **Professor:** Why don't you tell me about your project?
  Student: I want to study new approaches to bird migration.
- I am working on the lab project. I observed, diagrammed, and interpreted each stage of cell division ~
- That's what my research is about.

▶ **Example Question**

Script

Student: Well, the topic of my paper is monarch butterflies... You know, their migration patterns and the different routes they take.
Professor: Yes, I know.

Question

What is the topic of the biology paper?
Ⓐ What monarch butterflies look like
Ⓑ How monarch butterflies migrate
Ⓒ Where monarch butterflies live
Ⓓ How monarch butterflies communicate

> 이것을 듣고 답을 찾아라!
> paper의 주제를 묻는 문제이다. 따라서 'the topic of my paper ~'라는 표현을 들었다면 그 뒤에 나오는 내용을 주의 깊게 들어야 한다.

지문 해석
학생: 음, 제 보고서의 주제는 왕나비에요... 그 나비들의 이동 패턴과 그들이 가는 여러 다른 경로들 말이에요.
교수: 그래요, 알아요.

문제 해석 및 정답
생물학 보고서의 주제는?
Ⓐ 왕나비들의 생김새가 어떠한지
Ⓑ 왕나비들이 어떻게 이동하는지
Ⓒ 왕나비들이 어디에 사는지
Ⓓ 왕나비들이 어떻게 의사소통 하는지

어휘
migration 이동, 이주   route 경로   migrate 이동하다, 이주하다

03 Problem

1 문제의 핵심

Conversation 상황에서 발생할 수 있는 학생의 모든 문제점이 Problem 문제로 출제될 수 있다. 즉, 기숙사의 시설물 고장, 졸업학점 부족으로 졸업을 못하게 되는 문제, academic program에 지원시 필요한 일부 서류가 빠진 문제, 학생의 paper와 관련된 문제 등 다양한 Problem 문제가 대화 상황별로 출제된다.

2 문제의 예시

dorm	· What **problem** does the student have?
library	· What are two possible reasons why the man **cannot** find the book?
	· What is the potential **problem** with the available job in the library?
paper	· What is the professor's main **criticism** of the student's paper?
facility	· What **problem** concerning University Auditorium is mentioned?
class	· What does the student describe as **challenging** in his class?

3 100% 문제 공략법

학교 생활과 관련된 다양한 문제점들이 제시되므로, 각 상황별로 기존에 자주 출제되었던 문제점을 정리해두면 내용 예측이 가능해져 문제를 공략하기가 쉬워진다.

01 **dorm**: 시설물 고장, 소음 문제
02 **paper**: 필요한 자료가 없음, paper를 쓰는 방법을 모름
03 **roommate**: 정리를 안 함
04 **exam**: 점수가 생각보다 좋지 않음
05 **library**: 찾는 책이 없음
06 **group project**: 팀원이 자기 역할을 제대로 안 함

Tip 대화에서 문제점이 하나가 아니라 여러 개가 제시될 수도 있다. 이때 예를 들어 문제점이 세 가지 정도 나열된 후 그 중 한 문제점에 대해서만 상세하게 묻는 질문이 출제되면, 다른 두 문제점을 오답 보기로 제시하는 경우가 많으므로 주의하도록 한다.

4 대화 속 단서 표현

직접적으로 언급된 문제 표현(problem, trouble)이나 부정적인 표현에 주목한다.

dorm	· I have a problem. The door of my room is broken.
paper	· I don't know how to write up the research paper.
library	· I am having a hard time finding articles.
group project	· I am having trouble with my group project.
class	· I am a little overwhelmed by the size of this class.

▶ **Example Question**

Script

Professor: The point of the project is to see how pollution can spread and damage marine wildlife on the coast. The area will be very polluted and may smell like gasoline. You might get nauseous.

Student: Oh, that's not a problem.

P: Another thing is it's in a pretty remote location, so we'll have to travel by boat. Some students who have never been on boats at sea tend to get a little seasick. It's really hard to do anything when you're feeling dizzy on top of the smell.

S: I never thought about that, but I'm sure I'll manage.

Question

What are the problems the student may face during the field study?

ⓐ He may unintentionally damage the wild life.
ⓑ He may experience dizziness and nausea.
ⓒ He may have a hard time finding a boat to charter.
ⓓ He has to pay for his own transportation.

> **이것을 듣고 답을 찾아라!**
> 학생이 field trip을 갈 때 직면할 수 있는 문제점을 묻는 질문이다. 대화에 'nauseous', 'feeling dizzy' 같은 부정적 표현이 나왔으므로, problem이라는 표현이 직접적으로 언급되지 않아도 위 단어들이 학생이 겪을 문제점이라는 것을 잡아낼 수 있어야 한다.

지문 해석
교수: 프로젝트의 요점은 오염이 어떻게 퍼져나가 어떻게 해안가의 해양 야생동물들에게 피해를 주는지 알아보는 거예요. 그 지역은 심하게 오염이 되어서, 가솔린 같은 냄새가 날지도 몰라요. 속이 메스꺼워질 수 있고요.
학생: 아, 그건 문제되지 않아요.
교수: 또 다른 점은, 그곳이 꽤 외진 곳이라서 보트를 타고 가야 한다는 점이에요. 바다에서 보트를 한 번도 타보지 못한 일부 학생들은 약간 뱃멀미를 하기도 해요. 냄새에다가 어지럽기까지 하면 정말 아무것도 하기 힘들죠.
학생: 그런 건 생각해보지 못했는데, 하지만 견딜 수 있을 것 같아요.

문제 해석 및 정답
학생이 현장 연구에서 겪을지도 모르는 문제들은 무엇인가?
ⓐ 의도치 않게 야생 동물들에게 피해를 줄지도 모른다.
ⓑ 어지러움과 메스꺼움을 경험할지도 모른다.
ⓒ 전세 보트를 구하는 데 어려움을 겪을지도 모른다.
ⓓ 교통비를 스스로 지불해야 한다.

어휘
wildlife 야생동물   nauseous 메스꺼운   remote 외딴, 외진   get seasick 뱃멀미하다   on top of ~ …외에, …뿐 아니라   unintentionally 무심코   nausea 메스꺼움

04 Solution (Suggestion)

1 문제의 핵심

Conversation에서는 학생이 Problem 문제 유형에 해당하는 문제를 말하면 교수나 직원이 이를 해결하는 방법을 제시한다. 따라서 Solution 문제는 Problem 문제와 짝을 이루는 경우가 많으며 교수 또는 담당 직원의 제안을 잘 듣고 정답을 찾아야 한다.

2 문제의 예시

교수 · Why does the professor **suggest** that the student change the introduction of his paper?
· What does the professor **advise** the student to do in order to ~

직원 · What does the employee **suggest** the student do?
· What does the registrar **offer** to do for the student?
· What does the librarian **suggest** the student should do?

거절 · Why does the student **hesitate** before agreeing to the professor's request?

3 100% 문제 공략법

01 상황별 문제점을 인식하고, 그에 대한 해결책을 예측하여 듣는다.
02 최근에는 교수나 직원이 제안한 내용이 아니라, 위에 밑줄 친 문제처럼 교수의 제안이나 요청을 학생이 거절했을 때 그 이유를 묻는 문제가 출제되기도 한다. 따라서 제안이 언급되면 제안 내용만 듣지 말고 뒤에 이어지는 학생의 응답이 긍정적인지 부정적인지를 확인해야 하며, 특히 학생이 부정적인 응답을 할 때에는 그 이유도 함께 잘 들어두어야 한다.

Tip 여러 제안이 대화 중에 언급되었을 때는, 각 제안 내용을 구별하여 듣고 note-taking하여 문제에서 오답 보기로 출제될 내용을 걸러낼 수 있도록 대비한다.

4 대화 속 단서 표현

제안을 할 때 쓰이는 다양한 표현들이 정답을 찾는 단서가 된다.
· Why don't you ~ ?
· How about ~ ?
· Have you heard ~ ?
· You could ~
· You'd better ~ / You need to ~
· You would be better off v-ing.
· You might as well ~
· Make sure to / that ~

▶ **Example Question**

Script

Professor: Make sure you fill out your application as soon as you can. The deadline's in a week. Even though there's a deadline, it's always better to hand it in as soon as possible. You want to give a good impression, you know? And make sure you talk to your academic adviser before filling out the application.

Question

What does the professor suggest that the student do first?
- Ⓐ Rethink the countries he has chosen
- Ⓑ Gather information for the application
- Ⓒ Talk to an academic adviser
- Ⓓ Go to an exchange student conference

> 이것을 듣고 답을 찾아라!
> 'Make sure ~', 'You need to ~'와 같은 표현이 나오면 교수가 학생에게 무언가를 하도록 제안하는 것이므로, Suggestion 문제가 나올 것을 예측해서 그 뒤에 이어지는 'talk to ~' 부분을 note-taking해야 한다.

지문 해석
교수: 가능한 한 빨리 지원서를 작성하도록 해요. 마감이 일주일 후이니까요. 마감 기한이 있긴 하지만, 가능한 한 일찍 제출하는 것이 언제나 더 좋죠. 좋은 인상을 남기고 싶잖아요? 그렇죠? 그리고 지원서를 작성하기 전에 반드시 지도 교수님과 이야기를 나눠보도록 하고요.

문제 해석 및 정답
교수는 학생이 무엇을 먼저 해야 한다고 제안하는가?
- Ⓐ 그가 고른 나라에 대해 다시 생각해보기
- Ⓑ 지원서에 대한 정보를 모으기
- Ⓒ 지도 교수와 이야기하기
- Ⓓ 교환 학생 컨퍼런스에 참석하기

어휘
deadline 마감 기한　　hand in 제출하다　　impression 인상　　academic adviser 지도 교수　　exchange student 교환학생

05 Example

1 문제의 핵심

대화에서 앞서 언급된 문제점, 차이점, 장점 등에 대한 예가 제시된 경우, 왜 그 내용(예)을 언급했는지 묻는 문제 유형이다. Conversation에서 항상 출제되는 문제이며 특히 Why ~ metion ~? 질문의 80%가 이 유형에 해당된다.

2 문제의 예시

- **Why** does the student **mention** his previous jobs?
- **Why** does the student **mention** her roommate?
- **Why** does the student **mention** his job as a waiter?

3 100% 문제 공략법

대화에서 예를 제시할 때 for example 등의 단서 표현을 명확하게 사용하면 더할 나위 없이 좋겠지만, 요즘은 (특히 Conversation에서는) 이런 표현을 직접적으로 들려주는 경우가 흔치 않다. 따라서, 단서 표현이 나오지 않더라도 어떤 부분이 예시인지 알아들을 수 있어야 한다. 또한, 무엇에 대한 예시인지 파악하는 것도 중요하다. 이를 알면 문제 예측이 좀 더 쉬워진다.

Eg. 지난번에 study abroad program에 참여했을 때 다양한 문화권의 사람들을 만나서 많은 것을 배울 수 있어서 좋았다(장점). 예를 들어(단서 표현), 그 나라 전통 음식과 의상을 알게 되었다(장점의 예).

이 대화에서 출제될 수 있는 문제는 "Why does the student mention 전통음식 & 의상?"이다. 지문을 들을 때, study abroad program의 장점이 문제로 출제될 것을 먼저 예측하고, for example이라는 단서 표현을 통해 그 뒤에 바로 이어지는 내용은 앞에 언급된 장점의 예라는 것을 알 수 있어야 한다. 이와 같이 Example 문제 유형은 다른 문제 유형(여기에서는 Advantage 문제 유형)과 결합되어 출제되는 경향이 있다.

Tip Example 문제 유형에서는 지문에서 제시된 예와 관련하여 두 가지 이상의 내용이 언급된 경우, 이 예가 어떤 내용의 예시에 해당하는지 구별하는 것이 중요하다. 예와 함께 처음에 언급된 내용이 정답이라는 것을 기억해야 한다.

Eg. 교수: 잘 생긴 미국 영화배우는, 예를 들어 톰 크루즈가 있지요. 그는 무수히 많은 영화에 출연했고, 한국도 방문한 적이 있습니다.

교수가 톰 크루즈를 언급한 이유는?
- Ⓐ 잘 생긴 영화배우의 예
- Ⓑ 영화에 많이 출연한 영화배우의 예
- Ⓒ 우리나라에 방문한 적이 있는 영화배우의 예
- Ⓓ 자신과 얼굴이 비슷한 영화배우의 예

→ 지문에 A, B, C가 전부 언급되었지만 정답은 A이다. 교수가 처음에 언급한 의미가 정답이라는 것에 주의해야 한다.

4 대화 속 단서 표현

예를 나타내는 다양한 표현들이 단서 표현이 된다.

- for example, such as, like
- think of, imagine

▶ **Example Question**

Script

Employee: How can I help you today?

Student: I opened the window in my dorm room yesterday, but I can't seem to get it closed. I tried everything I could, I even asked my friend Bob who's on the wrestling team to try and shut it, but it just won't budge.

Question

Why does the student mention her friend Bob?
Ⓐ To recommend someone who can fix the heater
Ⓑ To explain that she is on the wrestling team
Ⓒ To suggest that her friend broke her window
Ⓓ To emphasize how difficult it is to close the window

> 이것을 듣고 답을 찾아라!
> 최근 Conversation의 Example 문제 유형은, for example과 같은 단서 표현이 언급되지 않고, 난이도도 높아지는 추세이다. "I can't seem to get it closed."에서 Problem 문제 유형의 단서 표현이 언급되면서 창문을 닫을 수 없다는 학생의 문제점이 먼저 제시되었다. 따라서 뒤이어 나오는 '운동선수인 친구에게까지 부탁했는데 할 수 없었다'는 내용은 화자의 어려움을 설명하는 예임을 알 수 있다.

지문 해석

직원: 무엇을 도와드릴까요?
학생: 제가 어제 제 기숙사 방 창문을 열었는데 그게 닫히지가 않아서요. 제가 할 수 있는 모든 걸 해보고, 심지어 레슬링 팀에 있는 친구 Bob에게 닫아봐 달라고 부탁까지 했지만, 꼼짝도 안 해요.

문제 해석 및 정답

학생이 친구 Bob을 언급한 이유는?
Ⓐ 히터를 수리할 수 있는 누군가를 추천하려고
Ⓑ 자신이 레슬링 팀의 일원이라는 것을 설명하려고
Ⓒ 친구가 자신의 창문을 깨뜨렸다는 것을 시사하려고
Ⓓ 창문을 닫는 것이 얼마나 어려운지 강조하려고

어휘

dorm(=dormitory) 기숙사   budge 약간 움직이다

06 Cause

1 문제의 핵심

Conversation에서 등장하는 다양한 상황과 관련된 중심 내용, 즉 특정 수업을 듣는 이유, 수업을 drop하는 이유, 특정 paper topic을 고른 이유, 수업이 취소된 이유 등 주로 이유를 묻는 문제 유형이다. 예를 들어 학생들이 기숙사에서 갑자기 이사를 나가는 상황의 대화라면, '이사에 대한 공지가 왜 미리 되지 않았는가?'와 같은 문제가 출제될 수 있다.

2 문제의 예시

- **Why** did the student choose the topic?
- **Why** does the student want to write for the campus newspaper?
- **Why** was the chemistry class canceled?
- What is **the main reason** the student is thinking of dropping the class?
- What are **two reasons** the student gives for choosing an elective in literature?

3 100% 문제 공략법

Cause 유형의 문제 역시 Conversation에서 자주 등장하는 상황별로 출제 가능성이 높은 이유를 미리 파악해 두는 것이 효과적이다.

01 part-time job: 지원한 이유, 그만두는 이유
02 class: 수강 신청한 이유, drop하는 이유, 수업이 취소된 이유
03 campus newspaper: 학교신문에 특정 기사를 쓰고 싶은 이유
04 paper: 특정 topic을 고른 이유

Tip 대화 중 이유가 두 가지 이상 제시될 때는 주의해야 한다. 예를 들어, 학생이 자신이 속한 팀의 보고서의 주제로 A라는 topic을 고른 이유 (이유 1)를 교수에게 설명한다. 그에 대해 교수는 다른 팀원들이 그 topic을 좋아하지 않으므로 B라는 topic으로 바꾸는 것이 어떻겠냐고 제안한다. 학생은 A topic으로 자료를 너무 많이 찾아 놓아서(이유 2) topic 변경이 불가하다고 대답을 한다. 이런 상황의 대화에서 학생이 A topic를 고른 이유를 묻는 문제가 출제될 때, 대화에서 언급된 이유 두 가지가 각각 정답(이유 1)과 오답(이유 2)으로 함께 출제된다.

4 대화 속 단서 표현

이유나 목적을 나타내는 표현을 단서로 정답을 찾을 수 있다.

- goal, purpose
- reason why ~
- That's because ~
- In order to ~
- What we are trying to do ~

▶ **Example Question**

Script

Student: Intro to European Literature isn't being offered anymore?
Employee: Yes, it's been canceled. That's just university policy whenever too few students register for a certain course. It's common sense really. The university can't afford to pay professors to lecture to an empty classroom. You see my point, don't you?

Question

Why was the literature class canceled?
Ⓐ The required number of registered students was not reached.
Ⓑ The professor who teaches the course demanded a pay raise.
Ⓒ The university changed its policy about required literature classes.
Ⓓ The designated classroom was not large enough for the class.

> **이것을 듣고 답을 찾아라!**
> 학생의 대사에서 수업과 관련된 문제가 생겼다는 것을 알 수 있다. 이런 경우, Problem이 무엇인지를 묻는 문제와 그 Problem을 해결하는 Solution 혹은 Problem이 발생한 Cause와 관련된 문제가 같이 출제될 수 있다. 따라서 먼저 문제점이 무엇인지 잘 들은 후 뒤에 나올 문제의 해결 방법이나 원인을 예측하여 들어야 한다. 위의 예처럼, Conversation에서는 수강 신청을 하는 이유, drop하는 이유 등을 묻는 문제가 자주 출제된다.

지문 해석
학생: 유럽 문학 개론 과정이 더 이상 제공되지 않는다고요?
직원: 네, 그 과정은 취소되었어요. 어떤 과정에 학생이 너무 적게 등록하면 언제든 그렇게 하는 것이 대학 정책이어서요. 일반적인 상식이죠. 텅텅 빈 강의실에서 강의를 하도록 교수들에게 비용을 지불할 여유가 대학에는 없으니까요. 무슨 말인지 알겠죠?

문제 해석 및 정답
문학 수업이 취소된 이유로 알맞은 것은?
Ⓐ 요구되는 등록 학생 수가 달성되지 못했다.
Ⓑ 그 과정을 가르치는 교수가 급여 인상을 요구했다.
Ⓒ 대학에서 필수 문학 수업에 대한 정책을 변경했다.
Ⓓ 지정된 교실이 그 수업에 충분할 만큼 크지 않았다.

어휘
policy 정책   register for ~ …에 등록하다   can't afford to ~ …할 (시간적·금전적) 여유가 없다   designated 지정된

Practice Questions I

[01 ~ 05] **Listen to a conversation between a student and a librarian. Then answer the questions.** MP3 04 정답 및 해석 p. 009

01 What is the conversation mainly about?
  Ⓐ Choosing a narrow topic for a report
  Ⓑ Finding information for a history class
  Ⓒ Using the library database to find books
  Ⓓ Transferring to the social sciences department

02 What does the student imply about the library's database?
  Ⓐ It is no longer available.
  Ⓑ It is going to be expanded.
  Ⓒ It is not intended for students.
  Ⓓ It is not functioning optimally.

03 What is the topic of the student's research project?
   Ⓐ Causes of the Great Depression
   Ⓑ The effect of Roosevelt's New Deal
   Ⓒ Differences in the Western and Eastern States
   Ⓓ Migration patterns of workers within the United States

04 What specific information about the Great Depression does the student need?
   Choose two answers.
   Ⓐ The number of migrants
   Ⓑ The percentage of lost jobs
   Ⓒ The geographic location of migrants
   Ⓓ The causes of worker migration
   Ⓔ Government projects in Western states

05 What will the student probably do next?
   Ⓐ Return the book to the library
   Ⓑ Go to the library computer lab
   Ⓒ Talk to his professor about his topic
   Ⓓ Go to the social sciences department

Similarity / Difference

1   문제의 핵심

주로 학생이 이전에 다녔던 학교와 지금 다니는 학교의 공통점/차이점 또는 지원할 프로그램의 공통점/차이점 등을 묻는 문제 유형이다. 가끔 몇몇 학생들간의 공통점/차이점이나 학생과 교수간의 공통점/차이점이 문제로 출제되기도 한다.

2   문제의 예시

- How is the language lab **different from** the library?
- What is **common between** the student and the professor?

3   100% 문제 공략법

대화에서 공통점이나 차이점이 언급된다면 Similarity / Difference 문제가 출제될 것임을 쉽게 예측할 수 있다. 대화 상황별로 자주 출제되는 이 유형의 문제를 확인해 두도록 한다.

01 library : transfer하기 이전의 학교와 현재 학교의 도서 대출방법의 차이점
02 scholarship : private school과 public school의 차이점 Eg. private school이 더 많이 지원해준다.
03 class : 고등학교에서는 소수의 학생들이 수업을 들었는데, 대학에서는 대형 강의가 많아 적응이 되지 않는다.

> **Tip** 공통점/차이점이 직접 언급되지 않고 정보를 종합해 유추해야 하는 경우도 있다. 예를 들어, 학생이 교수에게 자신이 독일에 살아본 적이 있고 독일어를 잘 해서 독일에 취직하고 싶다고 말을 하고 교수가 "나도 독일에 살아 봤다"라고 말한다면 쉽게 공통점을 파악할 수 있다. 하지만 학생이 독일에 살았다는 정보가 대화의 도입부에서 언급되고 교수가 "나도 살아봐서 아는데"라고 대화의 말미에 언급할 경우, 학생과 교수의 공통점을 쉽게 찾을 수 없는 고난이도의 문제가 된다.

4   대화 속 단서 표현

공통점/차이점을 나타내는 표현뿐 아니라 동감하는 표현도 단서가 된다.
- have a similar way of ~
- It goes the same with ~
- have in common
- different from ~
- Me, too.

▶ **Example Question**

Script

Student 1: Are you going to take summer school classes this year?
Student 2: Yeah, I have to. If I don't, I won't have enough credits to graduate on time.
S1: I have the same problem. This will be my second summer of taking classes. Anyway, I've got to run. My English class is going to start soon.

Question

What will the two students do this summer?
Ⓐ They will attend summer school.
Ⓑ They will look for part-time jobs.
Ⓒ They will graduate university.
Ⓓ They will teach English classes.

 이것을 듣고 답을 찾아라!
문제의 형태만 보아서는 다음에 무엇을 할 것인지를 묻는 Future Action 문제 유형으로 보이지만, 정답을 찾기 위해서는 두 학생 모두 'summer school class'를 듣는다는 내용을 들어야 한다. 따라서, 학생들간의 공통점에 대해 묻는 문제임을 알 수 있다.

지문 해석
학생 1: 너 올해 여름 학기를 들을 예정이니?
학생 2: 응, 그래야 해. 그러지 않으면 제때 졸업할 수 있는 충분한 학점이 안 되거든.
학생 1: 나도 같은 문제를 겪고 있어. 이번이 내가 수업을 듣는 두 번째 여름이 될 거야. 어쨌든, 서둘러야겠다. 영어 수업이 곧 시작할 거거든.

문제 해석 및 정답
두 학생이 이번 여름에 할 것으로 알맞은 것은?
Ⓐ **여름 학기를 들을 것이다.**
Ⓑ 아르바이트 일자리를 찾을 것이다.
Ⓒ 대학을 졸업할 것이다.
Ⓓ 영어 수업을 가르칠 것이다.

어휘
credit 학점

08 Advantage / Disadvantage

1 문제의 핵심

어떤 상황에 대한 장점/단점을 묻는 문제 유형이다. 주로 학교나 **academic program**을 비교하거나 기숙사나 **gym**과 같은 학교 시설물을 비교하는 대화에서 이 유형의 문제가 출제될 수 있으며 출제빈도가 매우 높다.

2 문제의 예시

- What does the professor emphasize as one **benefit** of taking a class?
- What is mentioned as an **advantage** of working on this project?
- What are the **disadvantages** of using pencils to advertise?

3 100% 문제 공략법

Advantage/Disadvantage 문제 유형은 상황별 대화 전개방식을 기억하면 쉽게 문제를 예측할 수 있어 점수 확보에 용이한 유형이다.

01 class/research: 이 class나 research에 참여하면 취직할 때나 대학원 진학 시 도움이 됨
02 field trip: 다녀오면 extra point를 부여함
03 part-time job: 도서관은 급여를 적게 주는데, 식당 serving은 급여가 높음
   원하는 시간을 선택해서 일할 수 있음
   TA(teaching assistant)를 하면 등록금이 면제됨
04 dorm: 전에는 4인 1실에 살았었는데 현재는 2인 1실에 살아서 좋음
   study lounge를 쓸 수 있거나 gym과 가까이 있어서 편리함
05 school: 학생 대 교수 비율이 높아서 학생들의 관심이 높음
   A학교가 B학교보다 특정 전공으로 유명하고 졸업생들도 많아서 사회 생활에 도움을 많이 받을 수 있음

Tip 대화에서는 한 가지의 주제에 관한 다양한 장단점이 언급될 수 있다. 장단점이 하나뿐일 때는 문제를 풀 때 쉽게 기억이 나겠지만, 두세 개 이상의 장단점이 언급되면 문제를 풀 때 혼동될 수 있으니 반드시 note-taking을 한다.

4 대화 속 단서 표현

장점이나 단점을 나타내는 표현들을 알아둔다.
- benefit, advantage, chance
- disadvantage, drawback

▶ **Example Question**

Script

Professor: To be honest, I've been thinking about offering extra credit to anyone who participates. It might be the only way I can get enough volunteers. The chance to earn extra credit would probably be enough to motivate a few more of my students.

Question

Which of the following is mentioned as an advantage of taking part in the project?
Ⓐ Off-campus travel expenses will be reimbursed.
Ⓑ Students will be excused early from their classes.
Ⓒ It takes place in a convenient, nearby location.
Ⓓ It can assist students in improving their class grade.

> 이것을 듣고 답을 찾아라!
> 프로젝트의 자원봉사자를 구하기 위해 교수가 추가 학점을 주는 방법을 고려하고 있다는 내용이므로, 학생 입장에서는 프로젝트에 참여해서 얻는 정보 외에 추가 학점이라는 이점이 생긴다는 것을 알 수 있다. 'chance', 'motivate' 등의 단서 표현을 놓치지 않아야 한다.

지문 해석
교수: 솔직히, 참가하는 학생에게는 추가 학점을 주려고 생각 중이에요. 그게 아마도 충분한 수의 지원자를 구할 수 있는 유일한 방법일지도 몰라요. 추가 학점을 얻을 수 있는 기회는 아마도 내 학생들 몇 명에게 동기를 부여하는 데 충분할 거예요.

문제 해석 및 정답
다음 중 프로젝트에 참여하는 것의 장점으로 언급된 것은?
Ⓐ 학교 밖으로의 여행 비용이 변제될 것이다.
Ⓑ 학생들은 수업에서 일찍 나올 수 있을 것이다.
Ⓒ 편리하고 가까운 위치에서 프로젝트가 이루어진다.
Ⓓ 학생들이 그 수업의 성적을 향상시키는 데 도움을 줄 수 있다.

어휘
extra 추가의   volunteer 자원봉사자   motivate 동기를 부여하다   expense 비용   reimburse 배상[변제]하다
assist 돕다

09 Future Action

1   문제의 핵심

학생의 다음 행동을 묻는 문제 유형이다. 대화에서 한 명의 화자가 상대방에게 무언가 제안을 하면 대화는 대체로 그 제안에 대한 긍정적 또는 부정적 응답으로 마무리된다. 제안에 대한 응답이 긍정적일 경우 제안 내용을 바탕으로 화자의 다음 행동을 예측하는 문제가 출제된다.

2   문제의 예시

- What will the student probably **do next**?
- What will the student probably **do** in **next** Tuesday's class?
- What does the professor want the student to **do next**?
- What **will** the applicants talk about?

3   100% 문제 공략법

교수나 담당 직원으로부터 어떠한 제안이 주어졌을 때 학생의 응답이 긍정인 경우, Future Action 문제가 출제될 수 있다.

> **Tip** 대화 중 여러 행동이 언급된 경우, 오답에 현혹되지 않도록 주의해야 한다. 예를 들어, 대화에서 학생이 밥을 먹고 나서 도서관에 가겠다고 말을 했다면, Future Action 문제에서는 보기가 '(A) 밥을 먹는다.' '(B) 도서관에 간다.'와 같이 제시된다. 이 경우 '다음에 할 것'을 묻는 문제이므로 (B)는 정답이 될 수 없고 (A)가 정답이다. 즉, 학생이 대화 직후 가장 먼저 할 행동을 답으로 고르면 된다.

4   대화 속 단서 표현

제안 표현과 이에 대한 긍정적 응답 표현이 단서이다.

제안 · Why don't you ~ ?

응답 · Sounds great.
 · I will.
 · I haven't thought about that.

▶ **Example Question**

`Script`

Professor: Exactly. Mmm… It's not on the reading list I gave you, but if you read Silliman's *The Alphabet*, you'll see what I mean. It's sort of… sort of in between traditional poetry and language poetry. Oh, and if you still don't get it, I have a lecture prepared on the topic. You'll be able to learn more in class.

Student: Thanks. I'll read it.

`Question`

What does the professor want the student to do next?
Ⓐ Set the date of the next writing conference
Ⓑ Go to a class about language poetry
Ⓒ Try to write a language poem himself
Ⓓ Read another language poem

 이것을 듣고 답을 찾아라 !

Future Action 문제 유형은 주로 대화의 끝부분에 단서가 나온다. 학생의 문제점에 대해 교수나 직원이 해결책을 제안할 때, 그에 대한 학생의 응답이 긍정적인지 아닌지를 듣는 것이 핵심이다. 예시 대화에서처럼 'I'll ~'이라고 학생이 긍정적인 응답을 할 경우 Future Action 문제의 정답으로 연결될 수 있기 때문이다.

지문 해석
교수: 맞아요. 음… 내가 준 읽기 자료 목록에는 없지만, Silliman의 시 〈알파벳〉을 읽어본다면, 내가 무슨 말을 하는지 알 수 있을 거예요. 그 시는… 전통적인 시와 언어시의 중간 정도에 있다고 보면 돼요. 아, 그래도 여전히 잘 모르겠으면, 그 주제에 관해 준비한 강의가 있어요. 수업 시간에 더 잘 알 수 있을 거예요.
학생: 감사합니다. 읽어보도록 할게요.

문제 해석 및 정답
학생이 다음에 할 일은?
Ⓐ 다음 writing conference 날짜를 정하기
Ⓑ 언어시에 관한 수업에 참석하기
Ⓒ 직접 언어시를 한 편 써보기
Ⓓ 또 다른 언어시를 읽어보기

어휘
conference 학회

Chapter I 047

10 Requirement

1 문제의 핵심

paper, part-time job, graduation, parking과 같은 다양한 상황에서 필요한 정보, 필요한 서류, 요구되는 절차 및 정책 등을 묻는 문제 유형이다.

2 문제의 예시

professor	· What information does the student still **need to** get from the professor?
paper	· What information **should** the student include in his report?
	· What are two of **the criteria** the professor will use to evaluate student's paper?
library	· What does the student **need to** do before he can use any rare books?
bookstore	· What is the bookstore's **policy** about giving refunds on books?

3 100% 문제 공략법

Conversation에서 다루고 있는 상황과 Requirement 문제는 논리적으로 연결되어 출제되는 경향이 있다. 아래의 상황 중 graduation 상황을 예로 든다면, 대화 중 credit이라는 말이 나오면 대부분 '졸업에 필요한 학점' 또는 '부족한 학점'에 관한 내용으로 연결되고, 그에 관한 Requirement 문제가 출제될 가능성이 높다.

- 01 **paper**: 보고서에 어떤 내용을 반드시 포함해야 하는가
- 02 **part-time job**: 지원 시 요구되는 서류
- 03 **graduation**: 졸업 시 요구되는 학점
- 04 **program**: 지원하려는 과에서 신청을 위해 요구하는 서류 (Eg. 토플점수, 성적증명서, 추천서 등)
- 05 **parking**: 학생은 몇 시부터 몇 시까지만 주차할 수 있다는 조건
- 06 **class**: prerequisite선수과목을 이수해야만 고급과목을 수강 신청할 수 있음

Tip research 참여의 경우에는 요구되는 서류나 절차뿐만 아니라, research에 참여할 수 있는 condition조건도 (Eg. 4학년 이상만 research에 참여할 수 있음) 자주 문제로 출제된다.

4 대화 속 단서 표현

필요나 의무를 나타내는 다양한 표현이 단서가 된다.

- policy, requirement
- It is necessary ~
- It is required to ~
- You need to do[have] ~

▶ **Example Question**

Script

Librarian: Okay. What type of demographics do you need? Do you need basic population statistics, like total population, male to female… and what not?
Student: Yeah. Population for sure, literacy rate and… uh… You know, like if women tend to live longer than men…

Question

What kind of information about European cities does the student need?
Choose two answers.
Ⓐ Average temperatures
Ⓑ Population
Ⓒ Size by area
Ⓓ Average lifespan of citizens

이것을 듣고 답을 찾아라!

도서관에서 자료를 찾을 때 도서관 사서가 "어떤 정보가 필요하니?"라고 물어보는 부분에서 Requirement 문제가 나올 것을 예측하고 정답을 들어야 한다. 학생이 필요한 정보가 한 가지가 아니라면 한 가지 이상의 답을 고르는 문제가 나올 수도 있다.

지문 해석
사서: 알겠어요. 어떤 종류의 인구 통계 자료가 필요한 거죠? 기본적인 인구 통계가 필요한가요? 총 인구, 남성 대 여성 등등 같은?
학생: 네. 인구는 물론 필요하고요, 문맹률과… 음… 여성이 남성보다 오래 사는 경향이 있다… 뭐 이런 거 있잖아요.

문제 해석 및 정답
유럽 도시들에 대해 학생이 필요로 하는 정보의 종류는? (두 가지 선택)
Ⓐ 평균 기온
Ⓑ 인구
Ⓒ 지역별 크기
Ⓓ 시민들의 평균 수명

어휘
demographics 인구 통계   statistics 통계, 수치   literacy rate 문맹률   life expectancy 기대수명   lifespan 수명

11 Opinion / Attitude

1 문제의 핵심

- 걱정/위로 type: 특정 상황에 대한 교수의 의견이나 학생의 태도를 묻는 문제로, 걱정이나 격려를 하는 부분에서 문제가 출제된다. 즉, 학생의 태도(걱정), 교수의 태도(학생을 안심시킴)에 관한 문제가 자주 출제된다.
- 긍정/부정 type: 특정 상황에 대한 태도가 긍정적인지 부정적인지를 묻는 문제이다. 예를 들어 교수가 "이 과목을 들으면 취직할 때 도움이 될 것 같다"라고 말한다면 교수는 그 과목에 대해 긍정적인 opinion을 갖고 있는 것이다. 반면 교수가 "수업에 자주 결석하면 성적에 도움이 안되겠지?"라고 말한다면 교수는 학생의 결석에 대해 부정적인 opinion을 갖고 있는 것이다.

2 문제의 예시

- How does the man **feel** at the end of the conversation?
- What is the man's **attitude** toward his new university?
- What is the professor's **opinion** of the other students in the woman's group?

3 100% 문제 공략법

대화를 들을 때 화자의 attitude가 긍정적인지 부정적인지를 파악해야 하며, 그에 대한 다른 화자의 반응이 긍정/부정/위로 중 어떤 것인지 주의하여 들어야 한다.

01 걱정/위로 type

  paper: 학생이 paper에 대해서 걱정함 (attitude: worry about)
  → 교수는 학생에게 할 수 있다고 격려함 (attitude: encouraging)
  Teaching Assistant(TA): 학생이 누구를 가르쳐 본 경험이 없어서 걱정함 (attitude: worry about)
  → 교수는 모두 처음엔 잘 못 한다고 하더니 나중엔 잘하더라고 격려함 (attitude: encouraging)

02 긍정/부정 type

  학생이 이 전공을 공부하면 취직이 잘 될 것 같다고 말함
  → 교수는 나도 이 전공을 공부하고 여러 곳에서 job offer를 받았다고 말함 (opinion: 긍정적/동의)

4 대화 속 단서 표현

걱정하는 표현과 이에 대해 격려하거나 공감하는 표현에 주목해야 한다.

- [걱정] worry about ~
- [걱정] I'm not sure if I can handle ~
- [격려] It is possible ~
- [격려] You are not the only one struggling with ~
- [공감] Yes, you are right.

▶ **Example Question**

Script

Employee: I mean, it is a well-known company, right? Hey, didn't you mention that you were an engineering major before you switched? That's great, because companies always prefer people with a computer background.

Question

What's the employee's attitude toward the student's prior major?
Ⓐ She is worried that it did not give him enough expertise.
Ⓑ She admires the way he made a difficult decision.
Ⓒ She believes that it was useless.
Ⓓ She thinks that it will help him get a position.

> 이것을 듣고 답을 찾아라!
> 학생의 전공이 구직 시 도움이 될 것 같다고 직원이 긍정적인 opinion을 나타내는 부분(That's great)에서 Opinion / Attitude 유형 문제와 연결될 것임을 예측할 수 있다.

지문 해석
직원: 유명한 회사잖아요? 이봐요, 학생이 전공을 바꾸기 전에 공학 전공이었다고 하지 않았나요? 그거 잘됐네요. 회사들은 항상 컴퓨터 관련 배경 지식이 있는 사람들을 선호하니까요.

문제 해석 및 정답
학생의 이전 전공에 대한 직원의 태도는?
Ⓐ 그에게 충분한 전문지식을 주지 못했다고 걱정한다.
Ⓑ 그가 어려운 결정을 내린 것을 칭찬한다.
Ⓒ 그것이 쓸모 없었다고 생각한다.
Ⓓ 그가 일자리를 구하는 데 도움이 될 것이라 여긴다.

어휘
switch 바꾸다   expertise 전문 지식[기술]

12 Replay Question (Headset)

1 문제의 핵심

본문의 일부를 다시 들려주고 화자의 의도를 묻는 문제 유형이다. 예를 들어, 교수가 "숙제를 안 내려거든 학교에 나오지 마"라고 말한 문장을 다시 들려주고 "학교에 나오지 마"가 의미하는 것을 묻는 문제의 경우, 문맥상 '교수는 학생이 숙제를 내기를 바란다'는 보기가 정답이 된다. 반면 대화의 문맥을 전혀 고려하지 않은 '교수는 학생이 학교에 나오지 않기를 바란다'는 보기는 오답이다. 즉, 화자의 의도를 문맥을 통해 정확하게 짚어내야 하는 문제이다.

2 문제의 예시

- Why does the man **say this**?
- What does the woman mean **when she says this**?
- What does the advisor imply **when she says this**?

3 100% 문제 공략법

01 Type 1

"Listen to part of conversation. Then answer the question."이라는 지시문이 나오고 지문의 특정 부분(보통 3~4문장 정도)을 다시 들려준다. 이후 "What does the professor mean when he says this?"라는 지시문이 나오고 앞에서 다시 들려주었던 부분 중 한 문장을 한 번 더 들려준다. 이런 유형의 문제는, 다시 들려준 내용의 문맥을 토대로 하여 문제로 출제된 문장의 의미/의도를 파악하는 문제이다.

02 Type 2

Type 1의 경우처럼 지문의 특정 부분을 다시 들려주지 않고, "What does the professor mean when she says this?"와 같은 지시문 뒤에 하나의 문장만 다시 들려주고 그 문장의 의미를 묻는다. 이런 유형의 문제는 본문 전체 내용을 토대로 주어진 문장의 의미를 파악하는 문제이다.

4 대화 속 단서 표현

Replay 문제 유형은 지문에 특정한 단서 표현이 없다. 단, 문제를 풀 때 문장 그대로의 1차적인 의미가 아니라 배경이 되는 문장 혹은 전체 지문의 내용을 토대로 화자의 진짜 의도를 파악해야 한다.

Eg. Man: Do you want to play tennis?

　　Woman: I have a headache.

What does the woman mean when she says this?

> I have a headache.

Ⓐ She is sick.
Ⓑ She doesn't want to play tennis.

→ 위 문제에서 정답은 (B)이다. 다시 듣기 문제는 문장의 문자 그대로의 의미를 나타낸 것은 오답이며 문맥상 화자의 의도가 정답이다.

▶ **Example Question**

Script

Professor: Definitely. I suggest you do some more research on your topic and find something slightly more specific that you can focus on.
Student: I've already done that. Well, I tried to, anyway. 🎧 To tell you the truth, it was just more than I could handle.

Question

What does the student mean when she says this?

To tell you the truth, it was just more than I could handle.

Ⓐ She could not understand the resources she used.
Ⓑ She did not have enough time to finish her project.
Ⓒ She found an overwhelming amount of information.
Ⓓ She has already submitted a new topic to the professor.

> 이것을 듣고 답을 찾아라!
> Replay Question 문제 유형은 기본적으로는 Imply 문제 유형의 성격을 강하게 지니고 있다. 다만, Replay Question의 경우 다시 들려주는 문장에 암시된 화자의 의도를 알아내는 것이 핵심이다. 연구 주제를 좀 더 구체화하기 위해 조사를 더 해 보라는 교수의 제안에, 이미 조사를 해 봤는데 자신이 다룰 수 있는 것보다 더 많은 내용을 찾았다는 학생의 대답은 문맥상 '자료의 양이 압도적으로 많다'는 것을 암시하고 있다.

지문 해석
교수: 물론이죠. 학생이 주제에 대해 조사를 좀 더 해서 초점을 맞출 수 있는 좀 더 구체적인 무언가를 찾아보았으면 좋겠네요.
학생: 이미 그렇게 했어요. 음, 어쨌든 그렇게 하려고 노력은 했지요. 사실대로 말씀 드리면, 제가 다룰 수 있는 것보다 너무 많았어요.

문제 해석 및 정답
학생이 다음과 같이 말할 때 의미하는 것은?

사실대로 말씀 드리면, 제가 다룰 수 있는 것보다 너무 많았어요.

Ⓐ 그녀는 자신이 이용한 자료를 이해하지 못했다.
Ⓑ 그녀는 프로젝트를 끝낼 충분한 시간이 없었다.
Ⓒ 그녀는 엄청난 양의 정보를 찾았다.
Ⓓ 그녀는 이미 교수에게 새로운 주제를 제출했다.

어휘
specific 구체적인   resource 자료   overwhelming 압도적인

Practice Questions II

[01 ~ 05] Listen to a conversation between a student and his zoology professor. Then answer the questions.

01 Why does the student visit his professor?
  Ⓐ He has a lot of extra time.
  Ⓑ He is interested in the zoology seminar.
  Ⓒ He wants to volunteer at the local park.
  Ⓓ He is looking for ways to improve his grade.

02 What does the professor suggest that the student do?
  Ⓐ Write a report on zoo keeping
  Ⓑ Help with household chores
  Ⓒ Rewrite his last report
  Ⓓ Drop a class to lighten his schedule

03 Why does the professor mention zookeepers?
- Ⓐ To recommend someone who can give career advice
- Ⓑ To explain what work is required
- Ⓒ To explain how to observe animals
- Ⓓ To emphasize the importance of feeding animals

04 What is mentioned as an advantage of the Volunteer and Observe program?
- Ⓐ Students can feed zoo animals.
- Ⓑ Students can receive hands-on experience.
- Ⓒ Students can visit the zoo whenever they like.
- Ⓓ Students can choose how much work to do.

05 How is the Volunteer and Observe program similar to the seminar?
- Ⓐ Both require an understanding of zoology.
- Ⓑ Both involve a significant amount of paperwork.
- Ⓒ Both give volunteers a chance to observe animals.
- Ⓓ Both take place during the same set schedule.

Conversation

Conversation Topics

Conversation Topics

(1) Instructor's Office Hours
학생이 교수님을 찾아가서 수업 내용(class) 중 이해가 안 되는 것에 대해 질문을 하거나, course grade, exam, field trip, paper, research, major와 관련된 내용을 상담하는 상황이 나온다.

(2) Service Encounters
학생이 class registrar office와 같은 대학 사무실이나 post office, gym과 같은 생활하면서 종종 가는 곳들을 방문하여 어떤 문제점에 관해 이야기를 하고, 담당자가 이에 대한 해결책을 제시하는 대화 상황이 주로 제시된다.

Chapter II

Conversation Topics

Unit 1
Instructor's Office Hours

01_ **Class**
02_ **Course Grade / Exam**
03_ **Field Trip**
04_ **Paper**
05_ **Project / Research**
06_ **Major**

Class

상황별 출제포인트
- ♀1 Difference
- ♀2 Solution (Suggestion)
- ♀3 Example
- ♀4 Problem
- ♀5 Opinion / Attitude

Situation 1. Literature Class

literature 수업에서, 셰익스피어 원작 작품을 공연에 올릴 때 기존의 모든 사람들은 원작과 똑같은 대사, 무대장치 등을 사용했는데, 어느 한 감독은 셰익스피어 원작을 다르게 해석하여 공연을 올렸다고 말한다. 다른 감독들은 등장인물에 대해서 성적인 묘사를 하지 않았지만 이 감독은 표현했고, 다른 감독들은 숲에서 요정이 등장하면 forest setting 숲 속 배경을 쓴 반면 이 감독은 종이로 무대장치를 만들었다.♀1 학생이 특정 작가의 연극에 대해서 paper보고서를 쓰고 싶은데 자료가 없다고 하자♀4 교수는 관련 논문이 도서관에 많이 있으니 reference참고문헌로 이용하라♀2고 조언한다.

→ conversation에서 문학작품을 소재로 하는 경우, lecture 지문과 마찬가지로 문학작품이나 작가 간의 차이점 등이 출제될 수 있다.

Situation 2. Biology Class

biology 수업 내용에 따르면, 나방이 말벌 색을 띄는 것처럼 다른 종족을 속이기 위해 위장하는 것은 많이 보았지만, frog처럼 같은 종족을 속이기 위해 위장하는 경우는 보지 못했다고 한다.♀3

→ 이와 같은 Example 문제가 종종 출제된다.

학생은 교수가 지난 수업시간에 언급한 game theory가 이해가 안 된다♀4고 말한다.

→ 학생이 수업내용을 이해하지 못해서 생기는 Problem 문제가 출제될 수 있다.

그러자, 교수는 computer 판매를 예로 들어 game theory를 설명한다. 컴퓨터 판매업자에게 경쟁자가 많아지면, 이윤이 적어지더라도 더 낮은 가격에 판매해 판매량을 늘리려고 한다. 이렇게 상황에 따라 살아남기 위한 방법이 바뀌듯이, biology에서의 game theory는 동물이 바뀐 환경에 어떻게 적응하는지를 보여 주는 것♀3이라고 설명한다. 학생이 자료조사를 할 때 통계를 내야 하는 것에 대해 걱정이 된다고 말하자, 교수는 학생에게 여기서 말하는 통계는 간단한 수준이니 걱정할 필요 없다♀5고 위로한다.

Situation 3. Marketing Class

대학원 또는 취직에 관심이 있는 학생이 어느 수업을 들으면 진로에 더 도움이 될지 조언을 구하는 상황이 출제된다. 예를 들어, marketing 전공으로 grad school대학원에 가고 싶은 학생이 PR(Public Relations)대외홍보 수업과 advertising광고 수업 중에 어떤 것을 듣는 게 더 좋을지♀4 문의한다. 교수는 두 과목의 차이점을 설명하고, 대학원 등록금이 비싸니 신중하게 고려하라고♀2 제안한다.

핵/심/표/현

- academic calendar   학사일정
- academic conference   학술회의
- approach   n. 접근법
- assign   v. 할당하다
- assignment   n. 과제물
- assure   v. 확신시키다
- attitude   n. 태도
- audit   v. 청강하다
- auditor   n. 청강자
- better off   더 좋은, 더 나은
- break   n. 휴식
- bulletin   n. 공시, 공고
- class discussion   토론 수업
- computer lab   n. 컴퓨터실
- consistency   n. 일정함
- contemporary   adj. 동시대의, 당대의
- content   n. 내용(물), 항목
- conventional   adj. 전통적인, 관례의
- criticize   v. 비난[비판]하다
- curriculum   n. 교과 과정
- deadline   n. 마감, 기한
- distribution   n. 분배, 배포
- emphasize   v. 강조하다
- excuse   v. 실례하다, 변명하다
- field trip   n. 현장 학습[연구]
- frustrate   v. 좌절시키다
- genre   n. 장르
- indicate   v. 가리키다, 암시하다
- interpretation   n. 해석, 설명
- lab report   연구실 보고서
- laboratory   n. 연구실, 실험실
- material   n. 자료
- mean   n. 평균
- miss   v. 놓치다
- notice   v. 알아차리다
- policy   n. 정책
- postpone   v. 미루다
- print-out   n. 프린트 물
- proposal   n. 제안
- protagonist   n. 주인공
- reinforce   v. 보강하다, 강조하다
- representative   n. 대표
- semester   n. 학기
- spring break   n. 봄방학
- subject matter   소재
- submit   v. 제출하다
- summer session   여름 학기[강좌]
- term   n. 용어
- term paper   n. 학기말 보고서
- thesis   n. 논문, 주제

Sample Questions

[01 ~ 05] **Listen to a conversation between a student and her film professor. Then answer the questions.** MP3 06   정답 및 해석 p. 014

Note-taking

- Problem:

- Requirement:

- Limitation:

- Requirement:

- Suggestion:

01 Why does the student go to see the professor about his cinema course?
   Ⓐ To tell him she's no longer interested in taking his course
   Ⓑ To ask about which advanced courses she has to take later
   Ⓒ To find out if she can take the course without getting credit
   Ⓓ To discuss how to improve her poor grades in his course

02 What characteristics of the course does the professor emphasize?
Choose two answers.
Ⓐ It is very demanding.
Ⓑ Too many students take it.
Ⓒ It cannot be audited by students.
Ⓓ It is a requirement for film majors.

03 According to the professor, what are the two disadvantages of auditing the film course? Choose two answers.
Ⓐ The student may not be able to take advanced film courses.
Ⓑ The student cannot get a good grade.
Ⓒ The student cannot attend the movie screenings.
Ⓓ The student cannot participate in class discussions.

04 What does the professor suggest the student do?
Ⓐ Audit his course to see if it interests her
Ⓑ Take the course when she is not so hectic
Ⓒ Concentrate on her work this semester
Ⓓ Think about what courses to take next year

Listen again to part of the conversation. Then answer the question. 🔊 MP3 06_1

05 What does the student imply about class discussions?
Ⓐ She thinks that they will be too difficult for students who audit the class.
Ⓑ She is afraid that there will be too many students talking at once.
Ⓒ She had thought that students who audit the class could take part in them.
Ⓓ She believes that the students who take the class for credit are selfish.

▶ **Question Review**

Introduction

Problem
수업을 듣고 싶지만 이미 15학점을 수강 신청 함

Requirement
학생에게 요구되는 것이 많음

Limitation / Headset
청강만 하는 학생은 토론 수업에 참여할 수 없음

Listen to a conversation between a student and her film professor.

Student(female): Professor Wooden?
Professor(male): Hi. You must be Louisa Smith. Come on in and have a seat.
S: Thanks.
P: So, you wanted to see me about the History of Cinema course? I'm assuming that you want to see if it would interest you.
S: Oh... No, I definitely want to take it. But, you know, the thing is, I'm already registered for 15 credits, and I don't know if I have space for another. I mean, I asked around and heard that your classes require a lot of reading, writing reports, and well... I guess I don't want too much on my plate.
P: All right, fair enough. What year are you in? Didn't you say you're in your first year?
S: Right.
P: Then, why don't you just take my class next year?
S: Well, I guess I could do that. But I really love film, and the high school I went to, they didn't teach cinema. I'd hate to wait another year.
P: Okay, but, **Q2-A** **I have to give you fair warning. This might be an introductory course, but it's going to take a lot of commitment on your part. You're going to have to come to the lectures and do the readings, and there are also weekly film screenings and four papers, not to mention the final exam.** But, then again, I'm sure you've already heard all about it.
S: Yeah, but... Actually, **Q1** **what I really wanted to find out is if I could maybe audit the class.** I don't really need the credits, you know? I thought it'd be nice just to listen to your lectures and see the films.
P: Oh, then that wouldn't be a problem at all. The lecture room is big enough. Even though there're a lot of students taking the class, there's usually enough room for auditors. If you audit, there won't be a final and you wouldn't have to write the papers either, but there's a catch. I find it funny, but, **Q3-D** **what I found bothers students, I mean, the ones who audit, the most is...** 🎧 **Q5** **well.. they can't participate in class discussions.**
S: Wait a minute. We can't?
P: I'm sorry, but that's the university policy. It's like that at most schools. I mean, it's a big class already, so if we let everyone participate and everyone starts talking...

S: Oh, sure. I guess that wouldn't be fair to the students who are actually taking the class for credit. Oh, wow… I need to think about this a little more…

P: Mmm-hmm. There's also something else you need to ponder about. Do you plan on taking advanced courses on film or even becoming a film major?

S: Yeah, I'm actually considering it.

P: Well, **Q2-D for most film courses, History of Cinema is a prerequisite course. You're going to have to take it.**

S: Oh, I had no idea. So, then, the question is, **Q3-A if I audit the class and don't take it for credit, would I still be able to take advanced film courses?**

P: Technically not. Well, there are some professors who might let you in, but I wouldn't count on it, you know, especially for those advanced classes. They fill up pretty quickly with people who have taken the prerequisites.

S: I see. So, then…

P: So, if you want to take more film courses in the future, you might want to just take my class for credit. You might be better off not auditing my class this semester. Of course, **Q4 if you're too busy, you might want to postpone it until you can handle it.**

S: Hmm… I'll have to think about this a little more. Anyway, thanks.

Requirement
History of Cinema는 film 과정을 듣기 위한 선수 과목

Suggestion
여유가 생기면 학점 과정으로 들으라고 제안

Practice Questions

[01 ~ 05] Listen to a conversation between a student and his English professor. Then answer the questions. 🔊 MP3 07 정답 및 해석 p. 015

Note-taking

01   What is the conversation mainly about?
   Ⓐ Experiences the student had with famous authors during a writing conference
   Ⓑ Different types of subject matter that language poets use
   Ⓒ The student's difficulties in understanding the point of language poetry
   Ⓓ The differences between a poem's language and its metaphors

02 According to the professor, how is language poetry different from traditional poetry?
   Ⓐ It relies on the reader's understanding of rhythm and mood.
   Ⓑ The poet has a specific purpose when writing it.
   Ⓒ There is more imagery used in it than in conventional poetry.
   Ⓓ It uses nothing but words to make readers decide what it is about.

03 What does the professor imply about language poets?
   Ⓐ They make their poems difficult to understand on purpose.
   Ⓑ They often use words that do not fit the context.
   Ⓒ They cover many different topics in their poems.
   Ⓓ They have a great understanding of the alphabet.

04 Why does the professor mention 'multicolored apple trees'?
   Ⓐ To point out the best way to understand Silliman's poetry
   Ⓑ To confirm that the student understood the reading
   Ⓒ To give an example of words used in language poetry
   Ⓓ To illustrate a technique used in traditional poetry

05 What will the student probably do next?
   Ⓐ Set the date of the next writing conference
   Ⓑ Go to a class about language poetry
   Ⓒ Try to write a language poem himself
   Ⓓ Read another language poem

02 Course Grade / Exam

상황별 출제포인트	Q1 Cause Q2 Result / Finding / Research Q3 Example Q4 Solution (Suggestion) Q5 Problem

Situation 1. Biology Exam

운동부 학생이 poor grade^{안 좋은 성적}를 받은 것을 보고 교수가 그 이유를 묻는 상황. 학생은 cell division^{세포 분열}에 관한 시험을 봤는데, cram^{벼락치기}을 했더니 시험 당일 답이 잘 기억나지 않았다고 말한다.^{Q1} 교수는 cram을 하면 brain^뇌에 input^{입력}이 잘 안되기 때문에, 하루에 6시간을 공부하는 것보다 하루에 1시간씩 6일간 공부하는 것이 더 좋다^{Q2}는 연구 결과에 대해 얘기한다. 교수는 학생에게 "너는 운동선수니까 muscle^{근육}을 brain이라고 생각해 봐.^{Q3} 운동연습을 시합 하루 전날에 몰아서 하면 안되겠지?"라고 말한다.
→ 이와 같이 시험을 잘 보지 못한 이유, 공부습관에 대한 연구 결과, 그리고 muscle처럼 예를 든 부분 등이 시험에 출제될 수 있다.

Situation 2. Exam Preview

교수가 marketing 과목 시험에 대한 preview^{예습}를 해 주는 상황. 교수는 fitness center^{헬스 클럽}를 예로 들면서, 요즘 fitness center가 많아지고 있는데 어떤 marketing strategy^{마케팅 전략}를 쓰면 customer^{고객}를 더 모을 수 있겠는지 묻는다. 집에는 구비할 수 없는 비싸고 좋은 장비를 설치해 사람을 모을 수 있을 것 같다,^{Q4} 또는 요가나 에어로빅과 같은 좋은 수업을 많이 개설하면 사람들이 더 많이 올 것 같다^{Q4}고 학생이 대답한다. 또한 교수는 도서관을 예로 들면서, 요즘은 인터넷으로 책을 많이 읽는데 저자 사인회 같은 행사를 유치하면 사람들을 도서관으로 오게 할 수 있다^{Q3}고 말한다. 그리고, 시험에서도 다른 상황에 적용 가능한 marketing strategy를 물을 것이니 이에 대비하라고 조언한다.

Situation 3. Final Exam

학생이 교수에게 final exam^{기말고사}에 대해서 문의하는 상황. 시험범위가 학기 중에 배운 모든 내용인지 아니면 mid-term exam^{중간고사} 이후부터 배운 내용인지 묻는다. 교수가 학기 중 배운 모든 것이 시험에 나온다고 하자, 학생은 중간고사 때 hydrological cycle^{물의 순환}의 개념을 이해하지 못해서 시험을 잘 보지 못했다고 말한다.^{Q5} 교수는 tutoring center^{과외 센터}에 가면 이 과목을 전공하는 대학원생들이 있으니 도움을 받을 수 있다^{Q4}고 조언한다.
→ 시험준비에 필요한 것이나 시험 전 학생이 겪는 문제, 또는 교수가 제시하는 해결 방안 등이 자주 출제된다.

핵/심/표/현

- academic dismissal　퇴학
- academic probation　유급
- academic warning　학사경고
- attendance　n. 출석
- basic course　기본 과정[과목]
- blue book　n. (청색 표지의) 대학 시험 답안 책자
- console　v. 위로하다
- course catalogue　과목 목록
- course syllabus　강의계획서
- credit course　학점 과정
- credit　n. (대학의) 학점
- department chair　학과장
- distinction　n. 구별
- extension　n. (마감 기한) 연장
- extracurricular activity　n. 과외[교과외] 활동
- final exam　기말시험
- formal compliant　정식 항의
- grade point average　평균 학점(=GPA)
- grade　n. 점수
- guideline　n. 지침, 안내 글
- handbook　n. 편람, 안내서
- manageable　adj. 관리[감당]할 수 있는
- marking scheme　평가[채점] 기준
- mid-term exam　중간고사
- mix-up　n. 혼동, 혼란
- non-credit course　무학점 과정
- official document　공문서
- optional class　교양 과목
- passing grade　합격 점수
- peer review　동료 평가
- prerequisite　n. 선수 과목(미리 수강해야 하는 과목)
- proctor　n. 시험 감독관
- refine　v. 다듬다
- register　v. 등록하다
- report card　성적표
- request　n./v. 요구[하다]
- required writing course　필수 작문 수업
- retake　v. 재수강하다
- sign up　v. 신청하다
- student rank　학년
- take-home exam　재택 시험
- intermediate level course　중급 과정[과목]
- transcript　n. 성적증명서
- true-false exam　T/F(오엑스)문제의 시험
- tutor　n. 과외교사
- verify　v. 증명하다
- workload　n. 학업량, 작업량

Sample Questions

[01 ~ 05] **Listen to a conversation between a student and a professor. Then answer the questions.** MP3 08   정답 및 해석 p. 018

Note-taking

- Problem 1:

- Requirement:

- Problem 2:

- Opinion:

- Problem 3:

01 Why does the student go to see the professor?
   Ⓐ To talk about report he is writing
   Ⓑ To discuss a grade he got on a paper
   Ⓒ To ask for advice on how to conclude a paper
   Ⓓ To explain why he did not finish a paper

02 According to the professor, what was wrong with the student's paper?
Choose two answers.
Ⓐ It only focused on a single topic.
Ⓑ It was plagiarized from other sources.
Ⓒ It did not include enough examples about birds.
Ⓓ It was missing a complete list of sources.
Ⓔ It did not include a proper conclusion.

03 What does the professor say about the style the student learned in his writing class?
Ⓐ It is not what she believes to be proper.
Ⓑ It is the required style at the school.
Ⓒ It would have improved his paper.
Ⓓ It is only good for introductions.

04 What will the professor do for the student?
Ⓐ She will explain to his parents what happened.
Ⓑ She will talk to the writing lecturer about his teaching methods.
Ⓒ She will grade the paper a second time.
Ⓓ She will grade another paper the student writes instead.

Listen again to part of the conversation. Then answer the question. 🔊 MP3 08_1

05 What does the professor imply when she says this?
Ⓐ The student should focus on the topic of the paper.
Ⓑ The student may have copied his material from a previous paper.
Ⓒ The student should do more research that is relevant to the paper.
Ⓓ The student could probably write another paper to get a better grade.

▶ **Question Review**

Introduction	**Listen to a conversation between a student and a professor.** **Professor(female):** Hey Brian, what can I help you with? **Student(male):** Professor Johnson. **Q1** I, uh… am coming from the computer lab. I just saw the grades you posted online, um… for the biology paper that was due this Tuesday.
Problem (1) 출처 목록이 빠짐 **Requirement** 보고서에 출처 목록이 포함되어야 함	P: I'm glad you're here. I looked at the paper you handed in… but some things just didn't add up. I mean, I saw the footnotes in the paper, but **Q2-D** I didn't see a full list of sources at the end of the paper. You have to include the sources for all your quotes, you know. That's why I was wondering if maybe some pages of your paper were missing. S: Oh! That page must have fallen off. I can get a copy of it to you by tomorrow.
Problem (2) 보고서가 열린 결론으로 끝남	P: Great. And while you're at it… **Q2-E** I think another page was missing too. I didn't really see a conclusion to the paper. Let's see… there we go… Yeah, you, you didn't tie up the ideas. You needed to have a paragraph that did that, that is, uh, unless you meant to leave the paper open-ended. S: Oh, I thought it had to be open-ended. You know that mandatory writing class all first-year students have to take? Well, I learned that a good conclusion should always raise new questions instead of just summarizing whatever was written in the paper. P: And that's what you attempted in your paper on bird migration for my class? S: Uh-huh. The instructor said that we should do it in all of our writing. So I just assumed it was a required way to write here, required at the university. I actually thought I was doing a good thing.
Opinion ◯ disagree	P: Well, **Q3** learning something in one course and implementing it in another is great, but, you see, the thing is, that's not the standard style of writing in this school. In fact, I find it hard to believe that that's what they teach in that writing class, because to be quite frank, I don't agree with that style of writing. I think that you'll find most of my peers, um, your other science professors, will agree with me. A good conclusion should primarily focus on tying up the ideas of the paper. S: Okay. Well, to tell you the truth, that's what I've always been taught too, but, um, this writing professor, he said that leaving the conclusion open-ended could be a better way to end a paper. P: Brian, I didn't know any of this when I graded your paper. I just couldn't grasp why the conclusion seemed… well, so illogical. You see, you have

Problem (3)
보고서의 주제와 무관한 내용이 많음

Headset

to summarize what has come before first. Then you might want to point to a new idea or question. But then again, you do risk introducing something irrelevant.
S: Irrelevant?
P: Yes! I mean, you have lots of nice examples about birds, but you also have a fairly lengthy section on butterflies at the end of the paper. I just didn't understand why you did that in a paper about bird migration. 🎧 **Q5 I mean, it's true that butterflies migrate too, but that's a totally different paper altogether.** But I get what you were trying to do now.
S: No, I know butterfly migration is different… No wonder I got such a poor grade. I can rewrite the paper if you'd like.
P: No, no, there's no need to. Look, **Q4 now that I know where you're coming from, I'll go over your paper again.**
S: Okay.
P: Let's meet again next week.

Practice Questions

[01 ~ 05] **Listen to a conversation between a student and his English professor. Then answer the questions.** MP3 09 정답 및 해석 p. 020

Note-taking

01 Why does the professor ask the student to come to her office?
Ⓐ To ask the student what he will do for spring break
Ⓑ To show the student how to choose a proper topic
Ⓒ To tell the student that he needs to improve his grade
Ⓓ To encourage the student to revise a paper he wrote

02 Why does the student hesitate before agreeing to the professor's request?
Ⓐ He is not sure his effort would be successful.
Ⓑ He is unclear about what the professor wants him to do.
Ⓒ He has too much of a workload related to school.
Ⓓ He does not have the motivation to write a better paper.

03 What does the professor suggest the student do to improve his paper?
Ⓐ Include more examples to illustrate the main point
Ⓑ Exclude excessive information that distracts readers
Ⓒ Cut out the unnecessary technology part on his paper
Ⓓ Give more details on technological terms that are difficult to follow

04 Why does the professor mention the number of pages on the assignment?
Ⓐ She thinks the paper was too long for the student to revise.
Ⓑ She believes the student's paper will be better if it's longer.
Ⓒ She wants to point the proper way to approach a paper.
Ⓓ She thinks the assignment was too difficult to finish on time.

05 In what way does the professor say the student should change the introduction of his paper?
Ⓐ To make it catch the reader's attention
Ⓑ To reflect changes made in the paper
Ⓒ To include more specific details
Ⓓ To correct spelling and grammar errors

03 Field Trip

상황별 출제포인트	♀1 **Problem** ♀2 **Solution (Suggestion)** ♀3 **Result / Finding / Research** ♀4 **Advantage**

Situation 1. Field Trip (1)

biology class^{생물 수업}에서 sea lion^{바다사자}을 보러 가는 field trip^{현장 학습}이 있는데, 학생의 physics class^{물리학 수업} 시험 날짜와 overlap^{겹치다}된다.♀1 물리학 교수가 field trip을 다른 날 가도 되는지 묻자, 학생이 동물 group^{무리}을 관찰하고 report paper^{보고서}를 제출하는 것으로 final exam을 대체하기 때문에 불가능하다고 대답한다. 그리고 biology class와 교수의 physics class를 동시에 듣는 학생이 많다고 말한다. 그렇다면 take-home exam^{재택 시험}을 내 줄 테니 field trip을 다녀와서 제출하라♀2고 교수가 제안한다.

→ 예시 상황에서는 언급되지 않았지만, **field trip 후 해야 할 연구 내용(Research)**에 대해서도 빈번하게 출제된다. 또한 **field trip**을 갈 때 발생하는 **문제점(Problem)**과 그 **해결 방법(Solution)**도 많이 출제되는 편이다.

Situation 2. Field Trip (2)

학생이 field trip에 참여해야 하는데, 경비가 개인 부담이라 걱정하고 있다. Michigan까지 one way ticket^{편도 승차권}은 살 수 있지만, round trip ticket^{왕복 승차권}은 비용이 만만치 않아서 가기 힘들다♀1고 학생이 교수에게 하소연한다. 교수는 Great lakes를 방문해서 주변 농경지에서 사용되는 pesticide^{살충제}가 호수에 미치는 영향♀3을 보기 위해 현지 답사를 가는 것이라고 말한다. 그리고 학생이 환경학과 대학원에 갈 계획이 있다면, 이 현장 학습이 대학원 진학에 도움이 많이 될 것♀4이라고 말한다. 교수는 학생에게, 학부생에게는 field trip^{현장 학습} grant^{지원금}가 많이 나오지 않지만, 지원금을 받을 수 있는지 알아 보겠다♀2고 얘기한다.

핵/심/표/현

- accompany   v. 동행하다, 함께 ...을 하다
- allocation   n. 할당, 분할
- assessment   n. 평가
- budge   v. 의견을 바꾸다
- car rental share   차 대여 요금 공동부담
- carpool   v. 승용차 함께 타기를 하다
- charter bus   전세버스
- coastline   n. 해안지대
- complete   v. 마치다, 끝내다
- depart   v. 출발하다, 시작하다
- designate   v. 지정하다, 지명하다
- destination   n. 도착지
- domestic   adj. 국내의
- expectation   n. 기대치, 예상
- explore   v. 탐험하다, 연구하다
- fare   n. 요금
- gather   v. 모이다, 모으다
- habitat   n. 서식지
- identify   v. 확인하다, 밝히다
- instruction   n. 지시, 설명
- investigate   v. 조사하다, 수사하다
- migration   n. 이주, 이동
- observation   n. 관찰
- observe   v. 관찰하다
- pollution   n. 오염
- potential   adj. 잠재적인
- preparedness   n. 준비된 상태, 준비성
- procurement   n. 입수, 획득
- provide   v. 제공하다
- recommend   v. 추천하다
- remote   adj. 외진, 외딴
- research assistant   연구 조교
- specimen   n. 표본, 견본
- teaching assistant   (대학의 수업) 조교
- teamwork   n. 협동심, 협동 작업
- traffic jam[congestion]   n. 교통 체증
- transportation   n. 교통수단
- unforeseen   adj. 예기치 않은, 뜻밖의
- volunteer   v. 자원 봉사하다   n. 자원 봉사(자)
- waiver form   포기 각서
- wildlife   n. 야생동물

Sample Questions

[01 ~ 05] **Listen to a conversation between a student and his environmental science professor. Then answer the questions.** MP3 10 정답 및 해설 p. 022

Note-taking

• problem:

• Research:

• Disadvantage:

• Suggestion:

• Advantage:

01   Why does the student go to see the professor?
        Ⓐ To ask about a class assignment
        Ⓑ To discuss ways to get extra credit
        Ⓒ To discuss ways to improve his grade
        Ⓓ To find out about a mid-semester project

02 What can be inferred about the students who participate in the field study?
   Ⓐ They have prior experience with similar work.
   Ⓑ They may initially know what they have to do.
   Ⓒ They are able to afford the trip on their own.
   Ⓓ They are willing to participate without credit.

03 What are the problems the student may face during the field study?
   Choose two answers.
   Ⓐ He may unintentionally damage the wildlife.
   Ⓑ He may experience dizziness and nausea.
   Ⓒ He may have a hard time finding a boat to charter.
   Ⓓ He has to pay for his own transportation.

04 What help does the professor offer the student?
   Ⓐ A free ride to the site
   Ⓑ Payment for his time
   Ⓒ A flexible work schedule
   Ⓓ An introduction to another student

05 What does the professor suggest to the student?
   Ⓐ He would be better off waiting until the next project.
   Ⓑ He might need to make his decision quickly.
   Ⓒ He should take his time before deciding.
   Ⓓ He can get more information at the career services office.

▶ **Question Review**

Introduction

Listen to a conversation between a student and his environmental science professor.

Student(male): Hi, >Q1> Professor Archer, you know how in class last week you said that you were looking for students who are interested in participating in your project on oyster habitats?

Professor(female): Of course. Are you thinking about it?

S: Yes, I am. It sounds really interesting, but, um… do I need to have any experience for these kinds of mid-semester projects?

Problem
field trip 경험이 전혀 없음

P: No, not really. I assume that most students taking introductory level classes would have little or no experience with field work, but that's okay.

S: Oh, good. That's a relief. Actually, that's why I want to participate in the project — to get experience.

P: I do, however, have to warn you about a few challenges you might face.

S: What do you mean?

Research
기름 유출이 해양 야생 동물에게 어떤 피해를 주는지를 연구

P: Well, as you know, we're studying the environmental impact on the coastline caused by commercial maritime activities. The area we're going to has been damaged by oil spills. The point of the project is to see how pollution can spread and damage marine wildlife on the coast. The area will be very polluted and may smell like gasoline. >Q3-B> **You might get nauseous.**

Disadvantage
(1) 메스껍고 뱃멀미를 겪을 수 있음

S: Oh, that's not a problem.

P: Another thing is it's in a pretty remote location, so we'll have to travel by boat. >Q3-B> **Some students who have never been on boats at sea tend to get a little seasick.** It's really hard to do anything when you're feeling dizzy on top of the smell.

S: I never thought about that, but I'm sure I'll manage.

P: Well, most do. And…

S: And?

P: Well, the university can only support the project to a certain extent, financially, I mean. They gave us enough funding to get a chartered boat and the equipment we'll be using, but I'm afraid the transportation costs, you know, getting to the harbor to take the boat, well, that's not part of the budget. >Q3-D> **You'll have to use your own money to travel there.**

(2) 학생이 교통비를 내야 함

S: Oh, no… I'm already short on cash… How much do you think it'll be?

P: Around 50 dollars or so… Tell you what. If that's too much for you, I'll

Suggestion

(1) 다른 학생 차량에 동승하도록 제안

(2) 결정을 서두르도록 제안

Advantage

참여한 학생에게 추가 학점을 주려고 고려 중

ask some students who might be driving there. Maybe you can carpool.

S: That'd be great. So… how many student volunteers are you looking for?

P: I'm shooting for seven or eight. ▶Q2 **I've asked for participants in all of the classes I teach. It's actually generated quite a lot of interest.** ▶Q5 **You might have to hurry up and decide.**

S: I really want to go, but it sounds like it could be a lot of work.

P: Well, ▶Q4 **I can introduce you to one of the students who has already been to the site. He can tell you how much work you should be expecting and what you'll be doing if you go there.** Just make sure you send me an email and ask for his contact info.

S: Thank you, I will.

P: Oh, and ▶Q2 **I've actually been considering offering extra credit for class because it is a lot of work. Extra credit is always a good incentive for students.** Why don't you ask the department office and ask if there's something you can do to get credit? You can always write a research paper or field report for a credit, you know.

S: That's a great idea!

P: Make sure you get back to me once you make your decision. I'll keep a spot open for you until next week, but I would appreciate it if you could tell me if you can't participate. Like I said, a lot of other students are interested. I also have an orientation next week. The time is still to be decided, but you should definitely check it out even if you decide not to go. There're a lot of things you can learn there.

S: Okay, I'll try to inform you of my decision as soon as possible. Thanks a lot for your time.

Practice Questions

[01 ~ 05] Listen to a conversation between a student and his English professor. Then answer the questions. ◀ MP3 11   정답 및 해석 p. 024

Note-taking

01 Which places does the student prefer the most? Choose three places and put them in order.

Scotland – Great Britain – France – Germany – Switzerland

02 What does the student imply when he mentions the French Literature class he is taking?
 Ⓐ He doesn't think he needs to go to France.
 Ⓑ He has excellent grades in his French class.
 Ⓒ He is very competent when it comes to French.
 Ⓓ He wants to learn more about France.

03 What does the professor say about the program in Scotland?
 Ⓐ It is suitable for people who are bilingual.
 Ⓑ It is more competitive than most students think.
 Ⓒ There are many problems related to its classes.
 Ⓓ Students cannot learn a foreign language in it.

04 What does the professor suggest that the student do first?
 Ⓐ Rethink the countries he has chosen
 Ⓑ Gather information for the application
 Ⓒ Talk to his academic adviser
 Ⓓ Go to an exchange student conference

Listen again to part of the conversation. Then answer the question. 🔊 MP3 11_1

05 Why does the professor say this?
 Ⓐ She believes that the student has good grades.
 Ⓑ She doesn't know about the student's grades.
 Ⓒ She is unfamiliar with the requirements.
 Ⓓ She doubts that the student is qualified.

04 Paper

상황별
출제포인트

Q1 **Purpose**
Q2 **Cause**
Q3 **Requirement (Condition) / Limitation**
Q4 **Problem (Worry About)**
Q5 **Solution (Suggestion)**
Q6 **Opinion (Positive / Negative)**
Q7 **Misunderstanding / Correction**
Q8 **Example**
Q9 **Difference**

Situation 1. Psychology Paper

교수는 학생들에게 4세 어린이를 관찰해서 cognitive development^{인지 발달} 이론에 대한 paper^{보고서}를 써 내라고 하면서, 관찰하는 방법에 focus^{초점}을 두고 설명한다. 여러 명의 아이들을 관찰하는 것이 아니고, 한 아이를 두 번 관찰해야만 한다.^{Q3} 교수는 4세 아이들은 인지발달 과정에서 ego-centric^{자아중심적}이 되고, 또한 상상력이 발달하여 장난감 비행기를 가지고 놀면서 마치 자신이 비행기 조종사인 것처럼 행동하기도 한다^{Q8}고 설명한다.

→ 이와 같은 예시 문제가 매우 자주 출제된다.

이에 학생은 "저처럼 처음 보는 사람도 4세 아이를 관찰할 수 있게 해 주나요?"^{Q4}라고 질문한다. 교수는 심리학과 사무실에 가면 관찰할 수 있는 아이의 부모님 명단이 있으니 가서 도움을 받으라^{Q5}고 말한다.

Situation 2. Literature Paper

학생은 교수가 지난번에 내 준 paper 작성 숙제를 어떻게 준비해야 할지 모르겠다^{Q4}고 고민을 상담한다. sci-fi와 science fiction novel^{공상 과학 소설}을 비교해 보는 것이 어떠냐고^{Q5} 교수가 제안하자 학생은 "둘 다 같은 거 아닌가요? 사전에도 scifi는 science fiction의 약자라고 나와 있는데요."라고 말한다. 대부분의 사람들이 그렇게 생각하지만, sci-fi는 외계인이 나와 인간과 전쟁하는 이야기같은 것이고, science fiction은 과학발달에 대한 인간의 고민이 들어간 것^{Q7}이라고 교수가 설명한다. 예를 들면, *Frankenstein*^{프랑켄슈타인}과 같은 소설이 여기에 해당된다. 즉, 과학발달에 대한 인간의 고뇌가 포함되어 있는지가 둘을 구분하는 기준^{Q9}이 된다고 설명한다.

핵/심/표/현

- abstract   n. (논문의) 개요, 초록
- accurately   adv. 정확하게, 정밀하게
- altogether   adv. 전적으로, 모두 함께
- attempt   v. 시도하다   n. 시도
- awkward   adj. 어색한, 민망한
- bibliography   n. 참고문헌[목록]
- conclusion   n. 결론
- convince   v. 설득하다
- critique   v. 비평하다
- deadline   n. 마감
- depth   n. 깊이
- disappointment   n. 실망, 좌절
- discuss   v. 논의하다
- distract   v. 방해하다, 산만하게 하다
- draft   n. 초안
- essay   n. 에세이, 논문
- fall behind   뒤처지다
- flow   n. 흐름
- footnote   n. 주석
- hand in   제출하다
- horrible   adj. 끔찍한
- illogical   adj. 비논리적인
- implement   v. 시행하다, 실시하다
- insight   n. 통찰력
- introduction   n. 도입
- include   v. 포함하다, 내재하다
- individually   adv. 개인적으로, 혼자서
- lengthy   adj. 너무 긴, 장황한
- method   n. 방법
- nod   v. 끄덕이다
- open-ended   adj. 열린 결말의
- organize   v. 정리하다
- plagiarize   v. 표절하다
- present   adj. 현재의, 지금의
- previous   adj. 이전의, 먼저의
- primarily   adv. 주로
- product   n. 생산물, 결과물; 상품
- proper   adj. 적절한, 제대로 된
- quote   n. 인용문
- rarely   adv. 드물게, 매우 가끔씩
- reference   n. 참고문헌[목록]
- relate   v. 연관되다
- relevant   adj. 연관성 있는
- responsible   adj. 책임이 있는
- revise   v. 수정하다
- schedule   n. 스케줄, 일정
- source   n. 자료(의 출처)
- submit   v. 제출하다
- summarize   v. 요약하다
- tangential   adj. 주제를 벗어난, 별로 관계가 없는
- thesis   n. 논문
- turn in   제출하다
- unnecessary   adj. 불필요한

Sample Questions

[01 ~ 05] **Listen to a conversation between a student and a professor. Then answer the questions.** MP3 12 정답 및 해석 p. 027

Note-taking

• Problem:

• Cause:

• Problem:

• Term / Origin:

01   What is the conversation mainly about?
   Ⓐ Methods for finding appropriate sources for a project
   Ⓑ Complaints the student received from research subjects
   Ⓒ Reasons the student is having difficulties with a project
   Ⓓ Ways to correctly conduct research for a project

02 Why did the student's group tell their subjects they were being watched?
Ⓐ The students who were being observed became angry at the group.
Ⓑ The group members did not know how to do the group project.
Ⓒ The library was not bright enough to make a proper observation.
Ⓓ The group members wanted to be courteous to the other students.

03 What can be inferred about the group project the student is participating in?
Ⓐ The other group members are too busy to help with it.
Ⓑ It will have inaccurate results if the methods do not change.
Ⓒ The professor does not approve of the topic they chose.
Ⓓ It is closely related to another psychology project.

04 Why does the professor mention lights?
Ⓐ To give an example of how productivity can be improved
Ⓑ To explain a point he made in a lecture about the Hawthorne effect
Ⓒ To reinforce his point about the proper way to observe subjects
Ⓓ To suggest a new topic for the group members to think about

Listen again to part of the conversation. Then answer the question. 🔊 MP3 12_1

05 Why does the student say this?
Ⓐ She is annoyed that she does not know what the Hawthorne effect is.
Ⓑ She is concerned that she missed an important point in class.
Ⓒ She is not sure if the professor is familiar with the Hawthorne effect.
Ⓓ She is suggesting the professor has mistakenly used the wrong term.

▶ **Question Review**

Introduction	Listen to a conversation between a student and a professor. **Student(female):** Hi, Professor Manning. **Professor(male):** Yes! Amy, what can I help you with today? I wanted to talk to you about something anyway. **S:** Yeah, I think I know what you wanted to talk about. Actually, that's why I'm here. **P:** What about the other members of your group? **S:** They are all finishing up a psychology project and are probably gonna be stuck in the library until tomorrow. **P:** Hmm... It'd be better if I talked to all of you... But I guess you'll have to relay the information.
Problem 프로젝트에서 부정적인 코멘트를 받음	**S:** Yeah. Well, as you probably know by now, **Q1** **I think we need a little more specific feedback on our project. I was kind of shocked to see your negative comments.** I really don't understand the comment about our research methods. It was something about how we have to change how we approach our subjects. I mean, you told us that we chose an excellent topic. I guess, I don't understand why we got such a negative comment. **P:** Well, there's nothing wrong with the topic, meaning it's still a very interesting topic to study. **Q1** **It's the way your group is going about doing the research that needs a little adjustment.** The topic you guys chose was how students are studying in the library, right? **S:** That's right. **P:** That's indeed an interesting topic, but the conclusions you came up with, well, you might have to look at them again. 🎧 **Have you ever heard of something called the Hawthorne effect?**
Headset	**S: Q5 Uh... Am I supposed to know what that is?** **P:** Ha ha... No, I haven't gone over it in class yet. We'll probably be covering it in about two weeks. Anyway, I looked at your report. You followed the typical procedures and observed the students that were studying in the study rooms in the campus library. But you also told them that you'd be observing them. Can I ask why you decided to do so?
Cause 학생들에게 관찰에 대해 말한 이유	**S: Q2 We didn't want to give students the wrong impression. Staring at someone who is concentrating is pretty rude**, isn't it?
Problem 관찰되고 있는 것을 알면 다르게 행동함	**P:** Yes, it is. **Q3 But that's exactly what the problem was. When the students you're observing know that they're being watched, they'll act differently. That's what the Hawthorne effect is.** **S:** Oh, so you mean we need to observe the students without them

Term / Origin

Hawthorne effect
용어와 기원을 설명

knowing?

P: Yes. ▶Q4◀ **The Hawthorne effect occurs when individuals modify, improve, their behavior in response to being observed.** The name comes from an electric factory called Hawthorne Works. There, **a researcher wanted to see how worker productivity changed depending on lighting conditions.** He thought productivity would increase when the lights were brighter. He started his observations and found that workers became more productive as they installed more lights. He decided it was true that workers worked better in a brighter environment.

S: Uh… What was the problem then?

P: The problem came about when he dimmed the lights to their original state. What do you think happened?

S: Did… the workers work harder than before? I mean, were they more productive even when the lights were dim?

P: Yes, exactly. The workers should have worked less when the lights became dimmer, but they didn't.

S: I guess the researcher made the same mistakes we did, huh?

P: Uh-huh. ▶Q4◀ **He told the workers that he'd be watching them. The workers acted differently from how they usually did and the researcher didn't get accurate results.**

S: I see what you mean… I'll make sure the group knows what we did wrong. But what about our grades? Can…

P: Don't sweat it. It's a mistake a lot of students who aren't familiar with observation methods make. Now that you know, I'll update the grade based on the new report your group makes.

Practice Questions

[01 ~ 05] Listen to a conversation between a student and his film professor. Then answer the questions. MP3 13 정답 및 해설 p. 029

Note-taking

01 Why does the student go to see the professor?
   Ⓐ To find out how to use different camera angles in tight spaces
   Ⓑ To request permission to postpone the due date of his paper
   Ⓒ To discuss a way of getting an actor for a scene
   Ⓓ To get help locating some information for his paper

02 What is the professor's attitude toward the student's film report?
  Ⓐ She doesn't think he needs to spend a lot of time writing it.
  Ⓑ She is surprised that he has finished most of it already.
  Ⓒ She dismisses his concerns as being unimportant.
  Ⓓ She is looking forward to seeing the results.

03 Why does the student mention a dancer?
  Ⓐ To point out one of the film angles he used
  Ⓑ To confirm that his way of filming a subject is correct
  Ⓒ To indicate that he could not finish the assignment in time
  Ⓓ To emphasize that student actors are unreliable

04 Why does the professor mention other artists?
  Ⓐ To suggest that looking at artists can give new insights
  Ⓑ To emphasize the importance of handing in assignments on time
  Ⓒ To point out that artists have a lot of time to spare
  Ⓓ To indicate her expectations for the amount of research to be done

Listen again to part of the conversation. Then answer the question. 🔊 MP3 13_1

05 Why does the professor say this?
  Ⓐ To indicate that a lot of time has passed during the conversation
  Ⓑ To suggest that the student may be late for his next class
  Ⓒ To be sure that the student understands what he has to do for the assignment
  Ⓓ To remind the student that he has not fulfilled his requirements yet

05 Project / Research

상황별 출제포인트
- Q1 **Purpose**
- Q2 **Cause**
- Q3 **Requirement (Condition) / Limitation**
- Q4 **Problem (Worry About)**
- Q5 **Solution (Suggestion)**
- Q6 **Opinion (Positive / Negative)**
- Q7 **Misunderstanding / Correction**
- Q8 **Example**
- Q9 **Difference**

Situation 1. Group Project

한 학생이 다른 학생들과 group project^그룹 프로젝트를 못 하겠다고 교수에게 complain^불평하다을 한다. 다른 학생들이 자료는 안 찾고 goof around^빈둥대다해서 자신이 혼자 자료를 다 찾아야 하기 때문에 project의 진행이 더디다^Q4고 말한다. 교수는 그 학생들을 전에 가르쳐 본 적이 있는데, 열심히 하는 학생이었다^Q6고 반박한다.

→ 이와 같이 학생들에 대한 교수의 opinion은 직접적으로 언급되지 않으니 놓치지 않도록 주의한다.

교수는 다른 학생들이 project에 관심이 없는 이유는 이 학생이 다른 사람들의 동의 없이 project 주제를 정했기 때문^Q2이니, 다시 회의를 해서 팀원 모두가 관심이 있는 주제를 찾아 보라고 권유한다.^Q5

→ **Conversation**에서는 문제가 발생한 이유(Cause)도 문제로 자주 출제되며, 그에 대한 **Solution (Suggestion)**을 묻는 문제도 나올 수 있다.

Situation 2. Film Project

film^영화 수업을 듣는 학생들에게 교수는 같은 장소를 촬영하도록 지시한다. 같은 장소를 촬영하게 하는 목적은 동일한 장소를 각 학생마다 어떻게 다르게 촬영하는지 보기 위함^Q1이라고 한다. 교수는 실제 영화감독이 촬영할 때는 예산, 장소, 시간 제한 등을 잘 고려해서 촬영한다^Q5고 덧붙인다.

핵/심/표/현

- adjustment   n. 조정, 조절, 수정, 보정
- analytical   adj. 분석적인
- appreciate   v. 감사히 여기다
- attend   v. 참가하다
- career   n. 직업, 사회생활[경력]
- comment   n. 의견 v. 언급하다
- commitment   n. 약속, 책무; 헌신
- concern   v. 우려[걱정]하다 n. 우려, 걱정
- contact information   연락처
- contradiction   n. 모순, 반박
- controversy   n. 논쟁, 논란
- criteria   n. 판단 기준
- decision   n. 결정
- department   n. 학과
- equipment   n. 장치, 장비
- evaluate   v. 평가하다
- experiment   n. 실험
- extra   adj. 추가의
- familiar   adj. 익숙한, 친숙한
- feedback   n. 피드백
- flexible   adj. 융통성 있는
- format   n. 포맷, 구성
- fund   n. 자금
- get a feel for ~   ...에 대한 감을 잡다
- hands-on experience   실제 체험
- impression   n. 인상
- in charge of ~   ...을 담당해서
- innovative   adj. 혁신적인
- joint research fellowship   공동연구
- lab study   실험실 실습
- material   n. 재료, 자료, 소재
- mention   v. 언급하다
- neglect   v. 게을리하다
- offer   n./v. 제안(하다)
- organize   n./v. 정리(하다)
- orientation   n. 오리엔테이션, 예비 교육
- overlap   v. 겹치다
- overwhelmed   adj. 압도된
- participate   v. 참가하다
- pile up   쌓이다
- procedure   n. 절차, 진행 과정
- productive   adj. 생산적인
- requirement   n. 필수 과목
- sorting   n. 구분, 분류
- specific   adj. 특정한, 구체적인
- suggest   v. 제안하다; 시사하다
- suppose   v. 추측하다
- take charge   떠맡다, 책임을 지다

Sample Questions

[01 ~ 05] Listen to a conversation between a student and a professor. Then answer the questions. MP3 14 정답 및 해석 p. 031

Note-taking

- problem:

- Attitude:

- Suggestion:

01 Why does the student go to speak with the professor?
    Ⓐ To discuss how to plan a budget
    Ⓑ To ask if she can become the leader of her group
    Ⓒ To get advice about a problem with her group project
    Ⓓ To find out if her group chose a good product for their presentation

02 Why does the student mention the budget?
  Ⓐ To show how they came up with the figures in their spreadsheet
  Ⓑ To explain that she did not have enough time to finish it
  Ⓒ To boast about the amount of work she has done
  Ⓓ To point out the problems related to her group

03 What is the professor's opinion about becoming a group leader?
  Ⓐ It's better to appoint someone else leader than to be the leader yourself.
  Ⓑ It's sometimes necessary to take charge of a group without holding a vote.
  Ⓒ Groups that get along well do better when nobody is named group leader.
  Ⓓ People who appoint themselves leader are usually the least qualified to lead.

04 What additional steps do the speakers discuss taking to help the group finish the project? **Choose two answers.**
  Ⓐ Voting to choose a group leader
  Ⓑ Dividing the tasks equally among everyone
  Ⓒ Sending out a schedule that sets due dates
  Ⓓ Cooperating to make sure everything gets done

Listen again to part of the conversation. Then answer the question. 🔊 MP3 14_1

05 What does the student imply when she says this?
  Ⓐ She suspects that the other group members do not care about the assignment.
  Ⓑ She thinks she has found a way to get the rest of the group to agree with her.
  Ⓒ She has seen the professor have similar problems with the other students.
  Ⓓ She feels she does not have the same ability to persuade people as the professor.

▶ **Question Review**

Introduction

Listen to a conversation between a student and a professor.

Student(female): Professor Moore, can I get a minute of your time?
Professor(male): Sure thing. What's going on, Becky?
S: Well, you know, the assignment – creating a marketing plan for a new product – (sigh) Well, my group just can't, we just don't…
P: Having trouble finding a product to talk about?
S: I wish that were the problem. We… we've actually found a pretty innovative product, but that's only a part of the process. **Q1** **When we have our meetings, we can't seem to focus on how to market the product…** We just seem to spend our time talking about whatever… things that are totally unrelated to the assignment. We don't even have a marketing plan yet. I'm really getting concerned that we'll all get horrible grades on this one. This project is a big portion of our total grade, you know.
P: Did you elect a leader?
S: No, not really… We kind of figured we didn't need one. Everyone works really hard. Plus, nobody was better qualified to be the team leader than anyone else.
P: All right, then how are you organizing the project?

Problem
project 진행이 더딤

S: Well, we've already divided up the tasks by picking what we preferred to do. It worked out okay. Well, at least it seemed like it did. Everyone wanted to be responsible for a different part, but we rarely talk about how much we've gotten done. We just don't know how much work is done individually. Everyone says they've done this much, but…
P: What about you? Have you finished your part?
S: Well, some of it. I finished what I could. **Q2** **I'm in charge of the budget, but I need a plan first to do it.** I even made the spreadsheet. We just have to plug in the numbers and we'll get the total budget. But I need input from the other members first. I need to know what type of advertising we'll do, where we'll do it, and how often we'll do it… things like that. **Q2** **There are a lot of decisions that I can't make by myself. We really need to talk to make a realistic budget.**

Headset Attitude
조원들이 과제에 큰 관심을 갖지 않음

P: 🎧 Hmm… What do the other group members think?
S: Well, I tried to talk to them and **Q5** **they kind of nodded their heads in agreement. You know, when people just look at you and start nodding…** But then we started talking about something else… Anyway, we aren't making any progress.
P: Maybe it's time to have a leader in the group. Why don't you take

charge?

S: No... I couldn't do that, I'd be appointing myself as the leader.

P: And... What's wrong with that?

S: First of all, we all agreed that a leader would be unnecessary.

P: Hey, you know, not all leaders are elected... You know, voted in by others. ▶Q3◀ **Some of the best leaders I've seen are people who realized there was a need for someone to take charge, to step up.** Although it can be awkward and uncomfortable, it can really be the difference between success and failure.

S: Hmm... You do have a point. ▶Q4-C◀ **Maybe I'll just hand out schedules**, you know, **with real deadlines**. The others might just follow them.

P: You know what? I bet that they'd actually be grateful. You can also find out how much each member has completed during the meetings. ▶Q4-D◀ **Just ask them to present what they have done, and if someone's really falling behind, the group can work together to get back on track.**

S: That sounds like a good idea. I'm thinking of giving it a shot.

P: Good luck.

Suggestion
학생에게 그룹 리더가 되라고 조언

Practice Questions

[01 ~ 05] **Listen to a conversation between a student and her biology professor. Then answer the questions.** MP3 15 정답 및 해석 p. 033

Note-taking

01 What is the conversation mainly about?
   Ⓐ How the student made a difficult career decision
   Ⓑ What the requirements are for a biochemistry class
   Ⓒ Whether the busy student can handle a fellowship
   Ⓓ Why the student didn't complete an assignment

02. What reason does the student give for not accepting the professor's request right away?
    Ⓐ She was tutoring members of the volleyball team.
    Ⓑ She did not understand the material taught in class.
    Ⓒ She had to apply to several graduate schools.
    Ⓓ She feared she'd be overwhelmed by the added work.

03. What is the professor's attitude toward the student's indecision?
    Ⓐ He thinks the student should ask a career counselor to help her.
    Ⓑ He thinks the student needs to think about her future.
    Ⓒ He thinks the student chose the wrong major.
    Ⓓ He thinks the student's worries are unnecessary.

04. Why does the professor mention a lab study project?
    Ⓐ To introduce the student to a professor in a different department
    Ⓑ To persuade the student to help him with an experiment
    Ⓒ To complain about the lack of labs in the biology department
    Ⓓ To offer the student a way to help her make a good decision

05. What will the student probably do after the volleyball tournament?
    Ⓐ Participate in a lab study
    Ⓑ Attend an orientation
    Ⓒ Study for her exams
    Ⓓ Write a paper on biochemistry

06 Major

상황별 출제포인트
- ♀1 Advantage
- ♀2 Solution (Suggestion)
- ♀3 Opinion (Agree / Disagree)
- ♀4 Requirement
- ♀5 Result / Finding / Research

Situation 1. Food Science Major

학생이 취직이 잘 될 것 같아♀1 food science^{식품과학} 전공을 선택했다고 말한다. 교수는 "맞아요, 나도 이 학교에 오기 전에 여러 곳에서 일했어요."♀3라고 대답한다. 교수는 이 전공을 공부하기 위해서는 physics^{물리}, chemistry^{화학}, engineering^{공학}, mathematics^{수학}과 같은 과목을 이수해야 한다♀4고 조언한다. 학생은 과학에 자신이 있다고 말하며, 현재 food packaging^{식품 포장}에 대한 연구♀5를 하고 있는데 어떤 방향으로 하면 좋을지 조언을 구하고 싶다고 말한다.

→ 전공 관련 대화에서는 특정 전공의 장단점, diploma^{전공학위}를 취득하기 위해 필요한 조건에 대한 문제도 자주 출제되는 편이다. 학생 의견에 찬성하거나 반대하는 교수의 Opinion은 주로 간접적으로 표현되기 때문에, 듣다가 놓치기 쉬우므로 주의해야 한다. 또한, Conversation과 Lecture 모두 study, research, experiment의 Result에 관한 내용은 문제로 많이 출제된다.

Situation 2. Choosing a Grad School

학생이 두 학교의 grad school^{대학원}에서 admission letter^{입학허가서}를 받고, 어느 학교를 가는 것이 좋겠는지 교수에게 상담하는 상황. A학교는 학교의 전체적인 평이 좋고, alumni^{졸업생}들이 장학금도 많이 지원해 준다.♀1 반면에 B학교는 A학교보다 덜 알려져 있지만, 학생이 전공하려는 biology^{생물} 학과의 인지도가 높아서♀1 그가 박사학위를 받아서 나중에 교수가 되고 싶다면 B학교가 더 나을 수도 있다♀2고 교수가 얘기해 준다.

핵/심/표/현

- academic advisor 지도교수
- advanced course 심화 과정[과목], 상급 과정[과목]
- advantage n. 이점, 장점
- alternative n. 대안, 대체 adj. 대신의
- alumni n. 동창생, 졸업생
- argue v. 논쟁하다
- bachelor's degree 학사 학위
- college n. (전문)대학, 단과 대학
- competitive adj. 경쟁이 치열한
- concrete adj. 짜임새 있는, 견고한
- course syllabus 강의계획서
- declare v. 선언하다, 선포하다
- dilemma n. 딜레마
- disadvantage n. 단점
- doctor's degree 박사 학위
- elective n. 선택 과목
- employee n. 직원
- employer n. 고용주
- employment n. 취업, 고용
- engineer n. 기술사, 공학자
- field n. 분야
- foundation course (대학의) 예비 과정[과목]
- graduation n. 졸업
- intermediate course 중급 과정[과목]
- intermediate level 중급 수준
- internship n. 인턴직
- interview n. 면접
- introduction course 입문 과정[과목]
- job opportunity 취직 기회
- master's degree 석사 학위
- objective n. 목표
- option n. 옵션, 선택권
- perceive v. 인식하다, 인지하다
- pointer n. 조언, 충고
- practical adj. 현실적인, 실용적인
- preparation n. 준비
- preparatory course 준비 과정[과목]
- reasoning n. 논리, 추론
- resume n. 이력서
- suitable adj. 알맞은
- undergrad n. 학부 과정(= undergraduate)
- upperclassman n. 상급생
- well-developed adj. 잘 쓰여진
- workplace n. 일터, 직장

Sample Questions

[01 ~ 05] **Listen to a conversation between a student and her philosophy professor. Then answer the questions.** MP3 16 정답 및 해석 p. 035

Note-taking

• Problem:

• Problem (Worry About):

• Opinion:

• Function / Advantage:

• Suggestion:

01 What is the conversation mainly about?
   Ⓐ When the deadline to change majors is
   Ⓑ Why the student should not change her major
   Ⓒ How the student can get more job opportunities
   Ⓓ How to study philosophy in graduate school

02 What does the professor imply about becoming an engineering major?
Ⓐ It doesn't make sense unless you already have a job.
Ⓑ It is the best way to establish a clear career goal.
Ⓒ It helps students develop very good analytical skills.
Ⓓ It is only suitable for students who have a specific goal.

03 Why does the professor talk about what was learned in philosophy class?
Ⓐ To make sure the student has been keeping up with the class material
Ⓑ To suggest that learning about Berkeley and Johnson is useless
Ⓒ To give an example of how philosophy is related to engineering
Ⓓ To show how philosophy majors can use what they learned in class

04 What does the student say about her career goal?
Ⓐ She wants to lead a company.
Ⓑ She hopes to become an engineer.
Ⓒ She doesn't have one.
Ⓓ She keeps changing her mind.

05 What is the student's initial opinion about the Berkeley argument?
Ⓐ She doesn't think it can be applied to the workplace.
Ⓑ She thinks that Berkeley had the correct opinion.
Ⓒ She thinks that Berkeley's views are outdated.
Ⓓ She thinks that it is very useful when in a disagreement.

▶ **Question Review**

Listen to a conversation between a student and her philosophy professor.

Student(female): Professor Tyler?
Professor(male): Hi, Lauren. Everything all right?
S: Well... I guess... but I thought I'd let you know that **Q1** **I've decided to change my major after this semester.**
P: What? Why? Don't you like philosophy?
S: Oh, no, don't get me wrong, I love philosophy. But I've got to be practical at the same time, too. I mean, taking philosophy classes is great, but I have to worry about getting a job after I'm done with college.
P: Oh, I see. Let me guess... People with a degree in philosophy just don't have anything to offer employers, right?
S: Hmm... kind of... right? A lot of my friends are either engineering or business majors. They have a career waiting for them, but I'm not too sure... if I can get a job with a philosophy degree.
P: If I had a nickel for every time I heard that... All right... **Q2** **studying applied sciences like engineering is great preparation to get a job, but that's only for people who already have career goals. If they know what they want to do, that's fine, but what about those who, well, don't have...** **Q4** Anyway, do you have any goals?
S: (Sigh) I don't have a clue.
P: So, for you, perhaps it's not the best option out there.
S: That's a good point.
P: **Q1** **With a major in philosophy, besides possibly studying even more and doing research at grad school, which, by the way, I think would be an excellent choice, you'll know plenty of things that can help you out in any field.**
S: Like what? The refuting of Berkeley's empiricism by Johnson?
P: Well, what did Johnson do exactly?
S: Well, you know. Berkeley claimed that we can't really know any object, physically, I mean. When we perceive an object, it's only our senses that perceive it, but that doesn't mean the actual physical matter exists. Johnson tried to refute the theory, right? He... He kicked a large stone and said that refuted Berkeley.
P: Very good, So... What do you think of that?
S: Well, not that I think Berkeley's right, either, but I also don't think that Johnson refuted anything. Berkeley would probably just say that Johnson still can't really know that the stone exists, he can only

---

Introduction

Problem
철학 전공으로 직업을 구하기 힘들 것 같아 전공을 바꾸려 함

Problem (Worry about)
직업 목표가 있다면 응용 과학을 전공하는 것이 좋지만, 아닌 경우의 학생을 걱정함

Opinion
❯ disagree

sense it. Seeing the stone, feeling the pain in his foot after kicking it, it's all still just based on his perceptions. Johnson still won't be able to say that he knows anything, well, other than what he feels and senses.

P: Do you know what you just did?

S: ▶Q5◀ Told you something that's totally useless anywhere but in a philosophy class?

P: No, you just showed me very well-developed analytical skills. You see, ▶Q3◀ **studying philosophy lets us critique other people's reasoning by making convincing arguments, and then summarizing and communicating those arguments very effectively. In life and in any field, these things are very important, you know?**

S: Okay, but, still… You don't see any jobs asking for reasoning and arguing skills.

P: Really? Well, I sure don't think so. I've read many articles written by the leaders of companies in all sorts of fields. One thing that always sticks out is how difficult it is to find employees who have those skills. Try going to the career services office. I'm sure they'll tell you the same thing.

S: Hmm… I guess you're right.

P: Also, while we're at it, have you given any thought about what to do this summer? Our department always has information about internships. It would give you some concrete experience to add to your resume.

S: That's an idea.

P: An internship is definitely a good first step.

Function / Advantage
철학은 추론과 논쟁 능력을 키워줌
회사 지도자들은 그런 인재를 찾고 있음

Suggestion
취업 서비스 사무실을 방문할 것 – 여름 인턴직 권유

Practice Questions

[01 ~ 05] **Listen to a conversation between a student and her art history professor. Then answer the questions.** MP3 17 정답 및 해석 p. 037

Note-taking

01 Why does the student go to see the professor?
   Ⓐ To get advice about what she should major in
   Ⓑ To find out why she received a bad grade on a paper
   Ⓒ To sign up for an art seminar that is being held next week
   Ⓓ To ask how to revise a paper she is writing

02 What didn't the student understand about her professor's written comments?
   Ⓐ Which art movement the professor wanted her to write about
   Ⓑ What the professor considers a weakness in her writing style
   Ⓒ Why the professor wanted her to write about technology and art
   Ⓓ What the professor meant by the term "generalized examples"

03 What does the professor say about avant-garde artists?
   Ⓐ They are affected by the development of photography.
   Ⓑ They studied both painting and photography.
   Ⓒ They favored portraits over traditional landscapes.
   Ⓓ They expressed themselves by painting in black and white.

04 Why does the professor mention the student's grades?
   Ⓐ To indicate that the student did not put enough effort into her paper
   Ⓑ To encourage the student to become an art major
   Ⓒ To suggest that the student could become a good artist
   Ⓓ To point out that the student should study harder for her exams

05 Why does the professor want the student to attend an art seminar?
   Ⓐ He does not want to go to the seminar by himself.
   Ⓑ He wants the student to meet other art professors.
   Ⓒ He believes going there will help the student choose a major.
   Ⓓ He wants more participants because the attendance will be low.

Unit 2
Service Encounters

01_ **Class / Credit / Transcript / Financial Aid**
02_ **Housing (Dorm)**
03_ **Library / Bookstore**
04_ **Part-time Job / Job Fair / Internship**
05_ **School Facility**
06_ **기타 (Miscellaneous)**

01 Class/Credit/Transcript/Financial Aid

상황별 출제포인트	♥1 Cause ♥2 Requirement ♥3 Problem ♥4 Solution (Suggestion) ♥5 Difference

Situation 1. Graduation Credit

학생이 졸업신청서를 내러 갔는데, credit^{학점}이 부족해서 졸업을 못한다는 사실을 알게 된다. physics department^{물리학과}에서는 졸업하려면 총 130학점이 필요^{♥2}한데, 이 학생은 3학점이 부족해 졸업을 못 한다.^{♥3} 당황한 학생이 그 이유를 알아 보니, 다른 학교에서 3학점짜리 과목을 수강한 후 학점을 transfer^{학점 옮기기}해 달라고 신청했으나 학점 관련 서류가 오지 않아서 3학점이 인정되지 않았기 때문이었다.^{♥1}

Situation 2. Credit Transfer

Northwestern University에서 marketing class^{마케팅 수업}를 들으려는 학생이 조언을 구하러 찾아온다. 교수는 학생에게, 수업을 잘 듣고 Northwestern University의 담당자에게 그가 들은 수업의 transcript^{성적표}를 반드시 우리 학교로 보내 달라고 요청해야 한다^{♥2}고 조언한다. 그 학교에서 이수한 3 credits^{3학점}가 그의 졸업 학점에 추가되어야 졸업 requirement credits^{요구 학점}가 충족되기 때문이다.

→ 학점 관련 대화에서는 필요한 절차나 서류로 인해 생기는 문제의 출제 빈도가 매우 높다. 이런 유형의 문제가 **Requirement** 유형이다.

Situation 3. Scholarship

한 학생이 A대학에서 B대학으로 transfer^{전학가다}를 했는데, 전에 다니던 A대학에서는 full scholarship^{전액 장학금}을 받았다고 한다. 입학성적도 좋았고, dean's list^{장학생 명단}에도 올라갔다. 그런데 이번 B학교에서는 장학금이 예전 학교에 비해 반 밖에 나오지 않아 걱정이다. 장학금으로는 tuition^{등록금}만 부담할 수 있고, room and board^{기숙사 숙식비}가 해결이 안된다.^{♥3} 이에 B학교 담당자는 A학교는 private school^{사립학교}이기 때문에 fund^{자금}가 많았을 것이고 alumni^{졸업생들}가 grant^{지원금}를 donate^{기부하다}하기도 하지만, B학교는 public school^{공립학교}이기 때문에 자금이 많지 않다고 설명한다.^{♥5} 그는 학생에게 part-time job^{아르바이트}을 찾아서 해결하는 편이 좋을 것 같다^{♥4}고 조언한다.

핵/심/표/현

- academic calendar 학사일정
- academic conference 학술회의
- academic record 학과 성적, 성적표
- academic warning 학사경고
- assignment n. 과제물
- attendance n. 출석
- balance n. 잔고, 지불 잔액
- blue book n. (청색 표지의) 대학 시험 답안 책자
- budget n. 예산
- catch up 따라잡다
- chairperson n. 의장, 회장
- course catalogue 수강 신청 안내서
- credit n. 학점
- curriculum n. 교과 과정
- deadline n. 마감 기한
- dean n. 학장
- dean's list n. 우등생 명단
- deposit n. 보증금
- diploma n. 졸업[수료]증
- dismissal n. 퇴학
- drop v. (수강을) 그만두다
- due date n. 만기일, 마감일
- elective n. 선택 과목
- eligible adj. 자격이 있는
- enroll in ~ …에 등록하다
- fail v. 낙제하다
- fieldwork n. 현장 연구
- fill out 작성하다
- forward v. (새 주소로) 다시 보내 주다
- grant n. 지원금
- group project 그룹 프로젝트[과제]
- loan period 대출 기간
- mailing address 우편주소
- merit-based scholarship 성적우수 장학금 (제도)
- mix-up n. (실수로 인한) 혼동
- payroll n. 지급명세서
- permission n. 허락, 허가, 승낙
- presentation n. 발표, 설명
- proctor n. 시험 감독관
- prospective student 입학 예정 학생
- register v. 등록하다, 가입하다
- registrar n. 교무과장
- report card n. 성적표
- required subject 필수 과목
- room and board 기숙사 숙식비
- savings account 예금통장
- scholarship n. 장학금
- selective adj. 선별적인, 선별 가능한
- summer school 여름[계절] 학교
- summer session 여름 학기 수업
- syllabus n. 강의 계획표
- tuition n. 등록금
- waive v. 면제하다, 포기하다
- wage n. 급여

Sample Questions

[01 ~ 05] Listen to a conversation between a student and a registrar. Then answer the questions. MP3 18 정답 및 해석 p. 040

Note-taking

- Problem:

- Purpose:

- Cause:

- Attitude:

- Suggestion:

- Future Action:

01 Why does the student go to the registrar's office?
  Ⓐ To confirm that she wants to accept a scholarship
  Ⓑ To find out why she can't register for classes
  Ⓒ To register for her general requirement classes
  Ⓓ To ask why her scholarship is smaller than her tuition

02 What can be inferred about the scholarship?
   Ⓐ It is only given to students in their fourth year of school.
   Ⓑ This is the first time she has been offered it.
   Ⓒ It does not apply to classes taken during the summer.
   Ⓓ There are many steps required to apply for it.

03 Why does the employee mention the post office?
   Ⓐ To confirm the student's new home address
   Ⓑ To indicate the reason why the student did not get the letter
   Ⓒ To suggest that the post office caused the problem
   Ⓓ To explain the best way to accept the scholarship

04 Why does the employee mention that the student is in her last year of school?
   Ⓐ To emphasize that the student needs to register quickly
   Ⓑ To introduce the classes the student needs to take in order to graduate
   Ⓒ To point out that the student will most likely be able to register for the classes she wants
   Ⓓ To encourage the student to take large classes that are not yet filled

05 What will the student most likely do next?
   Ⓐ Ask the biology professor if she can take her class
   Ⓑ Find out what classes she needs to graduate
   Ⓒ Visit the post office to pick up her undelivered mail
   Ⓓ Go online to change her personal information

▶ **Question Review**

Introduction

Problem
수업 등록 페이지에
접속할 수 없음

Purpose
최대한 많은 학생들이
받을 수 있도록 하기
위해 다른 장학금이
부담하지 않는 금액만
지불해줌

Cause
편지가 전 주소로 보내짐

Attitude
걱정 - 위로

Listen to a conversation between a student and a registrar.

Employee(male): May I help you?
Student(female): Yeah, um, I need to talk to you about my tuition.
E: Okay, what seems to be the problem?
S: Well, **Q1** **I tried to register for my classes, but I couldn't access the registration page.** I got a notice saying that I owed tuition. But, the thing is, I'm on a scholarship, so the tuition should have already been paid.
E: Okay. Let's see if we can figure this out. What's your name?
S: Lisa Johnson.
E: All right. I'm bringing up your information on the computer. Hmm… It looks like you're on hold because you didn't pay this semester's tuition.
S: Exactly! What's going on?
E: Hmm… **Q2** **It says that you were offered an academic merit scholarship… Did you get the letter?**
S: What do you mean?
E: **We sent you a letter asking for your confirmation that you would accept the scholarship.** This scholarship only covers the amount that isn't covered by other scholarships that students may be getting from other sources. We want to give out scholarships to as many students as possible, you know. I'm assuming that since you didn't send a confirmation letter back, the system went to the next person on the list.
S: What? No, I never received any letter from the school. When did you guys send it?
E: Let's see… Our system says that the letters were sent out on August 15th. Your letter was sent to 1023 Birch Street…
S: Oh, I moved to a different apartment this summer! The letter went to my old address.
E: Hmm… **Q3** **Did you go to the post office right after you moved?** You know, you can ask the post office to forward your letters to your new address for two months, just in case things like this happen. They also hold any letters that get sent back for two weeks. **I bet your letter was probably at the post office waiting for someone to pick it up… Well, before it got sent back to us.**
S: So does that mean I can't get the scholarship? What, uh, what should I do now? There's no way…
E: Hold on a second there, there's still time to confirm. Let me give you the form you need to fill out. Just fill it out on the back. Your balance will be settled after we process the papers. It usually just takes two days.

Suggestion

상급 수업은 정원이 빨리 차지 않으니 너무 걱정말라고 조언

S: That's great! Phew... But... two days... That's a long time. What if I can't register for the classes I want?

E: Hmm... I'm sorry but there's really nothing that I can do for you about that. But what I can do is look for vacant classes for you. **Q4** **It says that you're in your last year of school.** That's good. You really don't have to worry about the classes closing. **They're all upper level classes, meaning that students need a lot of prerequisites to take the classes. These classes generally don't fill up that quickly.**

S: What about my general requirements? I still need to take a few basic courses to graduate.

E: Let me check... Well, these classes are really big, and it seems that there's a lot of seats open for the Intro to Biology class. Do you need a basic science requirement?

S: Yeah, actually, I do.

E: Well, at this rate you should have no problem getting into that class. Even if you can't, you can explain your situation to the professor, I'm sure she'll let you in. We don't want anyone to miss graduation because they can't take a class, you know.

S: Thank you so much.

Future Action

학생 정보 페이지에서 주소 변경

E: **Q5** **Make sure you change your contact info before you do anything.** Once the papers go through, we still need to contact you as soon as possible. There still might be some classes that close if you're too late. **Go to the student information page on our website after logging in. You'll be able to change it from there.**

S: I'll get right on it.

Practice Questions

[01 ~ 05] **Listen to a conversation between a student and a registrar. Then answer the questions.** MP3 19 정답 및 해석 p. 041

Note-taking

01   Why does the student go to the registrar's office?
   Ⓐ To ask about the process of applying to a summer program
   Ⓑ To find out why an official document was not sent
   Ⓒ To see if she could look at her grades in her music courses
   Ⓓ To discuss a problem with her performance schedule

02 Why does the employee mention college music events?
    Ⓐ To acknowledge that the music program needs help
    Ⓑ To emphasize the importance of music in schools
    Ⓒ To explain why the transcript was not sent
    Ⓓ To indicate that he knows who the student is

03 Why does the employee mention the student handbook?
    Ⓐ To point out that the student should have known better
    Ⓑ To acknowledge that students do not read it
    Ⓒ To suggest that the student file a formal complaint
    Ⓓ To show that it is difficult to get transcripts

04 What does the employee imply when he points out that the student requested her transcript too late?
    Ⓐ The student has requested too many documents.
    Ⓑ The student should not be concerned about getting accepted to the summer program.
    Ⓒ The student should follow the guidelines set by the school.
    Ⓓ The student has no control over the computer problem.

05 Why will the employee attach a note to the student's transcript?
    Ⓐ To remind the student to submit it to the summer music program on time
    Ⓑ To inform his staff that it needs to be sent as soon as possible
    Ⓒ To prove that the procedures are included in the student handbook
    Ⓓ To explain the circumstances that caused it to be sent late

02 Housing (Dorm)

상황별 Q1 **Problem**
출제포인트 Q2 **Cause**
  Q3 **Solution (Suggestion)**
  Q4 **Disadvantage**

Situation 1. Broken Facility

heater난방기, closet door knob옷장 손잡이, bulb백열등 등 기숙사 비품의 파손 및 고장과 관련된 상황^{Q1}이나, 기숙사 근처에서 공사를 하여 소음이나 먼지 문제를 일으키는 상황^{Q1} 등이 대화의 주제로 자주 등장한다. 이런 내용과 관련하여 발생한 이유가 무엇이고 해결방법으로 무엇이 제시되었는지를 묻는 질문이 출제된다.

Situation 2. Lost ID Card

학생이 ID card학생증를 분실하여 기숙사에 들어갈 수 없다.^{Q1} 관리과에 문의하니 이름과 생년월일을 적으면 임시로 들어갈 수는 있으며, ID card를 reissue재발급하다하려면 20달러가 필요하고 다음 주 월요일에나 재발급이 된다고 한다. 재발급이 그렇게 늦어지면 불편하다^{Q4}고 학생이 말하니, 직원은 30달러를 내면 내일 받을 수도 있다는 다른 해결방법^{Q3}을 제시한다.

Situation 3. Meal Plan

학교나 기숙사에서는 한 학기 동안 필요한 식권을 meal plan식사 이용권으로 구입할 수 있다. 하루에 세 끼를 먹는 경우에는 full-time plan전체 이용을, 하루 한 끼나 두 끼만 먹는 경우에는 part-time plan부분 이용을 구입해서 사용하면 된다. 자주 출제되는 상황으로는, 학생이 full-time plan을 샀는데 도중에 part-time job 등을 하게 되어 기숙사에서 식사를 할 수 없게 되는^{Q1} 경우가 있다. 이 때 학교 담당자가 part-time meal plan으로 바꿔 주거나, 남은 금액만큼 다음 학기로 credit잔여분을 넘겨 주겠다(예를 들어, 이번 학기에 식사를 10번 놓쳤다면 다음 학기에 그만큼을 사용할 수 있도록 해 주는 것)^{Q3}고 제안하는 내용이 나온다.

핵/심/표/현

- administrator   n. 관리자
- amenity   n. 편의시설
- citation   n. 딱지; 소환장
- closet   n. 옷장
- common room   거실, 공용실
- compliant   adj. (법률을) 준수하는
- contract   n. 계약
- cooking appliance   요리도구
- corridor   n. 복도
- custodian   n. 건물 관리인
- decoration   n. 장식, 장식품
- dorm manager   기숙사 관리자
- dorm   n. 기숙사(= dormitory)
- dormitory dean   사감
- facility   n. 시설
- faucet   n. 수도꼭지
- fine   n. 벌금   v. 벌금을 부과하다
- fire code violation   소방법규 위반
- fire escape   비상 계단
- fitness center   n. 피트니스 센터(헬스클럽)
- fix   v. 고치다
- fraternity   n. (미국 대학의) 남학생 사교 클럽
- get cited   딱지를 떼다
- hazardous   adj. 위험한
- host family   n. 민박 가정
- ID card   n. 학생증
- inspection   n. 검사, 점검
- janitor   n. 수위
- landlord   n. 집주인
- laundry room   n. 세탁실
- leak   v. (물이) 새다
- lease   v. 임대[대여]하다
- maintenance office   관리실
- move-out notice   이사 공지
- occupant   n. 거주자, 점유자
- off-campus housing   교외 주거
- on-campus living   교내 주거
- rent   n. 집세, 방세
- repair   v. 고치다
- replace   v. 교체하다
- residence dining   기숙사 식당
- residence hall   기숙사 강당
- roommate   n. 룸메이트
- rusty   adj. 녹슨, 낡은
- security deposit   임대 보증금
- share   v. 공유하다
- smoke detector   연기 탐지기
- sorority   n. (미국 대학의) 여학생 클럽
- studio apartment   원룸형 아파트
- temperature   n. 온도, 기온

Sample Questions

[01 ~ 05] **Listen to a conversation between a student and a university employee. Then answer the questions.** 🔊 MP3 20   정답 및 해석 p. 044

Note-taking

• Problem (1):

• Example:

• Problem (2):

• Solution:

01 Why does the student go to see the employee?
   Ⓐ To tell him that her room is too cold to study in
   Ⓑ To ask if she can get her room's heater fixed
   Ⓒ To inform him that she is moving out of the dorm
   Ⓓ To complain about the view from her window

02 Why does the student mention her friend Bob?
   Ⓐ To recommend someone who can fix the heater
   Ⓑ To explain that he is on the wrestling team
   Ⓒ To suggest that her friend broke her window
   Ⓓ To emphasize how difficult it is to close the window

03 What can be inferred about the student's friend who is living off campus?
   Ⓐ She is annoyed about the delay in repairing the radiator.
   Ⓑ She moved out of the dorms due to a similar problem.
   Ⓒ She has enough room in her apartment for a guest.
   Ⓓ She used to be the student's roommate.

04 Why does the student mention the uneven heating in the dorms?
   Ⓐ To emphasize the seriousness of her problem
   Ⓑ To suggest that other radiators are broken
   Ⓒ To complain about the custodian's laziness
   Ⓓ To explain why she opened a window in her room

   Listen again to part of the conversation. Then answer the question. 🔊 MP3 20_1
05 What does the employee imply about the student's heater when he says this?
   Ⓐ It has broken down before.
   Ⓑ It is older than he expected.
   Ⓒ It may be severely damaged.
   Ⓓ It was broken due to misuse.

▶ **Question Review**

Problem (1)
창문이 안 닫힘

Example
최선을 다한 예

Problem (2)
히터가 고장 남

Headset

Solution
수리하는 동안 친구 집에서 거주

Listen to a conversation between a student and a university employee.

Student(female): Hi, um, is this the housing maintenance office?
Employee(male): Yep, it sure is! How can I help you today?
S: Oh, good. I opened the window in my dorm room yesterday, but I can't seem to get it closed. **Q2** **I tried everything I could, I even asked my friend Bob who's on the wrestling team to try and shut it, but it just won't budge.**
E: What? Why would you open a window in the middle of winter?
S: Oh, **Q4** **the heating is so uneven in the dorms that some students are freezing while others get too hot.** I guess I just ended up with one of the hotter rooms. **The students sometimes have to open the windows to get a good temperature.** I guess I just did the same.
E: Wow, I didn't know it was that bad. So, should I send someone to fix the window? I can have a custodian take a look at it and see if he can do something.
S: Thanks, **Q1** **but there's another reason why I'm here.**
E: Oh, what is it?
S: **I think the heater in my room is broken.** My room is a big mess. There's a pool of water next to the radiator.
E: Really? Are you sure it didn't leak because you opened the window?
S: 🎧Yeah, I saw steam coming out of the radiator, and the water that leaked was rusty.
E: **Q5** **Oh, rusty isn't good.** Wait a minute… So are you telling me that you slept in a room with a broken radiator with the window open?
S: Uh-huh. One night of sleeping in the cold is enough for me. That's why I came here. So, what can be done about it? How long would it take to fix?
E: Well, okay, the window won't take long, but the radiator is another story. **Q5** **The heaters are so old in the dorms, it might take a long time to fix it or we might have to replace the whole radiator.** I'm gonna have to check your room and call a few places to see how long it'll take. Do you want to come back a little later, maybe after you grab lunch?
S: Uh… Can you just give me a ballpark number? **Q3** **I'm about to call my friend who lives off campus. She told me that I could stay over until it gets fixed,** but I want to tell her how long I expect to stay there.
E: Hmm… Well… Today's Friday, so I won't be able to get anything done until Monday… Why don't you say it'll take about five days just to be

sure?

S: Okay, that's great. Thanks so much for your help.

E: No problem. I'll head over to your room soon to take a look.

Practice Questions

[01 ~ 05] Listen to a conversation between a student and a housing office administrator. Then answer the questions. MP3 21 정답 및 해석 p. 045

Note-taking

01   Why does the student go to the housing office?
   Ⓐ To ask about using an electric kettle
   Ⓑ To select new roommates for next year
   Ⓒ To pay a fine related to fire code violations
   Ⓓ To get an explanation of a citation he received

02. What does the employee imply about the school's citations?
  Ⓐ They will be updated and improved by the university soon.
  Ⓑ They are not supposed to be viewed by students who receive them.
  Ⓒ They are often given out to students who have messy dorm rooms.
  Ⓓ They explain violations in a manner many students don't understand.

03. What does the student imply about his roommates?
  Ⓐ They do not understand the importance of inspections.
  Ⓑ They do not get along with each other.
  Ⓒ They do a lot of cooking in the room.
  Ⓓ They plan to avoid paying the fine for their violations.

04. According to the employee, what will the students have to do if violations are found during the re-inspection?
  Ⓐ They will have to keep getting inspections until they are compliant.
  Ⓑ They will have to agree not to cook in their room anymore.
  Ⓒ They will each have to pay an equal share of the fine.
  Ⓓ They will all have to purchase new cooking appliances.

Listen again to part of the conversation. Then answer the question. 🔊 MP3 21_1

05. What does the employee imply when she says this?
  Ⓐ She does not believe that the student did anything wrong.
  Ⓑ She has dealt with this kind of situation many times.
  Ⓒ She suspects that the sticker was given by accident.
  Ⓓ She believes that the student has bad roommates.

03 Library / Bookstore

상황별
출제포인트
- Q1 Requirement
- Q2 Problem
- Q3 Solution (Suggestion)
- Q4 Advantage
- Q5 Cause

Situation 1. Extended Borrowing Privilege

　4학년 학생이 논문을 쓰기 위해 책을 빌린 후 extended borrowing privilege^{대출 기한 연장}를 한다. 최초의 대출 기한(예를 들어 4주)이 만료되었을 때 그 책을 찾는 다른 사람이 없다면 대출 기한을 연장할 수 있다고 사서가 설명해 준다. 그러나 대출 기한을 연장했더라도, 연장 기간 중에 다른 사람이 그 책을 찾으면 바로 return[drop off]^{반납하다}해야 하는 것이 도서관 policy^{방침}^{Q1}이다.

→ 도서관에서 일어나는 대화 상황에서는 도서관의 **rule**이나 **policy**에 관한 문제가 자주 출제된다.

Situation 2. Finding Articles

　학생이 도서관에서 심리학 관련 article^{기사}을 찾아야 하는데 어디에 있는지 잘 모르겠다^{Q2}며 librarian^{사서}에게 도움을 요청한다. 사서는 reference room^{참고문헌실}에 없으면, electric journal^{전자 신문}을 찾아 보라고^{Q3} 조언한다. electric journal을 사용하면 article abstract^{기사 요약문}만 검색할 수 있어서, 그 article 전체를 읽어야 할지 말지 빨리 판단할 수 있기 때문에 시간이 많이 save^{절약하다}된다.^{Q4}

→ 학생이 겪는 문제점 - 자료를 찾는 방법을 모름
　문제점에 대한 해결방안 제안 - **electric journal**을 사용하라고 제안
　제안한 방법의 장점 - 시간을 절약해 줌
　이와 같이 문제점, 해결방안, 장점 등이 모두 함께 문제로 출제될 수도 있다.

Situation 3. Reserve Material

　교수가 자신의 수업에 필요한 책이나 article을 도서관에 reserve^{예약하다}하여 수업을 듣는 학생들이 그 자료를 볼 수 있도록 하는 것을 reserve material^{예약 자료}이라고 한다. 여러 명의 학생들이 자료를 같이 봐야 하기 때문에, 도서관에서는 reserve material을 각 학생에게 최대 2시간 동안 대출해 주고 도서관 내에서만 보도록 하는^{Q1} policy를 갖고 있다.

핵/심/표/현

- abstract　n. (논문의) 개요, 초록
- appropriate　adj. 적합한, 알맞은
- archive　n. 기록 보관소
- article　n. 기사
- charge　v. 청구하다
- copy　n. (책의 한) 권, 부
- database　n. 데이터베이스
- delay　v. 늦어지다, 미뤄지다　n. 지연
- demographics　n. 인구 통계 (자료)
- electric journal　전자 신문
- fine　n. 벌금
- front cover　책 표지
- hardcover　n. 양장본(딱딱한 표지로 제본한 책)
- holding　n. 보유
- index　n. 색인
- inter-library loan　도서관 대 도서관으로 책을 빌리는 제도 (자신의 학교 도서관에 빌리고 싶은 책이 없으면 다른 학교 도서관에서 책을 빌려오는 시스템)
- journal　n. 일지, 일기
- librarian　n. 사서, 도서관원
- literature guide　문헌 지침[가이드]
- literature review　문헌 검토
- merchandise　n. 상품, 물품
- newspaper review　신문 논평
- out-of-date　adj. 낡은, 시대에 뒤진
- paperback　n. 페이퍼백 (얇은 종이로 표지를 제본한 싸고 간편한 책)
- photocopier　n. 복사기
- policy　n. 규율, 방침
- precaution　n. 예방, 주의, 대비
- publish　v. 출판[출간]하다
- purchase　v. 구매하다
- reference guide　참고문헌 안내
- reference　n. 참고, 관련, 인용
- refund　v. 환불[환급]하다　n. 환불(액)
- reliable　adj. 믿을 수 있는
- renew　v. 재개하다
- reserve　v. 예약하다
- secondhand　adj. 중고의
- source　n. (정보[자료]의) 출처
- statistics　n. 통계 (자료)
- stock　n. 재고
- store credit　n. 상점 크레딧 (상점에서 물건을 환불하려 할 때, 물건 값을 현금으로 환불해주지 않는 대신 물건 값을 상점의 채무로 처리하는 것)
- up-to-date　adj. 최신의
- video library　n. 비디오 라이브러리(비디오 작품을 수집, 보존하여 일반인에게 공개하는 영상 도서관)
- yearbook　n. 연감, 연보

Sample Questions

[01 ~ 05] Listen to a conversation between a student and his economics professor. Then answer the questions. MP3 22 정답 및 해석 p. 048

Note-taking

• Problem:

• Cause:

• Suggestion:

01 Why does the student go to see the professor?
    Ⓐ To discuss the relationship between hospitals and economics
    Ⓑ To apologize for dropping her class at the last minute
    Ⓒ To explain why he did not participate in a class discussion
    Ⓓ To suggest a new policy for the university bookstore

02 Why was the student unable to buy the book?
- Ⓐ He didn't know the book's title and author.
- Ⓑ The bookstore did not have enough copies.
- Ⓒ Too many students dropped the class.
- Ⓓ The professor did not ask for enough books.

03 What does the student suggest the professor do?
- Ⓐ Talk to the head of the department
- Ⓑ Talk to the bookstore manager again
- Ⓒ Ask another bookstore to sell the book
- Ⓓ Assign a different book for the next class

04 According to the professor, what should the student do before the next class?
- Ⓐ Look for another bookstore that sells the book
- Ⓑ Talk to his classmates about the contents of the book
- Ⓒ Apologize to the bookstore manager for his mistake
- Ⓓ Make copies of the material needed for class

Listen again to part of the conversation. Then answer the question. 🔊 MP3 22_1

05 Why does the student say this?
- Ⓐ To suggest that few students will attend the next class
- Ⓑ To express his frustration with the bookstore policy
- Ⓒ To assure the professor that he will get the book in time for class
- Ⓓ To suggest that he won't be able to participate in the class discussion

▶ **Question Review**

Introduction	**Listen to a conversation between a student and his economics professor.** **Professor(female):** Hello, John. Is something wrong? **Student(male):** I… I just wanted to say I'm sorry. **P:** What? Why? I don't think you have anything to apologize to me for. **S:** Well, **Q1 I wanted to talk to you about the class today. I really wasn't able to participate at all in the class discussion.** **P:** Yes… You did seem kind of quiet in class today. You're usually much more involved in the discussion. Were you just not interested in today's topic? **S:** Oh, no, that's not the case at all. The thing is… I really wanted to participate in class, I'm really interested in the relationship between healthcare and economics. I mean, it's really interesting how we can take the principles of economics and use them to see how efficient a hospital
Problem 책을 읽지 못해 토론 수업에 참여를 못 함	is. **Q1 Unfortunately, I didn't read the chapter, so I couldn't join the discussion.** **P:** What do you mean? How come you didn't read the material? Didn't I assign it last Thursday?
Cause 서점에 책이 다 팔리고 없어 구매를 못 함	**S:** Well, it's not like I didn't read the book, well, not on purpose anyway. **Q2 I couldn't buy the book at the university bookstore.** I mean, just in case you're wondering, it's not like I went there at the last minute, you know? **I went to the bookstore the day after you assigned the reading, but it was sold out.** **P:** You're kidding! Well, I understand your frustration! **S:** You do? Really? **P:** Yes, the university bookstore policy is very frustrating to the professors just as it is to the students. **S:** Wow, you mean there are other students like me? **P:** Unfortunately, yes. The bookstore has this policy to only order a certain amount of books. So when I request 50 books, they'll only stock 40. The manager says that it's because some students might drop the class. They don't want to have books that are unsold. They have a hard time getting rid of them, you know? So it's not like I can order a lot more than needed. But still, it's the university bookstore! The university bookstore. I mean, I try suggesting a different policy every semester, but they won't budge.
Suggestion / **Headset**	**S:** 🎧 Wow… **Q3 Did you try taking it up with the department chair? Wouldn't he have more of a say?**

학생은 교수에게
학과장과 얘기해볼 것을
제안

교수는 자신의 책을
복사할 것을 제안

P: That does sound like a good idea…
S: **Q5 Anyway, I'm giving you fair warning about the next class.** I won't be able to read the next chapter until I can get my hands on the book.
P: I see, I get your point. **Q4 Why don't you check again with the bookstore, and if they still don't have it, you can borrow my book to make copies.** I'll have to check with the other students just to make sure they all have their books. If not, I'll have to change the way we go about class. We might just talk about the material a few days later, once everyone has a chance to read it, you know.
S: Thanks so much! Now I don't feel quite so bad about my participation in class.

Practice Questions

[01 ~ 05] **Listen to a conversation between a student and a librarian. Then answer the questions.** 🔊 MP3 23 정답 및 해석 p. 050

Note-taking

01 What is the conversation mainly about?
   Ⓐ Methods for finding appropriate sources for a project
   Ⓑ Reasons the student is having difficulties with a project
   Ⓒ Criteria countries use to evaluate demographics
   Ⓓ Possible sources for the student's research project

02 What does the student say about the atlas he checked?
    Ⓐ It was too complicated to figure out.
    Ⓑ It did not list population statistics by city.
    Ⓒ It contained out-of-date information.
    Ⓓ It lacked information on Western Europe.

03 What kind of information about European cities does the student need?
    Choose two answers.
    Ⓐ Average temperatures
    Ⓑ Population
    Ⓒ Size by area
    Ⓓ Average lifespan of citizens

04 Where will the speakers look for the information the student needs?
    Ⓐ In the reference section
    Ⓑ In a different library
    Ⓒ In Professor Philips' office
    Ⓓ In the geography department

    Listen again to part of the conversation. Then answer the question. 🔊 MP3 23_1

05 Why does the librarian say this?
    Ⓐ She is surprised by the information the student needs.
    Ⓑ She is too busy to find the information for the student.
    Ⓒ She is not sure she can find the information.
    Ⓓ She is not sure she has heard the student correctly.

04 Part-time Job / Job Fair / Internship

상황별
출제포인트
- Q1 Requirement
- Q2 Problem (Worry About)
- Q3 Cause
- Q4 Solution (Suggestion)
- Q5 Advantage
- Q6 Disadvantage

Situation 1. Student Host

student host^{주최 학생가} prospective student^{입학 지망자}를 데리고 다니면서 campus^{교정} 안내를 해준다. 입학 지망 학생이 입학을 하면 part-time job^{아르바이트}으로 student host를 하고 싶은데, 주로 무슨 업무를 하게 되는지 ^{Q1} 묻는다. 또한 학생이 관련 경험이 없어서^{Q2} 걱정을 하자 student host가 경험이 있는 다른 학생을 만나 보라^{Q4}고 제안한다.

Situation 2. Part-time Job (1)

한 학생이 part-time job을 하고 있는데 band club^{밴드 동아리}에도 가입하고 싶다고 한다. 하지만 band club에 가입하면 일하는 시간과 겹쳐서 일을 하지 못하게 될 것 같아^{Q2} 걱정한다. 그러자, 담당 직원은 다른 학생과 shift^{교대 근무}를 바꿔서 일하는 건 어떠냐^{Q4}고 제안한다.

→ 예를 들어, 어떤 학생이 카페에 일자리가 있는지 문의하는 상황의 경우에는 serving^{손님 시중 들기} 경험이 있어야 한다는 자격 요건 (Requirement)이 언급된다. 이처럼 part-time job을 구하기 위해 갖추어야 할 요건을 묻는 문제가 자주 출제된다. 또한, 왜 이 직장에 지원했는지 혹은 왜 전 직장을 그만뒀는지 등을 묻는 문제도 출제된다.

Situation 3. Part-time Job (2)

part-time job을 구하러 student career center^{구직 상담 센터}를 방문한 학생에게, 직원은 chemistry lab^{화학 실험실}에서의 일자리를 제안하며 학생의 전공이 화학이니 도움이 많이 될 것^{Q5}이라고 말한다. 학생은 작년에 그 일을 해봤는데 보수가 너무 적었다^{Q6}며 거절한다. 등록금을 내야 하기 때문에 힘들어도 보수가 더 높은 food court^{푸드 코트, 식당}에서 serving을 하고 싶다고 하자, 직원이 일자리 찾는 것을 도와 준다.

→ part-time job 관련 대화에서는 일자리의 장단점(Advantage / Disadvantage) 문제가 많이 출제된다.

핵/심/표/현

- academic advisor 지도교수
- admission n. 입학
- advancement n. 진보, 향상
- advantage n. 이점, 우위
- alumni n. 졸업생들
- application n. 신청, 응시
- appointment n. 예약
- average n. 평균, 보통
- bachelor's degree 학사 학위
- campus activity 교내 활동
- career n. 경력, 직업
- career advisory service 직업 조언 서비스
- commencement ceremony 학위 수여식
- competitive adj. 경쟁적인
- coordinate v. 조정하다
- corporation n. (큰 규모의) 기업, 회사
- CV n. 이력서(= curriculum vitae)
- degree n. 학위
- double major 복수 전공
- drop out 중퇴하다
- employee n. 피고용인, 직원
- employer n. 고용주
- enhance v. 증가하다, 나아지다
- expertise n. 전문 지식[기술]
- firm n. 회사
- freshman n. (대학) 신입생
- full-time adj. 정규직의 adv. 정규직으로
- graduate v. 졸업하다
- internship program 인턴 프로그램
- interview n. 면접, 기자 회견
- job fair n. 직업 박람회
- junior n. (대학) 3학년생
- master program 석사 과정
- option n. 선택권
- part-time adj. 아르바이트의 adv. 아르바이트로
- position n. (사회적인) 위치
- prioritize v. 우선 순위를 매기다
- promotion n. 승진, 승급
- propose v. 제안하다
- qualification n. 자격, 자질
- qualified adj. 자격이 있는
- recruit v. 모집하다
- reject v. 거절하다
- requirement n. 자격요건
- resume n. 이력서
- scholarship/fellowship n. 장학금
- senior n. 졸업반 학생
- shift n. 교대 근무
- sophomore n. (대학) 2학년생
- specialization n. 전문화, 전문 과목[분야]
- study abroad n. 해외 연수
- transfer v. 전학하다, 전과하다

Sample Questions

[01 ~ 05] **Listen to a conversation between a student and an employee at the university center. Then answer the questions.** MP3 24 정답 및 해석 p. 052

Note-taking

- Disadvantage / Advantage:

- Requirement:

- Suggestion:

- Future Action:

01 Why does the student visit the employee?
   Ⓐ To learn about writing resumes
   Ⓑ To get a part-time job
   Ⓒ To get information about summer internships
   Ⓓ To ask about switching majors

02. What's the employee's attitude toward the student's prior major?
   Ⓐ She is worried that it did not give him enough expertise.
   Ⓑ She admires the way he made a difficult decision.
   Ⓒ She believes that it was useless.
   Ⓓ She thinks that it will help him get a position.

03. What does the student imply about the position at the convention center?
   Ⓐ It is too far away.
   Ⓑ It does not pay enough money.
   Ⓒ It suits his expertise.
   Ⓓ It is a position he wants.

04. What will the student probably do on Friday?
   Ⓐ Visit the employee again
   Ⓑ Talk to an academic counselor
   Ⓒ Attend a resume writing seminar
   Ⓓ Look for more summer internships

Listen again to part of the conversation. Then answer the question. 🔊 **MP3 24_1**

05. What does the student imply when he says this?
   Ⓐ He is worried that he will have to wait to get hired.
   Ⓑ He thinks the opportunity seems too good to be true.
   Ⓒ He doubts that he is qualified for the position.
   Ⓓ He is concerned that the position won't suit him.

▶ Question Review

Introduction
internship 정보를 얻고 싶어함

Listen to a conversation between a student and an employee at the university center.

Student(male): Hi, Q1 I was wondering if I could possibly get any information about internship opportunities for this summer.

Employee(female): Well, you've come to the right place. All right, take a seat. So, what are you interested in?

S: Um... I recently changed majors from computer engineering to international business, so I wanted to check out business internships.

E: Okay. So what year are you in?

S: I'm a sophomore.

E: Hmm... You do know that most companies want to hire interns who are finished with their junior year, right? I mean, most students start taking upper level classes in their field in the third year. Companies generally want interns that have a little more knowledge.

S: Yeah, I know, but I thought I might as well give it a shot. It's better just to ask, right?

E: True. Okay, let me check the system just to see if there are any spots available. Hmm... so business major... and... no experience requirements... Do you have any special skills? Or other requirements?

S: Well... I'm fluent in French, although I'm not sure that will help any... and I also want a full-time position where I can work 40 hours a week in the summer.

E: All right, the system shows two results.

S: Great, so give me the details.

E: There's a position at the town convention center coordinating business conventions.

S: That sounds interesting!

E: But...

S: But what?

Disadvantage / Advantage
낮은 급여 / 좋은 경험

E: The pay is a little lower than average... It'll give you good experience, but they pay a little over seven dollars an hour.

S: Q3 Seven dollars! I need to make enough money to pay rent... What about the other one?

Headset

E: 🎧 It's at JKJ Corporation.

S: Oh wow, that's a great company... Q5 but wait... what's the problem with that one?

Disadvantage / Advantage

E: Well, I wouldn't say it's a problem, but it's a pretty competitive position. I mean, it is a well-known company, right? Hey, Q2 didn't you

높은 경쟁률 / 학생의
컴퓨터 관련 배경 지식이
유리하게 작용

Requirement
이력서

Suggestion
이력서 쓰기 세미나에
참석할 것

Future Action
이력서를 쓴 후 같이 수정

mention that you were an engineering major before you switched? That's great, because companies always prefer people with a computer background.

S: Well, I guess I'll take my chances then. What do I need to do to apply?
E: First, you'll need to send me your resume or CV.
S: Actually, I don't have one yet…
E: That's okay. **Q4** **There's going to be seminar on how to write resumes this Friday at the campus business center. I suggest you go to the seminar to get some pointers.** In the meantime, why don't you write a basic resume, and we can have individual meetings so we can figure out what to put in and what to take out.
S: That sounds great! Thank you so much! So… can I stop by next week, Thursday? I'll have my resume ready by then.
E: Hmm… I have a spot available at 2 p.m. Does that sound good?
S: Super.

Practice Questions

[01 ~ 05] **Listen to a conversation between a student and an employee at the school radio station. Then answer the questions.** MP3 25 정답 및 해석 p. 054

Note-taking

01 Why does the student go to see the employee?
    Ⓐ To complain about the campus radio station
    Ⓑ To request a job application form
    Ⓒ To find out why he did not get a job
    Ⓓ To ask for a change in his radio show

02 Why did the employee reject the student's application?
   Ⓐ She did not like the student's attitude.
   Ⓑ She decided the student wasn't qualified.
   Ⓒ The student proposed the wrong kind of show.
   Ⓓ The student did not have enough experience.

03 What does the student want to do at the radio station?
   Ⓐ Play the music that students want
   Ⓑ Talk about topics that interest students
   Ⓒ Interview local student musicians
   Ⓓ Have a monthly debate about university policies

04 Why does the student mention that his major is communication arts?
   Ⓐ To emphasize his qualifications
   Ⓑ To explain his motivation to get the job
   Ⓒ To point out that he doesn't have experience
   Ⓓ To show how confusing the application form is

05 How does the employee probably feel at the end of the conversation?
   Ⓐ Annoyed that the student will not give up
   Ⓑ Impressed by the student's great idea
   Ⓒ Glad that the student is applying again
   Ⓓ Appreciative of the student's musical taste

05 School Facility

상황별 출제포인트	♀1 Problem ♀2 Cause ♀3 Solution (Suggestion) ♀4 Advantage ♀5 Disadvantage

Situation 1. Gym

학생이 gym체육관 open hours운영시간가 너무 짧아서 이용하기 쉽지 않다며♀1 운영시간을 늘려주면 좋겠다고 말한다. 직원은 gym 이용시간을 늘리면 직원들의 근무시간도 늘어나는데, budget예산이 한정되어 있어 이로 인한 비용 문제가 발생하기 때문에 안 된다♀2고 대답한다. 학생은 요가와 같은 수업을 discount할인해 주면 더 많은 학생들이 gym에 가입해서 재정 상태가 좋아지지 않겠냐♀3고 제안하고, 직원은 생각해 보겠다고 말한다.

→ 학생이 학교 시설에 대해서 불만을 제기하는 상황이 자주 출제된다.

Situation 2. Parking Lot

학생이 parking lot주차장을 사용하기 위해 parking permit주차증을 구입하러 왔는데, 지금 campus교내 parking lot은 renovation수리 중이라서 주차 가능한 장소가 lot F 밖에 없다♀1고 한다. lot F는 학생의 강의실에서 멀어서 shuttle bus셔틀 버스를 타고 가야 하지만,♀5 대신에 가격이 더 저렴한♀4 이점이 있다. 직원은 renovation이 끝나면 faculty교직원와 학생들 모두에게 인상된 parking fee주차요금를 받을 것♀5이라고 알려준다.

Situation 3. Listening Lab

학생이 listening lab시청각실에 갔는데 VCR(video cassette recorder)비디오 플레이어이 malfunction오작동한다.♀1 직원이 살펴 보더니 자신이 고칠 수는 없고 repair center수리 센터에 보내야 한다고 말한다. 학생은 video비디오를 빨리 시청하고 paper보고서를 써서 deadline마감 기한인 내일 모레까지 turn in제출하다해야 한다고 걱정한다. 학생은 이 과목에서 A를 받지 못하면 scholarship장학금을 못 받게 된다.♀2 다른 lab을 이용하는 방법을 생각해 보았지만 예약이 모두 끝나서 이용이 불가능하다. lab 직원은 video file이 Internet에도 있을 수 있으니 학생에게 직접 찾아보라고 하고, VCR이 수리되는 대로 학생에게 바로 연락을 주겠다♀3고 이야기한다.

→ 기계가 오작동하거나 그로 인해 학생이 불이익을 당하는 내용이 Problem 유형의 문제로 자주 출제된다.

핵/심/표/현

- administration office n. 행정실
- approval n. 승인
- auditorium n. 강당
- authorize v. 인가하다, 재가하다
- budget n. 예산
- cafeteria n. (셀프 서비스식의) 구내 식당
- campus job n. 교내 일자리
- campus restaurant 교내 식당
- choir n. 합창단
- chorus n. 합창(곡), 합창단 v. 합창하다
- committee n. 위원회
- construction n. 건설, 공사
- convenience store n. 편의점
- center for disability service 장애학생 지원 센터
- endorsement n. 승인
- equipment n. 장비, 용품
- facilities management 시설 관리
- faculty n. 교수진
- faculty only 교직원 전용
- feedback n. 피드백
- formality n. 형식상 절차
- gym n. 체육관, 경기장(= gymnasium)
- lab manager 연구실 관리자
- laboratory n. 연구실
- listening lab 시청각실
- malfunction n. 오작동 v. 오작동하다
- meal plan n. 식사 이용권
- medical insurance n. 의료보험
- parking fee n. 주차요금
- parking lot n. 주차장
- parking permit n. 주차증
- parking sticker n. 주차권
- parking ticket n. 주차 위반 딱지
- postal service n. 우편 제도
- radio station 라디오 방송국
- rehearsal n. 리허설
- renovation n. 개조, 보수
- reschedule v. 일정을 변경하다
- residence dining 기숙사 식당
- school fair 학교 바자회
- student club 학생 동아리
- student council 학생 자치회
- student health center 학교 보건소
- teaching assistant n. 조교
- wireless adj. 무선의

Sample Questions

[01 ~ 05] Listen to a conversation between a student and a professor. Then answer the questions. MP3 26 정답 및 해석 p. 056

Note-taking

- Disadvantage:

- Misunderstanding / Correction:

- Requirement:

- Difference:

- Suggestion:

01 Why does the student visit the professor?
   Ⓐ To complain about the computer center
   Ⓑ To explain why he handed his paper in late
   Ⓒ To give his opinion on the professor's class
   Ⓓ To discuss the direction of his paper

What is the professor's attitude toward the new printers?
Ⓐ She is surprised that the university bought them.
Ⓑ She feels that buying them was not a good use of university funds.
Ⓒ She thinks it is difficult to keep up with new technology.
Ⓓ She believes that they will be useful to her students.

Why does the professor mention her home printer?
Ⓐ To indicate that she did not know it was difficult for students to print
Ⓑ To offer an alternative to using the school's printers
Ⓒ To agree that the university printers are difficult to use
Ⓓ To emphasize that the student should not make excuses

Why does the professor mention that the sentences in *A Simple Heart* have great meaning?
Ⓐ To point out the best way to learn about the novel's protagonist
Ⓑ To reinforce Gustave Flaubert's stance on society
Ⓒ To give an example of contemporary French literature's style
Ⓓ To explain how the student should read Flaubert's novels

What did the professor and the student find interesting about Flaubert's writing style?
Ⓐ He criticized people using favorable language.
Ⓑ He created a slowly changing view of a character.
Ⓒ He allowed one of his main characters to die at the end.
Ⓓ He used language consistently across all of his novels.

▶ **Question Review**

Introduction	**Listen to a conversation between a student and a professor.**
Disadvantage 새 장비의 사용 방법이 까다로움	**Professor(female):** Brian! Finally… What took you so long? **Student(male):** Oh, I'm so sorry, the computer center… They brought in new printers. I mean, they're new, so they should be better, right? But I can't figure out how to use them… It seems like they're too complicated for ordinary people like me. P: Yeah, I know what you mean. **Q2** Every time the school brings in new equipment… It's a lot to learn, you know? S: Exactly, I mean, I can go to the library to make print-outs, but there're just so many people in line… It's impossible to print without waiting for about an hour. Of course, I can just go to the computer center next to the dorms, but the new printers… They just… I mean, I try to print using the wireless feature in the new printers, but the data never transfers properly. All I get is an error message. It's really frustrating. I mean, new technology is supposed to make things simpler, right?
Misunderstanding / Correction 학생들이 프린터기를 이용하는 게 그렇게 힘든지 몰랐음	P: Ha ha… **Q3** Really? It's that bad, huh? I mean, I just print everything at home… my printer is 10 years old and works fine. I just assumed that all students could use a printer better than I ever could. S: There are times when I have to drive off campus and pay for print-outs just because it's impossible to print at the computer center. **Q1** Anyway, here's the copy of the paper I wrote on *Three Tales* by Gustave Flaubert that you asked for. P: Okay, let's see. Right, "The True Meanings of Modern French Classics". Well, like I told you last week, it's a great topic for your paper, but have you… S: Yeah, do you mean look deeper into the first story, *A Simple Heart*?
Requirement 첫 이야기를 이해해야만 나머지 이야기들을 이해할 수 있음	P: Exactly. Even though it's a simple story, it sets the tone for the other stories, you know? **Q4** The sentences that are used in the story all have great meaning in them. Unless you properly understand the first of the three stories, you won't be able to truly figure out the meaning of the others. S: Well… I did some more reading and more research, and I think I figured some things out. P: Is it about the protagonist of the story, Félicité? Did you find anything about her? S: I don't know if it's something about her. Was I supposed to find out more about the character?

P: No, not at all, I'm just seeing if you really found what I wanted you to see.

S: Phew… that's a relief. Anyway, at first, I didn't really think much of the story, I mean, there's this servant who just dies at the end when she gets old. But then I noticed how the voice of the narrator changed throughout the novel.

P: Very good! So what did you realize?

S: Well, Flaubert seemed very critical of Félicité at first. She does sacrifice everything, even though she gets nothing in return. But as the story progresses, the words that are used to describe the character change. They become more and more positive. **Q5 It's really interesting. The words pretty much describe the same person, but they change so much.**

P: I know! That's why Flaubert's works are incredible! You see why I told you to look closely at the sentences?

S: Yeah, I just assumed that Flaubert was trying to be critical of people who sacrifice themselves for others, but when I realized how the narrator's voice changed, I came to the opposite conclusion.

P: Now you're on the right track. Why don't you take what you learned and see if it applies to the other two stories as well?

Difference
작가가 한 등장인물을 묘사하는 방식이 점점 긍정적으로 변화

Suggestion
다른 두 이야기도 살펴볼 것을 제안

Practice Questions

[01 ~ 05] **Listen to a conversation between a student and a receptionist at the administration office. Then answer the questions.** MP3 27 정답 및 해설 p. 057

Note-taking

01 Why does the student go to the office?
  Ⓐ To find out why she failed her biological sciences course
  Ⓑ To explain why she did not receive a grade in a class
  Ⓒ To complain about a poor grade she received
  Ⓓ To request a transcript of her grades from last semester

02 What can be inferred about the student's professor?
    Ⓐ He is not aware of the student's schedule.
    Ⓑ He does not tolerate sloppy research habits.
    Ⓒ He is understanding in regards to the student's situation.
    Ⓓ He has a bad relationship with the administration office.

03 What reasons does the student give to explain why her project failed?
    Choose two answers.
    Ⓐ She accidentally left a sample in her refrigerator.
    Ⓑ She could not catch a bus to go to the lab.
    Ⓒ The lab she worked in caught on fire.
    Ⓓ Nobody answered the phone at the lab when she called.

04 What does the employee imply about the school's buses?
    Ⓐ They should run every day.
    Ⓑ They often fail to arrive on schedule.
    Ⓒ They are more reliable than public transportation.
    Ⓓ Their weekly schedule is not known by many students.

05 What does the employee imply when he says this? 🔊 MP3 27_1
    Ⓐ He is worried that the student created a fire hazard.
    Ⓑ He thinks the research project must have been difficult.
    Ⓒ He thinks that watching a fire all night would be boring.
    Ⓓ He is annoyed that the student made such a silly mistake.

 기타 (Miscellaneous)

| 상황별
출제포인트 | Q1 Function
Q2 Advantage
Q3 Opinion / Attitude
Q4 Problem
Q5 Solution (Suggestion) |

Situation 1. Math Club

교수가 학생에게 수학에 관심이 있다면 math club^{수학 동아리}에 가입하라고 제안한다. math club에서는 수학에 뒤처진 학생에게 수학을 잘 하는 학생을 소개해 주어 수학 공부를 도와 주게 한다.^{Q1} 수학을 잘 하는 학생의 입장에서는 **teaching experience**^{교습 경험}가 생기기 때문에 grad school^{대학원} 진학에 도움이 될^{Q2} 것이라고 말한다.

→ **club**^{동아리} 관련 대화에서는 **club**의 목적이나 기능을 묻는 문제가 자주 출제된다.

Situation 2. Writing Club

교수가 글을 잘 쓰는 학생에게 writing club^{작문 동아리}에 가입하라고 제안한다. 학생은 writing club에 가입하면 어떤 활동을 하게 되는지^{Q1} 궁금해 한다.

→ **club**에서 어떤 활동을 하게 되는지를 묻는 문제도 **Function** 유형에 해당된다.

교수는 문학 교수를 초빙해서 세미나도 하고, 책을 정해서 읽은 후 감상문을 쓰고 발표하는 등 여러 가지 활동을 하게 된다고 설명한다. 학생은 자신에게 글 쓰는 재주가 있는지 의문이 들어 writing club에 들어갈 수 있을지 걱정한다.^{Q3}

→ 학생이 걱정하는 상황은 **Problem – Worry About** 문제로 출제될 수도 있으나, **Attitude(Positive / Negative)** 문제로도 출제될 수 있다.

Situation 3. Poetry Club

한 학생이 자신은 poem^시이 좋은데 시를 쓸 시간이 없다고 하자, 다른 학생이 시에 관심이 있으면 poetry club^{시 동아리}에 가입하는 것이 어떠냐고^{Q5} 제안한다. 그러자 학생은 관심은 정말 많은데 이번 학기에 수강하는 과목이 너무 많다^{Q4}고 대답한다.

→ 제안을 거절하는 이유를 완곡하게 돌려 말하고 있기 때문에 출제 포인트를 놓칠 우려가 있으니 유의해야 한다.

Situation 4. Concert Bus

학생들이 concert^{공연}에 가기 위해 차를 빌리려고 하는데, bus는 하루에 몇 시간만 이용하더라도 하루 요금을 받고, van^{승합차}은 시간제 요금을 받는다. 따라서 van이 더 경제적이다.^{Q2} bus는 대형 주차 공간이 필요한 반면, van은 concert hall^{콘서트 홀}의 주차장에 주차하기도 더 쉽다.^{Q2} 하지만, 학생의 수가 많기 때문에 van을 빌릴 경우 두 대를 빌려야 해서 기사가 두 명 필요하고, deposit^{예약금}을 조금 더 내야 한다. van 회사의 직원은 9시에 공연이 끝나면 van으로 다시 pick up^{태우러 가다/하러 갈} 테니 9시 10분까지 지정된 장소로 오라고 말한다. 학생은 공연이 길어질 수도 있고, 사람들이 많아 일행을 금방 찾지 못할 수도 있으니^{Q4} 9시 30분까지 만나는 것으로 하자고 말한다.

핵/심/표/현

- allegory n. 우화, 풍자, 비유
- autobiography n. 자서전
- accent n. 억양
- background n. 배경, 출신
- club n. 동아리
- committee n. 위원회
- commute v. 통학하다
- concurrent enrolment 동시 등록
- contaminate v. 오염시키다
- credit hour (학점 이수의) 단위 시간
- deposit n. 예약금
- dialect n. 사투리
- division n. 부, 분과, 반
- editorial n. 사설
- epilogue n. 에필로그, 종결 부분
- exchange student 교환 학생
- extension n. 기한 연장
- formula n. 공식
- honor roll n. 우등생 명단
- humanities course 인문계열 과정[과목]
- illogical adj. 비논리적인
- inspire v. 영감을 주다, 격려하다
- interdisciplinary adj. 여러 학문 분야가 관련된
- international student 국제 학생, 유학생
- invoice n./v. 청구서(를 보내다)
- legend n. (지도·도표 등의) 범례, 기호 설명표
- legislation n. 법률 제정
- literacy n. 글을 읽고 쓸 줄 아는 능력
- logical adj. 논리적인
- overdue v. 연체되다
- prologue n. 서막, 서언, 프롤로그
- proverb n. 속담
- quotation n. 인용
- radical adj. 근본적인, 급진적인
- review v. 검토하다, 심사하다
- serial n. 연재물
- ship v. 배송하다
- shipping fee n. 배송비
- wholesaler n. 도매업자

Sample Questions

[01 ~ 05] **Listen to a conversation between a student and an employee at the student activity center. Then answer the questions.** MP3 28 정답 및 해석 p. 060

Note-taking

• Advantage:

• Problem:

• Requirement / Cause:

• Suggestion:

• Attitude:

• Future Action:

01 Why does the student go to speak with the employee?
   Ⓐ To find out about joining a club
   Ⓑ To inquire about a French class
   Ⓒ To get help starting a new club
   Ⓓ To ask where a professor's office is

What does the employee say about clubs that have a professor's support?
Ⓐ They must bring in a letter signed by the professor.
Ⓑ They are eligible for full funding by the school.
Ⓒ They don't need to reserve a room in advance.
Ⓓ They tend to be approved more easily than other clubs.

What is the student's attitude toward using a shared room?
Ⓐ He thinks that it will help him find out about other clubs.
Ⓑ He considers it to be an acceptable alternative.
Ⓒ He is concerned that the other club members won't like it.
Ⓓ He is enthusiastic about it because the rooms are larger.

According to the employee, why can't the student get a private room?
Ⓐ There are too many members in his club.
Ⓑ The student wants to meet on weekends.
Ⓒ The student's club hasn't been approved.
Ⓓ Many clubs hold meetings on Fridays.

What is the student most likely to do next?
Ⓐ Request a letter from his professor
Ⓑ Reconfirm his room reservation
Ⓒ Fill out some application forms
Ⓓ Ask a committee to review his registration

▶ **Question Review**

Listen to a conversation between a student and an employee at the student activity center.

Student(male): This is the student activity center, right?
Employee(female): Uh-huh. How can I help you?

Introduction

S: Well, **Q1 I'm trying to start a new club.** During one of our conversations, my professor recommended that I start a French club. You know, so students can meet on a regular basis to practice speaking French and possibly meet French exchange students. **Q1 But I really don't know where to start.**

E: Well, you've definitely come to the right place. All right, well, first things first... You're going to need a leader. The form has to be filled out by the president. Who's going to be the club's president?

S: That'd be me. Kevin Williams.

E: Okay. You're going to have to fill this form out. It's good to hear that your professor told you to start the club. **Q2 Our committee always reviews the clubs that have a professor recommendation first, so it's much easier for them to get started,** you know?

Advantage
교수님 추천이 있는
신청서부터 검토함

S: That's good to hear. He told me the French department will give us its full support.

E: Great. The second thing you need is a location for your meetings and stuff. Do you guys have a place in mind?

S: Not really. I assumed I could reserve a place on campus through you guys. It would be great if we could just have a room to hold weekly meetings in.

E: Hmm... Let me check our system... What day will you guys be meeting on?

S: I'm thinking it would be best to meet on Fridays, since it's the end of the week.

Problem
원하는 요일에 쓸 수
있는 room이 없음

E: Uh-oh... There aren't any rooms available on Fridays. I guess all the clubs want to meet on that day. Hmm... The only days that you guys can meet regularly are Mondays and Thursdays.

S: Let's see... Mondays will probably be too tough... So... so... I guess... It'll have to be on Thursdays then.

**Requirement /
Cause**
등록된 동아리만
private room을 쓸
수 있음

E: All right then. I'll reserve a place on Thursdays for you... But **Q4 since your club isn't officially registered yet, we're not going to be able to get you a room all to yourselves.**

S: Wait, I thought...

Suggestion
shared room을 쓰도록 제안

E: Oh, you can still get a room. You'll just have to share it with some other clubs that may be meeting at the same time. In order to become a registered club, you'll need to fill out the forms I gave you and wait until your request is approved. Not that you would have been able to reserve a room on Fridays even if you were registered right now.

S: I see. Well… I'm not really sure what you mean by sharing a room.

E: Well, some rooms are private. One club, one room. But we also have large rooms that are broken up into three separate meeting spaces for three different clubs.

S: Oh. But there are dividers or walls, right?

E: Oh, yes. There will be a couple of dividers, so there's some privacy. Our shared rooms are currently filled up on Fridays too, but Thursdays will be fine.

Attitude
◎ agree

S: **Q3** **Okay, we can work with that then. I wouldn't want to start without a place to meet.**

E: Okay, here's another set of forms you have to fill out to reserve a shared room. But make sure you fill out the first form first.

S: So after we're registered, is there any chance we can get a private room for our meetings?

E: Well, that depends. If you want a private room on Fridays, probably not. The waiting list is really long. But another day may be possible.

Future Action
서류를 작성해옴

S: All right. **Q5** **I'll bring the forms back tomorrow.** Thanks so much for your help.

Practice Questions

[01 ~ 05] **Listen to a conversation between a student and an employee in the university bookstore. Then answer the questions.** MP3 29 정답 및 해석 p. 062

Note-taking

01 Why does the student need the employee's assistance?
   Ⓐ She does not know where to purchase a vase.
   Ⓑ She is trying to find a local crafts store.
   Ⓒ She needs to figure out what her assignment is.
   Ⓓ She is unsure how to sell an item she made.

02. What can be inferred about students who try to sell their items in the university bookstore?
   Ⓐ They must sell an item as part of an assignment.
   Ⓑ They will ask the store to sell their items if they know they can.
   Ⓒ They must be willing to get only a small amount of money.
   Ⓓ They can only sell items that can be sold by wholesalers.

03. What is the student's attitude toward her assignment?
   Ⓐ She feels that it is unfair for students who cannot use computers.
   Ⓑ She is optimistic that she can find a way to sell her vase.
   Ⓒ She is not confident that her vase will find a suitor.
   Ⓓ She thinks her vase will be sold faster than the vases made by her classmates.

04. What are two reasons why the student does not want to sell her vase on consignment? Choose two answers.
   Ⓐ She is not confident in her work.
   Ⓑ She does not know how to use computers.
   Ⓒ She has too much schoolwork to do.
   Ⓓ She does not have a proper means of transportation.

05. How does the student react to the information the employee gives her about the town fair? Choose two answers.
   Ⓐ She is embarrassed because she did not think of it herself.
   Ⓑ She thinks she'll be too busy with schoolwork during the fair.
   Ⓒ She is grateful that there is a way to complete her assignment.
   Ⓓ She is convinced that she can carry her vase to the fair.

Lecture

Lecture Question Types

Lecture Question Types

01. Main Idea
02. Function / Purpose
03. Problem
04. Solution (Suggestion)
05. Example
06. Cause & Effect
07. Similarity / Difference
08. Advantage / Disadvantage
09. Misunderstanding / Correction
10. Definition (Term) / Origin
11. Two Click / Three Click
12. Ordering
13. Matching
14. Opinion / Attitude
15. Replay Question (Headset)
16. Requirement (Condition)
17. Character
18. Imply / Infer

Chapter III

Lecture Question Types

01 Main Idea

1 문제의 핵심

수험자가 글 전체의 의도를 파악할 수 있는 능력이 있는지를 확인하는 문제이다. 글 전체를 통해서 교수가 전달하고 싶어 하는 메시지를 가장 잘 나타낸 보기를 고르는 것이 이 문제 유형의 핵심이다. 따라서 전체 글의 의도가 아닌, 글의 일부에서만 언급된 내용이 오답 보기로 등장하므로 주의해야 한다.

2 문제의 예시

- What is the lecture **mainly about**?
- What are the speakers **mainly talking about**?
- What is the **main purpose** of the lecture?

3 100% 문제 공략법

01 난이도가 하인 문제는 대부분 Lecture의 도입부에서 Main Idea에 대한 단서가 나오므로 초반에 집중하여 듣는 것이 중요하다. 예를 들어, 강의 초반에 "오늘은 A에 대해서 이야기하겠다"라고 언급한 뒤 그에 대해 강의를 이끌어 가는 식이다.

02 난이도가 중상인 문제는 Lecture의 도입부에 주제에 대한 단서가 broad하게 나오며, 전체 지문을 다 듣고 보기를 읽었을 때 지문에 언급된 내용이 크게 보기 (A)와 보기 (B)로 갈리는 경우이다. 이때는 (A)와 (B)의 내용을 혼합한 보기가 있는지 살펴보도록 한다. 두 가지 내용을 혼합한 보기가 없다면 좀 더 난이도가 높은 문제이며, 이때는 (A)와 (B) 내용 중 교수가 어떤 것에 더 focus를 두고 강의를 했는지를 생각하여 Main Idea에 더 가까운 답을 고르면 된다.

03 가장 난이도가 높은 문제는 Lecture에서 (A)에 대한 내용을 조금 언급한 후, (A)에 대한 예로 (B)를 언급하고 (B)에 대해 계속해서 이야기하는 것이다. (B)에 대한 내용이 더 많이 언급되었으므로 (B)가 강의의 Main Idea일 것 같지만, (B)는 (A)를 이해시키기 위한 예로 언급된 것이므로 Main Idea는 (A)가 된다.

Tip Main Idea 문제 유형은 전체 글의 의도를 묻는 문제이므로 부분적인 내용을 언급한 보기는 정답이 될 수 없다. 또한, 강의의 도입부에서 가장 많은 단서가 나오기는 하지만, 난이도가 높은 강의의 경우 지문 내용을 끝까지 들어야만 답을 찾을 수 있는 문제도 있으므로 항상 글의 전체 내용과 의도를 염두에 두고 문제를 풀어야 한다. 앞 부분에 등장한 단서만으로는 오답을 고르게 될 가능성이 있다.

4 강의 속 단서 표현

강의 도입부에서 강의의 주제를 언급하는 표현에 주목한다.
- Today, we are going to talk about ~
- I'd like to focus on ~

▶ **Example Question**

Script

Today, I want to talk about a kind of adaptation that takes place in places where temperatures and precipitation aren't constant. You know, in some places it sometimes rains a lot, and sometimes weeks can pass without any rain at all. So, plants that grow in these climates have evolved in various ways to cope with the dry season.

Question

What is the lecture mainly about?

Ⓐ The differences in how humans and plants release water
Ⓑ How plants sense and respond to dry seasons
Ⓒ Why plants need water to create energy
Ⓓ The process by which plants prevent the loss of water

> **이것을 듣고 답을 찾아라!**
> 'Today ~'라고 말한 뒤 강의의 주제를 명확하게 말해주는 경우도 있지만, 실제 시험에서는 명확하게 단서를 주지 않는 경우도 많으므로 도입부 전체를 잘 듣도록 한다. 처음에는 기온과 강수량이 일정하지 않은 곳을 먼저 언급한 후, '식물이 건기에 맞춰 진화하는 방식'을 언급한다. 여기서 강의의 Main Idea가 '동식물의 adaptation'과 관련된 것임을 예측하고 나머지 강의를 들으면 된다.

지문 해석
오늘은 기온과 강수량이 변하는 지역에서 생기는 적응 방법의 한 종류에 대해 이야기하고자 합니다. 알다시피, 어떤 지역은 가끔은 비가 엄청나게 내리고, 가끔은 비가 전혀 내리지 않은 채로 몇 주가 흐르기도 하지요. 그래서 이런 기후에서 자라는 식물들은 건기에 대처할 수 있도록 다양한 방식으로 진화해 왔습니다.

문제 해석 및 정답
강의의 주된 내용은?
Ⓐ 인간과 식물이 수분을 방출하는 방식의 차이
Ⓑ 식물이 건기를 감지하고 반응하는 방식
Ⓒ 식물이 에너지를 만들기 위해 물을 필요로 하는 이유
Ⓓ 식물이 수분 손실을 방지하는 과정

어휘
adaptation 적응   temperature 온도, 기온   precipitation 강수(량)   climate 기후   evolve 진화하다

02 Function / Purpose / Influence / Role / Usage

1 문제의 핵심

강의에 언급된 main topic의 기능, 역할, 목적, 영향력, 용도 등을 묻는 문제 유형이다. 예를 들어, 역사 지문에서는 어떤 사람의 업적(Eg. 토마스 제퍼슨의 업적)을 묻고, 제조법에 관한 지문에서는 만들어진 물건이 어떤 용도로 사용되는지를 묻는 문제가 출제될 수 있다. 또한 제도나 법과 관련된 강의에서는 그 목적 또는 기능을 묻는 문제가 자주 출제된다.

2 문제의 예시

- What is one **objective** of free trade measures? (제도의 목적)
- What was **the intent** of Act? (법안의 목적)
- What **purpose** does the dam serve? (댐의 목적)
- What is **the main function** of semiconductor switches? (반도체의 기능)
- What was Egyptian glass **used for**? (물건의 용도)
- What does the professor say about **Charles Dickens**? (사람의 역할)
- Why does the professor mention **Ken Nelson**? (사람의 역할)
- What **influence** did the fall of the Roman Empire have? (역사적 사건의 영향)
- What **influenced** the earliest American writers? (A가 B에게 미치는 영향)
- What is **the role** of photosynthesis in biological communities? (광합성의 기능)

3 100% 문제 공략법

각 주제별 예상가능한 논리 전개를 정리해두는 것이 좋다.

- 01 engineering: 제품의 기능 (Eg. 반도체의 기능, 숲의 정화 기능)
- 02 history: 사람의 업적/역할 (Eg. 조지 워싱턴의 업적)
- 03 act: 법의 목적/기능 (Eg. 독점방지법의 목적)
- 04 art: 예술 사조의 영향 (Eg. Cubism이 Surrealism에 영향을 줌)
- 05 botany: 특정 현상의 역할 (Eg. 광합성이 생태계에서 하는 역할)

Tip topic 별로 자주 출제되는 Function 문제 유형을 익히고, 그와 관련된 다양한 표현을 익혀두는 것이 중요하다. 또한, 자주 출제되는 오답 방식에 대해서도 알아두는 것이 좋다. 예를 들어, 지문에서 A 장비와 B 장비의 기능을 언급한 후 문제로 A 장비의 기능에 대해 물어봤을 때, B 장비의 기능이 오답 보기로 주어지는 경우가 많다. 따라서 각각의 기능을 구별해서 듣고 note-taking할 필요가 있다.

4 강의 속 단서 표현

목적이나 기능을 나타내는 명사와 동사 표현을 잘 알아두자.

- function, purpose
- help, make, enable, provide, influence, allow ~ to, used for ~
- application, practical uses

▶ **Example Question**

Script

Now, there are also some other ways that charcoal is used. You may own an air or water purifier with a charcoal filter. The charcoal used for filtration is called activated charcoal.

Question

Why does the professor mention air and water purifiers?
Ⓐ To introduce another function of charcoal
Ⓑ To give an example of how charcoal is made
Ⓒ To suggest a new way to utilize heat from charcoal
Ⓓ To illustrate how impurities are filtered from wood

 이것을 듣고 답을 찾아라!

Lecture의 topic이 특정 물건인 경우, 물건의 사용 목적이나 용도를 집중해서 들어야 한다. 'some other ways that charcoal is used'라는 부분에서 'used'를 듣고, 이어지는 강의에서 charcoal의 용도에 관한 내용이 언급될 것이며 용도를 묻는 문제가 출제될 것이라는 점을 예측할 수 있다. 그리고 바로 뒤 문장에서 'used for filtration'이라고 나오므로 정답은 (A)이다. 주의할 점은, 문제에서 'why mention ~'으로 물어봤지만 출제자가 묻고자 하는 내용이 'charcoal의 용도'이므로, 이 문제는 Example 문제로 분류하지 않고 Function 문제로 분류한다는 점이다.

지문 해석
자, 숯이 이용되는 다른 방식도 있습니다. 여러분은 숯 필터가 있는 공기 청정기나 정수기를 가지고 있을지도 모르겠네요. 여과에 사용되는 숯은 활성탄이라고 합니다.

문제 해석 및 정답
교수가 공기 청정기와 정수기를 언급한 이유는?
Ⓐ 숯의 또 다른 기능을 소개하려고
Ⓑ 숯이 어떻게 만들어지는지에 대한 예를 보여주려고
Ⓒ 숯의 열을 이용하는 새로운 방법을 제시하려고
Ⓓ 나무에서 불순물이 여과되는 방법을 예를 들어 설명하려고

어휘
charcoal 숯   purifier 정화 장치   filtration 여과   activated 활성화된   utilize 활용하다   impurity 불순물

03 Problem

1 문제의 핵심

강의에서 언급된 문제점에 대해 묻는 문제 유형이지만, problem이라는 단서 표현에만 의존해서 풀기에는 문제점의 주제나 문제를 나타내는 표현이 너무나 다양하다. 예를 들어, 동·식물학에서 problem이라는 단어를 직접적으로 쓰지 않고 endangered species 멸종위기의 종라는 말만 언급되었더라도, 그 자체가 problem이라는 것을 인지할 수 있어야 한다. 또한, 문제점이 언급된 후에는 그 종을 멸종위기에서 구하려는 사람들의 노력(Solution)이 언급될 가능성이 높다.

2 문제의 예시

- What was a **problem** with Wagner's theory?
- What are the two **main problems** solar power presents as an energy source?
- What were two **difficulties** the scientists had to overcome?
- What does the professor discuss Van Gogh's **difficulties** as a painter?
- What does the professor say about a **decrease** in the polar bear population?
- Why is it **impossible** to monitor most pieces of orbital debris?

3 100% 문제 공략법

각 주제별 강의의 논리 전개를 기억해야 한다. 대체로 문제가 언급되고 뒤이어 해결 방법이 제시되는 흐름이다. 예를 들어, disorder라는 주제에서는 병의 원인 다음으로 problem에 해당하는 병의 증상들이 나오고 그 후에는 병의 치료법이 언급되는 흐름으로 강의가 진행된다.

강의 주제별 대표적인 문제점들도 미리 파악해 두자.

01 science: 과학자들이 설명할 수 없거나 입증할 수 없는 문제
02 engineering: 비행기나 고층건물을 만들 때 발생하는 문제
03 zoology: 어떤 종이 멸종되거나 개체수가 줄어드는 문제
04 education: 유치원생들이 수업시간에 잘 집중하지 못하는 문제
05 environmental science: 환경 오염으로 발생하는 문제
06 disorder: 병의 증상
07 business: 소비자들이 어떤 상품이나 서비스를 외면하는 문제

4 강의 속 단서 표현

직접적으로 문제점을 나타내는 표현뿐 아니라 '불가능하다', '모른다' 등 부정적인 느낌의 표현도 단서가 된다.
- difficulties, problem, air pollution, endangered species
- can't explain ~, not possible to ~, we don't know ~,
- haven't been successful ~, fail to ~, no evidence to support the theory

▶ **Example Question**

Script

That's why it's important to have a good balance between two characteristics. In theory, it's simple. But in practice, companies haven't been successful at figuring out if the people they hire have those traits. Too many companies look for applicants with the same interests as very successful salespeople, and not for people with the best skills to do the job.

Question

What does the professor say about companies that hire salespeople?
Ⓐ They do not take interests of the applicants into account.
Ⓑ They fail to look at the sales abilities of the applicants.
Ⓒ They only seek out people who have empathy.
Ⓓ They scare away people who care about what they sell.

> **이것을 듣고 답을 찾아라!**
> 회사가 직원을 채용할 때 성공적이지 못하다는 'companies haven't been successful at'을 듣고 Problem 문제가 나올 것임을 예측할 수 있다. 지문에서는 직원을 뽑을 때 지원자의 관심사도 중요하지만 업무 능력을 보는 것이 중요한데 많은 회사들이 그 부분을 간과한다는 점을 지적하고 있다.

지문 해석
그것이 바로 두 가지 특징 간의 균형을 갖추는 것이 중요한 이유입니다. 이론적으로는 간단해요. 하지만 실제 상황에서는 회사들이 그들이 고용하는 사람들이 그런 특징들을 가지고 있는지를 알아내는 데 성공하지 못했습니다. 너무 많은 회사들이, 매우 성공적인 판매원과 같은 관심사를 가지고 있는 지원자들만을 찾고 있어요. 그 일을 할 수 있는 최고의 기술을 가진 사람들을 찾는 것이 아니고 말이죠.

문제 해석 및 정답
판매원을 고용하는 회사들에 대해 교수가 말한 것은?
Ⓐ 지원자들의 흥미를 고려하지 않는다.
Ⓑ 지원자들의 판매 능력을 보지 못한다.
Ⓒ 공감능력을 가진 사람들만을 찾는다.
Ⓓ 그들이 팔려는 것에 대해 신경 쓰는 사람들을 쫓아낸다.

어휘
trait 자질　　salesperson 판매원　　take ~ into account ...을 고려하다　　empathy 감정이입, 공감

04 Solution (Suggestion)

1 문제의 핵심

지문에서 언급된 문제점에 대한 Solution을 묻는 문제 유형이다. 강의의 흐름에 따라 문제점이 언급되면 자연스럽게 Solution이 따라서 언급되므로, Problem과 Solution 문제 유형은 함께 묶어서 공략하는 것이 좋으며, 이를 위해 각 주제별 출제 가능성이 높은 Problem과 Solution을 같이 정리해 두는 것이 좋다.

2 문제의 예시

engineering	· What are two **ways to increase the strength** rope made from fibers?
environmental science	· What does the professor say **people have done to help** polar bears survive?
botany	· When discussing needle-leaf tress, which of **adaptations to cold weather** does the professor mention?
disorder	· What can a patient **do to prevent** sleep attack?
architecture	· What factors can **prevent the building** from being damaged?

3 100% 문제 공략법

각 주제별 〈Problem – Solution〉 전개방식을 숙지한다.
- 01 engineering: 구조물을 만들 때 발생한 문제점의 해결 방법
- 02 zoology: 어떤 종이 멸종되거나 개체수가 줄어든 것에 대한 해결 방법
- 03 architecture: 건물이 손상되는 것을 막는 방법
- 04 environmental science: 환경 오염으로 발생하는 문제점의 해결 방법
- 05 disorder: 병의 치료법
- 06 business: 회사를 위기에서 구하는 방법, 매출이 급감했을 때 매출을 증가시키는 방법
- 07 theory: 한 이론의 증거가 부족할 때 제시되는 대체 이론

4 강의 속 단서 표현

문제점의 해결 방법을 나타내므로 단서 표현 중에는 '대안, 해결책' 또는 '막아준다, 증가시킨다' 등의 긍정적인 느낌의 표현들이 많이 있다.
- alternative, innovation
- in order to ~
- prevent, survive
- increase the strength of ~, adaptation to harsh environment

▶ **Example Question**

Script

But there was a problem. The engineers could not do anything about the soil because the tower had tilted too much. Removing the base soil to replace it with concrete would cause the tower to tumble.

So, in order to make the structure stable, the engineers used counterweights. After removing some soil, they used more than 800 tons of lead to raise one end of the base. They also removed the bells to make the tower lighter. Eventually, the tower was moved to a straighter angle.

Question

According to the professor, what did the engineers do to prevent the tower from falling before they stabilized the soil?

Ⓐ They added concrete to the base.
Ⓑ They made one side heavier.
Ⓒ They made the tower heavier.
Ⓓ They prevented tourists from visiting the tower.

○ 이것을 듣고 답을 찾아라!

　　콘크리트로 토양을 대체하기 위해 토양을 제거할 경우 사탑이 너무 기울어져 있어서 무너질 우려가 있다는 Problem이 언급된 후, 구조물을 안정적으로 유지하기 위해서 평형추를 달았다는 Solution이 제시되었다. 목적을 나타내는 in order to가 Solution을 제시하는 단서 표현으로 쓰인 것에 주목한다.

Tip tumble – to stable → counterweight 와 같이 〈Problem – Solution〉을 key word로 note-taking하는 것은 좋은 전략이다.

지문 해석
하지만 문제가 있었죠. 사탑이 너무나 많이 기울어져 있어서 공학자들은 토양에 아무것도 할 수가 없었습니다. 밑부분의 토양을 콘크리트로 교체하기 위해 제거하게 되면 사탑이 무너지게 될 것이었어요.
그래서, 구조물을 안정시키기 위해 공학자들은 평형추를 사용했습니다. 밑부분의 토양을 조금 제거한 후, 그들은 밑부분의 한쪽 끝을 올리기 위해 800톤이 넘는 납 덩어리를 이용했습니다. 그들은 또한 탑이 좀 더 가벼워지도록 종들도 없앴습니다. 마침내, 탑은 좀 더 수직 방향의 각도로 움직였습니다.

문제 해석 및 정답
교수에 의하면, 공학자들은 토대 부분의 토양을 안정화시키기 전에 탑이 쓰러지는 것을 막기 위해 무엇을 했는가?
Ⓐ 토대에 콘크리트를 추가했다.
Ⓑ **한쪽 면을 더 무겁게 했다.**
Ⓒ 사탑의 무게를 더 무겁게 했다.
Ⓓ 관광객들이 탑을 방문하는 것을 막았다.

어휘
tumble 폭삭 무너지다　　counterweight 평형추　　lead 납　　tilt 기울다　　stable 안정된

05 Example

1 문제의 핵심

강의에서 학생들이 이해하기 어려운 전문적인 내용이 언급될 때, 교수는 이해를 돕기 위해 예시를 많이 든다. 따라서, 어려운 단어가 많고 내용이 어려워 잘 들리지 않는 주제의 Lecture라 하더라도 예를 든 부분은 쉽게 이해할 수 있으므로, Example 유형은 조금만 연습하면 쉽게 점수를 딸 수 있는 문제이다. 또한, 강의 주제와 관계없이 자주 출제되는 유형이기도 하다.

2 문제의 예시

- Which of the following are **examples** of A?
- What **example** does the professor give of A?
- **Why** does the professor **mention** turtles?
- **Why** does the professor **mention** the wind?
  (정답 예시: **To provide an example** of how introduced species can be distributed)

3 100% 문제 공략법

01 강의에서 for example, for instance와 같은 단서 표현이 나오면 Example 문제로 연결될 것을 예측할 수 있다.

02 특별한 단서 표현 없이 다른 문제 유형과 연결하여 예가 제시되기도 한다. Advantage/Disadvantage의 예, Problem의 예, Solution의 예, Evidence의 예 등 거의 모든 유형과 Example 유형을 연결할 수 있다. 만약 자신이 Example 유형의 문제를 자주 틀린다면, 어떤 주제에서 어떤 유형과 결합된 Example 문제를 주로 틀리는지를 기억하여 유사한 문제를 많이 풀어 보도록 한다. (Eg. 과학 주제에서 Cause & Effect의 Example 문제 유형)

03 Example 문제이지만 example이 직접 언급되지 않고 'Why mention ~ ?'이라고 나오는 경우도 많으므로 유의한다.

4 강의 속 단서 표현

예시를 나타내는 부사 표현과 '상상하다' 류의 동사 표현이 정답을 찾는 단서가 될 수 있다.

- for example, for instance, such as, like
- imagine, think about[of]

▶ **Example Question**

Script

I'll give you an example of how this theory was applied. A volcanic eruption in 1883 on the island of Krakatoa decimated every living species.

Question

Why does the professor mention Krakatoa?

Ⓐ To illustrate an actual situation to which the equilibrium theory was applied
Ⓑ To demonstrate how a species can be wiped out by natural disasters
Ⓒ To show what type of island generally has higher extinction rates
Ⓓ To suggest that birds and butterflies can be used to predict immigration rates

 이것을 듣고 답을 찾아라!

강의에 'example'이라는 단서 표현이 나와서 예에 관해 묻는 질문이 나올 것임을 쉽게 예측할 수 있다. 따라서, 바로 뒤의 내용을 집중해서 들으면 'this theory'가 적용되는 예를 보여주기 위해 'Krakatoa 섬'을 언급한 것임을 알 수 있다.

지문 해석
이 이론이 어떻게 적용되었는지 예를 들어볼게요. 1883년 Krakatoa 섬에서 화산 폭발로 모든 생물이 죽었습니다.

문제 해석 및 정답
교수가 Krakatoa를 언급한 이유는?
Ⓐ 평형이론이 적용되었던 실제 상황의 예를 들어 설명하려고
Ⓑ 자연재해로 인해 한 종이 어떻게 멸종될 수 있는지 보여주려고
Ⓒ 어떤 종류의 섬이 일반적으로 더 높은 멸종률을 보이는지 알려주려고
Ⓓ 새와 나비가 이주율을 예측하는데 사용될 수 있다는 것을 암시하려고

어휘
volcanic eruption 화산 폭발   decimate 대량으로 죽이다   species 종(種)   equilibrium 평형[균형] 상태   extinction 멸종   immigration 이민   wipe out 완전히 파괴하다   natural disaster 자연 재해

06 Cause (Evidence) & Effect (Result / Finding / Research)

1   문제의 핵심

Cause & Effect는 인과관계에 대해 묻는 문제 유형으로, 대체로 과학분야의 주제에서 자주 출제된다. 이 외에 과학 분야에서 자주 출제되는 문제 유형으로는 Evidence증거와 Finding연구 결과 등이 있다. 예를 들어, 고생물학에서는 화석에 관한 연구 결과나 어떤 이론을 뒷받침하는 화석 증거에 대한 문제들이 출제된다.

2   문제의 예시

zoology	· **Why** do hibernating animals eat more before winter?
environmental science	· What **evidence** proves that the Mediterranean dried up in the past?
astronomy	· What are three **clues** relate to life on Mars?
Earth science	· What are **two factors** that decrease salinity of the Baltic Sea?
archaeology	· What is **indicated** by the size of knifes found in ruins?
psychology	· What does the professor say about the **results** of the brain research?
geology	· What does the presence of gypsum **indicate**?

3   100% 문제 공략법

각 주제별로 Cause & Effect 문제와 연계되는 강의의 논리 전개 방식을 미리 익혀 두면 문제 풀이에 도움이 된다.

01   astronomy: 화성에 생명체가 있다는 Evidence와 화성에 탐사선을 보낸 후의 Finding
02   Earth science: 낮에는 땅이 더워서 육지에는 저기압이 형성되고, 바다는 육지보다 서서히 온도가 올라가므로 육지보다는 온도가 차가워서 고기압이 형성된다. 따라서 낮에는 바다 쪽(고기압)에서 육지 쪽(저기압)으로 해풍이 분다. (Cause & Effect 유형)
03   geology: 지중해가 몇 백만 년 전에 말라서 바닥을 드러냈다는 증거가 있다. (Evidence 유형)

4   강의 속 단서 표현

인과관계를 나타내는 다양한 표현뿐 아니라 증거나 (연구의) 결과를 나타내는 표현들을 함께 알아 두어야 한다.

Cause & Effect	· the more ~ the less, that's because ~, that's why ~
Evidence	· evidence, clue, proof
Finding	· study, research, experiment
	· we can see clearly ~, from the fact that ~, found ~

▶ **Example Question**

Script

Archaeologists there found artifacts like tools and bones from land mammals – sufficient evidence to prove that its inhabitants were primarily land-dwelling hunter-gatherers.

Question

What is something that archaeologists would likely find in the archeological sites?

Ⓐ The bones of hunted animals
Ⓑ The remains of eaten fish
Ⓒ Fossilized shark teeth made into jewelry
Ⓓ Special equipment for shark fishing

> 이것을 듣고 답을 찾아라!
> 고고학 지문에서 고고학자들이 발견한 연구 결과와 그 연구 결과를 뒷받침할 수 있는 증거가 언급되면 Finding 문제와 Evidence 문제가 출제될 수 있다. 예시 지문에서는, 'found'란 동사와 'evidence'라는 명사가 각각 Finding과 Evidence 문제의 단서 표현으로 쓰였으며 이를 통해 쉽게 정답을 찾을 수 있다.

지문 해석
고고학자들은 그곳에서 도구들과 육지 포유류의 뼈와 같은 유물들을 발견했습니다. 즉, 그곳에 거주했던 사람들이 주로 육지에 사는 수렵채집민이라는 것을 증명하기에 충분한 증거들이지요.

문제 해석 및 정답
고고학자들이 고고학 유적지에서 찾을 가능성이 높은 것은?
Ⓐ 사냥된 동물들의 뼈들
Ⓑ 먹어 치운 물고기의 잔해들
Ⓒ 장신구로 만들어진 화석화된 상어 이빨
Ⓓ 상어 낚시를 위한 특수 장비

어휘
archaeologist 고고학자   artifact 인공품, 공예품   mammal 포유 동물   sufficient 충분한   inhabitant 주민
prmarily 주로   land-dwelling 육지에 거주하는   hunter-gatherer 수렵채집민   remains (pl.) 유적

07 Similarity / Difference

1   문제의 핵심

동물/물체/이론 등의 공통점과 차이점에 대해 질문하는 문제 유형이다. 두 가지 이상의 주제를 비교하는 강의에서 많이 볼 수 있는 문제 유형으로, Lecture 도입부에서 두 가지 topic이 언급되면 반드시 공통점/차이점 문제나 장단점 문제가 출제될 것을 예상하면서 듣는 것이 좋다. 대체로 자연적인 현상이나 동식물 등을 비교할 때는 공통점/차이점 문제가 많이 나오고, 사물을 비교할 때는 장단점 문제가 좀 더 자주 출제되는 경향이 있다.

2   문제의 예시

공통점
- What are two features that skunks and honey badgers **have in common**?
- What do beavers and their predators **have in common**?
- What is the **similarity** between migration and dormancy?

차이점
- Why are squirrels that live in the cold **different from** bears?
- What **difference** is there snow hydrology and other types of hydrology?
- In what two ways did art **change** in the Victorian era? (시대의 초기와 말기 비교)

3   100% 문제 공략법

각 주제별로 Similarity / Difference 문제로 출제될 수 있는 내용을 미리 숙지해 둔다.
01 botany: 동식물의 공통점과 차이점
02 engineering: 장비의 기능이나 디자인의 차이점
03 art: painting 스타일 비교, literature 작품 스타일 비교, 한 예술가의 작품 스타일의 변화
04 architecture: 건축 스타일의 변화
05 paleontology: 한 생명체의 오랜 기간에 걸친 진화 과정

4   강의 속 단서 표현

공통점과 차이점을 나타내는 표현에 주목한다. 또한 시대의 흐름에 따른 차이점을 설명할 때는 시대 표현 역시 정답을 안내하는 단서가 될 수 있다.

- have in common
- differ from, different from
- on the other hand, exception
- unique, unconventional, strange, weird, odd
- early, later, in the past, modern

▶ **Example Question**

Script

So just how does the way mandrills behave differ from the way other primates act? Well, in any given group of mandrills, the adults are likely to be predominantly female. The males in the group, on the other hand, will tend to be limited to the juvenile offspring of mature females.

Question

What is the main difference between mandrills and other primates?
Ⓐ Juvenile males and females form their own groups.
Ⓑ Mature males only mate with one female in the group.
Ⓒ Adult females greatly outnumber adult males in groups.
Ⓓ A single adult female usually leads groups of young males.

> **이것을 듣고 답을 찾아라!**
> 동물학 관련 지문에서는 다른 동물과의 공통점/차이점을 묻는 문제가 자주 출제된다. 예시 지문에서는 'differ from'이라는 단서 표현이 있어 차이점에 대한 문제가 출제될 것이 예측 가능하다.
> **Tip** 단서 표현을 들은 후에는 뒤에 나오는 내용을 'female ↑'와 같이 note-taking해 두어야 나중에 정답을 찾는 데 수월하다.

지문 해석
자, 개코원숭이가 행동하는 방식이 다른 영장류 동물들의 행동 방식과 어떻게 다를까요? 음, 어느 개코원숭이 무리이든 어른 개코원숭이들은 대부분 암컷일 가능성이 높습니다. 반면에, 무리 안의 수컷들은 어른 암컷의 어린 새끼들일뿐일 경향이 높지요.

문제 해석 및 정답
개코원숭이와 다른 영장류 동물들과의 주된 차이점은?
Ⓐ 어린 수컷들과 암컷들이 자신들만의 무리를 형성한다.
Ⓑ 어른 수컷은 무리 안의 암컷 한 마리와만 짝을 짓는다.
Ⓒ 무리 내 어른 암컷들은 어른 수컷들의 수를 훨씬 뛰어넘는다.
Ⓓ 어른 암컷 한 마리가 대개 어린 수컷들 무리를 이끈다.

어휘
mandrills 개코원숭이   primate 영장류   predominantly 대개, 대부분   juvenile 청소년의   offspring 새끼
outnumber ~보다 수가 더 많다

08 Advantage / Disadvantage

1 문제의 핵심

강의에 언급된 topic의 장단점에 대해 묻는 문제 유형으로, Similarity/Difference 문제 유형과 접근방식이 크게 다르지 않다. 두 가지를 비교하는 강의에서 자주 출제되는 문제 유형이며, Lecture 도입부에서 두 가지에 대한 언급이 나오면 공통점/차이점 혹은 장단점 문제가 나올 것을 예상하면서 들어야 한다.

2 문제의 예시

장점 (두 가지 대상 비교)
- What was an **advantage** of using clear glass **instead of** A?
- What is the primary **advantage** of this method **over** the other laboratory methods?

장점 (한 가지 대상의 장점)
- What is an **advantage** of oil ink?
- What are two **advantages** of wind turbines?
- In what ways was the project **successful**?

단점
- What is a potential **drawback** of A?

3 100% 문제 공략법

주제별 지문에서 출제 가능성이 높은 장단점 관련 내용들을 파악해 둔다.

01 chemistry / physics: A 실험 방법과 비교했을 때 B 실험 방법의 장점
02 history: 기록매체가 가죽에서 종이로 바뀌어서 더 가볍고, 저렴해졌다.
03 engineering: 이전 방법에 비해서 짧은 시간 내에 high quality의 물건을 만들 수 있다.
04 archaeology: A 방법을 통해 다른 방법보다 비교적 안전하게 유물을 발굴할 수 있다.
05 advertising: A 광고 방법은 가격과 시간 대비 TV 광고보다 더 좋다.

4 강의 속 단서 표현

장점과 단점을 직접적으로 나타내는 표현들과 긍정적 혹은 부정적 뉘앙스를 전달하는 표현들이 단서가 될 수 있다.

장점	• safer, attract more people
단점	• drawback, dangerous, risky, • susceptible to ~
장점 – 단점	• cheap – expensive, durable – fragile

▶ **Example Question**

Script

The gambrel roof doesn't just have one slope, like the Cape Cod roof does. No, it has two different sections with different slopes. At the very top section, the roof has a fairly flat angle, while the second part of the roof, the part that goes down to the first floor line... that has a very steep slope. Well, the advantage to the gambrel roof should be obvious. There's much more room on the second floor, so a person can stand up straight.

Question

What is the advantage of a gambrel roof?
(A) It has the same angle on both sides.
(B) It allows for many rooms on the second floor.
(C) It creates more space for people to stand.
(D) It has fewer maintenance issues.

○ 이것을 듣고 답을 찾아라!

건축물의 장단점 문제는 출제 가능성이 매우 높다. 지문에서는 'advantage'라는 단서 표현 뒤에 박공 지붕의 이점이 '공간(room)이 넓다'는 것이라고 나온다. 이때 room의 뜻을 오해하여 '방이 많다(many rooms)'는 오답 (B)를 선택하지 않도록 주의한다.

Tip 지문에서 'advantage'라는 단서 표현을 들으면, 간단히 'A'라고 note-taking한 뒤 장점인 'much more room'을 함께 적어 둔다.

지문 해석
박공 지붕은 케이프 코드 지붕처럼 하나의 경사만 있는 것이 아닙니다. 박공 지붕은 두 가지 경사가 있는 두 가지 다른 부분으로 구성되어 있어요. 꼭대기 부분에서는, 지붕이 꽤 평탄한 각도로 되어 있는 반면, 지붕의 두 번째 부분, 그러니까 1층의 내려가는 부분은... 매우 급격한 경사로 되어 있습니다. 음, 박공 지붕의 이점은 명백하죠. 2층의 공간이 훨씬 넓어져서, 사람이 똑바로 서 있을 수 있죠.

문제 해석 및 정답
박공 지붕(gambrel roof)의 이점은?
(A) 양쪽으로 같은 경사를 이루고 있다.
(B) 2층에 방을 많이 둘 수 있다.
ⓒ 사람들이 서 있을 공간을 더 만들어 준다.
(D) 유지 보수 관련 문제가 더 적다.

어휘
slope 경사면   advantage 이점   maintenance 유지, 보수   issue 문제

09 Misunderstanding / Correction

1 문제의 핵심

과학자들이 기존에 연구한 것과는 다른 새로운 사실을 발견한 내용이나 일반인들이 흔히 잘못 알고 있는 것을 교수가 정정해주는 내용이 지문에 나오면 이에 대해 묻는 문제 유형이다. Misunderstanding / Correction 문제는 새로운 발견이나 깨달음과 관련이 있기 때문에 "What is surprising ~ ?"으로 묻기도 하지만, "Why ~ mention ~ ?"으로 질문하기도 한다.

2 문제의 예시

- Why does the professor **mention** an oil pool?
  (정답 예시: **To clear up a misconception** about oil's appearance underground)
- Why is it **surprising** that many marine plants ~ ?
- What **surprises** the professor about hairless dogs?
- Why were the scientists **surprised** when they saw tubeworms in two and half kilometers bottom of the ocean?

3 100% 문제 공략법

Misunderstanding / Correction 유형과 관련이 있는 지문의 흐름은 대체로 반전 흐름이다. 즉 '~라고 생각했지만 ~였다'는 내용 전개가 나오면 이 유형 문제를 예측하고 대비해야 한다.

01 astronomy: 그 당시 사람들은 대부분 천동설이 맞다고 생각했지만, ~
02 biology: 바다 밑바닥에는 생명체가 없다고 과거에 믿었지만, ~
03 literature: 최초의 탐정소설은 A 소설로 알려져 있지만, ~
04 zoology: 사람들은 북극곰의 털이 하얀색이라 믿지만, ~

Tip 지문에서 '대부분 사람들이 A라고 믿고 있지만, 사실은 B이다.'라고 언급되고 잘못 알고 있는 것이 무엇인지 묻는 문제가 나오면, A가 정답으로 B는 오답 보기로 대체로 함께 선택지에 등장한다.

4 강의 속 단서 표현

반전 흐름이 핵심이므로 역접이나 대조를 나타내는 표현들이 이 유형의 단서 표현이 된다.
- Once we believed ~, but ~
- Originally we have believed ~, but ~
- surprising ~
- That's not the case at all.
- ~ seem out of this world, ~
- A is news to me.

▶ **Example Question**

Script

Global warming is making it harder for reindeer to survive. You'd think that if it were warmer during the winter, it'd be easier to survive, right? The thing is, the food reindeer eat, you know, lichen, is very sensitive to its environment. Even if there is a slight temperature drop of just two degrees Celsius, the algae won't be able to grow on fungus to create lichen.

Question

What does the professor say about global warming?
Ⓐ She believes it helps animals that live in cold climates.
Ⓑ She expects that it will get worse in the future.
Ⓒ She thinks that reindeer can easily adapt to it.
Ⓓ She feels it hurts reindeer more than people might think.

이것을 듣고 답을 찾아라!

'You'd think ~', 'The thing is ~ (또는 but ~)'라는 표현이 나오므로 Misunderstanding/Correction 유형의 문제가 나올 것을 예측할 수 있다. 'A라고 생각하지만, 그렇지 않고 B이다'에서 내용이 반전되는 부분인 B를 더 집중해서 들어야 한다.

Tip Misunderstanding/Correction 문제 유형의 약자인 MC를 note-taking해 둔다. global warming과 같이 자주 나오는 용어는 GW로 줄여서 적어두면 시간을 절약할 수 있다.
Eg. MC: GW – survive ↑ / but ↓ / ∵ (이유)

지문 해석

지구온난화로 인해 순록이 살아남는 것이 더 어려워지고 있습니다. 겨울 동안 더 따뜻하면 살아남기가 더 쉬워질 것 같죠? 문제는, 순록이 먹는 먹이, 즉 지의류 식물은 환경에 매우 민감하다는 것입니다. 기온이 단 섭씨 2도 정도만 떨어져도, 지의류 식물을 만들기 위한 조류가 균류 위에 자라지 않게 됩니다.

문제 해석 및 정답

지구온난화에 대해 교수가 말한 것은?
Ⓐ 추운 기후에 사는 동물들에게 도움이 된다고 생각한다.
Ⓑ 앞으로 더 악화될 것으로 예상한다.
Ⓒ 순록이 쉽게 지구온난화에 적응할 수 있다고 생각한다.
Ⓓ 사람들이 생각하는 것보다 훨씬 더 순록에게 해롭다고 생각한다.

어휘

reindeer 순록   lichen 지의류, 이끼   algae 말, 조류(藻類)   fungus 균류, 곰팡이류 (pl. fungi)

Practice Questions I

[01 ~ 06] Listen to part of a lecture in a business class. Then answer the questions.

MP3 30 정답 및 해석 p. 065

01 What is the lecture mainly about?
Ⓐ Guidelines for purchasing an established company
Ⓑ The advantages of having multiple partners invest in a business
Ⓒ Different ways that co-owners are responsible within a company
Ⓓ Business advice about how to avoid financial loss and bankruptcy

02 What is a risky aspect of a standard partnership?
Ⓐ One partner can make a decision without discussing it.
Ⓑ Bank loans might require the owners to make a profit quickly.
Ⓒ An owner could be less experienced than he or she claims.
Ⓓ Some investors may want to expand a business too rapidly.

03 Why does the professor mention a door manufacturing business?
   Ⓐ To explain why local companies need to do business with one another
   Ⓑ To show how one business created a strong base of loyal customers
   Ⓒ To present the case of a company that failed because of poor planning
   Ⓓ To emphasize that each person is required to pay the debts of a business

04 According to the lecture, what is needed to sell a business that is a standard partnership?
   Ⓐ Each partner must receive their full original investment.
   Ⓑ All of the partners have to agree to make the deal.
   Ⓒ One of the partners must remain with the business.
   Ⓓ Everything the company owes to creditors must be paid.

05 What is the professor's opinion of partnerships?
   Ⓐ Individuals should never enter into them.
   Ⓑ They are less risky compared to other ownership models.
   Ⓒ The proper kind depends on the specific circumstances.
   Ⓓ Being a general partner is better than being a limited partner.

06 What does the professor mean when he says this? 🔊 MP3 30_1
   Ⓐ He wants to emphasize the importance of getting approval by partners.
   Ⓑ He thinks partners should be aware of what the other is doing.
   Ⓒ He would like the students to read their textbooks before the class.
   Ⓓ He does not want to spend time discussing the transactions that need approval.

Practice Questions I

[07 ~ 11] Listen to part of a lecture in a geology class. Then answer the questions.

MP3 31   정답 및 해석 p. 067

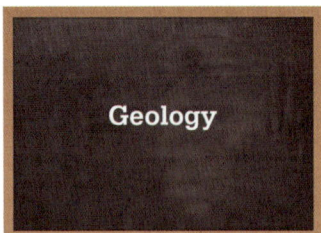 

07   What is the lecture mainly about?
   Ⓐ The breaking down of rock layers into sand
   Ⓑ The formation of deserts by wind systems
   Ⓒ The processes that create sand dunes
   Ⓓ The features of sand dunes in deserts

08   What is the process of saltation?
   Ⓐ Winds move grains of sand a short distance.
   Ⓑ Plants and rocks force dunes to split around them.
   Ⓒ Dunes flatten out over the surface of the desert.
   Ⓓ Sand grains hit the ground and push others forward.

09. According to the professor, what are two characteristics of a sand dune? **Choose two answers.**
    - Ⓐ Its weight causes it to change shape.
    - Ⓑ It moves upwind when the wind pushes it.
    - Ⓒ Its sides are unevenly formed.
    - Ⓓ Its shapes is symmetrical.
    - Ⓔ It does not stay in one place.

10. According to the professor, what causes a barchan dune to form?
    - Ⓐ Sand piling up downwind of an obstacle
    - Ⓑ Wind blowing from a single direction
    - Ⓒ Long, deep piles of sand gradually merging
    - Ⓓ Ridges in the desert being worn away by wind

11. Why does the professor mention snowstorms?
    - Ⓐ To point out a similar process
    - Ⓑ To explain how sandstorms form
    - Ⓒ To show how desert climates are changing
    - Ⓓ To suggest that sand dunes are uncommon

10 Definition (Term) / Origin

1 문제의 핵심

어떤 용어의 기원이나 정의에 대해 묻는 문제 유형이다. 용어에 대한 설명이 나올 때는 이 유형의 문제를 맞추기 위해서도 잘 들어야 하지만, 지문의 전체 내용을 이해하는 데도 큰 도움이 되므로 반드시 이해하고 넘어가야 한다.

2 문제의 예시

- **What is** renewable energy?
- **What is meant by** the term nest?
- What does **the word** *hula* **mean** in the Hawaiian language?
- What is **the meaning of** saltation?

3 100% 문제 공략법

Lecture를 듣다 보면 잘 모르는 전문 용어가 가끔씩 들려 당황하게 된다. 하지만 **TOEFL** 지문에서 전문 용어가 나오면 반드시 바로 뒤이어서 의미를 설명해 주거나 이해를 돕는 예시를 들어 주므로, 당황하지 말고 침착하게 다음 내용을 들어야 한다.

> **Tip** Definition / Origin 문제 유형은 주제에 관계없이 자주 등장하며, 긴 전체 지문의 내용을 다 이해하지 못하더라도 적절한 훈련만 되어 있으면 용어의 정의나 기원에 관한 설명만을 잡아내어 문제를 맞출 수 있다. 따라서, 특히 자신이 취약한 주제의 Lecture에서 점수를 확보할 수 있는 중요한 문제 유형이라고 할 수 있다.
> 또한, 어려운 여러 전문 용어를 무작정 외우려 하기보다는 강의 도중에 나오는 용어 설명 부분을 잘 이해할 수 있는 능력을 기르는 것이 우선시되어야 한다.

4 강의 속 단서 표현

용어의 기원이나 의미를 설명하는 표현에 주목해야 한다.

- name after ~, take one's name ~, what we call, refer to
- which means ~
- last time we defined ~

▶ **Example Question**

Script

Well, as I mentioned before about new forms of art... Well, it was no surprise that cubism was met with a healthy dose of skepticism. One critic dismissed Braque's works as a canvas filled with little cubes. Ironically, it was from the critic's harsh words that Cubism took its name.

Question

According to the professor, what are the origins of the term "Cubism"?

Ⓐ A famous artist's painting
Ⓑ A portrait by Georges Braque
Ⓒ Picasso's cubic drawings
Ⓓ A critic's comment

> 이것을 듣고 답을 찾아라!
> art 분야에서는 특정 화풍이나 문학 사조 등의 이름과 그 기원에 관한 문제가 자주 출제된다. 지문에서 'it was from'이나 'took its name' 같은 단서 표현을 들었다면, 그 이후의 내용만 주의 깊게 듣는다면 이 유형의 문제를 쉽게 풀 수 있다.

지문 해석
자, 새로운 형태의 미술에 대해 전에 내가 언급했던 것처럼... 음, 입체파가 적절한 양의 회의적 의견을 듣게 된 것은 놀라운 일이 아니었어요. 한 비평가는 Braque의 작품들이 작은 정육면체들로 가득 찬 캔버스일 뿐이라고 일축했지요. 아이러니하게도, 입체파가 그 이름을 얻은 것은 다름 아닌 그 비평가의 혹독한 비평에서였습니다.

문제 해석 및 정답
교수에 의하면, '입체파'라는 이름의 기원은 무엇인가?
Ⓐ 한 유명한 화가의 그림
Ⓑ George Braque의 자화상
Ⓒ Picasso의 정육면체 그림
Ⓓ 한 비평가의 언급

어휘
cubism 입체파   dose (어느 정도의) 양   skepticism 회의론   critic 비평가   dismiss 일축하다   cube 정육면체
portrait 초상화

11 Two Click / Three Click

1   문제의 핵심

답안으로 주어진 보기 중에서 2개나 3개의 정답을 고르는 문제 유형이다. 여기서 중요한 것은 정답의 수가 아니라, 이 유형이 앞에서 배운 문제 유형들로 출제된다는 점이다. 즉, Two Click / Three Click 유형 문제는 내용적으로는 앞서 나온 어느 유형이라도 될 수 있으며 출제빈도가 매우 높다. 최근에는 Main Idea 문제 유형에서도 두 가지의 정답을 고르는 문제가 출제되었다. (본 책에서는 종이책 방식을 감안하여 이 문제의 지시문 Click on two answers를 Choose two answers로 표기하였다.)

2   문제의 예시

- What are **two reasons** ~ ?
- What are **two advantages** ~ ?
- What **mistakes** does the professor imply ~ ? (Click on two answers.)
- Which of the following are **examples** ~ ? (Click on two answers.)
- What are **two conditions** ~ ?

3   100% 문제 공략법

Two Click / Three Click 유형의 문제를 푸는 핵심은 어떤 유형의 문제가 Two Click / Three Click 문제로 많이 출제되는지를 파악하는 것이다. 위에 나온 문제의 예시를 보면 (1) Cause, (2) Advantage / Disadvantag, (3) Problem, (4) Example 등의 문제임을 알 수 있다.

주의할 것은, 최근 출제경향을 보면 두 개의 정답 위치가 지문에서 나란히 있는 경우가 많지 않다는 것이다. 예를 들어, 식물학 강의에서, A 식물이 추운 곳에서 잘 견디는 이유를 지문 초반에 하나 언급한 뒤 지문이 끝날 때쯤 또 다른 이유 하나를 언급한다. 학생 입장에서는 두 정보를 연결시켜 기억하기도 힘들고 우선 순차적으로 note-taking한 후 이를 바탕으로 정답을 찾아야 하기 때문에 난이도가 매우 높은 문제가 될 수 있다.

4   강의 속 단서 표현

둘 또는 셋의 숫자와 관련된 표현이 단서가 될 수 있지만 이런 숫자 단서가 아예 나오지 않는 경우도 많다.

- There are two reasons ~
- two advantages, two conditions

> **Tip** two 또는 three 라는 단서 표현이 없어도, 앞에서 다뤘던 Cause 유형, Advantage / Disadvantage 유형, Problem 유형, 그리고 Example 유형과 관련된 모든 표현들이 Two Click / Three Click 문제 유형의 단서 표현이 될 수 있다.

▶ **Example Question**

Script

That's right. That means a high amount of carbon atoms are present in the atmosphere of Neptune. Combined with the crushing pressure and high temperatures, it is an ideal place for diamonds to form. So let's take a look at how it could happen.

Question

According to the professor, what are two conditions required to transform methane into diamonds? Choose two answers.

Ⓐ Hot temperatures
Ⓑ Cooled hydrocarbons
Ⓒ Pressurized methane liquid
Ⓓ High pressure

> **이것을 듣고 답을 찾아라!**
> astronomy나 geology 지문에서는 어떤 현상이 일어나는 조건이나 어떤 물질이 만들어지는 조건에 관한 문제가 많이 출제된다. 예시 지문에서 탄소에 높은 압력과 고온이 가해지면 다이아몬드가 형성될 수 있고 해왕성의 대기가 그에 가장 이상적인 장소라고 언급하였고, 다이아몬드의 형성 조건을 묻는 문제가 출제되었다. 그러나, 이 지문에는 two라는 단서 표현이 나오지 않았다. 따라서, 다이아몬드의 형성 조건이라는 것을 말해주는 'ideal place for diamonds to form'이라는 부분을 잡아낼 수 있어야 문제의 답을 모두 찾을 수 있다.

지문 해석
맞습니다. 그 말은, 해왕성의 대기에는 많은 양의 탄소 원자가 있다는 말입니다. 짓누르는 압력과 높은 기온이 결합하여, 해왕성은 다이아몬드가 형성되기에 이상적인 장소가 되지요. 그럼, 이런 일이 어떻게 일어날 수 있는지 살펴봅시다.

문제 해석 및 정답
교수에 의하면, 메탄이 다이아몬드로 변화하기 위해 필요한 두 가지 조건은 무엇인가? (두 가지 선택)
Ⓐ 높은 온도
Ⓑ 냉각된 탄화수소
Ⓒ 압축된 액체 메탄
Ⓓ 높은 압력

어휘
carbon 탄소   atom 원자   atmosphere 대기   Uranus 천왕성   Neptune 해왕성

12 Ordering

1 문제의 핵심

어떤 과정이나 사건, 제조법 등이 일어나는 순서를 묻는 문제 유형이다. 내용을 순서대로 정확히 기억해야 하기 때문에 난이도가 매우 높은 문제이지만, 다행히 출제 빈도는 매우 낮은 편이다. 최근에는 **TOEFL Listening Section**의 34문제 중에서 한 문제도 출제되지 않은 경우도 있었다. 목표점수가 25점 이하라면 우선순위가 높은 문제 유형은 아니며, 25점 이상으로 진입했을 때 공략하는 것이 바람직하다.

2 문제의 예시

- The woman described the process of making a digital artwork. Put the steps listed below in the correct order.

Step 1	
Step 2	
Step 3	

Ⓐ Make use of a computer ~
Ⓑ Construct a frame ~
Ⓒ Reproduce the artwork ~

3 100% 문제 공략법

각 주제별로 Ordering 문제로 출제될 수 있는 사건을 미리 확인해 둔다.
01 history: 어떤 역사적 사건이 일어난 순서
02 engineering: 조력발전이 일어나는 순서
03 art: 그림 그리는 순서, craft와 같은 공예품을 만드는 순서

4 강의 속 단서 표현

과정이나 순서를 열거하는 표현이 나오면 이 유형의 단서 표현이 될 수 있다.
- How is A made?
- First, second, third
- And then, Next
- process

▶ **Example Question**

Script

Let's start by looking at the process through which charcoal is created. One technique is to simultaneously bake wood and deprive it of oxygen. This can be accomplished by burying the wood in a fire pit, where there is little oxygen. And then, the wood must be baked at moderate temperature. This ensures that while the wood's carbon isn't burned off, a variety of unwanted substances, such as water and methane, are. In the end, the wood's volume will have been reduced to approximately one quarter of its original size.

Question

Put the sentences in the proper order of making a charcoal.
(　　) Ⓐ Undesirable elements are removed from the wood.
(　　) Ⓑ The wood is slowly burned at a medium temperature.
(　　) Ⓒ About 25 percent of the wood is left behind.
(　　) Ⓓ Wood is buried in a pit to limit its exposure to oxygen.

이것을 듣고 답을 찾아라 !

'process through which charcoal is created' 이후에 나오는 내용은 숯이 만들어지는 과정을 설명하므로 Ordering 문제가 나올 수 있다고 예측할 수 있다. 중간에 나오는 'And then', 'In the end'와 같은 단서 표현으로 순서를 정리하면서 note-taking해 두면 문제를 푸는 데 도움이 된다.

지문 해석
숯이 만들어지는 과정을 살펴보는 것으로 시작해보죠. 한 가지 기법은 나무를 굽는 동시에 목재에서 산소를 제거하는 것입니다. 이것은 나무를 화덕에 묻어서 이루어질 수 있는데, 화덕에는 산소가 거의 없기 때문이죠. 그 다음으로, 나무는 중간 정도의 온도로 구워져야 합니다. 그래야 나무의 탄소는 타버리지 않는 반면에 물이나 메탄 같은 여러 다양한 원치 않는 물질들은 타버리게 되지요. 마침내, 나무의 용적은 원래 크기의 약 4분의 1정도까지 줄어들게 됩니다.

문제 해석 및 정답
숯을 만드는 올바른 순서로 문장들을 놓으시오.
(D) Ⓐ 원치 않는 요소들이 나무에서 제거된다.
(B) Ⓑ 나무가 중간 온도에서 천천히 탄다.
(A) Ⓒ 나무의 약 25퍼센트만 남겨진다.
(C) Ⓓ 산소에의 노출을 제한하기 위해 나무가 화덕 안에 묻힌다.

어휘
charcoal 숯　　simultaneously 동시에　　deprive A of B A에게서 B를 빼앗다　　accomplish 성취하다, 해내다
fire pit 화덕　　moderate 보통의, 중간의　　ensure 보장하다　　carbon 탄소　　substance 물질　　volume 용적, 양
element 요소, 성분　　exposure 노출

13 Matching

1 문제의 핵심

지문에 나온 내용을 표(table)의 내용에 맞는 곳에 골라 넣는 문제 유형이다. Matching 문제도 Ordering 문제와 마찬가지로 많은 내용을 정확히 기억해야 하기 때문에 난이도가 높은 편이지만, 앞서 배운 유형들을 잘 공략한다면 이 문제도 잘 풀 수 있다. 아래의 문제의 예시에 나타난 것처럼, 이 문제는 형태적으로는 표 맞추기 형식을 띄고 있지만, 내용적으로는 Solution, Advantage/Disadvantage 유형의 문제이기 때문이다.

2 문제의 예시

- What does the professor suggest the student to include in her report? For each phrase below, place a checkmark in the "suggested" column or the "Not suggestion" column.
Click in the correct box for each phrase.

	Suggested	Not Suggested
The writer's personal letters		
Photos of the writer		
Writer's biography		

3 100% 문제 공략법

각 주제별로 이전에 출제된 내용을 알아 두면 도움이 된다.
01 astronomy: 탐사선을 보내서 알아낸 내용, 즉 연구 결과를 표와 매칭
02 painting: 그림의 특징을 표와 매칭, 또는 두 그림의 공통점/차이점을 표와 매칭
03 engineering: 특정 장비의 장단점 비교를 표와 매칭

4 강의 속 단서 표현

앞에서 배운 모든 문제 유형의 단서 표현이 Matching 문제 유형의 단서 표현이 될 수 있다. 예를 들어, 장단점을 묻는 표 문제는 cheap/expensive, durable/fragile과 같은 단어가 단서 표현이 되며, 특정 그림에 대한 강의에서 그 그림의 특징을 묻는 표 문제는 unique, distinctive와 같은 단어가 단서 표현이 된다.

▶ **Example Question**

Script

A man is suffering from a terrible headache and asks his doctor for aspirin. But the doctor gives him a sugar pill and tells him that it's an aspirin. If the man starts to feel better, we can attribute this to the placebo effect. Of course, the placebo doesn't have to be a pill. One study actually used the aroma of vanilla as a placebo for people with asthma. In another, the placebo for people experiencing knee problems was the suggestion that surgery had been performed when actually it had not.

Question

Based on the lecture, match each placebo to the problem it was used for.

Ⓐ Sugar pill
Ⓑ False surgery
Ⓒ The smell of vanilla

Asthma	Knee pain	Headache

> 🔍 **이것을 듣고 답을 찾아라!**
> 이 문제는 'placebo'의 몇 가지 다른 예를 들고 있으므로 Example 문제를 표 문제인 Matching 문제 유형으로 출제했다는 것을 알 수 있다. 따라서 표 문제도 문제가 무엇을 묻고 있는지를 정확히 이해해야 풀 수 있다.

지문 해석
한 남자가 끔찍한 두통을 앓고 있어서 의사에게 아스피린을 부탁합니다. 하지만 의사는 그에게 설탕으로 된 알약을 주고 그것이 아스피린 이라고 말합니다. 그 남자가 나아진다고 느끼기 시작한다면, 우리는 이것을 위약 효과 덕이라고 할 수 있습니다. 물론, 위약은 알약일 필요는 없습니다. 한 연구에서는 실제로 바닐라 향을 천식을 앓는 사람들에게 위약으로 사용하기도 했습니다. 또 다른 연구에서는, 무릎에 문제가 있는 사람들을 위한 위약으로 사실은 이루어지지 않은 수술이 행해졌다는 암시를 준 적이 있었죠.

문제 해석 및 정답
강의 내용에 기반하여, 각각의 위약을 그것이 사용된 문제점에 연결하시오.
Ⓐ 설탕 알약
Ⓑ 거짓 수술
Ⓒ 바닐라 냄새

천식	무릎 통증	두통
Ⓒ 바닐라 냄새	Ⓑ 거짓 수술	Ⓐ 설탕 알약

어휘
pill 알약   attribute A to B A를 B의 덕분으로 돌리다   aroma 향   asthma 천식

14 Opinion / Attitude

1 문제의 핵심

어떤 사안에 대한 교수나 학자, 평론가의 의견이나 태도(agree/disagree or positive/negative)에 관해 묻는 문제 유형이다. 강의자인 교수의 의견을 묻는 문제는, 교수의 독자적인 의견을 묻기도 하지만, 최근에는 다른 사람의 의견이 먼저 제시되고 그 의견에 대한 교수의 동의/반대 또는 긍정/부정 여부를 묻는 문제가 자주 출제되고 있다.

2 문제의 예시

science
- What is the professor's **opinion** regarding life on Mars?
  (opinion – agree/disagree)
- What is the professor's **attitude** concerning theory of mind in animals?
  (attitude – positive/negative)

art
- What is the professor's **opinion** of the criticism Wyeth received from fellow artists?

business
- What is one **viewpoint** expressed by advocates of the free trade system?
- What is the professor's **attitude** toward the free trade system?

3 100% 문제 공략법

각 주제별로 교수가 동의 혹은 반대하는 문제가 어떻게 출제되었는지 알아 두면 도움이 된다.
01 astronomy: 화성에 생명체가 있다는 주장에 교수가 동의/반대하는 의견을 제시
02 business: 자유무역제도는 특정.국가에 도움이 된다는 주장에 교수가 긍정/부정적 의견을 제시
03 art: 새로 등장한 화풍에 대한 비평가들의 의견에 교수가 동의/반대하는 의견을 제시

4 강의 속 단서 표현

동의를 나타내는 표현은 대체로 긍정적이고 반대를 나타내는 표현은 부정적이거나 극단적인 경향이 있다.

agree
- support, agree, believe, this is the one that I want to share with ~

disagree
- ridiculous, non-sense, far-fetched설득력 없는, wild터무니 없는, take issue문제삼다, naive순진한, 믿기 힘든, too optimistic너무 낙관적인

▶ **Example Question**

Script

So what does this tell us about architectural stabilization? Even though there may be a single cause, many combined steps have to be taken in order to solve the problem. While it is important to learn the various methods used to stabilize structures, we have to keep in mind that it is better to make things right the first time around by learning from mistakes of the past.

Question

What is the professor's opinion about using architectural stabilization techniques?
Ⓐ It helps historians learn more about great architects of the past.
Ⓑ It is never a good idea to tamper with a building's foundation.
Ⓒ It is more important to avoid making mistakes in the first place.
Ⓓ It can destroy the unique beauty of unconventional buildings.

> 이것을 듣고 답을 찾아라!
>
> 마지막에 나오는 'we have to keep in mind ~' 부분에서 교수의 의견이 제시된다는 것을 알 수 있다. 여기서는 교수의 독자적인 의견이 문제로 출제되었지만, 앞에 제시된 주장이나 의견에 대한 교수의 긍정/부정, 동의/반대 의견이 문제로 나오면 앞의 내용과 교수의 의견/태도를 종합하여 답을 선택해야 한다.

지문 해석
자, 이것은 우리에게 건축학적 안정화에 관해 무엇을 말해주나요? 원인은 한 가지이더라도 그 문제를 해결하기 위해서는 수많은 결합된 조치들이 취해져야 합니다. 구조물을 안정화시키는 데 사용되는 다양한 방법들을 배우는 것도 중요하지만, 우리는 과거의 실수들로부터 교훈을 얻음으로써 처음부터 일을 바르게 하는 것이 더 낫다는 것을 염두에 두어야 합니다.

문제 해석 및 정답
건축학적 안정화 기법을 사용하는 것에 대한 교수의 의견은?
Ⓐ 역사학자들이 과거의 위대한 건축가들에 대해 더 많이 배울 수 있도록 돕는다.
Ⓑ 어떤 건물의 토대에 손을 대는 것은 결코 좋은 생각이 아니다.
Ⓒ 애초에 실수를 피하는 것이 더 중요하다.
Ⓓ 색다른 건물들의 독특한 아름다움을 파괴할 수도 있다.

어휘
stabilization 안정화   historian 역사가   architect 건축가   tamper 손대다   foundation (건물의) 토대
unconventional 색다른, 독특한

15 Replay Question (Headset)

1 문제의 핵심

지문의 일부분을 다시 듣고, 그 중 한 문장의 문맥상 화자의 의도가 무엇인가를 파악하는 문제 유형이다.

2 문제의 예시

- **Listen again** to part of the conversation. Then answer the question.
  What does the professor[student] mean **when he says this**?
  Eg.

  > 학생: 이번 토플시험 점수가 나왔는데 목표점수보다 20점이나 부족해요.
  > 아버지: 잘~했다 ~ (B)
  > 문제 What does B mean when he says this?
  >   Ⓐ 아버지는 학생을 칭찬한다. (오답)
  >   Ⓑ 아버지는 학생을 비난한다. (정답)

'잘~했다~'라는 말의 의미를 묻는 문제이다. 이것은 아버지가 학생을 비난하려는 의도로 한 말이므로 말 그대로의 의미인 '아버지는 학생을 칭찬한다'는 보기는 오답이다.

3 100% 문제 공략법

Headset 유형은 두 가지 type으로 나누어진다. 각각의 type에 맞는 공략법을 알아 두도록 한다.

01 **Type 1** – 일부 문맥을 다시 들려주고, 그 중 한 문장에 나타난 화자의 의도를 묻는 유형

"Listen again to part of the lecture. Then answer the question."과 같은 지시문이 나오고 3~4 문장의 강의 일부분을 먼저 다시 들려준다.

이후 "What does the professor mean when he says this?"라는 지시문과 함께 앞서 들은 문맥 중 한 문장을 다시 한번 들려주고 그 의미를 묻는다. Type 1의 문제는 다시 들려준 일부 지문의 문맥을 바탕으로 주어진 문장의 의미를 찾아야 한다.

02 **Type 2** – 한 문장만 다시 들려주고 화자의 의도를 묻는 유형

Type 2의 문제는 "What does the professor mean when she says this?"라는 지시문이 나오고 문맥 없이 한 문장만 다시 들려준 후 화자의 의도를 묻는다. 따라서 이 지문 전체 내용을 바탕으로 화자의 의도를 알아내야 한다.

4 강의 속 단서 표현

Headset 문제는 지문을 통해 예측할 수 있는 별도의 단서 표현이 없다. 화자의 본래 의도를 정확하게 파악하기 위해 주어진 일부 지문이나 전체 지문의 핵심 내용을 이해하는 것이 중요하다.

▶ **Example Question**

Script

Professor: Remember our discussion last week? What did we talk about, Raymond?
Student: Well, we talked about the way pigments are analyzed. You know, the reasons it's done and the different methods used. You mentioned molecular spectroscopy and …
P: 🎧 Good, stop right there.

Question

Why does the professor say this?

> Good, stop right there.

Ⓐ To suggest that he is annoyed because the student is talking too much
Ⓑ To indicate that the student has mentioned what the professor wanted to hear
Ⓒ To show that the student has made a mistake that the professor will correct
Ⓓ To emphasize that the topic is too difficult to be explained in a single class

---

이것을 듣고 답을 찾아라!

Headset 문제에서 교수가 학생에게 질문했을 때 학생 말이 '맞다' 또는 '틀리다'란 의미를 지닌 교수의 응답이 자주 출제된다. 여기서의 'Good'은 '잘했다, 좋다'의 의미가 아닌, '맞았으니 그만 얘기해도 된다'는 뜻이 된다. 주의할 것은, 'stop right there'에 화자의 의중이 있다고 생각하면 (A)와 같은 오답 함정에 걸릴 수 있다.

지문 해석

강의의 일부분을 다시 듣고 질문에 답하시오.
교수: 지난 주에 논의했던 것 기억이 나나요? 우리가 무슨 이야기를 했었죠, Raymond?
학생: 음, 우리는 안료들이 분석되는 방식에 대해 이야기를 했어요. 분석을 해야 하는 이유와, 사용되는 여러 다른 방법들이요. 교수님이 분자 분광기에 대해 언급하셨고…
교수: 좋아요, 거기서 멈추죠.

문제 해석 및 정답

교수가 다음과 같이 말한 이유는?

> 좋아요, 거기서 멈추죠.

Ⓐ 학생이 너무 많이 말을 해서 자신이 짜증이 났다는 것을 암시하려고
Ⓑ 교수가 듣고 싶어 했던 것을 학생이 언급했다는 것을 나타내려고
Ⓒ 학생이 교수가 수정을 해줄 실수를 했다는 것을 나타내려고
Ⓓ 그 화제가 한 수업에서 설명되기에는 너무 어렵다는 것을 강조하려고

어휘

pigment 안료   analyze 분석하다   molecular spectroscopy 분자 분광기

16 Requirement (Condition)

1   문제의 핵심

어떠한 현상이 일어나기 위해 필요한 조건을 묻는 문제 유형이다. 예를 들어, 식물학에서 광합성을 하기 위해 식물이 필요한 것이나, 지질학/기상학에서 어떤 자연현상이 일어나는 데 필요한 조건 등을 묻는 문제가 자주 출제된다. Requirement 문제는 자연 현상뿐 아니라 제조법에 관한 Lecture에서도 자주 출제되는 문제 유형으로, 예를 들어, 유리를 만들기 위해서 필요한 조건에 대한 문제가 나올 수도 있다.

2   문제의 예시

- What **condition is needed** for slow wind to move sand?
- In addition to carbon dioxide and water, **what is needed** in the process of photosynthesis?

3   100% 문제 공략법

Requirement 유형은 지문에서 직접적으로 조건이 언급되면(Eg. 눈이 만들어질 때 꼭 필요한 두 가지 조건은 충분한 수분과 0도 이하의 온도이다.) 비교적 예측이 쉬운 편이지만, 똑같은 내용이라도 강의자가 돌려서 설명한다면(Eg. 대기 중에 수분이 많고 온도도 섭씨 0도 이하로 내려가니 눈이 만들어지기에 이상적이다.) 정답을 알아 차리기 어려울 수도 있다.

각 주제별로 출제 가능한 Requirement 문제를 살펴보자.
01   geology: sand dune이 만들어질 때 필요한 조건, 다이아몬드가 땅 속에서 만들어질 때 필요한 조건
02   meteorology: 번개가 만들어질 때 필요한 조건
03   business: salesperson이 성공하기 위해 필요한 조건
04   science/psychology: research를 할 때 전제되는 조건

4   강의 속 단서 표현

필요나 조건을 나타내는 표현들이 정답의 단서가 될 수 있다.
- occur when ~
- ~ is needed, ~ is required
- ~ must have
- necessary

▶ **Example Question**

Script

Salespeople must be ego-driven… That is, they need to have an intense drive to get things done, like a person who wants to be better than everyone else.

Question

According to the professor, what characteristic of ego-driven salespeople makes them good at what they do?

Ⓐ They are confident in their understanding of the product.
Ⓑ They can relate to the person buying the product.
Ⓒ They want to finish whatever they start.
Ⓓ They want to be better than their coworkers.

 이것을 듣고 답을 찾아라!

지문의 'they need to have ~'를 단서 표현으로 알아듣고, 그 후에 나오는 필요 조건을 주의해서 들어야 한다. necessary, required와 같은 Requirement 문제 유형의 단서 표현을 외워두면 정답을 찾기가 훨씬 더 수월해진다.

지문 해석
판매원들은 자아지향적이어야 합니다… 즉, 그들은 일을 완수하겠다는 강한 열망을 가지고 있어야 한다는 것입니다.

문제 해석 및 정답
교수에 의하면, 자아지향적인 판매원들의 어떤 특성이 그들이 하는 일을 잘하도록 만들어주는가?
Ⓐ 상품의 이해에 있어 자신감이 있다.
Ⓑ 상품을 사는 사람과 공감대를 형성할 수 있다.
Ⓒ 시작한 일이 무엇이건 그것을 끝내고 싶어 한다.
Ⓓ 동료들보다 뛰어나고 싶어 한다.

어휘
ego-driven 자아지향적인   intense 강렬한   drive 욕구

17 Character

1 문제의 핵심

음악, 문학, 그림, 공예품 등 예술 작품의 특징을 묻는 문제 유형이다. 그런데 각 예술 분야별로 '특징'을 표현하는 어휘가 다르므로 이 어휘들을 분류하여 정리할 필요가 있다. 예를 들어, 문학 작품에 주로 쓰이는 특징 관련 어휘로는 character, message 등이 있다.

2 문제의 예시

literature
- What was **distinctive** about Mark Twain's works?
- What does the professor say about **themes** of *Aucassin and Nicolette*?
- What does the professor say about the **main character** Sergeant Cuff?

dance
- Which of the following would be the most likely **theme** of a modern 'hula' dance?

music
- What are two **characteristics** of the musical form the class is studying?

painting
- What are two **features** of Van Gogh's painting?

3 100% 문제 공략법

Character 유형은 주로 예술 지문과 관련이 있으므로 이에 관한 배경지식이 있다면 큰 도움이 된다. 예를 들어, 문학 지문을 공략할 때는 문학 지문을 최소한 세 개 이상 읽고 문학 작품 관련 어휘와 표현 방법을 연구하도록 한다. 이렇게 대비하면, 실제 시험에서 다른 작품이 언급되어도 문학 작품의 '특징'을 나타내는 표현들에 익숙하기 때문에 훨씬 수월하게 이 유형의 문제를 풀 수 있다. 다른 분야도 같은 방법으로 공부하면 된다.

분야별 '특징' 관련 어휘

01 literature: character등장인물의 특징, subject matter소재, message저자가 전달하고자 하는 메시지
02 painting: shade명암, texture질감, hue색조, perspective관점
03 dance: theme주제, costume의상

4 강의 속 단서 표현

이 유형의 단서 표현은 주로 독특함이나 특이함을 강조하는 표현들이다.

- unique, unconventional, weird, odd
- departure from the past[tradition]
- deviate

▶ **Example Question**

Script

A look at her manuscripts will reveal that she[Emily Dickinson] often replaced traditional punctuation marks with dashes and used unconventional capitalization.

Question

According to the professor, what is an interesting aspect of Dickinson's poetry?
Ⓐ She did not use conventional punctuation.
Ⓑ She focused on the traditional aspects of poetry.
Ⓒ She wrote about ugliness rather than beauty.
Ⓓ She created the free verse style of poetry.

 이것을 듣고 답을 찾아라!
   Emily Dickinson의 시를 보면 보면 전통적인 문장부호를 대시로 바꾸고 전례 없는 대문자 사용을 했다는 내용이 나온다. 따라서 conventional한 시의 작법을 새로운 것으로 대체했다는 점이 Dickinson의 '특징'이 될 수 있다. 'unconventional'은 '전에 없었던 것'을 의미하므로, 이 단어가 Dickinson의 특징을 나타내는 단서 표현이다.

지문 해석
그녀의 원고를 한 번 보기만 해도, 그녀가 전통적인 구두점을 대시로 대체했고 관습에 사로잡히지 않고 대문자를 사용했다는 사실이 드러납니다.

문제 해석 및 정답
교수에 의하면, Dickinson의 시에서 흥미로운 점은 무엇인가?
Ⓐ 관습적인 구두법을 쓰지 않았다.
Ⓑ 시의 전통적인 측면들에 초점을 맞췄다.
Ⓒ 아름다움보다는 추악함에 대해 썼다.
Ⓓ 자유시를 창조했다.

어휘
manuscript 원고   punctuation mark 문장부호   unconventional 색다른, 독특한   capitalization 대문자 사용

Chapter III   197

18 Imply / Infer

1 문제의 핵심

Imply 문제는 지문에서 화자가 돌려서 한 말에 숨겨진 의도를 묻는 문제 유형이다. 한편, Infer 문제는 화자가 암시한 내용을 추론하는 문제 유형이다. 보여지는 문제 형태는 다르지만 숨은 뜻을 찾아낸다는 점에서 매우 유사한 문제 유형이다.

2 문제의 예시

Imply · What does the man **imply** when he says this?
· What does the professor **imply** about A?
Infer · What can be **inferred** about A?

3 100% 문제 공략법

Imply와 Infer 문제 유형은 다른 유형과 결합되어서 출제되는 편이다. 즉, Problem이나 Solution, Advantage / Disadvantage 등을 직접적으로 말하지 않고 돌려 말해 어떤 의미를 암시하거나, 암시한 내용을 수험자가 추론하도록 하는 것이 출제포인트이다. 따라서 대화의 문맥을 정확하게 이해하면 어떤 Imply / Infer 문제도 풀 수 있다.

Eg.

> **남자:** 너 토플 시험 잘 봤니?
> **여자:** 다음에 다시 봐야 할 것 같아.
>
> 문제: 여자가 암시하는 것은? → 여자는 시험을 잘 못 봤다.
> 문제: 여자에 대해서 추론할 수 있는 것은? → 여자는 시험을 잘 못 봤다.

여자는 '다음에 다시 봐야 할 것 같아'라는 말로 시험을 잘 보지 못했다는 사실을 암시하였고, 이 대사를 근거로 '여자가 시험을 잘 못 봤다'는 것을 추론할 수도 있다. 또한, 이와 관련하여 여자의 Problem에 대한 문제가 출제될 수도 있다. 이 유형의 문제를 자주 틀리는 수험자의 경우, 반드시 지문에서 답의 단서가 되는 부분을 찾아서 밑줄을 그은 후 어떻게 정보가 암시되어 있는지 생각해 보아야 한다.

4 강의 속 단서 표현

Imply / Infer 유형의 단서 표현은 없다. 문맥을 파악해야만 정답을 찾을 수 있다.

▶ **Example Question**

Script

I remember sticking a pencil inside the leaves of my first Venus flytrap. I was expecting to see it chomp down on my pencil… As you might expect, I was pretty disappointed.

Question

What does the professor imply about his childhood experience with Venus flytraps?

Ⓐ His expectations were unrealistic.
Ⓑ It was one of the best memories of his life.
Ⓒ He wishes he had taken better care of the plant.
Ⓓ It led him to become a botanist.

> 이것을 듣고 답을 찾아라!
> 'Venus flytrap(파리지옥풀)의 잎에 연필을 넣으면 잎이 연필을 물 줄 알았는데, 많이 실망했다.'라는 교수의 말이 암시하는 것은 '파리지옥풀이 연필을 물지 않았다'는 것이다. 이 부분은 교수의 예상과 달랐기 때문에 Misunderstanding/Correction 문제 유형으로도 출제될 수 있다. 따라서, 이 부분을 들을 때는 출제가능성이 높은 Misunderstanding/Correction 유형을 먼저 예측하면서 듣는 것이 좋으며, Imply 문제로 출제된다면, Imply 문제 유형의 공략법을 도입해서 정답을 찾으면 된다.

지문 해석
내가 처음 가졌던 파리지옥풀 잎사귀 안에 연필을 붙여봤던 기억이 나는군요. 나는 그 풀이 내 연필을 우적우적 씹어 먹을 것을 기대했지만… 여러분이 예상한 것처럼 난 꽤 실망했었죠.

문제 해석 및 정답
파리지옥풀에 얽힌 교수의 어릴 적 경험에 관해 그가 암시한 것은?
Ⓐ 그의 기대가 비현실적이었다.
Ⓑ 그의 인생에서 가장 좋은 추억들 중 하나이다.
Ⓒ 그 식물을 좀 더 잘 돌보았더라면 하고 바란다.
Ⓓ 그가 식물학자가 되도록 이끌었다.

어휘
Venus flytrap 파리지옥풀(끈끈이주걱)   chomp down 우적우적 먹다   botanist 식물학자

Practice Questions II

[01 ~ 05] **Listen to part of a lecture in a biology class. Then answer the questions.**

MP3 32　정답 및 해석 p. 068

01　Why does the professor tell a story about her brother?
　　Ⓐ To illustrate how a bad experience can be associated with food
　　Ⓑ To emphasize the importance of the findings of a psychologist
　　Ⓒ To show how certain foods can make people think they're sick
　　Ⓓ To explain how brain damage can affect the sense of taste

02　What does the professor say about the insular cortex?
　　Ⓐ It regulates body temperature.
　　Ⓑ It is needed to taste food.
　　Ⓒ It controls bodily movements.
　　Ⓓ It causes nausea.

03. According to the lecture, what causes a conditioned taste aversion?
- Ⓐ A feeling of sickness that linked to a certain food
- Ⓑ A problem with the way the brain processes taste information
- Ⓒ A lack of proper nutrition that causes the body to malfunction
- Ⓓ A specific poison that is found in small amounts in some foods

04. Why does the professor mention Pavlov?
- Ⓐ To point out that dogs are directly descended from wolves
- Ⓑ To illustrate how dogs associate food with a learned behavior
- Ⓒ To explain how dogs can discern which food is good and which is bad
- Ⓓ To show that dogs can learn to do tricks if given the proper food

05. What can be inferred from the coyote that buried the rabbit?
- Ⓐ Coyotes save food to eat at a later time.
- Ⓑ Coyotes are not affected by lithium.
- Ⓒ Coyotes do not have a sense of taste.
- Ⓓ Coyotes have empathy for one another.

Practice Questions II

[06 ~ 10] **Listen to part of a lecture in an art class. Then answer the questions.** 🔊 MP3 33

정답 및 해석 p. 070

06 What is the students' main complaint about using watercolors?
   Ⓐ Watercolors are so thin that they often drip down the paper.
   Ⓑ They have used watercolors too many times before.
   Ⓒ The colors turn brown after the paint dries.
   Ⓓ They can't change their mind or correct mistakes.

07 Why are landscapes mentioned?
   Ⓐ To contrast the appearance of oil and watercolor paints
   Ⓑ To explain the biggest disadvantage of watercolors
   Ⓒ To point out a common type of watercolor painting
   Ⓓ To show how difficult it is to paint with watercolors

08 What two points does the male student make about oil paints?
Choose two answers.
Ⓐ They dry more slowly than watercolors.
Ⓑ They don't blend together easily.
Ⓒ They can be used to create textures.
Ⓓ They are good for landscapes.

09 What does the female student say is an advantage of using watercolors for landscapes?
Ⓐ They show light and shadow well.
Ⓑ They cover up the whiteness of the paper.
Ⓒ They are easier to use when painting outdoors.
Ⓓ The colors blend together quickly and easily.

10 What will the class probably discuss next?
Ⓐ The reason they stopped using watercolors
Ⓑ The best methods of using acrylic paints
Ⓒ The differences between oils and acrylics
Ⓓ The problems with the texture of oil paintings

Lecture

Lecture Topics

Lecture Topics

- **Arts**: 건축, 도시설계, 공예품, 음악, 문학, 사진, 극장 등의 주제가 출제된다. 특정 예술의 기원, 화가의 기법 변화, 예술이 특정 시대에 발달한 이유, 문학작품의 특징 등은 자주 출제되는 문제이다.
- **Life Science**: 동물학, 식물학, 생태학, 생리학, 고생물학, 해양생물학 등의 주제가 출제된다. 동물의 의사소통 방법, 동식물의 환경 적응 방법, 화석에 대한 연구결과나 이론 등을 묻는 문제가 출제된다.
- **Physical Science**: 천문학, 지구과학, 공학, 화학, 물리학, 신경과학, 지질학 등의 주제가 출제된다. 출제 가능성이 높은 문제는, 별의 크기 비교, 개발된 물건의 용도, 새로운 원소 발견, 특정 기상현상의 조건 등이 있다.
- **Social Science**: 인류학, 고고학, 경제, 교육, 역사, 언어학, 심리학, 철학, 사회학 등의 주제가 출제된다. 특정 문명이 발달/멸망한 이유나 경제학 관련하여 회사의 위기와 탈출 방법에 대한 문제가 나온다.

Chapter IV

Lecture Topics

Unit 3
Arts

01_ **Architecture**
02_ **Art & Science**
03_ **Painting**
04_ **Literature**
05_ **Film & Theater History**
06_ **Photography**

01 Architecture

TOEFL에 나오는 architecture건축 분야의 강의는 크게 네 가지 유형으로 나뉜다. 첫 번째로는, 예술적인 측면에서 특정 건축물이나 건축가의 건축 특징과, 그 건축물이 무엇의 영향을 받았는지 또는 무엇에 영향을 주는지에 중점을 둔 강의가 있다. 두 번째로, 두 가지의 건축물을 비교하여 장단점이나 공통점, 혹은 차이점을 출제포인트로 연결시키는 강의가 있다. 세 번째는 도시나 shopping mall쇼핑몰을 설계할 때 고려해야 할 필수요소와 이를 적용했을 때의 장단점을 언급하는 강의로, 예술적인 측면이 아닌 공학적인 측면에서 주제에 대해 이야기한다. 마지막으로, 세 번째와 마찬가지로 공학적인 측면에서 접근하여, 건축물의 공학적인 문제점과 이를 해결할 수 있는 공법을 언급하는 Problem – Solution 전개방식의 강의도 종종 출제된다.

출제포인트
- Q1 Main Idea
- Q2 Function (Influence)
- Q3 Problem
- Q4 Solution (Suggestion)
- Q5 Example
- Q6 Cause (Evidence) & Effect (Result / Finding / Research)
- Q7 Similarity / Difference
- Q8 Advantage / Disadvantage
- Q9 Misunderstanding / Correction
- Q10 Definition (Term) / Origin
- Q11 Two Click / Three Click
- Q12 Ordering
- Q13 Matching
- Q14 Opinion / Attitude
- Q15 Headset
- Q16 Requirement (Condition)
- Q17 Character
- Q18 Imply / Infer

1 Frank Lloyd Wright 프랭크 로이트 라이트, 건축가

Frank Lloyd Wright는 미국의 유명한 건축가로, 초창기에는 미국식 집을 지었다. 그러나 일본에 다녀온 후 동양 건축 양식의 영향을 받은^{Q2} 집을 짓게 되는데, 그 결과가 그의 대표 건축물 중의 하나로 시카고에 위치한 Robie House이다. 일반적인 미국식 집은 Robie House보다 지붕이 높고 큰 창문이 있는 반면, Robie House는 작은 창문을 가지고 있다.^{Q7} Frank의 건축 특징 중 하나는 prairie style초원 양식인데, 이는 초원의 수평선과 집이 자연스럽게 조화를 이루는 것^{Q2}을 말한다. 수평선을 강조하였기 때문에 굴뚝을 기준으로 집의 평면이 방사형으로 뻗어 나가는 형태를 하고 있다. 또한, 안에서 밖은 잘 보이지만, 밖에서는 안이 잘 보이지 않도록 설계^{Q2}하였다.

Difference		Function
미국식 집의 특징 (1) 지붕이 높음 (2) 창문이 큼	→	Prairie Style의 특징 (1) 수평선 강조 (2) 밖에서 안이 안 보임

2 Shopping Mall 쇼핑몰

지난 50년간 미국 도시의 downtown시내에 위치한 상점들은 경제적 어려움을 겪었다.♀3 그 이유는 많은 사람들이 교외로 이사를 갔기 때문이다.♀6 많은 건축가들이 이에 대한 해결 방법을 모색하여 나온 해결책이 pedestrian mall보행자 전용 쇼핑몰[구역]♀4이다. mall을 설계할 때는 위치와 디자인의 두 가지 요소를 고려해야 한다.♀16 위치는 다시 두 가지 요소가 충족되어야 하는데, 대중교통과 가까워야 하고, 직장인들이 퇴근 후에 쉽게 들를 수 있어야 한다. 좋은 예로는 convention center컨벤션 센터가 있다.♀5 convention center는 업무시설과 호텔, 상점들이 같이 있기 때문에 사람들이 많이 모이고, 업무가 끝난 후 쇼핑하기에 좋다. mall 디자인에서 중요한 것은 예쁜 건물이 아니라, 동선을 잘 설계하여 사람들이 짧은 거리를 이동해 많은 상점들을 볼 수 있도록 하는 것이다.

Problem – Solution		Requirement		Example
도시 상점들이 어려움에 처함 – pedestrian mall	→	위치와 디자인 고려	→	convention center

핵/심/표/현

- achievement   n. 성과
- adornment   n. 장식품, 액세서리
- accumulate   v. 모으다
- aesthetic   adj. 미학의
- alignment   n. 가지런함
- approach   v. 접근하다 n. 접근법
- aquarium   n. 수족관
- architect   n. 건축가
- archive   n. 문서 보관소
- building technique   건축 기술
- by-product   n. 부산물
- canal   n. 운하
- castle   n. 성
- cathedral   n. 대성당
- ceiling   n. 천장
- celebrated   adj. 유명한
- chimney   n. 굴뚝
- coherence   n. 일관성
- collapse   v. 무너지다
- component   n. (건물의) 구성요소
- compose   v. (그림 등을) 구성하다
- construct   v. 건설하다
- converge   v. 집중하다, 모이다
- craft   n. 수공예
- deliver   v. 전달하다, 보도하다
- design element   디자인 요소
- design   n./v. 디자인(하다)
- doorway   n. 출입구
- downtown   n. 시내
- drainer   n. 배수구
- dwelling   n. 주거(지), 주택
- elaborate   adj. 정교한
- erect   v. 건립하다 adj. 똑바로 선
- evolve   v. 발달하다
- exterior   n. 외부, 외면
- external   adj. 외부의
- fabric weaving   천[직물] 짜기
- facade   n. 정면, 외관, 표면
- facilitate   v. ...을 수월하게 하다
- fiber   n. 섬유
- fire-prone   adj. 불에 잘 타는
- fire-resistant   adj. 불에 내성이 있는
- flat   n. 플랫, 아파트
- floor plan   평면도
- found   v. 설립하다
- fountain   n. 분수, (무엇의) 원천
- geometric   adj. 기하학적인
- Gothic   adj. (건축) 고딕 양식의
- guild   n. 조합, 협회
- household   n. 가족, 가구, 가정
- immense   adj. 굉장한, 막대한
- incorporate   v. 포함하다
- industrial   adj. 산업의, 공업의
- inhabitant   n. 주민, 거주자
- interior design   내부 디자인
- lime   n. 석회
- limitation   n. 한계
- local resident   지역 주민
- maintenance   n. 유지, 보수
- marble slab   대리석 판
- mat   n. 매트, 돗자리
- metal frame   금속 틀[구조]
- molten   adj. 녹은
- mortar   n. 모르타르 v. 회반죽(을 바르다)
- mosque   n. 모스크, 회교사원
- office building   사무실 빌딩

- parallel   v. 평행하다
- parchment   n. 양피지
- pastel   n. 파스텔(미술 재료)
- pedestal   n. (기둥·동상 등의) 받침대
- pedestrian mall   보행자 전용 쇼핑몰
- pioneer   n. 선구자
- pipeline   n. 수송관
- planetarium   n. 천문관
- plaster   n. 석고, 회반죽
- plywood   n. 합판
- pour   v. (액체 등을) 붓다
- practical application   n. 응용
- prototype   n. 원형; (구조물의) 모델
- public utility   공공시설
- pyramid   n. 피라미드
- reinforce   v. 강화하다
- replace A with B   A를 B로 대체하다
- residential area   거주 지역
- revolutionize   v. 혁신을 일으키다
- rural area   지방, 시골
- sculpture   n. 조각품, 조형물
- sewer   n. 하수구, 하수도
- shift   v. 이동하다
- skeleton   n. (건물의) 뼈대, 구조
- skim   v. 훑어보다
- skyscraper   n. 고층빌딩
- slope   n. 경사면
- sphinx   n. 스핑크스
- spice   v. 가미하다, 장식하다
- splint   n. 부목
- staircase   n. 계단
- steel girder   강철 대들보
- steel reinforcement   n. 철근
- steep   adj. 가파른, 급격한
- suburb   n. 교외, 외곽, 변두리
- susceptible   adj. 민감한
- tension   n. 팽팽함, 압력
- timber   n. (건설용) 목재
- transportation hub   교통 중심지
- underground   n. 지하
- withstand   v. 견디다

Sample Questions

[01 ~ 06] Listen to part of a lecture in an architecture class. Then answer the questions.

MP3 34   정답 및 해석 p. 073

Note-taking

- Difference:

- Main Idea:

- Role:

- Function/Advantage:

- Character:

- Difference/Disadvantage:

- Solution:

- Character:

- Problem – Soultion:

- Role:

- Term:

01   What aspect of design does the professor mainly discuss in the lecture?
Ⓐ The focus on worker safety in factory design
Ⓑ The evolution of design through technological advance
Ⓒ Developments in engineering that improved design
Ⓓ The different construction methods used in industrial design

02   According to the professor, how did Albert Kahn differ from Julius Kahn?
Ⓐ He believed that factories should have external decorations.
Ⓑ He felt that a building's strength was the most important thing.
Ⓒ He focused on finding ways to use trussed bars in residences.
Ⓓ He was more concerned with how his designs affected workers.

03 What does the professor imply about the factories built before the Kahn brothers?
Ⓐ If they had wide spaces made of concrete, they were in danger of collapsing.
Ⓑ They were designed to encourage workers to be as efficient as possible.
Ⓒ Many of them were elaborately designed to resemble churches.
Ⓓ Their spacious rooms were filled with lots of daylight.

04 What can be inferred about the factories designed by Albert Kahn?
Ⓐ They weren't able to handle new technology.
Ⓑ They tended to become local landmarks.
Ⓒ They were popular with the factory workers.
Ⓓ They had interiors that were extremely ornate.

05 According to the professor, what were the advantages of using the Kahn system?
Choose two answers.
Ⓐ Workplaces could be made brighter.
Ⓑ Factories could use more wood in their design.
Ⓒ Factories could be made less susceptible to fire.
Ⓓ Buildings could be built larger overall.

06 According to the professor, what is a similarity between the buildings designed by Albert Kahn and Thomas Wallis?
Ⓐ Their exterior designs were elaborate.
Ⓑ Their design benefited from the Kahn system.
Ⓒ Their windows were a major design theme.
Ⓓ Their geometric shapes resembled churches.

▶ Question Review

Introduction
현대 건축
Difference
18세기 건축 – 교회, 성
19세기 건축 – 주택
지역, 공장

Main Idea
공업 건축의 선구자들

Role
Kahn 형제:
– 회사 설립자
– 건축가 & 발명가
– 현대 건축에 혁신을
  일으킴

Function / Advantage
화재 방지, 넓은 작업
공간

Character
Julius Kahn
– trussed bar

Difference / Disadvantage
Kahn 이전에는 건축
재료로 나무를 써서 화재
에 취약함

Solution
콘크리트 구조물의 문제
점을 해결함

Listen to part of a lecture in an architecture class.

Professor(male): As we have been studying, architecture in the 18th century was focused on churches and castles. So, now let's move on to modern architecture, which evolved in the late 19th century. The focus of architecture shifted to residential areas and, more importantly, to factories, in a form known as industrial architecture. Architecture, which had always emphasized style, was beginning to take function into consideration.

Q1 **Today we're going to talk about how this form was developed by the pioneers of industrial architecture.** Companies in need of factories in the late 19th century did not usually hire architects, as many thought it was a waste of resources. But when Julius and Albert Kahn came on the scene, things started changing.

The brothers came to the United States in 1880 and founded the architectural firm, Albert Kahn Associates in Detroit, Michigan. Albert was an architect, and his brother was an inventor who developed an engineering system for building construction. They revolutionized modern architecture by developing a method of replacing wood with reinforced concrete in factory walls, roofs, and supports. This not only gave better fire protection, but it also allowed for a more open factory floor.

Now it's important to understand that each brother had different points of emphasis when approaching a design. It's the convergence or combination of their philosophies that really ushered in a new era of modern architecture. As an inventor, Julius Kahn was more interested in the practical application of his design. He was an engineer, not an architect. He focused on utilizing building materials and applying them to architecture. A very good example is the Kahn trussed bar (shown on screen). Buildings before the Kahn brothers had weaknesses in one way or another. **Q3** **Q5-C** **If the buildings were made of wood, they could have large work areas but would be susceptible to fire.** You can see how this would be a problem in factories with machines that run very hot. **Q3** **If the buildings were made of concrete, they could not have large areas because the concrete would be too heavy and bend the steel reinforcement.** Well, the Kahn system solved this problem by introducing extra steel beams bent at a 45-degree angle to distribute the stress put on steel reinforcements. With the additional strength of reinforced concrete beams, floor space could be increased.

Character

Albert Kahn:
공장 작업자에 초점을 맞춤 – 더 큰 창문

Problem – Solution

공장 작업장의 문제점: (어두운 조명) – 햇빛

Role

Thomas Wallis – Kahn의 bar를 도입하고 새로운 디자인을 창조함

Term

Art Deco style 용어 설명

Julius Kahn's older brother **Q2 Q4 Albert had a different point of focus. Instead of thinking about the work itself, he focused on the people doing the work.** An important factor in the workplace was the amount of light. You'll most likely agree that the days seem longer when you're working in a dimly lit room. **Q5-A So Albert focused on getting more daylight into the working areas.** He realized the importance of how people would feel inside the buildings he designed.

Using the Kahn trussed bar, Albert could incorporate larger windows into his designs. In 1905, he designed the Packard Plant Building #10 using reinforced concrete made with the Kahn system. The building itself had almost no decoration, but it featured large windows and a lot of floor space for the workers. This expression of function became the start of a new era of industrial design.

Although the Kahn brothers revolutionized factories, by the 1930s some companies wanted more than just a good factory to work in. They wanted to incorporate style… Not like the statues you see in medieval churches, but they didn't want their factories to look like simple rectangles. So a British architect named **Q6 Thomas Wallis started to incorporate more style into his factories.** The factories still needed to be efficient work places, so **he utilized the Kahn trussed bar in his design**. But for the exteriors of the buildings, he changed the direction of industrial design once more. He used Art Deco, a style that utilized bold geometric shapes and lines, as well as rich colors. Factories became not only places where people would work but also landmarks that stood out in the busy streets of the city.

Practice Questions

[01 ~ 06] **Listen to part of a lecture in an architecture class. Then answer the questions.**

MP3 35   정답 및 해석 p. 074

Note-taking

01   What is the main topic of the lecture?
   Ⓐ The standard types of housing frames
   Ⓑ The best construction methods for housing frames
   Ⓒ The most efficient roofing materials
   Ⓓ The features of different roof styles

02 Why does the professor mention houses that were built in Cape Cod?
    Ⓐ To describe the typical American house frame
    Ⓑ To explain the origins of a certain roof style
    Ⓒ To give an example of a modern house design
    Ⓓ To suggest that roofs were impractical in the past

03 What is the advantage of a gambrel roof?
    Ⓐ It has the same angle on both sides.
    Ⓑ It allows for many rooms on the second floor.
    Ⓒ It creates more space for people to stand.
    Ⓓ It has fewer maintenance issues.

04 What is a disadvantage of a Cape Cod house?
    Ⓐ Its second story rooms have low ceilings.
    Ⓑ Its flat roof makes it weaker.
    Ⓒ Its lower floor contains only one room.
    Ⓓ Its roof slopes steeply in both front and back.

05 What can be inferred about people who choose to live in lean-to houses?
    Ⓐ They prefer wide spaces to stand up and walk around.
    Ⓑ They are concerned about harsh climates.
    Ⓒ They prefer beautiful scenery around their houses.
    Ⓓ They want a bright interior.

06 What would an architect who applies the principle of "form follows function" do?
    Ⓐ Reflect an inhabitant's needs when designing the house
    Ⓑ Research the most popular housing styles in the area
    Ⓒ Select the materials for the house before the house is designed
    Ⓓ Choose inexpensive materials for the houses in cold, harsh climates

02 Art & Science

TOEFL에서 art & science예술과 과학 분야는 학생들에게 다소 생소할 수 있다. 이 분야 강의들의 강의 소재가 예술작품이기는 하지만, 도입부를 잘 들어 보면 강의의 Main Idea는 (천문학자, 화학자, 지질학자 같은 과학자들이) 각 과학 분야의 지식과 장비를 이용해서 특정 예술품을 연구하는 내용이다. 따라서, 출제포인트는 특정 예술품 자체가 아니라 작품에 대한 과학적인 연구 결과 또는 과학자들의 주장을 뒷받침하는 Evidence증거이다. 그러므로, 도입부를 잘 듣고 강의가 온전히 예술품에 대한 내용인지, 아니면 과학기술을 이용한 예술품 연구에 대한 내용인지를 구별하는 것이 관건이라 할 수 있다. art & science 분야에 속하는 강의라는 판단이 서면, 강의에서 언급된 예술작품이 아니라 연구나 연구결과, 과학 기술 등에 초점을 맞춰 note-taking을 해두어야 문제를 막힘 없이 풀 수 있기 때문이다.

출제포인트
- Q1 Main Idea
- Q2 Function (Application)
- Q3 Problem
- Q4 Solution (Suggestion)
- Q5 Example
- Q6 Cause (Evidence) & Effect (Result / Finding / Research)
- Q7 Similarity / Difference
- Q8 Advantage / Disadvantage
- Q9 Misunderstanding / Correction
- Q10 Definition (Term) / Origin
- Q11 Two Click / Three Click
- Q12 Ordering
- Q13 Matching
- Q14 Opinion / Attitude
- Q15 Headset
- Q16 Requirement (Condition)
- Q17 Character
- Q18 Imply / Infer

1 Spectroscopy 분광학

spectroscopy는 간단히 정의하면, 물질과 빛의 관계를 연구하는 학문Q10이다. 빛은 여러 색상을 띤 파장들로 구성되어 있으며 이 파장들이 spectrum스펙트럼을 구성한다. 스펙트럼은 색상들의 밴드, 즉 무지개와 비슷하다. 분광법은 artwork예술작품을 분석하는 데도 사용된다.Q2 예를 들어 한 박물관의 큐레이터가 Rembrandt렘브란트의 작품을 구입하려고 하지만 그림이 진품인지 아닌지를 정확하게 확인할 수 없다. 그 그림이 Rembrandt 작품인지를 판단하려면, 우선 그의 작품들의 특징, 즉 brush 기법과 주로 사용한 pigment색소(물감의 성분과 같은 것)를 수집해야 한다. 그림에 사용된 모든 색

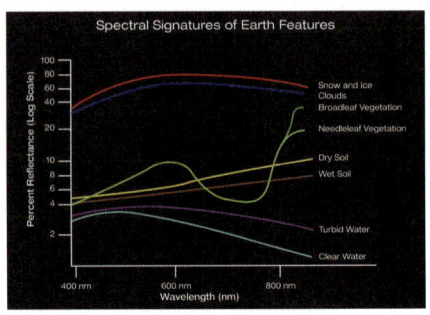

소가 Rembrandt가 살아있을 때 만들어진 것이어야만 진품으로 인정할 수 있다. 이것을 알아내는 데는 분광법이 필요하다. 물감의 성분마다 고유한 spectral line^{스펙트럼선}이 있기 때문에, 적외선 현미경을 사용해 분광법을 적용하면 적은 양의 물감으로도 각 색소의 성분을 알아낼 수 있다. 만일 색소 중 한 성분의 spectral line이 zinc^{아연}과 일치한 경우, zinc는 18세기 이전에는 발견되지 않았고 Rembrandt는 17세기에 살았기 때문에 그 작품은 진품이 아니라는 결론을 내릴 수 있다.^{Q6}

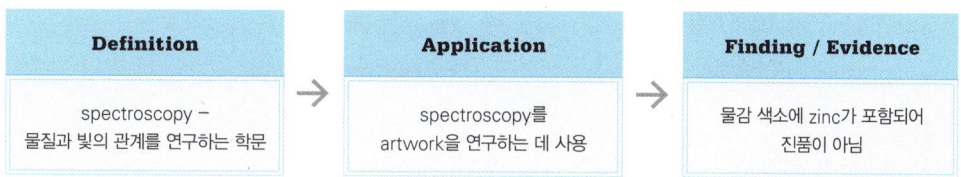

핵/심/표/현

- abstract art 추상 미술
- academy n. 학원
- adornment n. 장식품, 액세서리
- aesthetics n. (철학) 미학
- affordable adj. (가격이) 알맞은
- amateur n. 아마추어
- analyze v. 분석하다
- animator n. 만화 영화제작자
- appeal v. 흥미를 끌다
- art academy 미술 교육원
- art dealer n. 미술상, 화상
- art historian n. 미술사가
- artwork n. 미술품; 삽화
- autograph n. 자필 서명
- avant-garde n. 아방가르드(전위적인 사상)
- brush n. 붓
- brushstroke n. 붓 놀림, 필법
- bust n. 반신상, 흉상
- calligraphy n. 서법, 서예
- canvas n. 캔버스
- caricature n. 캐리커처
- cave art 동굴예술
- ceramics n. 도예
- charcoal drawing 목탄 미술
- clergy n. 성직자
- contemporary art 현대 미술
- convention n. 집회, 협의회
- critic n. 비평가, 비판가
- curator n. 큐레이터(전시 책임자)
- Dadaism n. 다다이즘
- decoration n. 장식
- drawing board 화판
- dusk n. 황혼
- emulsion n. (기름수지 등) 유액, 유화액
- engraving n. 조각법, 인쇄물
- equipment n. 도구
- era n. (특정)시대
- exhibition n. 전시회
- expose v. 노출하다, 알려지다
- exposure n. 노출
- fabric n. 천, 직물
- facial adj. 얼굴의
- fake adj. 가짜의
- fiber n. 섬유, 섬유질
- fine art n. 미술, 예술, 미술품
- figure n. 인물
- forge v. 위조하다
- framework n. 뼈대 작업, 틀 짜기
- gallery n. 갤러리, 전시관
- genuine adj. 진실된, 진짜의
- gesture n. 몸 동작, 신호
- handcraft v. 손으로 만들다
- high-tech adj. 첨단 기술의
- hone v. 연마하다, 갈다
- image n. 이미지, 그림
- Impressionism n. 인상파
- indigo n. 인디고, 남색
- ivory n. 아이보리
- knight n. (중세의) 기사
- landscape n. 풍경, 풍경화
- layer n. (페인트 등의) 층
- lead n. 납
- lightproof adj. 빛이 통하지 않는
- masterpiece n. 걸작, 명작
- minimalist n. 미니멀리스트
- monastery n. (주로 남자) 수도원

- mosaic   n. 모자이크
- mural painting   벽화
- nature scene   자연 풍경
- neoclassical   adj. 신고전주의의
- oil painting   n. 유화
- one-of-a-kind   adj. 특별한, 독특한
- ordinary   adj. 보통의
- original   adj. 원본의, 원래의
- ornamental   adj. 장식적인
- panorama   n. 전경
- paste   v. 붙이다
- perspective   n. 시각; 원근법
- pigment   n. 물감, 색소
- portrait   n. 초상화법, 인물 사진 기법
- posture   n. 자세, 포즈
- precision   n. 정확
- precursor   n. 선구자, 선배
- prehistory   n. 선사 시대
- printing press   인쇄기
- realism   n. 현실주의 미술
- realistic   adj. 현실적인, 사실적인
- repetitive   adj. 반복적인
- reproduction / replica   n. 복제, 복제품
- revolt   v. 반항하다 n. 반란, 저항
- salon   n. 살롱(과거 상류 가정 응접실에서 열리던 예술가들의 사교 모임)
- scene   n. 장면, 풍경
- sculptor   n. 조각가
- sculpture   n. 조각
- shoddy   adj. 조잡한, 싸구려의
- sketch   n. 스케치, 밑그림
- spectroscopy   n. 분광학
- split   v. 나누다
- standard   n./adj. 기준(의), 평균(의)
- statue   n. 동상
- tedious   adj. 지루한
- texture   n. 질감
- tribal art   부족 미술
- ventilate   v. 통풍시키다
- verify   v. 입증하다
- wave length   n. 파장
- work of art   미술 작품, 예술품

Sample Questions

[01 ~ 06] **Listen to part of a lecture in an Art & Science class. Then answer the questions.**

MP3 36 정답 및 해석 p. 077

Note-taking

• Main Idea:

• Correction:

• Research Method / Finding:

• Cause:

01 What is the purpose of the lecture?
   Ⓐ To explain the work of a famous European astronomer
   Ⓑ To show the early influences on Van Gogh's style
   Ⓒ To discuss astronomical themes in early modern art
   Ⓓ To show how art can be analyzed with astronomical principles

02 What does the professor say about most people's perception of Van Gogh?
   Ⓐ Their views on Van Gogh are generally correct.
   Ⓑ They do not give him enough credit for his accuracy.
   Ⓒ They think he depicted everyday life with great precision.
   Ⓓ They believe he was both an astronomer and an artist.

03 What does the professor mention as a method used to determine when *Starry Night* was painted?
   (A) Looking at other paintings from the period
   (B) Matching up its details with historical facts
   (C) Analyzing the positions of objects in the sky
   (D) Examining the pigments of the paints he used

04 Why does the professor point out the colors of Van Gogh's untitled painting?
   (A) To explain the source of debate regarding the painting
   (B) To illustrate how colors are used to analyze paintings
   (C) To give an example of Van Gogh's painting style
   (D) To indicate why scientists made an incorrect assumption

05 Why does the professor mention that Van Gogh was an Impressionist?
   (A) To give the reason why he was so interested in learning about astronomy
   (B) To explain why people don't expect his work to be scientifically accurate
   (C) To suggest that he lived during a time when little was known about science
   (D) To show why researchers have such a hard time analyzing his paintings

06 What does the professor imply about all the paintings discussed in the lecture?
   (A) Van Gogh paid great attention to his depiction of the night sky in them.
   (B) They would have had more value if they had included dates and locations.
   (C) They were painted by an artist who understood astronomy, not by Van Gogh.
   (D) Van Gogh painted them during the day and later added in the moon and stars.

Question Review

Listen to part of a lecture in an Art & Science class.

Professor(female): Last week, we talked about the methods used by astronomers to identify the movement of celestial bodies. In today's lecture, we'll be looking at the practical applications of this.

Calendars, for example, are the most obvious application. They're essentially just records of the regular movements of various celestial bodies through space. But I want to start today's discussion with a less obvious application.

Q1 **In recent years, astronomers have begun to get involved with the study and analysis of art.** It sounds really strange, I know. So, I'm assuming, **Q2 Q5** everyone knows Van Gogh, the famous artist. He was an Impressionist, meaning his paintings emphasized mood rather than realism, so you might not think that his artwork included accurate representations of the stars. But a group of astronomers from all over the United States took their knowledge of the movement of the stars and used it to analyze some of Van Gogh's paintings. It turns out that **Van Gogh's artwork was so accurate that the exact date that he created one of his paintings could be determined.** Let's take a look at a slide to get a better idea about the process of forensic astronomy.

I'm sure you're all familiar with this painting. It's Van Gogh's masterpiece, *Starry Night*. It's a painting of the view from his room in Saint-Remy-de-Provence, just before sunrise. Most people assumed that Van Gogh painted it from his imagination, but it turns out that wasn't the case.

The astronomer who studied it realized that the configuration of the stars in the painting was strikingly similar to scientific drawings of spiral nebulas. By using a university's planetarium computer projection, the astronomer found not only the exact year but the exact date and time of the painting – it was created between 3 and 4 a.m. on the morning of June 19, 1889.

Q3 So, how did they find this out? Well, first of all, they needed reference points. And indeed, the painting contained some. **Q6** Van Gogh had included a depiction of Venus, also known as the morning star, and a crescent moon. Their relative positions were checked against a computer simulation of the positions of these celestial bodies on various days during the period Van Gogh was thought to have painted *Starry Night* until an exact match was found.

Main Idea
천문학자들이 과학기술을 이용해서 예술작품 분석

Correction
인상파 화가라서 별을 정확하게 그리지 않았을 것이라고 추측했지만, 그렇지 않음

Research Method / Finding
반 고흐 그림 안의 행성과 달의 위치가 정확한 것으로 확인됨에 따라 반 고흐가 정확한 묘사를 했음을 알 수 있음

A similar tactic was used to determine the date he painted *White House at Night*. The painting shows a house at dusk, in a small town near Paris. Once again, Van Gogh had painted Venus into his night sky. But the astronomers noticed that it was brighter than usual. Rather than writing this off as a quirk of Van Gogh's imagination, they did some research and found out that Venus was indeed unusually bright in June of 1890. Later, a computer analysis of the stars and planets indicated it was painted on June 16, 1890, at approximately 7 p.m.

Now let's look at another painting, one that has been a great source of debate among art historians as to whether it was painted by Van Gogh or not. The painting is untitled, and since it contains no stars, there was no way to verify the date and time it was created using the method that was applied to *Starry Night*. However, by using historical knowledge, the shape of the mountains on the horizon, and a farmhouse in the painting, researchers were able to determine the approximate location of where it was painted – a hospital that Van Gogh had stayed in.

Q4 **Most assumed, because of the colors used in the painting... you see how the field is a golden color? Most assumed that the yellow object was the sun.** However, the path of the sun never actually corresponded with its position in the painting. This led to the realization that the object was actually the moon. Using the same computer program that was used to determine when *Starry Night* was painted, the researchers calculated that this untitled painting was created around 9 p.m. on July 13, 1889.

Cause
그림에 대해서 오판하게 된 이유

Practice Questions

[01 ~ 06] **Listen to part of a lecture in an Art & Science class. Then answer the questions.**

MP3 37

Note-taking

01 What is the main purpose of the lecture?
   Ⓐ To show how new technology can reveal more about art
   Ⓑ To illustrate the development of technology used to analyze art
   Ⓒ To explain the significance of the discovery of x-rays
   Ⓓ To explore the use of x-ray technology to create new art

02 According to the lecture, what did an art historian in Ohio discover about two famous paintings?
   Ⓐ They had not been painted by the same artist.
   Ⓑ An art dealer had tried to hide them.
   Ⓒ One was a copy of the other.
   Ⓓ They were once joined together.

03 Why does the professor mention painting over a hand?
   Ⓐ To emphasize the similarities of medical x-rays and x-radiography
   Ⓑ To help the students understand how x-rays work
   Ⓒ To give an example of an unusual painting technique
   Ⓓ To show how x-radiography creates different pigment types

04 What does the professor say about Van Gogh?
   Ⓐ He often painted portraits of his friends.
   Ⓑ He was cheated by dishonest art dealers.
   Ⓒ He practiced his skills over and over again.
   Ⓓ He painted over the canvases of other artists.

05 According to the professor, what are two things we can learn about painters through x-radiography? Choose two answers.
   Ⓐ Their changing social status
   Ⓑ Whether their paintings were forged
   Ⓒ How they improved their skills
   Ⓓ What their thought process was

Listen again to part of the lecture. Then answer the question. 🔊 MP3 37_1

06 Why does the professor say this?
   Ⓐ To suggest that she is annoyed because the student is talking too much
   Ⓑ To indicate that the student has mentioned what the professor wanted to hear
   Ⓒ To show that the student has made a mistake that the professor will correct
   Ⓓ To emphasize that the topic is too difficult to be explained in a single class

03 Painting

painting그림은 TOEFL에서 가장 많이 출제되는 Art 분야이다. 대개 특정 화풍을 처음 시작한 화가들과 관련된 문제나, 한 예술가의 작품 스타일의 변화, Influence(예술가가 무엇으로부터 영향을 받고, 무엇에 영향을 주었는지), Opinion(평론가들의 비평에 대한 교수의 의견)이 문제로 자주 출제된다. 강의는 주로 Origin화법의 기원에 대한 언급으로 시작하여 작품의 특징을 설명하고 그 작품이 무엇에 영향을 주었는지로 전개되는 방식이 있고, 또는 두 작가의 작품의 변화를 언급하며 둘의 차이점이나 공통점을 설명하는 방식도 있다. 두 가지 방식이 혼합된 강의가 나올 가능성도 있으니, 한 가지 방식으로만 단정짓지 말고 강의를 끝까지 주의해서 들어야 한다.

출제포인트
- Q1 Main Idea
- Q2 Function (Application)
- Q3 Problem
- Q4 Solution (Suggestion)
- Q5 Example
- Q6 Cause (Evidence) & Effect (Result / Finding / Research)
- Q7 Similarity / Difference
- Q8 Advantage / Disadvantage
- Q9 Misunderstanding / Correction
- Q10 Definition (Term) / Origin
- Q11 Two Click / Three Click
- Q12 Ordering
- Q13 Matching
- Q14 Opinion / Attitude
- Q15 Headset
- Q16 Requirement (Condition)
- Q17 Character
- Q18 Imply / Infer

1 Fresco 프레스코

르네상스 시대에는 벽이나 천장에 먼저 plaster석고를 바르고 그 위에 물감과 물을 섞어 그림을 그려서 말리는 그림 방식이 유행했다. 이 화법을 fresco라고 부른다. fresco painting에는 두 가지 방식, buon fresco와 secco fresco 방식이 있다.Q10 buon fresco는 석고가 마르기 전에 그림을 그리는 방식으로, 석고가 마르기 전에 그림을 완성해야 하기 때문에 화가가 그림을 그리다가 실수를 할 경우 수정이 거의 불가능하였다.Q8 secco fresco는 buon fresco와는 달리 이미 마른 석고에 그림을 그리는 방식Q7이라서 buon fresco의 문제점을 해결했다. 그러나, 이 방법도 drawback결점, 문제점이 있었는데, **buon fresco**만큼 그림이 오래 지속되지 않는 것[98]이었다. 그 이유는 **buon fresco**와는 다르게 물감이 석고와 단단하게 섞이지 않기 때문이었다. 그 예로 레오나르도 다빈치의 〈최후의 만찬〉은 **secco fresco** 방식[95]으로 그려졌는데, 완성된 지 20년이 지나면서부터 그림에 조금씩 손상이 가기 시작했다.

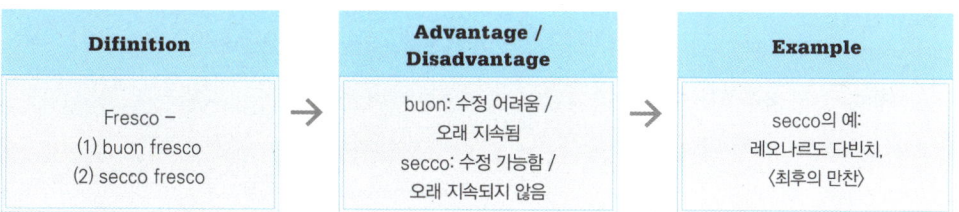

Difinition	Advantage / Disadvantage	Example
Fresco – (1) buon fresco (2) secco fresco	buon: 수정 어려움 / 오래 지속됨 secco: 수정 가능함 / 오래 지속되지 않음	secco의 예: 레오나르도 다빈치, 〈최후의 만찬〉

2 Cecilia Beaux 세실리아(미국 초상화가)

미국 초상화가인 **Cecilia Beaux**는 당대 최고의 초상화가로 알려졌으며, 루즈벨트 대통령 가족의 초상화도 그렸다.[95] 색상을 **contrast** 대조하다하는 것이 이 화가의 화법의 특징인데, 검은 색 배경에 흰색 옷을 입은 여인을 그려 넣는 방식 같은 것이다.[17] 이 화가의 그림은 **John Singer Sargent**를 연상케 한다. 두 화가의 작품을 보면 색을 사용하는 기술이 유사하다[97]는 것을 알 수 있다. 두 화가는 초상화를 사실적으로 그리는 데 중점을 두기보다 대상 인물의 감정 상태를 잘 파악해서 그리기 때문에 그림에 인물의 감정 상태가 나타나 있다. 이 화가처럼 본인만의 **insight** 통찰력, 이해을 가지는 것이 필요하다.[14]

Example	Character	Character/ Similarity	Opinion
화가의 지명도를 예로 설명 – 대통령 가족 초상화가	인물과 배경을 흑백을 써 contrast하는 기법	색 사용 기법이 John Singer Sargent와 유사함	자신만의 독특한 insight가 필요함

핵/심/표/현

- abrasive   adj. 연마재의
- ancient   adj. 고대의
- adopt   v. 채택하다
- approval   n. 승인, 동의, 허가, 찬성
- brushstroke   n. 붓 놀림
- canvas   n. 캔버스
- challenge   n. 어려움
- cite   v. 예로 들다, 말하다
- coincidentally   adv. 일치하게; 동시에 발생하는
- combining   n. 결합, 연합
- competitive   adj. 경쟁적인
- connection   n. 연결고리
- conservation   n. 보존, 보전
- contemporary art   현대 미술
- convey   v. (의미를) 전달하다
- cutout   n. 오려내기
- damaged   adj. 상처[상해]를 입은
- dating   n. 연대 결정
- decipher   v. 해독하다, 판독하다
- decline   n. 쇠퇴
- demonstrate   v. 설명하다, 증명하다
- departure   n. 벗어남, 일탈
- depiction   n. 묘사, 서술
- diagnose   v. (원인을) 진단하다
- dominant   adj. 우세한, 지배적인
- drawback   n. 결점, 문제점
- entitle   v. 제목을 붙이다
- enthusiast   n. 열렬한 팬
- eventually   adv. 결국에는, 서서히
- exhibit   v. 전시하다
- exposed   adj. 노출된
- extremely   adv. 극도로, 극히
- facet   n. 측면

- foreground   n. (그림의) 전경
- founder   n. 창설자
- fresco   n. 프레스코화[화법]
- hue   n. 색조
- inaccessible   adj. 접근하기 어려운
- inanimate   adj. 무생물의
- incentive   n. 장려금, 장려책
- influence   v. 영향을 미치다
- intangible   adj. 무형의
- intense   adj. 강렬한
- invention   n. 발명품
- limited   adj. 한정된
- medium   n. 매체
- multiple   adj. 다수의
- naked eye   육안
- norm   n. 표준, 규범
- obtain   v. 얻다, 얻어내다
- opulence   n. 부유함
- outline   v. 윤곽을 나타내다
- Paleolithic   adj. 구석기 시대의
- parchment   n. 양피지
- perform   v. 공연하다, 수행하다
- period   n. 기간, 연대
- perspective   n. 시각; 원근법
- pigment   n. 색소, 색깔
- plaster   n. 석고
- portrait   n. 초상화
- portray   v. 그리다, 묘사하다
- primary color   n. 원색
- progressive   adj. 진보적인, 진행되는
- radical   adj. 급진적인
- represent   v. 대표하다, 상징하다
- revival   n. 부활

- scholar   n. 학자
- scrape away   문질러 대다
- scribe   v. (…에) 새기다
- separate   v. 분리하다
- shade   n. 명암
- shallow   adj. 좁은, 얕은
- simultaneous   adj. 동시의
- skepticism   n. 회의론
- social hierarchy   n. 사회 계층
- sophisticated   adj. 정교한, 세련된
- specifically   adv. 특히, 구체적으로
- spectrum   n. 스펙트럼; 범위, 분광
- speculate   v. 심사 숙고하다
- still life   n. 정물화
- stretched   adj. 늘어난

- striking   adj. 빼어난
- superior   adj. 우월한
- supply   v. 제공하다
- surreal   adj. 초현실주의의
- symbolic   adj. 상징적인
- technique   n. 기술
- texture   n. (작품 등의) 질감
- to the extent of ~   …정도까지
- typically   adv. 일반적인, 전형적인
- uncommon   adj. 특이한
- unusual   adj. 평범하지 않은
- valued   adj. 가치 있는, 귀중한
- various   adj. 다양한
- vibrant   adj. 생기가 넘치는
- wipe out   지우다

Sample Questions

[01 ~ 06] Listen to part of a lecture in a contemporary art class. Then answer the questions. MP3 38 정답 및 해석 p. 082

Note-taking

- Main Idea:

- Difference:

- Example:

- Character:

- Origin / Example:

- (Name) Origin:

- Character:

- Differnece:

01   What is the lecture mainly about?
   Ⓐ Methods artists use to differentiate themselves
   Ⓑ The characteristics of a 19th century art movement
   Ⓒ Reasons why new art movements are met with skepticism
   Ⓓ Differences between Cubism and Romanticism

02   Why does the professor mention photographs?
   Ⓐ To contrast their content with that of Cubism
   Ⓑ To show how photographs influenced how painters painted portraits
   Ⓒ To suggest that Braque started Cubism due to his love for photography
   Ⓓ To introduce the origins of the Romantic movement

03 According to the professor, what characteristics of Cubism made it different from traditional art? Choose two answers.
   Ⓐ It replaced dull colors with brighter ones.
   Ⓑ It included more than what could be seen.
   Ⓒ It focused on surreal scenes from a fantasy world.
   Ⓓ It showed several sides of its subjects.

04 Why does the professor mention dice?
   Ⓐ To identify them as a tool Braque used for his paintings
   Ⓑ To point out that Braque's paintings looked like cubes
   Ⓒ To illustrate the uniqueness of Braque's painting style
   Ⓓ To give an example of a shape Braque used as a subject

05 According to the professor, what are the origins of the term "Cubism"?
   Ⓐ A famous artist's painting
   Ⓑ A portrait by George Braque
   Ⓒ Picasso's cubic drawings
   Ⓓ A critic's comment

06 What is the difference between Cubism and other art movements such as the Romantic Movement?
   Ⓐ Cubism was adopted by other mediums.
   Ⓑ Cubism was established much earlier.
   Ⓒ Cubism was influenced by traditional art.
   Ⓓ Cubism wasn't suitable for other mediums.

Question Review

Main Idea
현대 미술

Difference
너무 급진적임

Example
현대 미술이 어떻게 다른지 사진을 예로 들어 설명

Character
Braque의 특징
- 인상주의 화가
- 입체파(Cubism)

Origin / Example
Cubism이 어떻게 나오게 되었는지 주사위를 예로 들어 설명

Origin
Cubism이란 이름은 한 평론가의 언급에서 유래

Listen to part of a lecture in a contemporary art class.

Professor(female): As we have been studying, classic paintings, the traditional method, are based on what the naked eye can perceive, a copy of what we see through our eyes. But >Q1> **today, let's move on to modern art, also known as contemporary art. Modern art evolved in the early 19th century through the Avant-Garde movement, but in most cases audiences refused to accept it as art. It was too radical for their tastes.**

Student(male): Um… What made modern art so radical?

P: Well, the best way to explain this is by thinking of a photograph. >Q2> **Photographs capture a scene, but, in essence, the scene is what we see through our eyes. But, in the case of modern art, artists started experimenting by painting what can't be seen.** They looked at the intangible aspects of life – the things that cannot be touched. Say, for example, I was feeling really blue – depressed. Our eyes wouldn't be able to see it, but a painter might paint the whole canvas blue to express the feeling. The public was only accustomed to paintings that were real, so when they saw pictures that were beyond the norm, they were shocked. Now, a pioneer of modern art was Georges Braque, who was born in 1882. Braque was a house painter and decorator, but he quickly developed into an impressionistic painter. And by the age of 25, he started to develop his own unique style, which quickly became Cubism. Cubism was based on his new interest in geometry and, more importantly, simultaneous perspective. We know that there are other faces of an object even though we can only see one. For example, um… well… Name something that's shaped like a cube.

S: Uh… dice?

P: OK, >Q3-B> >Q4> **think about dice. Even though we can only see one dot, that doesn't mean the other faces, you know, with two, three, four, five, six dots don't exist. We simply can't see them. Well, Braque thought, "Well, why don't I draw the sides with two, three, four dots with the side that I can see?"** When this method of showing multiple facets of objects was combined with basic geometric shapes such as cubes, Cubism was born.

Well, as I mentioned before about new forms of art… Well, it was no surprise that Cubism was met with a healthy dose of skepticism. >Q5> **One critic dismissed Braque's works as a canvas filled with little cubes.**

Ironically, it was from the critic's harsh words that Cubism took its name. Now don't get me wrong here, Cubism wasn't totally free from the rules of traditional art. The artists continued to portray still lifes, human figures, and landscapes, all of which are part of reality. However, it is the way these subjects were presented that truly made Cubism unique.

Georges Braque also took another departure from the norm and de-emphasized the role of color, using dull colors such as greens, browns, and grays, even for people. I am pretty certain that none of us have green or gray skin. The subjects were also shown two-dimensionally, as if you were looking at them from straight on. But it was really hard to tell what exactly you were looking at because the other sides and angles of the subject were also shown. **Q3-D So, a violin would be painted in a way that showed the front, sides, and back simultaneously, in the shape of two-dimensional cubes. The paintings were quite striking indeed.**

Cubism was quite a departure from older artistic movements such as the Romantic movement. While the Romantic movement was something new in that it emphasized intense emotions, it still did not break the rules of art. What was painted was what could be seen. Romantic painters only painted one side, the side they could see. **Q6 This is probably why movements like Romanticism lent themselves to other mediums, such as music and literature, better than Cubism.** They were based on themes and emotions that could be found in reality. Cubism, on the other hand, was based on core principles that were primarily visual and were therefore not easily adopted by other mediums.

Character
기존 그림들과 차별화된 Braque의 시도
- 칙칙한 색
- 2차원적인 정육면체 형태

Difference
Romanticism은 다른 예술 분야에도 사용됨

Practice Questions

[01 ~ 06] **Listen to part of a lecture in an art history class. Then answer the questions.**

MP3 39   정답 및 해석 p. 083

Note-taking

01   What is the lecture mainly about?
    Ⓐ How artists choose their subjects
    Ⓑ The decline and revival of an art genre
    Ⓒ Different artistic styles in 17th-century Europe
    Ⓓ The differences between American and European artists

02   What does the professor mention as a reason for the popularity of still-life painting?
    Ⓐ The public had grown tired of landscapes.
    Ⓑ The paintings sold for a lot of money.
    Ⓒ The techniques required little time.
    Ⓓ The artists could control what they painted.

03 Why does the professor mention symbols?
   Ⓐ To compare Dutch paintings to American paintings
   Ⓑ To explain why historical paintings were popular
   Ⓒ To highlight a feature of some still-life paintings
   Ⓓ To describe the style of American folk artists

04 What does the professor say about still-life painting in the 19th century?
   Ⓐ It came back into style in Europe.
   Ⓑ It began to feature a lot of symbolism.
   Ⓒ It was only used to decorate furniture.
   Ⓓ It spread from America to Europe.

05 What is the professor's view of still-life paintings in America?
   Ⓐ She feels they are inferior to European paintings.
   Ⓑ She believes that most of them are too expensive.
   Ⓒ She considers some of them to be impressive.
   Ⓓ She thinks they use too many symbols.

Listen again to part of the lecture. Then answer the question. 🔊 MP3 39_1

06 Why does the student say this?
   Ⓐ To indicate that he does not understand the class material
   Ⓑ To refer to a well-known view about art
   Ⓒ To imply that still lifes should be considered modern art
   Ⓓ To indicate that he needs clarification about one point

04 Literature

TOEFL에서 literature문학 분야는 painting 분야와 강의 전개방식이나 문제유형이 비슷하게 출제되는 경향이 있다. 단, 작품의 특징을 언급할 때 내용과 표현이 다르므로 주의해서 듣는다면 구분할 수 있다. 두 분야 모두 특정 작품의 특징에 대해 이야기하는데, painting은 그림이 대상이므로 작품의 특징으로 주로 shade명암, texture물감의 질감, hue색조 등이 언급되는 반면, 문학에서는 작품의 character등장인물의 특징, 글을 통해 전달하고 싶은 메시지, 특정 작가의 작품에 자주 등장하는 시대적 배경이나 소재 등이 언급된다. 이는 강의의 주된 내용이자 출제포인트이기도 하니 유의해서 알아 두도록 한다.

출제포인트
- Q1 Main Idea
- Q2 Function (Application)
- Q3 Problem
- Q4 Solution (Suggestion)
- Q5 Example
- Q6 Cause (Evidence) & Effect (Result / Finding / Research)
- Q7 Similarity / Difference
- Q8 Advantage / Disadvantage
- Q9 Misunderstanding / Correction
- Q10 Definition (Term) / Origin
- Q11 Two Click / Three Click
- Q12 Ordering
- Q13 Matching
- Q14 Opinion / Attitude
- Q15 Headset
- Q16 Requirement (Condition)
- Q17 Character
- Q18 Imply / Infer

1 Detective Novel 탐정 소설

최초의 장편 탐정 소설은 *The Moonstone*이며, 그 뒤에 나온 소설들은 모두 같은 format형식에 따라 쓰여 졌다. 지금은 너무나 당연시 여기는 형식이지만, 그 origin기원은 *The Moonstone*인 것이다. Q10 이 소설에 등장하는 주인공은 다른 등장인물들과는 달리, 남들이 지나치는 사소한 특징들을 모두 기억하고 알아본다. 주인공은 경찰 수십 명을 동원하고도 찾지 못하는 범인을 범행 장소에서 발견된 약간의 페인트를 단서로 찾아낸다. Q17 이렇게 특출난 능력을 가진 주인공은 이후에 출판된 〈셜록 홈즈〉 같은 작품에도 똑같이 등장한다. Q7 탐정 소설의 주인공만이 이런 능력을 갖고 있으며 이를 통해 사건들을 해결하기 때문에 주인공이 부각된다.

이 탐정 소설의 주인공이 가지고 있는 다른 특징은 장미 향을 맡는 취미가 있는 것인데, Q17 이런 취미는 살인 사건과 같은 흉악한 범죄를 추적하고 범인을 잡는 일상에서 탈출하는 의미를 가진다. 이 특징 역시 〈셜록 홈즈〉에서 홈즈가 고상한 취미를 갖고 있는 것으로 유사하게 표현되었다.

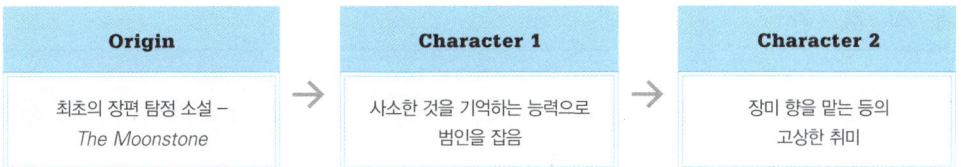

2 Postmodernism 포스트모더니즘

Postmodernism은 Realism현실주의과 Modernism모더니즘[현대주의] 이후에 Modernism의 반향으로 나타났다. 그러나 정확하게 언제 Postmodernism이 시작되었는지는 알 수 없다.♀3 Realism의 특징은 〈올리버 트위스트〉에서처럼 사람들의 힘들고 고된 일상생활을 그대로 생생하게 보여 주는 것이다.♀17 그 후에 나타난 Modernism은 사람들의 겉모습을 보여 주는 것을 넘어 사람들의 생각에 초점을 두게 된다.♀17 Modernism이 흥미로운 또 다른 이유는, 등장인물들 사이에 유대가 형성되어 있는 것이다.♀17 예를 들어, 처음에는 주인공들이 모르는 사람으로 만나서 서로 사랑하게 되지만, 알고 보니 어렸을 때 헤어진 동생이라는 사실을 알게 되어 서로 사랑할 수 없는 상황이 펼쳐지고, 그로 인해 갈등이 고조되는 전개방식♀5을 취한다. 이에 대한 반향으로 Postmodernism이 등장하게 되는데, Postmodernism은 인간의 우애 같은 것에 초점을 두기보다는 인생은 혼자서 살아가는 것이고 사람들이 그것을 받아들여야 한다는 메시지♀17를 전달한다.

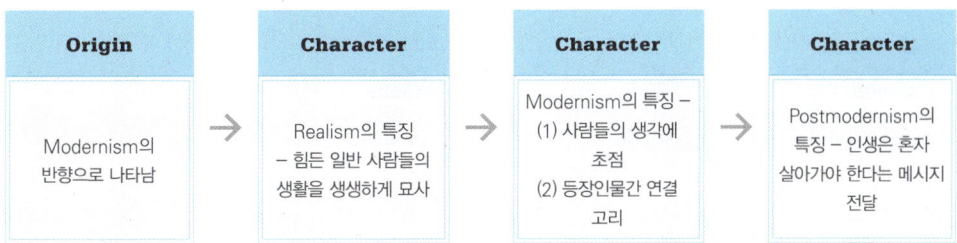

3 Autobiography자서전 vs. Memoir회고록

자서전과 회고록은 둘 다 작가가 작품의 주제라는 공통점♀7이 있다. 그러나, 자서전은 작가의 일대기를 다루고, 회고록은 작가의 특정 기간 동안의 일을 특정 주제의 관점에서 다룬다는 점에서 차이♀7, ♀10가 있다. 예를 들어 맥아더 장군의 유년기, 청소년기, 장군으로서의 업적을 서술했다면 자서전이고, 2차 세계대전에만 중점을 두고 기술했다면 회고록♀5이 된다. 어느 작가가 둘의 차이를 잘 요약했는데, 이에 따르면 자서전은 많은 연구와 검증을 기반으로 한 역사적 사실의 기록이고, 회고록은 한 사람이 특정 시기를 어떻게 기억하고 있는가에 기반을 둔 서술이므로 개인적인 생각을 적은 글♀7에 더 가깝다. 대개 회고록은 글을 전개하는 기법이 fiction소설과 유사하다. 그러나 자서전과 회고록의 전개가 미묘한 차이를 보일 때는 둘의 경계를 구별하는 것이 생각만큼 쉽지 않다.♀3

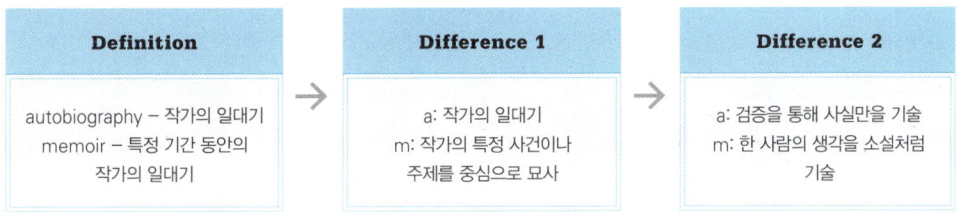

핵/심/표/현

- admire   v. 존경하다, 우러러보다
- agenda   n. 의제
- artistic   adj. 예술적인
- attest   v. 증명하다, 증언하다
- autobiography   n. 자서전
- awakening   n. 자각, 인식
- bestow   v. 수여하다, 주다
- boast   v. 뽐내다, 내세우다
- capitalization   n. 대문자 사용
- category   n. 분류, 카테고리
- character   n. 등장인물
- characterize   v. 특징을 나타내다, 규정하다
- circumstances   n. (주위의) 사정, 상황
- claim   v. 주장하다, 제기하다
- charity   n. 자선 단체
- community   n. 커뮤니티, 단체
- companion   n. 친구, 동료, 동반자
- concentration   n. 집중
- conflict   n. 논쟁, 다툼
- conform   v. 따르다, 순응하다
- consciously   adv. 의식적으로
- consequence   n. (발생한 일의) 결과, 벌
- conservative   adj. 보수적인
- conviction   n. 확신, 신념,
- creature   n. 생물, 생물체
- daring   adj. 모험적인, 대담한
- detective novel   탐정소설
- detractor   n. 폄하하는 사람
- distinctive   adj. 특이한
- defy   v. 저항하다
- depict   v. 묘사하다
- determination   n. 결심, 결의
- dweller   n. 거주자
- element   n. 구성 요소
- eliminate   v. 제거하다, 없애다
- epic poem   서사시
- espouse   v. (이념·사상 등을) 지지하다
- essentially   adv. 근본적으로, 본질적으로
- establish   v. 설립하다, 확립하다
- fiction   n. 소설
- fictitious   adj. 거짓의, 허구의
- fore-runner   n. 선구자
- format   n. 형식
- generalizable   adj. 일반화 할 수 있는
- ghetto   n. 빈민촌, 빈민가
- give in   굴복하다
- glimpse   v. 언뜻 보다 n. 언뜻 봄
- groundwork   n. 기초, 기본원리, 토대
- heritage   n. 유산, 전통
- humiliate   v. 굴욕[창피]을 주다
- indefinable   adj. 정의[설명] 할 수 없는, 애매한
- ideology   n. 이념, 사상
- implied   adj. 암시된, 함축된
- incline   v. 경향이 있다
- inflict   v. (부담·고통·타격 등을) 가하다
- insight   n. 통찰력
- intensely   adv. 강렬하게, 격렬히
- intrinsically   adv. 본질적으로
- justify   v. 정당화하다
- main feature   주요 기능[특징]
- medieval times   중세 시대
- memoir   n. 회고록
- metaphor   n. 은유, 암유
- migrate   v. 이주하다, 이동하다
- mindset   n. 사고방식
- motivation   n. 동기, 자극제

- mundane   adj. 일상적인
- nonfiction   n. 논픽션, 실화
- oral   adj. 입의, 구두의
- outburst   n. 폭발, 급격한 증가
- path   n. 길
- patriotic   adj. 애국적인
- personification   n. 의인화
- pitfall   n. 위험, 곤란
- plot   n. 줄거리
- poet   n. 시인
- Postmodernism   n. 포스트모더니즘
- profound   adj. 심오한
- prolific   adj. 다산의, 다작의
- punctuation   n. 구두법, 문장부호
- racial equality   인종 평등
- rapacious   adj. 탐욕적인, 욕심이 많은
- reaction   n. 반응, 반작용
- Realism   n. 현실주의
- rebirth   n. 갱생, 소생, 부활
- recall   v. 기억해내다
- recognize   v. 인정하다, 인식하다
- reflective   adj. 반영하는
- relevance   n. 연관성
- remarkable   adj. 대단한, 예외적인
- reputation   n. 명성
- rhyme   n. 각운
- sacrifice   n./v. 희생[하다]
- self-identity   n. 개성, 자아정체성
- settle   v. 정착하다, 자리잡다
- slavery   n. 노예제도
- spiritual   adj. 정신적인
- standout   n. 특출 난 것, 사람
- stanza   n. 스탠자(4행 이상의 각운이 있는 시구)
- storyteller   n. 이야기 작가
- struggle   v. 고생하다
- subject matter   소재
- synonymous   n. 동의어의, 뜻이 같은
- syntax   n. 구문론, 통사론
- take place   일어나다, 발생하다
- thread   n. 줄거리, 맥락
- transformation   n. 변화, 변신
- transition   n. 과도
- underestimate   v. 얕보다, 과소평가하다
- universal   adj. 전세계적인, 공통적인
- unprecedented   adj. 전례 없는
- unspecified   adj. 명시되지 않은
- verse   n. (시의) 연

Sample Questions

[01 ~ 06] Listen to part of a lecture in an American literature class. Then answer the questions. MP3 40 정답 및 해석 p. 086

Note-taking

• Main Idea:

• Character:

• Difference:

• Similarity:

• Opinion:

01 What is the purpose of the lecture?
   Ⓐ To explain how American poetry developed
   Ⓑ To introduce two unique American poets
   Ⓒ To give an example of modern poetry
   Ⓓ To show the effects of war on literature

02 According to the lecture, what is true about Dickinson?
   Ⓐ She was close friends with Whitman.
   Ⓑ She often edited the poetry of others.
   Ⓒ She was not famous when she was alive.
   Ⓓ She kept religious themes out of her poems.

03 According to the professor, what is an interesting aspect of Dickinson's poetry?
   Ⓐ She did not use conventional punctuation.
   Ⓑ She focused on the traditional aspects of poetry.
   Ⓒ She wrote about ugliness rather than beauty.
   Ⓓ She created the free verse style of poetry.

04 In what way was Whitman's poetry different from Dickinson's?
   Ⓐ It was more conservative due to his religious beliefs.
   Ⓑ It used a different technique to break away from tradition.
   Ⓒ It mainly focused on the everyday aspects of American life.
   Ⓓ It started a new genre of poetry instead of changing an old one.

05 According to the professor, what are the aspects do Whitman and Dickinson have in common? Choose two answers.
   Ⓐ They both found new ways to present common themes.
   Ⓑ They shared a fondness for writing very long stanzas.
   Ⓒ They each showed a religious influence in their work.
   Ⓓ They are both considered to be modern poets.

06 Why does the professor say this? 🔊 MP3 40_1
   Ⓐ To suggest that few students get enough sleep
   Ⓑ To identify an annoyance Dickinson most likely felt
   Ⓒ To show that Dickinson was an unusual person
   Ⓓ To reinforce the fact that Dickinson used common themes

▶ **Question Review**

Main Idea
남북전쟁 이후의 시인

Character
Emliy Dickinson –
죽은 뒤에야 대중에게 알려짐

작가의 특징
(1) 독특한 소재 – 일상적인 물건에서 의미를 찾음
(2) 독특한 언어
(3) 구두점 대신 대시를 사용
(4) 이례적인 대문자 사용

Headset

Listen to part of a lecture in an American literature class.

Professor(male): Following up on our class about post-colonial literature, let's focus on literature after the Civil War. Keep in mind, just like the post-colonial era, this was a period of transition and change for the people of the United States. There were changes in the political structure as well as in the mindset in the country. The age-old institutions and social norms of the country were changed in a span of few years. Like all forms of art, literature in this era adapted to these new ideas and paved the way for change.

I would like to take a look at poetry now. Sadly, there isn't a lot of poetry from this era. Most of the American poetry we know was published in the 20th century. But **Q1** **there were still prolific poets during this time, pioneers of a truly American form of poetry.**

So, **one of the first poets we're going to talk about is Emily Dickinson.** As she was a female writer, most of her works that were published during her lifetime were actually heavily edited. **Q2** **It wasn't until after her death that her truly artistic and radical style became evident. Her first volume of work was not published until 1890, four years after her death.** Despite this, she remains one of the most influential American poets.

What made Dickinson's poetry so unique was both the subject matter and language used. She didn't deviate much from traditional poetry, in the sense that there were verses and rhymes. She... uh... used perfect rhymes for lines two and four of her stanzas. What really makes Dickinson's poems interesting is her syntax. She did not follow the standard arrangement of words and phrases to form her sentences. A look at her manuscripts will reveal that **Q3** **she often replaced traditional punctuation marks with dashes and used unconventional capitalization.**

Her subject matter also made her poetry distinct from other poets' during her time. She searched for meaning in the common things in life, the familiar aspects that mostly go unnoticed. Think of an image like the loud ticking of a clock at night. **Q6** **This is something we generally don't notice, but we can identify with it nonetheless.** 🎧 You've all heard a clock at night, right? Her poems reveal a mind that was both serious and playful. It was the way she fused such mundane objects into her profound thoughts that made her one of the greatest poets in American history.

Character
Walt Whitman의 특징
(1) 자유시
(2) 전통적인 요소를 배제

Difference
Emily Dickinson은 구문을 통해, Walt Whitman은 전통적 요소를 배제해 전통 시와 차별화시킴

Similarity
종교의 영향이 시에 나타남

Opinion
◐ agree

>Q1> **Another poet I want to talk about is Walt Whitman.** He broke tradition, both in form and meaning, so radically that he shocked his generation and later generations as well. Even though he did not create it, he is often called the father of free verse, a type of poetry that does not rely on consistent patterns or rhymes. He was one of the first poets that did not rely on traditional poetry techniques. >Q4> **While Dickinson tried to break tradition through her syntax, Whitman did so with his lack of traditional elements.** In one of his most popular poems, he writes, "He turns his quid of tobacco while his eyes blur with the manuscript; The malformed limbs are tied to the surgeon's table." You can clearly see the lack of rhyme in his lines, but the way these words flow… No other poet could… the structure of his poems was truly remarkable.

The subject matter Whitman used was a brutally honest representation of everyday life. The line about limbs, it really isn't the fluffy, beautiful subject matter that most associate with poetry. His unfiltered nature led to many detractors, including Dickinson, but his influence is still felt today.

These two poets wrote about totally different subject matter and had different technical styles, >Q5-C> **but both showed the heavy influence of religion in their poetry, with various references to a divine power.** >Q5-D> **They are both also considered by many writers, including myself, to have been the first modern poets.**

Practice Questions

[01 ~ 06] **Listen to part of a lecture in an African–American history class. Then answer the questions.** MP3 41 정답 및 해석 p. 088

Note-taking

01 What is the lecture mainly about?
   Ⓐ The history of an African-American literary movement
   Ⓑ The problems faced by African-American authors
   Ⓒ The early origins of the Civil Rights Movement
   Ⓓ The portrayal of African Americans in literature

02 The professor mentions two prominent writers of the Harlem Renaissance. What were innovative features of their writing? Choose two answers.
   Ⓐ Incorporating new language to depict the feelings of African Americans
   Ⓑ Including more rhythmic elements to emphasize the culture of African Americans
   Ⓒ Combining traditional African-American music and poetry
   Ⓓ Exposing the public to an African-American lifestyle they were not familiar with

03 What point does the professor make about the geographic origins of the Harlem Renaissance?
   Ⓐ It was brought to America from Europe after World War I.
   Ⓑ It started in New York and spread to other northern cities.
   Ⓒ It began in rural areas of the southern United States.
   Ⓓ It was adopted from a similar movement in Jamaica.

04 What does the professor imply about the Niagara Movement?
   Ⓐ It didn't have much of an impact on African Americans.
   Ⓑ It was a forerunner of the Harlem Renaissance.
   Ⓒ It was attended by many Harlem Renaissance writers.
   Ⓓ It motivated African Americans to move to the North.

05 Why does the professor mention the writer W.E.B. Du Bois?
   Ⓐ To identify one of the figures who laid the foundation for the Harlem Renaissance
   Ⓑ To explain why African-American authors seldom wrote about their communities
   Ⓒ To illustrate how the great migration of African Americans to the North began
   Ⓓ To show that not all African-American authors supported the Harlem Renaissance

06 According to the professor, what may have contributed to the start of the movement?
   Ⓐ A mass migration of authors to northern cities
   Ⓑ Discrimination African-American soldiers faced in Europe
   Ⓒ Better educational opportunities for African Americans
   Ⓓ A desire by African Americans to be treated as equals

05 Film & Theater History

TOEFL에서 film & theater history영화 및 연극의 역사 분야에서는 특정 영화나 연극의 Origin, 연극의 흥망성쇠의 Cause 등을 묻는 문제가 종종 출제된다. 또한, 좋은 연극이나 영화가 되기 위해 꼭 필요한 요소들을 묻는 Requirement 문제 유형도 자주 출제된다.

출제포인트
- Q1 Main Idea
- Q2 Function (Application)
- Q3 Problem
- Q4 Solution (Suggestion)
- Q5 Example
- Q6 Cause (Evidence) & Effect (Result / Finding / Research)
- Q7 Similarity / Difference
- Q8 Advantage / Disadvantage
- Q9 Misunderstanding / Correction
- Q10 Definition (Term) / Origin
- Q11 Two Click / Three Click
- Q12 Ordering
- Q13 Matching
- Q14 Opinion / Attitude
- Q15 Headset
- Q16 Requirement (Condition)
- Q17 Character
- Q18 Imply / Infer

1 Underwater Documentary Film 수중 다큐멘터리 영화

Jean Painléve는 1920년대 film 제작자로, science과학와 fiction소설을 혼합한 독특한 film을 제작하였다.^Q18 그는 수중 촬영 영화의 선구자이기도 하다. 그는 해양생물과 관련된 영화를 많이 촬영했는데, 예를 들어, 연체동물을 촬영해 음악과 함께 연체동물의 움직임을 보여주어, 마치 연체동물이 춤을 추는 것 같은 장면을 연출했으며^Q5 narration내레이션을 통해 동물과 사람이 어떻게 다른지를 설명해 주었다. 그 당시 Jacques도 수중 촬영 영화를 만들었는데, 그는 Jean의 film과는 달리 다큐멘터리 방식의 film을 촬영하였다.^Q7 당시에는 science와 fiction을 혼합한 hybrid혼성체 방식은 대중들을 불편하게 했기 때문에 Jean은 유명해지지 못했다.^Q6

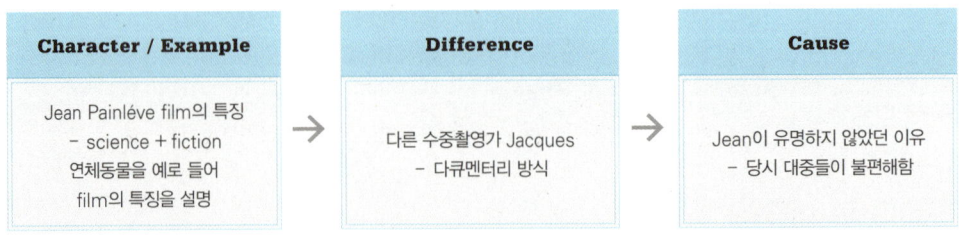

2 Nickelodeon 니켈로디언

nickelodeon은 1900년도 초에 유행했던 극장의 한 형태로, 그 이름은 입장료였던 5 cent 동전 nickel과 '고대 그리스의 극장'이라는 뜻의 odeon에서 유래했다.♀10 nickelodeon은 narrative film 서사 영화이 발달하면서 나타났으며,♀6 장르와 관계없이 짧은 영화를 많이 보여주는 것이 특징이었다. 이 극장의 형태는 큰 성공을 거두게 되는데, 가격이 싸고, 언제든지 원할 때 영화를 볼 수 있다는 편리성♀8 때문이었다. 그러나, 이후 다른 큰 극장과 plot 줄거리이 있는 더 긴 영화가 등장하기 시작하면서, 줄거리 없이 그냥 화면만 보여 주었던 nickelodeon은 쇠퇴기를 맞이하게 된다.♀6

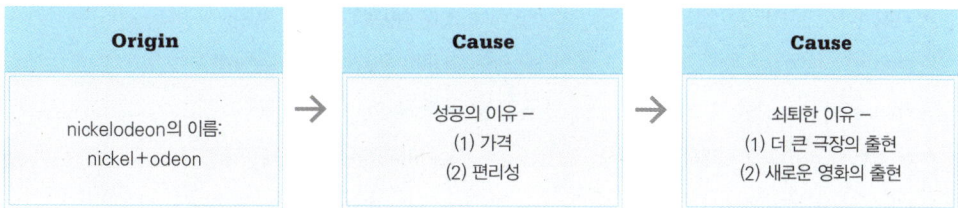

3 Well-made Play 잘 구성된 연극

19세기 유럽에 Realism 현실주의이 널리 퍼지면서 연극도 같이 성공하게 되었다. 인기 있는 연극은 모두 공통적인 요소들이 있었으며 이 성공요소들은 서로 논리적으로 연결되어 있다. 첫째가 logical exposition 논리적 설명♀16이다. 이전까지는 연사가 등장해 연극의 배경지식을 설명하는 방식이었는데, well-made play에서는 연사가 등장하지 않고 등장인물들의 대사가 이를 대신하게 된다. 예를 들어, 청소하는 사람들의 대사를 통해 주인공의 집안이나 등장인물의 성격을 알 수 있는 것이다.♀5 두 번째는 inciting incident 호기심을 일게 하는 사건♀16로, 특정 사건을 주인공은 모르지만 관객들만 알고 있는 것을 말한다. 예를 들어, 남자 주인공과 여자 주인공 집안 사이에 안 좋은 일이 생겼는데, 관객들은 그 사건에 대해 알고 있지만 정작 남녀 주인공은 그 사실을 모르는 상황이 연출된다. 따라서, 긴장감이 증폭되어 이를 지켜보는 관객들은 연극에 더욱 몰입하게 된다. 마지막으로, 극의 끝에는 happy ending 행복한 결말이 꼭 들어간다.♀16 관객들이 이를 좋아하기 때문이다.

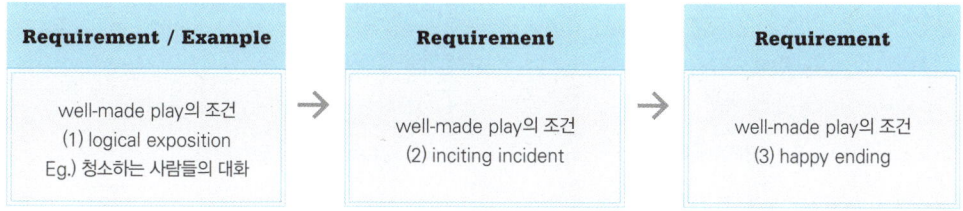

핵/심/표/현

- accessible   adj. (입장·권한 등이) 허락된
- acoustics   n. 음향시설
- acrobat   n. 곡예사
- apparent   adj. 분명히, 명백히, 확실히
- audience   n. 관람객, 방청객
- audition   n. 오디션
- characteristic   n. 특성, 특징
- cheerless   adj. 흥이 없는, 힘이 없는
- cinema   n. 영화관, 상영관
- classic   adj. 전형적인, 고전적인
- classify   v. 분류하다, 등급별로 정하다
- clown   n. 광대
- clumsy   adj. 서투른, 재치 없는
- coin   v. (새로운 낱말을) 만들다
- commercially   adv. 상업적으로
- component   n. 요소
- conservative   adj. 보수적인
- constrain   v. 제약[제한]하다
- contemplative   adj. 명상적인, 사색적인
- costume   n. 의상
- daydream   n. 몽상, 상상
- denouement   n. 대단원, 결말
- dimension   n. 차원
- disbelief   n. 불신, 의혹
- dramatic   adj. 극적인, 급격한
- dramaturge   n. 희곡 작가
- early version   초본, 이전 버전
- eccentric   adj. 별난, 괴짜스러운
- eliminate   v. 제거하다
- emotional   adj. 감정의, 정서의
- emotive   adj. 감정을 자극하는
- emphasis   n. 강조, 중점, 중시
- entertaining   adj. 재미있는

- erratic   adj. 불규칙한, 변덕스러운
- exposition   n. 전시회, 박람회
- fictional   adj. 소설의
- formula   n. 공식
- fortune   n. 운명
- identical   adj. 똑 같은
- illuminate   v. (빛으로) 비추다
- illusion   n. 환각, 환영
- imitation   n. 모조품, 모방
- immediately   adv. 즉각적으로, 당장
- immoral   adj. 부도덕한
- inappropriate   adj. 부적절한
- innocent   adj. 결백한, 순수한
- knack   n. 요령, 비결
- make up   화장을 하다
- mass   n. 대중
- minimal   adj. 최소의
- mime   n./v. 무언극(을 하다)
- minstrel   n. 음유 시인, 음악가
- motion picture   n. 영화
- mysterious   adj. 신비스러운
- narration   n. 내레이션, 설명 (부분)
- nightmare   n. 악몽
- notable   adj. 주목할 만한, 눈에 띄는
- obligatory scene   필수 장면
- odd   adj. 이상한, 특이한
- oppose   v. 반대하다
- optimal   adj. 최적의
- perception   n. 인식
- performance   n. 공연, 성과
- performer   n. 공연가, 연기자
- pioneer   n. 선구자
- playwright   n. 극작가, 각본가

- proceed   v. 진행하다, 절차를 밟아가다
- producer   n. 제작자, 연출가
- production   n. (영화연극 등의) 제작
- profanity   n. 신성 모독; 불경스런 말
- prop   n. 소도구
- puppeteer   n. 인형을 부리는[조종하는] 사람
- renowned   adj. 저명한, 유명한
- reverberate   v. (소리가) 울리다
- reversal   n. 반전, 전환
- rigid   adj. 엄격한, 융통성 없는
- sarcastic   adj. 빈정대는, 비꼬는
- scenery   n. 풍경, (무대의) 배경
- script   n. (연극 등의)대사
- sentimental   adj. 감상적인
- shame   n. 수치심, 부끄러움
- social climate   사회적 풍토
- spare   adj. 여분의, 남는
- stand out   눈에 띄다
- stereotype   n. 고정 관념
- stigma   n. 낙인, 오명
- subsequent   adj. 그 다음의, 차후의
- subtle   adj. 섬세한, 미세한
- suspend   v. 연기하다, 미루다
- suspicious   adj. 의심스러운, 의혹이 생기는
- tension   n. 긴장감
- traditional   adj. 전통적인, 관례적인
- tragedy   n. 비극
- unaffordable   adj. 감당할 수 없는 금액의
- uncanny   adj. 이상한, 묘한
- vagueness   n. 막연함
- versatile   adj. 다재다능한
- vulgar   adj. 저속한
- weird   adj. 이상한, 기이한

Sample Questions

[01 ~ 06] Listen to part of a lecture in a theater class. Then answer the questions.

🔊 MP3 42   정답 및 해석 p. 091

Note-taking

• Main Idea:

• Example:

• Difference:

• Requirement / Example:

• Difference:

• Requirement:

01 What is the lecture mainly about?
Ⓐ The problems faced by early stage productions
Ⓑ The need to improve costume design elements
Ⓒ The importance of visual design in modern theater
Ⓓ The influence of ancient Greek theater

02 What does the professor say about theater before the 20th century?
Ⓐ The concept of production design did not exist.
Ⓑ The audience did not pay attention to the sets.
Ⓒ Costume designers were highly respected.
Ⓓ People did not think production design was important.

03 Why does the professor mention a slammed door?
   Ⓐ To highlight the importance of acoustics
   Ⓑ To show how a door can be used as a prop
   Ⓒ To give an example of a set design challenge
   Ⓓ To point out a common production design error

04 According to the professor, how is a prop different from part of the set?
   Ⓐ It can be seen by the audience.
   Ⓑ It is picked up by an actor.
   Ⓒ It has some historical context.
   Ⓓ It is mentioned in the script.

05 According to the professor, what are some effects of costume design?
   Choose two answers.
   Ⓐ It can cause the audience to notice a character.
   Ⓑ It can make the lighting director's job much easier.
   Ⓒ It can allow the actors to better understand their roles.
   Ⓓ It can give the play the appearance of a specific era.

06 Why does the professor mention his experience as a lighting director?
   Ⓐ To emphasize that lighting was more difficult in the past
   Ⓑ To give a specific example of a modern lighting technique
   Ⓒ To describe the technology needed to light a stage well
   Ⓓ To show a common misconception about production design

▶ **Question Review**

Main Idea
프로덕션 디자인

Difference
20세기 이전에는 프로덕션 디자인에 신경을 많이 안 씀

Requirement / Example
세트 디자인에 고려해야 할 두 가지 조건을 예를 들어 설명
- 시각적 요소
- 기능적 측면

Difference
소도구와 세트의 차이

Listen to part of a lecture in a theater class.

Professor(male): Theater really isn't anything new. There has been some sort of theater that more or less resembles what we see now since the sixth century BC. I mean, the basic elements pretty much have stayed the same. Essentially, any type of play consists of actors acting out scenes that follow a storyline. But there is an aspect of modern theater that has evolved into something more. **Q1** **What I'm talking about is production design.**

Production design, of course, has always been an element of theater, but **Q2** **it wasn't until the 20th century that people really started to focus on it.** Basically, **Q1** **it concerns all of the visual elements of a play, such as the stage, the scenery, the costumes and the lighting.** And, in some cases, it even includes the sound.

The reason I say sound is included is the importance of having good acoustics… you know, so the audience can actually hear what is being said on the stage. We have the ancient Greeks to thank for the way theaters are now constructed for optimal acoustic qualities. These ancient architects considered how the human voice travels, as well as how it reverberates… you know, how it bounces off the walls… so that everyone in the theater would be able to hear the actors equally well. Today, sound quality has already been considered in the construction of most theaters, so it doesn't usually affect the design of the stage. But, as I said, it sometimes does.

Next up is set design. The set is essentially anything on the stage that is not a prop or part of a costume. **Q3** **Proper set design needs not only to consider the visual experience of the audience, but also to address some functional aspects. For example, there might be a scene in a play in which a door is slammed by an angry character.** The set designer needs to make sure that the door makes the appropriate sound when it is slammed and, at the same time, that the whole set doesn't come tumbling down.

Now, **Q4** **sometimes, parts of the set can be turned into props. The main difference between an object being part of the set or a prop is whether an actor picks it up or not.** So let's say there's a scene in which an angry character throws a chair and breaks it. The chair will be part of the set in the beginning of the scene but will become a prop the moment the actor grabs it.

Requirement 의상 디자이너는 연극의 역사적 맥락을 고려해야 함	The next key element of production design is the costumes. Costume designers must understand and accurately reflect the historical context of the play. This is especially important in plays that feature minimal set design – **Q5-D the costumes themselves are the main visual component that sets the historical period of the play.** **Q5-A Costumes can also be used to affect the way the audience perceives a character.** For example, a character whose hat is set at a slightly different angle than those of the rest of the cast will stand out from the crowd. The hat will catch the audience's attention, but they really won't know why. In other words, subtle costume design elements can have a strong effect on the perception of a character.
Requirement 조명 – 가장 중요한 요소	And finally, there's lighting. Lighting is the most important element of production design. I mean, you wouldn't be able to see a play without any lighting, would you? So lighting is crucial. It illuminates the action, and it can be used to control the mood of a scene. Early theaters were constrained by the limitations of candlelight. Today, however, the possibilities of what can be achieved with lighting are basically limitless. **Q6**
Example 교수의 조명 감독으로서의 과거 경험	**I remember being the lighting director of a production as a college student.** It was an old English play that had been revised to take place in modern-day New York. **Every time I started thinking about how difficult my job was, I reminded myself of all the lighting directors before me who didn't have a theater full of electric lights to work with. I mean, it must have been a whole different world.** Anyway, production design has clearly become an invaluable part of modern theater. Really, it's come to be as important to the success of a play as a good script and talented actors.

Practice Questions

[01 ~ 06] Listen to part of a lecture in a theater class. Then answer the questions.

MP3 43 정답 및 해석 p. 093

Note-taking

01 What does the professor mainly discuss?
   Ⓐ The differences between European and American theater
   Ⓑ The evolution of a new form of entertainment in America
   Ⓒ An American businessman's innovative circus
   Ⓓ The life of a popular 19th-century American actor

02 According to the professor, what changed in America after the Civil War?
   Ⓐ The country was devastated by the aftermath of the war.
   Ⓑ The American middle class had more money to spend.
   Ⓒ More Americans wanted to become members of the upper class.
   Ⓓ Most of the entertainment available became immoral.

03 What does the professor imply about the entertainment available for middle-class citizens in 19th-century America?
  Ⓐ It existed in many different forms.
  Ⓑ It was unaffordable to many.
  Ⓒ It was inappropriate for families.
  Ⓓ It copied European entertainment.

04 What does the professor say about the word "vaudeville"?
  Ⓐ It was mistranslated from a French phrase.
  Ⓑ It was chosen for its elegant sound.
  Ⓒ It came from the name of a French city.
  Ⓓ It probably doesn't have any real meaning.

05 According to the lecture, what are two notable features of American vaudeville?
  Choose two answers.
  Ⓐ It was identical to the French version of vaudville.
  Ⓑ It appealed to a wider audience than past forms of entertainment.
  Ⓒ It often made use of highly trained European stage actors.
  Ⓓ It was performed nonstop, so it could be enjoyed at any time.

06 Why does the professor mention audiences screaming at actors?
  Ⓐ To demonstrate a reason the middle class couldn't attend operas
  Ⓑ To show how people were encouraged to act at vaudeville shows
  Ⓒ To explain one of the changes Keith made to entertainment
  Ⓓ To illustrate how American audiences reacted to Keith's ideas

06 Photography

TOEFL에서 photography^{사진술} 분야는 사진기의 작동원리, 초기 카메라의 문제점, 그 이후 개선된 변화, 사진을 인화하는 기법 등의 내용이 출제된다.

출제포인트
- Q1 Main Idea
- Q2 Function (Role)
- Q3 Problem
- Q4 Solution (Suggestion)
- Q5 Example
- Q6 Cause (Evidence) & Effect (Result / Finding / Research)
- Q7 Similarity / Difference
- Q8 Advantage / Disadvantage
- Q9 Misunderstanding / Correction
- Q10 Definition (Term) / Origin
- Q11 Two Click / Three Click
- Q12 Ordering
- Q13 Matching
- Q14 Opinion / Attitude
- Q15 Headset
- Q16 Requirement (Condition)
- Q17 Character
- Q18 Imply / Infer

1 Pinhole Camera 핀홀[침공] 사진기

pinhole camera는 다음과 같은 원리로 작동한다. 촛불을 켜 놓고 바늘 구멍을 통해 초를 들여다 보면, 양초의 오른쪽 이미지는 왼쪽 편에, 양초의 왼쪽 이미지는 오른쪽 편에 보이게 된다. 이 원리를 이용하여 카메라를 만들 수 있다. 먼저 빛이 들어가지 않는 상자를 준비^{Q16} 한 뒤, 상자의 한 쪽 면에 작은 구멍을 뚫고 작은 구멍의 맞은편에 하얀 종이를 붙여 pinhole camera를 만들면, 하얀 종이에 나무의 상이 맺히게 된다.^{Q12} 이때, 그림에서 보이는 것처럼 나무의 상이 라인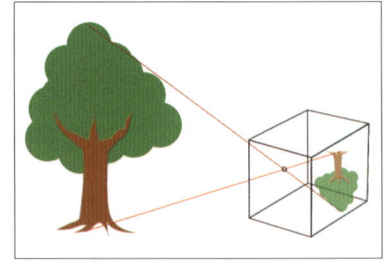
을 따라서 이동하여 상자의 뒤쪽에 맺히게 되므로, 피사체인 나무의 위아래와 좌우가 바뀌어 보이게 된다.^{Q6} 이것은 우리가 사물을 볼 때 물체의 상이 눈을 통과해서 망막에 맺히는 것과 똑같은 원리^{Q5}이다. 그러나, 눈의 시신경이 그 상을 보정하므로, 우리는 제대로 된 이미지를 볼 수 있게 된다.

Ordering		Cause & Effect		Example
핀홀 카메라 제작과정 (1) 빛이 들어가지 않는 상자 준비 (2) 한 쪽 면에 구멍 뚫기 (3) 구멍 맞은 편에 하얀 종이 붙이기	→	피사체의 상이 상자의 뒤쪽에 맺히므로 피사체의 위아래와 좌우가 바뀌어 보임	→	우리의 눈: 피사체가 망막에 맺히는 것과 같은 원리 – 시신경이 보정한 이미지를 뇌에 전달함

2 Taking a Picture of Moving Animals 움직이는 동물 사진 찍기

오늘날에는 사진 기술의 발달로 움직이는 순간을 사진으로 쉽게 찍을 수 있지만, 1800년대에는 사진 기술이 걸음마 단계에 있었기 때문에, '말이 달릴 때 4개의 말발굽이 동시에 공중에 떠 있을까?'와 같은 질문에 답변을 할 수 있는 사진을 얻을 수 없었다. 당시의 사진기는 셔터 스피드가 2~3초였기 때문에 빠르게 움직이는 동물을 찍으면 blur흐릿한 형체로 나왔다.♀3 셔터 스피드가 빨라질 경우에는 카메라 렌즈가 빛에 노출되는 시간이 짧아지기 때문에, 적은 광량(빛의 양)으로도 사진을 찍을 수 있는 기술이 필요하게 되었다. 이에, Edward라는 사진 작가가 캘리포니아에서 자금을 지원받아 이 문제를 해결할 수 있는 장비를 개발하게 되었고, 그로 인해 말의 네 발굽이 동시에 공중에 떠 있는 사진을 찍을 수 있게 되었다.♀4 이 작가는 motion picture영화를 처음 개발하여 film영화 (산업) 기술의 발달에도 기여하였다.♀2

Problem		Solution		Role
1800년대 사진기로는 움직이는 동물을 선명하게 찍을 수 없었음	→	빠른 셔터 스피드를 가진 장비 개발	→	motion picture 개발 – film 기술의 발달에도 기여

핵/심/표/현

- a mass of ~   다량[다수]의 ...
- acceptance   n. 수락, 허락
- accurate   adj. 정확한, 정밀한
- attach   v. 붙이다, 첨부하다
- attention   n. 주의, 주목
- blurry   adj. 흐릿한, 잘 안 보이는
- candidly   adv. 솔직히, 숨김 없이
- cardboard   n. 판지, 마분지
- celluloid   n. 셀룰로이드(과거 영화 필름에 쓰던 물질)
- chemical   n. 화학물질
- clarity   n. 선명도
- commence   v. 시작하다
- constitute   v. 구성하다, 이루다, 포함하다
- contact   v. 연락하다
- container   n. 상자, 용기
- criticism   n. 비판
- cumbersome   adj. 크고 무거운, 다루기 힘든
- daguerreotype   n. 은판 사진(법)
- declare   v. 선언하다, 선포하다
- dedicate   v. 헌신하다, 전념하다
- define   v. 윤곽[모양]을 분명히 나타내다
- develop   v. 현상하다
- device   장치, 기기, 기구
- discard   v. 버리다, 폐기하다
- display   v. 전시하다
- distort   v. 비틀다, 왜곡하다
- document   v. 기록하다
- dominate   v. 지배하다; (...의 가장 중요한 특징이 되다)
- duplicate   n. 사본
- elongate   v. 길게 늘이다
- enormous   adj. 거대한, 막대한
- envision   v. 상상하다, 마음 속에 그리다
- equipment   n. 장비
- essence   n. 본질, 정수
- expose   v. 노출시키다
- fairly   adv. 꽤, 상당히
- frame   n. 틀, 프레임
- framing   n. 구성, 틀 짜기
- frequent   adj. 꾸준히, 한결같이
- grainy   adj. 선명하지 못한
- illuminate   v. (...에 불을) 비추다
- image   n. 이미지, 영상
- imagine   v. 상상하다
- implement   v. 시행하다, 실시하다, 실행하다
- impress   adj. 인상적이다, 감동적이다
- improvise   v. 즉흥적으로 하다
- imprint   v. 새기다
- in a row   잇달아, 연이어, 일렬로
- instantly   adv. 즉시, ...하자마자, 즉각
- inspiration   n. 영감
- interpret   v. 해석하다
- iris   n. (카메라의) 조리개
- kit   n. 도구 (세트)
- medium   n. 매개, 매체
- mount   v. 끼우다, 고정시키다
- naked eye   육안
- negative   n. 음화, 원화
- notice   v. 주목하다
- notoriety   n. 악평, 악명
- novelty   n. 새로움
- persistent   adj. 끈질긴, 끊임없는
- photo paper   n. 인화지
- picturesque   adj. 생생한, 그림 같은
- pinhole camera   핀홀 카메라
- pixel   n. (사진의) 화소

- portrait   n. 인물 사진
- pose   v. 포즈를 취하다
- pressing   adj. 긴급한, 시급한, 절박한
- prestigious   adj. 일류의, 명성 있는
- primitive   adj. 초기의, 원시적 단계의
- print   v. 인화하다
- property   n. 속성, 특성
- publicize   v. 공표하다, 광고하다
- recognize   v. 인지하다, 인식하다
- reflect   v. 반사하다, 비추다
- refract   v. 굴절시키다
- replace   v. 교체하다, 대체하다
- representation   n. 표현, 표시, 설명
- resolution   n. 해상도
- selectively   adv. 선택적으로
- sensitive   adj. 민감한
- shutter   n. (사진기의) 셔터
- subject   n. 피사체
- subtlety   n. 미묘함; 중요한 세부 요소들
- surface   n. 겉(면)
- transform   v. 변화하다, 변신하다
- tripod   n. 삼각대
- tycoon   n. 거물
- undo   v. 원 상태로 되돌리다
- utilize   v. 이용하다
- vary   v. 가지각색이다, 다르다
- venue   n. 장소
- vivid   adj. 생생한

Sample Questions

[01 ~ 06] Listen to part of a lecture in a photography class. Then answer the questions.

MP3 44   정답 및 해석 p. 096

Note-taking

- Main Idea / Term:

- Problem:

- Solution:

- Disadvantage:

- Difference:

- Example:

- Role:

01   What is the lecture mainly about?
   Ⓐ How the idea for cameras was stolen from an inventor
   Ⓑ The developments that led to modern photography
   Ⓒ A comparison between different types of film
   Ⓓ The transition from black-and-white to color photography

02   What does the professor imply about the first forms of photography?
   Ⓐ They could not capture moving objects.
   Ⓑ They were used for scientific purposes.
   Ⓒ They needed dangerous chemicals.
   Ⓓ They could only be used indoors.

03 According to the lecture, what were two disadvantages of daguerreotypes?
Choose two answers.
- Ⓐ They were very expensive to make.
- Ⓑ They had a limited range of shades.
- Ⓒ They required a lot of paper.
- Ⓓ They could not be duplicated.

04 What did Talbot improve upon in his version of Daguerre's invention?
- Ⓐ His method captured more light.
- Ⓑ His method didn't require chemicals.
- Ⓒ His method used a different medium.
- Ⓓ His method created color images.

05 Why does the professor mention a leaf?
- Ⓐ To suggest that colors can be changed
- Ⓑ To give an example of a common image
- Ⓒ To explain the details of plant structure
- Ⓓ To illustrate the basic properties of Talbot's film

06 What does the professor imply about Nicéphore Niépce?
- Ⓐ He helped Talbot with his method.
- Ⓑ He stole his idea from Daguerre.
- Ⓒ He destroyed his own camera.
- Ⓓ He was not interested in fame.

▶ **Question Review**

Main Idea / Term
daguerreotype 용어 설명

Problem
초창기 사진의 문제점: 굉장히 오랫동안 자세를 취해야 했음

Solution
과정 개선

Disadvantage
– 사본을 못 만듦
– 해상도가 떨어짐

Difference
Talbot은 Daguerre와 다른 재료를 사용

Listen to part of a lecture in a photography class.

Professor(female): All right, let's get started. Are any of you familiar with the Q1 **daguerreotype process?** The term might not be familiar, **but it was one of the first processes created for making photographs. It was invented by a man named Louis Daguerre.**

Back in the early 1800s, photography wasn't even a term yet, although the concept did exist. Uh… Daguerre found a way to capture images that was related to the way certain chemicals react to light. This wasn't his idea but… we'll get to that later.

So, this is how the daguerreotype process worked. Daguerre used a copper plate that had been exposed to vapor given off by iodine crystals. Uh, what this did was make the copper light sensitive by forming a silver iodide surface. Now, at first this process took a very long time. Even though the plate was sensitive, it wasn't that sensitive. Q2 **The very first daguerreotype of a person shows a man getting his shoes polished. This was because he was one of the few people who would stay still long enough for the picture to be taken – about 10 minutes. Imagine saying "cheese" and then waiting ten minutes for the photographer to finish. It was a really long process.**

However, Daguerre later improved the process after realizing he could take daguerreotypes that were less defined in a shorter time. He would then make them clearer using chemicals. It was the first time that a picture was chemically developed. This cut down the exposure time significantly and led to the widespread use of Daguerre's method.

But, uh, there were a few issues. First, Q3-D **there was no practical way to make duplicates.** There was also Q3-B **the issue of detail. You can't expect a lot of resolution or clarity from early cameras, but, uh… most daguerreotypes were just black and white, with very little gray in between.** Um… The results were very primitive and weren't that much different from, let's say, a diploma that just has black letters printed on a white background.

 Q1 **Eventually, a British man named William Talbot got word of Daguerre's invention and started developing his own version, something he called the calotype process. His method, uh, is the method that most resembles how we develop film today.** The same elements that were present in daguerreotypes were present in Talbot's invention. I mean, um, there was a plate that was sensitive to light, but Q4 **unlike Daguerre, who used a metal-based plate, Talbot used paper,** and in the process he created the first form of film.

By using paper in his calotype, Talbot could make duplicates of photos and have greater control of the final product. He got his inspiration from a leaf. **Q5** **If you hold a leaf up to a bright light, its shadow won't be all black – you'll see different shades. Holes will be white, thin areas will be gray and the rest will be black.** When Talbot took a picture with his calotype, it would leave an imprint on the paper. But since the paper was sensitive to light, the darkest areas would actually become the brightest areas, and the brightest would become the darkest. Think about it – when light hit the paper, it caused a chemical reaction, causing that area to darken. **This created the exact opposite of what you would see in real life – therefore, the resulting image was called a negative.** In a negative of the sky, white clouds would be black and black birds would be white.

Of course, the negative was only the first step. Talbot used a method called contact printing to make the final picture. He first made the negative insensitive to light by chemically treating it, so no matter how much light it was exposed to, it wouldn't change. Then he put another light sensitive sheet right below it. Next, he turned on a really bright light. More light would go through the lighter areas and less light would go through the darker areas, thus reversing the process and creating a positive. These positives could be duplicated with ease. So if something went wrong during the process, it could just be done again.

Now, going back to what I mentioned earlier about where Daguerre got the idea for his process… It was from a man named Nicéphore Niépce, who is generally credited as being the inventor of photography. **Q6** **Niépce kept his research a secret and little was known about it until his death.** However, **he gave his ideas to Daguerre, who used them to create the daguerreotype process.**

Example
calotype 공정을 예를 들어 설명

Role
Niépce – 사진술의 창시자

Practice Questions

[01 ~ 06] Listen to part of a lecture in a photography class. Then answer the questions.

MP3 45 정답 및 해석 p. 097

Note-taking

01 What is the lecture mainly about?
   Ⓐ The problems with modern camera technology
   Ⓑ The history behind a new genre of photography
   Ⓒ The ways the government supports photographers
   Ⓓ The very first camera made for journalism

02 Why does the professor mention the newspaper?
   Ⓐ To give an example of digital photography
   Ⓑ To suggest an interesting article on camera technology
   Ⓒ To draw the students' attention to news photography
   Ⓓ To illustrate a problem with modern cameras

03 What does the professor say about cameras in the early 1900s?
   Ⓐ They could not be used indoors.
   Ⓑ They could not capture moving objects.
   Ⓒ They used lenses that were too heavy.
   Ⓓ They had to be moved around to work properly.

04 According to the professor, what two aspects of early cameras made them difficult to use? Choose two answers.
   Ⓐ The film used was too large.
   Ⓑ They were too expensive.
   Ⓒ They could not take landscape photos.
   Ⓓ Tripods were needed to hold them.

05 What did Dorothea Lange do differently than other photographers of her time?
   Ⓐ She used traditional equipment.
   Ⓑ She tried to capture candid emotions.
   Ⓒ She created beautifully posed portraits.
   Ⓓ She requested government support.

06 Why does the professor say this? 🔊 MP3 45_1
   Ⓐ To suggest that he has had a similar experience
   Ⓑ To emphasize the skill of modern photographers
   Ⓒ To show his admiration of traditional techniques
   Ⓓ To express empathy for photographers of the past

Unit 4
Life Science

01_ **Animal Communication**
02_ **Animal Adaptation**
03_ **Botany**
04_ **Ecology**
05_ **Physiology**
06_ **Paleontology**

 **Animal Communication**

TOEFL에서 animal communication^{동물의 의사소통} 분야는 특정 동물의 same species^{같은 종} 간의, 또는 같은 개체 그룹 간의 communication 방법과 기능에 대해서 자주 문제가 출제된다. 강의의 도입 부분에서 소재가 animal communication임이 확인되면, 모르는 동물이 언급되거나 강의 내용이 잘 들리지 않더라도 당황하지 말고, 이 topic의 핵심인 communication 방법과 기능에 focus를 두고 듣도록 한다.

출제포인트	Q1 Function
	Q2 Difference
	Q3 Similarity
	Q4 Example
	Q5 Finding

1 Dolphin Communication^{돌고래의 의사소통}

dolphin의 communication 방법은 three types^{세 종류로}, whistle, click, 그리고 bubble stream이 있다. whistle은 돌고래들끼리 소리를 내어 정확히 어떤 고래가 낸 신호인지 알아보는^{Q1} 방법으로, 이는 돌고래가 소리를 듣고 같은 무리 중 정확히 어느 고래가 낸 소리인지 identify^{알아내다}할 수 있다는 뜻이다. click은 sonar^{음파}를 쏴서 돌고래의 앞에 장애물이 있는 경우, 이를 피해갈 수 있게 하는^{Q1} 기능을 한다. click을 이용하기 위해, 돌고래들은 무리 이동을 할 때 서로 앞서거니 뒤서거니 하지 않고 나란히 이동하는 습성이 있다. 마지막으로, bubble stream은 고래의 숨 구멍에서 bubble^{공기방울}을 내는 방법인데, 이 방법 역시 공기방울을 통해 서로를 정확하게 확인하는 데 쓰인다^{Q1}고 한다.

→ 여기서 돌고래의 communication 기능들 간의 Difference와 Similarity 문제나 communication 방법을 설명하기 위한 Example 문제도 같이 출제될 수 있다.

Communication Method & Function	Communication Method & Function	Communication Method & Function
(1) whistle – 서로 identify	(2) click – 음파로 앞에 장애물 파악	(3) bubble stream – 서로 identify

2 Prairie Dog Communication 프레리 도그의 의사소통

과학자들의 연구결과에 따르면, prairie dog가 내는 소리에는 predator 포식 동물를 구별[Q1]할 수 있는 기능이 있다고 한다. prairie dog의 vocalization발성의 pitch음의 높고 낮음에 따라 보내는 신호가 다르다는 것이다. 예를 들어, prairie dog의 서식지 근처에 코요테가 접근했을 때와 사람이 접근했을 때 prairie dog가 내는 warning sound경고음의 pitch가 달라진다[Q4]는 것이 밝혀졌다.

Communication Method
pitch의 변화
Eg.) A동물 접근 – low pitch warning sign

→

Communication Method
pitch의 변화
Eg.) B동물 접근 – high pitch warning sign

3 Crocodile Vocalization 악어의 발성

crocodile은 vocalization을 이용해 물에 vibration진동을 일으켜 다른 악어들과 communication을 한다는 연구 결과가 있다. 악어는 10가지 이상의 다른 종류의 소리를 낼 수 있다고 한다. 진동으로 신호를 굉장히 멀리까지 보낼 수도 있는데, mating season짝짓기 시기에는 짝을 찾는 데 vocalization을 사용[Q1]하기도 하며, 기분이 좋지 않은 것을 다른 악어에게 표현[Q1]하거나, 새끼악어가 어미와 의사소통을 할 때도 vocalization을 사용[Q1]한다. 악어가 이렇게 정확하게 의사소통을 할 수 있는 것은 악어의 뇌가 굉장히 복잡한 구조를 가지고 있기 때문이다. 악어는 단순한 뇌 구조를 가지고 있는 다른 reptiles파충류보다, 오히려 개와 뇌 구조가 비슷[Q3]하다고 한다.

Communication Method & Function
vocalization
(1) 짝짓기 상대를 찾는 기능
(2) 기분, 감정 표현 기능
(3) 새끼와 어미가 의사소통하는 기능
Similarity – 파충류보다 개와 비슷한 구조의 뇌를 가짐

핵/심/표/현

- acoustic   adj. 청각의, 소리의
- acquire   v. 습득하다
- adulthood   n. 성인, 성년
- affect   v. 영향을 미치다
- aggressive   adj. 공격적인, 적극적인
- ahead   adv. 앞서, 앞에, 미리
- approach   v. 접근하다, 다가가다   n. 접근법
- artificial   adj. 인공의
- assumption   n. 가정, 추측
- attract   v. 유혹하다, 끌어들이다
- bellow   v. 우렁찬 소리를 내다
- blind   adj. 시각장애의, 안 보이는
- capable   adj. 능력이 있는
- chaotic   adj. 혼란스러운, 무질서한
- chorus   v. 합창하다
- cognitive   adj. 인식[인지]의
- continue   v. 계속하다
- coordinate   v. 조정하다
- cooperating   adj. 협력하는
- detect   v. 발견하다, 알아내다
- determine   v. 결정하다
- directed   adj. 지시된
- discreetness   n. 조심스러움, 신중함
- display   v. 보여주다, 표현하다
- distraction   n. 방해, 혼란
- distress   n. 고뇌, 골칫거리
- echo   n. 울림, 메아리
- echolocation   n. (초음파를 사용한 돌고래나 박쥐의) 반향 위치 측정
- ecosystem   n. 생태계
- engage   v. 관여하다, 참가하다
- exhausted   adj. 지친
- exploration   n. 탐사, 연구
- fascinating   adj. 매혹적인
- for instance   예를 들면
- frequency   n. 주파수
- generate   v. 발생시키다, 내다
- grooming   n. (동물의) 털 손질
- grunting   n. 꿀꿀거리는 소리
- hatchling   n. 갓 부화한 새[동물]
- hierarchy   n. 계급, 위계
- high frequency sound   고주파 소리
- hiss   v. 쉿 하는 소리를 내다
- hive   n. 벌집
- howl   n. 길게 울부짖는 소리
- imitate   v. 모방하다
- infinite   adj. 무한한
- infrasound   n. 초(超)저주파 음파
- insight   n. 통찰력
- intelligent   adj. 똑똑한, 총명한
- interact   v. 상호작용하다
- internal   adj. 체내의
- let out   (울음·신음소리 등을) 내다
- mammal   n. 포유동물
- mating   n. 짝짓기
- mimic   v. 흉내내다
- motionless   adj. 움직임이 없는[적은]
- moan   n. 신음 소리
- muffled cry   숨죽인[조용한] 울음
- nearby   adj. 근처의   adv. 근처에
- noteworthy   adj. 주목할 만한
- open-ended   adj. 제한[제약]을 두지 않은
- pitch   n. 음의 높이
- pollen   n. 꽃가루
- pollination   n. 수분(受粉)
- possess   v. 소유하다, 지니다

- precisely   adv. 정확히, 정밀하게
- presence   n. 존재
- pretend   v. ...인 척하다
- primitive   adj. 원시의, 원초적인
- pulse   n. 파동, 맥박
- reassurance   n. 안심시키기, 안심시키는 말[행동]
- reflection   n. 반사
- replicate   v. 복제[복사]하다
- reptile   n. 파충류
- sequence   n. 순서, 배열
- sibling   n. 형제 자매
- solitary   adj. 혼자 하는[사는]
- sonar   n. 음파
- sound wave   n. 음파
- spontaneously   adv. 자발적으로, 자연스럽게
- spread   v. 퍼지다, 전파되다
- squeaking   adj. 찍찍[삐걱]거리는
- squeal   v. (높고 길게) 소리를 지르다
- stationary   adj. 멈추어 있는, 가만히 있는
- stress   v. 강조하다
- swerve   v. 방향을 틀다, 벗어나다
- synchronize   v. 동시에 발생하다
- tendency   n. 경향, 추세
- trained   adj. 훈련된
- typical   adj. 전형적인, 통상적인
- ultrasonic   adj. 초음파의
- ultraviolet   n. 자외선
- unique   adj. 특이한, 유별난
- vibrate   v. 진동하다
- vigilant   adj. 바싹 경계하는, 방심하지 않는
- vision   n. 시야, 전망
- vocalization   n. 발성
- willing   adj. 기꺼이 하는, 꺼리지 않는

Sample Questions

[01 ~ 06] Listen to part of a lecture in a biology class. Then answer the questions.

MP3 46 정답 및 해석 p. 101

  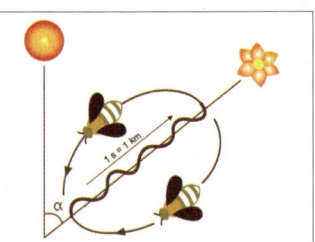

Note-taking

• Topic: • Cause & Effect:

• Function:

                                            • Function:

                                            • Opinion:

01 What is the lecture mainly about?
 Ⓐ The role of dancing in the lives of insects
 Ⓑ How honeybees coordinate activities within the hive
 Ⓒ Why honeybees only eat certain types of nectar
 Ⓓ The ways that bees communicate to locate food

02 What is the purpose of the waggle dance? Choose two answers.
 Ⓐ To indicate the direction of a food source
 Ⓑ To compete for limited food supplies
 Ⓒ To indicate the direction of sunlight
 Ⓓ To signify the distance to a food source
 Ⓔ To warn other bees of danger

03   What does the professor say about the sun?
     Ⓐ It helps the bees detect food on cloudy days.
     Ⓑ It indicates what time of day it is.
     Ⓒ It is used to identify the direction of a food source.
     Ⓓ It helps the bees find their nests easily.

04   What does the professor imply about the circle dance?
     Ⓐ It does not give information about distance.
     Ⓑ It helps bees synchronize their internal clocks.
     Ⓒ It serves a purpose similar to that of the waggle dance.
     Ⓓ It is another verbal language bees use to communicate.

05   What does the professor say is the relationship between the length of a bee's waggle and the location of the food source?
     Ⓐ The shorter the waggle, the closer the food source is to the hive.
     Ⓑ The longer the waggle, the closer the food source is to the sun.
     Ⓒ The longer the waggle, the farther the food source is from the sun.
     Ⓓ The shorter the waggle, the farther the food source is from the hive.

06   What is the professor's opinion towards honeybee dancing?
     Ⓐ He expects that other theories will be proposed.
     Ⓑ He suspects that it will evolve over time.
     Ⓒ He worries that it raises too many unanswerable questions.
     Ⓓ He feels that future research will give more information.

Unit 4_Life Science   275

▶ **Question Review**

Topic
꿀벌의 의사소통

Function
waggle dance로 먹이 공급원의 방향과 거리를 나타냄

태양의 방향은 waggle dance의 지표가 됨

Listen to part of a lecture in a biology class.

Professor(male): Okay, today let's look at an insect that plays an integral role in our environment and ecosystem through pollination. Of course, I'm talking about honeybees. Now, we tend to think of bees as insects that randomly fly from one flower to the next, gathering pollen to give to their queen. If anyone has seen a bee hive, in which direction do bees exiting the hive tend to fly?

Student(female): Which direction? They seemed to be flying off in all directions.

P: Exactly. That's because they're searching for new sources of food. But once they find one, **Q1** **they actually communicate with other members of the hive to explain the direction and distance of the food source.** They do this through a highly evolved and unique communication system known as "dance language." In other words, **they use dance as a form of communication.** So how do honeybees communicate with each other through dancing? Well, they use something called the waggle dance. They shake their bodies from side to side and go in circles like real dancers, but it's not for artistic purposes. All right, let's take a look at the slide. (show slide 1) The dance takes on the form of a figure eight, but the bee waggles in the section where the two circles overlap. The honeybee waggles its body from side to side as it moves forward in a straight line, then circles to the right, back to its starting point, waggles ahead again, and then circles to the left. This dance pattern is repeated a number of times. The foragers – the worker bees who seek pollen or nectar – search for food. When they find a food source, such as a blooming flower or an artificial food source, they'll fill their honey sac with nectar and return to the nest and perform this vigorous dance.

S: But how do bees know where to go from just a dance? I mean, I can see how the waggle dance can help bees tell each other about a food source, but it's really hard to believe that they can be that accurate.

P: That's a good point. Although it may seem like a random dance, **Q2** **the waggle dance does give very specific information about distance and direction of the food source. What the honeybee's waggle dance does is tell other bees where the food source is in relation to the sun.** The direction of the food source is actually shown by the angle of the straight line the bee waggles in. Of course, **Q3** there needs to be some sort of indicator – a reference point – to show the direction and in this case, it's the bearing of the sun and gravity. There's a relationship

between the angle of the dance on the vertical comb and the bearing of the sun with respect to the location of the food. So, if the sun and the food are in the same direction, the straight portion of the waggle dance is directed upward. If it is 90 degrees to the left of the sun, the honeybee will orient the straight portion of its dance to 90 degrees. (show slide 2)
S: But how do they always know where the sun is? I mean, the sun's position constantly changes, right? And what about cloudy days?
P: The bees have an internal clock that lets them, with great accuracy, figure out the position of the sun even in a dark hive. They also see ultraviolet light, which helps them find the exact angle of the sun. Now, the distance can also be shown by how long the bee waggles. ▶Q5 **If the duration is short, that means the food source is close by.** So, if a bee waggles in a straight line for two seconds, it tells other bees that the food source is about two kilometers away. Now, if a food source is so close that bees would not be able to tell the exact distance – let's say like 50 meters or so, the waggle shrinks and forms a different type of dance, called ▶Q4 **the circle dance, to indicate a nearby food source.** The first movement is two centimeters or more, and then the bee circles in the opposite direction. Once the circle dance has been performed, numerous other worker bees in the nest closely follow the dance, imitating the movement. Clearly, the dance language is an important survival strategy that has helped honeybees in their success as a species. ▶Q6 **Nevertheless, several serious questions remained unanswered, because researchers have yet to figure out how the bees can perceive the quantity and quality of the food from dance.** For our next class, I want you to read some of the additional materials that I have put on reserve in the library.

---

internal clock으로 어두운 곳에서도 태양의 위치를 확인

Cause & Effect
벌이 waggle하는 시간과 먹이까지의 거리와의 상관관계

Function
circle dance는 가까이에 있는 먹이 공급원을 나타냄

Opinion
벌이 먹이의 양과 질을 인지하는 방법은 연구가 더 필요함

Practice Questions

[01 ~ 06] Listen to part of a lecture in a biology class. Then answer the questions.

MP3 47   정답 및 해석 p. 102

Note-taking

01   What is the lecture mainly about?
   Ⓐ Various adaptations of humpback whales
   Ⓑ Different kinds of songs of humpback whales
   Ⓒ The evolution of animal vocalizations
   Ⓓ The unique characteristics of humpback whales songs

02   Why does the professor first mention bird songs?
   Ⓐ To explain the basic mechanism of animal songs
   Ⓑ To provide an example of other animals that use songs
   Ⓒ To give an example of non-communicative songs
   Ⓓ To illustrate the difference between humpback whales and other animals

03 What does the professor say about humpback whale song sequences?
Ⓐ They will not be used by other humpbacks far away.
Ⓑ They follow a pattern that is similar to those of birds.
Ⓒ They helps whales become accepted in a pod.
Ⓓ They are used to attract whales from other areas.

04 According to the professor, which of the following are characteristics of humpback whale songs? Choose two answers.
Ⓐ They have no real meaning.
Ⓑ They are unique to each group.
Ⓒ They last a short time.
Ⓓ They are adjusted over time.

05 Why does the professor mention the trombone and piano?
Ⓐ To compare whale songs to bird songs
Ⓑ To illustrate the complexity of humpback whale songs
Ⓒ To describe the way a whale's body makes sounds
Ⓓ To help explain the sounds humpbacks make

06 According to the lecture, which of the following is true about humpback whale songs?
Ⓐ They are similar to the songs of birds.
Ⓑ They are the same year after year.
Ⓒ They are not yet fully understood.
Ⓓ They are used to scare away predators.

02 Animal Adaptation

TOEFL에서 animal adaptation동물의 적응 방법 분야는 특정 동물이 predator포식동물에게 prey먹이가 되지 않기 위해서 camouflage보호색을 띠는 위장를 하는 방법, 또는 겨울에 극한의 기온에서 살아남기 위해 동물이 취하는 행동이나 서식 환경의 문제점 등이 문제로 자주 출제된다. 강의의 도입 부분에서 animal adaptation에 대한 내용임이 확인되면, 모르는 동물이 언급되거나 강의 내용이 잘 들리지 않더라도 당황하지 말고 이 topic의 핵심인 환경 적응 방법에 focus를 두고 듣도록 한다.

출제포인트
- **Q1 Problem**
- **Q2 Solution (Adaptation)**
- **Q3 Cause & Effect**
- **Q4 Example**
- **Q5 Misunderstanding / Correction**

1 Octopus문어

octopus는 predator로부터 몸을 숨기기 위해 chromatophore색소세포를 이용해 camouflage보호색을 띠는 위장Q2를 아주 잘 하는 동물이다. 또한, octopus는 몸 안에 internal skeleton내부 뼈이 없어Q3 malleable유연한하기 때문에, 모양을 자유자재로 바꾸어 아주 작은 틈 사이에 숨어 적으로부터 몸을 숨길 수 있다.Q2 문어는 적이 아주 가까이 접근해 미처 도망갈 시간이 없으면,Q1 ink jet먹물을 쏴 적의 시야를 가리고 잽싸게 도망가는Q2 등 여러 가지의 defense방어 수단을 가지고 있는 동물이다.

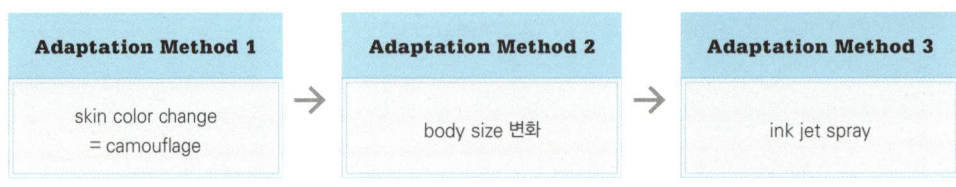

Adaptation Method 1	Adaptation Method 2	Adaptation Method 3
skin color change = camouflage	body size 변화	ink jet spray

2 Snowshoe hare눈신토끼

snowshoe hare가 털갈이를 할 때는 발에 있는 털부터 흰색으로 바뀐다. 봄, 가을에는 주위 환경에 보호색을 띄기 위해서 brown color갈색의 fur털가 나고, 눈이 내리는 겨울에는 적에게 노출되는 것을 피하기 위해서 흰색으로 fur change털갈이를 해 주위 환경과 비슷한 색으로 camouflage위장♀2를 한다. climate change기후 변화에 의해 토끼가 털갈이를 할 시기를 감지한다고 알고 있는 사람들이 많으나, 사실 토끼는 일조량, 즉, day-time낮에 해가 떠 있는 시간의 길이가 길어지고 짧아짐에 따라 털갈이를 할 시기임을 감지한다.♀5 미국 중서부나 동부는 4월에도 눈이 오는 경우가 가끔 있는데, 이때 이미 갈색으로 털갈이를 한 snowshoe hare들은 predator의 눈에 띌까 두려워 집 밖으로 나오지 못하기도 한다.

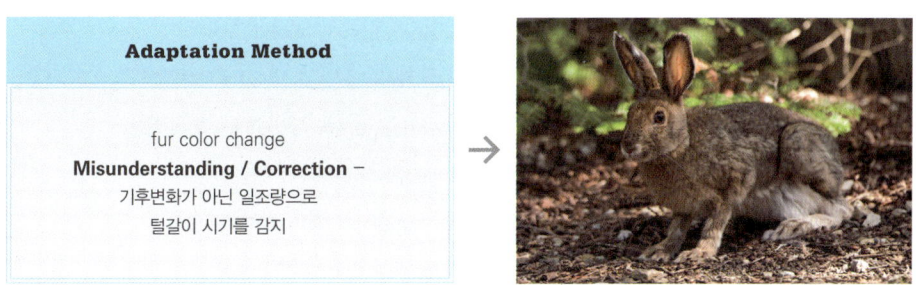

3 Green sea turtle푸른바다거북

green sea turtle은 sea grass거머리말를 주식으로 하는데, sea grass에는 cellulose섬유소가 많아 digestion소화이 잘 되지 않는다.♀1 그래서 green sea turtle은 같은 자리에서 돋아난 sea grass의 새순만 먹는다.♀2 young sea grass어린 거머리말는 mature sea grass다 자란 거머리말보다 상대적으로 cellulose 함유량이 적어서 소화가 잘 되기 때문이다. green sea turtle은 이렇게 young sea grass만을 섭취함으로써 소화시킬 수 있는 sea grass의 양을 최대한으로 늘리고 주어진 시간 내 energy intake에너지 섭취량도 최대한으로 늘릴 수 있다.♀3

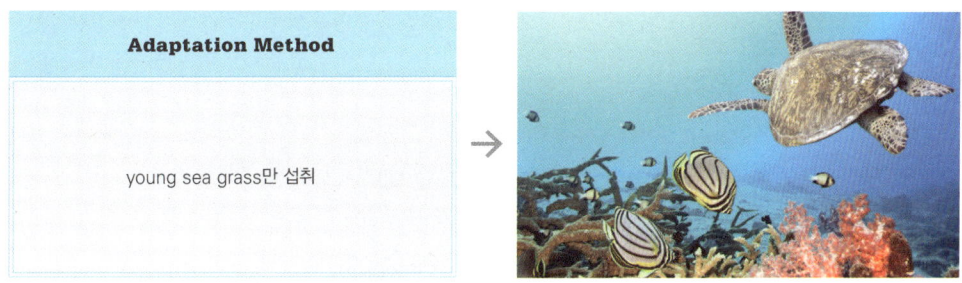

핵/심/표/현

- absorb   v. 흡수하다
- activity   n. 활동
- adapt   v. 적응하다, 맞추다
- adaptation   n. 적응 (방식)
- aspect   n. 측면, 양상
- bounce back   되살아나다, 회복하다
- burrow   v. 굴[은신처]을 파다 n. 굴
- calf   n. 새끼
- camouflage   n. (보호색이나 형태 등을 통한) 위장
- catalyst   n. 촉매(제), 계기, 자극
- ceremony   n. 식, 의식, 의례
- chlorophyll   n. 엽록소
- chloroplast   n. 엽록체
- chromatophore   n. 색소 세포, 색소체
- climate   n. 기후
- colonist   n. 외래 식물[동물]
- colonize   v. 대량 서식하다
- competition   n. (생존) 경쟁
- complex   adj. 복잡한
- conservation   n. 보존, 보전
- constantly   adv. 꾸준히, 계속해서
- constraint   n. 억제, 제약(이 되는 것)
- consume   n. 섭취하다
- contract   v. 수축하다, 압축하다
- courage   n. 용기, 대담함
- covering   n. 외피, 막
- crossbreed   n. 잡종 v. 이종 교배하다
- decompose   v. 분해되다, 부패되다
- degrade   v. 분해하다
- defense mechanism   방어 기제[기구]
- deforestation   n. 삼림 벌채
- dehydrate   v. 탈수되다
- density   n. (개체 수의) 밀도
- descendant   n. 자손, 후예
- destruction   n. 파괴, 붕괴
- determine   v. 결정하다, 결심하다
- digestive   adj. 소화의
- drag back   가지고 돌아가다
- edible   adj. 먹을 수 있는
- elements   n. 비바람, 폭풍우
- enable   v. …을 가능하게 하다
- endangered   adj. 멸종 위기에 처한
- environment   n. 환경
- escape   v. 벗어나다, 달아나다
- excess   v. 초과하다, 넘어서다
- fauna   n. (한 지역의) 동물상
- feed   v. 먹이를 주다, 부양하다
- fern   n. 양치식물
- fiber   n. 섬유질
- fledgling   n. (막 날기 시작한) 어린 새
- forage   v. 먹이를 찾아 다니다
- freshwater   adj. 민물의
- fungus   n. 균류, 곰팡이류
- graze   v. 풀을 뜯다
- habitat   n. 서식지
- harsh   adj. 매서운, 가혹한
- hemisphere   n. (지구의) 반구
- hibernation   n. 동면, 겨울잠
- immediate   adj. 즉각적인, 당장
- in response to ~   …에 대하여[응하여]
- individual   n. 개인 adj. 각각의
- mature   adj. 성숙한, 다 자란
- metamorphosis   n. 탈바꿈, 변태
- microbe   n. 미생물
- microclimate   n. 미기후
- mobility   n. 이동성

- moss n. 이끼
- nutrient n. 영양분, 영양소
- offspring n. 자식, 새끼
- organism n. 유기체, 생물
- papilla n. 유두, 작은 돌기
- parenting n. 육아
- passive adj. 수동적인, 소극적인
- perish v. 사라지다, 죽다
- permanent adj. 영구적인
- phenomenon n. 현상
- photolysis n. (식물) 광분해
- pigment n. (동·식물에 자연 상태로 존재하는) 색소
- poisonous adj. 독이 있는
- population n. 개체 수
- prefer v. 선호하다
- protection n. 보호, 방어
- rainfall n. 강수
- reproduce v. 번식하다
- reproductive adj. 번식(생식)의
- resemble v. …을 닮다, 비슷하다
- resource n. 자원, 재료
- respiration n. 호흡

- scarce adj. 부족한, 드문
- shelter n. 안식처, 은신처, 대피소
- slightly adv. 약간, 조금
- snapping adj. (동물이) 달려들어 무는
- soak up 빨아들이다, 흡수하다
- speckled adj. 반점이 있는, 얼룩덜룩한
- strategy n. 전략, 방법
- stream n. 강가, 개울가
- strengthen v. 강해지다, 견고해지다
- suitability n. 적합, 적당, 알맞음
- supplement v. 보충하다
- surpass v. (한계 등을) 초월하다, 넘어서다
- surroundings n. 환경
- temporary adj. 임시의
- territorial adj. 영토의, 영역의
- thrive v. 번창하다, 확장하다
- transition n. 변화, 변신
- trigger v. 유발하다, 일으키다
- vegetation n. 초목, 식물
- vulnerability n. 공격 당하기 쉬움, 약함
- yield v. 굴복하다, 따르다

Sample Questions

[01 ~ 06] **Listen to part of a lecture in a biology class. Then answer the questions.**

MP3 48   정답 및 해석 p. 105

Note-taking

• Main Idea:

• Example:

• Adaptation:

• Difference:

• Opinion:

01   What is the lecture mainly about?
      Ⓐ Typical features of reindeer that do not result from adaptation
      Ⓑ Various strategies used by reindeer to find food during the winter
      Ⓒ Interaction between reindeer and humans in the state of Alaska
      Ⓓ Characteristics that reindeer have developed in response to their environment

02   Why does the professor mention Alaska's climate?
      Ⓐ To describe typical climates in the northern hemisphere
      Ⓑ To explain the reason why reindeer live in the north
      Ⓒ To introduce the connection between environment and adaptations
      Ⓓ To talk about her past experiences as a field researcher

03 According to the professor, what is the purpose of reindeer's thick fur?
Ⓐ To help them walk on the ice
Ⓑ To hide them from predators
Ⓒ To block the wind and snow
Ⓓ To prevent lichen from growing on them

04 What point does the professor make about the special microbes that exist in reindeer digestive systems?
Ⓐ They come from a special fungus.
Ⓑ They change depending on the season.
Ⓒ They only exist during the winter.
Ⓓ They are poisonous to reindeer.

05 What can be inferred about reindeer?
Ⓐ They would starve in winter without lichen.
Ⓑ They often have moss growing on their fur.
Ⓒ They are endangered due to harmful microbes.
Ⓓ They are actually benefiting from global warming.

06 What does the professor say about global warming?
Ⓐ She believes it helps animals that live in cold climates.
Ⓑ She expects that it will get worse in the future.
Ⓒ She thinks that reindeer can easily adapt to it.
Ⓓ She feels it hurts reindeer more than people might think.

▶ **Question Review**

Introduction

Listen to part of a lecture in a biology class.

Professor(female): Now, Jonathan, **Q2** **you said you had been to Alaska,** right?

Student(male): Yeah. Actually, I lived there for a year because of my dad.

P: Great. So why don't you tell everybody what the winter was like there?

S: Hmm… **Q2** **The winter? Well, it's cold. I mean, it's really cold and a lot of snow out there.** There are winters and there are Alaskan winters. I don't understand how anything or anyone can live there.

Main Idea
환경에 대응하기 위한
적응 방법을 갖게 됨

P: Hah, I'd agree with you on that. I did field research up there a couple of winters ago, and it really was as bad as people say. **Q2 Q1** **In that sort of extreme environment, animals have to have certain adaptations – features, um… I mean, the physical or behavioral features of a species that help it survive or reproduce in its environment.** And adaptations in extreme environments like the northern hemisphere in the winter time… well, animals can have very interesting adaptations. **Q1**

Example

Take, for example, the reindeer.

Now, reindeer, tell me, how do you think they adapted to survive the harsh northern winters? I'll give you a hint – food is really scarce in winter. Reindeer have to go long distances when foraging for food.

S: Well, I don't know… Does that mean they have to move a lot? Do the adaptations have something to do with their legs?

P: Yes. That's exactly right. One major concern of reindeer is mobility. They have to continuously move from one place to another, even right after they give birth. So, one of their adaptations is that reindeer calves can walk as soon as they are born. You see, reindeer can't wait for their offspring to learn how to walk during the winter, or else… well, they'll starve to death. Another physical adaptation is the amount of fat on their legs. They have lots of it, so they do not have to spend as much energy to keep their extremities warm. When food is scarce, you want to be as efficient as possible, right? And speaking of warmth and efficiency, like other mammals that live in cold winter climates, **Q3** **they develop a thick layer of fur to protect them from the elements.** Now, I just talked about the adaptations that can be seen with the naked eye. What else? What other adaptations that can't be seen do you think reindeer have? Janathan?

Adaptation
(1) 태어나면서부터 걸을 수 있음

(2) 다리에 지방이 많음

(3) 두꺼운 털

S: Well, you mentioned food. I remember reading something about special food they eat that helps them survive.

(4) 계절에 따라 다른 먹이

Difference
다른 동물과 달리 소화기계에 특별한 미생물이 있음

Opinion
지구온난화가 동물에게 미치는 부정적인 영향
◉ Influence 문제로도 출제 가능

P: You're right. Reindeer also have adapted their diet to survive in the winter. Reindeer can eat a lot of different kinds of plants. Their diet consists of over a dozen plants, ferns, and fungi. But the most significant adaptation is their ability to eat lichens (shown on screen) in winter. Lichens are a sort of combination of algae and fungus. One kind, which looks sort of like thick fur, is commonly known as reindeer moss, because, you know, reindeer eat it. Lichen grows on rocks and branches and can be found relatively easily during the winter. This is an important adaptation because most animals cannot consume lichen. You see, lichen is actually poisonous to most animals, but **Q5 reindeer have special microbes in their digestive system that degrade the toxic compounds in lichen. So, even though food is scarce during the winter, reindeer still have an easier time finding food than other mammals do.** What makes this even more impressive is that reindeer don't eat that much lichen during the summer. Can anyone guess why?

S: Because... if they eat it all, they'll have nothing to eat during the winter?

P: That's correct. But it's how they do it, that's more impressive. **Q4 Their digestive system adjusts to the different months.** You see, reindeer mostly digest their food with the help of certain bacteria that live in their stomachs. During the summer, they will graze on herbs and leaves, and the bacteria that are helpful for digesting fiber will grow. While in the autumn, since there are no leaves, the bacteria that help them digest fungi will grow. And then in the winter, they can go right back to eating lichen. Of course, that's what's supposed to happen, but **Q6 global warming is making it harder for reindeer to survive.** You'd think that if it were warmer during the winter, it'd be easier to survive, right? The thing is, the food reindeer eat, you know, lichen, is very sensitive to its environment. Even if there is a slight temperature drop of just two degrees Celsius, the algae won't be able to grow on fungus to create lichen.

Practice Questions

[01 ~ 06] **Listen to part of a lecture in a biology class. Then answer the questions.**

MP3 49   정답 및 해석 p. 107

Note-taking

01   What is the lecture mainly about?
   Ⓐ The effects of global warming on fish and animals in the ocean
   Ⓑ How freshwater creatures deal with a changing environment
   Ⓒ The various stages in the formation of temporary ponds
   Ⓓ Methods of minimizing damage caused by global warming

02   What does the professor say about global warming's effect on animals that live in temporary ponds?
   Ⓐ It will double the number of endangered species.
   Ⓑ It will increase the number of animals living in temporary ponds.
   Ⓒ It will have little effect, as the animals will be able to adapt to it.
   Ⓓ It will decrease the amount of food available for the animals to eat.

03 According to the lecture, how do plants benefit the ecosystem?
- Ⓐ They provide a temporary shelter for hatchlings.
- Ⓑ They help the soil hold water for longer periods.
- Ⓒ They purify the water in temporary ponds.
- Ⓓ They provide nutrition to the soil.

04 According to the professor, how do animals survive when temporary ponds dry up? Choose two answers.
- Ⓐ They go underground.
- Ⓑ They live in plants.
- Ⓒ They move to lakes.
- Ⓓ They develop physical protection.

05 Why does the professor mention the fairy shrimp?
- Ⓐ To emphasize the role of plants in the ecosystem
- Ⓑ To give an example of an animal that uses a shell to survive
- Ⓒ To illustrate the diverse fauna in temporary ponds
- Ⓓ To help students understand arid environments

06 Why does the professor mention metamorphosis?
- Ⓐ To explain the damaging effect of global warming on frogs
- Ⓑ To show why some animals live a part of their lives in temporary ponds
- Ⓒ To illustrate how some animals survive when temporary ponds dry up
- Ⓓ To offer an example of plants that provide nutrients to the soil

03 Botany

TOEFL에서 botany^{식물학} 분야는 특정 식물이 사막과 같은 extreme environment^{가혹한 환경}에서 적응하는 방법(adaptation)에 대해 이야기한다. 예를 들어, cactus^{선인장}가 사막에서 살아남기 위해 증산작용(잎을 통해 식물의 수분이 증발하는 현상)을 최소화 하는 내용 등을 다루게 된다. 식물의 각 부분 명칭과 기능들을 설명하는 것도 botany 분야의 출제 범위에 속하며, deciduous tree^{낙엽수}나 evergreen tree^{상록수}, 또는 coniferous tree^{침엽수}와 같은 나무들의 특징을 설명하거나 비교하면서 유사점과 차이점에 관해 묻는 문제가 출제되기도 한다. 위에 언급된 내용은 식물학 강의에서 자주 출제되므로, 강의를 들을 때 그 부분에 유의해서 듣도록 한다.

출제포인트
- Q1 Problem
- Q2 Solution (Adaptation)
- Q3 Cause & Effect
- Q4 Example
- Q5 Misunderstanding / Correction
- Q6 Definition
- Q7 Function
- Q8 Similarity
- Q9 Difference
- Q10 Requirement (Condition)

1 Mangrove^{맹그로브}

mangrove는 아마존이나 동남아시아와 같은 tropical climate^{열대기후}에 habitat^{서식지}을 두고 있다. 물속에 root^{뿌리}를 내리고 서식하는 mangrove는 oxygen deficient mud^{산소가 부족한 진흙에 살기}Q1 때문에, breathing root^{숨쉬는 뿌리}를 물 밖으로 빼내어 나무에 산소를 공급Q2한다. 이것은 마치 dissolved oxygen^{용존산소량(물에 녹아있는 산소량)}이 부족한 물 속에 사는 물고기가 호흡을 하기 위해 주둥이를 물 밖으로 밀어내어 숨쉬는 것과 비슷Q8하다.

Adaptation Problem	→	Adaptation Solution
진흙 속에 산소가 부족		breathing root를 물 밖으로 빼내어 산소 공급

2 Plant Stem 식물 줄기

식물의 stem줄기은 물과 영양분을 수송하고 저장하는 두 가지의 역할⁹⁷을 한다. 식물은 photosynthesis광합성를 통해서 영양분을 얻는데, 광합성을 하려면 sunlight햇빛, CO₂, water가 필요⁹¹⁰하다. 이 과정에서 stem이 광합성에 필요한 물을 수송하고, 광합성에 의해 잎에서 만들어진 영양분을 이를 필요로 하는 식물의 각 부분으로 다시 수송하는 역할을 담당한다.

식물의 줄기 내부에는 vascular bundles관다발가 있는데, 이것은 마치 파이프⁹⁴처럼 앞서 언급한 물과 영양분을 수송하는 통로 역할을 한다. vascular bundles 안의 파이프 배열은 식물의 종류마다 조금씩 다르다. 줄기의 cross section단면도을 보면, 관다발들이 random무작위의하게 배열되어 있는 식물도 있고, ring반지처럼 circle원형 형태로 되어 있는 식물도 있다.⁹⁹

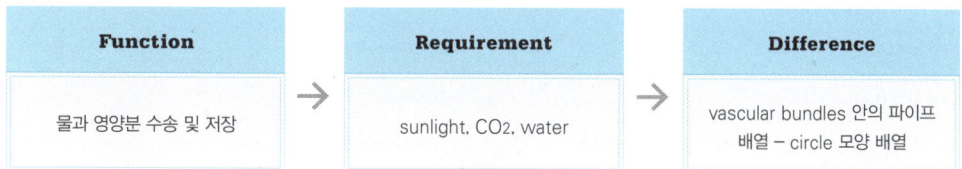

Function	Requirement	Difference
물과 영양분 수송 및 저장	sunlight, CO₂, water	vascular bundles 안의 파이프 배열 – circle 모양 배열

3 Leaves Color Change & Water Conservation 잎의 색상 변화 & 수분 보존

가을이 되면 deciduous tree낙엽수의 잎 색상이 변한다. 그 이유는 보통은 photosynthesis광합성를 통해 green pigment녹색 색소가 생성되는데 가을이 되면 amount of sunlight일조량이 줄어듦에 따라 색소의 가장 많은 부분을 차지하는 녹색 색소는 덜 생성되는 반면 노란색이나 빨간색 색소는 동일하게 만들어지기 때문이다.⁹³ 이 때문에 녹색 색소보다 노란색과 빨간색 색소가 더 많이 보이게 되어 단풍의 화려한 색이 만들어지는 것⁹³이다.

또한, 식물은 겨울이 되면 땅에서 수분을 흡수하기 어려워지기 때문에, 잎에서 transpiration증산작용이 계속해서 일어나면 문제⁹¹가 되므로 shedding잎을 떨어뜨리는 것을 해서 수분의 손실을 최대한 막는다.⁹²

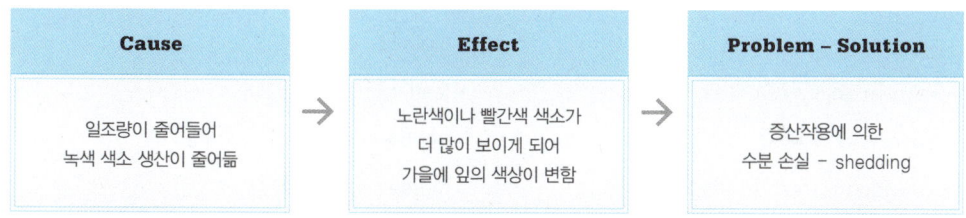

Cause	Effect	Problem – Solution
일조량이 줄어들어 녹색 색소 생산이 줄어듦	노란색이나 빨간색 색소가 더 많이 보이게 되어 가을에 잎의 색상이 변함	증산작용에 의한 수분 손실 – shedding

핵/심/표/현

- agriculture n. 농업
- annual adj. 연간의, 매년의
- aquatic adj. 수생의
- automatically adv. 자동적으로
- bark n. 나무 껍질
- barren adj. 메마른, 불모의
- blossom n./v. 꽃(을 피우다)
- bog n. 늪지, 습지
- botanist n. 식물학자
- botany n. 식물학
- branch n. 나무 가지
- bridging adj. 연결하는
- bud n. (식물의) 봉오리
- bundle n. 묶음
- cactus n. 선인장
- carbon dioxide n. 이산화탄소
- classification n. 분류, 등급
- climatic swing 기후의 변화
- cluster n. (꽃·열매의) 송이
- compost n. 퇴비, 두엄
- coniferous tree n. 침엽수
- conspicuous adj. 눈에 잘 띄는
- constriction n. 압축, 긴축, 수축
- convert v. 변환하다
- counterintuitive adj. 직관에 어긋나는
- cross section n. 단면도, 횡단면
- crown n. (산 등의) 꼭대기
- decay v. 부패하다
- deciduous tree n. 낙엽수
- deficient adj. 결핍된, 부족한
- dehydrate v. 건조시키다
- density n. 밀도
- deposit n. 침전물
- distinguishing adj. 특징적인, 특색 있는
- drought n. 가뭄
- emit v. 내다, 내뿜다
- endangered adj. 멸종 위기에 처한
- evaporate v. 증발하다
- evergreen tree n. 상록수
- exceptionally adv. 유별나게, 예외적으로
- extract v. 추출하다
- fade v. 시들다, 색이 바라다
- fertile adj. 비옥한
- fertilizer n. 비료
- fiber n. 섬유질
- forest n. 숲
- germinate v. 싹트다, 발아하다
- germination n. 발아
- granary[grain store] n. 곡창[곡물 저장고]
- grassland n. 초원, 풀밭
- horticulture n. 원예학
- humidity n. 습도
- husk n./v. (곡물의) 겉껍질(을 벗기다)
- immerse v. (액체 속에) 담그다
- infertile adj. 불모의
- infrared adj. 적외선의
- insecticide n. 살충제
- irrelevant adj. 관계없는, 연관이 없는
- lawn n. 잔디
- leaflet n. 전단, 인쇄물
- lumber n. 목재
- marsh n. 습지, 늪지대
- meadow n. 초원, 목초지
- microscopic adj. 아주 작은, 미시적인
- mutualism n. 상리 공생
- nestle up …에 바싹 파고들다

- obvious   adj. 명백한
- odor   n. 악취
- parasitic plant   n. 기생 식물
- peel off   껍질을 벗겨내다
- perennial   adj. 다년생의
- pesticide   n. 농약, 살충제, 구충제
- petal   n. 꽃잎
- photoreceptor   n. 광수용기[용체] (빛에 민감한 세포·조직)
- photosynthesis   n. 광합성
- pistil   n. (식물의) 암술
- prairie   n. 대초원
- precipitation   n. 강수(량)
- presumably   adv. 아마, 생각건대
- ranch   n. 목장, 농장
- range   n. 산맥; 범위
- release   v. 방출하다
- respiratory system   호흡기계
- respond   v. 반응하다, 응답하다
- retain   v. 유지하다, 보유하다
- rhizome   n. 뿌리줄기
- root   n. 뿌리
- seed dispersal   n. 종자분산
- seemingly   adv. 겉보기에는
- shedding   n. (잎·털·껍질 등을) 흘리기, 발산
- shrivel   v. 쪼글쪼글하게 만들다
- shrub   n. 관목, 키 작은 나무
- sprout   v. 싹트다, 발아하다
- stamen   n. (꽃의) 수술
- stem   n. (식물의) 줄기
- stimulate   v. 자극하다
- stomata   n. 기공
- subarctic   adj. 북극에 가까운
- symbiosis   n. 공생, 공존
- temperate   adj. (기후 등이) 온화한
- thrive   v. 번창하다
- transpiration   n. 증산작용(잎을 통해 수분이 증발하는 현상)
- tropical alpine region   열대 고산 지역
- tropical rainforest   열대 우림
- trunk   n. (나무의) 몸통
- twig   n. 어린[작은] 가지
- uproot   v. (나무 등을) 뿌리째 뽑다
- viable   adj. 독자 생존 가능한
- wetland   n. 습지
- wither   v. 시들다

Sample Questions

[01 ~ 06] Listen to part of a lecture in a botany class. Then answer the questions.

MP3 50 정답 및 해석 p. 110

Note-taking

- Main Idea:

- Similarity:

- Term:

- Problem / Disadvantage:

- Solution:

- Difference / Cause & Effect:

- Correction:

- Function:

- Result:

- Application:

01 What is the lecture mainly about?
   Ⓐ The differences in how humans and plants release water
   Ⓑ How plants sense and respond to dry seasons
   Ⓒ Why plants need water to create energy
   Ⓓ The process by which plants prevent the loss of water

02 According to the professor, what is a problem associated with the respiratory system of plants?
   Ⓐ Plants cannot breathe in carbon dioxide during the day.
   Ⓑ Too much air enters the cells of plant roots.
   Ⓒ Plants lose water through their respiratory openings.
   Ⓓ The size of the openings is too small.

03 Why does the professor mention sweat in humans?
Ⓐ To emphasize how strongly humans are affected by heat
Ⓑ To explain what happens when a plant's stomata close
Ⓒ To point out a common source of carbon dioxide
Ⓓ To contrast two similar processes in plants and humans

04 According to the professor, how does a plant typically react when it senses a prolonged period without rain?
Ⓐ It slows the growth of its roots and leaves.
Ⓑ It starts to emit a certain type of chemical.
Ⓒ It speeds up the process of photosynthesis.
Ⓓ It repeatedly opens and closes its stomata.

05 Why does the professor say that the reaction of plants to water shortages is counterintuitive?
Ⓐ The common belief is that plants need water to survive.
Ⓑ It is unusual for plants to perform photosynthesis at night.
Ⓒ Plants usually grow in areas with high levels of rainfall.
Ⓓ It doesn't make sense to lose water during a dry period.

06 What is the professor's opinion about understanding how plants adapt to periods of dryness?
Ⓐ It can be used to find ways to improve agriculture.
Ⓑ It is useless unless we understand the same process in humans.
Ⓒ It can help better understand the causes of global warming.
Ⓓ It is the key to ending the spread of desert environments.

▶ **Question Review**

Main Idea
건조한 지역에서 식물이
살아남는 방법

Similarity
사람과 식물의 공통점
(1) 영양분을 처리하기
    위해 기체를 마셔야
    함
(2) 호흡 구멍

Term
stomata 용어 설명

**Problem /
Disadvantage**
기공은 수분 손실을
야기함

Solution
시간대에 따라 기공을
열었다 닫았다 하며 수분
손실을 방지함

**Difference /
Cause & Effect**
더워서 수분 증발이 빠른

Listen to part of a lecture in a botany class.

Professor(female): **Q1** Today, I want to talk about a kind of adaptation that takes place in places where temperatures and precipitation aren't constant. You know, in some places it sometimes rains a lot, and sometimes weeks can pass without any rain at all. So, plants that grow in these climates have evolved in various ways to cope with the dry season.

In order to understand how these adaptations work, we first have to understand how plants create nutrition. I'm sure all of you know about photosynthesis, the process through which plants use light to convert carbon dioxide and water into energy. Just like humans have to breathe in oxygen to process nutrition, plants have to breathe in carbon dioxide. The similarities between humans and plants do not end there – both need a respiratory system to breathe in these gases. In order to breathe, humans need their mouths and nostrils, openings that allow fresh oxygen to enter the body. Plants have similar openings, albeit much tinier, called stomata (shown on screen). These tiny openings allow plants to exchange gases in cellular processes like photosynthesis. So plants breathe in carbon dioxide through stomata and release oxygen.

Now, **Q2** an unfortunate side effect of having these small openings is that it allows for water loss. We lose water through our sweat glands, but that's because we need to cool down. Plants, on the other hand, don't really need such a function, so they prefer to retain their water. This process of losing water is called transpiration.

Now, this water loss isn't a problem when it rains or humidity levels are very high. It really doesn't matter when it rains because their roots pick water right back up from the soil. And when it's humid, well, water just doesn't evaporate, so plants can minimize their water loss. However, things change when there are extended periods of dryness. Some plants have evolved a way to close these small pores as much as possible to prevent the loss of water. It's really incredible how plants have developed the ability to control these small holes in order to survive.

Plants control water loss by closing these openings depending on the time of day. Like I mentioned before, humidity matters, but so does the temperature. **Q3** We sweat a lot more when it's hotter. The reason is, well, because water evaporates at a much faster rate when it's hot. So you can think of plants as the exact opposite: they want to lose less water through evaporation, so they close their stomata during

낮에는 기공을 닫고, 밤에는 기공을 엶

Correction
잎이 아닌 뿌리가 기상 상태 변화를 감지
Function
뿌리가 잎으로 신호를 보냄

Result
guard cell에 대한 연구 결과는 아직 증명되지 않음

Application
기공에 대한 연구 내용을 농업에 응용 가능

the day. But at night, when it gets cooler, they open their stomata to breathe more air because there's less transpiration.

How exactly do these plants know when it's dry? Most people just assume that since the stomata are located on the leaves, the leaves can identify the weather conditions. But the part that actually identifies the humidity levels is in an unlikely place. It is the root system that sends a signal to the leaves, dictating whether or not the plant closes its stomata. **Q4 When the roots first sense a water shortage in the soil, they will release a type of acid that will make cells lose water. Q5 It's counterintuitive, I know, but when cells lose water, they start shrinking.** Stomata are surrounded by special cells called guard cells. When the roots release the signal, cells within the plant will start to lose water. These cells include the guard cells. Of all the cells that lose water, the guard cells affect the stomata the most. Once they start losing water, they will start to shrink, closing the opening in the process. Of course, this is what most botanists including myself believe, but there is still some debate about what exactly the guard cells do… There's still not enough proof. We only know how these special cells react.

What's important is that we continue to research how plants cope with different environments. Understanding how stomata work actually changes what goes on our dinner table. **Q6 What I mean is, by understanding stomata, plant breeders and farmers can find the species best suited to grow in high heat climates and during long droughts.** Knowing which species can control their openings will tell us what crops we have to grow to face food security challenges. As temperatures and carbon levels increase due to pollution and global warming, it is becoming crucial to understand how plants adapt to changing environments.

Practice Questions

[01 ~ 06] Listen to part of a lecture in a botany class. Then answer the questions. 🔊 MP3 51

정답 및 해석 p. 111

Note-taking

---

01 What is the lecture mainly about?
  Ⓐ Different plant species that prey on animals
  Ⓑ How insects are able to escape from Venus flytraps
  Ⓒ The reason so many plants are unable to grow in bogs
  Ⓓ How a type of plant has adapted to survive in harsh environments

02 According to the professor, what aspect of bogs makes it difficult for plants to grow in them?
  Ⓐ Their water levels rise and fall quickly.
  Ⓑ There are too many plants in a small area.
  Ⓒ Dead plants are turned into nutrition too slowly.
  Ⓓ The plants cannot get enough sunlight.

03 Why does the professor mention mousetraps?
   Ⓐ To emphasize how dangerous bogs can be
   Ⓑ To point out an error in the Latin name of Venus flytraps
   Ⓒ To explain one of the early uses of Venus flytraps
   Ⓓ To give an example of an environmental adaptation

04 What does the professor identify as the reason Venus flytraps evolved to eat insects?
   Ⓐ The use of fertilizers by early farmers
   Ⓑ Competition with stronger plants
   Ⓒ The lack of nitrogen in the soil of bogs
   Ⓓ Amino acids found only in insects

05 What does the professor imply about his childhood experience with Venus flytraps?
   Ⓐ His expectations were unrealistic.
   Ⓑ It was one of the best memories of his life.
   Ⓒ He wishes he had taken better care of the plant.
   Ⓓ It led him to become a botanist.

06 What does the professor say about the habitat of the Venus flytrap?
   Ⓐ It doesn't just include bogs.
   Ⓑ It is protected by scientists.
   Ⓒ It is spread across the globe.
   Ⓓ It is disappearing quickly.

04 Ecology

TOEFL에서 ecology생태학 분야는 biology생물학와 구별이 잘 되지 않을 정도로 유사한 부분이 많다. 그러나 굳이 구별을 해보면, ecology 분야에서는 생태계의 동식물이 ecosystem생태계에 미치는 영향에 대한 연구 내용이 가장 많이 출제된다. 또한, hunting사냥이나 development개발와 같은 인간 활동으로 인해 ecosystem에 어떤 변화가 생기는지, 이로 인해 동식물 개체 수 감소에 어떤 영향을 주고 어떤 변화가 일어나는지에 대한 문제도 출제된다.

ecology의 핵심은 interdependence상호 의존임을 기억하면 이해하기가 좀 더 수월해진다. 동식물의 행동이나 서식지가 ecosystem에 영향을 미치면, 이로 인해 생기게 되는 ecosystem의 변화가 또 다른 생명체의 개체 수에 영향을 미치게 된다는 이치이다. 앞에서 언급한 생물학과 관련된 내용에 ecology 강의에서 나오는 내용이 합쳐져 출제되는 경우도 많으므로, 도입 부분에서 알아채기 힘들 수 있다. 하지만, 대체적으로 출제포인트에 focus를 두고 강의를 들으면 큰 어려움 없이 문제를 풀 수 있을 것이다.

출제포인트
- Q1 **Problem**
- Q2 **Solution (Adaptation)**
- Q3 **Cause & Effect**
- Q4 **Example**
- Q5 **Misunderstanding / Correction**
- Q6 **Definition**
- Q7 **Function**
- Q8 **Similarity**
- Q9 **Difference (Change)**
- Q10 **Requirement (Condition)**
- Q11 **Influence**

1 Beavers비버

유럽인들이 미국에 정착하기 전 북미에는 beaver가 많이 살고 있었다. 그러나 유럽인들이 북미 지역에 정착하고 fur모피를 얻기 위한 목적으로 비버 사냥을 하기 시작하면서 개체 수가 많이 줄었다.

비버는 나뭇가지를 이용해서 dam댐을 만든다. 비버가 stream개울이나 river강에 만든 댐은 물이 흐르는 속도를 바꾼다. 즉, flowing water 흐르는 물에 still water고여있는 물가 생기는 것이다. 물이 고이면 부유물이 가라앉고 깨끗해져서 생명체가 살기에 더 좋은 조건이 갖추어 진다. 이로 인해 wetland습지가 더 생겨나고, 이로 인해 다양한 식물과 곤충이 살 수 있는 habitat서식지이 생긴다.Q3 즉, 비버가 만든 dam은 다양한 생명체가 공존할 수 있도록 하는 역할Q7을 하는 것이다. 그러나, 유럽인들의 비버 사냥으로 인해 비버 개체 수가 감소되고 이로 인해 wetland 또한 줄어들게 되므로, 그 곳에서 서식하던 많은 동식물들이 사라지는 현상이 발생하게 된다.Q11

Cause & Effect	Influence
비버가 만든 댐은 still water를 만들어 생명체 서식에 더 좋은 조건을 만들고, wetland를 만들어 다양한 생명체가 살 수 있도록 함	북미에 유럽인들이 정착하면서 fur를 목적으로 비버 사냥을 함 → 비버의 개체 수가 감소하여 ecosystem에 영향을 줌

2 Mangrove Trees 맹그로브 나무

mangrove tree는 다양한 종류의 생명체들에게 shelter^{주거지}를 제공⁹⁷ 해주며, 물 안에서 tangled^{얽힌} 뿌리는 흙이나 모래가 해안으로 쓸려 내려가는 것을 방지⁹⁷ 해주는 역할을 한다. 따라서 mangrove tree는 ecosystem의 keystone species^{핵심종}이다.

Influence
shelter 제공 해안선 토양 유실 방지

핵/심/표/현

- abundant   adj. 풍부한, 많은
- accumulate   v. 축적되다, 쌓이다
- agriculture   n. 농업
- artificially   adv. 인위적으로
- break down   분해하다
- cellulose   n. 섬유소
- clay   n. 진흙, 점토
- clogged   adj. 막힌
- clutter   v. (어수선하게) 채우다
- collapse   v. 붕괴되다, 무너지다
- colony   n. 군집
- condition   n. 조건, 상황, 상태
- creature   n. 생물, 생명체
- crucial   adj. 중요한, 주요한
- cultivate   v. 재배하다
- decimate   v. 대량으로 줄이다
- decomposition   n. 분해; 부패
- die out   멸종되다
- direct effect   직접적인 영향
- displacement   n. 이동
- diversification   n. 다양화
- ecologist   n. 생태학자
- ecology   n. 생태학
- ecosystem   n. 생태계
- emigrate   v. (다른 곳으로) 이민 가다, 이주하다
- enzyme   n. 효소
- equilibrium   n. 평형 상태
- excrete   v. 배설하다, 분비하다
- extinct   adj. 멸종한, 사라진
- extinction   n. 멸종
- fauna   n. (한 지역의) 동물상
- fertilizer   n. 비료
- food chain   n. 먹이사슬

- groundwater   n. 지하수
- habitat   n. 서식지, 서식환경
- habitat fragmentation   서식지 단편화
- harsh   adj. 가혹한, 매서운
- haul   v. (세게) 끌어당기다
- hibernate   v. 동면하다
- immigrate   v. 이주해오다
- inhabit   v. 살다
- interdependent   adj. 상호 의존의
- interlock   v. 서로 맞물리다
- isolated   adj. 외떨어진
- plentiful   adj. 풍부한, 많은
- interrelationship   n. 연관성
- interrupt   v. 방해하다, 끼어들다
- keystone   n. 핵심
- labeled   adj. (이름 등이) 표시된
- land phase   지면 단계
- landfill   n. 쓰레기 매립지
- landscape   n. 풍경
- mainland   n. 본토
- mate   n./v. 짝(짓기를 하다)
- mature   adj. 다 자란
- mechanism   n. (생물체 내에서 특정한 기능을 하는) 구조
- metabolize   v. 대사작용을 하다
- microbe   n. 미생물, 병원균
- microscopic organism   미생물
- migrate   v. 이주[이동]하다
- migration route   이주 경로
- minimal   adj. 최소의
- mollusc   n. 연체 동물
- natural disaster   자연 재해
- nectar   n. 과즙, 꿀
- nesting site   집터, 둥지

- nutrient   n. 영양소, 영양분
- ocean sediment   바다 침전물
- olfactory   adj. 후각의
- organism   n. 생물, 유기체
- osmosis   n. 삼투 (현상)
- paw   n. (동물의) 발
- permafrost   n. 영구 동토층
- pest   n. 해충
- pollen   n. 꽃가루
- pollinate   v. 수분하다
- preference   n. 선호(도)
- preservation   n. 보존, 보전
- prey   n. 먹이
- prime   adj. 가장 중요한, 기본적인
- quantity   n. 수, 양
- ratio   n. 비, 비율
- recycle   v. 재활용하다
- ritual   n. 전례, 절차
- saline   n./adj. 염분(이 함유된)
- scarcity   n. 부족, 결핍
- scent   n. 향
- sensory organ   감각기관
- settlement   n. 정착지
- shimmering   adj. 희미하게 빛나는
- soil   n. 흙, 땅
- submerge   v. 물 속에 잠기다
- survive   v. 살아남다
- swiftly   adv. 신속히, 즉시
- symbiotic relationship   공생 관계
- technically speaking   엄밀히 말하면
- threatened   adj. 멸종 위기에 직면한
- trail   v. (식물이) 땅에 붙어서 뻗어 나가다
- variable   n. 변수
- vice versa   adv. 반대의 경우도 같음
- weathered   adj. 풍화된
- wetland   n. 습지(대)
- wild environment   야생환경
- wildness   n. 야생(성)
- wilderness   n. 황야, 황무지
- wipe out   완전히 파괴하다

Sample Questions

[01 ~ 06] Listen to part of a lecture in an ecology class. Then answer the questions.

MP3 52 정답 및 해석 p. 115

Note-taking

- Main Idea:

- Example:

- Requirement / Condition:

- Cause & Effect:

- Limitation:

01 According to the professor, what factors determine the number of animals that live on an island? Choose two answers.
   Ⓐ The number of species that immigrate to the island
   Ⓑ The geographical size of the island
   Ⓒ The number of species that inhabit the mainland
   Ⓓ The distance from the island to the mainland
   Ⓔ The seasonal climate of the island

02 What does the professor say determines when the species on an island will reach equilibrium? Choose two answers.
   Ⓐ The rate at which the island's species die out
   Ⓑ The speed at which the island's species evolve
   Ⓒ The number of species that move to the island
   Ⓓ The ratio of predator to prey among the island's species

03 According to the professor, what is likely to happen if an island is overcrowded?
     Ⓐ The diversity of the island will increase.
     Ⓑ Certain species will move back to the mainland.
     Ⓒ The rate of extinction will increase.
     Ⓓ Species will stop evolving.

04 What does the professor consider to be a limitation of the equilibrium theory?
     Ⓐ The size of the island cannot be calculated.
     Ⓑ The type of species that will survive cannot be predicted.
     Ⓒ When certain species will become extinct cannot be determined.
     Ⓓ The theory cannot be applied to areas that are not islands.

05 Why does the professor mention Krakatoa?
     Ⓐ To illustrate an actual situation to which the equilibrium theory was applied
     Ⓑ To demonstrate how a species can be wiped out by natural disasters
     Ⓒ To show what type of island generally has higher extinction rates
     Ⓓ To suggest that birds and butterflies can be used to predict immigration rates

06 The professor discusses the process of reaching an equilibrium on Krakatoa. Put the steps in the correct order of events.
     Ⓐ The number of species reaches pre-eruption levels.
     Ⓑ The extinction rate of species increases.
     Ⓒ The diversification of species increases.
     Ⓓ Species emigrate from the mainland.

▶ **Question Review**

Main Idea
특정 환경에서의 종의 다양성을 설명할 수 있는 요인

Listen to part of a lecture in an ecology class.

Professor(female): Let's continue our discussion on species diversification. We've talked about specific adaptations animals make to survive in their respective environments. But today, let's focus on some other factors that can explain the diversity of species in certain environments. Jason, didn't you mention going on a family trip this summer?

Student(male): Yeah, my family traveled to Hawaii. It was great. I mean, there were so many things to see.

P: Did you notice anything about the animals?

S: Actually, yeah. There were so many different species, and they were all different on each island I visited.

P: We might not really give any thought to it, or automatically assume that the animals living on the islands just naturally evolved, but there are a number of different factors that determine the species we see today. Before we get into the details, let me introduce a new concept – biogeography. Anyone want to guess what it is?

S: Hmm… It just sounds like a combination of biology and geography…

P: That's correct. It's a theory that examines the richness of species in isolated geographic locations. Around 50 years ago, Robert MacArthur and E.O. Wilson created the equilibrium theory to explain how the diverse species on oceanic islands came to be. They basically stated that the number of species will eventually even out on a newly formed island. This is important because biologists can now estimate how long it will take for a community of different species to find their equilibrium. Of course, as the species adapt to their respective environments, the overall number of species will gradually increase over time, but having an approximate estimation of when equilibrium will be reached has many ecological implications. But before we get into those details, let's look at what may be needed to know the approximate number of animals that inhabit the island. Anybody have any ideas?

Requirement / Condition
종의 수를 결정하는 요소
– 섬의 위치와 크기

◉ 단서 표현: factor

S: Hmm… Wouldn't where the island is located matter? I mean, if it's too far away from the mainland…

P: Yes, location is a very important factor. Obviously, some animals can move from the mainland to nearby islands. The size of the island is just as important. There needs to be enough space for habitats and feeding. So, **Q1** **the number of animals that live on the island is primarily determined by space and distance.** You might think this also has something to do with the number of different species in the island, but

Cause & Effect
이주율과 멸종률이 같아지면 종의 수가 평형이 됨

surprisingly, it has little relation to it, meaning a large island doesn't necessarily have more diversification than one that is remote and small. That's where the theory of biogeographic equilibrium comes in. MacArthur and Wilson proposed that **Q2-C the rate of immigration and Q2-A the rate of extinction will even out, creating the equilibrium of species and thus determining the actual composition of the fauna.** Okay, let me explain. Let's say a new volcanic island were to rise out of the ocean. Some birds would begin to emigrate from the mainland to the island. Of course, as more and more species came in, fewer species would be left in the mainland to emigrate. Hence, the immigration rate would eventually decrease. Equally, the rate at which species might become extinct on the island would be related to the number of those that have become residents. And since the resources of an island are limited, as the number of resident species increased, the smaller and more prone to extinction their individual populations would likely become. **Q3 The extinction rate would slowly increase as the island became overcrowded with immigrating species.** This rate would increase until it finally met the decreasing immigration rate, creating an equilibrium. Yes, Sarah?

S(female): Um... Let me get this straight. So, we can know approximately how many species will become extinct by looking at the number of immigrating species?

Limitation
어떤 종이 살아남을지는 예측 못함

Example
Krakatoa island를 평형 이론 적용의 예로 둠

P: Precisely. But **Q4 there are limitations to this theory. Although we can predict the rates, we can't predict what types of species will end up surviving.** There are just too many variables that determine which species get to survive and which species become extinct. **Q5 I'll give you an example of how this theory was applied. A volcanic eruption in 1883 on the island of Krakatoa decimated every living species.** Yet within a few years, the number of birds and insects slowly increased. **Q6-D The same species of birds and butterflies that used to live on the island immigrated back to the island from the mainland.** As the years passed, **Q6-C the overall diversification increased.** However, once too many species had moved in, **Q6-B the number of bird and butterfly species that became extinct started to increase.** Just like the theory says. However, what scientists were surprised to find was that although some bird species successfully recolonized, some species that lived there before the eruption became extinct. So, **Q6-A the number of actual animals didn't change, nor did the degree of diversity** – what did change is which species survived. The size of the cast remained the same, but the actors changed.

Practice Questions

[01 ~ 06] **Listen to part of a lecture in an ecology class. Then answer the questions.**

MP3 53 정답 및 해석 p. 116

Note-taking

01 What is the lecture mainly about?
   Ⓐ New methods to reduce pollution
   Ⓑ The characteristics and ecological role of termites
   Ⓒ Common insect infestations and how to remove them
   Ⓓ Symbiotic relationships between insects and other organisms

02 What are the examples of symbiosis mentioned by the professor?
   Choose two answers.
   Ⓐ Recycling waste with termites
   Ⓑ Termite communication
   Ⓒ Exterminating termites with ants
   Ⓓ Termite digestion

03 What can be inferred from the way termites communicate?
   Ⓐ Each termite creates its own unique vibrations.
   Ⓑ They are able to communicate with some bees.
   Ⓒ Their sense of smell is stronger than their eyesight.
   Ⓓ They can recognize the sound of different enemies.

04 According to the professor, why were there termite wings in her house?
   Ⓐ An exterminator killed some termites by mistake.
   Ⓑ Reproductive termites swarmed in her home.
   Ⓒ Soldier termites ate some other insects.
   Ⓓ The termites left them there because of their scent.

05 What was the professor's attitude toward ridding her house of termites?
   Ⓐ She was surprised at the number of termites in her home.
   Ⓑ She was impressed by the effectiveness of the exterminators.
   Ⓒ She doubted that she could ever get rid of all the termites.
   Ⓓ She was concerned about its impact on the ecosystem.

06 According to the professor, what could decompiculture be used for?
   Ⓐ Protecting homes against termites
   Ⓑ Recycling soil and water
   Ⓒ Cleaning up certain types of pollution
   Ⓓ Helping with the production of paper

05 Physiology

TOEFL에서 physiology생리학와 health science건강학 분야는 신체 organ기관의 구조와 기능 등 우리의 건강과 관련된 내용을 다룬다. physiology에서 출제되었던 문제로는 eye lens수정체에 transparent cell투명한 세포이 있는 이유, joints관절의 작동 원리, sick building syndrome새 건물 증후군, separation anxiety disorder분리 불안 장애, insomnia불면증, hypersomnia과면증, child amnesia어린이 기억 상실 등이 있다.

physiology 분야는 평상시에 접하기 힘든 단어들이 많이 나와서 학생들이 난이도가 가장 높다고 생각하는 주제 중 하나이다. 그러나, 실제 TOEFL 시험에서는 간혹 어려운 주제가 나오긴 해도 심오한 수준의 깊이까지는 다루지 않으니, 출제포인트에 focus를 두고 강의를 듣는 법을 연습한다면 이 분야도 도전해 볼 만하다.

출제포인트

- 1 Problem
- 2 Solution (Adaptation)
- 3 Cause & Effect
- 4 Example
- 5 Misunderstanding / Correction
- 6 Definition
- 7 Function
- 8 Similarity
- 9 Difference (Change)
- 10 Requirement (Condition)
- 11 Influence

1 Hypersomnia과면증

sleep clinic수면 클리닉에는 insomnia patient불면증 환자가 대부분일 것이라 생각하지만, 사실은 hypersomnia과면증 환자들이 더 많다.♥5 과면증은 뇌에서 각성을 유지하는 호르몬 분비가 저하되어 발생♥3 한다는 것은 밝혀졌지만, 호르몬 분비가 왜 저하되는지는 아직 밝혀내지 못했다. 과면증은 10대에 발생하여 성인이 될 때까지 이어진다. 병의 symptom증상으로는 운전 도중 조는 것 말고도, 회의 중에 갑자기 잠이 들거나, 심한 경우는 길을 걷다가 잠에 빠지기도 한다.♥3 그렇지만, 이렇게 심한 증상이 나타나는 경우는 흔하지 않다. therapy치료법로는 drug약물 복용과 중간 중간 nap낮잠을 자는 방법♥2이 있지만, 완치는 되지 않는다.

Cause	Effect (symptom)	Solution (therapy)
뇌의 각성 호르몬 분비의 저하	운전, 회의 등 일상생활 중 갑작스러운 수면 상태 돌입	(1) 약물 복용 (2) 낮잠

2 Joints관절

관절은 우선 movable joint움직이는 관절와 immovable joint움직이지 않는 관절로 classified분류되는=된다.⁹⁶ 움직이지 않는 관절이라 하면 생소하게 느껴질 수 있지만 skull머리뼈이 여기에 해당된다.⁹⁴ 움직이는 관절은 hinge joint경첩 관절, ball and socket joint절구공이 관절, 그리고 pivot joint회전 관절로 분류된다.
hinge joint는 손가락 마디로, ball and socket joint는 어깨로, 그리고 pivot joint는 목을 예로 든다.⁹⁴ hinge joint와 pivot joint보다 ball and socket joint가 가장 많이 움직여지는⁹⁹ 관절이다.

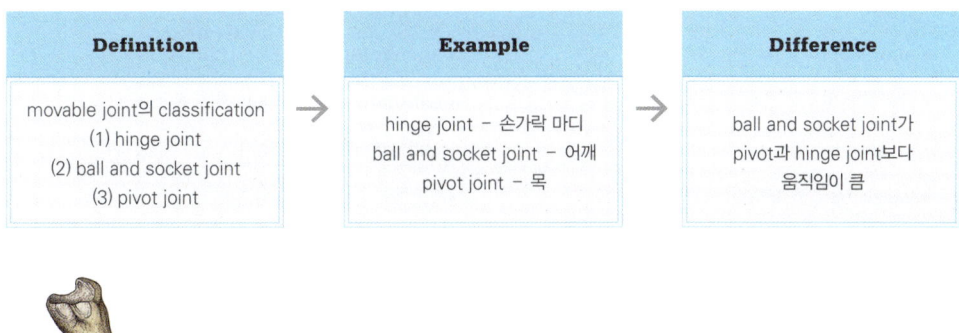

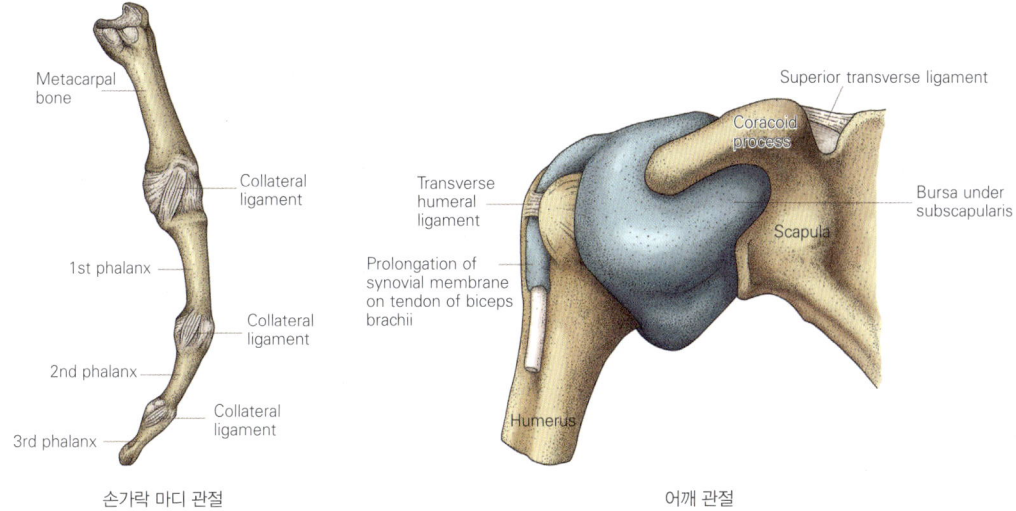

손가락 마디 관절   어깨 관절

핵/심/표/현

- abandon   v. 버리다, 포기하다
- adhesion   n. 접착
- alert   adj. 정신이 초롱초롱한
- amnesia   n. 기억 상실
- anatomize   v. 해부하다
- annihilation   n. 전멸, 소멸
- anticipate   v. 기대하다, 예상하다
- arrangement   n. 정리, 배열
- assemble   v. 모으다, 조합하다
- associate   v. 연상하다, 연관 짓다
- anxiety   n. 불안
- awareness   n. 의식
- cell   n. 세포
- chromosome   n. 염색체
- classification   n. 분류
- coexist   v. 공존하다
- color blindness   색맹
- complex   n. 복합체
- comprise   v. ...로 이루어지다
- conduct   v. 실시하다, 처리하다
- conjunction   n. 결합
- constitute   v. ...을 구성하다
- contravene   v. 위반하다, 위배하다
- correlation   n. 상관관계
- corresponding   adj. 상응하는, 일치하는
- deficient   adj. 부족한, 결핍된
- delicate   adj. 섬세한, 정교한
- deliberate   adj. 고의적인, 의도적인
- deserve   v. ...을 받을 만하다
- dichromatic   adj. 두 색을 가진, 2색성의
- differentiate   v. 차별하다, 구별하다
- disorder   n. 장애
- distinctive   adj. 독특한, 특징이 있는
- drug   n. 약물
- duplicate   v. 복제하다
- effective   adj. 효과적인
- efficiency   n. 효율성
- elevate   v. 향상시키다
- encounter   v. 마주치다, 접하다
- estimate   v. 추정하다, 예상하다
- exhaustion   n. 탈진
- figure out   이해하다, 해결하다
- free radical   활성산소
- friction   n. 마찰
- fudge   n./v. 날조(하다)
- function   n./v. 기능(하다)
- gene   n. 유전자
- handicap   n. 장애
- heart rate   n. 심박동수
- hemisphere   n. (뇌의) 반구
- hinder   v. 방해하다, 저해하다
- hollow   adj. 공허한, 속이 빈
- homogenous   adj. 동종의, 동질의
- human nature   사람의 본능
- hypersomnia   n. 과면증
- hypothesis   n. 가설
- in regard to ~   ...에 관해서(는)
- inactivity   n. 무활동, 정지
- incorporate   v. 포함[통합]하다
- independent   adj. 독립적인
- inherit   v. 유전되다, 물려받다
- insomnia   v. 불면증
- insulation   n. 절연(체), 단열(체)
- invasive   adj. 침입하는, 침략적인
- invertebrate   n. 무척추동물
- joint   n. 관절, 이음매

- junction   n. 접합[연결] 지점
- eyelid   n. 눈꺼풀
- locomotion   n. 이동, 보행
- looseness   n. 느슨함
- lubricate   v. 매끄럽게 하다, 기름을 치다
- majority   n. 과반수 이상, 대부분
- maneuvering   n. 능수능란함
- matching   adj. 어울리는, 조화로운
- mature   adj. 다 자란, 원숙한
- medicinal   adj. 치유력[약효]이 있는
- metabolism   n. 신진대사
- mimic   v. 흉내 내다, 흡사하다
- mutation   n. 돌연변이, 변화
- obsess   v. 사로잡다
- organ   n. 기관, 장기
- organizational   adj. 조직[구조]적인
- overreach   v. (지나치게 욕심을 내다가) 도를 넘다
- perceive   v. 인지[감지]하다
- physiology   n. 생리학
- periodically   adv. 주기적으로
- phase   n. 단계
- predetermine   v. 미리 결정하다
- presence   n. 존재
- principle   n. 원칙, 원리
- pristine   adj. 본래의, 자연 그대로의
- probability   n. 확률
- proportion   n. 비율, 비례, 부분
- rare   adj. 드문, 희귀한

- receptor   n. 감각기관
- refreshed   adj. (기분이) 상쾌한
- resistance   n. 저항
- retina   n. 망막
- skull   n. 두개골
- sensation   n. 감각
- severely   adv. 심하게
- separation   n. 분리
- sick building syndrome   새 건물 증후군
- simultaneously   adv. 동시에, 한번에
- somatic   adj. 신체의, 육체의
- stimulus   n. 자극
- suffering   n. 고통, 괴로움
- surgically   adv. 외과적으로
- suicidal   adj. 자멸[죽음]을 초래할, 몹시 위험한
- sustainable   adj. 유지[지속] 할 수 있는
- switch   v. 바꾸다, 전환하다
- symptom   n. 증상, 증세
- therapy   n. 치료법
- tone   n. (근육의) 긴장
- toxin   n. 독소
- treatment   n. 치료
- transparent   adj. 투명한
- trichromatic   adj. 3색의
- uniformity   n. 일치, 한결같음
- unwillingness   n. 본의 아님, 자발적이 아님
- vertebrate   n. 척추동물

Sample Questions

[01 ~ 06] Listen to part of a lecture in a physiology class. Then answer the questions.

MP3 54 정답 및 해석 p. 120

Note-taking

• Main Idea:

• Difference:

• Example:

• Function:

• Misunderstanding / Correction:

• Difference / Example:

• Function:

01 What does the professor mainly discuss?
  Ⓐ How animals adapt to their harsh environments
  Ⓑ Why inactivity is needed by animals and humans to survive
  Ⓒ The differences between the sleep patterns of mammals and birds
  Ⓓ The various processes and functions of sleep in humans and animals

02 According to the professor, why is the way dolphins sleep unusual?
  Ⓐ They do not need much sleep.
  Ⓑ They move very little when sleeping.
  Ⓒ They do not shut down their whole brain.
  Ⓓ They produce toxins in their body.

03 What is the professor's attitude towards the view that the main function of sleep is to allow the body to recover from physical activity?
    Ⓐ He feels that it is believed by many people.
    Ⓑ He is surprised that anyone would have that view.
    Ⓒ He doesn't think that it can fully explain why people sleep.
    Ⓓ He doubts that the body needs to recover from physical activity.

04 Why does the professor mention reptiles?
    Ⓐ To discuss different adaptations of sleep
    Ⓑ To help explain the purpose of sleep
    Ⓒ To give an example of animals that do not sleep
    Ⓓ To emphasize the superior intelligence of mammals

05 According to the hypotheses discussed by the professor, what determines how alert we feel?
    Ⓐ The type of situation we are in
    Ⓑ The rate of our metabolism
    Ⓒ The amount of sleep we get
    Ⓓ The amount of toxins in our brain

Listen again to part of the lecture. Then answer the question. 🔊 MP3 54_1

06 Why does the professor say this?
    Ⓐ To imply that humans should be more grateful
    Ⓑ To emphasize the importance of our possessions
    Ⓒ To indicate that humans are accustomed to a safe environment
    Ⓓ To imply that students who study sleep can apply for grant

▶ **Question Review**

Main Idea 수면 **Difference** 수면과 일반 휴식의 차이	**Listen to part of a lecture in a physiology class.** **Professor(male):** Okay, so last time, we covered how animals need a period of inactivity to recover. We learned that recovery is just as needed as eating. **Q1** Today, I'd like to take a look at a longer type of rest. Let's talk about sleep. I want to emphasize that **there's a difference between sleep and other forms of inactivity, like regular rest. Insects, for example, rest, but don't sleep.** Sleep is different in that the brain alters many of its usual activities, including its connection to the sensory and motor organs. Sleep makes animals shut those connections down. So, a sleeping animal can usually neither sense nor move. Well, I say usually because, well… well, we'll get to that in a minute. We all sleep – I mean, all invertebrates, animals and humans alike, need sleep to function properly. Now many of you may think that we become unconscious – just shut down everything except our vital organs – but we're only in a state of reduced awareness of our environment. 🎧 It's
Headset **Difference** 동물은 위험에 노출되어 있어 사람처럼 수면할 수 없음	fine for humans because most of us are lying down on a cozy bed in a room. But what if we didn't have a safe home, or room, to sleep in? What if we were out in the open? **Q6** **We take many things for granted,** but for animals in the wild, sleep, I mean, sleeping like we do, is simply not possible. Many animals are at risk of being attacked by predators, or sometimes they simply can't sleep the way we do because of their surroundings.
Example 환경 적응 방식의 예 – 돌고래는 뇌의 반구만 정지시킴	Take, for example, marine mammals like dolphins or whales. Compared to land mammals, dolphins have one huge difference – their environment. We all need to breathe, but dolphins live in water. This presents a big problem because dolphins need to swim up for air once in a while, meaning that they can't completely just shut off all movement and sensation. So their brains can't shut down completely. So, **Q2** **dolphins have adapted to their environment by shutting down one hemisphere at a time while sleeping.** This lets them swim up for air occasionally. That's why when we look at dolphins, we can't even tell that they're sleeping. The only way we can tell is by measuring their brain activity. Scientists were shocked to see that one half of the brain was active while the other was sleeping.
Function 수면의 기능 – 몸의 회복	So, **Q3** you might be wondering what exactly the function of sleep is. Most of us assume that it's a **mechanism to recover from physical activity.** I mean, when we sleep, the whole body rests – our muscles

Misunderstanding / Correction

일반적인 휴식으로도 몸을 쉬게 하고 에너지를 아낄 수 있음

lose their tone, they relax, and the body saves energy. But this can happen even during regular rest, when we're awake. This is probably what happens to insects when they rest. What I'm trying to say is, we don't sleep to rest our bodies. We could easily do this through regular conscious inactivity.

Studying the adaptations of dolphins really makes us think about the true purpose of... the benefits of sleep. You remember how dolphins allow just one hemisphere of their brains to sleep at a time? We say that dolphins are sleeping because we are looking at the brain. It's because of the unique pattern of brain activity, or inactivity, depending on how you look at it, which is a clue that sleep's function has to do specifically with the brain.

This explains why sleep can be observed more in mammals and birds than in reptiles. The brains of mammals are much more complex than those of other animals. **Q4** **A simpler brain, like a reptile's, doesn't need a lot of sleep. We can see from the correlation of brain size and the amount of sleep that sleep's most important function has something to do with benefiting the brain.**

Difference / Example

파충류처럼 더 단순한 뇌는 많은 수면을 필요로 하지 않음

But in what way? Well, we're not quite sure yet. One hypothesis is that sleep is needed to remove toxins. All living cells produce toxins as a result of metabolism. Like all cells, toxins called free radicals are produced as a result of metabolic functions of the brain. **Q5** **Sleeping supposedly allows the brain to remove these toxins. Without these toxins, we feel much more alert and energetic.** This explains why we are so refreshed after a night's sleep. Although... this might not always seem to be the case, especially in a biology class at 8 a.m. in the morning.

Function

수면의 목적 – 독소 제거

Practice Questions

[01 ~ 06] **Listen to part of a lecture in a physiology class. Then answer the questions.**

MP3 55 정답 및 해석 p. 121

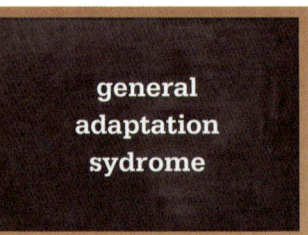

Note-taking

01 What is the lecture mainly about?
    Ⓐ The various medical definitions of stress
    Ⓑ The methods the body uses to handle stress
    Ⓒ The physical effects of stress on the human body
    Ⓓ The differences between mental and physical stress

02 What does the professor say about the body of a person who is embarrassed?
    Ⓐ It will enter an alert state.
    Ⓑ Its reaction will depend on the surrounding environment.
    Ⓒ It will experience physical pain.
    Ⓓ It will react in a similar manner to getting hurt physically.

03 In the study the professor mentions, what happened to mice that were occasionally put into situations that caused stress?
Ⓐ They suffered physical and mental damage.
Ⓑ They did not suffer physical or mental damage.
Ⓒ They became stronger and better able to handle stress.
Ⓓ They became weaker and less able to handle stress.

04 Why does the professor mention Nietzsche?
Ⓐ To give an example of a person who struggled with stress
Ⓑ To emphasize a prior point made about stress
Ⓒ To suggest a way to overcome stressful situations
Ⓓ To explain how people react to horrible situations

05 What does the professor imply about the alarm and resistance phases of the general adaptation syndrome?
Ⓐ They do not affect the body.
Ⓑ They are caused by mental stimuli.
Ⓒ They are the shortest stages of stress.
Ⓓ They are likely to be handled without damage.

06 What causes the body to enter the third stage of the general adaptation syndrome?
Ⓐ It loses its ability to deal with the stress.
Ⓑ It successfully deals with the first two stages.
Ⓒ It begins to experience an increased heart rate.
Ⓓ It no longer responds to any kind of stress.

06 Paleontology

TOEFL에서 paleontology고생물학 분야는 life science생명 과학의 토픽 중에서도 상당히 어려운 편에 속하며, 대개 debate토론 방식의 강의가 많이 출제된다. 예를 들어, 한 동물에 대한 연구 결과들의 증거가 상이할 경우, 각기 다른 주장에 대한 근거를 명시하며, 어느 쪽 주장이 더 타당한지 검토하는 전개방식의 강의가 나온다. 한편, 과거에 살았던 동물들이 어떻게 진화했는지에 대한 강의는 debate 방식이 아닌, 그들이 과거 살았던 지역이나 그 시기의 climate change기후 변화를 알 수 있는 evidence증거나 연구 결과로 교수가 설명하는 전개방식으로 진행되기도 한다.

출제포인트
- Q1 Problem
- Q2 Solution (Adaptation)
- Q3 Cause (Evidence) & Effect (Conclusion)
- Q4 Example
- Q5 Misunderstanding / Correction
- Q6 Definition (Theory)
- Q7 Function
- Q8 Similarity
- Q9 Difference (Change / Evolve)
- Q10 Requirement (Condition)
- Q11 Influence

1 Whale's Evolution 고래의 진화

모두가 알고 있듯이 고래는 mammal포유류이다. 따라서 분명 고래는 land-dwelling mammal육지에 사는 포유류이 aquatic mammal해양포유류로 evolve진화하다한 것이다.⁶ 이에 대한 증거로, 고대에 살았던 늑대의 화석 중에서 해양생물에서만 볼 수 있는 귀 구조를 가진 늑대 화석을 발견⁹³했다. 또한, 고래와 뼈대구조가 유사한 고대 해양생명체에서는 limb팔, 다리으로 보이는 4개의 작은 뼈가 발견⁹³됐다. 물론 이 생명체가 걸어 다녔을 거라고 볼 수는 없지만, 이는 4개의 다리를 가진 생명체가 수중생명체로 진화했다는 증거로 볼 수 있다. 따라서 고래가 늑대로부터 진화했다는 주장에 무게가 실린다. 하지만, DNA를 이용한 최근 연구에서, 놀랍게도 고래의 DNA가 늑대가 아닌 하마 쪽에 더 가깝다는 결과⁹³가 나왔다. 앞에서 언급한 고대 생명체의 화석과 고래의 DNA 검사 결과가 상반되기 때문에, 여전히 고래의 조상이 무엇인지에 대한 debate가 진행⁹³되고 있다.

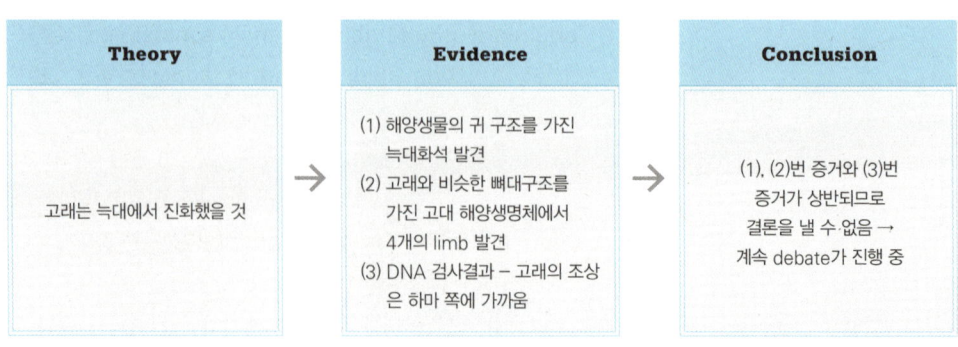

2 Amber호박

amber는 tree sap나무 수액이 딱딱하게 굳어서 만들어진 화석을 말한다.⁹⁶ 일반적으로 amber는 보석의 일종으로 알려져 있지만, 나무에 붙어있던 곤충이 같이 굳어져 화석이 된 경우, 고생물학자들에게는 더 없이 귀중한 연구자료가 된다. amber와 일반 화석의 차이로는, 일반 화석은 눌러서 평평해진 것인 반면, amber 안에 있는 화석은 수액이 곤충을 감쌀 때 3차원 형체 그대로 굳어 버리기 때문에 organic matter유기물가 그대로 보존된다.⁹⁹ 이를 통해 과학자들은 behavior fixity행동 불변라는 theory이론를 세우는데, 이 이론은 예를 들어 amber에 나비가 들어있다면,⁹⁴ 그 종류의 나비가 주로 꿀을 따라 가는 식물도 amber가 발견된 지역에 서식했을 것⁹⁶이라고 주장하는 것이다.

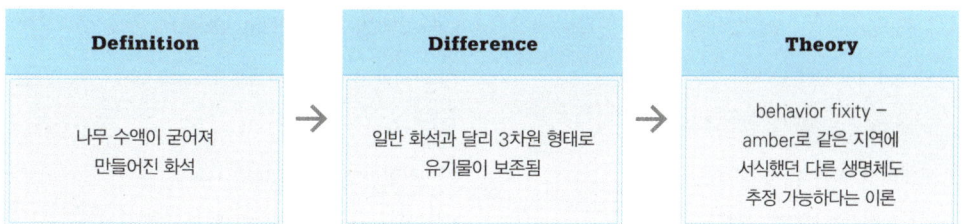

3 Dragonfly잠자리

Carboniferous Period석탄기에는 곤충이 진화하기 좋은 조건으로 인해, 날개 달린 곤충을 비롯해 많은 새로운 곤충들이 등장⁹¹⁰했다. 이 시기에는 fern양치식물과 같이 몸집이 커다란 식물이 등장하면서 photosynthesis광합성를 활발하게 하여 지구의 CO_2양이 많이 줄어든 대신 O_2 양이 증가하게 되었다. O_2 양이 증가하자, 대기의 밀도가 증가했고, 이는 다시 lift양력가 쉽게 생기게 하였다.⁹³ 그 당시 화석을 보고, paleontologist고생물학자들은 이런 조건이 형성된 후에 잠자리와 같은 곤충들에게 날개가 나타났다는 것을 밝혀내었다. 화석을 통해 밝혀낸 또 다른 사실은, 석탄기 초기에는 잠자리 날개가 fixed고정된 형태였는데, 석탄기 후반에는 folding접을 수 있는된 형태로 진화하였다는 것이다.⁹⁹

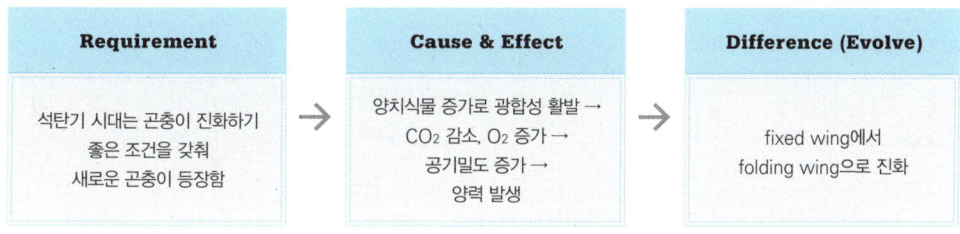

핵/심/표/현

- alternate   v. 번갈아 나오다
- amber   n. 호박
- aquatic   adj. 수생의
- Arctic   n./adj. 북극 대륙(의)
- Antarctic   n./adj. 남극 대륙(의)
- ashore   adv. 물가로[에]
- backbone   n. 척추
- balance   v. 균형을 잡다
- beak   n. (새의) 부리
- blend   v. 섞이다, 혼합되다
- blood vessel   n. 혈관
- brisk   adj. 활발한, 빠른
- brood   v. 알을 품다
- buried   adj. (땅에) 파묻힌
- canal   n. (체내의) 관
- capture   v. 획득하다, 포획하다
- cavity   n. 구멍
- circulatory system   순환계
- claw   n. 발톱
- cold-blooded   n./adj. 냉혈 동물(의)
- competing   adj. 상충되는
- conserve   v. 보존하다
- contrast   v. 대조하다, 비교하다
- contribute   v. 기여하다, 일조하다
- Cretaceous period   백악기
- crop   n. 농작물
- crushed   adj. 부서진, 으깨진
- debate   n./v. 논의[논쟁]하다
- devastate   v. 완전히 파괴하다
- Devonian period   데본기
- dig up   발굴하다, 파내다
- distinctive   adj. 특이한, 독특한
- distort   v. 왜곡하다
- draw the line   기준[한도]를 정하다
- elastic   adj. 탄력[신축성] 있는
- eliminate   v. 제거하다, 없애다
- entire   adj. 전부 다, 모든
- eucalyptus   n. 유칼립투스 (나무)
- evolution   n. 진화
- extinct   adj. 멸종된
- ferocious   adj. 사나운, 포악한
- fibrous   adj. 섬유로 된
- fin   n. 지느러미
- fine-grained   adj. 결이 고운
- firmly   adv. 확고히, 단호히
- fossil   n. 화석
- fossilize   v. 화석화하다
- give off   방출하다, 발산하다
- grain   n. 곡물, 낟알
- growth ring   n. 나이테
- hibernate   v. 동면하다
- hollow   adj. 속이 빈, 움푹 꺼진
- house   v. 수용하다
- impression   n. (세게 눌렀을 때 생기는) 자국
- imprint   v. 각인시키다
- impulse   n. 자극
- in conjunction with ~   …와 함께
- incline   v. …쪽으로 마음이 기울다
- initial   adj. 최초의, 처음의
- insulation   n. 단열
- internal organ   내장
- intimately   adv. 친밀하게; 직접적으로
- isolated   adj. 고립된, 격리된
- juvenile   adj. 청소년의
- limb   n. 팔, 다리
- limestone   n. 석회석

- living fossil 살아있는 화석
  (예를 들어 실러캔스와 같은 물고기는 4백만 년 전의 실러캔스의 화석의 뼈대구조나 모양이 현재의 모양과 매우 비슷하다. 일반적으로는 오랜 시간 동안 진화를 통해 많이 변하게 되지만, 실러캔스처럼 그렇지 않은 생명체를 '살아있는 화석'이라고 부른다.)
- lizard n. 도마뱀
- locate v. 찾아내다, 위치시키다
- maneuver v. 조종하다
- maple n. 단풍나무
- native n./adj. 원주민(의), 태생민(의)
- natural selection 자연 도태[선택]
- nerve n. 신경
- oak n. 참나무
- occasional adj. 가끔의
- orchid n. 난초
- organic matter 유기물
- ornamental adj. 장식적인
- ornithologist n. 조류학자
- outrun v. 넘어서다, …을 앞지르다
- paleontology n. 고생물학
- particle n. 입자
- permit v. 허용하다, 허가하다
- pine needle n. 솔잎
- polar region 극지방
- precision n. 정밀(성), 꼼꼼함
- prehistoric adj. 선사시대의
- proliferate v. (빠르게) 증식하다, 번식하다
- protrude v. 돌출되다, 튀어나오다
- quarry n. 채석장
- regulate v. 조절하다
- remnant n. 남은 부분, 나머지
- rotate v. 회전하다, 돌다
- sap n. 수액
- seal n. 바다표범
- skeleton n. 뼈
- snout n. (동물의) 코, 주둥이
- softwood n. 연질 목재
- spine n. 등뼈
- subsequent adj. 그 다음의, 차후의
- tetrapod n. 네발 짐승
- thawing n. 해동
- translocate v. 이동시키다, 바꾸어 놓다
- trawler n. 트롤선, 저인망 어선
- unearth v. 발굴하다; 밝혀내다
- vegetation n. 초목, 식물
- warm-blooded n./adj. 온혈 동물(의)

Sample Questions

[01 ~ 06] Listen to part of a lecture in a paleontology class. Then answer the questions.

MP3 56 정답 및 해석 p. 124

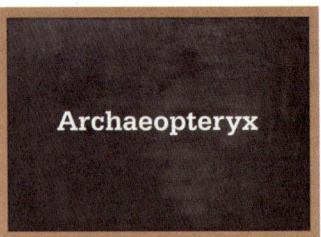

Note-taking

- Main Idea:

- Cause:

- Example:

- Debate:

- Difference:

- Opinion:

- Similarity:

- Finding:

01 What does the professor mainly discuss?
   Ⓐ Theories about where an ancient bird belongs in terms of evolution
   Ⓑ Features large birds must possess in order to be able to fly
   Ⓒ Different ideas about what the proper definition of a bird is
   Ⓓ Explanations of the evolutionary process that allowed modern birds to fly

02 Why does the professor mention the quarry in which the bird was found?
   Ⓐ To dispute the theories about Archaeopteryx held by ornithologists
   Ⓑ To present evidence that Archaeopteryx had the ability to fly
   Ⓒ To show that paleontologists can find fossils in a variety of places
   Ⓓ To point out why the Archaeopteryx fossil was so detailed

03 Why does the professor mention the *Mona Lisa*?
   Ⓐ He thinks that it is as beautiful as a finely detailed fossil.
   Ⓑ He believes it can be used to illustrate techniques of analyzing fossils.
   Ⓒ He feels that it and Archaeopteryx are perceived in similar ways.
   Ⓓ He wants to emphasize how rare well-preserved bird fossils are.

04 According to the professor, what characteristics are used to define birds?
   Choose two answers.
   Ⓐ A tail used for maneuvering
   Ⓑ The size of the beak
   Ⓒ The ability to fly
   Ⓓ The presence of feathers

05 What point does the professor make about paleontologists' view of Archaeopteryx?
   Ⓐ They don't think it is actually related to either dinosaurs or modern birds.
   Ⓑ They feel it represents an evolutionary link between birds and dinosaurs.
   Ⓒ They suspect it was the first bird to use its tail to maneuver while flying.
   Ⓓ They believe it was a dinosaur that used its feathers to attract mates.

06 What does the professor imply is a problem with the theory held by ornithologists?
   Ⓐ It may be disproved by recent findings.
   Ⓑ It was formed without any proper evidence.
   Ⓒ It only explains certain features of Archaeopteryx.
   Ⓓ It cannot be proved without fossils.

▶ **Question Review**

Listen to part of a lecture in a paleontology class.

Main Idea

Professor(male): Okay, during our last class we discussed birds – modern birds and their environment. **Q1** **But today, let's discuss a bird that is very ancient but very interesting nonetheless.** It's called Archaeopteryx (shown on screen). I know it's a difficult word, but all it means is "ancient wing." This ancient bird was first discovered in 1861 in Germany. It was a stroke of luck, really, especially from a paleontologist's point of view. It was found fossilized in a piece of stone taken from a quarry in Germany. What was surprising was that **Q2** **the bones were extremely well preserved.** It's really rare that the fragile bones of an ancient bird are found in such good condition. The details that were preserved were something else. You can even see the impressions of feathers on it.

Cause
화석이 채석장에서 발견되어 보존이 잘 됨

This was due to where the fossil was found. Like I mentioned before, the fossil was found in a quarry – a place where people cut stone. In this case, it was an exceptionally fine-grained limestone. **The fine particles that made the stone were so small, even smaller than the lines in a feather. This allowed even the smallest details to be imprinted.** Like I said, it's pretty rare. So we don't really have a lot of information, well, not any concrete information, about Archaeopteryx. So everyone has their own ideas. Hmm… it's like the *Mona Lisa*. I'm sure you've seen the painting yourselves or at least seen a copy of it, right? Well, one of the reasons why it's so famous is that **Q3** **everyone who sees the painting has a different opinion about it. They each understand the painting a little differently, according to their own biases.** Archaeopteryx is science's version of the *Mona Lisa*.

Example
보는 사람에 따라 견해가 다른 예

Ornithologists, the scientists who study modern birds, tend to see Archaeopteryx as an early ancestor of the birds we see today. On the other hand, you have paleontologists, scientists who study fossils and forms of ancient life, who tend to point out its similarities to some dinosaur species. They have a point, too. There is no beak and the tail is long and bony just like a reptile's – it's different from the short and stubby tail of a modern bird. Another distinct feature is the claws at the end of what are called "wing fingers." This too is a feature that is absent in most modern birds.

Now many of you might get the wrong impression that the debate has something to do with whether Archaeopteryx was a bird or not, but that's not what the debate is about. **Q4-D** **The ancient bird has feathers**

Difference
현대의 새에서 발견할 수 없는 특징
(1) 부리가 없음
(2) 길고 뼈로 된 꼬리
(3) 갈고리 발톱

Opinion
시조새가 새와 공룡 간의 연결점임

Similarity
현대의 새와의 유사점

Finding
깃털은 단지 장식용이거나 체온 유지용이었을 수 있음

and all creatures with feathers are classified as birds. So even though it doesn't have a beak, has a different tail and has claws on its wings, it's still a bird. **Q1** **The real debate is where Archaeopteryx fits in evolutionary terms.** For paleontologists who study the dinosaurs from a similar period, it's really nothing out of the ordinary... except for one major feature: its feathers.

Q5 **This feature has many paleontologists seeing Archaeopteryx in terms of its evolutionary relationships with dinosaurs and modern birds. They see it as a link between the two of them.** For the ornithologist, Archaeopteryx is the earliest bird on record, one with exceptional features. **Q4-C** **Ornithologists believe that the evolution of birds is closely linked to their ability to fly.** But Archaeopteryx doesn't have a bird-like tail, which is needed to maneuver in the air. It also has claws where modern birds would only have wings. These features really go against the notion that Archaeopteryx had the ability to fly. But at the same time, it did have some features like modern birds, so maybe it could take off, or at least get off the ground. However, we really don't have any evidence to conclusively prove that Archaeopteryx had the ability to fly.

As far as which view is correct, well, there really is no way of telling. However, **Q6** **the most recent research is based on some fossils discovered in China. Although it is far from being complete, it draws some compelling conclusions. These feathers might not have been used for flight at all.** They could have been for display, just like those of many modern animals... Nothing more than ornamental features to attract females. They could have been for insulation, too, as feathers are very useful for conserving body heat in cold temperatures. Just ask Canadian geese.

Practice Questions

[01 ~ 06] **Listen to part of a lecture in a paleontology class. Then answer the questions.**

MP3 57 정답 및 해석 p. 126

Note-taking

01 What is the lecture mainly about?
  Ⓐ Why most dinosaurs lived in warm regions of the world
  Ⓑ The features of dinosaur fossils that were found in polar regions
  Ⓒ Whether dinosaurs were able to regulate their body temperature
  Ⓓ The differences between warm- and cold-blooded dinosaurs

02 According to the professor, what caused the debate regarding dinosaurs?
  Ⓐ A fossil in unusually good condition was discovered.
  Ⓑ New fossil types were identified in tropical regions.
  Ⓒ Lizards were found living in cold regions.
  Ⓓ Fossils were unearthed in new areas.

03   What does the professor say about dinosaurs that lived in the Arctic region?
       Ⓐ They could not have survived unless they had been warm-blooded.
       Ⓑ They may have had a way of raising their body temperature when needed.
       Ⓒ They were able to survive because the Arctic was much warmer than it is today.
       Ⓓ They either hibernated or migrated during the colder months.

04   According to the professor, why does the presence of Haversian canals suggest that dinosaurs were endothermic?
       Ⓐ They act like the rings of trees.
       Ⓑ They house blood vessels.
       Ⓒ They allow for rapid body growth.
       Ⓓ They are found in some fish.

05   According to the professor, why are paleontologists having difficulty deciding whether dinosaurs were warm-blooded or not? Choose two answers.
       Ⓐ Dinosaur fossils mostly consist of bones rather than organs.
       Ⓑ The size of dinosaurs found in Antarctica differs from those found in Arctic regions.
       Ⓒ It is difficult to travel to extreme climates to uncover fossils.
       Ⓓ Analysis of dinosaur bones has resulted in contradictory findings.

06   What can be inferred about some species of sharks from the lecture?
       Ⓐ They can survive in cold water for short periods of time.
       Ⓑ They have fewer Haversian canals than other fish.
       Ⓒ They have ancestors that were warm-blooded.
       Ⓓ They are seldom found fossilized.

Unit 5
Physical Science

01_ **Astronomy**
02_ **Chemistry**
03_ **Earth Science**
04_ **Environmental Science**
05_ **Geology**
06_ **Engineering**

01 Astronomy

TOEFL에 자주 출제되는 astronomy천문학 분야의 주제로는 solar system태양계에 있는 planet행성, 태양계에서 화성과 목성 사이에 가장 많이 분포하고 있으며 행성보다 작은 단위인 asteroid소행성, 타원형 궤도를 그리며 태양계 안과 밖을 이동하는 comet혜성 등이 있다. 또한 행성에 대한 내용 외에도 별의 생성부터 소멸까지의 과정을 다룬 내용들도 등장한다. 천문학 용어에 약한 학생들은 천문학 관련 분야의 핵심 단어들을 먼저 익히고 강의를 들으면 더 수월할 것이다.

출제포인트
- Q1 Main Idea
- Q2 Function (Application)
- Q3 Problem
- Q4 Solution (Suggestion)
- Q5 Example
- Q6 Cause (Evidence) & Effect (Result / Finding / Research)
- Q7 Similarity / Difference
- Q8 Advantage / Disadvantage
- Q9 Misunderstanding / Correction
- Q10 Definition (Term) / Origin
- Q11 Two Click / Three Click
- Q12 Ordering
- Q13 Matching
- Q14 Opinion / Attitude
- Q15 Headset
- Q16 Requirement (Condition)
- Q17 Character
- Q18 Imply / Infer

1 Mars화성

최근 한 연구에 의하면, 화성이 예전에는 지금보다 더 습하고 온도가 따뜻해서 화성에 물이 모인 바다가 있었을 것[Q1]이라고 한다. 그 주장의 근거로, 화성에서 바다였을 것으로 추정되는 basin움푹 들어간 부분과, 해안선이라고 추정되는 부분과 평행한 terrace단구[Q6]를 들고 있다. 조수간만의 차이가 큰 바닷가를 보면 바닷물이 남긴 흔적을 통해 밀물이 어디까지 들어왔었는지를 알 수 있는데, 그 흔적을 terrace라고 한다. 화성의 basin에도 일정한 간격으로 terrace의 흔적이 있는데, 이것을 화성의 바닷물이 마른 증거로 보는 것이다. 화성에 바다가 있었을 것이라고 추정하는 또 다른 증거는 basin 가운데가 너무 flat평평한하고 smooth부드러운하다는 점인데, 대개 물이 있던 곳이 마르면 흙이 부드럽고 평평하게 된다.[Q6] 하지만, 이런 증거만으로는 화성에 바다가 있었다는 가설을 입증하기에 불충분하므로 더 많은 연구가 필요하다.

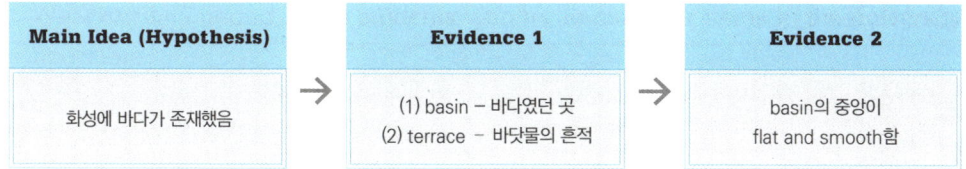

Main Idea (Hypothesis)	→	Evidence 1	→	Evidence 2
화성에 바다가 존재했음		(1) basin – 바다였던 곳 (2) terrace – 바닷물의 흔적		basin의 중앙이 flat and smooth함

2 Pluto^{명왕성}

최근 Pluto가 planet^{행성}의 자격을 박탈당했다. Pluto를 처음에 행성으로 분류했던 이유는 태양을 orbit^{공전하다}하며 atmosphere^{대기}가 있기 때문이었다.^{Q6, Q7} 그러나, 다른 천문학자들에 의해 Pluto를 reclassify^{재분류하다}해야 한다는 주장이 나오면서 controversy^{논쟁}가 생겼다.^{Q1} 그 이유는 Pluto의 orbit^{궤도}이 eccentric^{이상한}하기 때문이다.^{Q6} 다른 행성들은 태양을 circle^{원형} 모양으로 도는데, Pluto만 elliptical^{타원형의}한 모양으로 돈다.^{Q7}  또한, 수성, 금성, 지구와 같은 행성들은 작고 딱딱한 terrestrial planet^{지구형 행성}으로 돌과 금속의 composition^{구성}으로 되어 있으며, 천왕성이나 해왕성은 구성성분이 gas인데, Pluto만 구성성분이 ice이다.^{Q6, Q7} 이렇게, Pluto는 태양계의 다른 행성들과 궤도와 구성성분이 달라서 행성에서 제외되었다. 천체 망원경의 발달로, Neptune^{해왕성}과 Pluto 사이에서 작은 얼음 덩어리인 KBO(Kuiper Belt Object)^{카이퍼대 천체}라는 물질이 발견되는데, Pluto와 성분이 거의 일치한다. 그래서 Pluto가 행성의 조건에 더 부합한지, 아니면 커다란 KBO인지 논쟁이 되었지만, 지금은 더 이상 행성이 아닌 것으로 결론이 났다.

→ Lecture 중에 debate나 controversy란 단어가 나오면 논쟁의 이슈가 소개되고, 대개 두 개의 주장과 각 주장에 대한 evidence가 언급된다.

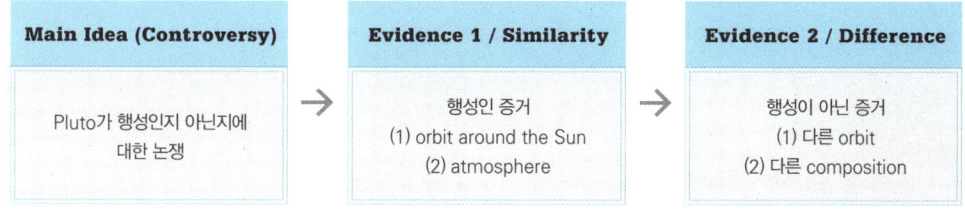

Main Idea (Controversy)	→	Evidence 1 / Similarity	→	Evidence 2 / Difference
Pluto가 행성인지 아닌지에 대한 논쟁		행성인 증거 (1) orbit around the Sun (2) atmosphere		행성이 아닌 증거 (1) 다른 orbit (2) 다른 composition

핵/심/표/현

- albedo   n. 알베도(달·행성이 반사하는 태양 광선의 비율)
- ambient light   주위 밝기, 환경광
- angle   n. (특정 시각에서의) 각도, 관점
- asteroid belt   소행성대
- asteroidal body   소행성체
- astrology   n. 점성술, 점성학
- astronaut   n. 우주 비행사
- astronomer   n. 천문학자
- astronomical observatory   천문대
- astronomical unit   천문 단위
- astronomy   n. 천문학
- astrophysics   n. 천체[우주]물리학
- atmospheric   adj. 대기의
- binary star   n. 연성(連星)
- bombardment   n. 충격, 포격, 폭격
- calculation   n. 계산, 견적
- celestial body   n. 천체
- chromosphere   n. 채층(태양 주위의 백열 가스층)
- comet   n. 혜성
- constellation   n. 별자리
- convection zone   대류층
- cosmic   adj. 우주의, 장대한
- cosmos / universe   n. 우주
- crater   n. 분화구
- crust   n. 지각, 표면
- diameter   n. 지름
- dust   n. 흙, 먼지
- dwarf (star)   n. 왜성
- electromagnetic radiation   전자기 방사선
- elongated   adj. 가늘고 긴
- emission   n. (기체 등의) 방출, 배출
- erupt   v. 분출하다
- evaporation   n. 증발
- flare   v. 확 타오르다
- galaxy / milky way   n. 은하계
- geocentric   adj. 지구를 중심으로 하는
- giant   adj. 매우 거대한[커다란]
- gravitation   n. 중력, 인력, 중력작용
- heliocentric   adj. 태양을 중심으로 하는
- high-resolution   adj. 고해상도의
- hydrogen   n. 수소
- infinite   adj. 무한한, 끝이 없는
- infrared ray   적외선
- interferometer   n. 간섭 관측기
- intergalactic   adj. 은하계 사이의
- interplanetary   adj. 행성간의
- interstellar   adj. 항성 간의, 별과 별 사이의
- intriguing   adj. 아주 흥미로운
- irregular   adj. 고르지 못한
- Jupiter   n. 목성
- leap year   n. 윤년
- length   n. 길이, 거리
- light year   n. 광년
- liquid   n. 액체
- lunar   adj. 달의
- Mars   n. 화성
- massive   adj. 거대한
- Mercury   n. 수성
- meteor   n. 유성, 별똥별
- meteor shower   n. 유성우
- meteorite   n. 운석
- meteoroid   n. 유성체, 운성체
- methane   n. 메탄
- microscopic   n. 매우 작은
- molecular   adj. 분자의

- nebula   n. 성운
- Neptune   n. 해왕성
- obscure   v. 보기 어렵게 하다
- observation   n. 관찰, 관측
- optical radiation   광학 방사선
- orbit   n./v. (행성 등의) 궤도(를 돌다)
- outburst   n. 폭발, 분출
- paradox   n. 역설, 모순
- periodic   adj. 주기적인
- permanent base   영구적 기지
- phase   n. 단계, 국면
- phases of the moon   달의 모양
- phenomenon   n. 현상
- photosphere   n. (태양·행성등의) 광구
- planet   n. 행성
- planetoid   n. 미행성
- Pluto   n. 명왕성
- pressurize   v. 압력을 가하다
- prolong   v. 연장시키다
- pseudoscience   n. 의사[사이비] 과학
- purified   adj. 정화된
- quasar   n. 준항성, 퀘이사
- reference   n. 참조, 참고
- rotate   v. (행성 등이) 회전하다, 자전하다
- Saturn   n. 토성
- solar   adj. 태양의, 태양열을 이용한
- solar eclipse   일식(日蝕)
- speck   n. 반점
- spew out   분출하다
- stellar   adj. 별의
- supernova   n. 초신성
- telescope   n. 망원경
- Uranus   n. 천왕성
- variable star   n. 변광성
- Venus   n. 금성

Sample Questions

[01 ~ 06] Listen to part of a lecture in an astronomy class. Then answer the questions.

MP3 58 정답 및 해석 p. 130

Note-taking

- Main Idea:

- Similarity:

- Advantage:

- Application:

- Condition:

- Result:

01 What is the lecture mainly about?
   Ⓐ The similarities between Neptune and Earth
   Ⓑ The composition of Neptune's atmosphere
   Ⓒ Atmospheric conditions that could form gems
   Ⓓ The weather conditions on Neptune's surface

02 Why does the professor mention a geology class?
   Ⓐ To make sure everyone understands the terms he is using
   Ⓑ To clarify the major difference between Neptune and Uranus
   Ⓒ To point out that geology can make the subject easier to understand
   Ⓓ To explain why Neptune's atmosphere contains large amounts of carbon

03 What does the professor imply when he mentions synthetic diamonds?
   Ⓐ The way the hypothesis suggests diamonds are being formed is not unrealistic.
   Ⓑ There are many practical uses for diamonds formed on other planets.
   Ⓒ Diamonds are very simple in terms of their basic molecular structure.
   Ⓓ The Earth is the only place with all the conditions needed to form diamonds.

04 According to the professor, what are two conditions required to transform methane into diamonds? Choose two answers.
   Ⓐ Hot temperatures
   Ⓑ Cooled hydrocarbons
   Ⓒ Pressurized hydrogen
   Ⓓ High pressure

05 What can be inferred from the experiment mentioned in the lecture?
   Ⓐ Coal crystals are present in the Earth's atmosphere.
   Ⓑ Neptune's atmospheric pressure is weaker than expected.
   Ⓒ It is impossible to make true synthetic diamonds.
   Ⓓ Diamonds found on Neptune would probably be black.

Listen again to part of the lecture. Then answer the question. MP3 58_1

06 Why does the professor say this?
   Ⓐ He wants to know if the student is paying attention.
   Ⓑ The student has not provided the answer he wants.
   Ⓒ He cannot recall what he wants to say next.
   Ⓓ He wants the student to do more research on the topic.

▶ **Question Review**

Main Idea
해왕성의 대기

Similarity
해왕성과 천왕성 간의 유사점

Headset

Advantage
지진학을 들었다면 다이아몬드의 구성 성분을 알 수 있음

Application
화학 지식을 합성 다이아몬드를 만드는 데 응용

Condition
다이아몬드가 만들어지려면 필요한 조건

Listen to part of a lecture in an astronomy class.

Professor(male): **Q1** Today I'd like to talk a bit more about the atmospheres of other planets, specifically about Uranus and Neptune. They're the seventh and eighth planets from the Sun and have very similar atmospheric conditions. So what do you know about the atmospheres of these planets?

Student 1(female): 🎧 Uh... They contain some of the same elements as the Earth's atmosphere... helium, hydrogen...

P: **Q6** What else?

S1: Hmm... **Oh! Methane!** Neptune and Uranus have a higher proportion of methane in their atmospheres, you know, when compared to other planets.

P: Good. **Q1** It's this methane I want to talk about. Because of it, on Neptune, there may literally be diamonds in the sky.

S1: What?

P: It might sound crazy, but it actually makes quite a bit of sense. This isn't about astronomy. It's basic geology we can study right here on Earth. **Q2** Has anyone taken Geology 101? If you have, then surely know what diamonds are made of. They're carbon atoms bonded together, right? Diamonds are essentially just carbon that has been subjected to extremely high pressure. **Q3** We can actually make synthetic diamonds by applying very high pressure to a gas mixture that contains carbon. So, for those of you who took chemistry, what is present in methane?

Student 2(male): Carbon!

P: That's right. That means a high amount of carbon atoms are present in the atmosphere of Neptune. Combined with the crushing pressure and high temperatures, it is an ideal place for diamonds to form. So let's take a look at how it could happen.

Although only pressure is needed to create diamonds from carbon, one thing must happen first in the case of methane: It has to be broken down into carbon atoms. Unlike diamonds, methane contains four hydrogen atoms per each carbon atom. So we first need to break them down into pure carbon. One of the ways this happens is through **Q4-A** **extreme temperatures, which just happen to be present in Neptune's atmosphere.** Although scientists don't know why Neptune is so hot, as it's much farther away from the Sun than the Earth, the high temperatures could break the methane into carbon and hydrogen.

While the carbon atoms float around, >Q4-D> **they could be pressurized by the enormous clouds that form in Neptune's atmosphere.** If the pressure was high enough, the carbon atoms would bond together to create diamonds. And just like it rains on Earth when water vapor gets heavy enough, the resulting diamonds would fall from the sky! It's quite intriguing indeed. You might think that this sounds like a fantasy, but scientists in California have proved it is possible. When Italian scientists first came up with this claim, there were obviously many skeptics.

S1: Yeah, I wouldn't have believed it either.

P: Well, a group of scientists in California tried to confirm these theoretical predictions in the lab, through a series of experiments. So here's what happened. The scientists used a device called an anvil, essentially an enormous press that pressurizes things, to squeeze liquid methane at a pressure that is many hundreds of thousands of times greater than the Earth's atmospheric pressure. Um… what am I missing…?

S2: Heat?

P: Yes, thanks. While pressurizing the methane, they used a laser beam to heat up the liquid to about 3,000 degrees Celsius. The high temperatures from the beam broke down the methane into hydrocarbons, which is what's used to make synthetic diamonds. As these hydrocarbons were subjected to high pressure, >Q5> **black specks began to form. When these specks were examined, their molecular structure was indeed the same as that of a diamond.**

S2: Black? I thought diamonds were white.

P: Well, diamonds actually come in many colors. Anyway, if the atmospheric conditions on Neptune are as we expect, we could get these same diamond flecks forming in the atmosphere. The researchers say that these crystals might even coalesce, just like ice in our own atmosphere, and produce a sort of diamond sleet or hail that would fall through the atmosphere and end up in a layer at the core of the planet. Can you imagine that? A layer of diamonds at the center of Neptune?

Result
분자 구조가 다이아몬드와 동일

Practice Questions

[01 ~ 06] **Listen to part of a lecture in an astronomy class. Then answer the questions.**

MP3 59   정답 및 해석 p. 131

Note-taking

01   What is the lecture mainly about?
   Ⓐ The life cycle of massive stars
   Ⓑ Ways of measuring the brightness of stars
   Ⓒ How binary stars create eclipses
   Ⓓ The characteristics of an unusual type of star

02   Why are the first four planets in our solar system mentioned?
   Ⓐ To say that the size of Eta Carinae is huge
   Ⓑ To say that their combined mass would equal a variable star's
   Ⓒ To say that they are the most affected by our Sun's eruptions
   Ⓓ To say that they are the same size as planets orbiting around Mira

03 What does the professor identify as the reason for the short lifespan of Eta Carinae?
    Ⓐ Its variable brightness
    Ⓑ Its massive size
    Ⓒ Its hot temperatures
    Ⓓ Its nearness to the Sun

04 Why does the professor mention candles?
    Ⓐ To explain how binary stars interact
    Ⓑ To show how quickly stars can die out
    Ⓒ To emphasize the brightness of Eta Carinae
    Ⓓ To illustrate the distance between two stars

05 According to the professor, what is the reason for Eta Carinae's variable brightness?
    Ⓐ It is larger than most stars.
    Ⓑ It consists of two stars.
    Ⓒ It experiences eclipses.
    Ⓓ It experienced a supernova.

Listen again to part of the lecture. Then answer the question. 🔊 MP3 59_1

06 What does the professor imply when he says this?
    Ⓐ The students aren't paying enough attention.
    Ⓑ It takes a lot of training to detect a variable star.
    Ⓒ Supernovas can be viewed with the naked eye.
    Ⓓ Mira is currently impossible to see from the Earth.

02 Chemistry

TOEFL에서 chemistry화학 분야는 자주 출제되지는 않지만, 출제가 될 경우 physics물리학처럼 물질의 특성에 대해 다룬다. 예를 들어, graphite흑연와 diamond다이아몬드의 결정구조의 차이점을 다루거나, 소금이 만들어질 때 필요한 조건 등이 출제된다. 또한, 만들어진 물질들이 어떤 용도로 쓰이는지에 대해서도 종종 출제된다. 지문 몇 개로 화학 분야의 모든 주제를 다룰 수는 없지만, 출제포인트에 focus를 두고 출제 가능성이 높은 지문과 연습 문제를 공부해 시험에 대비하도록 한다.

출제포인트
- Q1 Main Idea
- Q2 Function (Application)
- Q3 Problem
- Q4 Solution (Suggestion)
- Q5 Example
- Q6 Cause (Evidence) & Effect (Result / Finding / Research)
- Q7 Similarity / Difference
- Q8 Advantage / Disadvantage
- Q9 Misunderstanding / Correction
- Q10 Definition (Term) / Origin
- Q11 Two Click / Three Click
- Q12 Ordering
- Q13 Matching
- Q14 Opinion / Attitude
- Q15 Headset
- Q16 Requirement (Condition)
- Q17 Character
- Q18 Imply / Infer

1 Homogeneous Mixture동질 혼합물 vs. Heterogeneous Mixture이질 혼합물

화학에서는 한 물질이 solid고체, liquid액체, gas기체 중 한 상태를 띠고 있을 때, 이를 phase단계라고 부른다. 소금이 물에 녹으면 물에 섞인 소금의 결정이 보이지 않는 것처럼, 고체가 액체로 녹아 하나의 phase가 될 때 이런 solution용매을 homogeneous mixture라고 부른다.Q10 반면, 물과 기름이 섞일 때와 같이 그 경계를 구별할 수 있는 경우는 heterogeneous mixture라고 부른다.Q10 소금물과 같은 homogeneous mixture인 solution을 분리하는 데에는 distillation증류이 쓰이고, heterogeneous mixture를 분리하는 데에는 filtering여과이 쓰인다.Q7 또한, solution의 농도는 variable property가변성로 나타내는데, 예를 들어 coffee가 진한 정도를 variable property로 나타낼 수 있다.Q5

2 Periodic Table 주기율표

현재의 periodic table을 보면 43번 원소가 포함되어 있는데, early version초기 버전의 주기율표에는 43번 원소가 빠져 있었다.♀9 그래서 과학자들은 43번 원소도 분명히 존재했을 것이라고 생각하고 연구하기 시작했다.♀1 그 결과, A연구팀이 43번 원소를 발견했다고 주장했는데, 발견의 근거를 정확하게 보여 주지는 못했다.♀3 B연구팀은 43번 원소에 인공적으로 합성했다는 의미에서 technetium테크네튬이라는 이름을 붙였다.♀10 시간이 지난 후, B연구팀은 43번 원소가 자연적으로도 발생하는데 발생하자마자 decompose분해되다되기 때문에 예전에는 43번 원소가 없다고 생각했다는 사실을 알아냈다.

→ 특정 물질이 누구에 의해 어떻게 발견되었는지에 관한 문제가 자주 출제된다.

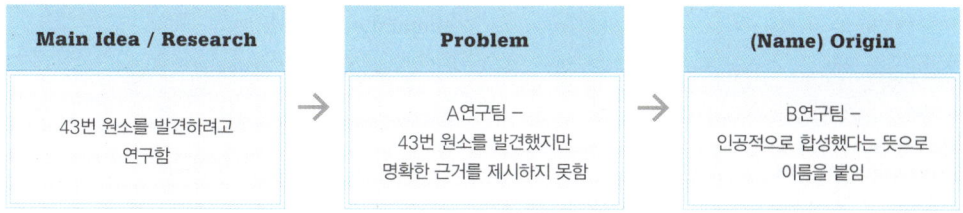

핵/심/표/현

- acid   n. 산, 산성물질
- activate   v. 활성화시키다
- adhere   v. 붙다
- advocate   v. 지지하다, 옹호하다
- ailment   n. 질병
- allotrope   n. 동소체
- alloy metal   합금
- aluminum   n. 알루미늄
- artificial   adj. 인조의
- atom   n. 원자
- atomic number   원자번호
- binding agent   결합 매개체[물]
- biochemistry   n. 생화학
- calcium   n. 칼슘
- carbohydrate   n. 탄수화물
- carbon   n. 탄소
- carbon dioxide   n. 이산화탄소
- carbonic acid   n. 탄산
- catch   n. (숨은) 단점, 함정
- charcoal   n. 숯
- chemical reaction   화학 반응
- chemist   n. 화학자, 약사
- compound   n. 화합물, 합성물
- conceptualize   v. 개념화하다
- conductor   n. (전기나 열의) 전도체
- constituent   n. 구성 요소
- copper   n. 구리
- cosmetic   n. 화장품
- crude oil   n. 원유
- cyclotron   n. 사이클로트론
- cylinder   n. 원통형 용기
- decay   v. 부패하다, 쇠퇴하다
- derivative   n. 파생물

- dissolve   v. 녹이다, 용해시키다
- durable   adj. 내구성이 있는
- dye   v. 염색하다, 물들이다
- elastic   adj. 탄력[신축성] 있는
- electron   n. 전자
- electrolysis   n. 전기 분해
- element   n. 원소
- excess   adj. 초과한
- flammable   adj. 가연성의
- gap   n. 틈, 간격
- gasoline   n. 휘발유
- hexagonal   adj. 육각형의
- hydrogen   n. 수소
- impurity   n. 불순물
- inauthentic   adj. 진짜가 아닌, 모조의
- ingredient   n. 재료, 성분
- inorganic chemistry   무기 화학
- insulator   n. 절연체
- intact   adj. 온전한
- ion   n. 이온
- iron   n. 쇠, 철
- isotope   n. 동위 원소
- lattice   n. 격자, 격자 모양의 것
- lead   n. 납
- liquefy   v. 액화하다, 액화시키다
- malleable   adj. 펴 늘일 수 있는
- material   n. 재료
- matter   n. 물질, 성분
- methane   n. 메탄
- minute   adj. 극히 작은, 미세한
- molecule   n. 분자
- neutron   n. 중성자
- nickel   n. 니켈

- nitrogen   n. 질소
- nucleus   n. 핵, 세포 핵
- ore sample   광물 샘플
- organic chemistry   n. 유기 화학
- organic material   n. 유기 물질
- oxide   n. 산화물
- oxidize   v. 산화시키다
- oxygen   n. 산소
- petroleum   n. 석유
- phosphorus   n. 인
- platinum   n. 백금
- polymerization   n. 중합
- property   n. 특징, 속성
- proton number   양성자 번호
- proton   n. 양성자
- purely   adv. 순수하게
- purifier   n. 정화 장치
- quantum   n. 양자
- radioactive   adj. 방사성[능]의

- reduction   n. (화학) 환원
- refine   v. 정제하다, 제련하다
- release   n. 방출, 유출
- residue   n. 잔여물
- resistant   adj. 저항력이 있는
- rust   n. 녹
- salinity   n. 염분, 염도
- silicon   n. 실리콘, 규소
- shifting   adj. 변하기 쉬운; 바뀌는
- sodium   n. 나트륨
- solution   n. 용액
- spherical   adj. 구형의, 구체의
- substance   n. 물질, 개체, 구성 요소
- sulfur   n. (유)황
- sulphide   n. 황화물
- synthesize   v. 합성하다
- synthetic   adj. 합성한, 인조의
- toxic   adj. 독성이 있는
- undesirable   adj. 원하지 않는

Sample Questions

[01 ~ 06] Listen to part of a lecture in a chemistry class. Then answer the questions.

MP3 60 정답 및 해석 p. 134

 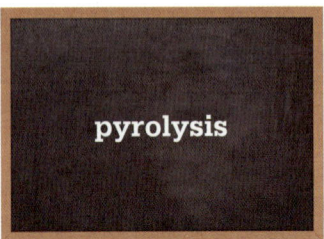

Note-taking

- Main Idea:
- Term:
- Cause:
- Ordering:
- Advantage:
- Cause & Effect:

- Advantage:
- Function:
- Difference:

01 What is the lecture mainly about?
 Ⓐ The types of woods that make the best charcoal
 Ⓑ How two different types of charcoal are created
 Ⓒ How carbon reacts with other gases
 Ⓓ The dangers of using wood as a cooking fuel

02 According to the professor, why is charcoal made in pits or ovens?
 Ⓐ To raise the temperature of the heat
 Ⓑ To avoid the release of carbon into the air
 Ⓒ To prevent injuries from the flames
 Ⓓ To lessen the amount of air present

03 What can be inferred about charcoal with a high water content?
- Ⓐ It will burn out more quickly.
- Ⓑ It will be better for filtration.
- Ⓒ It will produce more smoke.
- Ⓓ It will produce hotter temperatures.

04 According to the professor, what are the advantages of charcoal when it comes to cooking? Choose two answers.
- Ⓐ It removes excess water from the food.
- Ⓑ It retains high heat for longer periods.
- Ⓒ It can be used repeatedly.
- Ⓓ It creates less smoke.

05 Why does the professor mention air and water purifiers?
- Ⓐ To introduce another function of charcoal
- Ⓑ To give an example of how charcoal is made
- Ⓒ To suggest a new way to utilize heat from charcoal
- Ⓓ To illustrate how impurities are filtered from wood

06 What can be inferred about cooking charcoal?
- Ⓐ It is produced through a process that takes many years.
- Ⓑ It can be burned easily except in lower temperatures.
- Ⓒ It contains more toxic chemicals than a piece of wood.
- Ⓓ It has fewer holes in its surface than activated charcoal.

▶ **Question Review**

Main Idea
숯의 제조과정

Term
pyrolysis 용어 설명

Cause
산소 없이 나무를 태우기 위함

Ordering
숯 만드는 과정 – 산소 없이 태워 수분과 위험 물질을 태워 없앰

Advantage
숯의 장점
(1) 연기가 거의 없음

Listen to part of a lecture in a chemistry class.

Professor(female): So far we have been talking about carbon-based fuels. One of the most basic fuels is charcoal, which is primarily used for cooking in many parts of the world. Now, we have to think of why people cook with charcoal. It would be easier to use wood as a cooking fuel, right? I mean, essentially, that's where charcoal comes from. But the real reason lies in what is removed from wood when it turns into charcoal. To understand **Q1** **why charcoal is so effective when used as a cooking fuel, we must first look at how charcoal is made.** So, does anyone know how charcoal is made?

Student(male): Yeah, I remember reading that you have to burn wood to create charcoal. But what I don't get is… I mean, doesn't wood just turn into ash? I don't get how it stays intact.

P: That's a good question. The reason why the wood just doesn't burn away is because of the way it is baked. **Q1** **Charcoal is produced through slow pyrolysis (shown on screen). This is a method of heating wood in the absence of oxygen.** When organic materials such as wood are heated, they react with oxygen, causing a lot of the carbon in the material to be burned away. But what if we were to take oxygen out of the equation? That's the key to making charcoal. Through pyrolysis, char, a solid residue rich in carbon content, is created. The gas and liquid elements leave the wood, and a purer form of carbon is left behind. This is essentially what charcoal is. **Q2** **In order to burn wood without oxygen, the wood is buried in a pit or placed in specially designed kilns, a kind of oven.** This process also removes lots of undesirable elements from wood. For one thing, wood contains a lot of water, which can cause lower temperatures when the wood is burned. But when wood is heated without oxygen, the water molecules evaporate. And dangerous substances such as methane and hydrogen are also burned off. You'd be surprised at how much of these unneeded substances are present in wood. In the end, only about a fourth of the original volume of the wood is left. What's left is mostly carbon. Without these unwanted elements, charcoal has several advantages. For starters, **Q4-D** **it produces little smoke.** So, who likes to go camping?

S: I do, I just went the other weekend with my friends.

P: All right. So I assume you guys made a campfire. Tell me about the smoke.

Cause & Effect 나무의 불필요한 성분이 연기를 발생시킴	S: Hmm… Well, there was a lot of it, I had to move from one place to another to dodge it. P: That's because >Q3> **wood has a lot of unnecessary contents, such as water, gases, and what not. All of these things cause smoke. Believe it or not, the smoke that you see, well, a lot of that is actually vapor.** Some charcoal manufacturers use this as a way to improve their charcoal. Depending on how the charcoal is made, the amount of smoke it produces varies. Sometimes we want a little smoke to add that charcoal flavor we all enjoy.
Advantage 숯의 장점 (2) 나무보다 더 오래, 더 뜨겁게 연소	>Q4-B> **Another benefit is that charcoal burns longer, hotter, and more steadily than wood.** When charcoal is burned, oxygen molecules bond with the molecules of carbon, which forms new gases. These gases create scorching hot heat, rising up and cooking the food. The more carbon content there is to react with the oxygen, the more heat it can produce. So, naturally, since charcoal is basically the carbon left over from burnt wood, a given amount of charcoal will burn much longer than an equal amount of wood.
Function 숯의 또 다른 용도 – 물·공기 정화	Now, >Q5> **there are also some other ways that charcoal is used. You may own an air or water purifier with a charcoal filter.** The charcoal used for filtration is called activated charcoal. This type of charcoal is a little different from the charcoal we use for cooking. I mean, you could use cooking charcoal to filter things, but it wouldn't do too good of a job.
Difference 요리용 숯과 정화용 숯의 차이점 – 극대화된 숯의 흡수 성질	>Q6> **The biggest difference is that activated charcoal maximizes the absorption qualities of charcoal.** I mean, all types of charcoal have purifying capabilities, but it's best to maximize the surface area available for absorption and chemical reactions. So, how do we make this type of charcoal? We basically overcook it. Remember how charcoal is manufactured? Without oxygen, right? >Q1> **At the end of the process of manufacturing regular charcoal, we expose the charcoal to oxygen for a little while. This process is called activation…** exposing carbon to oxidizing air. This causes the oxygen to dig tiny holes in the surface of the charcoal. >Q6> **These tiny holes create a greater surface area, which maximizes the purifying qualities of the charcoal.**

Practice Questions

[01 ~ 06] Listen to part of a lecture in a chemistry class. Then answer the questions.

MP3 61   정답 및 해석 p. 136

Note-taking

01   What is the lecture mainly about?
   Ⓐ How a new kind of non-metal substance was invented
   Ⓑ The properties of a certain alloy made with two metals
   Ⓒ How the properties of metals can be changed with heat
   Ⓓ Different types of metal alloys and their applications

02   What can be inferred about nitinol?
   Ⓐ It will not bend as much as titanium.
   Ⓑ It will melt at lower temperatures.
   Ⓒ It will split into two metals when heated.
   Ⓓ It will bend more than titanium.

03 What does the professor imply about nitinol's "memory" ability?
   Ⓐ It is useful for weapons.
   Ⓑ It was not an intended function.
   Ⓒ It was copied from musical instruments.
   Ⓓ It can be found in many metals.

04 Why does the professor mention melting ice?
   Ⓐ To illustrate why heating changes a structure
   Ⓑ To demonstrate the different properties of different substances
   Ⓒ To give an example of molecular structural change
   Ⓓ To show how objects react when heated and cooled

05 According to the professor, what will happen if nitinol is bent while heated?
   Ⓐ It will become weak and break easily.
   Ⓑ It will bend more easily in the future.
   Ⓒ It will return to that shape when heated again.
   Ⓓ It will stay in that shape forever.

06 What does the professor mention as examples of practical uses of nitinol?
   Choose two answers.
   Ⓐ Making durable frames for glasses
   Ⓑ Coating missile cones with a strong substance
   Ⓒ Preventing ice cubes from melting quickly
   Ⓓ Creating braces that don't need to be tightened
   Ⓔ Keeping stainless steel from rusting easily

03 Earth Science

TOEFL에서 earth science지구과학 분야는 지구에서 벌어지는 특정 현상의 Cause원인과 Effect영향에 대해 강의하는 지문이 출제된다. 또한, 어려운 용어의 정의나, 원리를 쉽게 설명하기 위해 언급한 Example 문제가 자주 나온다. 어렵고 낯선 전문용어들 때문에 지문이 안 들린다고 너무 당황하지 말고, 침착하게 지구과학에서 자주 출제되는 출제포인트에 focus를 두고 지문을 이해하고 연습문제를 풀어보도록 한다.

출제포인트
- Q1 Main Idea
- Q2 Function (Application)
- Q3 Problem
- Q4 Solution (Suggestion)
- Q5 Example
- Q6 Cause (Evidence) & Effect (Result / Finding / Research)
- Q7 Similarity / Difference
- Q8 Advantage / Disadvantage
- Q9 Misunderstanding / Correction
- Q10 Definition (Term) / Origin
- Q11 Two Click / Three Click
- Q12 Ordering
- Q13 Matching
- Q14 Opinion / Attitude
- Q15 Headset
- Q16 Requirement (Condition)
- Q17 Character
- Q18 Imply / Infer

1 Sahara Desert 사하라 사막

몇천 년 전 사하라 사막은 풀이 나는 지역이었으며, 비록 열대 우림은 아니었지만 지금과는 굉장히 다른 환경을 가지고 있었다.^{Q9} 그 증거로, 그 지역 사람들이 그린 동굴 벽화에서 hippo하마 그림이 발견되었고, pollen꽃가루이 화석으로 발견되기도 하였다.^{Q6} 사하라 지역이 사막으로 변한 이유는 지구의 움직임과 관련이 있다.^{Q6} 여름과 겨울의 발생은 지구가 태양과 얼마나 가까이 있느냐에서 기인한다. Ice Age빙하 시대도 지구가 태양과 멀어지면서 발생한 것이다. 이런 지구 움직임의 변화로 monsoon우기, 장마이 이동한 것이 사하라 지역이 사막화된 이유이다.^{Q6} monsoon이 이동하니 비가 내리지 않았고, 따라서 식물이 죽어서 땅에 습기가 없어지고, 습기가 없어지니 구름을 만들 수 있는 수분이 없어 구름이 생기지 않는 cycle주기이 반복되어 사막화라는 결과를 낳았다.^{Q6} 한편, 사하라 지역에 비가 내리지 않는 drought가뭄이 장기화되자 사람들은 근처의 이집트로 이주하였는데,^{Q6} 이것을 Nile River나일강를 따라 형성된 이집트 문명 발전의 원동력으로 보는 사람들도 있다.

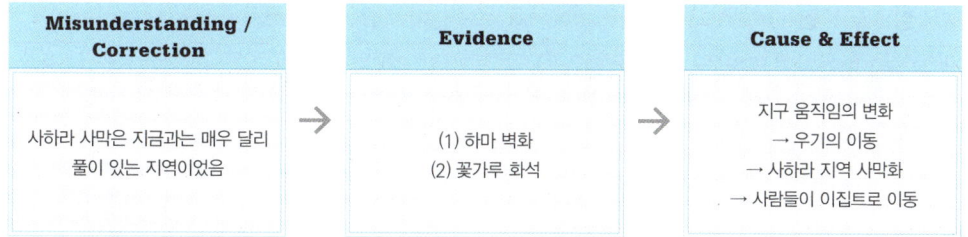

2 Coriolis Effect 코리올리 효과

Coriolis effect는 약간 생소한 주제일 수 있다. 만일 한 사람이 북극에 있다고 하고, 다른 한 사람은 북극에서 일직선으로 내려온 적도 지점에 있다고 상상해 보자.[95] 북극에 있는 사람이 적도에 있는 사람을 향해 미사일을 발사할 경우, 미사일은 그 사람에게 떨어지지 않고 (쏘는 사람 입장에서) 오른쪽으로 휜다. 미사일이 날아오는 동안 지구가 오른쪽으로 자전하여 적도에 있는 사람도 지구와 같이 움직였기 때문이다.[95, 96] 만일 반대로 적도에서 북극에 있는 사람에게 미사일을 쏜다고 가정하면, 마찬가지로 미사일은 똑바로 날아가지 않고 (쏘는 사람 입장에서) 왼쪽으로 휘는 것처럼 보인다. 이렇게 지구의 자전 때문에 경로가 휘어져 발생하는 편차를 **Coriolis effect**라고 한다.[96] 이 현상을 이해하는 것은 특히 일기예보를 할 때 매우 중요하다. 예를 들면, 북극에서 오는 찬 바람은 지구의 자전 현상 때문에 똑바로 밑으로 내려올 수 없게 되는데, 바람의 패턴은 날씨에 커다란 영향을 미치므로, 어느 지역의 정확한 날씨와 폭풍의 양상을 예상하기 위해서는 기상학자가 이 패턴을 이해해야만 한다.[92]

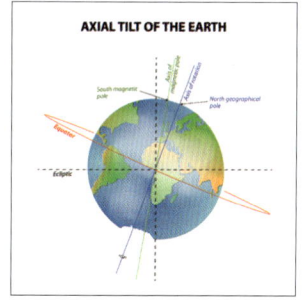

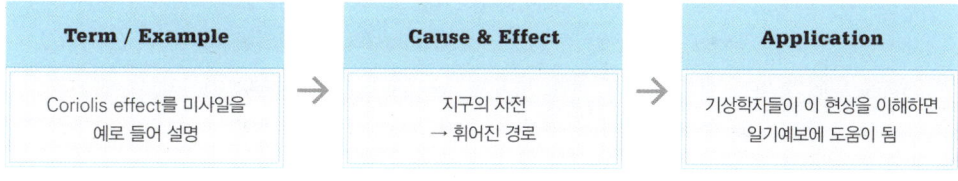

핵/심/표/현

- abrupt   adj. 갑작스런, 돌연한
- accelerate   v. 가속화하다
- accomplish   v. 달성하다, 성취하다
- align   v. 일직선으로 하다
- aquifer   n. 대수층(지하수를 품고 있는 지층)
- axis   n. 중심축
- barely   adv. 간신히, 가까스로
- bothersome   adj. 성가신, 귀찮은
- briefly   adv. 간단히
- climate change   기후 변화
- clockwise   adj./adv. 시계 방향의[으로]
- confirmation   n. 확인, 확답
- counter-clockwise   adj./adv. 시계 반대 방향의[으로]
- deficit   n. 부족
- devise   v. 궁리하다, 고안하다
- differentiate   v. 구분하다, 구별하다
- distribute   v. 분배하다
- documented   adj. 문서로 기록된
- drastic   adj. 과감한, 극단적인
- effect   n. 효과, 영향
- equator   n. 적도
- examine   v. 검사하다, 조사하다
- exploitation   n. 개발, 이용
- external   adj. 외부의
- flattened   adj. 반듯해진, 평평해진
- flourish   v. 번창하다, 번영하다
- fossilized   adj. 화석화된
- generate   v. 발생시키다
- glacier   n. 빙하
- global warming   지구 온난화
- gradual   adj. 서서히 일어나는, 점진[점차]적인
- gravity   n. 중력
- greenery   n. 푸른 나무
- hardened   adj. 딱딱하게 굳은
- harmless   adj. 무해한
- heavy machinery   중장비
- high tide   n. 만조, 밀물
- hydrothermal   adj. 열수의[에 의한]
- hypothesize   v. 가설[추측]을 세우다
- immobile   adj. 움직이지 않는
- impetus   n. 자극, 추동력
- indicate   v. 나타내다, 보여주다
- inertia   n. 관성
- intersection   n. 교점, 교차점
- layer   n. (지)층
- low tide   n. 간조, 썰물
- mass   n. 질량
- measurable   adj. 측정 가능한
- mobile   adj. 이동하는, 움직이는
- motion   n. 동작, 움직임
- natural forces   자연력
- occasional   adj. 가끔의
- occurrence   n. 발생
- orbit   v. 공전하다
- overnight   adv. 밤사이에, 밤 동안
- overview   n. 개요, 총람, 개관
- parameter   n. 매개 변수
- particularly   adv. 특히, 특별히
- permeate   v. 스며들다, 침투하다
- possibility   n. 가능성
- practically   adv. 사실상, 현실적으로
- prevail   v. 만연하다, 우세하다
- promising   adj. 유망한, 촉망되는
- proximity   n. 가까움
- refinement   n. 개선, 발전

- regardless   adv. 개의치 않고, 상관없이
- reshaping   n. 형성
- retain   v. 유지하다, 지속하다
- resistive force   저항력
- revolutionary   adj. 혁명적인
- rotate   v. 회전하다, 자전하다
- rotation   n. 자전
- satellite   n. 인공위성
- scattered   adj. 흩어진, 퍼져 있는
- screening   n. 심사, 선발
- slippery   adj. 미끄러운
- speculate   v. 추측하다
- spin   v. 돌다
- spiral   adj. 나선형의
- stationary   adj. 정지된
- surplus   n. 과잉
- swampy land   n. 늪 지대
- technical advance   기술 진보[발전]
- tidal range   n. 조차
- tide   n. 조수(밀물과 썰물)
- tiny   adj. 아주 작은
- tremendous   adj. 대단한, 엄청난
- underbrush   n. 덤불
- vast   adj. 방대한, 넓은 범위의
- vegetated   adj. 초목이 있는
- wetland   n. 습지
- widespread   adj. 널리 퍼진, 광범위한

Sample Questions

[01 ~ 06] Listen to part of a lecture in an earth science class. Then answer the questions.

MP3 62 정답 및 해석 p. 139

Note-taking

- Term:
- Main Idea:
- Research:
- Cause & Effect:
- Example:

- Cause & Effect:
- Finding:

01 What is the lecture mainly about?
  Ⓐ How to calculate the length of a day
  Ⓑ The effect of human activities on the length of a day
  Ⓒ How the rotational axis is affected by global warming
  Ⓓ The effects of global warming on the Earth's rotation

02 Why does the professor discuss the redistribution of water?
  Ⓐ To give an example of a problem associated with global warming
  Ⓑ To illustrate how a serious problem has been corrected
  Ⓒ To show how human activities can contribute to a shift in the Earth's mass
  Ⓓ To explain the relationship between the weight of water and the Earth's orbit

03 According to the professor, what do reservoirs have to do with the Earth's mass?
   Ⓐ They have distributed it evenly.
   Ⓑ They have increased it slightly.
   Ⓒ They have made it harder to measure.
   Ⓓ They have moved it closer to the Earth's axis.

04 What does the professor say about the length of a day?
   Ⓐ It has decreased greatly.
   Ⓑ It has gotten slightly shorter.
   Ⓒ It has increased a significant amount.
   Ⓓ It has caused global warming.

05 According to the professor, what do a skater and the earth have in common?
   Ⓐ They require external forces to spin faster.
   Ⓑ They can shift their center of mass to control their spin.
   Ⓒ They can only spin as fast as their weight will allow.
   Ⓓ They spin faster when their weight is closer to their axis.

06 Why does the professor mention atomic clocks?
   Ⓐ To give an example of a harmful human activity
   Ⓑ To explain how the speed of the Earth's rotation is measured
   Ⓒ To emphasize how little the length of a day has changed
   Ⓓ To introduce another problem caused by water redistribution

▶ **Question Review**

Listen to part of a lecture in an earth science class.

Professor(male): As we all know, the Earth rotates on its axis – the imaginary line that runs through the center of the Earth from the North Pole to the South Pole – while it orbits the Sun. The length of our days is calculated by this rotation. That is, the amount of time the Earth needs to spin completely around on its axis is called a day, which is 24 hours. Now, the original cause to this rotation is uncertain, but the continued rotation of the Earth is believed to be a product of inertia. Inertia, of course, is the tendency of objects to resist any changes to their state of motion – immobile objects tend to stay immobile, while those in motion tend to stay in motion. Some speculate that the Earth started spinning when our solar system was born, and, since there were no resistive forces trying to slow the Earth down, it keeps on spinning to this day.

Most of you might think that the length of a day has been the same since the Earth was formed, but what if I were to tell you that the time the Earth needs to spin completely can change? **Q1** **This is what I'd like to talk about today. Now, what if I were to also tell you that humans can actually change the speed of its rotation?** Of course, no single human being can have an effect on the Earth, but the combination of human activities over the past 50 years has actually made the Earth rotate faster, thus **Q4** **making our days literally shorter than they were a century ago.**

Student(female): But how do we know that the Earth is spinning faster?

P: We can figure the Earth's rotation speed through the use of satellites. We can send a signal to a stationary satellite and calculate the time the signal takes to come back. This way, we have an absolute reference. So, anyone have any idea on why the Earth is spinning faster?

S: Does it have to do with global warming? I mean, the North and South Poles are heavily affected by global warming, with glaciers melting and creating more water. Does that have anything to do with the axis? I mean, the axis can have an effect on rotational speed, right?

P: Well, the axis is not affected by human activities, but you are partially right in that water has something to do with it. **Q2** **Since the 1950s, human beings have made about 10,000 artificial reservoirs all over the world. This means a tremendous amount of water has been redistributed. I mean, water is incredibly heavy, and mass has a big effect on rotational inertia.** Most of the Earth's water was located near the equator, the midway point between the North and South Poles, meaning that

---

Term
inertia 용어 설명

Main Idea
인류 활동이 하루의 길이가 바뀌는 것에 영향을 미치는가

Research
인공위성을 통해 지구의 자전 속도를 측정

Cause & Effect
저수지로 인해 적도 부근의 물이 남쪽과 북쪽으로 재분배될 때 생기는 결과

most of the water was located in areas that are the farthest away from the Earth's axis. However, the construction of reservoirs has moved a lot of water to the northern and southern parts of the world. And hence... hence what?

S: The Earth's mass was redistributed.

P: That's right.

S: But what does that have to do with shorter days?

P: Okay, now, you are familiar with rotational inertia, right? The distribution of an object's mass has an effect on its center of mass and the speed at which it spins. Take figure skaters, for example. When an ice skater performs a spin, did you notice how **Q5** **they spin slowly with their legs and arms out but spin much faster as they pull their legs and arms closer to their bodies? They're not using any strength to move faster but are merely making their center of mass closer to their axis. This naturally makes them spin much faster.**

Q3 **When water was redistributed from equatorial regions to the north and south, the water got closer to the Earth's axis,** just like when skaters pull their arms closer. Naturally, since the Earth's mass becomes closer to its axis, the speed at which it spins will become faster. Now, we don't have to worry about any environmental effects like we do with global warming. **Q4 Q6** **Atomic clocks show that a day has decreased by about eight millionths of second. It's not significant enough to impact anything,** but this is the first time that any measurable result in the Earth's rotation has been seen as a result of human activities.

Example
질량과 회전체의 회전 속도와의 관계를 피겨 스케이트 선수를 예로 들어 설명

Cause & Effect
지구의 질량 재분배와 지구의 자전 속도와의 관계를 설명

Finding
환경에 영향이 없고, 아주 미묘한 변화임을 확인

Practice Questions

[01 ~ 06] **Listen to part of a lecture in an earth science class. Then answer the questions.**

MP3 63   정답 및 해석 p. 141

Note-taking

01 What is the lecture mainly about?
    Ⓐ Theories about why tidal ranges vary in certain seasons
    Ⓑ The information needed to accurately predict tides
    Ⓒ Environmental changes that occur following a high tide
    Ⓓ How to predict weather by looking at rainclouds

02 Why does the professor mention rainfall when mentioning tides?
    Ⓐ To suggest that both can be predicted in a similar way
    Ⓑ To imply that one is a natural force and the other is not
    Ⓒ To note that one needs to be predicted to predict the other
    Ⓓ To explain that causes of tides are known but not the causes of weather

03 According to the professor, what happens when the sun and moon are farthest from each other?
    Ⓐ The lowest tides are produced.
    Ⓑ Most tidal patterns are accelerated.
    Ⓒ The location of the high tide changes.
    Ⓓ Some of the highest tides of the year take place.

04 What can be inferred about tidal ranges?
    Ⓐ They cannot be predicted beforehand.
    Ⓑ They remain constant regardless of the sun's location.
    Ⓒ They affect the level of water during the high tide.
    Ⓓ They are affected by the location of the sun and moon.

05 According to the professor, why does the moon have a stronger effect on tides than the sun?
    Ⓐ It rotates around the earth.
    Ⓑ It is closer to the earth.
    Ⓒ It is illuminated by the sun.
    Ⓓ It has stronger gravity.

06 According to the professor, what is a use of tidal range predictions?
    Ⓐ They can provide data to calculate energy demand in advance.
    Ⓑ They can help fisheries predict the best time to catch fish.
    Ⓒ They can be used to find the proper locations for tidal energy plants.
    Ⓓ They can assist in measuring the orbiting speeds of the sun and moon.

04 Environmental Science

TOEFL의 environmental science환경 과학 분야에서는 alternative energy대체에너지에 관한 내용이 제일 많이 출제되었다. 지금까지 solar energy태양 에너지, wind energy풍력, wave energy파동 에너지, OTEC(ocean thermal energy conversion)햇빛에 의한 바닷물의 온도 변화 차이를 이용한 발전 등의 주제가 출제되었다. 강의의 전개방식이 조금씩 다르기는 해도, 석유나 석탄과 같은 fossil fuel화석 연료의 문제점 또는 대체에너지의 장단점을 논하는 지문이 자주 출제되고 있으며, 각 종류의 대체에너지를 만드는 과정을 소개하는 지문도 출제될 가능성이 있다. 또한, 자연 활동이나 인간의 활동에 의한 자연 변화가 동식물에 미치는 영향도 출제 가능성이 매우 높은 주제인데, 이런 주제의 강의에서는 자연 변화가 미치는 영향과 이를 해결하는 방법 등을 묻는 문제가 종종 출제된다.

출제포인트
- Q1 Main Idea
- Q2 Function (Application)
- Q3 Problem
- Q4 Solution (Suggestion)
- Q5 Example
- Q6 Cause (Evidence) & Effect (Result / Finding / Research)
- Q7 Similarity / Difference
- Q8 Advantage / Disadvantage
- Q9 Misunderstanding / Correction
- Q10 Definition (Term) / Origin
- Q11 Two Click / Three Click
- Q12 Ordering
- Q13 Matching
- Q14 Opinion / Attitude
- Q15 Headset
- Q16 Requirement (Condition)
- Q17 Character
- Q18 Imply / Infer

1 Humming Bird벌새

사람들이 humming bird의 서식지에 농사 지을 땅을 개간하고 가축을 키움으로써, 벌새의 서식지가 파괴되어 population개체 수가 줄어들었다.^{Q3} 그 해결방안으로, 벌새의 서식지를 보호하고 ecotourism생태 관광을 육성하는 방법^{Q4}이 있다. ecotourism의 예로는, 조류 서식지를 잘 보존하여 조류학자나 사진작가들이 연구나 촬영을 위해 이곳으로 몰려오면, 마을 차원에서 이들에게 숙식을 제공하여 생긴 수익을 조류 서식지를 더 잘 보호하는 데 쓰는 경우를 들 수 있다. 또한, 벌새를 잘 보호하기 위해서는 새에 대해서도 잘 알아야 하므로, 벌새의 이동 경로나 벌새가 서식하기 좋은 환경 등을 연구하여^{Q6} 유용한 정보로 활용하고 있다.

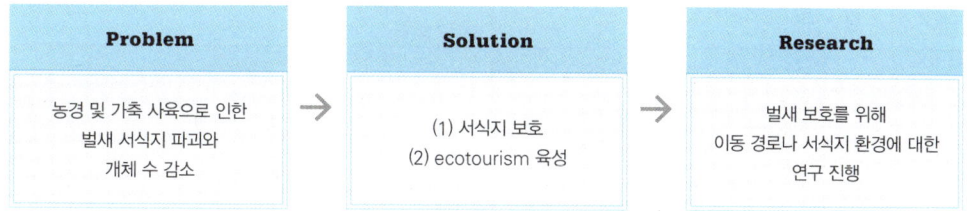

2 Tundra 툰드라

Alaska 지역의 tundra는 원래 평평한 지역으로, 매우 춥고 강수량이 없기 때문에 식물이 거의 살지 않는다. 하지만 최근 기후 변화로 인해 온도가 올라가면서 tundra에 shrub관목이 늘고 있다.[Q1] tundra는 매우 추워서 표토층이 두 겹으로 되어 있는데, 봄이 오면 위층의 땅은 녹지만 아래층의 땅은 녹지 않는 permafrost영구 동토(영원히 얼어 있는 땅)으로 남아 있다. 따라서 위층의 땅에는 shrub이 살 수 있는데, shrub은 키가 낮아 강한 바람이 불어도 괜찮고 뿌리를 깊게 내리지 않아서 permafrost까지 닿지 않기 때문이다.[Q6] 식물은 온도가 따뜻한 곳에서 더 잘 자라지만, 놀랍게도 tundra의 shrub은 겨울에 더 잘 자란다. 그 이유는 microbe미생물 때문이다. 겨울에 눈이 쌓이면 microbe가 서식하기에 좋은 조건이 되는데, 쌓인 눈 아래에서 microbe가 식물에 필요한 영양분을 많이 만들어 낸다. 이 때문에, shrub이 여름이 아닌 겨울에 오히려 더 잘 자랄 수 있는 것이다.[Q6]

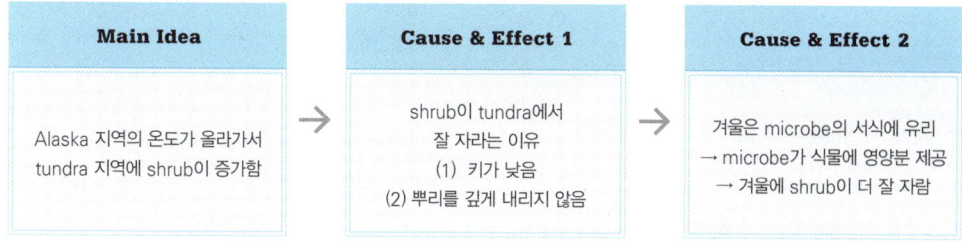

핵/심/표/현

- alternative energy 대체에너지
- atmosphere n. 대기
- avalanche n. 눈사태, 산사태
- beachfront n. 해변, 해안지대
- blizzard n. 눈보라, 폭설
- breeze n. 산들바람
- buffer n. 완충물
- capture v. 잡다, 포획하다
- carnivore n. 육식동물
- climate n. 날씨, 기후
- coastal zone 연안역
- cold front 한랭 전선, 한파
- complexity n. 복잡함
- compress v. 압축하다
- condensation n. (기체의) 응결
- constitute v. 구성하다
- convection current 대류
- decline v. 감소하다, 떨어지다
- Celsius degree n. 섭씨 온도
- delist v. (목록에서) 지우다
- devastation n. 황폐, 대대적인 파괴
- downpour n. 폭우, 호우
- droplet n. 작은 물방울
- dune n. 모래언덕, 사구
- dwindle v. 점차 감소하다
- encroach v. 침해하다, 잠식하다
- entangle v. 얽어 매다, 꼼짝 못하게 하다
- erosion n. 침식
- evaporation n. 증발
- excrete v. 배설하다, 분비하다
- Fahrenheit degree 화씨 온도
- feasible adj. 실현 가능한
- food chain n. 먹이사슬
- food web n. 먹이 그물
- forecast / predict v. (날씨) 예측[예보]하다
- frost n. 서리 v. 성에가 끼다
- funnel n. 깔때기 v. (깔대기 같이 좁은 공간 속을) 이동하다
- gale n. 강풍, 돌풍
- generator n. 발전기
- graze v. 풀을 뜯다[먹다]
- habitat n. 서식지
- hail n. 우박
- harness v. 이용하다
- herbivore n. 초식동물
- humid adj. 습한
- hygrometer n. 습도계
- impermeable adj. 불침투성의, (액체기체를) 통과시키지 않는
- inland adv. 내륙으로
- inshore adj. 연안의
- intervention n. 개입, 간섭
- ionosphere n. 이온층, 전리층
- lifespan n. 수명
- mesosphere n. (지구 대기의) 중간권
- microbe n. 미생물
- mist n. 안개 v. 흐려지다
- moist adj. 촉촉한, 습한
- moisture n. 수분, 습기
- monsoon n. 우기, 장마
- numerical adj. 숫자의, 수량의
- oceanography n. 해양학
- organism n. 유기체, 생물
- permafrost n. 영구 동토층
- photosynthesis n. 광합성
- precipitation n. 강수, 강수량

- predator   n. 포식자
- prevalent   adj. 널리 퍼진, 일반적인
- prey   n. 먹이, 먹잇감
- prolonged   adj. 장기간의
- promising   adj. 유망한
- recede   v. 물러나다, 멀어지다
- recycle   v. 재활용하다
- renewed   adj. 새로워진
- sandstorm   n. 모래폭풍, 황사
- saturate   v. 흠뻑 적시다, 포화시키다
- semiarid   adj. 반 건조의
- shower   n. 소나기
- shrub   n. 관목
- smog   n. 스모그, 연무
- snowstorm   n. 폭설, 눈보라
- solar energy   태양 에너지
- spell   v. (보통 나쁜 결과를) 가져오다, 의미하다
- stark   adj. 극명한; 냉혹한; 삭막한
- station   n. 정거장 v. 주둔시키다
- stratosphere   n. 성층권
- supportive   adj. 힘을 주는, 도와주는
- susceptible   adj. 민감한

- sustainable   adj. 지속 가능한
- temperature   n. 온도
- tempest   n. 사나운[거센] 태풍
- thaw   v. (얼음 등이) 녹다; 날이 해동하다
- thermometer   n. 온도계
- tidal   adj. 조수의
- tidal fluctuation   조석 변동
- tolerant   adj. 잘 견디는
- tornado   n. 토네이도, 회오리바람
- torrential   adj. 폭우가 내리는
- tracking   n. 추적
- troposphere   n. 대류권
- twister   n. 회오리바람, 토네이도
- typhoon   n. 태풍, 폭풍
- underlying   adj. 근본적인, 밑에 있는
- unsound   adj. 오류가 있는
- upper atmosphere   초고층 대기
- vegetation   n. 초목, 식물
- velocity   n. (빠른) 속도
- warm air mass   온난기단
- wave energy   파동[파력] 에너지
- wind energy   풍력

Sample Questions

[01 ~ 06] **Listen to part of a lecture in an environmental science class. Then answer the questions.** MP3 64 정답 및 해석 p. 144

Note-taking

• Attitude:

• Main Idea:

• Term:

• Example:

• Cause:

• Function:

• Opinion:

• Function:

• Problem:

01 What is the lecture mainly about?
   Ⓐ An efficient solution to the problem of beach erosion
   Ⓑ Reasons why the coast is unsuitable for development
   Ⓒ A comparison of the different types of sand found on beaches
   Ⓓ How the value of real estate changes depending on its location

02 What does the professor say about the trough?
   Ⓐ It is the closest zone to the beach.
   Ⓑ It protects the primary dune from the ocean.
   Ⓒ It is unable to withstand any human activity.
   Ⓓ It is stable enough to be built on.

03 Why does the professor mention walking on a peninsula?
    Ⓐ To reminds the students of the details of a field study
    Ⓑ To illustrate one of the different coastal zones
    Ⓒ To give an example of how shorelines change
    Ⓓ To show that beaches are environmentally sensitive

04 According to the professor, what possible problems can be caused by building on the primary dune? **Choose two answers.**
    Ⓐ The plants that live there will be killed.
    Ⓑ The groundwater will be polluted.
    Ⓒ The secondary dune will get bigger.
    Ⓓ The beach's sand will move inland.

05 What is the professor's attitude towards people who buy beachfront houses?
    Ⓐ He feels they are misunderstood.
    Ⓑ He believes they are foolish.
    Ⓒ He hopes they will protect inland areas.
    Ⓓ He thinks they are lucky.

06 Why does the professor mention his "dream house"?
    Ⓐ To illustrate the dangers of building on the beach
    Ⓑ To show a more positive view of coastal development
    Ⓒ To indicate that his home was affected by the changing coastline
    Ⓓ To give an example of environmentally responsible construction

▶ **Question Review**

Attitude
해변에 위치한 집을 사는 것은 현명한 생각이 아님

Main Idea
❋ 강의의 주제가 구체적이지 않으므로 이런 경우는 중반 이상까지 주의해서 들어봐야 알 수 있다.

Term
연안역
(1) 해변
(2) 모래언덕

모래언덕
(1) 1차 모래언덕
(2) 골(trough)
(3) 2차 모래언덕
(4) 뒤쪽 모래언덕

Example
해안선이 계속 변한다는 것을 교수의 개인적인 경험을 예로 들어 설명

Cause
연안역이 중요한 이유 – 연안지역 보호(완충장치 역할)

Listen to part of a lecture in an environmental science class.

Professor(male): All right, so let me tell you a little story about when I was looking for a house, uh... about 10 years ago. **Q5** **My two kids really wanted a beachfront house. They wanted to be as close to the beach as possible. I tried to explain to them that building near the beach just doesn't make sense.** But the kids still had that dream of living near the ocean. So, my wife and I looked at a few homes... Oh man, were they beautiful! I saw our family's dream house, but we couldn't afford it. But I think it was a blessing in disguise, I'll tell you why a little later... Uh, where was I? Oh, so we just ended up living in a house that's a 15-minute drive from the beach.

Student(female): Uh... Professor Jackson? **Q1** **Didn't you mention during our last class that building a house near the ocean just doesn't make any sense environmentally?**

P: Yes, that's right. It doesn't make sense. Let me start by explaining coastal zones. These zones start where ocean's waves break, but we're only going to talk about the zones that are on the land. The first zone is the beach, I'm sure you all know what that is. The second one is the dunes. Now, there are several dune zones. The primary dune is the closest to the water and is more fragile. The one right behind it is called the trough. Finally, you have two other dunes in the back, the secondary dune and the back dune. So let's talk about building on these zones. What do you think about building on the beach?

S: That wouldn't make much sense, would it?

P: I agree. You'd have to worry about the waves and tidal fluctuations. And, of course, sand isn't very supportive for building on. Not to mention the shifting shorelines. Do you remember when we went to the marine research center for our field project? **Q3** **We all took a long walk on that peninsula. Well, one of the older professors told me that it used to be an island. You couldn't walk there even about 30 years ago. So you see, shorelines are always moving and changing shape.**

Now, before we get to the next zone, let's talk about the environmental aspects. Why are these zones important?

S: Well, you mentioned during our last class that coastal areas protect inshore areas. You know, from floods, saltwater, and storms. They act as a sort of buffer zone.

P: Good. So going back to the other zones... uh... the primary dune.

Function
1차 모래언덕에는 초목이 살 수 있음

골(trough)은 휴양과 일부 건물 용도로 사용할 수 있음

Opinion
◎ disagree

Function
집을 짓기에 가장 좋은 장소 – 뒤쪽 모래언덕

Problem
해안가에 있는 dream house는 좋은 전망을 갖고 있지만 위험할 수 있음

Now you can't really build on that part. I mean, you can use the beach for recreation, but the primary dune really can't support any human activity. It's more sensitive than the beach. You might think dunes are just a bunch of sand that the wind blew into piles. But they can support vegetation. **Q4-A** **And when they're disturbed, the vegetation can't survive.** Now, this is a problem, because **Q4-D** **when there's no vegetation, there's nothing to hold the sand in place and the beach starts moving inland.** What I mean is, without a primary dune, all beaches are susceptible to erosion. **Q2** **The next zone is the trough. Now this area is a little more tolerant than the dunes in front of it. The ground is more stable and the vegetation is thicker. It can be used for recreation and some building.** We have to make sure not to pollute or damage the quality of the groundwater, but in general it's okay to build here.

S: So this is where we can start developing without any environmental concerns?

P: No. Just because we can build there doesn't mean we should. You can build a house that won't collapse, of course, but that wouldn't be a very responsible thing to do. Anyway, next we have the rest of the dunes. The secondary dune is the final defense against the sea, and since it has similar characteristics to the primary dune, nothing should be built there. The final zone is the back dune. It is more suitable for building than any of the zones I mentioned before. The first two areas I mentioned are the worst places to develop, but people… **Q6** **most people want to build on the beach and primary dune. They want that dream house, just like I wanted mine, right on the beach. The ocean view may be very nice, but in a few years, or even after a bad storm, your living room may be the water's edge. That's what happened to my dream house.** A storm caused the water's edge to move right up to the house. The water eventually receded, but the damage was done. The waves removed so much sand that the house is now unstable. That expensive and very beautiful house can no longer be lived in.

Practice Questions

[01 ~ 06] **Listen to part of a lecture in an environmental science class. Then answer the questions.** MP3 65　정답 및 해설 p. 145

Note-taking

01 What is the lecture mainly about?
   Ⓐ Reasons why wave energy is no longer being used
   Ⓑ Possible solutions to the problem of using wave energy
   Ⓒ The relationship between energy and the economy
   Ⓓ The similarities between solar power and wave energy

02 According to the professor, what led to the popularity of wave energy in the 1970s?
   Ⓐ More power was needed due to an economic depression.
   Ⓑ New wave energy technologies were being developed.
   Ⓒ The prices of oil and natural gas were increasing rapidly.
   Ⓓ Countries had established marine energy facilities.

03 What does the professor imply about solar energy?
   Ⓐ It is a potentially dangerous energy source.
   Ⓑ It has been scientifically proven to be unsound.
   Ⓒ It needs to be stored in a safe place.
   Ⓓ It is difficult to harness because it is spread out.

04 What are the two main problems of oscillating water columns?
   Choose two answers.
   Ⓐ Too many would have to be built.
   Ⓑ There hasn't been any research on them.
   Ⓒ Marine life could be harmed by them.
   Ⓓ They don't create enough energy.

05 What does the professor mean when she says this? 🔊 MP3 65_1
   Ⓐ She cannot remember what she wanted to say.
   Ⓑ The material is too difficult for the students.
   Ⓒ The number of waves is constantly changing.
   Ⓓ There is no need to know the precise amount.

Listen again to part of the lecture. Then answer the questions. 🔊 MP3 65_2
06 Why does the professor say this?
   Ⓐ Powerbuoys seem like an obvious idea.
   Ⓑ Too few people know about powerbuoys.
   Ⓒ Powerbuoys could harm the environment.
   Ⓓ There is already a device similar to powerbuoys.

05 Geology

TOEFL에서 geology지질학 분야는 continental drift대륙이동, plate tectonics판구조론와 같은 이론들이 강의의 주제로 등장한다. 강의는 주로 〈Theory이론 주장 - Evidence근거 - Theory Problem이론의 문제점 - Conclusion결론〉 순으로 전개된다. 그 밖에 classification of rocks암석의 분류에 대한 내용이나, lake호수, desert사막와 같은 topography지형가 만들어지는 과정들도 출제 범위에 속한다.

출제포인트
- Q1 Main Idea
- Q2 Function (Application)
- Q3 Problem
- Q4 Solution (Suggestion)
- Q5 Example
- Q6 Cause (Evidence) & Effect (Result / Finding / Research)
- Q7 Similarity / Difference
- Q8 Advantage / Disadvantage
- Q9 Misunderstanding / Correction
- Q10 Definition (Term) / Origin
- Q11 Two Click / Three Click
- Q12 Ordering
- Q13 Matching
- Q14 Opinion / Attitude
- Q15 Headset
- Q16 Requirement (Condition)
- Q17 Character
- Q18 Imply / Infer

1 Moving Rocks움직이는 바위

미국 California의 어느 평평한 지역에는 바위들이 움직여 지나간 긴 자국이 있다. 사람이나 동물이 움직인 흔적이 없으므로, 지질학자들은 무엇이 바위를 움직였을지에 대한 가설을 내놓았다. 첫 번째 가설은 바람에 의해서 움직였다는 것인데, 지그재그 방향으로 이동한 바위도 있고 바람의 방향과 반대로 이동한 바위도 있어 이 가설은 타당하지 않다.^Q3 두 번째 가설은 비가 내려서 미끄러워진 흙 위로 바람과 비가 바위를 움직였을 수 있다는 것인데, 그 지역에 이제껏 바위를 움직일 만큼 큰 바람이 분 기록이 없으므로 이 가설도 타당하지 않다.^Q3 마지막 가설은 지표면의 물이 얼어서 바위가 얼음 위를 미끄러졌다는 것이다. 하지만 얼음이 얼어도 바위가 미끄러져 이동할 가능성은 거의 없기 때문에^Q3 바위의 움직임에 대해서는 어떠한 결론도 나지 않은 상태이다.

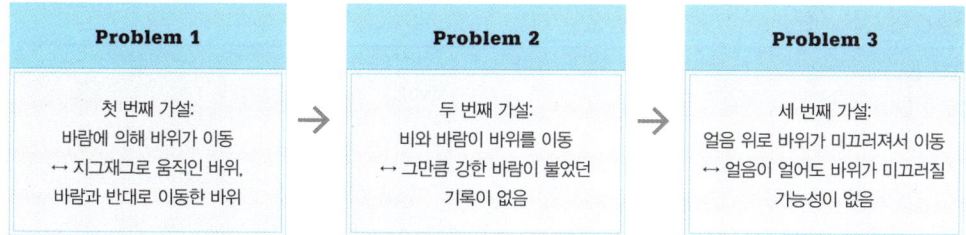

2 Lechuguilla Cave 레추길라 동굴

교수가 두 가지의 cave 형성 과정을 설명한다.^{Q1} 먼저 빗물에 의해 cave가 만들어질 수 있다. rainwater^{빗물}가 땅속으로 seep into^{스며들다}한 후 dead plant material^{죽은 식물}을 만나서 CO_2^{이산화탄소}를 흡수하면, 약한 산성을 띤 groundwater^{지하수}가 된다. 이 지하수가 물에 잘 녹는 성질을 가진 limestone^{석회암}을 만나게 되면, 석회암에 나 있는 많은 구멍으로 지하수가 들어가 석회암을 녹이면서 점점 구멍이 커져 cave가 형성된다.^{Q12} 그러나 Lechuguilla Cave는 생성 과정이 다르다. oil reservoir^{기름이 매장된 곳}에서 올라오는 강한 산성가스와 지하수가 만나면 물이 강한 산성을 띠게 되는데, 이 산성의 지하수가 석회암을 녹여 cave가 만들어지는 것이다.^{Q12} Lechuguilla Cave가 빗물에 의해 만들어지지 않았다는 증거로는, water track^{물이 흐른 흔적}이 없고, 빗물에 의해 만들어진 cave에는 존재하지 않는 gypsum^{석고}이 있다^{Q6}는 것이다. Lechuguilla Cave는 dormant cave^{성장을 중단한 동굴}로, 만일 Lechugullia Cave가 형성 과정 중에 있다면, 그곳에서 나오는 독성 가스로 인해 사람이 죽을 수도 있을 것이다.

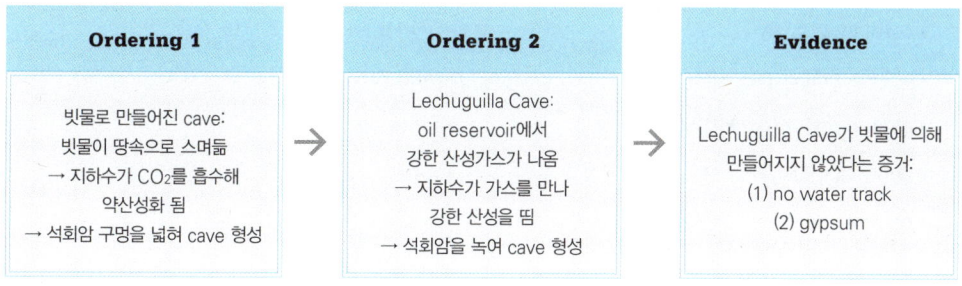

핵/심/표/현

- active volcano 활화산
- asthenosphere n. 암류권
- altitude n. 고도, 고지
- ascribe v. (원인을) …에 돌리다
- assumption n. 가정, 추측, 가설
- basalt n. 현무암
- basin n. 분지
- binocular n. 쌍안경
- calcite n. 방해석
- calamitous adj. 재앙을 초래하는
- carbonic acid 탄산
- cataclysm n. 대재앙, 대변동
- coincidence n. 우연
- combine v. 합치다, 결합시키다
- compact v. 다지다, 누르다
- configuration n. 배열, 배치
- continent n. 대륙
- continental crust 대륙 지각
- continental drift 대륙이동(설)
- continental island 대륙도 (대륙에 딸린 섬)
- continental shelf 대륙붕
- continental slope 대륙 사면
- contour n. 등고선
- convection n. 대류
- core n. (지구의) 중심 핵
- crust n. (지구의) 지각
- crystallize v. 결정체를 이루다[이루게 하다]
- dating n. 연도[연대] 결정
- debris n. 잔해, 부스러기
- decompose v. 분해시키다
- deformation n. 변형, 기형
- deposit n. 매장층, 광산 v. (서서히) 침전시키다
- depression n. 오목한[움푹한] 곳

- debris n. 잔해, 부스러기
- diameter n. 지름
- dormant volcano n. 휴화산
- drought n. 가뭄
- earthquake n. 지진
- ejecta n. 분출물
- elevation n. 고도, 해발 높이
- embed v. 끼워 넣다, 박아 넣다
- entirely adv. 완전히, 전적으로
- epicenter n. 진원지, 진앙
- epicentral adj. 진앙의
- erode v. 침식시키다, 부식시키다
- erosion n. 침식
- eruption n. 분화
- exclusive adj. 배타적인, 독점적인
- extinct volcano 사화산
- fault plane 단층면, 단층 지대
- fault zone 단층대
- force n. 압력, 힘
- formation n. 형성, 구성
- friction n. 마찰
- glacial adj. 빙하의
- glacial drift 빙하 이동
- glacial epoch 빙하기
- global warming 지구 온난화
- granite n. 화강암
- groundwater n. 지하수
- horizon n. 지평선, 수평선
- Ice Age 빙하기
- iceberg n. 빙산
- indentation n. (패인) 자국
- interglacial adj. 간빙기의, 빙하 시대 중간의
- intermittent volcano 간헐화산

- latitude n. 위도
- launch v. 발사하다
- lava n. 용암
- layer n. 층
- limestone n. 석회암
- lithosphere n. 암석권
- longitude n. 경도
- machinery n. 기계, 장치
- magma n. 마그마
- magnetic field n. 자기장
- magnitude n. 정도, 규모
- moraine n. 빙퇴석
- mountain range 산맥
- oceanic crust 대양 지각
- ooze v. (수분 등이) 새어[스며]나오다
- outermost adj. 가장 바깥쪽의
- particle n. 작은 조각, 입자
- physical evidence 물리적 증거
- plateau n. 고원
- plate tectonics 판구조론
- presence n. 존재, 있음
- pulverize v. 가루로 만들다
- quartz n. 석영
- radius n. 반지름
- rainwater n. 빗물
- reservoir n. 저수지

- rift / crack / split n. 균열, 틈, 분열
- rigid adj. 뻣뻣한, 단단한
- rim n. 가장자리, 테두리
- runoff n. 유출 액체, 땅 위를 흐르는 빗물
- scale n. 규모, 범위
- sedimentary rock n. 퇴적암
- seep v. 새다, 스며들다
- seismic adj. 지진의
- seismic intensity 지진 강도, 진도
- seismic wave 지진파(동)
- seismology n. 지진학
- seismometer n. 지진계
- slit n. (좁고 기다란) 구멍, 틈
- speculation n. 추측, 짐작
- squishy adj. 질척질척한
- stabilize v. 안정되다
- stereography n. 입체 화법, 사진술
- stratum n. 지층
- support v. 지지하다, 지원하다
- surge v. 급증하다, 급등하다
- susceptible adj. 민감한, 약한
- swirl v. 소용돌이치다
- terrain n. 지형
- topography n. 지형
- viscous adj. 점성의, 끈적끈적한
- weathering n. 풍화작용

Sample Questions

[01 ~ 06] Listen to part of a lecture in a geology class. Then answer the questions.

MP3 66 정답 및 해석 p. 148

Note-taking

• Main Idea:

• Origin:

• Example:

• Problem:

• Evidence:

• Term:

• Example / (Name) Origin:

01 What is the lecture mainly about?
   Ⓐ Why mountain ranges formed as the Earth cooled
   Ⓑ A giant continent that was formed by plate movement
   Ⓒ How a single land mass broke up into the current continents
   Ⓓ The reason that the Earth is slowly shrinking over time

02 According to Wegener's theory, what can be inferred about dinosaurs?
   Ⓐ They used land bridges to migrate to different continents.
   Ⓑ Most species are considered to be cold-blooded reptiles.
   Ⓒ They lived primarily in mountainous regions in Europe.
   Ⓓ Individual species weren't as widespread as their fossils indicate.

03 Why does the professor mention puzzle pieces?
   Ⓐ To illustrate the different layers of the Earth's mantle
   Ⓑ To describe the way the modern continents can be fit together
   Ⓒ To show how Wegener put together different pieces of evidence
   Ⓓ To suggest that Wegener's theory is missing something important

04 According to the professor, in what ways was Wegener wrong?
   Choose two answers.
   Ⓐ He did not understand the concept of tectonic plates.
   Ⓑ He thought that there was originally only one continent.
   Ⓒ He failed to recognize the importance of dinosaur fossils.
   Ⓓ He miscalculated the speed at which the continents move.

05 What important point does the professor make about magnetic minerals?
   Ⓐ They are used to make compass needles.
   Ⓑ They dictate the direction of lava flows.
   Ⓒ Their chemical make-up is the same in every continent.
   Ⓓ Their orientation can be used to prove that continental drift occurred.

06 What does the professor imply when he says this? 🔊 MP3 66_1
   Ⓐ The continents move faster than Wegener thought.
   Ⓑ Other geologists' views cannot explain continental drift.
   Ⓒ Wegener shared some views with other geologists of his time.
   Ⓓ The movement Wegener predicted is inconsistent with what we know now.

▶ **Question Review**

Main Idea 대륙이동설	**Listen to part of a lecture in a geology class.** **Professor(male):** Okay, today in class we're going to talk about a topic that most of you are familiar with… but, um, you may be unfamiliar with the details. **Q1** **What I'm talking about is the process that led to the current configuration of our continents.**
Origin 대륙이동설이 나오게 된 배경	First, I want to talk about Pangea. In 1915, a German scientist named Alfred Wegener came up with the theory that a single continent called Pangea once existed. This wasn't just a baseless claim. He developed the theory while studying the fossils of ancient freshwater reptiles. While these fossils were found everywhere, scientists had proved that the reptiles could only have lived in South America and Africa. **Q2** **While most scientists of his time believed that dinosaurs had moved from one continent to another via land bridges, he figured there had to be a better explanation of why certain fossils were so widespread.** The answer he came up with was continental drift.
Example Pangea의 모양을 설명하기 위해 퍼즐 조각으로 예를 들어 설명	**Q3** **The continental drift theory states that a single gigantic continent called Pangea slowly split into the continents that we know today. This would mean that the continents are like puzzle pieces.** And when we do try to put them together, they actually match up surprisingly well. Of course, this can't just be coincidence.
Problem Wegener theory의 문제점 **Headset**	While there is little disagreement today over the existence of Pangea, Wegener's theory of continental drift does have some errors. **Q4-A** **Wegener thought the continents plowed through the Earth's crust like ice breakers moving through the ice.** **Q4-D** **He also calculated the speed at which the continents moved as being about 250 millimeters per year.** 🎧 **Q6** This was because, at that time, geologists thought mountains were formed as the Earth cooled and shrank after forming. We all know this part of his theory is wrong. It was the giant tectonic plates themselves that moved. And we also now know that they moved about ten times more slowly than Wegener thought. But don't get the idea that his claim about continental drift was wrong. It is indeed correct. In fact, there is now physical evidence that this movement occurred.
Evidence 대륙이 움직였다는 증거 - 자성 광물	There are certain minerals in lava that are sensitive to magnetic fields. They'll align in the directions of our poles. Think of them as compass needles. These magnetic minerals lined up with the magnetic fields of the Earth as the lava hardened. **Q5** **So, we can be sure that the continents used to be in different positions because the orientation of these minerals varies depending on the time period.** The minerals

Term

plate tectonics 용어 설명

Example / (Name) Origin

conveyor belt 이름의 유래와 원리

in one layer of hardened lava might have a north-to-south orientation, while another layer on top, a layer that was formed many millions of years later, might have a northwest-to-southeast orientation. This is confirmation that the plates had moved.

The one issue scientists had with Wegener's claim was that he couldn't correctly explain what powered the movement. People just assumed that the continents moved because the earth shrank. Geologists now know that the Earth's outermost layer, the lithosphere, is divided into independently moving plates onto which the continents are embedded. The plates "float" on a layer called the asthenosphere. The theory that explains all of this is called the theory of plate tectonics.

Let's talk about the lithosphere, the outermost layer. Think of it as a rigid shell. This shell is broken up into seven or eight major plates. These are the parts that move around, and this movement creates mountains and earthquakes.

So how do these giant plates move? They move somewhat like items on top of a conveyor belt. Actually, that's the name of the principle used to predict where the plates will move next – the conveyor belt principle. To explain the movement, we must look at what's below the lithosphere, the asthenosphere. The asthenosphere is the top part of the Earth's mantle, and it's very viscous, meaning that it's like a thick liquid. Due to the pressure of the lithosphere, the asthenosphere gets incredibly hot. I'm sure you have seen how water moves when it boils… you know, how it kind of swirls. This is called convection. The same process happens in the asthenosphere. As the asthenosphere swirls, it carries the plates on top with it, thus moving them. Of course there are other factors at play, but their relationship to each other is unclear and still the subject of much debate.

Practice Questions

[01 ~ 06] **Listen to part of a lecture in a geology class. Then answer the questions.**

MP3 67 | 정답 및 해석 p. 150

Note-taking

01 What is the lecture mainly about?
   Ⓐ The effects of erosion on the Earth's surface
   Ⓑ Two different ways craters are formed
   Ⓒ Volcanic eruptions and their effects
   Ⓓ The formation of the Earth and the moon

02 According to the professor, why are few impact craters formed nowadays?
   Ⓐ Meteorites were formed millions of years ago.
   Ⓑ The moon acts as a shield against meteorites.
   Ⓒ The ground hardened as the Earth aged.
   Ⓓ The atmosphere burns up most meteorites.

03 According to the professor, why do most people fail to recognize impact craters? Choose two answers.
   Ⓐ The rim can be too far away.
   Ⓑ Craters are often located next to hills.
   Ⓒ Nature hides the crater's features.
   Ⓓ Houses are often built on top of them.

04 What does the professor imply about the surface of the moon?
   Ⓐ It has not been hit by a meteorite for a long time.
   Ⓑ It changes more slowly than that of the Earth.
   Ⓒ It cannot be clearly seen from the Earth.
   Ⓓ It has been altered by human activity.

05 What does the professor imply about the ejecta from craters?
   Ⓐ It appears the same regardless of the crater's origins.
   Ⓑ It is often too old to be analyzed properly by researchers.
   Ⓒ It only exists around craters formed by volcanic activity.
   Ⓓ It does not always point clearly to the cause of the crater.

06 What does the presence of glass-like debris near a crater indicate?
   Ⓐ The ejecta created long marks.
   Ⓑ The crater is unusually deep.
   Ⓒ Extreme amounts of heat were involved.
   Ⓓ A meteorite hit the Earth at a great velocity.

06 Engineering

TOEFL에서 engineering공학 분야는 어떤 structure구조물를 만들면서 발생하는 문제점과 이에 대한 해결방법이나, 구조물이 만들어진 후 발생하는 문제점과 이에 대한 해결방법에 focus를 둔 문제들이 출제된다. 강의 역시 〈Problem문제 – Solution해결방법〉 전개방식을 취하며, 구조물의 종류만 바꾸어서 출제되는 경향이 있다. 여기에 Problem 또는 Solution의 이해를 돕기 위해 언급한 Example이나 전문용어를 제대로 이해했는지 묻는 문제가 나오기도 한다.

출제포인트
- Q1 Main Idea
- Q2 Function (Application)
- Q3 Problem
- Q4 Solution (Suggestion)
- Q5 Example
- Q6 Cause (Evidence) & Effect (Result / Finding / Research)
- Q7 Similarity / Difference
- Q8 Advantage / Disadvantage
- Q9 Misunderstanding / Correction
- Q10 Definition (Term) / Origin
- Q11 Two Click / Three Click
- Q12 Ordering
- Q13 Matching
- Q14 Opinion / Attitude
- Q15 Headset
- Q16 Requirement (Condition)
- Q17 Character
- Q18 Imply / Infer

1   Eiffel Tower에펠탑

Eiffel Tower의 이름은 탑을 design설계하다한 Gustave Eiffel의 이름에서 유래했다.^{Q10} Gustave Eiffel은 세계에서 가장 높은 tower를 만들고 싶어 했지만, 탑을 높게 만들면 표면적이 늘어나는 문제^{Q3}를 해결해야만 했다. 그는 naked frame 프레임 노출 공법^{Q4}을 도입하여 이 문제를 해결했다. 또한 구조물을 더욱 견고하게 하기 위해서 frame을 lattice격자 모양^{Q4}으로 만들었다. 이로 인해 Eiffel Tower는 높지만 바람의 저항에 견딜 수 있는 프랑스의 landmark랜드마크가 되었다.

2 Brooklyn Bridge 브루클린교

Brooklyn Bridge는 미국 뉴욕의 Manhattan 과 Brooklyn을 연결하는 suspension bridge 현수교이다. 다리가 바다와 인접해 있어 강한 바람에 지속적으로 흔들리게 되면 다리가 무너질 수도 있기 때문에[Q3] John Augustus Roebling은 이 문제를 해결해야 했다. 강한 바람에도 잘 견디는 견고한 다리를 만들기 위해서 그는 twisted wirecables 꼬임 철선를 suspension bridge를 만드는데 도입[Q4]하였다. 그가 개발한 cable은 바람에 의한 문제점을 효과적으로 개선했다.

Problem	Solution
강한 바람에 다리가 흔들려 무너질 수 있음	twisted wire cables

3 Confederation Bridge in Canada 캐나다의 연방교

Confederation Bridge는 캐나다 본토의 New Brunswick와 인접한 Prince Edward Island를 연결하며, Northumberland Strait 해협을 가로지른다. 이 해협은 캐나다 최북단에 위치하고 있어 바닷물이 1년 중 6개월 정도나 얼어 있다. 따라서, 바닷물이 녹아 있는 6개월 동안 다리를 완공하기에는 공사 기간이 너무 짧았다.[Q3] 이 문제를 해결하기 위해, 다리 기둥과 같은 부품들을 육지에서 미리 만든 뒤 배로 날라 조립하는 방식[Q4]을 택하였다. 또한 해빙기에 녹은 얼음이 흘러 내려오면서 다리 기둥에 부딪혀 충격을 주거나 기둥 사이에 얼음 덩어리들이 끼어서 배의 운행을 막는 문제[Q3]가 생길 수 있었는데, 이를 해결하기 위해서 다리 기둥과 해수면이 접하는 부분을 conical shape 원뿔모양으로 만들었다.[Q4]

Problem	Solution
(1) 6개월간 얼어 있는 바다 – 짧은 공사 기간 (2) 얼음에 의한 충격	(1) 육지에서 미리 부품 제작 (2) conical shape의 다리 기둥

핵/심/표/현

- additional   adj. 추가의
- applied   adj. 응용의, 적용의
- apprentice   n. 견습생, 조수
- architect   n. 건축가
- architecture   n. 건축학
- asymmetry   n. 불균형, 비대칭
- atop   prep. 꼭대기에, 맨 위에
- base   n. 맨 아래 부분
- bear   v. 견디다, 참다
- breakthrough   n. 돌파구
- bungle   v. 엉망으로[서투르게] 하다
- canyon / gorge   n. 협곡
- circuit   n. 회로, 순환
- cling   v. 달라붙다, 집착하다
- collapse   v. 붕괴되다
- combination   n. 조합, 결합
- commence   v. 시작되다
- compact   v. (단단히) 다지다
- compartment   n. 칸, 구획
- corrective   adj. 수정의
- costly   adj. 많은 비용이 드는
- counteract   v. (악영향에) 대응하다
- crucial   adj. 중대한, 결정적인
- density   n. 밀도
- disperse   v. (넓은 지역으로) 흩다, 확산시키다
- dissipate   v. 소멸시키다
- economical   adj. 경제적인, 실속 있는
- efficiency   n. 효율성
- enlist   v. (협조, 참여를) 요청하여 얻다
- exert   v. 가하다, 행사하다
- existing   adj. 현존하는
- factor   n. 요인
- foundation   n. (건물의) 토대

- friction   n. 마찰
- gaseous   adj. 기체의, 가스의
- generate   v. 발생하다, 창출하다
- gist   n. 요지, 골자
- grand   adj. 웅장한
- grease   n. 기름, 윤활유
- halt   v. 중단시키다
- handle   v. 다루다, 처리하다
- hauling   n. 운반
- imbalance   n. 불균형
- improvement   n. 발전, 개선
- inefficient   adj. 비효율적인
- innovation   n. 혁신
- install   v. 설치하다
- integrate   v. 통합하다
- investigation   n. 수사, 조사, 탐사
- inward   adj. 안으로 향하는
- level   adj. 평평한
- lightweight   adj. 가벼운, 경량의
- limitless   adj. 무한한, 끝[한계]가 없는
- marble   n. 대리석
- marvelous   adj. 놀라운, 경이로운
- misconception   n. 오해, 잘못 이해함
- modify   v. 수정하다, 변경하다
- normalize   v. 정상화해[되]다
- noticeable   adj. 눈에 띄는, 뚜렷한
- obstacle   n. 장애, 방해물
- ongoing   adj. 계속 진행 중인
- outward   adj. 밖으로 향하는
- overcome   v. 극복하다, 이겨내다
- porous   adj. 다공성의
- potential   n. 가능성 adj. 잠재적인, 가능성이 있는
- pressurize   v. 압력을 가하다

- principle   n. 원리
- reinforce   v. (구조 등을) 보강하다
- relatively   adv. 상대적으로, 비교적
- remedy   v. 바로잡다, 개선하다
- render   v. …이 되게 만들다
- scheme   n. 계획, 책략
- solid   adj. 견고한
- sound   adj. 견고한, 안전한
- speculation   n. 추측, 짐작
- stabilization   n. 안정화
- stable   adj. 안정된
- steer   v. 조종하다, 이끌다
- storage   n. 저장(소), 보관(소)
- structural   adj. 구조상의, 구조물의
- structure   n. 구조물, 건축물
- substitute   n. 대체물

- symmetry   n. 균형, 대칭
- take ~ into account   …을 고려하다
- tamper   v. 손대다
- theoretically   adv. 이론적으로, 이론상
- tilt   v. 기울다 n. 기울기
- tourist attraction   n. 관광 명소
- track down   찾아내다, 감지하다
- tremendous   adj. 엄청난, 거대한
- tumble   v. 폭삭 무너지다
- unconventional   adj. 색다른, 독특한
- uneven   adj. 평평하지 않은
- upright   adj. 똑바른
- utilize   v. 활용하다, 이용[사용]하다
- variation   n. 변화, 변형
- water pressure   n. 수압
- wrap up   마무리[결론]를 짓다

Sample Questions

[01 ~ 06] **Listen to part of a lecture in an engineering class. Then answer the questions.**

MP3 68 정답 및 해석 p. 153

Note-taking

- Main Idea:

- Opinion:

- Difference / Problem:

- Solution:

- Cause:

- Solution:

- Advantage:

01 What is the main purpose of the lecture?
   Ⓐ To discuss the history of dams in the United States
   Ⓑ To explain the most effective ways to build with concrete
   Ⓒ To describe the innovative engineering of a large structure
   Ⓓ To talk about American architecture during the Great Depression

02 What is the professor's opinion of the Hoover Dam?
   Ⓐ He believes it threatens surrounding homes.
   Ⓑ He thinks it is a remarkable structure.
   Ⓒ He feels it helped America recover from the Great Depression.
   Ⓓ He doesn't believe it is as complex as people think.

03 Why does the professor mention the location of the Hoover Dam?
   Ⓐ To describe the effects of the area's climate
   Ⓑ To compare the physical differences of two rivers
   Ⓒ To explain where arch gravity dams can be built
   Ⓓ To emphasize the size of the Colorado River

04 According to the professor, why is the dam's arch shape important?
   Ⓐ It helps the dam disperse the weight of the water.
   Ⓑ It allowed the builders to make the dam taller.
   Ⓒ It allows the dam to fit inside a narrow canyon.
   Ⓓ It lets the water go around the dam easily.

05 What points does the professor make about the wide base of the Hoover Dam? **Choose two answers.**
   Ⓐ It allows the dam to disperse its weight across a larger area.
   Ⓑ It was necessary to build the dam in an arched shape.
   Ⓒ It made the dam very expensive to construct.
   Ⓓ It was needed to make the dam structurally sound.

   Listen again to part of the lecture. Then answer the question. 🔊 MP3 68_1
06 Why does the professor say this?
   Ⓐ To suggest there is a structural flaw in the dam
   Ⓑ To point out another interesting aspect of the dam
   Ⓒ To show the relationship between the dam and its size
   Ⓓ To emphasize the standard design of the dam's lower section

▶ **Question Review**

Main Idea ❍ 글의 전체에서 찾아야 한다. – Hoover Dam 에 쓰인 공학 기술에 대해 설명	**Listen to part of a lecture in an engineering class.** **Professor(male):** Now there are some pretty marvelous modern structures in this world. One of them can be found in the western United States, still providing power for thousands of homes. It makes this electricity by using the water from the Colorado River. Can anyone guess what it is? Yes, Anne? **Student 1(female):** Is it the Hoover Dam? **P:** That's right. Built during the Great Depression to create thousands of jobs, it was one of the largest dams in the world. In fact, when it was built in the 1930s it was the largest concrete structure in the world. Even though there have been grander and more complex structures built
Opinion ❍ positive (공학 기술이 인상적이라 생각함)	since then, **Q1 Q2 I still find the engineering behind the Hoover Dam to be quite impressive.** There are not many dams like it, even today. Now, can anyone guess what makes this structure so special? Ah, yes… Dan? **Student 2(male):** I remember reading about its shape. Most dams are straight, but the Hoover Dam is built like the letter U. **P:** Good! Now, can anyone guess why the architects decided to build the
Difference / Problem Hoover Dam의 독특한 모양 / 물의 압력을 지탱할 방법이 필요	dam in such an unconventional shape? **S1:** Does it have to do with the fact that the dam is blocking the Colorado River? I remember reading that it was the fifth-longest river in the United States. **P:** Exactly! Engineers and architects had to find a way to handle water pressure of up to 45,000 pounds per square foot. The Hoover Dam is what is called an arch gravity dam (shown on screen). Well, you know how you mentioned that the dam is built like the letter U? That's where
Solution (1) 아치 형태	the word "arch" in "arch gravity dam" comes from. **Q4 The arch shape allows the structure to support more weight.** The dam works just like arches that the Romans used to support heavy roofs and walls. The stones on top of the arch pressed down on it, but the shape distributed the pressure to the sides, which are much stronger. The same principle applies to arch gravity dams. The water pushes on the arch, but some of the pressure is moved to the canyon walls, so the dam does not have to support all of the massive weight. Yes, Dan? **S2:** If the design is so effective, how come other dams aren't built like arches? **P:** That's a good point. Take a look at the picture on the screen and note
Cause	**Q3** where the dam is located.

Headset

Hoover Dam만 아치 형태인 이유 – 댐의 위치

Solution

(2) 아랫부분을 윗부분 보다 두껍게 설계

Advantage

아랫부분을 더 두껍게 설계한 것의 장점

S2: It's in a… um, **well it looks like a gorge.**
P: Exactly! **Canyons are generally very narrow compared to other areas of rivers. An arch dam works best only in a narrow gorge with steep walls of rock.** Well, that's the "arch" part of "arch gravity dam." Let's look at the gravity part now. Let's see the picture again. ▶Q6▶ **Do you notice anything unusual about the base of the dam?** Anne?
S1: Yeah… It seems like… it's curved outward, almost like it's bending.
P: It is curved outward, but it's not bending. Actually, the base of the dam is almost as thick as it is tall. The base of the dam is more than 600 feet thick, while the top is less than 50 feet thick. This is why this is called a gravity dam. The dam is very heavy at its base, where the pressure of the water is at its greatest. Even though the arch shape can help distribute the pressure to the canyon walls, this is still not enough to hold back the tremendous amount of water. But the broad base makes it possible, dissipating the pressure over a larger area of the foundation. This design also has many other advantages. ▶Q5-A▶ **The dam has to support its own weight as well. You see, the taller the structure is, the more force there is being exerted on the base. The base has to be much thicker to hold the dam up. This explains why the top of the dam is very thin compared to its base.** ▶Q5-D▶ **Because the top part, which does not need to be as strong, is thinner, more structural force can be used to stop the water.** This design is also much more economical, since concrete is expensive. All in all, the Hoover Dam is still a modern structural masterpiece.

Practice Questions

[01 ~ 06] Listen to part of a lecture in an engineering class. Then answer the questions.

MP3 69 정답 및 해석 p. 155

Note-taking

01 What is the lecture mainly about?
   Ⓐ The history and design of leaning towers in Europe
   Ⓑ How the stability of a famous structure was improved
   Ⓒ The architectural methods used to build towers in the past
   Ⓓ The problems faced when building an unusually tall structure

02 According to the professor, what is the main cause of the Leaning Tower of Pisa's tilt?
   Ⓐ The soil beneath it was softer on one side.
   Ⓑ Lead was used to support one side of the tower.
   Ⓒ The tower was visited by too many tourists.
   Ⓓ A concrete foundation was built only on one side.

03. What problem did engineers face when stabilizing the tower?
   Ⓐ Tourists continued to visit it during the project.
   Ⓑ The bells atop the tower acted as counterweights.
   Ⓒ The base was damaged when they applied concrete.
   Ⓓ It would have fallen if soil was removed from beneath it.

04. According to the professor, what did the engineers do to prevent the tower from falling before they stabilized the soil?
   Ⓐ They added concrete to the base.
   Ⓑ They made one side heavier.
   Ⓒ They made the tower heavier.
   Ⓓ They prevented tourists from visiting the tower.

05. What does the professor say about the architect of the Leaning Tower of Pisa?
   Ⓐ There is no conclusive evidence as to the identity of the architect.
   Ⓑ There were actually two architects who worked together to design the tower.
   Ⓒ The presence of sculptures indicates that the architect was also an artist.
   Ⓓ The technology the architect used was not advanced enough to make a safe building.

06. What is the professor's opinion about using architectural stabilization techniques?
   Ⓐ It helps historians learn more about great architects of the past.
   Ⓑ It is never a good idea to tamper with a building's foundation.
   Ⓒ It is more important to avoid making mistakes in the first place.
   Ⓓ It can destroy the unique beauty of unconventional buildings.

Unit 6
Social Science

01_ **Anthropology**
02_ **Archaeology**
03_ **Business**
04_ **Education**
05_ **Psychology**
06_ **Sociology**

01 Anthropology

TOEFL에서 anthropology^{인류학} 분야는 남미의 3대 문명인 Maya, Inca, Aztec 문명에 대해 많이 출제되어 왔고, Sumerian 문명이나 북남미의 Native American^{북미 원주민}과 관련된 내용도 자주 나온다. 강의 내용과 관련해서, 특정 민족이 이루어낸 문명과 해당 문명이 발달했던 이유 또는 쇠퇴한 이유를 묻는 문제는 꼭 출제되는 편이다. 또한 이들이 겪은 변화와, 어떤 한 문명이 다른 문명에 미친 영향에 관한 문제도 자주 출제된다. 이 분야는 archaeology^{고고학}와 유사한 점이 많으므로 두 분야를 같이 공부하는 것도 좋은 전략이다.

출제포인트
- Q1 Main Idea
- Q2 Function (Influence)
- Q3 Problem
- Q4 Solution (Suggestion)
- Q5 Example
- Q6 Cause (Evidence) & Effect (Result / Finding / Research)
- Q7 Similarity / Difference
- Q8 Advantage / Disadvantage
- Q9 Misunderstanding / Correction
- Q10 Definition (Term) / Origin
- Q11 Two Click / Three Click
- Q12 Ordering
- Q13 Matching
- Q14 Opinion / Attitude
- Q15 Headset
- Q16 Requirement (Condition)
- Q17 Character
- Q18 Imply / Infer

1 Clovis People^{클로비스 사람들(시베리아에서 알래스카로 최초로 이주했다고 알려진 사람들)}

Clovis인이 북남미에 살았던 최초의 사람들이라는 가설이 틀릴 수 있다는 주장이 나왔으며, ^{Q3} 이를 뒷받침하는 증거들이 발견되었다. 우선, Clovis 지역 및 다른 지역에서 발견된 유물 중, Clovis 사람들이 북남미에 들어가서 살기 시작했다고 추정되는 연대보다 훨씬 더 오래 전 유물들이 발견되었다. 한 예로, Clovis 사람들은 11만 년 전에 북남미에 살았다고 추정되는데 그 지역에서 20만 년 전의 유물이 발견된 것이다. ^{Q6} 두 번째 증거는 언어학적 반박 근거이다. 이 사람들이 최초로 북남미에서 살기 시작한 사람들이라고 할 경우, 현재 북남미에서 사용되는 아주 많은 종류의 원주민 언어가 이들의 언어에서 분화되었어야만 한다. 하지만, 언어학자들은 하나의 언어가 완전히 다른 언어로 분화되는 데에 6천 년 정도가 걸린다고 보기 때문에, Clovis 사람들의 언어가 북남미에 현존하는 언어 수로 분화되는 데는 계산상 50만 년이 걸린다. 이는 Clovis 사람들이 11만 년 전에 처음 북남미로 이주했다고 보기 힘든 근거가 된다.^{Q6}

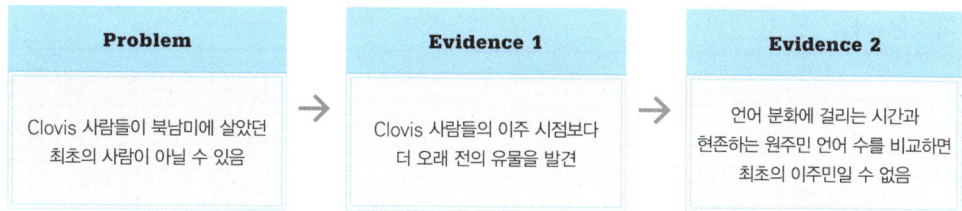

2 Aztec Civilization 아즈텍 문명

Aztec civilization은 남미의 3대 문명 중 하나이다. Aztec 사람들은 농사를 지을 땅이 부족해서, 반 수경재배형 식인 chinampa라는 경작 방식을 개발하여 많은 인구에게 필요한 식량을 조달했다. chinampa는 농사가 어려운 땅에서 Q3 적은 인원으로 많은 농작물을 재배할 수 있는 system 체계 Q4 이다. chinampa의 제작 과정은 다음과 같다. 먼저, 얕은 물 위에 막대로 경계선을 만들고 갈대를 십자형태로 엮어서 판을 만든다. 그 다음, 이 갈대판 위에 흙과 풀을 덮어서 경작지를 만든다. Q12 여기에서 주로 옥수수와 콩을 재배했는데, 이 두 곡식은 Aztec 사람들의 주요 단백질 공급원이었다. Q2

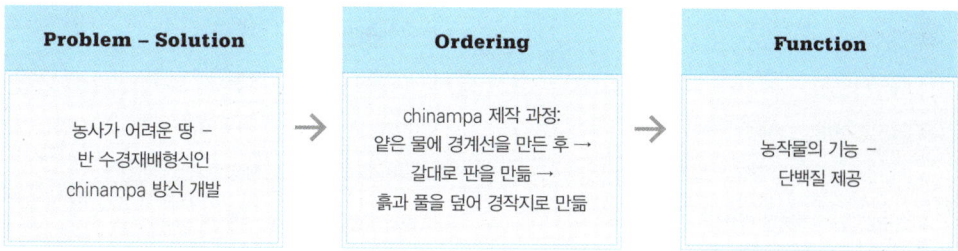

3 Native American 북미 원주민

북미 원주민 중 Iroquois 이로쿼이 부족은 나무껍질로 그릇을 만들어 사용했는데, 그 그릇은 물이 새지 않을 정도로 견고했다. Q17 이들의 주요 교통수단은 카누였으며, 카누를 타고 다니면서 서로 교역을 하였다. 카누 역시 너무나 정교하게 잘 만들어져서, Q8 후에 이주해 온 프랑스 사람들이 이에 감명을 받아 유사한 배를 만들 정도였다. Q2 Iroquois 부족이 카누로 이동한 경로는 너무나 광범위해서 오늘날 비행기로 2~3시간이 걸릴 정도의 거리 Q5 인데, 이런 거리를 카누로 이동했다는 것은 무척 놀라운 일이다.

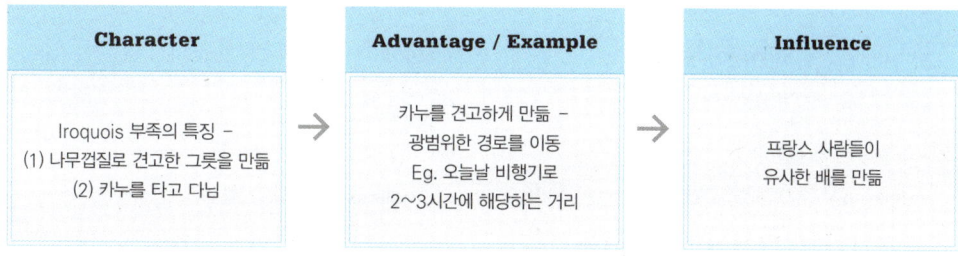

핵/심/표/현

- accreditation   n. 승인, 인가
- adhere   v. 들러붙다, 부착하다
- adopt   v. 채택하다
- agony   n. 고통
- agriculture   n. 농업
- anthropologist   n. 인류학자
- anthropology   n. 인류학
- arid   adj. 건조한
- armor   n. 갑옷
- artifact   n. 인공물, 공예품
- basic needs   기본 생필품[조건]
- boost   v. 신장시키다, 북돋우다
- cease   v. 중단하다
- centralize   v. 중앙집권화하다
- ceremonial   adj. 의식의
- civilization   n. 문명
- coin   v. 신조어를 만들다
- collective behavior   집단 행동
- compile   v. (여러 출처에서 자료를 따서) 엮다, 편집하다
- comprehend   v. 이해하다
- conduct   v. (열이나 전기를) 전도하다
- content   n. 속에 든 것들, 내용물
- contradict   v. 모순되다
- convincing   adj. 설득력 있는, 확실한
- critical   adj. 대단히 중요한
- crumble   v. 흔들리다, 무너지다
- crux   n. 가장 중요한 부분
- decline   v. 쇠퇴하다
- defender   n. 방어[옹호]자
- deforestation   n. 삼림 벌채, 삼림 파괴
- demise   n. 종말, 죽음
- deplete   v. 격감시키다
- desert   v. 버리다, 유기하다
- devour   v. 집어삼키다, 파괴하다
- discipline   n. 규율; 학과목
- disruption   n. 붕괴, 분열
- disturbance   n. 방해; 소란, 소동
- diverse   adj. 다양한, 여러 가지의
- domesticate   v. 길들이다, 사육하다
- downfall   n. 몰락, 전복
- drastic   adj. 급격한
- empirical   adj. 경험에 의거한, 실증적인
- erosion   n. 침식, 부식
- fallacy   n. (많은 이들이 옳다고 믿는) 틀린 생각
- farfetched   adj. 설득력 없는
- give rise to ~   …이 생기게 하다
- glorify   v. 찬미하다, 미화하다
- ground cover   n. 지피[지표] 식물
- hierarchy   n. 계급, 계층
- homage   n. 경의, 존경의 표시
- immense   adj. 엄청난, 어마어마한
- imprint   v. 각인시키다, 새기다
- infertile   adj. 메마른, 불모의
- intensify   v. 격렬해지다, 심해지다
- interconnected   adj. 상호 연결된
- interpretation   n. 해석, 설명
- invasion   n. 침입, 침략
- jade   n. 옥, 비취
- jargon   n. 전문어, 은어
- juvenile   adj. 청소년의
- lowland   n./adj. 저지대(의)
- middle class   n. 중산층
- millennium   n. 천년
- monument   n. 기념비
- mural   n. 벽화

- native   n./adj. 원주민(의), 본토(의)
- noble   n./adj. 귀족(의)
- nomadic   adj. 유목의, 방랑의
- official   n. 공무원
- overgrown   adj. (풀·잡초 등이) 마구 자란
- overpopulation   n. 인구 과잉[과밀]
- overthrow   v. 전복시키다
- peasant   n. 농민, 소작농
- piece together   (세부 사항들을) 종합하다
- pin ~ down   …을 정확히 밝히다[이해하다]
- pliable   adj. 휘기 쉬운, 유연한
- pottery   n. 도자기
- prehistory   n. 선사 시대
- prevalent   adj. 널리 퍼진, 유행하는
- rebellion   n. 반란
- relocate   v. 이동하다
- remarkable   adj. 훌륭한
- represent   v. 상징하다
- retreat   v. 후퇴하다
- ruins   n. 유적, 폐허
- sealed   adj. 봉인된, 포장된
- seemingly   adv. 겉보기에는, 외견상으로
- shortage   n. 부족, 결핍

- slash-and-burn-farming   n. 화전농법
- sophisticated   adj. 정교한, 복잡한
- sophistication   n. 세련됨, 정교함
- spark   v. 유발하다, 촉발시키다
- starvation   n. 굶주림, 기아
- stitched   adj. 꿰맨
- strain   n. 부담, 압박
- stretch   v. 늘이다, 늘어나다
- stunning   adj. 매우 놀라운
- suppress   v. 진압하다, 억누르다
- take action   행동을 취하다, 조치를 취하다
- temperament   n. 기질, 성질
- tension   n. 긴장, 갈등
- taxation   n. 조세, 세수
- topsoil   n. 표토
- transportation vessel   이동수단
- undertake   v. 떠맡다, 착수하다
- unravel   v. 흐트러지기 시작하다
- unrest   n. 국내의 불안
- vanish   v. 사라지다, 없어지다
- vulnerable   adj. 취약한, 영향 받기 쉬운
- warlike   adj. 호전적인

Sample Questions

[01 ~ 06] **Listen to part of a lecture in an anthropology class. Then answer the questions.**
MP3 70 정답 및 해석 p. 159

Note-taking

- Main Idea:

- Character:

- Function:

- Finding:

- Requirement:

- Function:

- Similarity:

- Evidence:

01 What is the lecture mainly about?
   Ⓐ The mysterious disappearance of the Olmec
   Ⓑ Sports played by ancient civilizations
   Ⓒ The characteristics of Olmec art
   Ⓓ The use of jaguars in ancient sculptures

02 What is surprising about the Olmec head sculptures?
   Ⓐ They resemble many different animals.
   Ⓑ They were made from stone not found in the region.
   Ⓒ They resemble other Mesoamerican sculptures.
   Ⓓ They were made with stone tools.

03 Why does the professor mention a ceremonial sport played by the Olmec civilization?
   Ⓐ To explain the connection between the Olmec and nearby civilizations
   Ⓑ To illustrate that cultural knowledge can help us understand art
   Ⓒ To support her point about the warlike qualities of the Olmec
   Ⓓ To emphasize that there is a lot that is unknown about the Olmec culture

04 According to the professor, why do jaguar features indicate a statue representing an Olmec ruler?
   Ⓐ The Olmec are known to have had a great fear of jaguars.
   Ⓑ Jaguars were an important part of Olmec culture.
   Ⓒ The Olmec hunted jaguars for food and sport.
   Ⓓ Jaguars were considered gods by the Olmec.

05 What can be inferred about the ceremonial ball game?
   Ⓐ It was a rough and violent sport.
   Ⓑ It was borrowed from European explorers.
   Ⓒ It was only played by Olmec rulers.
   Ⓓ It was played before hunting jaguars.

Listen again to part of the lecture. Then answer the question. 🔊 MP3 70_1
06 What does the professor mean when she says this?
   Ⓐ To explain why students should visit museums
   Ⓑ To indicate the difficulty of identifying ancient art
   Ⓒ To express her opinion about the quality of prehistoric art
   Ⓓ To make the point that Olmec art is very distinctive

▶ Question Review

Main Idea
Olmec 문명의 예술

Listen to part of a lecture in an anthropology class.

Professor(female): So, now that we've discussed how people in ancient Mesoamerican cultures shared technology, architecture, and art of thousands of years ago, **Q1 I'd like to talk about the art of one of these cultures, the Olmec civilization.** Well, the Olmec civilization began around 1200 BC and lasted for just 700 years. By 400 BC, Olmec society was gone. Today there just aren't many indicators of who exactly they were. So why does this matter in relation to art? Eric?

Student(male): Well, to analyze a work of art, you need to know something about the people who created it.

P: Precisely. Although we don't know much about the Olmec civilization, what we do know is that the people lived an agricultural lifestyle in small communities located in the swampy lowlands of southern Mexico. They raised turkeys, fished, and had an extensive trade network of valuable materials, such as jade. They also had a writing system. We know this because we see their writing on various pieces of their art, but **Q1 it's the art, not their writing, that they're known for.**

Character
Olmec 문명의 가장 널리 알려진 예술품

The Olmec created a vast range of artistic artifacts such as painted murals, fine pottery, and little figures carved out of jade. But their gigantic, stone sculptures of heads are their most famous works of art. Here's a picture of one (shown on screen). These heads are quite large, approximately three meters high. That's almost twice as tall as most of us. And they're almost just as wide as they are tall. They all look pretty similar, too. I mean, they all have similar features. Anyone want to try and describe the head? Yes?

S: It looks really round, with a broad nose, and the lips… they're very full, downturned lips. It kind of looks like it's frowning.

Headset

P: 🎧 These features you just mentioned, they're very distinctive. When you see one of these heads in a museum, you say **Q6 "Yeah, that's an Olmec all right." Q2 Another surprising aspect of these sculptures is their material. The heads were carved out of a very hard type of rock, but the Olmec people only used stone tools. They didn't have any metal tools.** Yet, only using stone, they created what many archaeologists consider to be the best quality sculptures in ancient Mesoamerica. It's remarkable when you think about the level of sophistication that was achieved with the most basic of tools.

Character
Olmec 문명의 놀라운 조각 기술 – 석기만으로 정교한 조각을 함

S: What's on the head? It doesn't look like hair. It kind of looks like a helmet.

Function
전쟁투구 외에 헬멧의 또 다른 용도

Finding
문화에 대한 이해를 통해서 예술품에 대한 또 다른 결론을 내릴 수 있음

Requirement
예술을 연구하기 위해서는 다른 분야에 대한 지식도 필요

Function
jaguar의 역할과 용도

Similarity
석조 두상의 입술과 jaguar 입술 간의 유사점

Evidence
중요한 사람을 상징한다는 근거

P: Ah, yes. **Q5** **Many view the helmet as a kind of armor, worn to fight wars. Helmets like these probably provided protection in battles, but most archaeologists and art historians think they were also used in sports… specifically, for a ceremonial ball game.** Olmec athletes played this game on courts using rubber balls. This brings up another interesting point. Let's say you've found an ancient sculpture in the jungle and a helmet is carved onto its head. If you didn't know anything about the culture it came from, you'd just probably assume it was used as protection during war. But, **Q3** **what if you knew that other ancient people in the area played a certain type of sport? What if you knew they wore protective equipment during the game? You'd naturally come to a different conclusion.** It might not be a sculpture of a warrior at all. It might be a sculpture of an athlete. **This is what I mean by knowing the culture to know about art.** To be an art historian, you must also have knowledge on other disciplines, such as anthropology and archaeology. Then you can see how different cultures have influenced one another and how these cultures are reflected in their artistic styles and symbols. In other words, you can't just study art. If you do, you might miss out on a valid interpretation of a work of art. You need to have something to relate the symbols in art to… uh… take the jaguar, for example.

Jaguars are commonly found in Olmec art. These large predatory cats were once found throughout the Americas. **Q4** **They were a very important part of Olmec culture and religion.** So it's not surprising that they are often in Olmec art. **Jaguars were often used to represent someone important, such as a ruler, in order to glorify them.** You can even see their influence on the stone heads. Can you see how the features sort of resemble a jaguar's?

S: Hmm… Well, the mouth, the way the lips are turned down… It sort of looks like the mouth of a jaguar.

P: Yes! This is one of the reasons why researchers believe this is a representation of one of the important rulers of the period. But whether these are supposed to be Olmec rulers or Olmec athletes, it's pretty clear from the similarities in their features that these are all Olmec works of art.

Practice Questions

[01 ~ 06] **Listen to part of a lecture in an anthropology class. Then answer the questions.**

MP3 71　정답 및 해석 p. 160

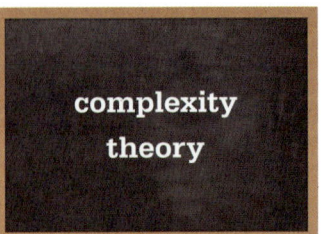

Note-taking

---

01 What is the lecture mainly about?
　Ⓐ The usefulness of archaeological evidence in assessing historical events
　Ⓑ Possible reasons for the sudden decline of population in a city
　Ⓒ Methods used by Greek historians to analyze past events
　Ⓓ The relationship between citizens and rulers in ancient Greece

02 Why does the professor mention Aristotle?
　Ⓐ To indicate that hypotheses of the Mycenaean collapse were created long ago
　Ⓑ To help explain the relationship between weather and declining populations
　Ⓒ To prove that the hypothesis related to climate change is wrong
　Ⓓ To show that a theory about the Mycenaean collapse may have some credibility

03 According to the professor, what evidence was used to prove that climate change did not cause the decline in population?
    Ⓐ There were many fallacies in ancient Greek historical records.
    Ⓑ The ruins of buildings destroyed in a foreign invasion were found.
    Ⓒ Cities near Mycenae seemed to be unaffected by drought.
    Ⓓ No records of the decline of agriculture exist.

04 Why does the professor discuss the complexity theory?
    Ⓐ To explain how theories from other fields can be applied to anthropology
    Ⓑ To prove that the city collapsed due to a foreign invasion
    Ⓒ To provide an alternative explanation to why Mycenae collapsed
    Ⓓ To show how complex relationship exist between events

05 What evidence suggests that Mycenae collapsed due to internal conflict?
    Ⓐ A palace in the city may have been burned down.
    Ⓑ Taxes do not seem to have been collected fast enough.
    Ⓒ The city was on the verge of becoming overpopulated.
    Ⓓ Farmers might have stopped farming for long periods.

Listen again to part of a lecture. Then answer the question. 🔊 MP3 71_1
06 Why does the professor say this?
    Ⓐ To imply that the complexity theory relies on other concepts
    Ⓑ To indicate that Mycenae wasn't supported by other cities
    Ⓒ To emphasize the problem with making hypotheses
    Ⓓ To help explain why the farmers became angry

02 Archaeology

TOEFL에서 archaeology고고학 분야는 다루어지는 내용이 인류학과 조금 다르다. 인류학에서는 주로 과거에 사람들이 어떻게 살았는지 설명한다. 이에 비해 고고학에서는, 과거 사람들의 유물을 발굴한 내용이나 발굴에 필요한 technology기술에 관한 내용, 예를 들어 x-ray엑스레이나 radar레이더와 같은 장비의 사용법과 방사선 동위원소에 의한 연대 추정법 등이 강의의 주요 주제가 된다. 고고학 분야에서 자주 출제되는 문제 유형으로는 발굴 장비의 기능, 과거 사람들의 생활방식에 대한 증거 등이 있다.

출제포인트
- Q1 Main Idea
- Q2 Function (Influence)
- Q3 Problem
- Q4 Solution (Suggestion)
- Q5 Example
- Q6 Cause (Evidence) & Effect (Result / Finding / Research)
- Q7 Similarity / Difference
- Q8 Advantage / Disadvantage
- Q9 Misunderstanding / Correction
- Q10 Definition (Term) / Origin
- Q11 Two Click / Three Click
- Q12 Ordering
- Q13 Matching
- Q14 Opinion / Attitude
- Q15 Headset
- Q16 Requirement (Condition)
- Q17 Character
- Q18 Imply / Infer

1 GPR(Ground Penetrating Radar)지표 투과 레이더

GPR은 땅을 파기 전에 어떤 유물이 어느 정도 깊이에 어떤 모양으로 묻혀 있는지를 미리 확인해Q4 주는 장비로, 발굴 도중 유물이 훼손되는 문제Q3를 해결해 준다. GPR은 레이더가 땅을 투과하여 가다가 땅속의 흙보다 밀도가 높은 물체에 부딪히면 다시 돌아오는 원리를 이용한다. 레이더의 복귀 정보에 따라 땅에 묻혀 있는 물질이 단순한 돌인지, 아니면 도자기와 같은 유물인지 알 수 있다.Q8 이것은 배나 비행기가 항해할 때 사용하는 레이더의 원리와 비슷하지만, GPR은 땅을 투과하는 점이 다르다. 단점은 땅속에 소금이나 진동과 같은 방해 요소가 있을 때는 땅속을 투과하는 해상도가 매우 낮아진다Q8는 점이다.

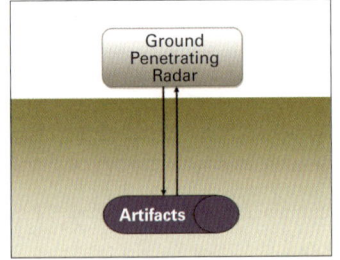

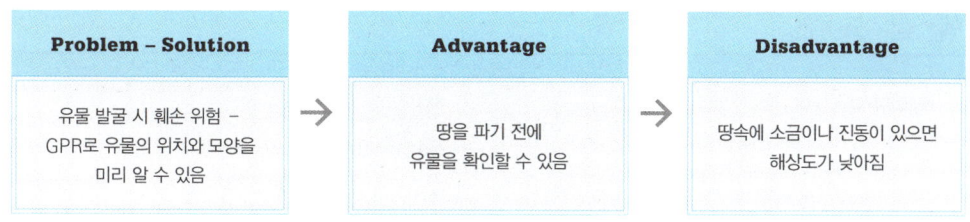

2 Passage Graves 통로 분묘

영국에서 발견된 Stonehenge 스톤헨지(영국에 있는 석기시대 원형 유적)의 용도에 관해서는 여러 가지 가설이 있다. 주로, 무덤의 용도 외에 살아있는 사람들을 위해 다른 목적으로 이용되지 않았는지에 대한 것이다. Stonehenge는 안으로 들어가는 입구가 좁은 통로로 되어 있어 passage grave라고도 불리며, Q10 그 안에서 두 가지 소리 현상을 경험할 수 있다. 첫 번째는 소리가 벽에 부딪쳐 다시 만나면서 발생하는 standing wave 정상파 현상이다. Q18 예를 들어, 바로 옆에서 드럼을 치면 소리가 거의 들리지 않다가 한 발짝만 뒤로 물러서면 귀청이 떨어져 나갈 것 같은 큰 소리로 들리는 현상이다. 두 번째는 resonance 공명 현상으로, 소리를 들을 수는 없지만 느낄 수는 있는 현상 Q18 이다. 이 두 가지의 특징으로 봤을 때, Stonehenge가 종교적인 용도 Q2로 사용되었을 가능성이 높다는 가설이 있다. 옛 사람들이 이런 현상을 경험했다면 소리로 인한 놀라운 체험이 종교적인 경외심으로 연결되었을 수 있기 때문이다. Q6 Stonehenge의 용도에 관한 또 다른 가설로는, 돌을 달력을 만드는 데 사용했을 것이라는 주장도 있다.

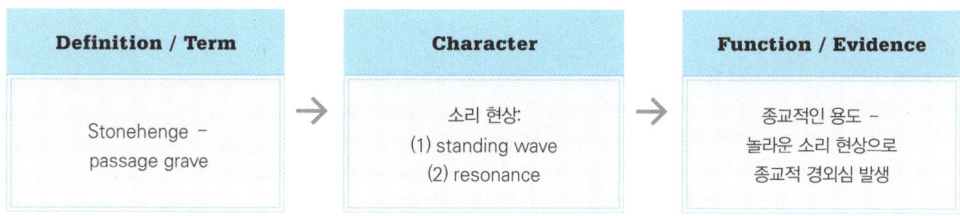

핵/심/표/현

- agitated   adj. 불안해하는, 동요하는
- alliance   n. 연합, 동맹
- anomaly   n. 변칙, 이례
- antique   n./adj. 골동품(의)
- antiquity   n. 고대, 아주 오래됨; 유물
- archaeologist   n. 고고학자
- archaeology   n. 고고학
- artifact   n. 인공물, 공예품
- Atlantic (Ocean)   n./adj. 대서양(의)
- be subject to ~   …의 대상이다
- boulder   n. 바위
- Bronze Age   n. 청동기 시대
- bury   v. 묻다, 파묻다
- canoe   n. 카누
- cave man   n. (석기 시대의) 혈거인
- chamber   n. (특정 목적용) 실(室)
- chanting   n. 찬팅(구호, 성가)
- chimney   n. 굴뚝
- citadel   n. 성채, 요새
- claim   n. 주장
- clan   n. 부족, 집단
- conductivity   n. 전도성
- container   n. 그릇, 용기
- covert   adj. 비밀의, 은밀한   n. 은신처
- cranial   adj. 두개골의
- ditch   n. 배수로
- domestication   n. 사육
- dwelling   n. 주거(지), 주택
- electromagnetic pulse   전자기파
- electromagnetism   n. 전자기
- elements   n. (pl.) 비바람, 폭풍우
- enclose   v. 에워싸다
- excavate   v. 발굴하다, 파다

- explorer   n. 탐험가
- extraordinary   adj. 기이한, 놀라운
- federation   n. 연방 국가, 연합
- fisherman   n. 어부
- fishing rod   n. 낚싯대
- fortification   n. 방어 시설, 요새화
- fortress   n. 요새, 성곽
- geophysicist   n. 지구 물리학자
- grave   n. 무덤
- grid   n. 격자, 격자무늬
- heterogeneous   adj. 이종(異種)의, 혼합의
- highland   n./adj. 산악 지대(의)
- homogeneous   adj. 동종[균질]의
- hook   n. 고리
- in light of ~   …을 고려하여
- Indian Ocean   n. 인도양
- indistinguishable   adj. 구분이 안 되는
- inhabit   v. 살다, 정착하다
- Iron Age   n. 철기 시대
- iron smelting   철 제련
- land-dwelling   adj. 육지에 거주하는
- lodge   v. …에 꽂히다
- massive   adj. 거대한, 엄청나게 큰
- Mesolithic   adj. 중석기 시대의
- Middle Stone Age   중석기 시대
- miraculous   adj. 기적적인
- myth   n. 신화; 근거 없는 믿음
- navigator   n. 항해사
- Neolithic   adj. 신석기 시대의
- New Stone Age   신석기 시대
- nomad   n. 유목민
- Nordic   adj. 북유럽 국가의
- Old Stone Age   n. 구석기 시대

- organic matter　유기물
- originate　v. 유래하다
- ornamental　adj. 장식용의
- overlapping　adj. 중복되는, 겹치는
- Pacific (Ocean)　n. 태평양
- Paleolithic　adj. 구석기 시대의
- passageway　n. 통로, 복도
- peat　n. 이탄
- penetrate　v. 관통하다, 통과하다
- plaster　n. 회[석고]반죽　v. 회반죽을 바르다
- pluck out　뽑다
- preserve　v. 보존하다
- primitive　adj. 원시의, 초기의
- proximity　n. 가까움, 근접
- reflect　v. 반사하다
- relic　n. 유물
- remains　n. 유적, 유해
- remote sensing tool　원격 감지 도구
- resistivity　n. 저항력
- resolution　n. 해상도
- resort to ~　...에 의존하다

- ritual　n. 의례, 의식
- rule out　배제하다
- rumble　v. 덜커덩거리며 나아가다
- saga　n. 영웅 전설
- saturated　adj. 흠뻑 젖은, 포화된
- shelter　n. 안식처, 대피소
- skull　n. 해골
- specialized　adj. 전문화된
- steadily　adv. 꾸준히, 변동 없이
- strand　v. 좌초시키다
- strategic　adj. 전략적인, 전략상 중요한
- sufficient　adj. 충분한
- systematically　adv. 체계적[조직적]으로
- tomb　n. 무덤
- trading　n. 교역
- transaction　n. 처리 (과정)
- transmit　v. 전송하다
- tribe　n. 부족
- utensil　n. 기구, 도구
- validity　n. 유효함, 타당성

Sample Questions

[01 ~ 06] **Listen to part of a lecture in an archeology class. Then answer the questions.**

MP3 72 정답 및 해석 p. 164

Note-taking

• Main Idea:

• Evidence:

• Cause:

• Correction:

• Term:

• Effect:

• Finding:

• Role:

01 What aspect of archeology in Iceland does the professor mainly discuss in the lecture?
   Ⓐ Similarities between remains in the Americas and Iceland
   Ⓑ How methods borrowed from geology are used to find ruins
   Ⓒ The strategy of locating artifacts based on traditional sagas
   Ⓓ Various materials used to build traditional Icelandic houses

02 According to the professor, why are the remains of old Icelandic houses difficult for archaeologists to find?
   Ⓐ They were built too long ago.
   Ⓑ They were made with a kind of soil.
   Ⓒ They are covered in thick layers of ice and snow.
   Ⓓ They were made of wood that has since decomposed.

03 Why does the professor mention Icelandic sagas and Viking explorers?
  Ⓐ To give an example of traditional Icelandic literature
  Ⓑ To suggest a reason why Icelandic houses were built with peat
  Ⓒ To point out why archeology was important in Iceland in the past
  Ⓓ To offer a reason why some people look for ruins in Iceland

04 According to the professor, what kind of data does the remote sensing tool provide?
  Ⓐ The magnetic forces created by metal artifacts
  Ⓑ The depth of where the remains are located
  Ⓒ The resistances of different materials
  Ⓓ The age of the remains it senses

05 What is the significance of the building that was found using the remote sensing tool?
  Ⓐ It showed that traditional archaeological methods are best.
  Ⓑ It provides evidence that an Icelandic legend may have been true.
  Ⓒ It was made from wood and stone rather than traditional peat blocks.
  Ⓓ It was the first Viking structure ever found in North America.

Listen again to part of the lecture. Then answer the question. 🔊 MP3 72_1
06 Why does the professor say this?
  Ⓐ To explain the primary problem faced by Icelandic geophysicists
  Ⓑ To emphasize the difference between Icelandic soil and North American soil
  Ⓒ To indicate that the experiment with the tool contained a crucial error
  Ⓓ To suggest that the tool would be useful for finding old Icelandic homes

▶ **Question Review**

Main Idea 유물 위치 및 연대 추정 기법	**Listen to part of a lecture in an archeology class.** **Professor(male):** Okay, we've been talking about some archeological findings related to the Clovis culture of North and South America. **Q1** **Now, let's concentrate on some techniques for locating and dating archaeological artifacts.** It'd be nice to just stroll in and investigate ruins, but, in some places, it's just too difficult to do so. So we have to resort to some special techniques. I want to take a look at a place far away from the Clovis culture and give an example from the country of Iceland. Now, um, Iceland is a volcanic island located in the Northern Hemisphere, and a tenth of it is covered by glaciers.
Evidence 이야기의 진위 여부를 확인할 증거 부족	One of the very first things that may come to mind about Iceland and other Nordic countries is the stories behind them. You've all heard of the Vikings, right? Icelandic sagas about the Vikings have intrigued people for ages, but we've always lacked hard evidence to support the validity of these claims. They seem more like legends. Historians, astronomers, navigators... They've all tried to find proof that people settled where the stories indicate. It's almost as if people are just drawn to try to verify the truth of these stories. We archaeologists too have been trying to locate dwellings, evidence of farming, iron smelting, or even animal domestication – anything that indicates the signs of early settlement.
Cause 확인하기 힘든 지역	Anyway, part of the reason why Icelandic sagas are only considered myths is the difficulty of verifying archeological facts in the areas in question. You might think that the weather or extreme amounts of ice are the problem, but you'd be surprised at the truth – it's actually the lack
Correction 날씨나 얼음이 아닌, 나무 부족 때문임	of trees. There just aren't any trees to hold down the soil, and so there's naturally a lot of erosion, especially from the highlands to lower coastal areas. Now, with so few trees available, most of the earliest dwellings in Iceland were made from peat. Peat, as you may remember, is airy soil
Term peat 용어 설명	that comes mainly from wetlands and bogs and contains a high amount of decayed organic matter. The early inhabitants of Iceland would compress peat and dry it, making it into big thick blocks that formed the walls of early Icelandic houses. **Q2** **Today, the remains of these houses are extremely difficult to find. Being made of soil, they are almost indis-**
Effect 나무가 부족해 peat으로 집을 지었기에 집의 유적이 남아있지 않음	**tinguishable from the soil around them.** However, a new method was developed by borrowing a modern technique used by geophysicists. So, how is this all related to Icelandic legends? Well, **Q3** **one of these Icelandic sagas tells of some Viking explorers who were probably the first Europeans to cross the Atlantic and live in North America.** It

Headset

was a Viking family from Iceland, uh, called Thorfinnson. They settled in North America for a few years, but then moved back to Iceland, which is not that far away. Naturally, **Q3** **there is a great interest in investigating Viking-era sites in Iceland,** especially in the place where the saga says this family finally settled.

Q4 **One team of archaeologists decided to use a remote sensing tool that relies on electromagnetism.** 🎧 Now this tool, which, as I mentioned before, is usually used by geophysicists, um, **mainly to distinguish between different materials that look the same to the naked eye but have different compositions.** **Q6** **Regular soil conducts electricity well, but walls made of peat, not so much.** The tool sends electromagnetic pulses into the ground and sensors pick up the speed at which the pulses come back. Um, electricity will travel faster or slower depending on the soil type. In this case, a faster signal will mean regular soil, while a slower one is a sign of peat. In this way, buried peat walls can be detected.

So anyway, the team wanted to investigate a site in Iceland that looks like the place where the old saga says the Thorfinnsons built their home.

Finding

연구팀이 원격감지장치를 이용해 유적지 발견

Q5 **Using this technique, the team found the remains of a large farmhouse. The dating of the building corresponded exactly to the time the Thorfinnson family would have lived there, according to the story.** The team is working to find other evidence, especially personal artifacts. Most people looking for the house thought it was most likely located right underneath a nearby museum. They assumed it had been damaged during the construction, but it was actually located in a nearby field. Without the remote sensing tool, this house might not have even been found forever.

Role

장비 없이는 불가능

Practice Questions

[01 ~ 06] **Listen to part of a lecture in an archeology class. Then answer the questions.**

MP3 73 | 정답 및 해석 p. 165

Note-taking

01   What does the professor mainly discuss?
   Ⓐ The role of evidence in dating archaeological sites
   Ⓑ Evidence that the inhabitants of NM1 were hunter-gatherers
   Ⓒ A debate about the origins of shark teeth found in NM1
   Ⓓ An example of early jewelry-making in South America

02   What can be inferred about the shark teeth found at NM1?
   Ⓐ They represent evidence of an ancient fishing people.
   Ⓑ They are representative of the art made in the Holocene era.
   Ⓒ They were actually found in a different region of Argentina.
   Ⓓ They are unique among the artifacts found at the site.

03 Why does the professor mention the equipment that ancient groups used to fish for sharks?
   Ⓐ To give evidence that the inhabitants of NM1 fished
   Ⓑ To suggest that a hypothesis is invalid
   Ⓒ To explain why shark teeth were found at the site
   Ⓓ To describe the habits of similar cultures

04 What is something that archaeologists would likely find in other archeological sites near NM1?
   Ⓐ The bones of hunted animals
   Ⓑ The remains of eaten fish
   Ⓒ Fossilized shark teeth made into jewelry
   Ⓓ Special equipment for shark fishing

05 According to the professor, why were there holes in the shark teeth?
   Ⓐ They were on the beach for a long time.
   Ⓑ They were damaged when the shark bit its prey.
   Ⓒ They were broken by a tool used to pull them out.
   Ⓓ They were used for ornamental purposes.

06 What does the professor believe is the most likely origin of the shark teeth?
   Ⓐ They were the result of trading.
   Ⓑ They were obtained through fishing.
   Ⓒ They were pulled from a shark's mouth.
   Ⓓ They were found inside a shark's prey.

03 Business

TOEFL에서 business경영학 분야는 수험자가 가장 어려워하는 분야 중 하나이다. 이 분야의 주제가 다양하기 때문이기도 하지만, 강의의 전개방식이 여러 번 바뀌기도 하기 때문이다. 예를 들어, 강의의 도입부분에서는 경영의 한 방법에 대해서 목적과 기능을 설명하며 마치 이것이 강의의 주된 내용인 것 같은 느낌을 준다. 하지만 곧이어, 회사에 특정 문제가 발생했을 때 그 방법을 적용해서 어떻게 해결할 수 있는지, 또 그 방법을 어떻게 세 가지로 구분하는지 등이 언급되며 내용이 여기저기로 뻗어나가기도 한다. 이 때문에 강의의 핵심을 잘못 이해하고 문제에 적용하려다가 정답을 찾지 못해 곤란해지는 일이 생긴다. 하지만 경영학 강의 지문의 이런 특징을 잘 이해하고, 각 문제 유형이 주제와 어떻게 결합되는지를 기억하면 실전에서 보다 수월하게 정답을 찾을 수 있다.

출제포인트
- Q1 Main Idea
- Q2 Function (Influence / Application)
- Q3 Problem
- Q4 Solution (Suggestion)
- Q5 Example
- Q6 Cause (Evidence) & Effect (Result / Finding / Research)
- Q7 Similarity / Difference
- Q8 Advantage / Disadvantage
- Q9 Misunderstanding / Correction
- Q10 Definition (Term) / Origin
- Q11 Two Click / Three Click
- Q12 Ordering
- Q13 Matching
- Q14 Opinion / Attitude
- Q15 Headset
- Q16 Requirement (Condition)
- Q17 Character
- Q18 Imply / Infer

1 Tariff관세

관세의 목적은 자국의 미약한 산업을 보호Q2하는 데 있다. 관세를 부여하게 되면 수입품의 판매가가 올라가므로, 국내 생산업자들의 제품에 가격경쟁력이 생겨서 소비자들이 국산품을 더 많이 소비하게 되고, 이로 인해 국내 산업을 발전Q8시킬 수 있다. tariff는 세금이기 때문에 정부 입장에서는 국가의 revenue수입가 증가Q8하는 이점도 있다. 그러나, 어떤 시장을 조기에 개방하고 어떤 시장을 장기적으로 보호해야 국가 이익에 더 도움이 될지 결정하는 것은 쉽지 않은 일이다.Q8

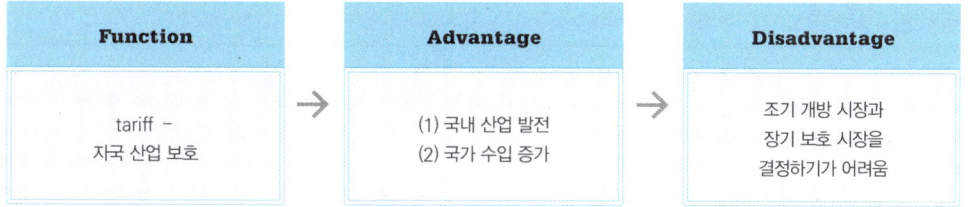

2 Segmentation 세분화

모든 잠재고객이 구매 능력이 있는 것이 아니므로, 물건을 판매할 때는 시장과 고객을 segment 부분로 나누어 공략해야 한다. ♥2 segmentation은 물건의 가격을 결정하고 광고 전략을 세우는 데 있어 비용과 노동의 측면에서 매우 효과적이다. ♥8 고가의 수입 차량을 예로 들어보면, 어느 연령대에서 가장 많이 구입하고 연령별로 어느 색상을 선호하는지 등의 demographics 인구통계를 이용한 classification 분류이 필요하다. ♥5 market segmentation 시장 세분화에는 고려해야 할 세 가지 조건이 있다. 첫 번째는 수익성이다. ♥16 많이 팔아도 수익이 많이 나지 않으면 아무런 의미가 없기 때문이다. 두 번째는 접근성이다. ♥16 segment 안에 들어가는 사람들이 누구나 상품에 접근하기 쉬워야 한다. 세 번째는 예측성이다. ♥16 잠재고객이 어느 정도인지 예측할 수 있어야 segmentation의 효과를 극대화할 수 있다.

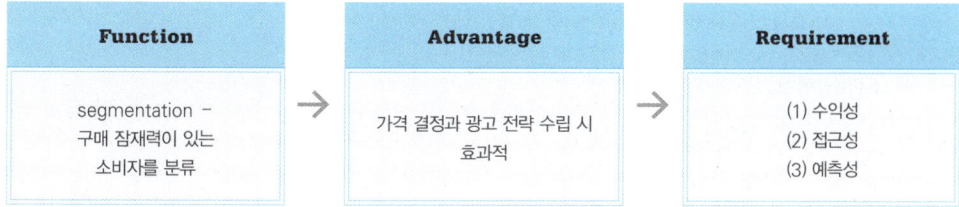

3 Opportunity Cost 기회비용

기회비용은 A와 B를 한꺼번에 할 수 없을 때, 둘 중 한 가지의 기회를 잃어 버리게 되는 것이다. ♥10 예를 들어, 영화(A)를 보고 싶은데 공부(B)도 해야 할 때, 둘 중 하나를 하게 되면 나머지 하나를 못하게 되는 것을 말한다. 산업을 예로 들어 보자. 바나나는 미국에서도 재배할 수 있지만, 남미 국가들의 기후가 더 좋고 노동력이 더 싸기 때문에 남미 국가들이 바나나 재배에 있어 absolute advantage 절대우위를 가지고 있다. 반면, 전자제품의 경우에는 미국이 기술력과 기반산업을 잘 갖추고 있기 때문에 절대우위를 가지고 있다. 미국이 바나나 재배를 선택한다면 전자제품 생산에서 얻을 수 있는 더 높은 수익을 놓칠 수 있다. 따라서, 미국은 전자제품을 생산하고 바나나는 남미 국가와의 무역을 통해 수입함으로써 기회비용을 방지한다. ♥6 기회비용 개념은 각 국가가 어떤 제품 생산에 주력하고 어떤 제품을 수입하는 것이 국가 경제에 도움이 되는지 판단하는 데 중요한 수단 ♥2이 된다.

Definition (Term)	Cause	Application
기회비용 – 선택으로 인한 기회 상실	trade를 하는 이유 – 기회비용 방지	어떤 제품을 수입할 것인지 결정하는 데 활용

핵/심/표/현

- absolute advantage 절대우위
- accordingly adv. 그에 맞춰
- accuse A of B B의 이유로 A를 비난[고소]하다
- acknowledge v. 인정하다
- adjust v. 조정하다
- adman n. 광고인
- advertisement n. 광고
- advertising plan 광고안
- affluence n. 풍요
- aggressive adj. 공격적인, 대단히 적극적인
- alliance n. 연합, 동맹
- annual budget 연간 예산
- attention-grabbing adj. 관심을 끄는
- auction n. 경매
- bank loan 은행대출
- be attributed to ~ ...에 기인하다
- bidder n. (경매) 가격 제시자
- billboard n. 광고판
- boom and bust 벼락 경기와 불경기의 교체, 일시적인 비정상적 호경기
- borrowing n. 대출, 차용(금)
- business owner n. 사업주
- client n. 고객
- collaborate v. 협력하다, 공동으로 작업하다
- collapse v. 붕괴하다, 무너지다
- commercial adj. 상업의
- commodity n. 상품, 물품
- comparative advantage 상대적 우위
- conflict n. 분쟁, 갈등
- consumerism n. 소비; 소비지상주의
- cost n. 값, 비용
- credit n. 신용 거래, 융자; 신용도
- criteria n. (pl.) 기준, 표준
- dealer n. 딜러, 중개인
- deliberately adv. 의도적으로
- demographics n. 인구 통계 (자료)
- direct mail n. 광고용 우편물
- disposable income 가처분 소득
- drive n. 욕구
- electronics n. 전자제품
- employer n. 고용주
- ensure v. 보장하다
- entrepreneur n. 기업가, 사업가
- expertise n. 전문 지식[기술]
- exploit v. 활용하다, 이용하다
- factual adj. 사실에 기반을 둔
- federal subsidy 연방 보조금
- financial assistance n. 융자, 대출
- flourish v. 번창하다, 번영하다
- flyer n. 전단
- fund n./v. 기금(을 대다)
- go hand in hand 관련되다; 함께 가다
- Great Depression 경제 대공황
- guarantee v. 보장하다
- income n. 소득
- Industrial Revolution 산업혁명
- industry cluster 산업 단지
- infrastructure n. 사회[공공] 기반 시설
- interplay n. 상호 작용
- invade privacy 사생활을 침해하다
- irrational adj. 비이성적인
- lucrative adj. 수익성이 좋은
- luxury n. 호화로움, 사치
- market research[survey] 시장조사
- market segmentation 시장 세분화
- maximize v. 극대화하다

- media   n. 대중 매체, 미디어
- merchandise   n. 물품, 상품
- merchant   n. 상인
- metropolitan   n./adj. 대도시(의)
- minimize   v. 최소화하다
- miss out on ~   ...을 놓치다
- monetary   adj. 화폐[통화]의
- mortgage   n. 대출, 융자, 저당
- native to ~   ...에 고유한
- opportunity cost   기회비용
- outdated   adj. 구식인
- outsource   v. 외부에 위탁하다
- packaging   n. 포장
- panic   n. 극심한 공포, 공황
- patron   n. 후원자
- patronage   n. 후원
- per capita   1인당
- persevere   v. 인내하며 계속하다
- personalize   v. (개인의 필요에) 맞추다
- potential customer   n. 잠재 고객
- poverty   n. 가난, 궁핍
- product   n. 생산품, 상품, 제품
- profit   n. 이익, 수익
- profitable   adj. 이익이 되는, 수익성이 있는
- promissory note   약속 어음
- prosper   v. 번영하다, 번창하다
- rent   v. 세내다, 임차하다; 집세, 임차료
- retail   n. 소매, 소매상
- revenue   n. (정부·기관의) 수익, 수입
- salesperson   n. 판매원
- scale   n. 규모, 범위
- segment   n. 부분
- significance   n. 의미, 중요성
- skilled labor   숙련공; 숙련 노동
- slogan   n. 구호
- slot   v. (가느다란 자리에) 넣다, 들어가다
- sort out   선별하다, 분류하다
- sponsor   n. 스폰서, 후원자
- statistics   n. 통계
- subsistence   n. 최저 생활
- tailor   v. 맞추다
- target age group   목표 연령대
- tariff   n. 관세
- tax   n. 세금
- taxation   n. 조세, 세수; 과세제도
- tax incentive   n. 세금 혜택, 감세 조치
- trademark   n. 상표
- trading route   n. 교역로, 통상로
- urbanization   n. 도시화
- utilize   v. 이용하다
- wholesale   adj. 도매의
- year-round   adj. 연중 계속되는

Sample Questions

[01 ~ 06] **Listen to part of a lecture in a business class. Then answer the questions.**

MP3 74 정답 및 해석 p. 169

Note-taking

- Correction / Finding:
- Main Idea:
- Requirement:
- Example:
- Role:

- Requirement:
- Disadvantage:

01 What is the lecture mainly about?
   Ⓐ Various methods of direct marketing
   Ⓑ Using direct mail successfully
   Ⓒ Ways to satisfy consumer demands
   Ⓓ How to develop products consumers want

02 What does the professor say about companies that use direct mail advertising?
   Ⓐ They need to spend more time preparing their ads.
   Ⓑ They should also use television advertising campaigns.
   Ⓒ They don't have to spend as much to make a profit.
   Ⓓ They utilize the newest technology in their ad campaigns.

03 Why does the professor mention sports cars?
   Ⓐ To illustrate the difficulty of knowing how some consumers will react to an ad
   Ⓑ To suggest it is important to ensure the quality of a product before advertising it
   Ⓒ To show how a poorly worded advertisement can have negative consequences
   Ⓓ To emphasize the need to find out who would be interested in certain products

04 What are the main roles of list sellers? Choose two answers.
   Ⓐ Hiring brokers to sell a company to potential buyers
   Ⓑ Obtaining and organizing information about consumers
   Ⓒ Analyzing which consumers would sell a company's product
   Ⓓ Checking to see which people buy the products of their clients

05 What does the professor imply about deciding when to send direct mail advertising?
   Ⓐ It should be decided by the list seller, not the company.
   Ⓑ It may be best to send the advertisements year-round.
   Ⓒ It is better to rely on research than on common sense.
   Ⓓ It is not a good idea to send direct mail during big events.

Listen again to part of the lecture. Then answer the question. 🔊 MP3 74_1

06 Why does the professor say this?
   Ⓐ To prove that people no longer use regular mail
   Ⓑ To point out that few people like receiving junk mail
   Ⓒ To point out that companies should send out lots of catalogues
   Ⓓ To emphasize that companies must identify relevant consumers

▶ **Question Review**

Correction / Finding
DM 광고가 TV 광고보다 이윤을 더 많이 창출한다는 연구결과

Main Idea
좋은 DM 광고 플랜

Requirement
사람들을 카테고리로 분류할 필요가 있음

Headset

Example
관심 없는 사람에게 보내는 걸 피해야 함 – 캠핑 차를 예로 들어 설명

Role
list seller의 역할

Listen to part of a lecture in a business class.

Professor(female): Let's get started. Um, last time we were talking about the need for advertising. Now, let's look at a method that might seem a little outdated but is very effective nonetheless. **Q1 We're going to talk about direct mail advertising.** This method of direct advertising involves mailing letters and catalogues directly to consumers. You might think that it would be very ineffective, but you'd be surprised at how much revenue can be attributed to direct mailing campaigns. In a recent study, **Q2 it was found that direct mail advertising generates about double the profit that advertising on television does.** That's right – every dollar spent on junk mail advertisements generates as much as ten dollars in sales while television advertising only generates half of that. **Even ads that use newer technology, such as email advertisements and website banner ads don't even come close to the revenue generated by direct mail advertising.**

Q1 But what does a good direct mail advertising plan look like? A good plan uses one of the basic techniques of direct marketing. The basis of this technique is a complex analysis of the purchasing habits of consumers – what products draw the attention of consumers, how a potential customer reacts to trends… But in order to do this, we first need to slot people into categories, such as occupation or age, as well as more refined categories. For example, people who have bought sedans, four-door cars, or vegetarians that eat out more than twice a week. Such precise labeling of people can save companies money. 🎧 **Q6 It's not like companies can send out a bunch of catalogues and assume everyone will want to take a look at them.** They have to carefully sort out what type of people would want to take a look at their specific catalogues. In other words, **Q3 companies need to avoid sending advertisements to consumers who will not be interested in their merchandise. You wouldn't want to try to sell a camping trailer to people who drive sports cars and live in a metropolitan city without any parking space.** So, now let's take a look at the detailed steps needed to create a successful mail advertising campaign, and how the analysis of consumers fits in with the way the campaign is conducted. The first step is obtaining information about the purchasing habits of people. Now, it would simply take too much of a company's resources to do this themselves, so the work is outsourced to list sellers. **Q4-B The list sellers are the ones who gather information about what consumers are interested in.** There are many methods of gaining this information, but many sellers keep this a secret for obvious reasons. The list buyer, in this case a company that wants to obtain a list of people to send its catalogues to, will request a list of people that meet a certain criteria. The list seller will either directly or indirectly sell a list of people who meet the criteria. I said indirectly because many companies go through list brokers. It's quite a complex process just to get the right information, huh?

Anyway, the next step is to send the flyers and catalogues through the mail. We can't just send anything and expect people to read it in great detail. People don't spend more than five seconds looking at one piece of junk mail. In response, marketers have developed attention-grabbing methods to catch a person's interest – tailoring their ads to individuals, for instance. More sales result from personalized appeals to consumers than from strictly factual ads. Some companies even employ hundreds of people to hand-write letters. One business actually deliberately adds crossed out mistakes to its letters to create a more personal touch.

Once the mail is sent, **Q4-D** **the list sellers gather more information about the consumers' response rate to the ads…** um… **This would include how many consumers actually order products from the catalogue.** It's the company's responsibility to give this information to the list sellers so the sellers can analyze it in order to improve the effectiveness of their lists in the future… because once the data is organized, the whole process is repeated.

Oh, I almost forgot! We can't forget that the timing of the mail is just as important as who it is sent to. Like, maybe you're advertising electronics, and you have been spending most of your budget during the winter holiday season, when people buy gifts for each other. Now, **Q5** **that would seem to be a great time to advertise, but that might be wrong.** Sometimes it might be better to send out a catalogue during a major sporting event like the Olympics. What's important is that just as a company carefully sorts out who to send their mail to, **the company must also conduct research on when having a mail advertisement campaign is more effective. You need to get the facts – facts that come from good research – to be certain, and to know for sure that you're getting your money's worth.**

One other thing that you might want to consider is how sending the mail will affect the image of a company – how a consumer might perceive a company that sends out junk mail. It's important to keep in mind that not everybody supports this very lucrative method of advertising. Although it is the list sellers that gather the personal information, people will question the company with its name on the catalogue. They may even accuse the company of invading their privacy. This too can be prevented with more research. So in order for any marketing campaign to be successful, we must keep in mind the need for proper research.

Requirement
우편 광고를 위한 최적의 시기 조사도 필요함

Disadvantage
고려해야 할 사항 – junk mail로 인한
(1) 회사 이미지 실추 가능성
(2) 사생활 침해로 비난 받을 가능성

Practice Questions

[01 ~ 06] **Listen to part of a lecture in a business class. Then answer the questions.**

MP3 75 정답 및 해석 p. 171

Note-taking

01 What is the lecture mainly about?
   Ⓐ The reasons people become salespeople
   Ⓑ Character traits of effective salespeople
   Ⓒ How to understand customer demands
   Ⓓ The secrets of getting the lowest price

02 According to the professor, what characteristic of ego-driven salespeople makes them good at what they do?
   Ⓐ They are confident in their understanding of the product.
   Ⓑ They can relate to the person buying the product.
   Ⓒ They want to finish whatever they start.
   Ⓓ They want to be better than their coworkers.

03 Why does the student mention buying a car?
  Ⓐ To prove that everyone has some empathy
  Ⓑ To point out the bad side of ego-driven salespeople
  Ⓒ To provide an example of an effective salesperson
  Ⓓ To request a clearer explanation from the professor

04 According to the professor, what problem will empathic salespeople face?
  Ⓐ They will be too honest about a product's faults.
  Ⓑ They will make customers feel bad for buying a product.
  Ⓒ They will lose sales to more aggressive salespeople.
  Ⓓ They will not feel good after making a sale.

05 What does the professor say about companies that hire salespeople?
  Ⓐ They fail to look at the sales abilities of the applicants.
  Ⓑ They do not take the interests of the applicants into account.
  Ⓒ They only seek out people who have empathy.
  Ⓓ They scare away people who care about what they sell.

06 Why does the professor say this? 🔊 MP3 75_1
  Ⓐ To ask students if they are familiar with art
  Ⓑ To acknowledge her lack of expertise in art
  Ⓒ To suggest that anyone can be a good salesperson
  Ⓓ To explain the importance of skill over interests

04 Education

TOEFL에서 education교육학 분야는 심리학과 결합된 교육심리학에 관한 지문이 출제되는 경우가 많다. 강의는 교사가 학생을 지도할 때 발생하는 문제점과 해결 방법을 차례대로 제시하는 〈Problem문제 - Solution해결 방법〉 전개방식이 주를 이룬다. 또한, 교육 혁신을 일으킨 인물이 제시한 새로운 교육 방식과 기존 교육 방식 간의 차이점, 또는 새로운 교육법의 장단점 및 그 교육법에 알맞은 교육 대상에 관한 문제 등이 출제되기도 한다.

출제포인트
- Q1 Main Idea
- Q2 Function (Influence)
- Q3 Problem
- Q4 Solution (Suggestion)
- Q5 Example
- Q6 Cause (Evidence) & Effect (Result / Finding / Research)
- Q7 Similarity / Difference
- Q8 Advantage / Disadvantage
- Q9 Misunderstanding / Correction
- Q10 Definition (Term) / Origin
- Q11 Two Click / Three Click
- Q12 Ordering
- Q13 Matching
- Q14 Opinion / Attitude
- Q15 Headset
- Q16 Requirement (Condition)
- Q17 Character
- Q18 Imply / Infer

1 Montessori몬테소리

이탈리아 교육자 Montessori는 발달장애 학생들을 가르쳐 일반인 학생들보다 더 좋은 성적을 받게 하는 기적을 일으켰다.Q18 그녀의 교육방식은 일반적인 교육방식과 차이가 있었다. 우선 선생님들의 역할이 달랐다. 일반 교실에서는 교사가 일방적으로 학생들에게 지식을 전달하는 반면, Montessori는 self-directed learning자기 주도형 학습법을 이용하여, 학생들이 각자 배우고 싶은 교구를 고르면 교사는 교구 사용법만 알려주고 학생이 스스로 학습하게 하였다.Q7 학생들이 스스로 선택한 교구로 학습하기 때문에 동기 부여 측면에서 굉장한 이점이 있었다.Q8 둘째는 교실 책상과 의자의 크기가 달랐다.Q7 Montessori는 아이들이 마음대로 움직일 수 있는 큰 책상에서 친구들과 삼삼오오 모여 앉아 이야기할 수 있도록 했다.Q8 세 번째. Montessori는 아이들에게 사회적인 역할 및 책임도 가르쳤다.Q7 상대방의 물건을 만질 때는 반드시 허락을 먼저 받게 하고, 교실을 어지럽혔을 경우 스스로 청소하게 하였다. 마지막으로, 아이들이 교구를 직접 만져 보면서 개념을 공부하기 때문에 학습 효과가 훨씬 좋았다.Q7, Q8 예를 들어, 나무 블록을 가지고 덧셈과 뺄셈의 개념을 배우는 것Q5은 좋은 학습 효과를 거두었다.

Character		Difference – Advantage
Montessori의 기적 – 발달장애 학생이 일반인 학생보다 좋은 성적을 받음	→	(1) 자기주도형 학습 – 동기 부여가 큼 (2) 가구 크기의 차이 – 삼삼오오 모여 이야기함 (3) 사회적 책임 교육 (4) 교구를 만지면서 학습 – 학습 효과 큼

2 Break Time 쉬는 시간

미국 초등학교의 수업 시간 구조를 연구한 결과, 각 학교가 경쟁적으로 더 많은 내용을 가르치려다 보니 수업 시간을 포함한 학습 시간을 늘리고 학생들이 휴식을 취할 수 있는 쉬는 시간은 점차 줄이고 있었다.♀93 하지만, 학생들에게 적당한 휴식 시간을 주는 것은 매우 중요하다.

8~10세 학생들을 관찰한 결과, 적당량의 휴식 시간을 가진 학생들이 쉬는 시간 이후에 수업 집중도가 좋아졌다는 연구결과가 있다.♀96, ♀98 또한 쉬는 시간에 날씨가 좋으면 아이들이 운동장에서 뛰어 노는데, 적당한 운동은 아이들이 건강한 신체를 갖는 데 도움이 된다.♀98 마지막으로, 쉬는 시간에 아이들은 어떻게 행동해야 하는지 서로 배울 수 있고, 어떻게 협력하면서 놀아야 하는지도 배울 수 있다.♀98 그러나, 쉬는 시간에 아이들이 놀다가 다칠 수도 있고 힘이 센 학생이 힘이 약한 학생을 괴롭힐 수도 있으므로, 교사는 쉬는 시간에도 지속적으로 아이들을 관찰해야 한다.♀16

Problem		Advantage		Requirement
수업 시간 증가로 쉬는 시간 감소	→	쉬는 시간의 장점 – (1) 집중력 향상 (2) 건강에 도움 (3) 학생들끼리 배움	→	교사의 지속적인 관찰

핵/심/표/현

- accelerate v. 가속화하다
- adopt n. 채택하다
- algebraic adj. 대수학의
- approach n. 접근(법)
- argument n. 주장, 논쟁
- assign v. 부여하다, 할당하다
- associate A with B A를 B와 관련시켜 생각하다
- attach v. 붙이다; 연관되다
- attempt v. 시도하다, 애써 해보다
- babbling adj. 재잘거리는; 옹알이하는
- board of directors n. 이사회, 경영진
- case study n. 사례 연구
- celebrated adj. 유명한, 저명한
- celebrity n. 유명 인사
- commonplace adj. 흔한, 널린, 다반사의
- communal adj. 공동의
- compliment n. 칭찬, 찬사
- comprehensive adj. 포괄적인, 종합적인
- compute v. 계산하다, 산출하다
- coordination n. (신체 동작의) 조정력
- corresponding adj. (...에) 해당하는, 상응하는
- counterintuitive adj. 반직관적인
- decision-making n. 의사 결정
- dedicate v. 헌신하다, 바치다, 전념하다
- directorship n. (회사의) 이사직
- disabled adj. 장애가 있는
- disillusion v. 환상을 깨뜨리다
- disruptive adj. 지장을 주는
- drive n. 욕구, 충동
- encourage v. 격려하다, 고무하다
- entity n. 독립체
- experimental adj. 실험적인, 실험의
- faculty n. 교수진
- figure out 생각해내다; 이해하다
- found v. 설립하다, 세우다
- get along with ~ ...와 잘 지내다
- govern v. 지배하다, 다스리다
- hands-on adj. 실천하는, 직접 해 보는
- have a say 발언권이 있다
- hierarchy n. 계급, 계층
- influential adj. 영향력 있는, 영향력이 큰
- initially adv. 처음에
- innate adj. 선천적인, 타고난
- institution n. 기관
- instill v. (생각을) 심어주다, 서서히 주입시키다
- instinct n. 본능, 직감
- institutionalized adj. 일상화된; 자활 능력이 결여된
- instruct v. 지시하다, 가르치다
- intellectual adj. 지적인
- interactive adj. 상호적인, 상호작용을 하는
- interdisciplinary adj. 학제간의(여러 학문 분야가 관련된)
- intuitively adv. 직감적으로
- kinetic adj. 운동의
- lengthen v. (시간·길이 등을) 늘리다
- live by ~ ...에 따라 살다
- maturity n. 성숙함, 원숙함
- merit n. 장점, 유익한 점
- mind-numbing adj. 지루한, 따분한
- motivation n. 동기, 자극
- occasional adj. 가끔의, 때때로의
- parlance n. 말투, 용어
- participant n. 참가자
- perspective n. 시각, 관점
- practical adj. 현실적인, 실질적인
- predetermined adj. 미리[사전에] 결정된
- prioritize v. 우선순위를 매기다

- priority   n. 우선 사항
- privilege   n. 특전
- profession   n. 직업
- progressive   adj. 진보적인, 혁신적인
- proponent   n. 지지자, 옹호자
- punishment   n. 벌, 처벌
- rank   v. 등급을 매기다
- reinforce   v. 강화하다
- reinforcer   n. 강화 인자
- remarkable   adj. 놀라운, 훌륭한
- revolutionary   adj. 획기적인
- reward   n./v. 보상(하다)
- self-directed   adj. 자기 주도적인
- stately   adj. 장엄한, 위엄이 있는
- stem from ~   …에서 유래하다, 근거하다
- systematic   adj. 체계적인, 조직적인
- tactile   adj. 촉감의, 촉감을 이용한
- unjust   adj. 부당한, 불공평한
- virtually   adv. 사실상
- warrant   v. 보장하다, 정당화하다
- well-behaved   adj. 품행이 바른

Sample Questions

[01 ~ 06] Listen to part of a lecture in an education class. Then answer the questions.

MP3 76   정답 및 해석 p. 174

Note-taking

• Main Idea:

• Influence:

• Role:

• Difference:

• Example:

01   What does the professor mainly discuss?
    Ⓐ Comparisons between traditional and modern approaches to education
    Ⓑ The possible reasons why Black Mountain College was shut down
    Ⓒ A progressive school that influenced the current university system
    Ⓓ The best ways for university students to participate in school activities

02   Why does the professor mention John Dewey's principles of education?
    Ⓐ To emphasize the need to gain more than just knowledge in school
    Ⓑ To explain the need for students to have a say in a school's decisions
    Ⓒ To describe the background of the founder of Black Mountain College
    Ⓓ To introduce the underlying philosophy of Black Mountain College

03 What differences between Black Mountain College and traditional colleges does the professor mention? Choose two answers.
   Ⓐ Black Mountain College did not offer science courses.
   Ⓑ Students at Black Mountain College were required to work.
   Ⓒ Everyone at Black Mountain College had an equal say in matters.
   Ⓓ Students in traditional colleges were considered equal to their professors.

04 According to the professor, what is true about the founder of Black Mountain College?
   Ⓐ He did not agree with the teaching methods of traditional schools.
   Ⓑ He believed students should be able to focus on specific subjects.
   Ⓒ He was disillusioned with John Dewey's principles of education.
   Ⓓ He wanted to give college students a place where they could work.

05 What can be inferred about Albert Einstein?
   Ⓐ He preferred teaching other professors to teaching students.
   Ⓑ He only taught at schools that limited their class sizes.
   Ⓒ He agreed with Black Mountain College's educational philosophy.
   Ⓓ He helped Black Mountain College become financially successful.

Listen again to part of the lecture. Then answer the question. 🔊 MP3 76_1

06 Why does the student say this?
   Ⓐ She believes that the professor should stop lecturing.
   Ⓑ She does not think she needs to learn about Black Mountain College.
   Ⓒ She does not know what she is expected to do in class.
   Ⓓ She does not understand what was unique about Black Mountain College.

▶ **Question Review**

Main Idea
특별한 교육법을 추구했던 한 대학

Listen to part of a lecture in an education class.

Professor(male): So, last week we started our unit on educational approaches. **Q1 Today, we'll be doing a case study about a college that attempted to provide a different type of teaching – Black Mountain College.** It was founded in 1933 in Black Mountain, North Carolina, but was... um... shut down in 1957.

Student(female): Why are we learning about a school that failed?

P: Oh, no. It may have failed, but it wasn't because of a lack of effort... It didn't do anything wrong, not anything wrong in the sense that it was a bad school. It was just too far ahead of its time. Its educational approach was too radical for the 1930s.

Anyway, what made this school so special was its views on what education should be. **Q2 It was founded on John Dewey's principles of education.** You remember these from last class, right? Dewey's main argument was that education and learning are social and interactive processes. He thought the school itself should be a social institution, where students could have the opportunity to interact with the curriculum, that they should have the opportunity to take part in their own learning.

Headset

S: 🎧 Uh, Professor Hill? What's so special about that? **Q6 I mean, aren't we having a class discussion right now?** Isn't that taking part in our learning?

P: Yes, indeed it is. That's why it's important to note what made Black Mountain College so special. Even though the philosophies behind it are commonplace today, they weren't during its time. **Q1 It was only after this type of school was established that other liberal arts colleges began to adopt many of the same principles.**

Influence
BMC가 다른 학교에 미친 영향

Let's take a look at what education was like when the college was founded. Most colleges were focused on giving students the specific knowledge needed to be successful in a certain profession. Colleges were there for professors to teach what they knew, and the students had no say on what they wanted to learn or needed to learn. However, the **Q4 founder of Black Mountain College, John Andrew Rice, had different ideas. He not only focused on learning school subjects, he also tried to accelerate the students' emotional and intellectual maturity. He didn't agree with traditional teaching methods which only focused on learning.** He thought learning and living were intimately connected. The school was unique in its communal methods. It was created as an

Role
설립자의 철학 – 교과과목 및 감성과 지성의 성장에도 관심

Difference
다른 교육기관과의 차이점
(1) 학생과 교수진이 일을 함

(2) 학생이 학교 운영에 참여

Example
영향력 있는 인사의 교육 참여 예

experiment of "education in a democracy," with the idea that creative arts and practical responsibilities were of equal importance to the development of the intellect. **Q3-B Everyone, faculty and students alike, participated in some form of work to help the college. This included working on a farm operated by the college, constructing buildings, doing maintenance work, serving meals, and so on.**

The school was also unique in its decision-making process. Traditionally, the students, faculty, and staff were all separate entities. Each student had a relationship with his or her professors but not with the staff that helped run the school. But because Black Mountain College was a small school, the three separate groups could elect leaders, and these leaders could meet to discuss the future of the school. **Q3-C Students had as much say in what direction the school should take as the professors who were teaching there.**

The largest impact of this college stemmed from the idea of interdisciplinary studies. Students were required to take a broad range of courses. So, a science major would also be required to take art classes to gain a broader perspective of life. By the 1940s, word of what was happening at Black Mountain College got out. Soon, the board of directors included many influential artists, writers, and scientists. **Q5 Even Albert Einstein was part of the board and gave lectures.**

However, the college was too experimental in nature, and by the 1950s it had run its course. Black Mountain College, a school that strongly influenced how modern education is conducted, closed its doors in 1957.

Practice Questions

[01 ~ 06] **Listen to part of a lecture in an educational psychology class. Then answer the questions.** MP3 77 정답 및 해석 p. 176

 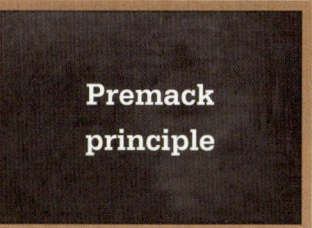

Note-taking

01   What is the lecture mainly about?
  Ⓐ Ways to encourage children to pay attention in class
  Ⓑ The best rewards for certain kinds of behavior
  Ⓒ The difficulties of teaching young children
  Ⓓ A method of encouraging good behavior in children

02   What does the professor say about a child who does the dishes?
  Ⓐ Children are very good at doing everyday chores.
  Ⓑ Children behave better when they can get a reward.
  Ⓒ Very few children listen to their parents.
  Ⓓ Children can quickly learn how to do certain tasks.

03 According to the professor, what does the Premack principle state?
Ⓐ When given a choice, people will only do what they want to do.
Ⓑ Certain kinds of activities are preferred to other kinds of activities.
Ⓒ The threat of punishment can be used to encourage good behavior.
Ⓓ All types of behavior can be encouraged or reinforced.

04 What can be inferred about children who receive toys as prizes for good behavior?
Ⓐ They will not continue to behave well in the long run.
Ⓑ They will begin to study for longer periods of time.
Ⓒ They will no longer need to be rewarded with reinforcers.
Ⓓ They will share their toys with kids who behave badly.

05 How were the children in the professor's elementary school classes rewarded?
Ⓐ They received time to study at the end of the day.
Ⓑ They were given toys and stickers.
Ⓒ They were given snacks to eat.
Ⓓ They were allowed to run around and scream.

06 What common classroom problem does the professor describe?
Ⓐ Some students cannot learn as quickly as others.
Ⓑ Certain students do not want to be in the classroom.
Ⓒ Students do not want to sit still and listen to the teacher.
Ⓓ Students cannot get along with their classmates.

05 Psychology

TOEFL에서 psychology^{심리학} 분야는 neuroscience^{신경과학}와도 관계가 있으며 뇌에 관한 지문이 가장 많이 나온다. 또한 인간의 능력을 특정 동물도 가지고 있는지 알아보기 위한 실험과 같은 case study^{사례 연구}가 강의에 자주 언급된다.

출제포인트
- ♀1 Main Idea
- ♀2 Function (Influence)
- ♀3 Problem
- ♀4 Solution (Suggestion)
- ♀5 Example
- ♀6 Cause (Evidence) & Effect (Result / Finding / Research)
- ♀7 Similarity / Difference
- ♀8 Advantage / Disadvantage
- ♀9 Misunderstanding / Correction
- ♀10 Definition (Term) / Origin
- ♀11 Two Click / Three Click
- ♀12 Ordering
- ♀13 Matching
- ♀14 Opinion / Attitude
- ♀15 Headset
- ♀16 Requirement (Condition)
- ♀17 Character
- ♀18 Imply / Infer

1 Memory^{기억}

sensory memory^{감각 기억}는 시각과 청각으로 받아들이는 external stimuli^{외부 자극}를 filtering^{걸러}해서 short-term memory^{단기 기억}로 보내 주는 역할을 한다.^{♀2} 매일 접하는 외부 자극들을 뇌가 모두 기억한다면 뇌의 용량이 금방 포화 상태가 될 것이다. 따라서, 뇌는 본인과 관련이 있거나 흥미롭다고 느끼는 정보만을 걸러서 short-term memory에 전달하고, 이 중 반복되는 정보는 long-term memory^{장기 기억}로 이동시킨다.^{♀12} long-term memory는 episodic memory^{일화 기억}와 semantic memory^{의미 기억}로 나뉘는데, 전자는 경험을 통해 보고 들은 정보가 오랫동안 기억되는 것을, 후자는 단순히 외운 것이 아니라 개념으로 이해한 정보가 오래 기억되는 것을 말한다. 기억을 떠올리는 방법에는, 예를 들어, 음악을 들을 때 이전에 들어본 적이 있다고 기억하는 recognition^{인식}과 알고 있는 정보를 기억해 주관적으로 말하는 recall^{상기}이 있다.^{♀10}

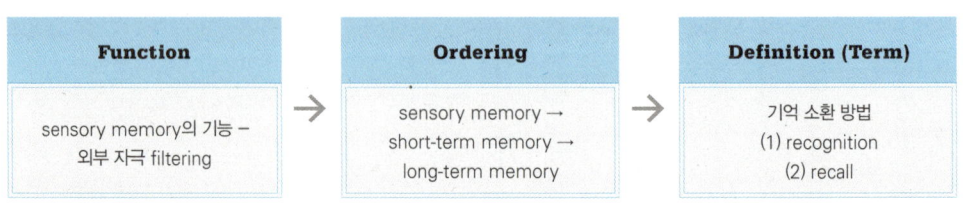

2 Object Permanence 대상 연속성

사람은 물체가 순간적으로 눈에 보이지 않게 되어도 그 대상이 없어지지 않고 연속적으로 존재한다는 것을 알고 있다. 예를 들어, 어린아이의 장난감을 빼앗아 등 뒤에 감추면, 아이는 등 뒤쪽으로 손을 뻗으며 다시 달라고 할 것이다. 눈에는 보이지 않는 장난감이 등 뒤에 있다는 것을 아는 능력 덕분이다. 이것이 object permanence이다. 동물도 이런 능력을 가지고 있는지에 대한 case study 사례 연구 Q1를 해 보았다. 원숭이에게 바나나를 보여준 뒤 감추면, 원숭이는 감춰둔 곳에 가서 바나나를 찾아냈다. 조금 더 복잡한 실험도 해 보았다. box 1과 box 2를 나란히 놓고, 바나나를 box 1에 넣는 것을 원숭이에게 보여준다. 그런 후, 원숭이의 눈을 가리고 바나나를 box 1에서 box 2로 옮긴 뒤, 원숭이의 눈가리개를 없애고 비어있는 box 1을 보여 주었을 때 원숭이가 box 2에서 바나나를 찾을 수 있는지를 알아보는 실험 Q12이다. 이 실험 결과를 통해, 동물도 대상 연속성이 있다는 것을 확인하였다. Q6

→ 이런 실험에 관한 강의에서는 그 결과를 반드시 들어야 한다. 결과를 토대로, 가설이 사실이라고 주장하는지 아닌지 끝까지 주의해서 듣도록 한다.

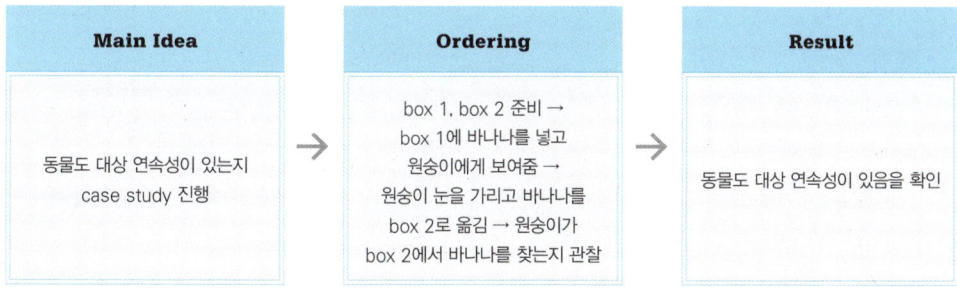

3 Blind Spot 사각지대

cognitive process 인식 과정는 과거에 대한 기억, 현재 인식하고 있는 정보, 미래에 대한 예측을 통해서 특정 정보나 지식을 이해하고 믿게 되는 과정이다. Q10 그런데, 이 세 가지 정보가 모두 정확할 것이라고 생각하는 데에는 문제가 있다. 첫째, 과거의 기억은 정확하지 않을 수 있다. Q3 예를 들어, 피실험자에게 과일 이름만 적힌 단어장 10개를 연속으로 보여 준 후 '딸기'와 '연필'이 쓰인 단어장을 보여주면, 피실험자는 앞서 본 단어장에 '딸기'는 있었지만 '연필'은 없었다고 답변한다. Q5 하지만, 사실 10장의 단어장에는 '딸기'와 '연필'이 모두 없었다. 즉, 피실험자는 같은 과일 종류인 '딸기'를 본 적이 없음에도 보았다고 잘못 기억하는 것이다. 둘째, perception 인식에도 문제가 생길 수 있다. Q3 다른 실험에서, "The Sun rises in the (   )."라는 문장을 다른 문장들과 섞어서 말한 후 피실험자들에게 east 동쪽라는 단어를 들었느냐고 물으면 대부분 들었다고 응답하는데, Q5 이는 blank 빈 부분을 자신의 인식을 이용해 알아서 채우는 현상이 발생했기 때문이다. 당연히 보거나 들었다고 인식하지만 사실이 아닌 경우를 심리학에서는 blind spot 사각지대이라고 한다. Q10 세 번째는, 예를 들어 음식점에서 주문할 때 샐러드에는 토마토가 당연히 들어갈 것이라고 기대하는 것이다. Q5, Q10 그러나 막상 나온 샐러드에 토마토가 없다면 실망하게 된다. 즉, 당연히 기대하는 것이 있는데 막상 그 기대에 못 미치는 상황이 발생하는 것은 미래상황 예측에 대한 blind spot이라고 볼 수 있다. Q10

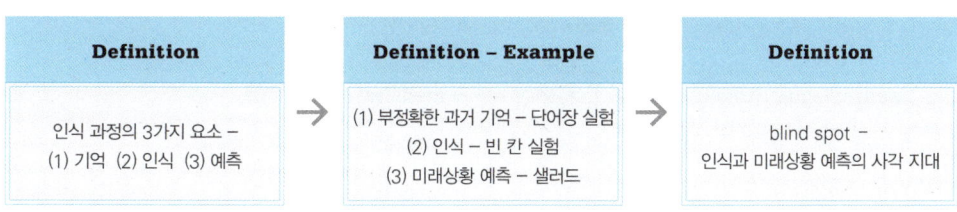

핵/심/표/현

- abnormal adj. 비정상적인
- account for ~ …을 설명하다, 해명하다
- acute adj. 극심한; 급성의
- ambivalent adj. 반대 감정이 병존하는
- amnesia n. 기억상실증
- anxiety n. 불안, 염려
- anxious adj. 불안해하는
- assess v. 평가하다
- attachment n. 애착
- attain v. 이루다, 획득하다
- beneficial adj. 유익한, 이로운
- bond n. 유대
- caregiver n. 돌보는 사람, 양육자
- classify v. 분류하다, 구분하다
- cognition n. 인식, 인지
- cognitive ability 인지적 능력
- conformity n. 따름, 순응
- confront v. 맞서다; 직면하다
- conscience n. 양심, 가책
- content adj. 만족하는
- cope v. 대처하다, 대응하다
- crawl v. 기어가다
- curiosity n. 궁금증, 호기심
- deceive v. 속이다
- deceptive adj. 속이는, 거짓말의
- deficiency n. 결핍(증), 부족
- developmental psychology 발달 심리
- diagnosis n. 진단
- diagnostic adj. 진단의
- diarrhea n. 설사
- disadvantage n. 불리한 점, 약점
- discern v. 알아차리다, 파악하다
- disinhibition n. (심리학) 탈억제 (효과), 탈제지

- disorder n. 장애
- displacement n. (정신분석) 전이
- display v. 드러내다, 보이다
- dissect v. 해부하다, 분석하다
- distracted adj. 방해되는, 산만한
- distraught adj. (흥분해서) 제정신이 아닌
- drawback n. 결점, 문제점
- egocentric adj. 자기중심적인, 이기적인
- equivalent adj. (가치, 중요도 등이) 동등한, 맞먹는
- exhibit v. 보이다, 드러내다
- filthy adj. 더러운, 역겨운
- generous adj. 너그러운, 넉넉한
- head-on adj. 정면으로 부딪친, 정면으로 대응하는
- identity n. 신원, 정체
- inconsistent adj. 내용이 다른[모순되는]
- infant n. 유아
- innate adj. 타고난, 선천적인
- insecure adj. 불안정한
- instigate v. 부추기다, 선동하다
- intention n. 의도
- intruder n. 불청객
- intuitive adj. 직관에 의한
- irrelevant adj. 관련 없는
- labyrinth n. 미로
- laryngeal adj. 후두의, 후두음의
- larynx n. 후두
- majority n. 다수, 대부분
- manifestation n. 징후, 나타남
- mature adj. 성장한, 성숙한
- maze n. 미로
- medicament n. 약물
- mental adj. 정신의, 마음의
- mental process (심리학) 정신(적) 과정, 심리 작용

- minority   n. 소수, 소수집단
- motivation   n. 동기, 자극
- nausea   n. 메스꺼움, 멀미
- newborn   n. 신생아
- nursling   n. (유모가 기르는) 유아, 젖먹이
- nurture   v. 양육하다, 보살피다
- objective   n. 목표, 목적 adj. 객관적인
- obsession   n. 집착, 강박 관념
- occurrence   n. (사건·일의) 발생, 나타남
- panic   n. (극심한) 공포, 공황
- permanence   n. 영속성, 영구성
- physical   adj. 육체적인, 신체적인
- primary   adj. 주된
- procedure   n. 절차
- provoke   v. 유발하다
- psychoanalysis   n. 정신 분석
- psychologist   n. 심리학자
- psychology   n. 심리학
- questionnaire   n. 설문지
- rational   adj. 이성적인
- reason   v. (논리적 근거에 따라) 판단하다, 추론하다
- reassure   v. 안심시키다, 진정시키다
- relaxation   n. 완화, 휴식
- relieve   v. 완화시키다, 안심시키다
- representation   n. 표현
- robust   adj. 원기 왕성한, 팔팔한
- routine   n. (판에 박힌) 일상
- secure   adj. 안정적인
- self-reliance   n. 자기 의존, 자립
- senior citizen   n. 고령자
- side effect   n. (약의) 부작용
- sign language   n. 수화
- somatic   adj. 신체의, 육체의
- spiritual   adj. 정신의, 영적인
- subjective   adj. 주관적인
- tactic   n. 전략, 작전
- temperament   n. 기질
- toddler   n. 걸음마를 걷는 아기

Sample Questions

[01 ~ 06] **Listen to part of a lecture in a developmental psychology class. Then answer the questions.** MP3 78 정답 및 해석 p. 178

Note-taking

- Main Idea:

- Term:

- Function:

- Opinion:

- Research:

- Example:

- Research:

01 What is the main purpose of the lecture?
   Ⓐ To discuss possible causes of developmental problems in infants
   Ⓑ To describe key characteristics needed to correctly raise a child
   Ⓒ To discuss the types of relationships between infant and caregiver
   Ⓓ To explain the various stages infants pass through as they grow up

02 According to the professor, what is the purpose of the Strange Situation Protocol?
   Ⓐ To help nurture proper development in infants with problems
   Ⓑ To diagnose the various development issues infants may have
   Ⓒ To determine whether an infant has a secure attachment
   Ⓓ To find out what kind of bonds infants develop with various people

03 What can be inferred about Mary Ainsworth's critics?
  Ⓐ They disagree with her methods more than her classifications.
  Ⓑ They reject the idea that infants form bonds with their caregivers.
  Ⓒ They feel that she should accept the Strange Situation Protocol.
  Ⓓ They believe she overemphasizes the comfort level of infants.

04 What is Jerome Kagan's view of Ainsworth's idea of attachment classifications?
  Ⓐ She fails to take into account the age of the infants.
  Ⓑ There are far more classifications than she has identified.
  Ⓒ Her ideas cannot be applied to cultures with different traditions.
  Ⓓ Other factors are more important in determining an infant's future.

05 What does the professor say about babies from other cultures?
  Ⓐ They are usually brought up in families with multiple caregivers.
  Ⓑ They are always classified as having a secure attachment.
  Ⓒ They may appear to be insecure because they are less dependent.
  Ⓓ They tend to form stronger attachments to their primary caregivers.

Listen again to part of the lecture. Then answer the question. 🔊 MP3 78_1

06 Why does the professor say this?
  Ⓐ He suspects the results do not accurately reflect the data.
  Ⓑ He doesn't think the students need to know all the details.
  Ⓒ He feels the students should participate in a similar study.
  Ⓓ He wants to emphasize the hardships of the researchers.

▶ **Question Review**

Main Idea 유아와 양육자 간의 유대	**Listen to part of a lecture in a developmental psychology class.** **Professor(male):** We've spent the last week talking about the psychological development of children in the early childhood years. **Q1** Now **I want to spend some time talking about the bond between an infant and the person who takes care of it, its caregiver.** Of course, in most cases it's usually a parent, but not all the time. In child development, this connection is what we call a bond attachment. Um… Attachment is the emotional relationship between the infant and the caregiver. It starts between the ages of two and seven months and gradually develops as the infant grows.
Term attachment 용어 설명	I should mention that not all babies experience positive attachment. If it is positive, we call it a secure attachment. But if not, it is referred to as an insecure attachment. But before we get into the details, I want to introduce an experiment done by the psychologist Mary Ainsworth. Ainsworth believed that an infant must develop a secure attachment with at least one primary caregiver to attain successful social and emotional development. This will allow the infant to explore the world knowing that it will always have a caregiver to rely on if needed. She assessed children by using something she called the "Strange Situation Protocol." Now, you have to keep in mind this wasn't a diagnostic tool, meaning it can't be used to determine if there's a problem with the
Function 실험의 목적 – 안정적인 애착을 가졌는지 아닌지를 판단	infant or not. **Q2** **It's a research tool to help classify whether the type of attachment the infant has is secure or insecure.** The Strange Situation Protocol involves a laboratory procedure that follows a set format. 🎧 A mother, her baby, and an experimenter enter the room. Then the experimenter leaves and a series of episodes occur. The baby is put in different situations. Sometimes the baby is left alone, sometimes the baby is with the caregiver, and sometimes the baby, the caregiver, and a stranger are together… Anyway, **Q6** **it's a pretty involved process. The results are what's important.** It's called the Strange Situation Protocol, well, because, as you can see, the baby is subject to a lot of situations it probably isn't familiar with. Okay, secure babies… when they're in the new room, they tend to explore the room, for toys, things to do… When the caregiver leaves, the baby only gets a little upset. When the caregiver comes back in, the baby is happy again and has some sort of positive interaction – the baby will smile or crawl towards the caregiver. Babies will show these signs if they have a secure attachment.

Opinion
교수 ◐ agree
비평가들 ◐ disagree

Research
다른 연구결과 (1)

다른 연구결과 (2)
Jerome Kagan의 주장

Example
주장을 설명하기 위한 예

Research
다른 연구결과 (3)

But what about insecure babies? As the name suggests, they are anxious from the moment they enter the new room. They won't look around or explore, and they might not even interact with the caregiver when he or she comes back. These babies seem confused, scared even, because they're insecure.

Although I myself agree with Ainsworth's ideas about development, it's important to note that **Q3 there are skeptics of the attachment theory and, more importantly, the Strange Situation Protocol. Critics complain that the lab environment is controlled and is therefore not an accurate representation of what happens in real life. Their argument is that the bond should be analyzed in a more natural situation – at home or someplace where the infant is comfortable.**

There have been some studies that show that a baby with an insecure attachment will display this insecurity later in life through its behavior. However, some say, the attachment really doesn't indicate what will happen in the baby's future. They say that you don't know if the baby is going to grow to be a content and confident adult. A researcher named Jerome Kagan believes that infants have the ability to adapt to different situations and can cope, in a positive way, with different styles of caregiving. **Q4 Kagan further believes that, in the long run, innate personality and temperament are more important than an infant's attachment to its caregiver.** Let's say a baby has a very low tolerance for stressful situations. The baby just doesn't know what to do when it doesn't get what it wants. That will affect what kind of adult the infant becomes more than attachment would.

Q5 Other researchers who have studied attachment in babies from different cultures have found differences in their behavior towards caregivers. While the Strange Situation Protocol might identify them as insecure, it could just be that the culture they come from encourages independence even in infants. But, I would like to point out that studies have shown that most babies fall into the category of having a secure attachment, even in other cultures.

Practice Questions

[01 ~ 06] **Listen to part of a lecture in a psychology class. Then answer the questions.**

MP3 79   정답 및 해석 p. 180

Note-taking

01   What is the purpose of the lecture?
   Ⓐ To introduce a new way of organizing belief structures in humans
   Ⓑ To show how animals can discern behavior through the actions of others
   Ⓒ To discuss whether a psychological ability can be observed in animals
   Ⓓ To explain the differences between the cognitive abilities of animals and humans

02   According to the professor, what type of behavior in animals suggests that they have a theory of mind?
   Ⓐ They communicate with each other.
   Ⓑ They attempt to deceive each other.
   Ⓒ They develop a social structure.
   Ⓓ They warn one another of danger.

03 According to the professor, why did the low-ranking vervet make the alarm call?
ⓐ It mistakenly believed that the new monkey was a predator.
ⓑ It wanted to prevent the new monkey from joining the group.
ⓒ It believed it could persuade the group to attack the new monkey.
ⓓ It didn't realize that the new monkey interpreted the alarm call differently.

04 What behavior of the vervet suggested that it might not have a theory of mind?
ⓐ It exhibited the same behavior when an actual leopard was present.
ⓑ It tried to deceive the others in order to protect its rank in the group.
ⓒ It only made an alarm call when no other vervets were present.
ⓓ It acted in a way that showed it knew there wasn't a leopard nearby.

05 What does the professor imply about observational studies of animals?
ⓐ They often produce contradictory evidence.
ⓑ They can be very difficult to carry out properly.
ⓒ They are an easier way to learn about humans.
ⓓ Different studies usually point to the same conclusion.

06 Based on the lecture, what cognitive ability do most children over the age of five have that younger children do not?
ⓐ They know how to instigate certain reactions in others.
ⓑ They are able to plan out their next action logically.
ⓒ They can discern the motivation behind the actions of others.
ⓓ They understand the link between actions and consequences.

06 Sociology

TOEFL에서 sociology사회학 분야는 학자들이 사회 현상에 대한 규칙을 발견하여 설명하는 내용이 나온다. 자주 출제되는 주제로는 social law사회제도와 social principle사회규칙 등이 있다. 강의 중 생소한 용어가 나오더라도, 대개 강의를 통해 용어의 개념부터 차근차근 설명해주므로 침착하게 들으면 된다. 특정 제도나 규칙이 어떻게 생겨났는지, 그 규칙이 어디에 적용되는지를 묻는 문제가 주로 출제되므로, 이에 focus를 두고 집중해서 듣는다.

출제포인트
- Q1 Main Idea
- Q2 Function (Application)
- Q3 Problem
- Q4 Solution (Suggestion)
- Q5 Example
- Q6 Cause (Evidence) & Effect (Result / Finding / Research)
- Q7 Similarity / Difference
- Q8 Advantage / Disadvantage
- Q9 Misunderstanding / Correction
- Q10 Definition (Term) / Origin
- Q11 Two Click / Three Click
- Q12 Ordering
- Q13 Matching
- Q14 Opinion / Attitude
- Q15 Headset
- Q16 Requirement (Condition)
- Q17 Character
- Q18 Imply / Infer

1   Meme밈(문화 전달 방식)

생명체는 DNA유전자를 통해서 후손들에게 필요한 정보를 전달하지만, 사회에서는 meme라는 전달방식을 통해 기술, 사고방식, 이야기, 노래 등을 전달한다. Q10 meme의 세 가지 요건인 지속성, 생산성, 정확성Q16이 충족되면 오랫동안 많은 사람들이 정확하게 정보를 전달받게 된다. 예를 들면, 어렸을 때 부모님이 불러 주었던 자장가는 자녀가 부모가 되어 자신의 자녀들에게 계속해서 불러 주기 때문에 첫 번째 요건인 지속성이 충족된다.Q5 두 번째 요건인 생산성은, 개구리가 알을 많이 낳아 개체보존을 최대한 유지하려고 노력하는 것처럼, 자장가도 많은 사람들에 의해 불림으로써 충족된다.Q5 세 번째 요건인 정확성은, 누군가 자장가의 가사를 틀리게 부르면 다른 사람이 틀린 가사를 지적하고 고쳐 주는 것에 의해 충족된다.Q5 이렇게 3가지 요건을 만족시킨다면, 자장가처럼 오랜 기간 동안 많은 사람들에 의해 정확한 정보가 전달된다.

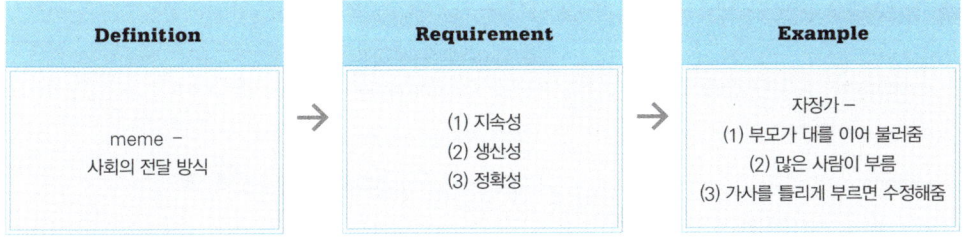

2 Bureaucracy 관료제도

관료제도는 현대적인 국가가 태동하면서 중앙정부가 강력한 행정부를 필요로 하여 생겨났으며,♡10 현재는 공공기관뿐만 아니라 회사와 같은 사설기관에도 널리 적용되고 있다. 관료제도는 위에서 내리는 지시를 조직의 담당자가 바로 이행하는 제도로, 분야별로 전문인력이 양성되어 효율성을 높인다는 장점♡8이 있지만, 담당자의 입장에서는 맡아 보지 않은 업무에 대해서는 잘 알지 못하는 단점♡8도 있다. 관료제도를 clear깨끗한하고 transparent투명한하게 운영하기 위해서는, rule규칙에 의해서만 제도를 운영♡17하고 담당자가 개인적인 감정에 따라 일 처리를 하지 않도록 해야 한다. 그러나 제도는 사람을 위해 만들어진 것이기 때문에, 사정에 따라서는 rule을 탄력적으로 적용할 수도 있어야 한다.

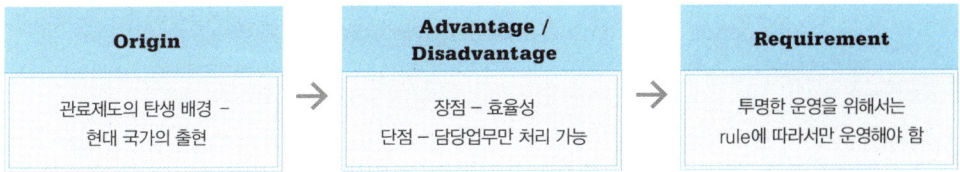

3 Guild 길드(기능인들의 조합)

사업장에 workers' union노동조합이 있듯이, 중세 시대에 공예품을 만드는 사람들인 craftspeople장인들에게는 guild가 있었다. union은 노동자들의 이익을 대변하는 역할을 하지만, guild는 instructional function교육적인 기능을 했다.♡2, ♡7 guild는 같은 기술을 가진 사람들이 모여서 물건을 만들기 시작하면서 생겨났다.♡10 최초의 guild는 중국의 한 왕조시대에 생겨났으며, 유럽에서는 로마에서 guild가 생겨난 뒤에 유럽 전역으로 퍼져나갔다. guild에서는 장인들이 모여서 기술을 share공유하다고 apprentice견습생를 훈련시켰다.♡8 또한 왕이나 정부로부터 독점권을 부여 받아 guild 외의 사람들이 유사한 제품을 만드는 것을 철저히 방지해 엄청난 부를 축적하였는데, 이 과정에서 많은 문제가 발생♡3하기도 했다. apprentice는 기술이 늘면 journeyman장인이 되어 여러 곳을 돌아다니면서 기술을 더 연마하여 master명수가 될 수 있었다.

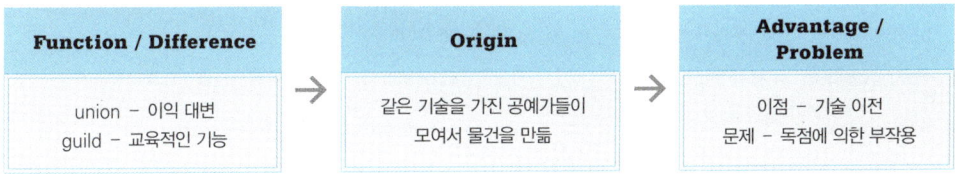

핵/심/표/현

- accuracy   n. 정확(성), 정확도
- acquaintance   n. 지인, 아는 사람
- alienate   v. 소원하게 만들다, 소외감을 느끼게 하다
- analogy   n. 비유, 유추
- aspect   n. 측면, 양상
- autonomy   n. 자율[자주]성
- be concerned with ~   ...에 관계가 있다
- buttress   v. 지지하다, 힘을 실어주다
- charity   n. 자선[구호] 단체
- chronic   adj. 장기간에 걸친, 만성적인
- commission   n. 위원회; 수수료
   v. (작품 등을) 의뢰하다, 주문하다
- communism   n. 공산주의 (체제)
- conducive   adj. ...에 도움이 되는, 공헌하는
- consensus   n. 의견 일치, 합의
- consequently   adv. 그 결과, 따라서
- contrariety   n. 반대, 불일치, 모순
- contribute   v. 기여하다
- convenience   n. 편리, 편의
- cortex   n. (대뇌)피질
- deduce   v. 추론하다, 연역하다
- disagreement   n. 의견 불일치
- displeasure   n. 불쾌감, 불만
- dominance   n. 지배, 우세
- duration   n. 지속 기간[시간]
- emerge   v. 나오다, 모습을 드러내다
- enormous   adj. 거대한, 막대한
- equation   n. 방정식, 등식
- equivalent   n. (...에) 상당[대응]하는 것
- exaggerate   v. 과장하다
- fecundity   n. 생산력; 다산
- fidelity   n. 충실함, 신의
- field of study   연구 분야
- framework   n. 뼈대, 틀, 체계
- glean   v. 얻다, 모으다
- groundbreaking   adj. 획기적인
- highlight   v. 강조하다
- impersonal   adj. 개인적인 것이 개입되지 않은
- implication   n. 영향, 결과
- indisputable   adj. 반론의 여지가 없는, 부인할 수 없는
- infallible   adj. 틀림없는, 절대 확실한
- intimate   adj. 친한, 친밀한
- involuntarily   adv. 모르는 사이에, 부지불식간에
- longevity   n. 장수, 오래 지속됨
- long-term   adj. 장기적인
- meme   n. 비유전적 문화 요소(유전자가 아닌 모방 등에 의해 다음 세대로 전달됨)
- misrepresentation   n. 와전, 그릇된 설명
- mistakenly   adv. 잘못하여, 실수로
- monumental   adj. 기념비적인, 엄청난, 대단한
- mundane   adj. 재미없는, 일상적인
- obscene   adj. 음란한, 외설적인
- ornate   adj. 화려하게 장식된
- outweigh   v. ...보다 대단하다[더 크다]
- paradigm   n. 모범, 전형적인 예
- pass on   넘겨주다, 물려주다
- presume   v. 추정하다, 여기다
- prompt   v. (행동·감정 등을) 일으키다, 유발하다
- prosecution   n. 고발, 기소
- purview   n. 범위, 권한
- rapacious   adj. 탐욕스러운, 욕심이 많은
- ratio   n. 비율, 비
- recall   v. 기억해 내다
- reclassify   v. 재분류하다
- regression   n. 퇴행, 퇴보, 회귀
- remark   n. 발언, 말

- reoccur   v. 다시 일어나다, 재발생하다
- replicate   v. 모사[복제]하다
- reproduce   v. 번식하다, 복제하다
- reputation   n. 명성
- ridicule   n. 조롱, 놀림
- rigorous   adj. 엄격한, 철저한
- search warrant   수색 영장
- sentenced   adj. 선고를 받은
- short-term   adj. 단기적인
- smuggle   v. 밀수[밀반입]하다
- stable   adj. 안정적인

- stay tuned   계속해서 주목하다
- subliminal   adj. 부지불식간에 영향을 미치는
- sue   v. 고소하다
- summarize   v. 요약하다, 간추리다
- superior   adj. 우월한, 보다 나은
- temporary   adj. 일시적인
- transmission   n. 전달, 전송
- treatment   n. 치료, 처치
- underlying   adj. 근본적인
- writ   n. (법원의) 영장

Sample Questions

[01 ~ 06] **Listen to part of a lecture in a sociology class. Then answer the questions.**

 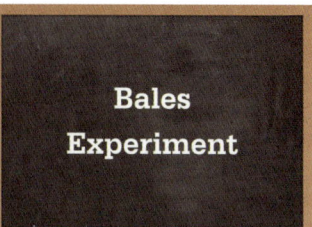

Note-taking

- Main Idea:

- Ordering:

- Character:

- Term / Example:

- Misunderstanding / Correction:

- Result:

- Ordering:

- Example:

01 What is the main purpose of the lecture?
 Ⓐ To illustrate the importance of working in groups
 Ⓑ To explain what makes groups successful
 Ⓒ To discuss Bales' views on productive discussions
 Ⓓ To point out the importance of focusing on a goal

02 What does the professor imply about the participants in the study?
 Ⓐ They were not as diverse as they should have been.
 Ⓑ They took part in the study involuntarily.
 Ⓒ They changed their behavior to satisfy Bales.
 Ⓓ They were not pleased with the results of the study.

03 According to the professor, which actions would Bales have classified as instrumental acts? Choose two answers.
   Ⓐ Voicing displeasure with the behavior of another person
   Ⓑ Praising a person about a proposed solution
   Ⓒ Suggesting a method of finding relevant information
   Ⓓ Compiling a list of reference material related to the problem

04 What is the professor's opinion of the results of the Bales Experiment?
   Ⓐ He doubts their accuracy.
   Ⓑ He finds them surprising.
   Ⓒ He is concerned about their implications.
   Ⓓ He does not understand them.

05 What can be inferred about the groups who tried to find the solutions before talking about the problem?
   Ⓐ They were the most effective at solving the problem.
   Ⓑ They displayed the highest levels of teamwork.
   Ⓒ They did not get along well with the other groups.
   Ⓓ They took a longer time to find a solution to the problem.

Listen again to part of the lecture. Then answer the question. 🔊 MP3 80_1

06 Why does the student say this?
   Ⓐ To imply that Bales failed to understand the motivations behind some behavior
   Ⓑ To suggest that the participants would have exhibited some negative behavior
   Ⓒ To demonstrate an obvious mistake in the categorizing method that Bales used
   Ⓓ To show that he thinks the professor is purposely holding back information

▶ **Question Review**

Main Idea
무엇이 그룹을 성공하게 하는가를 확인하는 실험

Ordering
실험 방법

Character
행동을 두 가지 범주로 분류

Term / Example
instrumental act 용어 설명과 그 예

expressive act의 예

Headset

Listen to part of a lecture in a sociology class.

Professor(female): Okay, I'm sure every one of you has worked in a group setting in one way or another, whether it was participating in a group project in school or planning a camping trip. And through those experiences, you've probably figured out at least some of the things that can make or break a group. Hmm... **Q1** **Today, I want to go over one experiment that was conducted to really figure out and pin down what makes groups successful.** It was done by a sociologist named Bales, so it is generally called the "Bales Experiment" (shown on screen). So what do you think makes groups successful?

Student(male): Teamwork? I mean, isn't that all that matters?

P: Yes, but how would you define teamwork?

S: Uh...

P: It's difficult, right? But that's exactly what Bales tried to do. The idea was to put small groups of people together... hmm... Well, **Q2** **he actually just used a bunch of male students from his university, for the sake of convenience.** Bales divided these guys, who had never met before, into groups. Then he made them solve all sorts of problems. When the students interacted, Bales and his assistant classified each aspect of their behavior or, uh, what Bales called their "various acts." These acts were put into different categories. So, after observing a lot of interaction, Bales hypothesized that every act, everything that the subjects did, fit into one of two basic categories – "expressive" or "instrumental."

Q3 **Instrumental acts were defined as any activity that had a direct impact on solving whatever problem the group faced. Giving information, making a suggestion, basically anything that was directly concerned with solving a problem and contributing to completing the task at hand,** like when a member said "Why don't we try to solve the problem this way?" or "Let's take a look at this." These would be considered instrumental acts. Of course, actions such as taking notes or writing up a report were considered instrumental, too.

Pretty much any other action was considered to be an expressive act. Comments and actions that had little to do with actually solving the problem at hand – things like "Thanks for the hard work guys" or "That's a great idea." 🎧 These would be considered expressive comments. Even joking around, for example, was considered expressive. Yes, Jerry?

S: But... You make it sound like Bales only observed positive behavior...

Q6 **That seems pretty unlikely.**
P: Actually, negative comments were considered to be expressive... negative expressives... such as when someone said "I can't work with you guys anymore!" So, now that we've gained a basic understanding of the underlying categories of Bale's experiment, let's talk about the conclusions he made. He was primarily interested in the ratio of instrumental and expressive acts that made a group most effective. What do you think?
S: Hmm... Wouldn't a group with a higher percentage of instrumental acts be the most successful?
P: That's the logical conclusion. I mean, if you think about it, the more instrumental acts there were, the more the group was working towards their goal, right? **Q4** **But that wasn't the case at all. The groups with the highest rates of instrumental behavior weren't very productive at all.** Instead, the most successful groups had, uh, had about a fifty-fifty ratio of instrumental and expressive acts. And their expressive acts were about one third negative and two thirds positive.

Bales also found a, um, reoccurring pattern in the way in which activities were carried out. Successful groups began their sessions by exchanging information about the problem, things like identifying the problem and the people involved in it and so on. After this information exchange, they used some of their time to voice their opinions, mainly about the causes of the problem. Then they made suggestions on how to solve the problem. Not all groups had this pattern. **Q5** **Some groups went the other way and started with trying to find solutions without first defining the problem at hand. They ended up with long periods of disagreement filled with negative expressive acts before moving on, wasting tons of time in the process.**

Misunderstanding / Correction
instrumental act가 많은 그룹이 꼭 성공적인 것은 아닌 것으로 결론

Result
50:50 비율의 그룹이 가장 성공적

Ordering
성공적인 그룹이 문제를 해결하는 순서

Example
성공적이지 못한 그룹의 예

Practice Questions

[01 ~ 06] **Listen to part of a lecture in a sociology class. Then answer the questions.**

MP3 81 정답 및 해석 p. 185

Note-taking

01 What is the lecture mainly about?
   Ⓐ The benefits of laughter
   Ⓑ Cultural variations in the use of laughter
   Ⓒ Different roles served by laughter
   Ⓓ The causes of laughter

02 According to the professor, in which situation would laughter be the least likely to occur?
   Ⓐ When a person is alone
   Ⓑ When a person does not understand a question
   Ⓒ When a person greets another person
   Ⓓ When a person wants to gain another's attention

03 According to the lecture, which is most likely to be true about people who laugh while speaking?
 Ⓐ They just thought of something funny.
 Ⓑ They want to move on to the next point.
 Ⓒ They do not have enough self-confidence.
 Ⓓ They are not interested in the conversation.

04 Why does the professor mention stand-up comedians?
 Ⓐ To give an example of something that makes people laugh
 Ⓑ To suggest that not all comedians are funny
 Ⓒ To explain the reason for using punctuation laughs
 Ⓓ To emphasize his point about laughing to get attention

05 What does the professor say about filler laughter?
 Ⓐ They occur in funny situations.
 Ⓑ They are a way of being polite.
 Ⓒ They are a way of getting a reaction.
 Ⓓ They are used to interrupt others.

Listen again to part of the lecture. Then answer the question. 🔊 MP3 81_1

06 Why does the professor say this?
 Ⓐ To indicate that laughter can help us avoid disagreements
 Ⓑ To explain the way people react when uncomfortable
 Ⓒ To help explain the role of filler laughter
 Ⓓ To ask the students for their opinion

TOEFL Listening

Actual Test

| TOEFL Listening | VOLUME | HELP | OK | NEXT |

Listening Section Directions

Please check to make sure your headset is on.
To change the volume level, click the icon in the upper right-hand corner of the screen.
Adjust the volume by moving the arrow on the volume indicator.
Click the volume icon again to close it.

This section uses conversations and lectures to test your listening skills.
It is divided into two parts that are timed separately. Each part contains a conversation and two lectures. You will listen to each one only once.
Each conversation or lecture will be followed by questions asking about the main idea and supporting details. Some may be related to a speaker's purpose or attitude. Be sure to answer the questions based on what you've heard.

Each question must be answered. After each answer, click "next". Then confirm your answer by clicking "ok". This will take you to the next question. Once you click "ok", you cannot go back and change your answer.
When taking an actual test, you will see the time remaining on a clock at the top of the screen.

Actual Test 1

Part 1 정답 및 해석 p. 189

[01 ~ 05] **Listen to a conversation between a student and a student housing employee. Then answer the questions.** MP3 82

TOEFL Listening

01 **Why does the student go to see the employee?**
Ⓐ To request a place to stay during the semester
Ⓑ To get interviewed for a job opening
Ⓒ To hand in an application for a job
Ⓓ To request more information about a job

02 **What reason does the student give for applying to become a resident assistant?**
Ⓐ He would like to stay in a room in the dorm.
Ⓑ He heard it paid better than other campus jobs.
Ⓒ He wants to help others the way that he was helped.
Ⓓ He has had problems getting along with other students.

03 **What is mentioned as a requirement of the job?**
Ⓐ Knowing how to make a study schedule
Ⓑ Having previously lived in the dorms
Ⓒ Having many acquaintances in the dorms
Ⓓ Submitting an essay about problem-solving

04 **What does the employee imply about the application process?**
Ⓐ There usually aren't enough people who apply for the position.
Ⓑ Applicants who don't meet all the requirements are not interviewed.
Ⓒ It takes place over a long period to ensure the best candidate is chosen.
Ⓓ The personalities of applicants are not as important as experience.

05 **What is the employee's attitude towards the student's story?**
Ⓐ She does not think that he is telling the truth.
Ⓑ She is not impressed by the solution he came up with.
Ⓒ She thinks that he should avoid his neighbors' problems.
Ⓓ She believes it could help him during his interview.

Part 1 정답 및 해석 p. 191

TOEFL Listening

[06 ~ 11] Listen to part of a lecture in an anthropology class. Then answer the questions. MP3 83

06 What is the lecture mainly about?
 Ⓐ Modern methods of dating artifacts made of metal
 Ⓑ The transition from the Bronze Age to the Iron Age
 Ⓒ Changing views on the start of the Iron Age in Africa
 Ⓓ The controversy caused by an archeological site in Turkey

07 What does the professor say about the Iron Age?
 Ⓐ It can be traced back to a single origin.
 Ⓑ It reached Africa later than other regions.
 Ⓒ It occurred at the same time as the Bronze Age.
 Ⓓ It started at different times in different regions.

08 According to the professor, how did scientists previously believe the Iron Age reached Africa?
 Ⓐ Turkey conquered African nations and brought them steel.
 Ⓑ North Africans obtained steel by trading with other civilizations.
 Ⓒ African civilizations copied the shape of iron tools from Europe.
 Ⓓ Sub-Saharan tribes learned how to make steel from maritime traders.

09 According to the professor, what are two methods used to trace the spread of iron usage? Choose two answers.
   Ⓐ Verifying the age of iron tools
   Ⓑ Finding different types of iron
   Ⓒ Matching the shapes of similar tools
   Ⓓ Checking historical records of commerce

10 What reasons does the professor give for the incorrect assumption regarding the Iron Age in Africa? Choose two answers.
   Ⓐ African civilizations traded with many other cultures.
   Ⓑ Civilizations in southern Africa did not use bronze tools.
   Ⓒ African people often migrated from place to place.
   Ⓓ Sub-Saharan Africa was geographically isolated.

11 According to the professor, what is the significance of the Nok culture site?
   Ⓐ It shows that African civilizations only knew how to make stone tools.
   Ⓑ It provided evidence of trade routes passing through the Sahara desert.
   Ⓒ It illustrates the dangers of introducing new technology to other cultures.
   Ⓓ It proved that not all civilizations evolved metalworking skills the same way.

Part 1 정답 및 해석 p. 193

TOEFL Listening   VOLUME HELP OK NEXT
PAUSE TEST   SECTION EXIT   HIDE TIME 03:30

[12 ~ 17] Listen to part of a lecture in a physics class. Then answer the questions.
🔊 MP3 84

  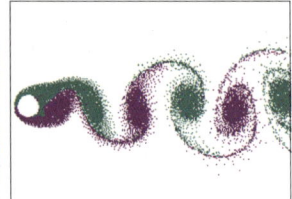

12   **What is the main purpose of the lecture?**
   Ⓐ To highlight the dangers caused by vortexes
   Ⓑ To show the many different states of fluids
   Ⓒ To discuss how moving fluids react to obstacles
   Ⓓ To explain how vortex streets were discovered

13   **What can be inferred about fluids that do not have a lot of velocity?**
   Ⓐ They are more likely to have obstacles in the path of their flow.
   Ⓑ The vortexes that occur in them cannot be seen with the naked eye.
   Ⓒ Their Reynolds numbers will be higher than those of fast-moving fluids.
   Ⓓ They are unlikely to create vortexes when impeded by an unmoving object.

14   **According to the professor, what created the vortexes seen in the picture?**
   Ⓐ The presence of thick clouds
   Ⓑ The presence of a mountain peak
   Ⓒ The difference in atmospheric pressure
   Ⓓ An airplane that passed through the clouds

15 According to the professor, why is it important to know where vortexes form?
 Ⓐ To predict changing weather conditions
 Ⓑ To avoid dangerous flying situations in these areas
 Ⓒ To study the cause of fast-moving winds
 Ⓓ To allow scientists to research viscous forces

16 What does the professor say about the swirls found in "Von Karman vortex streets"?
 Ⓐ They create forces that move outward.
 Ⓑ They will never form in fast-moving fluids.
 Ⓒ They will always move in a certain direction.
 Ⓓ They resemble a curtain that is split in two.

17 Why does the professor mention Leonardo da Vinci?
 Ⓐ To familiarize students with how science is used in art
 Ⓑ To point out that vortex streets can sometimes form in water
 Ⓒ To cite a prominent artist who depicted vortexes in his paintings
 Ⓓ To show that vortex streets were observed long before von Karman

Part 2 정답 및 해석 p. 197

TOEFL Listening

[01 ~ 05] Listen to a conversation between a student and her professor. Then answer the questions. 🔊 MP3 85

01   What is the problem the professor was addressing when the student came to his office?

Ⓐ He could not find a satisfactory way to schedule a movie screening in his class.

Ⓑ He was having trouble remembering the title of a movie he wanted to discuss.

Ⓒ He did not understand why the media center was asking him to return a movie.

Ⓓ He received a movie in a format that was different from the one he requested.

TOEFL Listening

02 **Why did the professor mention orchestra music?**
Ⓐ To explain the difference between video tapes and film reels
Ⓑ To suggest an alternative to attending the movie screening
Ⓒ To inform the student of the content of the film reel he borrowed
Ⓓ To describe the similarity between audio tapes and video tapes

03 **What can be inferred about the professor when he mentions keeping the film reel longer?**
Ⓐ He does not like following the university's rules.
Ⓑ He wants to return the film as soon as possible.
Ⓒ He has already watched the film several times.
Ⓓ He is not familiar with the media center's policies.

04 **What does the student imply when she mentions that many students want to spend time with their parents?**
Ⓐ Most professors cancel their classes during parent's week.
Ⓑ Students want to watch films with their families during parent's week.
Ⓒ Some students may miss the film if it's shown during parent's week.
Ⓓ The parents have traveled a long way to see their kids.

05 **What is the reason that the professor did not know it was parent's week?**
Ⓐ It is not an official academic event.
Ⓑ He lost the calendar the school gave him.
Ⓒ The university made a change in the academic calendar.
Ⓓ He is indifferent to his students' needs.

Part 2 정답 및 해석 p. 199

TOEFL Listening

[06 ~ 11] Listen to part of a lecture in an art history class. Then answer the questions.

🔊 MP3 86

06 What is the lecture mainly about?
  Ⓐ The shift of art from France to New York
  Ⓑ A famous European avant-garde artist
  Ⓒ The unusual style of a modern painter
  Ⓓ A modern method of painting portraits

07 According to the professor, what aspect of abstract expressionism was different from avant-garde art?
  Ⓐ It embodied a spirit of revolution.
  Ⓑ It broke the rules of traditional art.
  Ⓒ It took existing paintings and modified them.
  Ⓓ It portrayed things that could not be seen in reality.

08 What point does the professor make about Jackson Pollock during the period he was training as an artist?
  Ⓐ He painted the same work over and over again.
  Ⓑ He did not paint anything that stood out.
  Ⓒ He did not paint what most artists painted.
  Ⓓ He applied great force into his brush strokes.

09 According to the professor, what were two unique features of Pollock's painting technique? Choose two answers.
    Ⓐ He stood up when painting.
    Ⓑ He used a very small canvas.
    Ⓒ He laid the canvas on the floor.
    Ⓓ He used brushes with long handles.

10 What does the professor say about *Number 5*?
    Ⓐ It has a definite structure to it.
    Ⓑ It is a totally random work of art.
    Ⓒ It looked better once it was damaged.
    Ⓓ It has many lines and shapes that represent Pollock's feelings.

11 Why does the professor mention photographs?
    Ⓐ To stress the importance of realism in avant-garde art
    Ⓑ To explain an influence behind many of Pollock's works
    Ⓒ To point out a misconception about viewing Pollock's work
    Ⓓ To explain why the artistic community moved from Europe to the US

Part 2 정답 및 해석 p. 202

TOEFL Listening

[12 ~ 17] Listen to part of a lecture in a zoology class. Then answer the questions.

MP3 87

12. What does the professor mainly discuss?
    - Ⓐ Ways to protect migratory birds
    - Ⓑ Adaptations that allow birds to navigate
    - Ⓒ Methods of monitoring bird migration
    - Ⓓ Climate change and its effect on migration

13. Why does the professor mention the long distances migratory birds travel?
    - Ⓐ To show the adaptations that birds have
    - Ⓑ To explain why it is difficult to study some birds
    - Ⓒ To give an example of how satellites are used
    - Ⓓ To emphasize the need to preserve bird habitats

14. According to the professor, what are the disadvantages of ringing or banding birds? Choose two answers.
    - Ⓐ It is difficult to catch and band birds.
    - Ⓑ The bands sometimes harm the birds' legs.
    - Ⓒ The path of flying birds cannot be tracked.
    - Ⓓ It cannot give detailed information about bird habitats.

15 What does the professor say about using radar to observe migratory birds?
- Ⓐ It allows scientists to identify individual birds.
- Ⓑ It cannot track the path of birds that are flying.
- Ⓒ It is more effective during the day than at night.
- Ⓓ It can be used in conjunction with banding.

16 Why does the professor mention the bar-tailed godwit?
- Ⓐ To emphasize the importance of preserving bird habitats
- Ⓑ To illustrate the ability of scientists to track birds that can't fly
- Ⓒ To explain the limitations of using radar to track migratory paths
- Ⓓ To show that satellites can provide ornithologists with detailed data

17 What is the professor's opinion of technology used to study birds?
- Ⓐ It ultimately harms migratory birds.
- Ⓑ It is useful but has limitations.
- Ⓒ It produces inaccurate information.
- Ⓓ It creates more questions than it answers.

Actual Test 2

Part 1 정답 및 해석 p. 205

TOEFL Listening   VOLUME HELP OK NEXT
PAUSE TEST   SECTION EXIT

[01 ~ 05] Listen to a conversation between a student and his professor. Then answer the questions. 🔊 MP3 88

01   Why does the student go to see the professor?
   Ⓐ To ask about becoming a humanities major
   Ⓑ To get advice about what to do about his major
   Ⓒ To talk about the grade he received in his paper
   Ⓓ To get information about writing his senior thesis

02 What's the professor's attitude toward the student's dilemma?
- Ⓐ She does not think it is relevant to the class she teaches.
- Ⓑ She feels the student is making a big problem out of nothing.
- Ⓒ She believes that the student is not alone in his struggles.
- Ⓓ She thinks the student should spend more time thinking about it.

03 What does the professor imply about writers?
- Ⓐ Many of them cannot link points together.
- Ⓑ Many of them struggled to find a suitable major.
- Ⓒ They need to have knowledge about computers.
- Ⓓ They can generally major in anything they want.

04 Why does the professor suggest that the student write a research paper in his computer sciences class?
- Ⓐ Graduate schools require senior theses.
- Ⓑ The student needs extra credit to graduate.
- Ⓒ The student needs to verify what he wants to do.
- Ⓓ Professors favor students who write good papers.

05 What does the professor imply when she says this?
- Ⓐ More students should get jobs that are consistent with their field of study.
- Ⓑ Universities should do a better job of training students to succeed in their careers.
- Ⓒ Many graduates waste their potential when they get jobs that differ from their majors.
- Ⓓ Many professionals choose a field of work that is different from what they majored in.

Part 1 정답 및 해설 p. 207

TOEFL Listening

[06 ~ 11] Listen to part of a lecture in an English literature class. Then answer the questions. MP3 89

06 What is the lecture mainly about?
   Ⓐ How modern scientific developments affect literature
   Ⓑ A common misconception related to the title of a novel
   Ⓒ How writers sometimes gain inspiration from other writers
   Ⓓ An alternative explanation of the motivation behind a novel

07 Why does the professor mention the subtitle "the Modern Prometheus"?
   Ⓐ To explain why Shelley chose to write a horror novel
   Ⓑ To provide background information about the plot of the novel
   Ⓒ To point out why people view Shelley's inspiration in a certain way
   Ⓓ To show the similarities between Greek myths and *Frankenstein*

08 According to the professor, what caused the weather during Shelley's vacation to get worse?
   Ⓐ Ice in the Arctic had begun to melt.
   Ⓑ A volcanic eruption affected the atmosphere.
   Ⓒ A major climate shift had occurred.
   Ⓓ The Industrial Revolution created air pollution.

09 What does the professor think about the motivation behind *Frankenstein*?

Ⓐ It might be simpler than most people think.
Ⓑ It is a mystery that may never be solved.
Ⓒ It was a combination of many different things.
Ⓓ It was the opposite of what was once thought.

10 According to the professor, why do people believe that weather could have been Shelley's motivation? **Choose two answers.**

Ⓐ Many writers of the time were interested in the weather.
Ⓑ The novel's subtitle makes a reference to a Greek myth.
Ⓒ Shelley wrote a letter to her sister about the bad weather.
Ⓓ The weather becomes worse when the monster goes outside.

11 What does the professor imply when he says this? 🔊 MP3 89_1

Ⓐ Children like to watch horror movies.
Ⓑ Most people know who Frankenstein is.
Ⓒ The students should do their assignments.
Ⓓ Movies misrepresent the characters of the novel.

Part 1 정답 및 해석 p. 210

TOEFL Listening   VOLUME HELP OK NEXT
PAUSE TEST SECTION EXIT   HIDE TIME 03:30

[12 ~ 17] Listen to a part of lecture in a music history class. Then answer the questions. ◁ MP3 90

12 What does the professor mainly discuss?
    Ⓐ The popularity of guitar music
    Ⓑ The technical aspects of guitars
    Ⓒ The evolution of the modern guitar
    Ⓓ Different types of Spanish instruments

13 According to the professor, what distinguished the oud from other Middle Eastern stringed instruments?
    Ⓐ It was made out of wood.
    Ⓑ It was covered in animal hides.
    Ⓒ It did not have frets on its neck.
    Ⓓ It originated in another region.

14 What does the professor say about the Muslim people from North Africa?
    Ⓐ They played the guitar in a different way.
    Ⓑ They introduced the oud to Spain.
    Ⓒ They were among the first to modify the oud.
    Ⓓ They helped popularize the Spanish guitar in Africa.

15 **Why does the professor mention the tuning of the lute?**
  Ⓐ To show how the instrument evolved over time
  Ⓑ To emphasize the versatility of ancient instruments
  Ⓒ To point out what makes it similar to the guitar
  Ⓓ To explain a way of distinguishing the type of music played

16 **What does the professor say about the Spanish vihuela?**
  Ⓐ It looked very different from the oud and lute.
  Ⓑ It was widely used in many different countries.
  Ⓒ It was more difficult to play than the modern guitar.
  Ⓓ It looked and sounded like the modern guitar.

17 **Why does the professor mention Cupid?**
  Ⓐ To show how instruments were used in mythology
  Ⓑ To describe the appearance of another instrument
  Ⓒ To familiarize students with a common use of the guitar
  Ⓓ To point out that few other instruments are played with strings

Part 2 정답 및 해석 p. 213

TOEFL Listening

VOLUME HELP OK NEXT
PAUSE TEST SECTION EXIT

[01 ~ 05] Listen to a conversation between a student and her English professor. Then answer the questions. MP3 91

TOEFL Listening

01 Why did the professor ask the student to stop by his office?
    Ⓐ To talk about possibly becoming a guest speaker
    Ⓑ To inform her of an impending interview
    Ⓒ To inquire about a position in the literacy program
    Ⓓ To ask her to help write an article on English education

02 What kind of volunteer work did the student do?
    Ⓐ Giving lectures on early childhood literacy
    Ⓑ Reading books to elementary school children
    Ⓒ Writing articles for the campus newspaper
    Ⓓ Teaching adults how to expand their vocabulary

03 Why did the student start a literacy program?
    Ⓐ She had to do it as part of a class project.
    Ⓑ She needed experience before becoming a teacher.
    Ⓒ She wanted to teach children how to write.
    Ⓓ She noticed parents who could not read well.

04 What's the student's attitude towards the interview?
    Ⓐ She is excited because she will gain recognition.
    Ⓑ She is pleased because it will help the literacy program.
    Ⓒ She is convinced that it is unimportant.
    Ⓓ She is concerned that she might not be able to do it.

Listen again to part of the conversation. Then answer the question. 🔊 MP3 91_1

05 Why does the professor say this?
    Ⓐ He needs to apologize for not helping out with the literacy program.
    Ⓑ He wants to confirm what he already knows about the award.
    Ⓒ He does not agree with the student's view about the interview.
    Ⓓ He did not know that the award had anything to do with the program.

Part 2 정답 및 해석 p. 215

TOEFL Listening

[06 ~ 11] Listen to part of a lecture in a US history class. Then answer the questions.
🔊 MP3 92

06 What is the main purpose of the lecture?
  Ⓐ To discuss the differences in North American capital cities
  Ⓑ To illustrate the relationship between geography and politics
  Ⓒ To show why the United States was unable to create a special district
  Ⓓ To explain the events that led to the establishment of the United States' capital

07 According to the professor, why was the capital moved to Philadelphia?
  Ⓐ The first president was from the area.
  Ⓑ State representatives met regularly there.
  Ⓒ Bankers and merchants wanted it farther north.
  Ⓓ It was located in the center of the United States.

08 What does the professor imply about the federal government in its early stages?
  Ⓐ It wasn't as strong as some state governments.
  Ⓑ It was under attack by the governors of some states.
  Ⓒ It was structured to resemble the British political system.
  Ⓓ It did not have the power to make delegates meet regularly.

09 What reason does the professor give to explain why it was difficult to agree on a new location for the capital?
  Ⓐ The constitution had to be modified to specify a site.
  Ⓑ The capital needed to be easy to defend against enemy attacks.
  Ⓒ The Northern and Southern states had conflicting interests.
  Ⓓ The United States was growing in physical size at a rapid rate.

10 Why was the capital district located among the Southern states?
  Ⓐ Bankers wanted more economic power.
  Ⓑ The Southern states agreed to cover some debt.
  Ⓒ Slaves were needed to maintain the capital.
  Ⓓ The capital's construction was funded by agriculture.

11 Why does the professor mention the man who discovered the Americas?
  Ⓐ To give an example of a patriotic name
  Ⓑ To illustrate a disagreement between the states
  Ⓒ To show why it took a while to establish the capital's name
  Ⓓ To explain the origins of the capital city's original name

Part 2 정답 및 해석 p. 218

TOEFL Listening

[12 ~ 17] **Listen to part of a lecture in a theater class. Then answer the questions.**

🔊 MP3 93

12 **What does the professor mainly discuss?**
- Ⓐ A director who changed the way films are edited
- Ⓑ The differences between screen and stage acting
- Ⓒ Different methods of effectively depicting emotions
- Ⓓ The response of the audience in theatrical productions

13 **Why does the professor mention the criticism he received early on in his career?**
- Ⓐ To give an example of problems caused by unfriendly audiences
- Ⓑ To demonstrate the difficulties actors face when starting movie careers
- Ⓒ To illustrate the different acting methods needed for theater and film
- Ⓓ To show that he has had experience in both theater and cinema acting

14 **According to the professor, what was D.W. Griffith's contribution to acting?**
- Ⓐ He used close-ups to catch small gestures.
- Ⓑ He always filmed scenes in chronological order.
- Ⓒ He only used stage actors in all of his movies.
- Ⓓ He taught actors techniques appropriate for films.

15 What does the professor say about screen actors?
- Ⓐ They are more effective when they seem natural.
- Ⓑ They speak loudly to ensure they are heard clearly.
- Ⓒ They prefer to hide their emotions from the camera.
- Ⓓ They make gestures that are very different from real life.

16 What does the professor say is a difficulty sometimes faced by film actors?
- Ⓐ They can only film scenes one time.
- Ⓑ They have to act scenes out of order.
- Ⓒ They are not accepted by theater critics.
- Ⓓ They must play many different characters.

Listen again to part of the lecture. Then answer the question. 🔊 MP3 93_1

17 What does the professor mean when he says this?
- Ⓐ He wants to emphasize the importance of actors.
- Ⓑ He doesn't think theater actors are as talented as film actors.
- Ⓒ He does not want to spend time discussing the names of actors.
- Ⓓ He would like the students to give examples of some failed actors.

커넥츠 영단기
eng.conects.com

영단기 토익 교재

입문서

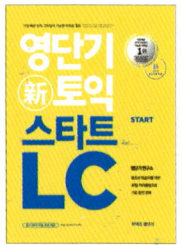  

영단기 신토익 스타트 LC 영단기 신토익 스타트 RC 영단기 영문법 스타트

기본서

목표 점수 800+ | 목표 점수 900+

기적의 토익 LC 기적의 토익 RC 영단기 토익 LC 영단기 토익 RC 영단기 토익 기출보카

필기노트 | LC+RC 통합 기본서

영단기 700+ 기적의 필기노트 영단기 토익 만점자 필기노트 PART 5 문법 영단기 토익 LC+RC 700+한 달에 끝내기 정재현 토익 똑똑한 기본서 LC+RC

기술서/요약서

영단기 토익 기술 LC 영단기 토익 기술 실전문제집 LC 영단기 토익 기술 RC 영단기 토익 기술 실전문제집 RC 영단기 신토익 LC 20일 속성 영단기 신토익 RC 20일 속성

파트별 교재

| 영단기 2기적 토익 LC | 영단기 2기적 토익 PART 5&6 | 영단기 2기적 토익 PART 7 | 영단기 토익 PART 7 유형별 공식 40 |

실전모의고사

| 단기 신토익 LC+RC 빈출모의고사 | 영단기 토익 실전 1000제 1 LC | 영단기 토익 실전 1000제 1 RC | 영단기 토익 실전 1000제 2 LC | 영단기 토익 실전 1000제 2 RC |

영단기 오픽 & 토익스피킹 교재

| 영단기 OPIc | 영단기 OPIc 실전모의고사 | 영단기 토익스피킹 | 영단기 토익스피킹 기술 | 영단기 토익스피킹 실전모의고사 |

영단기 지텔프 교재

| 현 지텔프 Level 2 | 지텔프 기출문제 Level 2 | 지텔프 독해 유형별 기출문제 Level 2 | 지텔프 문법 유형별 기출문제 Level 2 |

커넥츠 영단기
eng.conects.com

전략이 있는 토플

영단기
TOEFL
LISTENING

정답 및 해석

영단기 연구소

eng.conects.com

커넥츠 영단기

영단기 TOEFL LISTENING

정답 및 해석

커넥츠 영단기

Diagnostic Test

01 B	02 C	03 D	04 A	05 C	06 B	07 C	08 B, D	09 A	10 C	11 D	12 B	13 C	14 D
15 A, C	16 C	17 C											

본문 p. 020 ~ 025

[01 ~ 05] Listen to a conversation between a student and a librarian. 🔊 MP3 01

Student(male): Hello, um… Can you help me find something?

Librarian(female): That's why I'm here! What can I help you find?

S: **Q1** I need to find a book for a research project I'm doing with my professor. It's related to the psychological development phases in children. I'm supposed to check out a book about the experiments done on children to prove that the stages of cognitive development actually exist.

L: Do you know the title?

S: Actually, I forgot it. That's why I need your help.

L: Okay, let me check. Cognitive development… experiments… Oh, here we go! There's a book about the experiments done by Jean Piaget. Does that ring a bell?

S: Yes! That's the book I need. Where can I get it?

L: It's on the third floor, in the reference section. But, if you don't mind me asking, are you a graduate student?

S: No… I'm a senior. Why? Does it matter?

L: Well, **Q2** the books in the reference section can only be checked out by grad students. If you're an undergrad, you can look at them in the library, but you can't take them home. I'm sorry, but that's the university policy.

S: Oh, no… **Q3** They're doing renovations on the third floor. It'll be too loud for me to concentrate on anything with all that construction going on. Besides, my professor told me to bring it to him.

L: Well, there's nothing I can do about it. Rules are rules.

S: Isn't there anything you can do? I mean, can't you make an exception just this one time? My professor will be upset if I don't bring that book to him.

L: He probably doesn't know that that book is in the reference section, or maybe he just doesn't know the library policy. But, you know, professors can borrow any reference books they want.

S: 🎧 You want me to ask him to come down here himself? I don't know… **Q5** That's asking a lot. He's really busy.

L: Oh, professors send their research assistants to check out books all the time. Here's a request form. **Q4** He can just fill it out, and then you can check the book out for him. Technically, you won't be the one checking out the book, so it will be okay.

S: Oh, okay. That should work.

L: It might be a bit of a hassle for you to go back and forth with the request form, but if that's not a problem…

S: No, I don't mind. Thanks for the suggestion. You've been really helpful!

해석 학생과 사서간의 다음 대화를 들으시오.

학생(남자): 안녕하세요, 음… 제가 뭘 좀 찾는 걸 도와주실 수 있으신가요?

사서(여자): 그래서 제가 여기 있는 거죠! 뭘 찾는 걸 도와드릴까요?

학생: 제가 교수님과 하고 있는 연구 프로젝트를 위해 책을 찾아야 하는데요. 아이들의 심리적 발달 단계들에 관한 것이에요. 인지적 발달의 단계들이 실제로 존재한다는 것을 증명하기 위해 아이들에게 행해진 실험들에 관한 책을 대출해야 하는데요.

사서: 제목을 아세요?

학생: 사실, 그걸 잊어버렸어요. 그래서 도움이 필요한 거고요.

사서: 좋아요. 확인해보도록 하죠. 인지적 발달이라… 실험… 아, 여기 있네요! Jean Piaget에 의한 실험들에 대한 책이 하나 있어요. 들어본 적 있는 거 같나요?

학생: 네! 그게 제가 필요한 책이에요. 어디서 구할 수 있죠?

사서: 3층 참고도서 섹션에 있어요. 그런데 제가 물어봐도 괜찮다면, 혹시 대학원생인가요?

학생: 아니요… 4학년인데요. 왜요? 그게 중요한가요?

사서: 음, 참고도서 섹션의 책들은 대학원생들만 대출할 수 있어요. 학부생이라면, 도서관 내에서는 그 책들을 볼 수 있지만 집으로 가져갈 수

는 없어요. 미안하지만, 그게 학교 규정이라서요.
학생: 오, 이런… 3층은 내부수리를 하고 있던데요. 그 공사가 진행되는 와중에 뭔가에 집중하기에는 너무 시끄러울 것 같은데요. 게다가, 교수님께서 그 책을 가져다 달라고 하셨어요.
사서: 음, 제가 해드릴 수 있는 것이 없어요. 규칙은 규칙이니까요.
학생: 뭔가 해주실 수 있는 게 없을까요? 그러니까, 이번 한번만 예외로 해주시면 안되나요? 그 책을 가져다 드리지 않으면 교수님께서 기분 상해하실 텐데요.
사서: 교수님이 아마도 그 책이 참고도서 섹션에 있다는 것을 모르실 거예요. 아니면 아마도 도서관 규칙을 잘 모르시던지요. 하지만, 있죠, 교수님들은 원하시는 참고도서를 아무거나 빌릴 수 있어요.
학생: 저보고 교수님께 직접 이곳까지 오시라고 부탁 드리라는 말씀이신가요? 잘 모르겠어요… 그건 좀 과도한 부탁 같아서요. 교수님이 정말 바쁘시거든요.
사서: 아, 교수님들은 항상 연구 조교들을 보내 책을 대출해가세요. 여기 신청서가 있어요. 교수님은 이걸 작성만 하시면 돼요. 그리고 나서 학생이 교수님을 위해 그 책을 대출할 수 있는 거죠. 엄밀히 따지면, 학생이 책을 대출하는 사람은 아닌 게 되니까, 그건 괜찮을 거예요.
학생: 아, 좋아요. 그러면 되겠군요.
사서: 신청서를 가지고 왔다 갔다 하는 것이 학생에게는 좀 번거로운 일이 될 수는 있겠지만, 그게 문제가 안 된다면…
학생: 네, 괜찮아요. 제안해주셔서 감사해요. 정말로 도움이 되었어요!

Ⓦ cognitive [kɑ́gnitiv] 인지적인   ring a bell 들어본 적이 있는   reference [réfərəns] 참고도서   senior [síːnjər] (대학교) 4학년, (고등학교) 3학년   checked out 대출된   renovation [rènəvéiʃən] 내부수리   make an exception 예외를 허락하다   hassle [hǽsl] 번거로움

01 학생이 사서를 찾아간 이유는?
Ⓐ 제목으로 책을 찾는 법을 문의하려고
Ⓑ 제목을 잊어버린 책을 찾는 데 도움을 구하려고
Ⓒ 참고도서 섹션에서 공부해도 되는지 알아보려고
Ⓓ 도서관 공사가 언제 끝날지 알아보려고

02 사서가 참고도서 섹션의 책들에 대해 말한 것은?
Ⓐ 새로운 장소로 옮겨졌다.
Ⓑ 교수에 의해서만 대출이 가능하다.
Ⓒ 학부생은 그 책들을 집에 가져갈 수 없다.
Ⓓ 그 책들 중 어떤 것도 현재 이용할 수 없다.

03 도서관이 내부수리를 하고 있다는 것에 대해 학생이 언급한 이유는?
Ⓐ 대학 규정이 불공평하다고 생각한다.
Ⓑ 그것 때문에 그의 프로젝트가 지연될까 봐 걱정한다.
Ⓒ 사서의 말이 잘 안 들린다.
Ⓓ 그 소음이 집중을 방해할 것이라 생각한다.

04 사서는 학생이 무엇을 하도록 제안하는가?
Ⓐ 교수를 대신해서 책을 빌리기
Ⓑ 교수에게 규정에 대해 불만을 제기하도록 부탁하기
Ⓒ 책을 대출할 연구 조교를 찾기
Ⓓ 학생을 위해 교수가 책을 빌리도록 하기

대화의 일부분을 다시 듣고 질문에 답하시오. 🔊 **MP3 01_1**

> S: You want me to ask him to come down here himself? I don't know… That's asking a lot. He's really busy.
> L: Oh, professors send their research assistants to check out books all the time.

05 학생이 다음과 같이 말한 이유는?

> That's asking a lot.

Ⓐ 추가적인 허가를 받아야 해서 짜증이 나 있다.
Ⓑ 교수님이 너무 많은 책을 대출했다고 생각한다.
Ⓒ 교수님에게 또 다른 일을 하도록 부탁하지 말아야 한다고 생각한다.
Ⓓ 자신이 해야 하는 일들 중 몇 가지를 잊어버릴까 봐 걱정이 된다.

[06 ~ 11] Listen to part of a lecture in a psychology class. 🔊 MP3 02

Professor(male): Here's a question: What are most patients at sleep clinics being treated for? I bet most of you are thinking the answer is insomnia. Well, although **Q6** **there are many people who suffer from insomnia, the majority of patients at sleep clinics are suffering from a disorder related to excessive sleep.** This problem is so widespread that it even has a name. It's called hypersomnia.

As I said, this disorder is related to getting too much sleep. While most insomniacs can somehow manage to make it through the day and function at slightly non-optimal levels, **Q7** **patients with hypersomnia aren't so lucky. Not only do they have a hard time with desk jobs, in some professions they can present a danger to themselves and others.** People who suffer from hypersomnia can't resist the urge to sleep during the day. Imagine if you were in a business meeting with your boss and you just fell asleep when he was talking. Or if you were shopping at the supermarket and fell asleep in front of the cashier. And of course there are even more dangerous situations… Think about people who operate heavy machinery, for instance. What if a crane operator suddenly fell asleep while operating a 20-story-tall crane? Falling asleep in this kind of situation could obviously be life-threatening.

Another kind of excessive sleep disorder is narcolepsy, which is caused by an inability to create enough of a neurotransmitter that promotes wakefulness. We all stay awake because our nervous system constantly tells us to stay alert. Most people have enough of these transmitters to stay awake for most of the day. But without these neurotransmitters that tell you to stay awake… Well, you get the idea, right?

Q8-B The primary symptom of narcolepsy is excessive daytime sleepiness, which is called EDS for short. Remember the stages of sleep we learned about? One of them is the rapid eye movement, or REM, stage. In narcolepsy patients, REM sleep occurs almost immediately after falling asleep. **Q9** **It may not be apparent in childhood, because most children take naps during the day and generally fall asleep quickly anyway.** But when a narcoleptic person reaches his or her teen years, EDS will become apparent, and the symptom will continue throughout the person's life. When someone who suffers from narcolepsy gets the urge to fall asleep, we call it a sleep attack. These attacks may occur as often as 15 to 20 times during the course of a day and can result in anywhere from a few seconds to several hours of deep sleep.

REM sleep is also the stage in which **Q8-D** we sometimes experience muscle paralysis. This is a big problem for people with narcolepsy because it can cause them to suffer from something called cataplexy (shown on screen). This is defined as the **sudden loss of voluntary muscle control.** When people experience cataplexy, they go limp and are unable to move even though they're awake. According to studies, about 70% of narcolepsy patients experience this symptom.

Sadly, there is no cure for narcolepsy. However, **Q11** **EDS can be controlled with medication** that causes the nervous system to release the alerting agents that keep people from falling asleep. In other word, **the medication keeps the patients alert because their nervous systems can't do it alone.** But although it can control EDS, this medication can't prevent cataplexy. **Q10** **To control that symptom, patients must take a different type of medication.** It induces deep sleep at night, which reduces the chances of losing muscle control during the day.

해석 심리학 수업의 다음 강의 일부를 들으시오.

교수(남자): 질문 하나 할게요. 수면 클리닉의 대부분의 환자들은 무엇 때문에 치료를 받고 있을까요? 여러분 대부분은 그 답이 불면증이라고 생각할 거라 확신합니다. 음, 불면증으로 고생하고 있는 많은 사람들이 있긴 하지만, 수면 클리닉의 대다수 환자들은 과도한 수면과 관련된 장애로 고통 받고 있습니다. 이 문제는 너무나 널리 퍼져 있어서 이름도 붙여졌지요. 과면증이라고 불립니다.

말했듯이, 이 장애는 잠을 너무 많이 자는 것과 관련이 있습니다. 대부분의 불면증 환자들이 어느 정도는 낮 시간을 견뎌내고 약간 덜 최적화된 수준으로 기능을 할 수 있는 반면, 과면증 환자들은 그렇게 운이 좋지는 않습니다. 그들은 책상 앞에 앉아 일을 하는 데 어려움을 겪을 뿐만 아니라, 어떤 직종들에서는 자신들은 물론 다른 사람들에게 위험을 초래할 수도 있습니다. 과면증을 겪는 사람들은 낮 시간 동안 잠이 오는 충동에 저항할 수가 없습니다. 상사와 함께 업무 회의를 하는데 상사가 이야기하는 동안 여러분이 잠들었다고 상상해보세요. 아니면, 슈퍼마켓에서 장을 보다가 계산대 점원 앞에서 잠이 들어버린 거죠. 물론, 훨씬 더 위험한 상황들도 있지요... 예를 들어 중장비를 작동시키고 있는 사람들을 생각해보세요. 기중기 운전사가 20층 높이의 기중기를 작동시키는 도중 갑자기 잠이 들게 된다면요? 이런 종류의 상황에서 잠에 빠지는 것은 분명 생명에 위협이 될 수도 있습니다.

또 다른 종류의 과도한 수면 장애는 기면증으로, 각성을 촉진시켜주는 신경 전달 물질을 충분히 만들지 못해서 생깁니다. 우리는 모두 우리의 신경 체계가 우리에게 깨어 있도록 끊임없이 명하기 때문에 깨어 있습니다. 대부분의 사람들은 낮 동안은 대부분 깨어 있을 수 있도록 이러한 전달 물질들을 충분히 가지고 있습니다. 하지만, 깨어 있도록 명령하는 이러한 신경 전달 물질이 없는... 음, 이해가 가죠?

기면증의 주된 증상은 낮 동안의 과도한 졸림(excessive daytime sleepiness)으로, 줄여서 EDS라고 불립니다. 우리가 배웠던 수면의 단계를 기억하나요? 그 단계들 중 하나는 급속 안구 운동, 즉 REM 단계입니다. 기면증 환자들에게, REM 수면은 잠이 들자마자 거의 즉시 발생합니다. 대부분의 어린이들이 낮 시간에 낮잠을 자는 데다가 대개 빨리 잠이 들기 때문에 기면증은 아동기에는 분명하게 나타나지 않을지도 모릅니다. 하지만 기면증을 앓는 사람이 십대가 되면, EDS가 분명해지고 그 증상은 그 사람의 일생 동안 계속됩니다. 기면증을 앓는 사람에게 잠에 빠져들려는 충동이 생길 때, 우리는 그것을 수면 발작이라고 부릅니다. 이러한 발작은 하루 동안 15에서 20 차례나 자주 발생할 수도 있으며, 몇 초에서 몇 시간 동안의 숙면을 야기할 수 있습니다.

REM 수면은 또한 우리가 가끔씩 근육 마비를 경험하는 단계이기도 합니다. 이것은 기면증 환자들에게는 큰 문제인데, 그것이 그들에게 탈력 발작이라고 불리는 것을 겪도록 할 수도 있기 때문입니다. (화면에 보여준다) 탈력 발작은 수의근 조절의 갑작스런 상실이라고 정의됩니다. 탈력 발작을 겪을 때, 사람들은 깨어 있음에도 불구하고 축 늘어지고 움직일 수 없게 됩니다. 연구에 의하면, 기면증 환자들의 약 70퍼센트가 이 증상을 경험한다고 합니다.

안타깝게도, 기면증은 치료제가 없습니다. 하지만, EDS는 신경계로 하여금 잠에 빠져드는 것을 막아주는 경계 물질을 방출하도록 만드는 약물을 통해 제어될 수 있습니다. 즉, 환자들의 신경계가 혼자서는 할 수 없기 때문에 약물이 환자들로 하여금 깨어 있도록 유지시켜 주는 것이죠. 하지만 이 약이 EDS를 제어할 수는 있다 하더라도, 탈력 발작을 막지는 못합니다. 그 증상을 제어하기 위해서는, 환자들은 다른 종류의 약을 먹어야만 합니다. 그 약은 밤에 숙면하도록 유도하는데, 이것이 낮 시간 동안의 근육 제어 능력 상실의 가능성을 줄여주는 것이죠.

ⓦ insomnia [insάmniə] 불면증　patient [péiʃənt] 환자　sleep clinic 수면 진료소(클리닉)　hypersomnia [hàipərsάmniə] 과면증　disorder [disɔ́ːrdər] (신체 기능의) 장애　optimal [άptəməl] 최적화된, 최상의　heavy machinery 중장비　life-threatening [laif-θrétniŋ] 생명이 위험한　narcolepsy [nάːrkəlèpsi] 기면증　neurotransmitter [njùərоutrænsmítər] 신경 전달 물질　symptom [símptəm] 증상　muscle paralysis 근육 마비　cataplexy [kǽtəplèksi] 탈력 발작　limp [limp] 기운이 없는, 축 처진　induce [indjúːs] 유도하다

06 강의의 주요 목적은?
Ⓐ 불면증의 증상들을 설명하려고
Ⓑ 과도한 수면 장애들에 대해 묘사하려고
Ⓒ 수면의 대체 가능한 정의를 주려고
Ⓓ 사람들이 잠을 자는 데 어려움을 겪는 이유를 논의하려고

07 교수에 의하면, 과면증이 불면증보다 더 심각한 문제로 간주되는 이유는?
Ⓐ 매우 어린 아이들에게 더 흔하게 발생하는 경향이 있다.
Ⓑ 신체적인 질병이라기보다는 정신적인 질병이다.
Ⓒ 사람들로 하여금 정상적으로 기능하는 데 더 어려움을 겪게 한다.
Ⓓ 늘어난 수면 때문에 사람들이 건강을 유지하지 못하게 한다.

08 기면증을 겪는 사람들의 흔한 증상으로 언급된 것은? (두 가지 선택)
Ⓐ 깊은 수준의 수면을 이룰 수 없다.
Ⓑ 낮 시간 동안 깨어 있을 수 없다.
Ⓒ 짧은 시간 동안만 잘 수 있다.
Ⓓ 깨어 있는 동안 근육 제어 능력을 잃는다.

09 교수에 의하면, 아이들의 기면증을 진단하는 것이 어려운 이유는?
Ⓐ 아이들은 대개 낮 시간 동안 낮잠을 잔다.
Ⓑ 아이들은 거의 수면 장애를 경험하지 않는다.
Ⓒ 아이들은 근육 마비를 경험하지 않는다.
Ⓓ 아이들은 REM 수면 단계에 도달하지 않는다.

10 교수가 기면증 치료에 관해 말한 것은?
Ⓐ 최고의 치료법은 그냥 일찍 잠자리에 드는 것이다.
Ⓑ 의사의 도움 없이도 대개 치료될 수 있다.
Ⓒ 여러 다른 증상들은 별개로 치료되어야 한다.
Ⓓ 기면증을 앓는 사람들을 도울 방법은 아무것도 없다.

11 교수에 의하면, 기면증 환자들이 수면 발작을 방지하기 위해 할 수 있는 것은?
Ⓐ 스트레스가 되는 사회 상황을 피하기
Ⓑ 낮 시간 동안 여러 번 낮잠을 자기
Ⓒ 매일 밤 여덟 시간씩 잠자기
Ⓓ 깨어 있게 해주는 약을 복용하기

[12 ~ 17] Listen to part of a lecture in a US history class. 🔊 MP3 03

Professor(male): All right... So, continuing on with our Wild West theme, **Q12** **we're going to talk about transportation.** As we learned last week, gold was discovered in California in 1848. **Q13** **That led to the Gold Rush of 1849, and by 1860 the region's population had grown to 380,000.** So all these **Q12** **people who lived in California needed a way to reach their family, friends, and business partners who lived out east. Also, the government needed to find a way to transport mail**... to, um, establish a reliable postal service across the country. However, since there weren't any roads that led all the way to California, the government thought it would be best to sign a contract with the Pacific Mail Steamship Company after California became the 31st state in 1850.

Student(female): 🎧 **Q17** **Did you say steamships?**

P: Yes, I did. The first official mail service provided by the government was seagoing. Ships carried the mail south, from New York to Panama. This was before the Panama Canal was constructed, so the mail had to be unloaded and carried across the narrow strip of land there. Then it was loaded onto new ships, which sailed north to San Francisco. Now, there were a few issues with this service. **Q14** **If you think the mail is too slow nowadays, you should definitely be glad you didn't live in California back then. It took a month and a half for the mail to arrive.** Not only did the mail service need to be faster, it also had to be cheaper and rely less on middlemen. The process of sending mail was just too complicated.

S: Couldn't they use the railway? Didn't you mention that gold was transported to the east on the railroad?

P: Well, at the time we're talking about, the transcontinental railroad was still in the planning stages. So, to remediate the situation, a faster stagecoach line was proposed. Anyone who's seen a western will probably be familiar with stagecoaches. These were vehicles pulled by horses. They mostly carried people, but they could also carry freight, including mail. The Butterfield Overland Mail Company won the government contract to operate the western stagecoach service. In 1858, the first stagecoach carried mail along a southern route. But there were a few problems with this method, too. I mean, it was faster than going through Panama – sending mail only took three weeks. And the use of stagecoaches definitely improved the roads in the U.S. But there just weren't enough routes. Also, barges had to **Q15-A** **carry the stagecoaches across rivers in places where there weren't bridges.** And **Q15-C** **not all of the roads could support these big, heavy vehicles.** The routes themselves were a matter of great debate because the Northern States wanted a northern route while the Southern States wanted a southern route. This was made worse by the fact that everyone expected that the first transcontinental railroad line would eventually be built along the same route. A man named William H. Russell thought he had a better way to deliver mail using a much shorter route. He believed that by following a different route across the middle of the country, he could get the mail to California in less than two weeks. Russell had owned a stagecoach company but realized he could not compete unless he had a government contract. So, in order to attract business, he created the famous Pony Express. The Pony Express could deliver the mail in roughly half the time that stagecoaches could. Russell relied on hundreds of fast horses and riders. Single, lightweight riders carried the mail at galloping speeds. Of course the horses would tire out quickly, but there were more than 150 relay stations on the route to the West. When a rider's horse was exhausted, he would stop at the next relay station, where fresh horses would be waiting. The rider would simply get off the tired horse and jump onto one with a fresh set of legs. **Q16** This new way of transporting mail was impressively fast. A transcript of President Lincoln's inaugural address was delivered in just seven and a half days. Sadly, the company couldn't last. A telegraph line across the United States was completed just a year and a half later. Pony Express riders could only carry small pieces of mail, and that's essentially what telegraphs did. Therefore, the company lost most of its business almost instantly. Russell sold the company to a bank, and the Pony Express became nothing more than a legend. Although it operated for only about a year and a half, it proved that a year-round route to the West was possible. This helped railway planners find an ideal route, and a few years later, when the railway was completed, stagecoach mail service became a thing of the past as well.

해석 미국사 수업의 다음 강의 일부분을 들으시오.

교수(남자): 좋아요... 자, 서부 시대 주제를 계속해서, 운송에 대해 이야기를 해보도록 하지요. 지난주에 배웠듯이, 1848년에 캘리포니아에서 금이 발견되었습니다. 그것이 1849년의 골드 러시를 가져왔고, 1860년 쯤에는 캘리포니아 지역의 인구가 38만 명까지 늘어났습니다. 그래서 이제 캘리포니아에 사는 이 모든 사람들은 동쪽에 살고 있던 가족들, 친구들, 사업 동료들과 연락을 할 방법이 필요하게 되었지요. 또, 정부 역시 우편물을 보낼 방법을 찾아야 했습니다... 음, 전국에 걸쳐 믿을 수 있는 우편 서비스를 확립하기 위해서요. 하지만, 캘리포니아까지 죽 이어진 도로가 아무것도 없었기 때문에, 1850년에 캘리포니아가 미국의 31번째 주가 된 후, 정부는 **Pacific Mail Steamship Company**(태평양 우편 증기선 회사)와 계약을 맺는 것이 가장 좋을 것이라고 생각했습니다.

학생(여자): 증기선이라고 하셨어요?

교수: 그래요. 정부에 의해 제공된 최초의 우편 서비스는 항해를 통한 것이었어요. 배들이 우편물을 남쪽으로, 그러니까 뉴욕에서 파나마로 실어 날랐죠. 이것은 파나마 운하가 지어지기 전이어서, 우편물은 그곳에서 내려져 좁고 길쭉한 육지를 지나 옮겨져야 했습니다. 그리고 나서 우편물은 샌프란시스코를 향해 북쪽으로 항해했던 새로운 배들에 실어졌지요. 자, 이 우편 서비스에는 몇 가지 문제점이 있었습니다. 여러분이 만일 요즘 우편이 너무 느리다고 생각한다면, 그 당시 캘리포니아에 살고 있지 않았던 것에 분명 기뻐해야 할 거예요. 우편물이 도착하는 데 한달 반이나 걸렸거든요. 우편 서비스는 더 빨라질 필요가 있었을 뿐만 아니라, 요금도 더 저렴해져야 했고 중개인들에 덜 의존해야 할 필요도 있었습니다. 우편물을 보내는 과정은 너무 복잡했어요.

학생: 철도를 이용하면 안 됐나요? 금이 철도로 동쪽으로 수송되었다고 하지 않으셨어요?

교수: 음, 우리가 이야기하고 있는 당시에는, 대륙 횡단 철도는 아직 기획 단계였습니다. 그래서, 상황을 개선하기 위해서, 좀 더 빠른 역마차 노선이 제안되었었죠. 서부 영화를 본 적이 있는 사람이라면 역마차가 아마 익숙할 것입니다. 역마차는 말이 끄는 교통수단이었죠. 역마차는 주로 사람을 날랐지만, 우편물을 포함한 화물을 나르기도 했습니다. **Butterfield Overland Mail Company**(버터필드 오버랜드 우편 회사)가 서부의 역마차 서비스를 운영하는 계약을 정부로부터 땄습니다. 1858년에, 첫 역마차가 남쪽 노선을 따라 우편물을 수송했습니다. 하지만 이 방법에도 몇 가지 문제점이 있었지요. 그러니까, 파나마를 통해 가는 것보다는 빠르긴 했죠... 우편물을 보내는 데 삼 주밖에 걸리지 않았으니까요. 그리고 역마차를 이용하는 것은 미국 도로들을 분명 향상시켰습니다. 하지만, 충분한 노선이 없었어요. 또한, 다리가 없는 곳에서는 바지선이 역마차를 실어 강을 건너야 했습니다. 그리고 모든 도로가 이 크고 무거운 운송수단을 견뎌낼 수 있었던 것도 아니고요. 노선 자체들도 엄청난 논쟁 거리였는데, 북부 주들은 북부 노선을 원했고 남부 주들은 남부 노선을 원했기 때문입니다. 모든 사람들이 최초의 대륙 횡단 철도 노선이 결국 같은 노선을 따라 만들어질 것이라고 기대했다는 사실로 인해 이 상황은 더욱 나빠졌습니다. **William H. Russell**이라는 이름의 한 남자는 훨씬 더 짧은 노선을 이용하여 우편물을 배달할 수 있는 더 나은 방법이 있다고 생각했습니다. 그는 미국의 중앙을 가로지르는 다른 노선으로 가로 가는 방법을 통해, 캘리포니아에 우편물을 2주 안에 배달할 수 있을 것으로 생각했습니다. Russell은 역마차 회사를 소유하고 있었지만, 정부 계약을 따지 않고서는 경쟁을 할 수 없다는 것을 깨달았습니다. 그래서, 사업을 유치하기 위해, 그는 그 유명한 **Pony Express**(포니 익스프레스사(社))를 만들어냈습니다. **Pony Express**는 역마차의 약 절반 정도 되는 시간에 우편물을 배달할 수 있었습니다. Russell은 수백 마리의 빠른 말과 기수들에 의존했습니다. 한 명의 체중이 가벼운 기수가 빠른 속도로 우편물을 날랐습니다. 물론, 말들은 금방 지쳤겠지만, 서부로 가는 길에는 150개가 넘는 중계소들이 있었습니다. 한 기수의 말이 녹초가 되면, 그 기수는 생생한 말들이 기다리고 있던 다음 중계소에 멈추곤 했죠. 기수는 지친 말에서 내려 생기 넘치는 다리를 가진 말에 올라타기만 하면 되었습니다. 이러한 새로운 방식의 우편 배송

은 굉장히 빨랐죠. 링컨 대통령의 취임연설 원고는 불과 7일 반 만에 배달되었습니다. 안타깝게도, 그 회사는 오래 지속되지 못했습니다. 고작 일년 반 뒤에 미국 전역에 전신선이 완성되었거든요. Pony Express는 크기가 작은 우편물만을 나를 수 있었는데, 그것은 기본적으로 전보가 하는 일이었습니다. 따라서, Pony Express는 거의 즉각적으로 대부분의 거래처를 잃게 되었지요. Russell은 회사를 한 은행에 팔았고, Pony Express는 전설에 불과한 것이 되어버렸습니다. 비록 일년 반 정도만 운영이 되었지만, Pony Express는 서부로의 연중 노선이 가능하다는 것을 증명했습니다. 이는 철도 기획자들이 이상적인 노선을 찾는 데 도움이 되었고, 몇 년 후 철도가 완성되었을 때, 역마차 우편 서비스 역시 과거의 산물이 되었습니다.

W reliable postal service 믿을 수 있는 우편 서비스   contract [kántrækt] 계약   steamship [stíːmʃip] 증기선   seagoing [síːgóuiŋ] 항해(용)의   unload [ʌnlóud] (화물을) 내리다   narrow strip of land 좁고 길쭉한 땅   middleman [mídlmæn] 중개인   transcontinental railroad 대륙횡단철도   remediate [rimíːdiət] 개선하다, 치유하다   stagecoach [stéidʒkòutʃ] 역마차   freight [freit] 화물   barge [baːrdʒ] 바지선   lightweight [láitwèit] 경량의   galloping [gǽləpiŋ] 급속히 진행되는   inaugural address 취임연설   year-round [jíər-áund] 연중 계속되는   telegraph [téligræf] 전신(전보)

12 강의의 주된 내용은?
Ⓐ 미국인들이 서쪽으로 이동한 이유들
Ⓑ 미국 우편 서비스의 역사
Ⓒ 운송 기술의 발달
Ⓓ 사람들을 미국 전역으로 나르는 가장 빠른 방법

13 교수에 의하면, 전국적인 우편 시스템이 필요했던 이유는?
Ⓐ 사람들이 캘리포니아에서 금을 보내야 했다.
Ⓑ 지역 우편 시스템들의 대다수가 실패했었다.
Ⓒ 캘리포니아의 인구가 급속히 증가했다.
Ⓓ 캘리포니아가 공식적으로 미국의 일부가 되었다.

14 캘리포니아로의 최초의 우편 서비스에 대해 교수가 말한 것은?
Ⓐ 그것이 캘리포니아를 살기 좋지 않은 지역으로 만들었다.
Ⓑ 오늘날의 우편 시스템과 매우 유사했다.
Ⓒ 우편물을 배달하는 데 많은 사람들이 필요하지 않았다.
Ⓓ 목적지에 도달하는 데 오랜 시간이 걸렸다.

15 교수에 의하면, 우편물을 역마차로 배달할 때 사람들이 겪었던 문제점은? (두 가지 선택)
Ⓐ 몇몇 강 위에는 다리가 놓여있지 않았다.
Ⓑ 역마차를 만드는 데 비용이 너무 많이 들었다.
Ⓒ 역마차들은 일부 도로들을 이용할 수 없었다.
Ⓓ 역마차들은 승객들과 우편물을 둘 다 나를 수는 없었다.

16 교수가 링컨의 취임 연설을 언급한 이유는?
Ⓐ 대통령 연설의 중요성을 설명하려고
Ⓑ 새 전보 시스템이 어떻게 사용되었는지 예를 들려고
Ⓒ Pony Express가 우편물을 배달했던 속도를 증명하려고
Ⓓ 어떤 종류의 우편물이 Pony Express에 의해 배달될 수 없었는지 알려주려고

17 학생이 다음과 같이 말할 때 의미하는 것은? ◁ MP3 03_1

> Did you say steamships?

Ⓐ 학생은 교수가 실수로 스스로의 말에 모순되는 말을 했다고 생각한다.
Ⓑ 학생은 교수가 언급한 배의 종류를 잘 알지 못한다.
Ⓒ 학생은 미국 내에서 우편물을 배달하는 데 배가 사용되었다는 것에 놀랐다.
Ⓓ 학생은 증기선으로 우편물을 배달하기로 한 정부의 결정에 동의하지 않는다.

Chapter 1. Conversation Question Types

Practice Questions I

본문 p. 040

| 01 B | 02 D | 03 B | 04 A, E | 05 B |

[01 ~ 05] Listen to a conversation between a student and a librarian. 🔊 MP3 04

Librarian(male): What can I do for you?
Student(female): Um… **Q1** I need to find some books about the Great Depression. It's for my US history class.
L: Well, you've come to the right place. But before I help, do you mind me asking if you've tried using the computers in the reference center? It's not that I don't want to help you, but you can find articles and books in the library's database pretty quickly.
S: I've tried to find the book on the computers in the reference section, but I'm just getting overwhelmed by the results. I mean, **Q2** I get so many results that I just can't find what I need. The database is great when I can think of the proper key words, but sometimes it just gives too many results.
L: I know what you mean. You're not the first student to have this problem. All right, then let's get started. So what specifically are you looking for?
S: **Q3** I need to find some information on the consequences and results of Roosevelt's 'New Deal.'
L: Oh, I see. Well, that's a rather broad topic.
S: Yeah, I guess it is. That's probably why I'm getting too many results.
L: Why don't you try to narrow it down a bit? I know it can be hard, but can you give me something more specific?
S: Hmm… Well, I suppose what I really care about is the impact it had on the population that moved west to get new jobs. So I should probably start by finding out **Q4-A** how many migrants moved from the Eastern states to the West. How about searching for census information from before and after the New Deal for the Western States? You know, Utah, Arizona, New Mexico, and um… Nevada.
L: OK, that's much better. Let me check… Here we go. You can get the census information from the National Archives. It's not a book but you should be able to print out the information in the computer lab. So, what else do you need?
S: **Q4-E** I also need information on specific government projects. The ones that were part of the New Deal. I'm probably going to need to know how many jobs were made available.
L: OK. Then why don't we look up "New Deal" and "jobs"? Oh, here we go. There's a book that goes into the specifics of the New Deal. I'm sure you could find your information there, but…
S: What?
L: We don't have the book here. You'll have to go to the social sciences department to get it. Here's a reference number to help you find it there.
S: Um… Where exactly should I go?
L: The main offices of the social sciences department are on the 3rd floor of Emerson Hall. They keep a small library there. It's pretty far away, **Q5** so you should probably go to the computer lab first. You know where the computer lab is right?
S: Yeah, I go there all the time to do my homework. **I guess I'll stop by before going to the social sciences department.** Thanks a lot.

해석 학생과 사서간의 다음 대화를 들으시오.

사서(남자): 무엇을 도와드릴까요?
학생(여자): 음… 대공황에 대한 책을 좀 찾아야 하는데요. 미국사 수업을 위해서요.
사서: 음, 잘 찾아왔어요. 하지만 돕기 전에, 자료관에 있는 컴퓨터를 사용해본 적이 있는지 물어봐도 될까요? 돕고 싶지 않아서가 아니라, 도서관의 데이터베이스에 있는 기사들과 책들을 꽤 빨리 찾을 수 있거든요.
학생: 자료실에 있는 컴퓨터에서 그 책을 찾으려고 애써봤는데, 그 결과물에 압도됐거든요. 제 말은, 너무 많은 결과물이 나와서, 제가 뭘 필요로 하는지 찾을 수가 없어요. 데이터베이스는 제가 적절한 키워드를 생각해 낼 수 있을 때는 아주 좋은데, 가끔은 너무 많은 결과물을 가져다

주거든요.

사서: 무슨 말인지 알겠어요. 학생이 이런 문제를 겪고 있는 학생 중 처음은 아니거든요. 좋아요, 그럼 시작해보죠. 구체적으로 무엇을 찾고 있는 거죠?

학생: 루즈벨트의 '뉴딜' 정책의 중요성과 결과에 대한 정보를 좀 찾아야 해요.

사서: 아, 알겠어요. 음, 그건 좀 넓은 주제네요.

학생: 네, 그런 것 같아요. 그게 아마 제가 너무 많은 결과물을 얻은 이유일 거예요.

사서: 주제를 좀 좁혀보면 어때요? 그게 힘든 건 알지만, 좀 더 구체적인 뭔가를 말해볼 순 없나요?

학생: 음… 음, 아마도 제가 정말 관심이 있는 것은, 그 정책이 새 일자리를 구하기 위해 서부로 이주를 한 인구에 미친 영향에 대한 것 같아요. 그래서 아마도 얼마나 많은 이주자들이 동부 주(州)에서 서부 주로 이동했는지를 알아보는 것으로 시작해야 할 것 같아요. 서부 주들에서의 뉴딜 정책 이전과 이후의 인구 조사 정보를 검색해보면 어떨까요? 유타, 아리조나, 뉴멕시코, 그리고 음… 네바다 같은 곳이요.

사서: 좋아요, 훨씬 낫네요. 어디 봅시다…. 나왔네요. 국가기록원에서 인구 조사 정보를 구할 수 있어요. 책은 아니지만, 컴퓨터실에서 그 정보를 인쇄할 수는 있을 거예요. 그럼, 또 어떤 게 필요하죠?

학생: 구체적인 정부 프로젝트들에 대한 정보도 필요해요. 뉴딜의 일환인 프로젝트들이요. 얼마나 많은 일자리가 가능하게 되었는지 알아야 할 것 같아요.

사서: 좋아요. 그럼 '뉴딜'과 '일자리'로 검색해보면 어때요? 아, 여기 있네요. 뉴딜 정책의 세부사항에 대해 다룬 책이 있어요. 거기서 학생이 필요한 정보를 찾을 수 있을 거예요. 하지만…

학생: 왜요?

사서: 여기에는 그 책이 없어요. 그 책을 구하려면 사회과학 학과로 가야 할 거예요. 그곳에서 그 책을 찾을 수 있도록 도와줄 참고도서 번호가 여기 있어요.

학생: 음… 정확히 어디로 가야 하죠?

사서: 사회과학 학과 사무실은 Emerson 홀의 3층에 있어요. 거기에 작은 도서관을 가지고 있지요. 그곳이 꽤 머니 아마 컴퓨터실에 먼저 가야 할 거예요. 컴퓨터실이 어디인지는 알죠?

학생: 네, 숙제를 하러 그곳에 항상 가요. 사회과학 학과에 가기 전에 들러야겠네요. 감사합니다.

Ⓦ Great Depression (미국) 대공황 reference [réfərəns] 참고, 참조 overwhelmed [òuvərhwélmd] 압도된 specifically [spisífikəli] 구체적으로 consequence [kánsəkwèns] 중요성, 결과 impact [ímpækt] 영향 population [pàpjuléiʃən] 인구 migrant [máigrənt] 이주자 census [sénsəs] 인구 조사 National Archives 국가기록원

01 대화의 주된 내용은?
Ⓐ 보고서를 위한 한정된 주제 고르기
Ⓑ 역사 수업을 위한 정보 찾기
Ⓒ 책들을 찾기 위해 도서관 데이터베이스를 사용하기
Ⓓ 사화과학 학과로 전과하기

02 도서관의 데이터베이스에 대해 학생이 암시하는 것은?
Ⓐ 더 이상 이용 가능하지 않다.
Ⓑ 확장될 것이다.
Ⓒ 학생들을 위한 것이 아니다.
Ⓓ 최적으로 기능하지 않는다.

03 학생의 연구 프로젝트의 주제는?
Ⓐ 대공황의 원인
Ⓑ 루즈벨트의 뉴딜 정책의 영향
Ⓒ 서부와 동부 주(州)들의 차이점들
Ⓓ 미국 내에서의 노동자들의 이주 패턴들

04 학생이 필요로 하는, 대공황에 대한 구체적인 정보는 무엇인가? (두 가지 선택)
Ⓐ 이주자들의 수
Ⓑ 실직률
Ⓒ 이주자들의 지리적 위치
Ⓓ 노동자 이주의 원인들

Ⓔ 서부 주(州)들에서의 정부 프로젝트들

05 학생이 다음에 할 일은?
Ⓐ 도서관에 책 반납하기
Ⓑ 도서관의 컴퓨터실에 가기
Ⓒ 주제에 관해 교수와 이야기하기
Ⓓ 사회과학 학과에 가기

ⓢ Practice Questions II

본문 p. 054

| 01 D | 02 A | 03 B | 04 D | 05 A |

[01 ~ 05] Listen to a conversation between a student and his zoology professor. ◁) MP3 05

Student(male): Hello, Professor Jenkins. Do you have a minute?
Professor(female): Of course, I was expecting you to come by. You wanted to talk to me about your grades?
S: Yeah, that's right. ▶Q1 **I've been wondering what I can do to make up for the bad mid-term grade I got.**
P: Hmm… Well, your grade certainly can use some help. I mean, you do seem very active in class. I assumed you understood all the material pretty well.
S: To tell you the truth, I do. But I just couldn't find the time to memorize all the terms. I was taking a lot of classes, but I realized I couldn't handle all of them at once. I dropped a class, so my schedule is more manageable now. But I need to find a way to make up for my bad grades. Is there anything I can do for your class? Like some extra credit work?
P: Well… ▶Q2 **Have you heard about the Volunteer and Observe program?**
S: Actually, no… But I'd love to hear the details.
P: Well, the program essentially involves going to the local zoo and helping the zoo staff while studying the daily routines of some animals. It requires some basic zoology knowledge, but ▶Q3 **you'd mostly be doing chores such as feeding and cleaning. But that will give you the chance to observe the animals very closely.** Um… **You can think of it as being a zookeeper, but without the dangerous parts,** of course. You won't be asked to feed any predators or do anything risky. ▶Q2 **At the end of the program you can write a paper** and submit it.
S: Wow, that seems like a very interesting program… But it also seems like a lot of work. I mean, volunteering and writing a paper seems like a lot to do.
P: I see. Well, you can just volunteer without writing the paper. You'll still get some extra credit, but it obviously won't be as much. ▶Q4 **That's actually one of the advantages of this program. You can do as much as your workload allows.**
S: That's great, but are there any other programs? I just want to see what all my options are.
P: Hmm… You can also help out at the annual zoology seminar. ▶Q5 **It's similar to the volunteer program in that, well, it's volunteer work for extra credit and it requires a background in zoology.** You'd still have to work hard, but not with animals, and you wouldn't be required to write a paper at the end. Another difference is that with the zoo program, you can work whenever you'd like as long as you're there for three hours a week. But the seminar has set dates. You'd have to make sure they don't conflict with your schedule.
S: Do you have the dates?
P: Sure, wait a minute… Oh, here we go. There's an orientation next week, on Thursday at 6 p.m. And then the seminar is from the 15th to the 17th. You'll have to be present from 4 p.m. to 9 p.m. on those three days.
S: Oh, I see. In that case, it looks like I'll have to volunteer at the zoo.

해석 학생과 동물학 교수간의 다음 대화를 들으시오.
학생(남자): 안녕하세요, Jenkins 교수님. 혹시 시간 있으세요?

교수(여자): 그럼요. 학생이 들르기를 기다리고 있었어요. 내게 성적에 대해 이야기하고 싶어 했죠?

학생: 네, 맞아요. 제가 받았던 형편없는 중간 고사 성적을 벌충하기 위해 뭘 할 수 있을지 궁금해서요.

교수: 음... 음, 학생의 성적은 분명 도움이 좀 필요하긴 하네요. 그러니까 내 말은, 학생은 수업 때 무척 능동적으로 보이는데 말이죠. 수업 자료를 매우 잘 이해하고 있다고 생각했어요.

학생: 솔직히 말씀 드리면, 맞아요. 하지만 그 모든 용어들을 외울 시간을 낼 수가 없었어요. 수업을 많이 듣고 있었는데, 그 모든 수업들을 한꺼번에 다룰 수 없다는 걸 깨달은 거죠. 수업 하나를 취소해서, 이제 제 스케줄을 좀 더 잘 관리할 수 있게 되었어요. 하지만 제 안 좋은 성적을 보충할 방법을 찾아야 해요. 교수님 수업을 위해 제가 할 수 있는 일이 있을까요? 추가 학점 작업 같은 거 말이에요.

교수: 음... 자원봉사 및 관찰 프로그램에 대해 들어본 적이 있나요?

학생: 사실, 아뇨... 하지만 자세한 내용을 들어보고 싶어요.

교수: 음, 그 프로그램은 기본적으로는 지역 동물원에 가서 동물원 직원들이 몇몇 동물들의 일상 생활을 연구하는 것을 돕는 활동을 포함해요. 약간의 기본적인 동물학 지식이 필요하긴 하지만, 학생은 먹이를 주거나 청소를 하는 등의 허드렛일을 주로 하게 될 거예요. 하지만 그 일은 학생에게 동물들을 매우 가까이서 관찰할 수 있는 기회를 주겠죠. 음... 그 일을 동물원 관리인이 되는 일, 물론 위험한 부분이 없는 일 말이죠. 그런 일로 여겨도 될 거예요. 포식 동물에게 먹이를 주거나 어떤 위험한 일을 하도록 요구 받지는 않을 거예요. 프로그램 말미에는 보고서를 써서 제출하면 되는 거죠.

학생: 와, 매우 흥미로운 프로그램 같아 보이는데요... 하지만 일이 많을 것 같기도 하네요. 그러니까, 자원봉사에 보고서까지 쓰는 것은 일이 많은 것 같아 보여요.

교수: 알겠어요. 음, 보고서를 쓰지 않고 자원봉사만 해도 돼요. 그래도 추가 학점을 좀 받긴 하겠지만, 분명 (보고서까지 쓰는 것 만큼) 그렇게 많이 받지는 못할 거예요. 그게 사실 이 프로그램의 장점들 중 하나거든요. 학생의 작업량이 허용하는 만큼만 일을 해도 돼요.

학생: 그건 멋지군요, 다른 프로그램은 없나요? 그냥 가능한 모든 선택 사항들을 알고 싶어서요.

교수: 음... 매년 열리는 동물학 세미나에서 도움을 줄 수도 있어요. 그 일은, 음, 추가 학점을 받기 위한 자원봉사 일이고 동물학에 배경 지식이 있어야 한다는 점에서는 그 자원봉사 프로그램과 비슷해요. 열심히 일해야 하긴 하지만 동물을 대하는 건 아니고, 끝에 보고서를 쓸 필요도 없어요. 또 다른 차이점은 동물원 프로그램은 일주일에 세 시간을 동물원에 있기만 하면 언제든 일을 할 수 있다는 거예요. 하지만 세미나는 정해진 날짜가 있지요. 그 날짜들이 학생의 일정과 겹치지 않는지 확인해야 할 거예요.

학생: 그 날짜들을 알 수 있을까요?

교수: 그럼요. 잠시만요... 아, 여기 있네요. 다음주에 오리엔테이션이 있어요. 목요일 오후 6시예요. 그리고 나서 세미나는 15일부터 17일까지고요. 그 3일간 오후 4시부터 밤 9시까지 자리를 지켜야 할 거예요.

학생: 아, 알겠습니다. 그런 경우라면, 동물원에서 자원봉사를 해야 할 것 같아요.

Ⓦ make up for 벌충하다. 만회하다 term [tə:rm] 용어 manageable [mǽnidʒəbl] 관리[감당]할 수 있는 extra [ékstrə] 추가 credit [krédit] 학점 volunteer [vὰləntíər] 자원봉사(자), 자원봉사 하다 essentially [isénʃəli] 기본[본질]적으로 involve [inválv] 수반하다. 포함하다 daily routine 평범한 일상 zoology [zouáləchi] 동물학 chore [tʃɔ:r] 정기적으로 하는) 일 zookeeper [zú:ki:pər] 동물원 사육사[관리인] predator [prédətər] 포식 동물 workload [wə́:rkloud] 업무량, 작업량 annual [ǽnjuəl] 매년의, 연례의 conflict [kənflíkt] 상충하다

01 학생이 교수를 방문한 이유는?
Ⓐ 여유 시간이 많다.
Ⓑ 동물학 세미나에 관심이 있다.
Ⓒ 지역 공원에서 자원봉사를 하고 싶어 한다.
Ⓓ 자신의 성적을 향상시킬 방법을 찾고 있다.

02 교수가 학생에게 제안한 것은?
Ⓐ 동물 관리에 대한 보고서 쓰기
Ⓑ 집안일 돕기
Ⓒ 마지막 보고서를 다시 쓰기
Ⓓ 일정을 가볍게 하기 위해 수업을 하나 취소하기

03 교수가 동물원 관리인을 언급한 이유는?
Ⓐ 직업에 관한 조언을 줄 수 있는 사람을 추천하려고
Ⓑ 무슨 일이 요구되는지를 설명하려고
Ⓒ 동물을 어떻게 관찰하는지 설명하려고

Ⓓ 동물들에게 먹이를 주는 것의 중요성을 강조하려고

04 자원봉사 및 관찰 프로그램의 이점으로 언급된 것은?
Ⓐ 동물원의 동물들에게 먹이를 줄 수 있다.
Ⓑ 실제 경험을 쌓을 수 있다.
Ⓒ 언제든 원할 때 동물원을 방문할 수 있다.
Ⓓ **얼마나 많은 양의 일을 할지 선택할 수 있다.**

05 자원봉사 및 관찰 프로그램은 세미나와 어떻게 유사한가?
Ⓐ **둘 다 동물학에 대한 이해를 필요로 한다.**
Ⓑ 둘 다 상당한 양의 서류작업을 포함한다.
Ⓒ 둘 다 자원봉사자들에게 동물들을 관찰할 수 있는 기회를 준다.
Ⓓ 둘 다 똑같이 정해진 일정에 일어난다.

Chapter 2. Conversation Topics

Unit 1. Instructor's Office Hours

01 / Class

Sample Questions
본문 p. 062

01 C **02** A, D **03** A, D **04** B **05** C

해석 학생과 영화학 교수 간의 다음 대화를 들으시오. ◁) MP3 06

학생(여자): Wooden 교수님?

교수(남자): 안녕하세요, Louisa Smith죠. 들어와 앉아요.

학생: 감사합니다.

교수: 영화사 수업에 관해 나를 보고자 했다고요? 그 과정이 학생한테 괜찮을지 문의하려고 보자고 한 것 같군요.

학생: 아… 아뇨, 그 과정은 확실히 수강하길 원해요. 하지만, 실은 제가 이미 15학점을 등록해서 더 수강을 할 여유가 될지 모르겠어요. 그러니까 제 말은, 주변에 좀 물어봤는데 교수님 수업은 읽을 자료와 보고서 작성이 많다고 들어서요… 음… 할 일이 너무 많아지는 건 원치 않거든요.

교수: 알겠어요, 괜찮아요. 몇 학년이죠? 일 학년이라고 하지 않았던가요?

학생: 맞습니다.

교수: 그러면 내 수업을 그냥 내년에 듣지 그래요?

학생: 그게, 그렇게 해도 될 것 같긴 해요. 하지만 저는 정말 영화를 좋아하는데, 제가 다녔던 고등학교에서는 영화를 가르치지 않았거든요. 일 년 더 기다리는 건 싫을 것 같아요.

교수: 알겠어요. 하지만 미리 어느 정도 경고는 해야겠네요. 이 수업이 개론 과정이기는 하지만, 학생이 해야 할 일들이 많을 거예요. 강의에 매번 참석해야 하고, 자료도 읽어야 할 것이고, 매 주 영화 상영에 네 번의 보고서 제출, 그리고 물론 기말고사도 있을 거예요. 뭐, 하지만, 이미 그건 다 들어서 알고 있을 것 같네요.

학생: 네, 하지만… 사실 제가 정말 알아보고 싶었던 건 혹시 청강이 가능한가요. 실제 학점이 필요한 건 아니니까요. 교수님 강의를 듣고 영화를 보는 것만으로도 좋을 것 같거든요.

교수: 아, 그렇다면 그건 전혀 문제가 되지 않아요. 강의실이 충분히 크거든요. 많은 학생들이 수업을 듣긴 하지만, 대개 청강자들을 위한 여유는 있어요. 학생이 청강을 한다면, 기말고사도 없을 거고 보고서도 쓸 필요가 없어요. 하지만 한 가지 문제가 있죠. 좀 우습긴 하지만, 내가 알기로 학생들, 그러니까, 청강하는 학생들에게 제일 문제가 되는 것이… 음… 청강자들은 토론 수업에 참여할 수 없다는 점이에요.

학생: 잠깐만요. 참여할 수 없다고요?

교수: 미안하지만, 그게 대학 정책이에요. 대부분의 대학들도 다 그렇죠. 그러니까, 원래도 사람이 많은 수업인데 모두가 참여할 수 있게 허용하고, 모두가 이야기를 하기 시작한다면…

학생: 아, 물론이죠. 그건 학점을 위해 실제로 수업을 듣는 학생들에게 공평하지 않겠죠. 아, 이런… 좀 더 생각해봐야겠네요.

교수: 그래요. 학생이 고려해봐야 할 또 다른 점이 있어요. 영화 쪽 상급 과목을 듣거나 영화 전공을 할 계획이 있나요?

학생: 네, 실제로 그걸 고려 중이에요.

교수: 음, 대부분의 영화 과목들에 있어 영화사는 필수 과목이에요. 반드시 들어야 할 거예요.

학생: 아, 전혀 몰랐어요. 그럼, 궁금한 게, 제가 청강만 하고 학점 이수를 하지 않아도 영화 상급 과목을 들을 수 있나요?

교수: 엄밀히 따지면 안 되죠. 음, 어떤 교수들은 학생 같은 사람을 들여보내 줄지도 모르지만, 확신할 순 없어요. 특히 그런 상급 과목들 같은 경우는 말이죠. 그런 수업들은 필수 과목들을 들은 사람들로 꽤 빨리 정원이 차거든요.

학생: 알겠어요. 그러면…

교수: 그러니, 앞으로 영화 수업을 더 듣고 싶다면, 내 수업을 학점 이수로 들어야 할 거에요. 이번 학기에 내 수업을 청강으로 듣지는 않는 편이 나을 것 같네요. 물론, 학생이 너무나 바쁘다면, 감당할 수 있을 때까지 수강을 미루는 편이 나을 테고요.

학생: 음… 좀 더 생각해봐야겠어요. 어쨌든 감사합니다.

W register for ~ …에 등록하다 on one's plate (…을) 해야 할 의무가 있는, 하기로 되어 있는 warning [wɔ́ːrniŋ] 경고 introductory [ìntrədʌ́ktəri] 입문자들을 위한 film screening 영화 상영 audit [ɔ́ːdit] 청강하다 auditor [ɔ́ːditər] 청강생 catch [kætʃ] (숨은) 문제점, 애로점 ponder [pándər] 숙고하다 advanced [ədvǽnst] 상급의 prerequisite [pri(ː)rékwizit] 선수과목 technically [téknikəli] 엄밀히 따지면 count on ~ …을 믿다 better off 더 좋은, 더 나은 postpone [poustpóun] 미루다

01 학생이 교수의 영화 수업에 관해 그를 찾아간 이유는?

Ⓐ 그의 수업을 듣는 것에 더 이상 관심이 없다는 것을 말하려고

- Ⓑ 나중에 어떤 상급 과목을 들어야 하는지 문의하려고
- Ⓒ 학점을 이수하지 않고 그 수업을 들을 수 있는지 알아보려고
- Ⓓ 그의 수업에서의 자신의 안 좋은 성적을 어떻게 향상시킬 수 있을지 상의하려고

02 교수가 강조한 수업의 특징은 무엇인가? (두 가지 선택)
- Ⓐ 요구되는 것이 많다.
- Ⓑ 너무 많은 학생들이 그 수업을 듣는다.
- Ⓒ 청강이 불가능하다.
- Ⓓ 영화 전공자들에게 필수 과목이다.

03 교수에 의하면, 영화 수업을 청강하는 것의 두 가지 단점은 무엇인가? (두 가지 선택)
- Ⓐ 영화 상급 과목을 들을 수 없을지도 모른다.
- Ⓑ 좋은 성적을 받을 수 없다.
- Ⓒ 영화 상영에 참석할 수 없다.
- Ⓓ 토론 수업에 참여할 수 없다.

04 교수가 학생에게 제안한 것은?
- Ⓐ 흥미로운지 알아보기 위해 그의 수업을 청강하기
- Ⓑ 많이 바쁘지 않을 때 그 수업을 수강하기
- Ⓒ 이번 학기에는 그녀의 공부에 집중하기
- Ⓓ 내년에 무슨 수업을 들을지 생각해보기

대화의 일부분을 다시 듣고 질문에 답하시오. 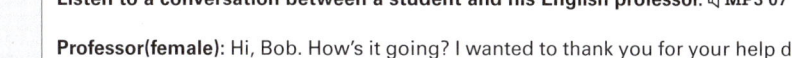 MP3 06_1

> P: Well… they can't participate in class discussions.
> S: Wait a minute. We can't?
> P: I'm sorry, but that's the university policy. It's like that at most schools. I mean it's a big class already, so if we let everyone participate and everyone starts talking…
> S: Oh, sure. I guess that wouldn't be fair to the students who are actually taking the class for credit.

05 토론 수업에 대해 학생이 암시하는 것은?
- Ⓐ 청강하는 학생들에게는 토론이 너무 어려울 것이라고 생각한다.
- Ⓑ 너무 많은 학생들이 한 번에 말을 할까 봐 걱정한다.
- Ⓒ 청강을 하는 학생들도 토론에 참여할 수 있을 것으로 생각했었다.
- Ⓓ 학점 이수를 위해 수업을 듣는 학생들이 이기적이라고 생각한다.

≥ Practice Questions   본문 p. 066

| 01 C | 02 D | 03 B | 04 C | 05 D |

Listen to a conversation between a student and his English professor. MP3 07

Professor(female): Hi, Bob. How's it going? I wanted to thank you for your help during the writing conference last week. Your assistance definitely made it a better experience for everyone.

Student(male): Thanks. It really was my pleasure to help out. It's not every day you get the chance to meet best-selling authors and learn writing skills. It was awesome. But I started to wonder about something after the conference.

P: What was it?

Introduction	S: Well, when I was doing the reading, you know, the reading you assigned in the class, **Q1** **I read something about language poetry.** P: Yes, that would be in the reading… What about it?
Problem 읽은 내용이 이해가 안됨	S: Uh… well, **I don't get it.** I mean, isn't poetry about language anyway? Poems are written using words or… language, right? I don't get why there's a whole new genre in poetry when poetry uses language anyway. P: Well, in a way, it might just seem like regular poetry, meaning that it is generally short, but **Q2** **the approach is totally different.** Instead of relying on traditional poetry techniques like you learned in class, you know, mood, rhythm, imagery, things of that sort, **language poetry relies on the words themselves.** S: Well, that's what I read, and I looked at one of the language poems in the reading, I think it was by Ron Silli… P: Ron Silliman? S: Yeah, that was it. Anyway, I just couldn't understand his poem at all. To be honest, it didn't even seem like a poem to me. P: Hmm… Okay, Bob, what's the first thing you think about when you read something? S: Uh… P: We look at the author's, or in this case, the poet's intention. We ask ourselves "Why did this poet write the poem?" S: Hmm… Yeah, come to think of it, that's right. But, I still don't understand the intention of a language poem… It just seems like meaningless mumbo jumbo.
Purpose 언어시는 의도가 없음	P: **Q3** That's actually exactly the point of language poetry. **The poet doesn't have an intention. There's no hidden agenda in language poems.** Language poets **use interesting and sometimes offbeat words. By doing so they draw the attention of the reader to the words that are used.** **Q2** **It's up to the reader to decide what the word means and why it was written that way.** Okay, so, think of an apple tree. **Q4** **What comes to mind when I say** multicolored apple tree?
Example 다색 사과나무로 예를 듦	S: Uh… apple trees don't have that many colors… Oh, so **because multicolored is an interesting way to describe an apple tree, I'm supposed to be drawn to that word.** P: That's correct. Then what exactly is multicolored? What does it mean? Does it have just one meaning? S: No, I mean, it can mean a lot of things to a lot of people. So, you mean to tell me that there can be many interpretations of the same poem and that's what the poets want?
Suggestion 또 다른 언어시를 읽어볼 것을 제안	P: Exactly. Mmm… **Q5** **It's not on the reading list I gave you, but if you read Silliman's *The Alphabet*, you'll see what I mean.** It's sort of… sort of in between traditional poetry and language poetry. Oh, and if you still don't get it, I have a lecture prepared on the topic. You'll be able to learn more in class. S: Thanks. I'll read it. P: Glad I could help. Oh, and by the way, could you help out at the next writing conference, you know, the one next month? S: Sure thing.

해석 학생과 영문학 교수 간의 다음 대화를 들으시오.
교수(여자): 안녕, Bob. 어떻게 지내요? 지난주 있었던 writing conference 때 도와주어서 고마웠어요. 학생이 도와주어 확실히 conference가 모두에게 더 좋은 경험이 되었을 거예요.
학생(남자): 감사합니다. 도울 수 있어서 좋았어요. 베스트셀러 작가들을 만나서 글쓰기 기술에 대해 배울 수 있는 기회를 갖는 게 매일 오는 게 아니잖아요. 정말 좋았어요. 하지만 conference가 끝난 뒤에 뭔가 궁금해지기 시작했어요.

교수: 그게 뭐였죠?

학생: 음, 읽기 자료를 읽다가, 교수님이 수업 시간에 내주신 자료 말이에요. 언어시(language poetry)에 대해 뭔가 읽었거든요.

교수: 그래요. 읽기 자료 중에 그게 있을 거예요... 그게 왜요?

학생: 아... 음, 잘 모르겠어요. 그러니까 제 말은, 시는 어쨌든 언어가 아닌가요? 시는 단어들, 즉... 언어를 사용해서 쓰여지잖아요? 시는 어쨌든 언어를 사용하는데 어째서 시에 언어라는 새로운 장르가 있는지 모르겠어요.

교수: 음, 어떤 면에서는 언어시는 일반 시처럼 보일 수도 있어요, 일반적으로 짧다는 점에서요. 하지만 접근법이 완전히 달라요. 수업 시간에 배운 전통적인 시 기법들, 그러니까, 분위기, 리듬, 형상화, 뭐 그런 것들에 의존하는 대신, 언어시는 단어 그 자체에 의존해요.

학생: 음, 그게 제가 읽은 내용이에요. 그리고 읽기 자료에 있는 언어시 중 하나를 봤는데, 그게 아마 Ron Silli...

교수: Ron Silliman의 시요?

학생: 네, 그거예요. 어쨌든, 그의 시를 전혀 이해할 수가 없더라고요. 솔직히 말씀 드리면, 제겐 그게 시처럼 보이지도 않았어요.

교수: 음... 알겠어요, Bob, 학생이 무언가를 읽을 때 가장 먼저 생각하는 것은 뭐죠?

학생: 어...

교수: 우리는 작가의, 아니 이 경우에는 시인의 의도를 보죠. 우리는 스스로에게 "이 시인이 왜 이 시를 썼을까?"하고 묻게 돼요.

학생: 음... 네, 생각해보니, 맞는 것 같아요. 하지만, 저는 여전히 언어시의 의도를 이해하지 못하겠어요... 언어시는 그저 횡설수설하는 것 같아만 보여요.

교수: 실제로 그게 바로 언어시의 핵심이에요. 시인은 의도를 가지고 있지 않죠. 언어시에는 숨은 의도 같은 것이 없어요. 언어시 시인들은 흥미롭고 가끔은 색다른 단어들을 사용하죠. 그렇게 함으로써 그들은 독자의 주의를 시에 사용된 단어에 돌려요. 그 단어가 무슨 의미인지, 그리고 그 단어가 왜 그런 방식으로 사용되었는지는 독자가 결정하도록 두는 거죠. 좋아요, 그럼 사과 나무를 떠올려봅시다. 내가 다색(多色)의 사과 나무라고 말한다면 머리 속에 어떤 생각이 드나요?

학생: 음... 사과 나무들은 그렇게 많은 색깔이 없으니까... 아, '다색'이 사과 나무를 묘사하는 흥미로운 방식이기 때문에 제가 그 단어에 주목을 하게 되는 거군요.

교수: 맞아요. 그럼 '다색'이라는 것이 정확히 뭔가요? 그게 의미하는 것이 뭐죠? 단지 한 가지 의미만 있나요?

학생: 아뇨, 제 말은, 그것은 많은 사람들에게 여러 가지 뜻을 의미할 수 있어요. 그럼, 같은 시에 대해 많은 해석들이 있을 수 있고, 그것이 시인들이 바라는 거라는 말씀이세요?

교수: 맞아요. 음... 내가 준 읽기 자료 목록에는 없지만, Silliman의 시 <알파벳>을 읽어본다면, 내가 무슨 말을 하는지 알 수 있을 거예요. 그 시는... 전통적인 시와 언어시의 중간 정도에 있다고 보면 돼요. 아, 그래도 여전히 잘 모르겠으면, 그 주제에 관해 내가 준비한 강의가 있어요. 수업 시간에 더 많이 배울 수 있을 거예요.

학생: 감사합니다. 읽어보도록 할게요.

교수: 도움이 되어 기쁘네요. 아, 그나저나, 다음 writing conference 때에도 도와줄 수 있나요? 다음 달에 있는 거 말이에요.

학생: 물론이죠.

Ⓦ conference [kánfərəns] 학회　assign [əsáin] 부과하다　genre [ʒáːŋrə; F ʒáːr] 장르　approach [əpróutʃ] 접근법　mumbo jumbo (아무 의미 없는) 복잡하기만 한 말　hidden agenda 숨은 의도　offbeat [ɔ́(ː)fbíːt] 색다른　multicolored [mʌ̀ltikʌ́lərd] 여러 색의　interpretation [intə̀ːrpritéiʃən] 해석

01 대화의 주제는?
Ⓐ 학생이 writing conference에서 유명한 작가들과 겪은 경험
Ⓑ 언어시 시인들이 다루는 여러 가지의 소재
Ⓒ 언어시의 핵심을 이해하는 데 있어 학생이 겪는 어려움
Ⓓ 시의 언어와 비유 간의 차이점

02 교수에 따르면, 언어시는 전통적인 시와 어떻게 다른가?
Ⓐ 언어시는 리듬과 분위기에 대한 독자의 이해에 의존한다.
Ⓑ 시인은 언어시를 쓸 때 특정한 목적을 가지고 있다.
Ⓒ 전통적인 시보다 언어시에 더 많은 형상화가 쓰인다.
Ⓓ 단어들만 써서 그 시가 무엇에 관한 것인지 독자가 결정하도록 한다.

03 교수가 언어시 시인들에 대해 암시하는 것은?
Ⓐ 그들은 일부러 자신들의 시를 이해하기 어렵게 만든다.

Ⓑ 그들은 종종 문맥에 어울리지 않는 단어들을 사용한다.
Ⓒ 그들은 시에서 여러 가지 다른 주제들을 다룬다.
Ⓓ 그들은 알파벳에 대한 뛰어난 이해를 가지고 있다.

04 교수가 '다색(多色)의 사과 나무'를 언급한 이유는?
Ⓐ Silliman의 시를 이해하는 가장 좋은 방법을 알려주려고
Ⓑ 학생이 읽기 자료를 이해했는지 확인하려고
Ⓒ 언어시에 쓰인 단어들의 예시를 들려고
Ⓓ 전통적인 시에 쓰인 기법을 설명하려고

05 학생이 다음에 할 일은?
Ⓐ 다음 writing conference 날짜를 정하기
Ⓑ 언어시에 관한 수업에 참석하기
Ⓒ 직접 언어시를 한 편 써보기
Ⓓ 또 다른 언어시를 읽어보기

02 / Course Grade, Exam

Sample Questions
본문 p. 070

01 B   02 D, E   03 A   04 C   05 A

해석 학생과 교수 간의 다음 대화를 들으시오. ◁ MP3 08
교수(여자): 안녕, Brian. 무엇을 도와줄까요?
학생(남자): Johnson 교수님. 음... 컴퓨터실에서 오는 길인데요. 교수님께서 인터넷에 올리신 성적을 방금 봤어요. 음... 이번 화요일 마감이었던 생물학 보고서 성적 말이에요...
교수: 나를 찾아와서 기쁘네요. 학생이 제출한 보고서를 봤어요... 하지만 뭔가 앞뒤가 맞지 않더군요. 그러니까, 보고서의 각주는 봤는데, 보고서 말미에 있어야 하는 출처자료의 완전한 목록이 없었어요. 알다시피, 인용한 것은 모두 출처를 포함시켜야 해요. 그래서 보고서의 몇몇 페이지가 누락되었나 하고 궁금했어요.
학생: 오! 그 페이지가 떨어져 나갔나 봐요. 내일까지 복사본을 가져다 드릴게요.
교수: 좋아요. 그리고 보고서 이야기를 하는 김에... 다른 페이지도 누락된 것 같아요. 내가 보고서의 결론 부분을 제대로 보지 못했는데. 어디 봅시다... 여기 있네요... 그래요, 학생은 아이디어를 모아서 마무리 짓지 않았어요. 아이디어를 모아주는 문단이 있어야 하는데, 즉, 음, 보고서를 일부러 열린 결론으로 남겨놓으려고 한 것이 아니라면 말이죠.
학생: 아... 열린 결론이어야 한다고 생각했어요. 일 학년이 모두 들어야 하는 필수 작문 수업 아시죠? 음, 거기서 좋은 결론은, 보고서에 쓰여 있는 것들을 그냥 요약만 하는 것 대신에 항상 새로운 질문을 제기해야 한다고 배웠거든요.
교수: 그것을 내 수업의 새의 이동에 관한 보고서에 시도해본 거란 말이죠?
학생: 네. (작문 수업) 선생님이 모든 글에 그렇게 해야 한다고 하셨어요. 그래서, 저는 그게 여기, 그러니까, 대학에서 요구되는 글쓰기 양식이라고 생각한 거죠. 전 사실 잘했다고 생각했거든요.
교수: 음, 한 수업에서 무언가를 배워 그걸 다른 수업에 써보는 것은 아주 좋아요. 하지만, 있죠, 문제는, 그게 우리 학교에서 쓰는 규범적인 글쓰기 방식이 아니라는 점이에요. 사실, 그게 작문 수업에서 가르치는 것이라는 게 믿기지 않네요. 왜냐면, 솔직히 말하면, 나는 그런 글쓰기 양식에 동의하지 않거든요. 대부분의 내 동료들, 그러니까, 학생의 다른 과학 과목 교수들도 내 말에 동의할 거라는 걸 알게 될 거예요. 좋은 결론은 보고서의 아이디어들을 모아서 정리하는 데에 주로 초점을 맞춰야 해요.
학생: 알겠습니다. 음, 솔직히 말씀 드리면, 그게 제가 늘 배워왔던 것이긴 해요. 하지만, 음, 이 작문 교수님은, 결론을 열어 두는 것이 보고서를 마무리 짓는 더 좋은 방식일 수 있다고 하셨어요.
교수: Brian, 내가 학생의 보고서를 채점할 때는 이런 것에 대해 전혀 몰랐어요. 난 그저, 왜 결론이... 음, 그렇게 비논리적인지 이해가 되지 않

았죠. 알다시피, 먼저 앞에 나온 내용을 요약하고, 그리고 나서 새로운 생각이나 질문을 언급하는 것이 좋아요. 하지만, 그렇다 하더라도, 학생은 상관없는 내용을 도입하는 위험을 무릅쓰고 있어요.
학생: 상관이 없다고요?
교수: 네! 그러니까 내 말은, 학생이 새에 관한 좋은 예들을 많이 보여주고 있지만, 보고서 말미에 나비에 관해 꽤 장황하게 적어놓기도 했더군요. 새의 이동에 관한 보고서에 왜 그렇게 했는지 이해를 못하겠더군요. 그러니까, 나비도 이동을 하는 건 사실이긴 하지만, 그렇게 되면 완전히 다른 보고서가 되죠. 하지만 이제는 학생이 무엇을 하려 했는지 이해가 되네요.
학생: 아뇨, 저도 나비의 이동이 다른 건 알아요… 제가 그렇게 형편 없는 성적을 받은 게 당연하네요. 교수님께서 원하신다면 보고서를 다시 써올 수 있어요.
교수: 아니, 아니, 그럴 필요는 없어요. 있죠, 내가 이제 학생의 상황을 알게 되었으니, 보고서를 다시 살펴보도록 할게요.
학생: 알겠습니다.
교수: 다음 주에 다시 보도록 하죠.

🆆 computer lab 컴퓨터실 due [djuː] …하기로 예정된 hand in 제출하다 footnote [fútnòut] 주석 quote [kwout] 인용문 open-ended [oupən-ended] 열린 결말의 mandatory [mǽndətɔ̀ːri] 의무적인 raise questions 의문을 제기하다 attempt [ətémpt] 시도하다 migration [maigréiʃən] 이주 primarily [práimərəli] 주로 grasp [græsp] 이해하다, 파악하다 risk v-ing 과감히 …을 하다, …의 위험을 무릅쓰다 lengthy [léŋkθi] 너무 긴, 장황한

01 학생이 교수를 찾아간 이유는?
Ⓐ 자신이 쓰고 있는 보고서에 대해 이야기하려고
Ⓑ 보고서에 받은 성적에 대해 논의하려고
Ⓒ 보고서를 마무리하는 방법에 대해 조언을 청하려고
Ⓓ 보고서를 끝내지 못한 이유를 설명하려고

02 교수에 따르면, 학생의 보고서에서 잘못된 것은 무엇인가? (두 가지 선택)
Ⓐ 한 가지 주제에만 초점을 맞췄다.
Ⓑ 다른 자료들을 표절했다.
Ⓒ 새에 대한 충분한 예시를 들지 않았다.
Ⓓ 완전한 출처자료 목록이 빠져 있다.
Ⓔ 제대로 된 결론을 포함하지 않았다.

03 학생이 작문 수업에서 배운 방식에 관해 교수가 언급한 것은?
Ⓐ 자신이 생각하기에는 바르지 않다고 생각한다.
Ⓑ 학교에서 요구되는 방식이다.
Ⓒ 학생의 보고서를 향상시켰을 것이다.
Ⓓ 도입부분에만 좋다.

04 교수가 학생에게 해줄 일은?
Ⓐ 무슨 일이 있었는지 그의 부모에게 설명해줄 것이다.
Ⓑ 작문 교수에게 그의 교수법에 대해 이야기를 할 것이다.
Ⓒ 보고서를 다시 한 번 채점할 것이다.
Ⓓ 학생이 대신 쓸 다른 보고서를 채점할 것이다.

대화의 일부분을 다시 듣고 질문에 답하시오. 🔊 **MP3 08_1**

> I mean, it's true that butterflies migrate too, but that's a totally different paper altogether.

05 교수가 다음과 같이 말할 때 암시하는 것은?
Ⓐ 학생은 보고서의 주제에 초점을 맞춰야 한다.
Ⓑ 학생은 이전 보고서에서 자료를 베껴왔을지도 모른다.
Ⓒ 학생은 보고서와 관련된 것에 대해 더 많이 연구해야 한다.
Ⓒ 학생이 더 나은 성적을 받기 위해서 아마 보고서를 하나 더 써야할지도 모른다.

Practice Questions

본문 p. 074

01 D   02 C   03 B   04 C   05 B

Introduction

Listen to a conversation between a student and his English professor. 🔊 MP3 09

Student(male): So, Professor Livingston, you wanted to see me? **Q1** **Your notes on the paper I wrote about the history of photography said that you wanted to see me about it.** I thought I'd done a pretty good job, but I am a little disappointed about my grade.
Professor(female): Oh, you did a pretty good job. But if I told you that something could be excellent, would you settle for pretty good?
S: Well, no…
P: Exactly!
S: Are you telling me that… that I could get a better grade?
P: Oh, sorry! It's not about your grade. **Q1** **It's… I think you could gain a lot of insight by revising it.**

Attitude
보고서를 수정할 시간이 없어서 걱정함

S: **Q2** **You mean, rewriting it? The whole thing? My plate is already pretty full as it is. There are deadlines and exams… I really… don't know if I can give any time to it, if any, actually.**
P: I understand it's a busy time, with spring break coming up next week. It's up to you. But with just a little bit of effort, you can really turn this around.

Problem
너무 여러 다른 내용이 들어감

S: No… yeah… I mean, after reading your comments, I… I can definitely see what the problem is. There're just too many things going on.
P: Yeah. It does get carried away and takes the focus off of the assignment. I understand that they're related, but it just branches out a little too much.
S: So I should cut out the technology part?

Suggestion
관련 없는 내용은 삭제할 것

P: Oh no, that's actually a part that you need – history and technology are related. I think it's the depth that you have to worry about. **Q3** **I wouldn't take the whole part out. But anything unrelated to how photography developed has no place in the paper.** All that tangential material about different technologies applied to camera sensors and such just distracts from the flow.
S: Yeah, I always want to put in everything I know. I never know where to draw the line.
P: That's something all writers struggle with. But it's also something you can learn to fix. You're going to have to practice it, and if you just cut out the… um…
S: The stuff about applied technology. But won't the paper be too short?
P: See, that's actually the point I wanted you to think about. **Q4** **What were your thoughts when I asked for a 20-page paper?**
S: Uh… to write a good paper…
P: No, what did you really think? You can be honest, it's okay.
S: Twenty pages…
P: Exactly. **Q4** **A lot of writers, especially students, write everything they know because, well… they have to get the pages filled up. If that becomes a habit, you'll never learn how to write a well-structured paper.** A short, well-structured paper is always better than a long paper that goes all over the place.
S: So, all I have to do is delete those sections?

Suggestion
불필요한 내용 삭제 후 보고서 서론 부분을 수정할 것

P: Not so fast. That's the first thing you'll do, but you'll have to go back and revise the rest, to see how the contents flow. And, of course, **Q5 you'll have to revise the introduction so it describes what you do in the body of the paper accurately**. But I think it's manageable. Just remember to be focused on the task at hand. How's tomorrow sound? Noon okay?

S: Um… I have so much… er… wow… but I'll try. Are you sure you won't give me a better…

P: Ha ha! Well, I can't, but if you learn how to write a focused essay, you'll be able to make up for it later, trust me.

해석 학생과 영문학 교수 간의 다음 대화를 들으시오.

학생(남자): Livingston 교수님, 저를 보자고 하셨죠? 사진의 역사에 대해 제가 썼던 보고서에 교수님이 남기신 메모에, 제 보고서와 관련해 저를 봤으면 하신다고 써있었어요. 전 제가 꽤 잘 썼다고 생각했는데, 성적이 조금 실망스럽네요.

교수(여자): 아, 꽤 잘 썼어요. 그런데 만일 내가 무엇인가가 훌륭해질 수 있다고 한다면, 학생은 '꽤 잘한' 것에 그냥 만족할 건가요?

학생: 음, 아뇨…

교수: 바로 그거예요!

학생: 교수님 말씀은… 제가 더 좋은 성적을 받을 수 있다는 말씀이세요?

교수: 아, 미안해요! 성적에 대한 말이 아니에요. 그러니까… 내 생각엔 학생이 보고서를 수정함으로써 많은 통찰력을 얻을 수 있을 것 같아요.

학생: 보고서를 다시 쓰라는 말씀이세요? 전체를요? 전 이미 할 일이 정말 많은데요. 과제 마감일들도 있고 시험도 있고… 정말이지… 보고서에 할애할 시간이 있을지 정말 모르겠어요, 만일 실제로 시간이 좀 난다 해도 말이에요.

교수: 봄방학이 다음 주라 바쁜 때인 건 이해해요. 학생에게 달렸죠. 하지만, 약간의 노력만으로 이 보고서를 정말 향상시킬 수 있어요.

학생: 아뇨… 네… 그러니까 제 말은, 교수님의 코멘트를 읽고 난 후에… 문제가 뭔지 확실히 알았어요. 너무 많은 내용들이 있는 거죠.

교수: 그래요. 딴 길로 새는 바람에 과제의 초점이 벗어났어요. 그것들이 관련이 있는 것은 이해하지만, 내용이 너무 가지를 많이 치고 있어요.

학생: 그럼 제가 기술 부분을 삭제해야 하나요?

교수: 오, 아니에요. 그건 사실 학생에게 필요한 부분이에요. 역사와 기술은 연관되어 있으니까요. 학생이 염려해야 하는 부분은 깊이예요. 나라면 전체 부분을 들어내지는 않겠어요. 하지만 사진이 어떻게 발달했는지와 관련 없는 것은 보고서에 들어갈 자리가 없어요. 카메라 센서에 적용된 여러 다른 기술과 관련 없는 모든 자료나 그러한 것들은 흐름에서 벗어나게 할 뿐이에요.

학생: 네, 저는 항상 제가 아는 모든 걸 넣고 싶어 해요. 어디에서 선을 그어야 할지 정말 모르겠어요.

교수: 그건 모든 글 쓰는 사람들이 고군분투하는 점이에요. 하지만 그건 또한 학생이 배워서 고칠 수 있는 것이기도 하죠. 학생은 그걸 연습해야 하는데, 그 부분은… 그냥 삭제하게 되면…

학생: 적용된 기술에 관한 부분이요. 하지만 보고서가 너무 짧아지지 않을까요?

교수: 봐요, 그게 사실 내가 학생이 생각해보기를 원했던 요점이에요. 내가 20페이지 분량의 보고서를 쓰라고 했을 때 학생은 어떤 생각이 들었어요?

학생: 음… 좋은 보고서를 쓰라고…

교수: 아니, 실제로 어떤 생각이 들었냐고요. 솔직히 말해도 돼요. 괜찮으니까.

학생: 20페이지라는…

교수: 바로 그거예요. 글을 쓰는 많은 사람들, 특히 학생들은, 자신이 아는 모든 것을 써요. 왜냐하면, 음… 페이지 분량을 채워야 하니까요. 그게 습관이 되면, 잘 구성된 보고서를 쓰는 법을 결코 배울 수 없을 거예요. 짧으면서 구성이 잘 된 보고서는 횡설수설하는 긴 보고서보다 언제나 더 나은 법이죠.

학생: 그럼, 그 부분들을 삭제하기만 하면 되는 건가요?

교수: 잠깐 기다려봐요. 그건 학생이 해야 할 첫 번째 일이긴 하지만, 학생은 다시 앞으로 돌아가서 내용이 어떻게 흘러가는지 보고, 나머지를 수정해야 해요. 그리고 물론, 학생이 보고서 본론에서 무엇을 설명하는지 정확히 나타내기 위해 서론 부분도 수정해야 할 거고. 하지만 이 정도는 감당할 수 있을 거라 보는데요. 다루고 있는 과제에 초점을 맞추는 것을 꼭 기억하세요. 내일은 어때요? 정오쯤이면 괜찮겠어요?

학생: 음… 제가 할 일이 너무… 어… 이런… 하지만 노력해볼게요. 정말 제게 더 나은… 주시진 않으실 건가요…

교수: 하하! 이런, 그럴 순 없어요. 하지만 학생이 초점이 맞춰진 보고서를 쓰는 법을 배운다면, 나중에 이 보고서 성적을 만회할 수 있을 거예요. 내 말을 믿어봐요.

W insight [ínsàit] 통찰력　revise [riváiz] 수정하다　deadline [dédlàin] 마감　turn around 호전시키다　branch out 확장하다

tangential [tændʒénʃəl] 별로 관계가 없는　distract [distrǽkt] 집중이 안되게 하다　draw the line 한도를 정하다　manageable [mǽnidʒəbl] 관리[감당]할 수 있는

01 교수가 학생에게 자신의 사무실로 찾아오라고 한 이유는?
Ⓐ 학생이 봄방학 때 무엇을 할 것인지 물어보려고
Ⓑ 학생에게 올바른 주제를 선택하는 법을 알려주려고
Ⓒ 학생이 성적을 향상시켜야 할 필요가 있다고 말해주려고
Ⓓ 학생이 쓴 보고서를 수정하도록 권고하려고

02 학생이 교수의 요청에 동의하기 전에 망설인 이유는?
Ⓐ 자신의 노력이 성공을 거둘지 확신할 수 없다.
Ⓑ 교수가 자신에게 무엇을 하기 원하는지 분명히 알지 못한다.
Ⓒ 학교와 관련된 작업량이 너무 많다.
Ⓓ 더 나은 보고서를 써야 할 동기가 없다.

03 보고서를 향상시키기 위해서 교수가 학생에게 제안한 것은?
Ⓐ 요점을 잘 보여주는 더 많은 예시를 넣기
Ⓑ 독자의 주의를 산만하게 하는 과도한 정보를 배제하기
Ⓒ 보고서에서 불필요한 기술에 대한 부분을 삭제하기
Ⓓ 이해하기 어려운 기술적 용어에 대해 세부 정보를 더 주기

04 교수가 과제의 페이지 수를 언급한 이유는?
Ⓐ 학생이 수정하기에는 보고서가 너무 길다고 생각한다.
Ⓑ 학생의 보고서가 더 길면 더 나을 것이라 생각한다.
Ⓒ 보고서에 접근하는 올바른 방법을 알려주고 싶어 한다.
Ⓓ 제시간에 끝내기에는 과제가 너무 어려웠다고 생각한다.

05 교수는 학생에게 어떤 방향으로 보고서의 서론을 바꿔야 한다고 제안하는가?
Ⓐ 읽는 사람의 관심을 끄는 쪽으로
Ⓑ 보고서에 바뀐 부분을 반영하는 쪽으로
Ⓒ 더 구체적인 세부사항들을 넣는 쪽으로
Ⓓ 철자와 문법 오류를 수정하는 쪽으로

03 / Field Trip

≷ Sample Questions

본문 p. 078

| 01 D | 02 D | 03 B, D | 04 D | 05 B |

해석 학생과 환경 과학 교수 간의 다음 대화를 들으시오. 📢 MP3 10
학생(남자): 안녕하세요, Archer 교수님. 지난주 수업시간에 교수님이 교수님의 굴 서식지 프로젝트에 참가하는 데 관심이 있는 학생들을 구하신다고 말씀하신 것 알고 계시죠?
교수(여자): 물론이죠. 그것에 대해 생각해 보고 있어요?
학생: 네, 정말 괜찮을 것 같아요. 하지만 음… 이런 종류의 학기 중 프로젝트를 하려면 경험이 있어야 하나요?
교수: 아뇨, 그렇진 않아요. 입문 단계 수업을 듣는 대부분의 학생들은 현장 연구 경험이 거의 없거나 아예 없을 거라고 생각하지만, 그건 괜찮아요.

학생: 아, 다행이네요. 사실, 제가 프로젝트에 참여하고자 하는 것도 그 이유이거든요. 경험을 쌓는 거요.

교수: 하지만, 학생이 접하게 될지도 모르는 몇 가지 어려운 사항들에 대해 미리 주의를 주어야 할 것 같아요.

학생: 무슨 말씀이시죠?

교수: 음, 알다시피, 우리는 바다에서의 영리활동이 해안 지대에 미치는 환경적 영향을 연구할 거잖아요. 우리가 가는 지역은 기름 유출로 피해를 입었어요. 프로젝트의 요점은, 오염이 퍼져나가 어떻게 해안가의 해양 야생동물들에게 피해를 주는지 알아보는 거예요. 그 지역은 심하게 오염이 되어서, 가솔린 같은 냄새가 날지도 몰라요. 속이 메스꺼워질 수도 있고요.

학생: 아, 그건 문제되지 않아요.

교수: 또 다른 점은, 그곳이 꽤 외진 곳이라서 보트를 타고 가야 한다는 점이에요. 바다에서 보트를 한 번도 타보지 못한 일부 학생들은 약간 뱃멀미를 하기도 해요. 냄새에다가 어지럽기까지 하면 정말 아무것도 하기 힘들죠.

학생: 그런 건 생각해보지 못했는데, 하지만 견딜 수 있을 것 같아요.

교수: 음, 대부분 그래요. 그리고...

학생: 또 있나요?

교수: 음, 대학에서는 이 프로젝트를 어느 정도까지만 지원해줄 수 있어요. 경제적으로 말이죠. 학교에서 우리에게 전세 보트와 우리가 사용할 장비들을 구하는 데 필요한 자금 지원은 해줬지만, 교통비는, 그러니까, 보트를 타기 위해 항구까지 오는 교통비는, 예산에 포함되지 않아요. 자비로 항구까지 와야 할 거예요.

학생: 오, 이런... 원래도 돈이 부족한데... 얼마 정도가 들 거라 생각하세요?

교수: 한 50달러쯤... 있잖아요. 그 금액이 부담스러우면, 거기까지 차를 몰고 갈지도 모르는 학생들에게 한번 물어볼게요. 아마 같이 타고 갈 수 있을 거예요.

학생: 그러면 좋겠네요. 그럼... 자원 학생을 몇 명이나 구하시는 거예요?

교수: 일곱 여덟 명 정도 구하는 중이에요. 내가 가르치는 모든 수업에서 지원자를 요청했거든요. 실제로 관심들을 꽤 보이더라고요. 학생도 서둘러 결정을 내려야 할지도 몰라요.

학생: 저도 정말 가고 싶어요, 하지만 일이 많을 것 같기도 하네요.

교수: 음, 그곳에 이미 다녀와본 적이 있는 학생들 중 한 사람을 소개해줄 수 있어요. 그 학생이 그곳에 가게 되면 어느 정도의 일을 예상해야 할지, 그리고 무슨 일을 하게 될지 학생에게 말해줄 수 있을 거예요. 꼭 내게 이메일을 보내서 그 학생의 연락처를 묻도록 해요.

학생: 감사합니다. 그렇게 할게요.

교수: 아, 그리고 사실 프로젝트가 일이 많기 때문에 추가 학점을 줄 것을 고려 중이에요. 추가 학점은 항상 학생들에게 좋은 인센티브가 되니까요. 학과 사무실에 문의해보고 (추가) 학점을 받기 위해 학생이 할 수 있는 것이 있는지 문의해보는 게 어때요? 학점을 위해 연구 보고서나 현장 학습 보고서를 써도 되니까요.

학생: 그거 좋은 생각이네요!

교수: 결정을 내리게 되면 꼭 나를 다시 찾아와요. 다음 주까지는 학생을 위해 자리를 하나 남겨둘게요, 하지만 만일 참가할 수 없다면 내게 알려주면 고맙겠어요. 말했듯이, 다른 많은 학생들이 관심 있어 하거든요. 또, 다음 주에 오리엔테이션이 있어요. 시간은 아직 정해야 하지만, 가지 않기로 결정한다 해도 반드시 한번 와보도록 해요. 거기서 배울 수 있는 것들이 많거든요.

학생: 알겠습니다. 가능한 한 빨리 제 결정을 교수님께 알려드리도록 할게요. 시간 내 주셔서 감사합니다.

ⓦ **field work** 현장 연구 **coastline** [kóustlàin] 해안지대 **commercial** [kəmə́ːrʃəl] 상업적인 **maritime** [mǽritàim] 바다의 **wildlife** [wáildlàif] 야생동물 **nauseous** [nɔ́ːʃəs] 메스꺼운 **remote** [rimóut] 외딴, 외진 **get seasick** 뱃멀미하다 **funding** [fʌ́ndiŋ] 지원금 **chartered** [tʃɑ́ːrtərd] 전세 낸 **budget** [bʌ́dʒit] 예산 **short on ~** ...이 부족하여 **carpool** [carpuːl] 카풀(승용차 함께 타기)을 하다 **volunteer** [vὰləntíər] 자원자 **shoot for ~** ...을 달성하려 애쓰다 **incentive** [inséntiv] 장려책

01 학생이 교수를 찾아간 이유는?
Ⓐ 수업 과제에 대해 문의하려고
Ⓑ 추가 학점을 받는 방법에 대해 논의하려고
Ⓒ 학점을 향상시킬 수 있는 방법에 대해 논의하려고
Ⓓ 학기 중 프로젝트에 대해 알아보려고

02 현장 연구에 참가하는 학생들에 대해 추론할 수 있는 것은?
Ⓐ 이전에 비슷한 연구를 해본 경험이 있다.
Ⓑ 무엇을 해야 하는지 처음부터 잘 알 것이다.
Ⓒ 여행 경비를 스스로 부담할 수 있다.
Ⓓ 학점 없이도 기꺼이 참여할 것이다.

03 학생이 현장 연구에서 겪을지도 모르는 문제들은 무엇인가? (두 가지 선택)
Ⓐ 의도치 않게 야생동물들에게 피해를 줄지도 모른다.
Ⓑ 어지러움과 메스꺼움을 경험할지도 모른다.
Ⓒ 전세 보트를 구하는 데 어려움을 겪을지도 모른다.
Ⓓ 교통비를 스스로 지불해야 한다.

04 교수가 학생에게 제의한 도움은?
Ⓐ 현장까지의 차량 무료 탑승
Ⓑ 학생의 시간에 대한 비용 지불
Ⓒ 조정 가능한 연구 스케줄
Ⓓ 다른 학생 소개

05 교수가 학생에게 제안한 것은?
Ⓐ 다음 프로젝트까지 기다리는 것이 나을 것이다.
Ⓑ 결정을 빨리 내려야 할지도 모른다.
Ⓒ 결정하기 전에 충분히 시간을 가져야 한다.
Ⓓ 취업 사무실에서 더 많은 정보를 구할 수 있다.

Practice Questions
본문 p. 082

| 01 France – Scotland – Switzerland | 02 C | 03 D | 04 C | 05 D |

Introduction

Listen to a conversation between a student and his English professor. 🎧 MP3 11

Student(male): Professor Williamson?
Professor(female): Yes, Adam. I was expecting you. So did you give what I told you some thought?
S: As a matter of fact, I did. I'm definitely looking forward to being a part of the study abroad program. I have a lot of countries in mind, but I think I've got them prioritized.
P: Great. I remember studying abroad when I was an undergrad. It was a great experience. Glad you decided to apply. So, what countries were you looking into going to? Where do you want to go?
S: Oh… if it were as easy as just picking and going…
P: Ha ha ha, I know, but that's why you're here. So…
S: 〔Q1〕 **The first place I had in mind is Paris, France.** I really want to study there. I think it'd be great.

Headset

P: 🎧 But… It's a pretty competitive program. A lot of students are going to apply. Are you sure? 〔Q5〕 **Don't you need good grades to get accepted?**
S: I know, I might not have the best grades, but I still have something up my sleeve! You know, 〔Q2〕 **I'm perfectly fluent in French.** I think I can make up for my grades during the interview.
P: You do have a point. I forgot your French was good. Knowing the language in the country you're applying to go to is definitely an advantage.
S: Yeah, I'm kind of counting on it. 〔Q2〕 **I'm even taking Advanced French Literature this semester.**

Example
상급 프랑스 문학 수업을 예로 들어 설명

P: Great! But keep in mind it's still very competitive. Were you thinking of any other places? Just in case.
S: Of course, 〔Q1〕 **I would love to go to France, but I really think Scotland is a great**

Cause
새로운 언어를 배울 수 없어 지원자가 많지 않음

place too. I wouldn't mind going there at all.

P: Oh, Scotland! I heard that it's a beautiful place. All the students who went there loved it, but strangely, **Q3** **the competition isn't as fierce for some reason. I'm assuming that's probably because most students who study abroad want to enhance their foreign language skills.** I guess the same goes for Great Britain too. **You really wouldn't be learning a new language if you went there.** Do you have any other places in mind?

S: Well, if the first two don't work out, **Q1** **I'm thinking Switzerland is another option.**

P: The competition for that program is pretty tough, too. But then again, you're also fluent in German, right?

S: Yes, I am.

P: If you know German and French, that gives you a pretty good chance.

S: That's good to hear.

Suggestion
신청서 작성 전 지도 교수와 이야기할 것

P: Make sure you fill out your application as soon as you can. The deadline's in a week. Even though there's a deadline, it's always better to hand it in as soon as possible. You want to give a good impression, you know? And **Q4** **make sure you talk to your academic adviser before filling out the application.** You have to know what classes to take. You wouldn't want to go to a school where you can't take the classes you need.

S: Oh no… My adviser… I tried talking to her yesterday, so I could fill out the application form, but she's at a conference.

P: When's your adviser going to come back?

S: Not until next week.

P: Oh, that's not good… do you think you can make the deadline?

S: She did say that she'd be back on Tuesday, and I made an appointment so I can meet her as soon as she comes back, but…

P: Don't worry too much about it, I'll make sure I leave a note to the people reviewing your application. I'm sure they'll understand. And it really isn't a big deal, as long as you can hand it in by the deadline.

해석 학생과 영문학 교수 간의 다음 대화를 들으시오.

학생(남자): Williamson 교수님?

교수(여자): 아, Adam. 기다리고 있었어요. 내가 말했던 것에 대해 생각 좀 해봤어요?

학생: 사실, 해봤어요. 제가 해외 유학 프로그램에 참여할 수 있기를 정말 고대하고 있어요. 여러 나라들을 마음에 두고 있긴 한데, 우선 순위를 매긴 것 같아요.

교수: 잘됐네요. 내가 학부생일 때 해외에서 공부했던 기억이 나네요. 정말 좋은 경험이었어요. 지원하기로 결심했다니 기쁘네요. 그럼, 어느 나라들을 가고자 살펴보던 중이에요? 어디를 가고 싶어요?

학생: 아… 그냥 골라서 가기만 하면 되는 것처럼 쉽기만 하다면…

교수: 하하하, 알아요. 하지만 그래서 여기 온 거잖아요. 그럼…

학생: 마음에 둔 첫 번째 장소는 프랑스 파리에요. 저는 정말 그곳에서 공부하고 싶어요. 정말 멋질 것 같아요.

교수: 하지만… 파리는 경쟁률이 무척 센 프로그램이에요. 많은 학생들이 지원을 할 거예요. 확실한가요? 합격하려면 성적이 좋아야 하지 않나요?

학생: 알아요. 제 성적이 가장 좋지는 않을지도 모르지만, 제게는 비장의 무기가 있어요! 있죠, 제가 프랑스어를 유창하게 구사하거든요. 면접 때 제 성적을 그걸로 만회할 수 있을 것 같아요.

교수: 일리 있는 말이네요. 학생이 프랑스어를 잘한다는 걸 잊고 있었어요. 가려고 지원하는 나라의 언어를 안다는 것은 분명히 이점이 되지요.

학생: 네, 그것에 기대보는 중이에요. 이번 학기에는 상급 프랑스 문학 수업도 듣고 있어요.

교수: 좋아요! 하지만 여전히 경쟁률이 매우 세다는 것을 기억해 둬요. 다른 장소도 생각해봤나요? 만약을 위해.

학생: 물론이죠. 정말 프랑스에 가고 싶긴 하지만, 스코틀랜드도 멋진 곳이라고 생각해요. 거기 간다 해도 정말 괜찮을 것 같아요.

교수: 아, 스코틀랜드! 그곳은 무척 아름다운 곳이라 들었어요. 거기 간 학생들이 모두 무척 좋아했어요. 하지만 이상하게도, 무슨 이유인지 경쟁률이 그다지 세지 않던데요. 내 추측으로는 아마도 해외에서 공부하는 대부분의 학생들은 그들의 외국어 능력을 향상시키기 원해서인 것 같네요. 영국도 마찬가지고요. 그곳에 가면 새로운 언어를 배울 수 없을 거예요. 마음에 둔 다른 곳은 있나요?

학생: 음, 처음 두 곳이 안 된다면, 다른 한 가지 선택은 스위스예요.

교수: 그 프로그램의 경쟁률도 꽤 세요. 하지만 또 한편으로는, 학생은 독일어에도 능하잖아요. 맞죠?

학생: 네, 그래요.

교수: 독일어와 프랑스어를 모두 안다면, 가능성이 꽤 있을 거예요.

학생: 그 말을 들으니 기쁘네요.

교수: 가능한 한 빨리 지원서를 작성하도록 해요. 마감이 일주일 후이니까요. 마감 기한이 있긴 하지만, 가능한 한 일찍 제출하는 것이 언제나 더 좋죠. 좋은 인상을 남기고 싶잖아요, 그렇죠? 그리고 지원서를 작성하기 전에 반드시 지도 교수님과 이야기를 나눠보도록 하고요. 어떤 수업들을 들을지 알아야 하니까요. 필요한 수업들을 들을 수 없는 학교에 가고 싶진 않을 테니까요.

학생: 오 이런... 제 지도 교수님이... 지원서를 작성할 수 있도록 어제 그분과 이야기를 나눠보려고 했는데, 컨퍼런스에 참석 중이시더라고요.

교수: 언제 돌아오시는데요?

학생: 다음 주에나 오셔요.

교수: 이런, 그건 좋지 않은데... 마감 기한에 맞출 수 있을 것 같아요?

학생: 교수님이 화요일에 오신다고 말씀하셔서, 오시는 대로 만나 뵐 수 있도록 약속을 잡긴 했어요. 하지만...

교수: 너무 걱정하지 말아요. 학생의 지원서를 검토하는 사람들에게 메모를 남겨 놓을게요. 그들이 이해해줄 거예요. 마감 기한까지만 제출한다면 그다지 큰 문제도 아니까요.

Ⓦ look forward to v-ing ...하기를 고대하다   prioritize [pràiɔ́:rətàiz] 우선순위를 매기다   undergrad [ʌ́ndərgræ̀d] 학부생   competitive [kəmpétitiv] 경쟁이 치열한   have something up one's sleeve 해결책이 있다, 비책을 가지고 있다   fluent [flú(:)ənt] 유창한   make up for ~ ...을 만회하다   advantage [ədvǽntidʒ] 이점   count on ~ ...을 믿다   fierce [fiərs] 격렬한   enhance [inhǽns] 향상시키다   impression [impréʃən] 인상   academic adviser 지도 교수

01 학생이 가장 선호하는 장소는 어디인가? 세 장소를 골라서 순서대로 배열하시오.

스코틀랜드 – 영국 – 프랑스 – 독일 – 스위스

France
Scotland
Switzerland

02 학생이 자신이 듣고 있는 프랑스 문학 수업을 언급했을 때 그가 암시하는 것은?
Ⓐ 프랑스에 갈 필요가 없다고 생각한다.
Ⓑ 프랑스어 수업에서 뛰어난 성적을 받는다.
Ⓒ 프랑스어에 능숙하다.
Ⓓ 프랑스에 대해 더 배우고 싶다.

03 스코틀랜드에서의 프로그램에 대해 교수가 말한 것은?
Ⓐ 이중언어를 쓰는 사람들에게 적합하다.
Ⓑ 대부분의 학생들이 생각하는 것보다 더 경쟁률이 세다.
Ⓒ 그 프로그램의 수업과 관련된 문제가 많다.
Ⓓ 학생들은 그 프로그램에서 외국어를 배울 수 없다.

04 교수는 학생이 무엇을 먼저 해야 한다고 제안하는가?
Ⓐ 그가 고른 나라에 대해 다시 생각해보기
Ⓑ 지원서에 대한 정보를 모으기
Ⓒ 지도 교수와 이야기하기
Ⓓ 교환 학생 컨퍼런스에 참석하기

대화의 일부분을 다시 듣고 질문에 답하시오. ◁) MP3 11_1

P: But... It's a pretty competitive program. A lot of students are going to apply. Are you sure? Don't you need good grades to get accepted?
S: I know, I might not have the best grades, but I still have something up my sleeve!

05 교수가 다음과 같이 말한 이유는?

> Don't you need good grades to get accepted?

Ⓐ 교수는 학생의 성적이 좋다고 생각한다.
Ⓑ 교수는 학생의 성적에 대해 잘 모른다.
Ⓒ 교수는 자격 요건에 대해 잘 모른다.
Ⓓ 교수는 학생이 자격이 된다고 생각하지 않는다.

04 / Paper

⇘ Sample Questions

본문 p. 086

| 01 D | 02 D | 03 B | 04 C | 05 B |

해석 학생과 교수 간의 다음 대화를 들으시오. ◁) MP3 12

학생(여자): 안녕하세요, Manning 교수님.
교수(남자): 그래요! Amy, 오늘은 무엇을 도와줄까요? 어쨌든 학생과 이야기를 할 사안이 있기는 했어요.
학생: 네, 교수님이 저와 무엇에 대해 이야기하고 싶어 하셨는지 알 것 같아요. 사실, 그게 제가 여기 온 이유예요.
교수: 학생 그룹의 다른 조원들은요?
학생: 모두 심리학 프로젝트를 마무리 짓는 중이라서 내일까지는 도서관에 콕 박혀 지낼 거예요.
교수: 음... 모두에게 이야기를 하면 더 좋겠지만... 학생이 정보를 전달해줘야 할 것 같네요.
학생: 네, 음, 지금쯤 아마 교수님이 알고 계시지만, 저희는 프로젝트에 대해서 좀 더 구체적인 피드백이 필요한 것 같아요. 저는 교수님의 부정적인 코멘트를 보고 조금 충격을 받았어요. 저희 연구 방법에 대한 코멘트를 잘 이해하지 못하겠고요. 저희가 연구대상에게 접근하는 방식을 바꿔야 한다는 것에 대한 거였는데요. 그러니까 제 말은, 교수님은 저희가 훌륭한 주제를 골랐다고 하셨잖아요. 저희가 왜 그렇게 부정적인 코멘트를 받았는지 이해가 안 가요.
교수: 음, 주제에는 잘못된 것이 없어요, 연구하기에 여전히 매우 흥미로운 주제라는 말이지요. 조정이 좀 필요한 곳은 학생의 그룹이 연구를 진행하는 방식이에요. 학생 그룹에서 고른 주제는 학생들이 도서관에서 어떻게 공부를 하는가였지요, 맞나요?
학생: 맞아요.
교수: 그건 정말 흥미로운 주제예요. 하지만 여러분이 도출한 결론은, 음, 여러분은 그걸 다시 살펴봐야 할지도 몰라요. 혹시 호손 효과(Hawthorne effect)라고 불리는 것에 대해 들어본 적이 있나요?
학생: 음... 그게 무언지 알고 있어야 하나요?
교수: 하하... 아니, 그건 아직 수업에서 다루지 않았어요. 이 주쯤 후에 아마 수업에서 다룰 거예요. 어쨌든, 여러분의 보고서를 봤어요. 전형적인 절차를 잘 따라서 학교 도서관의 스터디룸에서 공부하고 있는 학생들을 관찰했더군요. 하지만, 그 학생들에게 여러분이 그들을 관찰할 거라는 것도 말했더군요. 왜 그렇게 하기로 결정했는지 물어봐도 될까요?
학생: 학생들에게 나쁜 인상을 주기 싫었어요. 집중하고 있는 사람을 지켜보는 건 꽤 무례한 일이잖아요, 그렇지 않나요?
교수: 맞아요. 하지만 그 점이 바로 문제가 되었어요. 여러분이 관찰하고 있는 학생들이 자신들이 관찰되고 있다는 걸 알면, 그들은 다르게 행동하거든요. 그게 호손 효과예요.
학생: 아, 그럼 교수님 말씀은, 저희가 학생들이 모르게 관찰을 해야 한다는 말씀이세요?

교수: 그래요. 호손 효과는, 관찰 당하는 것에 대한 반응으로 사람들이 자신의 행동을 바꿀 때, 즉 개선시킬 때 생겨요. 그 이름은 Hawthorne Works라는 전기 공장에서 왔어요. 그곳에서, 한 연구가가 조명 상태에 따라 작업자들의 생산성이 어떻게 달라지는지를 알고 싶어 했어요. 그는 조명이 더 밝으면 생산성이 증가할 것이라고 생각했지요. 그는 관찰을 시작했고, 조명을 더 많이 설치하자 작업자들의 생산성이 더 좋아졌다는 것을 알아냈어요. 그는 작업자들이 더 밝은 환경에서 일을 더 잘하는 것이 사실이었다고 결론 내렸어요.

학생: 음... 그러면 문제가 뭐였지요?

교수: 문제는 그가 조명을 다시 원래 상태로 낮추었을 때 발생했어요. 무슨 일이 일어났을 거라 생각되나요?

학생: 작업자들이 전보다 더 열심히 일했나요? 그러니까, 조명이 어둑한 데도 생산성이 더 나아졌나요?

교수: 네, 바로 그거에요. 조명이 어두워지면 작업자들이 일을 덜 열심히 했어야 했는데, 그렇지 않았죠.

학생: 그 연구가가 저희가 한 것과 같은 실수를 한 거군요?

교수: 그래요. 그는 작업자들에게 자신이 그들을 지켜볼 거라고 말했어요. 작업자들은 그들이 평소에 하던 것과 달리 행동했고, 연구자는 정확한 결과를 얻지 못했죠.

학생: 무슨 말씀이신지 알겠어요... 저희가 뭘 잘못했는지 조원들이 알게 할게요. 하지만 저희 성적은요? 성적을...

교수: 속 태우지 말아요. 관찰 방법에 익숙하지 않은 많은 학생들이 하는 실수니까. 이제 알았으니, 학생의 그룹에서 새로 쓸 보고서를 토대로 성적을 다시 올리도록 할게요.

Ⓦ relay [ríːlèi] (정보 등을) 전달하다   specific [spisífik] 구체적인   negative [négətiv] 부정적인   approach [əpróutʃ] 접근하다   adjustment [ədʒʌ́stmənt] 수정, 조정   procedure [prəsíːdʒər] 절차   observe [əbzə́ːrv] 관찰하다   in response to ~ ...에 응하여   productivity [pròudʌktívəti] 생산성   dim (빛의 밝기를) 낮추다; (빛이) 어둑한

01 대화의 주제는?
Ⓐ 프로젝트를 위한 적절한 자료를 찾는 방법들
Ⓑ 학생이 연구 대상으로부터 받은 불평들
Ⓒ 학생이 프로젝트와 관련해 어려움을 겪는 이유들
Ⓓ 프로젝트를 위해 정확하게 연구를 수행하는 방법들

02 학생의 그룹이 실험 대상자들에게 그들이 관찰되고 있다는 것을 말한 이유는?
Ⓐ 관찰되고 있는 학생들이 그룹에게 화를 냈다.
Ⓑ 조원들이 그룹 프로젝트를 하는 법을 몰랐다.
Ⓒ 도서관이 제대로 된 관찰을 하기에 충분히 밝지가 않았다.
Ⓓ 조원들이 다른 학생들에게 예의를 지키기 원했다.

03 학생이 참여하고 있는 그룹 프로젝트에 대해 추론할 수 있는 것은?
Ⓐ 다른 조원들은 너무 바빠서 그것을 도울 수 없다.
Ⓑ 방법을 바꾸지 않는다면 부정확한 결과를 얻게 될 것이다.
Ⓒ 교수는 그들이 고른 주제를 승인하지 않는다.
Ⓓ 다른 심리학 프로젝트와 긴밀한 연관이 있다.

04 교수가 조명을 언급한 이유는?
Ⓐ 생산성이 어떻게 향상될 수 있는지 예시를 들려고
Ⓑ 호손 효과에 대해 강의에서 자신이 제시한 요점을 설명하려고
Ⓒ 실험 대상을 관찰하는 올바른 방법에 대한 자신의 주장을 보강하려고
Ⓓ 조원들이 생각해봐야 할 새로운 주제를 제안하려고

대화의 일부분을 다시 듣고 질문에 답하시오. 🔊 MP3 12_1

> P: Have you ever heard of something called the Hawthorne effect?
> S: Uh... Am I supposed to know what that is?

05 학생이 다음과 같이 말한 이유는?

> Uh... Am I supposed to know what that is?

Ⓐ 호손 효과가 무엇인지 몰라서 짜증이 나 있다.
Ⓑ 강의에서 중요한 점을 놓쳤을까 걱정하고 있다.
Ⓒ 교수가 호손 효과에 대해 잘 알고 있는지 확신할 수 없다.
Ⓓ 교수가 실수로 잘못된 용어를 썼다는 것을 암시하고 있다.

≋ Practice Questions

본문 p. 090

| 01 B | 02 D | 03 C | 04 B | 05 D |

Introduction	**Listen to a conversation between a student and his film professor.** 🔊 **MP3 13** **Student(male):** Hi, Professor Peterson. Do you have a minute? **Professor(female):** Yes, of course, Tom. How's your film report going? Did you film your subjects from different perspectives just like in your storyboard? I really think your take on using different camera angles to show mood is a great experiment. You'll really learn a lot from it. **S:** Yes! It was difficult finding the right angle in such a tight space, but it really worked out well. There are a lot of interesting perspectives and scenes in the film. I'm quite excited about it.
Attitude 교수는 결과물을 기대하고 있음	**P:** Ah, that's great. ▶Q2◀ **I'll be interested to see how it all came out.** So, where's your follow-up report? I don't think I received yours yet. **S:** No, I'm sorry. Actually, I still haven't gotten around to finishing it. That's why I'm here.
Headset	**P:** 🎧 ▶Q5◀ **You do know that the paper is due today by noon, don't you? It's 10 o'clock already.**
Problem dance scene을 아직 찍지 못함	**S:** ▶Q1◀ **I know it's a little last minute, but can I get an extension?** I still need to film a dance scene. ▶Q3◀ **The dancer that was supposed to show up bailed on me at the last minute. She said that she had to go to recital practice, so I couldn't shoot the scene. Unfortunately, I really need this scene to complete the detailed analysis of my camera perspectives in my report.** I just want to write a very good paper, you know? **P:** You know my policy about late work. The deadline was already pushed back when the school was closed during the snowstorm last week. That gave you an extra day. **S:** I know, but… **P:** You had plenty of time to plan and film whatever you needed to do for the report. And you can't always count on getting every scene you want. These things happen all the time in tight filming schedules. But there's always something else you can do instead of just waiting around. **S:** You're right. I should have had an alternative plan. (sighs)
Example 다른 화가들을 예로 들어 마감을 지키는 것의 중요함을 설명	**P:** I know I might sound harsh, but credibility is really important in the art world. ▶Q4◀ **There's always a deadline that filmmakers and artists alike have to meet.** Painters might seem like they have all the time in the world to make whatever they like, but the reality is that they have deadlines, too. **What I'm trying to say is you need to get in the habit of meeting your deadlines no matter what.** **S:** Well, it's not like I didn't write the paper at all. I wrote all the sections except for the one about the scene I'm missing. **P:** Whether or not you turn your assignment in by the deadline is up to you. **S:** But… the last scene is a big part of my paper, I don't know if I'll get a good grade.

P: You know the policy, Tom. I'll dock half a grade for every day it's late. If you think you'll be better off handing in a late assignment, be my guest. The bottom line is that there are no extensions no matter what. Think of this as a life lesson that will eventually help you in your professional career.
S: Okay. Thanks for your time, Professor.

해석 학생과 영화학 교수 간의 다음 대화를 들으시오.
학생(남자): 안녕하세요, Peterson 교수님. 잠시 시간이 되시나요?
교수(여자): 네, 물론이죠, Tom. 영화 보고서는 어떻게 되어가고 있나요? 학생의 스토리보드처럼 그대로 대상들을 다른 시점으로 촬영했나요? 학생이 분위기를 보여주기 위해 여러 다른 카메라 앵글을 사용해서 찍은 것은 대단한 실험이라고 생각해요. 거기서 정말 많은 것을 배우게 될 거예요.
학생: 맞아요! 그렇게 좁은 공간에서 올바른 앵글을 찾아내는 건 힘들었지만, 정말이지 잘 진행되었어요. 영화에 흥미로운 시점들과 장면들이 많아요. 그것에 무척 신이 나요.
교수: 아, 그거 멋지네요. 그게 모두 어떻게 나왔는지 보고 싶네요. 그럼, 후속 보고서는 어디 있죠? 학생 걸 아직 받지 못한 것 같은데.
학생: 네, 죄송해요. 사실, 그 보고서를 끝마칠 짬을 아직 내지 못했어요. 그래서 찾아 뵌 거고요.
교수: 보고서가 오늘 정오까지인 건 알지요? 벌써 10시인데.
학생: 좀 막판에 말씀 드리는 것이라는 건 알지만, 기한을 좀 연장 받을 수 있을까요? 아직 댄스 장면을 촬영해야 하거든요. 나타나기로 했던 댄서가 마지막 순간에 바람을 맞혔어요. 그녀가 발표회 연습에 가야 한다고 해서 그 장면을 찍지 못했거든요. 불행히도, 제 보고서의 카메라 시점들에 대한 세부적인 분석을 마치기 위해서는 이 장면이 정말 필요해요. 저는 정말 좋은 보고서를 쓰고 싶거든요.
교수: 늦게 제출하는 과제물에 대한 내 정책을 알잖아요. 지난주 눈보라로 학교가 쉬었을 때 마감이 이미 미뤄졌었어요. 그걸로 하루를 더 벌었잖아요.
학생: 알아요, 하지만…
교수: 학생은 보고서를 위해 해야 하는 것이 무엇이건 계획을 하고 촬영을 할 충분한 시간이 있었어요. 그리고 항상 자기가 원하는 모든 장면을 찍을 거라고 기대해서는 안돼요. 이런 일들은 빡빡한 촬영 스케줄에서는 언제나 일어나거든요. 하지만 그냥 기다리기만 하는 것 대신에 학생이 할 수 있는 무언가가 언제나 있어요.
학생: 교수님 말씀이 맞아요. 대안이 되는 다른 계획을 세웠어야 했는데 말이죠. (한숨)
교수: 가혹하게 들릴 거라는 건 알지만, 예술계에서는 신뢰성이 정말 중요해요. 영화제작자들과 예술가들은 모두 지켜야 할 마감이 항상 있어요. 화가들은 그들이 원하는 것을 뭐든지 만들 수 있는 시간이 마음껏 있는 것처럼 보일지는 모르지만, 현실은, 그들도 마감이 있다는 거예요. 내가 말하고자 하는 건, 학생이 무슨 일이 있어도 마감을 지키는 습관을 들여야 한다는 겁니다.
학생: 음, 제가 보고서를 하나도 쓰지 않거나 한 건 아녜요. 제가 못 찍은 그 장면에 대한 부분만 제외한 모든 부분들을 써놨어요.
교수: 학생이 과제를 마감 기한까지 제출할 건지 말 건지는 학생에게 달렸어요.
학생: 하지만… 그 마지막 장면은 제 보고서의 큰 부분이라서, 제가 좋은 성적을 받을 수 있을지 모르겠어요.
교수: 규정을 알잖아요, Tom. 나는 하루 늦을 때마다 반등급을 감점해요. 과제를 늦게 제출하는 것이 더 나을 것 같다고 생각되면, 그렇게 해요. 핵심은, 무슨 일이 있어도 기한 연장은 안 된다는 거예요. 이걸 학생의 전문적인 경력에 있어 학생에게 결국은 도움이 될 일생의 교훈으로 여기도록 해요.
학생: 알겠습니다. 시간 내주셔서 감사 드려요, 교수님.

W follow-up [fálou-ʌp] 후속 조치   extension [iksténʃən] 기한 연장   bail on 약속을 어기다, 바람을 맞히다   count on ~ …을 기대하다   dock [dɑk] …을 빼다[감하다]   bottom line 핵심, 요점

01 학생이 교수를 찾아간 이유는?
Ⓐ 좁은 공간에서 여러 다른 카메라 앵글을 사용하는 법을 알아보려고
Ⓑ **보고서 마감 날짜를 연기해달라고 허락을 요청하려고**
Ⓒ 한 장면을 위한 배우를 구하는 방법에 대해 논의하려고
Ⓓ 보고서를 위한 몇 가지 정보의 위치를 찾는 데 도움을 구하려고

02 학생의 영화 보고서에 대한 교수의 태도는?
Ⓐ 학생이 보고서를 쓰는 데 많은 시간을 보낼 필요가 없다고 생각한다.
Ⓑ 학생이 보고서의 대부분을 이미 끝내서 놀랐다.

Ⓒ 학생의 염려를 중요하지 않다고 일축한다.
Ⓓ 그 결과를 보기를 고대하고 있다.

03 학생이 댄서를 언급한 이유는?
Ⓐ 자신이 사용한 영화 앵글들 중 하나를 알려주려고
Ⓑ 자신이 대상을 촬영한 방식이 옳다는 것을 확인시켜 주려고
Ⓒ 과제를 제때 끝낼 수 없었다는 것을 나타내려고
Ⓓ 학생 배우들은 신뢰할 수 없다는 것을 강조하려고

04 교수가 다른 화가들을 언급한 이유는?
Ⓐ 화가들을 보는 것이 새로운 통찰력을 줄 수 있다는 것을 제안하려고
Ⓑ 과제를 시간에 맞게 제출하는 것의 중요성을 강조하려고
Ⓒ 화가들은 쓸 수 있는 시간이 많다는 것을 알려주려고
Ⓓ 이루어진 연구의 양에 대한 자신의 기대를 나타내려고

대화의 일부분을 다시 듣고 질문에 답하시오. ◁) MP3 13_1

You do know that the paper is due today by noon, don't you? It's 10 o'clock already.

05 교수가 다음과 같은 말을 하는 이유는?
Ⓐ 대화 도중에 많은 시간이 지나갔다는 것을 나타내려고
Ⓑ 학생이 다음 수업에 늦을지도 모른다는 것을 암시하려고
Ⓒ 과제를 위해 학생이 무엇을 해야하는지 이해하고 있다는 것을 확인하려고
Ⓓ 학생이 과제를 아직 수행하지 않았다는 것을 상기시키려고

05 / Project, Research

≈ Sample Questions
본문 p. 094

01 C   02 D   03 B   04 C, D   05 A

해석 학생과 교수 간의 다음 대화를 들으시오. ◁) MP3 14
학생(여자): Moore 교수님, 잠시 시간 좀 되시나요?
교수(남자): 물론이죠. 무슨 일이에요, Becky?
학생: 저기, 있죠, 그 과제, 신제품을 위한 마케팅 플랜을 세우는 거요... (한숨) 음, 저희 그룹이, 아니 저희가 할 수가...
교수: 이야기할 만한 제품을 찾는 게 어려운가요?
학생: 그게 문제면 좋겠어요. 저희는... 저희는 사실 꽤 혁신적인 제품을 찾긴 했는데, 그건 과정의 그저 한 부분일 뿐이라서요. 저희는 모임을 할 때면, 그 제품을 어떻게 마케팅 해야 할지에 초점을 맞출 수 없는 것 같아요... 저희는 그냥 이것저것, 그러니까 과제와 아무 관련도 없는 것들에 대해서만 이야기하느라 시간을 보내는 것 같아요. 저희는 심지어 아직 마케팅 플랜도 세우지 못했어요. 저는 이번 과제에서 저희 모두 끔찍한 점수를 받을 것 같아 정말 걱정이 돼요. 아시다시피 이 프로젝트가 저희 전체 성적에 큰 부분을 차지하잖아요.
교수: 리더를 뽑았나요?
학생: 아뇨, 그렇진 않아요... 저희는 리더가 필요치 않다고 생각했어요. 모두 정말 열심히 준비하는데다, 누구도 다른 누구보다 더 리더가 될 만한 자격이 있지 않았거든요.
교수: 좋아요, 그러면 학생의 팀은 프로젝트를 어떻게 준비하고 있지요?
학생: 음, 저희는 각자 뭘 하고 싶어 하는지 선택해서 할 일을 이미 나누어뒀어요. 그건 잘 진행되었고요, 음, 적어도 그런 것 같아 보였죠. 모두

가 각자 다른 부분에 대해 책임을 맡고자 하긴 했지만, 저희는 얼마큼 끝냈는지에 대해서는 서로 거의 이야기를 나누지 않아요. 개인적으로 얼마큼씩 일을 해놨는지는 서로 모르는 거죠. 모두들 자기들이 이만큼 했다고 말을 하긴 하지만…

교수: 학생은 어때요? 학생이 담당한 부분은 끝냈나요?

학생: 음, 일부는요. 제가 할 수 있는 건 끝냈어요. 저는 예산을 담당하는데, 예산을 짜려면 먼저 플랜이 필요해요. 전 심지어 스프레드 시트도 만들었어요. 몇몇 셀에 수치를 집어넣기만 하면 전체 예산이 나와요. 하지만, 우선 입력할 수치를 다른 조원들에게 받아야 해요. 우리가 어떤 종류의 광고를 할 건지, 어디에 광고를 할 건지, 얼마나 자주 광고를 할 건지를… 그런 것들을 제가 알아야 한다고요. 제가 혼자서는 할 수 없는 결정들이 많아요. 현실적인 예산을 짜기 위해서 저희는 정말 이야기를 나눠야 해요.

교수: 음… 다른 조원들은 어떻게 생각하나요?

학생: 음, 그들과 이야기를 해보려 애썼고, 그들도 동의하며 고개를 끄덕였어요. 그거 있잖아요, 그냥 상대 얼굴만 보고 고개를 끄덕이기 시작하는 거요… 하지만 그리고 나서 저희는 또 다른 것에 대해 이야기를 하기 시작했어요… 어쨌든, 저희는 진전이 전혀 없어요.

교수: 아무래도 그룹 내에 리더를 둘 때인 것 같네요. 학생이 담당해보지 그래요?

학생: 아뇨… 저는 그럴 수 없어요. 제 자신을 리더로 임명하는 그런 거 말이에요.

교수: 그게 뭐가 어때서요?

학생: 우선, 저희는 모두 리더가 필요하지 않을 거라고 동의했거든요.

교수: 있죠, 모든 리더들이 다른 이들에 의한 투표로만 선출되는 건 아녜요. 내가 지금까지 본 최고의 리더들 중 일부는 책임을 질 누군가가, 앞으로 나설 누군가가 필요하다는 것을 깨달은 사람들이었죠. 그게 어색하고 불편할 수는 있겠지만, 그것이 실제로 성공과 실패를 가르게 될 수 있어요.

학생: 음… 교수님 말씀도 일리가 있어요. 아무래도 제가 그냥 일정을 나누어 줄까 봐요. 실제 마감이 있는 일정이요. 조원들은 그냥 그 일정을 따를지도 몰라요.

교수: 그거 알아요? 내가 장담하건대, 분명 그들은 고마워할 거예요. 또 회의 동안 각 조원이 얼만큼 완료했는지를 알 수도 있을 거고요. 그들에게 완료한 부분을 보여달라고 부탁하고, 누군가 일정에 뒤쳐져 있다면 그룹 전체가 같이 힘을 합쳐서 제대로 해나가면 돼요.

학생: 그거 좋은 생각인 것 같네요. 한번 해보도록 할게요.

교수: 행운을 빌어요.

W innovative [ínəvèitiv] 혁신적인   concerned [kənsə́ːrnd] 걱정되는   qualified [kwάləfàid] 자격이 있는   individually [ìndəvíʤuəli] 개인적으로   in charge of ~ …을 담당해서   input [ínpùt] 투입, 입력   progress [prάgres] 진전, 진척   take charge 떠맡다, 책임을 지다   step up 앞으로 나오다   awkward [ɔ́ːkwərd] 어색한   grateful [gréitfəl] 고마워하는   fall behind 뒤떨어지다   give it a shot 시도해보다

01 학생이 교수와 이야기하러 간 이유는?
Ⓐ 예산을 짜는 방법에 대해 상의하려고
Ⓑ 자신이 그룹의 리더가 될 수 있을지 물어보려고
Ⓒ 그룹 프로젝트와 관련된 문제에 대한 조언을 구하려고
Ⓓ 자신의 그룹이 프레젠테이션에 괜찮은 상품을 골랐는지 알아보려고

02 학생이 예산을 언급한 이유는?
Ⓐ 스프레드시트에 넣은 수치를 어떻게 산출했는지 보여주려고
Ⓑ 그것을 끝낼 만한 충분한 시간이 없었다는 것을 설명하려고
Ⓒ 자신이 끝낸 일의 양을 자랑하려고
Ⓓ 자신의 그룹과 관련된 문제를 알려주려고

03 그룹 리더가 되는 것에 대한 교수의 의견은?
Ⓐ 자신이 리더가 되는 것보다 다른 누군가를 리더로 임명하는 것이 더 낫다.
Ⓑ 가끔은 투표를 통하지 않고도 그룹을 책임지는 것이 필요하다.
Ⓒ 서로 잘 지내는 그룹들은 아무도 그룹 리더로 임명되지 않을 때 더 잘한다.
Ⓓ 자신을 리더로 임명하는 사람들은 대개 그룹을 이끌기에 가장 자격이 없는 사람들이다.

04 그룹이 프로젝트를 끝내는 데 도움을 주기 위해 취해야 할 추가적인 조치들로 두 사람이 논의하고 있는 것은? (두 가지 선택)
Ⓐ 그룹 리더를 뽑기 위해 투표하기
Ⓑ 모두에게 업무를 공평하게 나누기
Ⓒ 마감이 있는 일정을 나누어주기
Ⓓ 모든 것이 완료되었는지 확인하기 위해 협력하기

대화의 일부분을 다시 듣고 질문에 답하시오. ◁ MP3 14_1

P: Hmm... What do the other group members think?
S: Well, I tried to talk to them and they kind of nodded their heads in agreement. You know, when people just look at you and start nodding... But then we started talking about something else... Anyway, we aren't making any progress.

05 학생이 다음과 같이 말할 때 암시하는 것은?

They kind of nodded their heads in agreement. You know, when people just look at you and start nodding.

Ⓐ 다른 조원들이 과제에 신경을 쓰지 않는다고 생각한다.
Ⓑ 그룹의 나머지 사람들이 자신에게 동의하도록 할 방법을 찾았다고 생각한다.
Ⓒ 교수가 다른 학생들과 비슷한 문제를 겪고 있는 것을 보았다.
Ⓓ 자신이 교수처럼 사람들을 설득할 만한 동일한 능력을 가지고 있지 않다고 생각한다.

≋ Practice Questions

본문 p. 098

| 01 C | 02 D | 03 B | 04 D | 05 B |

Introduction

Listen to a conversation between a student and her biology professor. ◁ MP3 15

Stduent(female): Professor Johnson? You wanted to see me?
Professor(male): Oh, Clara! Good. Yes, come and sit down... So, Q1) **have you given some thought to what I was talking to you about the other day?** I mean, I'm still waiting for an answer.
S: Well, I've been thinking about it a lot lately... **but I'm still not sure yet.**
P: What? Do you mind if I ask you why?

Cause
배구팀 주장이라 할 일이 많음

S: The thing is... I mean, Q2) **I'm the captain of the school's volleyball team right now, and you know how these things go. I have to go to practice every day**, and I have to call the other members to check up on how they're doing and such. There's a volleyball tournament starting next month and well... there are a lot of times when I'm just in the gym.
P: Oh, wow. I actually didn't know that you were part of the volleyball team. I heard our team is pretty good.
S: Thanks.
P: But how's your schoolwork going? You shouldn't neglect your studying, you know? You are a student after all. How well are you following the class?
S: Q2) **The schoolwork is not too much of a problem.** Well, **it could be if I had more to do,** but as of now, I think I've found a good balance between doing homework and papers and studying for exams.
P: But... You're going to get too busy if you add on the fellowship I was telling you about the other day.
S: I hate to say this, but yeah... I don't think I'll be able to handle the workload. I mean, going to all the meetings and writing the reports on top of volleyball and my classes seems a little too difficult.

Advantage
연구 조교 경험은 대학원 진학에 도움이 됨

P: I understand that you're busy, but Q3) **you should really think about how it will help your career. I mean, you wanted to go to grad school, right? Getting experience as a research assistant will really help boost your resume, you know?**

Suggestion
단기 실험실 연구에 지원해 어떤지 미리 경험해볼 것을 제안

Requirement
오리엔테이션 참가 필요

S: That's why I can't say no. I mean, I'm busy, but at the same time, this is too good of an opportunity to miss. I really don't know what to do.

P: Okay. I understand a joint research fellowship with the biochemistry lab is very time consuming – with all the experiments and reports you'll have to do – so why don't you get a taste of what it's like first?

S: I thought once I made a commitment, I had to stay with the program? Can I just quit in the middle if I can't handle it?

P: Oh, no. Q4 **Why don't you sign up for a short lab study with Professor Adams in the biochemistry department? You'll get a feel for what it's like to apply your knowledge in a lab environment.** We really don't have that many labs in the biology department, you know? **Once you get some hands-on experience, you might want to take a chance.**

S: That sounds like a great idea! So when does it start?

P: Q5 Well, it starts in April, but there's an orientation in a month. **Can you make it?**

S: Hmm... well, the tournament is going to start... oh... can I get the date?

P: Yeah, **it's on the 20th.** On...Thursday.

S: That's great! **The volleyball tournament will be over by then!** I can't wait!

해석 학생과 생물학 교수 간의 다음 대화를 들으시오.

학생(여자): 안녕하세요. Johnson 교수님? 저를 보자고 하셨어요?

교수(남자): 아, Clara! 잘됐네요. 맞아요, 와서 앉아요... 자, 내가 일전에 말한 것에 대해 생각을 좀 해봤나요? 아직 답을 기다리고 있어서요.

학생: 음, 요즘 많이 생각해봤는데요... 아직 잘 모르겠어요.

교수: 뭐라고요? 이유를 물어봐도 될까요?

학생: 문제는... 그러니까, 제가 지금 학교 배구팀의 주장이라, 어떤지 아시잖아요. 매일 연습에 가야 하고, 다른 선수들이 어떻게 하고 있는지 뭐 그런 것들을 확인하기 위해 선수들에게 전화를 해야 해요. 다음달에 시작하는 배구 대회도 있어서, 음... 그냥 체육관에 있는 시간이 많아요.

교수: 아, 이런. 학생이 배구팀인지는 몰랐어요. 우리 학교 팀이 무척 잘한다고는 들었는데.

학생: 감사합니다.

교수: 하지만 학교 공부는 어떻게 되어 가고 있어요? 공부를 소홀히 해서는 안되잖아요? 어쨌든 본분은 학생이니까요. 수업은 어떻게 따라가고 있나요?

학생: 학교 공부는 큰 문제는 아니에요. 음, 할 일이 더 많아지면 문제가 될 수도 있겠지만, 지금으로서는, 숙제와 보고서, 시험 공부를 하는 것 사이에 균형을 잘 잡고 있는 것 같아요.

교수: 하지만... 내가 일전에 말한 장학 프로그램 일을 더한다면 너무 바빠질 텐데.

학생: 이렇게 말하기는 싫지만, 맞아요... 그 일들을 감당할 수 있을 것 같지는 않아요. 배구와 제 수업뿐만 아니라, 회의에 다 참석하고 보고서들을 써야 하는 건 좀 너무 어려울 것 같아요.

교수: 학생이 바쁜 건 이해하지만, 조교 일이 학생의 경력에 얼마나 도움이 될 지 잘 생각해봐야 해요. 내 말은, 학생은 대학원에 가고 싶어 했잖아요, 맞죠? 연구 조교로서 경험을 쌓는 것은 학생 이력서를 향상시키는 데 정말 도움이 될 거예요.

학생: 그래서 제가 거절을 못하는 거예요. 그러니까, 너무 바쁘긴 하지만, 또 한편으로는, 이게 놓치기에는 너무 좋은 기회라서요. 어떻게 해야 할지 정말 모르겠어요.

교수: 알겠어요. 생화학 실험실에서의 공동 연구 조교는 시간 소모가 무척 클 거라는 건 이해해요, 학생이 해야 하는 그 모든 실험들과 보고서가 있으니 말예요. 그럼 조교 생활이 어떨지 먼저 조금 맛보기를 해보는 건 어때요?

학생: 제가 일단 하기로 하면, 프로그램이 끝날 때까지 계속 해야만 하는 줄 알았는데요? 제가 감당할 수 없으면 중간에 그만두어도 되나요?

교수: 아, 안돼죠. 생화학 학과의 Adams 교수가 하는 단기 실험실 연구에 신청해보는 게 어때요? 학생의 지식을 실험실 환경에 적용하는 게 어떤 건지에 대해 감을 좀 잡을 수 있을 거예요. 생물학과에는 실험실이 그렇게 많지는 않잖아요? 실제 경험을 좀 해보게 되면, 기회를 잡고 싶어질지도 몰라요.

학생: 그거 좋은 생각 같아요! 그럼 그건 언제 시작하죠?

교수: 음, 4월에 시작하지만, 한 달 후에 오리엔테이션이 있어요. 시간 되겠어요?

학생: 음... 저기, 대회가 곧 시작할 거라... 아... 날짜를 알 수 있을까요?

교수: 그럼요. 20일이네요. 목요일이에요.

학생: 잘됐네요! 배구 대회는 그때쯤이면 끝날 거예요. 기대되네요!

🅦 neglect [niglékt] 등한하다, 도외시하다   fellowship [félouʃip] 장학 프로그램   workload [wɜ́ːrkloud] 학업량   research assistant 연구 조교   boost [buːst] 신장시키다   résumé [rézumèi] 이력서   time consuming 시간 소모가 큰   commitment [kəmítmənt] 약속   sign up for ~ …을 신청하다   biochemistry [bàioukémistri] 생화학   get a feel for ~ …에 대한 감을 잡다   hands-on experience 실제 체험

01 대화의 주제는?
Ⓐ 학생이 어떻게 어려운 직업적 결정을 내렸는지
Ⓑ 생화학 수업의 필요 요건들이 무엇인지
Ⓒ 바쁜 학생이 장학 프로그램 일을 감당할 수 있는지
Ⓓ 학생이 과제를 왜 완료하지 못했는지

02 교수의 요청을 바로 수락하지 못하는 것에 대해 학생이 내세운 이유는?
Ⓐ 배구팀의 학생들을 지도하고 있다.
Ⓑ 수업에서 배운 내용을 이해하지 못했다.
Ⓒ 여러 대학원에 지원해야 했다.
Ⓓ 추가되는 일을 감당하지 못할까봐 두려웠다.

03 학생의 망설임에 대한 교수의 태도는?
Ⓐ 학생이 직업 상담가에게 도움을 청해야 한다고 생각한다.
Ⓑ 학생이 자신의 미래에 대해 생각해야 한다고 생각한다.
Ⓒ 학생이 잘못된 전공을 선택했다고 생각한다.
Ⓓ 학생의 걱정이 불필요하다고 생각한다.

04 교수가 실험실 연구 프로젝트를 언급한 이유는?
Ⓐ 학생에게 다른 학과의 교수를 소개해주려고
Ⓑ 학생에게 자신의 실험을 도와달라고 설득하려고
Ⓒ 생물학과에 실험실이 부족한 것에 대해 불평하려고
Ⓓ 학생이 좋은 결정을 내릴 수 있도록 도와줄 방법을 제안하려고

05 배구 대회 후에 학생이 할 일은?
Ⓐ 실험실 연구에 참가하기
Ⓑ 오리엔테이션에 참석하기
Ⓒ 시험 공부하기
Ⓓ 생화학에 관해 보고서 쓰기

06 / Major

≋ Sample Questions
본문 p. 102

| 01 B   02 D   03 D   04 C   05 A |

해석 학생과 철학과 교수 간의 다음 대화를 들으시오. 🔊 MP3 16
학생(여자): Tyler 교수님?
교수(남자): 안녕, Lauren. 잘 지내요?
학생: 음... 그런 것 같아요... 그런데 교수님께는 알려드려야 할 것 같아서요... 이번 학기가 끝나면 전공을 바꾸기로 했어요.

교수: 뭐라고요? 왜요? 철학이 마음에 안 드나요?

학생: 아, 아뇨, 오해하지 마세요. 저는 철학이 정말 좋아요. 하지만 동시에 현실적이어야 할 필요도 있어서요. 제 말은, 철학 수업들을 듣는 것은 좋지만, 대학을 마치고 나서 일자리를 구하는 것에 대해서도 걱정해야 해요.

교수: 아, 알겠어요. 짐작해 볼게요... 철학 학위를 가지고 있는 사람들은 고용주들에게 제공할 것이 없다. 이런 거죠?

학생: 음... 말하자면요, 아닌가요? 많은 제 친구들은 공학 전공이거나 경영 전공이에요. 그 애들은 곧 직장을 얻을 테지만, 저는 잘 모르겠어요... 철학 전공으로 일자리를 구할 수 있을지 말이에요.

교수: 그런 이야기를 정말 많이 들어요... 좋아요... 공학 같은 응용 과학을 공부하는 것은 일자리를 얻기에 아주 좋은 대비책일 수는 있지만, 그건 이미 진로에 대한 목표가 있는 사람들을 위한 거예요. 그 사람들이 자신이 뭘 하고 싶은지를 안다면, 상관없죠. 하지만, 음, 목표가 없는 사람들은 어떨까요? 어쨌든, 학생은 목표가 있나요?

학생: (한숨) 전혀 모르겠어요.

교수: 자 그럼, 학생에게는, 그것이 아마 최선의 선택은 아닐 거예요.

학생: 좋은 지적이세요.

교수: 철학을 전공하면, 아마 대학원에서 더 공부하고 연구를 하는 것 외에도, 그런데 내 생각엔 그게 아주 훌륭한 선택인 것 같긴 하지만, 학생은 어느 분야에서건 자신에게 도움을 줄 수 있는 많은 것들을 알게 될 거예요.

학생: 어떤 것 말씀이세요? Berkeley의 경험론을 Johnson이 반박한 것 같은 거 말씀이세요?

교수: 글쎄, Johnson이 정확히 뭘 했죠?

학생: 음, 그러니까, Berkeley는 우리는 어떠한 물체도 실제로 알 수 없다고 주장했어요. 물리적으로 말이죠. 우리가 어떤 물체를 인식할 때, 그것을 감지하는 것은 우리의 감각일 뿐이고, 하지만 그게 실제 물리적인 물질이 존재하는 것을 의미하는 것은 아니라고 말이죠. Johnson은 그 이론을 반박하려고 했어요, 그렇죠? 그는... 그는 큰 돌을 발로 차고 그것이 Berkeley를 반박하는 것이라고 말했어요.

교수: 아주 좋아요, 그래서... 학생은 그것에 대해 어떻게 생각해요?

학생: 음, 저도 Berkeley가 옳다고 생각하는 것은 아니지만, Johnson이 무언가를 반박했다고도 생각하지는 않아요. Berkeley는 아마도 그냥 그렇게 말할 거예요. Johnson은 여전히 그 돌이 존재하는 것을 실제로 알 수 없다고, 그는 그것을 그저 감각을 통해 느낄 뿐이라고 말이죠. 돌을 보고, 그걸 발로 찬 뒤에 발에 통증을 느끼는 것, 그건 모두 여전히 그냥 그의 자각에 근거한 것일 뿐이잖아요. Johnson은 여전히 그가 무언가를 안다고 말할 수 없을 거예요. 그러니까, 그가 느끼고 감지하는 것 외에는 말이죠.

교수: 학생은 방금 자신이 무슨 일을 했는지 알아요?

학생: 철학 수업을 제외하고는 어디에서도 전혀 쓸모가 없는 무언가를 말씀 드린 거요?

교수: 아니, 학생은 방금 내게 매우 잘 다듬어진 분석 능력을 보여줬어요. 있죠, 철학을 공부하는 것은 우리가 설득력 있는 주장을 하고 그런 주장들을 매우 효과적으로 요약하고 전달함으로써 다른 사람들의 추론을 비판하도록 해주죠. 인생에서, 그리고 어떤 분야에서든, 이러한 것들은 매우 중요해요.

학생: 알겠어요, 하지만, 여전히... 추론과 논쟁 능력을 요구하는 일자리는 어디에서도 볼 수 없잖아요.

교수: 정말 그런가요? 글쎄, 난 정말이지 그렇게 생각하지 않아요. 나는 최근에 여러 분야의 회사 지도자들이 쓴 많은 기사들을 읽어봤어요. 항상 눈에 띄는 한 가지가, 그런 기술들을 가지고 있는 직원들을 찾는 것이 얼마나 어려운가 하는 것이에요. 취업 서비스 사무실에 한번 가봐요. 분명 그들도 똑같은 말을 해줄 거예요.

학생: 음... 교수님 말씀이 맞는 것 같아요.

교수: 그리고, 이 이야기를 나누는 김에, 이번 여름에 뭘 할 건지 생각해 봤나요? 우리 과는 항상 인턴직에 대한 정보를 가지고 있어요. 그게 학생이 이력서에 더할 구체적인 경험을 좀 쌓을 수 있도록 해줄 거예요.

학생: 그거 좋은 생각이네요.

교수: 인턴쉽은 분명 좋은 첫 단계가 될 거예요.

Ⓦ semester[siméstər] 학기   practical[præktikəl] 실용적인   applied science 응용 과학   grad school 대학원(= graduate school)   refuting[rifjú:tiŋ] 반론, 반박   empiricism[empírisìzm] 경험[실증]주의   physically[fízikəli] 신체적으로   analytical[æ̀nəlítikəl] 분석적인   critique[krití:k] 비평하다   reasoning[rí:zəniŋ] 추리, 추론   convincing[kənvínsiŋ] 설득력 있는   argument[á:rgjumənt] 논쟁; 주장   stick out 눈에 띄다   concrete[kànkrí:t] 구체적인

01 대화의 주제는?
Ⓐ 전공을 바꿀 수 있는 마감 시한이 언제인지
Ⓑ 왜 학생이 전공을 바꾸지 말아야 하는지
Ⓒ 학생이 어떻게 더 많은 일자리 기회를 가질 수 있는지
Ⓓ 대학원에서 어떻게 철학을 공부할지

02 공학 전공자가 되는 것에 대해 교수가 암시하는 것은?
Ⓐ 이미 일자리를 가지고 있지 않는 이상 말이 되지 않는다.
Ⓑ 분명한 직업 목표를 세우는 가장 좋은 방법이다.
Ⓒ 학생들이 매우 뛰어난 분석 능력을 발달시키는 데 도움이 된다.
Ⓓ 구체적인 목표를 가지고 있는 학생들에게만 적합하다.

03 철학 수업시간에 배웠던 것에 대해 교수가 이야기하는 이유는?
Ⓐ 학생이 수업 자료를 잘 따라가고 있는지 확인하려고
Ⓑ Berkeley와 Johnson에 대해 배우는 것은 쓸모가 없다는 것을 시사하려고
Ⓒ 철학이 어떻게 공학과 관련이 있는지 예시를 들려고
Ⓓ 철학 전공자들이 수업에서 배운 것을 어떻게 사용할 수 있는지 알려주려고

04 학생이 자신의 직업 목표에 대해 말한 것은?
Ⓐ 회사를 이끌고 싶어 한다.
Ⓑ 엔지니어가 되기를 희망한다.
Ⓒ 목표가 없다.
Ⓓ 계속해서 마음이 바뀐다.

05 Berkeley 논쟁에 대한 학생의 최초 의견은?
Ⓐ 직장에서 적용될 수 없다고 생각한다.
Ⓑ Berkeley가 올바른 의견을 가졌다고 생각한다.
Ⓒ Berkeley의 견해는 시대에 뒤떨어졌다고 생각한다.
Ⓓ 이견이 있을 때 매우 유용할 것으로 생각한다.

Practice Questions

본문 p. 106

| 01 B | 02 D | 03 A | 04 B | 05 C |

Introduction

Listen to a conversation between a student and her art history professor. 🔊 MP3 17

Student(female): Professor Evans, can I steal a bit of your time?
Professor(male): Sure, Erika. What can I do for you?
S: Well… I guess I thought I was doing really well in your class. But suddenly I'm not so sure.
P: **Q1** Ah… You must be referring to your report.
S: Yeah. **I expected a much better grade. I wanted to find out what I did wrong.** I thought I did a good job of explaining the relationship between radical art movements and technology after the Industrial Revolution. But **Q2** **you wrote that I used generalized examples. I'm not sure what you mean.**
P: Well, you made a common mistake that a lot of students make. You generalized too much. So, when you wrote about the Avant Garde movement and how the development of photography could have had something to do with it, I wanted you to give me a specific example. Um… for instance, you could have written about **Q3** **how Cubism was developed by Braque and Picasso and what aspects of photography may have made them paint that way.**
S: I'm not sure I follow you. I thought I did a good job of giving examples. I mentioned how traditional portraiture didn't have much of a foothold in art because photography

Problem
교수가 쓴 'generaized examples'의 의미를 이해하지 못함

Requirement 더 세부적인 예시가 필요	took its place and that it made artists paint in a different way. P: Yes, but the specifics are missing. You should have been more detailed… um, like mentioning that photography was only black and white, and how painters like, um, like Matisse, painted in an Impressionist style that emphasized vibrant colors. That way you could have given an even better analysis by comparing black and white to colors… you know, what the power of colors enabled the artist to paint. S: Oh, now I see. P: Judging by ▶Q4◀ **your exam grades, I think you had the knowledge.** You just didn't apply it. Um… which brings me to another point. **Have you ever considered becoming an art major? You've taken three of my classes, and your grades are excellent in all of them.** Even though you didn't get the grade you probably wanted on this paper, **your grades show that you have a lot of potential.** S: Wow… I've, uh… I've actually never thought about it. But I really have enjoyed your classes.
Suggestion art seminar 참석 권유	P: Then ▶Q5◀ why don't you go to the art seminar that's being held next week? A lot of alumni will be there. **You can ask a lot of questions about what art majors can do when they graduate.** I'll be there too, just in case you're worried about being there all alone.

해석 학생과 예술사 교수 간의 다음 대화를 들으시오.

학생(여자): Evans 교수님, 잠시 시간 되세요?
교수(남자): 그럼요, Erika. 무슨 도움이 필요해요?
학생: 음… 저는 교수님 수업에서 제가 정말 잘하고 있다고 생각했는데, 갑자기 잘 모르겠어요.
교수: 아… 학생의 보고서에 대해 말하는 거군요.
학생: 네. 저는 훨씬 더 좋은 성적을 기대했었어요. 제가 뭘 잘못 한 건지 알고 싶었어요. 저는 산업 혁명 후의 급진적인 미술 운동과 기술 간의 관계를 잘 설명했다고 생각했어요. 하지만 교수님은 제가 일반화된 예를 들었다고 쓰셨더라고요. 그게 무슨 뜻인지 잘 모르겠어요.
교수: 음, 학생은 많은 학생들이 저지르는 흔한 실수를 한 거예요. 너무 일반화를 시킨 거죠. 자, 학생이 아방가르드 운동에 대해서, 그리고 사진의 발달이 어떻게 그것과 관련이 있을 수 있었는지에 대해서 썼을 때, 나는 학생이 구체적인 예를 들기를 바랐어요. 음… 예를 들어, Braque와 Picasso에 의해 어떻게 입체파가 발전될 수 있었는지에 대해, 그리고 사진의 어떤 측면들이 그들로 하여금 그런 방식으로 그림을 그리게 했을지에 대해 쓸 수도 있었겠죠.
학생: 제가 잘 이해하고 있는지 모르겠네요. 저는 예를 잘 들었다고 생각했어요. 저는 사진이 초상화법의 자리를 차지했기 때문에 전통적인 초상화법이 어떻게 미술에 기반을 잃게 되었는지에 대해, 그리고 그것이 화가들로 하여금 다른 방식으로 그림을 그리도록 만들었다는 것을 언급했어요.
교수: 그래요. 하지만 구체적인 것들이 빠졌죠. 학생은 좀 더 세부적으로 들어갔어야 했어요… 음, 사진은 흑백일 뿐이었다는 것과, 음, 어떻게 Matisse 같은 화가들이 생생한 색을 강조했던 인상파 스타일로 그림을 그렸는지를 언급하는 것 같은 것 말이죠. 그런 식으로 흑백과 컬러를 비교함으로써 훨씬 더 나은 분석을 할 수 있었겠죠… 색깔의 힘이 화가들로 하여금 무엇을 그릴 수 있게 해주었는지 말이에요.
학생: 아, 이제 알겠어요.
교수: 학생의 시험 성적으로 봐서는, 학생이 그런 지식을 갖고 있었다고 생각해요. 그저 그걸 적용하지 않았을 뿐이죠. 음… 그게 또 다른 점을 언급하게 하는데, 혹시 미술 전공을 고려해본 적이 없나요? 학생은 내 수업 세 개를 들었고 그 수업 모두에서 성적도 뛰어나요. 이 보고서에는 원했던 성적을 받지 못했을지 모르지만, 학생의 성적으로 보면 잠재력이 뛰어나 보여요.
학생: 와… 저는, 어… 사실 한번도 그것에 대해 생각해 본 적이 없어요. 하지만 교수님 수업은 정말 즐겁게 들었어요.
교수: 그럼 다음 주에 열릴 미술 세미나에 가보는 게 어때요? 많은 졸업생들이 거기 올 거예요. 미술 전공자들이 졸업하게 되면 무엇을 할 수 있는지에 대해 많은 질문을 해 볼 수 있죠. 나도 거기 갈 거고요. 학생이 거기 혼자 있게 될까 염려할 경우에 대비해서 말이죠.

Ⓦ refer [rifə́ːr] 언급하다   Industrial Revolution 산업혁명   portraiture [pɔ́ːrtritʃər] 초상화   foothold [fúthòuld] 거점, 기반
vibrant color 선명한 색   alumni [əlʌ́mnai] 동창생

01 학생이 교수를 찾아간 이유는?
Ⓐ 무엇을 전공해야 할지에 대한 조언을 얻으려고

ⓑ 보고서에 왜 안 좋은 성적을 받았는지 알아보려고
ⓒ 다음 주에 열릴 미술 세미나에 신청하려고
ⓓ 자신이 쓰고 있는 보고서를 어떻게 고쳐야 할지 문의하려고

02 교수가 쓴 의견에 대해 학생이 이해하지 못했던 것은?
ⓐ 교수가 어떤 미술 운동에 대해 쓰기를 자신에게 바랬는지
ⓑ 교수가 어떤 것이 그녀의 작법에 있어 약점이라고 여기는지
ⓒ 교수가 왜 자신에게 기술과 미술에 대해 쓰기를 바랬는지
ⓓ 교수가 '일반화된 예'라는 용어로 의미한 것이 무엇이었는지

03 교수가 아방가르드 화가들에 대해 말한 것은?
ⓐ 그들은 사진의 발달에 영향을 받았다.
ⓑ 그들은 회화와 사진을 모두 연구했다.
ⓒ 그들은 전통적인 풍경화보다 초상화를 더 선호했다.
ⓓ 그들은 흑백으로 그림을 그림으로써 자신들을 표현했다.

04 교수가 학생의 성적을 언급한 이유는?
ⓐ 학생이 보고서에 충분한 노력을 기울이지 않았다는 것을 나타내려고
ⓑ 학생에게 미술 전공을 하도록 격려하려고
ⓒ 학생이 좋은 예술가가 될 수 있을 것이라는 점을 암시하려고
ⓓ 학생이 시험공부를 더 열심히 해야 한다는 것을 지적하려고

05 교수가 학생이 미술 세미나에 참석하길 원한 이유는?
ⓐ 교수는 혼자 세미나에 가고 싶지 않다.
ⓑ 교수는 학생이 다른 미술 교수들을 만나보기 원한다.
ⓒ 교수는 세미나에 가는 것이 학생이 전공을 정하는 데 도움이 될 것이라 생각한다.
ⓓ (세미나의) 참석률이 낮을 것이기 때문에 교수는 더 많은 참가자를 원한다.

Chapter 2. Conversation Topics
Unit 2. Service Encounters

01 / Class, Credit, Transcript, Financial Aid

Sample Questions
본문 p. 112

01 B **02** B **03** B **04** C **05** D

해석 학생과 교무과 직원 간의 다음 대화를 들으시오. ◁ MP3 18

직원(남자): 무엇을 도와드릴까요?

학생(여자): 네, 음, 제 학비에 대해 이야기를 좀 하고 싶어서요.

직원: 네, 무슨 문제인가요?

학생: 음, 수업 등록을 하려고 했는데, 등록 페이지에 접속할 수가 없어요. 학비가 미납되었다는 공지를 받았고요. 그런데, 실은, 저는 장학금을 받고 있어서 학비가 이미 지불되었어야 하는데요.

직원: 알겠습니다. 처리할 수 있는지 한번 알아보죠. 이름이 뭔가요?

학생: Lisa Johnson이요.

직원: 알겠습니다. 컴퓨터에 학생 자료를 띄우고 있어요. 음... 학생이 이번 학기 학비를 내지 않아서 보류가 된 상태로 보이네요.

학생: 그렇다니까요! 무슨 일인 거죠?

직원: 음... 학생이 성적우수 장학금을 제의 받았었다고 되어 있네요... 편지를 받았나요?

학생: 무슨 말씀이에요?

직원: 장학금을 수락하겠다는 학생의 확인을 부탁하는 편지를 학교에서 보냈었네요. 이 장학금은, 학생들이 다른 곳에서 받고 있을지도 모르는 다른 장학금이 부담해주지 않는 금액만 지불하도록 되어 있어요. 알다시피, 우리는 가능한 한 많은 학생들에게 장학금을 나누어주고 싶거든요. 학생이 확인 편지를 보내지 않아서, 전산상 목록에 있는 다음 학생에게로 넘어간 것 같아요.

학생: 뭐라고요? 아니에요. 저는 학교에서 어떤 편지도 받은 적이 없어요. 언제 그걸 보내셨는데요?

직원: 어디 보죠... 전산 자료에 따르면 편지들이 8월 15일에 발송되었다고 되어 있네요. 학생의 편지는 1023 Birch가(街)로...

학생: 아, 여름에 다른 아파트로 이사를 했어요! 예전 주소로 갔나 봐요.

직원: 음... 이사를 한 후에 바로 우체국에 갔나요? 그러니까, 우체국에 두 달간 학생의 우편물을 새 주소로 전달해주도록 부탁할 수 있어요. 이런 일이 일어날 때를 대비해서 말이죠. 우체국에서는 반송된 우편물들을 2주간 보관해주기도 해요. 분명 그 편지도 우체국에서 누군가 가져가기를 바라며 보관되어 있었을 거예요... 음, 학교로 다시 반송되기 전까지 말이죠.

학생: 그러면 제가 장학금을 받을 수 없다는 말씀이세요? 아, 그럼, 그럼 어떻게 하죠? 방법이 없는...

직원: 잠시만요. 확인을 할 시간이 아직 있어요. 학생이 써야 하는 양식을 하나 줄게요. 뒷면을 작성해서 제출하세요. 학교에서 서류를 처리하고 나면 잔고가 제대로 정산될 거예요. 대개 이틀 정도 걸리죠.

학생: 그거 잘됐네요! 휴우... 하지만... 이틀이면... 좀 오래 걸리네요. 제가 원하는 수업에 등록할 수 없게 되면 어쩌죠?

직원: 음... 미안하지만 그 부분은 제가 어떻게 해드릴 수 있는 게 없어요. 하지만 학생을 위해 자리가 있는 수업을 찾아봐 줄 수는 있어요. 마지막 학년이라고 되어 있네요. 잘됐어요. 수업 마감에 대해서는 걱정할 필요가 없겠네요. 다 상급 수업들이니, 그 수업들을 들으려면 선수 과목을 많이 들어두었어야 하거든요. 이런 수업들은 대개 그렇게 빨리 정원이 차지는 않아요.

학생: 제 일반 필수 과목들은요? 졸업하려면 아직 몇 가지 기본 과목들을 들어야 하는데요.

직원: 한번 체크해볼게요... 음, 이 수업들은 정원이 많은, 무척 큰 강의들이고, 생물학 개론 수업은 아직 자리가 많아 보여요. 기초 과학 필수 과목도 들어야 하나요?

학생: 네, 사실 그래요.

직원: 음, 지금 속도라면 그 수업에 들어가는 데에도 문제가 없을 것 같네요. 못 들어간다 하더라도, 교수님께 학생의 사정을 설명 드리면 받아주실 거예요. 수업 하나를 못 들어서 졸업을 못하게 되면 안되니까요.

학생: 정말 감사합니다.

직원: 뭐든 하기 전에 일단 학생 연락처부터 반드시 바꾸도록 하세요. 서류가 처리되는 대로, 학교에서 학생에게 가능한 한 빨리 연락을 해야 하니까요. 만일 너무 지체되면 마감되어 버리는 수업들이 생길지도 몰라요. 로그인 한 후에 학교 웹사이트의 학생 정보 페이지를 여세요. 거기서 학생 연락처를 바꿀 수 있어요.

학생: 지금 바로 할게요.

W tuition [tjuːíʃən] 등록금   registration [rèdʒistréiʃən] 등록   notice [nóutis] 알림, 통지   owe [ou] (돈을) 빚지고 있다   scholarship [skάlərʃip] 장학금   figure out 알아내다   on hold 보류된, 연기된   academic merit 학문적 이점[장점]   forward [fɔ́ːrwərd] (이사간 새

주소로 우편물들을) 다시 보내주다   fill out 작성하다   balance [bǽləns] 잔고, 잔액   settle [sétl] 정산하다   vacant [véikənt] 비어 있는
contact info[information] 연락처

01 학생이 교무처를 찾아간 이유는?
Ⓐ 장학금을 수락하고 싶다는 것을 확인시켜 주려고
Ⓑ 수업 등록을 할 수 없는 이유를 알아보려고
Ⓒ 일반 필수 과목들을 등록하려고
Ⓓ 장학금이 학비보다 더 적은 이유를 문의하려고

02 장학금에 대해 추론할 수 있는 것은?
Ⓐ 4학년 학생들에게만 수여된다.
Ⓑ 학생은 그 장학금을 처음 제안 받았다.
Ⓒ 여름에 수강한 수업에는 적용되지 않는다.
Ⓓ 장학금을 신청하는 데 요구되는 절차가 많다.

03 직원이 우체국을 언급한 이유는?
Ⓐ 학생의 새 집 주소를 확인하려고
Ⓑ 학생이 편지를 받지 못한 이유를 나타내려고
Ⓒ 우체국이 문제를 발생시켰다는 것을 시사하려고
Ⓓ 장학금을 수락하는 가장 좋은 방법을 설명하려고

04 학생이 마지막 학년이라는 것을 직원이 언급한 이유는?
Ⓐ 학생이 빨리 등록해야 한다는 것을 강조하려고
Ⓑ 학생이 졸업하기 위해 들어야 하는 수업들을 알려주려고
Ⓒ 학생이 원하는 수업들을 등록할 수 있는 가능성이 높다는 것을 알려주려고
Ⓓ 아직 정원이 차지 않은 큰 규모의 수업들을 듣도록 학생에게 권하려고

05 학생이 다음에 할 일은?
Ⓐ 생물학 교수에게 수업을 들어도 되는지 묻기
Ⓑ 졸업하기 위해 어떤 수업들을 들어야 하는지 알아보기
Ⓒ 우체국에 가서 그녀에게 배달되지 않은 우편물을 찾아오기
Ⓓ 인터넷에 접속해 개인 정보를 변경하기

Practice Questions

본문 p. 116

| 01 B | 02 D | 03 A | 04 C | 05 D |

Introduction	Listen to a conversation between a student and a registrar. 🔊 MP3 19 **Employee(male):** Hello, may I help you? **Student(female):** Yeah, um, **Q1** I think there's been some kind of mix-up with my transcript. **E:** Okay, and your name is? **S:** Adams. Melissa Adams.
Cause 학교 음악 행사에서 학생이 연주하는 것을 봄	**E:** Oh, yes. Melissa Adams. **Q2** You're the violinist. My wife and I went to the concert you had at the Student Union last weekend. You were great. **S:** Oh, uh… thanks! **E:** You're welcome. **We love going to college music events. The holiday pageant, the spring concert, the senior recitals… we go to all of them.** **S:** Hey, thanks so much. The music program needs all the support it can get. But…

uh... what about my transcript?

E: Oh! Of course, I'm sorry, I got a little carried away there. Um, you'll need to be a little bit more specific about your problem. What's the mix-up?

S: Well, I'm applying to the summer music program at City University, and they want to know what music classes I've taken and the grades I got in them. Anyway, **Q1** **I just received an email saying that the school didn't get my transcript yet.**

E: Hmm... Okay, let's pull up your file. Uh, when did you request it?

S: I think I put in the request in... early March. So, three weeks ago, maybe?

E: Okay... Okay, yeah, I see here that you emailed us on March 3rd.

S: That sounds about right.

E: Okay, I see what happened. For one thing, transcript requests have to either be in person or by regular mail. See, we need your signature, and we can't get that with email.

S: But...

E: So, you'll need to fill out a request form today and sign it. And your transcript will go out in the mail in about two days. When's your deadline?

S: Last week! But nobody told me...

E: (mutters something unintelligible) The transcript should get there by the end of the week. I suggest you contact the school and just explain that there's been a delay. Make sure you tell them that the transcript is on its way.

S: But nobody told me I had to sign anything!

E: Actually, **Q3** **it says it quite clearly that a signature is required for all transcript requests in the student handbook. As you know, the handbook contains all the school policies.**

S: Oh, this is so unfair... Nobody reads the handbook!

E: Yeah, I know, but even if you had followed procedures, our computer system was down for the whole week at the end of February, and that created a terrible backlog. We're still catching up. **Q5** **I'll attach a note to your transcript explaining all of that for you, and all we can do is hope that they'll be understanding.**

S: But what if they're not? I mean, the computer problem's not my fault.

E: Look, I'm really sorry to break it to you, but I mean, **Q4** **you should never wait until the last minute to request these sorts of things.** The way I look at it, the computer problem only made a bad situation even worse. Either way, the transcript would have never made it by the deadline anyway. **That's why we say to allow at least three weeks for transcript delivery.** So, let's just do what we can and hope for the best, okay?

Problem
성적 증명서가 아직 도착하지 않음

Requirement
서류에 사인이 필요함

Attitude
상황에 안타까워 함

Requirement
성적 증명서 발송은 적어도 3주 이전에 신청해야 함

해석 학생과 교무과 직원 간의 다음 대화를 들으시오.

직원(남자): 여보세요, 무엇을 도와드릴까요?

학생(여자): 네, 음, 제 성적 증명서에 약간 혼동이 생긴 것 같아서요.

직원: 알겠습니다. 학생 이름이...?

학생: Adams예요. Melissa Adams.

직원: 아, 네, Melissa Adams. 그 바이올린 연주자군요. 지난 주말에 아내와 학생회에서 열린 학생의 연주회에 갔었어요. 멋지던데요.

학생: 아, 네... 감사합니다!

직원: 천만에요. 우린 학교 음악 행사에 가는 걸 정말 좋아해요. 휴일 음악대회나 봄 연주회, 졸업 연주회 등... 우리는 전부 참석하죠.

학생: 아, 정말 감사합니다. 음악 행사는 응원이 많이 필요해요. 그런데... 음... 제 성적 증명서는...?

직원: 아! 그렇죠. 미안해요. 딴 길로 샜네요. 음, 문제점을 좀 더 자세히 말해 주어야겠어요. 잘못된 것이 무엇이죠?

학생: 저기, City 대학에서 열리는 여름 음악 프로그램에 지원을 하려고 하는데, 그쪽에서 제가 어떤 음악 수업들을 들었고 그 수업에서 어떤 성

적을 받았는지 알고 싶어 해요. 그런데, 방금 그쪽 학교에서 제 성적 증명서를 아직 받지 못했다는 이메일을 받았어요.

직원: 음... 알겠어요. 학생 파일을 좀 불러올게요. 음, 언제 성적 증명서를 요청했지요?

학생: 신청을... 3월 초에 한 것 같아요. 그게 삼 주 전이죠, 아마?

직원: 알겠어요... 자, 네, 저희에게 3월 3일에 이메일을 보낸 것이 보이네요.

학생: 맞는 것 같아요.

직원: 좋아요. 무슨 일인지 알겠네요. 우선, 성적 증명서는 직접 방문해서 신청하거나 우편으로 신청해야 해요. 보세요, 학생 서명이 필요하거든요. 그건 이메일로는 받을 수가 없고요.

학생: 하지만...

직원: 그러니, 오늘 신청 양식을 작성해서 서명을 해야 할 거예요. 그러면 학생의 성적 증명서는 약 이틀 정도 후에 우편으로 발송될 거고요. 지원 마감이 언제죠?

학생: 지난주요! 하지만 아무도 제게...

직원: (알아들을 수 없는 말을 중얼거린 뒤) 성적증명서는 이번 주 말경에 도착할 거예요. 학교에 연락해보고 증명서가 지연되었다고 설명하는 것이 좋겠네요. 성적 증명서가 가는 중이라고 반드시 말해두고요.

학생: 하지만 아무도 제가 무언가에 서명을 해야 했다고 말해주지 않았어요!

직원: 사실, 모든 성적 증명서를 요청할 때 서명이 필요하다는 건 분명히 명시되어 있어요. 학생 편람에 말이죠. 알다시피, 편람에는 모든 학교 규정이 들어 있어요.

학생: 이런, 이건 너무 불공평해요... 편람을 읽어보는 사람은 아무도 없다고요!

직원: 그래요, 알아요, 하지만 학생이 절차를 따랐다 하더라도, 학교 전산이 2월 말에 한 주 내내 다운됐었어요. 그 때문에 엄청나게 일들이 밀렸고요. 아직도 밀린 일들을 처리 중이에요. 학생을 위해, 학생 성적 증명서에 이 모든 걸 설명하는 메모를 붙여 둘게요. 저희가 해드릴 수 있는 건 그쪽 학교에서 이해해주기를 바라는 것뿐이에요.

학생: 하지만 그쪽에서 받아들여주지 않는다면요? 제 말은, 전산 문제는 제 잘못이 아니잖아요.

직원: 있죠, 이런 말을 해서 정말 미안하지만, 절대로 이런 종류의 일들을 막판까지 미루어두었다 요청해서는 안 돼요. 제가 보기엔, 전산 문제는 안 좋은 상황을 더 나쁘게 만들었을 뿐이에요. 어느 쪽이든, 증명서는 어쨌든 지원 마감 전까지 도착하지 못 했을 거예요. 그게 학교에서 성적 증명서 발송에 적어도 3주의 시간을 두라고 말하는 이유에요. 자, 우리가 할 수 있는 것들을 다 해보고 최선을 결과를 바래봅시다. 알겠죠?

🅦 **registrar** [rédʒistrər] 교무과장 **mix-up** [miks-ʌp] 혼동 **transcript** [trǽnskript] 성적 증명서 **pageant** [pǽdʒənt] 야외극 **recital** [risáitəl] 발표회, 연주회 **request** [rikwést] 요청하다; 요청 **in person** 직접 **signature** [sígnətʃər] 서명 **student handbook** 학생 편람 **backlog** [bǽklɔ(:)g] 밀린 일 **catch up** 따라잡다

01 학생이 교무처를 방문한 이유는?
ⓐ 여름 수업에 지원하는 절차에 대해 문의하려고
ⓑ 공식적인 서류가 왜 발송되지 않았는지 알아보려고
ⓒ 자신의 음악 수업 성적을 볼 수 있을지 알아보려고
ⓓ 자신의 연주회 일정에 생긴 문제점에 대해 논의하려고

02 직원이 대학 음악 행사들을 언급한 이유는?
ⓐ 음악 프로그램에 도움이 필요하다는 사실을 인정하려고
ⓑ 학교에서의 음악의 중요성을 강조하려고
ⓒ 성적 증명서가 발송되지 않은 이유를 설명하려고
ⓓ 학생이 누구인지 안다는 것을 나타내려고

03 직원이 학생 편람을 언급한 이유는?
ⓐ 학생이 좀 더 잘 알고 있었어야 했다는 것을 지적하려고
ⓑ 학생들이 그것을 읽지 않는다는 것을 인정하려고
ⓒ 학생이 공식적인 항의를 해야 한다는 것을 시사하려고
ⓓ 성적 증명서를 떼는 것이 어렵다는 것을 보여주려고

04 학생이 성적 증명서를 너무 늦게 요청했다는 것을 지적할 때 직원이 암시하는 것은?
ⓐ 학생은 너무 많은 서류를 요청했다.
ⓑ 학생은 여름 프로그램에 합격하는 것에 대해 염려하지 말아야 한다.
ⓒ 학생은 학교에서 정한 지침을 따라야 한다.

Ⓓ 학생은 컴퓨터 문제에 대해 할 수 있는 것이 없다.

05 직원이 학생의 성적 증명서에 메모를 붙여둘 이유는?
Ⓐ 학생에게 여름 음악 프로그램에 제때 제출하도록 상기시키려고
Ⓑ 그의 직원들에게 가능한 한 빨리 발송이 되어야 한다는 것을 알려주려고
Ⓒ 학생 편람에 그 절차들이 포함되어 있다는 것을 증명하려고
Ⓓ 성적 증명서가 늦어지게 된 상황을 설명하려고

02 / Housing (Dorm)

Sample Questions 본문 p. 120

01 B   02 D   03 C   04 D   05 C

해석 학생과 대학 직원 간의 다음 대화를 들으시오. ◁) MP3 20

학생(여자): 안녕하세요. 음, 여기가 기숙사 관리사무실인가요?
직원(남자): 네, 그렇습니다! 무엇을 도와드릴까요?
학생: 아, 잘됐네요. 제가 어제 제 기숙사 방 창문을 열었는데 그게 닫히지가 않아요. 제가 할 수 있는 모든 걸 해보고, 심지어 레슬링 팀에 있는 친구 Bob에게 닫아봐 달라고 부탁까지 했지만, 꼼짝도 안 해요.
직원: 뭐라고요? 어째서 한겨울에 창문을 열어둔 거죠?
학생: 아, 기숙사 내에 난방이 고르지 않아서 어떤 학생들은 너무 춥고 어떤 학생들은 너무 더워요. 저는 좀 더 더운 방으로 배정받은 것 같아요. 학생들은 적정한 온도를 유지하기 위해 가끔씩 창문을 열어야 해요. 저도 그렇게 한 거고요.
직원: 이런, 그렇게 심한 줄 몰랐네요. 그러면, 창문을 수리하러 사람을 보낼까요? 관리인에게 가서 살펴보고 무언가 할 수 있을지 알아보도록 해 줄 수 있어요.
학생: 감사합니다. 하지만 제가 여기 온 이유가 하나 더 있어요.
직원: 아, 그게 뭐죠?
학생: 제 방의 히터가 고장 난 것 같아요. 방이 엉망진창이에요. 라디에이터 옆에 물웅덩이가 생겼거든요.
직원: 그래요? 창문을 열어두어서 샌 건 아니고요?
학생: 네, 라디에이터에서 증기가 나오는 걸 봤고, 새어 나온 물이 녹슨 물이었어요.
직원: 이런, 녹슨 물은 좋지 않은데. 잠깐만요... 그럼 학생은 라디에이터가 고장 난 방에서 창문을 열어둔 채로 잤단 말이에요?
학생: 네. 덜덜 떨며 자는 건 하루면 충분할 것 같아요. 그래서 여기 찾아온 거고요. 그러면, 어떻게 해주시는 거죠? 수리하는 데 얼마나 걸릴까요?
직원: 음, 알겠어요. 창문은 오래 걸리지 않겠지만, 라디에이터는 또 다른 문제네요. 기숙사의 히터들이 너무 오래되어서 수리하는 데 오래 걸릴 수도 있고, 아니면 라디에이터 자체를 교체해야 할지도 몰라요. 제가 학생 방을 살펴보고 몇 군데 전화해서 얼마나 걸릴지 알아봐야 할 것 같네요. 조금 있다가 다시 오겠어요? 점심 먹은 후에 어때요?
학생: 음... 대략적인 기간이라도 알려주실 수는 없나요? 학교 밖에서 거주하는 친구에게 전화를 하려던 참인데요, 그 애가 수리가 끝날 때까지 자기 집에 와서 지내도 된다고 했는데, 거기서 얼마나 머물게 될지 말해주고 싶어서요.
직원: 음... 그러면... 오늘이 금요일이라, 월요일까지는 아무것도 할 수가 없으니... 혹시 모르니 5일 정도 걸릴 거라고 하면 어떨까요?
학생: 좋아요. 그거 괜찮겠네요. 도와주셔서 감사합니다.
직원: 천만에요. 곧 학생 방을 살펴보러 건너갈게요.

Ⓦ maintenance [méintənəns] 유지, 보수   dorm [dɔːrm] 기숙사   budge [bʌdʒ] 약간 움직이다   uneven [ʌníːvən] 고르지 않은   freeze [friːz] 추워 죽을 지경이다   end up (with) 결국 (어떤 처지에) 처하게 되다   temperature [témpərətʃər] 기온, 온도   custodian [kʌstóudiən] 관리인   leak [liːk] 새다   rusty [rʌ́sti] 녹이 슨   replace [ripléis] 교체하다   ballpark [bɔ́ːlpɑːrk] 대략적인 액수[양]   off campus 교외에서

01 학생이 직원을 찾아간 이유는?
Ⓐ 자신의 방이 공부하기에 너무 춥다고 말하려고
Ⓑ 자신의 방에 있는 히터를 수리 받을 수 있을지 문의하려고
Ⓒ 기숙사에서 이사를 나간다는 것을 알리려고
Ⓓ 창문으로 보이는 전망에 대해 불평하려고

02 학생이 친구 Bob을 언급한 이유는?
Ⓐ 히터를 수리할 수 있는 누군가를 추천하려고
Ⓑ 자신이 레슬링 팀의 일원이라는 것을 설명하려고
Ⓒ 친구가 자신의 창문을 깨뜨렸다는 것을 시사하려고
Ⓓ 창문을 닫는 것이 얼마나 어려운지 강조하려고

03 학교 밖에서 사는 학생의 친구에 관해 추론할 수 있는 것은?
Ⓐ 라디에이터를 수리하는 것이 지연되어 짜증이 나 있다.
Ⓑ 비슷한 문제로 기숙사에서 이사 나갔다.
Ⓒ 그녀의 집에 손님이 있을 만한 충분한 공간이 있다.
Ⓓ 학생의 룸메이트였다.

04 학생이 기숙사의 고르지 않은 난방에 대해 언급한 이유는?
Ⓐ 자신의 문제의 심각성을 강조하려고
Ⓑ 다른 라디에이터들도 고장 났다는 것을 암시하려고
Ⓒ 관리인의 게으름에 대해 불평하려고
Ⓓ 방의 창문을 연 이유를 설명하려고

대화의 일부분을 다시 듣고 질문에 답하시오. 🔊 MP3 20_1

S: Yeah, I saw steam coming out of the radiator, and the water that leaked was rusty.
E: Oh, rusty isn't good. Wait a minute… So are you telling me that you slept in a room with a broken radiator with the window open?

05 직원이 다음과 같이 말할 때 학생의 히터에 대해 암시하는 것은?

Oh, rusty isn't good.

Ⓐ 전에도 고장 난 적이 있다.
Ⓑ 그가 생각하는 것보다 더 오래되었다.
Ⓒ 심하게 손상되었을지도 모른다.
Ⓓ 잘못 사용해서 고장이 났다.

≫ Practice Questions

본문 p. 124

| 01 D | 02 D | 03 A | 04 C | 05 B |

| Introduction | Listen to a conversation between a student and a housing office administrator. 🔊 MP3 21

Student(male): Excuse me, Q1 I'm here about a fire code violation. There was an inspection yesterday morning and we got cited.
Administrator(female): Okay, first, I'm going to need your name.
S: Jason Grant. |

Headset

Problem
딱지 내용을 이해 못함

Cause
numerical code system을 사용해 일반인은 이해할 수 없음

Problem
룸메이트들이 화재 안전 검사의 중요성을 이해 못함

Requirement
비상 계단 입구를 치우고, 모든 조리 기구를 없애야 함

Problem
거주자 모두 벌금을 내야 함

A: Jason Grant… Okay. There we go. Let's see… We had an inspection yesterday, and, oh, here are the violations. You were issued a warning. So, what's the problem? I mean, there's other…

S: Well, that's the thing. I wasn't responsible for the citations. My other roommates… All four of us share a common room and…

A: 🎧 **Q5** Uh-huh. Yeah, I know. And you want to know why your name is on the citation even though you didn't do anything wrong.

S: Um… I don't think I did. I mean, the things on this citation – **Q2** I can't even understand what they mean. How am I supposed to know what I did wrong when I can't even understand the citation?

A: That's because they use a numerical code system. Hmm… Let's take a look. It looks like several violations. There's an electric cooking appliance of some kind… And… there were also clothes and paper stacked all over the place?

S: Yeah, I guess my roommates can get kind of messy, but I don't think it was to the point that the room was dangerous. Right?

A: Well, believe me, we've seen worse, I'm sure, but in this case, it looks like it was bad enough to be considered hazardous.

S: (Deep sigh) That does sound like our room. But it's still not fair! I'm not the one who makes a mess, you know. I cleaned the room the day before it was inspected.

A: Well, it clearly wasn't tidy when the inspectors came.

S: **Q3** You know, my roommates are first-year students. I tried telling them what the fire inspection was all about, but, honestly, I don't think it got through. I can't believe we all have to pay when they're the ones responsible.

A: Hold on there. You know that you do have a chance to correct the problems before getting fined, right? There's a re-inspection in two weeks, so let's talk about what you need to get done. All right? First, the fire escape has to be clear. Second, no cooking appliances are allowed. I'm talking about hotplates, microwave ovens and such. They can trigger the smoke detectors. We don't allow cooking in the dorm rooms under any circumstances.

S: Does that mean my kettle has to go?

A: It certainly does.

S: Well… I guess it's not all on my roommates after all. Um, anyway, what happens if we're not in the room when the inspectors come?

A: There's no need to worry. We have a passkey. Of course, we'll tell you in advance that we'll be there. You'll know that we were there by the yellow slip we'll leave on your door. Now, if the room is compliant, you'll see this yellow slip. If it's red, it means you're still violating the fire code. **Q4** You'll have to pay a fine that will be equally distributed between all of the room's occupants.

S: But…

A: That's because we have no way of knowing who's actually violating the rules.

S: Well, I guess my roommates and I are going to have a meeting tonight.

해석 학생과 기숙사 관리인 간의 다음 대화를 들으시오.

학생(남자): 실례합니다. 소방법규 위반 때문에 왔는데요. 어제 아침에 점검이 있었고, 저희가 딱지를 받았어요.

관리인(여자): 알겠어요. 우선, 학생 이름이 필요해요.

학생: Jason Grant예요.

관리인: Jason Grant라… 아, 여기 있네요. 어디 보죠… 어제 점검을 했고, 아, 여기 위반사항이 있네요. 경고장도 받았군요. 그런데, 문제가 뭐죠? 그러니까, 다른…

학생: 음, 바로 그거에요. 저는 딱지를 받은 데에 대한 책임이 없어요. 제 다른 룸메이트들이… 저희는 넷이 거실을 같이 쓰는데요, 그런데…
관리인: 아, 네, 알겠어요. 학생은 아무것도 잘못한 것이 없는데 딱지에 왜 학생 이름이 올라 있는지 알고 싶은 거죠.
학생: 음… 잘못한 것이 있다고 생각하지는 않아요. 그러니까, 딱지에 써있는 것들… 전 그것들이 무슨 뜻인지 이해조차 못하겠어요. 딱지 내용이 이해조차 안 되는 상황에서 제가 뭘 잘못했는지 어떻게 알 수 있겠어요?
관리인: 그건 그들이 숫자 코드 시스템을 사용하기 때문이에요. 음… 어디 봅시다. 여러 위반 사항이 있는 것 같네요. 전기 취사용품 같은 것이 있었고… 그리고… 의류와 종이들이 사방에 쌓여 있기도 했네요?
학생: 예, 제 룸메이트들이 좀 지저분할 수는 있지만 그게 방이 위험한 정도까지는 아니라고 생각하는데요. 아닌가요?
관리인: 글쎄, 있죠, 분명 더 심한 경우도 보긴 했지만, 이 경우는 위험하다고 여겨질 만큼 충분히 안 좋은 상태였다고 보여지네요.
학생: (깊은 한숨) 그건 정말 저희 방 얘기 같기는 하네요. 하지만 그래도 불공평해요! 어지른 사람은 제가 아니에요. 점검 받기 전날 저는 방을 치웠다고요.
관리인: 글쎄요, 점검원들이 갔을 때는 분명 깨끗하지 않았어요.
학생: 보시다시피, 제 룸메이트들은 일 학년이에요. 그 애들에게 화재 안전검사가 뭔지 말해주었는데, 솔직히 잘 전달되지는 않은 것 같아요. 그 애들에게 책임이 있는데 우리 모두 다 벌금을 내야 한다니 믿을 수가 없어요.
관리인: 잠시만요. 벌금을 부과 받기 전에 문제점들을 시정할 기회가 있다는 것은 알죠? 2주 후에 재점검이 있어요. 그러니 그 전에 무엇을 해야 하는지 이야기해보죠. 어때요? 첫째, 비상 계단은 비워져 있어야 해요. 둘째, 취사용품은 쓸 수 없어요. 전열기나 전자레인지 같은 것들 말이죠. 그런 것들은 화재 경보기를 작동시킬 수 있어요. 저희는 어떤 상황에서도 기숙사 방 안에서 조리하는 것을 허용하지 않아요.
학생: 그 말은 제 주전자를 없애야 한다는 건가요?
관리인: 틀림없이 그래야 해요.
학생: 음… 그럼 전부 제 룸메이트들 탓인 건 아닌 거네요. 음, 어쨌든, 점검원들이 올 때 저희가 방에 없으면 어떻게 하죠?
관리인: 걱정할 필요 없어요, 저희가 열쇠를 가지고 있으니까. 물론, 저희가 갈 거라고 미리 알려드리긴 할 거예요. 우리가 문에 남겨둘 노란색 종이로 우리가 다녀갔다는 걸 알 수 있을 거예요. 자, 방이 규칙을 준수한 상태면, 이 노란색 종이가 있을 거예요. 만일 종이가 빨간색이면, 그건 학생들이 아직도 소방법규를 위반하고 있다는 뜻이에요. 방을 같이 쓰는 모든 입주자에게 균등하게 부과되는 벌금을 내게 될 겁니다.
학생: 하지만…
관리인: 그건 누가 실제로 규칙을 위반했는지 저희가 알 수 없기 때문이에요.
학생: 음, 제 룸메이트들과 오늘 밤에 회의를 좀 해봐야겠네요.

🅦 administrator [ədmínəstrèitər] 관리자　fire code 소방 규정　violation [vàiəléiʃən] 위반　get cited 딱지를 받다　issue a warning 경고하다　citation [saitéiʃən] 딱지; 소환장　numerical code 숫자 코드　stacked [stækt] 잔뜩 쌓인　hazardous [hæzərdəs] 위험한　get through 전달되다　fine [fine] 벌금; 벌금을 부과하다　fire escape 비상 계단　trigger [trígər] 작동시키다　smoke detector 연기 탐지기　circumstances [sə́ːrkəmstænsiz] (pl.) 상황　passkey [pǽski:] 마스터 키　in advance 미리　compliant [kəmpláiənt] (법률을) 준수하는　distribute [distríbju(ː)t] 나누어주다　occupant [ákjəpənt] 거주자

01 학생이 기숙사 사무실을 찾아간 이유는?
　Ⓐ 전기 주전자를 사용하는 것에 대해 문의하려고
　Ⓑ 내년을 위한 새 룸메이트들을 선정하려고
　Ⓒ 소방법규 위반과 관련된 벌금을 내려고
　Ⓓ 자신이 받은 딱지에 대한 설명을 들으려고

02 직원이 학교의 딱지에 관해 암시하는 것은?
　Ⓐ 대학에 의해 곧 갱신되고 개선될 것이다.
　Ⓑ 딱지를 받은 학생들은 볼 수 없도록 되어 있다.
　Ⓒ 기숙사 방을 지저분하게 쓰는 학생들에게 종종 주어진다.
　Ⓓ 많은 학생들이 이해하지 못하는 방법으로 위반사항을 설명하고 있다.

03 학생이 그의 룸메이트들에 대해 암시하는 것은?
　Ⓐ 점검의 중요성을 이해하지 못한다.
　Ⓑ 서로 잘 지내지 못한다.
　Ⓒ 방에서 조리를 많이 한다.
　Ⓓ 위반사항에 대해 벌금을 내지 않으려 한다.

04 직원에 의하면, 재점검 동안 위반사항이 발견될 경우 학생들이 하게 될 일은?
Ⓐ 법규를 준수할 때까지 계속해서 점검을 받아야 할 것이다.
Ⓑ 방 안에서 더 이상 조리하지 않는 데 동의해야 할 것이다.
Ⓒ 각자 똑같은 금액의 벌금을 내야 할 것이다.
Ⓓ 모두 새 조리도구들을 구입해야 할 것이다.

대화의 일부분을 다시 듣고 질문에 답하시오. ◁ MP3 21_1

> Uh-huh. Yeah, I know. And you want to know why your name is on the citation even though you didn't do anything wrong.

05 직원이 다음과 같이 말할 때 암시하는 것은?
Ⓐ 직원은 학생이 아무것도 잘못한 것이 없다고 생각하지 않는다.
Ⓑ 직원은 이런 종류의 상황을 많이 겪었다.
Ⓒ 직원은 딱지가 실수로 발부되었다고 생각한다.
Ⓓ 직원은 학생이 안 좋은 룸메이트들과 지낸다고 생각한다.

03 / Library, Bookstore

Sample Questions
본문 p. 128

01 C   02 B   03 A   04 D   05 D

해석 학생과 경제학 교수 간의 다음 대화를 들으시오. ◁ MP3 22

교수(여자): 안녕, John. 무슨 문제가 있나요?
학생(남자): 저... 죄송하다고 말씀 드리고 싶어서요.
교수: 뭐라고요? 왜요? 나한테 사과할 만한 일이 없는 것 같은데요.
학생: 저기, 오늘 수업에 대해 말씀 드리고 싶었어요. 토론 수업에 전혀 참여를 할 수가 없었거든요.
교수: 그래요... 오늘 수업 때 좀 조용해 보이긴 했어요. 학생은 대개 토론에 훨씬 더 참여하는 편이니까요. 오늘 수업 주제가 흥미롭지 않았나요?
학생: 아, 아닙니다. 그래서가 아녜요. 실은... 수업에 정말 참여하고 싶었어요. 저는 의료 서비스와 경제학의 관계에 관심이 정말 많거든요. 그러니까, 어떻게 경제학의 원칙들을 가져다 그것들을 병원이 얼마나 효율적인지를 알아보는 데 이용할 수 있는지가 정말 흥미로워요. 불행히도, 제가 그 부분을 읽지 못해서, 토론에 참여할 수가 없었어요.
교수: 무슨 소리에요? 어째서 수업자료를 읽지 않은 거죠? 내가 지난주 목요일에 내주지 않았나요?
학생: 저기, 그러니까, 어쨌든 책을 일부러 안 읽은 것은 아니에요. 학교 서점에서 책을 사지 못했어요. 그러니까 제 말은, 혹시 궁금해 하실까봐 말씀 드리면, 막판에 닥쳐서 서점에 가거나 한 건 아니고요. 교수님이 읽기 과제를 내주신 다음날 서점에 갔었는데 책이 다 팔리고 없었어요.
교수: 정말이에요? 이런, 얼마나 상심했을지 알겠네요!
학생: 예? 정말이요?
교수: 그래요. 학교 서점 정책은 학생들뿐만 아니라 교수들에게도 똑같이 무척 불만스러워요.
학생: 와, 저 같은 학생들이 또 있단 말씀이세요?
교수: 불행히도 그래요. 우리 학교 서점은 특정 분량의 책만 주문하는 그런 정책이 있어요. 그래서 내가 50권을 요청하면 40권만 가져다 두죠. 점장 말로는, 일부 학생들이 수강을 취소할지도 몰라서 그렇다는데. 팔리지 않은 책들을 가지고 있기는 싫은 거죠. 알다시피, 남은 책을 처분하기가 어려우니까요. 그러니 필요한 양보다 내가 훨씬 더 많이 주문할 수 있거나 할 수가 없어요. 하지만, 그래도 학교 서점이잖아요! 학교 서점이라고요. 내가 학기마다 다른 정책을 제안해보지만, 그들은 꿈쩍도 안 하더라고요.
학생: 와... 혹시 학과장님께 말씀해 보셨어요? 그분 말씀이 좀 더 힘이 있지 않을까요?

교수: 그거 좋은 생각인 것 같네요...
학생: 어쨌든, 교수님께 다음 수업에 대한 말씀도 미리 드리려고요. 제가 책을 구할 때까지는 다음 부분도 읽을 수 없을 거예요.
교수: 알겠어요, 무슨 말인지 알겠어요. 서점에 다시 한번 더 확인해보고, 그래도 없으면 내 책을 빌려가서 복사해도 돼요. 다른 학생들도 책을 다 구했는지 확인해봐야겠네요. 아니라면, 수업 진행을 바꿔야 할 것 같아요. 그 내용에 대해서는 며칠 뒤에 이야기해야 할지도 모르겠네요, 모두가 그걸 읽은 다음에 말이죠.
학생: 정말 감사합니다! 이제야 수업 참여에 관해 기분이 좀 나아졌네요.

Ⓦ on purpose 일부러, 의도적으로   at the last minute 마지막 순간에   stock [stɑk] 재고품; (판매할 상품을 갖춰두고) 있다   drop [drɑp] 그만두다   take something up with somebody (문제를 해결하거나 도움을 줄 수 있을) ...에게 ~에 대해 이야기하다   department chair 학과장   have a say 발언권이 있다   get one's hands on ~ ...을 손에 넣다

01 학생이 교수를 찾아간 이유는?
Ⓐ 병원과 경제학의 관계에 대해 논의하려고
Ⓑ 막판에 교수의 수업 수강을 취소한 것에 대해 사과하려고
Ⓒ 토론 수업에 참여하지 못한 이유를 설명하려고
Ⓓ 대학 서점을 위한 새로운 정책을 제안하려고

02 학생이 책을 살 수 없었던 이유는?
Ⓐ 학생이 책의 제목과 저자를 몰랐다.
Ⓑ 서점에 책이 충분히 없었다.
Ⓒ 너무 많은 학생들이 수업 수강을 취소했다.
Ⓓ 교수가 필요한 만큼의 책을 충분히 주문하지 않았다.

03 학생이 교수에게 하도록 제안한 것은?
Ⓐ 학과장에게 이야기해보기
Ⓑ 서점 점장과 다시 이야기해보기
Ⓒ 다른 서점에 그 책을 판매하도록 요청하기
Ⓓ 다음 수업에 다른 책을 배정하기

04 교수에 따르면, 학생이 다음 수업 전에 해야 할 일은?
Ⓐ 그 책을 파는 다른 서점을 찾아보기
Ⓑ 책의 내용에 대해 수업을 같이 듣는 학생들과 이야기해보기
Ⓒ 그의 실수에 대해 서점 점장에게 사과하기
Ⓓ 수업에 필요한 자료를 복사하기

대화의 일부분을 다시 듣고 질문에 답하시오. 🔊 MP3 22_1

> S: Wow... Did you try taking it up with the department chair? Wouldn't he have more of a say?
> P: That does sound like a good idea...
> S: Anyway, I'm giving you fair warning about the next class. I won't be able to read the next chapter until I can get my hands on the book.

05 학생이 다음과 같이 말한 이유는?

> Anyway, I'm giving you fair warning about the next class.

Ⓐ 다음 수업에 참여할 학생이 거의 없다는 것을 시사하려고
Ⓑ 서점 정책에 대한 불만을 표현하려고
Ⓒ 교수에게 자신이 수업에 맞춰 책을 구할 것이라는 확신을 주려고
Ⓓ 토론 수업에 참여할 수 없을 것이라는 점을 암시하려고

≽ Practice Questions

본문 p. 132

01 D	02 B	03 B, D	04 A	05 C

Introduction	**Listen to a conversation between a student and a librarian.** 🔊 MP3 23 **Librarian(female):** Hello, there. What can I help you with? **Student(male):** **Q1** Well, I'm looking for a reference book. **L:** Okay. Do you know the title? **S:** Uh… well, the things is, I'm not exactly sure what the title is. Uh… **Q3-B** I'm looking for books about European demographics. **L:** Okay. What type of demographics do you need? Do you need basic population statistics, like total population, male to female… and what not? **S:** Yeah. Population for sure, literacy rate and… uh… You know, **Q3-D** like if women tend to live longer than men… **L:** You mean life expectancy by gender? **S:** Yeah, things like that. **L:** All right. Hmm… You can probably get most, if not all, of the information you want from an atlas. They're in the refren…
Misunderstanding / Correction 국가별 자료가 아닌 도시별 자료가 필요함 **Headset**	**S:** Uh… Sorry to cut you off, **Q2** but I looked in an atlas, and everything was divided by country. I'm kind of looking for it by city, you know? **L:** Oh, okay. **S:** Do you know where I can find statistics by city? **L:** Hmm… By city, huh? 🎧 Were you looking for a particular region? Eastern Europe? Western Europe? Scandinavia? **S:** Nope. I pretty much need the whole thing. **L:** **Q5** All of Europe. Hmm… You know what, if you tell me **Q1** why you're looking for this information, I can help you a little more. **S:** Sure thing. Well… it's a geography class with Professor Philips. I have to analyze trends in urban areas like population, economic and social indicators… that sort of thing. **L:** Hmm… Did you check out the *Demographic Yearbook*? I know it's… it's probably not going to give you information city by city, but… **S:** Yeah, it's only by country. **L:** Oh, so you already looked at it, huh? Well, let me just double-check to make sure… (Pause) Yeah, population… by country. Okay. Hmm… Do you… I mean, did the professor mention anything about where to look? For demographic information by city… I mean… **S:** No, he didn't mention anything in particular. I figured I'd just come here and find it without a hitch. **L:** Unfortunately, that's not going to happen. I mean, there's one for cities in North America, but that probably won't do you any good. **S:** No, not really.
Suggestion reference room에서 찾아볼 것	**L:** Well, tell you what, **Q4** let's look around the reference section and see if we can find anything.

해석 학생과 사서 간의 다음 대화를 들으시오.
사서(여자): 안녕하세요, 무엇을 도와드릴까요?

학생(남자): 아, 참고 도서를 찾고 있는데요.
사서: 네, 제목을 알고 있나요?
학생: 음... 저기, 문제는, 제목이 뭔지 정확히 잘 모르겠어요. 음... 유럽의 인구 통계에 대한 책들을 찾고 있는데요.
사서: 알겠어요. 어떤 종류의 인구 통계 자료가 필요한 거죠? 기본적인 인구 통계가 필요한가요? 총 인구, 남성 대 여성 등등 같은?
학생: 네, 인구는 물론 필요하고, 문맹률과... 음... 여성이 남성보다 오래 사는 경향이 있다... 뭐 이런 거 있잖아요.
사서: 성별에 따른 평균 수명 말이죠?
학생: 네, 그런 것이요.
사서: 알겠어요. 음... 학생이 원하는 정보의 대부분을, 전부는 아니더라도, 지도 책에서 찾을 수 있을지 몰라요. 지도 책들은 참고 도서...
학생: 음... 말을 잘라 죄송하지만, 지도 책을 보기 했는데 모든 게 국가별로 나뉘어져 있었어요. 저는 도시별로 된 것을 찾고 있는데.
사서: 아, 알겠어요.
학생: 도시별로 된 통계 자료를 어디에서 찾을 수 있는지 아시나요?
사서: 음... 도시별로요? 어느 특정한 지역을 찾고 있었나요? 동유럽? 서유럽? 스칸디나비아?
학생: 아니요. 모두 다 필요해요.
사서: 유럽 전체라. 음... 있죠, 이 정보를 왜 찾고 있는지를 제게 말해주면 좀 더 잘 도와줄 수 있을 것 같은데요.
학생: 물론이죠. 음... Philips 교수님의 지리학 수업인데요. 인구나 경제적, 사회적 지표 같은, 도시 지역들의 경향들을 분석해야 해요.
사서: 음... 〈인구 연보〉는 살펴봤나요? 제가 알기로는 그건... 아마도 도시별로 정보가 나와 있지는 않을 테지만, 그래도...
학생: 네, 그건 그냥 국가별이에요.
사서: 아, 그럼 이미 그걸 살펴봤군요? 음... 제가 한번 더 체크해볼게요... (잠시 후) 그렇지, 인구... 국가별. 좋아요. 음... 학생이... 아니, 교수님이 어디에서 찾아보라고 언급하신 것이 있나요? 도시별 인구 통계 정보 말이에요.
학생: 아뇨. 아무것도 특별히 말씀하시진 않았어요. 그냥 저는 여기 오면 쉽게 찾아질 거라 생각했어요.
사서: 불행히도, 그렇지 않을 것 같네요. 음... 북미의 도시들에 관한 것은 한 권 있는데, 그건 아마 학생에게 도움이 되지 않을 것 같네요.
학생: 네, 별로요.
사서: 음, 있죠, 참고 도서 섹션을 둘러보고 거기에서 뭐라도 찾을 수 있을지 한번 봅시다.

Ⓦ reference book 참고도서　demographics [dìːməɡrǽfiks] 인구 통계　statistics [stətístiks] 통계, 수치　literacy rate 문맹률　life expectancy 기대수명　atlas [ǽtləs] 지도 책　geography [dʒiáɡrəfi] 지리학　analyze [ǽnəlàiz] 분석하다　trend [trend] 추세, 경향　urban [ə́ːrbən] 도시의　indicator [índəkèitər] 지표　yearbook [jíərbùk] 연감, 연보　without a hitch 술술, 거침없이

01 대화의 주제는?
Ⓐ 프로젝트를 위한 적절한 자료를 찾는 방법들
Ⓑ 학생이 프로젝트에 어려움을 겪는 이유들
Ⓒ 인구 통계를 평가하기 위해 나라들이 사용하는 기준들
Ⓓ 학생의 연구 프로젝트에 쓸 수 있는 자료들

02 점검해본 지도 책에 대해 학생이 말한 것은?
Ⓐ 이해하기에 너무 어려웠다.
Ⓑ 인구 통계 자료가 도시별로 되어 있지 않다.
Ⓒ 오래된 정보가 담겨 있다.
Ⓓ 서유럽에 대한 정보가 부족했다.

03 유럽 도시들에 대해 학생이 필요로 하는 정보의 종류는? (두 가지 선택)
Ⓐ 평균 기온
Ⓑ 인구
Ⓒ 지역별 크기
Ⓓ 시민들의 평균 수명

04 학생이 필요로 하는 정보를 찾기 위해서 화자들이 찾아볼 곳은?
Ⓐ 참고 도서 섹션
Ⓑ 다른 도서관
Ⓒ Philips 교수의 사무실
Ⓓ 지리학과

대화의 일부분을 다시 듣고 질문에 답하시오. ◁› MP3 23_1

L: Were you looking for a particular region? Eastern Europe? Western Europe? Scandinavia?
S: Nope. I pretty much need the whole thing.
L: All of Europe. Hmm…

05 사서가 다음과 같이 말한 이유는?

All of Europe. Hmm…

Ⓐ 학생이 필요로 하는 정보에 놀랐다.
Ⓑ 너무 바빠서 학생을 위해 정보를 찾아줄 수 없다.
Ⓒ 그 정보를 찾을 수 있을지 확신하지 못한다.
Ⓓ 학생의 말을 제대로 들었는지 확신하지 못한다.

04 / Part-time Job, Job Fair, Internship

◈ Sample Questions
본문 p. 136

01 C 02 D 03 B 04 C 05 D

해석 대학 센터에서의 학생과 직원 간의 다음 대화를 들으시오. ◁› MP3 24

학생(남자): 안녕하세요, 이번 여름 인턴 자리에 대한 정보를 얻을 수 있는지 궁금한데요.
직원(여자): 음, 잘 찾아왔어요. 자, 앉으세요. 어떤 분야에 관심이 있지요?
학생: 음… 제가 최근에 컴퓨터 공학에서 국제 경영으로 전공을 바꿔서, 경영 쪽 인턴 자리를 알아보고 싶어요.
직원: 좋아요. 몇 학년이죠?
학생: 2학년이요.
직원: 음… 대부분의 회사들이 3학년을 마친 인턴들을 고용하고 싶어 한다는 것은 알고 있죠? 대부분의 학생들은 3학년부터 자기 분야의 상급 수업들을 듣기 시작하잖아요. 회사들은 대개 (자기 분야의) 지식이 좀 더 있는 인턴들을 원하기 마련이에요.
학생: 네, 알아요. 하지만 한번 시도해보는 것도 좋겠다고 생각했어요. 일단 물어는 보는 게 더 낫잖아요?
직원: 맞아요. 좋아요. 가능한 자리가 있는지 전산 자료를 한번 볼게요. 음… 경영 전공에… 유 경험자 조건이 없는 것으로… 무슨 특별한 기술이 있나요? 아니면 다른 자격 요건이라도?
학생: 음… 도움이 될지는 모르겠지만 프랑스어에 유창하고요… 여름방학 때 주당 40시간을 일할 수 있는 정규직 자리를 원해요.
직원: 좋아요. 전산에 두 개가 뜨네요.
학생: 잘됐네요, 자세히 좀 말해주세요.
직원: 타운 컨벤션 센터에서 비즈니스 컨벤션 일정을 조정해주는 자리가 하나 있고요.
학생: 그거 재미있을 것 같네요!
직원: 하지만…
학생: 하지만, 왜요?
직원: 급여가 평균보다 조금 낮네요… 좋은 경험이 되긴 하겠지만, 시간당 7달러가 조금 넘는 금액이에요.
학생: 7달러라고요! 집세를 낼 만큼은 벌어야 하는데… 다른 하나는 어떤 건가요?
직원: JKJ 기업이에요.
학생: 와, 무척 좋은 회사잖아요… 하지만 잠시만요… 거긴 어떤 문제가 있죠?
직원: 음… 문제랄 것까지는 아니지만 굉장히 경쟁이 치열한 자리라서요. 유명한 회사잖아요? 이봐요, 학생이 전공을 바꾸기 전에 공학 전공이었다고 하지 않았나요? 그거 잘됐네요. 회사들은 항상 컴퓨터 관련 배경 지식이 있는 사람들을 선호하니까요.

학생: 음, 그러면 운에 맡겨봐야겠네요. 지원하려면 제가 뭘 해야 하죠?
직원: 우선, 제게 이력서를 보내주세요.
학생: 사실, 아직 없는데요...
직원: 괜찮아요. 이번 금요일에 학교 비즈니스 센터에서 이력서 쓰는 법에 대한 세미나가 있을 예정이에요. 거기 참석해서 조언을 좀 구해보세요. 그동안은 기본적인 이력서를 써보면 어때요? 그리고 함께 뭘 더 추가하고 뭘 삭제할지 상의할 수 있도록 개별 미팅을 가지면 될 거요.
학생: 그거 좋네요! 정말 감사합니다! 그러면... 다음 주 목요일에 들러도 될까요? 그때까지 이력서를 준비해 올게요.
직원: 음... 오후 2시에 시간이 비는데, 괜찮나요?
학생: 좋습니다.

ⓦ **sophomore** [sάfəmɔ̀ːr] 대학 2학년생 **requirement** [rikwáiərmənt] 자격요건 **full-time position** 정규직 **coordinate** [kouɔ́ːrdineit] 조직하다, 편성하다 **switch** [switʃ] 바꾸다 **CV**(= curriculum vitae) 이력서 **pointer** [pɔ́intər] 충고, 조언

01 학생이 직원을 방문한 이유는?
Ⓐ 이력서 쓰는 법에 대해 배우려고
Ⓑ 아르바이트 일자리를 구하려고
Ⓒ 여름 인턴 자리에 대한 정보를 구하려고
Ⓓ 전공을 바꾸는 것에 대해 문의하려고

02 학생의 이전 전공에 대한 직원의 태도는?
Ⓐ 그에게 충분한 전문지식을 주지 못했다고 걱정한다.
Ⓑ 그가 어려운 결정을 내린 것을 칭찬한다.
Ⓒ 그것이 쓸모 없었다고 생각한다.
Ⓓ 그가 일자리를 구하는 데 도움이 될 것이라 여긴다.

03 컨벤션 센터의 일자리에 대해 학생이 암시하는 것은?
Ⓐ 너무 멀다.
Ⓑ 급여가 충분치 않다.
Ⓒ 자신의 전문지식과 맞다.
Ⓓ 자신이 원하던 자리이다.

04 학생이 금요일에 할 일은?
Ⓐ 직원을 다시 방문하기
Ⓑ 학업 상담사와 이야기하기
Ⓒ 이력서 쓰기 세미나에 참석하기
Ⓓ 여름 인턴 자리를 더 찾아보기

대화의 일부분을 다시 듣고 질문에 답하시오. 🔊 MP3 24_1

> E: It's at JKJ Corporation.
> S: Oh wow, that's a great company... but wait... what's the problem with that one?

05 학생이 다음과 같이 말할 때 암시하는 것은?

> But wait... what's the problem with that one?

Ⓐ 채용되기를 기다려야 할 것 같아 걱정이 된다.
Ⓑ 그 기회가 너무 좋아서 사실이 아닐 것 같다.
Ⓒ 그 자리에 자격이 될지 확신하지 못한다.
Ⓓ 그 자리가 자신에게 맞지 않을까 봐 염려스럽다.

Practice Questions
본문 p. 140

01 C   02 C   03 B   04 B   05 A

Introduction

Listen to a conversation between a student and an employee at the school radio station. 🔊 MP3 25

Student(male): Excuse me, ma'am. My name is Eric, Eric Grant. I recently applied to the radio station, but my application was rejected.

Employee(female): Okay. So what can I do for you?

S: **Q1** Well, I was wondering why my application was rejected.

E: Okay, let me check your application. Your last name is Grant, right?

S: Yeah.

E: Okay, Grant… There we go, I remember this application.

S: Was there something wrong with it? Did I miss something?

E: Hmm… You didn't miss anything, per se… I mean, you wrote everything down, but the part about what kind of show you wanted to do… You proposed a talk show, right?

S: That's right. I've been talking to a lot of my friends lately, and they all seem to think that the station needs something fresh, you know? Something different. So I thought **Q3** I'd apply to the radio station and start a talk show, where students can call in and discuss campus related things like dorm food and club meetings.

Funciton
토크쇼를 하고 싶어 함

Cause
음악 프로그램에 맞지 않아 거절함

E: Well, that's great and all, but **Q2** the thing is… our position was for a music program. The campus radio station is a music station, and **I don't think a talk show would fit in**. When I saw your application, I didn't even really consider it because… well… **you applied for the wrong job.**

S: I knew it was a long shot, but if I just had the chance… Students really want to talk about campus issues, you know? They want to know what's going on on campus.

E: Okay, let's say that you had gotten the job. A talk show would be really hard to manage. If we receive phone calls from students, we really don't know what the students are going to say and ask. We don't even know if what you say will follow university policy. There are so many variables that go into having a talk show, to be quite honest. I don't even think we have the manpower to pull it off. Anyway, there's a student council meeting every month. Any student can attend and voice their opinions there. I really can't see why we would need a radio show that does the same thing.

Cause
실제 라디오 방송국에서 일하기 전에 관련 경험이 필요해서 지원함

S: **Q4** The thing is… I really want to get some experience under my belt before I work at an actual radio station. I'm a communication arts major, and **I really want and need to get this job**. It'd be great if I can have another chance.

E: Hmm… Well, there's still two more weeks before the deadline, and we really haven't found any candidates who are qualified for the job, so I guess you can apply again. But this time you need to write about what you can contribute with a music program – what kind of music you're going to play, how you're going to split the program… Just make sure it's related to music.

Suggestion
지원서를 다시 쓸 것을 제안

S: I'll do that for sure, but can I add in some call-in phone interviews into the programming? Of course they'll be about music.

E: **Q5** Why don't you just fill out a new application form first? We can talk about details later.

S: All right. Thanks.

해석 교내 라디오 방송국에서의 학생과 직원 간의 다음 대화를 들으시오.

학생(남자): 실례합니다. 제 이름은 Eric, Eric Grant인데요. 일전에 방송국에 지원을 했는데 탈락했어요.
직원(여자): 알겠습니다. 무엇을 도와드릴까요?
학생: 저, 제 지원이 불합격된 이유가 궁금해서요.
직원: 알겠어요. 지원서를 한번 살펴볼게요. 성이 Grant라고 했죠?
학생: 네.
직원: 그래요, Grant라... 여기 있네요. 이 지원서 기억이 나요.
학생: 지원서에 잘못된 것이 있었나요? 제가 뭔가 빠뜨렸나요?
직원: 음... 빠뜨린 것은 없어요, 그 자체로는요. 그러니까, 빠짐없이 작성은 했지만, 어떤 프로그램을 하고 싶은지에 대한 부분에... 토크쇼를 제안했네요? 맞나요?
학생: 맞아요. 최근에 많은 친구들과 이야기를 해봤는데, 모두가 방송국에 뭔가 신선한 게 필요하다고 생각하는 것 같아요. 뭔가 다른 거 말이에요. 그래서 생각했죠, 방송국에 지원해서 토크쇼를 만들자 하고 말이죠. 학생들이 전화를 걸어, 기숙사 음식이나 동아리 모임 같은 캠퍼스 관련 이야기를 나누는 쇼 말이에요.
직원: 음, 그건 좋은데, 문제는... 저희가 낸 공고는 음악 프로그램 자리였어요. 학교 방송국은 음악 방송국인데 토크쇼는 거기에 맞지 않을 것 같아요. 제가 학생 지원서를 봤을 때는, 사실 거의 고려조차 하지 않았어요... 왜냐면... 음... 맞지 않는 곳에 지원을 했으니까요.
학생: 가능성이 별로 없을 거라는 건 알았지만, 만일 기회가 있기만 하다면... 학생들은 학교에서 일어나는 일들에 대해 정말 이야기를 나누고 싶어 하잖아요. 학생들은 캠퍼스에 무슨 일이 일어나는지 알고 싶어 해요.
직원: 알겠어요. 그걸로 채용이 되었다고 합시다. 하지만 토크쇼는 운영하기가 정말 어려울 거예요. 학생들에게서 전화를 받게 되면, 그들이 무슨 이야기를 하고 무슨 질문을 던질지 알 수가 없다고요. 심지어 학생이 이야기하는 내용이 대학 규정에 맞을지도 알 수 없고요. 솔직히, 토크쇼에는 변수가 너무 많아요. 우리가 토크쇼를 해낼 수 있는 인력이 있는 것 같지도 않고요. 어쨌든, 매달 학생회가 열리는데, 학생이라면 누구나 참석해서 자신의 의견을 낼 수 있어요. 그것과 똑같은 일을 하는 라디오 프로그램이 왜 필요한지 이해가 안 가네요.
학생: 그러니까... 저는 실제 라디오 방송국에서 일하기 전에 정말이지 경험을 좀 쌓고 싶어요. 저는 커뮤니케이션 아트 전공이라 이 일을 꼭 하고 싶고 해야만 해요. 기회를 한 번 더 갖게 된다면 정말 좋을 거예요.
직원: 음... 마감까지 아직 2주가 남았고, 자리에 적합한 후보를 아직 찾지 못했으니, 다시 지원해봐도 좋아요. 하지만, 이번에는, 학생이 음악 프로그램에 어떤 기여를 할 수 있는지를 써야 해요. 어떤 종류의 음악을 틀 것인지, 프로그램을 어떻게 나누어 구성할 것인지... 반드시 음악과 관련해서 쓰도록 해야 해요.
학생: 그렇게 할게요. 하지만 제가 방송에 전화 인터뷰 같은 것을 추가해도 될까요? 물론 음악에 관한 내용으로요.
직원: 우선 새 지원서부터 쓰는 게 어때요? 자세한 사항은 나중에 얘기해도 되요.
학생: 알겠습니다. 감사합니다.

Ⓦ pse se 그 자체로는 a long shot 거의 승산 없는 것 variable [vέ(:)əriəbl] 변수 manpower [mǽnpàuər] 인력 pull something off (힘든 것을) 해내다, 성사시키다 student council 학생회 voice [vɔis] (말로) 나타내다, 표하다 under one's belt 이미 겪은 candidate [kǽndidèit] 후보자, 지원자 contribute [kəntríbjuːt] 기여하다 call-in [mi-lɔːd] 시청자 전화 참가 프로그램

01 학생이 직원을 찾아간 이유는?
Ⓐ 학교 라디오 방송국에 대한 불만을 말하려고
Ⓑ 일자리 지원서를 요청하려고
Ⓒ 자신이 채용이 되지 않은 이유를 알려고
Ⓓ 자신의 라디오 프로그램에 변경을 요청하려고

02 직원이 학생의 지원서를 탈락시킨 이유는?
Ⓐ 직원이 학생의 태도를 좋아하지 않았다.
Ⓑ 직원은 학생이 자격이 되지 않는다고 결정했다.
Ⓒ 학생이 엉뚱한 종류의 프로그램을 제안했다.
Ⓓ 학생에게 충분한 경험이 없었다.

03 학생이 라디오 방송국에서 하고 싶어 하는 것은?
Ⓐ 학생들이 원하는 음악을 틀어주기
Ⓑ 학생들에게 흥미로운 주제에 대해 이야기하기
Ⓒ 지역 학생 음악가들을 인터뷰하기

Ⓓ 대학 정책들에 대해 매달 토론을 열기

04 학생이 자신의 전공이 커뮤니케이션 아트라고 언급한 이유는?
Ⓐ 자신이 자격이 된다는 것을 강조하기 위해서
Ⓑ 일자리를 얻고자 하는 자신의 동기를 설명하려고
Ⓒ 자신이 경험이 없다는 점을 설명하려고
Ⓓ 지원서가 얼마나 혼동되는지 알려주려고

05 직원이 대화 말미에 아마도 느낀 감정은?
Ⓐ 학생이 포기하지 않아 짜증이 남
Ⓑ 학생의 뛰어난 아이디어에 감탄함
Ⓒ 학생이 다시 지원할 것이라 기쁨
Ⓓ 학생의 음악적 취향에 감사함을 느낌

05 / School Facility

≳ Sample Questions 본문 p. 144

| 01 D | 02 C | 03 A | 04 D | 05 B |

해석 학생과 교수 간의 다음 대화를 들으시오. ◁ MP3 26

교수(여자): Brian! 드디어... 왜 이리 오래 걸렸나요?
학생(남자): 아, 정말 죄송해요. 컴퓨터 센터에... 새 프린터기가 들어와서요. 그러니까, 새 기계니까 더 좋아야 하잖아요? 그런데 그 기계를 어떻게 사용해야 하는지를 모르겠어요... 저 같은 보통 사람들이 쓰기에는 너무 복잡한 것 같아요.
교수: 그래요, 무슨 말인지 알겠어요. 학교가 새 장비를 들여올 때마다... 배워야 할 게 많죠, 그렇죠?
학생: 정말 그래요. 제 말은, 인쇄를 하러 도서관에 가도 되지만, 줄 서서 기다리는 사람들이 너무 많아서요... 한 시간 정도 기다리지 않고서는 인쇄를 할 수가 없어요. 물론, 그냥 기숙사 옆에 있는 컴퓨터 센터에 가도 되긴 하지만, 새 프린터기들은... 정말이지... 있죠. 새 프린터기에 있는 무선 기능을 이용해서 인쇄하려고 했는데, 데이터가 한 번도 제대로 전송되지 않는 거예요. 계속 에러 메시지만 뜨고요. 정말 답답해요. 신기술은 일을 더 쉽게 만들어 주기 위한 거잖아요, 아닌가요?
교수: 하하... 정말이요? 그 정도로 심한가요? 나는 인쇄를 모두 집에서 해서... 내 프린터기는 10년이나 됐지만 잘 작동해요. 학생들이 모두 프린터기를 내가 사용할 수 있는 것보다 더 잘 사용하고 있을 줄 알았는데.
학생: 가끔씩은 컴퓨터 센터에서 인쇄를 할 수가 없어서 학교 밖으로 차를 타고 나가서 돈을 지불하고 인쇄를 해야 할 때도 있어요. 어쨌든, 여기 교수님께서 요청하셨던, Gustave Flaubert의 〈Three Tales〉에 대해 쓴 제 보고서의 사본이에요.
교수: 좋아요. 어디 봅시다. 자, '근대 프랑스 고전학의 진정한 의미'라. 내가 지난주에 말했듯이, 학생의 보고서를 위한 아주 좋은 주제예요. 하지만...
학생: 네, 첫 번째 이야기인 〈A Simple Heart〉에 대해 더 깊이 고찰했는지를 물으시는 건가요?
교수: 맞아요. 그게 단순한 내용이기는 하지만, 나머지 이야기들을 위한 분위기를 잡아주거든요. 그 이야기에 쓰인 문장들은 모두 그 안에 엄청난 의미를 지니고 있어요. 그 세 이야기들 중 첫 번째 것을 제대로 이해하지 못하게 되면, 다른 이야기들의 의미도 제대로 파악할 수 없게 될 거예요.
학생: 음... 분명 더 읽어보고 조사도 더 해봤고요, 그래서 몇 가지를 알아낸 것 같기도 해요.
교수: 이야기의 주인공인 Felicité에 대한 건가요? 그녀에 대해 뭔가 알아냈나요?
학생: 이게 그녀에 대한 건지는 잘 모르겠어요. 그 캐릭터에 대해 제가 좀 더 알아냈어야 했나요?
교수: 아니, 그렇지 않아요. 내가 학생이 보았으면 했던 것을, 학생이 정말 찾아냈나 알아보려는 거예요.
학생: 휴... 그럼 안심이네요. 어쨌든, 처음에는, 저는 그 이야기를 중요하게 생각하지는 않았어요. 제 말은, 끝에 그녀가 나이가 들자, 그냥 죽어버리는 하인이 나오잖아요. 그런데 그리고 나서, 저는 소설 전반적으로 해설자의 톤이 어떻게 바뀌는지를 알아차렸어요.

교수: 아주 좋아요! 그래서 뭘 깨달았나요?
학생: 음, Flaubert는 처음에는 Felicité에 대해 매우 비판적인 것처럼 보였어요. 그녀는 아무것도 돌려받지 못하는데도 불구하고 모든 걸 희생하잖아요. 하지만, 이야기가 진전되면서 그 캐릭터를 설명하는 데 쓰이는 단어들이 바뀌어요. 점점 더 긍정적인 단어들로요. 정말 흥미롭더군요. 그 단어들이 같은 사람을 묘사하는데도, 굉장히 많이 바뀌더라고요.
교수: 맞아요! 그게 Flaubert의 작품들이 뛰어난 이유이죠! 이제 왜 내가 학생에게 문장들을 면밀히 살펴보라고 했는지 알겠죠?
학생: 네, 전 그저 Flaubert가 다른 사람들을 위해 자신을 희생하는 사람들에 대해 비판적이 되려고 한다고만 생각했어요. 하지만 해설자의 톤이 어떻게 바뀌는지 깨닫고 나서는, 정반대의 결론에 이르렀어요.
교수: 이제 올바른 방향으로 가고 있네요. 그럼 배운 것을 가지고 그게 다른 두 이야기에도 적용되는지 살펴보는 게 어때요?

Ⓦ complicated [kɑ́mpləkèitid] 복잡한   print-out [print-aut] 인쇄물   wireless [wáiərlis] 무선의   transfer [trǽnsfər] 옮기다, 전송하다   protagonist [proutǽɡənist] 주인공   relief [rilíːf] 안도, 안심   narrator [nǽreitər] (소설의) 서술자   critical [krítikəl] 비판적인, 비난하는   sacrifice [sǽkrəfàis] 희생하다   on the right track 올바른 방향인

01 학생이 교수를 찾은 이유는?
Ⓐ 컴퓨터 센터에 대해 불평하려고
Ⓑ 보고서를 왜 늦게 제출했는지 설명하려고
Ⓒ 교수의 수업에 대한 자신의 의견을 이야기하려고
Ⓓ 자신의 보고서의 방향에 대해 논의하려고

02 새 프린터기에 대한 교수의 태도는?
Ⓐ 대학에서 새 프린터기를 구입해서 놀랐다.
Ⓑ 프린터기를 구매한 것은 대학 기금을 유용하게 사용한 것이 아니라고 생각한다.
Ⓒ 신기술을 따라잡는 것은 힘들다고 생각한다.
Ⓓ 새 프린터기들은 학생들에게 도움이 될 것이라고 생각한다.

03 교수가 자신의 집 프린터기를 언급한 이유는?
Ⓐ 학생들이 인쇄를 하는 데 어려움이 있다는 것을 몰랐다는 것을 나타내려고
Ⓑ 학교 프린터기를 이용하는 것에 대한 대안을 제안하려고
Ⓒ 학교의 프린터기가 이용하기 어렵다는 것에 동의하려고
Ⓓ 학생이 변명을 하지 말아야 한다는 것을 강조하려고

04 〈A Simple Heart〉의 문장들에 중요한 의미가 있다고 교수가 언급한 이유는?
Ⓐ 소설의 주인공에 대해 알 수 있는 가장 좋은 방법을 알려주려고
Ⓑ 사회에 대한 Gustave Flaubert의 입장을 강화하려고
Ⓒ 현대 프랑스 문학의 스타일에 대한 예를 들려고
Ⓓ 학생이 Flaubert의 소설들을 어떻게 읽어야 하는지 설명하려고

05 Flaubert의 작법에 대해 교수와 학생이 흥미롭다고 느낀 것은?
Ⓐ 그는 호의적인 말을 쓰는 사람들을 비판했다.
Ⓑ 그는 한 등장인물에 대해 서서히 바뀌는 관점을 만들어 냈다.
Ⓒ 그는 주요 등장인물들 중 한 명을 끝에 죽게 했다.
Ⓓ 그는 그의 모든 소설에 언어를 일관적으로 사용했다.

≫ Practice Questions   본문 p. 148

| 01 B | 02 C | 03 B, D | 04 D | 05 A |

| Introduction | Listen to a conversation between a student and a receptionist at the administration office. ◁ MP3 27

Student(female): Excuse me, I received an email from the administration office saying |

that **Q1** **I didn't get a grade for the biological sciences course I took this semester. I'm here to explain my situation.**

Employee(male): Okay. What's your name?

S: Sarah, Sarah Johnson.

E: All right, I'm bringing up your records on the computer. Hmm… Yeah, your professors submitted your grades for all your other classes, but the biological sciences grade is missing. We just wanted to double check with you just in case something was wrong. There are times when professors forget to submit a final grade, or something goes wrong while processing all the documents. There are a lot of grades, you know?

S: Well, that's not the case at all. I mean, something went wrong, but it's not because something's wrong with the system. I, I still don't have a grade.

E: What? What do you mean? What happened?

S: Oh, I'll tell you what happened. I was doing some research on the RP73 genome and how it can be used for medical purposes if only the proteins can be refined. Anyway, that was part of my final research project.

E: Well, research projects are common… So what went wrong? I mean… That's why you still don't have a grade yet, right?

S: Exactly! I have to heat the sample up at a very low temperature for a long time and then cool it down in the fridge to get the RP73 protein out. Well, since I had to heat the sample overnight, I thought I'd just leave it there and come back the next day.

E: 🎧 **Q5** **You mean to tell me you left a fire unattended for the whole night?**

S: Oh, no… It's not what you think, students do it all the time. We don't use an actual flame to heat things up. Anyway, I tried to go back to the lab the next day, but it was just one of those days. I started up my car… or at least attempted to, but it just wouldn't start.

E: Why didn't you just take the bus?

S: That's the thing, it was a Saturday, but I didn't realize the bus wasn't running!

E: Ah. **Q4** **They really need to make the bus schedules easier for students to access.** So you waited at the bus stop?

S: Yes! **Q3-B** **I waited for about two hours! How was I supposed to know that the campus bus stops running during the weekends?** **Q3-D** **I tried calling someone at the lab, but no one would pick up because it was the weekend.** By the time I finally arrived at the lab, the sample had melted too much and I couldn't use it.

E: Did you talk to your professor about it?

S: Of course I did. He told me I could do it again, but I had to study for my other finals. I wouldn't be able to study for my finals if I had to stay at the lab all day. So **Q2** **he told me I could finish the project and hand it in after my finals were over.**

E: I see. But you're supposed to send us a notification if one of your grades is going to be delayed. It happens more than you think. But I understand that you wouldn't have known. I guess that goes for a lot of students.

S: Sorry about that.

E: Oh, no, no need to be sorry. So, we should be expecting your grade soon, right?

S: Yeah. I actually handed the report in yesterday. Is there anything else that I have to do?

E: No, not really. All we can do is wait. If we don't get a grade by the end of the week, we'll let you know.

S: Oh, I hope that doesn't happen.

해석 학생과 행정실 접수 담당 직원 간의 다음 대화를 들으시오.

학생(여자): 실례합니다. 제가 이번 학기에 들은 생물과학 수업의 성적이 나오지 않았다고 행정실로부터 이메일을 받았는데요. 제 상황을 설명드리러 왔어요.

직원(남자): 알겠습니다. 이름이 어떻게 되나요?

학생: Sarah, Sarah Johnson이에요.

직원: 알겠습니다. 학생의 기록을 컴퓨터에 띄울게요. 음… 네, 교수님들께서 학생의 다른 수업 성적들은 모두 제출하셨는데, 생물과학 성적은 없네요. 혹시 무언가 잘못된 게 있을지도 몰라서 학생에게 한번 더 확인하고 싶었어요. 가끔 교수님들이 최종 성적을 제출하는 것을 잊거나, 서류들을 처리하는 도중에 무언가 잘못될 때도 있거든요. 알다시피, 성적이 정말 많잖아요?

학생: 음, 제 경우는 전혀 그런 게 아녜요. 제 말은, 잘못된 것이 있긴 했지만, 전산 시스템에 문제가 있어서 그런 건 아녜요. 제가 아직 성적을 받지 못한 거예요.

직원: 네? 무슨 말이에요? 무슨 일이 있었죠?

학생: 아, 무슨 일인지 말씀 드릴게요. 저는 RP73 게놈과, 그 단백질이 정제될 수 있기만 하다면 RP73 게놈이 어떻게 의료 목적으로 쓰일 수 있는지에 대해 연구를 하던 중이었어요. 어쨌든, 그게 제 최종 연구 프로젝트의 한 부분이었죠.

직원: 음, 연구 프로젝트는 흔히 있는 거죠… 그런데 뭐가 잘못된 거죠? 그러니까… 그게 학생이 아직 성적을 받지 못한 이유라는 거죠?

학생: 맞아요! RP73 단백질을 추출하기 위해서는 샘플을 무척 낮은 온도에서 오랜 시간 동안 열을 가한 뒤 냉장고에서 식혀야 해요. 음, 샘플을 밤새 데워야 했기 때문에, 저는 그냥 그걸 놔두고 다음 날 다시 오려고 했어요.

직원: 밤새 불을 방치해두었다고 말하는 거예요?

학생: 아, 아뇨… 생각하시는 그런 게 아녜요. 학생들은 늘 그렇게 해요. 저희는 열을 가하기 위해서 실제 불꽃을 사용하지는 않거든요. 어쨌든, 다음날 실험실에 다시 가려고 했는데, 일이 잘 안 풀리는 날이었던 거죠. 차 시동을 걸었는데… 아니, 걸어보려고 했는데, 시동이 걸리지 않더라고요.

직원: 그냥 버스를 타지 그랬어요?

학생: 그게 문제에요. 토요일이었는데, 버스가 다니지 않는다는 걸 알아차리지 못했던 거죠!

직원: 아, 정말이지 학생들이 버스 운행표를 찾아보기 더 쉽게 만들어야 해요. 그래서 버스 정류장에서 기다렸어요?

학생: 네! 두 시간이나 기다렸다고요! 학교 버스가 주말에는 운행을 중단한다는 걸 제가 어떻게 알 수 있었겠어요? 실험실에 있는 누구와라도 전화 통화를 하려고 해봤는데, 주말이라서 아무도 받지 않았어요. 마침내 제가 실험실에 도착했을 때는, 샘플이 너무 많이 녹아서 쓸 수가 없게 되었어요.

직원: 그것에 대해 교수님께 말씀 드렸나요?

학생: 물론 했죠. 교수님께서는 제가 다시 해도 된다고 하셨지만, 저는 다른 기말고사 공부를 해야 했어요. 하루 종일 실험실에 있어야 한다면 기말고사 공부를 할 수 없을 테니까요. 그래서 교수님은 기말고사가 모두 끝난 후에 프로젝트를 끝내고 제출해도 된다고 하셨어요.

직원: 알겠어요. 하지만 학생 성적들 중 하나가 지연될 예정이었다면, 학생이 저희에게 알려줘야 해요. 이런 일은 학생이 생각하는 것보다 더 많이 생겨요. 하지만 학생이 몰랐을 거라는 건 이해해요. 많은 학생들도 그럴 거라 생각되고요.

학생: 죄송합니다.

직원: 아, 아녜요. 미안해할 건 없고요. 그럼 학생 성적이 곧 나올 거라 생각하면 되는 거죠?

학생: 네. 사실 어제 보고서를 제출했어요. 제가 또 해야 할 게 있을까요?

직원: 아뇨, 없어요. 기다리기만 하면 돼요. 이번 주 말까지 저희가 성적을 받지 못하면, 그때 학생에게 알려줄게요.

학생: 아, 그런 일이 없기를 바라요.

🅦 receptionist [risépənist] 접수 담당자   administration office 행정실   genome [dʒíːnoum] 게놈   protein [próutiːn] 단백질   refine [rifáin] 정제하다   unattended [ʌ̀nəténdid] 지켜보는/돌보는 사람이 없는   flame [fleim] 불꽃   delay [diléi] 지연시키다

01 학생이 행정실을 찾은 이유는?
Ⓐ 자신이 왜 생물과학 수업에서 낙제를 했는지 알아보려고
Ⓑ 자신이 왜 한 수업에서 성적을 받지 못했는지 설명하려고
Ⓒ 자신이 받은 안 좋은 성적에 대해 불만을 제기하려고
Ⓓ 지난 학기의 성적 증명서를 요청하려고

02 학생의 교수에 관해 추론할 수 있는 것은?
Ⓐ 학생의 일정에 관해 알지 못한다.
Ⓑ 엉성한 연구 습관을 봐주지 않는다.
Ⓒ 학생의 상황에 관해 이해심이 많다.

Ⓓ 행정실과 관계가 나쁘다.

03 학생이 자신의 프로젝트가 실패한 이유를 설명하기 위해 제시한 이유는? (두 가지 선택)
Ⓐ 실수로 샘플을 냉장고에 넣어두었다.
Ⓑ 실험실로 가는 버스를 타지 못했다.
Ⓒ 학생이 작업했던 실험실에 불이 났다.
Ⓓ 학생이 실험실에 전화를 했을 때 아무도 전화를 받지 않았다.

04 직원이 학교 버스에 대해 암시한 것은?
Ⓐ 버스가 매일 운행되어야 한다.
Ⓑ 버스는 종종 운행 스케줄대로 도착하지 않는다.
Ⓒ 대중교통보다 훨씬 더 신뢰할 수 있다.
Ⓓ 주간 운행 스케줄이 많은 학생들에게 알려져 있지 않다.

05 직원이 다음과 같이 말할 때 암시하는 것은? ◁ **MP3 27_1**

| You mean to tell me you left a fire unattended for the whole night? |

Ⓐ 학생이 화재 위험 상황을 만들었다고 걱정한다.
Ⓑ 연구 프로젝트가 매우 힘들었을 것이라고 생각한다.
Ⓒ 밤새 불을 지켜보는 것은 지루할 것이라고 생각한다.
Ⓓ 학생이 그렇게 어리석은 실수를 해서 짜증이 났다.

06 / 기타 (Miscellaneous)

≋ Sample Questions
본문 p. 152

| 01 C 02 D 03 B 04 C 05 C |

해석 학생 활동 센터에서의 학생과 직원 간의 다음 대화를 들으시오. ◁ **MP3 28**

학생(남자): 여기가 학생 활동 센터죠?
직원(여자): 네, 무엇을 도와드릴까요?
학생: 저기, 제가 새 동아리를 만들어 보려고 하는데요. 교수님과의 대화 중에, 교수님이 제게 프랑스어 동아리를 시작해볼 것을 권유하셨어요. 그러니까, 학생들이 정기적으로 모여서 프랑스어로 말하기 연습도 하고, 기회가 되면 프랑스에서 온 교환학생들을 만날 수도 있게 말이죠. 하지만 어디서부터 시작해야 할지 모르겠어요.
직원: 음… 잘 찾아오셨어요. 좋아요. 그럼, 중요한 것부터 하죠… 먼저 리더가 필요해요. 회장이 양식을 작성해야 하고요. 누가 동아리 회장이 될 예정이죠?
학생: 제가 될 거예요. Kevin Williams요.
직원: 좋아요. 학생은 이 양식을 작성해야 할 거예요. 교수님이 동아리를 해보라고 하셨다는 말을 들으니 좋네요. 우리 위원회는 항상 교수 추천을 받은 동아리들을 먼저 심사하거든요. 그래서 그런 동아리들이 시작하기가 훨씬 쉬워요.
학생: 그거 다행이네요. 교수님께서, 프랑스어 학과에서 저희에게 전폭적인 지원을 해줄 거라고 하셨어요.
직원: 좋아요. 두 번째로 필요한 건 모임 등을 위한 장소예요. 생각해 둔 장소가 있나요?
학생: 아뇨. 여기를 통해 학교 안에 있는 장소를 하나 예약할 수 있을 거라 생각했는데요. 주간 모임을 열 수 있는 방이 있으면 정말 좋을 것 같은데요.
직원: 음… 전산을 한번 살펴볼게요… 무슨 요일에 모임을 가질 예정이죠?
학생: 금요일에 모이는 것이 가장 좋을 것 같아요. 주의 마지막 날이니까요.

직원: 이런... 금요일에는 사용 가능한 장소가 없네요. 모든 동아리가 그날 모이고 싶어 하는 것 같아요. 음... 학생의 동아리가 정기적으로 모일 수 있는 유일한 날은 월요일과 목요일이에요.

학생: 잠시만요... 월요일은 너무 힘들 것 같고... 그럼... 그러면... 아마... 목요일로 해야겠네요.

직원: 좋아요. 목요일로 장소를 예약해 둘게요... 하지만 학생의 동아리가 아직 공식적으로 등록이 되지 않았으니, 학생의 동아리에게만 독점적으로 공간을 줄 수는 없을 거예요.

학생: 잠시만요, 저는...

직원: 아, 여전히 방을 쓸 수는 있어요. 다만, 같은 시간에 모일지도 모르는 다른 동아리들과 방을 나누어 써야 할 거예요. 등록된(허가 받은) 동아리가 되려면, 제가 드린 양식을 먼저 작성하고 요청이 승인될 때까지 기다려야 할 거예요. 지금 등록이 되어 있다고 하더라도 금요일에는 예약을 할 수 없었을 거예요.

학생: 알겠습니다. 음... 방을 나누어 쓴다는 게 정확히 뭔지 모르겠네요.

직원: 음, 어떤 방들은 개인적으로 쓸 수 있어요. 한 동아리가 한 방을 쓰는 거죠. 하지만 세 개의 동아리를 위한 세 개의 개별적인 모임 공간으로 나누어 쓸 수 있는 큰 방들도 있지요.

학생: 아, 하지만 파티션이나 벽 같은 건 있겠죠?

직원: 아, 그럼요. 파티션이 몇 개 있을 거라서, 개인적인 공간이 될 거예요. 나누어 쓰는 방들도 현재 금요일은 다 찼는데, 목요일은 괜찮을 것 같아요.

학생: 좋아요, 그 정도면 될 것 같아요. 모일 장소도 없이 동아리를 시작하고 싶진 않으니까요.

직원: 좋아요. 나누어 쓰는 방을 예약하기 위해 작성해야 할 또 다른 서류들이 여기 있어요. 하지만 우선 첫 번째 양식을 먼저 작성하도록 하세요.

학생: 그럼, 저희가 등록이 되고 나면, 개별 모임 공간을 구할 수 있는 가능성이 있을까요?

직원: 음, 그건 상황에 따라 달라요. 만일 금요일에 개별 공간을 원한다면, 아마 가능성이 없을 거예요. 대기 목록이 무척 길거든요. 하지만 다른 날이라면 가능할지도 몰라요.

학생: 알겠습니다. 내일 서류들을 다시 가져올게요. 도와주셔서 감사합니다.

Ⓦ on a regular basis 정기적으로   exchange student 교환학생   committee [kəmíti] 위원회   review [rivjúː] 검토하다   officially [ɔ(ː)fíʃəli] 공식적으로   register [rédʒistər] 등록하다   private [práivit] 개인 소유의   divider [diváidər] 칸막이

01 학생이 직원을 찾아간 이유는?
Ⓐ 동아리에 가입하는 것에 대해 알아보려고
Ⓑ 프랑스어 수업에 대해 문의하려고
Ⓒ 새 동아리를 시작하는 데 도움을 얻으려고
Ⓓ 교수님의 사무실이 어디인지 문의하려고

02 교수의 지원을 받는 동아리들에 대해 직원이 이야기한 것은?
Ⓐ 교수의 서명이 있는 편지를 가져와야 한다.
Ⓑ 학교에서 전액 지원을 받을 자격이 된다.
Ⓒ 미리 방을 예약할 필요가 없다.
Ⓓ 다른 동아리들에 비해 더 쉽게 승인을 받는 경향이 있다.

03 나누어 쓰는 방을 사용하는 것에 대한 학생의 태도는?
Ⓐ 다른 동아리들에 대해 아는 데 도움이 될 것이라 생각한다.
Ⓑ 수용 가능한 대안이라고 생각한다.
Ⓒ 동아리 멤버들이 좋아하지 않을까 봐 걱정한다.
Ⓓ 그 방들이 더 크기 때문에 그것에 열성적이다.

04 직원에 따르면, 학생이 개별 공간을 쓸 수 없는 이유는?
Ⓐ 학생의 동아리에 회원이 너무 많다.
Ⓑ 학생이 주말에 모임을 하고 싶어 한다.
Ⓒ 학생의 동아리는 승인을 받지 않았다.
Ⓓ 많은 동아리들이 금요일에 모인다.

05 학생이 다음에 할 일은?
Ⓐ 그의 교수에게 편지 요청하기

Ⓑ 모임 장소 예약을 재확인하기
Ⓒ 몇 가지의 신청서 작성하기
Ⓓ 위원회에게 자신의 등록 신청을 검토해달라고 부탁하기

⇘ Practice Questions
본문 p. 156

| 01 D | 02 B | 03 C | 04 A, D | 05 B, C |

Introduction

Listen to a conversation between a student and an employee in the university bookstore. ◁ MP3 29

Employee(male): Hi, what can I help you with today?

Student(female): Hi, um, I wanted to see if, um, ▶Q1◀ you would buy this vase from me?

E: Excuse me?

S: Well, um, is it possible for the bookstore to purchase a vase I made in class? You know, to sell to other students?

E: Uh… Well… I don't think we can purchase products that are made by students. We can only resell things we get from one of our designated wholesalers. ▶Q2◀ If we were to buy this vase from you, then what's to stop other students from trying to sell their things to us?

S: Um… Couldn't you just only do this for me as a one-time deal? I promise I won't ever ask again.

E: I'm sorry, but if we buy something from you, then another student will ask, and another… You see my point, right? If we say yes to you, then we have to say yes to everyone.

Cause
자신이 만든 작품을 파는 것이 과제임

S: (Sigh) I see your point. Well, the thing is, it wasn't my idea to sell this… ▶Q1◀ I'm an art major, and my sculpting professor gave us an assignment to sell an item we made in class. He told us that we have to be confident enough to sell what we make to anyone, but this is a little bit too much for me.

E: Oh… That must be tough. Let's see… Did you try selling it online? I mean, a lot of people auction things off on the Internet. I'm sure you'd be able to find a buyer that way.

S: Unfortunately, I don't know much about computers. I mean, I'm really horrible with computers. I wouldn't know where to start. Even if I could somehow post this online, I wouldn't know how to ship it. It's really fragile, you know? What if it breaks on the way there?

Suggestion
위탁 판매를 제안

E: Hmm… You have a point… Hey! ▶Q4◀ What about selling it on consignment?

S: On consignment? You mean you'd display it in the bookstore and take a commission if it sells?

E: Well, not here. But I know a place downtown that sells crafts… It's called… uh… Emporium. Yeah, that's right. You can ask them to display it for you. If a customer likes your vase and buys it, they'll take a cut. If it doesn't sell… well… they'll ask you to take it back.

Attitude – Worry About
아무도 사가지 않을까 염려함

S: Oh… ▶Q3◀ ▶Q4-A◀ I don't know if I can do that… I mean, if nobody liked what I made… I'd be crushed… I'm too scared to leave it there. And besides, ▶Q4-D◀ there's no way to take this vase downtown. I don't own a car, and it's too heavy for me to

Suggestion
town fair에서 팔아볼 것을 제안

Attitude
❯ positive

Requirement
form만 작성하면 됨

carry it on a bus.

E: Hmm… I just thought of something else. Q5 **What about the town fair?** It takes place next weekend. I mean, there's going to be an open market for people like you who want to sell what they made.

S: Q5-C **That sounds like a great idea.** I didn't even know there would be an open market. So what do I have to do?

E: I think you have to call City Hall to get the details, but one of my friends said that she only had to fill out a form with what she was going to sell. They took care of the rest. Hey, they might even send some people to help carry the vase to the market. Since you don't have a car and all…

S: Wow, thank you so much… but… Q5-B **I do have a lot to do… I can't just sit around all day and wait until someone buys this…** Hmm… I guess I'll just have to do my work while I'm at the market.

해석 대학 서점에서의 학생과 직원 간의 다음 대화를 들으시오.

직원(남자): 안녕하세요, 무엇을 도와드릴까요?

학생(여자): 안녕하세요. 음, 혹시 서점에서 제 꽃병을 사주실 수 있을까 해서요.

직원: 뭐라고요?

학생: 저기, 음, 제가 수업시간에 만든 꽃병을 서점에서 사주실 수 있을까요? 그러니까, 다른 학생들에게 판매하도록요.

직원: 음… 그게… 저희는 학생들이 만든 제품을 구매할 수 없어요. 저희는 지정된 도매업체들 중 한 곳에서 받은 물건들만 다시 팔 수 있거든요. 저희가 학생으로부터 이 꽃병을 산다면, 다른 학생들 역시 저희에게 물건을 판매하려는 걸 저희가 어떻게 막겠어요?

학생: 음… 저를 위해 이번 한 번만 그렇게 해주시면 안될까요? 다시는 부탁 드리지 않는다고 약속할게요.

직원: 죄송해요. 하지만 저희가 학생으로부터 무언가 사게 되면, 다른 학생, 또 다른 학생이 계속 그런 요구를 해올 거예요… 제 말 이해하시겠죠? 지금 학생의 요청을 수락한다면, 모두의 요청을 수락해야 하잖아요.

학생: (한숨) 무슨 말씀이신지 알겠어요. 사실은… 이걸 판매하는 건 제 생각이 아니었어요… 저는 미술 전공 학생인데, 조각 교수님께서 저희에게 수업시간에 만든 것을 판매해보라는 과제를 내주셨어요. 교수님은 저희가 만든 것을 누구에게든 팔 수 있을 만큼 저희가 자신감이 있어야 한다고 하셨는데, 이건 제게 너무 힘이 드네요.

직원: 아… 그거 정말 힘들겠네요. 어디 보죠… 인터넷으로 파는 건 시도해봤어요? 그러니까, 많은 사람들이 인터넷에 물건들을 경매로 내놓잖아요. 그런 식으로 구매자를 구할 수 있을 것 같은데요.

학생: 불행히도, 제가 컴퓨터에 대해 잘 모르거든요. 제 말은, 저는 컴퓨터에 정말 서툴러요. 어디서부터 시작해야 할지 모르겠어요. 제가 어떻게든 이걸 인터넷에 올린다 하더라도, 어떻게 배송을 해야 할지도 모르고요. 아시다시피, 정말 깨지기 쉽잖아요. 배송되는 도중에 깨지기라도 하면 어떡하죠?

직원: 음… 일리가 있네요. 아! 위탁 판매를 해보는 건 어때요?

학생: 위탁 판매요? 서점에 제 물건을 진열하고, 물건이 팔리면 수수료를 받아가시겠다는 건가요?

직원: 음, 저희가 아니고요. 하지만 시내에 공예품을 파는 장소를 한 군데 알아요… 거기 이름이… 음… Emporium이에요. 그래요, 맞아요. 거기에 학생의 꽃병을 진열해달라고 부탁하면 돼요. 손님이 학생의 꽃병이 마음에 들어 구매하게 되면, 거기서 자기 몫을 제할 거예요. 팔리지 않으면… 음… 학생에게 도로 가져가라고 할 거고요.

학생: 아… 제가 그렇게 할 수 있을지 모르겠네요… 그러니까 제 말은, 만일 아무도 제가 만든 것을 좋아하지 않으면… 전 완전히 좌절하게 될 거예요… 무서워서 꽃병을 맡길 수가 없을 것 같아요. 게다가, 이 꽃병을 시내까지 가져갈 방법이 없어요. 저는 차가 없는데다, 버스로 옮기기에는 너무 무겁거든요.

직원: 음… 방금 다른 생각이 났어요. 시 박람회는 어때요? 다음 주말에 열릴 예정인데요. 그러니까, 학생처럼 자기가 만든 것들을 팔고 싶어하는 사람들을 위해 열리는 장터가 있을 거예요.

학생: 그거 좋은 생각 같네요. 열린 장터가 있을 거라는 건 몰랐어요. 그럼 제가 뭘 해야 할까요?

직원: 자세한 정보를 구하려면 시청에 전화를 해야 하겠지만, 제 친구 말에 의하면, 무엇을 팔 예정인지에 대해 서류만 작성하면 됐다고 해요. 그들이 나머지를 다 처리해줬고요. 있죠, 아마 꽃병을 장터까지 옮겨줄 사람들을 보내줄지도 몰라요. 학생이 차가 없고 하니까…

학생: 와, 정말 고맙습니다… 하지만… 할 게 많아서… 하루 종일 앉아서 누군가 이걸 사가기를 기다릴 수가 없는데… 음… 장터에 앉아 있는 동안 작업을 해야 할 수 밖에 없겠네요.

Ⓦ designated [dézigneitid] 지정된   wholesaler [hóulsèilər] 도매업자   auction off 경매로 처분하다   ship [ʃip] 배송하다   fragile [frǽdʒəl] 깨지기 쉬운   on consignment 위탁 판매로   display [displéi] 전시하다   commission [kəmíʃən] 수수료   craft [kræft] 공예   take a cut 몫을 가져가다   crushed [krʌʃt] 짓밟힌 기분이 드는   fair [fɛər] 축제 마당   open market 열린 장터

01 학생이 직원의 도움을 필요로 하는 이유는?
Ⓐ 꽃병을 어디에서 구입해야 하는지 모른다.
Ⓑ 지역의 공예품 가게를 찾으려 애쓰는 중이다.
Ⓒ 자신의 과제가 무엇인지 알아내야 한다.
Ⓓ 자신이 만든 제품을 어떻게 팔아야 할지 모른다.

02 자신의 물품을 대학 서점에서 판매하려 하는 학생들에 대해 추론할 수 있는 것은?
Ⓐ 과제의 일부로 한 가지 품목을 판매해야 한다.
Ⓑ 부탁해도 된다는 것을 알면 자신의 물품들을 가게에 팔아달라고 부탁할 것이다.
Ⓒ 기꺼이 적은 금액의 돈을 받으려 할 것이다.
Ⓓ 도매업자들이 판매한 물품들만 팔 수 있다.

03 자신의 과제에 대한 학생의 태도는?
Ⓐ 컴퓨터를 쓸 수 없는 학생들에게는 불공평하다고 느낀다.
Ⓑ 자신의 꽃병을 판매할 방법을 찾을 수 있다고 낙관하고 있다.
Ⓒ 자신의 꽃병을 구매할 사람을 찾을 수 있을 거라고 자신하지 않는다.
Ⓓ 같은 수업을 듣는 친구들이 만든 꽃병보다 자신이 만든 것이 더 빨리 판매될 것이라 생각한다.

04 학생이 꽃병을 위탁 판매 하고 싶어 하지 않는 두 가지 이유는? (두 가지 선택)
Ⓐ 자신의 작품에 자신이 없다.
Ⓑ 컴퓨터를 사용하는 법을 모른다.
Ⓒ 해야 할 학교 공부가 너무 많다.
Ⓓ 마땅한 운송 수단이 없다.

05 시 박람회와 관련해 직원이 준 정보에 대해 학생이 보이는 반응은? (두 가지 선택)
Ⓐ 자신이 먼저 그 생각을 하지 못해서 부끄러워한다.
Ⓑ 박람회 기간 동안 학교 공부로 너무 바쁠 것이라고 생각한다.
Ⓒ 자신의 과제를 마칠 수 있는 방법이 있어 감사해한다.
Ⓓ 꽃병을 장터까지 가지고 갈 수 있다고 확신한다.

Chapter 3. Lecture Question Types

Practice Questions I

본문 p. 178 ~ 181

| 01 C | 02 A | 03 D | 04 B | 05 C | 06 D | 07 C | 08 A | 09 C, E | 10 B | 11 A |

[01 ~ 06] Listen to part of a lecture in a business class. 🔊 MP3 30

Professor(male): During our last class we talked about sole proprietorship, which is, as I'm sure you remember, a business with a single owner. **Q1 In this class, let's discuss partnerships, a business ownership model that involves two or more co-owners who share the profits and the losses.** The most basic partnership structure is called the standard partnership. In this structure, each owner can act on behalf of the business – they can open a bank account, buy assets, conduct everyday business, and whatnot for the partnership. One of the advantages is that the partners can help each other run the business. **Q2 But it can also be very risky because one partner does not have to consult with the other when making decisions.** So, it goes without saying that it's important to really trust your partner. There's also another type of partnership known as a 'limited partnership,' but we'll talk more about it later.

We also have to keep in mind that **Q3 all partners are held accountable for the partnership's debts in standard partnerships**. This means that every partner is personally liable for these debts. Their own house, money, and whatever personal assets they hold can be taken to pay any debts that the partnership cannot cover. This applies to situations where another partner's actions put the company in debt. **Q3 Let's say that you created a partnership that manufactures doors. If your partner goes out and buys a lot of wood on credit, you're just as responsible for paying for the wood as your partner is.** If you make doors with the wood and sell them to a builder, and then the builder goes out of business before paying you for the doors… Well, you still have to pay for the wood, even though it was bought by your partner. And if the business fails, you are legally responsible to pay off any debt.

However, it's not like partners can do anything they want. **Q4 There are a small number of activities that require the approval of all partners. For example, a partner can't just sell the business.** 🎧 **Q6 There are other transactions that need partner's approval, but you can just consult your textbook if you're interested in what they are.**

As I mentioned earlier, the other type of partnership, a limited partnership, is different from a standard partnership. For starters, there are two different types of partners. One type is called a general partner – these partners are in charge of running the business and share in its profits and losses. They are essentially like partners in a standard partnership. General partners are also personally liable. The other type is a limited partner. These partners invest money into the business but cannot participate in its operation. They share profits, but if the business loses money, their personal assets are protected. They can only lose the money they put into the business. **Q5 Now, is one type of partnership better than the other? Well, it all comes down to what's needed.** Sometime the benefits of being free to act on behalf of the business outweigh the risks. However, except for a limited number of specific businesses, I would actually prefer a limited liability partnership. We'll start discussing what that is next week.

해석 경제학 수업의 다음 강의 일부분을 들으시오.

교수(남자): 지난 시간에는 개인 기업, 그러니까, 여러분이 기억할 것이라 생각하는데, 소유주가 한 명인 기업을 말하죠. 그것에 대해 이야기했습니다. 오늘 수업에서는 동업, 즉 이익과 손실을 공유하는 두 명 이상의 공동 소유자를 포함하는 사업 소유 모델에 대해 이야기해보죠. 가장 기본적인 동업 구조는 무한 책임 회사라고 불립니다. 이 구조에서는 각각의 소유자가 회사를 대표하여 행동을 취할 수 있습니다. 즉, 그들은 은행 계좌를 개설하고, 자산을 구입하고, 매일 매일의 일을 수행하고, 동업을 위해 이런 저런 일들을 할 수 있습니다. 이 모델의 장점 중 하나는 동업자들이 사업을 운영하는 데 있어 서로서로를 도울 수 있다는 점이지요. 하지만 이 모델은 한 동업자가 결정을 내릴 때 다른 동업자와 협의를 할 필요가 없기 때문에 매우 위험할 수도 있습니다. 그래서, 상대 동업자를 진실로 신뢰하는 것이 중요한 것은 말할 필요도 없지요. '유한 책임 회사'라고 알려진 또 다른 유형의 동업도 있는데, 그것에 대해서는 나중에 다루도록 하지요.

우리는 또한 무한 책임 회사에서는 모든 동업자들에게 동업에 얽힌 빚에 대한 책임이 지워진다는 것을 명심해야 합니다. 이 말은 즉, 모든 동업자들이 개인적으로 이러한 빚을 지불할 의무가 있다는 뜻입니다. 그들이 보유하고 있는 개인의 집, 돈, 그리고 어떠한 개인적 자산이든, 동업에 의해 감당할 수 없는 어떤 종류의 빚이라도 그 빚을 지불하기 위해 뺏길 수도 있습니다. 여러분이 문을 제조하는 동업을 시작했다고 해봅시다. 여러분의 동업자가 나가서 외상으로 목재를 많이 사게 되면, 여러분도 그 동업자와 마찬가지로 그 목재에 대해 비용을 지불할 책임을 똑같이 갖게 됩니다. 그 목재로 문을 만들어서 건축 회사에 판매한다면, 그리고 나서 그 건축 회사가 여러분에게 문 대금을 지급하기 전에 파산을 한다면... 음, 여러분은 여전히 그 목재 비용을 지불해야 하지요. 비록 동업자가 목재를 사기는 했지만 말이죠. 그리고 사업이 실패하게 되면, 여러분은 어떠한 빚이라도 갚아야 할 법률상의 책임을 지게 됩니다.

하지만, 동업자들이 자신들이 원하는 대로 아무거나 할 수 있는 것은 아닙니다. 모든 동업자들의 승인을 필요로 하는 몇 가지 활동들이 있지요. 예를 들어, 동업자 혼자서는 회사를 매각할 수 없습니다. 동업자의 승인을 필요로 하는 다른 거래들이 있지만, 그것들이 어떤 것들인지 관심이 있다면 교과서를 살펴보도록 하세요.

앞서 언급했던 것처럼, 다른 종류의 동업인 유한 책임 회사는, 무한 책임 회사와는 다릅니다. 우선, 동업자의 두 가지 다른 유형이 있습니다. 한 가지 유형은 무한 책임 사원이라고 불립니다. 이런 동업자들은 사업을 운영하는 것을 담당하고 손익을 서로 나누어 갖습니다. 그들은 본질적으로는 무한 책임 회사의 파트너들과 같습니다. 무한 책임 사원들은 또한 개인적으로 법적 책임을 집니다. 다른 유형은 유한 책임 사원입니다. 이런 동업자들은 사업에 자금을 투자하지만 그 운영에는 참여하지 않습니다. 그들은 이익은 나누지만, 회사가 금전적 손실을 보게 되면 유한 책임 사원들의 자산은 보호받습니다. 그들은 사업에 투자한 돈을 잃을 뿐입니다. 자, 어느 한 유형의 동업이 다른 유형보다 나은가요? 음, 그건 결국 무엇이 필요한지에 귀결됩니다. 가끔은 회사를 대표해 자유롭게 활동하는 이점이 위험보다 더 큽니다. 하지만, 제한된 수의 특정 회사들을 제외하고서는, 나라면 사실 유한 책임 동업을 선호할 겁니다. 그게 무엇인지 다음 주에 다뤄보도록 하지요.

Ⓦ sole proprietorship 개인 기업, 개인 사무소   partnership [pάːrtnərʃip] 동업   profit [prάfit] 이익, 수익   on behalf of ~ ...을 대표하여   asset [ǽset] 자산   whatnot [hwάtnɑːt] ...인가 원가(부정확한 것을 말할 때 사용)   consult with ~ ...와 협의하다   it goes without saying that ~ ...은 말할 나위도 없다   hold someone accountable for A ...에게 A의 책임을 지우다[묻다]   debt [det] 빚   be liable for A A의 지불 의무가 있다   manufacture [mæ̀njufǽktʃər] 제조[생산]하다   on credit 외상으로, 신용 대출로   go out of business 폐업하다   legally [líːɡəli] 법률상   approval [əprúːvəl] 승인   transaction [trænsǽkʃən] 거래, 매매, 처리   consult [kənsʌ́lt] (정보를 얻기 위해 무엇을) 찾아보다, 참고하다   in charge of ~ ...을 맡아서[담당해서]   share in ~ ...을 서로 나누다   come down to ~ 결국 ...이 되다   outweigh [autwéi] ...보다 더 크다   limited liability (부채에 대한) 유한 책임

01 강의의 주된 내용은?
Ⓐ 기반이 탄탄한 회사를 구입하는 것을 위한 가이드라인
Ⓑ 여러 동업자들을 회사에 투자하도록 하는 것의 이점
Ⓒ 한 회사 내에서 공동 소유자들이 책임을 지는 다양한 방법
Ⓓ 재정적 손실과 파산을 피하기 위한 방법에 대한 사업적 조언

02 무한 책임 회사의 위험한 면은?
Ⓐ 한 명의 동업자가 논의 없이 결정을 내릴 수 있다.
Ⓑ 은행 대출로 인해 회사 소유자들이 빨리 수익을 내야 할지도 모른다.
Ⓒ 한 명의 소유자가 자신이 주장한 것보다 경험이 부족할 수 있다.
Ⓓ 일부 투자자들이 사업을 너무 빨리 확장하기를 바랄 수도 있다.

03 교수가 문 제조 회사를 언급한 이유는?
Ⓐ 현지 회사들이 왜 서로 거래를 해야 하는지를 설명하려고
Ⓑ 한 회사가 어떻게 튼튼한 단골 고객 기반을 구축하는지를 보여주려고
Ⓒ 형편 없는 계획으로 인해 실패한 회사의 예를 제시하려고
Ⓓ 각자 회사의 빚을 지불하도록 요구 받는다는 것을 강조하려고

04 강의에 의하면, 무한 책임 회사를 매각하는 데 필요한 것은 무엇인가?
Ⓐ 각 동업자가 각자의 원래 투자금 전액을 받아야 한다.
Ⓑ 모든 동업자들이 (매각) 거래를 하도록 동의해야 한다.
Ⓒ 동업자 중의 하나가 회사에 남아야 한다.
Ⓓ 채권자에게 회사가 빚진 모든 것이 지불되어야 한다.

05 동업에 대한 교수의 의견은?
Ⓐ 개인들은 동업에 참여해서는 안 된다.
Ⓑ 다른 소유 모델에 비해 덜 위험하다.
Ⓒ 올바른 종류(의 동업)는 특정 상황에 달려 있다.
Ⓓ 무한 책임 동업자가 되는 것이 유한 책임 동업자가 되는 것보다 더 낫다.

06 교수가 다음과 같이 말했을 때 의미하는 것은? 🔊 MP3 30_1

> There are other transactions that need partner's approval, but you can just consult your textbook if you're interested in what they are.

Ⓐ 교수는 동업자들로부터 승인을 받는 것의 중요성을 강조하고 싶어한다.
Ⓑ 교수는 동업자들은 상대가 무엇을 하고 있는지를 알고 있어야 한다고 생각한다.
Ⓒ 교수는 학생들이 수업 전에 교과서를 읽어오기를 바란다.
Ⓓ 교수는 승인이 필요한 거래에 대해 이야기하는 데 시간을 할애하고 싶어하지 않는다.

[07 ~ 11] Listen to part of a lecture in a geology class. 🔊 MP3 31

Professor(female): So, we've been discussing deserts for the past week. In our previous discussion, we defined a desert as being any region that has less than 25 centimeters of rain per year. Temperatures also play a role in defining what a desert is. Desert temperatures fluctuate greatly from very high during the day to very cold at night. This has to do with the dry desert air. We also talked about how wind contributes to the formation of deserts, and, um, today ▶Q7◀ **I want to talk about another way the wind affects the deserts – the formation of sand dunes.**

Sand dunes are formed when the wind moves grains of sand, slowly creating the hilly features that are a common sight in deserts. There are two ways that dunes are created. ▶Q8◀ **The first is called saltation. This is a process in which the wind lifts sand grains into the air and carries them for a short distance before gravity pulls them down.** Now the second way the wind moves the sand is through a process called creep. When the wind drops the sand grains, the force of the sand that hits the ground pushes other sand grains forward. When there's an obstacle, such as a rock or a plant, the sand piles up on the downwind side. As more wind blows, the dunes grow in height, and as the dune moves around the obstacle even more grains are moved. Um... ▶Q11◀ **An example of a similar phenomenon can be seen after a snowstorm. Snowdrifts form when the blowing snow is stopped by an obstacle such as a car or a fence.** The more snow that gets blown towards the obstacle, the higher the snowdrift will be.

▶Q9-E◀ **When the dune reaches a certain size, it begins to move downwind.** Some dunes move as much as 35 meters per year. Generally, smaller dunes will move faster than larger ones because, well, there's just not as much sand to move. ▶Q9-C◀ **The wind gives all dunes an asymmetrical shape when viewed from the side.** The side that faces the wind is always longer and is less steep than the other side. Sand dunes can also vary in shape when looked at from above. Some dunes are curved, while others are straighter and look like ridges. ▶Q10◀ **One classic shape can be observed in the barchan dune. This dune, which is created when wind constantly blows from one direction only,** has a crescent shape.

해석 지질학 수업의 다음 강의 일부분을 들으시오.

교수(여자): 자, 지난 주에는 사막들에 대해 논의를 했습니다. 지난 논의에서 우리는 사막을 일년에 비가 25센티미터 이하로 오는 지역으로 정의 내렸습니다. 기온 역시 사막이 무엇인지를 정의 내리는 데 역할을 합니다. 사막의 기온은 낮 동안에 매우 높은 것부터 밤에는 매우 낮은 것까지 엄청나게 오르락내리락 합니다. 이것은 건조한 사막 공기와 관련이 있습니다. 우리는 또한 바람이 어떻게 사막의 형성에 기여하는지에 대해 이야기를 하기도 했었죠. 그리고, 음, 오늘은 바람이 사막에 영향을 미치는 또 다른 방식에 대해 이야기하고자 합니다. 바로 사구의 형성입니다. 사구는 바람이 모래 알갱이들을 움직여, 사막에서 흔히 보이는 광경인 언덕 모양을 천천히 만들어낼 때 형성됩니다. 사구가 만들어지는 방식에는 두 가지가 있습니다. 첫 번째는 도약(saltation)이라고 불립니다. 이것은 바람이 모래 알갱이들을 공중으로 들어올려, 중력에 의해 떨어지기 전에 짧은 거리를 이동시키는 과정입니다. 자, 바람이 모래를 옮기는 두 번째 방식은, 포행(creep)이라고 불리는 과정을 통해서입니다. 바람이 모래 알갱이들을 떨어뜨릴 때, 땅을 치는 모래의 힘이 다른 모래 알갱이들을 앞으로 밀어내게 됩니다. 바위나 식물과 같은 장애물이 있을 때는, 모래는 바람이 부는 쪽으로 쌓이게 됩니다. 바람이 더 불면서, 사구의 높이는 높아지고, 사구가 그 장애물 주위로 움직임에 따라 더 많은 모래 알갱이들이 움직이죠. 음... 비슷한 현상의 예는 눈보라 후에 볼 수 있겠군요. 날리고 있는 눈이 차나 담장과 같은 장애물에 의해 저지되었을 때 눈더미들이 형성되지요. 그 장애물 쪽으로 더 많은 눈이 날려올수록, 그 눈더미는 더 높아질 것입니다.

사구는 일정 크기에 다다르면, 바람이 부는 방향으로 움직이기 시작합니다. 어떤 사구들은 일년에 35미터만큼이나 움직이기도 합니다. 일반적으로는, 작은 사구들이 큰 사구들보다 더 빨리 움직이는데, 왜냐하면, 음, 움직일 모래가 그만큼 많지 않기 때문입니다. 바람은, 옆에서 봤을 때 모든 사구로 하여금 비대칭적인 모양을 갖게 합니다. 바람을 마주하는 면이 항상 반대 쪽보다 더 길고 경사가 덜합니다. 사구들은 또한 위에서 봤을 때 다양한 모양을 갖고 있기도 합니다. 어떤 사구들은 휘어진 모양인 반면, 또 어떤 사구들은 좀 더 일직선 모양에 산등성이 같이 보이기도 합니다. 한가지 전형적인 (사구의) 형태는 바르칸형 사구(barchan dune)에서 관찰할 수 있습니다. 바람이 끊임없이 한 방향에서만 불어올 때 형성되는 이 사구는, 초승달 모양을 하고 있습니다.

W fluctuate [flʌ́ktʃueit] 변동[등락]을 거듭하다   contribute [kəntríbjuːt] 기여하다, 이바지하다   sand dune 사구, 모래언덕   grain [grein] 알갱이   gravity [ɡrǽvəti] 중력   obstacle [ábstəkl] 장애물   phenomenon [finámənàn] 현상   snowdrift [snóudrìft] 바람에 날려 쌓인 눈더미   downwind [daunwind] 바람을 타고, 바람 부는 방향으로   asymmetrical [èisəmétrikəl] 비대칭의   ridge [ridʒ] 산등성이   steep [stiːp] 가파른, 비탈진   crescent [krésnt] 초승달 모양

07 강의의 주된 내용은?
Ⓐ 암석층이 모래로 부서지는 것
Ⓑ 바람의 시스템에 의한 사막 형성
Ⓒ 사구가 만들어지는 과정들
Ⓓ 사막에 있는 사구의 특징들

08 도약(saltation) 과정은 무엇인가?
Ⓐ 바람으로 인해 모래 알갱이가 짧은 거리를 이동한다.
Ⓑ 식물과 바위가 그것들 주위로 사구가 나뉘어지도록 만든다.
Ⓒ 사구가 사막 표면에 걸쳐 차츰 평평해진다.
Ⓓ 모래 알갱이들이 땅을 쳐서 다른 모래 알갱이들을 앞으로 밀어낸다.

09 교수에 의하면, 사구의 두 가지 특성은 무엇인가? (두 가지 선택)
Ⓐ 사구의 무게가 그 형태를 바뀌도록 만든다.
Ⓑ 바람이 사구를 밀어내면 바람을 거슬러 움직인다.
Ⓒ 옆면들은 균형이 맞지 않게 형성된다.
Ⓓ 모양들이 대칭적이다.
Ⓔ 한 장소에 머무르지 않는다.

10 교수에 의하면, 바르칸형 사구를 형성하도록 만드는 것은 무엇인가?
Ⓐ 어떤 장애물에서 바람 방향으로 쌓이는 모래
Ⓑ 한 방향에서만 불어오는 바람
Ⓒ 서서히 합쳐지는 길고 깊은 모래 더미들
Ⓓ 바람에 의해 깎여 나가고 있는 사막의 능선들

11 교수가 눈보라를 언급한 이유는?
Ⓐ 비슷한 과정을 언급하려고
Ⓑ 모래 폭풍이 어떻게 형성되는지 설명하려고
Ⓒ 사막의 기후가 어떻게 바뀌는지 보여주려고
Ⓓ 사구가 흔하지 않다는 것을 암시하려고

Practice Questions II

본문 p. 200 ~ 203

| 01 A | 02 C | 03 A | 04 B | 05 D | 06 E | 07 C | 08 A, C | 09 A | 10 C |

[01 ~ 05] Listen to part of a lecture in a biology class. ◁ MP3 32

Professsor(female): Today let's take a look at one way animals form their eating habits. **Q1** I'll start off with **a story about my brother James.** When he was about six years old, he had some peanuts during an airplane flight. But shortly after he ate them, he became airsick. Since that time he has refused to eat peanuts. He knows that it wasn't the peanuts that made him sick, but he still doesn't eat them today. **Q1** What my **brother experienced was a phenomenon known as conditioned taste aversion.** **Q3** This phenomenon is related to the way people associate nausea, or other illnesses, with the taste of a food they ate around the same time. The associated food is then avoided, often forever. The thing is, conditioned taste aversion also occurs in animals. If a wild animal that eats spoiled or poisoned food becomes ill but survives, it will refuse to eat that kind of food again. A Russian psychologist, **Q4** Ivan Pavlov, laid the foundation for this area of research. You might have heard of him. He's the one who experimented with dogs that learned to associate the sound of a bell with food, which is another type of biologically-based learning.

So, what makes animals avoid certain foods this way? What happens inside the brain? Well, evidence suggests a specific part in the brain keeps track of these taste aversions: **Q2** the insular cortex. This is the part of the brain that is used by animals to control physical motions and perceive different degrees of pain. In an experiment with rats, the rats with a damaged insular cortex could not form taste aversions.

Scientists have used their knowledge of conditioned taste aversions to keep wild predators away from livestock. In one case, lithium was injected into sheep carcasses. When wolves that lived nearby ate this meat, the lithium made them nauseous and dizzy. Afterwards, the wolves refused to eat the meat of other sheep, even when it hadn't been injected with anything. Even though it was the lithium that made the wolves sick, the wolves associated their sickness with sheep meat. It may seem cruel, but it's a good alternative to killing them.

These studies have led to further investigations in regards to how animals communicate about food aversions. **Q5** In another study, a coyote that ate part of a rabbit injected with lithium covered the remaining meat with dirt. Scientists speculate that covering the carcass was a way of alerting other coyotes that the meat was bad.

해석 생물학 수업의 다음 강의 일부분을 들으시오.

교수(여자): 오늘은 동물들이 식습관을 형성하는 하나의 방식을 살펴보도록 합시다. 제 남동생 James에 대한 이야기로 시작할게요. 그가 여섯 살 무렵이었을 때, 그는 비행기를 타던 중에 땅콩을 좀 먹었습니다. 하지만 땅콩을 먹자마자, 그는 비행기 멀미를 하게 되었습니다. 그 때 이후로, 그는 땅콩 먹는 것을 거부해왔지요. 그는 아팠던 것이 땅콩 때문이 아니었다는 것을 알지만, 요즈음 여전히 땅콩을 먹지 않습니다. 내 남동생이 경험한 것은 조건부 맛 기피라고 알려진 현상입니다. 이 현상은 사람들이 메스꺼움이나 다른 질병들을 같은 시기에 먹었던 음식의 맛과 결부시키는 방식과 관련이 있습니다. 그리고 나서 결부된 음식을 피하게 되고, 종종 평생 피하게 되지요. 조건부 맛 기피는 동물에게도 일어납니다. 상하거나 독이 든 음식을 먹은 야생 동물이 병이 났다가 살아 남게 되면, 그 동물은 그런 종류의 음식을 다시는 먹지 않으려 합니다. 러시아의 심리학자 Ivan Pavlov는 이런 연구 분야의 토대를 놓았지요. 여러분은 아마도 그의 이름을 들어본 적이 있을 것입니다. 그는 종 소리를 음식에 결부시키는 법을 배우게 된 개들을 가지고 실험을 한 사람인데요, 그것은 생물학에 바탕을 둔 또 다른 학습 유형입니다.

자, 무엇이 동물들로 하여금 특정한 음식을 이런 식으로 피하게 만드는 것일까요? 그 동물들의 뇌 속에서는 무슨 일이 일어나는 걸까요? 음, 뇌의 특정 부분이 계속해서 이러한 맛 기피 현상을 유지하도록 한다는 증거가 있습니다. 바로 섬피질이지요. 이곳은 동물들이 몸의 움직임을 조절하고 여러 다른 정도의 고통을 인지하는 데 사용되는 뇌의 부분입니다. 쥐를 상대로 한 어떤 실험에서, 섬피질에 손상을 입은 쥐들은 맛 기피를 형성하지 못했습니다.

과학자들은 포식동물들을 가축으로부터 떼어 놓기 위해 조건부 맛 기피에 대한 지식을 이용했습니다. 한 경우에는, 리튬이 양의 사체에 주입되었습니다. 근처에 사는 늑대들이 이 고기를 먹었을 때, 리튬이 그 늑대들로 하여금 메스껍고 어지럽게 만들었지요. 그 후로, 그 늑대들은 다른 양의 고기를 먹는 것을 거부했습니다. 아무것도 주입되지 않았는데도 말이지요. 늑대들을 아프게 만든 것은 리튬이었지만, 늑대들은 그 질병을 양고기에 결부시켜 생각했습니다. 좀 잔인하게 보일 수는 있겠지만, 늑대들을 죽이는 것에 대한 좋은 대안이었지요.

이런 연구들은 동물들이 음식 기피에 대해 어떻게 의사소통하는지에 관해 더 깊은 연구를 이끌었습니다. 또 다른 연구에서는, 리튬이 주입된 토끼의 일부를 먹은 코요테 한 마리가 남은 고기를 흙으로 덮어버렸습니다. 과학자들은 (토끼의) 사체를 덮어버린 것이 다른 코요테들에게 그 고기가 상했다는 것을 경고하기 위한 하나의 방법이라고 추측합니다.

W airsick [ɛərsik] 비행기 멀미를 하는 phenomenon [finámənàn] 현상 conditioned taste aversion 조건부 맛 기피 associate A with B A를 B와 관련시켜 생각하다 nausea [nɔ́ːziə] 메스꺼움 spoil [spɔil] 상하다 keep track of ~ ~을 파악하고[계속 알고] 있다 insular cortex 섬피질 predator [prédətər] 포식 동물 livestock [laivztɑːk] 가축 lithium [líθiəm] 리튬 inject [indʒékt] 주사하다, 주입하다 carcass [kàːrkəs] (큰 동물의) 시체 alternative [ɔːltə́ːrnətiv] 대안, 선택 가능한 것 investigation [invèstəgéiʃən] 연구, 조사 dirt [dəːrt] 흙 speculate [spékjulèit] 추측하다, 짐작하다 alert [ələ́ːrt] (위험을) 알리다

01 교수가 자신의 남동생에 대한 이야기를 한 이유는?
- **(A) 나쁜 경험이 어떻게 음식과 결부될 수 있는지 예를 들려고**
- (B) 한 심리학자의 연구 결과의 중요성을 강조하려고
- (C) 특정 음식들이 어떻게 사람들로 하여금 자신이 아프다고 생각하게 만드는지 보여주려고
- (D) 뇌 손상이 어떻게 미각에 영향을 미치는지 설명하려고

02 섬피질에 대해 교수가 이야기한 것은?
- (A) 체온을 조절한다.
- (B) 음식의 맛을 보기 위해 필요하다.
- **(C) 신체 움직임을 조절한다.**
- (D) 메스꺼움을 유발한다.

03 강의에 따르면, 조건부 맛 기피를 유발하는 것은 무엇인가?
- **(A) 특정 음식과 관련된 아픈 느낌**
- (B) 뇌가 맛 정보를 처리하는 방식에 생기는 문제점
- (C) 신체가 제대로 기능하지 못하도록 만드는 적절한 영양의 부족
- (D) 몇몇 음식에서 소량으로 발견되는 특정한 독

04 교수가 Pavlov를 언급한 이유는?
- (A) 개들이 늑대의 직계 후손이라는 점을 지적하려고
- **(B) 개들이 음식을 어떻게 학습된 행동과 결부시키는지 예를 들려고**
- (C) 개들이 어떻게 음식이 좋고 나쁜지를 구별하는지 설명하려고
- (D) 적절한 음식이 주어지면 개들이 묘기 부리는 법을 배울 수 있다는 것을 보여주려고

05 토끼를 물은 코요테에 대해 추론할 수 있는 것은?
- (A) 코요테들은 나중에 먹기 위해 먹이를 저장한다.
- (B) 코요테들은 리튬에 영향을 받지 않는다.
- (C) 코요테들은 미각을 가지고 있지 않다.
- **(D) 코요테들은 서로 공감을 한다.**

[06 ~ 10] Listen to part of a lecture in an art class. 🔊 MP3 33

Professor(female): Over the past couple of days we've been working with watercolors. But some of you have complained that watercolors are difficult to paint with and have requested that we try another medium. That's fine. To be honest, I'm pleased with the results of our first watercolor assignment. But I'm curious... What exactly is so difficult about painting with watercolors? Marcus?

Student 1(male): Well, um, this is the first time I've tried watercolors. I mean, don't get me wrong, I've been painting for a while, but most of the time I usually paint with oils. It's just what I'm comfortable with. But when I paint with watercolors, it just seems like I have to use a completely different method. Every time I try, I just can't seem to make anything turn out the way I envisioned it. To make matters worse, **Q6** **it's pretty much impossible to go back and make changes if you want to tweak something a little.**

Student 2(female): Yeah, I've been running into the same problem. With watercolors, I can't make changes or fix the mistakes that I made. On top of that, I realized that I have to be really careful about using just the right amount of paint. When I use too much, everything just turns into a brown muddy mess. It's just awful.

P: I certainly think those are all valid arguments against using watercolors. **Watercolors are one of the most unforgiving pigments to work with.** You can always use a primer or layer the paint when using oils or acrylics, but you can't use either of those methods with watercolors. You have to apply thin washes of color directly on blank paper. You also have to avoid mixing colors or you'll get the muddy effect that Lydia just mentioned. But this is related to one of the great benefits of using watercolors. Light can pass right through the thin layers of paint and reflect the whiteness of the paper. So, with this in mind, let's talk about what type of scenes are usually painted using watercolors. Anybody?

S2: Q7 I see a lot of outdoor scenes, mostly landscapes that have been painted with watercolors. I guess it's because Q9 watercolors do have a certain way of capturing different shades of light and shadow. There are just so many combinations of colors in nature. I think watercolors are a really good medium to express them. I have to be honest with you, even though it's really frustrating to use watercolors, I've kind of enjoyed it.

S1: I agree with the points you made, but I still enjoy using oils much more than watercolors.

P: OK, fair enough. But did you ever think about… Well, maybe you're just not used to watercolors yet. Why don't you tell me what you like about oils?

S1: First of all, Q8-A **oil paints dry much more slowly than watercolors,** which basically dry instantly. That lets me blend colors at my own pace. Even if I make a mistake, it's really not that big of a deal. I can always go back and paint over it. And most importantly, Q8-C **when I'm painting with oils,** there are just more ways to express myself. I'm not limited to just using colors. **I can also use texture.** I can apply thick coats of color, one over the other. These layers can turn into really interesting textures that affect the appearance of the painting. That's just something that I can't do using watercolors.

P: Very interesting! It seems like you've put a lot of thought into this topic. The good news is that we won't be using watercolors anymore. Q10 **Starting tomorrow we'll switch to a different medium.** But we won't be using oil paints. Instead, **we're going to switch over to acrylics.** I'm assuming a lot of you have worked with acrylic paints before. So, **now let's talk about the pros and cons of working with acrylics, as compared to working with oils.**

해석 미술 수업의 다음 강의 일부분을 들으시오.

교수(여자): 지난 며칠 동안 우리는 수채화 물감으로 작업을 해봤습니다. 하지만 여러분들 중 일부는 수채화 물감을 이용해서 그리는 것이 어렵다고 불평해왔고 다른 재료로 작업해보자고 요청했습니다. 괜찮습니다. 솔직히 말해, 나는 우리의 첫 수채화 과제 결과에 만족하니까요. 하지만 궁금해요… 정확히 무엇이 수채화 물감으로 그림을 그리는 것을 그렇게 어렵게 만드나요? Marcus?

학생 1(남자): 저, 음, 이번에 제가 수채화 물감을 처음으로 사용해본 것인데요. 그러니까, 오해는 마시고요, 저는 그림을 오랫동안 그려왔는데, 대부분은 대개 유화 물감으로 그림을 그리거든요. 유화 물감이 제가 편하게 느끼는 재료라서요. 하지만 수채화 물감으로 그림을 그릴 때는, 완전히 다른 방법을 사용해야 하는 것만 같아요. 제가 그림을 그려볼 때마다, 어떤 것도 제가 마음속에 그렸던 방식대로 나오지 않는 것 같아요. 설상가상으로, 무언가 조금 수정하고 싶은 경우, 되돌아가서 수정을 하는 것이 거의 불가능해요.

학생 2(여자): 맞아요. 저도 같은 문제에 부딪혀 왔어요. 수채화 물감으로는, 수정을 하거나 이미 한 실수를 고칠 수가 없어요. 게다가, 물감의 양을 딱 맞게 써야 하는 것에도 정말 주의를 해야 한다는 것을 깨달았어요. 너무 많이 사용하면, 모든 게 그냥 갈색의 탁한 엉망진창으로 되어버리거든요. 정말 끔찍해요.

교수: 그 내용들이 모두 수채화 물감을 사용하는 것에 대한 정당한 반론이라고 생각해요. 수채화 물감은 작업하기에 가장 힘든 안료들 중 하나이죠. 유화 물감이나 아크릴 물감으로 작업할 때는 언제나 프라이머(밑칠 페인트)를 사용하거나 덧칠할 수 있지만, 수채화 물감으로는 그런 방법 중 어떤 것도 사용할 수가 없어요. 빈 종이 위에 얇게 색을 곧바로 칠해야 하죠. 또, 색을 섞는 것을 피해야 하는데, 그렇지 않으면 Lydia가 방금 언급했던 탁한 효과를 겪게 됩니다. 하지만 이것이 수채화 물감을 사용하는 것의 큰 이점들 중 하나와 관련되어 있어요. 빛은 얇은 물감층을 곧바로 투과할 수 있어서, 종이의 흰 색이 비치지요. 자, 이 점을 염두에 두고, 어떤 종류의 풍경들이 대개 수채화 물감으로 그려지는지에 대해 이야기해보도록 합시다. 누구 말해볼 사람 있나요?

학생 2: 저는 수채화 물감으로 그려진 많은 야외 장면들, 대부분은 풍경들을 봤어요. 여러 다른 빛의 음영과 그늘을 포착하는 특정한 방식을 수채화 물감이 분명 가지고 있어서 그런 듯 해요. 자연에는 너무나 많은 색의 조합이 있어요. 제 생각엔 수채화 물감이 그 색의 조합들을 나타내기 위한 정말 좋은 도구인 것 같아요. 솔직히 말씀 드리면, 수채화 물감을 사용하는 것이 정말 좌절스럽기는 하지만, 어느 정도는 즐겁기도 했어요.

학생 1: 나도 네 주장에 동의하지만 난 여전히 수채화 물감보다는 유화 물감을 사용하는 것이 훨씬 더 좋아.

교수: 자, 좋아요. 하지만 이렇게 생각해 본 적이… 음, 아마도 여러분은 아직 수채화 물감에 익숙하지 않은 건지도 모르죠. 유화 물감의 무엇이 좋았는지 말해볼까요?

학생 1: 우선, 유화 물감은 기본적으로 즉시 마르는 수채화 물감보다 훨씬 더 늦게 말라요. 그게 제가 제 속도에 맞게 색상을 섞을 수 있게 해주고요. 실수를 한다 하더라도, 그리 큰 문제는 아니에요. 언제든 다시 돌아가서 그 위에 색을 칠할 수 있거든요. 그리고 가장 중요한 것은, 유화 물감으로 그림을 그릴 때는 제 자신을 표현할 수 있는 더 많은 방법들이 있어요. 그저 색상을 사용하는 것에만 제한되지 않아요. 질감을 사용할 수도 있거든요. 색을 두껍게 여러겹 칠할 수 있어요. 이런 층들은 그림의 모습에 영향을 주는 정말 흥미로운 질감들로 나타낼 수 있지요. 그건 수채화 물감을 사용해서는 할 수 없는 것이에요.

교수: 무척 흥미롭네요! 학생이 이 주제에 관해 생각을 많이 한 것 같네요. 좋은 소식은, 우리가 더 이상 수채화 물감을 사용하지 않을 것이라는 점입니다. 내일부터는 다른 도구로 바꿀 거예요. 하지만 유화 물감을 사용하지는 않습니다. 대신, 아크릴 물감으로 넘어갈 예정이에요. 여러분 중 많은 이들이 전에 아크릴 물감을 사용해봤을 것이라 생각합니다. 그럼, 이제 유화 물감으로 작업하는 것과 비교하여 아크릴 물감으로 작업하는 것의 찬반 양론에 대해 이야기해보죠.

Ⓦ watercolor [wɔ́:tərkʌlər] 수채화, 수채화 물감   medium [mí:diəm] 수단, 도구   oils [ɔil] (pl.) 유화 물감   envision [invíʒən] 마음속에 그리다[상상하다]   tweak [twi:k] 수정하다, 변경하다   on top of that 그뿐 아니라, 그외에   muddy [mʌdi] 탁한   valid [vǽlid] 타당한   argument against ~ ...에 대한 반론   unforgiving [ʌnfərgíviŋ] 힘든   pigment [pígmənt] 안료, 물감 재료   primer [prímər] 프라이머, (밑칠) 페인트   layer [leiə] 층, 막   acrylic paint 아크릴 물감   wash [waʃ] (물감의) 얇은 막[겹]   reflect [riflékt] 비추다, 나타나다   capture [kǽptʃər] 포착하다   texture [tékstʃər] 질감   coat [kout] 칠   pros and cons 찬반 양론

06 수채화 물감을 이용하는 것에 대한 학생들의 주된 불평은?
Ⓐ 수채화 물감은 너무 묽어서 종종 종이 위로 뚝뚝 떨어진다.
Ⓑ 학생들은 전에 수채화 물감을 너무 많이 사용했다.
Ⓒ 물감이 마르고 나면 색상들이 갈색으로 변한다.
Ⓓ 마음을 바꾸거나 실수를 고칠 수 없다.

07 풍경이 언급된 이유는?
Ⓐ 유화 물감과 수채화 물감의 외양을 대조하려고
Ⓑ 수채화 물감의 가장 큰 단점을 설명하려고
Ⓒ 수채화 그림의 일반적인 유형을 지적하려고
Ⓓ 수채화 물감으로 그림을 그리는 것이 얼마나 어려운지를 보여주려고

08 남학생이 유화 물감에 대해 이야기한 두 가지 요점은? (두 가지 선택)
Ⓐ 유화 물감은 수채화 물감보다 더 느리게 마른다.
Ⓑ 유화 물감은 서로 쉽게 섞이지 않는다.
Ⓒ 유화 물감은 질감을 만들어내는 데 사용될 수 있다.
Ⓓ 유화 물감은 풍경을 그리는 데 좋다.

09 풍경을 그리는 데 수채화 물감을 사용하는 것의 이점으로 여학생이 말한 것은?
Ⓐ 수채화 물감은 빛과 그림자를 잘 보여준다.
Ⓑ 수채화 물감은 종이의 흰 색을 덮어 버린다.
Ⓒ 야외에서 그림을 그릴 때 수채화 물감이 사용하기 더 쉽다.
Ⓓ 색상들이 빠르고 쉽게 서로 섞인다.

10 다음 수업에서 다뤄질 내용은?
Ⓐ 수채화 물감 사용을 중단한 이유
Ⓑ 아크릴 물감을 사용하는 가장 좋은 방법들
Ⓒ 유화 물감과 아크릴 물감의 차이점들
Ⓓ 유화 그림들의 질감에 얽힌 문제점들

01 / Architecture

Sample Questions

본문 p. 212

| 01 B | 02 D | 03 A | 04 C | 05 A, C | 06 B |

해석 건축학 수업의 다음 강의 일부분을 들으시오. MP3 34

교수(남자): 지금까지 공부한 대로, 18세기의 건축은 교회와 성에 중점을 두었죠. 자, 이제 현대 건축으로 넘어가보죠. 현대 건축은 19세기 후반에 발달했지요. 건축의 초점이 주택 지역으로, 그리고 더욱 중요하게는, 공업 건축의 형태로 알려진 공장으로 옮겨갔습니다. 언제나 양식을 강조해왔던 건축이 기능을 고려하기 시작한 것입니다.

오늘은 이 형태가 공업 건축의 선구자들을 통해 어떻게 발전되어 왔는지에 대해 이야기해보도록 합시다. 19세기 후반에 공장이 필요했던 회사들은 대개 건축가들을 고용하지 않았습니다. 많은 이들이 그것은 자원 낭비라고 생각했기 때문이죠. 하지만 Julius Kahn과 Albert Kahn이 등장하자, 상황이 바뀌기 시작했죠.

이 두 형제는 1880년에 미국에 와서 미시간주의 디트로이트에 Albert Kahn Associates라는 건축 회사를 세웠습니다. Albert는 건축가였고, 그의 동생(Julius)은 건축을 위한 공학 시스템을 개발한 발명가였습니다. 그들은 공장의 벽과 지붕, 그리고 버팀대에 쓰이는 목재를 철근 콘크리트로 대체하는 방법을 개발함으로써 현대 건축에 혁신을 일으켰습니다. 이 방법은 화재 방지도 더 잘 될 뿐만 아니라, 더 확 트인 작업 현장을 만들어 주었죠.

자, 디자인에 접근하는 데 있어 이 두 사람이 서로 다른 주안점을 가지고 있었다는 것을 이해하는 것이 중요합니다. 현대 건축의 새 시대를 열었던 것은 다름 아닌 이 둘의 철학의 수렴 또는 조합 덕분입니다. 발명가로서 Julius Kahn은 자신의 디자인의 실제적 응용에 더 관심이 있었어요. 그는 건축가가 아닌 공학자였으니까요. 그는 건축 자재를 사용하는 것과, 그것들을 건축에 응용하는 것에 주력했어요. 이것의 좋은 예로는 Kahn의 트러스 바(trussed bar)가 있죠. (화면에 보여준다) Kahn 형제 이전의 건축은 어느 쪽으로든 취약점이 있었습니다. 건물이 목재로 지어지면, 작업 현장을 넓게 만들 수는 있지만 화재에 취약하겠죠. 기계들이 매우 뜨겁게 작동되는 공장에서 이것이 왜 문제가 되는지는 여러분이 잘 알 수 있겠지요. 만일 건물이 콘크리트로 지어지게 되면, 콘크리트가 너무 무거워서 철근을 휘게 만들기 때문에 작업 현장을 넓게 만들 수가 없습니다. 음, Khan의 시스템은 철근에 가해지는 압력을 분산시키기 위해 45도 각도로 휘어진 추가 철제 빔을 도입하여 이 문제를 해결했습니다. 철근 콘크리트 빔이 힘을 보강해 주어, 작업 공간을 더 넓힐 수 있었습니다.

Julius Khan의 형인 Albert는 다른 주안점을 가지고 있었습니다. 그는 작업 자체에 대해 생각하는 대신, 그 작업을 하는 사람들에 초점을 맞췄습니다. 작업 공간에서 중요한 한 가지 요소는 빛의 양이었습니다. 불빛이 어두운 공간에서 일을 할 때는 하루가 더 길게 느껴진다는 것에 대부분 동의할 겁니다. 그래서, Albert는 작업 공간에 햇빛이 더 많이 들어오도록 하는 데 초점을 두었습니다. 그는 자신이 디자인한 건물 안에서 사람들이 어떻게 느끼는지의 중요성을 깨달았습니다.

Kahn 트러스 바를 이용하여, Albert는 자신의 디자인에 전보다 더 큰 창문을 포함할 수 있게 되었습니다. 1905년에 그는 Kahn 시스템으로 만들어진 철근 콘크리트를 사용하여, Packard 공장 건물 10번을 설계했습니다. 건물 자체에는 장식이 거의 없었지만, 작업자들을 위한 큰 창문들과 많은 작업 공간이 있었습니다. 이러한 기능의 표현이 산업 디자인의 새 시대의 시작을 연 것이죠.

Kahn 형제가 공장 건물들에 혁신을 불러 일으키긴 했지만, 1930년대가 되자 몇몇 회사들은 일하기 좋은 공장 이상의 것을 원했습니다. 그들은 스타일을 추가하고 싶어했지요… 중세 교회에 있는 조각상 같은 것을 원한 것은 아니었지만, 그들은 공장이 단순한 직사각형처럼 보이는 것을 원하지는 않았어요. 그래서 Thomas Wallis라는 이름의 한 영국인 건축가는 그가 디자인한 공장에 스타일을 더하기 시작했습니다. 공장은 여전히 효율적인 작업 공간도 되어야 했기 때문에, 그는 그의 디자인에 Kahn 트러스 바를 이용했습니다. 하지만 그가 만든 건물 외관은 산업 디자인의 방향을 한 번 더 바꾸어 놓았습니다. 그는 아르 데코 스타일, 즉 풍부한 색채뿐만 아니라 대담한 기하학적인 무늬들과 선들을 사용했던 스타일을 그의 건물 디자인에 사용했습니다. 공장은 사람들이 일을 하는 공간일 뿐만 아니라 도시 번화가에서 눈에 확 띄는 랜드마크가 되었습니다.

W evolve [ivάlv] 발달하다　shift [ʃift] 이동하다　residential [rèzidénʃəl] 주택지의　industrial [indΛstriəl] 산업의, 공업의　take ~ into consideration …을 고려하다　pioneer [pàiəníər] 선구자　architect [άːrkitèkt] 건축가　found [faund] 설립하다　revolutionize [rèvəljúːʃənàiz] 혁신을 일으키다　replace A with B A를 B로 대체하다　reinforce [rìːinfɔ́ːrs] 강화하다　convergence [kənvə́ːrdʒəns] 집중 philosophy [filάsəfi] 철학　usher ~ in …이 도입되게 하다　practical application 응용　susceptible [səséptəbl] 민감한　steel reinforcement 철근　dimly [dímli] 흐릿하게　incorporate [inkɔ́ːrpəreit] (일부로) 포함하다　exterior [ikstí(ː)əriər] 외부, 외면　geometric [dʒìːəmétrik] 기하학적인

01 교수가 강의에서 주로 다루고 있는 디자인 측면은?
Ⓐ 공장 디자인에 있어 작업자 안전에 주력
Ⓑ 기술적 진보를 통한 디자인의 진화

Ⓒ 디자인을 향상시킨 공학에서의 발전
Ⓓ 산업 디자인에 사용된 여러 다른 건축 방법

02 교수에 의하면, Albert Kahn은 어떤 점에서 Julius Kahn과 달랐는가?
Ⓐ 공장에 외부 장식이 있어야 한다고 생각했다.
Ⓑ 건물의 강도가 가장 중요한 것이라고 생각했다.
Ⓒ 트러스 바를 주택에 사용할 수 있는 방법을 찾는 것에 주력했다.
Ⓓ 자신의 디자인이 작업자들에게 어떻게 영향을 미치는지에 더 관심을 가졌다.

03 Kahn 형제 이전에 지어진 공장들에 대해 교수가 암시한 것은?
Ⓐ 공장에 콘크리트로 된 넓은 공간이 있었다면 공장이 무너질 위험이 있었다.
Ⓑ 작업자들이 가능한 한 효율적일 수 있도록 만들어졌다.
Ⓒ 많은 공장들이 교회처럼 정교하게 디자인되었다.
Ⓓ 빛이 많이 드는 넓은 작업 공간을 가지고 있었다.

04 Albert Kahn이 디자인한 공장들에 대해 추론할 수 있는 것은?
Ⓐ 새로운 기술을 다룰 수 없었다.
Ⓑ 지역 랜드마크가 되는 경향이 있었다.
Ⓒ 공장 작업자들에게 인기가 있었다.
Ⓓ 내부가 굉장히 화려하게 장식되어 있었다.

05 교수에 의하면, Kahn 시스템을 사용하는 이점은 무엇인가? (두 가지 선택)
Ⓐ 작업 공간이 더 밝아질 수 있었다.
Ⓑ 공장 설계에 목재를 더 많이 쓸 수 있었다.
Ⓒ 공장이 화재에 덜 취약할 수 있었다.
Ⓓ 건물이 전체적으로 더 크게 지어질 수 있었다.

06 교수에 의하면, Albert Kahn과 Thomas Wallis에 의해 디자인된 건물들의 유사점은 무엇인가?
Ⓐ 외관 디자인이 정교했다.
Ⓑ 건물 디자인이 Kahn 시스템의 혜택을 입었다.
Ⓒ 창문이 중요한 설계 주제였다.
Ⓓ 기하학적 모양들이 교회와 유사했다.

Practice Questions

본문 p. 216

01 D   02 B   03 C   04 A   05 D   06 A

Main Idea
건물 디자인에서 지붕의 중요성

Listen to part of a lecture in an architecture class. ◁ MP3 35

Professor(male): **Q1** Today, I'd like to talk a bit about the importance of roofs when it comes to the design of buildings. Let's take a look at common residential architecture in the United States. I think we're all familiar with it, wouldn't you say? Well, although we may not pay much attention to the design of our homes, there's definitely a relationship between the function of a structure and its style or form. I'd like to take a look at the style of roofs to show how their function and form are related. But before we get into the details, let's think about the most common type of house in the US. Does anybody know what it is?

Student 1(male): Yeah, isn't it the framed house?

P: You're right! Most of the houses we see in the suburbs are first made with a wooden frame, a skeleton, and then walls and plywood sheets and shingles are bolted onto

	the frame, making the houses we are so familiar with. **Q1 But I want to focus on the roof.** You see, although the type of roof on a house may seem like a simple design choice, you'll see that they are carefully chosen designs that serve a specific function. **I'll talk about three different types of roof designs as examples.** Okay, first, there's the Cape Cod roof. Has anyone heard of it? **Student2(female):** Hey, that's the kind of house my parents live in. I remember them saying something about living in a Cape Cod. I always found it odd that they said that, because my parents don't live anywhere near Cape Cod.
Origin Cape Cod란 이름은 지역 이름에서 유래	**P:** You bring up a good point. **Q2 Cape Cod is located in the northeast of the United States.** For those of you who don't know where Cape Cod actually is, it's a peninsula, a narrow strip of land with three sides touching the water, in Massachusetts. **Many of the first houses built in the region during the 1600 were built in this particular style and the name of the place became the name of the style.** Anyway, is anyone from the northeast? How's the weather there? **S1:** Freezing in the winter… It's windy on the coast and the snow…
Function / Advantage Cape Cod roof – 겨울에 지붕 위에 눈이 쌓이는 것을 방지함	**P:** That's right. So let's take a look at the picture (shown on screen) and see what kind of function this style of roof serves. Take a look at the steep angle of the roof and notice how low it is to the ground. The steep angle helps keep off the snow that can accumulate during the winter. You know how heavy snow can get when it's packed. It's low to the ground because the compact structure will also help the house withstand the strong winds from the ocean. Now, this is great for houses out in the open, but anyone see a limitation to this design?
Disadvantage Cape Cod roof – 경사면이 급해서 2층 공간이 부족	**S2: Q4 Well, it seems kinda inefficient…** I mean, my room was on the second floor, but I used to bump my head on the ceiling all the time. **P:** Exactly! See **how the steep angle of the roof gives little room to stand?** In order to get a little more ceiling space, we can use a gambrel roof (shown on screen). Let's take a look at a picture. The gambrel roof doesn't just have one slope, like the Cape Cod roof does. No, it has two different sections with different slopes. At the very top section, the roof has a fairly flat angle, while the second part of the roof, the part that goes down to the first floor line… that has a very steep slope. Well, **Q3 the advantage to the gambrel roof should be obvious. There's much more room on the second floor, so a person can stand up straight.**
Advantage gambrel roof – 2층 공간이 더 생겨서 사람이 일어설 수 있음	Finally, there's a type of roof based on form more than function. Now, I don't mean that it's useless, but what I mean is sometimes the form becomes the function. Let's take a look at lean-to roofs (shown on screen). A lean-to house has two stories in front, but only one story in back. Let's take a look at a diagram. There's a long, sloping roof from front to back, connecting the first and second floor. So there's not as much space to walk around as with a gambrel-roof house. But the **Q5 main advantage of the lean-to roof is that it allows you to have a number of windows on the roof. There's really not that much function other than the fact that you get a lot of light,** but it's a different type of roof that suits a different taste.
Advantage lean-to roof – 창문이 많아 실내가 밝음	
Opinion 건축가들은 form과 function을 둘 다 고려해야 함	**Q6 Form following function is something we always talk about and consider. The design of a building should be based on the needs of the people who use it.** So architects always have to think about the people who'll actually be living in the house, even if it is something as simple as choosing what type of roof to build.

해석 건축학 수업의 다음 강의 일부분을 들으시오.

교수(남자): 오늘은, 건물 디자인에 있어 지붕의 중요성에 대해 조금 이야기해 보려고 합니다. 미국의 일반적인 주거 건축을 한번 살펴보죠. 우리 모두 그것에 익숙한 것 같은데, 그렇지 않나요? 음, 우리는 아마 우리가 사는 집의 디자인에 주의를 그다지 많이 기울이지 않을지도 모르지만, 한 구조물의 기능과 그 스타일, 또는 형태 간에는 분명히 관련이 있습니다. 기능과 형태가 어떻게 관련이 있는지 알려주기 위해 지붕들의 스타일을 살펴보고자 합니다. 하지만 자세한 내용을 다루기 전에, 미국에서 가장 흔한 주택 종류를 한번 생각해보죠. 그게 뭔지 아는 사람 있나요?

학생 1(남자): 네, (판자를 댄) 목조 가옥 아닌가요?

교수: 맞아요! 우리가 교외에서 보는 대부분의 주택들은 목재 프레임, 즉 뼈대가 먼저 만들어지고, 그 다음 벽과 합판들, 그리고 지붕널들을 프레임 위에 접합하면, 우리에게 익숙한 집이 만들어집니다. 하지만, 저는 지붕에 주목하고 싶습니다. 집에 있어 지붕의 종류는 그저 단순한 디자인 선택 사항처럼 보일 수도 있겠지만, 지붕은 특정한 기능을 수행하는, 주의 깊게 선택된 디자인이라는 점을 여러분은 알게 될 겁니다. 예로, 세 가지 다른 종류의 지붕에 대해 이야기해보죠. 좋아요, 먼저, 케이프 코드(Cape Cod) 지붕입니다. 들어본 적이 있는 사람 있나요?

학생 2(여자): 아, 저희 부모님이 사시는 집이 그런 종류예요. 부모님이 케이프 코드에서 사시는 것에 대해 뭔가 이야기하셨던 게 기억이 나요. 저는 부모님이 그런 말씀을 하시는 게 이상하다고 항상 생각했었죠. 부모님은 케이프 코드 근처 어디에서도 사시지 않거든요.

교수: 좋은 지적이에요. 케이프 코드는 미국 북동부에 있는 지역이에요. 케이프 코드가 실제 어디에 있는지 모르는 사람들에게 말해주자면, 그곳은 메사추세츠 주(州)에 있는 반도, 즉 삼면이 물로 둘러싸인 좁은 띠 모양의 땅이에요. 1600년대에 그 지역에 처음 세워진 집 중 많은 수가 이 특정한 스타일로 지어졌고, 그 지역의 이름이 그 스타일의 이름이 되었지요. 어쨌든, 북동부 지역에서 온 사람 있나요? 그곳 날씨는 어떤가요?

학생 1: 겨울에 굉장히 추워요... 해안가는 바람이 많이 불고요, 눈이...

교수: 맞아요. 자, 사진을 살펴보고 이 스타일의 지붕이 어떤 종류의 기능을 수행하는지 살펴봅시다. (화면에 보여준다) 지붕의 급격한 경사를 보세요, 그리고 지붕이 땅 쪽으로 얼마나 낮은지도 살펴보세요. 이 급격한 경사는 겨울 동안 지붕에 쌓일 수 있는 눈을 피할 수 있게 해 줍니다. 눈이 다져지면 얼마나 무거워질 수 있는지 알고 있지요? 이 지붕은 땅 쪽으로 낮게 되어 있는데, 이 조밀한 구조가 집이 바다로부터 불어오는 강한 바람을 견딜 수 있도록 해주기도 하기 때문입니다. 자, 이런 지붕은 탁 트인 장소에 있는 주택에는 매우 좋죠. 하지만 이 디자인의 한계를 아는 사람 혹시 있나요?

학생 2: 음, 조금 비효율적인 것 같아요... 그러니까 제 말은, 제 방은 2층에 있었는데, 항상 천장에 머리를 부딪히곤 했거든요.

교수: 바로 그거예요! 지붕의 급격한 경사 때문에 (2층에는) 서 있을 만한 공간이 거의 없는 것을 알겠죠? 천장 공간을 조금 더 내기 위해, 우리는 박공 지붕(gambrel roof) 방식을 써도 됩니다. (화면에 보여준다) 사진을 한번 보죠. 박공 지붕은 케이프 코드 지붕처럼 하나의 경사만 있는 것이 아닙니다. 박공 지붕은 두 가지 경사가 있는 두 가지 다른 부분으로 구성되어 있어요. 꼭대기 부분에서는, 지붕이 꽤 평탄한 각도로 되어 있는 반면, 지붕의 두 번째 부분, 그러니까 1층으로 내려가는 부분은... 매우 급격한 경사로 되어 있습니다. 음, 박공 지붕의 이점은 명백하죠. 2층의 공간이 훨씬 넓어져서, 사람이 똑바로 서 있을 수 있죠.

마지막으로, 기능보다는 형태에 더 기반을 둔 종류의 지붕이 있습니다. 이 지붕이 쓸모 없다는 말이 아닙니다. 제 말은, 가끔은 형태가 기능이 되기도 한다는 것이죠. 부섭 지붕(lean-to roof)을 살펴보도록 하죠. (화면에 보여준다) 부섭 지붕으로 된 집은 앞쪽은 2층으로 되어 있지만, 뒤쪽은 1층으로 되어 있습니다. 도표를 살펴보죠. 앞에서 뒤쪽으로 향하는 길고 경사진, 1층과 2층을 연결하는 지붕이 있습니다. 그래서, 부섭 지붕으로 된 집은 박공 지붕처럼 걸어다닐 수 있는 공간이 많지는 않습니다. 하지만 부섭 지붕의 가장 주된 이점은 지붕에 창문을 많이 만들 수가 있다는 점이죠. 빛이 많이 들어온다는 사실 외에는 그다지 많은 기능은 없는 편이지만, 다른 취향에 맞춘, 다른 종류의 지붕인 셈이죠. 기능을 따르는 형태는 우리가 항상 이야기하고 또 고려해야 하는 것입니다. 건물 디자인은 그 건물을 사용하는 사람들의 필요에 근거를 두어야 합니다. 그래서 건축가들은 언제나 그 집에 실제로 살게 될 사람들을 생각해야 하죠. 비록 그것이 어떤 종류의 지붕을 선택할까 하는 단순한 것이라 할지라도 말이죠.

W residential architecture 주거용 건축 suburb [sʌ́bərb] 교외 skeleton [skélitən] 뼈대, 골격 plywood [pláiwùd] 합판 shingle [ʃíŋl] 지붕널 bolt [boult] (볼트로) 접합하다 peninsula [pənínsələ] 반도 strip [strip] 좁고 기다란 육지 steep [sti:p] 가파른, 급격한 keep off 멀리하다, 피하다 accumulate [əkjúːmjəlèit] 모으다, (서서히) 늘어나다 pack [pæk] (눈·흙을) 다지다 compact [kə́mpækt] 조밀한 withstand [wiðstǽnd] 견디다 limitation [lìmətéiʃən] 한계 bump [bʌmp] 부딪치다 slope [sloup] 경사면 suit one's taste ...의 취향에 맞다

01 강의의 주된 내용은?
Ⓐ 주택 뼈대의 기본적인 종류들
Ⓑ 주택 뼈대를 위한 최고의 건축 방법들
Ⓒ 가장 효율적인 지붕용 자재들
Ⓓ 여러 다른 지붕 스타일의 특징들

02 교수가 케이프 코드(Cape Cod)에 지어진 집들에 대해 언급하는 이유는?
Ⓐ 전형적인 미국 주택의 뼈대에 대해 설명하려고

Ⓑ 어떤 지붕 스타일의 기원에 대해 설명하려고
Ⓒ 현대 주택 디자인의 예를 들려고
Ⓓ 지붕이 과거에는 비실용적이었다는 것을 암시하려고

03 박공 지붕(gambrel roof)의 이점은?
Ⓐ 양쪽으로 같은 경사를 이루고 있다.
Ⓑ 2층에 방을 많이 둘 수 있다.
Ⓒ 사람들이 서 있을 공간을 더 만들어 준다.
Ⓓ 유지 보수 관련 문제가 더 적다.

04 케이프 코드(Cape Cod) 주택의 단점은?
Ⓐ 2층 방들의 천장이 낮다.
Ⓑ 평평한 지붕은 주택을 더 약하게 만든다.
Ⓒ 아래층에는 방이 하나밖에 없다.
Ⓓ 앞쪽과 뒤쪽 모두 지붕의 경사가 급격하다.

05 부섭 지붕(lean-to roof) 주택에 살기를 원하는 사람들에 관해 추론할 수 있는 것은?
Ⓐ 일어서서 걸어 다닐 수 있는 넓은 공간을 선호한다.
Ⓑ 혹독한 기후에 대해 걱정한다.
Ⓒ 집 주변의 아름다운 경치를 선호한다.
Ⓓ 더 밝은 실내를 원한다.

06 '형태는 기능을 따른다'라는 원칙을 적용하는 건축가가 할 일은?
Ⓐ 집을 설계할 때 거주하는 사람들의 요구를 반영하기
Ⓑ 해당 지역에서 가장 인기 있는 주택 스타일을 연구하기
Ⓒ 집이 설계되기 전에 집의 자재를 선택하기
Ⓓ 춥고 혹독한 기후에 지어지는 집에는 저렴한 자재를 선택하기

02 / Art & Science

≥ Sample Questions 본문 p. 222

| 01 D | 02 B | 03 C | 04 D | 05 B | 06 A |

해석 예술과 과학 수업의 다음 강의 일부분을 들으시오. ◁) MP3 36

교수(여자): 지난주에는 천체들의 움직임을 알아내기 위해 천문학자들이 사용한 방법들에 대해 이야기했습니다. 오늘 강의에서는 이것의 실제 적용에 대해 살펴보려고 합니다.

예를 들어, 달력은 가장 분명한 적용 예입니다. 달력은 본질적으로는 다양한 천체들이 우주를 규칙적으로 움직이는 것에 대한 기록입니다. 하지만 나는 오늘 토론을 좀 덜 분명한 적용 예로 시작해보고 싶네요.

최근, 천문학자들은 미술 연구와 분석에 관여하기 시작했습니다. 정말 이상하게 들리긴 하죠. 자, 여러분 모두 유명한 화가인 반 고흐에 대해 잘 알고 있을 걸로 생각합니다. 그는 인상파 화가였죠. 그 말은 즉, 그의 그림들이 사실성보다는 감정을 강조했다는 뜻입니다. 따라서 여러분은 그의 작품이 별들의 정확한 묘사를 포함했다고 생각하지 못할지도 모릅니다. 하지만 미국 전역에서 모인 한 무리의 천문학자들이 별들의 움직임에 대한 그들의 지식을 반 고흐의 그림들 중 일부를 분석하는 데 사용했습니다. 그 결과, 반 고흐의 그림들은 너무나 정확해서 그의 그림들 중 하나를 그린 정확한 날짜까지 알아낼 수 있었다는 것이 드러났습니다. 슬라이드를 보고 법의학 천문학 과정에 대한 감을 더 잡아보도록 합시다. 여러분은 모두 이 그림을 잘 알고 있을 것입니다. 이것은 반 고흐의 대작인 〈별이 빛나는 밤에〉입니다. 프랑스 상레미 지역의 그의 방에서, 일출 직전에 본 광경을 그린 그림이지요. 대부분의 사람들은 반 고흐가 이 그림을 그의 상상으로 그렸을 걸로 생각했지만, 그렇지 않았습니다.

이 그림을 연구했던 천문학자는, 그림에 있는 별들의 배치가 나선 은하의 학술 묘사와 놀라울 정도로 유사하다는 것을 깨달았습니다. 한 대학의 천문관 컴퓨터 투영을 이용하여, 그 천문학자는 그림의 정확한 년도뿐만 아니라 정확한 날짜와 시간도 알아내었습니다. 그 그림은 1889년 6월

19일 새벽 3시에서 4시 사이에 그려졌습니다.
자, 그들은 이것을 어떻게 알아냈을까요? 음, 우선, 그들은 기준이 필요했습니다. 그리고 사실, 그 그림에 일부 기준이 포함되어 있었죠. 반 고흐는 샛별이라고도 알려져 있는 금성과 초승달의 모습을 담았습니다. 그 두 별의 상대적인 위치들은, 반 고흐가 〈별이 빛나는 밤에〉를 그렸을 것으로 생각되는 시기 동안 다양한 날의 이 천체들의 위치에 대한 컴퓨터 시뮬레이션에 대조되었습니다. 정확한 매치가 찾아질 때까지요.
비슷한 전략이 그가 〈밤의 하얀 집〉을 그렸던 날짜를 결정하는 데에도 이용되었습니다. 그 그림은 파리 근처에 있는 한 작은 도시에 있는, 저녁 무렵의 한 집을 보여줍니다. 여기에도, 반 고흐는 밤하늘에 금성을 그려 넣었습니다. 하지만 천문학자들은 그 별이 보통 때보다 더 밝다는 것을 알아차렸습니다. 이것을 그저 반 고흐의 상상의 일환이라고 치부하지 않고, 그들은 조사를 하여 금성이 1890년 6월에 실제로 유별나게 밝았다는 사실을 알아냈습니다. 후에, 별들과 행성들에 대한 컴퓨터 분석을 통해 그 그림이 1890년 6월 16일, 오후 약 7시쯤에 그려졌다는 것이 밝혀졌죠.
자, 이제 또 다른 그림을 살펴봅시다. 반 고흐가 그렸는가 아닌가 하는 것에 대해 미술사가들 사이에서 엄청난 논쟁 거리가 되어왔던 그림입니다. 그 그림은 제목이 붙여져 있지 않은데요. 그 그림에는 별이 없기 때문에 〈별이 빛나는 밤에〉에 적용되었던 방법을 사용해서 그 그림이 그려진 날짜와 시간을 입증할 방법이 없었습니다. 하지만, 역사적인 지식과 지평선 위의 산들의 모양, 그리고 그림 속의 농가를 통해, 연구가들은 그 그림이 그려졌던 대략의 장소를 밝혀낼 수 있었습니다. 반 고흐가 머물렀던 병원이었지요.
대부분의 사람들이 생각하기로는, 그 그림에 사용되었던 색상들로 인해… 들판이 금색인 것이 보이죠? 대부분의 사람들은 노란색 물체가 태양일 것으로 생각했습니다. 하지만, 태양의 행로는 실제로 결코 그림 속의 자리와 일치하지 않았습니다. 이것은 그 물체가 실제로는 달이었다는 깨달음으로 이어졌습니다. 〈별이 빛나는 밤에〉가 언제 그려졌는지를 밝혀내는 데 사용되었던 컴퓨터 프로그램을 이용하여, 연구가들은 이 제목 없는 그림이 1889년 7월 13일 밤 9시 경에 그려졌다는 것을 계산해냈습니다.

ⓦ celestial body 천체   essentially [əsénʃəli] 본질적으로   Impressionist [impréʃənist] 인상주의 화가   forensic [fərénsik] 법의학적인   masterpiece [mǽstərpi:s] 걸작, 명작   configuration [kənfìgjəréiʃən] 배열, 배치   strikingly [stráikiŋli] 두드러지게   spiral nebula 나선선 성운   planetarium [plæ̀nitɛ́(:)əriəm] 천체 투영관   projection [prədʒékʃən] 투영, (투사된) 영상   reference point 기준   crescent moon 초승달   tactic [tǽktik] 전략, 작전   dusk [dʌsk] 황혼   a quirk of 운명의 일격[장난]   verify [vérəfai] 확인하다, 입증하다   correspond with ~ …와 부합하다, 일치하다

01 강의의 목적은?
Ⓐ 유럽의 유명한 한 천문학자의 업적을 설명하려고
Ⓑ 반 고흐의 스타일에 미친 초기 영향을 보여주려고
Ⓒ 초기 근대 미술에서의 천문학 주제에 대해 논의하려고
Ⓓ 어떻게 미술이 천문학 원리에 의해 분석될 수 있는지 보여주려고

02 반 고흐에 대한 대부분의 사람들의 인식에 대해 교수가 말한 것은?
Ⓐ 반 고흐에 대한 그들의 견해는 대개 올바르다.
Ⓑ 그의 정확성에 대해 충분히 인정하지 않는다.
Ⓒ 매일의 일상을 매우 정확하게 묘사했다고 생각한다.
Ⓓ 반 고흐가 천문학자이자 예술가였다고 생각한다.

03 〈별이 빛나는 밤에〉가 언제 그려졌는지를 밝혀내기 위해 사용된 방법에 대해 교수가 언급한 것은?
Ⓐ 그 시대의 다른 그림들을 살펴보기
Ⓑ 그 그림의 세부사항들을 역사적 사실들과 맞춰보기
Ⓒ 하늘의 물체들의 위치를 분석하기
Ⓓ 그가 사용했던 물감의 안료들을 검사하기

04 교수가 반 고흐의 제목 없는 그림의 색상에 대해 지적한 이유는?
Ⓐ 그 그림과 관련된 논쟁의 원인을 설명하려고
Ⓑ 그림들을 분석하는 데에 색상이 어떻게 사용되는지 설명하려고
Ⓒ 반 고흐의 그림 스타일의 예를 들려고
Ⓓ 과학자들이 왜 부정확한 추측을 했었는지 나타내려고

05 반 고흐가 인상주의 화가였다는 것을 교수가 언급한 이유는?
Ⓐ 그가 왜 천문학에 대해 배우는 것에 관심이 많았는지를 가르쳐주려고
Ⓑ 사람들이 왜 그의 작품이 과학적으로 정확할 것으로 기대하지 않는지를 설명하려고
Ⓒ 그가 과학에 대해 거의 알려지지 않았던 때에 살았다는 것을 암시하려고

Ⓓ 연구가들이 그의 그림을 분석하는 데 왜 그렇게 고생했는지 알려주려고

06 강의에서 언급된 모든 그림들에 대해 교수가 암시한 것은?
Ⓐ 반 고흐는 그 그림들에서 밤 하늘을 묘사할 때 엄청난 주의를 기울였다.
Ⓑ 그 그림들이 날짜와 위치에 대한 내용을 포함했더라면 더 가치가 있었을 것이다.
Ⓒ 그 그림들은 반 고흐가 아닌, 천문학을 이해했던 한 화가에 의해 그려졌다.
Ⓓ 반 고흐는 그 그림들을 낮에 그렸고, 이후에 달과 별들을 추가했다.

❧ Practice Questions

본문 p. 226

| **01** A | **02** D | **03** B | **04** C | **05** C, D | **06** B |

Listen to part of a lecture in an Art & Science class. 🔊 MP3 37

Professor(female): Let's continue our discussion on how works of art are analyzed. So, does anyone remember what we went over during our last class?

Student(male): We talked about how different pigments are analyzed. You mentioned something about lead-based pigments and… uh… carbon-based pigments. How, uh… art historians can analyze paintings without taking samples. So they don't have to scratch expensive pieces of art.

P: Good! Well, today we're going to build off of that knowledge and expand it. I'm sure you've heard of x-rays. Well, **Q1** **in the past, this relatively modern technology was only used in hospitals and dentists' offices. But now it's widely used in the study of works of art**. Can anyone guess why?

S: Is it because a lot of artwork gets damaged? I mean, x-rays are used when people break their bones, right?

P: Hmm… sort of. That's not the reason I was referring to, but x-rays can be used to learn more about damaged artwork. In one case, there were two separate paintings by the same artist. But an art historian in Ohio suspected that they were parts of the same painting, which had been cut in half by a dishonest art dealer hoping to double his money. **Q2** **X-rays revealed several hidden figures that had been painted over by the artist. Well, those figures were split between the two canvases, proving that the two paintings were once one**. But the main purpose of using x-rays, which is called x-radiography, is to examine the progress of the work. You know how some of you, uh… when you paint a picture, you make a sketch with a pencil first, and then you just paint over it. Well, x-radiography can be used to see the pencil marks. 🎧 Remember our discussion last week? What did we talk about, Raymond?

S: Well, we talked about the way pigments are analyzed. You know, the reasons it's done and the different methods used. You mentioned molecular spectroscopy and…

P: **Q6** Good, stop right there. We learned about molecular spectroscopy, which essentially analyzes the fibers used in pigments to tell them apart. The reason why I mention this is that x-radiography uses the same principles. X-rays can capture what can't be seen or analyzed just by looking at the surface. So, because these pigments have different atomic structures, we can use a certain type of film that will only pick up signs of certain pigments. This is how it works. **Q3** What shows up on x-ray photographs is basically whatever blocks the x-rays themselves from going through the film. Imagine if you painted over your hand on top of a piece of paper. Once you lifted your hand, you'd see an image of it in the area that hadn't been painted. With x-rays, we

Main Idea
과학기술이 예술에 어떻게 적용되는가

Misunderstanding / Correction
x-ray로 예술 작품의 진행상황을 확인
Headset

Example
x-ray의 원리를 예를 들어 설명

Unit 3_Arts_정답 및 해석 | 079

Finding
*Patch of Grass*에서 한 네덜란드인 소작농의 초상을 발견

Cause
그림을 캔버스 위에 덧칠하는 이유

Finding
*The Blue Boy*에서는 흰색 개를 잔디와 바위로 덮어 그림

can use different wavelengths and film to filter out what we want to see. X-rays have led to some very impressive discoveries. ▶Q5-C◀ For example, we can see how an artist developed, or honed, a specific skill. X-rays of Van Gogh's *Patch of Grass* revealed a portrait of a Dutch peasant. ▶Q4◀ **He had painted a series of peasant's heads as a means of perfecting his control of color and light.** It is thought that this was a part of that series. And x-rays of the Picasso painting *The Blue Room* uncovered a bearded man wearing a jacket and bow tie. Many artists painted over their canvases, I guess even now, to save money. Therefore, examining artwork this way can be quite enlightening.

▶Q5-D◀ **We can also gain insight into how an artist's thinking developed and changed during the process of painting a picture.** *The Blue Boy* by Thomas Gainsborough shows an aristocratic young man. But according to historians, the subject was actually the son of one of Gainsborough's merchant friends who wanted his boy to look like he was from a wealthy upper-class family. In a portion where there is now just grass and rocks, x-rays revealed a fluffy white dog prancing around his feet. The artist probably thought this would ruin the aristocratic illusion he was looking for and eventually just painted over it.

해석 예술과 과학 수업의 다음 강의 일부분을 들으시오.

교수(여자): 미술 작품들이 어떻게 분석되는지에 대해 논의를 계속하도록 하죠. 자, 지난 수업시간에 무엇을 얘기했는지 기억하는 사람 있나요?

학생(남자): 여러 다른 안료들이 어떻게 분석되는지에 대해 이야기했어요. 납을 원료로 한 안료들과… 음… 탄소를 원료로 한 안료들에 대해서도 뭔가 말씀하셨고요. 어떻게… 음… 미술사가들이 샘플을 채취하지 않고도 그림을 분석할 수 있는지도요. 그래서 값비싼 미술 작품에 손상을 입히지 않아도 된다고요.

교수: 좋아요! 음, 오늘은 그 지식에 더하여 그것을 확장해볼 겁니다. 여러분 모두 엑스레이에 대해 들어봤을 것으로 생각합니다. 음, 과거에는, 이런 비교적 현대적인 기술은 병원과 치과에서만 사용되었었죠. 하지만 이제는 엑스레이가 미술 작품들의 연구에도 널리 쓰이고 있습니다. 어째서인지 짐작가는 사람 있나요?

학생: 많은 예술품이 손상을 입어서가 아닌가요? 제 말은, 엑스레이는 사람이 뼈가 부러졌을 때 사용되잖아요?

교수: 음… 그럴 수도 있죠. 그게 내가 언급하려던 그 이유는 아니지만, 엑스레이는 손상된 미술품에 대해 더 알고자 하기 위해 쓰일 수도 있어요. 한 예로, 같은 화가에 의해 그려진 두 가지 별개의 그림들이 있었습니다. 하지만 오하이오주의 한 미술사가는 그 그림들이 같은 그림의 부분들이라고 의심했는데, 그 그림은 돈을 두 배로 벌고자 했던 한 부정직한 미술상에 의해 반으로 잘려진 것이었습니다. 엑스레이를 통해, 화가가 덮어 씌워 그렸던 여러 숨겨진 인물들도 드러났습니다. 음, 그 인물들은 두 개의 캔버스로 나뉘었는데, 그것이 그 두 그림이 한 때는 하나였다는 것을 증명하는 것이었습니다. 하지만 엑스레이를 사용하는 주된 목적은, 그것은 x-radiography라고 불리는데, 그 작품의 진전을 살펴보기 위함입니다. 여러분 일부는… 음… 여러분이 그림을 그릴 때는, 먼저 연필로 스케치를 하고, 그 위에 색을 칠하죠. 음, x-radiography는 연필 자국을 살펴보는 데 쓰일 수 있습니다. 지난주에 논의했던 것 기억이 나나요? 우리가 무슨 이야기를 했죠, Raymond?

학생: 음, 우리는 안료들이 분석되는 방식에 대해 이야기를 했어요. 분석을 해야 하는 이유와, 사용되는 여러 다른 방법들이요. 교수님이 분자 분광기에 대해 언급하셨고…

교수: 좋아요, 거기서 멈추죠. 우리는 분자 분광기에 대해 배웠는데, 그것은 안료에 사용된 섬유들을 구분하기 위해 그것들을 본질적으로 분석하는 기기이죠. 이것을 언급하는 이유는, x-radiography가 똑같은 원리들을 사용하기 때문입니다. 엑스레이는 표면만 봐서는 보이거나 분석할 수 없는 것들을 잡아낼 수 있습니다. 자, 이 안료들이 서로 다른 분자 구조들을 갖고 있기 때문에, 우리는 특정 안료들의 흔적만을 잡아내는 일종의 필름을 사용할 수 있습니다. 그게 작용하는 방식은 이렇습니다. 엑스레이 사진들에 나타나는 것은, 기본적으로 그것이 무엇이건 엑스레이 자체가 필름을 투과하는 것을 막는 것입니다. 여러분이 종이 위에 손을 놓고 그림을 그린다고 상상해보세요. 손을 들면, 색칠이 되지 않은 곳에 여러분의 손의 이미지를 보게 될 것입니다. 엑스레이로는, 보고 싶은 것을 걸러 내기 위해서 우리는 여러 다른 파장들과 필름을 사용할 수 있어요. 엑스레이는 몇 가지 매우 중요한 발견을 이끌기도 했습니다. 예를 들어, 우리는 어떤 화가가 어떻게 특정한 기술을 발전시켰는지, 즉 연마했는지 알 수 있습니다. 반 고흐의 〈풀밭〉을 엑스레이로 보자, 한 네덜란드인 소작농의 초상이 드러났습니다. 그는 색상과 빛에 대한 자신의 통제를 완벽히 하기 위한 방법으로, 일련의 소작농의 얼굴 그림들을 그렸던 것이죠. 이 그림 역시 그 연작들 중 한 부분이었다고 생각됩니다. 그리고 피카소의 그림 〈푸른 방〉의 엑스레이는 재킷과 나비넥타이를 하고 있는, 수염이 있는 한 남자의 모습을 드러냈습니다. 많은 화가들이, 돈을 아끼기 위해 캔버스 위에 그림을 덮어 그렸죠, 심지어 요즘에도 그렇다고 생각되지만요. 따라서, 미술 작품을 이런 식으로 검사하면 새로운 사실을 아는 데 매우 도움이 될 수 있습니다.

우리는 또한 한 그림을 그리는 과정 동안 한 화가의 사고가 어떻게 진전되고 바뀌었는지에 대한 통찰을 얻을 수도 있습니다. **Thomas Gainsborough**의 〈파란 옷을 입은 소년〉에는 한 귀족 청년이 나옵니다. 하지만 미술사가들에 의하면, 그 모델은 사실은 자신의 아들이 부유한 상류층 가족 출신처럼 보이기를 원했던, Gainsborough의 상인 친구들 중 한 명의 아들이었습니다. 지금은 그냥 잔디와 바위가 있는 부분에서, 엑스레이는 털이 수북한 흰 색 개 두 마리가 그의 발 주변을 뛰어다니고 있는 모습을 드러냈습니다. 화가는 아마도 이것이 자신이 바라던 귀족적 환상을 망칠지도 모른다 생각해서 결국 그 위에 덮어 그렸을지도 모르죠.

Ⓦ work of art 미술 작품, 예술품   pigment [pígmənt] 안료   lead [led] 납   carbon [káːrbən] 탄소   relatively [rélətivli] 비교적   figure [fígjər] 인물   split [split] 나누다   molecular spectroscopy 분자 분광기   fiber [fáibər] 섬유, 섬유질   atomic structure 분자 구조   wavelength [wéivleŋθ] 파장   filter out 걸러내다   hone [houn] 연마하다, 갈다   portrait [póːrtreit] 초상화   peasant [pézənt] 소작농   as a means of ~ ~의 수단으로   bearded [bíərdid] 수염이 있는   enlightening [inláitniŋ] 계몽적인   gain insight into ~ ~에 대한 식견을 갖다   aristocratic [ərìstəkrǽtik] 귀족의   upper-class [ʌpə(r)-klǽs] 상류층의   fluffy [flʌ́fi] 솜털의   prance around 뛰어다니다

01 강의의 주된 목적은?
Ⓐ **새로운 기술이 어떻게 미술에 대해 더 많은 것을 밝혀내는지 보여주려고**
Ⓑ 미술을 분석하는 데 사용되는 기술의 발달을 설명하려고
Ⓒ 엑스레이 발견의 중요성을 설명하려고
Ⓓ 새로운 예술을 창조하기 위한 엑스레이 기술 사용에 대해 탐구하려고

02 강의에 의하면, 오하이오의 한 미술사가는 두 점의 유명한 그림에서 무엇을 발견했는가?
Ⓐ 그 그림들은 같은 화가에 의해 그려지지 않았다.
Ⓑ 한 미술상이 그 그림들을 숨기려 했다.
Ⓒ 한 그림은 다른 하나의 복제품이었다.
Ⓓ **그 그림들은 한때 하나로 붙어 있었다.**

03 교수가 손 위에 그림을 그리는 것을 언급한 이유는?
Ⓐ 의료용 엑스레이와 x-radiography 간의 유사성을 강조하려고
Ⓑ **학생들이 x-ray가 작용하는 방식을 이해하도록 도우려고**
Ⓒ 독특한 그림 기법의 예를 들려고
Ⓓ x-radiography가 어떻게 여러 다른 안료 유형들을 만들어내는지 보여주려고

04 반 고흐에 대해 교수가 말한 것은?
Ⓐ 그는 종종 친구들의 초상을 그렸다.
Ⓑ 그는 부정직한 미술상들에게 속았다.
Ⓒ **그는 자신의 기술을 여러 번 반복해서 연습했다.**
Ⓓ 그는 다른 화가들의 캔버스 위에 그림을 그렸다.

05 교수에 의하면, x-radiography를 통해 화가들에 대해 배울 수 있는 두 가지는 무엇인가? (두 가지 선택)
Ⓐ 그들의 변화하는 사회적 지위
Ⓑ 그들의 그림이 위조되었는지 아닌지
Ⓒ **어떻게 그들의 기술을 향상시켰는지**
Ⓓ **그들의 사고 과정이 어땠는지**

강의의 일부분을 다시 듣고 질문에 답하시오. 🔊 **MP3 37_1**

> P: Remember our discussion last week? What did we talk about, Raymond?
> S: Well, we talked about the way pigments are analyzed. You know, the reasons it's done and the different methods used. You mentioned molecular spectroscopy and…
> P: Good, stop right there.

06 교수가 다음과 같이 말한 이유는?

> Good, stop right there.

Ⓐ 학생이 너무 많이 말을 해서 자신이 짜증이 났다는 것을 암시하려고
Ⓑ 교수가 듣고 싶어 했던 것을 학생이 언급했다는 것을 나타내려고
Ⓒ 학생이 교수가 수정해 주어야 할 실수를 했다는 것을 나타내려고
Ⓓ 그 화제가 한 번의 수업에서 설명되기에는 너무 어렵다는 것을 강조하려고

03 / Painting

Sample Questions

본문 p. 232

| 01 B | 02 A | 03 B, D | 04 C | 05 D | 06 D |

해석 현대 미술 수업의 다음 강의 일부분을 들으시오. ◁ MP3 38

교수(여자): 우리가 지금까지 공부해왔던 것처럼, 고전 회화들, 즉 전통적인 방식은 육안으로 인식할 수 있는 것에 기반합니다. 즉 우리가 눈을 통해 보는 것들을 모사하는 것이죠. 하지만 오늘은, 컨템포러리 아트라고도 알려져 있는, 현대 미술로 넘어가보죠. 현대 미술은 아방가르드 운동을 통해 19세기 초에 발달되었습니다. 하지만 대부분의 경우, 사람들은 이를 예술로 받아들이기를 거부했지요. 그들의 취향에는 너무나 급진적이었기 때문입니다.

학생(남자): 음... 현대 미술이 무엇 때문에 그렇게 급진적이 된 건가요?

교수: 음, 이걸 설명할 수 있는 가장 좋은 방법은 사진에 대해 생각해보는 거예요. 사진은 한 장면을 포착하지만, 본질적으로 그 장면은 우리가 눈을 통해 보는 것입니다. 하지만, 현대 미술의 경우는, 우리가 볼 수 없는 것을 그림을 통해 실험하기 시작했어요. 그들은 삶의 무형적인 측면, 즉 만질 수 없는 측면을 보았죠. 예를 들어, 내가 만일 정말 우울하다고 해봅시다. 우리의 눈은 그것을 볼 수 없지만, 화가들은 그 감정을 표현하기 위해 캔버스 전체를 파란색으로 칠할지도 모르죠. 대중은 사실적인 그림에만 익숙해 있었기 때문에, 일반적인 것을 넘어선 그림들을 보았을 때, 그들은 충격을 받았죠.

자, 현대 미술의 선구자는 George Braque로, 그는 1882년에 태어났습니다. Braque는 도장공이자 도배공이었지만, 급새 인상주의 화가로 발전했습니다. 그리고 25세가 되던 때, 그는 자신만의 독특한 스타일을 발전시키기 시작했는데, 그 스타일은 곧 입체파(Cubism)가 되었습니다. 입체파는 기하학에 대한, 그리고 더 중요하게는, 동시 시각에 대한 그의 새로운 관심에 기반했습니다. 우리는 어떤 물체의 한 측면만 볼 수 있다 하더라도, 다른 측면들이 존재한다는 것을 알고 있지요. 예를 들어, 음... 음... 아무거나 정육면체 모양을 한 것을 말해보세요.

학생: 어... 주사위요?

교수: 맞아요. 주사위를 한번 생각해봅시다. 우리에겐 점 하나만 보이더라도, 그게 다른 면들, 그러니까 점 두 개, 세 개, 네 개, 다섯 개, 여섯 개가 있는 다른 면들이 존재하지 않는다는 의미는 아니지요. 우리는 그 면들을 그저 볼 수 없을 뿐이에요. 음. Braque는 "글쎄, 내가 볼 수 있는 면과 점 두 개, 세 개, 네 개가 있는 면들을 같이 그리면 어떨까?"하고 생각했죠. 물체의 여러 면들을 보여주는 이런 방식이 정육면체 같은 기본적인 기하학 형태와 결합했을 때, 입체파가 탄생한 것입니다.

자, 새로운 형태의 미술에 대해 전에 내가 언급했던 것처럼... 음, 입체파가 적절한 양의 회의적 의견을 듣게 된 것은 놀라운 일이 아니었어요. 한 비평가는 Braque의 작품들이 작은 정육면체들로 가득 찬 캔버스일 뿐이라고 일축했지요. 아이러니하게도, 입체파가 그 이름을 얻은 것은 다름 아닌 그 비평가의 혹독한 비평에서였습니다. 자, 오해는 말고요. 입체파는 전통 회화의 규칙에서 완전히 벗어난 것은 아니었습니다. 입체파 화가들은 계속해서 현실세계의 일부인 정물과 인물, 경치를 묘사했습니다. 그러나, 입체파를 정말 독특하게 만들어준 것은 이런 대상들이 나타내어진 방식입니다.

George Braque가 표준으로부터 일탈을 했던 또 한 가지 점은, 녹색, 갈색, 회색 등의 칙칙한 색을 써서 색의 역할을 덜 강조한 것이었습니다. 심지어 사람을 그릴 때 조차도요. 나는 우리 중 그 누구도 녹색이나 회색 피부를 가진 사람이 없다고 확신해요. 그림의 대상들은 또한 마치 바로 전면에서 그것들을 보듯이 이차원적으로 그려지기도 했습니다. 하지만 그 대상의 다른 면들과 각도들도 보여지고 있기 때문에, 우리가 보고 있는 것이 정확히 무엇인지 알기는 정말 어려웠죠. 그래서, 바이올린은 앞과, 양 옆, 그리고 뒷모습이 동시에 보이는 식으로, 2차원적인 정육면체의 형태로 그려지는 것이죠. 그 그림들은 실제로 굉장히 놀라운 것이었습니다.

입체파는 낭만주의 같은 이전의 예술 운동에서 꽤 일탈한 것이었습니다. 낭만주의도 그림에서 격렬한 감정을 강조했다는 점에서 새로운 것이긴 했지만, 낭만주의는 여전히 미술의 규칙을 깨지는 않았어요. 그림으로 그려진 것들은 눈으로 볼 수 있는 것들이었죠. 낭만주의 화가들은 한 가지 면, 즉 자신들이 볼 수 있었던 면만을 그렸을 뿐이에요. 그것이 아마도 입체파보다 낭만주의 같은 운동들이 음악과 문학 같은 다른 매체에도 채택된 이유일 것입니다. 그것들은 실제 세계에서 찾을 수 있는 주제와 감정들에 기반을 두었기 때문이죠. 반면에 입체파는 주로 시각적인 핵심 원칙에 기반을 두었고, 따라서 다른 매체들에 의해 쉽게 채택되지 않았던 겁니다.

W naked eye 육안   contemporary art 현대미술   evolve [iválv] (서서히) 발달시키다   radical [rǽdikəl] 급진적인, 과격한   in essence 본질적으로   intangible [intǽndʒəbl] 무형의   norm [nɔːrm] 표준, 규범   impressionistic [imprèʃənístik] 인상파의   simultaneous [sàiməltéiniəs] 동시의   perspective [pərspéktiv] 원근법   multiple [mʌ́ltipl] 다수의   facet [fǽsit] 측면   dose (어느 정도의) 양   skepticism [sképtisizəm] 회의론   dismiss [dismís] 일축하다   portray [pɔːrtréi] 그리다, 묘사하다   still life 정물화   departure (일상 등으로부터의) 벗어남, 일탈   two-dimensionally 이차원적으로   striking [stráikiŋ] 빼어난   intense [inténs] 강렬한   medium [míːdiəm] 매체   adopt [ədápt] 채택하다

01 강의의 주된 내용은?
Ⓐ 화가들이 자신들을 차별화시키는 방법들
Ⓑ 한 19세기 예술 운동의 특징들
Ⓒ 새로운 예술 운동이 회의론을 마주치게 되는 이유
Ⓓ 입체파와 낭만주의 간의 차이점들

02 교수가 사진을 언급한 이유는?
Ⓐ 사진의 내용을 입체파와 대조하여 설명하려고
Ⓑ 사진이 어떻게 화가들이 자화상을 그리는 것에 영향을 주었는지 보여주려고
Ⓒ Braque가 사진에 대한 애정으로 인해 입체파를 시작했다는 것을 암시하려고
Ⓓ 낭만주의 운동의 기원을 소개하려고

03 교수에 의하면, 입체파의 어떤 특성이 전통적인 미술과 차이를 보였는가? (두 가지 선택)
Ⓐ 칙칙한 색상을 더 밝은 색상들로 대체했다.
Ⓑ 볼 수 있는 것 이상의 것을 포함시켰다.
Ⓒ 환상의 세계의 초현실적인 장면들에 초점을 맞추었다.
Ⓓ 대상의 여러 면들을 보여주었다.

04 교수가 주사위를 언급한 이유는?
Ⓐ Braque가 그림에 사용했던 도구라는 것을 알려주려고
Ⓑ Braque의 그림이 정육면체처럼 보였다는 것을 알려주려고
Ⓒ Braque의 독특한 그림 기법을 설명하려고
Ⓓ Braque가 대상으로 사용한 모양의 예를 들려고

05 교수에 의하면, '입체파'라는 이름의 기원은 무엇인가?
Ⓐ 한 유명한 화가의 그림
Ⓑ George Braque의 자화상
Ⓒ Picasso의 정육면체 그림
Ⓓ 한 비평가의 언급

06 입체파와 낭만주의 같은 다른 예술 운동의 차이점은?
Ⓐ 입체파는 다른 매체에 의해 채택되었다.
Ⓑ 입체파가 훨씬 이전에 확립되었다.
Ⓒ 입체파는 전통적인 예술의 영향을 받았다.
Ⓓ 입체파는 다른 매체에 적합하지 않았다.

≋ Practice Questions

본문 p. 236

| 01 B | 02 D | 03 C | 04 A | 05 C | 06 D |

Main Idea
정물화

Listen to part of a lecture in an art history class. ◁ MP3 39

Professor(female): **Q1** Today I'd like to spend some time talking about **still-life paintings.** As you all probably know, still lifes are paintings of inanimate objects. It

Cause
정물화가 인기 있는 이유
– 선택 사항이 많음

Headset

wasn't until the 17th century that still-life painting first became regarded as a genre of western art. >Q2< **One of the reasons why it gained so much popularity with artists, especially during that time, and in places like the Netherlands is, um, making a realistic painting of things that exist in front of you is a very flexible art form.** 🎧 >Q6< Painting things like books, fruit, or other objects that are placed on a table gives you a lot of options.

Student(male): What do you mean by options? Do you mean that they could depict the objects in whatever way they wanted? That sounds like a feature of modern art. I don't remember learning that it started that early.

P: You're right, it didn't. I'm not talking about how the artists painted still lifes. >Q2< **I'm talking about how you could arrange the inanimate objects, um… depending on the shapes and texture you were interested in.** It's different from painting landscapes in that you're creating and designing the scene as well. Painting is like a second step; the first is organizing what you're going to paint. In early still lifes from the Netherlands, you see a lot of elaborate tables filled with fine silver and fruit placed in expensive china. The whole scene conveys a sense of opulence and pleasure. In other still-life paintings, >Q3< **symbols were added. So along with the objects I mentioned, there might be an hourglass, or even a skull, on the table. These represented the temporary nature of things. My point is that the painters could choose what to include, as well as comment on life if they desired to do so.** But >Q1< by the 18th century, things had changed in Europe. Young artists were being taught that the quality of a painting hinged largely on its subject matter. So **artists believed that literary and historical subjects, uh… were inherently superior to still lifes. So, still-life painting was relegated to a supporting role in art,** meaning that most paintings from the 18th century showed scenes from literature and history. You'd have a bunch of people in the foreground, and in a small portion of the painting you'd have a still life of some food. The only other way still life was used was for the decoration of furniture or other household objects, if it was even used at all. Finally, though, >Q1< >Q4< **in the 19th century, still-life painting regained its status in European art and once again became a popular style with artists.** It was around this time that the genre spread across the Atlantic, to here in the United States. But it was popular primarily with painting enthusiasts and folk artists, people who were amateurs and produced art as a hobby or as part of a school curriculum, not as a profession. Um… One of the reasons why still lifes were popular with folk artists was that they could be made using a technique called stencil painting. You all know what stencils are, right?

S: Yes, I remember using them when I was a kid. They were cutouts of objects that you could use to draw things.

P: That's correct. The stencils you used were probably made of plastic, but back then they would cut objects out of a piece of cloth… let's say a bunch of leaves, for instance. You would place the stencil over the canvas and trace the shape onto the paper. After you had an outline, you could paint in the colors you wanted. This is useful for people who can't draw well free-hand… it lets them make realistic-looking objects. Now don't get me wrong, that doesn't mean the artists were untalented… >Q5< **I find some of their work to be pretty amazing. I mean, look at some of the stencil paintings from the 1800s and you'll see what I mean. Um… I recently saw a piece at an auction that sold for hundreds of thousands of dollars.** It had shading that gave it a three-dimensional look and bold colors that gave it a fresh, vibrant appearance. Still

Character
정물화는 원하는 사물을 배열하여 표현할 수 있음

Limitation
부활했지만 아마추어들에게만 국한됨

Cause
정물화가 민족 예술가들에게만 인기 있었던 이유
– stencil을 사용해 쉽게 그릴 수 있음

Opinion / Attitude
일부 미국 정물화는 꽤 놀랍다고 생각함

lifes like the one I saw, uh… symbolized the abundance that people sought after in their lives. It told them that their hard work would lead to a better life. Unlike, uh… the hourglasses or skulls I mentioned earlier. Uh, you don't see those sorts of symbols in American still lifes.

해석 미술사 수업의 다음 강의 일부분을 들으시오.

교수(여자): 오늘은 정물화에 대해 이야기할까 합니다. 여러분 모두 아마 알고 있듯이, 정물화는 생명이 없는 물체들을 그린 그림입니다. 17세기가 되어서야 정물화는 처음으로 서양화의 한 장르로 여겨졌습니다. 정물화가 화가들에게, 특히 그 시대 그리고 네덜란드 같은 곳에서, 그렇게 많은 인기를 얻었던 이유들 중 하나는, 음, 자신 앞에 존재하는 물건들에 대한 사실적인 그림을 그리는 것이 매우 융통성 있는 예술 형태이기 때문입니다. 탁자 위에 놓인 책이나 과일, 또는 다른 물체들을 그리는 것에는 많은 선택 사항이 있다는 것이죠.

학생(남자): 선택 사항이라니 무슨 뜻이죠? 화가들이 원하는 방식대로 그 물체들을 묘사할 수 있었다는 말씀이신가요? 그건 현대 미술의 특징처럼 들리는데요. 그게 그렇게 일찍 시작했다고 배운 기억은 없는데요.

교수: 맞아요, 그렇게 일찍 시작하지 않았죠. 나는 화가들이 정물을 어떻게 그렸는지에 대해 이야기하고 있는 것이 아니에요. 내가 말하는 바는, 생명이 없는 물체들을 어떻게 배열할 수 있었는지에 대한 겁니다. 음… 관심 있는 형태와 질감에 따라서 말이죠. 그것은 여러분이 장면을 만들어내고 디자인하기도 한다는 점에서, 풍경을 그리는 것과 다릅니다. 그림을 그리는 것은 두 번째 단계인 셈이죠. 첫 단계는 무엇을 그릴지 조직하는 것입니다. 네덜란드의 초기 정물화 그림들에서는, 은 제품들과 비싼 자기 위에 놓인 과일들로 가득한, 공을 들인 식탁들을 많이 보게 될 겁니다. (그림의) 전체 장면은 풍요로움과 쾌락을 전달하지요. 다른 정물화 그림들에서는, 상징들이 추가되었습니다. 그래서 내가 언급했었던 물체들과 함께, 식탁 위에 모래시계나, 심지어 해골이 있을지도 모르죠. 이것들은 사물의 일시적 속성을 나타냈습니다. 요점은, 화가들이 원하면, 그들은 인생에 대한 견해뿐만 아니라 무엇을 추가할지 선택할 수 있었다는 것입니다. 하지만 18세기경, 유럽에서의 상황이 변했습니다. 젊은 화가들은 그림의 질은 전적으로 그 소재에 달려 있다고 배우게 되었습니다. 그래서 화가들은 문학과 역사적 소재들이, 음… 본질적으로 정물화보다 우월하다고 생각했지요. 그래서, 정물화 그림은 미술에서 조연급으로 밀려나게 되었고, 이는 18세기의 대부분의 그림들은 문학과 역사의 장면들을 나타냈다는 것을 의미합니다. (그런 그림들에는) 전경에는 한 무리의 사람들이 있고, 그림의 작은 부분에 약간의 음식이 있는 정물이 있을 겁니다. 정물이 사용되었던 유일한 다른 방법은, 가구의 장식이나 다른 가재도구들의 장식을 위한 것이었죠, 만일 사용되기라도 했다면 말이죠. 하지만, 마침내 19세기에, 정물화는 유럽 미술에서 다시 그 지위를 찾고 다시 한번 화가들 사이에 인기 있는 양식이 되었습니다. 이 장르가 대서양을 건너 이곳 미국에 넘어온 것은 바로 이 시기 즈음이었습니다. 하지만 정물화는 주로 그림 애호가들과 민속 예술가들, 즉 직업이 아닌 취미나 학교 커리큘럼의 일부로 그림을 그렸던 아마추어인 사람들에게만 인기가 있었습니다. 음… 정물화가 민속 예술가들에게 인기가 있었던 이유들 중 하나는, 정물화가 스텐실 그림이라고 불리는 기법을 이용해서 만들어질 수 있었기 때문입니다. 여러분 모두 스텐실이 뭔지 알지요?

학생: 네, 어렸을 때 그걸 이용해봤던 기억이 나요. 그림을 그리는 데 사용되는, 물건 모양을 따라 오려진 것들이었어요.

교수: 맞아요. 학생이 사용했던 스텐실은 아마도 비닐로 만들어졌을 거예요. 하지만 옛날에는 천 조각에 물체의 모양을 잘랐죠… 예를 들어, 한 무더기의 잎사귀들이라고 해봅시다. 스텐실을 캔버스 위에 놓고 그 모양을 따라 종이 위에 그리는 거죠. 윤곽을 그리고 나면, 원하는 색상으로 칠할 수 있었어요. 이것은 손으로 그림을 잘 그리지 못하는 사람들에게 유용하지요… 사실처럼 보이는 물체들을 그릴 수 있게 해주니까요. 자, 오해하지는 마세요. 그게 그 화가들이 재능이 없었다는 말은 아닙니다… 그들 작품 중 일부는 무척이나 놀라워요. 내 말은, 1800년대의 스텐실 그림들 중 몇 개를 보면 내가 말하는 것을 이해할 겁니다. 음… 나는 최근에 한 경매에서 몇 십만 달러에 팔린 작품 하나를 본 적이 있어요. 그 작품에는 3차원 느낌을 주는 음영이 쓰였고, 그 작품에 신선하고 생기가 넘치는 모습을 선사하는 대담한 색상들도 쓰였어요. 내가 본 것과 같은 정물화는, 음… 사람들이 인생에서 추구했던 풍요로움을 상징했습니다. 그 작품은 사람들에게, 그들의 노고가 더 나은 삶으로 이끌어 줄 것이라고 말했습니다. 내가 앞서 언급했던, 음… 모래시계나 해골과는 달리 말이죠. 음, 그런 종류의 상징들은 미국의 정물화에서는 볼 수 없습니다.

Ⓦ still-life [stíl-láif] 정물(화)의   inanimate [inǽnəmit] 무생물의   flexible [fléksəbl] 융통성 있는   texture [tékstʃər] 질감   elaborate [ilǽbərit] 정성을 들인   fine silver 순은   china [tʃáinə] 도자기   convey [kənvéi] (의미를) 전달하다   opulence [ápjuləns] 부유함   skull [skʌl] 해골   hinge on ~ …에 달려 있다   inherently [inhí(:)ərəntli] 본질적으로   superior [sju(:)pí(:)əriər] 우월한   relegate [réləgèit] 격하시키다   foreground [fɔ́:rgràund] 전경   status [stéitəs] 지위   enthusiast [inθjú:ziæst] 열광적인 팬   profession [prəféʃən] 직업   cutout [kʌ́tàut] 오려내기   outline [áutlàin] 윤곽을 나타내다   freehand [fríːhænd] 손으로만 그린   three-dimensional [θrí:-diménʃənl] 3차원의   vibrant [váibrənt] 생기가 넘치는   abundance [əbʌ́ndəns] 풍부

01 강의의 주된 내용은?
Ⓐ 화가들이 어떻게 소재를 고르는지
Ⓑ 한 미술 장르의 쇠퇴와 부활
Ⓒ 17세기 유럽에서의 여러 다른 미술 양식들
Ⓓ 미국과 유럽 화가들간의 차이점들

02 정물화의 인기에 대한 이유로 교수가 언급한 점은?
Ⓐ 대중이 풍경화에 질려했다.
Ⓑ 정물화 그림들은 비싼 가격에 팔렸다.
Ⓒ (정물화) 기법들은 시간이 많이 걸리지 않았다.
Ⓓ 화가들은 자신이 그리는 것을 조절할 수 있었다.

03 교수가 상징을 언급한 이유는?
Ⓐ 네덜란드 그림과 미국 그림을 비교하려고
Ⓑ 역사적인 그림들이 왜 인기가 있었는지를 설명하려고
Ⓒ 일부 정물화 그림들의 특징을 강조하려고
Ⓓ 미국 민속 예술가들의 양식을 묘사하려고

04 19세기 정물화에 대해 교수가 말한 것은?
Ⓐ 유럽에서 다시 유행했다.
Ⓑ 많은 상징들을 나타내 보이기 시작했다.
Ⓒ 가구를 장식하기 위해서만 사용되었다.
Ⓓ 미국에서 유럽으로 퍼져 나갔다.

05 미국의 정물화에 대한 교수의 견해는?
Ⓐ 유럽의 그림들보다 못하다고 생각한다.
Ⓑ 대부분 너무 비싸다고 생각한다.
Ⓒ 일부는 인상적이라고 생각한다.
Ⓓ 너무 많은 상징을 사용한다고 생각한다.

강의의 일부분을 다시 듣고 질문에 답하시오. 🔊 **MP3 39_1**

> **P:** Painting things like books, fruit, or other objects that are placed on a table gives you a lot of options.
> **S:** What do you mean by options? Do you mean that they could depict the objects in whatever way they wanted? That sounds like a feature of modern art. I don't remember learning that it started that early.

06 학생이 다음과 같이 말한 이유는?

> I don't remember learning that it started that early.

Ⓐ 자신이 수업 자료를 이해하지 못하고 있다는 것을 나타내려고
Ⓑ 미술에 관해 잘 알려진 견해를 언급하려고
Ⓒ 정물화가 현대 미술로 간주되어야 한다는 것을 암시하려고
Ⓓ 어떤 점에 대해 설명이 필요하다는 것을 나타내려고

04 / Literature

⋟ Sample Questions

본문 p. 242

| 01 B | 02 C | 03 A | 04 B | 05 C, D | 06 D |

해석 미국 문학 수업의 다음 강의 일부분을 들으시오. 🔊 **MP3 40**

교수(남자): 탈식민지 문학에 대한 수업 내용에 이어서, 남북전쟁 이후의 문학에 초점을 맞춰보도록 하죠. 탈식민지 시대와 마찬가지로, 이 시기 역시 미국 사람들에게 있어 과도와 변화의 시기였다는 것을 염두에 두세요. 미국인들의 사고방식뿐만 아니라 정치 구조에도 변화들이 있었습니다. 미국의 오래된 제도들과 사회적 규범들이 몇 년이라는 시간 안에 변화되었죠. 모든 유형의 예술처럼, 이 시대의 문학도 이러한 새로운 발상

에 맞추고 변화를 위한 길을 닦아나갔죠.

이제 시를 살펴보고 싶네요. 슬프게도, 이 시대의 시는 많지가 않습니다. 우리가 알고 있는 대부분의 미국 시들은 20세기에 출간되었습니다. 하지만 이 시기에도 작품을 많이 냈던 시인들이 있긴 합니다. 진정한 미국 시 양식의 선구자들이었죠.

자, 우리가 다룰 첫 시인들 중 한 명은 Emily Dickinson입니다. 그녀는 여성 작가였기 때문에, 그녀가 살아 있는 동안 발표되었던 대부분의 그녀의 작품들은 사실상 심하게 편집되었습니다. 그녀가 사망하고 나서야 비로소 그녀의 진정한 예술적, 그리고 급진적인 스타일이 분명해졌지요. 그녀의 첫 작품집은 그녀가 사망한 4년 후인 1890년이 되어서야 출판되었습니다. 그럼에도 불구하고, 그녀는 가장 영향력 있는 미국 시인 중 한 명으로 남아 있습니다.

Dickinson의 시를 그렇게 특별하게 만들었던 것은 시의 소재와 사용된 언어 둘 다였습니다. 그녀는 전통적인 시에서 그다지 많은 일탈을 하지는 않았습니다. 연이 있고 각운이 있다는 점에서는 말이죠. 그녀는… 음… 자신의 스탠자(4행 이상의 각운이 있는 시구)의 2행과 4행에 완벽한 각운을 썼습니다. Dickinson의 시들을 정말로 흥미롭게 만드는 것은 그녀의 구문입니다. 그녀는 문장들을 구성하는 데 있어 일반적인 단어와 구 배열을 따르지 않았습니다. 그녀의 원고를 한 번 보기만 해도, 그녀가 전통적인 구두점을 대쉬로 대체했고 관습에 사로잡히지 않고 대문자를 사용했다는 사실이 드러납니다.

그녀가 사용한 소재 역시 그녀의 시를 그 시대의 다른 시인들과 뚜렷이 다르게 만들어주었습니다. 그녀는 생활 속의 흔한 물건들, 즉 대부분은 눈치채지 못하고 넘어가는 익숙한 측면들에서 의미를 찾았습니다. 밤에 큰 소리로 째깍거리는 시계 소리 같은 이미지를 생각해보세요. 이것은 우리가 대개 잘 알아차리지 못하는 것이지만, 그럼에도 불구하고 우리는 그것에 공감할 수 있습니다. 여러분 모두 밤에 시계 소리를 들어본 적이 있지 않나요? 그녀의 시들은 진지하기도 하고 장난기 많은 마음을 드러내기도 합니다. 그녀를 미국 역사상 가장 위대한 시인들 중 하나로 만들었던 것은 바로 그녀가 그러한 일상적인 물체들을 그녀의 심오한 생각에 결합시켰던 방법에 있습니다.

내가 다루고 싶은 다른 한 명의 시인은 Walt Whitman입니다. 그는 전통을, 형식적 그리고 의미적 측면에서 모두, 매우 급진적으로 깨서 그 세대 사람들과 이후 세대 사람들 또한 충격에 빠뜨렸습니다. 비록 그가 창시자는 아니었지만, 그는 일정한 패턴이나 각운에 의존하지 않는 유형의 시인 자유시의 아버지라고 종종 불립니다. 그는 전통적인 시 기법에 의존하지 않는 최초의 시인들 중 하나였습니다. Dickinson이 그녀의 구문을 통해 전통을 깨려고 애쓴 반면, Whitman은 전통적인 요소들을 없애서 전통을 깼죠. 그의 가장 유명한 시들 중 하나에서 그는 다음과 같이 썼습니다. '원고를 보느라 눈이 침침해지자 씹는 담배를 찾는다. 기괴한 모양의 사지들이 의사의 수술대에 묶여 있다.' 여러분은 그의 행들에 각운이 없다는 것을 분명히 알 수 있을 겁니다. 하지만 이 단어들이 흘러가는 방식은… 다른 시인들은 아무도 할 수 없는… 그의 시들의 구조는 정말로 놀라웠습니다.

Whitman이 사용했던 소재들은 매일매일의 삶에 대한 인정사정 없이 정직한 구현이었습니다. 사지에 관한 행은, 대부분의 사람들이 시에 어울린다고 생각하는 솜털같이 아름다운 소재는 아니죠. 그의 걸러지지 않은 본성은 Dickinson을 포함해 그의 시에 대해 폄하하는 많은 이들을 낳았지만, 그의 영향력은 오늘날에도 여전히 느껴집니다.

이 두 시인은 완전히 다른 소재에 대해서 시를 썼고, 서로 다른 기법들을 가지고 있었습니다. 하지만 둘 다 시에서 신의 권능에 대한 다양한 언급을 하며 강한 종교의 영향을 보여 주었습니다. 또한 그들 둘 다, 나를 포함한 많은 작가들로부터 최초의 근대적 시인으로 여겨지고 있어요.

ⓦ post-colonial [poustkəlóuniəl] 식민지로부터 독립 후의　Civil War 미국 남북 전쟁　transition [trænzíʃən] 과도　mindset [máindset] 사고방식　pave the way for (~) …을 위한 길을 닦다　prolific [prəulífik] 다작의　subject matter 소재　deviate from ~ …에서 일탈하다　verse [vəːrs] (시의) 연　rhyme [raim] 각운　stanza [stǽnzə] 스탠자(4행 이상의 각운이 있는 시구)　syntax [síntæks] 구문론, 통사론　punctuation mark 문장부호　capitalization [kæpətəlizéiʃən] 대문자 사용　unnoticed [ʌnnóutist] 간과되는　ticking [tíkiŋ] 째깍거림　fuse [fjuːz] 융합하다　mundane [mʌ́ndein] 일상적인　profound [prəfáund] 심오한　free verse 자유시　quid [kwid] 씹는 담배　malformed [mælfɔ́ːrmd] 기형인　limb [lim] 팔, 다리　unfiltered [ʌnfíltərd] 여과되지 않은　detractor [ditrǽktər] 폄하하는 사람　divine power 신의 권능

01 강의의 목적은?
Ⓐ 미국 시가 어떻게 발전했는지 설명하려고
Ⓑ 두 명의 독특한 미국 시인을 소개하려고
Ⓒ 현대 시의 예를 들려고
Ⓓ 전쟁이 문학에 끼친 영향을 보여주려고

02 강의에 의하면, Dickinson에 관해 사실인 것은?
Ⓐ Whitman과 절친한 친구였다.
Ⓑ 종종 다른 이의 시를 편집했다.
Ⓒ 살아 있는 동안은 유명하지 않았다.
Ⓓ 자신의 시가 종교적인 테마에 영향받지 않게 했다.

03 교수에 의하면, Dickinson의 시에서 흥미로운 점은 무엇인가?
- Ⓐ 관습적인 구두법을 쓰지 않았다.
- Ⓑ 시의 전통적인 측면들에 초점을 맞췄다.
- Ⓒ 아름다움보다는 추악함에 대해 썼다.
- Ⓓ 자유시를 창조했다.

04 Whitman의 시는 어떤 면에서 Dickinson의 시와 달랐는가?
- Ⓐ 그의 종교적인 믿음 때문에 더 보수적이었다.
- Ⓑ 전통을 깨기 위해 다른 기법을 사용했다.
- Ⓒ 미국인들의 삶의 일상적인 측면들을 주로 강조했다.
- Ⓓ 예전 시를 바꾸는 대신 새로운 장르의 시를 시작했다.

05 교수에 의하면, Whitman과 Dickinson이 공통으로 가진 측면은 무엇인가? (두 가지 선택)
- Ⓐ 일반적인 주제를 제시하는 새로운 방법들을 발견했다.
- Ⓑ 매우 긴 스탠자를 쓰는 것을 선호했다.
- Ⓒ 각자의 작품에 종교적인 영향을 나타냈다.
- Ⓓ 둘 다 현대 시인으로 여겨진다.

06 교수가 다음과 같이 말한 이유는? 🔊 **MP3 40_1**

> You've all heard a clock at night, right?

- Ⓐ 충분한 수면을 취하는 학생이 거의 없다는 것을 암시하려고
- Ⓑ Dickinson이 아마도 느꼈을 짜증을 말해주려고
- Ⓒ Dickinson은 독특한 사람이었다는 것을 알려주려고
- Ⓓ **Dickinson이 흔한 주제를 사용했다는 사실을 강조하려고**

≋ Practice Questions
본문 p. 246

| 01 A | 02 C, D | 03 B | 04 B | 05 A | 06 D |

Listen to part of a lecture in an African-American history class. 🔊 MP3 41

Professor(male): So, I just finished reading your papers on African-American culture. At first I was surprised that none of you discussed the Harlem Renaissance. Then I remembered that I haven't really covered that subject in depth. **Q1** The Harlem Renaissance was an unprecedented cultural movement that spanned the 1920s and had a profound impact not only on American culture and history but abroad as well. It introduced a significant period that emphasized self-identity as well as group consciousness among black people around the world.

Many aspects of culture developed during this movement, but I'd like to focus on the literary awakening that occurred among African Americans. It was characterized by an assertiveness on their part, and by an outburst of creativity never seen before. Some of the better known writers of the Harlem Renaissance include Langston Hughes and Claude McKay.

Langston Hughes was one of the earliest innovators of a new literary art called jazz poetry. Hughes wanted to somehow capture the folk traditions of his people and incorporate them into new forms... Basically, he wanted to create, to improve upon conventional forms. He wanted to create literature that was more reflective of the heritage of his people. **Q2-C** He incorporated many forms of African-American mu-

Main Idea
할렘 르네상스
Origin
– 전례가 없던 문화 운동

Character
작가의 특징
– innovator
◐ 'The first(최초의)', 'incorporate A into B(A에 B를 접목하다)' 와 같은 표현을 잘 들어야 한다.

sic, such as spirituals, jazz and blues, into his poetry. He was also the first person to write a gospel play.

As for Claude McKay, he was a Jamaican immigrant who published a bestselling novel, *Home to Harlem*, in 1928. Unlike Hughes, McKay focused on contemporary Harlem lifestyles. He wrote about the street life in Harlem in an attempt to capture the energetic and intense spirit of African Americans in the United States. **Q2-D** *Home to Harlem* gained substantial readership as the details of African American life in New York City was largely unknown to the general public.

Q3 As its name suggests, the movement was centered in Harlem, a neighborhood in New York City, which was at the time one of the largest cosmopolitan communities in the world. But as the works of pioneers influenced more and more African Americans across the United States, **the movement spread to other cities, especially in the urban north,** including Washington, D.C., Chicago, and even Cleveland, Ohio. Because of this, the Harlem Renaissance was sometimes referred to as "the New Negro Renaissance." At that time, "negro" was considered an acceptable term, but, of course, we no longer use it today.

Q4 Q5 **W.E.B. Du Bois, a prolific author and intellect, is considered by some to be one of the initiators of the renaissance.** The exact beginnings of the movement, however, are debatable. Historians have traditionally dated the start of the movement to the 1920s, but some feel that the sudden blossoming of literature at that time had its root in the earlier work of Du Bois. He published *The Souls of Black Folk*, one of the first works to explore black identity, in 1903. He emphasized the dual standard of African Americans, calling it "a sense of always looking at oneself through the eyes of others."

Q4 **In 1906, Du Bois organized a meeting in the town of Niagara Falls.** It included various leaders from African-American communities and had the goal of advocating the end of racial, social and economic discrimination of African Americans. **This was the beginning of the so-called Niagara Movement, which led to the formation of a number of civil rights organizations.**

Another factor in the development of the Harlem Renaissance, the great migration, began at the turn of the century and lasted well into the 1930s. More than one million African Americans left the rural communities of the southern United States and moved to northern cities such as New York, Chicago, and Cleveland. There were many reasons for this, but, for the most part, they left in search of a better life. There was a labor shortage in these cities, so African Americans from the South moved to them seeking better economic opportunities. The inherent and widespread discrimination in the South didn't help either.

Sadly, the treatment they received wasn't that much different in the North. Racial inequality existed everywhere in the U.S. Even African-American WWI veterans faced it when they returned home in 1918. But, having risked their lives for their country, they were no longer willing to accept second-class citizenship. **Q6** **They began to advocate for equality and become more assertive, often defying the oppressive behavior of whites. This created a mood that can be considered another early factor in the formation of the Harlem Renaissance.**

Origin
할렘 르네상스가 시작된 곳 – 뉴욕의 할렘

Role
선도자

Origin
정확한 시작 시점이 논쟁

Problem
미국 흑인들에 대한 차별이 만연함

Origin
평등에 대한 갈망이 할렘 르네상스의 원동력이 됨

해석 미국 흑인 역사 수업의 다음 강의 일부를 들으시오.

교수(남자): 자, 미국 흑인 문화에 관한 여러분의 보고서를 모두 읽었습니다. 처음에는 할렘 르네상스에 대해 다룬 사람이 아무도 없다는 것에 놀랐습니다. 그런데 내가 그 주제를 깊이 다룬 적이 없었다는 것이 기억났어요. 할렘 르네상스는 1920년대에 걸쳐 일어난, 전례가 없던 문화 운동이었고, 미국 문화와 역사뿐만 아니라 해외에까지 커다란 영향을 주었던 운동이었습니다. 이 운동은 전세계 흑인들 사이에 집단의식뿐만 아니라 자아 정체성을 강조했던 중요한 시기를 시작시켰지요.

이 운동이 진행되는 동안 문화의 많은 측면들이 발전했지만, 나는 미국 흑인들 사이에 일어났던 문학적 각성에 초점을 맞추고 싶습니다. 그것은 그들에게는 자기 주장으로 특징지어지며, 또한 이전에는 보지 못했던 창의성의 폭발로 특징지어집니다. 할렘 르네상스 작가 중 좀 알려진 몇몇 이들로는 Langston Hughes와 Claude McKay를 들 수 있습니다.

Langston Hughes는 재즈 시(jazz poetry)라고 불리는 새로운 문학 예술의 초기 창시자 중의 한 명이었습니다. 그는 흑인들의 민속 전통을 포착하여 이를 새로운 형식들에 접목시키고자 했습니다... 기본적으로, 그는 전통적인 형식을 더 향상시키고 싶어 했지요. 그는 흑인들의 유산을 더 잘 반영하는 문학을 만들고 싶어 했습니다. 그는 흑인 음악의 많은 형식들, 즉 영가, 재즈, 블루스 같은 것들을 그의 시에 접목시켰습니다. 그는 또한 최초로 가스펠 연극을 쓴 사람이기도 했습니다.

Claude McKay는 1928년에 베스트셀러 소설 〈홈 투 할렘〉을 출간한 자메이카 이민자였습니다. Hughes와는 달리, McKay는 동시대의 할렘의 생활양식에 초점을 맞췄습니다. 그는 미국에 사는 활기차고 강력한 미국 흑인들의 정신을 포착하려는 시도로, 할렘 거리에서의 삶에 대해 썼습니다. 뉴욕시에 사는 흑인들의 상세한 내용이 일반 대중들에게는 대체로 알려져 있지 않았기 때문에, 〈홈 투 할렘〉은 상당한 독자층을 얻게 되었습니다.

그 이름이 나타내듯이, 이 운동은 뉴욕시의 동네인 할렘이 중심이 되었습니다. 뉴욕은 그 당시 세계에서 가장 큰 국제적인 지역사회의 하나였지요. 하지만 선구자들의 작품들이 미국 전역의 점점 더 많은 흑인들에게 영향을 미치면서, 그 운동은 다른 도시들, 특히 워싱턴, 시카고를 포함한 북부 도시들과 심지어 오하이오의 클리브랜드까지 퍼져 나갔습니다. 이 때문에, 할렘 르네상스는 가끔씩 '뉴 니그로 르네상스'라고 불리기도 했습니다. 그 당시는 '니그로'가 사회적으로 용인되는 용어였지만, 물론 이제는 더 이상 쓰지 않습니다.

다작 작가이자 지식인인 W.E.B. Du Bois는 일부 사람들에 의해 이 르네상스의 선도자 중의 한 명으로 여겨집니다. 하지만 이 운동의 정확한 시초에 대해서는 여전히 논란이 있습니다. 역사학자들은 전통적으로 이 운동의 시작을 1920년대로 잡지만, 일부는 그 당시의 문학의 갑작스러운 번창이 Du Bois의 초기 작품에 그 뿌리를 두고 있다고 생각합니다. 그는 1903년에 〈흑인의 영혼〉을 출간했는데, 그것은 흑인의 정체성을 탐구한 최초의 작품 중 하나였습니다. 그는 미국 흑인들의 이중잣대를 강조하며, 그것을 '다른 사람들의 눈을 통해서 항상 자신을 바라보는 의식'이라고 불렀습니다.

1906년, Du Bois는 나이아가라 폭포 마을에서 한 회합을 조직했습니다. 그 회합은 다른 미국 흑인 공동체들의 다양한 지도자들로 구성되었으며, 미국 흑인들에 대한 인종적, 사회적, 경제적 차별의 종지부를 지지하는 것을 목표로 하였습니다. 이것이 소위 나이아가라 운동이라고 불리는 운동의 시작이었는데, 이는 수많은 민권 단체들의 형성으로 이어졌습니다.

할렘 르네상스의 발전에 있어 또 다른 요인이었던 흑인 대이동은, 19세기 말에 시작해서 1930년대에 이르기까지 이어졌습니다. 백만 명 이상의 흑인들이 미국 남부의 시골 공동체를 떠나 뉴욕, 시카고, 클리브랜드 같은 북쪽의 도시들로 이주했습니다. 이런 대이동에는 많은 이유들이 있었지만, 대개 그들은 더 나은 삶을 찾아 떠났습니다. 이런 도시들에는 인력이 부족했고, 그래서 남부에서 온 흑인들은 더 나은 경제적 기회를 찾아 그 도시들로 이주했지요. 남부의 내재된, 그리고 널리 퍼진 차별 역시 별 도움이 되지 못했습니다.

안타깝게도, 그들이 받았던 처우는 북부에서도 그다지 많이 다르지 않았습니다. 인종적 불평등은 미국 전역에 만연해 있었습니다. 심지어 제1차 세계대전 흑인 참전 용사들도 1918년에 전쟁에서 돌아왔을 때 그 점을 직면했지요. 하지만, 나라를 위해 목숨을 걸었던 그들은 더 이상 2등 시민 취급을 받아들일 수 없었습니다. 그들은 평등을 주장하기 시작했고, 더 적극적이 되었습니다. 종종 백인들의 억압적인 행동에 저항하면서 말이죠. 이것이 할렘 르네상스의 형성에 있어 또 다른 초기 요인으로 여겨지는 분위기를 형성했죠.

🆆 unprecedented [ʌnprésidèntid] 전례 없는　span [spæn] (얼마의 기간에) 걸쳐 이어지다　self-identity [sélf-aidéntəti] 개성, 자아 정체성　group consciousness 집단 의식　awakening [əwéikəniŋ] 자각, 인식　characterize [kǽriktəràiz] 특징짓다　assertiveness [əsə́ːrtivnes] 자기 주장　outburst [áutbə̀ːrst] 폭발, 급격한 증가　innovator [ínəvèitər] 혁신자　reflective [rifléktiv] 반영하는　heritage [héritidʒ] 유산, 전통　spiritual [spíritʃuəl] 정신적인　contemporary [kəntémpərèri] 동시대의　cosmopolitan [kɑ̀zməpɑ́litən] 세계적인　be referred to as ~ ...로 불리다　blossoming [blɑ́səmiŋ] 개화　discrimination [diskrìmənéiʃən] 차별　civil right 민권　inequality [ini(ː)kwɑ́ləti] 불평등　defy [difái] 저항하다　oppressive [əprésiv] 억압적인

01 강의의 주된 내용은?
ⓐ 미국 흑인 문학 운동의 역사
ⓑ 미국 흑인 작가들이 직면했던 문제들
ⓒ 민권 운동의 초기 기원
ⓓ 문학에 나타난 미국 흑인들에 대한 묘사

02 교수는 할렘 르네상스의 두 주요 작가를 언급하고 있다. 그들의 글에 있어 혁신적인 특징은 무엇인가? (두 가지 선택)
ⓐ 미국 흑인들의 감정을 묘사하기 위해 새로운 언어를 접목시키기
ⓑ 미국 흑인들의 문화를 강조하기 위해서 더 리듬감 있는 요소를 포함시키기

Ⓒ 전통적인 흑인 음악과 시를 결합시키기

Ⓓ 대중들에게 잘 알려지지 않았던 미국 흑인들의 생활방식을 대중들에게 노출시키기

03 할렘 르네상스의 지리적 기원에 대해서 교수가 지적하는 점은?

Ⓐ 제1차 세계대전 후에 유럽에서 미국으로 전해졌다.

Ⓑ 뉴욕에서 시작되어 다른 북부 도시들로 퍼져나갔다.

Ⓒ 미국 남부의 시골 지역에서 시작되었다.

Ⓓ 자메이카에서의 유사한 운동으로부터 차용되었다.

04 나이아가라 운동에 대해 교수가 암시하는 것은?

Ⓐ 미국 흑인들에게 그다지 큰 영향을 미치지 않았다.

Ⓑ 할렘 르네상스의 전신이 되었다.

Ⓒ 많은 할렘 르네상스 작가들이 참가했다.

Ⓓ 미국 흑인들이 북부로 이주하도록 동기를 부여했다.

05 교수가 작가 W.E.B. Du Bois를 언급한 이유는?

Ⓐ 할렘 르네상스를 위한 기반을 세운 인물들 중 하나를 알려주려고

Ⓑ 왜 흑인 작가들이 자신들의 공동체에 대한 글을 거의 쓰지 않았었는지를 설명하려고

Ⓒ 미국 흑인들의 북부로의 대이동이 어떻게 시작되었는지를 설명하려고

Ⓓ 모든 미국 흑인 작가들이 할렘 르네상스를 지지하지는 않았다는 것을 알려주려고

06 교수에 의하면, 할렘 르네상스의 시작에 기여했을 것은 무엇인가?

Ⓐ 작가들의 북부 도시들로의 대거 이주

Ⓑ 미국 흑인 병사들이 유럽에서 직면했던 차별

Ⓒ 미국 흑인들을 위한 더 나은 교육 기회들

Ⓓ 평등하게 대우받고 싶다는 미국 흑인들의 열망

05 / Film & Theater History

Sample Questions

본문 p. 252

01 C   02 D   03 C   04 B   05 A, D   06 A

해석 연극 수업의 다음 강의 일부분을 들으시오. ◁ MP3 42

교수(남자): 연극은 실제로 전혀 새로운 것이 아닙니다. 기원전 6세기경부터, 우리가 지금 보는 것과 거의 닮은 일종의 연극이 있어왔죠. 내 말은, 기본 요소들은 어느 정도 똑같았다는 것입니다. 본질적으로, 어떤 종류의 연극이건 어떤 줄거리를 따르는 장면들을 연기하는 배우들로 구성됩니다. 하지만 더 나아간 어떤 것으로 진화한, 현대 연극의 한 측면이 있지요. 내가 말하고자 하는 것은 프로덕션 디자인입니다.

프로덕션 디자인은 물론, 항상 연극의 한 요소였지요. 하지만 20세기가 되어서야 비로소 사람들은 실제로 그것에 초점을 맞추기 시작했습니다. 기본적으로, 프로덕션 디자인은 무대, 무대 장치, 의상, 그리고 조명과 같은 연극의 모든 시각적 요소들과 관련되어 있습니다. 그리고, 어떤 경우는, 심지어 음향도 포함하지요.

음향이 포함된다고 말한 이유는, 좋은 음향시설을 갖추는 것의 중요성 때문입니다… 관객이 무대에서 하는 말을 실제로 들을 수 있게 하기 위해서 말이지요. 우리는 최적의 음질을 위해 현재의 극장들이 지어진 방식에 관해서 고대 그리스인들에게 고마워해야 합니다. 이 고대 건축가들은 사람의 목소리가 어떻게 전달되는지도 고려했습니다. 목소리가 어떻게 울리는지 뿐만 아니라 말이죠… 즉, 목소리가 벽에 어떻게 반사되는지 말입니다. 극장 안의 모든 사람들이 배우들의 목소리를 똑같이 잘 들을 수 있도록 말이에요. 오늘날, 음질은 대부분의 극장 건축에 있어 이미 고려의 대상이 되어 있고, 그래서 음질은 무대 디자인에는 대개 영향을 미치지 않습니다. 하지만, 말한 대로, 가끔씩은 음질이 무대 디자인에 영향을 줍니다.

다음으로는 세트 디자인입니다. 세트는 본질적으로는 소도구나 의상의 일부가 아닌, 무대 위의 모든 것을 말합니다. 올바른 세트 디자인은 관객들의 시각적 경험을 고려해야 할 뿐만 아니라 일부 기능적인 측면들도 다루어야 할 필요가 있습니다. 예를 들어, 한 연극에서, 화난 등장인물이 문을 쾅 닫는 장면이 있을 수 있습니다. 세트 디자이너는 문이 쾅 하고 닫힐 때 적절한 소리를 내도록 해야 하는 동시에, 무대 전체가 무너

져 내리지 않도록 해야 합니다.

자, 가끔씩은, 세트의 일부가 소도구가 될 수도 있습니다. 세트의 일부분이 되는 물체와 소도구와의 주된 차이점은, 배우가 그것을 들어올리느냐 아니냐 하는 것입니다. 그래서, 한 화난 등장인물이 의자를 던져 부수는 장면이 있다고 해봅시다. 의자는 장면 초반에는 세트의 일부분이었지만, 배우가 그것을 들어올리는 순간 소도구가 되는 것입니다.

프로덕션 디자인의 다음 주요 요소는 의상입니다. 의상 디자이너들은 그 연극의 역사적 맥락을 이해하고 올바르게 반영해야 합니다. 이것은 최소한의 세트 디자인을 갖춘 연극들에서 특히 중요합니다. 의상 그 자체가 연극의 역사적 시기를 설정해주는 주요한 시각 요소이기 때문이지요. 의상은 또한 관객들이 어떤 등장인물을 인지하는 방식에 영향을 미치는 데에도 쓰일 수 있습니다. 예를 들어, 나머지 등장인물들의 모자와는 조금 다른 각도로 모자를 쓴 등장인물은 (배우들) 무리에서 눈에 띄겠죠. 그 모자는 관객들의 주목을 끌겠지만, 관객들은 왜 그런지는 실제로 알지 못할 것입니다. 다시 말해, 미묘한 의상 디자인 요소들이 등장인물을 인식하는 데에 큰 영향을 미칠 수 있는 것입니다.

그리고 마지막으로, 조명이 있지요. 조명은 프로덕션 디자인에 있어 가장 중요한 요소입니다. 조명 없이는 연극을 볼 수 없잖아요, 안 그럴까요? 따라서 조명은 매우 중요합니다. 조명은 동작을 비춰주고, 장면의 분위기를 조절하는 데 쓰일 수도 있습니다. 초기 극장들은 촛불이라는 제한에 얽매일 수 밖에 없었습니다. 하지만 오늘날에는, 조명에 의해 얻어질 수 있는 가능성들은 기본적으로 무한하죠. 내가 대학생 때 어떤 작품의 조명 감독을 했던 것이 기억나네요. 현대의 뉴욕에서 일어나는 일로 각색이 되었던 옛 영국 연극이었죠. 내 일이 얼마나 힘든지 생각이 나려 할 때마다, 나는 쓸 수 있는 전구들로 극장이 가득차 있지 않던 때의, 이전의 모든 조명 감독들을 내 자신에게 상기시켰습니다. 그건 정말 전혀 다른 세상이었을 거에요.

어쨌든, 프로덕션 디자인은 분명히 현대 극장에 있어 중요한 부분입니다. 정말로, 프로덕션 디자인은 좋은 극본과 재능 있는 배우들만큼이나 연극의 성공에 중요해졌습니다.

Ⓦ element [éləmənt] 요소　concern [kənsə́ːrn] ...에 관한[관련된] 것이다　acoustics [əkúːstiks] 음향시설　optimal [áptəməl] 최적의　reverberate [rivə́ːrbəreit] (소리가) 울리다　bounce [bauns] 튀다　prop [prɑp] 소도구　address [ədrés] 다루다　slam [slæm] (문을) 쾅 닫다　tumble [tʌ́mbl] 폭삭 무너지다　minimal [mínəməl] 최소의　component [kəmpóunənt] 요소　stand out 쉽게 눈에 띄다　perception [pərsépʃən] 인식　illuminate [ilj́úːmineit] 비추다　constrain [kənstréin] (...하는 것을) 제한[제약]하다　script [skript] 대본

01 강의의 주된 내용은?
Ⓐ 초기 연극 작품들이 직면했던 문제점들
Ⓑ 의상 디자인 요소들을 향상시켜야 하는 필요성
Ⓒ 현대 극장에서의 시각적 디자인의 중요성
Ⓓ 고대 그리스 극장의 영향

02 교수가 20세기 이전의 연극에 대해 이야기한 것은?
Ⓐ 프로덕션 디자인이라는 개념이 존재하지 않았다.
Ⓑ 관객들은 세트에 주의를 기울이지 않았다.
Ⓒ 의상 디자이너들은 매우 존경을 받았다.
Ⓓ 사람들은 프로덕션 디자인이 중요하다고 생각하지 않았다.

03 교수가 쾅 닫힌 문에 대해 언급한 이유는?
Ⓐ 음향의 중요성을 강조하려고
Ⓑ 문이 어떻게 소도구로 쓰일 수 있는지 알려주려고
Ⓒ 세트 디자인의 어려움의 예를 들려고
Ⓓ 흔한 프로덕션 디자인 실수를 지적하려고

04 교수에 의하면, 소도구는 세트의 일부분과 어떻게 다른가?
Ⓐ 관객들이 볼 수 있다.
Ⓑ 배우가 들어올린다.
Ⓒ 어느 정도 역사적 맥락을 가지고 있다.
Ⓓ 극본에 언급된다.

05 교수에 의하면, 의상 디자인의 영향의 일부는 무엇인가? (두 가지 선택)
Ⓐ 관객들이 한 등장인물에 주목하게 할 수 있다.
Ⓑ 조명 감독의 일을 훨씬 더 쉽게 만들어 줄 수 있다.
Ⓒ 배우들이 자신의 역할을 더 잘 이해하도록 해줄 수 있다.

Ⓓ 연극에 어느 특정한 시대의 모습을 줄 수 있다.

06 교수가 조명 감독으로서의 경험을 언급한 이유는?
Ⓐ 과거에는 조명 작업이 훨씬 더 어려웠다는 것을 강조하려고
Ⓑ 현대 조명 기법의 특정한 예를 들려고
Ⓒ 무대를 잘 밝히기 위해 필요한 기술을 묘사하려고
Ⓓ 프로덕션 디자인에 대한 일반적인 오해를 알려주려고

Practice Questions

본문 p. 256

| 01 B | 02 B | 03 C | 04 D | 05 B, D | 06 C |

Main Idea
사회 변화로 인한 새로운 연극 등장

Cause
미국 중산층의 수입 급증으로 극장이 발달하게 됨

Limitation
일반인들의 엔터테인먼트
– 공연 내용이 아이들에게 적합하지 않음

– 일반인들의 극장 이용의 사회적 장벽

Difference
프랑스 극장과의 차이점

Origin
vaudeville 단어의 유래

Listen to part of a lecture in a theater class. 🎧 MP3 43

Professor(female): As we have seen, theater can be affected by technological advancements. This clearly occurred in Europe during the 18th century, when productions became increasingly complex and entertaining. But **Q1** **in today's class I'll be discussing how socioeconomic factors can also have an impact on theater. Let's start by talking about how a new genre of theater was born from a new audience that was created by a change in the social climate.**

Q2 **After the American Civil War in the late 19th century, the income of the country's middle class soared to unprecedented levels. A lot more people had money, and they wanted to spend it on leisure activities. This provided the perfect environment for the growth of the entertainment industry.** But before we get into the details, let's get a little more information about the state of entertainment at that time.

Most of the entertainment in the United States was classified as either high or low. The aristocrats, the upper class, had access to all sorts of entertainment, such as opera, ballet, concerts and, to a certain extent, plays. **Q3** **However, for the rest of the population, entertainment venues were limited. Most entertainment took place in circuses or saloons, bars with a small stage for performers.** Let me just tell you, I'd never take my kids to one of those shows. **These performances were often vulgar, or even violent, and were therefore considered immoral by many.**

So, we have two situations going on here. The masses had more money and wanted to spend it, but there was nothing to spend it on. People from the middle and lower classes couldn't simply attend operas and ballets, as there were too many social barriers, and, besides, they just weren't interested in that sort of thing. This is the situation that a man named Benjamin Franklin Keith decided to take advantage of. He started out owning a circus but later expanded into theaters. The Bijou Theater was the first theater built by Keith, and it started a new movement in the entertainment industry.

Keith started a new kind of theater, called American vaudeville (shown on screen). I say "American" vaudeville because it was different from the vaudeville in French theater. In fact, the two forms of vaudeville really had nothing to do with each other. **Q4** **Some say the term comes from the French for "voice of the city," but chances are it was merely coined because of its vagueness.**

Anyway, Keith's approach to theater was very simple: Make it available to everyone. One of the ways he achieved this was by having shows constantly running in his theaters. A performance would be made up of a series of separate acts. Um... These

Difference
다른 미국 극장들과의 차이점

Change
어린이들도 볼 수 있게 됨

Role
Keith의 업적 –
고급과 저급 엔터테인먼트의 간극을 메움

unrelated acts would be grouped together to create a common theme. So if one were to walk into one of Keith's theaters, they could watch the show without having to know what had happened before. **Q5-D** **Whenever a member of the audience arrived, that would be when the show started.** People from all classes suddenly had an entertainment venue they could enjoy just by walking into the theater. This was very different from the high forms of entertainment, which required invitations and reservations sometimes weeks in advance.

Another way Keith changed entertainment was through his emphasis on cleanliness and order. He strictly forbade the use of vulgarity of all forms. No act could use profanity and the costumes were very conservative. He enforced this throughout all his theaters. **Q5-B** **He did this to eliminate the stigmas associated with low forms of entertainment, so that they could appeal to women and children as well as men.** Unlike the shows in saloons, Keith's vaudville performances could be attended by the entire family.

His emphasis on order applied to the audience as well. Audience members were forbidden from doing anything at the end of a show except clapping politely. This was very different from earlier audiences. **Q6** Many of them included people who would scream at the actors, throw bottles, and even climb up onto the stage. By putting an end to this behavior, Keith bridged the gap between high and low entertainment, which had grown increasingly wider in the years following the Civil War. Vaudeville continued to be the main source of entertainment for the masses until the 1920s, when cinemas started taking over. Make sure you do your required reading about early American cinema for the next class.

해석 연극 수업의 다음 강의 일부분을 들으시오.

교수(여자): 우리가 살펴본 바와 같이, 연극은 기술적 진보에 의해 영향을 받을 수 있습니다. 이는 18세기 동안 유럽에서 분명하게 발생했는데, 이 시기에는 연극 제작이 엄청나게 복잡해지고 재미있어졌습니다. 하지만 오늘 수업에서는 사회경제적인 요인이 어떻게 연극에도 영향을 줄 수 있는지에 대해 논의하도록 하겠습니다. 사회적 분위기의 변화로 인해 생긴 새로운 관객들로부터 어떻게 새로운 장르의 연극이 탄생했는지에 대해 이야기하는 걸로 시작해봐요.

19세기 후반에 있었던 미국의 남북전쟁 이후, 미국 중산층의 수입은 전례가 없는 수준으로 급증했습니다. 훨씬 더 많은 사람들이 돈을 가지게 되었고, 그들은 그 돈을 여가 활동에 쓰고 싶어 했지요. 이것이 엔터테인먼트 산업의 성장을 위한 완벽한 환경을 제공했습니다. 하지만 세부사항에 대해 이야기하기 전에, 그 당시의 엔터테인먼트 업계의 상황에 대해 조금 더 정보를 나눠봅시다.

미국의 대부분의 엔터테인먼트는 고급 또는 저급 중 하나로 분류되었습니다. 상류층인 귀족들은 모든 종류의 엔터테인먼트를 이용할 수 있었습니다. 오페라, 발레, 콘서트, 그리고 얼마간은 연극 같은 것에도 말이죠. 하지만, 나머지 사람들에게 있어 엔터테인먼트 장소들은 제한적이었습니다. 대부분의 엔터테인먼트들은 서커스나 살롱, 즉 공연자들을 위한 작은 무대가 있는 술집에서 이루어졌지요. 자, 그런데 말이죠, 저라면 제 아이들을 그런 쇼에는 절대 데려가지 않을 겁니다. 이러한 공연들은 종종 저속하거나 심지어 폭력적이기도 했고, 따라서 많은 사람들에게 부도덕적으로 여겨졌습니다.

자, 이제 두 가지 상황이 있네요. 대중은 돈이 더 많아져 그걸 쓰고 싶어 하지만, 그 돈을 쓸 곳이 없다는 것이죠. 너무 많은 사회적 장벽이 있어서, 중산층과 하류층 사람들은 오페라나 발레를 관람할 수 없었고, 게다가, 그들은 그런 종류의 것들에는 관심도 없었습니다. 이때 Benjamin Franklin Keith라는 이름의 한 남자가 이 상황을 활용하기로 합니다. 그는 서커스장을 소유하는 걸로 시작하여 나중에는 극장들로 확장해나갔습니다. Bijou 극장은 Keith에 의해 지어진 최초의 극장이었습니다. 그리고 그 극장은 엔터테인먼트 업계에 새로운 움직임을 일으켰습니다. Keith는 미국 보드빌(American vaudeville)이라고 불리는 새로운 종류의 연극을 시작했습니다. (화면에 보여준다) '미국' 보드빌이라고 말한 이유는 그것이 프랑스 극장의 보드빌과는 달랐기 때문입니다. 사실, 그 두 유형의 보드빌은 서로 그다지 연관이 없습니다. 어떤 사람들은 그 용어가 '시의 목소리(voice of the city)'라는 프랑스어에서 유래했다고 말하지만, 아마도 보드빌은 그저 그 말이 가진 모호함 때문에 만들어졌을 겁니다.

어쨌든, 연극에 대한 Keith의 접근법은 매우 간단했습니다. 모든 사람이 이용 가능하도록 만들자는 것이었죠. 그가 이것을 달성했던 방법들 중 하나는 그의 극장들에서 쇼들이 끊임없이 공연되도록 하는 것이었습니다. 하나의 공연은 일련의 별개의 파트들로 구성되었죠. 음... 이런 서로 관련 없는 파트들은 한데 묶여서 공통의 테마를 만들었습니다. 그래서 Keith의 극장 중 한 곳에 들어가면, 사람들은 그 전에 무슨 내용이 있었는지를 알 필요 없이 쇼를 볼 수 있었습니다. 관객들 중 아무나 한 사람이 오기만 하면, 그때 쇼가 시작되었죠. 갑자기 모든 계층의 사람들이, 극장 안으로 걸어 들어가기만 하면 즐길 수 있는 엔터테인먼트 장소를 갖게 되었습니다. 이 점이, 초대장과 가끔은 몇 주나 앞선 예약이 필요했던 고급 유형의 엔터테인먼트들과 무척 달랐습니다.

Keith가 엔터테인먼트를 변화시킨 또 다른 방식은, 청결과 질서에 대한 그의 강조를 통해서였습니다. 그는 모든 유형의 저속함을 사용하는 것을 엄격히 금지했습니다. 어떠한 파트도 비속함을 담을 수 없었고, 의상들도 매우 보수적이었습니다. 그는 이것을 그의 모든 극장에 걸쳐 실시했습니다. 그는 저급한 유형의 엔터테인먼트에 결부되어 있던 낙인을 제거하기 위해 이렇게 했고, 그래서 이런 엔터테인먼트들이 남성뿐 아니라 여성들과 아이들에게도 어필할 수 있었습니다. 살롱에서의 쇼와는 달리, Keith의 보드빌 공연들은 가족 전체가 관람할 수 있었던 거지요. 질서에 대한 Keith의 강조는 관객들에게도 적용되었습니다. 관객들은 쇼 말미에 정중하게 박수를 치는 것을 제외하고는 아무것도 하지 못하도록 금지당했습니다. 이것은 이전의 관객들과는 매우 다른 것이었지요. 그들 대부분은 배우들에게 소리를 지르고, 병을 던지고, 심지어 무대에 올라가기도 했었으니까요. 이런 행동에 종지부를 찍음으로써, Keith는 고급 엔터테인먼트와 저급 엔터테인먼트의 사이의 간극을 메웠는데, 이 간극은 남북전쟁 이후 수 년에 걸쳐 매우 벌어져 있던 상태였습니다. 보드빌은 1920년대에 영화가 이를 대체하기 시작하기 전까지 계속해서 대중들에게 주요한 엔터테인먼트 원천이었습니다. 다음 수업을 위해 미국의 초기 영화에 대한 필수 읽기자료를 반드시 읽어오도록 하세요.

ⓦ production [prədákʃən] (영화·연극 등의) 제작   entertaining [èntərtéiniŋ] 재미있는   socioeconomic [sòusiouèkənámik] 사회 경제적인   social climate 사회적 풍토   income [ínkʌm] 소득   soar [sɔːr] 급등[급증]하다   classify [klǽsəfài] 분류하다   vulgar [vʌ́lgər] 저속한   immoral [imɔ́(ː)rəl] 부도덕한   mass [mæs] 대중   barrier [bǽriər] 장벽, 장애물   coin [kɔin] (새로운 낱말을) 만들다   vagueness [véignis] 막연함   profanity [prəfǽnəti] 신성 모독; 비속함[불경스런] 말   conservative [kənsə́ːrvətiv] 보수적인   enforce [infɔ́ːrs] 집행[실시]하다   eliminate [ilíminèit] 제거하다   stigma [stígmə] 낙인, 오명   bridge the gap 간극을 메우다

01 교수가 주로 논의하고 있는 것은?
Ⓐ 유럽과 미국 연극 간의 차이점들
Ⓑ 미국에서의 새로운 형태의 엔터테인먼트의 진화
Ⓒ 한 미국인 사업가의 혁신적인 서커스
Ⓓ 한 인기 있는 19세기 미국 배우의 삶

02 교수에 의하면, 남북전쟁 후의 미국에는 어떤 변화가 있었는가?
Ⓐ 나라가 전쟁 후유증으로 인해 황폐화되었다.
Ⓑ 미국 중산층은 쓸 돈이 더 많이 생겼다.
Ⓒ 더 많은 미국인들이 상류층의 구성원이 되고 싶어 했다.
Ⓓ 이용 가능한 대부분의 엔터테인먼트들이 비도덕적이 되었다.

03 19세기 미국의 중산층 시민들이 이용 가능했던 엔터테인먼트에 대해 교수가 암시한 것은?
Ⓐ 여러 다른 형태로 존재했다.
Ⓑ 많은 사람들이 감당할 수 없는 비용이었다.
Ⓒ 가족에게는 부적절했다.
Ⓓ 유럽의 엔터테인먼트를 모방했다.

04 교수가 '보드빌'이라는 단어에 관해 말한 것은?
Ⓐ 한 프랑스어 구절을 잘못 번역한 것이다.
Ⓑ 그 단어의 고상한 발음 때문에 선택되었다.
Ⓒ 프랑스의 한 도시 이름에서 유래했다.
Ⓓ 아마도 어떠한 실질적인 의미를 가지고 있지는 않을 것이다.

05 강의에 의하면, 미국 보드빌의 눈에 띄는 두 가지 특징은 무엇인가? (두 가지 선택)
Ⓐ 프랑스 버전의 보드빌과 동일했다.
Ⓑ 이전의 엔터테인먼트 형태들에 비해 더 넓은 관객층에게 어필했다.
Ⓒ 종종 매우 잘 훈련된 유럽의 무대 배우들을 섭외했다.
Ⓓ 중단 없이 공연되어서 아무때나 즐길 수 있었다.

06 배우들에게 소리를 지르는 관객들을 교수가 언급한 이유는?
Ⓐ 중산층 사람들이 오페라를 관람할 수 없었던 이유를 실증하려고
Ⓑ 보드빌 쇼에서 사람들이 어떻게 행동하도록 장려되었는지를 보여주려고

ⓒ Keith가 엔터테인먼트에 가져온 변화 중 하나를 설명하려고
ⓓ 미국 관객들이 Keith의 발상에 어떻게 반응했는지를 예를 들어 보여주려고

06 / Photography

≋ Sample Questions

본문 p. 262

01 B   02 A   03 B, D   04 C   05 D   06 D

해석 사진 수업의 다음 강의 일부분을 들으시오. ◁ MP3 44

교수(여자): 좋아요. 시작합시다. 여러분 중 은판 사진법(daguerreotype) 공정을 알고 있는 사람이 있나요? 그 용어가 익숙하지 않을지도 모르지만, 이는 사진을 만들기 위해 만들어졌던 최초의 공정들 중 하나였습니다. 그것은 Louis Daguerre라는 이름의 한 남자에 의해 발명되었습니다.

1800년 초에는, 사진이라는 단어조차 없었습니다. 그런 개념이 존재하긴 했지만요. 음… Daguerre는 특정 화학약품들이 빛에 반응하는 방식에 관련된, 이미지들을 포착하는 방법을 발견했습니다. 이것이 그의 발상은 아니었지만… 그건 잠시 후 이야기하도록 하지요.

자, 이것이 은판 사진법이 작용되는 방식입니다. Daguerre는 요오드 결정체가 내뿜는 증기에 노출되었던 구리판을 사용했습니다. 음, 이것이 한 일은, 요오드화은 표면을 형성하게 함으로써 구리를 빛에 민감하게 만드는 것이었지요. 자, 처음에 이 공법은 시간이 매우 오래 걸렸습니다. 판이 민감하긴 했지만, 그렇게 많이 민감하지는 않았거든요. 인물을 찍은 가장 첫 은판 사진을 보면, 한 남자가 신발을 (다른 사람을 시켜) 닦고 있습니다. 이것은 그가 사진이 찍힐 동안 충분히 오래 머물러 있을 수 있었던, 그러니까 약 10분 정도 말이죠, 몇 안 되는 사람들 중 하나였기 때문입니다. '치즈'라고 말하면서, 사진사가 작업을 끝낼 때까지 10분 동안 기다리는 것을 상상해 보세요. 정말 오래 걸리는 공법이었지요.

하지만, Daguerre는 나중에, 더 짧은 시간에 덜 명확한 은판 사진들을 찍을 수 있다는 것을 깨달은 후에, 그 공법을 더 발전시켰습니다. 그리고 나서 그는 그 사진들을 화학약품들을 이용해서 더 선명하게 만들었습니다. 그것이 바로 사진이 화학적으로 현상되었던 첫 순간이었습니다. 이것은 노출 시간을 상당히 많이 단축시켰고, Daguerre의 방법이 널리 사용되게 해주었습니다.

하지만, 음, 몇 가지 문제가 있었지요. 우선, 복사품을 만들 수 있는 실용적인 방법이 없었습니다. 세부 양식에 대한 문제도 있었죠. 초기 카메라에서 해상도나 선명도를 많이 기대할 수는 없었지만, 음… 대부분의 은판 사진들은 그저 흑백으로 된, 간간히 아주 약간의 회색이 들어간 사진과 다르지 않았죠. 음… 그 결과는 무척 원시적이었고, 음, 말하자면, 흰색 바탕에 검은 글자로 인쇄된 졸업장과 별로 다를 바가 없었습니다.

결국, William Talbot이라는 이름의 한 영국 남자가 Daguerre의 발명품에 대한 이야기를 듣고, 캘러타이프(calotype) 공정이라고 이름을 붙인 자신의 버전을 개발하기 시작했습니다. 그의 방식은, 음 오늘날 필름을 현상하는 방식과 가장 닮은 것이었습니다. 은판 사진법에 나타났던 동일한 요소들이 Talbot의 발명품에도 있었습니다. 그러니까, 음, 빛에 민감한 판이 있었지요. 하지만 금속판을 사용했던 Daguerre와는 달리, Talbot은 종이를 이용해서, 그 과정에서 최초의 필름 형태를 만들었습니다.

그의 캘러타이프에서 종이를 사용함으로써, Talbot은 사진의 복사판을 만들 수 있었고 최종 결과물을 매우 잘 제어할 수 있었습니다. 그는 나뭇잎에서 그 영감을 얻었습니다. 나뭇잎을 잡아 밝은 빛에 가져다 올리면, 그 그림자는 모두 검은 색은 아닐 것입니다. 각기 다른 음영을 보게 될 거예요. 구멍이 있는 부분들은 하얗게 나오고, 얇은 부분들은 회색으로, 그리고 나머지는 검은 색으로 보일 것입니다. Talbot이 그의 캘러타이프로 사진을 찍었을 때, 그것은 종이에 각인을 남기게 됩니다. 하지만, 종이가 빛에 민감했기 때문에, 가장 어두운 부분이 실제로는 가장 밝은 부분이 되고, 가장 밝은 부분은 가장 어두운 부분이 되는 거지요. 생각해 보세요. 빛이 종이에 비출 때, 빛은 화학작용을 일으켜, 그 부분을 어둡게 만듭니다. 이것은 실생활에서 우리가 보는 것과 정확히 반대되는 것을 만듭니다. 따라서, 그 결과로 나타나는 이미지는 네거티브(음화, 원화)라고 불렸죠. 하늘을 찍은 네거티브에서는, 흰색 구름은 검은 색으로, 검은 새들은 흰색으로 나타냅니다.

물론, 네거티브는 그저 첫 단계일 뿐이었습니다. Talbot은 최종 사진을 만들기 위해 밀착인화법이라고 불리는 방식을 사용했습니다. 그는 먼저 네거티브를 화학적으로 처리를 해서 빛에 민감하지 않게 만들었습니다. 그래서 아무리 많은 빛에 네거티브가 노출이 되어도 네거티브가 변하지 않게 되었지요. 그리고 나서 그는 그 바로 밑에, 빛에 민감한 또 다른 종이 한 장을 두었습니다. 다음으로, 그는 매우 밝은 등을 켰습니다. 더 밝은 부분으로는 더 많은 빛이 투과하고, 더 어두운 부분으로는 더 적은 빛이 투과하여, 공법을 뒤집어 포지티브(양화)를 만든 것입니다. 이 포지티브들은 쉽게 복제될 수 있었습니다. 그래서 그 과정 중 무언가가 잘못되었다면, 다시 하면 그만이었죠.

이제, Daguerre가 어디서 공법의 아이디어를 얻었는가에 대해 내가 앞서 언급했던 것으로 돌아가보죠… 그것은 Nicéphore Niépce라는 이름의 한 남자로, 이 사람은 일반적으로 사진술의 창시자로 여겨집니다. Niépce는 자신의 연구를 비밀로 했기 때문에, 그의 연구는 그가 죽을 때까지 거의 알려지지 않았습니다. 하지만, 그는 자신의 모든 아이디어를 Daguerre에게 넘겼고, Daguerre는 그것들을 은판 사진법 공정을 만드는 데에 사용했습니다.

W daguerreotype [dəgériətàip] 은판 사진(법)　chemical [kémikəl] 화학물질　copper [kápər] 구리, 동　expose [ikspouz] 노출시키다　vapor [véipər] 증기　iodine [áiədàin] 요오드　crystal [krístəl] 결정체　sensitive [sénsətiv] 민감한　polish [páliʃ] 광을 내다　define [difáin] 윤곽(모양)을 분명히 나타내다　develop [divéləp] 현상하다　significantly [signífikəntli] 상당히　duplicate [djúːplikət] 사본　resolution [rèzəljúːʃən] 해상도　clarity [klǽrəti] 선명도　primitive [prímitiv] 초기의, 원시적 단계의　inspiration [ìnspəréiʃən] 영감　imprint [ímprint] 새기다　negative [négətiv] 음화, 원화　reverse [rivə́ːrs] 뒤집다　credit A as B A를 B로 여기다

01 강의의 주된 내용은?
Ⓐ 한 발명가로부터 카메라의 아이디어가 어떻게 도난 당했는지
Ⓑ 현대 사진술로 이어진 발전
Ⓒ 여러 다른 종류의 필름간의 비교
Ⓓ 흑백 사진에서 컬러 사진술로의 전환

02 최초의 사진 형태에 대해서 교수가 암시한 것은?
Ⓐ 움직이는 물체를 포착하지 못했다.
Ⓑ 과학적인 목적으로 사용되었다.
Ⓒ 위험한 화학약품들이 필요했다.
Ⓓ 실내에서만 이용될 수 있었다.

03 강의에 의하면, 은판 사진법의 두 가지 단점은 무엇인가? (두 가지 선택)
Ⓐ 만들기에 비용이 너무 많이 들었다.
Ⓑ 음영의 범위가 한정되어 있었다.
Ⓒ 종이를 많이 필요로 했다.
Ⓓ 사본을 만들 수 없었다.

04 Talbot이 Daguerre의 발명품에 대한 자신의 버전에서 향상시킨 점은?
Ⓐ 더 많은 빛을 포착했다.
Ⓑ 화학약품이 필요하지 않았다.
Ⓒ 다른 매개체를 이용했다.
Ⓓ 컬러 이미지를 만들었다.

05 교수가 나뭇잎을 언급한 이유는?
Ⓐ 색상들이 변할 수 있다는 것을 알려주려고
Ⓑ 일반적인 이미지의 예를 들려고
Ⓒ 식물 구조의 세부 사항을 설명하려고
Ⓓ Talbot의 필름의 기본적 속성들을 예를 들어 설명하려고

06 Nicéphore Niépce에 대해 교수가 암시한 것은?
Ⓐ 그는 Talbot의 방법에 도움을 주었다.
Ⓑ 그는 Daguerre에게서 아이디어를 훔쳤다.
Ⓒ 그는 자신의 카메라를 부쉈다.
Ⓓ 그는 명성에 관심이 없었다.

≋ **Practice Questions**　　　　　　　　　　　　　　　　　　　본문 p. 266

| 01 B | 02 C | 03 B | 04 A, D | 05 B | 06 D |

Listen to part of a lecture in a photography class. 🔊 MP3 45

Main Idea
사진의 새로운 접근법

Professor(male): **Q1** Today I want to talk about how a new approach to photography developed. You see, when photography first started, most photographers photographed landscapes or created portraits. The photography scene was quite different

Introduction
다큐멘터리 사진 →
사진 보도

from what it is today. ▶Q2 **Did anyone read the newspaper before coming here?**
Student(female): I did. Why? Was there an article about photography?
P: Oh, no. I just wanted to ask what you saw on the front page.
S: Uh… I guess it was just the same old talk about politics, with a big picture of a local politician in the middle.
P: That's right. Now, you might not realize it, but ▶Q2 **there were no photographs in early newspapers. It wasn't until the 1930s that papers started utilizing photographs on a regular basis. This new type of photography was called documentary photography.** As the name suggests, it involves documenting the lives of others. This has since branched out into photojournalism, which is what you see in the papers today. But before we get into that, let's talk about the changing technology that was responsible for the development of this new genre. So, photographs in the past, daguerreotypes, they… Okay, that's going too far back. Let's talk about film cameras in the early 1900s. Most cameras had a couple issues they needed to overcome. For starters, the lenses used did not let much light in. Now, this is a problem because in order to take a picture, the film must absorb light. So if only a little light is getting in, it takes a lot longer to absorb enough. Have you ever seen any old pictures taken at night? How did they look?
S: They were really blurry.

Requirement
삼각대 필요

Problem
대상이 가만히 있어야만
사진을 찍을 수 있음

P: Yes. That's because there wasn't enough light, so the photographer probably moved around a bit while waiting for the film to absorb it. When this process takes a long time, the camera and the subject have to stay still. Therefore, ▶Q4-D **most early cameras required a tripod, a kind of stand to hold them up.** This held the camera still, but ▶Q3 **photographers could only photograph subjects that weren't moving, such as landscapes and people who were sitting down.**
S: Couldn't they just have used film that was more sensitive? I remember reading something about film technology, um, how it developed at a really rapid pace in the late 1800s.

Limitation
필름이 너무 커 다루기가
까다로움

P: That's correct, but the problem with film at that time was that it was really cumbersome to use, even if it was sensitive. You see, the more sensitive film is, the grainier the photos. There was just too much loss of detail. The only way to counter this was to use big film. I mean, ▶Q4-A **this film was huge, more than 30 times larger than the film we use today…** if we even use film at all, with everything going digital these days. Anyway, using large film meant that ▶Q6 **a photographer had to slide each sheet of film into a film holder individually. After the film was in place, each film holder was then mounted on to the camera to take a photo.** 🎧 I can only imagine what photographers of that time had to go through.

Headset

Advantage
카메라 기술의 발전에 따
라 더 빨리 사진을 찍을 수
있게 됨

But the technology gradually changed. As lenses began to let in more light, people could take pictures faster. And film became more sensitive… and more importantly, it could be rolled and loaded to the camera. So, a photographer could take multiple shots without having to mount the film holder every time a picture was taken.
Now that we've gone over the technical details, let's talk about one of the very first documentary photographers, Dorothea Lange. She was one of the first photographers to use new camera technology to her advantage. She set out to document people who had left their farms to migrate to California. A lot of photographers were out of work at the time, due to the Great Depression. So the government hired them to document what was going on in the western states. Unlike most photographers,

Differnece
Lange의 사진이 다른 사진작가의 것과 다른 점
- 인물의 감정 포착

who held on to old habits, Lange took full advantage of the new technology. Instead of taking pictures of barren fields and abandoned farmhouses, **Q5 she took pictures of people and tried to capture their emotions**.

With the new cameras, she could take her photos candidly, without the subjects even knowing they were being photographed. This new type of photography was very powerful. Unlike posed portrait photographs, her photos showed raw emotion. Okay, let's see an example. It's called *Migrant Mother*. I'm sure you've all seen it one time or another. Look at the mother. She is supporting her children, but she has a far-off stare that shows the anxiety she is experiencing. This picture was so powerful that when it was published, the government rushed 10,000 kilograms of food to the camp. Today photojournalists still try to capture the essence of important situations, allowing people all around the world to know what others are experiencing.

해석 사진 수업의 다음 강의 일부분을 들으시오.

교수(남자): 오늘은 사진술에 있어 새로운 접근법이 어떻게 발전했는지에 대해 이야기를 하고 싶습니다. 여러분도 알다시피, 사진술이 처음 시작했을 때, 대부분의 사진사들은 풍경을 찍거나 인물사진을 만들었습니다. 그런 사진술 상황은 오늘날과는 꽤 다른 것이었죠. 수업에 오기 전에 신문을 읽은 사람이 있나요?

학생(여자): 저요. 왜 그러시죠? 사진에 대한 기사라도 있었나요?

교수: 오, 아니에요. 1면에서 무엇을 보았는지 그냥 묻고 싶어서요.

학생: 음... 그냥 정치에 대한 뻔한 오래된 이야기였던 것 같아요. 가운데에 지역 정치인의 사진이 크게 한 장 있었고요.

교수: 맞아요. 자, 여러분은 알아차리지 못할지도 모르지만, 초기 신문에는 사진이 없었습니다. 1930년대가 되서야 비로소 신문들은 정기적으로 사진을 이용하기 시작했어요. 이러한 새로운 유형의 사진은 다큐멘터리 사진이라고 불렸죠. 그 이름이 나타내듯이, 다큐멘터리 사진은 다른 사람들의 삶을 기록하는 것을 수반하죠. 이것은 그 이후로 사진 보도로 뻗어 나갔는데, 사진 보도는 여러분이 요즘 신문에서 보는 것을 말하죠. 하지만 그것에 대해 이야기하기 전에, 이런 새 장르의 발전의 원인이 된 변화하는 기술에 대해 이야기를 해보도록 하지요. 자, 과거의 사진이었던 은판 사진은... 자, 그건 너무 옛날이군요. 1900년대 초의 필름 카메라에 대해 이야기해보죠. 대부분의 카메라는 극복해야 할 한 두 가지 문제점들이 있었습니다. 우선, 사용되었던 렌즈들은 빛을 그다지 많이 받아들이지 못했습니다. 자, 이것은 문제가 되었는데, 왜냐하면 사진을 찍기 위해서는 필름이 빛을 흡수해야 하기 때문입니다. 그래서 빛이 아주 조금만 들어오게 되면, 충분한 만큼의 빛을 흡수하는 데 훨씬 더 오래 걸리죠. 밤에 찍힌 옛날 사진을 본 적이 있나요? 어떻던가요?

학생: 정말 흐릿했어요.

교수: 그래요. 빛이 충분하지 않아서예요. 그래서 사진사는 아마도 필름이 빛을 흡수하는 것을 기다리는 동안 약간 움직였을지도 모릅니다. 이런 과정이 오래 걸리게 되면, 카메라와 피사체가 가만히 머물러 있어야만 하지요. 따라서, 대부분의 초기 카메라들은 카메라를 지탱해주는 일종의 받침대인 삼각대가 있어야 했습니다. 삼각대가 카메라를 가만히 잡아주긴 했지만, 사진사들은 풍경이나 앉아 있는 사람들과 같은, 움직이지 않는 피사체만을 찍을 수 있었죠.

학생: 좀 더 민감한 필름을 사용할 수도 있지 않았나요? 필름 기술에 대한 무언가를 읽었던 기억이 나는데. 음, 필름 기술이 1800년대 후반에 어떻게 아주 급속한 속도로 발전했는지에 대한 것이었어요.

교수: 맞아요. 하지만 그 당시 필름에 관한 문제점은, 필름이 민감했다 하더라도 필름을 사용하기에 정말 크고 무거웠다는 것이었어요. 필름이 더 민감할수록, 사진은 더 거칠어집니다. 세부적인 요소들이 너무 많이 사라지게 되지요. 이에 대항하는 유일한 방법은 큰 필름을 사용하는 것이었습니다. 그러니까, 이 필름은 정말 컸는데, 우리가 오늘날 이용하는 필름의 30배나 더 컸어요... 우리가 필름을 사용한다 하더라도 말이죠, 모든 것이 디지털화된 요즘 세상에 말이에요. 어쨌든, 큰 필름을 사용한다는 것은 사진사가 각각의 필름 낱장을 필름 꽂이 안으로 하나하나 밀어넣어야 했다는 걸 의미합니다. 필름이 준비가 된 뒤에, 사진을 찍기 위해 각각의 필름 꽂이가 카메라에 장착되게 됩니다. 그 당시의 사진사들이 어떤 일을 겪어야 했을지 그저 상상만 될 뿐이네요.

하지만 기술은 점차 변화했습니다. 렌즈가 더 많은 빛을 받아들임에 따라, 사람들은 사진을 더 빨리 찍을 수 있게 되었지요. 그리고 필름은 좀 더 민감해졌습니다... 그리고 더 중요한 것은, 필름이 말려서 카메라에 들어갈 수 있게 되었습니다. 그래서, 사진사들은 사진 한 장을 찍을 때마다 필름 꽂이를 장착시켜야 할 필요 없이 여러 장의 사진을 찍을 수 있었습니다.

기술적인 세부 사항들에 대해 다루었으니, 아주 초기의 다큐멘터리 사진사 중의 한 명이었던 Dorothea Lange에 대해 이야기해봅시다. 그녀는 새로운 카메라 기술을 자신에게 유리하게 사용했던 최초의 사진사들 중 하나였습니다. 그녀는 캘리포니아로 이주하기 위해 자신의 농장을 떠났던 사람들을 기록하기 시작했습니다. 많은 사진사들이 그 당시 대공황으로 인해 실직 중이었습니다. 그래서 정부는 서부에 있는 주(州)들에서 무슨 일이 일어나고 있는지를 기록하게 하기 위해 그들을 고용했습니다. 옛날 습관을 고수하던 대부분의 사진사들과는 달리, Lange

는 새로운 기술을 충분히 이용했습니다. 황폐한 들판과 버려진 농가들의 사진을 찍는 대신, 그녀는 사람들의 사진을 찍었고 그들의 감정을 포착하려는 시도를 했죠.

새로운 카메라를 이용하여, 그녀는 피사체들이 자신이 사진에 찍히고 있다는 것을 모르는 채로 거리낌 없이 사진을 찍을 수 있었습니다. 이런 새로운 유형의 사진은 매우 영향력이 컸습니다. 포즈를 취한 인물 사진들과는 달리, 그녀의 사진들은 날 것 그대로의 감정을 보여주었습니다. 좋아요, 예를 하나 봅시다. 이것은 <이주자 어머니>라고 불립니다. 여러분 모두 한 번쯤은 이것을 본 적이 있을 걸로 생각됩니다. 어머니를 보세요. 그녀는 아이들을 부양하고 있지만, 그녀가 겪고 있는 불안을 보여주는, 아득한 시선을 띠고 있습니다. 이 사진은 너무나 영향력이 커서, 이 사진이 발표되었을 때, 정부는 그 캠프로 1만 킬로그램의 음식을 서둘러 보냈습니다. 오늘날 보도 사진가들은 여전히, 다른 사람들이 어떤 일을 겪고 있는지 전세계의 사람들로 하여금 알게 하기 위해, 중요한 상황들의 정수를 포착하기 위해 애를 쓰고 있습니다.

W utilize [júːtəlàiz] 이용하다   document [dάkjəmənt] 기록하다   branch out into ~ ...로 확장하다   blurry [bláːri] 흐릿한   tripod [tráipɑd] 삼각대   cumbersome [kʌ́mbərsəm] 크고 무거운, 다루기 힘든   grainy [gréini] 선명하지 못한   counter [káuntər] (악영향에) 대응하다   individually [ìndəvídʒuəli] 개별적으로   mount [maunt] 끼우다, 고정시키다   to one's advantage ...에게 유리하게   migrate [máigreit] 이주하다   barren [bǽrən] 척박한, 황량한   abandoned [əbǽndənd] 버려진   candidly [kǽndidli] 솔직히, 숨김 없이   pose [pouz] 포즈를 취하다   anxiety [æŋzáiəti] 불안   essence [ésəns] 본질, 정수

01 강의의 주된 내용은?
(A) 현대 카메라 기술에 관한 문제점들
(B) 새로운 장르의 사진술에 얽힌 역사
(C) 정부가 사진가들을 후원하는 방법들
(D) 저널리즘을 위해 만들어진 최초의 카메라

02 교수가 신문을 언급한 이유는?
(A) 디지털 사진의 예를 들려고
(B) 카메라 기술에 대한 흥미로운 기사를 제안하려고
(C) 학생들의 관심을 뉴스 사진으로 돌리려고
(D) 현대 카메라에 관한 문제점을 예를 들어 설명하려고

03 1900년대 초의 카메라에 대해 교수가 말한 것은?
(A) 실내에서는 이용될 수 없었다.
(B) 움직이는 물체를 포착할 수 없었다.
(C) 너무 무거운 렌즈를 사용했다.
(D) 제대로 작동하기 위해서는 이리저리 움직여져야 했다.

04 교수에 의하면, 초기 카메라들의 어떤 두 가지 측면이 카메라를 이용하기 어렵게 만들었는가? (두 가지 선택)
(A) 사용된 필름이 너무 컸다.
(B) 가격이 너무 비쌌다.
(C) 풍경 사진들을 찍을 수 없었다.
(D) 카메라를 고정시키기 위해 삼각대가 필요했다.

05 Dorothea Lange는 그 시대의 다른 사진가들과 무엇을 다르게 했는가?
(A) 전통적인 장비를 사용했다.
(B) 솔직한 감정들을 포착하려고 애썼다.
(C) 아름답게 포즈를 취한 인물 사진을 만들어냈다.
(D) 정부의 후원을 요청했다.

06 교수가 다음과 같이 말한 이유는? 🔊 **MP3 45_1**

I can only imagine what photographers of that time had to go through.

(A) 자신도 비슷한 경험을 했다는 것을 시사하려고
(B) 현대 사진가들의 기술을 강조하려고
(C) 전통적인 기법에 대한 자신의 감탄을 나타내려고
(D) 과거의 사진가들에 대한 공감을 표현하려고

Chapter 4. Lecture Topics Unit 4. Life Science

01 / Animal Communication

Sample Questions
본문 p. 274

| 01 D | 02 A, D | 03 C | 04 C | 05 A | 06 D |

해석 생물학 수업의 다음 강의 일부분을 들으시오. ◁) MP3 46

교수(남자): 좋아요. 오늘은 수분(受粉)을 통해 우리 환경과 생태계에 필수불가결한 역할을 하는 곤충에 대해 살펴보죠. 물론, 꿀벌을 이야기하는 것이죠. 자, 우리는 벌을 이 꽃에서 저 꽃으로 제멋대로 날아다니면서 꽃가루를 모아 여왕벌에게 가져다 주는 곤충으로 생각하는 경향이 있지요. 벌집을 본 사람이 있다면, 벌집에서 나온 벌들이 어느 방향으로 날아가는 경향이 있는 것 같나요?

학생(여자): 어느 방향이요? 모든 방향으로 막 날아다니는 것 같아 보이는데요.

교수: 맞아요. 그건 그들이 새로운 먹이 공급원을 찾고 있기 때문이에요. 하지만 일단 먹이 공급원을 찾게 되면, 그들은 실제로 그 먹이 공급원까지의 거리와 방향에 대해 설명하기 위해 벌집의 다른 벌들과 의사소통을 합니다. 벌들은 '춤 언어'라고 알려진, 상당히 진화되고 독특한 의사소통 체계를 통해 의사소통을 합니다. 다시 말해, 벌들은 의사소통의 한 형태로서 춤을 사용하는 거예요. 그러면, 꿀벌들은 어떻게 춤을 통해 서로 의사소통을 하는 걸까요? 음, 그들은 '8자춤'이라고 불리는 것을 이용합니다. 그들은 진짜 댄서들처럼 몸을 양쪽으로 흔들면서 원을 그립니다. 하지만 예술적 목적을 위해서가 아니죠. 좋아요, 슬라이드를 한번 봅시다. (슬라이드 1을 보여준다) 춤은 숫자 8자의 형태를 띠지만, 벌은 두 원이 겹치는 부분에서 몸을 흔들죠. 벌은 일직선으로 앞으로 움직이면서 몸을 좌우로 흔들고, 그 후 오른쪽으로 원을 그려 시작점으로 돌아가고, 다시 앞으로 몸을 흔들며 움직이고, 그리고는 왼쪽으로 원을 그립니다. 이런 춤 패턴이 여러 번 반복됩니다. 일벌, 즉 꽃가루나 꿀을 찾는 일벌들은 먹이를 찾습니다. 활짝 핀 꽃이나 인공적인 먹이 공급원 같은 것들을 찾으면, 그들은 꿀 주머니에 꿀을 가득 채우고 둥지로 돌아와 이 격렬한 춤을 춥니다.

학생: 하지만 벌들이 춤만으로 어디로 가야 하는지 어떻게 알지요? 제 말은, 8자춤으로 벌들이 서로 먹이 공급원에 대해 알려줄 수 있다는 것은 알겠지만, 그 춤 동작이 그렇게 정확할 수 있다는 것은 믿기가 정말 어려워요.

교수: 좋은 지적이에요. 비록 마음대로 추는 춤 같이 보일 수는 있겠지만, 8자춤은 실제로 먹이 공급원까지의 거리와 방향에 대한 매우 구체적인 정보를 제공합니다. 꿀벌의 8자춤은 다른 벌들에게 먹이 공급원이 태양과 관련하여 어디에 있는지를 알려주는 역할을 해요. 먹이 공급원의 방향은 실제로 벌이 몸을 흔드는 직선의 각도로 나타내어질 수 있어요. 물론, 방향을 알려주는 일종의 지표, 즉 기준이 필요하죠. 이 경우에는 태양의 방향과 중력이에요. 먹이의 위치에 있어, 수직으로 쌓인 벌집 통 위에서 추는 춤의 각도와 태양의 방향 간에는 연관성이 있습니다. 그래서, 태양과 먹이가 같은 방향에 있으면, 8자춤의 직선 부분이 위쪽 방향을 향합니다. 먹이가 태양의 왼쪽으로 90도에 위치하면, 벌 춤의 직선 부분을 90도 방향을 향하게 맞춥니다. (슬라이드 2를 보여준다)

학생: 하지만 벌은 태양이 어디에 있는지 항상 어떻게 알죠? 태양의 위치는 계속해서 변하잖아요? 게다가 구름이 낀 날에는요?

교수: 벌은 심지어 어두운 벌집 안에서조차 태양의 위치를 아주 정확하게 알 수 있게 해주는 체내 시계를 가지고 있어요. 벌은 또한 자외선을 볼 수도 있는데, 자외선은 벌이 태양의 정확한 각도를 알 수 있도록 도와줍니다. 자, 먹이까지의 거리는 벌이 얼마나 오래 몸을 흔드는가에 의해서도 알 수 있습니다. 몸을 흔드는 시간이 짧으면, 먹이 공급원이 가까이 있다는 뜻이지요. 그래서, 만일 벌이 직선으로 2초간 몸을 흔들면, 그것은 다른 벌들에게 먹이 공급원이 약 2킬로미터쯤 떨어져 있다는 것을 말해주는 것입니다. 자, 만일 먹이 공급원이 너무 가까이 있어서 벌이 정확한 거리를 알려줄 수 없다면, 음, 약 50미터라고 해보죠, 8자 모양이 줄어들면서 원춤이라고 불리는 다른 종류의 춤을 추게 됩니다. 근처에 있는 먹이 공급원을 나타내기 위해서요. 첫 움직임은 약 2센티미터 정도이고, 곧 벌은 반대방향으로 원을 그립니다. 원춤을 추고 나면, 둥지에 있던 다른 수많은 일벌들이 그 동작을 모방하며 가까이에서 춤을 따라 합니다. 확실히, 춤 언어는 꿀벌이 하나의 종으로 성공적으로 살아남을 수 있게 해준 중요한 전략입니다. 그럼에도 불구하고, 여러 중요한 의문들이 풀리지 않은 채 남아 있습니다. 벌들이 어떻게 춤을 통해 먹이의 양과 질에 대해 인지할 수 있는지를 연구자들이 아직 알아내지 못했기 때문이지요. 다음 수업까지, 내가 도서관에 예약해 둔 몇 가지 추가 자료들을 여러분이 읽어오기를 바랍니다.

Ⓦ integral [íntəgrəl] 필수적인   ecosystem [ékousìstəm] 생태계   pollination [pὰlənéiʃən] 수분(受粉)   pollen [pálən] 꽃가루   hive [haiv] 벌집   waggle [wǽgl] 흔들거리다   overlap [óuvərlæ̀p] 겹치다, 포개지다   forager [fɔ́(:)ridʒər] 약탈자, 먹이를 찾는 자   nectar [néktər] 꿀   artificial [ὰ:rtəfíʃəl] 인공의   honey sac 꿀 주머니   vigorous [vígərəs] 활발한, 격렬한   in relation to ~ …에 관하여; …와 비교하여   indicator [índəkèitər] 지표   gravity [grǽvəti] 중력   vertical [vɚ́:rtikəl] 수직의   comb [koum] 벌집   bearing [bέ(:)əriŋ] 방향, 방위   with respect to ~ …에 대하여   orient [ɔ́:riənt] …을 향하게 하다   internal [intɚ́:rnəl] 체내의   ultraviolet light 자외선   imitate [ímitèit] 모방하다

01 강의의 주된 내용은?
Ⓐ 곤충의 삶에서 춤이 차지하는 역할
Ⓑ 꿀벌이 벌집 안에서 활동을 조정하는 방법

Ⓒ 꿀벌이 특정 종류의 꿀만 섭취하는 이유
Ⓓ 벌이 먹이의 위치를 찾아내기 위해 의사소통하는 방법들

02 8자춤의 목적은? (두 가지 선택)
Ⓐ 먹이 공급원의 방향을 나타내려고
Ⓑ 제한된 먹이 공급을 위해 경쟁하려고
Ⓒ 햇빛의 방향을 나타내려고
Ⓓ 먹이 공급원까지의 거리를 나타내려고
Ⓔ 다른 벌들에게 위험을 경고하려고

03 교수가 태양에 대해 말한 것은?
Ⓐ 구름 낀 날에 벌이 먹이를 발견할 수 있도록 돕는다.
Ⓑ 하루 중 어느 때인지를 알려준다.
Ⓒ 먹이 공급원의 방향을 식별하는 데 이용된다.
Ⓓ 벌이 둥지를 쉽게 찾을 수 있도록 해준다.

04 원춤에 대해 교수가 암시하는 것은?
Ⓐ 거리에 대한 정보는 제공하지 않는다.
Ⓑ 벌들의 체내 시계를 동시에 작동하도록 돕는다.
Ⓒ 8자춤과 비슷한 목적을 수행한다.
Ⓓ 벌이 의사소통을 하는 데 사용하는 또 다른 음성 언어이다.

05 벌이 몸을 흔드는 길이와 먹이 공급원의 위치 간의 관계에 대해 교수가 말한 것은?
Ⓐ 더 짧게 흔들수록, 먹이 공급원이 벌집과 더 가까이 있다.
Ⓑ 더 길게 흔들수록, 먹이 공급원이 태양과 더 가까이 있다.
Ⓒ 더 길게 흔들수록, 먹이 공급원이 태양에서 더 멀리 있다.
Ⓓ 더 짧게 흔들수록, 먹이 공급원이 벌집에서 더 멀리 있다.

06 벌의 춤에 대한 교수의 의견은?
Ⓐ 다른 이론들이 제기될 것으로 기대한다.
Ⓑ 시간이 흐름에 따라 진화할 것이라고 생각한다.
Ⓒ 답을 찾을 수 없는 궁금증을 너무 많이 제기한다고 우려한다.
Ⓓ 앞으로의 연구가 더 많은 정보를 줄 것이라 생각한다.

Practice Questions   본문 p. 278

| 01 D | 02 B | 03 A | 04 B, D | 05 D | 06 C |

Introduction

Difference / Example
새와 혹등고래 노래의 차이점

Listen to part of a lecture in a biology class. ◁ **MP3 47**

Professor(female): We've been discussing animal communication. Um, today, we're going to talk about marine mammals, mainly the humpback whale (shown on screen). Now, we know that these whales make a wide range of communicative sounds. These sounds are also called songs. Of course, **Q2** **another animal comes to mind when we think of songs – birds.** We also define the many vocalizations of birds as songs. But, **bird songs are quite different from the songs of humpbacks.** For starters, what we consider to be a humpback whale song is a repetitive cycle of complex arrangements that last up to 30 minutes each. These magical songs travel for great distances through the world's oceans. These sequences of moans, howls, cries, and other noises are quite complex and often continue for hours on end. The songs of the two

Main Idea / Difference 다른 동물과의 차이점 (1) 동료들에게 배움 (2) 소리가 진화함 **Conclusion** 소리의 정확한 의미는 모름 **Difference** 노래가 불려지는 장소에 따라 노래가 조금씩 다름 이동한 지역의 고래 무리의 노래를 따라 부름 **Example** 지역마다 고래의 노래 순서가 다른 것을 예를 들어 설명 **Difference** 노래가 점차 진화함 **Difference / Example** 높낮이가 다른 음의 예로는 트롬본, 동음의 예로는 피아노 **Opinion** 혹등고래의 노래는 자연의 경이로움	animals are quite different, but there's actually a much bigger, more startling, **Q1 difference I want to talk to you about today. While most birds learn their vocalizations from their parents, humpback whales learn from their peers.** What I mean is, while other animals learn a set of sounds from their parents to communicate with and use the same sounds for the rest of their lives, **the sounds of a humpback whale evolve – slight variations in their songs occur each year.** We… **Q6 we still don't know their precise meanings – partly, I suppose, because we haven't really tried that hard to figure them out,** but we do know that humpback whales use vocalizations as a way of communicating with one another. Well, there are many theories about the meanings of the variety of sounds humpback whales make, but the way these animals acquire the ability to communicate is fascinating. So, how do we know that humpbacks learn songs from their peers? Well, there are a couple of clues. First of all, humpbacks sharing the same ocean basin also share similar songs. **Q4-B What's more, the songs that whales sing are different depending on the location they are sung.** Whales living on one side of the ocean will bellow different songs from those on the other side. Now, what's interesting is that if a male from one side should move to the other and have contact with a new group of males, the male will pick up songs from the new group. Let's say that a group of whales repeat a series of sounds. Okay, so, for example, if a group of whales in the Indian Ocean made a moan, a howl, and a moan. The new whale will listen to the sounds and start making a song in the same sequence. In this case, a moan, a howl, and a moan. So, **Q3 the whole group in that area will all be making the same moan, howl, and moan, while another pod of whales in the Pacific, the other side of the world, would be singing a totally different combination of sounds.** From this, we can see that whales have the ability to follow and mimic one another. So, whales in different groups sing different songs… But something more astounding was discovered in a recent research expedition in the Pacific Ocean – whales have the ability to refine their music in great detail. All the whales in an area sing virtually the same song at any point in time, but **Q4-D the song constantly and slowly evolves.** **Q5 The sequence of sounds differs, but so does the frequency – the pitch may go up and down like the sweeping sound made by a trombone or stay the same like the notes played on a piano.** Another factor in songs is the amplitude – the sounds might get louder or quieter. Over the course of a month, a particular phrase in the song that started as a sweeping sound, or a sound in which the pitch starts low and goes up, will slowly flatten and turn into a constant note. Another phrase might get steadily louder. So, the song slowly evolves through a process in which every whale learns a note and its volume from another. Humpbacks seem to change their songs consistently, meaning that every whale in the pod will be making the same sounds despite these numerous and subtle revisions. There are many different ways animals can communicate, but humpback whales are a real wonder of nature. The beautiful sound they make slowly evolves over time as whales travel and interact, just like the language of humans.

해석 생물학 수업의 다음 강의 일부분을 들으시오.

교수(여자): 지금까지 동물들의 의사소통에 대해 이야기해봤습니다. 음, 오늘은 해양 포유류, 주로 혹등고래에 대해 이야기해보려고 합니다. (화면에 보여준다) 자, 우리는 혹등고래가 광범위한 의사소통용 소리를 낸다는 것을 압니다. 이런 소리 또한 노래라고 불립니다. 물론, 노래를 생각하면 또 다른 동물이 생각나죠. 바로 새입니다. 우리는 새가 내는 많은 발성 역시 노래로 정의합니다. 하지만 새의 노래는 혹등고래의 노래와는 꽤 다릅니다. 우선, 우리가 혹등고래의 노래로 여기는 것은, 한 번에 30분까지 지속되는 복잡한 배열의 반복된 주기를 가지고 있죠. 이런 신기한 노래는 엄청난 거리를 이동하여 전세계 바다로 전달됩니다. 이런 연속된 신음 소리, 울부짖는 소리, 외치는 소리, 기타 다른 소리들은 굉장히 복잡하며, 종종 몇 시간 동안이나 끊임없이 계속됩니다. 새와 혹등고래의 노래는 굉장히 다르지만, 사실 오늘 여러분에게 말해주고 싶은, 훨씬 더 크고, 더 놀라운 차이점이 있습니다. 대부분의 새가 부모 새에게 발성을 배우는 것에 반해, 혹등고래는 동료들에게 배웁니다. 그러니까, 다른 동물들이 의사소통을 하기 위해 부모에게 일련의 소리를 배우고 일생 내내 같은 소리를 사용하는 것에 반해, 혹등고래의 소리는 진화한다는 것이죠. 그들의 노래에는 해마다 조금씩의 변화가 생깁니다.

우리는 아직 혹등고래 노래의 정확한 의미를 알지 못합니다. 부분적으로는 말이죠. 왜냐하면 그 노래들의 정확한 의미를 파악하기 위해 그다지 열심히 연구하지는 않았거든요. 하지만, 혹등고래가 서로서로 의사소통을 하기 위해 발성을 사용한다는 점은 분명히 알고 있습니다. 음, 혹등고래가 내는 다양한 소리들의 의미에 대한 이론들은 많지만, 혹등고래가 의사소통을 하는 능력을 습득하는 방법이 무척이나 매혹적입니다. 그럼, 혹등고래가 동료로부터 노래를 배운다는 것을 어떻게 알 수 있을까요? 음, 몇 가지의 실마리가 있습니다. 우선, 같은 해양 분지를 공유하는 혹등고래들은 비슷한 노래를 부릅니다. 게다가, 고래들이 부르는 노래는 노래가 불려지는 장소에 따라 다릅니다. 이쪽 바다에 사는 고래들은 바다 저쪽에 사는 고래들과 다른 소리를 내죠. 자, 흥미로운 점은, 만일 수컷 고래 한 마리가 이쪽 바다에서 저쪽 바다로 가서 새로운 수컷 무리들을 만나게 되면, 그들로부터 새 노래들을 배운다는 점입니다.

한 무리의 고래들이 일련의 소리를 반복해 낸다고 해보죠. 좋아요. 그럼 예를 들어, 인도양의 한 고래 무리가 신음 소리, 울부짖는 소리, 그리고 신음 소리의 순으로 소리를 냈다고 해보죠. 새로운 고래는 그 소리를 듣고 같은 순서로 노래를 부르기 시작합니다. 이 경우는, 신음 소리, 울부짖는 소리, 그리고 신음 소리의 순서가 되겠죠. 그래서, 그 지역의 무리 전체는 똑같이 신음 소리, 울부짖는 소리, 그리고 신음 소리의 순서대로 소리를 내게 됩니다. 반대쪽 세상에 있는, 태평양의 또 다른 고래 무리가 완전히 다른 조합의 소리를 내는 반면에 말이죠. 이를 통해, 우리는 혹등고래가 서로를 따르고 모방하는 능력이 있다는 것을 알 수 있습니다.

자, 서로 다른 무리의 고래는 서로 다른 노래를 부릅니다... 하지만 태평양에서의 최근 한 탐사 연구에서 훨씬 더 믿기 어려운 사실이 발견되었습니다. 혹등고래에게는 노래를 매우 상세하게 갈고 닦을 수 있는 능력이 있다는 것이죠. 한 지역의 모든 고래들은 어느 한 시점에는 사실상 같은 노래를 부릅니다. 하지만 그 노래는 계속해서 그리고 천천히 진화하지요.

소리의 순서는 노래마다 다르지만, 주파수도 다릅니다. 소리의 높이는 트롬본이 내는 스위핑 사운드(밀거나 당겨서 내는 소리)처럼 오르락 내리락 할 수도 있고, 피아노가 내는 음들처럼 똑같을 수도 있습니다. 노래의 또 다른 점은 진폭으로, 소리는 점점 더 커질 수도 작아질 수도 있습니다. 한 달이라는 시간 동안, 스위핑 사운드로 시작한 노래의 특정 구절, 혹은 낮게 시작해서 올라가는 음은, 천천히 낮아지고 일정한 음으로 바뀌게 됩니다. 노래의 다른 구절은 차츰 커질 수도 있고요.

그래서, 고래의 노래는 모든 고래들이 다른 고래로부터 음과 음량을 배워가는 과정을 통해 천천히 진화합니다. 혹등고래들은 노래를 끊임없이 바꾸는 것처럼 보이는데, 이는 이런 끊임없고 미묘한 수정들이 있음에도 불구하고 무리 안의 모든 고래들이 같은 소리를 내게 될 것이라는 것을 의미합니다. 동물들이 의사소통을 하는 다른 여러 가지의 방법들이 있지만, 혹등고래는 진정한 자연의 신비입니다. 그들이 내는 아름다운 소리는, 사람의 언어와 마찬가지로 고래가 이동하고 소통하면서 시간의 흐름에 따라 천천히 진화하니까요.

Ⓦ vocalization [vòukəlizéiʃən] 발성   repetitive [ripétitiv] 반복적인   sequence [síːkwəns] 순서   moan [moun] 신음 소리   howl [haul] 길게 울부짖는 소리   cry [krai] 외침   on end 계속   startling [stάːrtliŋ] 아주 놀라운   variation [vɛ̀əriéiʃən] 변화, 차이   precise [prisáis] 정확한   acquire [əkwáiər] 습득하다   ocean basin 해양 분지   bellow [bélou] 우렁찬 소리를 내다   a pod of ~ ... 한 무리   mimic [mímik] 흉내를 내다   astounding [əstáundiŋ] 믿기 어려운   refine [rifáin] 개선하다, 갈고 닦다   virtually [və́ːrtʃuəli] 사실상   frequency [fríːkwənsi] 주파수   pitch [pitʃ] 음의 높이   note [nout] 음   amplitude [ǽmplitjùːd] 진폭   flatten [flǽtən] 납작하게 만들다   subtle [sʌ́tl] 미묘한   interact [ìntərǽkt] 상호작용하다

01 강의의 주된 내용은?
Ⓐ 혹등고래의 다양한 적응 방법
Ⓑ 혹등고래가 내는 여러 다른 종류의 노랫소리
Ⓒ 동물 발성의 진화
Ⓓ 혹등고래 노래의 독특한 특징들

02 교수가 처음에 새의 지저귐에 대해 언급한 이유는?
Ⓐ 동물 노래의 기본적인 방법에 대해 설명하려고
Ⓑ 노래를 이용하는 다른 동물들의 예를 주려고
Ⓒ 의사소통용이 아닌 노래의 예를 들려고
Ⓓ 혹등고래와 다른 동물들간의 차이를 예를 들어 설명하려고

03 교수가 혹등고래의 노래 순서에 대해 말한 것은?
Ⓐ 멀리 있는 다른 혹등고래들에 의해서는 사용되지 않을 것이다.

Ⓑ 새의 노래 패턴과 유사한 것을 따른다.
Ⓒ 고래가 한 무리 속에 받아들여지는 데 도움이 된다.
Ⓓ 다른 지역의 고래를 끌어모으는 데 쓰인다.

04 교수에 따르면, 다음 중 혹등고래 노래의 특징은? (두 가지 선택)
Ⓐ 실제로는 아무 의미가 없다.
Ⓑ 각 무리에 따라 독특하다.
Ⓒ 지속되는 시간이 짧다.
Ⓓ 시간이 흐름에 따라 조정된다.

05 교수가 트롬본과 피아노를 언급한 이유는?
Ⓐ 고래의 노래를 새의 노랫소리와 비교하려고
Ⓑ 혹등고래 노래의 복잡성을 설명하려고
Ⓒ 고래의 몸이 소리를 만드는 방식을 묘사하려고
Ⓓ 혹등고래가 내는 소리를 설명하는 것을 도우려고

06 강의에 따르면, 다음 중 혹등고래 노래에 관해 사실인 것은?
Ⓐ 새의 노랫소리와 유사하다.
Ⓑ 매년 똑같다.
Ⓒ 아직 완전히 알지 못한다.
Ⓓ 포식동물을 쫓아버리기 위해 사용된다.

02 / Animal Adaptation

≋ Sample Questions

본문 p. 284

| 01 D | 02 C | 03 C | 04 B | 05 A | 06 D |

해석 생물학 수업의 다음 강의 일부분을 들으시오. ◁ MP3 48

교수(여자): 자, Jonathan, 알래스카에 가 본 적이 있다고 했죠?
학생(남자): 네, 사실 저는 아버지 때문에 거기서 일 년 동안 살았어요.
교수: 좋아요. 그러면, 모두에게 그곳의 겨울이 어땠는지 말해주는 게 어때요?
학생: 음... 겨울이요? 음, 추워요. 그러니까, 그곳은 정말 춥고 눈이 많이 와요. 겨울이 있고 알래스카 겨울이 따로 있어요. 그곳에서 어떻게 사람이나 무언가가 살 수 있는지 잘 모르겠어요.
교수: 하하, 그 점에 있어서는 나도 같은 생각이에요. 몇 년 전 겨울에 그곳에서 현장 연구를 한 적이 있는데, 정말 사람들이 말하는 것처럼 끔찍했죠. 그런 극한의 환경에서, 동물들은 어떤 적응을, 그러니까 특징을 가져야 해요, 음... 그러니까, 그런 환경 속에서 살아남거나 번식을 할 수 있도록 도와주는, 한 종(種)의 신체적 또는 행동적 특징을 가져야 하지요. 그리고 겨울철의 북반구 같은 극한의 환경에서의 적응은... 음, 동물들은 매우 흥미로운 적응 방식을 보일 수 있어요. 순록을 예로 들어보죠.
자, 순록이라, 말해보세요, 여러분은 순록이 어떤 방법으로 혹독한 북쪽의 겨울을 살아남도록 적응했다고 생각하나요? 힌트를 하나 주도록 하죠. 겨울에는 먹이가 매우 부족해요. 순록은 먹이를 찾아 다닐 때 먼 거리를 이동하죠.
학생: 음, 잘 모르겠어요... 많이 움직여야 한다는 건가요? 적응 방식이 순록의 다리와 관련이 있나요?
교수: 그래요. 바로 그거예요. 순록에 있어 가장 중요한 것은 이동성이에요. 그들은 이곳 저곳으로 끊임없이 이동해야 해요. 심지어 새끼를 낳은 직후조차도요. 그래서, 순록의 적응 방법 중 하나는, 순록의 새끼는 태어나자마자 걸을 수 있다는 점이에요. 알다시피, 순록은 겨울에는 새끼들이 걷는 법을 배울 때까지 기다릴 수가 없어요, 그렇지 않으면... 음, 굶어 죽게 되지요. 순록의 또 다른 신체적 적응 방법은 순록의 다리에 있는 지방의 양입니다. 순록의 다리에는 지방이 많아서, 사지를 따뜻하게 하느라 에너지를 많이 소모하지 않아도 되지요. 먹이가 부족할 때는 가능한 한

효율적이어야 하잖아요, 그렇죠? 보온과 효율성 이야기가 나왔으니 하는 말이지만, 추운 겨울 기후에서 사는 다른 포유류들처럼, 순록은 비바람으로부터 자신을 보호하기 위해 두꺼운 겹으로 된 털을 발달시켰어요. 자, 지금까지는 육안으로 볼 수 있는 적응 방법에 대해서만 말을 했는데, 그 외에 어떤 것들이 있을까요? 눈에 보이지 않는 어떤 적응 방법을 순록이 가지고 있다고 생각하나요? Jonathan?

학생: 음, 먹이에 대해 말씀하셨잖아요. 순록이 살아남을 수 있도록 도와주는 특별한 먹이에 관한 무언가를 읽었던 기억이 나요.

교수: 맞아요. 순록은 겨울에 살아남기 위해 먹이를 또한 조정했죠. 순록은 여러 가지 다른 종류의 식물을 먹을 수 있어요. 그들의 먹이는 열 종류가 넘는 식물, 양치식물, 그리고 균류 등으로 이루어져 있지요. 하지만, 순록의 가장 중요한 적응 방법은 겨울에 지의류 식물을 먹을 수 있는 능력에 있습니다. (화면에 보여준다) 지의류 식물은 일종의 균류와 조류(藻類)의 결합물입니다. 그 중 두꺼운 털처럼 보이는 한 종류는, 흔히 순록 이끼라고 불리는데, 알다시피, 순록이 먹기 때문이지요. 이 지의류 식물은 바위와 나뭇가지 위에 자라고 겨울 동안 비교적 쉽게 찾을 수 있습니다. 이것은 중요한 적응 방법인데, 대부분의 동물들은 지의류 식물을 섭취하지 못하기 때문입니다. 지의류 식물은, 사실 대부분의 동물들에게 독이 되지만, 순록은 그들의 소화기계에 지의류 식물에 있는 독성 화합물을 분해해주는 특별한 미생물을 가지고 있습니다. 그래서, 겨울에는 먹이가 부족하지만, 순록은 다른 포유류들에 비해 어렵지 않게 먹이를 찾죠. 더 인상적인 점은, 순록이 여름에는 지의류 식물을 그만큼 많이는 먹지 않는다는 것입니다. 이유가 뭔지 추측할 수 있는 사람 있나요?

학생: 그건... 그걸 다 먹어버리면 겨울에 먹을 것이 없어서인가요?

교수: 맞아요. 하지만 순록이 어떻게 그렇게 하는지, 그것이 더 인상적입니다. 그들의 소화기는 계절이 달라짐에 따라 조절이 됩니다. 순록은 주로 그들의 위에 사는 특정한 박테리아의 도움으로 먹이를 소화시킵니다. 여름에 순록은 풀과 나뭇잎을 뜯어 먹으니, 섬유질을 소화시키는 데 도움이 되는 박테리아가 자라나죠. 가을 동안에는, 나뭇잎이 없기 때문에, 균류를 소화시키는 것을 돕는 박테리아가 자라게 되죠. 그리고 겨울에는, 순록은 다시 지의류 식물을 먹는 상황으로 돌아가게 됩니다. 물론, 원래는 그렇게 되어야 하는데, 지구온난화로 인해 순록이 살아남는 것이 더 어려워지고 있습니다. 겨울 동안 더 따뜻하면 살아남기가 더 쉬워질 것 같지요? 문제는, 순록이 먹는 먹이, 즉 지의류 식물은 환경에 매우 민감하다는 것입니다. 기온이 단 섭씨 2도 정도만 떨어져도, 지의류 식물을 만들기 위한 조류가 균류 위에 자라지 않게 됩니다.

W adaptation [ædəptéiʃən] 적응 reproduce [rìːprədjúːs] 번식하다 hemisphere [hémisfiər] (지구의) 반구 scarce [skɛərs] 부족한, 드문 forage [fɔ́(ː)ridʒ] 먹이를 찾다 mobility [moʊbíləti] 이동성 calf [kæf] 새끼 (pl. calves) offspring [ɔ́(ː)fspriŋ] 새끼 extremities [ikstréməṭiz] (pl.) 사지 elements [éləmənts] (pl.) 비바람, 폭풍우 diet [dáiət] 식사 fern [fəːrn] 양치식물 fungus [fʌ́ŋgəs] 균류, 곰팡이류 (pl. fungi) lichen [láikən] 지의류, 이끼 algae [ǽldʒiː] 말, 조류(藻類) moss [mɔ(ː)s] 이끼 consume [kənsjúːm] 섭취하다 poisonous [pɔ́izənəs] 독성이 있는 microbe [máikroub] 미생물 digestive system 소화기 계통 degrade [digréid] (화학적으로) 분해하다 toxic compound 독성 화합물 graze [greiz] 풀을 뜯다 fiber [fáibər] 섬유질

01 강의의 주된 내용은?
Ⓐ 적응 방법에 기인하지 않은 순록의 전형적인 특징들
Ⓑ 겨울에 먹이를 찾기 위해 순록이 사용하는 다양한 전략들
Ⓒ 알래스카 주(州)에서의 순록과 사람 사이의 상호 작용
Ⓓ 순록이 환경에 대응하여 발전시킨 특징들

02 교수가 알래스카의 기후에 대해 언급한 이유는?
Ⓐ 북반구의 전형적인 기후에 대해 설명하려고
Ⓑ 순록이 북쪽에 사는 이유를 설명하려고
Ⓒ 환경과 적응 방법 간의 관계에 대해 소개하려고
Ⓓ 현장 연구가로서의 자신의 과거 경험에 대해 이야기하려고

03 교수에 따르면, 순록의 두꺼운 털의 목적은?
Ⓐ 얼음 위에서 걷는 것을 돕기 위해
Ⓑ 포식자들로부터 숨기 위해
Ⓒ 바람과 눈을 막기 위해
Ⓓ 몸 위에 지의류 식물이 자라나는 것을 막기 위해

04 순록의 소화기계에 존재하는 특별한 미생물에 대해 교수가 언급한 점은?
Ⓐ 특별한 균류에서부터 온다.
Ⓑ 계절에 따라 바뀐다.
Ⓒ 겨울에만 존재한다.
Ⓓ 순록에게 해롭다.

05 순록에 대해 추론할 수 있는 것은?

(A) 지의류 식물 없이는 겨울에 굶어 죽을 것이다.
(B) 종종 털 위에 이끼가 자란다.
(C) 해로운 미생물 때문에 멸종 위기에 처해 있다.
(D) 실제로는 지구온난화의 혜택을 받고 있다.

06 지구온난화에 대해 교수가 말한 것은?

(A) 추운 기후에 사는 동물들에게 도움이 된다고 생각한다.
(B) 앞으로 더 악화될 것으로 예상한다.
(C) 순록이 쉽게 지구온난화에 적응할 수 있다고 생각한다.
(D) 사람들이 생각하는 것보다 훨씬 더 순록에게 해롭다고 생각한다.

Practice Questions

본문 p. 288

| 01 B | 02 C | 03 D | 04 A, D | 05 B | 06 B |

Listen to part of a lecture in a biology class. ◁ MP3 49

Introduction

Main Idea
민물 환경에 사는 생물들의 적응 방법

Professor(female): Okay, in our last class, we talked about oceans and other large bodies of water, and how the creatures that live in them adapt to changes in the ecosystem, such as those caused by global warming. **Q1** Today, we'll be talking about freshwater environments and the adaptive abilities of the organisms that live in them.

You're probably assuming we'll be talking about larger bodies of fresh water, such as lakes. We'll actually be talking about smaller bodies of water: ponds. There are ponds that are permanent; that is, they never dry up. But today, we'll be looking at a type of fresh water that isn't permanent… I'm talking about temporary ponds.

Misunderstanding / Correction
임시 연못에 사는 생물의 수가 많음

Temporary ponds are small bodies of water that change seasonally. In the wet months, the summer, there is a lot of rainfall, so the ponds fill up. However, in the dry months of the winter, the water dries up. So, we're looking at small bodies of water that disappear but reappear in the same area. Well, you might think that there are not that many organisms that can survive in such bodies of water… but there are a surprising number of diverse organisms that live in these environments. Well… Of course, large animals like fish won't be able to survive, so most of the life is limited to smaller organisms. **Q2** So how strong is global warming's effect on these animals? Not so strong, actually… In fact, these animals are surprisingly good at adapting to their environment.

Cause & Effect
환경 변화에 생물이 잘 적응해서 큰 영향 없음

Well… To see how these ponds affect the ecosystem, let's start by taking a look at the plants that live in and around them. During the winter, many plants grow where the body of water would be because the soil is more fertile. Grazing animals will then migrate to the area to eat the vegetation. However, during the summer months, when the ponds form, not all the plants will be able to survive under the water. Well, **Q3** what happens to these plants is that they die and decompose, providing nutrients to the life forms that live in the water.

Function
물 속에서 죽은 식물은 분해되어 영양분이 됨

So, let's talk about the animals that use these nutrients to live… There are two types of animals that live in temporary ponds. One type would be animals that stay in the

Adaptation
임시 연못 안 동물의 적응법 두 가지

Example
껍질을 사용하는 동물 – 민물새우

Term
metamorphosis 용어 설명

Adaptation / Example
일시적으로 임시 연못에 사는 동물의 적응법
Eg.) 개구리

pond all their life, while the other type would be animals that only live there for a certain period. You might be wondering how the first type, you know, the type that lives in ponds even when they're dry, survives, but it is fairly simple. **Q4-A** **These animals have two ways to survive during the dry months. One way is to burrow deep into the soil when the ponds are dry.** They will stay burrowed until the water returns. Most of these animals are very small… They're mostly worms or insects.

Q4-D **Another way animals survive is through physical adaptations. They develop a form of protection for when there is no water.** What I mean is that they use shells or hard coverings to protect themselves. An example of this type of animal is the **Q5** fairy shrimp. This type of shrimp lives inside an egg, which is a type of shell, when the water disappears. This egg holds enough water and nutrients for the fairy shrimp to survive for up to 10 years.

Now, some animals only live a part of their lives in temporary ponds. These animals have distinct stages. Every time the animal changes into a new form, it has to go through what we call a metamorphosis (shown on screen). **Q6** **During a metamorphosis, the animal totally changes in form.** For example, frogs begin their lives as tadpoles, which need to be in water. They then go through a metamorphosis, slowly developing legs and lungs, and eventually becoming adult frogs. **Some frogs live in temporary ponds during their tadpole stage and then move to larger, more permanent bodies of water.** This makes sense because temporary ponds are an excellent environment for tadpoles to grow in. You see, as I mentioned before, **these ponds are safer because, unlike permanent ponds, they contain no predators or large animals like fish that can eat tadpoles.** So, there, the likelihood of surviving is much higher. Once they grow large enough, they can move to a permanent source of water without the same danger of being eaten.

해석 생물학 수업의 다음 강의 일부분을 들으시오.

교수(여자): 자, 지난 시간에는 바다와 같은 거대한 수역들에 대해, 그리고 그 속에서 사는 생물들이 어떻게 지구온난화와 같은 생태계 변화에 적응하는지에 대해 이야기 해보았습니다. 오늘은, 민물 환경과 그 안에 사는 생물들의 적응 능력에 대해 이야기해보죠.

여러분은 아마도 우리가 호수처럼 좀 더 커다란 민물 수역에 대해 이야기할 걸로 생각할지도 모르겠군요. 사실, 그보다 더 작은 수역인 연못에 대해서 이야기를 할 겁니다. 영구적인 연못들, 즉 결코 마르지 않는 연못들이 있기는 합니다. 하지만, 오늘은 영구적이지 않은 민물의 한 종류에 대해 살펴보도록 할 것입니다… 임시 연못을 얘기하는 것이죠.

임시 연못은 계절에 따라 변하는 작은 수역입니다. 우기인 여름에는 비가 많이 내려 연못에 물이 찹니다. 하지만, 건기인 겨울에는 물이 말라버리죠. 자, 우리는 동일한 지역에 사라졌다가 다시 생겨나는 작은 수역을 살펴보고 있습니다. 글쎄요, 여러분은 이런 수역에서 생존할 수 있는 생물이 그다지 많지 않다고 생각할지 모르겠군요… 하지만 이런 환경에서 살고 있는 다양한 생물체들은 놀라울 만큼 많아요. 아… 물론 물고기처럼 큰 동물들은 살아 남을 수 없겠지요. 그래서 (이런 수역에 사는) 대부분의 생물들은 더 작은 생물들로 한정됩니다. 그러면 지구온난화가 이런 동물들에게 미치는 영향은 얼마나 강할까요? 실제로 그렇게 강하지는 않습니다… 사실, 이런 동물들은 놀라우리만치 환경에 적응을 잘 합니다. 음… 이러한 연못들이 생태계에 어떻게 영향을 미치는지를 보기 위해, 그런 연못들 속과 주변에 사는 식물들에 대해 살펴보는 것으로 시작해봅시다. 겨울 동안, 물이 있었던 곳에는 많은 식물들이 자랍니다. 그곳의 토양이 더 비옥하기 때문이지요. 그리고 방목 가축들이 이 지역으로 그 초목을 먹기 위해 이주해 옵니다. 하지만, 연못이 만들어지는 여름에는, 그 식물들 모두가 물 속에서 생존할 수 있는 것은 아닙니다. 음, 이 식물들에게 일어나는 일은, 그들이 죽어 분해되면서 물 속에 사는 생명체들에 영양분을 제공하게 되는 것이죠.

그럼, 살아 남기 위해 이런 영양분을 이용하는 동물들에 대해서 이야기해봅시다… 임시 연못에 사는 동물에는 두 가지 유형이 있습니다. 한 유형은 일생 동안 연못 안에서 사는 동물들이고, 또 다른 유형은 특정 기간 동안만 그곳에 사는 동물들입니다. 여러분은 첫 번째 유형의 동물, 즉 심지어 연못이 말랐을 때조차 연못 안에서 일생을 사는 유형들이 어떻게 생존하게 되는지 궁금하겠지만, 그것은 매우 간단합니다. 이런 동물들은 건기 동안 생존을 위해 두 가지 방식으로 적응합니다. 한 가지 적응 방법은 연못이 말랐을 때 땅 속 깊이 굴을 파는 것입니다. 그들은 물이 돌아올 때까지 잠복해 있습니다. 이런 동물들은 대부분 아주 작은 것들입니다… 대부분 벌레나 곤충이지요.

동물들의 또 다른 생존 방법은 신체적 적응을 통한 것입니다. 그들은 물이 없을 때를 대비해 보호의 한 형태를 발달시키죠. 그 말은 즉, 그들이 스스로를 보호해 줄 딱딱한 껍질이나 덮개를 사용한다는 말입니다. 이런 유형의 동물의 예로는 '민물새우'가 있습니다. 이 새우들은 물이 사라지면,

껍데기의 일종인 알 속에서 삽니다. 이 알은 민물새우가 10년까지 생존할 수 있을 만큼의 충분한 물과 영양분을 담고 있어요.

자, 어떤 동물들은 일생 중 일부 동안만 임시 연못 속에서 삽니다. 이런 동물들은 뚜렷한 단계를 가지고 있습니다. 이런 동물들은 새로운 형태로 변화할 때마다 우리가 '변태'라고 부르는 과정을 거쳐야 합니다. (화면에 보여준다) 변태를 하는 동안, 이런 동물들은 완전히 형태가 변합니다. 예를 들어, 개구리는 물 속에 있어야 하는 올챙이로서 삶을 시작합니다. 그들은 그리고 나서 변태를 거치죠. 천천히 다리와 폐를 발달시키고, 결국 성체 개구리가 됩니다. 일부 개구리들은 올챙이 단계에서 임시 연못 안에서 살다가, 더 크고 더 영구적인 수역으로 이동해 갑니다. 이것은 매우 타당한데요, 임시 연못은 올챙이가 자라기에 탁월한 환경이기 때문이지요. 이전에도 언급했듯이, 이런 연못들에는 영구 연못과는 달리 올챙이를 잡아먹을 수 있는 포식동물이나 물고기 같은 큰 동물이 없기 때문에 더 안전합니다. 그래서 그곳에서의 생존 가능성은 훨씬 높습니다. 일단 충분히 자라고 나면, 잡아 먹히는 것과 같은 위험성이 없는 영구적인 수역으로 이동할 수 있습니다.

Ⓦ body of water (바다·호수 등의) 수역 freshwater [fréʃwɔːtər] 민물[담수]의 adaptive [ədǽptiv] 적응의, 적응할 수 있는 organism [ɔ́ːrgənìzəm] 유기체, 생물 pond [pɑnd] 연못 permanent [pə́ːrmənənt] 영구적인 temporary [témpərèri] 임시의 seasonally [síːzənəli] 계절에 따라 rainfall [réinfɔ̀ːl] 강우(량) fertile [fə́ːrtl] 비옥한 vegetation [vèdʒitéiʃən] 초목, 식물 decompose [dìːkəmpóuz] 분해되다, 부패되다 nutrient [njúːtriənt] 영양분, 영양소 burrow [bə́ːrou] 굴을 파다 adaptation [ædæptéiʃən] 적응 covering [kʌ́vəriŋ] 외피, 막 metamorphosis [mètəmɔ́ːrfəsis] 탈바꿈, 변태 tadpole [tǽdpòul] 올챙이 predator [prédətər] 포식동물 likelihood [láiklihùd] 가능성

01 강의의 주된 내용은?
Ⓐ 지구온난화가 바다에 사는 물고기와 동물들에 미치는 영향
Ⓑ 민물 생물들이 변화하는 환경에 대처하는 방식
Ⓒ 임시 연못 형성의 다양한 단계들
Ⓓ 지구온난화로 인한 피해를 최소화하는 방법들

02 지구온난화가 임시 연못에 사는 동물들에게 미치는 영향에 대해 교수가 말한 것은?
Ⓐ 멸종 위기 종의 수를 두 배로 늘릴 것이다.
Ⓑ 임시 연못에 사는 동물들의 수를 증가시킬 것이다.
Ⓒ 그 동물들은 적응을 할 수 있기 때문에, 영향이 거의 없을 것이다.
Ⓓ 그 동물들이 먹을 수 있는 먹이의 양을 감소시킬 것이다.

03 강의에 따르면, 식물이 생태계에 도움을 주는 방법은?
Ⓐ 갓 태어난 새끼를 위한 임시 보호처가 된다.
Ⓑ 토양이 더 오랜 기간 동안 물을 담고 있을 수 있도록 도와준다.
Ⓒ 임시 연못 안의 물을 정화시킨다.
Ⓓ 토양에 양분을 제공한다.

04 교수에 따르면, 임시 연못이 말랐을 때 동물들이 생존하는 방식은? (두 가지 선택)
Ⓐ 땅 속으로 들어간다.
Ⓑ 식물 속에서 산다.
Ⓒ 호수로 이동한다.
Ⓓ 신체적 보호를 발달시킨다.

05 교수가 민물새우를 언급한 이유는?
Ⓐ 생태계에서의 식물의 역할을 강조하려고
Ⓑ 생존하기 위해 껍질을 사용하는 동물의 예를 들려고
Ⓒ 임시 연못 속의 다양한 동물군을 설명하려고
Ⓓ 건조한 환경에 대한 학생들의 이해를 도우려고

06 교수가 변태를 언급한 이유는?
Ⓐ 지구온난화가 개구리에게 미치는 치명적인 결과를 설명하려고
Ⓑ 왜 일부 동물들은 일생의 일부를 임시 연못 속에서 사는지를 알려주려고
Ⓒ 임시 연못이 말랐을 때 일부 동물들이 어떻게 생존하는지 설명하려고
Ⓓ 토양에 양분을 제공하는 식물들의 예를 들려고

03 / Botany

Sample Questions
본문 p. 294

01 B   02 C   03 D   04 B   05 D   06 A

해석 식물학 수업의 다음 강의 일부분을 들으시오. MP3 50

교수(여자): 오늘은 기온과 강수량이 변하는 지역에서 생기는 적응 방법의 한 종류에 대해 이야기하고자 합니다. 알다시피, 어떤 지역은 가끔은 비가 엄청나게 내리고, 가끔은 비가 전혀 내리지 않은 채로 몇 주가 흐르기도 하지요. 그래서 이런 기후에서 자라는 식물들은 건기에 대처할 수 있도록 다양한 방식으로 진화해 왔습니다.

이러한 적응 방법이 어떻게 작용하는지 이해하려면, 식물이 영양분을 만드는 방법을 먼저 이해해야 합니다. 여러분 모두가 광합성, 즉 식물이 빛을 이용해서 이산화탄소와 물을 에너지로 변환하는 과정에 대해 알고 있을 겁니다. 인간이 영양분을 처리하기 위해 산소를 들이마시는 것처럼, 식물은 이산화탄소를 들이마셔야 합니다. 인간과 식물의 유사성은 거기서 끝나지 않습니다. 양쪽 모두 이런 기체들을 들이마시기 위한 호흡기를 필요로 합니다. 숨을 쉬기 위해, 인간은 입과 콧구멍, 즉 신선한 산소가 몸으로 들어올 수 있도록 해주는 구멍들이 필요합니다. 식물들도 비록 훨씬 작긴 하지만, 기공이라고 불리는 비슷한 구멍들을 가지고 있습니다. (화면에 보여준다) 이 작은 구멍들은 식물이 광합성과 같은 세포 과정에 있어 기체들을 주고 받을 수 있도록 합니다. 그래서 식물들은 기공을 통해 이산화탄소를 들이마시고 산소를 배출합니다.

자, 이런 작은 기공들로 인해 생기는 유감스러운 부작용은, 기공 때문에 수분이 손실된다는 것입니다. 우리는 땀샘을 통해서 수분을 손실하는데, 이는 몸을 식힐 필요가 있기 때문이지요. 반면, 식물은 그런 기능이 필요하지는 않아서, 수분을 보유하고 있는 것을 더 선호합니다. 수분을 손실하는 이런 과정을 증산이라고 합니다.

자, 이런 수분 손실은 비가 오거나 습도가 매우 높을 때는 문제가 되지 않습니다. 뿌리가 토양에서 곧바로 물을 흡수하기 때문에, 비가 올 때는 정말 아무 문제가 되지 않죠. 그리고 습할 때는, 음, 물이 증발하지 않으므로 식물은 수분 손실을 최소화할 수 있습니다. 하지만, 건기가 계속되면 상황이 달라지죠. 몇몇 식물들은 수분이 손실되는 것을 막기 위해서 이 작은 구멍들을 최대한 많이 닫을 수 있는 방법을 발달시켰습니다. 식물들이 생존을 위해서 어떻게 이런 작은 구멍들을 통제하는 능력을 발달시켰는지는 정말로 믿기 힘들 정도로 굉장하죠.

식물들은 하루의 시간대에 따라 기공을 닫아 수분 상실을 조정합니다. 앞에서 말한 것처럼, 습도가 문제가 되지만, 기온도 마찬가지로 문제가 됩니다. 우리는 날이 더워지면 땀을 훨씬 더 많이 흘립니다. 그 이유는, 음, 더울 때 물이 더 빠른 속도로 증발하기 때문입니다. 자, 식물은 정확히 이와 반대라고 생각할 수 있습니다. 식물들은 증발을 통한 수분 손실을 더 적게 하고 싶기 때문에, 낮에는 기공을 닫습니다. 하지만 서늘해지는 밤에는, 증산작용이 덜 되기 때문에, 식물은 기공을 열어 더 많은 공기를 들이마십니다.

식물들은 어떻게 건조한 때를 정확히 알까요? 대부분의 사람들은, 기공이 잎사귀에 있기 때문에 잎사귀가 기상 상태를 확인할 수 있다고 추측합니다. 하지만, 실제로 습도를 알아차리는 부위는 전혀 생각지도 못했던 곳에 있습니다. 식물이 기공을 닫아야 하는지 아닌지 명령을 내리는 신호를 잎사귀에 보내는 것은 바로 뿌리입니다. 뿌리가 먼저 흙에 수분이 부족한 것을 감지하면, 뿌리는 세포들이 수분을 잃도록 만드는 일종의 산(酸)을 방출합니다. 언뜻 납득이 되지 않지요? 압니다. 하지만 세포들이 수분을 잃게 되면, 세포가 수축하기 시작합니다. 기공은 공변세포라고 하는 특별한 세포로 둘러싸여 있습니다. 뿌리가 신호를 보내면, 식물 속의 세포들은 수분을 잃기 시작합니다. 이 세포들 중에는 공변세포들이 포함되어 있습니다. 수분을 잃는 세포들 중에 공변세포가 기공에 가장 많이 영향을 미칩니다. 일단 수분을 잃기 시작하면, 공변세포들은 그 과정 속에서 구멍을 닫으면서 수축을 하기 시작합니다. 물론 이것이 나를 비롯한 대부분의 식물학자들이 믿는 바이지만, 정확히 공변세포가 하는 일에 대해서는 여전히 논쟁이 있습니다... 증거가 아직 충분하지 않기 때문이죠. 우리는 이 특별한 세포가 어떻게 반응하는지만 알고 있을 뿐입니다.

중요한 것은, 우리가 식물이 다른 환경에 어떻게 대처하는지를 계속해서 연구한다는 점입니다. 기공이 어떻게 작용하는가를 이해하는 것이 실제로 우리의 저녁 식탁을 바꿉니다. 이 말은, 기공에 대해 이해를 함으로써, 식물을 기르는 사람들과 농부들이 높은 기온의 기후와 긴 가뭄 속에서 재배하기 최적인 종을 찾을 수 있다는 말입니다. 어떤 종이 기공을 조종할 수 있는지를 알면, 식량 안보의 과제에 직면하기 위해 어떤 곡물을 길러야 할지를 알 수 있게 될 겁니다. 오염과 지구온난화로 인해 기온과 탄소 농도가 높아짐에 따라, 변화하는 환경에 식물들이 어떻게 적응하는지를 이해하는 것이 매우 중요해지고 있습니다.

W precipitation [prisìpitéiʃən] 강수(량)   photosynthesis [fòutəsínθisis] 광합성   convert [kánvərt] 변환하다   carbon dioxide 이산화탄소   respiratory system 호흡기계   nostril [nástrəl] 콧구멍   albeit [ɔːlbíːit] 비록 ...일지라도   stomata [stóumətə] 기공   cellular [séljələr] 세포의   release [rilíːs] 방출하다   side effect 부작용   sweat gland 땀샘   retain [ritéin] 유지하다   transpiration [trænspəréiʃən] 증산, 김내기   humidity [hjuːmídəti] 습도   evaporate [ivǽpərèit] 증발하다   minimize [mínəmàiz] 최소화하다   pore [pɔːr] (피부의 땀구멍 같은) 구멍   unlikely [ʌnláikli] 예상 밖의   counterintuitive [kàuntərintʃúːitiv] 직관에 어긋나는   breeder [bríːdər] 사육자   drought [draut] 가뭄

01 강의의 주된 내용은?
Ⓐ 인간과 식물이 수분을 방출하는 방식의 차이
Ⓑ 식물이 건기를 감지하고 반응하는 방식
Ⓒ 식물이 에너지를 만들기 위해 물을 필요로 하는 이유
Ⓓ 식물이 수분 손실을 방지하는 과정

02 교수에 의하면, 식물의 호흡기계와 관련된 문제점은?
Ⓐ 식물은 낮 동안에는 이산화탄소를 들이마실 수 없다.
Ⓑ 너무 많은 공기가 식물의 뿌리 세포로 들어간다.
Ⓒ 식물은 호흡 구멍을 통해서 수분을 빼앗긴다.
Ⓓ 구멍들의 크기가 너무 작다.

03 교수가 인간의 땀을 언급한 이유는?
Ⓐ 인간이 열에 얼마나 큰 영향을 받는지를 강조하려고
Ⓑ 식물의 기공이 닫히면 어떤 일이 일어나는지 설명하려고
Ⓒ 흔한 이산화탄소 공급원을 알려주려고
Ⓓ 식물과 인간의 두 가지 유사한 작용을 대조하려고

04 교수에 의하면, 비가 오지 않는 오랜 기간을 감지할 때 식물이 일반적으로 반응하는 방식은?
Ⓐ 뿌리와 잎의 성장을 늦춘다.
Ⓑ 특정 유형의 화학물질을 방출하기 시작한다.
Ⓒ 광합성 과정을 가속화한다.
Ⓓ 기공을 반복적으로 열었다 닫았다 한다.

05 수분 부족에 대한 식물의 반응이 잘 납득이 되지 않을 것이라고 교수가 말하는 이유는?
Ⓐ 식물이 생존하기 위해서는 수분을 필요로 한다는 것이 일반적인 믿음이다.
Ⓑ 식물이 밤에 광합성을 하는 것은 흔치 않은 일이다.
Ⓒ 식물들은 대개 강수량이 많은 지역에서 자란다.
Ⓓ 건기에 수분을 손실하는 것은 말이 되지 않는다.

06 식물이 건기에 적응하는 방식에 대한 이해에 관한 교수의 의견은?
Ⓐ 농업을 향상시키는 방법들을 찾는 데 쓰일 수 있다.
Ⓑ 인간에게서 동일한 과정을 알아내지 못한다면 쓸모가 없다.
Ⓒ 지구온난화의 원인을 더 잘 이해하는 데 도움을 줄 수 있다.
Ⓓ 사막 환경의 확산을 끝내는 열쇠이다.

≋ Practice Questions

본문 p. 298

| 01 D | 02 C | 03 B | 04 C | 05 A | 06 D |

| **Main Idea**

Term
bog의 용어 설명 | Listen to part of a lecture in a botany class. ◁ MP3 51

Professor(male): Okay, **Q1** today we are going to continue our discussion on plant life in wet environments. I'd like to talk about bogs in particular. Bogs are among the least inviting environments for plants. They are a deposit of dead plant material, often from moss. The soil in bogs, which is also called peat, is very infertile.
Student(female): What do you mean by infertile? If bogs are made of dead plants, shouldn't there be more nutrition? Isn't compost a type of fertilizer?
P: Well, that's a good point. It's true that dead plants are a good source of nutrition… Well, in normal types of soil, that is. What really sets bogs apart is the type of wa- |

Problem – Solution
늪지의 토양이 산성이고 죽은 식물이 잘 부패되지 않아, 영양분을 만들 수 없음

Name Origin
flytrap의 어원 설명

Requirement / Problem – Solution
필요한 영양분을 얻지 못해 벌레를 잡아 먹도록 진화

Misunderstanding
잎으로 먹이를 '무는' 것이 아닌, 끈적이는 물질에 달라붙은 곤충 위로 잎을 닫음

ter at the surface. In bogs, this water is acidic. Also, **Q2 plants have to decay to create nutrition. But the soil in bogs is so saturated that the decaying of plants occurs more slowly.** Plants have to decay to create nutrition, but this just isn't possible in bogs. So the plants in bogs need to adapt to the environment to survive. Today we're going to talk about one plant that thrives in this environment. Can anyone guess what it is?

S: Is it the Venus flytrap?

P: That's right, I'm sure all of you have heard of the Venus flytrap. These carnivorous plants have captured the imagination of many, including myself when I was a child. I once thought that these were gigantic plants that captured wild animals. The funny thing is, the name, well, the Latin name, actually implies that these plants are animal eaters. **Q3 The "flytrap," part of the name comes from the Latin word "muscipula," which means "mousetrap," rather than "muscicapa," which actually means "flytrap."** But somehow, the botanists who first studied these plants came up with the correct English name we know today. Anyway, the concept of a plant that feeds on insects is quite intriguing, really. Most insects are supposed to eat plants, not the other way around, right? Well, **Q1 this plant has evolved to survive in the tough conditions presented by bogs.**

Okay, first we must understand the soil in bogs a little better. Oh, but before we get into that, do you remember the first paper I made you guys write, about the nutrients plants need?

S: Yeah, I remember. Plants need phosphorus, magnesium, potassium, and uh... oh yeah, nitrogen.

P: Very good. As I mentioned earlier, the soil in bogs is acidic, and minerals and other nutrients are scarce as a result. This includes nitrogen. Believe it or not, Venus flytraps get most of their energy from photosynthesis, just like normal plants. Most of us like to think of the plant as a vicious predator, but this just isn't the case. But plants need to make amino acids, the basic building blocks of protein that cells are made of. In order to do so, **Q4 they need a steady source of nitrogen, which just isn't available in Venus flytrap habitats. So, they needed to find nutrition elsewhere, and that source became small insects.**

Insects are an excellent source of the nitrogen and protein plants need to survive. But it took a while for these plants to evolve the ability to catch insects. You might just assume that Venus flytraps "bite" their prey by using their leaves that are shaped like mouths, but this is far from the truth. These leaves, which are called snap traps, have a sticky substance inside them that keeps the insects from escaping. So, the modern Venus flytrap has two mechanisms to hold its prey – the insects stick to the leaves and the leaves also clamp down on the insects, they, uh... close to prevent the insects from escaping. But ancient flytraps only had the sticky substance, not the closing mechanism... This allowed too many insects to get away. In order to make sure the insects wouldn't escape, they needed to close their leaves. As flytraps evolved, they developed the ability to close their leaves faster. Today they have a relatively fast closing speed.

Venus flytraps also needed a way to discern prey from other objects, such as rain. So they developed special sensors called trigger hairs. These hairs can sense a moving object. When an insect is stuck to a leaf, it will start thrashing about. That's when the plant will know it has caught an insect. **Q5 I remember sticking a pencil inside the**

연필을 먹어 치울 줄
알았으나 아니었음

Problem
서식지가 줄어듦
Solution
늪지 보호, 통제된 화재

leaves of my first Venus flytrap. I was expecting to see it chomp down on my pencil… As you might expect, I was pretty disappointed.

This brings me to my next point. When I had a Venus flytrap, I had no idea that its numbers were decreasing. Sadly it was due to the fact that people were removing Venus flytraps from their natural habitat and selling them in plant stores. To make things worse, **Q6** the habitat of Venus flytraps is shrinking. Today, less than 10 percent of their habitat remains. The key to survival for Venus flytraps in the wild lies in protecting wetlands and setting controlled fires. Experts also stress that you shouldn't buy any Venus flytraps unless you can be sure they didn't come from the wild.

해석 식물학 수업의 다음 강의 일부분을 들으시오.

교수(남자): 자, 오늘 우리는 습한 환경 속에 사는 식물에 대한 논의를 계속하겠습니다. 특히 늪지에 대해서 이야기하려 합니다. 늪지는 식물에게는 제일 매력적이지 않은 환경입니다. 늪지는 죽은 식물들의 퇴적물, 종종 이끼로부터 나온 퇴적물입니다. 이탄(泥炭)이라고도 불리는, 늪지의 토양은 매우 척박합니다.

학생(여자): 척박하다니 무슨 말이죠? 늪지대가 죽은 식물들로 이루어져 있다면 양분이 더 많아야 하지 않나요? 퇴비는 비료의 한 유형이잖아요?

교수: 음, 좋은 지적이에요. 죽은 식물이 훌륭한 영양원이라는 것은 사실이지요… 음, 보통 유형의 토양에서는 그렇습니다. 늪지대를 실상 다르게 만드는 것은, 표면에 있는 물의 유형입니다. 늪에서는 이 물이 산성이죠. 또한, 영양분이 생기기 위해서는 식물이 부패해야만 합니다. 하지만 늪의 토양은 너무나 포화된 상태여서, 식물의 부식이 훨씬 더디게 일어납니다. 식물은 양분을 만들어내기 위해서 부식이 되어야만 하는데, 늪에서는 이것이 가능하지 않게 되는 겁니다. 그래서 늪지대의 식물들은 살아남기 위해서 이런 환경에 적응해야 합니다. 오늘 수업에서는 이런 환경에서 번성하고 있는 식물에 대해 이야기할 거예요. 그게 뭔지 맞춰볼 사람 있나요?

학생: 파리지옥풀인가요?

교수: 맞아요. 분명 여러분 모두 파리지옥풀에 대해 들어본 적이 있을 겁니다. 이 식충식물은 어린 시절의 나를 포함해 많은 사람들의 상상력을 사로잡았지요. 나는 한때 파리지옥풀이 야생동물을 잡아 먹는 거대한 식물이라고 생각한 적이 있습니다. 재미있는 것은, 그 이름, 음, 라틴어로 된 그 이름이 실제로 이 식물이 동물을 먹는다는 뜻을 내포하고 있다는 것입니다. 파리지옥풀 이름의 일부인 flytrap은 실제로 '파리통'을 뜻하는 이름인 'muscicapa'가 아닌, '쥐덫'이라는 뜻의 라틴어 'muscipula'에서 유래했습니다. 하지만 어째서인지, 이 식물을 처음 연구한 식물학자들이 오늘날 우리가 알고 있는 올바른 영어 이름을 만들어 냈습니다. 어쨌든, 곤충을 먹는 식물이라는 개념은 정말이지 매우 흥미롭습니다. 대부분의 곤충들이 식물을 먹도록 되어 있지, 그 반대는 아니잖아요? 그렇죠? 그런데, 이 식물은 늪이 만든 이 험한 환경 속에서 생존하기 위해 진화를 해왔습니다.

좋아요, 우선 우리는 늪지대의 토양에 대해서 좀 더 이해를 해야 합니다. 아, 하지만 그 전에, 내가 여러분에게 쓰라고 했던 첫 번째 보고서를 기억합니까? 식물들이 필요로 하는 양분에 대한 것이었죠.

학생: 예, 기억나요. 식물들이 인, 마그네슘, 칼륨, 그리고 어… 아, 네, 질소를 필요로 한다는 거요.

교수: 아주 좋아요. 앞서 언급한 것처럼, 늪의 토양은 산성이고, 그 결과 무기물과 다른 영양분이 매우 부족합니다. 여기에는 질소도 포함돼요. 믿기 힘들겠지만, 파리지옥풀은 대부분의 에너지를 보통 식물들처럼 광합성으로 얻습니다. 우리들 대부분은 이 식물을 사악한 포식자로 생각하기 쉽지만, 사실은 그렇지 않습니다. 하지만 식물들은 세포를 구성하는 단백질의 기본 구성 요소인 아미노산을 만들어야 합니다. 그렇게 하려면, 그들은 안정적인 질소 공급원을 필요로 하는데, 파리지옥풀의 서식지에서는 이것이 전혀 가능하지 않습니다. 그래서 파리지옥풀은 다른 곳에서 양분을 얻어야만 했고, 작은 곤충들이 그 공급원이 되어버린 거죠.

곤충은 식물이 생존하기 위해 필요로 하는 질소와 단백질의 탁월한 공급원입니다. 하지만 이런 식물들이 곤충을 잡는 능력을 진화시키는 데에는 오랜 시간이 걸렸죠. 여러분은 파리지옥풀이 입처럼 생긴 잎사귀를 이용해서 먹이를 '문다'고 추측할지도 모르겠으나, 이는 사실과 전혀 다릅니다. 포획망(snap trap)이라고 불리는 이 잎사귀들은 그 안에 곤충이 도망가지 못하게 하는 끈적거리는 물질이 있습니다. 자, 현대의 파리지옥풀은 먹이를 잡아두는 두 가지 장치를 가지고 있습니다. 곤충들이 잎사귀에 달라 붙게 되고, 잎사귀들은 또한 곤충을 확 조이게 되는 것이죠. 음… 곤충이 도망가는 것을 방지하기 위해 잎을 닫는 거죠. 하지만 고대의 파리지옥풀은 잎을 닫는 장치 없이, 끈적거리는 물질만 가지고 있었습니다. 이로 인해 너무 많은 곤충들이 도망갈 수 있었죠. 곤충이 도망갈 수 없도록 하기 위해서, 파리지옥풀은 잎을 닫아야 했습니다. 파리지옥풀이 진화함에 따라, 그들은 잎을 더 빨리 닫는 능력을 발달시켰습니다. 오늘날 파리지옥풀은 입을 닫는 속도가 비교적 빠릅니다.

파리지옥풀에게는 먹이를 빗물과 같은 다른 물질과 구별하는 방법도 필요했습니다. 그래서 그들은 감각 촉수라고 하는 특별한 센서를 발달시켰습니다. 이 촉수들은 움직이는 물체를 감지할 수 있지요. 곤충이 잎에 달라붙게 되면 그 곤충은 몸부림치기 시작합니다. 그때가 바로 파리지옥풀이 곤충을 잡았다는 것을 알게 되는 거죠. 내가 처음 가졌던 파리지옥풀 잎사귀 안에 연필을 붙여봤던 기억이 나는군요. 나는 그 풀이 내 연필을 우적우적 씹어 먹을 것을 기대했지만… 여러분이 예상한 것처럼, 난 꽤 실망했었죠.

이제 다음 단계로 넘어가죠. 내가 파리지옥풀을 갖고 있을 때에는 그들의 개체 수가 줄어들고 있다는 것을 몰랐어요. 슬프게도, 그것은 많은 이들이 파리지옥풀을 그들의 자연서식지에서 가져다가 식물 가게에 팔았기 때문입니다. 설상가상으로, 파리지옥풀의 서식지는 줄어들고 있습니다. 오늘날에는 그들 서식지의 10% 이하만이 남아 있습니다. 야생에서 파리지옥풀의 생존의 핵심은, 늪지를 보호하고 통제 가능한 불을 놓는 데 있습니다. 전문가들은 또한, 파리지옥풀이 야생에서 오지 않았다는 확신이 없는 한 파리지옥풀을 사지 말아야 한다고 강조합니다.

ⓦ bog [bɑg] 늪지, 습지 inviting [inváitiŋ] 매력적인 deposit [dipázit] 침전물 peat [piːt] 토탄, 이탄 infertile [infə́ːrtəl] 불모의 compost [kámpoust] 퇴비, 두엄 fertilizer [fə́ːrtəlàizər] 비료 set apart 다르게 만들다 acidic [əsídik] 산성의 saturated [sǽtʃərèitid] 포화된 decay [dikéi] 부패하다 thrive [θraiv] 번창하다 intriguing [intríːgiŋ] 아주 흥미로운 phosphorus [fásfərəs] 인 magnesium [mægníːziəm] 마그네슘 potassium [pətǽsiəm] 칼륨 nitrogen [náitrədʒən] 질소 mineral [mínərəl] 무기물 vicious [víʃəs] 포악한 amino acid 아미노산 snap [snæp] 덥석 물다 trap [træp] 덫, 올가미 sticky [stíki] 끈적이는 mechanism [mékənìzəm] 방법 [매커니즘], 구조 clamp down on ~ ...을 꽉 조이다 discern A from B B에서 A를 구별하다 trigger [trígər] 방아쇠 thrash about 몸부림치다 chomp [tʃamp] 쩝쩝 먹다 wetland [wétlænd] 습지

01 강의의 주된 내용은?
Ⓐ 동물을 먹고 사는 여러 가지의 다른 식물종들
Ⓑ 곤충이 파리지옥풀로부터 빠져나올 수 있는 방법
Ⓒ 많은 식물들이 늪지에서 자랄 수 없는 이유
Ⓓ 한 식물 종류가 혹독한 환경 속에서 살아남기 위해 적응한 방법

02 교수에 의하면, 늪지의 어떤 면 때문에 식물들이 그 속에서 자라기 어렵다고 하는가?
Ⓐ 수위가 빨리 오르락 내리락 한다.
Ⓑ 좁은 지역에 식물이 너무 많다.
Ⓒ 죽은 식물들이 너무 느리게 양분으로 변한다.
Ⓓ 식물들이 충분한 햇빛을 받을 수 없다.

03 교수가 쥐덫을 언급한 이유는?
Ⓐ 늪지가 얼마나 위험할 수 있는지를 강조하려고
Ⓑ 파리지옥풀의 라틴어 이름에 생긴 오류를 알려주려고
Ⓒ 파리지옥풀의 초기 쓰임새들 중 하나를 설명하려고
Ⓓ 환경 적응의 예를 들려고

04 파리지옥풀이 곤충을 먹도록 진화한 이유로 교수가 발견한 것은?
Ⓐ 초기 농부들에 의한 비료 사용
Ⓑ 더 강한 식물들과의 경쟁
Ⓒ 늪지의 토양에 부족한 질소
Ⓓ 곤충에서만 발견되는 아미노산

05 파리지옥풀에 얽힌 교수의 어릴 적 경험에 관해 그가 암시한 것은?
Ⓐ 그의 기대가 비현실적이었다.
Ⓑ 그의 인생에서 가장 좋은 추억들 중 하나였다.
Ⓒ 그 식물을 좀 더 잘 돌보았더라면 하고 바란다.
Ⓓ 그가 식물학자가 되도록 이끌었다.

06 교수가 파리지옥풀의 서식지에 대해서 말한 것은?
Ⓐ 단지 늪지만 포함되지는 않는다.
Ⓑ 과학자들에 의해 보호된다.
Ⓒ 전세계에 퍼져 있다.
Ⓓ 빠른 속도로 사라져가고 있다.

04 / Ecology

≋ Sample Questions

본문 p. 304

| 01 B, D | 02 A, C | 03 C | 04 B | 05 A | 06 D-C-B-A |

해석 생태학 수업의 다음 강의 일부분을 들으시오. ◁) MP3 52

교수(여자): 종의 다양성에 대한 논의를 계속하죠. 우리는 동물들이 각각의 환경 속에서 생존하기 위해 하는 특정한 적응 방법들에 대해서 이야기 했습니다. 하지만 오늘은, 특정한 환경 속에서의 종의 다양성을 설명할 수 있는 몇 가지 다른 요인들에 초점을 맞춰봅시다. Jason, 이번 여름에 가족 여행을 다녀왔다고 하지 않았나요?

학생(남자): 예, 저희 가족은 하와이로 여행을 다녀왔어요. 정말 좋았어요. 그러니까, 볼 거리가 정말 많았어요.

교수: 동물들에 대해 뭔가 알아차린 게 있나요?

학생: 사실, 그랬어요. 상당히 많은 여러 가지의 종들이 있었고, 제가 방문했던 각 섬마다 모두 달랐어요.

교수: 우리는 그에 대해서 별로 아무런 생각을 하지 않거나, 또는 그 섬들에서 살고 있는 동물들이 그냥 자연적으로 진화한 것이라고 무의식적으로 추측할 수도 있습니다. 하지만, 우리가 오늘날 보는 종들을 결정짓는 많은 다른 요인들이 있습니다. 더 자세히 들어가기 전에, 생물지리학이라는 새로운 개념을 소개하도록 하지요. 이것이 무엇인지, 추측해 볼 사람 있습니까?

학생: 음... 생물학과 지리학이 결합된 것처럼 들리는데요...

교수: 맞습니다. 지리적으로 고립된 장소에서의 종들의 풍부함에 대해 연구하는 이론이지요. 약 50년 전, Robert MacArthur와 E.O. Wilson은 어떻게 대양도에 다양한 종들이 살게 되었는지를 설명하기 위해서 평형이론을 만들었습니다. 이들은 기본적으로, 새롭게 형성된 섬에서도 종들의 수가 결국에는 안정될 것이라고 주장했습니다. 이것은 매우 중요한데, 서로 다른 종들로 이루어진 공동체가 평형을 이루는 데 얼만큼의 시간이 걸릴지를 생물학자들이 이제 예상할 수 있기 때문입니다. 물론, 종들이 각각의 환경에 적응을 하게 되면서, 종들의 전반적인 수는 시간이 지나면서 서서히 증가하게 될 것입니다. 하지만, 언제 평형이 이루어질지에 대한 대략의 추정치를 가지고 있다는 것은 많은 생태학적인 의미를 가지고 있습니다. 하지만, 이런 세부 사항으로 들어가기 전에, 섬에 서식하는 동물들의 대략적인 수를 알기 위해 필요할지 모르는 것들에 대해 살펴 봅시다. 의견이 있는 사람이 있을까요?

학생: 음... 섬이 어디에 위치해 있는가가 중요하지 않을까요? 그러니까, 섬이 본토에서 너무 멀리 떨어져 있다면...

교수: 그래요. 위치는 매우 중요한 요인이지요. 분명, 어떤 동물들은 본토에서 근처의 섬으로 이동해갈 수 있습니다. 섬의 크기도 그와 마찬가지로 중요하죠. 서식지와 먹이를 위한 충분한 공간이 있어야만 하죠. 그래서, 섬에 사는 동물들의 수는, 공간과 거리에 의해서 주로 결정됩니다. 여러분은 아마도 이것이 그 섬에 사는 여러 다른 종들의 수와도 관련이 있다고 생각할지도 모르겠지만, 놀랍게도, 그것과는 거의 관련이 없습니다. 즉, 큰 섬이 외딴 곳에 있는 작은 섬보다 반드시 더 다양한 종을 가지고 있지는 않다는 말입니다. 여기서 생물지리학적 평형이론이 나오게 됩니다. MacArthur와 Wilson은 (동물들의) 이주율과 멸종률이 균등하게 되어 종의 평형을 만들게 되고, 그럼으로써 실제 동물군의 구성을 결정하게 된다는 점을 제시했습니다. 좋아요, 설명을 해 볼게요. 새로운 화산섬이 바다에서 솟아오른다고 해 봅시다. 몇몇 새들이 본토에서 이 섬으로 이주하기 시작할 겁니다. 물론, 점점 더 많은 종들이 들어옴에 따라, 본토에는 이주해 나갈 종들이 점점 더 적어질 겁니다. 그렇기 때문에, 새 섬으로의 이주율은 결국 감소하게 되죠. 마찬가지로, 종들이 그 섬에서 멸종하는 비율은, 그곳에 터를 잡은 동물들의 수와 관련이 있게 될 겁니다. 그리고, 섬의 자원은 한정되어 있기 때문에, 터를 잡은 종들의 수가 증가할수록 그들 각각의 개체 수는 점점 더 줄어들고 멸종하기 쉽게 될 가능성이 있어요. 섬으로 이주해 들어오는 종들로 인해 섬이 점점 과밀화됨에 따라, 멸종률은 서서히 증가할 것입니다. 이(멸종) 비율은 줄어드는 이주율과 마침내 만나게 될 때까지 계속 증가하여, 결국 평형이 이루어지는 것이지요. 네, Sarah?

학생(여성): 음... 확실히 해 볼게요. 그럼, 이주해오는 종들의 수를 살펴봄으로써, 얼마나 많은 종이 멸종할지를 대강 알 수 있다는 건가요?

교수: 바로 그렇습니다. 하지만 이 이론에는 한계가 있습니다. 그 비율을 예측할 수 있긴 하지만, 우리는 어떤 종이 생존해 남을지는 예측할 수 없습니다. 어떤 종이 생존하게 되고, 어떤 종이 멸종하게 될지를 결정하는 데는 변수가 너무 많아요. 이 이론이 어떻게 적용되었는지 예를 들어 볼게요. 1883년 Krakatoa 섬에서 화산 폭발로 모든 생물이 죽었습니다. 하지만 몇 년 안에, 조류와 곤충의 수가 서서히 증가했습니다. 그 섬에 살았던 같은 종의 새와 나비가 본토에서 다시 그 섬으로 이주해 온 것이지요. 몇 년이 지나자, 전체적인 다양성이 증가했습니다. 하지만, 일단 너무 많은 종들이 이주해 오면서, 멸종하는 새와 나비 종의 수가 늘어나기 시작했어요. 이론대로 말이죠. 하지만, 과학자들이 발견하고 깜짝 놀란 것은, 비록 일부 조류 종들이 성공적으로 재정착하긴 했지만, 폭발 전에도 그곳에 살았던 어떤 종들은 멸종했다는 겁니다. 그래서 실제 동물들의 수는 변하지 않았고, 다양성의 정도도 마찬가지였습니다. 변화한 것은 어떠한 종들이 살아남았는가 하는 것입니다. 배역의 수는 동일했지만, 배우가 바뀐 셈이죠.

Ⓦ diversification [divə̀ːrsəfəkéiʃən] 다양화   respective [rispéktiv] 각각의   combination [kàmbənéiʃən] 조합[결합](물)   isolated [áisəlèitid] 외떨어진   equilibrium [ìːkwəlíbriəm] 평형[균형] 상태   even out 안정되다   estimate [éstimət] 추산[추정]하다   implication [impləkéiʃən] 영향, 결과; 암시   inhabit [inhǽbit] 살다   mainland [méinlænd] 본토   extinction [ikstíŋkʃən] 멸종   composition [kὰmpəzíʃən] 구성   fauna [fɔ́ːnə] (한 지역의) 동물상   emigrate [éməgrèit] (다른 나라로) 이주하다   prone to ~ ...하기 쉬운   variable [vέː(ː)əriəbl] 변수   volcanic eruption 화산 분화   decimate [désəmèit] 대량으로 죽이다   recolonize [riːkάlənaiz] 다시 식민지화하다

01 교수에 의하면, 한 섬에 사는 동물들의 수를 결정하는 요인은? (두 가지 선택)
Ⓐ 섬으로 이주해오는 종들의 수
Ⓑ 섬의 지리학적 크기
Ⓒ 본토에 사는 종들의 수
Ⓓ 섬에서 본토까지의 거리
Ⓔ 섬의 계절적 기후

02 한 섬에서 종들이 평형을 이루는 시기를 결정짓는 것으로 교수가 말한 것은? (두 가지 선택)
Ⓐ 그 섬의 종들이 멸종하는 비율
Ⓑ 그 섬의 종들이 진화하는 속도
Ⓒ 그 섬으로 이동하는 종들의 수
Ⓓ 그 섬의 종들 중 포식자 대 먹잇감의 비율

03 교수에 의하면, 섬이 과도하게 밀집될 경우 일어날 일은?
Ⓐ 그 섬의 (종의) 다양성이 증가할 것이다.
Ⓑ 특정 종들이 본토로 다시 이주해 갈 것이다.
Ⓒ 멸종률이 증가할 것이다.
Ⓓ 종들이 진화를 멈출 것이다.

04 교수가 평형이론의 한계로 여기는 것은?
Ⓐ 섬의 크기는 계산할 수 없다.
Ⓑ 어떤 종류의 종들이 생존할지 예측할 수 없다.
Ⓒ 특정 종들이 언제 멸종할지 결정할 수 없다.
Ⓓ 섬이 아닌 지역들에는 적용될 수 없다.

05 교수가 Krakatoa를 언급한 이유는?
Ⓐ 평형이론이 적용되었던 실제 상황을 예로 들어 설명하려고
Ⓑ 자연재해로 인해 한 종이 어떻게 멸종될 수 있는지를 보여주려고
Ⓒ 어떤 종류의 섬이 일반적으로 더 높은 멸종률을 보이는지를 알려주려고
Ⓓ 새와 나비가 이주율을 예측하는 데 사용될 수 있다는 것을 암시하려고

06 교수는 Krakatoa에서 평형에 이르는 과정에 대해 논의하고 있다. 각 단계를 일이 일어난 순서대로 놓으시오.

Ⓓ 종들이 본토에서 이주한다.
Ⓒ 종들의 다양성이 증가한다.
Ⓑ 종들의 멸종률이 증가한다.
Ⓐ 종의 수는 화산 폭발 전의 수준에 이르게 된다.

≥ Practice Questions

본문 p. 308

01 B   **02** A, D   **03** C   **04** B   **05** D   **06** C

	Listen to part of a lecture in an ecology class. 🔊 MP3 53
Main Idea 흰개미의 특징과 역할	**Professor(female):** When we think of termites, we tend to focus on the fact that they're pests that damage our homes. So Q1 **I think you'd be surprised to learn that they are incredibly important to the ecosystem** and unbelievably interesting as well. Now,

Function
죽은 목재를 먹음으로써 recycling을 도움

Term
cellulose 용어 설명

Problem – Solution
cellulose를 소화 못 시킴 – 미생물이 cellulose를 분해

Condition / Requirement
흰개미와 미생물의
➧ 공생 관계 → 빈출

Difference / Function
벌은 시각에, 흰개미는 후각에 의존
냄새로 먹이 공급원을 알림

Evidence
흰개미 날개는 흰개미의 침입을 의미

Impact
흰개미가 생태계에 미치는 영향

---

as you all know, they eat a lot of wood. But we have to be a little more specific about what type of wood they eat. They eat dead wood, from dead trees in forests, or plant waste. Their consumption of wood is almost like, well, recycling. **Q1** **Termites recycle wood and are in turn turning waste into soil.**

The termite's major source of nutrition comes from cellulose – you know, the chemical found in cell walls of plants, leaves, trees, and grasses. However, termites can't actually digest this complex sugar. To be more specific, they don't have the right enzymes in their digestive systems to metabolize it, meaning they can't get the nutritional benefits of cellulose. You might wonder how termites can live off of cellulose when they can't digest it, but the answer is quite simple. They have a special relationship with protozoa and bacteria. These actually live inside termites, in their digestive systems. **Q2-D** **These microscopic organisms break down the cellulose enough to release its nutritional benefits to the termites. Without these organisms, termites would starve. This is a very obvious instance of a symbiotic relationship** – two different species live together, and it benefits one or both of them.

Another interesting aspect of termites is their social structure. They live in colonies, just like bees or ants. Now, about the colonies. Each colony is started by a pair of termites that mate and produce more termites. Termites in a colony are divided into castes, each of which performs a specific function. There're the reproductives, which breed, gatherers, which collect food to feed the colony, and soldiers, which defend the colony from predators such as ants. As you can imagine, thousands of termites each performing a specific job must have a way of communicating with one another. Unlike bees, which use visual cues, **Q3** **termites use their olfactory senses.** That is, they use specific scents that are unique to their respective colony to communicate. **When a worker finds a new food source, for example, it will leave a trail of scent so that others can follow.**

Scents also play an important role for soldiers. When they detect an unfamiliar scent, they will switch to an aggressive mode. Let's say an ant is near the colony. Ants have a distinct smell that can be sensed by soldier termites nearby. Once the scent is picked up, the termites will start defending their colony. Termites also communicate through sound. They literally sound the alarm by banging their heads against the tunnels of their nest. Other termites can feel the vibrations through special sensory organs on their legs and will help the soldiers defend their colony.

So, what about the reproductives? **Q4** **Only termites that can reproduce have wings. This allows them to fly to a new location, find a mate, and establish a new colony.** Eventually, a colony will swarm in enormous numbers to form new colonies. **These termites wings actually break off once they land.** This swarming… **it's actually how I knew I had a termite infestation in my house a few years back.** Ugh… A pretty amazing sight but definitely not something I ever wanted to see in my house. I found so many wings on the floor and window sills… Even though I had mixed feelings about it, I had to call an exterminator to get rid of them.

Q5 **You might wonder why I even had to think twice, but the fact is that termite colonies are crucial to the ecosystem.** Remember what I said about recycling? **They not only create new soil but are themselves a major food source for various species of reptiles and birds. They're part of the food chain, and it will definitely have an impact if they are removed from the ecosystem.** Of course, I had to get rid of them or else I would have lost my home, but we should always think of ways to preserve ecosys-

Term
decompiculture 용어 설명
Function
쓰레기를 분해해주는 생물을 배양하는 것
Opinion
◎ positive

tems whenever possible. This reminds me of an article I wanted to talk about. **Q6** A fellow professor recently coined the term "decompiculture" (shown on screen). This is a combination of decomposition and agriculture. **The idea behind this term is that humans should focus on cultivating organisms that decompose our waste... that is, organisms that feed on the waste that humans create and dump into landfills and water sources.** In other words, **Q2-A** we can remove what is essentially just pollution by feeding it to organisms like termites. Imagine sawmills and paper mills... termites could definitely help reduce waste there. When you think about it, it's actually **another type of symbiosis, except this time it's between humans and termites.**

해석 생태학 수업의 다음 강의 일부분을 들으시오.

교수(여자): 흰개미라고 하면, 우리는 그것들이 집에 손상을 주는 해충들이라는 사실에 초점을 두는 경향이 있습니다. 그래서, 흰개미들이 생태계에 매우 중요한 존재이며 또한 아주 흥미로운 존재이기도 하다는 것을 알게 된다면 여러분은 아마 놀랄 거예요. 자, 여러분이 모두 알다시피, 흰개미는 나무를 많이 먹지요. 하지만, 우리는 그들이 어떤 종류의 나무를 먹는지를 좀 더 구체적으로 살펴봐야 합니다. 그들은 숲의 죽은 나무나 공장 폐기물에서 나오는 죽은 목재를 먹습니다. 이들이 목재를 먹는 것은 마치, 음, 재활용이나 마찬가지인 셈이죠. 흰개미는 목재를 재활용하고 결국 쓰레기를 토양으로 바꿉니다.

흰개미의 주요 영양원은 셀룰로오스(섬유소)에서 나옵니다. 식물, 잎사귀, 나무, 그리고 잔디의 세포 벽에서 발견되는 화학 물질 말이지요. 하지만, 흰개미는 사실 이런 복합당을 소화시키지는 못합니다. 더 구체적으로 말하면, 그들의 소화기 계통에는 이를 대사시키는 적절한 효소가 없다는 말이에요. 즉, 흰개미는 셀룰로오스로 영양 보충을 하지 못한다는 뜻이죠. 그럼, 소화도 시키지 못하는데, 흰개미는 어떻게 셀룰로오스를 주식으로 할 수 있는지 궁금하겠지요. 하지만 답은 아주 간단합니다. 그들은 원생동물과 박테리아와 특별한 관계를 가지고 있습니다. 이들은 사실 흰개미의 내부, 그들의 소화기 계통에 살고 있어요. 이 미생물들은 흰개미에게 영양 보충을 시켜줄 만큼 충분히 작게 셀룰로오스를 부숩니다. 이 미생물들이 없다면, 흰개미는 굶어 죽을 겁니다. 이것은 공생 관계의 아주 명확한 예입니다. 다른 두 개의 종들이 함께 살면서, 한 쪽 또는 양쪽 모두에게 도움이 되는 것이지요.

흰개미의 또 다른 흥미로운 점은 그들의 사회적 구조입니다. 그들은 벌이나 개미처럼 군집을 이루어 삽니다. 자, 군집에 대해 이야기해보죠. 각각의 군집은, 짝짓기를 해서 더 많은 흰개미들을 낳는 한 쌍의 흰개미에 의해 시작됩니다. 한 군집의 흰개미들은 계급이 나뉘는데, 각 계급은 특정한 기능을 수행합니다. 새끼를 낳는 번식 계급, 무리를 먹이기 위한 먹이를 모으는 채집자들, 그리고 개미 같은 포식자들로부터 무리를 보호하는 병정들이 있지요. 여러분이 생각하는 것처럼, 각자 특정한 임무를 수행하는 수천 마리의 흰개미들은 서로서로 의사소통을 할 수 있는 방법을 가지고 있어야만 합니다. 시각적인 신호를 이용하는 벌과는 달리, 흰개미들은 후각을 이용합니다. 즉, 그들은 의사소통을 하기 위해 각각의 무리에게만 있는 특정 향기를 이용합니다. 예를 들어 한 일개미가 새로운 먹이 공급원을 발견하면, 그 개미는 향기로 자국을 남겨 다른 흰개미들이 따라올 수 있도록 합니다.

냄새는 병정개미들에게도 중요한 역할을 합니다. 병정개미는 낯선 향을 감지하면, 공격 모드로 전환합니다. 한 일반 개미가 흰개미 무리 가까이에 있다고 해봅시다. 일반 개미들은 가까이 있는 병정 흰개미가 감지할 수 있는 뚜렷한 향을 가지고 있습니다. 향을 맡게 되면, 흰개미들은 군집을 방어하기 시작합니다. 흰개미들은 또한 소리로도 의사소통을 합니다. 그들은 둥지 안의 터널에 머리를 부딪혀서 말 그대로 경보음 소리를 냅니다. 다른 흰개미들은 다리에 있는 특별 감각기관을 통해서 그 진동을 느낄 수 있고, 병정개미들이 군집을 방어하는 것을 돕습니다.

자, 번식을 담당하는 흰개미는 어떨까요? 번식을 할 수 있는 흰개미만이 날개가 있습니다. 이로 인해 그들은 새로운 장소로 날아가서, 짝을 찾고, 새로운 군집을 만들 수 있게 되지요. 결국, 엄청난 숫자의 떼가 이동을 해 새로운 군집들을 만들게 됩니다. 흰개미의 날개는 일단 그들이 땅에 내리고 나면 떨어져 나갑니다. 이렇게 떼를 지어 다니는 것은... 몇 년 전에 우리 집이 흰개미에게 습격당한 것을 알게 된 것도 사실 그 때문이었죠. 으... 매우 놀라운 광경이긴 했지만, 분명 우리 집에서 다신 보고 싶지는 않은 것이었죠. 바닥과 창틀에서 너무 많은 날개를 발견했어요... 흰개미에 대해 착잡한 감정을 느끼긴 했지만, 그것들을 없애기 위해 해충 구제업자를 부를 수밖에 없었죠.

여러분은 내가 왜 (흰개미를 죽이는 것에 대해) 심사 숙고해야 했는지 궁금하겠지만, 사실 흰개미 군집은 생태계에 매우 중요한 것입니다. 재활용에 대해서 말한 것 기억나나요? 흰개미는 새로운 토양을 만들 뿐만 아니라 파충류와 조류의 다양한 종에게 주요 먹이 공급원이 되기도 합니다. 그들은 먹이 사슬의 한 부분으로, 생태계에서 제거된다면 분명히 생태계에 영향을 미칠 거예요. 물론, 나는 흰개미를 제거해야 했어요. 그렇지 않으면 내 집을 잃어버릴 수도 있었으니까요. 하지만 우리는 가능하면 생태계를 보존할 수 있는 방법에 대해 항상 생각해야 합니다. 여기서 말하고 싶은 기사가 하나 생각나는군요. 한 동료 교수가 최근 'decompiculture'라는 신조어를 만들어냈습니다. (화면에 보여준다) 이것은 decomposition(분해)과 agriculture(농업)를 결합한 말입니다. 이 용어의 이면에는, 인간은 우리의 쓰레기를 분해하는 생물들을 배양하는 데 초점을 두어야 한다는 생각이 담겨 있어요... 즉, 인간이 만들어내고 매립지나 수원에 버린 쓰레기를 먹는 생물들을 말이에요. 다시 말해, 우리는 본질적으로는 그저 오염물질뿐인 것들을, 흰개미와 같은 생물들에게 먹임으로써 제거할 수 있는 것입니다. 제재소와 제지 공장을 생각해 보세요... 흰개미는 그곳의 쓰레기를 줄이는 데 분명 도움이 될 것입니다. 생각해 보면, 그것은 사실 또 다른 유형의 공생 관계입니다. 이번은 사람과 흰개미 간의 관계라는 것뿐이지요.

 pest [pest] 해충   cellulose [séljəlòus] 섬유소   digest [dáidʒest] 소화시키다   complex sugar 당질 복합체   enzyme [énzaim] 효소   metabolize [mətǽbəlàiz] 대사작용을 하다   protozoa [pròutəzóuə] 원생동물   microscopic organism 미생물   break down 분해하다   instance [ínstəns] 예   symbiotic relationship [rìléiʃənʃìp] 공생 관계   colony [káləni] 군집   mate [meit] 짝짓기를 하다; 짝   caste [kæst] 계층   gatherer [gǽðərər] 채집하는 자   cue [kju:] 신호   olfactory sense 후각   scent [sent] 향   sensory organ 감각기관   swarm [swɔ:rm] 떼를 지어 다니다   windowsill [wíndousìl] 창틀   exterminator [ikstə́:rmənèitər] 해충 구제업자   decomposition [dì:kɑmpəzíʃən] 분해; 부패   cultivate [kʌ́ltəvèit] 재배하다   landfill [lǽndfìl] 쓰레기 매립지   sawmill [sɔ́:mìl] 제재소   paper mill [mil] 제지공장

01 강의의 주된 내용은?
Ⓐ 오염을 줄이는 새로운 방법
Ⓑ 흰개미의 특징과 생태학적 역할
Ⓒ 흔한 해충 침입과 해충을 제거하는 방법
Ⓓ 곤충과 다른 생물 간의 공생 관계

02 교수가 언급한 공생 관계의 예는? (두 가지 선택)
Ⓐ 흰개미로 쓰레기를 재활용하기
Ⓑ 흰개미의 의사소통
Ⓒ 개미로 흰개미를 박멸하기
Ⓓ 흰개미의 소화

03 흰개미가 의사소통하는 방법에서 추론할 수 있는 것은?
Ⓐ 각각의 흰개미는 자신만의 독특한 진동을 만든다.
Ⓑ 흰개미는 일부 벌과 의사소통을 할 수 있다.
Ⓒ 흰개미의 후각은 시력보다 강하다.
Ⓓ 흰개미는 서로 다른 적들의 소리를 인식할 수 있다.

04 교수에 의하면, 교수의 집에 흰개미의 날개가 있었던 이유는?
Ⓐ 해충 구제업자가 실수로 일부 흰개미를 죽였다.
Ⓑ 번식을 담당하는 흰개미들이 교수의 집에 떼를 지어 있었다.
Ⓒ 병정 흰개미들이 다른 곤충을 먹었다.
Ⓓ 흰개미들이 자신들의 냄새를 위해 그곳에 남겨두었다.

05 자신의 집에서 흰개미를 제거하는 것에 대한 교수의 태도는?
Ⓐ 집에 들끓는 흰개미의 수에 깜짝 놀랐다.
Ⓑ 해충 구제업자들의 효과적인 작업에 감명받았다.
Ⓒ 흰개미를 모두 없앨 수 있을지 의심스러워했다.
Ⓓ 흰개미 박멸이 생태계에 끼칠 영향에 대해 염려했다.

06 교수에 의하면, decompiculture가 쓰일 수 있는 곳은?
Ⓐ 흰개미로부터 집을 보호하기
Ⓑ 토양과 물을 재활용하기
Ⓒ 특정 종류의 오염물질을 청소하기
Ⓓ 종이 생산을 돕기

05 / Physiology

Sample Questions

본문 p. 314

01 D　**02** C　**03** A　**04** B　**05** D　**06** C

해석 생리학 수업의 다음 강의 일부분을 들으시오. MP3 54

교수(남자): 자, 지난 시간에는 동물들이 회복을 하기 위해 휴식 기간이 필요한 것에 대해 다루어봤습니다. 먹는 것만큼이나 회복도 중요하다는 것을 배웠지요. 오늘은 더 긴 종류의 휴식에 대해 살펴보고자 합니다. 수면에 대해 이야기해보죠. 수면과 다른 형태의 무활동, 즉 일반적인 휴식 같은 것 사이에는 차이점이 있다는 것을 강조하고 싶습니다. 예를 들어, 벌레는 쉬기는 하지만 수면을 취하지는 않죠. 수면은 뇌가 감각기관과 운동기관과의 연결을 포함한 많은 평상시의 활동들을 변화시킨다는 점에서 차이가 있습니다. 수면은 동물들로 하여금 그러한 연결들을 정지시키도록 하지요. 그래서, 잠을 자고 있는 동물들은 대개 감각을 느끼지도, 움직이지도 않습니다. 음, 내가 대개라고 말한 것은, 음... 음, 그건 잠시 후에 이야기하도록 하지요.

우리는 모두 잠을 잡니다. 그러니까, 모든 무척추동물들, 즉 동물들과 사람들 모두 제대로 작동을 하기 위해서는 똑같이 잠을 자야만 합니다. 이제 여러분 중 많은 사람들은 (수면을 할 때) 우리가 무의식이 된다고 생각할지도 모릅니다. 생명 유지에 필수적인 기관들을 제외한 모든 것이 정지한다고요. 하지만, 우리는 그저 주위 환경에 대한 의식이 감소한 상태에 있는 것일 뿐입니다. 사람은 그래도 괜찮습니다. 우리는 대부분 방 안의 안락한 침대에 누워 있으니까요. 하지만 우리가 잠을 잘 수 있는 안전한 집이나 방이 없다면 어떨까요? 우리가 탁 트인 야외에 있다면 어떨까요? 우리는 많은 것들을 당연히 여기고 살고 있지만, 야생에 있는 동물들에게 잠은, 즉 우리처럼 수면하는 것은 가능하지 않습니다. 많은 동물들은 포식동물에 의해 공격을 받을 위험에 처해 있거나, 때로는 오로지 주변 환경 때문에 사람이 자는 것처럼 잘 수 없기도 합니다.

돌고래나 고래와 같은 해양 포유류들을 예로 들어보죠. 육지 포유류와 비교했을 때, 돌고래는 한 가지 큰 차이점을 가지고 있습니다. 바로 그들의 환경이지요. 우리는 모두 숨을 쉬어야 하는데, 돌고래는 물 속에서 살고 있습니다. 이는 큰 문제점을 제기하는데, 돌고래가 숨을 쉬기 위해 가끔씩 헤엄쳐 올라와야 한다는 것이지요. 즉, 돌고래는 모든 움직임과 감각을 완전히 차단시킬 수는 없다는 거지요. 그래서 돌고래의 뇌는 완전히 정지할 수 없습니다. 그래서, 돌고래는 잠을 자는 동안 한 번에 뇌의 한 쪽 반구만 정지시키는 방법으로 환경에 적응해 왔습니다. 이를 통해 돌고래는 가끔씩 숨을 쉬러 헤엄쳐 올라올 수 있는 것이죠. 그래서 우리는 돌고래를 볼 때, 그들이 자고 있는지를 알 수조차 없습니다. 우리가 (돌고래가 자고 있는지를) 알 수 있는 유일한 방법은 돌고래의 뇌 활동을 측정하는 방법 뿐이지요. 과학자들은 돌고래의 뇌의 절반 한 쪽이 자고 있는 동안 다른 한 쪽이 깨어 있었다는 것을 알게 되고는 놀라워했죠.

자, 여러분은 아마도 수면의 정확한 기능이 뭔지 궁금해지겠죠. 대부분의 사람들은 수면은 신체적 활동으로부터 회복하기 위한 장치라고 추측합니다. 즉, 우리가 수면을 취할 때는 몸 전체가 쉬게 되죠. 근육은 수축을 풀고 이완되며, 몸은 에너지를 아끼지요. 하지만 이런 것들은 우리가 깨어 있는 동안 일반적인 휴식을 취할 때도 일어날 수 있습니다. 곤충들이 쉬고 있을 때도 아마 이런 일이 일어날 겁니다. 내가 말하고자 하는 것은, 우리는 몸을 쉬게 하기 위해 잠을 자는 것이 아니라는 점이에요. 그것은 우리가 의식이 있는 상태에서의 일반적인 무활동을 통해서도 쉽게 할 수 있습니다.

돌고래의 적응 방법에 관한 연구를 통해 우리는 수면의 진정한 목적... 즉 수면의 이점에 대해 생각해볼 수 있습니다. 돌고래가 한 번에 뇌의 한 쪽 반구만을 잠재운다는 것을 기억하지요? 돌고래가 잠을 자고 있다고 말할 수 있는 것은, 돌고래의 뇌를 보고 있기 때문입니다. 그것은 뇌의 활동, 또는, 어떻게 보면, 무활동의 독특한 패턴 때문인데요, 그것이 바로 수면의 기능이 구체적으로 뇌와 관련이 있다는 것의 실마리가 됩니다. 이는 왜 수면이 파충류에 비해 포유류와 조류에서 더 많이 관찰될 수 있는지를 설명합니다. 포유류의 뇌는 다른 동물들의 뇌보다 훨씬 더 복잡합니다. 파충류의 뇌처럼 좀 더 단순한 뇌는 많은 수면을 필요로 하지 않습니다. 우리는 뇌의 크기와 수면의 양과의 상관관계를 통해, 수면의 가장 중요한 기능은 뇌에 이로움을 주는 것과 관련이 있다는 것을 알 수 있습니다.

하지만, 어떤 식으로일까요? 음, 우리는 아직 확실히 알지 못합니다. 한 가지 가설은, 수면이 독소를 제거하기 위해 필요하다는 것입니다. 모든 살아 있는 세포들은 신진대사의 결과로 독소가 생깁니다. 모든 세포처럼, 뇌의 대사 작용의 결과로 활성산소라고 불리는 독소가 생겨나지요. 수면은 아마도 뇌가 이러한 독소들을 제거하도록 해주는 것으로 생각됩니다. 이런 독소가 없을 때 우리는 훨씬 더 정신이 초롱초롱하고 에너지가 넘칩니다. 이것이 우리가 하룻밤 자고 나면 상쾌한 기분이 드는 이유이지요. 비록... 항상 그렇진 않을 수도 있겠지만요. 특히 오전 8시에 하는 생물학 수업의 경우는 말이지요.

ⓦ **inactivity** [inǽktivəti] 무활동, 정지　**alter** [ɔ́:ltər] 바꾸다　**motor organ** 운동 기관　**invertebrate** [invə́:rtəbrit] 무척추동물　**vital organ** 생명 유지에 필수적인 중요 기관　**awareness** [əwɛ́ərnis] 의식　**take ~ for granted** ...을 당연히 여기다　**sensation** [senséiʃən] 감각　**hemisphere** [hémisfiər] (뇌의) 반구　**tone** [toun] (근육의) 긴장　**correlation** [kɔ̀(:)rəléiʃən] 상관관계　**hypothesis** [haipάθisis] 가설　**toxin** [tάksin] 독소　**metabolism** [mətǽbəlìzəm] 신진대사　**free radical** 활성산소　**supposedly** [səpóuzidli] 아마　**alert** [ələ́:rt] 정신이 초롱초롱한　**refreshed** [rifréʃt] (기분이) 상쾌한

01 교수가 주로 다루고 있는 주제로 알맞은 것은?
Ⓐ 동물이 혹독한 환경에 적응하는 방법
Ⓑ 동물과 사람이 생존하는 데 있어 휴식이 필요한 이유
Ⓒ 포유류와 조류의 수면 패턴간의 차이점들
Ⓓ 사람과 동물의 다양한 수면 과정과 기능

02 교수에 의하면, 돌고래의 수면 방식이 특이한 이유는?
Ⓐ 돌고래는 잠을 많이 잘 필요가 없다.
Ⓑ 돌고래는 자는 동안 거의 움직이지 않는다.
Ⓒ 돌고래는 뇌 전체를 정지시키지 않는다.
Ⓓ 돌고래는 몸에서 독소를 만들어낸다.

03 수면의 주된 기능이 신체를 육체적 활동으로부터 회복시키기 위한 것이라는 관점에 대한 교수의 태도는?
Ⓐ 많은 사람들이 그렇게 믿는다고 생각한다.
Ⓑ 누군가 그런 관점을 가지고 있을 수 있다는 것에 놀란다.
Ⓒ 그 관점은 사람들이 수면을 취하는 이유를 완전히 설명하지 못한다고 생각한다.
Ⓓ 몸이 신체적 활동으로부터 회복해야 할 필요가 있다고 생각하지 않는다.

04 교수가 파충류를 언급한 이유는?
Ⓐ 수면의 여러 가지 적응 방식에 대해 논의하려고
Ⓑ 수면의 목적을 설명하는 것을 도우려고
Ⓒ 잠을 자지 않는 동물들의 예를 들려고
Ⓓ 포유류의 우월한 지능을 강조하려고

05 교수가 논의한 가설에 따르면, 우리가 얼마나 정신이 맑은지를 결정하는 것은?
Ⓐ 우리가 처한 상황의 종류
Ⓑ 우리의 신진대사율
Ⓒ 우리가 취하는 수면의 양
Ⓓ 뇌 속의 독소의 양

강의의 일부분을 다시 듣고 질문에 답하시오. 🎧 MP3 54_1

> It's fine for humans because most of us are lying down on a cozy bed in a room. But what if we didn't have a safe home, or room, to sleep in? What if we were out in the open? We take many things for granted, but for animals in the wild, sleep, I mean sleeping like we do, is simply not possible.

06 교수가 다음과 같이 말한 이유는?

> We take many things for granted.

Ⓐ 사람들은 더 감사함을 느껴야 한다는 것을 시사하려고
Ⓑ 우리의 재산의 중요성을 강조하려고
Ⓒ 사람은 안전한 환경에 익숙해져 있다는 것을 나타내려고
Ⓓ 수면을 연구하는 학생들은 보조금을 신청할 수 있다는 것을 시사하려고

❧ Practice Questions

본문 p. 318

01 C **02** D **03** C **04** B **05** D **06** A

Listen to part of a lecture in a physiology class. 🔊 MP3 55

Professor(male): Last week, we covered some theories about how the body reacts to physical stimuli. But, as you are probably all aware, our bodies react significantly to psychological stimuli as well. **Q1** **I'm sure you've all heard that stress plays a significant role in most major human disorders. Well, I'm going to discuss that in today's class.** But first, I want to come up with a proper definition of stress to prevent any confusion. Stress is a very widely used word… I mean, you can say that you were stressed out by the papers that I assigned you last week. But I want to be a little more specific about what stress is: It's the way the body reacts to different demands.

Student(female): I'm confused. We're talking about mental stimuli, right? Your definition makes it seem like stress is more like something physical.

P: Good point! I want to make a distinction between the causes of stress and what constitutes as a stressful situation. **Q1** **The definition of stress that I'm talking about today has nothing to do with what caused it. Rather, it's all about the result that occurs in our bodies.** So even if it's a physical stimulus, like breaking your arm when falling down a flight of stairs, or a mental stimulus, like someone talking about something foolish you once did, these are only factors that might or might not cause stress. What's important here is the reaction our body has, such as an increased heart rate, as a response to these stimuli. If our heart rate increases, that's what we call stress. If it doesn't, if our body doesn't react in any way, then it's not stress.

S: So we should try to avoid stress, right? To stay healthy?

P: Hmm… Now, most people, like you, think of stress as something to be avoided. But, actually, stress isn't necessarily harmful. I remember reading **Q3** **a study that dealt with young mice that were subjected to stressful situations**. Most would assume that these mice lived horrible lives and died quickly, but, uh, **the mice improved their ability to deal with stressful situations** compared to mice that had not been exposed to occasional stress. It also turns out, as the mice matured, **Q3** **the ones exposed to stress grew bigger and stronger than the unexposed mice.** So, I guess **Q4** Nietzsche was right when he said, "What doesn't kill you makes you stronger." **Being exposed to stressful situations helps our body adapt and become stronger,** so it's not necessarily bad.

But exposure to long periods of stress is potentially harmful to both animals and humans. The body's overall reaction to stress is referred to as the general adaptation syndrome (shown on screen). There are multiple phases in which our bodies react to exposure to stress. We must understand these phases to truly understand what effects stress has on our bodies.

So, the first phase is the alarm phase. This is the phase when a person would experience a reaction of alarm. Suppose someone experiences something physically or emotionally traumatic. He or she would experience a number of physical changes including the ones I mentioned – the heart beating faster, for example.

If the stress continues for a long time, the second phase, resistance, takes place. During this stage, a person has the greatest ability to endure the stressful situation. Depending on a person's strength and how well rested they are, **Q5** **this stage could last for days or months without causing harm.**

I am sure you all can recognize times in your life **when you have experienced the alarm and resistance stages. And you probably were successful in dealing with the**

3단계

Similarity
다양한 스트레스 원인에 대한 비슷한 몸의 반응

stress. And soon you got back to normal. But, **Q6** **if the stress does not end, you will eventually reach the third stage – exhaustion. In the exhaustion stage, the body no longer has the ability to handle the stress and will become weaker and weaker.** Now, these stages are known as the general adaptation syndrome because it applies to every possible stressful situation. **Q2** **Regardless of what the situation is, whether it's embarrassment or a broken arm, if it is stressful, the body will react the same way.** Now doctors will not argue against the principle idea of the general adaptation syndrome. Continuing periods of stress can result in exhaustion, in turn resulting in physical and mental harm.

해석 생리학 수업의 다음 강의 일부분을 들으시오.

교수(남자): 지난주에는 몸이 물리적 자극들에 어떻게 반응하는지에 관한 몇 가지 이론들을 다루었습니다. 하지만 여러분이 아마 모두 알고 있듯이, 우리의 몸은 심리적인 자극들에도 상당히 반응을 보이죠. 여러분은 모두, 사람들이 겪는 대부분의 주요 장애에 있어 스트레스가 중요한 역할을 한다는 것을 들어봤을 겁니다. 음, 오늘 수업에서는 그에 대해 논의하려 합니다. 하지만 우선, 혼란을 방지하기 위해, 스트레스에 대한 올바른 정의를 내리고 싶군요. 스트레스는 무척 폭넓게 쓰이는 단어입니다... 여러분은 제가 지난주에 숙제로 내준 보고서 때문에 스트레스를 받았다고 말을 할 수도 있지요. 하지만 나는 스트레스가 무엇인지에 대해 좀 더 구체적으로 말하고 싶습니다. 스트레스는 여러 다른 요구에 신체가 반응하는 방식을 얘기합니다.

학생(여자): 좀 혼동되네요. 저희는 정신적 자극에 대해 이야기하고 있는 거 아닌가요? 교수님의 정의에 따르면 스트레스는 신체적인 무언가에 더 가까운 것 같은데요.

교수: 좋은 지적이에요! 스트레스의 원인들과 무엇이 스트레스가 되는 상황을 이루는가를 구분해야겠네요. 내가 오늘 말하는 스트레스의 정의는 무엇이 그 스트레스를 유발했는지와는 아무런 관계가 없어요. 그보다는, 우리 신체에서 일어나는 결과에 관한 것이죠. 그래서 예를 들어, 층계에서 굴러 떨어지면서 팔이 부러진다거나 하는 신체적 자극이건, 아니면 누군가가 여러분이 예전에 했던 어리석은 일에 대해 이야기를 하는 것과 같은 정신적인 자극이건, 이런 것들은 스트레스를 유발할 수도, 유발하지 않을 수도 있는 요인일 뿐이죠. 여기서 중요한 것은 우리의 몸이 보이는 반응인데요, 이런 자극들에 대한 반응으로 심박수가 증가하는 것 같은 것들 말입니다. 심박수가 증가하면, 그것이 우리가 스트레스라고 부르는 것입니다. 심박수가 증가하지 않으면, 즉 우리 몸이 어떤 식으로든 반응하지 않으면, 그것은 스트레스가 아닌 것이지요.

학생: 그러면 우리는 스트레스를 피해야 하는 거죠? 건강을 유지하기 위해서 말이에요.

교수: 음... 자, 학생처럼 대부분의 사람들은, 스트레스를 피해야 하는 것으로 여기죠. 하지만 사실 스트레스는 반드시 해롭지만은 않습니다. 어떤 연구에 대해 읽은 적이 있었는데, 그 연구에서는 어린 쥐들을 스트레스 상황을 겪게 두었습니다. 대부분의 사람들은 이 쥐들이 끔찍한 삶을 살고 금새 죽었을 것이라 생각하겠지만, 이 쥐들은 때때로 스트레스에 노출된 적이 없었던 쥐들에 비해 스트레스 상황에 대처하는 능력을 향상시켰습니다. 또한, 쥐들이 성장하면서, 스트레스에 노출된 쥐들이 그렇지 않은 쥐들보다 더 크고 강하게 자랐다는 것이 밝혀졌죠. 니체가 말했던, '죽지 않으면 강해진다'라는 말이 옳았던 거죠. 스트레스 상황에 노출되는 것은 우리 몸을 적응하게 하고 더 강하게 만들기 때문에 반드시 나쁜 것만은 아닙니다.

하지만 오랜 기간 동안 스트레스에 노출되는 것은 동물에게나 사람에게나 모두 잠재적으로 해를 끼칩니다. 스트레스에 대한 신체의 전반적인 반응은 범적응 증후군(화면에 보여진다)이라고 불리는데요. 우리 몸이 스트레스에 노출됐을 때 반응하는 데에는 여러 단계가 있습니다. 스트레스가 우리 몸에 어떠한 영향을 끼치는지를 제대로 이해하기 위해서는 이런 단계들을 이해해야 합니다.

자, 첫 번째 단계는 경계 단계입니다. 경보라는 반응을 경험하는 단계죠. 누군가 신체적으로나 정신적으로 굉장한 충격이 되는 무언가를 겪는다고 가정해보죠. 그 사람은 내가 언급했었던 것들, 예를 들어 심장이 두근거리는 것 등을 포함한 많은 신체적 변화들을 겪을 겁니다.

그 스트레스가 오랫동안 지속되면, 두 번째 단계인 저항이 시작되죠. 이 단계에서는, 스트레스 상황을 견딜 수 있는 최대한의 능력을 갖게 됩니다. 각 개인의 힘과 얼마나 잘 쉬었는지 정도에 따라, 이 단계는 해를 끼치지 않은 채로 며칠 또는 몇 달 동안 지속될 수 있습니다.

여러분 모두 여러분 인생에서 경계 단계와 저항 단계를 경험했던 때를 알 수 있을 거라 생각해요. 여러분은 아마도 그 스트레스를 잘 이겨냈겠죠. 그리고는 금새 정상 상태로 돌아왔을 거고요. 하지만, 만일 스트레스가 끝나지 않는다면, 결국에는 세 번째 단계인 탈진에 도달하게 됩니다. 탈진 단계에서는, 신체는 더 이상 스트레스를 다룰 수 있는 능력이 없어, 점점 더 쇠약해지게 됩니다.

자, 이런 단계들은 범적응 증후군으로 알려져 있는데, 이는 그것이 온갖 가능한 스트레스 상황에 적용되기 때문입니다. 그 상황이 무엇이건 간에, 즉 그것이 창피함이건, 팔이 부러진 것이건 간에, 그것이 스트레스가 되는 상황이라면 신체는 같은 방식으로 반응할 거예요. 이제는 의사들도 범적응 증후군의 원리에는 반론을 펴지 못할 것입니다. 오랜 기간 동안의 스트레스는 탈진으로 이어질 수 있고, 결국 이는 신체적, 정신적 피해로 이어질 수 있습니다.

Ⓦ stimulus [stímjələs] 자극 (pl. stimuli) psychological [sàikəládʒikəl] 정신[심리]의 disorder [disɔ́rdər] (신체 기능의) 장애, 이상

demand [diménd] 요구(되는 일들)   make a distinction 구별하다   constitute ~을 구성하다   a flight of stairs 한 줄로 이어진 계단   heart rate 심박동수   not necessarily 반드시[꼭] ~은 아닌   be subjected to ~ ~을 받다   mature [mətʃúər] 다 자란, 원숙한   potentially [pəténʃəli] 잠재적으로   be referred to as ~ ~로 불리다   phase [feiz] 단계   alarm [əláːrm] 경보, 경고 신호   traumatic [trɔːmǽtik] 대단히 충격적인   resistance [rizístəns] 저항   exhaustion [igzɔ́ːstʃən] 탈진

01 강의의 주된 내용은?
(A) 스트레스에 대한 다양한 의학적 정의들
(B) 신체가 스트레스를 다루기 위해 사용하는 방법들
(C) 스트레스가 인간의 몸에 끼치는 신체적 영향들
(D) 정신적 스트레스와 육체적 스트레스 간의 차이점

02 부끄러움을 느끼는 사람의 몸에 대해 교수가 말한 것은?
(A) 경계 상태에 들어갈 것이다.
(B) 신체의 반응은 주변 환경에 따라 다를 것이다.
(C) 신체적 통증을 경험할 것이다.
(D) 신체적으로 부상을 입을 때와 유사한 방식으로 반응할 것이다.

03 교수가 언급한 연구에서, 스트레스를 유발하는 환경에 가끔씩 놓인 쥐들에게 생긴 일은?
(A) 신체적 정신적 손상을 입었다.
(B) 신체적 또는 정신적 손상을 입지 않았다.
(C) 더 튼튼해지고 스트레스를 더 잘 견딜 수 있게 되었다.
(D) 더 약해지고 스트레스를 더 못 견디게 되었다.

04 교수가 니체를 언급한 이유는?
(A) 스트레스로 고생한 사람의 예를 들려고
(B) 스트레스에 관해 이전에 언급한 의견을 강조하려고
(C) 스트레스 상황을 극복하는 방법을 시사하려고
(D) 사람들이 끔찍한 상황에 어떻게 반응하는지를 설명하려고

05 범적응 증후군의 경계 단계와 저항 단계에 관해 교수가 암시한 것은?
(A) 신체에 영향을 미치지 않는다.
(B) 정신적 자극에 의해 유발된다.
(C) 스트레스 단계 중 가장 짧다.
(D) 해를 입지 않고 다뤄질 수 있는 가능성이 있다.

06 무엇이 신체가 범적응 증후군의 세 번째 단계에 접어들도록 하는가?
(A) 스트레스에 대처하는 능력을 상실한다.
(B) 첫 두 단계에 성공적으로 대처한다.
(C) 심박수 증가를 경험하기 시작한다.
(D) 더 이상 어떠한 종류의 스트레스에도 반응하지 않는다.

06 / Paleontology

≋ Sample Questions   본문 p. 324

| 01 A | 02 D | 03 C | 04 C, D | 05 B | 06 A |

해석 고생물학 수업의 다음 강의 일부분을 들으시오. MP3 56

교수(남자): 자, 지난 시간에 우리는 새에 대해서 논의를 했습니다. 현대의 새들과 그 환경에 대해서 말이죠. 하지만 오늘은 아주 오래 전의 새이기는 하나 매우 흥미로운 새에 대해서 이야기 해 봅시다. 시조새라고 불리는 새입니다. (화면에 보여준다) 어려운 단어라는 건 알지만, 그건 그저 '고대의 날개'라는 뜻일 뿐입니다. 이 고대의 새는 1861년 독일에서 처음 발견되었습니다. 그것은 정말 행운이었지요. 특히 고생물학자의 관점에서는 말이죠. 이 새는 독일의 한 채석장에서 채취된 돌 한 조각에 화석화된 채로 발견되었습니다. 놀라운 것은, 뼈가 매우 잘 보존되어 있었다는 점입니다. 고대 새의 연약한 뼈가 그렇게 양호한 상태로 발견되는 것은 정말로 드문 일입니다. 보존된 세세한 부분들 역시 또 다른 희귀한 점이었죠. 돌 위에 깃털 자국까지 있는 것을 볼 수 있습니다.

이것은 화석이 발견된 장소 때문입니다. 언급했던 바와 같이, 이 화석은 채석장에서 발견되었습니다. 돌을 잘라내는 곳이죠. 이 경우에는 그 돌이 입자가 매우 고운 석회암이었습니다. 돌을 구성하는 미세 입자가 아주 작았어요. 깃털의 선들보다도 훨씬 작았죠. 이런 미세 입자가 가장 작은 세부적인 것들까지도 (돌에) 새겨질 수 있도록 한 것입니다. 앞서 말한 것처럼, 이런 것은 매우 희귀합니다. 그래서 우리는 시조새에 대한 많은 정보, 음, 어떤 구체적인 정보도 가지고 있지 않습니다. 그래서 모두가 각자 다른 생각들을 가지고 있지요. 음... 마치 〈모나리자〉같다고 할 수 있겠군요. 여러분 모두 그 그림을 직접 보았거나 적어도 복제품을 본 적이 있을 것 같은데요, 그렇지요? 이 그림이 그렇게 유명한 이유 중의 하나는, 그림을 보는 사람 각자가 그 그림에 대해 각각 다른 의견을 갖고 있기 때문입니다. 사람들은 각각 자신이 가진 성향에 따라 그 그림을 조금씩 다르게 이해합니다. 시조새는 〈모나리자〉의 과학 버전이라고 할 수 있겠네요.

현대의 새들을 연구하는 과학자들인 조류학자들은, 시조새를 오늘날 우리가 보는 새들의 초기 조상으로 보는 경향이 있습니다. 반면에, 화석과 고대 생물을 연구하는 과학자들인 고생물학자들은, 시조새와 일부 공룡과의 유사성들을 지적합니다. 그들의 말도 일리가 있습니다. 시조새는 부리가 없고, 마치 파충류의 꼬리처럼 꼬리가 길고 뼈로 이루어져 있습니다. 현대의 새들이 가진 짧고 뭉툭한 꼬리와는 다른 모양이지요. 또 다른 뚜렷한 특징은 '날개 손가락(wing fingers)'이라고 불리는 것의 끝에 달린 갈고리 발톱입니다. 이것 역시 현대의 새들에게는 없는 특징입니다. 이제 여러분은 이 논쟁이 시조새가 조류였느냐 아니었느냐에 관한 것이라는 잘못된 인상을 받을지도 모르겠지만, 논쟁은 그것에 관한 것이 아닙니다. 이 고대의 새는 깃털이 있었고, 깃털이 있는 모든 생물은 새로 분류됩니다. 그래서 부리가 없고, 다른 꼬리를 갖고 있으며, 날개에 갈고리 발톱이 있다고 해도, 이것은 새입니다. 진정한 논쟁은, 진화적인 관점에 있어 시조새가 어디에 적합하게 들어가는가 하는 것입니다. 비슷한 시기의 공룡을 연구하는 고생물학자들에게 이것은 평범하기 그지없는 것입니다... 가장 큰 특징을 제외하면 말입니다. 이 시조새의 깃털이죠. 이 특징은 많은 고생물학자들로 하여금 시조새를 공룡과 현대 조류의 진화론적 관계의 관점에서 보도록 했습니다. 시조새를 둘 사이의 연결점으로 보는 것이지요. 조류학자들에게 있어 시조새는 예외적인 특징들을 가진, 기록상 최초의 새입니다. 조류학자들은 새의 진화가 그들의 비행 능력과 긴밀한 관련이 있다고 여깁니다. 하지만 시조새는 새처럼 생긴 꼬리가 없는데, 그것은 공중에서 비행을 조종하는 데 필요한 것입니다. 또, 현대의 새라면 날개만 있어야 할 자리에 시조새는 갈고리 발톱까지 갖고 있지요. 이런 특징들은 시조새가 비행 능력이 있었다는 개념에 반하는 것입니다. 하지만 동시에, 시조새는 현대의 새와 동일한 특징들도 분명 갖고 있어서 아마도 이륙을 할 수 있었거나, 적어도 땅에서 발을 뗄 수 있었을 정도는 되었을지도 모릅니다. 하지만 우리는 시조새가 비행 능력을 가지고 있었다고 결정적으로 증명할 수 있는 어떤 증거도 실제로는 가지고 있지 않습니다.

어떤 견해가 맞느냐에 관해 알 수 있는 것은 아무것도 없습니다. 하지만 가장 최근의 한 연구는 중국에서 발견된 몇몇 화석에 기반을 두고 있습니다. 비록 결코 완벽하지는 않지만 그 연구는 몇가지 설득력 있는 결론을 끌어냈습니다. 이 깃털들은 비행에 전혀 사용되지 않았을지도 모른다는 것입니다. 시조새의 깃털은, 현대의 많은 동물들의 깃털처럼 그저 전시용이었을 수도 있습니다... 암컷을 유혹하기 위한 장식적인 특징에 불과하다는 것이죠. 깃털은 또한 단열을 위해 쓰였을지도 모릅니다. 깃털은 추운 기온에서 체온을 보존하는 데 매우 효과적인 방법이니까요. 캐나다의 거위들에게 한 번 물어보세요.

Ⓦ paleontologist [peiliəntàlədʒist] 고생물학자   fossilize [fásəlàiz] 화석화하다   quarry [kwɔ́(ː)ri] 채석장   impression [impréʃən] (세게 눌렀을 때 생기는) 자국   fine-grained [fine-ɡreind] 결이 고운   limestone [láimstòun] 석회석   particle [páːrtikl] 입자   imprint [imprínt] 각인시키다   bias [báiəs] 편견, 편향   ornithologist [ɔ̀ːrnəθάlədʒist] 조류학자   beak [biːk] 부리   bony [bóuni] 뼈가 다 드러나는, 앙상한   stubby [stʌ́bi] 뭉툭한, 짤막한   claw [klɔː] 발톱   evolutionary [èvəlúːʃənèri] 진화의   maneuver [mənúːvər] 조종하다   conclusively [kənklúːsivli] 결정적으로   compelling [kəmpéliŋ] 주목하지않을수없는   ornamental [ɔ̀ːrnəméntəl] 장식적인   insulation [ìnsjəléiʃən] 단열   conserve [kənsə́ːrv] 보존하다

01 강의의 주된 내용은?
Ⓐ 한 고대의 새가 진화의 관점에서 어디에 속하는지에 관한 이론들
Ⓑ 거대한 새들이 날 수 있기 위해 갖춰야만 하는 특징들
Ⓒ 새에 대한 올바른 정의가 무엇인지에 대한 여러 의견들
Ⓓ 현대의 새를 날 수 있게 해준 진화 과정에 대한 설명들

02 교수가 새가 발견되었던 채석장을 언급한 이유는?
Ⓐ 시조새에 대한 조류학자들의 이론을 반박하려고

Ⓑ 시조새에게 비행 능력이 있었다는 증거를 보여주려고
Ⓒ 고생물학자들이 다양한 장소에서 화석을 찾을 수 있다는 것을 보여주려고
Ⓓ 시조새의 화석이 그렇게 세밀하게 남아있었던 이유를 알려주려고

03 교수가 〈모나리자〉를 언급한 이유는?
Ⓐ 그 그림이 세밀한 부분들을 가진 화석만큼이나 아름답다고 생각한다.
Ⓑ 화석을 분석하는 기술들을 설명하기 위해 쓰일 수 있다고 생각한다.
Ⓒ 그 그림과 시조새는 비슷한 식으로 여겨진다고 생각한다.
Ⓓ 잘 보존된 새의 화석이 얼마나 희귀한지를 강조하고 싶어 한다.

04 교수에 따르면, 새를 정의하기 위해서 사용된 특징들은? (두 가지 선택)
Ⓐ 조종에 사용되는 꼬리
Ⓑ 부리의 크기
Ⓒ 비행 능력
Ⓓ 깃털의 존재

05 시조새에 대한 고생물학자들의 견해에 대해서 교수가 지적하는 점은?
Ⓐ 그들은 시조새가 공룡 또는 현대 새와 실제로 관련이 있다고는 생각하지 않는다.
Ⓑ 그들은 시조새가 새와 공룡 간의 진화적 관련을 나타낸다고 생각한다.
Ⓒ 그들은 시조새가 비행 도중에 조종을 위해 꼬리를 사용한 최초의 새라고 생각한다.
Ⓓ 그들은 시조새가 짝을 유인하기 위해 깃털을 사용했던 공룡이었다고 생각한다.

06 조류학자들이 주장하는 이론의 문제점으로 교수가 암시한 것은?
Ⓐ 최근의 발견으로 반박될 수도 있다.
Ⓑ 적절한 증거 없이 형성되었다.
Ⓒ 시조새의 특정 특징들만을 설명할 수 있다.
Ⓓ 화석 없이는 결코 증명될 수 없다.

≋ Practice Questions

본문 p. 328

| 01 C | 02 D | 03 B | 04 C | 05 A, D | 06 A |

Listen to part of a lecture in a paleontology class. ◁ MP3 57

Professor(male): Well, I'm sure you have all seen pictures, um… well, illustrations of dinosaurs ever since you were little kids. What do they look like?

Student(female): Giant lizards.

P: Exactly. They look like giant reptiles, and reptiles are cold-blooded animals. Today, I thought we'd talk about some of the reasons why some scientists believe dinosaurs could actually be warm-blooded animals. To be more exact, **Q1** **let's talk about the debate as to whether dinosaurs were endothermic or ectothermic.** Endothermic animals, of course, are warm-blooded, meaning they can manage their own body heat, while ectothermic animals are cold-blooded, meaning their body temperature is dependent on their surroundings.

You see, until recently most paleontologists just assumed dinosaurs were ectothermic animals. After all, the bulk of the dinosaur fossils found were in areas that had climates similar to tropical areas – areas that cold-blooded animals have no problems thriving in. The features of their fossils also closely resemble those of modern reptiles. However, uh, recent findings of new fossils have led to a whole host of discov-

Main Idea
공룡이 온혈 동물일 수도 있었다는 주장

Term
endothermic과 ectothermic 용어 설명

Correction

| 공룡이 외온성 동물이 아닐 수도 있음

Debate
공룡이 냉혈 동물인지 온혈 동물인지

Finding / Evidence
극지방에서 화석들이 발견됨

Finding
체온 유지 능력을 가지고 있었을 것

Difference
물고기, 상어와 온혈 동물 간의 차이점

Research
결정적인 증거를 찾지 못함

Evidence
canal – rapid growth → warm-blooded의 증거

growth ring – 여름에는 빨리 자랐다 겨울에는 천천히 자람 → cold-blooded의 증거

eries about dinosaurs… with one result being that now even the generally accepted idea that dinosaurs were cold-blooded is being challenged.

S: So what caused this debate? I mean, haven't fossils been around for ages? It's really difficult to believe that any new findings could suddenly change people's minds.

P: Well, actually, there are several findings that have caused this great debate, ▶Q2 **the first of which involves where some fossils have been found.** What are some animals that come to mind when you think of the North Pole and the South Pole?

S: Uh… Penguins, polar bears, and seals…

P: Okay, so these animals are all…

S: Endotherms. So what do they have to do with dinosaurs?

P: These days, ▶Q2 **more and more fossils are being uncovered in the polar regions.** These so-called "polar dinosaurs" have made a group of paleontologists believe that dinosaurs were warm-blooded. I mean, temperatures are extreme in polar regions, and all the modern animals that cope with these temperatures are warm-blooded. ▶Q3 **So many scientists have come to the conclusion that these polar dinosaurs must have had the ability to maintain their body heat to survive in the frigid Arctic and Antarctic regions.**

S: Couldn't they just have migrated or hibernated like modern animals and reptiles?

P: That's the argument that some make, although it does seem quite unlikely. You see, the fossils that were uncovered near the South Pole are fossils of very small dinosaurs. They are so small, in fact, that there would have been no way for them to cross the then shallow waters that separated Antarctica from the mainland. Even if the dinosaurs were large, like Edmontosaurus, there's no way that juvenile, newly born, dinosaurs could make the journey.

S: But… aren't fish cold-blooded, too? They don't seem to have a problem surviving in cold water.

P: Exactly. That's why it's still up for debate. ▶Q6 **Fish like tuna and some shark species have the ability to raise their body temperature… Not to maintain it the way that warm-blooded animals do, but enough to survive in harsh conditions.** Maybe dinosaurs had the same ability, but there's really no way of knowing. It's really difficult to find organs that are properly fossilized, and finding a specific organ that helped maintain body temperature, well… that's probably just not possible.

S: Can't we just look at what's left of dinosaurs and try to figure it out that way?

P: You bring up a good point. ▶Q5-C **Although flesh is rarely fossilized, bones are relatively better preserved.** Some paleontologists wanted to study dinosaurs bones at a more microscopic level to find more conclusive evidence, but ended being even more puzzled. ▶Q5-D **They found two competing pieces of evidence. Basically, the two pieces of evidence found contradicted each other.** The bones of dinosaurs contain something called Haversian canals. ▶Q4 **These canals house nerves and blood vessels that allow the animal to grow quickly regardless of outside temperature, and rapid body growth is a characteristic of endothermy.** However, the growth rings found in dinosaur bones told a different story. These rings are similar to rings you see in trees. The varying widths of these growth rings indicate that dinosaurs grew quickly in the summer and slowly in the winter, a characteristic also found in reptiles, which are, of course, cold-blooded.

S: So, what do you think? Warm-blooded or cold-blooded?

P: Well, there's still no conclusive evidence that can prove anything. You can't rule out the possibility that some dinosaur species were endothermic while others were ectothermic. There's still a lot of information that needs to be unearthed.

해석 고생물학 수업의 다음 강의 일부분을 들으시오.

교수(남자): 자, 모두들 어렸을 때부터 공룡의 그림들... 그러니까, 공룡 일러스트들을 봤을 거라 생각합니다. 공룡이 어떻게 생겼나요?

학생(여자): 거대한 도마뱀처럼요.

교수: 맞아요. 공룡은 거대한 파충류처럼 생겼죠. 파충류는 냉혈 동물이고요. 오늘은, 일부 과학자들이 어째서 공룡이 사실은 온혈 동물이었을 수도 있다고 생각하는지 그 이유 몇 가지에 대해 이야기해보는 것이 좋을 것 같습니다. 좀 더 정확히 말하자면, 공룡이 내온성(endothermic) 동물이었는지 외온성(ectothermic) 동물이었는지에 대한 논쟁에 대해 이야기해보자는 것이죠. 내온성 동물은 물론 온혈 동물들로, 스스로의 체온을 조절할 수 있다는 뜻인 반면, 외온성 동물들은 냉혈 동물들로, 체온이 주변 환경에 의존한다는 뜻입니다.

자, 최근까지 대부분의 고생물학자들은 공룡이 외온성 동물일 것이라고만 추측했습니다. 결국, 많은 공룡 화석들이 열대 지역, 즉 냉혈 동물들이 번성하는 데 아무 문제가 없는 지역과 비슷한 기후를 가진 곳에서 발견되었으니까요. 공룡 화석의 특징들 역시 현대 파충류들의 특징들과 흡사하게 닮았습니다. 하지만, 음, 새로운 화석들에 대한 최근의 연구들은 공룡에 대한 수많은 새로운 발견들을 이끌어냈습니다... 그 중 한 가지 결과는, 공룡이 냉혈 동물이었다는, 일반적으로 받아들여지고 있는 생각에조차 이제 이견이 제시되고 있다는 것입니다.

학생: 무엇이 이런 논쟁을 불러일으킨 거죠? 공룡 화석은 수 세기 동안 존재하지 않았나요? 어떤 새로운 발견이 갑자기 사람들의 생각을 바꿀 수 있다는 것은 믿기가 어렵네요.

교수: 음, 사실, 이런 엄청난 논쟁을 불러일으킨 몇 가지 연구결과들이 있어요. 그 중 첫 번째는 일부 화석이 어디에서 발견되었는가에 대한 것이죠. 여러분은 북극과 남극을 생각할 때 어떤 동물들이 생각나나요?

학생: 아... 펭귄, 북극곰, 그리고 물개...

교수: 좋아요. 그럼 이 동물들은 모두...

학생: 내온성 동물이죠. 그런데, 그 동물들이 공룡과 무슨 관계가 있죠?

교수: 최근, 점점 더 많은 (공룡) 화석들이 극지방에서 발견되고 있어요. 이런 소위 '극지방 공룡들'로 인해, 일부 고생물학자들은 공룡이 온혈 동물이었다고 생각하게 되었지요. 그러니까, 극지방의 기후는 매우 극심한데, 이런 기후를 견디는 현대 동물들은 모두 온혈 동물들이잖아요. 그래서 많은 과학자들은 이런 극지방 공룡들이 몹시 추운 북극과 남극 지방에서 살아남을 수 있도록 체온을 유지할 수 있는 능력을 분명 가지고 있었을 것이라는 결론을 내리게 되었죠.

학생: 공룡들이 현대 동물들과 파충류들처럼 그냥 이주를 하거나 동면을 했을 수도 있지 않나요?

교수: 일부는 그런 주장을 하기도 했습니다. 비록 그럴 가능성은 거의 없지만요. 남극 근처에서 발견된 화석들은 매우 작은 공룡들의 화석이었습니다. 그 공룡들은 너무나 작아서, 사실, 남극과 본토를 갈라놓았던 그 당시 얕은 바다를 건널 수 있는 방법이 없었을 것입니다. 만일, (북극 지방에서 발견된 공룡 화석인) 에드몬토사우르스처럼 공룡의 크기가 컸다 하더라도, 어린 공룡이나 갓 태어난 공룡들이 그런 여정을 할 수 있었을 리가 없어요.

학생: 하지만... 물고기도 냉혈 동물이 아닌가요? 물고기는 차가운 물에서 살아남는 데 아무런 문제가 없는 것 같은데요.

교수: 맞아요. 그게 아직도 논쟁 중인 이유이죠. 참치나 일부 상어 종 같은 물고기들은 체온을 올리는 능력이 있어요... 온혈 동물들이 체온을 유지하는 것과 같은 방식은 아니지만, 극한 환경에서 살아남기에는 충분한 정도로는 말이지요. 아마 공룡도 같은 능력을 가지고 있었을지도 몰라요. 하지만 그걸 알 수는 없어요. 제대로 화석화된 (공룡의) 장기를 발견하는 건 정말 어려운데다 체온을 유지하는 데 도움이 되었던 특정 장기를 찾는 것은, 음... 그건 아마도 불가능하다고 봐야죠.

학생: 그냥 공룡의 남은 부분을 보고 알아내 볼 수는 없나요?

교수: 좋은 지적이에요. 비록 공룡의 살은 거의 화석화되지 않았지만, 뼈는 상대적으로 잘 보존이 되었어요. 몇몇 고생물학자들은 더 결정적인 증거를 찾기 위해 더 미세한 수준으로 공룡의 뼈를 연구하고 싶어 했지만, 더 큰 혼란에 빠지고 말았죠. 두 가지 상충하는 증거를 찾은 거예요. 기본적으로, 발견된 두 가지 증거들은 서로를 반박했어요. 공룡의 뼈에는 하버스관(Haversian canal)이라고 불리는 것들이 들어 있어요. 이 관에는 그 동물이 외부 기온과 관계 없이 빨리 성장할 수 있도록 해주는 신경과 혈관이 들어가 있죠. 그리고, 빠른 성장은 내온성 동물의 특징이죠. 하지만, 공룡 뼈에서 발견된 나이테들은 전혀 다른 이야기를 했어요. 이 나이테들은 나무에서 볼 수 있는 것과 비슷합니다. 이 나이테들의 다양한 너비는, 공룡들이 여름에는 빨리 자랐다가 겨울에는 천천히 자랐다는 것을 나타내죠. 이는 파충류들에게서도 발견되는 특징인데, 파충류는 물론 냉혈 동물이지요.

학생: 그럼, 교수님은 어떻게 생각하세요? 온혈 동물, 아니면 냉혈 동물이요?

교수: 음, 아직은 어떤 것도 증명할 수 있는 결정적인 증거가 없어요. 어떤 공룡 종은 내온성인 반면 어떤 공룡 종은 외온성이었을 가능성을 배제할 수 없죠. 여전히 발견되어야 할 정보가 많이 남아 있어요.

lizard [lízərd] 도마뱀   cold-blooded [kould-bládid] 냉혈 동물(의)   warm-blooded [wɔːrm-bládid] 온혈 동물(의)   endothermic [èndouθɔ́ːrmik] 내온성의   ectothermic [èktəθɔ́ːrmik] 외온성의   the bulk of ~ ...의 대부분   seal [siːl] 바다표범   polar region 극지방   extreme [ikstríːm] 극심한   frigid [frídʒid] 몹시 추운   Arctic [áːrktik] 북극 대륙(의)   Antarctic [æntáːrktik] 남극 대륙(의)   hibernate [háibərnèit] 동면하다   juvenile [dʒúːvənàil] 청소년의   microscopic [màikrəskápik] 미세한   puzzled [pʌ́zld] 어리둥절한   competing [kəmpíːtiŋ] 상충되는   contradict [kàntrədíkt] 모순되다   canal [kənǽl] (체내의) 관   house [haus] 수용하다   nerve [nəːrv] 신경   blood vessel 혈관   growth ring 나이테   unearth [ʌnə́ːrθ] 발굴하다; 밝혀내다

01 강의의 주된 내용은?
Ⓐ 대부분의 공룡이 따뜻한 지역에서 살았던 이유
Ⓑ 극지방에서 발견된 공룡 화석들의 특징들
Ⓒ 공룡이 체온을 조절할 수 있었는지 아닌지
Ⓓ 온혈 공룡과 냉혈 공룡 간의 차이점들

02 교수에 의하면, 무엇이 공룡에 관한 논쟁을 야기했는가?
Ⓐ 대단히 상태가 좋은 화석이 발견되었다.
Ⓑ 새로운 화석 종류들이 열대지방에서 확인되었다.
Ⓒ 도마뱀들이 추운 지방에서 사는 것이 발견되었다.
Ⓓ 화석들이 새로운 지역에서 발굴되었다.

03 교수가 북극 지방에서 살았던 공룡에 대해 말한 것은?
Ⓐ 온혈 동물이 아니었다면 살아남지 못했을 것이다.
Ⓑ 필요 시 체온을 올릴 수 있는 방법을 가지고 있었을지도 모른다.
Ⓒ 북극이 오늘날보다 훨씬 더 따뜻했기 때문에 살아남을 수 있었다.
Ⓓ 날씨가 추운 달에는 동면을 하거나 이주를 했다.

04 교수에 의하면, 하버스관의 존재가 공룡이 내온성 동물이었다는 것을 암시하는 이유는?
Ⓐ 하버스관은 나이테와 같은 역할을 한다.
Ⓑ 하버스관은 혈관을 담고 있다.
Ⓒ 하버스관은 급격한 성장을 가능하게 한다.
Ⓓ 하버스관은 몇몇 어류에서 발견된다.

05 교수에 의하면, 고생물학자들이 공룡이 온혈 동물인지 아닌지 결정하는 것에 어려움을 겪는 이유는? (두 가지 선택)
Ⓐ 공룡의 화석은 대개 장기보다는 뼈로 이루어져 있다.
Ⓑ 남극에서 발견된 공룡의 크기는 북극 지방에서 발견된 것과 다르다.
Ⓒ 화석을 발굴하기 위해 극한 기후로 여행을 가는 것이 어렵다.
Ⓓ 공룡 뼈의 분석은 서로 상충하는 연구 결과를 낳았다.

06 강의에서 언급된 일부 상어 종에 관해 추론할 수 있는 것은?
Ⓐ 짧은 기간 동안 차가운 물에서 생존할 수 있다.
Ⓑ 다른 물고기들보다 더 적은 수의 하버스관을 가지고 있다.
Ⓒ 온혈 동물이었던 조상이 있다.
Ⓓ 좀처럼 화석화된 상태로 발견되지 않는다.

Chapter 4. Lecture Topics　　Unit 5. Physical Science

01 / Astronomy

≋ Sample Questions　　본문 p. 336

| 01 C | 02 C | 03 A | 04 A, D | 05 D | 06 B |

해석 천문학 수업의 다음 강의 일부분을 들으시오. ◁› MP3 58

교수(남자): 오늘은 다른 행성들의 대기, 구체적으로는 천왕성과 해왕성에 대해 좀 더 이야기를 하고 싶습니다. 천왕성과 해왕성은 태양에서 일곱 번째, 여덟 번째 떨어진 행성들로, 매우 유사한 대기 조건을 가지고 있습니다. 자, 이 행성들의 대기에 대해 무엇을 알고 있나요?

학생 1(여자): 음... 지구 대기의 요소들과 똑같은 일부 요소들이 포함되어 있는데... 헬륨, 수소...

교수: 또 뭐가 더 있나요?

학생 1: 음... 아! 메탄이요! 천왕성과 해왕성은 다른 행성들과 비교해서 대기에 매우 높은 비중의 메탄을 가지고 있어요.

교수: 좋아요. 내가 이야기하고 싶은 것은 바로 이 메탄입니다. 메탄 때문에, 해왕성에서는 말 그대로 하늘에 다이아몬드가 있을 수도 있습니다.

학생 1: 네?

교수: 미친 소리처럼 들릴지 모르지만, 실제로 매우 일리가 있는 말입니다. 이것은 천문학이 아니에요. 우리가 여기 이 지구에서 연구할 수 있는 기본적인 지질학이죠. 지질학 개론 수업을 수강했던 학생 혹시 있나요? 만일 수업을 들었다면, 다이아몬드가 무엇으로 만들어졌는지 분명히 알고 있겠지요. 다이아몬드는 탄소 원자들이 한데 결합된 것입니다. 그렇지요? 다이아몬드는 본질적으로는 극도의 높은 압력을 받은 탄소일 뿐입니다. 우리는 실제로 탄소를 포함하고 있는 기체 혼합물에 매우 높은 압력을 가해 합성 다이아몬드를 만들 수도 있습니다. 그렇다면, 화학 과목을 들은 여러분들, 메탄에는 무엇이 들어 있나요?

학생 2(남자): 탄소요!

교수: 맞습니다. 그 말은, 해왕성의 대기에는 많은 양의 탄소 원자가 있다는 말입니다. 짓누르는 압력과 높은 기온이 결합하여, 해왕성은 다이아몬드가 형성되기에 이상적인 장소가 되지요. 그럼, 이런 일이 어떻게 일어날 수 있는지 살펴봅시다.

탄소에서 다이아몬드를 만들려면 압력만 필요하긴 하지만, 메탄의 경우에는 먼저 일어나야 할 일이 한 가지 있습니다. 메탄이 탄소 원자로 분해되어야 하는 것입니다. 다이아몬드와 달리, 메탄은 탄소 원자 하나당 수소 원자 네 개를 포함하고 있습니다. 그래서 우리는 먼저 그것들을 순수한 탄소로 분해해야 합니다. 이렇게 하기 위한 방법 중 하나는 극한의 온도를 통해서입니다. 해왕성의 대기에서는 우연히도 그것이 존재하지요. 과학자들은 해왕성이 지구보다 태양에서 훨씬 더 멀리 떨어져 있는데도 해왕성이 어떻게 그렇게 뜨거울 수 있는지 알지 못하긴 하지만, 높은 기온은 메탄을 탄소와 수소로 분리할 수 있을 것입니다.

탄소 원자들이 떠돌아 다니는 동안, 그것들은 해왕성의 대기에 형성되는 거대한 구름에 의해 압력을 받을 수 있습니다. 압력이 충분히 높다면, 탄소 원자들은 한데 엉겨 붙어 다이아몬드를 만들 것입니다. 그리고 수증기가 충분히 무거워지면 지구에 비가 내리는 것과 마찬가지로, 그 결과로 생겨난 다이아몬드들이 하늘에서 떨어질 것입니다! 정말로 흥미롭지요. 여러분에게는 이것이 마치 공상처럼 들릴지 모르지만, 캘리포니아의 과학자들은 이것이 가능하다는 것을 증명해 보였습니다. 이탈리아 과학자들이 처음 이런 주장을 했을 때는, 분명 회의론자들이 많이 있었습니다.

학생 1: 예, 저도 믿지 않았을 거예요.

교수: 음, 캘리포니아의 한 무리의 과학자들은 이러한 이론적인 예측들을 실험실에서의 일련의 실험을 통해서 확인하기 위해 노력했습니다. 자, 다음과 같은 일이 있었지요. 그 과학자들은 본질적으로 물건들에 압력을 가하는 거대한 압축 기계인, 모루라고 불리는 한 기구를 이용했습니다. 지구의 대기 압력보다 수십만 배나 더 큰 압력으로 액체 메탄을 압착하기 위해서죠. 음... 뭔가 빠졌는데...

학생 2: 열이요?

교수: 그래요. 고마워요. 메탄을 압축하는 동안, 그들은 레이저 빔을 이용해서 액체 메탄에 섭씨 3천도 정도까지 열을 가했습니다. 레이저 빔에서 나오는 고온이 메탄을 탄화수소로 분해했는데, 이것이 합성 다이아몬드를 만들 때 사용되는 것이지요. 이 탄화수소가 높은 압력을 받으면, 검은 점들이 생기기 시작합니다. 이 점들을 검사하자, 분자 구조가 실제로 다이아몬드의 분자 구조와 동일했습니다.

학생 2: 검은 색이요? 다이아몬드는 하얗다고 생각했는데요?

교수: 음, 실제로 다이아몬드는 여러 색이 있습니다. 어쨌든, 해왕성의 대기 조건이 우리가 예상한 대로라면, 우리는 대기 중에 형성된 이런 똑같은 다이아몬드 부스러기들을 얻을 수 있습니다. 연구원들은 이런 결정체들이 지구의 대기 중에 있는 얼음처럼 결합하여, 대기에서 떨어져 내려 그 행성의 중심부에 쌓이는 일종의 다이아몬드 눈 또는 우박이 될지도 모른다고 말합니다. 상상이 되나요? 해왕성의 중앙에 쌓인 다이아몬드 층이?

Ⓦ astronomy [əstránəmi] 천문학　atmosphere [ǽtməsfiər] 대기　Uranus [júː)ərənəs] 천왕성　Neptune [néptjuːn] 해왕성　hydrogen [háidrədʒən] 수소　methane [méθein] 메탄　proportion [prəpɔ́ːrʃən] 비율, 비중　literally [lítərəli] 말 그대로　carbon [káːrbən] 탄소　atom [ǽtəm] 원자　bond [band] 결합하다　synthetic [sinθétik] 합성의, 인조의　mixture [míkstʃər] 혼합물　pressurize [préʃəràiz] 압력을 가하다　vapor [véipər] 증기　intriguing [intríːgiŋ] 아주 흥미로운　theoretical prediction 이론적 예측　speck [spek] 반점   molecular [moulékjələr] 분자의   fleck [flek] 부스러기   coalesce [kòuəlés] 합치다   sleet [sli:t] 진눈깨비

01 강의의 주된 내용은?
Ⓐ 해왕성과 지구의 유사점
Ⓑ 해왕성의 대기의 조성
Ⓒ 보석을 형성할 수 있는 대기 조건
Ⓓ 해왕성 표면의 기상 조건

02 교수가 지질학 수업을 언급한 이유는?
Ⓐ 모두가 자신이 사용하는 용어를 이해하고 있는지 확실히 하려고
Ⓑ 해왕성과 천왕성의 주요한 차이를 명확히 하려고
Ⓒ 지질학이 이 주제를 더 쉽게 이해하게 해줄 수 있다는 점을 지적하려고
Ⓓ 해왕성의 대기가 많은 양의 탄소를 포함하고 있는 이유를 설명하려고

03 교수가 합성 다이아몬드를 언급할 때 암시하는 것은?
Ⓐ 가설에서 다이아몬드가 형성되는 것을 시사하는 방식은 비현실적이지 않다.
Ⓑ 다른 행성들에서 형성된 다이아몬드들은 많은 실용성이 있다.
Ⓒ 다이아몬드는 그 기본적인 분자 구조의 관점에서 보면 매우 단순하다.
Ⓓ 지구는 다이아몬드가 형성되는 데 필요한 모든 조건을 갖춘 유일한 장소이다.

04 교수에 의하면, 메탄이 다이아몬드로 변화하기 위해 필요한 두 가지 조건은 무엇인가? (두 가지 선택)
Ⓐ 높은 온도
Ⓑ 냉각된 탄화수소
Ⓒ 압축된 수소
Ⓓ 높은 압력

05 강의에서 언급된 실험에서 추론할 수 있는 것은?
Ⓐ 석탄 결정체들이 지구의 대기에 존재한다.
Ⓑ 해왕성의 대기 압력은 예상보다 약하다.
Ⓒ 진정한 합성 다이아몬드를 만드는 것은 불가능하다.
Ⓓ 해왕성에서 발견되는 다이아몬드들은 아마도 검은 색일 것이다.

강의의 일부분을 다시 듣고 질문에 답하시오. ◁ MP3 58_1

> S: Uh… They contain some of the same elements as the Earth's atmosphere… helium, hydrogen…
> P: What else?

06 교수가 다음과 같이 말한 이유는?

> What else?

Ⓐ 학생이 주의를 기울이고 있는지 알고 싶어 한다.
Ⓑ 학생이 그가 원하는 대답을 제시하지 않았다.
Ⓒ 자신이 다음에 무슨 말을 하려고 하는지 기억할 수 없다.
Ⓓ 학생이 그 주제에 관해 연구를 더 하기를 바란다.

≧ Practice Questions

본문 p. 340

01 D   **02** A   **03** B   **04** C   **05** B   **06** D

Main Idea
격변 변광성

Listen to part of a lecture in an astronomy class. 🔊 MP3 59

Professor(male): All right, we've been talking about supernovas, but >Q1> **today I want to focus on something similar... similar but different – cataclysmic variable stars.** These are stars that create an immense burst of light, then slowly fade back to their normal brightness.

One of the most famous variable stars is called Mira. It was discovered in the 16th century by a German astronomer who was using it as a reference for what he thought was Mercury. As he looked for his reference star, he noticed it had faded from view. He actually thought it was a supernova, but after about four months he saw it again. This was the first recording of a variable star. Even today Mira appears and disappears on a regular cycle of eleven months.

However, not all variable stars completely disappear from view. Eta Carinae is probably the best-known of a type of variable stars called luminous blue variables. These stars are extremely rare – only six of them are known to exist. >Q2> **One of the reasons Eta Carinae is considered special is its massive size and brightness.** If Eta Carinae took the place of the Sun, it would swallow up Mercury, Venus, Earth, and Mars – four planets! >Q3> **It's so massive that its lifespan is relatively short. Remember, in our last class, we learned that most massive stars only last a few million years,** which is probably why luminous blue variables like Eta Carinae are so rare. Small stars like the Sun can last for billions of years.

Cause & Effect
큰 별들은 수명이 짧아 희귀함

Eta Carinae was long known to be a variable star. But in the mid-1800s it started to increase in brightness. It had done this before, but this time it started to get brighter and brighter. It became the second brightest star observed from Earth. The brightest star, Sirius, was only slightly brighter but almost 1,000 times closer to the Earth. >Q4> **Imagine seeing a candle that seemed to be 15 meters away, only to find out it was about 10 kilometers away. That's how bright Eta Carinae was.**

Example
얼마나 밝은 별인지 촛불을 예로 들어 설명

Eta Carinae slowly dimmed again, and by the 20th century it was no longer visible to the naked eye. However, the star has continued to vary in brightness ever since, but it has never come close to its peak of the 1800s. Astronomers believe that at its peak, the star had a stellar near-death experience. Scientists call these outbursts supernova impostor events. They look like supernovas, but stop short of actually destroying the star.

Cause & Effect
밝아졌다 어두워졌다하는 이유

>Q5> **So that explains why it was so bright. But why did it reappear? Well, Eta Carinae looks like it's blinking because it's something called a binary star.** Well, technically, we should say "stars" because, like the name suggests, it actually consists of two stars that orbit around a common center of mass. So what happens is actually very similar to a solar eclipse. When the moon blocks the Sun, what happens? We can't see the brightness of the Sun until the moon passes by. The supernova-like event occurred on only one of the two stars that make up Eta Carinae. When that star erupted, it spewed out immense clouds of gases and dust, obscuring its brightness. But just like eclipses don't last forever, the other star naturally orbited around to where we could see it again. In other words, >Q5> **the periodic decreases in brightness are caused by one star passing in front of the other. The darker star in front blocks the brightness of the one in back.** 🎧 Today Mira continues to appear and disappear on a regular 11-month cycle. I just checked its schedule this morning. >Q6> **Don't bother getting your telescopes out for another seven months.**

Headset

Anyway, Eta Carinae is not only interesting because of its past, but also because of what it may hold for us in the future. It's one of the closest stars to Earth that will likely become a supernova in the near future. But, of course, in astronomical terms, the near future can mean millions of years.

해석 천문학 수업의 다음 강의 일부분을 들으시오.

교수(남자): 자, 우리는 초신성에 대해 이야기를 해봤습니다. 하지만 오늘은 그와 유사한 어떤 것에 초점을 맞추고 싶군요... 유사하지만 다른 것이지요. 바로 격변 변광성입니다. 격변 변광성은 엄청난 양의 빛을 만들어내고는 원래의 밝기로 서서히 돌아가는 별입니다.

가장 유명한 변광성의 하나는 미라라고 불립니다. 미라는 16세기에, 수성이라고 생각했던 별에 대한 기준으로서 미라를 사용했던 한 독일 천문학자에 의해 발견되었습니다. 그는 기준이 되는 그 별을 찾았을 때, 그 별이 시야에서 사라져버린 것을 알아차렸습니다. 그는 사실 그 별이 초신성이라고 생각했지요. 하지만, 4개월 후 그는 그 별을 다시 보게 되었습니다. 이것이 변광성에 대한 최초의 기록이었습니다. 심지어 오늘날에도 미라는 11개월이라는 규칙적인 주기로 나타났다가 사라집니다.

하지만, 모든 변광성들이 시야에서 완전히 사라지는 것은 아닙니다. 에타 카리네는 밝은 청색 변광성이라고 불리는 변광성의 한 유형 중 아마도 가장 잘 알려진 별일 겁니다. 밝은 청색 변광성들은 매우 드문 별로서, 단 6개만이 존재한다고 알려져 있습니다. 에타 카리네가 특별하게 여겨지는 이유들 중 하나는, 그 별의 거대한 크기와 밝기입니다. 만일 에타 카리네가 태양을 대신하게 된다면, 그 별은 수성, 금성, 지구, 화성, 이렇게 네 행성을 삼켜버릴 겁니다! 이 별은 크기가 너무 거대해서 수명은 비교적 짧습니다. 기억하세요, 지난 시간에 우리는 대부분의 거대한 별들은 수백만 년밖에 지속되지 않는다고 배웠지요. 이것이 아마도 에타 카리네같은 밝은 청색 변광성들이 그토록 드문 이유일 겁니다. 태양과 같은 작은 별들은 수십억 년 동안 지속될 수 있습니다.

에타 카리네는 오랫동안 변광성으로 알려져 있었습니다. 하지만 1800년대 중반에 에타 카리네의 밝기가 증가하기 시작했습니다. 전에도 그랬던 적이 있었지만, 이번에는 점점 더 밝아지기 시작했지요. 에타 카리네는 지구에서 관측되는 두 번째로 가장 밝은 별이 되었습니다. 가장 밝은 별인 시리우스는 에타 카리네보다 아주 살짝만 더 밝을 뿐이었는데, 시리우스는 지구에 거의 천 배나 더 가까이 있습니다. 촛불이 15미터 정도 떨어져 있는 것 같이 보였는데, 실은 그것이 10킬로미터나 떨어져 있다는 것을 알아 차렸다고 생각해보세요. 그것이 바로 에타 카리네의 밝기였습니다. 에타 카리네는 다시 천천히 희미해져, 20세기경에는 더 이상 육안으로는 볼 수가 없었습니다. 하지만 그 별은 그 이후로도 계속 밝기가 변화했습니다. 하지만, 다시는 1800년대의 (밝기의) 정점에는 결코 이르지 못했죠. 천문학자들은 에타 카리네가 정점을 찍었을 때에, 그 별이 임사 체험을 했다고 생각합니다. 과학자들은 이런 갑작스런 폭발을 초신성 위장 현상이라고 부릅니다. 그 별들은 초신성처럼 보이지만, 실제 별이 파괴되기 직전에 멈추는 것이지요.

자, 그것이 에타 카리네가 왜 그렇게 밝았는지를 설명해 주고 있습니다. 하지만 그 별이 왜 다시 나타났을까요? 음, 에타 카리네는 연성(binary star)이라고 불리는 것이라서, 깜박거리는 것처럼 보입니다. 음, 원칙적으로는 '별들(stars)'이라고 해야 합니다. 왜냐면, 그 이름이 나타내듯이, 연성은 사실 하나의 공통된 물체의 중심 주변을 공전하는 두 개의 별들로 구성되어 있기 때문입니다. 그래서 실제 일어나는 일은 사실상 일식과 매우 유사합니다. 달이 태양을 가릴 때 어떤 일이 일어나나요? 우리는 달이 지나갈 때까지 태양의 밝은 빛을 볼 수 없습니다. 초신성처럼 보이는 현상은 에타 카리네를 구성하는 두 별 중의 하나에만 일어났습니다. 한 별이 분출했을 때, 방대한 양의 가스와 먼지 구름을 뿜어내며 빛을 가렸습니다. 하지만 일식이 영원히 지속되지 않는 것처럼, 다른 한 별은 자연적으로 우리가 그 별을 다시 볼 수 있는 곳으로 공전을 했지요. 다시 말해, 밝기가 주기적으로 감소한 것은 한 별이 다른 별의 앞으로 지나가면서 발생하는 것입니다. 앞에 있는 더 어두운 별이 뒤에 있는 별의 밝은 빛을 가리는 거지요. 오늘날 미라는 계속해서 11개월 주기로 사라졌다 다시 나타났다를 반복합니다. 나는 오늘 아침에도 미라의 일정을 점검했습니다. 앞으로 7개월간은 굳이 여러분의 망원경을 꺼내지 않아도 됩니다.

어쨌든, 에타 카리네는 그 과거로 인해 흥미로울 뿐만 아니라, 그 별이 우리에게 앞으로 가져올 것 때문에도 흥미롭습니다. 에타 카리네는 가까운 미래에 초신성이 될 가능성이 있는, 지구에서 가장 가까운 별들 중 하나이기 때문이지요. 하지만, 물론, 가까운 미래는 천문학적 용어로는 수백만 년을 의미할 수도 있겠지요.

W supernova [sjuːpərnóuvə] 초신성 cataclysmic [kætəklízmik] 격변하는 variable star 변광성 immense [iméns] 어마어마한 astronomer [əstránəmər] 천문학자 reference [réfərəns] 참고, 참조 massive [mǽsiv] 거대한 lifespan [láifspæn] 수명 peak [piːk] 최고점 stellar [stélər] 별의 near-death experience 임사 체험 outburst [áutbəːrst] 폭발, 분출 impostor [impástər] 위장, 사기꾼 binary star 연성(連星) solar eclipse 일식(日蝕) erupt [irʌ́pt] 분출하다 spew out 분출하다 obscure [əbskjúər] 보기 어렵게 하다 periodic [pìəriádik] 주기적인 telescope 망원경

01 강의의 주된 내용은?
Ⓐ 거대한 별들의 생명 주기
Ⓑ 별들의 밝기를 측정하는 방법들
Ⓒ 연성이 식(蝕)을 만드는 방법

Ⓓ 한 독특한 유형의 별의 특징들

02 태양계의 첫 네 개의 행성이 언급된 이유는?
Ⓐ 에타 카리네의 크기가 거대하다는 것을 말해주려고
Ⓑ 그 행성들의 합친 질량이 변광성과 동일할 것이라는 것을 말해주려고
Ⓒ 그 행성들이 태양 폭발로 가장 많은 영향을 받는다는 것을 말해주려고
Ⓓ 그 행성들이 미라 주위를 공전하는 행성들과 같은 크기라는 것을 말해주려고

03 에타 카리네의 짧은 수명의 이유로 교수가 말한 것은?
Ⓐ 다양한 밝기
Ⓑ 거대한 크기
Ⓒ 뜨거운 온도
Ⓓ 태양과 가까운 거리

04 교수가 촛불을 언급한 이유는?
Ⓐ 연성이 서로 어떻게 상호작용하는지를 설명하려고
Ⓑ 별들이 얼마나 빨리 죽는지 보여주려고
Ⓒ 에타 카리네의 밝기를 강조하려고
Ⓓ 두 별 사이의 거리를 예를 들어 설명하려고

05 교수에 의하면, 에타 카리네의 밝기가 변하는 이유는 무엇인가?
Ⓐ 대부분의 별보다 크다.
Ⓑ 두 별로 이루어져 있다.
Ⓒ 식(蝕)을 겪는다.
Ⓓ 초신성을 경험했다.

강의의 일부분을 다시 듣고 질문에 답하시오. ◁» MP3 59_1

> Today Mira continues to appear and disappear on a regular 11-month cycle. I just checked its schedule this morning. Don't bother getting your telescopes out for another seven months.

06 교수가 다음과 같이 말할 때 암시하는 것은?

> Don't bother getting your telescopes out for another seven months.

Ⓐ 학생들이 충분히 주의를 기울이지 않고 있다.
Ⓑ 변광성을 발견하는 데는 많은 훈련이 필요하다.
Ⓒ 초신성들은 육안으로 볼 수 있다.
Ⓓ 미라는 현재 지구에서 볼 수 없다.

02 / Chemistry

Sample Questions
본문 p. 346

01 B   02 D   03 C   04 B, D   05 A   06 D

해석 화학 수업의 다음 강의 일부분을 들으시오. ◁» MP3 60

교수(여자): 지금까지 우리는 탄소를 기반으로 한 연료들에 대해서 이야기 해왔습니다. 이 중 가장 기본적인 연료의 하나는 숯으로, 세계의 많은 곳에서 주로 요리에 사용되고 있지요. 자, 사람들이 왜 숯으로 요리를 하는지를 생각해봐야 합니다. 요리용 연료로서 목재를 사용하는 것이 더 쉬울 텐데요, 그렇지요? 그러니까, 본질적으로는, 숯은 나무에서 생기니까요. 하지만 진정한 이유는 나무가 숯으로 바뀔 때 무엇이 제거되는가에 있습니다. 숯이 요리용 연료로 사용될 때 왜 그렇게 효과적인지를 이해하기 위해서는, 먼저 숯이 어떻게 만들어지는지를 살펴봐야 합니다. 자, 숯이 어떻게 만들어지는지 아는 사람 있습니까?

학생(남자): 예, 숯을 만들려면 나무를 태워야 한다는 것을 읽은 기억이 납니다. 하지만 이해가 안 되는 것이... 그러니까, 그럼 나무가 그냥 재로 변하지 않나요? 어떻게 나무가 온전하게 유지되는지 이해가 안 가요.

교수: 좋은 질문입니다. 나무가 다 타버리지 않는 이유는 나무가 구워지는 방식 때문입니다. 숯은 느린 열분해를 통해 만들어집니다. (화면에 보여준다) 이것은 산소가 없는 상황에서 나무에 열을 가하는 방법입니다. 나무와 같은 유기 물질이 열을 받게 되면, 그 물질들은 산소와 반응하여 그 물질 안의 많은 탄소가 타버리게 됩니다. 하지만, 이 등식에서 산소를 빼면 어떻게 될까요? 그것이 숯을 만드는 핵심이죠. 열분해를 통해 탄소함유량이 높은 응고 물질인 목탄(char)이 만들어집니다. 나무에서 기체와 액체 성분이 빠져나가고, 더 순수한 형태의 탄소만 남게 되는 것이지요. 이것이 본질적으로 숯이라는 겁니다. 나무를 산소 없이 태우기 위해서는, 나무를 구덩이에 묻거나 특별히 고안된 일종의 오븐인 가마에 넣어야 합니다. 이 과정은 또한 나무에서 바람직하지 않은 모든 성분을 제거해줍니다. 그 하나로, 나무는 수분을 많이 함유하고 있는데, 이는 나무가 탈 때 온도를 떨어뜨릴 수 있습니다. 하지만 나무가 산소 없이 열을 받게 되면, 물 분자가 증발하게 됩니다. 그리고 메탄이나 수소 같은 위험 물질들도 타서 사라집니다. 여러분이 나무에 이런 불필요한 물질들이 얼마나 많이 있는지를 알게 되면 놀랄 거예요. 결국에는, 나무의 원래 부피의 4분의 1만이 남게 됩니다. 남겨지는 것은 대부분 탄소입니다. 이런 원치 않은 성분들이 없어지면, 숯은 여러 가지 이점을 갖게 됩니다. 우선, 숯은 연기가 거의 나지 않습니다. 자, 캠핑 좋아하는 사람 있나요?

학생: 저요. 요전번 주말에도 친구들과 갔습니다.

교수: 좋아요. 그러면 학생과 친구들은 캠프파이어를 만들었을 거라 추측되는군요. 연기에 대해서 말해보세요.

학생: 흠... 음, 연기가 많이 났어요. 연기를 피하려고 이곳 저곳으로 움직여야 했지요.

교수: 그건 나무가 물, 가스들, 그 밖에 기타 등등 불필요한 내용물들을 많이 갖고 있기 때문입니다. 이 모든 것들이 연기를 만들죠. 믿기 힘들겠지만, 여러분이 보는 연기는, 음, 그 중 상당 부분이 사실 증기입니다. 몇몇 숯 제조공장에서는 이것을 자신들의 숯을 향상시키는 방법으로 이용하기도 하지요. 숯이 만들어지는 방법에 따라, 숯이 내는 연기의 양이 달라집니다. 가끔은 우리 모두가 즐기는 숯의 풍미를 더하기 위해서, 약간의 연기가 있었으면 하기도 하지요.

숯의 또 다른 장점은 숯이 나무보다 더 오래, 더 뜨겁게, 더 꾸준하게 탄다는 것입니다. 숯이 탈 때는, 산소 분자가 탄소 분자와 결합하여 새로운 가스들을 만듭니다. 이 가스들은 타는 듯이 뜨거운 열을 만들며, 온도가 올라 음식을 익힙니다. 산소와 반응하는 탄소 함유량이 더 많을수록, 더 많은 열을 낼 수 있습니다. 그래서, 당연히, 숯은 본질적으로 타버린 나무에서 남은 탄소이기 때문에, 주어진 양의 숯은 당연히 동일한 양의 나무보다 훨씬 더 오래 타게 됩니다.

자, 숯이 이용되는 다른 방식도 있습니다. 여러분은 숯 필터가 있는 공기 청정기나 정수기를 가지고 있을지도 모르겠네요. 여과에 사용되는 숯은 활성탄이라고 합니다. 이런 종류의 숯은 요리를 할 때 사용하는 숯과는 조금 다릅니다. 그러니까, 요리용 숯을 여과시키는 데 사용할 수도 있겠지만, 그렇게 잘 작용하지는 않을 겁니다. 가장 큰 차이점은, 활성탄은 숯의 흡수하는 성질을 극대화했다는 것입니다. 즉, 모든 종류의 숯은 정화 능력을 갖고 있긴 하지만, 표면적을 흡수와 화학 반응에 적합하도록 최대화하는 것이 가장 좋지요.

그렇다면 이런 종류의 숯은 어떻게 만들까요? 기본적으로 과도하게 태우면 됩니다. 석탄이 어떻게 제조되는지 기억나나요? 산소 없이였지요? 일반 숯을 제조하는 마지막 과정에서, 숯을 잠시 산소에 노출시킵니다. 이 과정을 활성화라고 부릅니다... 탄소를 산화시키는 공기에 노출시키는 것이지요. 그렇게 하면, 산소가 숯의 표면에 미세한 구멍들을 파게 됩니다. 이렇게 작은 구멍들은 숯의 표면적을 더 크게 만들어, 숯의 정화 성질을 최대화 시키게 됩니다.

Ⓦ fuel [fjú(ː)əl] 연료 charcoal [tʃɑ́ːrkòul] 숯 ash [æʃ] 재 intact [intǽkt] 온전한 pyrolysis [paiərɑ́lisis] 열분해 absence [ǽbsəns] 부재 organic material 유기 물질 equation [ikwéiʒən] 방정식 char [tʃɑːr] 숯이 되다 residue [rézidjùː] 잔여물 pit [pit] (크고 깊은) 구덩이 kiln [kiln] 가마 undesirable [ʌndizáiərəbl] 원하지 않는 flavor [fléivər] 운치, 멋 scorching [skɔ́ːrtʃiŋ] 몹시 뜨거운 react [riǽkt] 반응하다 purifier [pjú(ː)rifàiər] 정화 장치 filtration [filtréiʃən] 여과 activated [ǽktəvèitid] 활성화된 maximize [mǽksəmàiz] 극대화하다 chemical reaction 화학 반응 expose [ikspóuz] 노출시키다 oxidize [ɑ́ksidàiz] 산화시키다

01 강의의 주된 내용은?
Ⓐ 최상의 숯을 만드는 나무의 종류
Ⓑ **두 가지 다른 종류의 숯이 어떻게 만들어지는지**
Ⓒ 탄소가 다른 가스들에 어떻게 반응하는지
Ⓓ 요리 연료로 나무를 사용하는 것의 위험성

02 교수에 의하면, 숯을 구덩이나 오븐에서 만드는 이유는 무엇인가?
Ⓐ 열의 온도를 높이기 위해
Ⓑ 공기 중으로 탄소가 배출되는 것을 막기 위해
Ⓒ 불꽃으로 인한 부상을 방지하기 위해
Ⓓ 존재하는 공기의 양을 줄이기 위해

03 수분 함유량이 높은 숯에 관해 추론할 수 있는 것은?
Ⓐ 더 빨리 타버릴 것이다.
Ⓑ 여과에 더 좋을 것이다.
Ⓒ 연기가 더 많이 날 것이다.
Ⓓ 더 뜨거운 온도를 만들어 낼 것이다.

04 교수에 의하면, 요리에 있어 숯의 장점은 무엇인가? (두 가지 선택)
Ⓐ 음식에서 과도한 수분을 제거한다.
Ⓑ 더 오랜 기간 높은 열을 유지한다.
Ⓒ 반복해서 사용할 수 있다.
Ⓓ 연기가 덜 난다.

05 교수가 공기 청정기와 정수기를 언급한 이유는?
Ⓐ 숯의 또 다른 기능을 소개하려고
Ⓑ 숯이 어떻게 만들어지는지에 대한 예를 보여주려고
Ⓒ 숯의 열을 이용하는 새로운 방법을 제시하려고
Ⓓ 나무에서 불순물이 여과되는 방법을 예를 들어 설명하려고

06 요리용 숯에 관해 추론할 수 있는 것은?
Ⓐ 수년이 걸리는 과정을 통해 만들어진다.
Ⓑ 더 낮은 온도에서를 제외하고는 더 쉽게 탄다.
Ⓒ 나무보다 독성 화학물질이 더 많이 함유되어 있다.
Ⓓ 활성탄보다 표면에 더 적은 개수의 구멍이 있다.

Practice Questions

본문 p. 350

| 01 B | 02 D | 03 B | 04 C | 05 C | 06 A, D |

Main Idea
합금 – 서로 다른 물질의 조합으로 더 좋은 금속을 만듦

Purpose
합금을 만드는 목적

Role
해군 연구원이 발명함

Listen to part of a lecture in a chemistry class. 🔊 MP3 61

Professor(female): So, we've been talking about the properties of metals. As I mentioned in yesterday's class, **Q1** **today I'm going to discuss alloy metals and how the properties of two metals can be combined to create a better substance.** So, an alloy is essentially two or more metals, or a metal and non-metal, that are combined to make a new material. One of the most common alloys we see is stainless steel. It's a combination of iron and carbon. As you probably know, iron rusts. So to prevent it from rusting, it is heated to bond with carbon, thus making a rust-proof, durable material. This would be an example of a metal and non-metal alloy.
Now, I want to focus on an alloy created with two metals. It's called nitinol (shown on screen). Its other name is nickel titanium. It is roughly a half-and-half mix of these two metals. It was made by a naval researcher who wanted to develop a better missile nose cone, one that could better resist heat and fatigue and be more flexible. **Q2** **A problem with strong metals like titanium is that they are subject to cracking. And

Difference 다른 금속과의 차이점 – 강하지만 탄력이 있음	the problem with malleable ones like nickel is that they're just not strong enough. He basically needed a metal that was strong but elastic, more flexible than other compounds with the same strength. He soon found his answer by combining nickel and titanium.
(Name) Origin 형상기억합금 이름의 기원	There is actually another name for nitinol – memory metal. There is a bit of story behind this name. Um… The person who made nitinol was showing some of its properties to his colleagues. First ▶Q3 **he demonstrated its elastic properties by bending some wire into a folded accordion shape. Then, one of his colleagues, presumably to check the heat resistant properties of the metal, held a lighter up to it. Much to everyone's surprise the accordion-shaped strip started returning to its original shape until it was straight again.** So, let's take a look at how this property works. This kind of transformation is called martensitic transformation. This is when, depending on a particular factor, a structure can have two forms. So in low temperatures, the molecular structure of nitinol would sort of be like a cube. However, when heat is applied, these small molecules will transform into more complicated structures. ▶Q4 **So depending on the temperature, the molecules will have different forms. It's similar to melting ice.** When solids become liquids, the arrangement of their molecules will change. So, when it's below freezing, water's molecules will change their arrangement. But once it warms up, they will return to their original arrangement.
Example 형상기억합금의 모양이 바뀌는 이유(결정 구조가 바뀌는 것)를 melting ice로 예를 들어 설명	
Cause & Effect 열을 가하면 원래 모양 으로 다시 돌아감	To apply this to metal, we must first define the original shape. This is the shape it assumes when it is heated. ▶Q5 **So if you change the shape of nitinol when it's hot, that's the shape it will return to every time it's heated.** The metal will "remember" the shape at a molecular level. So you can bend it into any position, but once you heat it up, it will go back to its original shape.
Application 형상기억합금의 용도 와 응용 (1) 안경테 (2) 치아 교정기	The potential applications for nitinol were realized immediately, but it took a while for technology to develop enough to make nitinol widely adaptable. It was actually 40 years before it could be ▶Q6-A **applied to practical uses, such as making durable eyeglass frames.** Has anyone accidently stepped on their glasses before? If the frames are made of nitinol, heating them up a little will make them go back to their original shape. There are ▶Q6-D **medical applications as well. Nitinol is used to make braces, the wires used to straighten teeth.** A very thin wire is heated and formed into the shape the orthodontist wants the patient's teeth to assume. Next, it is cooled down and bent around the patient's actual teeth. People have warm bodies, so the natural heat from the mouth will make the wire try to go back to its original shape, gently and constantly putting pressure on the teeth to help straighten them. This saves the patient the hassle of having to go to the orthodontist all the time to get the wires tightened.

해석 화학 수업의 다음 강의 일부분을 들으시오.

교수(여자): 자, 지금까지 금속의 속성에 대해서 이야기 했습니다. 어제 수업에서 말한 것처럼, 오늘은 합금들에 대해, 그리고 어떻게 두 금속의 속성이 결합하여 더 좋은 물질을 만드는지에 대해서 논의해보려고 합니다. 자, 합금은 본질적으로는 새로운 물질을 만들기 위해 결합한 둘 이상의 금속들, 또는 금속과 비금속입니다. 우리가 아는 가장 흔한 합금은 스테인리스 스틸입니다. 이것은 철과 탄소의 결합체입니다. 여러분이 아마 알고 있듯이, 철은 녹이 슬지요. 그래서 철이 녹이 스는 것을 막기 위해, 탄소와 결합하도록 철에 열을 가해 녹이 슬지 않고 내구성이 있는 물질이 만들어지는 것입니다. 이것은 금속과 비금속 합금의 한 가지 예가 되겠군요.

자, 이제 두 가지 금속으로 만들어지는 합금에 초점을 맞춰보겠습니다. 니티놀이라고 하는 것입니다. (화면에 보여준다) 또 다른 이름으로는 니켈 티타늄이라고 하지요. 이 두 가지 금속을 대략 반반 혼합한 것입니다. 이것은 더 좋은 미사일 노즈콘(원추형 앞부분), 즉 열과 마모에 더 잘 견딜 수 있고 더 유연한 노즈콘을 개발하고자 했던 한 해군 연구원에 의해 만들어졌습니다. 티타늄 같은 강한 금속의 한 가지 문제점은 금이 가기 쉽다는 것입니다. 또한 니켈처럼 가단성이 있는 금속들의 문제점은 충분히 강하지 않다는 것이었지요. 그는 기본적으로 강하지만 탄력 있는, 즉 같은 강도를 지닌 다른 합성물들보다 더 유연한 금속이 필요했습니다. 그는 니켈과 티타늄을 결합시켜 곧 그 답을 찾았지요.

니티놀에는 실제로 또 다른 이름이 있습니다. 형상기억합금입니다. 이 이름에는 얽힌 이야기가 있습니다. 음... 니티놀을 만든 사람은 동료들에게 그 금속의 속성 중 일부를 보여주고 있었습니다. 먼저 그는 철사를 접힌 아코디언 형태로 구부려서 니티놀의 탄력성을 보여주었지요. 그리고 나서, 그의 동료 중의 한 명이, 아마도 그 금속의 내열성을 점검해보기 위해서, 그 금속에 라이터를 가져다 댔습니다. 모두가 놀랍게도, 아코디언 모양의 철사가 원래의 모습인 일직선으로 돌아가기 시작한 것입니다.

자, 이런 속성이 어떻게 작용하는지 살펴봅시다. 이 변형은 마르텐사이트 변형이라고 합니다. 이것은, 어떤 특정 요인에 따라, 한 구조가 두 가지 형태를 가질 때를 말합니다. 그래서 낮은 온도에서는 니티놀의 분자 구조가 일종의 정육면체 모양과 같습니다. 하지만 열이 가해지면, 이 작은 분자들은 더 복잡한 구조로 변형됩니다. 그래서 온도에 따라, 분자들은 다른 형태를 가지게 됩니다. 녹는 얼음과 비슷하다고 볼 수 있겠군요. 고체가 액체가 될 때, 그 분자들의 배열이 바뀝니다. 그래서, 기온이 영하로 내려가면, 물의 분자들의 배열이 바뀌지요. 하지만 기온이 다시 오르면, 물 분자들은 원래의 배열로 돌아가게 됩니다.

이것을 금속에 적용하기 위해서는, 먼저 원래의 형태를 정의해야 합니다. 원래의 모양은 그것이 열을 받았을 때 취하는 형태입니다. 그래서 뜨거울 때 니티놀의 모양을 바꾸면, 니티놀이 열을 받을 때마다 그 모양으로 돌아가는 형태가 되는 것입니다. 그 금속은 분자 수준에서 그 형태를 '기억'하는 것이지요. 그래서 여러분은 그것을 어떤 형태로든 구부릴 수 있지만, 일단 그것에 열을 가하게 되면, 그것은 원래의 모습으로 돌아갑니다. 니티놀의 잠재적인 응용은 즉각적으로 실현되었지만, 니티놀을 널리 적용할 수 있게끔 기술이 발달되는 데에는 시간이 좀 걸렸습니다. 사실상 40년이 지나서야 니티놀은 내구성 있는 안경테를 만드는 것 같은 실용적인 사용에 적용될 수 있었지요. 전에 실수로 안경테를 밟은 적이 있었던 사람이 있나요? 만일 그 안경테가 니티놀로 만들어져 있다면, 그것에 약간만 열을 가하면 안경테가 원래의 형태로 돌아갈 것입니다.

(니티놀의) 의료적인 응용 영역도 있습니다. 니티놀은 치아 교정기, 즉 치아를 바르게 하는 데 쓰이는 철사를 만드는 데 사용됩니다. 매우 얇은 철사에 열을 가해 교정사가 환자의 치아가 취했으면 하는 모양으로 만듭니다. 다음으로, 그 철사를 냉각시켜 환자의 실제 치아 주위를 둘러 구부려 뜨립니다. 사람의 몸은 따뜻해서, 입에서 나오는 자연적인 열로 인해 철사는 원래의 형태로 돌아가려고 하게 됩니다. 부드럽게, 그리고 끊임없이 치아에 압력을 가해 치아가 바르게 되도록 하면서요. 이로 인해 환자는 매번 철사를 조이기 위해 교정사를 찾아가야 하는 불편을 줄일 수 있게 됩니다.

Ⓦ property [práp∂rti] 속성   alloy   metal 합금   combination [kàmbinéi∫∂n] 결합(물), 조합(물)   iron [ái∂rn] 철   rust [rʌst] 녹슬다   rust-proof [rʌ́st-pru:f] 녹 방지 처리를 한   durable [djú(:)∂r∂bl] 내구성이 있는   naval [néiv∂l] 해군의   fatigue [f∂ti:g] (금속 등의) 약화   flexible [fléks∂bl] 신축성 있는   crack [krǽk] 금이 가다, 부서지다   malleable [mǽli∂bl] 펴 늘일 수 있는   elastic [ilǽstik] 탄력 있는, 신축성 있는   compound [kámpaund] 복합체, 화합물   demonstrate [dém∂nstrèit] 입증하다, 보여주다   presumably [prizjú:m∂bli] 아마, 짐작컨대   resistant [rizíst∂nt] 저항력이 있는   transformation [trænsf∂rméi∫∂n] 변화   brace [breis] 치아교정기   orthodontist [ɔ̀:rθ∂dántist] 치과 교정 전문의   hassle [hǽsl] 귀찮은 상황

01 강의의 주된 내용은?
Ⓐ 새로운 종류의 비금속 물질이 어떻게 발명됐는지
Ⓑ 두 가지 금속으로 만들어진 어떤 합금의 속성들
Ⓒ 열이 가해지면 어떻게 금속의 속성들이 바뀔 수 있는지
Ⓓ 여러 다른 종류의 금속 합금과 그들의 응용

02 니티놀에 대해 추론할 수 있는 것은?
Ⓐ 티타늄만큼 잘 구부러지지 않을 것이다.
Ⓑ 더 낮은 온도에서 녹을 것이다.
Ⓒ 열이 가해지면 두 개의 금속으로 나누어질 것이다.
Ⓓ 티타늄보다 더 많이 구부러질 것이다.

03 니티놀의 '기억' 능력에 대해 교수가 암시한 것은?
Ⓐ 무기를 만드는 데 유용하다.
Ⓑ 의도했던 기능이 아니었다.
Ⓒ 악기에서 본뜬 것이었다.
Ⓓ 여러 금속에서 발견될 수 있다.

04 교수가 녹는 얼음을 언급한 이유는?
Ⓐ 열이 구조물을 변화시키는 이유를 설명하려고
Ⓑ 서로 다른 물질들의 다른 속성을 실증하려고

ⓒ 분자 구조 변화의 예를 주기 위해

ⓓ 물체들에 열이 가해졌을 때와 냉각되었을 때 반응하는 방식을 보여주려고

05 교수에 의하면, 니티놀에 열을 가하는 동안 구부려 놓으면 무슨 일이 일어나겠는가?

Ⓐ 약해지고 쉽게 부러질 것이다.

Ⓑ 앞으로 더 쉽게 구부러질 것이다.

Ⓒ 다시 열을 받으면 그 형태로 돌아갈 것이다.

Ⓓ 그 형태를 영원히 유지할 것이다.

06 니티놀의 실용적 사용의 예로서 교수가 언급한 것은? (두 가지 선택)

Ⓐ 내구성 있는 안경테 만들기

Ⓑ 강한 물질로 미사일 콘을 코팅하기

Ⓒ 각얼음이 빨리 녹는 것을 방지하기

Ⓓ 조일 필요가 없는 치아 교정기 만들기

Ⓔ 스테인리스 스틸이 쉽게 녹이 스는 것을 막기

03 / Earth Science

≫ Sample Questions

본문 p. 356

| 01 B | 02 C | 03 D | 04 B | 05 D | 06 C |

해석 지구과학 수업의 다음 강의 일부분을 들으시오. ◁ **MP3 62**

교수(남자): 우리 모두가 알고 있듯이, 지구는 태양 주위를 돌면서, 지구 중심을 북극에서 남극으로 가로지르는 상상의 선인 자전축을 중심으로 자전합니다. 하루의 길이는 이 자전에 의해 계산되지요. 즉, 지구가 자전축을 중심으로 완전히 한 바퀴 도는 데 필요한 시간의 양을 하루라고 부르고, 이는 24시간입니다. 자, 이런 자전의 원래 원인은 불명확하지만, 계속되는 지구의 자전은 관성의 산물로 생각되고 있습니다. 관성은, 물론, 물체들이 그들의 움직임 상태에 대한 어떠한 변화도 거부하려는 경향을 말합니다. 움직이지 않는 물체들은 움직이지 않는 채로 있으려 하고, 움직이고 있는 물체들은 계속해서 움직이려는 경향 말입니다. 어떤 이들은 지구는 우리 태양계가 탄생했을 때 돌기 시작했고, 지구가 도는 속도를 늦추게 할 어떤 저항력도 없었기 때문에 지구가 오늘날까지 계속해서 돈다고 생각합니다.

여러분 대부분은 하루의 길이가 지구가 처음 만들어졌을 때부터 계속 같았다고 생각할지도 모르겠지만, 내가 여러분에게 지구가 완전히 한 바퀴 도는 데 필요한 시간은 바뀔 수 있다고 말한다면 어떨까요? 이것이 내가 오늘 다루고자 하는 내용입니다. 자, 내가 또 여러분에게, 인류가 지구의 자전 속도를 실제로 바꿀 수 있다고 말한다면 어떨까요? 물론, 사람 한 명이 지구에 영향을 끼칠 수는 없지만, 지난 50년간의 인류 활동들의 조합은 실제로 지구가 더 빨리 돌도록 만들었습니다. 그 결과 우리의 하루가 백 년 전보다 말 그대로 더 짧아졌지요.

학생(여자): 하지만 지구가 더 빨리 돌고 있다는 것을 우리가 어떻게 알 수 있지요?

교수: 지구의 자전 속도는 인공위성을 사용해서 알 수 있어요. 정지해 있는 위성에 신호를 보내서, 그 신호가 다시 돌아오는 데 걸리는 시간을 계산하는 거지요. 이 방법으로 절대 기준이 생기지요. 자 그럼, 지구가 왜 더 빨리 돌고 있는지에 대해 의견이 있는 사람 있나요?

학생: 지구 온난화와 관련이 있나요? 제 말은, 북극과 남극이 지구 온난화로 큰 영향을 받고 있잖아요. 빙하들이 녹아서 물이 더 생겨나는 것 말이에요. 그게 자전축과 어떤 관련이라도 있지 않을까요? 그러니까, 자전축이 자전 속도에 영향을 미칠 수 있잖아요, 아닌가요?

교수: 글쎄, 자전축은 인류 활동의 영향을 받지는 않지만, 물이 그것과 관련이 있다는 점에서 학생 말은 부분적으로 맞아요. 1950년대 이후로, 사람들은 전세계에 만여 개나 되는 인공 저수지를 만들기 시작했어요. 이는 엄청난 양의 물이 세계 곳곳에 재분배되었다는 뜻입니다. 그러니까, 물은 엄청나게 무거운데, 질량은 회전 관성에 큰 영향을 미칩니다. 지구의 물의 대부분은 남극과 북극의 사이의 중간 지점에 있는 적도 근처에 있었는데, 이는 대부분의 물이 지구의 자전축에서 가장 멀리 떨어진 지역에 위치해 있었다는 말입니다. 하지만, 저수지들의 건설로 인해 많은 양의 물이 지구 북쪽과 남쪽 지방으로 이동되게 되었지요. 그래서 그 결과, 어떤 일이 생겼을까요?

학생: 지구의 질량이 다시 분배되었어요.

교수: 맞아요.

학생: 하지만 그게 하루의 길이가 줄어든 것과 무슨 관련이 있는 거죠?

교수: 좋아요, 자, 회전 관성에 대해서는 잘 알고 있지요? 어떤 물체의 질량 분포는 그 물체의 질량 중심과 그것이 회전하는 속도에 영향을 미쳐요. 피겨 스케이트 선수를 예로 들어보죠. 스케이트 선수가 회전을 할 때, 그들이 팔과 다리를 밖으로 뻗으면 천천히 돌지만 팔과 다리를 몸에 가까이 붙이면 훨씬 빨리 도는 것을 알아차린 적이 있나요? 그들은 더 빨리 돌기 위해 어떤 힘도 사용하지 않아요, 단지 질량 중심을 축에 더 가깝게 할 뿐이죠. 이것이 자연적으로 회전을 더 빨리 하게 해줘요.

물이 적도 지역에서부터 북쪽과 남쪽으로 재분배되면서, 물이 지구의 중심축에 더 가까워졌어요. 스케이트 선수들이 팔을 몸 쪽으로 더 가까이 당긴 것처럼 말이죠. 당연히, 지구의 질량이 중심축 쪽에 더 가까워졌기 때문에, 지구가 회전하는 속도는 더 빨라지게 되지요.

자, 우리가 지구 온난화에 대해 걱정하는 것만큼 (빨라진 지구의 자전 속도의) 환경적 영향에 대해 걱정할 필요는 없어요. 원자 시계에 따르면 하루가 백만 분의 팔 초 정도 줄어들었다고 해요. 이 정도는 어떤 것에 영향을 미칠 만큼 중요하지는 않지만, 이것은 인류 활동의 결과로 지구의 자전에 조금이라도 측정 가능한 결과를 보여준 최초의 사례이기는 합니다.

Ⓦ rotate [róuteit] 회전하다   axis [ǽksis] 중심축   imaginary [imǽdʒənèri] 상상의   orbit [ɔ́ːrbit] 공전하다   rotation [routéiʃən] 자전
spin [spin] 돌다   inertia [inə́ːrʃə] 관성   immobile [imóubl] 움직이지 않는   speculate [spékjəlèit] 추측하다   resistive force 저항력
have an effect on ~ ...에 영향을 미치다   satellite [sǽtəlàit] 인공위성   stationary [stéiʃənèri] 정지된   global warming 지구 온난화
glacier [gléiʃər] 빙하   reservoir [rézərvwàːr] 저수지   tremendous [triméndəs] 엄청난   redistribute [riːdistríbjuː)t] 재분배하다
mass [mæs] 질량   equator [ikwéitər] 적도   atomic clock 원자시계   measurable [méʒərəbl] 측정 가능한

01 강의의 주된 내용은?
Ⓐ 하루의 길이를 어떻게 측정하는지
Ⓑ 인류 활동이 하루의 길이에 미친 영향
Ⓒ 자전축이 지구 온난화에 의해 어떻게 영향을 받는지
Ⓓ 지구 온난화가 지구의 자전에 미치는 영향

02 교수가 물의 재분배에 대해 논의한 이유는?
Ⓐ 지구 온난화와 관련된 한 문제점에 대한 예를 들려고
Ⓑ 한 심각한 문제가 어떻게 바로 잡아질 수 있는지 예를 들어 설명하려고
Ⓒ 인류의 활동이 지구의 질량 변화에 어떻게 영향을 줄 수 있는지 보여주려고
Ⓓ 물의 중량과 지구의 궤도 간의 관계를 설명하려고

03 교수에 의하면, 저수지들은 지구의 질량과 어떤 관계가 있는가?
Ⓐ 지구의 질량을 고르게 분배했다.
Ⓑ 지구의 질량을 조금 증가시켰다.
Ⓒ 지구의 질량을 측정하기 더 어렵게 만들었다.
Ⓓ 지구의 질량을 지구의 중심축에 더 가깝게 움직였다.

04 교수가 하루의 길이에 대해 말한 것은?
Ⓐ 많이 줄어들었다.
Ⓑ 약간 짧아졌다.
Ⓒ 상당한 만큼 증가했다.
Ⓓ 지구 온난화를 유발했다.

05 교수에 의하면, 스케이트 선수와 지구 사이의 공통점은 무엇인가?
Ⓐ 더 빨리 돌기 위해서 외부의 힘이 필요하다.
Ⓑ 회전을 조정하기 위해 질량의 중심을 바꿀 수 있다.
Ⓒ 중량이 허용하는 만큼만 빨리 돌 수 있다.
Ⓓ 중량이 중심축에 더 가까울 때 더 빨리 돈다.

06 교수가 원자 시계를 언급한 이유는?
Ⓐ 유해한 인류 활동의 예를 들려고
Ⓑ 지구의 자전 속도가 어떻게 측정되는지를 설명하려고
Ⓒ 하루의 길이가 거의 변하지 않은 것을 강조하려고
Ⓓ 물의 재분배로 인해 유발되는 또 다른 문제를 소개하려고

Practice Questions

01 B 02 A 03 D 04 D 05 B 06 C

Main Idea

Difference
조수와 날씨의 차이점

Example
예측이 가능한 또 다른
예 – 강우량
Cause
조수를 예측할 수 있는
이유

Requirement
조수 예측에 필요한 조건
– 달과 태양의 위치

Term
tidal range 용어 설명

Cause & Effect
태양과 달이 일직선상에
있는 경우 조수가 크고,
태양과 달이 수직으로 있
는 경우는 조수가 작음

Listen to part of a lecture in an earth science class. ◁ MP3 63

Professor(female): **Q1** Okay, today we are going to continue our discussion of the earth's natural forces, and we are going to start by talking about tides. Now, we all know that it's impossible to accurately predict the weather. As much as we can try and predict precipitation by studying cloud formations and air pressure, we simply cannot be accurate. Sometimes clouds just disappear for no apparent reason or air pressure just doesn't stay constant. But what we can predict, in great detail and accuracy, is the times and heights of tides. We can not only predict tomorrow's tides, but we can also predict each day's tides years in advance.

Q2 We can predict tides in advance by understanding the principle behind what causes them, just as we can predict rainfall, although to a lesser extent, by understanding what makes rainclouds. Tides are the combined result of the strong gravitational pull of the moon and the weaker pull of the sun. We know that the moon and the earth both follow a circular path and that the length of time it takes for each to make one full orbit does not change. That's why we can predict tides accurately.

Q1 So, how do scientists calculate tides? **Q4** There are two critical factors to consider when predicting tides – the location of the moon and the location of the sun. Let's take a look at what we need, first. The two parts that make up a tide chart are height and time. Now let's start with height. The height of the tide is actually the difference between what we call a low tide – when the water levels are lowest – and high tide – when the water levels are highest. This is also called the tidal range, which varies depending on what time of the month and year it is.

Okay, so let's look at the position of the moon and how it affects tides. Now, **Q5** the location of the moon will have the largest impact on tides because of its proximity to the earth. The gravity of the moon causes a high tide both in the area directly below the moon and on the opposite side of the earth. Low tides, on the other hand, are on the sides of the earth 90 degrees away from the moon in either direction. So, the water closest to the moon and the water on the opposite end of the earth will experience high tides due to the moon's gravitational pull.

Now let's look at the location of the sun. Although the sun is much larger and has a much stronger gravitational pull than the moon, it does not affect tides as much due to its distance. When the water directly below the sun is at a low tide, the sun will actually pull up some of the water, making the difference between low tide and high tide smaller. However, when the sun and moon align, the gravitational pull will be at its greatest, making the tidal range the widest. We can clearly see that when gravitational forces are working together, they create the largest tides, and when they work against each other, the opposite occurs.

As you can imagine, the height and time of tides are inseparable because the relative locations of the sun and moon depend on the time of day. Let's think about full moons and new moons. We know that a full moon will occur every 29.53 days. So how's this related to tidal heights? **Q3** A full moon occurs when the moon is completely illuminated by the sun, meaning that the sun and moon are located at opposite ends, you know, as far away from each other as possible. We also know that a new moon –

Application
조수를 예측하는 기술이 무엇에 사용되는가

which occurs when the sun and moon are located on the same side of the earth – will occur in between the 14th and 15th days. **These two times would be when the tides are the highest**. So by knowing the time it takes for the moon and sun to overlap, we can predict when the highest tides will be. We can then predict tides years in advance because although the sun and moon follow different orbiting paths, we can also calculate when they will overlap the most.

There are quite a few exciting possibilities for predicting tidal range. Here is one that comes to mind... You know there's a need to find alternative energy sources. And tidal energy is becoming a hot issue in terms of alternative energy. However, energy plants must always figure out how much energy can be distributed at any given time. Generate too much energy, and it will be wasted. Generate too little, and thousands of homes could be left in the dark. Without a method to predict the difference in tidal heights, there would be no way of planning in advance. However, **Q6 by knowing the variations many years beforehand, energy companies can prepare for energy surpluses and deficits beforehand**. Also, companies can plan where to build tidal turbines in areas where the variation meets the overall energy demand.

해석 지구과학 수업의 다음 강의 일부분을 들으시오.

교수(여자): 자, 오늘은 지구의 자연적 힘에 대한 논의를 계속하겠습니다. 조수 이야기로 시작해 보죠. 자, 우리는 모두 날씨를 정확히 예측하는 것이 불가능하다는 것을 알고 있죠. 구름층과 기압을 연구해서 강수를 예측하려 많이 노력할 수는 있지만, 정확할 수는 없습니다. 때때로 구름이 명확한 이유 없이 그냥 사라져 버리거나, 기압도 일정하게 유지되지 않습니다. 하지만, 우리가 아주 세부적이고 정확하게 예측할 수 있는 것이 있으니, 그것은 조수의 때와 높이입니다. 우리는 내일의 조수를 예측할 수 있을 뿐만 아니라, 수년 동안의 매일의 조수도 미리 예측할 수 있습니다. 우리는 조수를 일으키는 원인 뒤에 놓인 원리를 이해함으로써 조수를 미리 예측할 수 있습니다. 비록 그것보다는 좀 덜 정확하지만, 비구름을 형성하는 것들을 이해함으로써 강우를 예측하는 것과 마찬가지로 말이죠. 조수는 달의 강한 인력과 그보다는 약한 태양의 인력이 결합한 결과입니다. 우리는 달과 지구가 모두 원형 경로를 따른다는 것과, 달과 지구가 각각 하나의 완전한 궤도를 도는 데 걸리는 시간이 변하지 않는다는 것을 알고 있습니다. 그것이 우리가 조수를 정확하게 예측할 수 있는 이유입니다.

그렇다면, 과학자들은 어떻게 조수를 계산할까요? 조수를 예측할 때 고려해야 할 두 가지 핵심적인 요인들이 있습니다. 바로 달의 위치와 태양의 위치이죠. 우선, 우리가 필요한 것을 살펴 봅시다. 조수 차트를 구성하는 두 부분은 높이와 시간입니다. 높이부터 보도록 하죠. 조수의 높이는 사실 간조, 즉 물의 높이가 가장 낮을 때와, 만조, 즉 물의 높이가 가장 높을 때의 차이를 말합니다. 이것은 조차라고도 하는데, 일 년 중 몇 월의 언제쯤이냐에 따라 달라집니다.

좋아요, 이제 달의 위치와 그것이 조수에 어떻게 영향을 미치는지를 살펴봅시다. 자, 달의 위치는 조수에 가장 큰 영향을 미치는데, 그것은 달의 지구와의 근접성 때문입니다. 달의 인력은 달 바로 밑에 있는 지역과 지구 반대편 쪽에 모두 만조를 일으킵니다. 반면에 간조는 달에서 90도 각도로 떨어진 지구의 양쪽에서 일어납니다. 자, 달에 가장 가까이 있는 물과 지구의 반대쪽 끝에 있는 물이 달의 인력 때문에 만조를 경험하는 것이죠. 이제, 태양의 위치를 살펴보죠. 태양이 달보다 훨씬 크고 더 강한 인력을 가지고 있기는 하지만, 그 거리 때문에 조수에는 그만큼 큰 영향을 주지 않습니다. 태양 바로 아래쪽의 물이 간조일 때, 태양은 사실상 물을 조금 끌어올려 간조와 만조 사이의 차이를 더 적게 만들어줍니다. 하지만, 태양과 달이 일직선으로 있을 때는, 인력이 가장 커지게 되므로 조차가 가장 크게 벌어지게 됩니다. 두 가지 중력의 힘이 함께 작용할 때는 가장 큰 조수를 만들고, 두 중력이 서로 상반되게 작용하면 반대의 일이 일어난다는 것을 분명히 알 수가 있지요.

여러분이 상상할 수 있듯, 조수의 높이와 때는 서로 불가분의 관계에 있는데, 이는 태양과 달의 상대적인 위치가 시간대에 따라 다르기 때문입니다. 보름달과 초승달을 생각해 봅시다. 보름달은 29.53일에 한 번씩 나타난다는 것을 알고 있지요. 그러면, 이것이 조수의 높이와 어떤 관계가 있을까요? 보름달은 달이 태양에 의해 완전히 비춰질 때 생깁니다. 즉, 태양과 달이 서로 정반대쪽에, 서로에게서 가능한 한 가장 멀리 위치하는 것이죠. 우리는 또한 초승달, 즉 태양과 달이 지구의 같은 쪽에 위치해 있을 때 발생하는 초승달이 14번째 날과 15번째 날 사이에 나타난다는 것도 알고 있습니다. 이 두 때가 조수가 가장 높을 때입니다. 그래서 달과 태양이 겹쳐지는 데 걸리는 시간을 알면, 언제 가장 높은 조수가 일어날지를 예측할 수 있는 것이죠. 그러면 태양과 달이 서로 다른 궤도를 따라 돈다고 해도 언제 그 둘이 가장 겹쳐지는지를 계산할 수 있기 때문에 우리는 몇 년 앞서 조수를 예측할 수 있는 것입니다.

조차를 예측하는 데에는 꽤 많은 흥미로운 가능성들이 있습니다. 그 중 하나가 떠오르는군요... 우리가 대체 에너지원을 찾아야 한다는 것을 여러분도 알고 있겠죠. 그리고 조수 에너지는 대체 에너지 측면에서 매우 뜨거운 이슈가 되고 있습니다. 하지만 발전소들은 어떠한 주어진 시간 안에 얼마나 많은 에너지가 배분될 수 있을지를 항상 파악해야 합니다. 너무 많은 에너지를 만들어내면 에너지를 낭비하게 되고, 에너지를 너무 적게 만들어내면, 수천 곳의 가정이 어둠 속에 남겨질 테니까요. 조수 높이의 차이를 예측하는 방법 없이는, 미리 계획을 세울 방법이 없을 것입니다다. 하지만 몇 년 미리 변화를 알아 놓음으로써, 에너지 회사들은 에너지 과잉과 부족을 미리 대비할 수 있습니다. 또한, 회사들은 그 변화가 전반적인 에너지 수요를 충족시키는 지역에서 어디에 조수 작용에 의한 터빈을 지을지를 계획할 수도 있습니다.

Ⓦ natural forces 자연력   tide [taid] 조수(밀물과 썰물)   gravitational pull 중력   low tide 썰물, 간조   high tide 밀물, 만조   tidal range 조차   proximity [prɑksíməti] 가까움   gravity [grǽvəti] 중력   align [əláin] 일직선으로 하다   inseparable [inséparəbl] 불가분한   full moon 보름달   new moon 초승달   alternative energy 대체에너지   distribute [distríbju(ː)t] 분배하다   generate [dʒénərèit] 발생시키다   surplus [sə́ːrplʌs] 과잉   deficit [défisit] 부족분   beforehand [bifɔ́ːrhænd] 미리   tidal turbine 조수작용에 의한 터빈

01 강의의 주된 내용은?
Ⓐ 조차가 특정 계절에 따라 변화하는 이유에 대한 이론들
Ⓑ 조수를 정확하게 예측하는 데 필요한 정보
Ⓒ 만조에 따라 발생하는 환경적 변화들
Ⓓ 비구름을 관찰하여 날씨를 예측하는 방법

02 교수가 조수를 언급하면서 강우를 언급한 이유는?
Ⓐ 둘 다 비슷한 방식으로 예측될 수 있다는 것을 암시하려고
Ⓑ 하나는 자연의 힘이고 다른 하나는 그렇지 않다는 것을 암시하려고
Ⓒ 하나를 예측하기 위해서는 다른 하나도 예측되어야 한다는 것에 주목하려고
Ⓓ 조수의 원인은 알려져 있지만 날씨의 원인은 그렇지 않다는 것을 설명하려고

03 교수에 의하면, 태양과 달이 서로 가장 멀리 떨어져 있을 때 발생하는 일은 무엇인가?
Ⓐ 간조가 생긴다.
Ⓑ 대부분의 조수 패턴들이 가속화된다.
Ⓒ 조수의 위치가 변한다.
Ⓓ 연중 가장 높은 조수의 일부가 발생한다.

04 조차에 대해 추론할 수 있는 것은?
Ⓐ 미리 예측할 수 없다.
Ⓑ 태양의 위치에 상관없이 언제나 일정하다.
Ⓒ 만조 동안 물의 높이에 영향을 준다.
Ⓓ 태양과 달의 위치에 영향을 받는다.

05 교수에 의하면, 달이 태양보다 조수에 더 강한 영향을 미치는 이유는 무엇인가?
Ⓐ 지구 주위를 돈다.
Ⓑ 지구에 더 가깝다.
Ⓒ 태양 빛을 받는다.
Ⓓ 더 강한 중력을 가지고 있다.

06 교수에 의하면, 조차 예측은 무엇에 사용되는가?
Ⓐ 에너지 수요를 미리 계산하기 위한 데이터를 제공할 수 있다.
Ⓑ 어업 관계자들이 물고기를 잡을 가장 최적의 시간을 예측하는 데 도움이 된다.
Ⓒ 조수 에너지 발전소를 지을 올바른 장소를 찾는 데 사용될 수 있다.
Ⓓ 태양과 달이 궤도를 도는 속도를 측정하는 것을 도울 수 있다.

04 / Environmental Science

Sample Questions

01 B   02 D   03 C   04 A, D   05 B   06 A

해석 환경 과학 수업의 다음 강의 일부분을 들으시오. ◁) MP3 64

교수(남자): 좋아요, 그럼 내가 집을 구하던 때에 대한 이야기를 조금 해보죠. 음... 약 10년 전쯤이에요. 내 두 아이들은 해변에 있는 집을 정말로 원했어요. 그 애들은 가능한 한 해변과 가까이 있고 싶어 했지요. 나는 아이들에게 해변에 가까이 있는 건물을 짓는 말도 안된다는 것을 설명하려고 노력했어요. 하지만 아이들은 여전히 바다 근처에 사는 꿈을 갖고 있었어요. 그래서 아내와 나는 몇몇 집들을 살펴 봤는데... 세상에, 정말 아름답더군요! 우리 가족이 꿈에 그리던 집을 봤지만, 우리는 그 집을 살 금전적 여유가 없었습니다. 하지만 나는 그것이 불행을 가장한 축복이었다고 생각합니다. 왜 그런지는 잠시 후에 말해주도록 하지요... 음, 무슨 이야기를 하고 있었죠? 아, 그래서 우리는 결국 해변에서 차로 15분 떨어진 한 집에서 살게 되었습니다.

학생(여자): 음... Jackson 교수님? 교수님은 지난 시간에 바다 근처에 집을 짓는 것은 환경적으로 전혀 말이 안된다고 말씀하시지 않으셨던가요?

교수: 그래요, 맞습니다. 말도 안되지요. 연안역(costal zones)에 대해 설명하는 걸로 시작해보도록 하죠. 이런 연안역들은 파도가 부서지는 곳부터 시작됩니다. 하지만 우리는 육지에 있는 지역에 대해서만 이야기를 해볼 겁니다. 첫 번째 지역은 해변입니다. 여러분 모두 해변이 뭔지 알지요. 두 번째 지역은 모래언덕 지역입니다. 자, 여러 모래언덕 지역들이 있는데요. 1차 모래언덕은 물과 가장 가깝고, 더 약합니다. 바로 그 뒤에 있는 것은 골(trough)이라고 불립니다. 마지막으로, 그 뒤 쪽에는 다른 두 모래언덕들이 있습니다. 2차 모래언덕과 뒤쪽 모래언덕이죠. 자, 그러면 이 지역에 건물을 짓는 것에 대해 이야기해 봅시다. 해변에 건물을 짓는 것에 대해 어떻게 생각하나요?

학생: 이치에 좀 맞지 않는 것 같아요, 그렇지 않나요?

교수: 내 생각도 그래요. 파도와 조석 변동을 걱정해야 하겠죠. 그리고, 물론, 모래는 그 위에 건물을 지을만큼 그다지 힘이 있지도 않고요. 변화하는 해안선은 말할 것도 없죠. 우리가 현장 프로젝트로 해양 연구 센터에 갔던 것을 기억하나요? 우리는 모두 그 반도 위를 따라 오래 걸었죠. 음, 연세가 더 드신 교수님들 중 한 분이 내게 그곳이 예전에는 섬이었다고 말씀하셨어요. 30년 전만 하더라도 그곳을 걸을 수 없었다고요. 따라서, 해안선은 언제나 움직이고 모양이 변하고 있습니다. 자, 다음 지역으로 넘어가기 전에, 환경적 측면들에 대해서 이야기 해보죠. 이런 지역들이 왜 중요할까요?

학생: 음, 교수님께서 지난 시간에 해안 지역은 안쪽 연안지역을 보호한다고 하셨잖아요. 홍수, 바닷물, 그리고 폭풍우 같은 것에서 말이에요. 해안 지대는 일종의 완충지대 역할을 해요.

교수: 좋아요. 그럼 다른 지역들로 돌아가서... 음... 1차 모래언덕이죠. 이곳에는 정말로 건물을 지을 수 없습니다. 그러니까, 그 해변을 휴양을 위해서 이용할 수는 있지만, 1차 모래언덕은 실제로 어떠한 인간 활동도 버틸 수 없습니다. 그곳은 해변보다 더 민감합니다. 여러분은 모래언덕은 그저 바람으로 인해 쌓인 한 무더기의 모래 더미라고 생각할지도 모릅니다. 하지만, 이런 모래언덕들은 초목을 품을 수 있습니다. 그런데 그것들을 건드리면 초목이 생존할 수 없습니다. 자, 여기에 문제점이 있습니다. 초목이 없기 때문에, 모래를 그 자리에 지탱해 줄 것이 아무것도 없고 해변이 내륙 쪽으로 이동하기 시작합니다. 내 말은, 1차 모래언덕 없이는 모든 해안들은 침식이 되기 쉽다는 것입니다. 다음 지역은 골(trough)입니다. 이 지역은 그 앞에 있는 모래언덕보다는 조금 더 저항력이 있습니다. 지반은 더 안정적이고 초목이 더 무성합니다. 이곳은 휴양과 일부 건물 용도로 사용될 수 있습니다. 지하수의 수질을 오염시키거나 손상을 주지 않도록 해야 하지만, 일반적으로는 이곳에 건물을 짓는 것은 괜찮습니다.

학생: 그럼, 이곳이 아무런 환경적 염려 없이 개발을 할 수 있는 시작 지점인가요?

교수: 아니에요. 그곳에 건물을 지을 수 있다는 것이 꼭 그렇게 해야 한다는 의미는 아닙니다. 물론 무너지지 않는 집을 지을 수는 있겠지만, 그것은 그다지 책임감 있는 행동이 아닐 겁니다. 어쨌든, 다음으로 나머지 모래언덕들이 있습니다. 2차 모래언덕은 바다에 맞서는 최종의 방어선이고, 1차 모래언덕과 유사한 특징들을 가지고 있기 때문에 이곳에도 아무 것도 지어서는 안됩니다. 마지막 지역은 뒤쪽 모래언덕으로, 이곳은 내가 앞서 언급했던 다른 어떤 지역들보다도 더 건물을 짓는 데 적합한 곳입니다. 언급했던 처음의 두 지역은 개발하기에 최악의 장소이지만, 사람들은... 대부분의 사람들은 해변과 1차 모래언덕 위에 집을 짓고 싶어 합니다. 그들은 내가 꿈꿨던 것과 같은 꿈의 집을 원하는 거지요. 해변 바로 위에 있는 집 말입니다. 바다를 바라보는 조망은 무척 멋지겠지만, 몇 년 후에, 또는 심한 폭풍우가 친 다음이면, 여러분의 거실이 바로 물가가 될 수도 있습니다. 그것이 내가 꿈에 그리던 집에 일어났던 일입니다. 폭풍우가 물가를 바로 그 집 앞으로 옮겨왔던 것이지요. 물은 결국 빠져나갔지만, 집은 피해를 입게 되었습니다. 물이 모래를 너무 많이 휩쓸고 가버려서, 그 집은 지금 불안정한 상태입니다. 그 비싸고 무척 아름다운 집은 이제 아무도 살 수 없는 집이 되어 버렸어요.

Ⓦ **beachfront** [bíːtʃrʌnt] 해변, 해안지대   **blessing in disguise** 변장한 축복(문제인 줄 알았던 것이 뜻밖의 좋은 결과를 가져온 것)   **end up v-ing** 결국 ...하게 되다   **coastal zone** 연안역   **dune** [djuːn] 모래언덕, 사구   **tidal fluctuation** 조석 변동   **supportive** [səpɔ́ːrtiv] 힘

을 주는, 도와주는 shifting [∫íftiŋ] 이동하는 inshore [ínʃɔːr] 연안의 buffer [bʌ́fər] 완충물 vegetation [vèdʒitéiʃən] 초목, 식물 inland [ínlænd] 내륙으로 susceptible [səséptəbl] 민감한 erosion [iróuʒən] 침식 tolerant [tɑ́lərənt] 잘 견디는 groundwater [gráundwɔ̀ːtər] 지하수 collapse [kəlǽps] 붕괴되다 defense [diféns] 방어 recede [resíːd] 물러나다, 멀어지다

01 강의의 주된 내용은?
Ⓐ 해안 침식 문제에 대한 효과적인 해결책
Ⓑ 해안이 개발에 부적절한 이유들
Ⓒ 해변에서 발견되는 다양한 종류의 모래들의 비교
Ⓓ 위치에 따라 어떻게 부동산의 가치가 바뀌는지

02 교수가 골(trough)에 관해 말한 것은?
Ⓐ 해변에 가장 가까운 지역이다.
Ⓑ 바다로부터 1차 모래언덕을 보호한다.
Ⓒ 어떠한 인간 활동도 견뎌낼 수 없다.
Ⓓ 위에 건물을 지을 수 있을 만큼 충분히 안정적이다.

03 교수가 반도 위의 산책을 언급한 이유는?
Ⓐ 학생들에게 현장 연구의 세부내용을 상기시키려고
Ⓑ 여러 다른 연안역 중 하나를 예를 들어 설명하려고
Ⓒ 해안선이 어떻게 바뀌는지에 대한 예를 제시하려고
Ⓓ 해변이 환경적으로 민감한 곳이라는 것을 보여주려고

04 교수에 의하면, 1차 모래언덕에 건물을 지을 때 유발될 수 있는 문제점은 무엇인가? (두 가지 선택)
Ⓐ 그곳에 사는 식물들이 죽을 것이다.
Ⓑ 지하수가 오염될 것이다.
Ⓒ 2차 모래언덕이 더 커질 것이다.
Ⓓ 해변의 모래가 내륙 쪽으로 움직일 것이다.

05 해안가 집을 사는 사람들에 대한 교수의 태도는?
Ⓐ 그들이 오해를 받고 있다고 생각한다.
Ⓑ 그들이 어리석다고 생각한다.
Ⓒ 그들이 내륙 지역을 보호하기를 바란다.
Ⓓ 그들이 운이 좋다고 생각한다.

06 교수가 자신의 '꿈에 그리던 집'을 언급하는 이유는?
Ⓐ 해변에 건물을 짓는 것의 위험성을 예를 들어 설명하려고
Ⓑ 해안가 개발에 대한 더 긍정적인 관점을 보여주려고
Ⓒ 자신의 집이 변화하는 해안선에 의해 영향을 받았다는 것을 나타내려고
Ⓓ 환경적으로 책임감 있는 건축의 예를 들려고

Practice Questions

본문 p. 370

| 01 B | 02 C | 03 D | 04 A, C | 05 D | 06 A |

Listen to part of a lecture in an environmental science class. 📢 MP3 65

Main Idea
대체에너지: 파력 에너지

Professor(female): All right, **Q1** let's continue our discussion of alternative energy sources and move on to another potential alternative energy source: wave energy. The ocean has a virtually limitless supply of energy, but as with all other alternative energy sources, **the problem has always been how we can harness its power.**

Headset	There's clearly a lot of power available. Think about the number of waves that crash into shorelines around the world every second of every day. 🎧 **Q5** Of course I don't know the exact number, but you get my point, right? According to some estimates, ocean waves around the world could hold up to 10 trillion watts of energy. But scientists are still trying to create an effective method of capturing all of this energy.
Cause 파력 에너지에 관심을 다시 갖게 된 이유	The first method of capturing energy from ocean waves dates back to the late 1700s, but there really wasn't anything substantial developed. But then, **Q2** **in the 1970s, there was a renewed interest in wave energy. Oil and natural gas, fossil fuels, were still plentiful, but they were growing more and more expensive.** These economic factors made alternative energy sources like wave energy a hot topic. In 2003, the first marine energy test facility was established in the United Kingdom, and it has since kick started the wave energy industry.
	All right then, let's shift our focus to some new methods of harnessing the power of waves. There haven't been many large scale projects, so let's just take a look at the most promising ideas.
Cause & Effect 진동수주의 작동 원리	In, um, 1990, a wave generator called the oscillating water column was created by a team of engineers. The way it works is quite simple. As waves enter into concrete compartments, they cause the water level to rise. The rising water compresses the air inside each compartment, forcing it to pass through a small vent. This movement of air causes a motor to turn, driving a generator that produces electricity. So, the waves push the air up a tube, and the air will push a turbine as it tries to get out. It's quite an intriguing idea. These columns could be installed virtually anywhere – on the shore or in deeper waters offshore.
Disadvantage 진동수주의 단점 (1) 경제적이지 않음 **Similarity** 파력 에너지와 태양 에너지 간의 유사한 문제점	But there are some issues that need to be overcome. Mainly, it's simply not economically feasible for most countries to adopt this method. As I mentioned before, there's a vast amount of potential energy in waves, **Q3** but it's just like sunlight. **It's not concentrated in one place. The same problem that plagues solar power affects oscillating water columns.** **Q4-A** We'd just need to install too many of them, and that's a problem.
Disadvantage 진동수주의 단점 (2) 해양 생물에 영향을 미침	There are also environmental issues. **Q4-C** **A lot of noise is produced as air is pushed through the turbines. This could potentially affect birds and other marine animals.** There hasn't been any research conducted on the effects of prolonged noise on marine wildlife, so we don't know its true effects. Marine life can also get trapped or entangled in the air chambers.
Headset / Solution 진동수주의 대안 – 파워부이(동력부표)	🎧 Another alternative is something called a powerbuoy. As the name suggests, it's a device that floats on the water and captures energy from the waves. **Q6** **I'm not sure why nobody thought of it earlier.** It really does make sense when you think about it. You see a lot of buoys floating around in harbors, bouncing up and down on the waves. They might as well harness that energy, right? The powerbuoy houses turbines that move as the buoy rises and falls. When a wave passes, the buoy will go up, and as it goes down, water will rush up to the turbine, causing it to turn. This is one idea that I personally subscribe to. It's pretty much just a buoy, and, although it does have some environmental impact, it's far less than that of other alternatives.

해석 환경 과학 수업의 다음 강의 일부분을 들으시오.

교수(여자): 자, 대체에너지원에 대한 논의를 계속 이어서, 또 다른 잠재적 대체에너지원인 파력 에너지로 넘어갑시다. 바다는 사실상 끝이 없는 에너지 공급을 해주지만, 다른 모든 대체에너지원처럼, 언제나 문제는 어떻게 그 힘을 활용하는가에 있습니다.

분명, 이용 가능한 힘이 많이 있지요. 매일 매 초마다 전 세계의 해안가에 부딪치는 파도들의 수를 생각해보세요. 물론 그 정확한 수는 알지 못하지만, 내가 무엇을 말하려고 하는지 알겠지요? 어떤 추정치에 따르면, 전 세계 바다의 파도는 10조 와트만큼의 에너지를 가지고 있을지도 모릅니다. 하지만 과학자들은 여전히 이 모든 에너지를 얻을 수 있는 효과적인 방법을 만들기 위해 노력하고 있습니다.

바다의 파도에서 에너지를 얻기 위한 최초의 방법은 1700년대 후반으로 거슬러 올라갑니다만, 실제로 어떤 상당한 것이 개발되지는 않았습니다. 하지만, 1970년대에, 파력 에너지에 대한 관심이 다시 생겨났지요. 기름과 천연 가스, 화석 연료는 여전히 풍부했지만, 그것들은 점점 더 비싸졌습니다. 이러한 경제적 요인들이 파력 에너지와 같은 대체에너지원을 뜨거운 관심의 주제로 만들었습니다. 2003년에, 최초의 해양 에너지 시험 시설이 영국에 설립되었고, 그것은 그 이후로 파력 에너지 산업에 시동을 걸게 되었습니다.

자, 그럼 초점을 파도의 동력을 이용하는 몇 가지 새로운 방법들로 옮겨 봅시다. 큰 규모의 프로젝트가 많이 없었던 터라, 그냥 가장 전도유망한 발상을 살펴보도록 하죠.

음… 1990년에, 진동수주라고 불리는 파도 발생기가 한 공학자들 팀에 의해 개발되었습니다. 그것이 작동하는 방식은 매우 간단합니다. 콘크리트실 안으로 파도가 들어오면, 물의 높이가 올라갑니다. 올라간 물은 각 콘크리트실 안의 공기를 압축하여, 그 공기가 작은 통풍구를 통과해 지나가도록 합니다. 이런 공기의 움직임은 모터를 돌게 하여 전기를 만들어내는 발전기를 가동시킵니다. 그러니까, 파도가 공기를 튜브 위로 밀어 넣고, 그 공기는 빠져 나오려고 하는 도중에 터빈을 밀게 되는 거지요. 매우 흥미로운 발상입니다. 이런 기둥들은 사실상 어디에나 설치될 수 있습니다. 해안가나 해안에서 멀리 떨어진 더 깊은 물 속에도 말이지요.

하지만, 극복해야 할 문제들이 있습니다. 우선, 대부분의 국가들이 이 방법을 채택하기에는 이 방법이 경제성이 낮다는 점입니다. 앞서 언급했던 것처럼, 파도에는 거대한 양의 잠재 에너지가 있지만, 파도는 햇빛과 같습니다. 한 장소에 집중되지 않는다는 것이지요. 태양 에너지에서 골치 아팠던 똑같은 문제가 진동수주에도 영향을 미치는 것입니다. 우리는 너무 많은 진동수주들을 설치해야 하고, 그것이 문제가 되죠.

또 환경적인 문제도 있습니다. 공기가 터빈을 통해 밀고 나가면서 많은 소음이 생깁니다. 이것은 새와 다른 해양 동물들에게 잠재적으로 영향을 줄 수 있습니다. 오래 지속되는 소음이 해양 생물에게 미치는 영향에 대해서 진행된 연구가 없어서, 우리는 진동수주의 진정한 영향력을 알 수 없습니다. 해양 생물들이 또한 공기실 안에 갇히거나 걸러질 수도 있고요.

또 다른 대안은 파워부이(동력부표)라고 불리는 것입니다. 그 이름이 나타내듯이, 파워부이는 물 위에 떠서 파도로부터 에너지를 얻는 장치입니다. 아무도 왜 더 일찍 이것을 생각해내지 못했는지 모르겠어요. 생각해보면 상당히 그럴듯합니다. 여러분은 항구에서 파도에 따라 위아래로 튕겨대며 여기 저기 떠다니는 부표들을 많이 보았겠지요. 그것들도 그 에너지를 활용하는 거 아니겠어요? 파워부이는 부표가 오르락 내리락 할 때 움직이는 터빈을 탑재하고 있습니다. 파도가 지나가면 부표가 올라가고, 부표가 내려가면서 물이 터빈으로 밀려 들어와 터빈을 돌게 만듭니다. 이것은 내가 개인적으로 지지하는 한 발상입니다. 이것은 단순한 부표와 상당히 비슷합니다. 비록 이것도 일부 환경적인 영향은 분명 있지만, 이것은 다른 대안들의 환경적 영향보다는 훨씬 적습니다.

Ⓦ wave energy 파동 에너지   harness [háːrnis] 이용하다   trillion [tríljən] 1조   date back to ~ (역사가) …까지 거슬러 올라가다   renewed [rinjúːd] 새로워진   fossil fuel 화석 연료   kick start 시동을 걸다   promising [prάmisiŋ] 유망한   generator [ʤénərèitər] 발전기   oscillate [άsəlèit] 진동하다   compartment [kəmpάːrtmənt] 칸, 격실   compress [kəmprés] 압축하다   vent [vent] 통풍구, 환기구   turbine [tə́ːrbin] 터빈   offshore [ɔ(ː)ʧɔ̀ːr] 연안의   feasible [fíːzəbl] 실현 가능한   plague [pleig] 괴롭히다, 성가시게 하다   prolonged [prəlɔ́(ː)ŋd] 장기간의   trap [træp] 가두다   entangle [intǽŋgl] 얽어매다, 꼼짝 못하게 하다   buoy [búːi] 부표   subscribe to ~ …에 동의하다

01 강의의 주된 내용은?
Ⓐ 파력 에너지가 더 이상 사용되지 않는 이유들
Ⓑ 파력 에너지를 이용하는 것에 대한 문제의 가능한 해결책들
Ⓒ 에너지와 경제의 관계
Ⓓ 태양 에너지와 파력 에너지간의 유사점들

02 교수에 의하면, 1970년대에 파력 에너지의 인기를 이끈 것은 무엇인가?
Ⓐ 경제침체로 인해 더 많은 에너지가 필요하게 되었다.
Ⓑ 새로운 파력 에너지 기술들이 개발되고 있었다.
Ⓒ 석유와 천연 가스의 가격이 급격히 오르고 있었다.
Ⓓ 여러 국가들이 해양 에너지 시설들을 설립했다.

03 태양 에너지에 대해 교수가 암시하는 것은?
Ⓐ 잠재적으로 위험한 에너지원이다.
Ⓑ 부적절하다고 과학적으로 증명되었다.
Ⓒ 안전한 장소에 저장되어야 한다.
Ⓓ 퍼져 있어서 이용하기가 어렵다.

04 진동수주의 두 가지 주요 문제점은 무엇인가? (두 가지 선택)
- (A) 너무 많은 진동수주가 지어져야 할 것이다.
- (B) 진동수주에 대한 연구가 전혀 없었다.
- (C) 진동수주로 인해 해양 생물들이 피해를 입을 수 있다.
- (D) 진동수주는 충분한 에너지를 만들어내지 못한다.

05 교수가 다음과 같이 말할 때 의미하는 것은? 🔊 MP3 65_1

> Of course I don't know the exact number, but you get my point, right?

- (A) 자신이 무슨 말을 하고 싶어 했는지 기억하지 못한다.
- (B) 자료가 학생들에게 너무 어렵다.
- (C) 파도의 수는 계속해서 바뀐다.
- (D) 정확한 양을 알 필요는 없다.

강의의 일부분을 다시 듣고 질문에 답하시오. 🔊 MP3 65_2

> Another alternative is something called a powerbuoy. As the name suggests, it's a device that floats on the water and captures energy from the waves. I'm not sure why nobody thought of it earlier.

06 교수가 다음과 같이 말한 이유는?

> I'm not sure why nobody thought of it earlier.

- (A) 파워부이가 확실한 방안인 것 같다.
- (B) 파워부이에 대해 아는 사람이 너무 적다.
- (C) 파워부이는 환경에 해를 줄 수 있다.
- (D) 파워부이와 유사한 장치가 이미 있다.

05 / Geology

≽ Sample Questions
본문 p. 376

| 01 C | 02 D | 03 B | 04 A, D | 05 D | 06 C |

해석 지질학 수업의 다음 강의 일부분을 들으시오. 🔊 MP3 66

교수(남자): 자, 오늘 수업에서는 여러분 대부분에게 익숙한 주제에 대해 이야기를 해보도록 하겠습니다… 하지만, 음, 여러분은 아마도 그 세부 사항들에 대해서는 익숙하지 않을지도 모르겠군요. 내가 말하려고 하는 것은, 대륙들을 현재의 배치로 이끈 과정에 대한 것입니다.

우선, 판게아(Pangea)에 대해서 이야기하고 싶군요. 1915년에, Alfred Wegener라는 이름의 한 독일 과학자가, 판게아라고 불리는 단 하나의 대륙이 한때 존재했었다는 이론을 들고 나왔습니다. 이것은 그냥 근거 없는 주장이 아니었습니다. 그는 고대 담수 파충류들의 화석을 연구하는 과정에서 이 이론을 발달시켰습니다. 이 화석들은 어디에서건 발견되었던 반면에, 과학자들은 그 파충류들이 남미와 아프리카에서만 살 수 있었을 것임을 증명했습니다. Wegener 시대의 대부분의 과학자들이 공룡들이 육교를 통해서 한 대륙에서 다른 대륙으로 이동했다고 생각했던 반면에, Wegener는 왜 어떤 화석들은 그렇게 널리 퍼져 있었는지에 대한 더 나은 설명이 있어야 한다고 생각했습니다. 그가 내세운 답은 대륙 이동이었습니다.

대륙이동설은 판게아라고 불리는 하나의 거대한 대륙이 천천히 쪼개져 오늘날 우리가 알고 있는 대륙들이 되었다고 말합니다. 이것은 대륙들이 퍼즐 조각들과 같다는 것을 의미할 겁니다. 그리고 대륙들을 한데 맞춰보려 애를 써보면, 대륙들은 실제로 놀랍게도 잘 맞춰집니다. 물론, 이것은 단순한 우연의 일치가 아닙니다.

판게아의 존재에 대해서는 오늘날 이견이 거의 없지만, Wegener의 대륙이동설은 분명 몇 가지 오류가 있습니다. Wegener는 쇄빙선이 얼음을 뚫고 움직이는 것과 마찬가지로, 대륙들이 지구의 지각을 밀치며 움직인다고 생각했습니다. 그는 또한 대륙들이 움직인 속도를 일 년에 250 밀리미터 정도라고 계산하기도 했습니다. 이것은 그 당시에, 지구가 형성된 이후에 냉각되고 수축하면서 산들이 만들어졌다고 지질학자들이 생각했기 때문입니다.

우리는 모두 그의 이론의 이런 부분이 잘못되었다는 것을 알고 있습니다. 움직였던 것은 거대한 지질구조판들 그 자체였습니다. 그리고 우리는 지질구조판들이 Wegener가 생각한 것보다 열 배 더 느리게 움직인다는 것도 알고 있습니다. 하지만 대륙 이동에 관한 그의 주장이 틀렸다는 생각을 갖지는 마십시오. 그의 주장은 사실 맞습니다. 실제로, 이제는 이런 움직임이 일어났다는 물리적 증거가 있죠.

용암 속에는 자기장에 민감한 어떤 광물들이 있습니다. 그 광물들은 지구의 양 극 방향으로 일직선으로 나열됩니다. 그것들을 나침반의 바늘이라고 생각하세요. 이런 자성 광물들은 용암이 굳어지면서 지구의 자기장과 함께 일렬로 정렬되었습니다. 그래서, 이러한 광물들의 방향이 시대에 따라 다르기 때문에, 우리는 대륙들이 한때 다른 위치에 있었다는 것을 확신할 수 있습니다. 굳어진 용암의 한 층에 있는 광물들은 북에서 남쪽 방향으로 향하는 반면, 수백만 년 후에 형성된 맨 위의 또 다른 층(의 광물들)은 북서쪽에서 남동쪽 방향으로 향하고 있을지도 모르는 거지요. 이것이 바로 판들이 이동했다는 것을 확인해 주는 것입니다.

과학자들이 Wegener의 주장에 대해 가졌던 한 가지 문제점은, 대륙 이동의 동력이 무엇이었는지를 그가 명확히 설명할 수 없었다는 점입니다. 사람들은 그저 땅이 수축했기 때문에 대륙들이 이동했다고만 추측했습니다. 지질학자들은 이제, 지구의 가장 바깥 층인 암석권이, 독립적으로 움직이는 판들로 나뉘어져 있다는 것을 알고 있습니다. 그 판들 위에 대륙들이 끼워져 있는 것이고요. 그 판들은 암류권이라고 불리는 층 위에 '떠다닙니다.' 이 모든 것을 설명해주는 이론은 판구조론이라고 불립니다.

가장 바깥 층인 암석권에 대해 이야기해 봅시다. 그것을 단단한 껍데기라고 생각해보세요. 이 껍데기가 7~8개의 큰 판들로 부서져 나옵니다. 이것들이 이리저리 움직여 다니는 부분입니다. 그리고 이 움직임이 산과 지진 등이 생겨나게 하지요.

그러면, 이런 거대한 판들이 어떻게 움직일까요? 이 판들은 마치 컨베이어 벨트 위에 놓여진 물건들과 같이 움직입니다. 사실, 그것이 판들이 다음에 이동할 곳을 예측하는 데 사용되는 원리의 이름이기도 합니다. 바로 컨베이어 벨트 원리이지요. 그 움직임을 설명하기 위해서는, 우리는 암석권 아래에 있는 것인 암류권을 살펴보아야 합니다. 암류권은 지구의 맨틀의 가장 윗부분으로, 매우 점성이 강합니다. 즉 끈적한 액체 같은 것입니다. 암석권의 압력 때문에, 암류권은 엄청나게 뜨겁습니다. 여러분은 물이 끓을 때 어떻게 움직이는지 본 적이 있지요... 물이 어떻게 소용돌이치는지 말입니다. 이것을 대류라고 합니다. 이와 똑같은 과정이 암류권에서 일어납니다. 암류권이 소용돌이를 일으키면서 그 위의 판들을 나르게 되고, 그래서 그 판들을 이동시킵니다. 물론 다른 요인들도 작용을 하긴 하지만, 그것들의 상호 관계는 명확하지 않고 여전히 많은 논쟁의 주제가 되고 있습니다.

Ⓦ configuration [kənfìgjəréiʃən] 배열, 배치   continent [kάntinənt] 대륙   baseless [béislis] 근거 없는   freshwater [fréʃwɔ̀ːtər] 민물의   continental drift 대륙이동설   coincidence [kouínsidəns] 우연   plow through ~ ...을 애써서 가다   crust [krʌst] (지구의) 지각   ice breaker 쇄빙선   tectonic plate 지질구조판   physical evidence 물리적 증거   lava [lάːvə] 용암   magnetic field 자기장   pole [poul] (지구의) 극   orientation [ɔ̀ːriəntéiʃən] 방향   outermost [áutərmòust] 가장 바깥쪽의   lithosphere [líθəsfìər] 대륙권, 암석권   embed [imbéd] 끼워 넣다, 박아 넣다   asthenosphere [æsθénəsfìər] 암류권   plate tectonics 판구조론   viscous [vískəs] 점성의, 끈적끈적한   swirl [swəːrl] 소용돌이치다   convection [kənvékʃən] 대류

01 강의의 주된 내용은?
Ⓐ 지구가 냉각되면서 왜 산맥이 형성됐는지
Ⓑ 판의 움직임으로 형성된 하나의 거대한 대륙
Ⓒ 하나의 땅덩어리가 어떻게 현재의 대륙들로 나누어졌는지
Ⓓ 지구가 시간이 흐르면서 천천히 줄어드는 이유

02 Wegener의 이론에 의하면, 공룡들에 관해 추론할 수 있는 것은 무엇인가?
Ⓐ 다른 대륙으로 이주하기 위해 육교를 이용했다.
Ⓑ 대부분의 종은 냉혈 파충류로 여겨진다.
Ⓒ 유럽의 산악 지대에 주로 살았다.
Ⓓ 각각의 종들은 그 화석들이 나타내는 것처럼 널리 퍼져 있지는 않았다.

03 교수가 퍼즐 조각을 언급한 이유는?
Ⓐ 지구의 맨틀의 여러 다른 층들을 예를 들어 설명하려고
Ⓑ 현재의 대륙들이 서로 들어맞는 방식을 묘사하려고
Ⓒ Wegener가 어떻게 여러 다른 증거들을 한데 모았는지를 보여주려고

Ⓓ Wegener의 이론이 무언가 중요한 것을 빠뜨렸다는 것을 암시하려고

04 교수에 의하면, Wegener가 틀린 점은 무엇인가? (두 가지 선택)
Ⓐ 그는 지질구조판의 개념을 이해하지 못했다.
Ⓑ 그는 원래 하나의 대륙만이 있었다고 생각했다.
Ⓒ 그는 공룡 화석들의 중요성을 인식하지 못했다.
Ⓓ 그는 대륙들이 움직이는 속도를 잘못 계산했다.

05 교수가 자성 광물들에 대해 말한 중요한 점은?
Ⓐ 나침반 바늘을 만드는 데 사용된다.
Ⓑ 용암이 흐르는 방향을 가리킨다.
Ⓒ 그 광물들의 구성 성분은 모든 대륙에서 동일하다.
Ⓓ 그 광물들의 방향은 대륙 이동이 발생했다는 것을 증명하는 데 쓰일 수 있다.

06 교수가 다음과 같이 말할 때 암시하는 것은? ◁ MP3 66_1

> This was because, at that time, geologists thought mountains were formed as the earth cooled and shrank after forming.

Ⓐ 대륙들은 Wegener가 생각했던 것보다 더 빠르게 움직인다.
Ⓑ 다른 지질학자들의 견해로는 대륙 이동을 설명할 수 없다.
Ⓒ Wegener는 그 당시의 다른 지질학자들과 일부 견해를 같이 했다.
Ⓓ Wegener가 예측했던 움직임은 우리가 지금 알고 있는 것과 모순된다.

◈ Practice Questions
본문 p. 380

| 01 B | 02 D | 03 A, C | 04 B | 05 D | 06 C |

Main Idea
분화구는 어떻게 만들어지는가

Cause
(1) 운석의 충돌에 의해서 만들어짐

분화구를 알아보기 힘든 이유

Listen to part of a lecture in a geology class. ◁ MP3 67

Professor(female): Over the past two weeks we've been going over the processes that shape the Earth's surface. We learned about weathering, plate movement, and erosion. **Q1** In today's class we're going to look at craters. In particular, I'll be explaining how these bowl-shaped depressions are formed.

One way craters are formed is through meteorite impact. The craters that are formed this way are called impact craters. When a large meteorite, a body of solid matter falling from space at immense speeds, reaches the Earth, the high velocity impact compresses a large area of rock. The force with which the meteorite pushes downward is so great that it pulverizes the rock almost immediately after the strike, creating that wide circular crater that we all know.

You don't have to worry too much about new impact craters being formed. Most of the craters that are found on Earth were created millions of years ago, when our solar system was being formed. **Q2** These days, when a meteorite is approaching the Earth, our atmosphere acts as a shield: The friction created as the meteorite goes through the atmosphere will burn up the meteorite until it is too small to create a noticeable crater or just make it disappear altogether.

But what about all the impact craters that were formed a long time ago? You might wonder why you've never come across one. Craters on the Earth's surface are generally not noticeable. **Q3-A** Even if you were standing inside a large impact crater, you wouldn't know it. They are so wide that you would just assume that the crater rim was just some hills in the distance. Some impact craters can reach upwards of 100 kilometers in diameter. **Q3-C** Also, the forces of nature, wind, rivers, and precipitation can wear away evidence of a crater, while vegetation often grows over it. There are just a lot of things that make craters difficult to see.

So, if you want to see impact craters, you should look at the moon. Most of the craters on the moon are impact craters formed by meteorites that slammed into the lunar surface millions of years ago. **Q4** Since there is hardly any weathering on the moon, they can be seen clearly, even with a set of toy binoculars. Many of these craters are landmarks and are named after different people, everyone from an American astronaut to an ancient Greek philosopher.

Okay, what else? Oh! **Q1** Another common way craters are formed is through volcanic activity. These volcanic craters are the results of magma bursting through the Earth's crust through openings we call vents. When the high-pressure lava erupts through the surface, a tremendous amount of gas and heat is released at the same time. The resulting explosion spews out a large amount of rock, and, when the vent opening stabilizes, it leaves an indentation.

Impact and volcanic craters have similar features, beyond the circular shape all craters have. Since there are enormous amounts of energy at play, both methods of formation cause a lot of rock to be launched outward from the ground – this rock is called ejecta.

So, how do we know, what caused specific craters? There are pretty obvious clues, especially in volcanic craters, since many of them are still active. But often the only clue that geologists have is the ejecta from the impact. When a meteorite impacts the Earth, most of the ejecta creates something called an ejecta blanket. About half of the debris from the Earth and the meteorite falls within an area that extends to about twice the radius of the crater. But as I mentioned before, some ejecta can fly much further than that.

So, **Q5** there are some cases when we just don't know what caused the crater. For example, numerous long marks that look like craters are found scattered around the Argentinean plains. Some of these marks are over one kilometer long. Many scientists have debated the true cause of these craters because the debris found nearby contains contradictory evidence of their origins. **Q6** Its glass-like features suggest that it came from incredibly hot temperatures, a common characteristic of debris from volcanic eruptions... meteorite ejecta rarely contains glass. But some metals that were found in the debris were not from the Earth. Scientists continue to be perplexed by the situation.

해석 지질학 수업의 다음 강의 일부분을 들으시오.

교수(여자): 지난 2주간, 우리는 지구의 표면을 만드는 과정들에 대해 다루었습니다. 풍화작용, 판의 이동, 그리고 침식에 대해 배웠지요. 오늘 수업에서는 분화구에 대해 살펴보겠습니다. 특히, 이런 그릇 모양으로 움푹 패인 곳들이 어떻게 형성되는지에 대해 설명하도록 하겠습니다. 운석이 형성되는 한 가지 방법은 운석 충돌을 통해서입니다. 이런 방식으로 생긴 분화구들은 충돌 분화구라고 불립니다. 어떤 큰 운석, 즉 우주에서 엄청난 속도로 떨어지는 고체 덩어리가 지구에 도달할 때, 그 고속 충격이 넓은 암석 지역을 꽉 누르게 됩니다. 운석이 아래로 미는 힘은 너무나 커서, 충돌 바로 직후에 암석을 가루로 만들어 우리가 모두 알고 있는 원형의 넓은 분화구를 만들게 됩니다.

새 충돌 분화구들이 생기는 것에 대해 여러분은 너무 걱정을 하지 않아도 됩니다. 지구에서 발견되는 대부분의 분화구들은 수백만 년 전, 우리 태양계가 형성되고 있을 때 만들어졌습니다. 요즘은, 운석이 지구에 접근하고 있어도 우리의 대기가 방패 역할을 합니다. 즉 운석이 대기를 통과하면서 생기는 마찰 저항이 운석을 태워버려서, 운석은 너무 작아져 눈에 띌 만한 분화구를 만들 수 없거나 그냥 사라져 버리게 됩니다.

하지만 오래 전에 형성된 모든 충돌 분화구들은 어떨까요? 여러분은 왜 그런 것들을 하나도 보지 못했는지 궁금할 것입니다. 지구 표면의 분화구들은 대개는 눈에 확 띄지가 않습니다. 여러분이 거대한 충돌 분화구 내부에 서 있다 하더라도, 여러분은 그것을 전혀 알지 못할 겁니다. 그

달에 있는 분화구가 변화하지 않는 이유

(2) 화산 활동에 의해서 만들어짐

Similarity
impact crater와 volcanic crater의 분출물

Term
ejecta 용어 설명

Evidence
파편의 유리와 같은 특징이 있다는 것은 당시 굉장히 뜨거웠다는 증거

런 분화구들은 너무나 넓어서, 여러분은 분화구의 가장자리가 멀리 있는 언덕들일 뿐이라고 생각하게 될 겁니다. 어떤 충돌 분화구들은 지름이 100킬로미터 이상 뻗어 있기도 합니다. 또한, 자연의 힘, 즉 바람, 강, 그리고 강수가 분화구의 증거를 닳아 없앨 수도 있습니다. 식물들이 종종 그 위에 자라기도 하고 말이죠. 분화구를 보기 어렵게 하는 것들은 너무나 많습니다.

자, 충돌 분화구를 보고 싶다면, 달을 보면 됩니다. 달 표면의 대부분의 분화구는 수백만 년 전에 달 표면을 강타한 운석들로 인해 형성된 충돌 분화구입니다. 달에는 풍화작용이 거의 없어서 그 분화구들이 명확히 보이는 것이지요. 심지어는 장난감 망원경으로도 말입니다. 이런 많은 분화구들은 (달의) 주요 지형이고, 미국 우주인부터 고대 그리스 철학가에 이르는 많은 사람들의 이름을 따서 이름이 붙여졌습니다.

자, 또 뭐가 있나요? 애! 분화구가 만들어지는 또 다른 일반적인 방식은 화산 활동을 통한 것입니다. 이러한 화산 분화구들은 우리가 vent라고 부르는 구멍을 통해서 지구의 지각을 뚫고 터져 나오는 마그마로 인한 결과입니다. 높은 압력의 용암이 표면을 통해 분출되면, 엄청난 양의 가스와 열이 동시에 방출됩니다. 이로 인한 폭발로 엄청난 양의 암석들이 분출되고, vent 구멍이 안정되면 움푹 들어간 자국이 남습니다. 충돌 분화구와 화산 분화구는, 다른 모든 분화구들이 가지고 있는 원형 형태를 제외하고도 매우 유사한 특징들을 가지고 있습니다. 엄청난 양의 에너지가 작용하기 때문에, 두 가지 형성 방법은 모두 많은 양의 암석들을 땅에서 밖으로 쏟아져 나오게 만듭니다. 이러한 암석을 분출물이라고 부릅니다.

그렇다면, 무엇이 특정한 분화구를 만드는지 우리는 어떻게 알 수 있을까요? 꽤 명확한 단서들이 있습니다. 특히 화산 분화구들의 경우에는 말이지요. 많은 수가 여전히 활화산이라서요. 하지만 종종 지질학자들이 가진 유일한 단서의 하나는, 충돌에서 나온 분출물입니다. 운석이 지구에 충돌할 때, 대부분의 분출물은 분출물 덮개라고 불리는 것을 만듭니다. 지구와 운석에서 나오는 파편의 약 절반 정도가 분화구 반경의 약 두 배 정도에 이르는 지역 안으로 떨어져 내립니다. 하지만 이전에 말했듯이, 일부 분출물은 그보다 훨씬 더 멀리까지 날아갈 수 있습니다.

자, 무엇이 그 분화구를 만들었는지 알 수 없는 몇몇 경우들도 있습니다. 예를 들어, 분화구처럼 보이는 수많은 긴 자국들이 아르헨티나 평원 주위에 흩어져 발견되었습니다. 이 자국들 중 일부는 길이가 1킬로미터에 달합니다. 많은 과학자들이 이 분화구들의 실제 원인에 대해 논쟁을 벌였는데, 이는 근처에서 발견된 파편들이 파편의 기원이 되는 곳에 대해 상반되는 증거를 포함하고 있었기 때문입니다. 파편의 유리 같은 특징들은 그 파편이 엄청나게 뜨거운 온도에서 나왔다는 것을 나타내는데, 이는 화산 폭발에서 나온 파편이 가장 흔히 보이는 특징이지요... 운석 분출물이 유리를 포함하는 경우는 매우 드뭅니다. 하지만 이 파편들에서 발견된 일부 금속들은 지구의 것이 아니었습니다. 과학자들은 이 상황에 계속해서 당혹해 하고 있습니다.

Ⓦ weathering [wéðəriŋ] 풍화작용 erosion [iróuʒən] 침식 crater [kréitər] 분화구 depression [dipréʃən] 움푹한 곳 meteorite [míːtiəràit] 운석 velocity [vəlásəti] 속도 pulverize [pʌ́lvəràiz] 가루로 만들다 solar system 태양계 shield [ʃiːld] 방패 friction [fríkʃən] 마찰 rim [rim] 가장자리, 테두리 upwards of ~ ...의 이상 diameter [daiǽmitər] 지름 wear away 차츰 닳게 만들다 lunar [lúːnər] 달의 binocular [bináykjələr] 쌍안경 volcanic activity 화산 활동 crust [krʌst] (지구의) 지각 erupt [irʌ́pt] 분출하다 spew out 분출하다 stabilize [stéibəlàiz] 안정되다 indentation [ìndentéiʃən] (패인) 자국 launch [lɔːntʃ] 발사하다 ejecta [idʒéktə] 분출물 debris [dəbríː] 잔해, 부스러기 radius [réidiəs] 반지름 contradictory [kɑ̀ntrədíktəri] 모순되는 perplexed [pərplékst] 당혹한

01 강의의 주된 내용은?
Ⓐ 침식이 지구 표면에 미치는 영향
Ⓑ 분화구가 형성되는 두 가지 다른 방법들
Ⓒ 화산 분출과 그 영향들
Ⓓ 지구와 달의 형성

02 교수에 의하면, 오늘날에는 충돌 분화구가 거의 생기지 않는 이유는 무엇인가?
Ⓐ 운석들이 수백만 년 전에 만들어졌다.
Ⓑ 달이 운석을 막는 방패 역할을 한다.
Ⓒ 지구가 나이가 들면서 땅이 단단해졌다.
Ⓓ 대기가 대부분의 운석들을 태워버린다.

03 교수에 의하면, 대부분의 사람들이 충돌 분화구를 알아차리지 못하는 이유는 무엇인가? (두 가지 선택)
Ⓐ (분화구의) 가장자리가 너무 멀리 있을 수 있다.
Ⓑ 분화구가 종종 언덕 옆에 위치해 있다.
Ⓒ 자연이 분화구의 특징들을 숨긴다.
Ⓓ 간혹 집들이 그 위에 지어진다.

04 달의 표면에 대해 교수가 암시하는 것은?
Ⓐ 오랫동안 운석이 강타하지 않았다.
Ⓑ 지구의 표면보다 더 느리게 변화한다.

Ⓒ 지구에서 뚜렷하게 보이지 않는다.
Ⓓ 인류의 활동으로 변화가 생겼다.

05 분화구에서 나온 분출물에 대해 교수가 암시하는 것은?
Ⓐ 분화구의 기원에 상관없이 똑같아 보인다.
Ⓑ 종종 너무 오래 되어서 연구원들이 제대로 분석할 수 없다.
Ⓒ 화산 활동에 의해 형성된 분화구 주위에서만 존재한다.
Ⓓ 분화구의 원인을 언제나 분명히 알려주는 것은 아니다.

06 분화구 근처의 유리 같은 파편의 존재가 나타내는 것은?
Ⓐ 분출물이 긴 자국들을 만들었다.
Ⓑ 분화구가 비정상적으로 깊다.
Ⓒ 엄청난 양의 열이 수반되었다.
Ⓓ 운석이 엄청난 속도로 지구를 강타했다.

06 / Engineering

≋ Sample Questions 본문 p. 386

| 01 C | 02 B | 03 C | 04 A | 05 A, D | 06 B |

해석 공학 수업의 다음 강의 일부분을 들으시오. ◁ MP3 68

교수(남자): 이 세상에는 몇몇 굉장히 멋진 현대 건축물들이 있습니다. 그 중 하나를 미국 서부에서 찾아볼 수 있는데, 이것은 여전히 미국의 수천 가정에 전력을 공급하고 있습니다. 그것은 콜로라도 강의 물을 이용하여 이 전기를 만듭니다. 그게 무엇인지 아는 사람이 있나요? 그래요, Anne?

학생 1(여자): 후버댐인가요?

교수: 맞아요. 대공황 시기 때 일자리 수천 개를 창출하기 위해 지어진 후버댐은 세계에서 가장 큰 댐 중 하나입니다. 사실, 1930년대에 그 댐이 지어졌을 시기에는 후버댐은 세상에서 가장 큰 콘크리트 구조물이었어요. 그 이후로 더 거대하고 더 복잡한 구조물들이 있어 왔지만, 나는 여전히 후버댐에 쓰인 공학 기술이 굉장히 인상적이라고 생각합니다. 오늘날에조차, 후버댐과 같은 댐은 많지 않습니다. 자, 무엇이 후버댐을 그렇게 특별하게 만드는지 추측해볼 사람이 있나요? 아... 그래요, Dan?

학생 2(남자): 댐의 모양에 대해 읽었던 기억이 나요. 대부분의 댐들은 일직선이지만, 후버댐은 U자처럼 지어졌어요.

교수: 좋아요! 그러면, 건축가들이 이 댐을 왜 그런 독특한 모양으로 짓기로 했는지 아는 사람이 있나요?

학생 1: 그건 그 댐이 콜로라도 강을 막고 있다는 사실과 관련 있지 않나요? 콜로라도 강이 미국에서 다섯 번째로 긴 강이라는 것을 읽었던 기억이 나요.

교수: 바로 그거에요! 공학자들과 건축가들은 1평방 피트당 4만 5천 파운드에 달하는 수압을 다룰 수 있는 방법을 찾아야만 했어요. 후버댐은 아치 중력 댐이라고 불리는 댐이에요. (화면에 보여준다) 음, 댐이 U자처럼 지어졌다고 말했었죠? 그것이 '아치 중력 댐'의 '아치(arch)'라는 말이 생긴 이유입니다. 아치 형태는 구조물이 더 많은 하중을 지탱할 수 있게 해주죠. 이 댐은 로마인들이 무거운 지붕과 벽들을 지탱하기 위해 사용했던 아치와 똑같은 작용을 합니다. 아치의 꼭대기에 있는 돌들이 아치를 위에서 내리 누르지만, 아치 형태가 그 압력을 아치의 양 끝 부분으로 분산시키는데, 그 양쪽 끝은 훨씬 더 강하지요. 같은 원리가 아치 중력 댐에도 작용합니다. 물살이 아치 부분을 밀지만, 그 수압의 일부는 협곡 벽으로 전해져서 댐이 그 엄청난 하중을 다 지탱할 필요가 없게 되는 것입니다. 네, Dan?

학생 2: 그 설계가 그렇게 효과적이라면 어째서 다른 댐들은 아치 형태로 지어지지 않은 거죠?

교수: 좋은 지적이에요. 화면의 사진을 보고 댐이 어디에 위치해 있는지 살펴보도록 하죠.

학생 2: 댐이 있는 곳이... 음, 협곡처럼 보이는데요.

교수: 바로 그거에요! 협곡들은 강의 다른 지역에 비해 일반적으로 매우 좁지요. 아치형 댐은 가파른 암석 벽이 있는 좁은 협곡에서 가장 큰 효력을 발휘합니다. 음, 그곳이 '아치 중력 댐'의 '아치' 부분이 되는 것이지요. 이제 중력 부분을 살펴봅시다. 사진을 다시 보도록 하죠. 댐의 아

랫부분에 무언가 특이한 것이 있는 것을 알아챘나요? Anne?

학생 1: 네... 마치... 바깥쪽으로 휘어져 있는 것 같아요. 구부러진 것처럼요.

교수: 바깥쪽으로 휘어져는 있지만 구부러지지는 않았어요. 사실, 댐의 아랫부분은 그 높이만큼이나 두껍습니다. 댐의 아랫부분은 두께가 600피트가 넘어요, 반면에 윗부분은 그 두께가 50피트도 되지 않지요. 이것이 후버댐이 중력 댐이라고 불리는 이유입니다. 후버댐은 아랫부분이 매우 무거운데, 그곳은 수압이 최대로 작용하는 곳입니다. 비록 아치 형태가 수압을 협곡 벽 쪽으로 분산시키는 데 도움이 되긴 하지만, 이것으로는 여전히 그 엄청난 양의 물을 저지할 만큼 충분하지는 않아요. 하지만, 넓은 아랫부분이 그것을 가능하게 해주지요. 수압을 아랫부분의 더 넓은 면적으로 나누어 줄어들게 하면서 말입니다. 이런 디자인은 다른 많은 장점들도 있어요. 후버댐은 그 자체의 중량을 지탱해야 하기도 합니다. 알다시피, 구조물이 높을수록 아랫부분에 가해지는 힘은 더 많아집니다. 댐의 아랫부분은 댐을 지탱할 수 있도록 훨씬 더 두꺼워야 합니다. 이것이 댐의 윗부분이 아랫부분에 비해 매우 얇은 이유입니다. (아랫부분만큼) 튼튼해야 할 필요가 없는 윗부분이 더 얇기 때문에, 더 많은 구조적인 힘이 물을 멎게 하는 데 쓰일 수 있습니다. 콘크리트가 비싸기 때문에, 이런 (점점 가늘어지는) 디자인은 또한 훨씬 경제적이기도 하지요. 대체적으로, 후버댐은 여전히 현대 건축의 걸작품입니다.

Ⓦ marvellous [mɑ́ːrvələs] 놀라운, 경이로운   structure [strʌ́ktʃər] 건축물, 구조물   Great Depression (미국의) 대공황   water pressure 수압   square foot 평방 피트   gravity [grǽviti] 중력   distribute [distríbju(ː)t] 나누어주다   canyon [kǽnjən] 협곡   gorge [gɔːrdʒ] 협곡   base [beis] 맨 아래 부분   outward [áutwərd] 밖으로 향하는   dissipate [dísəpèit] 소멸시키다   foundation [faundéiʃən] 토대   exert [igzə́ːrt] 가하다, 행사하다   economical [ìːkənámikəl] 경제적인, 실속 있는

01 강의의 주요 목적은?
Ⓐ 미국의 댐들의 역사를 논의하려고
Ⓑ 콘크리트로 건설하는 가장 효과적인 방법들을 설명하려고
Ⓒ 어떤 거대한 구조물의 혁신적인 공학을 설명하려고
Ⓓ 대공황 시기의 미국의 건축에 대해 말하려고

02 후버댐에 대한 교수의 의견은?
Ⓐ 주변 가정에 위협이 된다고 생각한다.
Ⓑ 뛰어난 구조물이라고 생각한다.
Ⓒ 미국이 대공황에서 회복하는 데 도움이 되었다고 생각한다.
Ⓓ 사람들이 생각하는 것만큼 복잡하지는 않다고 생각한다.

03 교수가 후버댐의 위치를 언급한 이유는?
Ⓐ 그 지역의 기후의 영향을 나타내려고
Ⓑ 두 강의 물리적 차이를 비교하려고
Ⓒ 아치 중력 댐이 지어질 수 있는 장소를 설명하려고
Ⓓ 콜로라도 강의 규모를 강조하려고

04 교수에 의하면, 댐의 아치 형태가 중요한 이유는 무엇인가?
Ⓐ 그것이 댐이 물의 무게를 분산시키는 데 도움이 된다.
Ⓑ 그것이 건축자들이 댐을 더 높게 만드는 것을 가능하게 했다.
Ⓒ 그것이 댐이 좁은 협곡에 들어맞도록 해준다.
Ⓓ 그것이 물이 댐 주위를 쉽게 흐르도록 해준다.

05 후버댐의 넓은 아랫부분에 대해 교수가 지적하는 점은? (두 가지 선택)
Ⓐ 댐의 중량을 더 넓은 면적으로 퍼뜨리도록 해준다.
Ⓑ 댐을 아치 형태로 짓기 위해 필요했다.
Ⓒ 그것 때문에 댐을 건설하는 데 비용이 많이 들었다.
Ⓓ 댐을 구조적으로 튼튼하게 만들기 위해 필요했다.

강의의 일부분을 다시 듣고 질문에 답하시오. ◁ MP3 68_1

> Well, that's the "arch" part of "arch gravity dam." Let's look at the gravity part now. Let's see the picture again. Do you notice anything unusual about the base of the dam? Anne?

06 교수가 다음과 같이 말한 이유는?

> Do you notice anything unusual about the base of the dam?

Ⓐ 댐에 구조적 결함이 있다는 것을 암시하려고
Ⓑ 댐의 또 다른 흥미로운 면을 지적하려고
Ⓒ 댐과 댐의 크기 간의 관계를 알려주려고
Ⓓ 댐의 아랫 부분의 일반적인 디자인을 강조하려고

≈ Practice Questions
본문 p. 390

| 01 B | 02 A | 03 D | 04 B | 05 A | 06 C |

Listen to part of a lecture in an engineering class. ◁ MP3 69

Professor(female): Okay, let's get started by talking about mistakes. Sometimes even the greatest architects make crucial mistakes, failing to take into account all of the different factors involved in constructing large buildings. In order to solve these problems, it is necessary to modify, or improve existing structures.

One of the methods used to do so is called architectural stabilization. It involves improving the foundation of an existing structure by stabilizing the levelness of the structure – making it stand up straight. Of course, it's better for the structure to be built on a proper foundation to start with. And in order for any structure to be stable, the ground beneath it must be stable. That's why engineers and architects take great lengths to ensure that the ground is stable before construction starts.

Term
architectural stabilization 용어 설명

Requirement
토대가 평평해야 함

Main Idea
건축공학의 문제점
⟨Problem – Solution⟩

But **Q1** **what if the engineers make a mistake and start building on unstable ground? Or what if too much weight is added to the structure? The building will no longer be level. In these situations, structural engineers are needed to stabilize the foundation of the building and the ground it rests on.**

Example
문제점의 구체적인 예시
– 피사의 사탑

Let me give you an example. I'm sure you've heard about the Leaning Tower of Pisa, which is located in central Italy. The tower is a huge tourist attraction and tens of thousands of people visit it every year. As you probably know, its popularity is due to the way it tilts. But this was not part of the tower's design. Rather, it was a result of mistakes made by the original architect.

Problem
진짜 건축가를 확인하기 어려움

Actually, **Q5** there is a little controversy regarding who the actual architect was. Some historians believe it was the famous sculptor Bonanno Pisano. But most think Diotisalvi is the designer because of his other work in Pisa during that period. However, he signed all of his works. The absence of a signature by Diotisalvi in the bell tower leads to further speculation.

Anyway, to get back to my point, the tower was built on unstable subsoil. It had already begun to tilt by the time the second floor was completed. Construction was halted and could not commence until the ground became stable. As a matter of fact, it was 100 years before construction started again. When the tower was finished, a bell chamber was installed on the top floor. The heavy bells caused the tower to tilt even further.

Even though engineers at that time believed that the tower would be stable, it continued to lean more and more until it reached the point where it was in danger of collapsing. Can you imagine the damage that could be caused by a seven-story building

Cause & Effect
사탑이 기우는 이유

Problem
밀도가 낮은 땅을 다지기 위한 시공법의 문제점

Solution
평행추

Opinion
문제가 발생하고 나서 해결하는 것보다 시공 전에 확인해서 문제점이 없도록 주의해야 함

made of solid marble and granite falling over?

The tower, however, did not fall, remaining upright for centuries. But in 1990 the tower was closed to the public due to safety concerns. The Italian government enlisted the help of engineers, mathematicians, and historians to solve the problem. They first had to find out what was causing the tower to lean. Engineers took soil samples from around the tower to figure out the soil density. If the soil was not evenly dense across the whole base, this would be the reason why the tower was tilting. Eventually, the **Q2 engineers confirmed that the tilt was accelerating due to the softer soil on the lower side.** Although the base soil is believed to have originally been level, it did not compact at the same rate. **As the soil on one side was more porous, it compacted more quickly, causing the ground to become uneven.**

After the engineers found the cause, they sought to remedy the situation by making the density equal, removing the porous soil, and replacing it with denser material. **Q3 But there was a problem. The engineers could not do anything about the soil because the tower had tilted too much. Removing the base soil to replace it with concrete would cause the tower to tumble.**

So, **Q4 in order to make the structure stable, the engineers used counterweights. After removing some soil, they used more than 800 tons of lead to raise one end of the base. They also removed the bells to make the tower lighter.** Eventually, the tower was moved to a straighter angle.

Next, the engineers removed the weak soil and reinforced the ground with concrete to prevent it from sinking again. When they were finished, they deemed the tower to be stable for at least another 300 years. After a decade of corrective reconstruction and stabilization efforts, the tower was reopened to the public on December 15, 2001. So what does this tell us about architectural stabilization? Even though there may be a single cause, many combined steps have to be taken in order to solve the problem. While it is important to learn the various methods used to stabilize structures, **Q6 we have to keep in mind that it is better to make things right the first time around by learning from mistakes of the past.**

해석 공학 수업의 다음 강의 일부분을 들으시오.

교수(여자): 좋아요. 실수에 대해 이야기하는 것으로 수업을 시작해보죠. 가끔은 위대한 건축가들조차도 중대한 실수를 저지릅니다. 큰 건물들을 지을 때 수반되는 여러 다른 요인들을 모두 고려하지 못해서 말이지요. 이러한 문제들을 해결하기 위해서는, 기존 구조물들을 변경하거나 개선시키는 것이 필요합니다.

그렇게 하기 위해 쓰이는 방법들 중 하나는 건축학적 안정화라고 불립니다. 그것은 구조물의 수평을 안정화시킴으로써 기존의 구조물의 토대를 향상시키는 것을 포함합니다. 즉 구조물을 똑바로 서도록 만드는 것입니다. 물론, 처음부터 구조물이 올바른 토대 위에 지어지는 것이 더 좋지요. 그리고 어떤 구조물이든 안정적으로 서 있기 위해서는, 그 밑에 있는 땅이 안정적이어야 합니다. 그것이 공학자들과 건축가들이 건축이 시작되기 전에 땅이 안정적인지 확인하기 위해 많은 노력을 하는 이유입니다.

하지만 만일 공학자들이 실수를 해서, 불안정한 토대 위에 짓게 되면 어떨까요? 또는 구조물에 너무 많은 하중이 더해지게 되면 어떻게 될까요? 그 건물은 더 이상 반듯할 수 없겠죠. 이런 상황들에서는, 그 건물의 토대와 그것이 서 있는 땅을 안정화시키기 위해서 구조 공학자들이 필요합니다.

예를 하나 들어보지요. 여러분은 이탈리아 중부에 있는 피사의 사탑에 대해 들어봤을 것입니다. 이 사탑은 엄청난 관광지여서 해마다 수많은 사람들이 사탑을 찾습니다. 여러분이 아마 알고 있듯이, 이 사탑의 인기는 그것이 기울어진 방식 때문이지요. 하지만, 이것은 이 사탑의 설계의 일부가 아니었습니다. 그보다는, 원래 건축가의 실수로 인한 결과였지요.

사실, 사탑의 실제 건축가가 누군지에 관해서는 약간의 논란이 있습니다. 몇몇 역사가들은 유명한 조각가인 Bonanno Pisano가 지었다고 생각합니다. 하지만, 대부분의 사람들은 Diotisalvi가 설계자라고 생각합니다. 그 시기 피사 지역에서의 그의 다른 작품들 때문이지요. 하지만, 그는 그의 모든 작품에 서명을 남겼습니다. (피사의 사탑의) 종루에 Diotisalvi의 서명이 없다는 사실이 더 많은 추측들을 불러 일으키게 되었습니다.

어쨌거나, 본론으로 돌아와서, 사탑은 불안정한 하층토 위에 지어졌습니다. 탑은 이층이 지어졌을 때쯤 이미 기울기 시작했습니다. 건축은 중단되었고, 지반이 안정화 될 때까지는 다시 착수될 수 없었습니다. 사실, 다시 건축이 재개될 때까지는 100년이나 걸렸습니다. 탑이 완성되었을 때, 꼭대기 층에 종이 있는 방이 설치되었습니다. 무거운 종들로 인해 사탑은 더욱 더 기울어지게 되었지요.

당시의 공학자들은 탑이 안정화될 것이라고 생각했지만, 탑은 계속해서 점점 더 기울어져 무너질 위기에 처할 지경까지 되었습니다. 단단한 대리석과 화강암으로 만들어진 7층 높이의 건물이 무너질 때 생길 수 있는 피해를 상상할 수 있겠습니까?

하지만 사탑은 무너지지는 않았습니다. 선 채로 수세기 동안 남아 있었죠. 하지만 1990년에, 사탑은 안전 우려로 인해 일반인들의 출입이 금지되었습니다. 이탈리아 정부는 문제를 해결하기 위해 공학자들과 수학자들, 그리고 역사가들의 도움을 요청했습니다. 그들은 우선 무엇이 탑을 기울어지게 했는지를 알아내야 했습니다. 공학자들은 토양의 밀도를 알아보기 위해 탑 주변의 토양 샘플을 채취했습니다. 만일 토양이 전체 밑부분에 걸쳐 고른 밀도를 보이지 않는다면, 이것이 사탑이 기울고 있는 이유가 될 것입니다. 마침내, 공학자들은 더 낮은 부분의 부드러운 토대 때문에 탑의 기울기가 가속화되고 있다는 것을 확인했습니다. 밑부분의 토양은 원래 수평이라고 여겨졌지만, 같은 비율로 빽빽하지가 않았습니다. 한쪽 면의 토양이 더 구멍이 많아서, 그쪽이 더 빨리 다져지게 되어 땅이 고르지 않게 되어 버린 것이죠.

공학자들은 원인을 발견한 후, 밀도를 똑같이 하고 다공성 토양을 제거한 뒤 그 자리에 밀도가 더 높은 물질로 교체하는 방법을 써서 그 상황을 해결하려 시도했습니다. 하지만 문제가 있었죠. 사탑이 너무나 많이 기울어져 있어서 공학자들은 토양에 아무것도 할 수가 없었습니다. 밑부분의 토양을 콘크리트로 교체하기 위해 제거하게 되면 사탑이 무너지게 될 것이었어요.

그래서, 구조물을 안정시키기 위해 공학자들은 평행추를 사용했습니다. 밑부분의 토양을 조금 제거한 후, 그들은 밑부분의 한쪽 끝을 올리기 위해 800톤이 넘는 납 덩어리를 이용했습니다. 그들은 또한 탑이 좀 더 가벼워지도록 종들도 없앴습니다. 마침내, 탑은 좀 더 수직 방향의 각도로 움직였습니다.

다음으로, 공학자들은 약한 토양을 제거하고, 다시 가라앉는 것을 막기 위해 콘크리트로 땅을 강화했습니다. 작업이 끝났을 때, 그들은 사탑이 앞으로 최소 300년 정도는 안정적일 것이라고 생각했습니다. 십 년에 걸친 수정 복원 작업과 안정화 노력 끝에, 사탑은 2001년 12월 15일에 다시 대중에게 공개되었습니다.

자, 이것은 우리에게 건축학적 안정화에 관해 무엇을 말해주나요? 원인은 한 가지이더라도 그 문제를 해결하기 위해서는 수많은 결합된 조치들이 취해져야 한다는 점입니다. 구조물을 안정시키는 데 사용되는 다양한 방법들을 배우는 것도 중요하지만, 우리는 과거의 실수들로부터 교훈을 얻음으로써 처음부터 일을 바르게 하는 것이 더 낫다는 것을 염두에 두어야 합니다.

Ⓦ take into account ...을 고려하다 factor [fǽktər] 요인 existing [igzístiŋ] 현존하는 stabilization [stèibəlizéiʃən] 안정화 foundation [faundéiʃən] (건물의) 토대 levelness [lévəlnəs] 수평임, 평평함 tilt [tilt] 기울다 speculation [spèkjəléiʃən] 추측, 짐작 halt [hɔːlt] 중단시키다 commence [kəméns] 시작되다 chamber [tʃéimbər] 실(室) collapse [kəlǽps] 붕괴되다 marble [mάːrbl] 대리석 granite [grǽnit] 화강암 upright [ʌ́prait] 똑바른 enlist [inlíst] (협조·참여를) 요청하여 얻다 density [dénsəti] 밀도 accelerate [əksélərèit] 가속화하다 compact [kəmpǽkt] (단단히) 다지다 porous [pɔ́ːrəs] 다공성의 uneven [ʌníːvən] 평평하지 않은 remedy [rémədi] 개선하다 tumble [tʌ́mbl] 폭삭 무너지다 counterweight [káuntərwèit] 평형추 deem [diːm] (...로) 여기다 corrective [kəréktiv] 수정의

01 강의의 주된 내용은?
Ⓐ 유럽의 기울어지는 탑들의 역사와 설계
Ⓑ 한 유명한 구조물의 안정성이 어떻게 향상되었는지
Ⓒ 과거에 탑을 설계하는 데 사용되었던 건축 방법들
Ⓓ 한 대단히 높은 구조물을 지을 때 직면한 문제점들

02 교수에 의하면, 피사의 사탑이 기울어지게 된 주요 원인은 무엇인가?
Ⓐ 밑에 있는 토양의 한쪽 면이 더 부드러웠다.
Ⓑ 탑의 한쪽을 지지하기 위해 납이 사용되었다.
Ⓒ 너무 많은 관광객들이 사탑을 방문했다.
Ⓓ 콘크리트로 된 토대가 한쪽에만 만들어졌다.

03 사탑을 안정화할 때 공학자들이 직면한 문제점은?
Ⓐ 관광객들이 프로젝트 중에도 계속해서 사탑을 방문했다.
Ⓑ 탑 위의 종들이 평행추 역할을 했다.
Ⓒ 콘크리트를 발랐을 때 아랫부분이 손상되었다.
Ⓓ 토양을 밑에서 제거할 경우 탑이 무너질 것이었다.

04 교수에 의하면, 공학자들은 토대 부분의 토양을 안정화시키기 전에 탑이 쓰러지는 것을 막기 위해 무엇을 했는가?
- Ⓐ 토대에 콘크리트를 추가했다.
- **Ⓑ 한쪽 면을 더 무겁게 했다.**
- Ⓒ 사탑의 무게를 더 무겁게 했다.
- Ⓓ 관광객들이 탑을 방문하는 것을 막았다.

05 피사의 사탑을 지은 건축가에 대해 교수가 말한 것은?
- **Ⓐ 건축가의 신원에 관해서는 어떠한 결정적인 증거도 없다.**
- Ⓑ 사실은 두 명의 건축가가 사탑을 설계하기 위해 함께 작업했다.
- Ⓒ 조각들의 존재는 그 건축가가 예술가이기도 했다는 것을 나타낸다.
- Ⓓ 그 건축가가 사용했던 기술은 안전한 건물을 만들기에는 충분히 선진화되지 않았다.

06 건축학적 안정화 기법을 사용하는 것에 대한 교수의 의견은?
- Ⓐ 역사학자들이 과거의 위대한 건축가들에 대해 더 많이 배울 수 있도록 돕는다.
- Ⓑ 어떤 건물의 토대에 손을 대는 것은 결코 좋은 생각이 아니다.
- **Ⓒ 애초에 실수를 피하는 것이 더 중요하다.**
- Ⓓ 색다른 건물들의 독특한 아름다움을 파괴할 수도 있다.

Chapter 4. Lecture Topics

Unit 6. Social Science

01 / Anthropology

Sample Questions

본문 p. 398

| 01 C | 02 D | 03 B | 04 B | 05 A | 06 D |

해석 인류학 수업의 다음 강의 일부분을 들으시오. ◁》 MP3 70

교수(여성): 자, 고대 메소아메리카 문화의 사람들이 수천 년 전의 기술과 건축, 그리고 예술을 어떻게 공유했는지에 대해 논의했으니, 이제는 이 문화 중 하나인 올멕 문명의 예술에 대해서 이야기하고자 합니다. 음, 올멕 문명은 기원전 약 1200년경에 시작되어, 단지 700년 정도만 지속되었습니다. 기원전 400년경, 올멕 사회는 사라졌습니다. 오늘날 그들이 정확히 어떤 사람들이었는지를 알려주는 지표들은 많지 않습니다. 자, 왜 이것이 예술과 관련해서 중요할까요? Eric?

학생(남성): 음... 어떤 예술 작품을 분석하기 위해서는, 그것을 창조한 사람들에 대해 뭔가 알아야 하잖아요.

교수: 정확해요. 우리는 올멕 문명에 대해서 많은 것을 알지는 못하지만, 우리가 알고 있는 사실은, 그 사람들이 남부 멕시코의 늪지대가 많은 저지에 위치한 작은 공동체 속에서 농경생활을 했다는 것입니다. 이들은 칠면조를 키웠고, 낚시를 했고, 옥과 같은 귀중품 거래를 위한 광범위한 교역망도 가지고 있었습니다. 그들에게는 또한 문자도 있었지요. 여러 예술 작품에서 이들의 문자를 볼 수 있기 때문에 이것을 알 수 있습니다. 하지만 그들이 유명한 것은, 그들의 문자가 아니라 바로 그들의 예술 때문입니다.

올멕 사람들은 채색된 벽화, 고급 도자기, 옥으로 조각한 작은 상들과 같은 광범위한 예술 공예품들을 만들었습니다. 하지만 그들의 거대한 석조 두상들이 그들의 가장 유명한 예술품입니다. 이게 그 중 하나의 사진입니다. (화면에 보여준다) 이 두상들은 아주 커서, 대략 3미터 정도의 높이입니다. 우리 대부분의 키보다 거의 두 배나 되는 높이지요. 그리고 거의 그들의 높이만큼이나 너비도 넓습니다. 또한 그들은 모두 꽤 비슷하게 생겼습니다. 즉, 모두 비슷한 특징들을 가지고 있다는 말입니다. 두상을 한번 설명해 볼 사람 있나요? 네.

학생: 정말 둥글고, 코는 넓고, 입술은... 매우 두꺼운데 밑으로 처진 입술이네요. 어떻게 보면 인상을 쓰고 있는 것처럼 보여요.

교수: 학생이 방금 언급한 특징들은 매우 독특합니다. 박물관에서 이들 두상 중 하나를 보게 되면, 여러분은 이렇게 말할 거예요. "아, 틀림없이 올멕이다." 이 조각상들의 또 다른 놀라운 점은 재료입니다. 이 두상들은 매우 단단한 유형의 바위를 깎아 만든 것인데, 올멕인들은 석기만을 사용했습니다. 그들은 철기가 없었어요. 하지만, 그들은 돌만을 이용해서 많은 고고학자들이 고대 메소아메리카에서 최상의 품질의 조각상으로 여기는 작품을 만들어낸 것입니다. 가장 기본적인 도구들을 가지고 얻어낸 정교함의 수준을 생각하면 정말 놀라운 일이지요.

학생: 머리 위에는 뭔가요? 머리카락 같지는 않아요. 헬멧처럼 보이는데요?

교수: 아, 맞아요. 많은 사람들은 그 헬멧을 전쟁에서 싸우기 위해 입는 일종의 갑옷 같은 것이라 생각합니다. 이런 헬멧은 아마도 전투에서 그들을 보호해주긴 하겠지만, 대부분의 고고학자들과 미술사가들은 이 헬멧들이 스포츠에서도 사용되었을 것이라고 생각합니다... 구체적으로 말하면, 의식적 성격을 가진 구기종목과 같은 데에서 말이지요. 올멕 선수들은 고무공을 이용하여 코트에서 이런 경기를 했습니다. 여기서 또 다른 흥미로운 점이 등장합니다. 여러분이 정글에서 고대 조각상을 하나 발견했는데, 헬멧이 그 머리 위에 조각되어 있었다고 해봅시다. 여러분이 그 조각상이 만들어진 문화에 대해 아무것도 모른다면, 여러분은 그저 그것이 전쟁 중의 보호를 위해서 사용되었을 것이라고 추측을 할 겁니다. 하지만 여러분이 그 지역의 다른 고대인들이 특정 종류의 스포츠를 했다는 것을 알게 되면 어떨까요? 그들이 경기를 하는 동안에 보호 장비를 착용했다는 것을 알게 된다면요? 여러분은 당연히 다른 결론에 도달하겠지요. 그것은 전사의 조각상이 아닐 수도 있습니다. 아마도 운동선수의 조각상일 수도 있는 것이죠. 이것이 바로 예술을 알기 위해 문화를 안다는 것의 의미입니다. 미술사가가 되려면 여러분은 인류학과 고고학 같은 다른 학문들에 대한 지식도 가지고 있어야 합니다. 그렇게 되면 여러분은 다른 문화들이 어떻게 서로에게 영향을 주고, 이런 문화들이 어떻게 그들의 예술 양식과 상징에 반영되었는지를 알 수 있습니다. 다시 말해, 여러분은 그저 예술만을 연구해서는 안됩니다. 그렇게 하면, 여러분은 한 예술품의 타당한 해석을 놓칠 수도 있습니다. 여러분은 예술에서의 상징들을 관련시킬 무언가가 필요할 것 같네요... 음... 재규어를 예로 들어보죠. 재규어는 올멕 예술에서 흔히 발견됩니다. 이 커다란 포식성 고양이류 동물은 한때 미대륙 전역에서 발견되었습니다. 재규어는 올멕 문화와 종교에서 매우 중요한 부분이었습니다. 그래서 이들의 예술에 재규어가 종종 나타난다는 것은 놀라운 일이 아니지요. 재규어는 통치자와 같은 중요한 사람들을 칭송하기 위해 그들을 나타내는 데에 종종 이용되었습니다. 심지어 석조 두상에서도 이들의 영향을 볼 수 있습니다. 두상의 특징들이 재규어와 다소 닮아있는 것을 알아볼 수 있나요?

학생: 음... 음, 입이요, 입술이 아래로 말려 내려간 방식이... 약간 재규어의 입처럼 보이네요.

교수: 맞아요! 이것이 많은 연구자들이 이 두상이 그 시기의 중요한 통치자 중의 한 명을 나타낸다고 생각하는 이유 중 하나입니다. 하지만, 이 두상들이 올멕의 통치자이건 올멕의 운동선수들이건 간에, 두상의 특징들의 유사성들로 인해 이것이 모두 올멕의 예술품이라는 것은 매우 분명합니다.

Ⓦ ancient [éinʃənt] 고대의   civilization [sìvəlizéiʃən] 문명   swampy [swάmpi] 습지의, 늪지대   lowland [lóulənd] 저지대   jade [dʒeid] 옥, 비취   artifact [άːrtəfækt] 인공물, 공예품   mural [mjúə(ː)rəl] 벽화   pottery [pάtəri] 도자기   sculpture [skΛ́lptʃər] 조각   frown [fraun] 찡그리다 remarkable [rimάːrkəbl] 훌륭한 sophistication [səfìstəkéiʃən] 세련됨, 정교함 armour [άːrmər] 갑옷 ceremonial [sèrəmóuniəl] 의식의 discipline [dísəplin] 학문 anthropology [ænθrəpάlədʒi] 인류학 represent [rèprizént] 상징하다 glorify [glɔ́ːrəfài] 찬미하다, 미화하다

01 강의의 주된 내용은?
Ⓐ 올멕인들의 불가사의한 사라짐
Ⓑ 고대 문명에서 행해졌던 스포츠
Ⓒ 올멕 예술의 특징들
Ⓓ 고대 조각에서 표범의 쓰임

02 올멕 두상 조각들에 관한 놀라운 점은?
Ⓐ 여러 많은 동물들을 닮았다.
Ⓑ 그 지역에서 발견되지 않는 돌로 만들어졌다.
Ⓒ 다른 메소아메리카 조각들과 닮았다.
Ⓓ 석기로 만들어졌다.

03 교수가 올멕 문명에서 행해진 의식적 성격의 스포츠를 언급한 이유는?
Ⓐ 올멕 문명과 인근의 문명들 간의 연관성을 설명하려고
Ⓑ 문화적인 지식이 우리가 예술을 이해하는 데 도움이 될 수 있다는 것을 설명하려고
Ⓒ 올멕 문명의 호전적 특성에 관한 자신의 의견을 지지하려고
Ⓓ 올멕 문명에 관해 알려지지 않은 것이 많다는 것을 강조하려고

04 교수에 의하면, 재규어의 특징들이 올멕의 통치자를 상징한다는 것을 나타내는 이유는 무엇인가?
Ⓐ 올멕 사람들은 재규어를 매우 두려워했던 것으로 알려져 있다.
Ⓑ 재규어는 올멕 문화의 중요한 한 부분이었다.
Ⓒ 올멕 사람들은 식량과 재미를 위해 재규어를 사냥했다.
Ⓓ 재규어는 올멕 사람들에게 신으로 여겨졌다.

05 의식적 성격의 구기종목에 관해 추론할 수 있는 것은?
Ⓐ 거칠고 난폭한 경기였다.
Ⓑ 유럽의 탐험가들에게서 전수받았다.
Ⓒ 올멕의 통치자들에 의해서만 이루어졌다.
Ⓓ 재규어를 사냥하기 전에 진행되었다.

강의의 일부분을 다시 듣고 질문에 답하시오. 🔊 MP3 70_1

> These features you just mentioned, they're very distinctive. When you see one of these heads in a museum, you say "Yeah, that's an Olmec all right."

06 교수가 다음과 같이 말했을 때 의미하는 것은?

> Yeah, that's an Olmec all right.

Ⓐ 학생들이 왜 박물관을 방문해야 하는지 설명하려고
Ⓑ 고대 예술을 확인하는 것의 어려움을 나타내려고
Ⓒ 선사시대 예술의 질에 대한 자신의 의견을 나타내려고
Ⓓ 올멕 예술은 매우 독특하다는 주장을 하려고

❧ Practice Questions 본문 p. 402

| 01 B | 02 D | 03 C | 04 C | 05 A | 06 D |

Main Idea
위대한 문명이 멸망한 이유

Hypothesis
멸망한 이유에 대한 가설
(1) 기후 변화

Evidence
아리스토텔레스의 언급

기후 변화 가설을 반박하는 근거

Problem
멸망 이유를 한 가지로 단정하기 어려움

Requirement
원인을 알아내기 위해서는 관련이 있는 여러 사건들을 분석해야 함

Term
complexity theory 용어 설명

Evidence
complexity theory와 관련하여 증거 설명

Headset

Listen to part of a lecture in an anthropology class. 🔊 MP3 71

Professor(male): One of the big questions sometimes asked when we look at archaeological sites is Q1 "Why did this great civilization collapse?" Well, today, I'd like to talk about an ancient Greek city that existed 2,500 years ago called Mycenae. This city was located about 90 kilometers southwest of Athens. Mycenae was one of the major centers of Greek civilization in the second millennium BC. However, by 1200 BC, its power had declined, and during the 12th century BC Mycenaean collapsed entirely. We are left to wonder – **what caused a city with a population of more than 30,000 to decline so suddenly?** There have been a few hypotheses, all still hotly debated.

One hypothesis is that the climate caused the destruction. When you think about it, Mycenae was very much a city based on agriculture. Any slight change in climate could have had a significant impact on its crops. Q2 **This hypothesis is consistent with ancient Greek historical records. According to accounts made by Aristotle, a drastic change in climate occurred in the area.** In a matter of a few years, the once plentiful rain ceased and Mycenae became a barren land. Q3 **However, the cities near Mycenae showed no signs of a severe drought.** Even if there was a drought, it probably wasn't that problematic. These other cities continued to thrive during the period Aristotle mentioned. It's highly unlikely that a change in climate severe enough to destroy a large city would impact only one city. So it's more likely that this city collapsed due to another reason.

You see, Q4 **when we study the collapse of a civilization or any moment in history, it's really difficult to pin the reasons down to one simple element.** As with a lot of things with life, a historical event is almost always going to be a combination of a number of factors. So, what do we do when we want to analyze what really happened? History is a train of events. **In order to carefully analyze all the factors related to an event as complicated as the demise of a great city, we need to look at all the events that are linked together. Let me introduce you to a term – the "complexity theory."** (shown on screen) This theory was actually first developed by mathematicians and scientists who wanted to investigate how relationships between parts give rise to collective behavior and how this system interacts with its environment.

So, like the name suggests, these relationships are so complex that even the slightest change in one factor can cause everything to crumble. This could have been the case in Mycenae. Even though everything seemed fine, one small disruption may have caused everything to quickly fall apart.

Let's look at two pieces of evidence while thinking about the complexity theory. Okay, first, Q5 **ruins of a palace have been uncovered, and in these ruins there were traces of a fire.** Mycenae had a complex social structure. Since there were palaces, we know that there were officials and guards. But we also know that the area was mostly agricultural, so there would have to have been farmers. And these farmers would have been paying taxes to the officials. Such a system of taxation would have likely been a source of tension. Any small changes, either in the amount of taxes being paid or in the farmers' perception of the system, could have led to drastic consequences.

🎧 So let's imagine the farmers began to grumble that the system was unfair. It doesn't seem farfetched. To the farmers, the officials and guards probably just seemed to be taking their hard-earned money. I mean, Q6 **would you like it if you did all the work in a group project?**

So, **Q5 angry farmers could have started a rebellion to overthrow their government, causing the guards and officials to retreat to the palace. The farmers then may have attacked the palace, burning it to the ground.** And in the midst of all this civil unrest, it wouldn't be surprising if the majority of the city's civilian population relocated to other regions.

To be honest, I really don't know if this hypothesis is right. But it does show one very possible way the social structure of Mycenae could have unraveled.

해석 인류학 수업의 다음 강의 일부분을 들으시오.

교수(남자): 고고학적 유적지들을 살펴볼 때 우리가 종종 하는 중요한 질문들 중 한 가지는 "이 위대한 문명이 어째서 붕괴했는가?"입니다. 음, 오늘은, 미케네(Mycenae)라고 불린, 2천 5백 년 전에 존재했던 고대 그리스의 도시에 대해 이야기해보죠. 이 도시는 아테네의 남서쪽 방향으로 90킬로미터 떨어진 곳에 위치했었습니다. 미케네는 기원전 제2천년기(기원전 2000년~기원전 1000년) 때 그리스 문명의 중심지 중 한 곳이었습니다. 하지만, 기원전 1200년경 미케네의 권력은 쇠퇴했고, 기원전 12세기에 미케네는 완전히 몰락했습니다. 우리는 이 점이 궁금합니다. 무엇이 3만 명이 넘는 인구를 가진 도시를 그렇게 갑자기 몰락시켰을까? 몇 가지 가설이 있습니다. 그것들 모두 여전히 뜨거운 논쟁의 대상이지요.

한 가지 가설은 기후가 파멸을 유발했다는 것입니다. 생각해보면, 미케네는 농업에 기반을 둔 도시였습니다. 기후에 아주 약간의 변화만 있어도 미케네의 곡물에 엄청난 영향을 미칠 수 있었을 것입니다. 이 가설은 고대 그리스의 역사적 기록들과 일치하기도 합니다. 아리스토텔레스(Aristotle)의 말에 따르면, 기후에 있어 급격한 변화가 그 지역에 발생했었다고 합니다. 몇 년 사이에, 한때는 풍부했던 강수가 멎고 미케네는 척박한 땅이 되어 버렸습니다. 하지만, 미케네 인근 도시들은 심한 가뭄을 겪었던 징후가 없었습니다. 가뭄이 있었다 하더라도, 아마도 그렇게 문제가 되지는 않았던 것으로 보입니다. 이런 다른 도시들은 아리스토텔레스가 언급했던 그 시기 동안 계속해서 번영했기 때문이죠. 한 거대한 도시를 멸망시킬 만큼 심각한 기후 변화가 그저 한 도시에만 영향을 미칠 가능성은 거의 없습니다. 그래서 미케네는 다른 이유에 의해 몰락했을 가능성이 더 높습니다.

한 문명의 몰락이나 역사상의 어떤 순간에 대해 연구를 할 때는, 그 이유들을 한 가지 단순한 요소로 분명히 정의 내리기는 매우 어렵습니다. 인생의 많은 일들과 마찬가지로, 한 가지 역사적 사건은 거의 항상 수많은 요인들의 조합입니다. 그러면, 실제 무슨 일이 일어났는지를 분석하고 싶을 때 우리는 무엇을 해야 할까요? 역사는 사건들의 연속입니다. 한 거대한 도시의 종말과 같은 복잡한 사건과 관련된 모든 요인들을 주의 깊게 분석하기 위해서는, 우리는 서로 관련이 되어 있는 모든 사건들을 살펴보아야 합니다. 용어 하나를 알려드리죠. '복잡성 이론'이라는 것입니다. (화면에 보여준다) 이 이론은 사실, 부분들간의 관계가 어떻게 집단 행동을 일으키는지와 이런 시스템이 그 환경과 어떻게 상호작용하는지를 조사하고 싶어 했던 수학자들과 과학자들에 의해 처음 전개되었습니다.

자, 그 이름이 암시하듯이, 이러한 관계들은 너무나 복잡해서, 한 가지 요인에 가장 작은 변화만 있어도 모든 것이 무너질 수 있습니다. 미케네가 이러한 경우였을 수도 있지요. 모든 것이 괜찮아 보였더라도, 하나의 작은 분열이 모든 것을 빠르게 허물어뜨렸을지도 모릅니다.

복잡성 이론에 대해 생각하며 두 가지 증거를 살펴보도록 하죠. 좋아요, 우선, 궁전의 유적들이 발굴되었는데, 이 유적들에서 화재의 흔적이 있었습니다. 미케네는 복잡한 사회 구조를 가지고 있었습니다. 궁전들이 있었기 때문에 우리는 관리들과 경비들이 있었다는 것을 압니다. 하지만 우리는 또한 그 지역이 대부분 농경 문화였다는 것도 알고 있기 때문에, 그곳에는 농부들도 있었어야만 하죠. 그리고 이런 농부들은 관리들에게 세금을 내고 있었겠지요. 그런 징세 시스템은 갈등의 이유가 되었을 가능성이 있습니다. 내고 있던 세금의 양이나 그 시스템에 대한 농부들의 인식에 생긴 어떤 작은 변화들이 극단적인 결과로 이어졌을 수도 있습니다. 자, 농부들이 시스템이 불공평하다고 불평하기 시작했다고 상상해봅시다. 설득력이 없지는 않죠. 농부들에게 있어, 관리들과 경비들은 아마도 그들이 힘들게 번 돈을 그냥 가져가는 것처럼만 보였을 것입니다. 그러니까, 그룹 프로젝트에서 여러분 혼자 일을 다 해야 하면 그게 좋을까요?

그래서, 분노한 농부들이 정부를 전복시키기 위해 반란을 시작했을 수도 있습니다. 경비들과 관리들이 궁 안으로 후퇴하도록 만들면서 말이죠. 농부들은 그리고 나서는 궁을 공격해 불태워버렸을지도 모릅니다. 그리고 나라가 불안한 상태인 가운데, 미케네 시의 주민의 대다수가 다른 지역들로 이주해갔다고 해도 놀라울 일은 아닐 테지요.

솔직히, 나도 이 가설이 맞는지 잘 모르겠습니다. 하지만 그것은 미케네의 사회 구조가 흐트러졌을 수도 있는 하나의 매우 가능성 있는 방식을 보여주는 것은 사실입니다.

ⓦ millennium [miléniəm] 천년   decline [dikláin] 쇠퇴하다   drastic [dræstik] 급격한   cease [si:s] 중단하다   problematic [pràblə mætik] 문제가 있는(많은)   pin ~ down ...을 정확히 밝히다(이해하다)   a train of ~ 일련의 ...   give rise to ~ ...이 생기게 하다   collective behavior 집단 행동   crumble [krʌ́mbl] 흔들리다, 무너지다   disruption [disrʌ́pʃən] 붕괴, 분열   ruins [rú(:)inz] (pl.) 폐허, 유적   official [əfíʃəl] 공무원, 관리   taxation [tækséiʃən] 조세, 세수   tension [ténʃən] 긴장, 갈등   grumble [grʌ́mbl] 투덜거리다   farfetched [fɑ́:rfétʃt] 설득력 없는   rebellion [ribéljən] 반란   overthrow [òuvərθróu] 전복시키다   retreat [ritrí:t] 후퇴하다   civil unrest 국내의 불안   majority [mədʒɔ́(:)rəti] 다수   civilian [sivíljən] 민간인   relocate [rilòukéit] 이동하다   unravel [ʌnrǽvəl] 흐트러지기 시작하다

01 강의의 주된 내용은?
Ⓐ 역사적 사건들을 평가하는 데 있어 고고학적 증거의 유용성
Ⓑ 한 도시에서의 급작스런 인구 감소에 대한 가능성 있는 이유들
Ⓒ 과거 사건들을 분석하기 위해 그리스 역사가들이 사용했던 방법들
Ⓓ 고대 그리스에서 시민과 통치자들간의 관계

02 교수가 아리스토텔레스를 언급한 이유는?
Ⓐ 미케네의 몰락에 대한 가설들이 오래 전에 생겼다는 것을 나타내려고
Ⓑ 날씨와 인구 감소 간의 관계를 설명하는 데 도움을 주려고
Ⓒ 기후 변화에 관련된 가설이 틀리다는 것을 증명하려고
Ⓓ 미케네의 몰락에 대한 한 이론이 신빙성이 있을지도 모른다는 것을 보여주려고

03 교수에 의하면, 기후 변화가 인구 감소를 유발하지 않았다는 것을 증명하기 위해 사용된 증거는 무엇인가?
Ⓐ 고대 그리스의 역사 기록들에 많은 오류들이 있었다.
Ⓑ 외부 침입으로 인해 파괴된 건물들의 유적이 발견되었다.
Ⓒ 미케네 인근의 도시들은 가뭄에 영향을 받지 않은 것처럼 보였다.
Ⓓ 농경 쇠퇴에 대한 어떤 기록도 존재하지 않는다.

04 교수가 복잡성 이론을 논의한 이유는?
Ⓐ 다른 분야의 이론이 어떻게 인류학에 적용될 수 있는지를 설명하려고
Ⓑ 미케네가 외부 침략으로 인해 몰락했다는 것을 증명하려고
Ⓒ 미케네가 왜 몰락했는지에 대한 대안이 되는 설명을 제공하려고
Ⓓ 사건들 간에 복잡한 관계가 어떻게 존재하는지 보여주려고

05 어떤 증거가 미케네가 내부 갈등으로 인해 몰락했다는 것을 암시하는가?
Ⓐ 도시 안의 궁전이 불탔을지도 모른다.
Ⓑ 세금이 충분히 빨리 거두어졌을 것으로 보이지 않는다.
Ⓒ 도시가 인구 과잉 직전이었다.
Ⓓ 농부들이 오랜 기간 동안 농사짓기를 중단했을지도 모른다.

강의의 일부분을 다시 듣고 질문에 답하시오. 🔊 MP3 71_1

> So let's imagine the farmers began to grumble that the system was unfair. It doesn't seem farfetched. To the farmers, the officials and guards probably just seemed to be taking their hard-earned money. I mean, would you like it if you did all the work in a group project?

06 교수가 다음과 같이 말한 이유는?

> Would you like it if you did all the work in a group project?

Ⓐ 복잡성 이론이 다른 개념들에 의존한다는 것을 암시하려고
Ⓑ 미케네가 다른 도시들의 지원을 받지 않았다는 것을 나타내려고
Ⓒ 가설을 만드는 것에 관한 문제점을 강조하려고
Ⓓ 농부들이 분노한 이유를 설명하는 데 도움이 되려고

02 / Archaeology

Sample Questions

01 B 02 B 03 D 04 C 05 B 06 D

해석 고고학 수업의 다음 강의 일부분을 들으시오 ◁) MP3 72

교수(남자): 자, 우리는 지금까지 북미와 남미의 클로비스 문화와 관련된 몇몇 고고학적 연구 결과들에 대해서 이야기했습니다. 이제, 고고학적 유물들의 위치와 연대를 알기 위한 몇 가지 기법들에 집중해 봅시다. 그저 슬슬 걸어 들어가서 유적들을 조사한다면 좋겠지만, 어떤 장소들은 그렇게 하기에 너무 어렵습니다. 그래서 우리는 몇몇 특수 기법들에 의존해야 합니다. 클로비스 문화에서 훨씬 더 떨어진 한 장소인 아이슬란드를 예로 들어보고 싶군요. 자, 음, 아이슬란드는 북반구에 위치한 화산섬으로서, 섬의 10분의 1이 빙하로 뒤덮여 있습니다.

아이슬란드와 다른 북유럽 국가들에 대해서 가장 처음 생각날지도 모르는 것들은 그 국가들에 얽힌 이야기들입니다. 모두들 바이킹에 대해서 들어보았겠죠, 그렇죠? 바이킹에 관한 아이슬란드의 무용담들은 사람들에게 오랫동안 흥미를 불러일으켰지만, 우리에게는 이런 주장들에 대한 타당성을 지지해주는 견고한 증거가 항상 부족했습니다. 그 이야기들은 전설 쪽에 더 가까워 보였지요. 역사가, 천문학자, 항해자... 이들은 모두 그 이야기들이 가리키는 곳에서 사람들이 정착했다는 증거를 찾으려고 노력해 왔습니다. 사람들은 마치 이 이야기들의 진실을 확인하기 위해 이끌리는 것 같습니다. 우리 고고학자들 역시 주택들, 농경의 증거, 철 제련, 또는 동물을 길렀던 증거라도 찾으려고 노력해 왔습니다. 초기 정착의 흔적을 가리키는 그 어떤 것이라도 말이지요.

하여간, 아이슬란드 무용담이 신화로만 여겨지는 이유 중에는, 논의되고 있는 지역들에서의 고고학적 사실을 입증하는 것이 어려운 이유도 있습니다. 여러분은 날씨나 극심한 얼음의 양이 문제가 될 것이라 생각할지도 모르겠군요. 하지만 여러분이 사실을 알게 되면 놀랄 겁니다. 사실은 나무 부족이 문제거든요. 토양을 움직이지 않게 잡아주는 나무가 하나도 없어서, 자연적으로 침식이 많이 일어나게 됩니다. 특히 고지대부터 낮은 해안 지역으로의 침식이 말이죠. 자, 이용 가능한 나무가 거의 없는 상태에서, 아이슬란드의 가장 초기 주택의 대부분은 이탄으로 만들어졌습니다. 여러분이 기억하듯이, 이탄은 주로 습지나 늪지에서 나오는 바람이 잘 통하는 토양으로, 상당한 양의 부식된 유기물을 포함하고 있습니다. 아이슬란드의 초기 거주민들은 이탄을 압축해서 건조시켜, 초기 아이슬란드 주택들의 벽을 형성하는 크고 두꺼운 벽돌들을 만들었습니다. 오늘날, 이러한 주택들의 유적은 찾기가 매우 어렵습니다. 흙으로 만들어졌기 때문에, 이런 집들은 주변에 있는 토양들과 거의 구별이 되지 않기 때문입니다. 하지만, 지구물리학자들이 이용하는 현대 기법을 빌려, 새로운 방법이 개발되었습니다.

자 그럼, 이 모든 것들이 아이슬란드 전설과 어떤 연관이 있을까요? 음, 이런 아이슬란드 무용담 중 하나는 대서양을 횡단하여 북미지역에 거주했던 아마도 최초의 유럽인들이었던 바이킹 탐험가들에 대한 이야기를 알려줍니다. 그들은 Thorfinnson이라는 이름의, 아이슬란드에서 온 바이킹 가족이었어요. 그들은 몇 년간 북미에 정착했지만, 그리고는 그다지 멀리 떨어져 있지 않았던 아이슬란드로 다시 돌아갑니다. 당연히, 아이슬란드에 있는 바이킹 시대의 장소들에 대한 큰 흥미가 생겨납니다. 특히 이 가족이 마침내 정착했다고 말하는 장소에서 말이지요.

고고학자들로 이루어진 한 팀은 전자기에 의존하는 원격감지장치를 이용하기로 했습니다. 이 기기는, 좀전에 말했듯이, 대개는 지구물리학자들이 사용하는 것으로, 음, 육안으로는 똑같이 보이지만 서로 다른 성분을 가진 다른 물질들을 구별하는 데 주로 쓰입니다. 일반 토양은 전기를 잘 전도시키지만, 이탄으로 만든 벽은 그다지 그렇지 않습니다. 이 기기는 땅속으로 전자기파를 보내고, 센서가 그 전자기파들이 되돌아오는 속도를 측정합니다. 음, 전기는 토양의 유형에 따라 더 빠르게 또는 더 느리게 이동하지요. 이 경우에는, 더 빠른 신호는 일반 토양을 의미하는 반면, 더 늦은 신호는 이탄을 나타냅니다. 이런 식으로, 땅속에 묻힌 이탄 벽들이 감지될 수 있지요.

그래서 여하간, 그 팀은 오래된 무용담에서 Thorfinnson 가족들이 집을 지었다고 말하는 장소처럼 보이는 아이슬란드의 한 장소를 조사하고 싶었습니다. 이 기법을 이용해서, 그 팀은 커다란 농가의 유적을 발견했습니다. 그 건물의 연대는 이야기에 나온 대로, Thorfinnson 일가가 그곳에 살았을 것으로 추정되는 시기와 정확하게 일치했습니다. 그 팀은 다른 증거들, 특히 개인적인 유물들을 찾기 위해 작업을 하고 있습니다. 그 집을 찾는 대부분의 사람들은 그 집이 아마도 근처에 있는 박물관의 바로 아래에 위치해 있을 것으로 생각했습니다. 그들은 집이 (박물관의) 건축 과정에서 부서졌을 것이라고 추측했지만, 사실 그 집은 근처의 밭에 위치해 있었습니다. 원격감지장치가 없었더라면, 이 집은 영원히 발견되지 못했을지도 모릅니다.

W locate [lóukeit] 정확한 위치를 찾아내다 date [deit] 연대를 추정하다 artifact [ά:rtəfǽkt] 인공물, 공예품 stroll [stroul] 산책하다 resort to ~ ...에 의존하다 Nordic [nɔ́:rdik] 북유럽 국가의 Icelandic [aislǽndik] 아이슬란드의 saga [sά:gə] 영웅 전설 validity [vəlídəti] 유효함, 타당성 navigator [nǽvigèitər] 항해자 dwelling [dwélin] 주거(지), 주택 iron smelting 철 제련 domestication [dəmèstikéiʃən] 사육 myth [miθ] 신화, 미신 highland [háilənd] 산악 지대(의) organic matter 유기물 remains [riméinz] (pl.) 유적 indistinguishable [ìndistíŋgwiʃəbl] 구분이 안 되는 geophysicist [dʒì:oufíziksist] 지구물리학자 the Atlantic 대서양 remote sensing tool 원격감지장치 electromagnetism [ilèktroumǽgnətìzəm] 전자기 conduct [kəndʌ́kt] (열이나 전기를) 전도하다 electromagnetic pulse 전자기파

01 교수가 강의에서 주로 논의하고 있는 아이슬란드 고고학의 측면은?
Ⓐ 미대륙과 아이슬란드 유적 사이의 유사점들
Ⓑ 지질학에서 빌려온 방법들이 유적을 발견하는 데 어떻게 사용되는지
Ⓒ 전통적인 무용담을 기반으로 유물들의 위치를 찾는 전략
Ⓓ 전통적인 아이슬란드 주택을 짓는 데 사용된 다양한 재료들

02 교수에 의하면, 고대 아이슬란드 주택들의 유적을 고고학자들이 찾기 어려운 이유는 무엇인가?
Ⓐ 너무 오래 전에 지어졌다.
Ⓑ 흙의 한 종류로 만들어졌다.
Ⓒ 얼음과 눈으로 이루어진 두꺼운 층으로 덮여 있다.
Ⓓ 이후에 분해되어 버린 나무로 만들어졌다.

03 교수가 아이슬란드 무용담과 바이킹 탐험가들을 언급한 이유는?
Ⓐ 전통적인 아이슬란드의 문학에 대한 예를 주려고
Ⓑ 아이슬란드 주택들이 이탄으로 지어진 이유를 제시하려고
Ⓒ 과거에 아이슬란드에서 고고학이 중요했던 이유를 나타내려고
Ⓓ 일부 사람들이 아이슬란드에서 유적들을 찾는 이유를 제시하려고

04 교수에 의하면, 원격감지장치가 제공하는 자료의 종류는 무엇인가?
Ⓐ 금속 유물들이 만들어내는 자기력
Ⓑ 유적들이 위치한 곳의 깊이
Ⓒ 여러 다른 물질들의 저항
Ⓓ 그 장치가 감지하는 유적의 연대

05 원격감지장치를 이용하여 발견된 건물의 중요성은?
Ⓐ 전통적인 고고학적 방법들이 최고라는 것을 보여주었다.
Ⓑ 아이슬란드 전설이 사실이었을지도 모른다는 증거를 제공한다.
Ⓒ 전통적인 이탄 벽돌보다는 나무와 돌로 만들어졌다.
Ⓓ 북미지역에서 발견되었던 최초의 바이킹 건축물이었다.

강의의 일부분을 다시 듣고 질문에 답하시오. ◁ **MP3 72_1**

> Now this tool, which, as I mentioned before, is usually used by geophysicists, um, mainly to distinguish between different materials that look the same to the naked eye but have different compositions. Regular soil conducts electricity well, but walls made of peat, not so much.

06 교수가 다음과 같이 말한 이유는?

> Regular soil conducts electricity well, but walls made of peat, not so much.

Ⓐ 아이슬란드의 지구물리학자들이 직면한 주된 문제를 설명하려고
Ⓑ 아이슬란드와 북미의 토양의 차이점을 강조하려고
Ⓒ 그 장치를 사용한 실험에 중대한 오류가 있었다는 것을 나타내려고
Ⓓ 그 장치가 오래된 아이슬란드 주택들을 찾는 데 유용할 것이라는 점을 나타내려고

⦿ Practice Questions

본문 p. 412

01 C　**02** D　**03** B　**04** A　**05** D　**06** C

Main Idea
고고학자들이 새로운 증거가 나타났을 때 사고하는 방식

Finding
NM1 지역 사람들은 주로 육지에 거주한다는 증거를 발견하고 결론내림

Evidence
위의 결론을 반박하는 증거 발견 – 상어 이빨

Evidence
상어를 잡았다는 증거 부족

Problem
첫 번째 가설의 문제점 – 어업의 흔적 없음

두 번째 가설의 문제점 – 긁힌 자국이 없음

세 번째 가설
(One-step process)

Function
장식용

네 번째 가설
(Two-step process)

Listen to part of a lecture in an archeology class. 🔊 MP3 73

Professor(male): I'm sure you'll all agree that archaeologists are a lot like detectives. It's their job to piece together evidence in order to come up with a conclusion. In today's lecture, I want to go over the process, um, the thought process that goes through an archaeologists' mind when he or she is presented with new evidence. So, to give you an example, **Q1** **I'm going to talk about an archaeological site in Argentina called NM1.** For your information, that's short for "Nutria Mansa One." The site was dated to Holocene period, about six to ten thousand years ago, and is located in Argentina, southeast of Buenos Aries and about four kilometers north of the Atlantic coastline. **Q4** **Archaeologists there found artifacts like tools and bones from land mammals – sufficient evidence to prove that its inhabitants were primarily land-dwelling hunter-gatherers.** But **Q1 Q2** **there was a surprising finding that sort of confused everyone – two teeth of a great white shark.**

Since the archaeologists were presented with evidence that contradicted their findings, they had to ask the question, "How did these hunter-gatherers get the shark teeth?" The first thing they looked at was the location of the site. Remember how I told you it's only four kilometers away from the coast? So, they started to seek additional clues as to whether they were shark fishers or something that would indicate that they caught other fish – fish bones, some fishing equipment, something like that... **Q3** **If they were fishermen, we'd expect to find fossilized fish bones at the site, but there's no evidence of anything like that. You have to keep in mind, we're talking about a great white shark. I mean, this isn't just some fish you catch with a fishing rod and hook. They are very large and aggressive animals; you'd need some specialized equipment.** There have been many artifacts found in other places that suggest that ancient groups from coastal regions fished for sharks. So, we do know that some ancient people used sharks as a food source. But, nothing resembling anything like that was found at the site. So even though there was the proximity to water, we had to rule out that the inhabitants of the site were fishers.

Since the most likely hypothesis was ruled out, archaeologists considered four other hypotheses. The first hypothesis was that they could have gotten the teeth through trading. But archaeologists ran into another problem. Remember what I said about artifacts that indicate a fishing culture? Well, **Q4** **there was no evidence to be found in any of the other sites around NM1.**

The archeologists moved on to the next hypothesis – that the teeth were just found on the beach. Someone could have picked up a couple of teeth that were just lying there. It's not uncommon for shark teeth to be found on beaches, but when taking a closer look at the teeth, there were no scratches or portions that were worn off. This makes it highly unlikely that they were just found at the beach, where they would have been exposed to the elements.

Of course, some thought the teeth had come directly from the shark's mouth. A shark could have washed up on shore, and the inhabitant could have just plucked the teeth out. This makes sense, as the **Q5** **only sign of damage are the holes used to attach them to a necklace.** But it's important not to jump to conclusions. Just because they had no damage doesn't mean they came directly from a shark's mouth. It only means they weren't subject to the harsh environment of the beach.

Let's try and think of another possible theory. What if the great white bit into something? Sharks have hundreds of teeth, and they easily break off. The teeth could have

– One-step process 보다 더 많은 가정이 포함됨

been lodged into its prey, but the prey could have somehow gotten away. It's really difficult to survive a shark bite, so the wounded prey could have died and ended up on the beach with the teeth still in it. And when someone saw it, they would have pulled the teeth out.

So we're left with two likely hypotheses. **Q6** **The first is a one-step process… A shark gets stranded on the beach, and when it is lying there, someone could have just pulled the teeth out.** Even today, it's not uncommon to see sharks beached on the Argentinean coastline. The next is the two-step process in which the shark bites its prey, and the prey escapes with the teeth still lodged in it, only to end up on a beach. What you believe is the correct hypothesis is up to you, but remember my talk about Occam's razor? You know, **Q6** the principle that among competing hypotheses, the one with the fewest assumptions should be selected. In this particular case, that principle clearly points to the hypothesis I support.

Opinion
교수는 추측이 가장 적은 가설을 지지함

해석 고고학 수업의 다음 강의 일부분을 들으시오.

교수(남자): 여러분 모두 고고학자들이 탐정과 많이 비슷하다는 것에 동의할 거라 생각합니다. 결론을 내기 위해 증거들을 한데 모아 붙이는 것이 고고학자들의 일입니다. 오늘 강의에서는 그 과정, 그러니까 고고학자들이 새로운 증거를 제시 받을 때 그들의 마음속을 지나가는 사고 과정을 살펴보고자 합니다.

자, 예를 들기 위해서, NM1이라고 불리는 아르헨티나의 한 고고학 유적지에 대해서 이야기하려고 합니다. 참고로, NM1은 'Nutria Mansa One'의 줄임말입니다. 이 장소의 연대는 대략 6천 년에서 1만 년 전까지 거슬러 올라간 완신세로, 아르헨티나의 부에노스 아이레스 남동쪽에 있으며 대서양 해안에서 북쪽으로 약 4킬로미터 떨어진 곳에 있습니다. 고고학자들은 그곳에서 도구들과 육지 포유류의 뼈와 같은 유물들을 발견했습니다. 즉, 그곳에 거주했던 사람들이 주로 육지에 사는 수렵채집민이라는 것을 증명하기에 충분한 증거들이죠. 하지만 모두를 혼란스럽게 만든 또 다른 놀라운 발견이 있었습니다. 대백상어의 이빨 두 개를 발견한 것입니다.

그들의 연구 결과와 상반된 증거를 제시 받았기 때문에, 고고학자들은 이런 질문을 할 수 밖에 없었습니다. "이 수렵채집민들은 어떻게 상어 이빨을 갖게 되었을까?" 그들이 처음 살펴본 것은 유적지의 위치였습니다. 그곳이 해안에서 불과 4킬로미터밖에 떨어지지 않은 곳이라고 했던 것 기억나지요? 그래서 학자들은 그들이 상어잡이였는지, 또는 그들이 다른 물고기를 잡았었는지를 보여줄 수 있는 무언가들에 대한 추가적인 단서들을 찾기 시작했습니다. 물고기의 뼈, 낚시 장비 등등 같은 것들 말이지요… 그들이 어부라면, 유적지에서 화석화된 물고기 뼈를 찾을 것이라 기대하겠지만, 그런 증거는 전혀 없었습니다. 우리가 대백상어에 대해서 말하고 있다는 것을 염두에 두어야 합니다. 즉, 대백상어는 낚시대와 갈고리로 잡을 수 있는 그런 물고기가 아니라는 말입니다. 대백상어는 매우 크고 공격적인 동물로, 특수 장비가 필요합니다. 다른 지역에서는 해안 지역에 사는 고대 집단들이 상어를 잡았다는 것을 시사하는 많은 유물들이 발견되었습니다. 그래서, 우리는 일부 고대인들이 상어를 식량원으로 사용했다는 것을 알고 있지요. 그러나 그것과 닮은 어떤 것도 그 유적지에서 발견되지 않았습니다. 그래서 비록 물가와 가깝긴 해도, 유적지의 거주자들이 어부였을 거라는 점은 제외시켜야 했습니다.

가장 그럴듯한 가설이 제외되었기 때문에, 고고학자들은 다른 네 가지 가설들을 고려했습니다. 첫 번째 가설은 그들이 교역을 통해서 상어 이빨을 얻었을 것이라는 겁니다. 하지만 고고학자들은 또 다른 문제에 봉착했습니다. 어업 문화를 나타내는 유물들에 대해서 말했던 것 기억하나요? NM1 주변의 다른 유적지들 중 어느 곳에서도 그런 증거가 발견되지 않았습니다.

고고학자들은 두 번째 가설로 넘어갔습니다. 그 이빨들은 그냥 해안가에서 발견된 것뿐이라는 것이죠. 누군가가 거기에 그냥 놓여져 있던 이빨 몇 개를 주웠을 수도 있습니다. 해안가에서 상어 이빨이 발견되는 것이 드문 일은 아니지만, 이빨을 자세히 살펴보면, 긁힌 자국이나 닳은 부분들이 없었습니다. 이는 그 이빨들이 해변에서 그냥 발견되었을 가능성이 거의 없다는 것을 말해줍니다. 해변에서는 이빨들이 비바람에 노출되었을 테니까요.

물론, 어떤 이들은 이빨이 상어의 입에서 바로 얻어진 것이라고 생각하기도 했습니다. 상어 한 마리가 해안가로 떠내려와 거주자들이 이빨을 뽑아냈을 수도 있지요. 이것은 말이 됩니다. 유일한 손상의 흔적이 그 이빨들을 목걸이에 부착하기 위해 사용된 구멍뿐이니까요. 하지만 성급하게 결론을 내리지 않는 것이 중요합니다. 아무런 손상이 없다는 것이, 그 이빨들이 상어의 입에서 바로 얻어진 것이라는 뜻은 아니기 때문이지요. 이는 단지 이빨이 해안의 거친 환경에 노출되지 않았었다는 것을 의미할 뿐입니다.

또 다른 가능한 이론을 생각해 봅시다. 대백상어가 무언가를 물었다면 어떻게 될까요? 상어들은 수백 개의 이빨을 가지고 있는데, 이빨들은 쉽게 빠집니다. 이빨이 먹이에 박혔는데, 먹이가 어찌해서 도망가버렸을 수도 있지요. 상어에게 물리고 생존하기란 정말 어려운 일이어서, 부상을 입은 먹이는 이빨이 박힌 채로 죽어서 해안가로 밀려오게 되었을지도 모릅니다. 그리고 누군가가 그것을 보고 이빨을 빼냈을 수도 있습니다. 자, 이제 우리에게는 두 가지 그럴듯한 가설만 남아 있습니다. 첫 번째는 한 단계 과정입니다… 상어가 해안가에 밀려왔을 때, 누군가가 이빨을 뽑았을 수 있습니다. 오늘날에도, 아르헨티나 해안가에서는 표류한 상어를 보는 것이 드문 일은 아닙니다. 다음은 두 단계 과정으로, 상어가 먹

이를 물고, 그 먹이가 이빨이 박힌 채로 도망가서 해안가에서 죽는 것입니다. 어떤 것이 맞는 가설이라고 믿는지는 여러분에게 달린 일이지만, 오컴의 면도날(절감의 법칙)에 대해서 내가 이야기했던 것을 기억하나요? 상충하는 많은 가설 속에서는 가장 적은 가정을 가진 가설이 선택되어야 한다는 원칙 말입니다. 이 특정한 경우에서는, 그 원칙은 분명 내가 지지하는 가설을 가리키고 있습니다.

Ⓦ piece together (세부 사항들을) 종합하다   land-dwelling [lǽnd-dwélɪŋ] 육지에 거주하는   hunter-gatherer [hʌ́ntə(r)-ɡǽðərər] 수렵채집민   contradict [kɑ̀ntrədíkt] 모순되다   fishing rod 낚싯대   resemble [rɪzémbl] 유사하다   rule out 배제하다   wash up on ~ …로 밀어 올리다   pluck out 뽑다   strand [strǽnd] 좌초시키다   lodge [lɑʤ] …에 꽂히다   principle [prínsəpl] 원칙, 원리   competing [kəmpíːtɪŋ] 상충하는   assumption [əsʌ́mpʃən] 가정

01 교수가 주로 논의하고 있는 것은?
Ⓐ 고고학적 유적지의 연대를 밝히는 데 있어 증거의 역할
Ⓑ NM1의 거주민들이 수렵채집인이었다는 증거
Ⓒ NM1에서 발견된 상어 이빨의 기원에 대한 논쟁
Ⓓ 남미의 초기 장신구 제작의 예

02 NM1에서 발견된 상어 이빨에 관해 추론할 수 있는 것은?
Ⓐ 고대 어업인들의 증거를 나타낸다.
Ⓑ 완신세기 시대에 만들어진 예술의 대표작이다.
Ⓒ 실제로는 아르헨티나의 다른 지역에서 발견되었다.
Ⓓ 그 유적지에서 발견된 유물 중에서 독특한 것이다.

03 고대 집단이 상어를 잡을 때 사용했던 장비를 교수가 언급한 이유는?
Ⓐ NM1의 거주민들이 낚시를 했다는 증거를 제시하려고
Ⓑ 어떤 가설이 타당하지 않다는 것을 시사하려고
Ⓒ 상어 이빨이 유적지에서 발견된 이유를 설명하려고
Ⓓ 유사한 문화의 습성들을 묘사하려고

04 고고학자들이 NM1 근처의 다른 고고학 유적지들에서 찾을 가능성이 높은 것은?
Ⓐ 사냥된 동물들의 뼈들
Ⓑ 먹어 치운 물고기의 잔해들
Ⓒ 장신구로 만들어진 화석화된 상어 이빨
Ⓓ 상어 낚시를 위한 특수 장비

05 교수에 의하면, 상어 이빨에 구멍이 있었던 이유는?
Ⓐ 이빨이 오랜 기간 동안 해변에 있었다.
Ⓑ 상어가 먹이를 물었을 때 이빨이 손상되었다.
Ⓒ 이빨을 뽑을 때 사용되었던 도구에 의해 부서졌다.
Ⓓ 이빨은 장식용의 목적으로 사용되었다.

06 교수가 생각하는 가장 가능성 높은 상어 이빨의 기원은?
Ⓐ 교역의 결과이다.
Ⓑ 고기잡이를 통해 얻은 것이다.
Ⓒ 상어에게서 뽑은 것이다.
Ⓓ 상어의 먹이 안에서 발견되었다.

03 / Business

Sample Questions

01 B   02 C   03 D   04 B, D   05 C   06 D

해석 경영학 수업의 다음 강의 일부분을 들으시오. ◁) MP3 74

교수(여자): 시작하죠. 음, 지난 시간에는 광고의 필요성에 대해 이야기했습니다. 이제 조금은 구식인 것 같아 보이긴 하지만 그래도 매우 효과적인 한 가지 방법에 대해 살펴보죠. 다이렉트 메일 광고(DM 광고)에 대해 이야기 해볼 겁니다. DM 광고에는 편지와 카탈로그를 고객들에게 곧바로 보내는 것이 수반됩니다. 여러분은 그것이 매우 효과가 없을 것 같다고 생각할지도 모르지만, 얼마나 많은 수익이 DM 활동으로 생기는지 알게 되면 놀랄 것입니다. 최근의 한 연구에 따르면, DM 광고가 TV광고보다 두 배의 수익을 낸다는 것이 밝혀졌습니다. 맞아요. 정크 메일 광고에 쓰인 1달러가 10달러어치 판매를 일으키는 것이죠. TV 광고는 그 절반밖에 수익을 내지 못하는 반면에 말이죠. 이메일 광고나 웹사이트 배너 광고 등과 같은 좀 더 새로운 기술을 사용하는 광고들도 DM 광고가 내는 수익에 근접하지조차 못합니다.

그러면 좋은 DM 광고 플랜은 어떤 것일까요? 좋은 플랜은 다이렉트 마케팅의 기본적인 기법들 중 하나를 사용합니다. 이 기법의 기반은 고객들의 구매 습관에 대한 복잡한 분석입니다. 어떤 상품이 고객들의 관심을 끄는지, 잠재 고객이 트렌드에 어떻게 반응하는지 등등에 대한 것이죠... 하지만 이를 위해서는, 먼저 사람들을 카테고리에 넣어야 하죠. 직업이나 나이뿐만 아니라 더 미세한 카테고리에 넣어야 합니다. 예를 들어, 문 4개짜리 차인 세단형 자동차를 산 사람들, 또는 일주일에 두 번 이상 외식을 하는 채식주의자들과 같이 말이죠. 사람들에게 그런 정밀한 라벨을 붙여 분류하는 것이 회사로 하여금 돈을 절약하게 해줍니다. 회사들이 그냥 카탈로그를 한 묶음 보내서 모든 사람들이 그걸 들여다볼 것이라고 생각하는 건 아닌 거죠. 회사는 어떤 종류의 사람들이 그들의 특정한 카탈로그를 보고 싶어 할지 주의 깊게 분류해야 합니다. 다시 말해, 회사들은 그들의 상품에 관심이 없는 고객들에게 광고를 보내는 걸 피해야 하는 거죠. 스포츠카를 몰고, 주차할 곳 하나 없는 대도시에 사는 사람들에게 캠핑 차를 팔려고 노력하진 않을 테니까요.

자, 이제 성공적인 DM 광고 활동을 하기 위해 필요한 세부적인 단계들과, 고객 분석이 그런 활동들이 실행되는 방식에 어떻게 맞아 들어가는지를 살펴봅시다. 첫 번째 단계는 사람들의 구매 습관에 대한 정보를 얻는 것입니다. 이것을 회사들이 자체적으로 하기에는 너무 많은 회사 자원이 들어가기 때문에, 이 일은 외부의 목록 판매자들에게 위탁됩니다. 목록 판매자들은 고객들이 무엇에 관심이 있는지에 관한 정보를 모아주는 사람들입니다. 이런 정보를 구하는 방법은 여러 가지가 있지만, 많은 목록 판매자들은 명백한 이유로 그걸 기밀로 하고 있지요. 목록 구매자는, 이 경우에는 카탈로그를 보내고자 하는 대상들의 목록을 구하려는 회사 말이죠, 그들은 특정 기준에 부합하는 사람들의 목록을 요청합니다. 목록 판매자들은 그 기준에 부합하는 사람들 목록을 직접 또는 간접적으로 판매합니다. 간접적이라고 말한 것은, 많은 회사들이 목록 브로커를 통하기 때문입니다. 올바른 정보를 받는 데만도 무척 복잡한 과정이지요?

어쨌든, 다음 단계는 광고지나 카탈로그를 우편을 통해 발송하는 것입니다. 그냥 아무거나 보내놓고는 사람들이 그것을 아주 상세하게 읽을 것이라 기대해서는 안됩니다. 사람들은 정크 메일 하나를 보는 데 5초 이상의 시간을 들이지 않습니다. 이에 대응하여, 마케터들은 사람들의 관심을 끌기 위해, 주의를 붙잡는 방법들, 예를 들면 그들의 광고를 개인에게 맞추어 조정하는 것 같은 방법들을 발전시켰습니다. 완전히 사실만 명시한 광고보다는 고객에게 개인적으로 어필을 하는 광고로 더 많은 판매를 불러일으킬 수 있습니다. 어떤 회사들은 심지어 손으로 편지를 쓰도록 수백 명의 사람들을 고용하기도 합니다. 한 회사는 실제로 사람의 손길이 들어간 느낌을 좀 더 주기 위해, 일부러 선으로 찍찍 지운 실수를 포함시키기도 합니다.

일단 우편물이 발송되고 나면, 목록 판매자들은 광고에 대한 고객들의 반응률에 관한 정보를 더 모으게 됩니다... 음... 얼마나 많은 고객들이 실제로 카탈로그에 있는 상품을 주문하는지도 여기에 포함되지요. 목록 판매자들이 자신의 목록의 효과성을 앞으로도 향상시킬 수 있기 위해 그 정보를 분석할 수 있도록, 이런 정보를 목록 판매자들에게 주는 것은 그 (광고를 하는) 회사의 몫이죠... 왜냐하면 일단 데이터가 정리되고 나면, 전체 과정이 다시 반복되기 때문이에요.

아, 이걸 빼먹을 뻔 했네요! 우편물이 누구에게 보내지는지 못지 않게, 우편물의 시기도 그만큼 중요하다는 것을 잊지 말아야 합니다. 여러분이 전자제품을 광고하고 있다고 합시다. 여러분은 (광고의) 예산 대부분을 사람들이 서로 선물을 주고 받는 겨울 연휴 기간에 써왔고요. 자, 겨울 연휴 기간은 광고를 하기에 아주 좋은 때처럼 보일지도 모릅니다. 하지만 틀릴 수도 있어요. 가끔은 올림픽과 같은 굵직한 스포츠 행사 때 카탈로그를 보내는 것이 더 나을지도 모릅니다. 중요한 것은, 회사는 우편물을 보낼 대상을 주의 깊게 분류하는 것만큼이나, 언제 우편 광고 활동을 하는 것이 더 효과적인지에 대해서도 조사를 해야 한다는 것입니다. 돈을 들인 만큼 효과가 있는지를 확신하기 위해, 그리고 알기 위해서 사실들, 즉 좋은 조사를 통해 나온 사실들을 얻어야 합니다.

또 한 가지 살펴봐야 할 것은, 우편물을 보내는 것이 회사의 이미지에 어떻게 영향을 미치냐 하는 것입니다. 고객이 정크 메일을 보내는 회사에 대해 어떻게 인지하는가 하는 것 말입니다. 모두가 이 수익성 높은 광고 방법을 지지하는 것은 아니라는 점을 기억해야 합니다. 개인 정보를 모으는 것은 목록 판매자들이지만, 사람들은 카탈로그에 자기의 이름이 있는 것에 대해 (우편물을 보낸) 회사에 캐물을 것입니다. 그들은 심지어 사생활을 침해했다고 그 회사를 비난할지도 모릅니다. 이것 역시 더 많은 조사를 통해 방지될 수 있습니다. 따라서, 어떠한 마케팅 활동이건 그것이 성공적이려면, 우리는 올바른 조사의 필요성을 반드시 염두에 두어야 합니다.

Ⓦ outdated [autdéitid] 구식인　nonetheless [nÀnðəlés] 그렇기는 하지만　direct mail 광고용 우편물　revenue [révənjùː] 수익, 수입　be attributed to ~ ...에 기인하다　profit [práfit] 이익, 수익　slot [slɑt] (가느다란 자리에) 넣다, 끼워 넣다　refined [rifáind] 엄밀한, 세밀한　metropolitan [mètrəpálitən] 대도시(의)　conduct [kándəkt] 시행하다　outsource [áutsɔːrs] 외부에 위탁하다　criteria [kraití(ː)əriə] (pl.) 기준, 표준　flyer [fláiər] 전단　in response to ~ ...에 대응하여　attention-grabbing 관심을 끄는　tailor [téilər] 맞추다　personalize [pə́ːrsənəlàiz] (개인의 필요에) 맞추다　deliberately [dilíbəritli] 의도적으로　cross out 선을 그어 지우다　personal touch 개인적인 손길[느낌]　lucrative [lúːkrətiv] 수익성이 좋은　accuse A of B B의 이유로 A를 비난[고소]하다　invade privacy 사생활을 침해하다

01 강의의 주된 내용은?
Ⓐ 다이렉트 마케팅의 다양한 방법들
Ⓑ 다이렉트 메일을 성공적으로 사용하기
Ⓒ 고객 요구를 만족시키는 방법들
Ⓓ 고객들이 원하는 상품을 개발하는 방법

02 DM 광고를 사용하는 회사들에 관해 교수가 말한 것은?
Ⓐ 광고를 준비하는 데 더 많은 시간을 써야 한다.
Ⓑ TV 광고도 활용해야 한다.
Ⓒ 수익을 내기 위해 그렇게 많은 돈을 쓰지 않아도 된다.
Ⓓ 광고 활동에 최신 기법을 사용한다.

03 교수가 스포츠카를 언급한 이유는?
Ⓐ 일부 고객들이 광고에 어떻게 반응하는지를 아는 것이 어렵다는 것을 예를 들어 설명하려고
Ⓑ 어떤 상품을 광고하기 전에 품질을 보장하는 것이 중요하다는 것을 시사하려고
Ⓒ 서툴게 쓰여진 광고 메시지가 어떤 부정적 결과를 낳을 수 있는지를 보여주려고
Ⓓ 누가 특정 상품에 관심이 있을지를 알아내야 할 필요성을 강조하려고

04 목록 판매자들의 주요 역할은? (두 가지 선택)
Ⓐ 회사를 잠재 고객들에게 팔 브로커를 고용하기
Ⓑ 고객들에 대한 정보를 구하고 조직하기
Ⓒ 어떤 고객들이 회사의 상품을 팔 것인지를 분석하기
Ⓓ 어떤 사람들이 그들의 의뢰자의 상품을 사는지를 점검하기

05 언제 DM 광고를 발송할 것인지 결정하는 것에 관해 교수가 암시한 것은?
Ⓐ 회사가 아닌 목록 판매자들에 의해 결정되어야 한다.
Ⓑ 광고를 연중 내내 보내는 것이 가장 좋을 것이다.
Ⓒ 상식보다는 조사에 의존하는 것이 더 좋다.
Ⓓ 큰 행사 기간 동안 DM을 보내는 것은 좋은 생각이 아니다.

강의의 일부분을 다시 듣고 질문에 답하시오. 🔊 MP3 74_1

> It's not like companies can send out a bunch of catalogues and assume everyone will want to take a look at them. They have to carefully sort out what type of people would want to take a look at their specific catalogues. In other words, companies need to avoid sending advertisements to consumers who will not be interested in their merchandise.

06 교수가 다음과 같이 말한 이유는?

> It's not like companies can send out a bunch of catalogues and assume everyone will want to take a look at them.

Ⓐ 사람들이 더 이상 일반 우편을 사용하지 않는다는 것을 증명하려고
Ⓑ 정크 우편물을 받는 것을 좋아하는 사람이 거의 없다는 것을 지적하려고
Ⓒ 회사들이 많은 카탈로그를 보내야 한다는 것을 지적하려고
Ⓓ 회사들이 적절한 고객층을 알아내야 한다는 것을 강조하려고

Practice Questions

본문 p. 422

| 01 B | 02 D | 03 B | 04 C | 05 A | 06 D |

Listen to part of a lecture in a business class. MP3 75

Main Idea
좋은 판매원이 되기 위한 특성

Professor(female): Okay, as we've talked about, a key aspect of successfully selling a product is getting a sense of whether the customer really wants it. But, sometimes, what it really boils down to is the person who is actually selling the product. **Q1 Today, I want to talk about the traits that make a successful salesperson.** Can anybody describe an effective salesperson? What type of person is probably the most successful salesperson?

Student(male): I'd say effective salespeople truly believe in the products they sell. They should really believe that what they're selling is a good value.

P: That's a good point… That's definitely important. Just like a product can be perceived based on its packaging and how it's advertised, perceptions can be changed by a salesperson who clearly has a firm belief in a product. But there are certain characteristics of people that make them more likely to have a successful sales career. It's true that sales and the product go hand in hand, but there are some characteristics that salespeople must have. What are some words that come to mind when you think about salespeople?

Requirement
필요한 자질 (1)
- 자아지향적

S: Confidence? I mean, a guitar salesperson can't be shy or be afraid of selling guitars, right?

P: Very good. But where does confidence come from? What are more detailed characteristics that make up a confident salesperson? The answer to these questions is simple. First, **Q2 salespeople must be ego-driven… That is, they need to have an intense drive to get things done, like a person who wants to be better than everyone else.** When ego-driven salespeople sell a certain product, they will feel that they are better than all the other salespeople. This motivation to become better gives a salesperson the drive to sell a product.

Disadvantage / Example
자아지향적인 판매원의 안 좋은 예

S: **Q3 Isn't that a little dangerous? What if the salesperson is a little too aggressive? I remember when I was buying my first car. I just felt like the salesperson was trying too hard, I felt really uncomfortable,** you know. I mean, I ended up buying the car, so I guess it worked, but I don't think I'd ever go to that dealer again.

P: That's a very good point. Although confidence is important, it's also important to have the ability to understand what the customer is feeling. He did ultimately sell you a car, so I'm sure he felt really good about it, but you see, he also lost a future customer and maybe a lot of potential customers too. Would you recommend the salesperson to any of your friends who were thinking of buying a car?

S: Probably not.

P: Exactly. Ego-driven salespeople may persevere and sell the product, but they'll miss out on a lot of chances.

Requirement
필요한 자질 (2)
- 공감

Definition
empathy의 정의

Disadvantage
공감을 하는 판매원의 안 좋은 예

Problem
회사들의 직원 채용 시 문제점

Headset

That brings me to the next characteristic of a successful salesperson, empathy. A person who is empathic is capable of feeling what another person feels. An empathic salesperson can understand what the customer needs and can listen to people, offering products or services that are relevant to them. For example, um… Let's say a mother went to a clothing store for babies. An empathic salesperson would probably ask how the mother feels and talk about the child a little bit. He would relate to the customer before making the sale. And if the customer didn't respond, he would try to figure out the reason and adjust his approach accordingly. In the case of the car dealer, he wouldn't have pushed you as hard if he was more of an empathic person.

S: Wouldn't an empathic salesperson just be better then? It's hard to believe that a salesperson who understands customers can be any worse than a salesperson who just wants to be better than other people.

P: Well, a lot of people believe that, but when you think about it, an empathic salesperson would not only understand the customer, **Q4** **he'd also be concerned about his fellow employees… let's say an ego-driven coworker who is also a salesperson.**

S: Ah… He'd lose a lot of sales to his coworkers.

P: Exactly. That's why it's important to have a good balance between two characteristics. In theory, it's simple. But in practice, **Q5** **companies haven't been successful at figuring out if the people they hire have those traits. Too many companies look for applicants with the same interests as very successful salespeople, and not for people with the best skills to do the job.** 🎧 **Q6** Rembrandt had an assistant that shared his interest in the interplay between shadow and light, but does anyone remember his name?

해석 경영학 수업의 다음 강의 일부분을 들으시오.

교수(여자): 좋아요, 지금까지 이야기했듯이, 성공적인 상품 판매의 핵심 측면은, 고객이 정말로 그것을 원하는지에 대한 감을 잡는 것입니다. 하지만, 가끔은, 정말 핵심이 되는 문제는, 실제로 그 상품을 파는 사람이기도 합니다. 오늘은, 성공적인 판매원을 만드는 자질들에 대해 이야기하고 싶습니다. 유능한 판매원에 대해 설명할 수 있는 사람이 있나요? 어떤 유형의 사람이 가장 성공적인 판매원일까요?

학생(남자): 유능한 판매원은 자신이 파는 물건을 진심으로 믿어요. 판매원은 자신이 파는 것이 좋은 가치가 있다고 정말로 믿어야 해요.

교수: 좋은 지적이에요… 그건 분명 중요하죠. 어떤 상품이 그 포장이나 광고되는 방식을 기반으로 인식되는 것과 마찬가지로, 그런 인식들은 상품에 대한 굳건한 믿음을 갖고 있는 판매원에 의해서도 바뀔 수 있어요. 하지만 사람들이 성공적인 판매 경력을 가질 수 있는 가능성을 높여줄 수 있는 어떤 특징들이 있기는 하지요. 판매량과 상품이 관련이 있긴 하지만, 판매원이 반드시 지녀야 하는 어떤 특징들이 있다는 말이에요. 여러분이 판매원을 생각할 때 떠오르는 단어들에는 어떤 게 있나요?

학생: 자신감이에요? 그러니까, 기타를 파는 판매원이라면, 수줍어하거나 기타를 파는 것에 대해 두려워하면 안되잖아요?

교수: 아주 좋아요. 하지만 자신감은 어디서 오는 걸까요? 자신감이 넘치는 판매원을 만드는 더 상세한 특징들은 어떤 것일까요? 이 질문들에 대한 답은 간단합니다. 우선, 판매원들은 자아지향적이어야 합니다… 즉, 그들은 일을 완수하겠다는 강한 열망을 가지고 있어야 한다는 것입니다. 자신이 다른 누구보다도 더 나은 사람이고 싶어 하는 사람처럼요. 자아지향적인 판매원들이 어떤 물건을 팔면, 그 사람들은 다른 판매원들보다 자신이 더 낫다고 생각합니다. (더 나은 사람이 되고 싶다는) 이런 동기 부여가, 물건을 팔려는 욕구를 판매원에게 가져다주는 것이죠.

학생: 그건 좀 위험하지 않나요? 만일 판매원이 지나치게 적극적이면 어떻게 하죠? 제 첫 차를 사던 때가 기억나요. 판매원이 너무 애쓰는다는 느낌이 들어서 정말 불편했거든요. 그러니까, 뭐 결국 제가 차를 샀으니 효과가 있었다고 볼 수는 있겠지만, 그 딜러를 다시 찾아갈 것 같지는 않아요.

교수: 매우 좋은 지적이에요. 자신감이 중요하기는 하지만, 고객이 어떻게 느끼는지를 이해하는 능력을 가지는 것도 또한 중요합니다. 그 사람은 결국에는 학생에게 차를 팔았고, 그로 인해 기분은 무척 좋았겠지만, 알다시피 그는 앞으로의 고객을 하나 잃었고, 아마도 더 많은 잠재고객들까지 놓쳤을 수도 있죠. 학생은 차를 살 생각이 있는 친구들에게 그 판매원을 추천하겠어요?

학생: 아마도 아니겠죠.

교수: 바로 그거에요. 자아지향적인 판매원들은 인내를 갖고 상품을 팔 수 있을지도 모르죠. 하지만 그들은 많은 기회들을 놓칠 것입니다. 이제 내가 다루고자 하는, 성공적인 판매원의 다음 특징으로 넘어가게 되네요. 바로 공감입니다. 공감을 하는 사람은 다른 사람이 느끼는 것을 느낄 수 있는 능력이 있습니다. 공감을 하는 판매원은 고객이 무엇을 필요하는지를 이해할 수 있고 사람들의 말에 귀를 기울이며 그들에게 적절한 상품이나 서비스를 제공합니다. 예를 들어, 음… 한 어머니가 아기 옷을 사기 위해 옷가게에 갔다고 해봅시다. 공감을 하는 판매원은 아마도

어머니의 기분을 묻고 아이에 대해 조금 이야기를 할 것입니다. 판매를 하기 전에 고객과 관계를 맺고자 하려는 것이지요. 만일 고객이 그것에 응답하지 않으면, 그는 그 이유를 파악하려 애쓰고 그에 맞춰 접근법을 조정할 것입니다. 자동차 판매원의 경우에는, 그 사람이 조금만 더 공감을 하는 사람이라면 그렇게 강하게 몰아 부치지 않았을 것입니다.

학생: 그러면, 공감을 하는 판매원이 더 나은 거 아닌가요? 고객들을 이해하는 판매원이 다른 사람들보다 더 월등해지려고만 하는 판매원보다 나쁠 수도 있다고는 생각되지 않는데요.

교수: 음, 많은 사람들이 그렇게 생각하지요. 하지만 생각해보면, 공감을 하는 판매원은 고객을 이해하는 것뿐만 아니라 동료 직원에 대해서도 염려를 할 거에요... 자아지향적 판매원 동료가 있다고 한번 해보죠.

학생: 아... 그런 사람은 동료들에게 매출을 많이 뺏길 수도 있겠군요.

교수: 바로 그거에요. 그것이 바로 두 가지 특징 간의 균형을 갖추는 것이 중요한 이유입니다. 이론적으로는 간단해요. 하지만 실제 상황에서는 회사들이 그들이 고용하는 사람들이 그런 특질들을 가지고 있는지를 알아내는 데 성공하지 못했습니다. 너무 많은 회사들이, 매우 성공적인 판매원과 같은 관심사를 가지고 있는 지원자들만을 찾고 있어요. 그 일을 할 수 있는 최고의 기술을 가진 사람들을 찾는 것이 아니고 말이죠. 렘브란트에게는 그림자와 빛의 상호작용에 대한 그의 관심을 공유했던 조수가 있었지만, 그의 이름을 기억하는 사람이 있기나 한가요?

Ⓦ aspect [金spekt] 측면   trait [treit] 자질   salesperson [séilzpə̀ːrsən] 판매원   packaging [pǽkidʒiŋ] 포장(재)   advertise [金dvərtàiz] 광고하다   go hand in hand 관련되다; 함께 가다   make ~ up ...을 이루다, 형성하다   ego-driven [íːgou-drívən] 자아지향적인   drive [draiv] 욕구   motivation [mòutəvéiʃən] 동기   dealer [díːlər] 딜러, 중개인   persevere [pə̀ːrsəvíər] 인내하며 계속하다   miss out on ~ ...을 놓치다   empathy [émpəθi] 감정이입, 공감   adjust [ədʒʌ́st] 조정하다   accordingly [əkɔ́ːrdiŋli] 그에 맞춰   assistant [əsístənt] 조수   interplay [íntərplèi] 상호작용

01 강의의 주된 내용은?
Ⓐ 사람들이 판매원이 되는 이유들
Ⓑ 유능한 판매원이 가진 성격적 자질들
Ⓒ 고객의 요구를 이해하는 방법
Ⓓ 최저 가격을 얻는 비결

02 교수에 의하면, 자아지향적인 판매원들의 어떤 특성이 그들이 하는 일을 잘하도록 만들어주는가?
Ⓐ 상품의 이해에 있어 자신감이 있다.
Ⓑ 상품을 사는 사람과 공감대를 형성할 수 있다.
Ⓒ 시작한 일이 무엇이건 그것을 끝내고 싶어 한다.
Ⓓ 동료들보다 뛰어나고 싶어 한다.

03 학생이 차를 구입했던 것을 언급한 이유는?
Ⓐ 모두가 약간의 공감능력이 있다는 것을 증명하려고
Ⓑ 자아지향적인 판매원들의 안 좋은 면에 대해 지적하려고
Ⓒ 유능한 판매원의 예를 제공하려고
Ⓓ 교수에게 좀 더 분명한 예를 요청하려고

04 교수에 의하면, 공감을 잘 하는 판매원들이 직면하는 문제점은 무엇인가?
Ⓐ 상품의 결점에 대해 너무 정직할 것이다.
Ⓑ 고객이 상품을 사는 것에 대해 기분이 좋지 않게 만들 것이다.
Ⓒ 좀 더 적극적인 판매원들에게 판매를 뺏길 것이다.
Ⓓ 판매한 후 기분이 좋지 않을 것이다.

05 판매원을 고용하는 회사들에 대해 교수가 말한 것은?
Ⓐ 지원자들의 판매 능력을 보지 못한다.
Ⓑ 지원자들의 흥미를 고려하지 않는다.
Ⓒ 공감능력을 가진 사람들만을 찾는다.
Ⓓ 그들이 판매하는 것에 대해 신경을 쓰는 사람들을 쫓아낸다.

06 교수가 다음과 같이 말한 이유는? 🔊 MP3 75_1

> Rembrandt had an assistant that shared his interest in the interplay between shadow and light, but does anyone remember his name?

- Ⓐ 학생들이 예술에 대해 잘 알고 있는지 물어보려고
- Ⓑ 자신이 예술에 전문 지식이 부족하다는 것을 인정하려고
- Ⓒ 누구든지 좋은 판매원이 될 수 있다는 것을 암시하려고
- Ⓓ 흥미보다 능력이 중요하다는 것을 설명하려고

04 / Education

Sample Questions
본문 p. 428

01 C **02** D **03** B, C **04** A **05** C **06** D

해석 교육학 수업의 다음 강의 일부분을 들으시오. 🔊 MP3 76

교수(남자): 자, 지난주에는 교육 접근법에 관한 단원을 배우기 시작했죠. 오늘은, 다른 유형의 교습 방식을 시도했던 대학에 관한 사례 연구를 다루려 합니다. Black Mountain 대학이죠. 이 대학은 1933년 노스캐롤라이나 주의 Black Mountain에 설립되었습니다. 하지만… 음… 1957년에 문을 닫았죠.

학생(여자): 실패한 학교에 대해 왜 배우는 거죠?

교수: 아, 아니에요. 그 학교가 실패를 했을지는 모르지만, 그건 노력 부족 때문은 아니었어요… 학교가 잘못한 것은 아무것도 없었죠. 안 좋은 학교였느냐 하는 의미에서는 어떤 것도 잘못된 것이 없다는 말이죠. 이 학교는 시대를 너무 앞서 갔을 뿐이었죠. 그 학교의 교육 접근법은 1930년대로서는 너무 급진적이었어요.

어쨌든, 이 학교를 그렇게 특별하게 만들었던 것은, 교육이 어떠해야 하는가에 대한 그 학교의 관점이었습니다. 이 학교는 John Dewey의 교육철학을 바탕으로 설립되었어요. 지난 수업 시간에 그것들에 대해 배웠던 것 기억하죠? Dewey의 주된 논거는 교육과 학습은 사회적이고 상호작용적인 과정이라는 것이었습니다. 그는 학교는 그 자체로 학생들이 교육과정과 상호작용을 할 기회를 가질 수 있는 사회적인 기관이어야 하고, 학생들은 스스로의 학습에 참여할 기회를 가져야 한다고 생각했습니다.

학생: 음, Hill 교수님? 그게 뭐가 그렇게 특별한가요? 그러니까 제 말은, 저희도 지금 토론 수업을 하고 있지 않나요? 그것도 저희가 학습에 참여하는 게 아닌가요?

교수: 네, 참여하는 것이 맞지요. 그것이 바로 무엇이 Black Mountain 대학을 그렇게 특별하게 만들었는지에 주목해야 하는 중요한 이유입니다. 그 바탕이 되는 철학들은 오늘날에는 흔한 것이지만, 그 당시에는 그렇지 않았어요. 이런 유형의 학교가 설립되고 난 후에야 다른 인문과학 대학들이 그 학교와 같은 원칙들 중 많은 것을 받아들이기 시작했습니다.

이 학교가 설립되었을 때의 교육이 어떠했었는지 한번 살펴보도록 하지요. 대부분의 대학은 학생들에게 어떤 직종에서건 성공하는 데 필요한 특정 지식을 주는 것에 초점을 맞추었습니다. 학교는 교수들이 자신들이 아는 것을 가르치기 위해 존재할 뿐이었고, 학생들은 자신들이 무엇을 배우고 싶은지, 또는 무엇을 배워야 하는지에 대해 발언권이 없었습니다. 하지만, Black Mountain 대학의 창립자인 John Andrew Rice는 다른 생각을 가지고 있었습니다. 그는 교과과목을 배우는 것에 초점을 맞추었을 뿐만 아니라, 학생들의 정서적, 지적 성장을 가속화하는 것에도 애를 썼습니다. 그는 학습에만 초점을 두는 기존의 교습 방식에 동의하지 않았습니다. 그는 학습과 삶은 밀접하게 연결되어 있다고 생각했습니다.

Black Mountain 대학은 그 학교의 공동 방식에 있어 독특했습니다. 이 학교는 창조 예술과 실질적인 책무는 지식인의 발달에 있어 똑같이 중요하다는 생각을 바탕으로 하여 '민주주의 속의 교육'의 실험의 장으로 만들어졌습니다. 교수진과 학생 모두 학교를 돕기 위한 작업들에 똑같이 참여했습니다. 여기에는 학교에서 운영하는 농장에서의 작업, 건물을 짓는 일, 유지보수 작업을 하는 것, 식사 나르기 등등이 포함되었습니다.

이 학교는 의사 결정 과정에 있어서도 독특했습니다. 전통적으로는, 학생들과 교수진, 학교 직원들은 모두 개별적인 독립체들이었습니다. 각 학생은 교수와는 관계가 있었지만, 학교 운영을 돕는 직원과는 관계를 맺지 않았죠. 하지만 Black Mountain 대학은 작은 학교여서, 이 독립적인 세 집단에서 리더들을 선출할 수 있었고, 이 리더들이 모여 학교의 미래에 대해 논의할 수 있었습니다. 학생들은 그들을 가르치는 교수

와 마찬가지로 학교의 발전 방향에 대해 동등한 발언권을 행사할 수 있었습니다.

이 대학이 끼친 가장 큰 영향은 학문간 연구라는 개념에서 기인합니다. 학생들은 광범위한 코스들을 수강하도록 요구 받았습니다. 그래서, 과학 전공의 학생은 인생에 대한 더 넓은 관점을 얻기 위해 예술 과목들을 수강하도록 요구 받았지요. 1940년대쯤에는 Black Mountain 대학에서 일어나고 있던 일들이 밖으로 퍼져 나갔습니다. 곧, 이사회에는 많은 영향력 있는 예술가, 작가, 과학자들이 포함되었습니다. 심지어 알버트 아인슈타인도 이사회의 일원이었고 강의도 했습니다.

하지만, 이 대학은 본질적으로 너무 실험적이었고, 1950년대 들어 자연히 사라지게 되었습니다. 현대 교육이 어떻게 실행되는지에 강력한 영향을 미쳤던 Black Mountain 대학은 1957년에 문을 닫았습니다.

Ⓦ found [faund] 설립하다 interactive [intəræktiv] 상호작용을 하는 institution [instɪtjúːʃən] 기관 commonplace [kάmənplèis] 아주 흔한 profession [prəféʃən] 직업 accelerate [əksélərèit] 가속화하다 intellectual [intəléktʃuəl] 지적인 intimately [íntəmətli] 친밀히, 직접적으로 communal [kəmjúːnəl] 공동의 faculty [fǽkəlti] 교수진 entity [éntəti] 독립체 stem from ~ …에서 생겨나다[기인하다] interdisciplinary [intərdísəplənèri] 여러 학문 분야가 관련된 board of directors 이사회, 경영진 run its course 자연히 사라지다

01 교수가 주로 논의하고 있는 것은?
Ⓐ 전통적인 교육 접근법과 현대 교육 접근법 간의 비교
Ⓑ Black Mountain 대학이 문을 닫은 가능성 있는 이유들
Ⓒ 현재의 대학 시스템에 영향을 미쳤던 진보적인 한 학교
Ⓓ 대학 학생들이 학교 활동에 참여하기 위한 가장 좋은 방법들

02 교수가 John Dewey의 교육 원칙들을 언급한 이유는?
Ⓐ 학교에서 단순한 지식 이상의 것을 얻어야 하는 필요성을 강조하려고
Ⓑ 학생들이 학교의 결정에 발언권이 있어야 하는 필요성을 설명하려고
Ⓒ Black Mountain 대학 창립자의 배경을 설명하려고
Ⓓ Black Mountain 대학의 근본적 철학을 소개하려고

03 Black Mountain 대학과 전통적인 대학들의 차이점으로 교수가 언급한 것은? (두 가지 선택)
Ⓐ Black Mountain 대학은 과학 수업을 제공하지 않았다.
Ⓑ Black Mountain 대학의 학생들은 일을 하도록 요구 받았다.
Ⓒ Black Mountain 대학의 모든 이들은 문제에 관해 동등한 발언권을 가졌다.
Ⓓ 전통적인 대학의 학생들은 교수와 동등하게 간주되었다.

04 교수에 의하면, Black Mountain 대학의 창립자에 대해 사실인 것은?
Ⓐ 기존 학교들의 교습 방법에 동의하지 않았다.
Ⓑ 학생들이 특정 과목들에 집중할 수 있어야 한다고 믿었다.
Ⓒ John Dewey의 교육 철학에 대한 그의 환상이 깨졌다.
Ⓓ 대학 학생들에게 그들이 일할 수 있는 장소를 주고 싶어 했다.

05 Albert Einstein에 관해 추론할 수 있는 것은?
Ⓐ 학생들을 가르치는 것보다 다른 교수들을 가르치는 것을 더 선호했다.
Ⓑ 반 크기에 제한을 둔 학교들에서만 가르쳤다.
Ⓒ Black Mountain 대학의 교육 철학에 동의했다.
Ⓓ Black Mountain 대학이 재정적으로 성공하도록 도왔다.

강의의 일부분을 다시 듣고 질문에 답하시오. 🔊 MP3 76_1

> Uh, Professor Hill? What's so special about that? I mean, aren't we having a class discussion right now? Isn't that taking part in our learning?

06 학생이 다음과 같이 말한 이유는?

> I mean, aren't we having a class discussion right now?

Ⓐ 교수가 강의를 멈춰야 한다고 생각한다.

Ⓑ Black Mountain 대학에 대해 배워야 한다고 생각하지 않는다.
Ⓒ 자신이 수업에서 무엇을 하도록 기대되는지 알지 못한다.
Ⓓ 무엇 때문에 Black Mountain 대학이 특별한지 이해하지 못한다.

≋ Practice Questions

본문 p. 432

| 01 D | 02 B | 03 B | 04 A | 05 D | 06 C |

Term
reinforcer 용어 설명

Origin
Premack principle
이름의 기원
◐ theory, principle이 언급되면 그 정의를 잘 들어야 한다.

Example
reinforcer를 설명하기 위한 예

Example
적용 실패의 예

Limitation
prize는 일시적 행동에만 효과가 국한됨

Listen to part of a lecture in an educational psychology class. ◁ MP3 77

Professor(female): As we talked about earlier, ▶Q1◀ the term "reinforcer" refers to something that makes someone more likely to do what you want them to do. So, for example, ▶Q2◀ if a child gets rewarded for doing the dishes, it is more likely that he'll want to do the dishes again in the future. So, rewards, prizes, privileges, compliments – anything that encourages a particular type of behavior. ▶Q1◀ If we learn to use these reinforcers effectively, we can get children to behave in a way that's appropriate for learning. Yet, we first need to understand the theories behind the reinforcement theory.

Let's start with the Premack principle (shown on screen). ▶Q3◀ The Premack principle is named after David Premack, who developed his theory in the 1960s. It is based on the fact that we all rank activities based on the perceived value we associate with them. Now, knowing that hierarchy is important, we can figure out the corresponding reinforcers depending on the person.

For example, I have two daughters, and I want them to read at least 30 minutes a day. Unfortunately, what child likes reading books? The older one loves listening to music, so I will tell her that she can download one song for every chapter she reads in her book. But the younger one doesn't listen to music at all. In her case, letting her download music wouldn't do anything at all. I would have to tell her she can go play with her friends once she's finished her reading. Premack's idea was, when you're using reinforcers, you need to know the values that other people, in my case, my girls, attach to various activities. You need to attach a higher value reinforcer if you want to encourage a low value activity.

So, how do we apply this to a classroom full of people? If everyone has different priorities, just like the case in my daughters, then we have to find a common activity that the group would prioritize. So, for example, think about a group of nine-year-olds. ▶Q6◀ **Running around and just playing with friends is probably the one thing every child that age wants to do.** Even if there is a large group of children, there will always be some activities that virtually all of them love.

But a lot of teachers fail to use reinforcers. Instead, they just tell their students to sit down as soon as class starts. These teachers are just following their first instinct, but, as you can see, **sitting down still is not a high ranking activity for children.** So, these teachers need a reinforcer. Now, we can use stickers or little plastic toys for rewards, ▶Q4◀ **but prizes only work for occasional activities. Prizes will eventually stop being special, but sitting quietly is something teachers want children to do quite often.** It might sound counterintuitive, but ▶Q5◀ **we can actually just let them run around as a reward for sitting still.** It sounds weird that a disruptive behavior – running around in the middle of class – can be used as a way to get children to sit down

Application / Example
초등학생에게 적용해서 성공한 예

quietly and concentrate, but in fact, play time can be a highly effective reinforcer.

Q5 **When I was teaching elementary school, I had a lot of success with this technique.** You start with equal amounts of time sitting and running, and then you start making the sitting time a little bit longer and the running around time a little bit shorter. As weeks go by, you keep lengthening the amount of time your class spends sitting and listening, and you gradually reduce the amount of time spent running and playing. It's remarkable, but by the end of the school year, you wind up with a classroom full of really well-behaved nine-year-olds. Even though some principles may seem counterintuitive, we must have an understanding of what works in the classroom to become efficient educators.

해석 교육 심리학 수업의 다음 강의 일부분을 들으시오.

교수(여자): 우리가 전에 이야기를 나누었듯이, '강화 인자'라는 용어는 어떤 사람에게 당신이 원하는 것을 하도록 할 가능성을 높여주는 무언가를 말합니다. 자, 예를 들면, 아이가 설거지를 한 대가로 보상을 받게 된다면, 그 아이는 앞으로 다시 설거지를 하고 싶어 할 가능성이 더 높습니다. 보상, 상, 특권, 칭찬 등 어떤 특정 유형의 행동을 하도록 격려하는 것은 무어라도 (강화 인자에) 해당되지요. 이 강화 인자들을 효과적으로 사용하는 법을 배운다면, 우리는 아이들을 학습에 적합한 방식으로 행동하도록 만들 수 있습니다. 하지만, 우선 강화 인자 이론에 얽힌 이론들을 이해해야 할 필요가 있겠군요.

Premack 원칙부터 시작해봅시다. (화면에 보여준다) Premack 원칙은 1960년대에 이 이론을 발전시킨 David Premack의 이름을 따서 지어졌습니다. 이 이론은, 우리는 모두 활동들에 관련을 지은 지각 가치에 근거하여 활동들의 순위를 매긴다는 사실에 근거를 두고 있습니다. 자, 서열이 중요하다는 것을 알고 있으므로, 우리는 사람에 따라 해당하는 강화 인자들을 파악할 수 있습니다.

예를 들어, 내게는 두 딸이 있는데, 나는 그 애들이 매일 최소 30분간 독서를 하기를 원합니다. 불행히도, 어떤 아이들이 독서를 좋아하겠어요? 큰딸은 음악을 듣는 것을 좋아해서, 나는 그 애에게 책의 각 챕터를 읽을 때마다 노래 하나를 다운받을 수 있다고 말할 겁니다. 하지만 작은딸은 음악을 전혀 듣지 않아요. 그 애의 경우에는, 음악을 다운받게 하는 것은 아무 도움이 되지 않지요. 그 애에게는 독서를 끝내면 친구들과 나가 놀 수 있다고 말해야 할 겁니다. Premack의 발상은, 강화 인자를 사용할 때는 다른 사람들, 내 경우에는 내 딸들이겠죠, 그들이 여러 다양한 활동들에 부여한 가치들을 알아야 한다는 것이었습니다. 낮은 가치의 활동을 장려하고 싶다면 더 높은 가치의 강화 인자를 부여해야 하는 것이죠. 그럼, 사람들로 가득한 교실에는 이것을 어떻게 적용할까요? 모두가 서로 다른 우선순위들을 가지고 있다면, 내 딸들의 경우처럼 말이에요, 그렇다면 그 무리가 우선시할 공통적인 활동을 발견해야 합니다. 자, 예를 들어, 아홉 살짜리들의 무리를 생각해봅시다. 친구들과 뛰어다니고 그냥 놀기만 하는 것이 아마도 그 나이의 모든 아이들이 하고 싶어 하는 한 가지일 겁니다. 큰 무리의 아이들이 있다 해도, 사실상 모두가 좋아하는 어떤 활동들이 항상 있기 마련이죠.

하지만 많은 교사들이 강화 인자를 사용하는 것에 실패합니다. 대신, 그들은 수업이 시작하자마자 그저 학생들에게 앉으라고 말할 뿐이죠. 이런 교사들은 자신들의 첫 직감을 따를 뿐이지만, 여러분도 알 수 있듯이, 아이들에게는 얌전히 앉아 있는 것이 높은 순위의 활동이 아닙니다. 그래서, 이런 교사에게는 강화 인자가 필요합니다. 자, 우리는 보상으로 스티커나 작은 플라스틱 장난감들을 사용할 수도 있겠지만, 상품은 가끔씩 있는 활동에만 효과를 볼 수 있습니다. 결국에는 상품이 더 이상 특별하게 느껴지지 않을 것이지만, 얌전히 앉아 있는 것은 교사들이 꽤 자주 아이들에게 원하는 것이거든요. 직관에 어긋나는 것처럼 들릴지도 모르겠지만, 우리는 사실 얌전히 앉아 있는 것에 대한 보상으로 아이들을 마음대로 뛰어다니도록 내버려두어도 됩니다. 수업 중에 뛰어다니는 것과 같이 지장이 되는 행동이 아이들이 얌전히 앉아서 집중하도록 하는 방법으로 쓰일 수 있다는 것이 이상하게 들리겠지만, 사실은, 놀이 시간은 매우 효과적인 강화 인자가 될 수 있습니다.

내가 초등학교에서 교사를 했을 때 이 기법으로 많은 성공을 거두었죠. 앉아 있는 시간과 뛰어다니는 시간을 똑같이 해서 시작한 뒤에, 앉아 있는 시간을 조금 더 길게, 그리고 뛰어다니는 시간은 조금 더 짧게 만드는 겁니다. 몇 주가 흐르는 동안, 반 아이들이 앉아서 수업을 듣는 시간의 양을 조금씩 늘리고, 뛰어다니고 노는 시간의 양은 점차 줄이는 거죠. 놀랍게도, 학년 말쯤에는, 매우 바르게 행동하는 아홉 살짜리들로 가득 찬 교실을 볼 수 있게 될 것입니다. 몇몇 원칙들이 직관에 어긋나 보이기는 하겠지만, 우리는 효과적인 교육자가 되기 위해서 교실에서 어떤 것들이 작용을 하는지에 대한 이해를 할 필요가 있습니다.

W reinforcer [reinfɔ́ːrsər] 강화 인자   reward [riwɔ́ːrd] 보상하다; 보상   privilege [prívəliʤ] 특권   compliment [kɑ́mpləmənt] 칭찬   rank [ræŋk] 등급을 매기다   perceived [pərsíːvd] 인지된   hierarchy [háiərɑ̀ːrki] 계급, 계층   corresponding [kɔ̀(ː)rispɑ́ndiŋ] (…에) 해당하는, 상응하는   prioritize [praiɔ́ːrətàiz] 우선순위를 매기다   instinct [ínstiŋkt] 본능, 직감   disruptive [disrʌ́ptiv] 지장을 주는   gradually [grǽdʒəwəli] 점차

01 강의의 주된 내용은?
Ⓐ 아이들에게 수업에 주의를 기울이도록 권고하는 방법들

Ⓑ 특정한 유형의 행동에 가장 좋은 보상들
Ⓒ 어린이들을 가르치는 것의 어려움
Ⓓ **아이들이 좋은 행동을 하도록 권장하는 하나의 방법**

02 설거지를 하는 아이에 대해 교수가 말한 것은?
Ⓐ 아이들은 매일 하는 집안일에 매우 능하다.
Ⓑ **아이들은 보상을 받을 수 있을 때 더 잘 행동한다.**
Ⓒ 부모의 말을 듣는 아이들은 거의 없다.
Ⓓ 아이들은 특정 과제를 하는 법을 빨리 배울 수 있다.

03 교수에 의하면, Premack 원칙이 말하는 것은?
Ⓐ 선택이 주어졌을 때, 사람들은 자신이 하고 싶은 것만 할 것이다.
Ⓑ **어떤 종류의 활동들은 다른 종류의 활동보다 더 선호된다.**
Ⓒ 처벌의 위협은 좋은 행동을 권장하기 위해 쓰일 수 있다.
Ⓓ 모든 종류의 행동들은 권장되거나 강화될 수 있다.

04 좋은 행동에 대한 상품으로 장난감을 받는 아이들에 대해 추론할 수 있는 것은?
Ⓐ **장기적으로는 계속해서 잘 행동하지 않을 것이다.**
Ⓑ 더 오랜 기간 동안 공부하기 시작할 것이다.
Ⓒ 더 이상 강화 인자로 보상을 받을 필요가 없을 것이다.
Ⓓ 안 좋게 행동하는 아이들과 장난감을 공유할 것이다.

05 교수가 가르쳤던 초등학교 반 아이들은 어떻게 보상을 받았는가?
Ⓐ 하루가 끝날 때 공부할 시간이 주어졌다.
Ⓑ 장난감과 스티커를 받았다.
Ⓒ 먹을 간식을 받았다.
Ⓓ **뛰어 다니고 소리를 지르도록 허락 받았다.**

06 교수가 설명하는 교실에서의 흔한 문제점은?
Ⓐ 일부 아이들은 다른 아이들만큼 빨리 배우지 못한다.
Ⓑ 어떤 학생들은 교실에 있고 싶어 하지 않는다.
Ⓒ **학생들은 얌전히 앉아서 교사의 말을 듣고 싶어 하지 않는다.**
Ⓓ 학생들은 반 친구들과 잘 어울리지 못한다.

05 / Psychology

Sample Questions

본문 p. 438

01 C   02 C   03 A   04 D   05 C   06 B

해석 발달 심리학 수업의 다음 강의 일부분을 들으시오. ◁) MP3 78

교수(남자): 지난주는 초기 유년 시기의 아이들의 심리적 발달에 대해 이야기 해보았습니다. 이제는 유아와 그 아이를 돌보는 사람, 즉 양육자 (caregiver)와의 유대에 대해 이야기하고 싶습니다. 물론, 대부분의 경우에 있어 양육자는 부모이지만, 항상 그렇지는 않습니다. 아이의 발달에 있어, 이런 관계는 우리가 애착 유대라고 부르는 것입니다. 음... 애착은 유아와 양육자 간의 정서적 관계입니다. 애착은 태어난지 2개월에서 7개월 사이에 시작하며, 유아가 자라남에 따라 점차 발달합니다.

모든 아기들이 긍정적인 애착을 경험하는 것은 아니라는 점을 언급해야 할 것 같네요. 애착이 긍정적일 경우, 우리는 그것을 안정적인 애착이라 부릅니다. 하지만 그렇지 않은 경우는 불안정한 애착이라고 불립니다. 하지만 상세 내용으로 들어가기 전에, 심리학자 Mary Ainsworth에 의해 실시된 한 실험을 소개하고 싶습니다. Ainsworth는 성공적인 사회적, 정서적 발달을 하기 위해서는, 아기가 최소한 한 명의 주 양육자와 안정적인 애착을 발달시켜야 한다고 생각했습니다. 이것은 유아가 필요할 때 의지할 수 있는 양육자가 항상 있다는 것을 아는 가운데 세상을 탐구할 수 있도록 해줍니다.

그녀는 '낯선 상황 프로토콜'이라 부르는 것을 사용하여 아이들을 평가했습니다. 자, 이것은 진단 도구가 아니었다는 것을 염두에 두어야 합니다. 즉, 이것은 유아에게 문제가 있느냐 아니냐를 결정하는 데 쓰일 수 없다는 뜻입니다. '낯선 상황 프로토콜'은 유아가 가지고 있는 애착의 유형이 안정적인지 불안정적인지 분류하는 데 도움을 주기 위한 연구 도구일 뿐입니다.

'낯선 상황 프로토콜'은 정해진 형식을 따르는 실험실에서의 절차를 수반합니다. 어머니와 아기, 그리고 실험자가 방에 들어갑니다. 그리고 나서 실험자가 나가고, 일련의 상황들이 발생합니다. 아기는 여러 다른 상황에 놓여집니다. 가끔은 아기가 혼자 남겨지기도 하고, 가끔은 양육자와 있기도 하며, 또 가끔은 아기와 양육자, 그리고 한 낯선 사람이 함께 있기도 합니다... 어쨌든, 꽤 복잡한 과정입니다. 중요한 것은 바로 그 결과입니다. '낯선 상황 프로토콜'이라고 불리는 이유는, 음, 여러분이 알 수 있듯이, 아기가 아마도 익숙하지 않은 여러 낯선 상황에 처하기 때문입니다. 자, 안정 애착을 가진 아기들은... 새로운 방에 놓여지면 이런 아이들은 방을 탐구하는 경향이 있습니다. 장난감이나 할 일을 찾아서요... 양육자가 떠나면, 아기는 약간 당황할 뿐입니다. 양육자가 다시 돌아오면, 아기는 다시 행복해지고 긍정적인 상호관계 같은 것을 보이죠. 미소를 짓거나 양육자를 향해 기어가거나 하면서요. 아기들은 안정 애착을 가지고 있을 경우 이런 신호들을 보입니다.

하지만 불안정한 아기들은 어떨까요? 그 이름이 시사하듯이, 그런 아기들은 새로운 방에 들어오는 순간부터 불안해합니다. 그들은 주위를 둘러보거나 탐구하려 하지 않고, 양육자가 돌아왔을 때 그들과 심지어 상호작용조차 하지 않을지도 모릅니다. 이런 아기들은 불안정함을 느끼기 때문에 혼란스러워 보이고, 심지어는 겁을 먹은 것처럼 보이기도 합니다.

나 역시 발달에 대한 Ainsworth의 생각에 동의하긴 하지만, 애착 이론에, 특히 더 중요하게는, '낯선 상황 프로토콜'에 이견을 갖는 사람들이 있다는 것을 알아두어야 합니다. 비판가들은, 실험실 환경이 통제된 것이고 따라서 실제 생활에서 일어나는 것의 정확한 구현이 아니라고 항의합니다. 그들의 주장은, 그런 유대는 집이나 유아가 편안함을 느끼는 장소 같은, 좀 더 자연스러운 상황에서 분석되어야 한다는 것입니다. 불안 애착을 가진 아기는 살면서 나중에 행동을 통해 이 불안정함을 내보이게 된다는 것을 보여주는 연구가 일부 있어 왔습니다. 하지만, 어떤 사람들은, 애착이 그 아기의 미래에 무슨 일이 일어날지를 실제로 나타내주지는 않는다고 말합니다. 그 아기가 만족스럽고 자신감 넘치는 어른으로 자랄지 어떨지 우리는 알 수 없다고 그들은 말합니다. Jerome Kagan이라는 이름의 한 연구가는, 유아들은 여러 다른 상황에 적응할 수 있는 능력을 가지고 있고, 여러 다른 종류의 양육에 긍정적인 방식으로 대처할 수 있다고 생각합니다. Kagan은 더 나아가, 결국에는, 타고난 성격과 기질이 양육자에게 보이는 애착보다 더 중요하다고 생각합니다. 어떤 아기가 스트레스 상황에 내성이 매우 낮다고 한번 해보죠. 그 아기는 자신이 원하는 것을 얻지 못할 때 무엇을 해야 할지 모를 뿐입니다. 그것이 그 아기가 어떤 종류의 어른이 될지에 애착보다 더 영향을 주는 것이죠. 여러 다른 문화권의 아기들의 애착을 연구해온 다른 연구가들은 양육자들에 대한 아기들의 행동에 있어 차이점들을 발견했습니다. 낯선 상황 프로토콜이 그 아기들을 불안하다고 알려줄 수는 있겠지만, 그것은 그들의 문화권에서 아기때부터조차 독립성을 권장하기 때문일 수도 있다는 것입니다. 하지만, 연구들에서 대부분의 아기들은, 심지어 다른 문화권의 아기들도, 안정적인 애착을 가진 범주에 속한다는 것을 말해주고 싶습니다.

Ⓦ developmental psychology 발달 심리 bond [bɑnd] 유대 infant [ínfənt] 유아, 아기 caregiver [kɛ́ərgìvər] 돌보는 사람, 양육자 attachment [ətǽtʃmənt] 애착 positive [pɑ́zitiv] 긍정적인 secure [sikjúər] 안정적인 attain [ətéin] 이루다, 획득하다 assess [əsés] 평가하다 diagnostic [dàiəgnɑ́stik] 진단의 experimenter [ikspérəmèntər] 실험자 crawl [krɔːl] 기어가다 anxious [ǽŋkʃəs] 불안해하는 content [kəntént] 만족하는 innate [inéit] 타고난, 선천적인 temperament [témpərəmənt] 기질

01 강의의 주요 목적은?
Ⓐ 유아들의 발달 문제의 가능한 원인들을 논의하려고
Ⓑ 아이를 올바로 키우기 위해 필요한 주요 특성들을 설명하려고
Ⓒ 유아와 양육자 간의 관계 유형에 대해 논의하려고
Ⓓ 유아들이 자라면서 거쳐가는 다양한 단계들을 설명하려고

02 교수에 의하면, 낯선 상황 프로토콜의 목적은 무엇인가?
Ⓐ 문제가 있는 유아들에 있어 올바른 발달을 육성하는 데 도움을 주려고
Ⓑ 유아들이 가지고 있을지도 모르는 다양한 발달 문제들을 진단하려고
Ⓒ 유아가 안정적인 애착을 가지고 있는지 확인하려고
Ⓓ 유아들이 다양한 사람들과 어떤 종류의 유대를 발달시키는지 확인하려고

03 Mary Ainsworth에 비판적인 사람들에 대해 추론할 수 있는 것은?
Ⓐ 그녀의 분류법보다는, 그녀의 (실험) 방법에 동의하지 않는다.

Ⓑ 유아들이 양육자와 유대를 형성한다는 생각을 거부한다.
Ⓒ 그녀가 낯선 상황 프로토콜을 받아들여야 한다고 생각한다.
Ⓓ 그녀가 유아들의 안도 수준을 지나치게 강조한다고 생각한다.

04 애착 분류에 관한 Ainsworth의 생각에 대한 Jerome Kagan의 관점은?
Ⓐ 그녀는 유아들의 나이를 고려하는 데 실패했다.
Ⓑ 그녀가 확인한 것보다 훨씬 많은 분류가 있다.
Ⓒ 그녀의 생각은 다른 전통을 가진 문화에는 적용될 수 없다.
Ⓓ 한 유아의 미래를 결정하는 데에는 다른 요인들이 더 중요하다.

05 교수가 다른 문화권의 아기들에 대해 말한 것은?
Ⓐ 대개 여러 양육자들이 있는 가족 안에서 양육된다.
Ⓑ 항상 안정적인 애착을 가지고 있는 것으로 분류된다.
Ⓒ 덜 의존적이기 때문에 불안정하게 보일지도 모른다.
Ⓓ 주 양육자들과 더 강한 애착을 형성하는 경향이 있다.

강의의 일부분을 다시 듣고 질문에 답하시오. 🔊 **MP3 78_1**

A mother, her baby, and an experimenter enter the room. Then the experimenter leaves and a series of episodes occur. The baby is put in different situations. Sometimes the baby is left alone, sometimes the baby is with the caregiver, and sometimes the baby, the caregiver, and a stranger are together... Anyway, it's a pretty involved process. The results are what's important.

06 교수가 다음과 같이 말한 이유는?

It's a pretty involved process. The results are what's important.

Ⓐ 결과가 자료를 정확하게 반영하지 않는다고 생각한다.
Ⓑ 학생들이 모든 세부사항을 알 필요가 있다고 생각하지 않는다.
Ⓒ 학생들이 유사한 연구에 참여해야 한다고 생각한다.
Ⓓ 연구가들의 고생을 강조하고 싶어 한다.

≽ Practice Questions

본문 p. 442

| 01 C | 02 B | 03 B | 04 D | 05 A | 06 C |

Term
theory of mind 용어 설명

Difference
3살 이하는 마음 theory of mind를 가지고 있지 않음

Function
theory of mind의 기능

Listen to part of a lecture in a psychology class. 🔊 **MP3 79**

Professor(male): I've previously explained that the term "theory of mind" refers to the ability to realize that people have different beliefs... um, that we don't all necessarily believe the same things. It's the cognitive ability to recognize that others have knowledge, ideas,... beliefs that may be different from our own. Basically, we say that people have a theory of mind when they are able to recognize that others may have different beliefs than they do. It might seem like an irrelevant fact, but newborns, uh, ▶Q6◀ **infants don't seem to have it. This ability seems to develop somewhere between the ages of three and five. Once we have a theory of mind, we can recognize what motivates other people and can sometimes predict the next action they will take in certain situations.**

Main Idea
동물도 theory of mind가 있는가

Evidence
원숭이도 theory of mind가 있다는 증거

Findings / Cause
서열이 낮은 원숭이가 거짓 경보 울음을 낸 이유

Evidence
원숭이가 theory of mind가 있다는 것에 반하는 증거

Problem
theory의 문제점

Q1 Now, the question for us today is whether animals have a theory of mind. Researchers accept the likelihood that monkeys have a theory of mind because they're social animals that live in groups. Naturally, primates like monkeys would benefit from the ability to understand motivations and predict what other monkeys will do next. Now, we're assuming that animals have beliefs. Perhaps not as complex as our beliefs, but we're... Well, we're inferring beliefs from behavior. Animals act a certain way for a reason, not just from instinct, but because of their knowledge and because they have reasoned that a particular course of action would be beneficial. **Q2** Now, one type of evidence which proves that humans have a theory of mind is deceptive behavior. Intending to deceive someone requires knowing that they can have different beliefs than you do.

Researchers discovered just this type of behavior in vervet monkeys while observing them in West Africa. Vervets live in social groups, and occasionally a new member will try to join an established group. The researchers noticed that when a new male would try to become a member of one particular group, a certain low-ranking male would make a false alarm call that a leopard was approaching the group. When this happened, all the group members and the visitor would retreat into the trees to safety right away. **Q3** It's pretty obvious why a low-ranking monkey would do this. Our friend would have had little interest in seeing a new male member, who would almost certainly outrank him, join the group. And this tactic did stop that from happening.

We can infer the monkey had a belief from its behavior. The vervet knew no leopard existed, but he also knew that other monkeys would believe that there was a leopard. He realized the others would have a different belief than he had. Researchers have interpreted the monkey's behavior as an understanding of other vervets' minds and their probable reactions.

However, this monkey's behavior after the false alarm makes it a little more difficult for this interpretation to stick. You see, after the alarm call, our friend then came down from his own tree, crossed over to the tree of the visitor, the one who wanted to join the group, and issued the false alarm call again, possibly to really give the message to the intruder. **Q4** The problem is, if he really did have a theory of mind, he would have realized that climbing down from his tree would show the others that he was aware that there was no leopard around. This might be evidence against the theory that this particular monkey had a theory of mind. He could have just simply learned to associate the false alarm calls with the action of the other monkeys retreating into the trees. He could have just learned to provoke a reaction without really understanding the motivation behind the other monkeys' behavior.

Q5 As often the issue with observational studies, we don't really know which interpretation is right. There's always evidence that is inconsistent with a hypothesis, just like in this case. Observers might start out believing that animals have a theory of mind due to observations or evidence that corresponds to their hypothesis. But there's always going to be other observations that tell another story. Skeptics can and will always find an alternative interpretation by using these inconsistencies.

해석 심리학 수업의 다음 강의 일부분을 들으시오.
교수(남자): '마음 이론'이라는 용어는 사람들이 서로 다른 믿음들을 가지고 있다는 것을 깨닫는 능력을 말하는 것이라고 이전 시간에 설명했습니다... 음, 그러니까, 우리가 모두 같은 것만을 믿지는 않는다는 것이죠. 마음 이론은, 다른 사람들이 우리와는 다를 수 있는 지식, 생각... 신념을 가지고 있다는 것을 깨닫는 인지적 능력입니다. 기본적으로, 사람들이 다른 이들은 자신이 가진 것과는 다른 믿음을 가지고 있을지도 모른다고 깨달을 수 있을 때 우리는 그들이 마음 이론을 가지고 있다고 말합니다. 연관이 없어 보일 수도 있겠지만, 신생아, 음, 유아들은 마음 이론을 가지

고 있는 것 같지 않아 보입니다. 이 능력은 3살에서 5살 사이의 언제쯤엔가 생성되는 것으로 보입니다. 우리가 마음 이론을 가지고 있으면, 우리는 사람들이 무엇에 동기를 부여 받는지 깨달을 수 있고, 가끔은 특정 상황에서 그들이 취할 다음 행동을 예상할 수도 있습니다.

그럼, 우리가 오늘 알아보고자 하는 것은, 과연 동물들도 마음 이론을 가지고 있는가 하는 것입니다. 연구자들은 원숭이가 마음 이론을 가지고 있을 가능성을 인정하는데, 원숭이는 무리로 모여 사는 사회적인 동물이기 때문입니다. 당연히, 원숭이 같은 영장류들은 동기를 이해하는 능력과, 다른 원숭이들이 다음에 무엇을 할지를 예상하는 능력을 통해 이득을 볼 것입니다. 자, 동물들이 믿음이 있다고 가정해봅시다. 아마도 인간의 믿음만큼 복잡하지는 않겠지만, 우리는… 음, 우리는 행동으로부터 믿음을 유추합니다. 동물들은 이유가 있어 특정 방식으로 행동합니다. 그저 본능에 의해서만은 아닌, 그들의 지식으로 인해, 그리고 특정한 일련의 행동이 유익할 것이라고 생각했기 때문에 그렇게 행동하는 것이지요. 자, 인간이 마음 이론을 가지고 있다는 것을 증명하는 한 가지 유형의 증거는, 바로 속이는 행동입니다. 다른 이를 속이려고 의도하는 것은, 다른 사람들이 나와 다른 믿음을 가지고 있을 수도 있다는 것을 알고 있어야 하기 때문입니다.

연구자들은 서아프리카에서 버빗(vervet)원숭이를 관찰하는 동안 바로 이런 유형의 행동을 발견했습니다. 버빗원숭이들은 사회적 집단을 이루어 살아가는데, 때때로 새로운 멤버가 기존 그룹에 들어가고자 합니다. 연구자들은, 새로운 수컷이 한 특정 그룹의 일원이 되려고 애쓸 때, 서열이 낮은 한 수컷이 표범이 그룹 쪽으로 다가오고 있다고 알리는 거짓 경고 울음을 내는 것을 알아챘습니다. 이런 일이 일어났을 때, 그룹 내 모든 원숭이들과 새 원숭이는 안전한 곳을 찾아 즉시 나무 속으로 숨었습니다. 서열이 낮은 원숭이가 왜 이러한 일을 하는지는 다분히 명백합니다. 이 친구는 아마도 자신보다 분명 서열이 높은 새 수컷이 그룹에 끼는 것을 보고싶지 않았을 것입니다. 그리고 이런 술책은 그러한 일이 일어나는 것을 방지했지요.

우리는 그 원숭이의 행동을 통해 그 원숭이가 어떤 믿음을 가지고 있었다는 것을 유추할 수 있습니다. 그 버빗원숭이는 표범이 없다는 것을 알고 있었지만, 또한 다른 원숭이들은 표범이 있다고 믿을 것이라는 것도 알고 있었습니다. 그 원숭이는 다른 원숭이들이 자신과는 다른 믿음을 가지고 있다는 것을 알고 있었지요. 연구자들은 그 원숭이의 행동을 다른 버빗원숭이들의 마음과 가능성 있는 반응들에 대한 이해라고 해석했습니다. 하지만, 가짜 경보 이후의 그 원숭이의 행동은 이런 해석을 유지하기에 조금 어렵게 만들었습니다. 그러니까, 경고 울음 후에, 이 친구는 자기가 있던 나무에서 내려와, 새로 온 원숭이의 나무로 옮겨갔습니다. 그 그룹에 끼고 싶어 했던 그 원숭이에게 말이죠. 그리고는 다시 거짓 경고 울음소리를 냈습니다. 아마도 진짜 그 불청객에게 메시지를 전하기 위해서 말입니다. 문제는, 만약 그 원숭이가 진짜 마음 이론을 가지고 있다면, 그는 자기가 나무에서 내려온 것이 자신이 주변에 표범이 없다는 것을 알고 있었다는 것을 다른 원숭이들에게 알려주는 것이라는 점을 깨달았을 거라는 점입니다. 이것은 이 특정 원숭이가 마음 이론을 가지고 있었다는 이론에 반하는 증거가 될지도 모릅니다. 그 원숭이는 그저 거짓 경고 울음을 다른 원숭이들이 나무 속으로 숨는 행동과 결부짓는 법을 배웠을 뿐일 수도 있습니다. 다른 원숭이들의 행동 뒤에 있는 동기를 실제 이해하지 않은 채, 어떤 반응을 일으키는 법을 그냥 배웠던 것일지도 모르는 것이지요.

관찰 연구들에 관해 종종 있는 문제점과 마찬가지로, 우리는 어떤 해석이 맞는 건지 실제로는 알지 못합니다. 가설과 불일치하는 증거들은 항상 존재하죠. 이 경우처럼 말이에요. 관찰자들은 관찰이나 그들의 가설에 상응하는 증거로 인해 동물들이 마음 이론이 있다고 믿기 시작할 수도 있습니다. 하지만 언제나 또 다른 이야기를 말해주는 다른 관찰 내용들이 있기 마련이지요. 회의론자들은 이러한 불일치들을 이용하여 대안이 되는 해석들을 찾을 수 있고, 항상 찾을 것입니다.

Ⓦ refer to ~ …을 나타내다   cognitive ability 인지적 능력   newborn [njúːbɔːrn] 신생아   likelihood [láiklihùd] 가능성, 가망   primate [práimèit] 영장류   infer [infə́ːr] 추론하다   instinct [ínstiŋkt] 본능   reason [ríːzən] (논리적 근거에 따라) 판단하다   deceptive [diséptiv] 속이는, 거짓말의   established [istǽbliʃt] 확실히 자리를 잡은   false alarm 거짓 경보   retreat [ritríːt] 후퇴하다   stick [stik] 받아들여지다, 인정받다   intruder [intrúːdər] 불청객   provoke [prəvóuk] 유발하다   alternative [ɔːltə́ːrnətiv] 대안이 되는

01 강의의 목적은?
Ⓐ 사람들의 신념 체계를 구성하는 새로운 방식을 소개하려고
Ⓑ 동물들이 다른 동물들의 행동을 통해 어떻게 행동을 식별하는지 알려주려고
Ⓒ 어떤 한 심리적 능력이 동물들에게서도 관찰될 수 있는지를 논의하려고
Ⓓ 동물과 인간의 인지 능력의 차이를 설명하려고

02 교수에 의하면, 동물들의 어떤 유형의 행동이 그들이 마음 이론을 가지고 있다는 것을 시사하는가?
Ⓐ 서로서로 의사소통을 한다.
Ⓑ 서로를 속이려는 시도를 한다.
Ⓒ 사회적 구조를 발달시킨다.
Ⓓ 서로 위험을 경고한다.

03 교수에 의하면, 서열이 낮은 버빗원숭이가 경고 울음을 낸 이유는 무엇인가?
Ⓐ 실수로 새 원숭이가 포식자라고 생각했다.
Ⓑ 새 원숭이가 그 그룹에 끼는 것을 막고 싶어 했다.

ⓒ 그룹이 새 원숭이를 공격하도록 설득할 수 있다고 생각했다.
ⓓ 새 원숭이가 경고 울음을 다르게 해석했다는 것을 깨닫지 못했다.

04 버빗원숭이의 어떤 행동이 그 원숭이가 마음 이론을 가지고 있지 않을지도 모른다는 것을 시사했는가?
ⓐ 실제 표범이 있었을 때와 똑같은 행동을 보여주었다.
ⓑ 그룹 내에서의 자신의 서열을 지키기 위해서 다른 원숭이들을 속이려 했다.
ⓒ 다른 버빗원숭이들이 없었을 때만 경고 울음을 냈다.
ⓓ 근처에 표범이 없다는 것을 자신이 알고 있다는 것을 보여주는 행동을 했다.

05 동물들의 관찰 연구에 관해 교수가 암시한 것은?
ⓐ 종종 상반되는 증거를 낳는다.
ⓑ 제대로 수행하기가 매우 어렵다.
ⓒ 사람에 대해서 알 수 있는 더 쉬운 방법이다.
ⓓ 여러 다른 연구들은 대개 같은 결론을 가리킨다.

06 강의에 따르면, 5세 이상의 대부분의 아이들은 그보다 어린 아이들이 가지고 있지 않은 어떤 인지적 능력을 가지고 있는가?
ⓐ 그들은 다른 사람들에게 특정 반응들을 부추기는 방법을 안다.
ⓑ 그들은 자신의 다음 행동을 논리적으로 계획할 수 있다.
ⓒ 그들은 다른 사람들의 행동 뒤에 있는 동기를 파악할 수 있다.
ⓓ 그들은 행동과 결과 사이의 관계를 이해한다.

06 / Sociology

Sample Questions
본문 p. 448

| 01 B | 02 A | 03 C, D | 04 B | 05 D | 06 B |

해석 사회학 수업의 다음 강의 일부분을 들으시오. ◁ MP3 80

교수(여자): 자, 여러분 모두가 학교 그룹 프로젝트에 참여하는 것이건 캠핑 여행을 계획하는 것이건 어떤 식으로든 그룹 환경에서 일을 해본 적이 있을 거라 생각합니다. 그리고 그런 경험들을 통해 여러분은 그룹을 만들거나 갈라지게 만들 수 있는 것들 중 최소한 몇 가지는 파악했을 거고요. 음... 오늘은 무엇이 그룹을 성공적으로 만드는지를 실제로 알아내고 정확히 밝히기 위해 실시된 한 실험에 대해 다루어보려고 합니다. 그 실험은 Bales라는 이름의 한 사회학자에 의해 이루어졌고, 그래서 그것은 일반적으로 'Bales 실험'이라고 불립니다. (화면에 보여준다) 그러면, 여러분은 무엇이 그룹을 성공적으로 만든다고 생각하나요?

학생(남자): 팀워크요? 그러니까, 그게 가장 중요한 것 아닌가요?

교수: 네, 그런데 팀워크를 어떻게 정의할 건가요?

학생: 음...

교수: 어렵죠? 하지만 그것이 Bales가 해보려 애썼던 바로 그것입니다. 그의 발상은 여러 그룹의 사람들을 만들어보는 것이었습니다... 흠... 자, 그는 편의상, 사실 그의 대학에 다니는 다수의 남학생들을 이용했습니다. Bales는 전에 서로 만난 적이 없었던 이 학생들을 여러 그룹으로 나누었죠. 그리고 나서, 그는 그들에게 모든 종류의 문제들을 해결하도록 했습니다. 학생들이 상호작용을 했을 때, Bales와 그의 조수는, 음, Bales가 그들의 '다양한 행동'이라고 불렀던, 학생들의 행동의 모든 측면들을 분류했습니다. 이런 행동들은 여러 다른 범주들로 나뉘었습니다. 그래서, 수많은 상호작용을 관찰한 뒤에, Bales는 모든 행동, 즉 실험대상자들이 했던 모든 것들이 두 가지 기본 범주 중 하나에 들어맞았다는 가설을 제기했습니다. '표현적인' 또는 '수단적인' 것으로 말이죠.

수단적인 행동들은, 그 그룹이 처한 어떤 문제든지 그것을 해결하는 데 직접적인 영향이 있었던 활동으로 정의 내릴 수 있었어요. 정보를 제공하는 것, 제안을 하는 것 등, 기본적으로 문제를 해결하는 것과 주어진 과제를 완료하는 데 기여하는 것에 직접적으로 관련이 있는 어떤 것이든 말이지요. 예를 들면 한 사람이 "문제를 이런 식으로 해결해보면 어떨까?"라던지 "이걸 한번 살펴보자."라고 말한 것들을 들 수 있죠. 이런 것들이 수단적인 행동으로 간주될 수 있을 것입니다. 물론, 메모를 한다거나 보고서를 작성하는 것 같은 행동들도 역시 수단적인 행동으로 간주되었습니다. 그 외의 어떤 다른 행동들은 모두 표현적인 행동으로 간주되었습니다. 실제 주어진 문제를 해결하는 것과 거의 관계가 없었던 코멘트와 행동들, 예를 들면 "열심히 해주어 고마워." 또는 "그거 좋은 생각이다." 같은 말들이죠. 이런 것들은 표현적인 코멘트로 간주될 수 있습니다. 예를 들어, 농담 같은 말들도 표현적인 행동으로 간주되었습니다. 그래요, Jerry?

학생: 하지만... 교수님 말씀대로라면 Bales는 긍정적인 행동들만 관찰했던 것처럼 들리는데요... 그랬을 가능성은 거의 없어 보이는데요.

교수: 사실, 부정적인 코멘트들도 표현적인 것으로 간주되었습니다... 부정적인 표현 행동이죠... 누군가 "너희들과는 더 이상 같이 일을 못하겠어!"라고 말했을 때 같은 거죠. 자, 이제 Bale의 실험에 있어 근본적인 범주들에 대한 기본적인 이해가 생겼으니, 그가 내린 결론에 대해 이야기를 해보죠. 그는 한 그룹을 가장 효과적으로 만들었던 수단적인 행동과 표현적인 행동의 비율에 주로 관심이 있었습니다. 여러분 생각은 어떤가요?

학생: 음... 수단적인 행동의 비율이 더 높은 그룹이 가장 성공적이지 않을까요?

교수: 그게 논리적인 결론이죠. 내 말은, 생각해보면, 더 많은 수단적인 행동이 있었을수록 그 그룹이 목표에 더 가까워지지 않았겠어요? 하지만 전혀 그렇지 않았습니다. 가장 높은 비율의 수단적인 행동을 가졌던 그룹들은 그다지 생산적이지 않았어요. 대신, 가장 성공적인 그룹들은, 음, 약 50대 50의 비율로 수단적인 행동과 표현적인 행동을 나타냈지요. 그리고 그들의 표현적인 행동들은 약 1/3 정도가 부정적이고 2/3가 긍정적인 것들이었어요.

Bales는 또한, 음, 활동들이 수행되는 방식에 있어 재반복되는 패턴을 발견하기도 했습니다. 성공적인 그룹들은, 문제와 그 문제에 관련된 사람들을 확인하는 등등과 같은, 문제에 대한 정보를 주고받는 것으로 회의를 시작했습니다. 이런 정보 교환 후에, 그들은 자신들의 의견을 내는 데 시간을 좀 할애했지요. 주로 문제의 원인에 대한 의견에 대해서요. 그리고 나서 그들은 문제를 어떻게 해결할 것인지 제안을 했습니다. 모든 그룹들이 이런 패턴을 가지고 있지는 않았어요. 어떤 그룹들은 반대 방식으로 해서, 주어진 문제를 먼저 규정하지 않고 해결점을 찾는 걸로 시작했지요. 그들은 더 나아가기 전에, 부정적인 표현적 행동들로 가득 찬, 의견 불일치로 긴 시간을 보내게 되었습니다. 그 과정에서 엄청난 시간을 낭비하면서요.

Ⓦ a bunch of ~ 다수의...   for the sake of ~ ...을 위해   convenience [kənvíːnjəns] 편리, 편의   hypothesize [haipάθisàiz] 가설을 세우다   be concerned with ~ ...와 관계가 있다   contribute [kəntríbjuːt] 기여하다   underlying [Àndərlàiiŋ] 근본적인   ratio [réiʃou] 비율   productive [prədΛktiv] 생산적인   reoccur [riːəkə́ːr] 다시 일어나다, 재발생하다

01 강의의 주된 목적은?
Ⓐ 그룹으로 일하는 것의 중요성을 예를 들어 설명하려고
Ⓑ 무엇이 그룹을 성공적으로 만드는지 설명하려고
Ⓒ 생산적인 토론에 대한 Bales의 관점들을 논의하려고
Ⓓ 목표에 집중하는 것의 중요성을 지적하려고

02 연구의 참가자들에 대해 교수가 암시한 것은?
Ⓐ 그랬어야 하는 것만큼 다양하지는 않았다.
Ⓑ 비자발적으로 연구에 참가했다.
Ⓒ Bales를 만족시키기 위해 그들의 행동을 바꾸었다.
Ⓓ 연구 결과에 기쁘지 않았다.

03 교수에 의하면, Bales가 수단적 행동으로 분류했을 행동들은 무엇인가? (두 가지 선택)
Ⓐ 다른 사람의 행동에 불만족을 나타내기
Ⓑ 제안된 해결책에 관해 어떤 사람을 칭찬하기
Ⓒ 관련 있는 정보를 찾는 방법을 제안하기
Ⓓ 그 문제와 관련 있는 참고 자료 목록을 편집하기

04 Bales 실험의 결과에 관한 교수의 의견은?
Ⓐ 그 결과의 정확성을 의심한다.
Ⓑ 그 결과들이 놀랍다고 생각한다.
Ⓒ 그 결과들의 영향에 대해 염려한다.
Ⓓ 그 결과들을 이해하지 못한다.

05 문제에 대해 이야기를 나누기 전에 해결점을 찾으려 했던 그룹들에 대해 추론할 수 있는 것은?
Ⓐ 문제를 해결하는 데 가장 효과적이었다.
Ⓑ 가장 높은 수준의 팀워크를 보여주었다.

ⓒ 다른 그룹들과 잘 어울리지 못했다.
ⓓ 문제의 해결점을 찾는데 더 오랜 시간이 걸렸다.

강의의 일부분을 다시 듣고 질문에 답하시오. 🔊 MP3 80_1

P: These would be considered expressive comments. Even joking around, for example, was considered expressive. Yes, Jerry?
S: But… You make it sound like Bales only observed positive behavior… That seems pretty unlikely.
P: Actually, negative comments were considered to be expressive… negative expressive…

06 학생이 다음과 같이 말한 이유는?

That seems pretty unlikely.

ⓐ Bales가 어떤 행동 뒤에 숨은 동기들을 이해하지 못했다는 것을 암시하려고
ⓑ 참가자들이 약간의 부정적 행동을 보였을 것이라는 점을 시사하려고
ⓒ Bales가 이용한 분류 방법에 있는 명백한 실수를 증명하려고
ⓓ 교수가 고의로 정보를 숨기고 있다고 생각한다는 것을 알려주려고

Practice Questions

본문 p. 452

01 C 02 A 03 B 04 D 05 B 06 C

Main Idea 웃음의 여러 다른 역할	**Listen to part of a lecture in a sociology class.** 🔊 MP3 81 **Professor(male):** Have you ever heard a person give a long speech? Perhaps at some point the speaker suddenly laughed, even though nothing funny had been said. ▶Q1◀ **This is what I want to talk about today – laughter.**
Condition 웃음이 일어나는 조건	Laughter is a type of group behavior. If you think about it, when's the last time you laughed when you were watching TV or reading a book alone? ▶Q2◀ **You generally don't laugh unless there is someone else around.** Now, in a typical social situation, most people assume people laugh when something funny is said. This is true to a certain extent. We all laugh at jokes or funny stories. Ha ha.
Correction 웃음은 웃긴 일이 있을 때만 발생하는 것이 아님	Do any of you notice what I just did? I just laughed, although most of you probably didn't catch it. I didn't say anything funny, and this class definitely isn't a joke. Like I said, a lot of people mistakenly assume that during a typical conversation, people only laugh because somebody said something funny. But you may be surprised to find out that ▶Q1◀ **most conversational laughter occurs in a different kind of situation.** Most laughter is actually the oral equivalent of punctuation at the end of a spoken sentence. For that reason, this type of laughter is called the punctuation effect. Punctuation comes at the end of sentences or clauses. But, since we can't use commas or periods in speech, we use laughter instead. ▶Q3◀ **When I just laughed, I did it to pause and then go deeper into the subject… sort of like a period at the end of a sentence.**
Function / Example 웃음의 다른 기능과 예 – 구두점 역할 구두점 역할의 또 다른 기능 – 청중의 주의 유지	This sort of thing was highlighted by a scientific study of laughter that showed that it only interrupted phrases 8 out of 1,200 times. Clearly, there's a specific purpose of laughter. Okay, what else? **The punctuation effect isn't just used as a way to go from one point to another.** It also serves another very important purpose. Listening to a long lecture is very grueling for a lot of people – not just for the speaker but for the listeners as

Example
구두점 역할의 웃음이 가진 또 다른 기능을 코미디언을 예로 들어 설명

well. **Q4** **Even a stand-up comedian who tells funny stories has a hard time keeping the audience engaged.** So you might notice that comedians, when they talk, they laugh, too. **This is to punctuate a point they were making, but it also serves to keep the attention of the listeners.** People will laugh to make sure they maintain dominance over their listeners, so that everyone stays tuned in. You may not even notice it, but when a person laughs, your brain picks up the subliminal stimuli. That is, it's something that we don't consciously think about, but we perceive it nonetheless. Our brains process information without knowing it. So, even though we may not notice it, our brains are wondering, without any will on our own part, "Why is this person laughing?" We think without even knowing that we're thinking. This process keeps us engaged in conversations focused on the speaker.

Function
filler laughter의 기능

Headset

Laughter also has a strong effect on the mood of a group situation. That's why it is sometimes used in response to pretty mundane remarks. You know, someone will say, "See you later," and one or more people will laugh. **Q5** **This way of laughing, to keep the situation positive, is also known as filler laughter.** It is mostly used in impersonal conversations. 🎧 We have been trained to connect conversation with positive reactions. Sometimes **Q6** we just can't say "yes" all the time, you know? By giving a small chuckle or a little laugh, we show the other person that we understand the context of the interaction… or at least give them the impression that we do. **Q5** **Sometimes we laugh because we don't have a clue what the other person is saying but we want to be polite to them.** So we hide our cluelessness with laughter. The point is, it's important to understand the role of laughter in group settings. Sometimes, the things we do mean more than what's on the surface.

해석 사회학 수업의 다음 강의 일부분을 들으시오.

교수(남자): 어떤 사람이 긴 연설을 하는 것을 들어본 적이 있나요? 아마도 어떤 지점에서, 연사는 아무것도 웃긴 말을 하지 않았음에도 갑자기 웃음을 터뜨렸을 겁니다. 이것이 오늘 내가 다루고 싶은 것입니다. 웃음이지요.

웃음은 일종의 그룹 행동입니다. 한번 생각해보면, 여러분은 혼자서 TV를 보거나 책을 읽을 때 언제 마지막으로 웃음을 터뜨렸나요? 우리는 누군가 다른 이가 주위에 있지 않으면 일반적으로 웃지 않습니다. 자, 일반적인 사회적 상황에서는, 대부분의 사람들은, 사람들이 무언가 웃긴 것이 말해졌을 때 웃는다고 생각합니다. 이는 어느 정도는 사실입니다. 우리는 모두 농담이나 재미있는 이야기에 웃지요. 하하.

내가 방금 무슨 일을 했는지 알아차린 사람이 있나요? 나는 방금 웃었습니다. 여러분 대부분은 아마 알아차리지 못했겠지만요. 나는 웃긴 이야기를 하지도 않았고, 이 수업도 분명 농담이 아닙니다. 말했듯이, 많은 사람들은 전형적인 대화 중에, 누군가 웃긴 이야기를 했기 때문에만 사람들이 웃는다고 잘못 생각합니다. 하지만 여러분은 대부분의 대화 중 웃음이 여러 다른 종류의 상황에서 발생한다는 것을 알게 되면 놀랄 것입니다. 대부분의 웃음은 실제로는 구어 문장의 끝에 쓰이는 구어의 구두점 역할을 합니다. 그런 이유로, 이런 유형의 웃음은 구두점 효과라고 불립니다. 구두점은 문장이나 절의 끝에 오지요. 하지만, 구어에서는 쉼표나 마침표를 사용할 수 없기 때문에, 우리는 대신 웃음을 사용하는 것입니다. 방금 내가 웃었을 때, 나는 잠시 쉬었다가 주제로 깊이 들어가기 위해 웃었던 것입니다… 문장 끝에 있는 마침표와 같은 거지요. 이런 것은, 1,200번의 웃음 중 단 8번만이 말을 중간에 중단시켰다는 것을 보여준, 웃음에 대한 한 과학적 연구에 의해 주목을 받았습니다. 분명, 웃음의 구체적인 목적이 있는 것이지요.

자, 또 무엇이 있을까요? 구두점 효과는 한 주장에서 다음 주장으로 넘어가는 방법으로만 쓰이지는 않습니다. 구두점 효과는 또 다른 매우 중요한 목적을 수행하기도 하지요. 긴 강의를 듣는 일은 많은 이들에게 매우 힘든 일입니다. 말하는 사람뿐만 아니라 청자들에게도 그렇지요. 심지어 웃긴 이야기를 말해주는 스탠드업 코미디언조차 청중들을 계속해서 주의를 기울이게 만드는 데 어려움을 느낍니다. 자, 여러분은 코미디언들이 말을 할 때 그들도 역시 웃는다는 것을 알아차릴지도 모르겠군요. 이것은 그들이 말하고 있던 내용을 마치기 위함이지만, 또한 청중들의 주의를 유지하려는 목적도 수행합니다. 사람들은 청자들에 대한 자신들의 (관심) 지배를 유지하기 위해 웃기도 하는 것이지요. 그렇게 해서 모두가 귀기울여 듣도록 하기 위해서요. 여러분은 그것을 알아차리지 못할지도 모르지만, 어떤 사람이 웃을 때 여러분의 뇌는 의식하의 자극을 받게 됩니다. 다시 말해, 그것은 우리가 의식적으로는 생각하지 않는 무언가이지만, 우리는 그럼에도 불구하고 그것을 인지하는 것이지요. 우리의 뇌는 알아차리지도 못하는 가운데 정보를 처리합니다. 그래서, 비록 우리가 알아차리지 못할지도 모르지만, 우리의 뇌는 스스로의 어떠한 의지 없이도 "이 사람은 왜 웃을까?"라고 궁금해하는 것입니다. 스스로 생각을 하고 있다는 것을 알지도 못한 채 생각을 하는 것이죠. 이런 과정은 우리로 하여금 말하는 사람에게 초점을 맞춘 대화에 계속 주의를 기울이도록 합니다.

웃음은 또한 그룹 상황의 분위기에 큰 영향을 미치기도 합니다. 그것이 가끔씩 웃음이 매우 일상적인 말들에 대한 응답으로 사용되는 이유입니다. 자, 누군가가 "나중에 보자."라고 말을 하면 다른 한 사람 또는 더 많은 사람들은 웃습니다. 이런 방식의 웃음, 즉 그 상황을 긍정적으로 유지하기 위한 웃음은 필러 웃음이라고도 알려져 있습니다. 필러 웃음은 개인적인 것이 개입되지 않은 대화에 주로 쓰입니다. 우리는 대화를 긍정적인 반응들로 이어나가도록 훈련 받아 왔습니다. 가끔씩은 늘 "그래요."라고만 대답할 수는 없지 않나요? 조금씩 하고 웃거나 조금 웃음소리를 내는 것으로, 우리는 상대방에게 우리가 그 상호작용의 맥락을 이해하고 있다는 것을 보여주거나… 아니면 최소한 우리가 그렇게 하고 있다는 인상을 줍니다. 때때로 우리는 상대방이 말하는 것이 무엇인지 전혀 모르지만 공손하고 싶어서 웃기도 합니다. 그렇게 우리는 웃음으로 어리둥절함을 숨기는 거죠. 요점은, 그룹 상황에서 웃음의 역할을 이해하는 것이 중요하다는 점입니다. 가끔씩, 우리가 하는 행동들은 그 표면에 드러난 것보다 더 많은 의미를 나타냅니다.

Ⓦ mistakenly [mistéikənli] 잘못하여, 실수로   oral [ɔ́(ː)rəl] 구어의   equivalent [ikwívələnt] (…에) 상당[대응]하는 것   punctuation [pʌ̀ŋktʃuéiʃən] 구두점   clause [klɔːz] 절   highlight [háilàit] 강조하다   interrupt [ìntərʌ́pt] 중단시키다   phrase [freiz] 구, 구절   grueling [grúː(ː)əliŋ] 대단히 힘든   engage [ingéidʒ] (관심을) 사로잡다, 끌다   dominance [dámənəns] 지배, 우세   stay tuned 계속해서 주목하다   subliminal stimuli 의식하의 자극   remark [rimάːrk] 발언   filler [fílər] 채우기 위한 것   impersonal [impə́ːrsənəl] 특정 개인과 상관없는   chuckle [tʃʌ́kl] 싱긋 웃기   cluelessness [klúːlisnəs] 아무 것도 모르는

01 강의의 주된 내용은?
Ⓐ 웃음의 이점
Ⓑ 웃음을 사용하는 것에 있어 문화적 차이
Ⓒ 웃음이 수행하는 여러 다른 역할
Ⓓ 웃음의 원인들

02 교수에 의하면, 어떤 상황에서 웃음이 일어날 가능성이 가장 적겠는가?
Ⓐ 혼자 있을 때
Ⓑ 어떤 질문을 이해하지 못할 때
Ⓒ 다른 사람을 맞이할 때
Ⓓ 다른 사람의 주의를 얻고자 할 때

03 강의에 의하면, 말하는 도중에 웃는 사람들에 대해 가장 사실일 것 같은 것은?
Ⓐ 방금 무언가 웃긴 것을 떠올렸다.
Ⓑ 다음 주제로 넘어가고 싶어 한다.
Ⓒ 충분한 자신감이 없다.
Ⓓ 대화에 관심이 없다.

04 교수가 스탠드업 코미디언을 언급한 이유는?
Ⓐ 사람들을 웃게 하는 무언가의 예를 들려고
Ⓑ 모든 코미디언이 웃기지는 않는다는 것을 시사하려고
Ⓒ 구두점 웃음을 사용하는 이유를 설명하려고
Ⓓ 주의를 끌기 위해 웃는 것에 관한 자신의 주장을 강조하려고

05 교수가 필러 웃음에 대해 말한 것은?
Ⓐ 웃긴 상황에서 발생한다.
Ⓑ 공손하고자 하는 하나의 방법이다.
Ⓒ 반응을 얻으려 하는 하나의 방법이다.
Ⓓ 다른 사람들의 말을 끊는 데 쓰인다.

강의의 일부분을 다시 듣고 질문에 답하시오. 🔊 MP3 81_1

> We have been trained to connect conversation with positive reactions. Sometimes we just can't say "yes" all the time, you know? By giving a small chuckle or a little laugh, we show the other person that we understand the context of the interaction.

06 교수가 다음과 같이 말하는 이유는?

> We just can't say "yes" all the time, you know?

Ⓐ 웃음은 우리가 의견 불일치를 피하는 것을 도울 수 있다는 점을 나타내려고
Ⓑ 사람들이 불편함을 느낄 때 반응하는 방식을 설명하려고
Ⓒ 필러 웃음의 역할을 설명하는데 도움을 주려고
Ⓓ 학생들의 의견을 묻기 위해

Actual Test 1

Part 1

| 01 D | 02 C | 03 B | 04 B | 05 D | 06 C | 07 D | 08 B | 09 A, C | 10 B, D | 11 D | 12 C | 13 D | 14 B |
| 15 B | 16 C | 17 D | | | | | | | | | | | |

본문 p. 456 ~ 461

[01 ~ 05] Listen to a conversation between a student and a student housing employee. 🔊 MP3 82

Student(male): Hi. I'm here because I saw your notice in the campus newspaper.

Employee(female): I'm sorry, but I don't think we have any more rooms available this semester. You might want to check the off-campus housing listings if you need a place to stay.

S: Oh, no. **Q1** **I meant the other notice, about the job opening for a resident assistant. I'm really interested in the position.** **Q2** **I'd love to be able to help the students who live in the dorms. I had a really tough time during my freshman year, but my resident assistant helped me get adjusted.** But I have a few questions.

E: Okay. What do you need to know?

S: First, It'd be nice to know the process. I mean, what do I have to do to apply? And any tips that you might have would be appreciated.

E: Well, you have to submit your resume and an application form first. After we've received all the applications, there's the application screening. Then we interview the candidates who have passed the initial qualifications. The hourly pay is pretty high compared to other jobs, and you get a free room. So there's a ton of applicants, and we only have so much time we can spend on interviews.

S: Fair enough. So do you have any pointers?

E: Well, like it says in the notice, **Q3** **you need to have lived in the dorms for at least a year.** You'd be surprised at the number of applicants who forget to make note of it on their application forms. **Q4** **If you forget, you won't even get a chance to get interviewed.**

S: I'll make sure to include that information. And… well, I know it might be a little too early to ask, but what do you look for in the interviews?

E: Well, we pay attention to the obvious things, like being friendly and having an open personality. That's actually really important, because talking to the residents is one of the main things a resident assistant does. And we also look for the ability to solve problems.

S: You know, I actually helped solve a problem my neighbors were having last year.

E: Did you?

S: Yeah. My neighbors didn't really respect each other's schedules, so they had friends over all the time. Do you know what I mean? Like, if one of my neighbors was studying, the other one would be playing video games with friends in the room. And when the other one wanted to go to bed, his roommate would usually be chatting with his friends in the room.

E: That actually happens a lot. So what did you do?

S: I had had enough of their constant arguing, so I made a schedule for them. I put it up on their wall, and they'd mark it when a visitor was coming. It made things much easier for them.

E: **Q5** **You should probably mention that in your interview.** That is, if you pass the application screening.

S: Well, I really hope I do. Thanks for your advice!

해석 학생과 학생 주거 담당 직원간의 다음 대화를 들으시오.

학생(남자): 안녕하세요. 학교 신문의 공고를 보고 왔는데요.

직원(여자): 미안하지만, 이번 학기에는 더 이상 이용 가능한 방들이 없을 것 같아요. 머물 곳이 필요하다면 교외 주거 목록들을 확인해봐야 할 것 같네요.

학생: 아, 아녜요. 다른 공지를 말씀 드린 건데요. 기숙사 조교 일자리에 대한 거요. 그 자리에 정말 관심이 있거든요. 제가 기숙사에 사는 학생들을 도울 수 있었으면 해요. 저는 일학년 때 정말 힘든 시간을 보냈지만, 제 기숙사 조교가 제가 적응하도록 도와주었어요. 그런데 몇 가지 질문사항이 있어요.

Actual Test 1_정답 및 해설 | 189

직원: 좋아요. 무엇을 알고 싶죠?

학생: 우선, 절차를 알 수 있으면 좋겠어요. 제 말은, 지원하려면 뭘 해야 하나요? 그리고 조언도 해주신다면 고맙겠습니다.

직원: 음, 학생의 이력서와 지원서를 우선 제출해야 해요. 우리가 지원서를 다 받은 뒤에, 지원서 심사가 있을 거예요. 그리고 나서 첫 자격조건들을 통과한 지원자들의 면접을 볼 거구요. 시간 당 급여가 다른 일들에 비해 꽤 높은데다, 방을 무료로 쓸 수 있어요. 그러니 어마어마한 지원자들이 몰릴 거고, 우리는 면접에 할애할 수 있는 시간이 별로 없어요.

학생: 좋아요. 조언해주실 것이 있으신지요?

직원: 음, 공지에 나온 것처럼, 기숙사에 최소한 일 년 정도 살았어야 해요. 지원서에 그것에 대해 적어두는 것을 잊어버리는 지원자들의 수를 보면 아마 놀랄 걸요. 적는 걸 잊어버린다면, 면접을 볼 기회조차 없을 거예요.

학생: 반드시 그 정보를 포함시키도록 할게요. 그리고... 음, 여쭤보기에 좀 너무 이를지도 모른다는 건 알지만, 면접에서는 어떤 걸 보시나요?

직원: 음, 분명한 것들에 유의해 보죠. 우호적인 성격인지, 열린 성품을 가지고 있는지 같은 것들이요. 기숙사 학생들과 이야기하는 것은 기숙사 조교가 하는 주요한 일들 중 하나이기 때문에, 그게 실제로 정말 중요하거든요. 그리고 또 문제 해결 능력을 보기도 해요.

학생: 있죠, 저는 실제로 작년에 제 옆 방 학생들이 겪고 있던 문제를 해결하는 데 도움을 주기도 했어요.

직원: 그랬어요?

학생: 네, 제 옆 방 학생들이 서로의 일정을 그다지 존중하지 않아서 항상 친구들을 데려오곤 했었어요. 무슨 말인지 아시죠? 그러니까, 옆 방 학생 중 하나가 공부를 하고 있으면 다른 한 명이 방 안에서 친구들과 비디오 게임을 하고 있곤 했어요. 그리고 다른 한 명이 잠자리에 들고 싶어 할 때, 그의 룸메이트는 대개 방 안에서 친구들과 수다를 떨곤 했고요.

직원: 그런 일들은 실제 많이 일어나죠. 그래서 어떻게 했어요?

학생: 그 애들의 끊임없는 논쟁에 질려서, 그들을 위해 일정을 짜줬어요. 그 일정을 그 애들 벽에 붙여 놓고, 방문자가 오게 되면 거기에 표시를 하곤 했죠. 그게 그 애들의 상황을 훨씬 더 수월하게 만들었죠.

직원: 아마도 그걸 면접에서 언급하는 것이 좋겠어요. 그러니까, 지원서 심사를 통과하면 말이죠.

학생: 음, 정말 그렇게 되길 바라요. 조언 감사 드립니다!

ⓦ off-campus house (학)교외 거주지   resident assistant 기숙사 조교   resume [rizúːm] 이력서   application [ӕpləkéiʃən] 지원서   candidate [kӕndidèit] 지원자   qualification [kwὰləfikéiʃən] 자격조건   open personality (생각·태도가) 열려있는 성격   application screening 지원서 심사   put A up on ~ A를 ...에 걸어 놓다

01 학생이 직원을 찾아간 이유는?
Ⓐ 학기 중에 머물 장소를 요청하려고
Ⓑ 비어 있는 일자리에 면접을 보려고
Ⓒ 일자리에 지원서를 제출하려고
Ⓓ 일자리에 대한 더 많은 정보를 요청하려고

02 학생이 기숙사 조교가 되기 위해 지원하려는 이유로 제시한 것은?
Ⓐ 기숙사 방에서 살고 싶어 한다.
Ⓑ 다른 캠퍼스 내 일자리들보다 급여가 더 좋다는 것을 들었다.
Ⓒ 자신이 도움을 받은 방식대로 다른 이들을 돕고 싶어 한다.
Ⓓ 다른 학생들과 잘 지내는 데 문제를 겪어 왔다.

03 그 일자리의 필요조건으로 언급된 것은?
Ⓐ 공부 일정을 짜는 법에 대해 알기
Ⓑ 이전에 기숙사에 살아보았기
Ⓒ 기숙사 안에 지인들이 많기
Ⓓ 문제 해결에 관한 에세이를 제출하기

04 지원 절차에 관해 직원이 암시하는 것은?
Ⓐ 그 자리에 지원하는 사람들이 대개 충분히 많지 않다.
Ⓑ 모든 요구조건들을 충족시키지 않는 지원자들은 면접을 보지 않는다.
Ⓒ 최고의 지원자가 선택되도록 하기 위해 오랜 기간에 걸쳐 이루어진다.
Ⓓ 지원자들의 성격은 경험만큼 중요하지는 않다.

05 학생의 이야기에 대한 직원의 태도는?
Ⓐ 학생이 진실을 말하고 있다고 생각하지 않는다.
Ⓑ 학생이 만들어낸 해결책에 감명을 받지 않았다.
Ⓒ 학생이 이웃 학생들의 문제를 회피해야 한다고 생각한다.
Ⓓ 학생의 면접에 그것이 도움이 될 것이라 생각한다.

[06 ~ 11] Listen to part of a lecture in an anthropology class. 🔊 MP3 83

Professor(female): Okay, so we all know that the Iron Age brought about a significant change in societies and led to the start of many great civilizations. **Q6** **Since there's really no way of knowing how exactly the Iron Age started in specific continents, we can only rely on archaeological evidence.** Does anyone remember when the Iron Age started?

Student(male): Wait… I thought you said that the Iron Age started at vastly different times in different places.

P: Very good. That is correct. However, historians generally say that the Early Iron Age started around 1300 BC. As we've learned, **Q7** **the Bronze Age was superseded by the Iron Age in many continents. It would be nice to just assume that the use of iron started with a single origin and spread throughout the world, but this is clearly not the case.** So we have to look at how the Iron Age started in each region. The Iron Age in Asia, for example, had very different origins than the Iron Age in Europe. Anyway, **Q6** **the region we're going to focus on in this class is the Middle East and Africa.** Most believe that the Iron Age in that region originated somewhere in modern Turkey. The oldest known steel artifacts in that region date back to sometime around 1800 BC. This is used as evidence to prove that steel manufacturing started around that time and spread throughout the region. Clearly something as revolutionary as steel would spread incredibly quickly, especially once people found out that steel was easier to make than bronze, not to mention much stronger if manufactured properly. It was only a matter of time before every major civilization adopted it. Historians assume that the use of iron in Africa started in the northern region, which is in close proximity to Turkey, and spread throughout the rest of the continent. All the artifacts that have been unearthed in North Africa seem to confirm this. Can anyone tell me how we would know this?

S: Is it the shape? I mean, if iron artifacts had a distinct shape in one region and the same shape was found in another, wouldn't that indicate it had spread from the first region to the second?

P: Yes, shape is a very good indicator. But how would we know which artifact was made first? You know, so we could determine the direction in which the use of iron spread.

S: I guess we'd have to **Q9-A** date the tools somehow.

P: Exactly. But that can't be the only indicator. We need more proof. An older tool could have just been traded for, so we need more evidence to really see when iron started to become widely used in the region. Archaeologists **Q9-C** have to find evidence of metalworking – evidence that can prove that iron was melted and formed into whatever tools the civilization needed. The artifacts in North Africa that were made with iron were all more recent than the ones found in the Middle East and Near East regions. Also, there was no evidence that North Africans could form iron before civilizations in Turkey. So **Q8** we were under the assumption that the Iron Age started in Turkey and spread to Africa through trade. However, recent discoveries have proven that this assumption could be incorrect. Africa is a large continent. What we didn't consider were the civilizations south of the Sahara.

S: Why not? I mean, like you said, Africa is a really large continent.

P: That's a good question. First of all, **Q10-D** it was very difficult for traders to pass through the Sahara desert, and maritime trading really wasn't widespread until the Middle Ages. Also, **Q10-B** only stone tools were found south of the Sahara… There wasn't any evidence that civilizations in the area could make bronze tools. So people thought it was an unlikely place for the Iron Age to start. Most anthropologists just assumed that the Iron Age followed the Bronze Age. However, recent findings have proven that the Iron Age in Sub-Saharan Africa started long before iron spread to North Africa. In an excavation of a site once inhabited by the Nok culture, iron tools were found alongside numerous pieces of pottery and organic remains, such as plant matter. When the plant remains were dated, archaeologists were startled to find out that the site dated back to a time long before iron was traded to North African civilizations. **Q11** This finding obviously changed the way we view the Iron Age in Sub-Saharan Africa. There simply wasn't a Bronze Age in that region. Stone tools were used in conjunction with steel tools, as there wasn't a transition period like in other civilizations.

해석 인류학 수업의 다음 강의 일부를 들으시오.

교수(여자): 좋아요. 이제 우리 모두는 철기시대가 사회에 있어 중대한 변화를 가져왔고 여러 많은 위대한 문명들의 시작을 이끌었다는 것을 알고 있습니다. 특정한 대륙에서 철기시대가 정확하게 어떻게 시작되었는지를 알 수 있는 방법이 없기 때문에, 우리는 고고학적 증거에 의존할 수밖에 없습니다. 철기시대가 언제 시작했는지 기억하는 사람이 있나요?

학생(남자): 잠시만요... 교수님이 철기시대는 여러 다른 장소에서 엄청나게 다른 시기에 시작했다고 말씀하셨던 걸로 기억하는데요.

교수: 아주 좋아요. 그게 맞습니다. 하지만, 역사가들은 일반적으로, 초기 철기시대가 기원전 약 1300년경에 시작되었다고들 말합니다. 우리가 배운 대로, 청동기시대는 여러 많은 대륙들에서 철기시대에 의해 대체되었습니다. 철기의 사용이 단 하나의 기원에서 시작해서 전세계로 퍼져나갔다고 그냥 생각하면 좋겠지만, 분명 그렇지는 않습니다. 그래서 우리는 각 지역에서 철기시대가 어떻게 시작되었는지를 살펴 보아야 합니다. 예를 들어, 아시아 대륙에서의 철기시대는 유럽 대륙에서와는 매우 다른 기원을 가지고 있습니다. 어쨌든, 오늘 수업에서 초점을 맞출 지역은 중동과 아프리카입니다. 대부분의 사람들은 그 지역에서의 철기시대가 현대의 터키 지방의 어딘가에서 시작했다고 생각합니다. 그 지역에서 가장 오래된 것으로 알려진 철기 유물은 기원전 약 1800년경 언제쯤인가로 거슬러 올라갑니다. 이것은 강철 제조가 그 시기 즈음에 시작해서 그 지역 일대로 퍼져나갔다는 것을 증명하는 증거로 쓰이고 있습니다. 분명, 강철처럼 획기적인 무언가는 엄청나게 빨리 퍼져나갔겠죠. 특히 사람들이 강철은 청동보다 만들기에 훨씬 쉽다는 것을 알아차리게 되면 말이죠. 올바로 제조되기만 하면 청동보다 훨씬 더 강한 것은 말할 것도 없고요. 모든 주요 문명들이 철기를 받아들이는 것은 시간 문제일 뿐이었습니다. 역사가들은 아프리카 지역에서의 철기 사용이 터키와 매우 근접한 북부 지역에서 시작되어 대륙 나머지 전체로 퍼져나갔다고 추측합니다. 북부 아프리카에서 발굴되어온 모든 유물들이 이것을 확인시켜줍니다. 우리가 이걸 어떻게 아는지 말해줄 수 있는 사람 있나요?

학생: 모양 때문인가요? 그러니까, 한 지역의 철기 유물들이 독특한 모양을 띠고 있고, 같은 모양이 다른 지역에서 발견되었다면, 그게 그 철기가 첫 번째 지역에서 두 번째 지역으로 퍼져나갔다는 것을 나타내는 게 아닌가요?

교수: 그래요. 모양은 아주 좋은 지표가 되지요. 하지만 어느 유물이 처음 만들어진 건지 어떻게 알 수 있을까요? 철기 사용이 어느 방향으로 퍼져나갔는지를 결정할 수 있게 말이지요.

학생: 어떻게든 그 도구들의 연대를 추정해야 할 것 같아요.

교수: 바로 그겁니다. 하지만 그것이 유일한 지표가 될 수는 없어요. 더 많은 증거가 필요합니다. 더 오래된 도구가 거래되었을 수도 있으니, 언제 철기가 그 지역에 널리 퍼지기 시작했는지를 실제로 보여주는 더 많은 증거가 필요해요. 고고학자들은 금속 세공, 즉 철이 녹여져 그 문명에서 필요로 했던 어떤 도구로라도 만들어졌다는 것을 증명할 수 있는 증거를 찾아야 합니다. 철로 만들어졌던 북아프리카의 공예품들은 모두 중동과 근동 지역들에서 발견된 것들보다 더 최근의 것이었습니다. 또한, 북아프리카인들이 터키 문명 이전에 철을 만들 수 있었다는 증거도 없습니다. 따라서 우리는 철기시대가 터키에서 시작하여 교역을 통해 아프리카로 퍼져 나갔을 것이라는 가정을 했지요. 하지만, 최근의 발견에 의하면 이런 가정이 틀릴 수도 있다는 것이 증명되었습니다. 아프리카는 큰 대륙이에요. 우리가 고려하지 못했던 점은 사하라 사막 남쪽의 문명들이었습니다.

학생: 왜 고려하지 못했죠? 그러니까 제 말은, 교수님께서 말씀하셨다시피, 아프리카는 정말로 큰 대륙이잖아요.

교수: 좋은 질문이에요. 우선, 상인들이 사하라 사막을 건너는 것은 매우 어려운 일이었고, 해양 무역은 중세대까지는 그다지 널리 퍼져 있지 않았습니다. 또한, 사하라 사막 남쪽에서는 석기 도구들만 발견되었어요... 그 지역의 문명들이 청동기를 만들 수 있었다는 어떠한 증거도 없었지요. 그래서 사람들은 그곳이 철기시대가 시작하기에는 가능성이 적은 지역이라고 생각했던 거죠. 대부분의 인류학자들은 그저 철기시대가 청동기시대의 뒤를 이었다고만 추측했을 뿐이에요. 하지만, 최근 연구들은 사하라 사막 이남 지역에서의 철기시대가, 철이 북부 아프리카로 퍼져 나가기 오래 전에 시작되었다는 것을 증명했습니다. 한때 노크(Nok) 문화 사람들이 살았었던 한 유적지의 발굴에서, 철기들이 여러 도자기류나 식물 같은 유기적 잔존물과 함께 발견되었습니다. 식물 찌꺼기의 연대를 측정했을 때, 고고학자들은 그 유적지의 연대가 철이 북부 아프리카 문명으로 교역이 되었던 때보다 더 오래 전으로 측정된 것을 알고 놀랐습니다. 이 발견은 우리가 사하라 사막 이남 지역에서의 철기시대를 바라보는 방식을 확실히 바꾸었습니다. 그 지역에서는 청동기시대가 아예 없었던 거죠. 석기들은 철기들과 함께 쓰였는데, 이는 다른 문명들에서처럼 (청동기시대라는) 과도기가 없었기 때문입니다.

W Iron Age 철기시대　archaeological [à:rkiəládʒikəl] 고고학적　supersede [sù:pərsí:d] 대체하다　Bronze Age 청동기시대　artifact [á:rtəfækt] 유물　manufacture [mænjufǽktʃər] 제조하다　adopt [ədápt] 도입하다　proximity [praksíməti] 가까움　unearth [ʌnə́:rθ] 발굴하다　indicator [índikèitər] 지표　metalworking [métlwə̀:rkiŋ] 금속세공술　civilization [sìvəkizéiʃən] 문명　maritime trading 해양 무역　widespread [waidspred] 널리 퍼진　excavation [èkskəvéiʃən] 발굴　pottery [pátəri] 도기[도자기]　organic remains 유기적 잔존물　startled [stá:rtld] 놀란　in conjuction with ~ ...와 함께

06 강의의 주된 내용은?
Ⓐ 금속으로 만들어진 공예품들의 연대를 측정하는 현대적 방법들
Ⓑ 청동기시대에서 철기시대로의 이행
Ⓒ 아프리카에서 철기시대의 시작에 대한 관점 변화
Ⓓ 터키의 한 고고학 유적지에서 유발된 논란

07 철기시대에 관해 교수가 말한 것은?
Ⓐ 단 하나의 기원으로 거슬러 올라갈 수 있다.
Ⓑ 다른 지역들보다 아프리카에 늦게 도달했다.
Ⓒ 청동기시대와 같은 때에 발생했다.
Ⓓ 여러 다른 지역에서 여러 다른 때에 시작했다.

08 교수에 의하면, 과학자들이 이전에는 철기시대가 어떻게 아프리카에 도달했다고 생각했는가?
Ⓐ 터키가 아프리카 국가들을 점령해서 그들에게 철기를 가져다 주었다.
Ⓑ 북아프리카인들이 다른 문명들과의 교역을 통해 철기를 얻었다.
Ⓒ 아프리카 문명들이 유럽에서 온 철기들의 모양을 본떠 만들었다.
Ⓓ 사하라 사막 이남 지역의 부족들이 해양 무역상들로부터 철기를 만드는 법을 배웠다.

09 교수에 의하면, 철기 사용의 확산을 추적하는 데 사용된 두 가지 방법은? (두 가지 선택)
Ⓐ 철기의 연대를 확인하기
Ⓑ 다른 유형의 철기를 발견하기
Ⓒ 비슷한 도구들의 모양을 맞춰보기
Ⓓ 무역의 역사적 기록들을 확인하기

10 아프리카에서의 철기시대에 관한 부정확한 가정의 이유로 교수가 제기한 것은? (두 가지 선택)
Ⓐ 아프리카의 문명들은 다른 많은 문화들과 교역을 했다.
Ⓑ 남부 아프리카의 문명들은 청동기를 사용하지 않았다.
Ⓒ 아프리카 사람들은 종종 이곳 저곳으로 이주해 다녔다.
Ⓓ 사하라 사막 이남 지역의 아프리카는 지리적으로 고립되어 있었다.

11 교수에 의하면, 노크 문화 유적지의 중요성은 무엇인가?
Ⓐ 아프리카의 문명들이 석기를 만드는 법만 알고 있었다는 것을 알려준다.
Ⓑ 사하라 사막을 건너는 무역로의 증거를 제공한다.
Ⓒ 새로운 기술을 다른 문화들에 전하는 것의 위험성을 보여준다.
Ⓓ 모든 문명들이 같은 방식으로 금속세공 기술을 진화시키지 않았다는 것을 증명한다.

[12 ~ 17] Listen to part of a lecture in a physics class. ◁ MP3 84
Professor(male): **Q12** Today we'll be talking about how fluids move when they are blocked at a single point. Most of you might assume we're only talking about liquids when we use the term fluid, but in the context of fluid flow we also have to include air. I'll get to that part later. So, what are the two possible states of a fluid?
Student(female): It can either be still or moving.
P: Yes, exactly. Most of the fluids we see are in constant motion. Even if we can't see this, we can feel it. We can, um, feel the current of the water when swimming or the wind in our face when walking. These are very large bodies of fluids, and our eyes alone can rarely observe how fluids move on a larger scale. But this changes once a moving fluid is disturbed by an object. The direction of the fluid is altered, as is its rotation. So, what we often see, just behind the obstacle, is a circular swirl called a vortex.
S: Yeah, I remember seeing those swirls when I rowed a boat in the lake last summer. They formed just behind the oars. But how come we don't see them more often?
P: That's a very good question. In order to better understand these vortexes, we need to learn about something called the Reynolds number. This is the ratio between the inertial forces and the viscous forces. These are the two types of forces present in fluids. Inertial forces are created by something in motion – it can be

either the fluid or the obstacle… or, in some cases, both. In your case, it was the oar that was moving. Viscous forces, on the other hand, depend on how easily a liquid can flow. What I mean is… Well, water can flow much more quickly than something sticky like syrup. But in today's class I want to focus on the inertial forces. Anyway, the ratio between these two has to be within a certain range for vortexes to form. **Q13** **If you moved your oar very slowly, you wouldn't see a swirl because the ratio of the inertial force would be smaller compared to the water's viscous forces.** But let's say that the water was moving very quickly. It would create its own inertial force, so even if you just stuck your oar in the water, a vortex would form.

Now, let's take a look at a picture of how fluids react to obstacles on a larger scale (shown on screen). Our atmosphere is a large body of fluid that is constantly moving. **Q14** **When large mountains, like the one you see in the bottom of the picture, impede the movement of fast-moving winds, you can see that several vortexes are formed.** It's a lot easier to see these swirls when clouds are present in the atmosphere, but the swirling occurs whether they are there or not. That is, as long as there's a strong enough wind, the Reynolds number is in the range in which these vortexes are formed. Now, **Q15** **it's really important to calculate the range and speed of these vortexes because you definitely don't want to get caught flying through these things. It can be quite dangerous.** The turbulence that is created by these swirls is immense and sometimes unpredictable, so we need to carefully calculate the conditions in which these swirls are formed for our safety. The physics behind fluid dynamics is quite stunning visually. You might think the clouds would just split like a curtain, but moving fluids actually have a tendency to form two rows of vortexes that alternate in direction. There's actually a name for this phenomenon: a "von Karman vortex street." This was named after Theodore von Karman, a scientist who described these swirls in the atmosphere in the mid-20th century. He found that **Q16** **the outer portion of fluid that hits the obstacle moves faster than the inner portion. So, the outer portion pushes the inner portion, creating the direction of the swirl. That's why vortex streets curve inward.**

S: Was von Karman really the first one to observe this? I mean, I understand that it might be difficult to see vortexes in the atmosphere, but they form in other fluids too, don't they?

P: Yes, you bring up a good point. **Q17** **This phenomenon was actually discovered a long time ago. von Karman was just the first to explain it. There's actually evidence that Leonardo da Vinci observed and sketched it.** In a picture he drew of a bridge, you can clearly see a vortex street formed by the water flowing around the bridge's columns.

서, 노를 그냥 물 안에 넣어두기만 해도 소용돌이가 생길 것입니다.

자, 더 대규모로 유체가 장애물들에 어떻게 반응하는지에 대한 사진을 보도록 합시다. (화면에 보여준다) 대기는 끊임없이 움직이고 있는 많은 양의 유체입니다. 여러분이 사진 아랫부분에서 보는 것과 같은 큰 산들이 빠르게 움직이는 바람의 움직임을 방해하게 되면, 여러 소용돌이들이 형성되는 것을 볼 수 있습니다. 대기에 구름들이 있을 때는 이 소용돌이를 보는 것이 훨씬 더 쉽지만, 구름들이 있건 없건 간에 소용돌이는 발생합니다. 즉, 충분히 강한 바람만 있다면, 레이놀즈 수는 이러한 소용돌이가 형성되는 범위 안에 있는 것이지요. 자, 이러한 소용돌이들의 범위와 속도를 계산하는 것은 정말 중요합니다. 분명 여러분은 이런 소용돌이 속으로 비행하고 싶지 않을 것이기 때문이지요. 그건 매우 위험할 수 있습니다. 이런 소용돌이들로 인해 생기는 난기류는 엄청나고 가끔은 예측 불가능해서, 우리는 안전을 위해서 이런 소용돌이들이 형성되는 조건들을 주의 깊게 계산해야 합니다.

유체 역학에 숨은 물리학은 시각적으로 매우 멋집니다. 여러분은 구름들이 커튼처럼 그냥 나뉘어진다고 생각할지도 모르지만, 움직이는 유체들은 사실 방향이 번갈아 바뀌는 2열의 소용돌이들을 형성하는 경향이 있습니다. 실제로 이런 현상에 대한 이름이 있는데, '본 카르만 소용돌이 길'이 바로 그것입니다. 이 이름은 20세기 중반에 대기에서의 이러한 소용돌이들을 묘사했던 과학자인 Theodore von Karman의 이름을 따서 만들어졌습니다. 그는 장애물을 치는 유체의 바깥쪽 부분이 안쪽 부분보다 더 빨리 움직인다는 것을 발견했습니다. 그래서, 바깥 부분이 안쪽 부분을 밀어내고, 소용돌이의 방향을 만들게 되는 것이죠. 그것이 소용돌이 길이 안쪽으로 휘어지는 이유입니다.

학생: von Karman이 정말 그것을 관찰했던 최초의 사람이었나요? 제 말은, 대기에서 소용돌이를 보는 것이 어려울 수는 있지만, 소용돌이는 다른 유체들에서도 형성되잖아요, 아닌가요?

교수: 맞아요, 좋은 지적이에요. 이런 현상은 사실 오래 전에 발견되었습니다. Von Karman은 그것을 처음으로 설명한 사람이었을 뿐이지요. 사실 레오나르도 다빈치가 그것을 관찰하고 스케치했다는 증거도 있습니다. 그가 다리를 그렸던 한 그림에서, 다리의 기둥 주변을 흐르는 물에 의해 만들어진 소용돌이 길을 분명히 볼 수 있습니다.

Ⓦ fluid [flúːid] 유체　liquid [líkwid] 액체　current [kə́ːrənt] 해류, 기류　alter [ɔ́ːltər] 바뀌다　rotation [routéiʃən] 회전, 순환　swirl [swəːrl] 빙빙 돌다　vortex [vɔ́ːrteks] 소용돌이　row a boat (노로) 배를 젓다　oar [ɔːr] 노　ratio [réiʃou] 비율　inertial force 관성력　viscous force 점성력　sticky [stíki] 끈적거리다　impede [impíːd] 방해하다　atmosphere [ǽtməsfiər] 대기　turbulence [tə́ːrbjuləns] 난기류　immense [iméns] 엄청난　unpredictable [ʌnpridíktəbl] 예측이 불가능한　dynamic [dainǽmik] 역학(관계)　inward [ínwərd] 안쪽으로 향한　column [kɑ́ləm] 기둥

12 강의의 주요 목적은?
Ⓐ 소용돌이에 의해 유발되는 위험들을 강조하려고
Ⓑ 유체의 여러 다른 상태들을 보여주려고
Ⓒ 움직이는 유체들이 장애물들에 어떻게 반응하는지 논의하려고
Ⓓ 소용돌이 길이 어떻게 발견되었는지 설명하려고

13 그다지 빠른 속도를 지니지 않은 유체들에 대해 추론할 수 있는 것은?
Ⓐ 그 유체들이 흘러가는 길에 장애물들이 있을 가능성이 높다.
Ⓑ 그 유체들에서 발생하는 소용돌이들은 육안으로는 볼 수 없다.
Ⓒ 그것들의 레이놀즈 수는 빨리 움직이는 유체들의 레이놀즈 수보다 높을 것이다.
Ⓓ 그 유체들은 움직이지 않는 물체에 의해 방해를 받을 때 소용돌이를 일으키지 않을 것이다.

14 교수에 의하면, 사진에 나온 소용돌이를 만든 것은?
Ⓐ 두터운 구름들의 존재
Ⓑ 산봉우리의 존재
Ⓒ 기압의 차이
Ⓓ 구름을 통과한 비행기

15 교수에 의하면, 소용돌이가 어디에 형성되는지를 아는 것이 중요한 이유는?
Ⓐ 변화하는 기상 상태를 예측하기 위해서
Ⓑ 그 지역에서의 위험한 비행 상황을 피하기 위해서
Ⓒ 빠른 속도로 움직이는 바람의 원인을 연구하기 위해서
Ⓓ 과학자들이 점성력에 대해 연구하는 것을 허용하기 위해서

16 '본 카르만 소용돌이 길'에서 발견된 소용돌이들에 대해 교수가 말한 것은?

Ⓐ 바깥쪽으로 움직이는 힘을 만들어낸다.
Ⓑ 빨리 움직이는 유체들에서는 절대로 형성되지 않을 것이다.
Ⓒ 항상 특정한 방향으로 움직일 것이다.
Ⓓ 반으로 나뉜 커튼의 모양과 닮았다.

17 교수가 레오나르도 다빈치를 언급한 이유는?

Ⓐ 학생들에게 과학이 어떻게 예술에서 사용되는지를 알려주려고
Ⓑ 소용돌이 길이 가끔씩 물에서도 형성될 수 있다는 것을 지적하려고
Ⓒ 자신의 그림에 소용돌이들을 묘사한 유명한 화가를 인용하려고
Ⓓ 소용돌이 길이 von Karman보다 훨씬 이전에 관찰되었다는 것을 보여주려고

Part 2

| 01 D | 02 A | 03 D | 04 C | 05 A | 06 C | 07 D | 08 B | 09 A, C | 10 A | 11 C | 12 C | 13 B | 14 A, C |
| 15 D | 16 D | 17 B |

[01 ~ 05] Listen to a conversation between a student and her professor. 🔊 MP3 85

Professor(male): Hey, Michelle! Come on in. Sorry to keep you waiting.
Student(female): That's okay. It wasn't a problem.
P: Good. You remember the film I was talking about in class the other day? The one that I was going to show you guys this week in class? It's really been a handful. I requested the film from the media center and guess what they sent me?
S: Uh...
P: **Q1** **They sent me a video tape! Can you believe it? There's a reason why I asked for the film reel.**
S: Yeah...
P: **Q2** **Looking at a tiny television compared to a large screen with the movie projected on it, it's too much of a different experience.** How are you supposed to experience a film that was designed to be watched at the cinema in a tiny little box? **It's like listening to recorded music when you can listen to an orchestra that's playing right in front of you.** The immersion is totally different, you know. It took me forever to persuade the media center to give me the reel. I had to explain why I needed to show the reel film version of the film. Oh goodness. I don't know why they just didn't give it out in the first place. Anyway… sorry about that. So what can I do for you? I kind of went off track there.
S: Oh no, don't worry about it. It's actually about the film that you were talking about.
P: Really? What about it?
S: You know how you said you'd be showing it to us this Friday?
P: Yes. Is there a problem with that?
S: Well… actually it's parent's week this week. A lot of parents come in on Friday night and that's when the class is. **Q4** **A lot of other students want to spend time with their parents, like me, you know?** It's that time when everyone is kind of getting homesick. So, **I was wondering, do you think we can watch the film in next week's class?**
P: Hmm… well, I understand where you're coming from, but I went through a lot of trouble to get this film. **Q3** **I don't know if the media center will let me keep for any longer.**
S: I would hate to miss the film. I was really looking forward to it. A lot of my friends who are taking the class are in the same boat. Is there any other way we can watch the film?
P: You can always watch the video tape, but like I said, watching a film is about the experience not just about the picture, you know? You want to be immersed in it.
S: Exactly, so can you please show it next week?
P: Sorry, the movie screening was already on the syllabus. It's been there since the beginning of the semester. It might sound harsh, but **Q5** **I didn't even know that it was parent's week. You know, it's not even on the academic calendar.** I mean, if I'd known… then… you get what I mean.
S: Yes, you're right.
P: If it's not a problem, then what about inviting your parents to the screening class? We do have a large lecture hall. I'm sure we'll have enough seats for everyone to sit in. Think of it as a welcoming movie, although I'm not sure if some of the parents would like watching a movie after driving for 10 hours.
S: That sounds like an idea. Thanks for understanding.

해석 학생과 교수간의 다음 대화를 들으시오.
교수(남자): 안녕, Michelle! 들어와요. 기다리게 해서 미안해요.

학생(여자): 괜찮습니다. 오래 기다리지 않았어요.

교수: 다행이네요. 내가 일전에 수업시간에 말했던 영화 기억하죠? 이번 주에 수업에서 보여주려고 했던 영화 말이에요. 그게 정말 까다로웠어요. 미디어 센터에 그 영화를 요청했었는데, 그쪽에서 내게 뭘 보내줬는지 알아요?

학생: 음...

교수: 비디오 테이프를 보내줬어요! 믿을 수 있겠어요! 내가 릴 필름으로 된 영화를 요청한 데는 이유가 있는데 말이죠.

학생: 예...

교수: 큰 스크린에 영화를 쏘아서 보는 것에 비해 작은 TV모니터로 보는 건... 그건 너무나 다른 경험이라고요. 극장에서 관람되도록 만들어진 영화를 어떻게 작은 TV상자로 경험할 수 있겠어요? 그건 마치 우리 바로 앞에서 연주하는 오케스트라의 음악을 들을 수 있는 상황에서 녹음된 음악을 듣는 것과 같고요. 몰입도가 완전히 다르잖아요. 릴 필름 버전을 달라고 미디어 센터를 설득하는 데는 정말 오래 걸렸어요. 그 영화를 릴 필름 버전으로 보여줘야 하는 이유를 설명해야 했죠. 오, 이런. 그들이 왜 처음부터 그 버전으로 주지 않았는지 모르겠어요. 어쨌든... 미안해요. 자, 내가 뭘 도와줘야 하죠? 본론에서 좀 벗어났었네요.

학생: 아, 괜찮아요. 염려하지 마세요. 사실 교수님께서 말씀하시던 영화에 관한 거였어요.

교수: 그래요? 뭔데요?

학생: 그 영화를 저희에게 이번 금요일에 보여주시겠다고 말씀하셨잖아요?

교수: 네. 무슨 문제라도 있나요?

학생: 음... 사실 이번 주가 부모 주간이라서요. 많은 부모님들이 금요일 밤에 오실 건데, 교수님 수업이 그때예요. 다른 많은 학생들도 저처럼 부모님과 시간을 보내고 싶어 하고요. 모두가 향수병 같은 거에 걸릴 때잖아요. 그래서, 영화를 다음주 수업 때 보면 안될까 궁금해서요.

교수: 음... 그게, 말하려는 바는 이해하지만, 이 영화를 구하는 데 내가 너무 고생을 해서요. 미디어 센터에서 내가 영화를 더 오래 가지고 있게 해줄지 잘 모르겠네요.

학생: 영화를 못 보게 되는 건 싫어요. 그 영화를 정말 고대하고 있었거든요. 수업을 듣는 많은 제 친구들도 같은 상황이고요. 저희가 영화를 볼 수 있는 다른 방법이 없을까요?

교수: 비디오 테이프는 언제든 볼 수 있지만, 아까도 말했듯이, 영화를 본다는 것은 그저 장면에 관한 게 아니라 경험과 관계된 거잖아요. 모두들 영화 속에 몰입되고 싶을 거라고요.

학생: 맞아요. 그러니 다음주에 보여주실 수는 없나요?

교수: 미안해요. 영화 상영은 이미 강의계획표에 나와 있어요. 학기 초부터 강의계획표에 나와 있었고요. 좀 가혹하게 들릴지는 모르겠지만, 난 부모 주간인지조차 몰랐어요. 알다시피, 학사 일정에도 나와 있지 않잖아요. 내 말은, 내가 만일 알고 있었더라면... 그랬다면... 무슨 말인지 알겠죠?

학생: 네, 교수님 말씀이 맞아요.

교수: 혹시 문제가 안 된다면, 부모님을 영화 상영 수업에 초대하면 어때요? 우리 강의실이 넓잖아요. 모두 앉을 수 있는 충분한 좌석이 있을 거예요. 환영의 뜻으로 보는 영화로 생각하자고요. 10시간 넘게 운전한 몇몇 부모님들이 영화를 보고 싶어하는지는 잘 모르겠지만요.

학생: 그거 좋은 생각 같아요. 이해해주셔서 감사합니다.

Ⓦ **film reel** 릴 필름 **immersion** [imə́ːrʒən] 몰입도 **go off track** 본론에서 벗어나다 **parent's week** 부모 주간 **get homesick** 향수병을 앓다 **in the same boat** 같은 상황이다 (비유적) **movie screening** 영화 상영 **syllabus** [síləbəs] 강의계획표 **harsh** [haːrʃ] 가혹한 **academic calendar** 학사 일정

01 학생이 교수를 찾아 왔을 때 교수가 설명한 어려움은?
Ⓐ 수업 시간에 영화 상영 시간을 잡을 만족스러운 방법을 찾을 수 없었다.
Ⓑ 다루고 했던 영화의 제목을 기억하는 데 힘이 들었다.
Ⓒ 미디어 센터가 자신에게 영화를 반납하라고 하는 이유를 이해할 수 없었다.
Ⓓ 영화를 자신이 요청했던 것과 다른 포맷으로 받았다.

02 교수가 오케스트라 음악을 언급한 이유는?
Ⓐ 비디오 테이프와 릴 필름의 차이를 설명하려고
Ⓑ 영화 상영에 참석하는 것에 대한 대안을 제시하려고
Ⓒ 자신이 빌린 릴 필름 영화의 내용에 대해 학생에게 알려주려고
Ⓓ 오디오 테이프와 비디오 테이프 간의 유사성을 설명하려고

03 교수가 릴 필름을 더 오래 가지고 있는 것에 대해 언급할 때 교수에 관해 추론할 수 있는 것은?
Ⓐ 대학의 정책을 준수하는 것을 좋아하지 않는다.
Ⓑ 영화를 가능한 빨리 반납하고 싶어 한다.
Ⓒ 그 영화를 이미 여러 번 보았다.
Ⓓ **미디어 센터의 규정에 대해 잘 알지 못한다.**

04 많은 학생들이 부모와 시간을 보내고 싶어 한다고 언급할 때 학생이 암시하는 것은?
Ⓐ 대부분의 교수들은 부모 주간에 수업을 취소한다.
Ⓑ 학생들은 부모 주간에 가족과 함께 영화를 보고 싶어 한다.
Ⓒ **부모 주간에 영화 상영이 있을 경우 일부 학생들은 수업을 빠질지도 모른다.**
Ⓓ 부모들은 아이들을 보기 위해서 먼 거리를 여행했다.

05 교수가 부모 주간임을 몰랐던 이유는?
Ⓐ **공식적인 학사 행사가 아니다.**
Ⓑ 학교에서 준 달력을 분실했다.
Ⓒ 학교에서 학사 일정을 변경했다.
Ⓓ 학생들의 필요에 무관심하다.

[06 ~ 11] Listen to part of a lecture in an art history class. 🔊 MP3 86

Professor(female): Okay, last week we talked about the avant-garde artists in Europe. This week, let's shift our focus to a similar movement here in the United States. A dominant movement started in the late 40s and 50s. It would later be called Abstract Expressionism. So, does anyone remember what the avant-garde painters stood for?

Student(male): Um… Wasn't it sort of like a revolution? They wanted to be free from the limiting rules of traditional art.

P: Very good. The avant-garde artists and abstract expressionists shared a spirit of revolt against tradition and a belief that art should be spontaneous and free. What was different about Abstract Expressionism was that ▶Q7◀ **it was basically an attempt by the artists to convey their thoughts in an abstract way. They didn't care about painting familiar subject matter or things you could actually see in the real world.** They used huge canvases, which itself was a break from tradition, and the way they painted was different too. It was common among artists to apply paint to their canvases very rapidly and with great force.

S: So you're saying that the artists just tried to convey their feelings, right? I remember you saying that the avant-garde artists were radical, but the subjects they painted really didn't differ from traditional art.

P: Exactly! Let's look at the work of probably ▶Q6◀ the most popular American abstract expressionist, Jackson Pollock. ▶Q8◀ **When Pollock was training as an artist, there was, um, nothing, well, at least not in his works, that would suggest he would be seen as an artistic revolutionary.** In the 1930s, he studied at the Art Students League, a popular art school in New York City. However, 10 years later, ▶Q6◀ he changed the way people create art. Anyone have any idea what I'm talking about?

S: You must mean the drip style he used.

P: Yes. He used something he called the "pour and drip technique." Instead of using a traditional easel, ▶Q9-C◀ he would lay his canvas, which was basically the size of a wall, on the floor ▶Q9-A◀ so he could move around it. Then he poured and dripped his paint onto the canvas. When Pollock worked, he moved around a lot more than traditional painters, and many came to call his style "action painting." This term almost suggests that the process of creating the painting was as important as the painting itself. A lot of people would go to watch him create his paintings at his studio, dripping and pouring paint or any other material he thought could convey his thoughts onto the canvas. You might assume his works were completely random… um, just wild and chaotic, without any order… but the truth is that Pollock was in full control of his materials and his paintings. Pollock's methods were truly revolutionary and shocked the art world. Creating a painting without touching the canvas with a brush was unheard of. Plus, the canvases he used were so massive that they seemed like murals more than anything else. A good example of his technique is a painting simply named *Number 5*, which Pollock painted twice in 1948.

S: Did you just say twice?

P: Yes, I'll get to that in just a minute. At first glance, it just looks like a mess of tangled lines, like a bird's nest. But if you see it in person, or even look at it closely, you'll understand why Pollock is known as a pioneer. **Q10** **Beneath the initial chaos, there's really a definite structure and meaning to it.** If it were random, it just wouldn't be as appealing as it is. So, anyway, the first version was actually damaged when it was being shipped to the buyer, so Pollock painted a new painting, assuming the owner would never know. But the owner could tell it was a different painting. However, he liked it nonetheless, and later said it had added depth when compared to the original.

S: I remember reading something about how Pollock's work should be looked at, um... Well, since he was looking down when he painted them, we should be looking down at them as well. But when we go to a museum, they're hung on a wall, so we really don't get to fully experience Pollock's work.

P: Hmm... Those people might have a point, but **Q11** **think about photography. Just because the photographer took a picture of the sky, it doesn't mean we have to hang the photograph on the ceiling. I personally believe it doesn't matter how you look at Pollock's works... The angle just doesn't matter.** Initially his works were misunderstood, not understood at all, but Pollock's work became so influential that the artistic community shifted its attention from Paris, which had been the center of the art world, to New York, the city Pollock painted in. He caused a shift in the center of contemporary art, and that really is a reflection of his greatness.

해석 미술사 수업의 다음 강의 일부분을 들으시오.

교수(여자): 좋아요, 지난 주에는 유럽의 아방가르드(전위파) 화가들에 대해 이야기했죠. 이번 주에는, 이곳 미국에서의 유사한 한 운동으로 초점을 옮겨봅시다. 한 주도적인 운동이 1940년대 후반과 1950년대에 시작되었습니다. 그것은 후에 추상적 표현주의라고 불리게 되었지요. 자, 아방가르드 화가들이 무엇을 나타냈는지 기억하는 사람이 있나요?

학생(남자): 음... 혁명 같은 것이 아니었나요? 그들은 전통적인 미술의 제한된 규칙들로부터 자유롭고 싶어 했잖아요.

교수: 아주 좋아요. 아방가르드 화가들과 추상적 표현주의 화가들은 전통에 대한 반발심과, 예술은 즉흥적이고 자유로워야 한다는 신념을 공유했지요. 추상적 표현주의가 달랐던 점은, 그것이 기본적으로 화가들이 자신들의 생각들을 추상적인 방법으로 전달하기 위한 시도였다는 것입니다. 그들은 익숙한 소재나 실생활에서 실제 볼 수 있는 것들을 그리는 것에는 관심이 없었어요. 그들은 큰 캔버스를 사용했는데, 그 자체가 전통으로부터의 탈피였고, 그들이 그림을 그린 방식 역시 달랐어요. 화가들 사이에서는 캔버스에 물감을 매우 빨리, 그리고 엄청난 힘으로 칠하는 것이 흔한 일이었죠.

학생: 그럼 교수님 말씀은, 그 화가들이 자신의 감정을 전달하기 위해 애를 쓴 것이라는 거군요? 아방가르드 화가들이 급진적이긴 했지만 그들이 그린 대상은 전통적인 미술과는 그다지 다르지 않다고 교수님께서 말씀하신 것이 기억나요.

교수: 바로 그거에요! 아마도 가장 유명한 미국 추상적 표현주의 화가일 Jackson Pollock의 작품을 살펴보도록 하죠. Pollock이 화가로 수련을 하고 있던 때에는, 그가 예술적 혁명가로 비칠 것이라는 것을 나타내는 것은 아무것도, 음, 적어도 그의 작품들에서는 아무것도 없었습니다. 1930년대에 그는 뉴욕 시에 있는 유명한 예술학교인 Art Students League에서 수학했습니다. 하지만, 10년 후, 그는 사람들이 미술 작품을 만드는 방식을 바꾸어 놓았습니다. 무슨 말인지 아는 사람 있나요?

학생: 그가 사용했던 (물감을 떨어뜨리는) 드립 방식을 말씀하시는 거군요.

교수: 맞아요. 그는 자신이 '쏟아 붓고 뚝뚝 떨어뜨리는 기법'이라고 부른 것을 사용했습니다. 전통적인 이젤을 사용하는 대신, 그는 캔버스 주변을 돌아다닐 수 있도록, 기본적으로 벽 크기에 달하는 캔버스를 바닥에 눕혀놓았습니다. 그리고 나서 그는 캔버스 위에 물감을 붓고 떨어뜨렸어요. Pollock은 작업을 할 때, 전통적인 화가들보다 훨씬 더 많이 돌아다녔고, 그래서 많은 사람들은 그의 스타일을 '액션 페인팅'이라고 부르게 되었지요. 이 용어는 작품을 만드는 과정이 작품 그 자체만큼 중요하다는 것을 나타낸다고 할 수 있습니다. 그가 물감이나 혹은 그가 생각하기에 자신의 생각을 잘 전달할 수 있는 다른 어떤 재료들을 캔버스에 떨어뜨리고 부으면서 그림을 그리는 것을 지켜보려 많은 사람들이 그의 화실을 찾아갔습니다. 여러분은 그의 작품들이 완전히 무작위이고... 음, 아무 규칙도 없이 그냥 거칠고 혼돈 상태일 뿐인 것으로 생각할지도 모르지만... 사실 Pollock은 자신의 재료들과 작품들을 완전히 통제하고 있었습니다. Pollock의 방법들은 정말이지 혁명적이었고 예술계를 충격에 빠뜨렸어요. 캔버스에 붓을 대지 않고 그림을 그리는 것은 들어본 적이 없는 것이었습니다. 게다가, 그가 사용했던 캔버스들은 너무나 거대해서 어느 무엇보다도 벽화처럼 보였습니다. 그의 기법에 관한 좋은 하나의 예는 그냥 〈Number 5〉라고만 이름 지어진 한 작품으로, Pollock이 1948년에 두 번을 그린 작품입니다.

학생: 두 번이라고 하셨어요?

교수: 그래요. 잠시 후에 그 이야기를 하도록 할게요. 처음 봐서는, 그 그림은 새 둥지처럼 뒤엉킨 선들로 된 엉망진창처럼 보이기만 합니다. 하지만 그 그림을 직접 본다면, 또는 그 그림을 가까이서 본다면, 여러분은 Pollock이 어째서 선구자라고 불렸는지 이해할 겁니다. 처음의 혼돈 밑에, 분명한 구성과 그것에 부여된 의미가 실제로 있습니다. 그 그림이 마구잡이라면, 그렇게 호소력이 있지는 않겠지요. 그래서, 어쨌든, 첫 번째 버전은 구매자에게 배송되는 도중 실제로 훼손되어서, Pollock은 그림 주인이 절대 알지 못할 것이라 생각하며 새 그림을 그렸습니다. 하지만 주인은 그것이 다른 그림이라는 것을 알 수 있었지요. 하지만, 그는 그럼에도 불구하고 그 그림을 좋아했고, 나중에 말하기를 원작에 비교해서 깊이가 더해졌다고 했습니다.

학생: Pollock의 작품을 어떻게 감상해야 하는지에 대해 뭔가 읽은 기억이 나요. 음... 그러니까, 그가 그림을 그릴 때 아래를 내려다보고 있었기 때문에, 우리도 그림을 아래로 내려다봐야 한다고요. 하지만 미술관에 가면 그림이 벽에 걸려 있어서 Pollock의 작품을 제대로 경험할 수 없어요.

교수: 음... 그렇게 말하는 사람들도 일리는 있을지 모르지만, 사진을 생각해보세요. 사진작가가 하늘의 사진을 찍었다고 해서 우리가 그 사진을 천장에 걸 필요는 없는 거죠. 나는 개인적으로 우리가 Pollock의 작품들을 어떻게 보느냐는 중요치 않다고 생각해요... 각도는 중요하지 않아요. 처음에 그의 작품들은 잘못 이해되었지만, 실은 전혀 이해 받지 못했었죠, Pollock의 작품은 너무나 영향력이 커서, 미술계는 그들의 관심을 예술계의 중심이었던 파리에서 Pollock이 작업을 했던 도시인 뉴욕으로 돌렸습니다. 그는 현대 미술의 중심의 이동을 초래했고, 그것은 실제로 그의 위대함을 반영하는 것입니다.

Ⓦ avant-garde [əvàːnt-gáːrd] 아방가르드(전위적인 사상)   Abstract Expressionism 추상적 표현주의   stand for ~ ...을 상징하다, 대표하다   revolt [rivóult] 반발, 반란   spontaneous [spantéiniəs] 즉흥적인   revolutionary [rèvəlúːʃənèri] 혁명적인, 혁명가   pour [pɔːr] 붓다   drip [drip] 뚝뚝 떨어뜨리다   easel [íːzəl] 이젤 (받침대)   chaotic [keiátik] 혼돈의, 혼돈 상태의   in control of ~ ...을 제어하고 있는   unheard of 전례가 없는   mural [mjúərəl] 벽화   mess of tangled line 뒤엉킨 선들로 이루어진 엉망인 상태   influential [ìnfluénʃəl] 영향력있는   artistic community 미술 공동체   contemporary art 현대 미술   reflection [riflékʃən] 반영

06 강의의 주된 내용은?
Ⓐ 프랑스에서 뉴욕으로의 예술의 이동
Ⓑ 한 유명한 유럽인 아방가르드 화가
Ⓒ 한 현대 화가의 독특한 스타일
Ⓓ 초상화를 그리는 현대 기법

07 교수에 의하면, 추상적 표현주의의 어떤 측면이 아방가르드 미술과 달랐는가?
Ⓐ 혁명 정신을 구현했다.
Ⓑ 전통 미술의 규칙을 깼다.
Ⓒ 기존 그림들을 이용하여 그것들을 변화시켰다.
Ⓓ 현실에서 볼 수 없었던 것들을 묘사했다.

08 화가 수업을 받던 시기의 Jackson Pollock에 대해 교수가 지적한 점은?
Ⓐ 그는 같은 작품을 계속해서 반복해 그렸다.
Ⓑ 그는 전혀 눈에 띌 만한 것을 그리지 않았다.
Ⓒ 그는 대부분의 화가들이 그린 것을 그리지 않았다.
Ⓓ 그는 붓질에 엄청난 힘을 가했다.

09 교수에 의하면, Pollock의 회화 기법의 두 가지 독특한 특징은? (두 가지 선택)
Ⓐ 그림을 그리는 동안 서 있었다.
Ⓑ 매우 작은 캔버스를 사용했다.
Ⓒ 캔버스를 바닥에 두었다.
Ⓓ 손잡이가 긴 붓들을 사용했다.

10 교수가 〈Number 5〉에 대해 말한 것은?
Ⓐ 분명한 구성이 있다.
Ⓑ 완전히 무작위로 그려진 작품이다.
Ⓒ 손상되었을 때 더 좋아 보였다.
Ⓓ Pollock의 감정을 나타내는 많은 선들과 형태들이 있다.

11 교수가 사진을 언급한 이유는?
Ⓐ 아방가르드 미술에서의 사실성의 중요성을 강조하려고
Ⓑ Pollock의 많은 작품들의 영향력에 대해 설명하려고
Ⓒ Pollock의 작품을 감상하는 것에 대한 오해를 지적하려고
Ⓓ 예술계가 유럽에서 미국으로 이동한 이유를 설명하려고

[12 ~ 17] Listen to part of a lecture in a zoology class. 🔊 MP3 87

Professor(female): Okay, well, last time we talked about the physiological adaptations birds have made in order to migrate. **Q12** **In today's class, let's take a look at how we can track the routes that these birds take during migration.** But first let's recap. What do we mean by migration? Larry?

Student(male): Well, it's basically a movement from one region to another in a regular fashion. Mostly, uh… according to the season.

P: Right! As we talked about during the last class, **Q13** **birds migrate very long distances** – sometimes over a thousand kilometers. **So accurately mapping out these migration routes has long posed a challenge to ornithologists.** Excessive development in bird habitats has threatened many migratory bird species. It's imperative that we learn which bird populations go where so we can help preserve their habitats. Since the same bird species can migrate to several areas, sometimes several thousands of kilometers apart, it's important to accurately track which specific birds fly where. The oldest method was developed in about 1560. English scientists marked swans with a nick – a small scratch – on the beak. But a more efficient method of marking birds was developed by a scientist named Hans Mortensen in 1899. The process was called ringing, although nowadays many ornithologists call it banding. As the name suggests, ringing involved putting a ring around a bird's leg. On this ring, there would be a specific number for each individual bird, as well as some information, such as the bird's age, sex, and wing and tail length. To get all that information on a slim ring is difficult, which is why thicker bands are now more commonplace… hence the alternative name "banding." One of the main advantages of banding is that each and every bird can be individually identified. This makes it the most accurate way of mapping the habitats of certain birds. Scientists can closely monitor each bird's migration habits. But **Q14-A** **capturing birds isn't easy,** so instead of banding an entire flock, scientists usually randomly select a few birds from the group. Probably the biggest limitation is that **Q14-C** **there is no way for ornithologists to track the actual movement of birds. They can't check the bands while the birds are flying** – they have to wait until they come back to their habitats.

S: Can't we use technology to track them while they fly?

P: That's actually my next point. We can use radar to detect birds. Radar sends out a signal and waits for it to bounce back. If there's something in the air, then the signal will tell the radar the size and speed of the object. This method is also very useful for tracking birds that migrate during the night. Cuckoos that migrate from England to various African countries have been tracked this way. But there are limitations to radar. It is only useful for birds in flight and it's very difficult to discern which bird is which when there are many birds flying together. Actually, **Q15** **scientists have combined ringing with radar to more accurately track migrating birds.** Can anyone guess how?

S: Um… When the birds are on the ground, ornithologists check the rings or bands. But they use radar to track birds that are flying. Right?

P: Exactly. This use of radar lessens the limitations of banding.

S: Professor… I understand how radar can track flying birds. But how can it tell which bird is which?

P: Well, that problem is actually solved by another type of technology. Scientists fit small transmitters into the rings. **Q16** **These transmitters send out a signal that satellites can pick up. The satellites can then track the bird's movement in the air and on the ground.** As long as there is a clear line of sight from the sky, **we can know exactly where each specific bird is.** In fact, since satellites are in space, birds can be observed from the start of their migration all the way to their destination. Scientists have made some startling discoveries this way. **For example, a bird called the bar-tailed godwit has been observed flying more than 11,000 kilometers,**

from Alaska to New Zealand, without taking a break for food or drink. Q17 **There's still a lot we need to learn about migration, things we can't currently figure out, even with all the technology available to us. But science is definitely moving in the right direction.**

해석 동물학 수업의 다음 강의 일부분을 들으시오.

교수(여자): 좋아요. 음, 지난 시간에는 이동을 하기 위해 새들이 겪어 온 신체적 적응에 대해 이야기했지요. 오늘 수업에서는, 이 새들이 이동할 때 택하는 경로를 우리가 어떻게 추적할 수 있는지에 대해 살펴보도록 합시다. 하지만 먼저 요약을 해보도록 하지요. 이동이 의미하는 것이 뭔가요? Larry?

학생(남자): 음, 이동은 기본적으로 정기적인 방식으로 한 지역에서 다른 지역으로 이동하는 것을 의미해요. 대개는, 음... 계절에 따라서요.

교수: 맞아요! 우리가 지난 시간에 이야기한 것처럼, 새들은 무척 먼 거리를 이동하지요. 가끔은 천 킬로미터가 넘게도요. 그래서 이런 이동 경로 지도를 정확하게 만드는 것은 조류학자들에게는 오랫동안 도전적인 일이었습니다. 새들의 서식지에서의 과도한 개발은 많은 철새 종들에게 위협이 되었습니다. 그들의 서식지를 보존할 수 있도록 하기 위해 어떤 새 개체군들이 어디로 가는지를 아는 것은 필수적입니다. 같은 새 종들이 여러 지역으로 이동할 수 있기 때문에, 가끔씩은 수천 킬로미터 떨어진 곳들로 말이지요, 그래서 어떤 특정한 새들이 어디로 비행해 가는지를 정확히 추적하는 것이 중요합니다. 가장 오래된 (추적) 방법은 약 1560년경에 개발되었습니다. 영국 과학자들이 백조들의 부리에 새긴 자국, 즉 작게 긁어둔 표시를 남겼습니다. 하지만 새들에게 더 효과적으로 표식을 남기는 방법이 Hans Mortensen이라는 이름의 과학자에 의해 1899년에 개발되었습니다. 그 과정은 고리 채우기(ringing)라고 불렸습니다. 요즘은 많은 조류학자들이 그것을 밴드 채우기(banding)라고 부르지만요. 그 이름이 의미하듯이, 고리 채우기는 새의 다리에 고리를 채우는 것을 수반했습니다. 이 고리 위에는 그 새의 나이, 성별, 그리고 날개와 꼬리의 길이와 같은 정보뿐만 아니라 각각의 새에 붙여진 특정한 번호가 있었습니다. 가는 고리 위에 그 모든 정보를 싣는 것은 어려운데, 그래서 지금은 더 두꺼운 밴드들이 더 흔히 이용됩니다... 그래서 대체된 이름인 '밴드 채우기'가 되었지요. 밴드 채우기의 주된 이점 중 하나는, 각각의 새들을 개별적으로 식별할 수 있다는 것입니다. 이 점이 밴드 채우기를 특정 새들의 서식지 지도를 만드는 가장 정확한 방법이 될 수 있게 합니다. 과학자들은 각 새들의 이동 습성을 면밀히 관찰할 수 있습니다. 하지만 새들을 포획하는 것이 쉽지는 않아서, 전체 무리에 밴드를 채우는 대신, 과학자들은 대개 그 그룹에서 몇몇 새들만을 무작위로 선택합니다. 아마도 (밴드 채우기의) 가장 큰 제약은, 조류학자들이 새들의 실제 이동을 추적할 방법이 없다는 점일 것입니다. 과학자들은 새들이 날고 있는 동안에는 밴드를 점검할 수 없으니까요. 그들은 새들이 서식지로 돌아올 때까지 기다려야 합니다.

학생: 새들이 나는 동안 과학기술을 이용해서 추적할 수는 없나요?

교수: 사실 그것이 다음에 나올 내용입니다. 우리는 새들을 추적하기 위해 레이더를 이용할 수 있어요. 레이더는 신호를 보내고 그 신호가 다시 튕겨져 돌아오기를 기다리지요. 공중에 무언가 있다면, 그 신호는 레이더에게 그 물체의 크기와 속도를 알려줍니다. 이 방법은 또한 밤 시간 동안 이동을 하는 새들을 추적하는 데에도 매우 유용합니다. 영국에서 여러 다른 아프리카 국가들로 이동하는 뻐꾸기들은 이런 방식으로 추적을 받았지요. 하지만 레이더에도 제약이 있습니다. 비행 중인 새들에게만 유용할 뿐, 많은 새들이 한데 날고 있을 때에는 어느 새가 어느 새인지를 구별하는 것이 무척 어렵다는 것입니다. 사실, 과학자들은 철새들을 좀 더 정확히 추적하기 위해 고리 채우기와 레이더를 결합해 사용해왔습니다. 어떻게 그렇게 하는지 추측할 수 있나요?

학생: 음... 새들이 땅 위에 있을 때는, 조류학자들이 고리나 밴드를 점검해요. 하지만 새들이 날고 있을 때는 레이더를 이용해서 추적하는 거죠. 맞나요?

교수: 바로 그거에요. 레이더의 이런 사용법은 밴드 채우기의 한계를 줄여주지요.

학생: 교수님... 레이더가 비행 중인 새들을 추적할 수 있다는 것은 이해했는데요. 하지만 어느 새가 어느 새인지는 레이더가 어떻게 구별하지요?

교수: 음, 그 문제는 사실 다른 종류의 기술에 의해 해결됩니다. 과학자들은 작은 송신기를 고리 안에 넣습니다. 이 송신기들이 위성이 수신할 수 있는 신호를 보내지요. 위성은 그리고 나서 공중과 땅 위에서 새들의 움직임을 추적합니다. 하늘에서 지켜보는 확실한 시선이 있는 한, 우리는 각 특정한 새들이 정확히 어디에 있는지 알 수 있는 것이죠. 사실, 위성은 우주에 있기 때문에, 새들은 그들의 이동 시작부터 목적지까지 내내 관찰될 수 있습니다. 과학자들은 이런 방식으로 몇몇 놀라운 발견을 이루어냈어요. 예를 들어, 큰뒷부리도요라고 불리는 한 새는 알래스카에서 뉴질랜드까지, 음식을 먹거나 물을 마시기 위해 쉬는 일 없이 11,000 킬로미터 넘게 비행한 것이 관찰되었습니다. 새의 이동에 관해서는 여전히 알아야 할 것들이 많습니다. 이용할 수 있는 그 모든 과학 기술로도 현재 파악할 수 없는 것들이 말이지요. 하지만 과학은 분명 바른 방향으로 나아가고 있습니다.

W physiological adaptation (생리적) 신체적 적응　migrate [máigreit] 이동하다, 이주하다　ornithologist [ɔ̀ːrnəθάlədʒist] 조류학자　habitat [hǽbitæt] 서식지　threaten [θrétn] 위협하다　imperative [impérətiv] 긴요한　swan [swan] 백조　nick [nik] 새긴 자국/흠집　beak [biːk] 부리　bounce [bauns] 튀다, 튕기다　track [træk] 추적하다　transmitter [trænsmítər] 송신기　satellite [sǽtəlàit] 위성　destination [dèstənéiʃən] 목적지　Bar-tailed Godwit (조류) 큰뒷부리도요

12 교수가 주로 논의하는 것은?
Ⓐ 철새들을 보호하는 방법들
Ⓑ 새들이 길을 찾을 수 있도록 해주는 적응방식들
Ⓒ 새의 이동을 관찰하는 방법들
Ⓓ 기후 변화와 그것이 (새의) 이동에 미치는 영향

13 철새가 여행하는 긴 거리에 대해 교수가 언급한 이유는?
Ⓐ 새들이 가진 적응 방식을 보여주려고
Ⓑ 일부 새들을 연구하는 것이 왜 어려운지 설명하려고
Ⓒ 위성이 어떻게 사용되는지 예를 들려고
Ⓓ 새의 서식지를 보호할 필요성을 강조하려고

14 교수에 의하면, 새에게 고리나 밴드를 채우는 것의 단점은? (두 가지 선택)
Ⓐ 새를 잡아서 밴드를 채우는 것이 어렵다.
Ⓑ 밴드가 가끔씩 새의 다리에 상처를 입히기도 한다.
Ⓒ 비행중인 새들의 경로를 추적할 수가 없다.
Ⓓ 새의 서식지에 대해 자세한 정보를 줄 수 없다.

15 철새를 관찰하기 위해 레이더를 사용하는 것에 관해 교수가 말한 것은?
Ⓐ 과학자들이 각각의 새들을 식별할 수 있게 해준다.
Ⓑ 날고 있는 새들의 경로를 추적할 수는 없다.
Ⓒ 밤 보다는 낮에 더 효과적이다.
Ⓓ 밴드 채우기와 결합하여 사용될 수 있다.

16 교수가 큰뒷부리도요를 언급한 이유는?
Ⓐ 새들의 서식지를 보존하는 것의 중요성을 강조하려고
Ⓑ 날 수 없는 새들을 추적하는 과학자들의 능력의 예를 들려고
Ⓒ 이동 경로를 추적하는 데 레이더를 사용하는 것의 한계를 설명하려고
Ⓓ 위성이 조류학자들에게 상세한 데이터를 제공할 수 있다는 것을 알려주려고

17 새를 연구하는 데 사용된 기술에 대한 교수의 의견은?
Ⓐ 결국 철새들에게 해가 된다.
Ⓑ 유용하지만 한계도 있다.
Ⓒ 부정확한 정보를 만든다.
Ⓓ 해답보다 더 많은 질문들을 불러일으킨다.

Part 1

| 01 B | 02 C | 03 D | 04 C | 05 D | 06 C | 07 C | 08 B | 09 A | 10 C, D | 11 D | 12 C | 13 A | 14 B |
| 15 C | 16 D | 17 B |

본문 p. 468 ~ 473

[01 ~ 05] Listen to a conversation between a student and his professor. ◁ MP3 88

Student(male): Professor Johnson, there's something that's been on my mind.

Professor(female): Okay... Does it have to with the final exam?

S: Well, sort of... I'm worried about my grades.

P: Hmm... I don't think you have to worry about your research paper. It was excellent. I think I gave you a pretty good grade, if I remember correctly.

S: It's not my grade in your class. It's the humanities classes that I'm taking. The thing is, I've been sitting here thinking, and I'm just not sure what to do after I graduate. I mean, I've been studying humanities for a while, but it's not like I really like it. I think my grades sort of reflect that. **Q1** **I'm thinking I might have picked the wrong major.**

P: I see. So what year are you in?

S: I'm in my fourth year!

P: Um... you do know it's kind of late to switch majors, don't you? I mean, if you want to graduate on time. I do, however, understand the situation you're in.

S: Really? Did you switch majors, too?

P: Luckily, I never had to. **Q2** **But a lot of students are in the same boat as you.** All the students I've met with the same problem had one thing in common – they really didn't have an idea of what they were good at. And sadly, a lot of students don't understand or know what they want until after a few years of studying.

S: Yeah...

P: I read your paper, and I thought it was excellent. The material that you put in, how you reflected what you learned in class... it was all there. But what got my attention most was how you linked all the points together in one coherent piece. Believe it or not, not a lot of students in any of my classes can do that. I really think you have a lot of potential as a writer. **Q3** **Have you ever thought about a career in writing? You wouldn't even have to switch majors.**

S: Wow, thanks for the compliment! But... I really like computers. Actually, I'm really passionate about programming. It wasn't even part of my studies, I just took a programming course for my general requirements, and I ended up loving it. But...

P: But... you don't think you'll be able to graduate on time, right? Humanities and computer sciences are totally different fields.

S: Exactly.

P: Okay, I see what your dilemma is. How about this then – Are you taking any classes related to programming or engineering?

S: I'm taking an artificial intelligence class this semester.

P: Have you thought about writing a research paper on it? **Q4** **If you really like doing it, then at least you'll have an idea of what field suits you best.** Even if a paper isn't required for the class, I'm sure you can talk to your professor about it. There's generally a policy about giving extra credit for personal research projects related to class. So it could help you with your grades too. Tell me how the writing goes. You're a very talented writer, and if you like computers, I think it'll turn out well. You always have the option to write your senior thesis on computers too, even though it isn't part of your major.

S: But what about my current major? I'll graduate with a degree in something I don't even like all that much.

P: 🎧 **Q5** Well, if everyone got hired or went to graduate school based solely on their majors... Let's just

say the world would be a very different place. Why don't you try what I suggested first? You can always go to graduate school for computer sciences. Coming from a different background might actually help your chances. And you can always write research papers on computers to prepare for graduate school. It's almost finals time, so why don't you focus on finishing your preparation and that paper I talked to you about? Afterwards, try making a list of what you can do. Write down all your options, and then we'll talk about it some more.
S: Thanks.

해석 학생과 교수간의 다음 대화를 들으시오.
학생(남자): Johnson 교수님, 제가 계속 생각해오던 것이 있어요.
교수(여자): 좋아요... 기말고사에 관한 것인가요?
학생: 음, 그런 셈이에요... 제 성적에 대해 걱정이 되요.
교수: 음... 학생 연구 보고서에 대해 걱정할 필요는 없을 것 같은데요. 아주 뛰어났거든요. 꽤 좋은 점수를 준 것 같은데, 내가 맞게 기억하고 있다면 말이에요.
학생: 교수님 수업에서의 성적 때문이 아니고요. 제가 지금 수강하고 있는 인문학 수업들 때문에요. 문제는, 여기 앉아 생각해봤는데요, 졸업한 뒤에 무엇을 해야 할지 정말 모르겠어요. 그러니까, 저는 한동안 인문학을 공부했는데, 인문학을 그다지 좋아하는 것 같지 않아요. 제 성적이 어느 정도 그런 걸 반영하고 있는 것 같고요. 잘못된 전공을 선택했는지도 모르겠다는 생각이 들어요.
교수: 알겠어요. 몇 학년이죠?
학생: 4학년이요.
교수: 음... 전공을 바꾸기에는 조금 늦었다는 것을 알고 있지요? 내 말은, 제때 졸업하려면 말이에요. 하지만, 학생이 처한 상황을 이해는 합니다.
학생: 정말이요? 교수님도 전공을 바꾸셨나요?
교수: 운 좋게도, 나는 그럴 필요는 없었어요. 하지만 많은 학생들이 학생과 같은 처지에 있죠. 같은 문제로 내가 만나온 모든 학생들은 한 가지 공통점을 가지고 있었어요. 바로 자신들이 무엇을 잘하는지에 대해 잘 알지 못했다는 것이죠. 그리고 안타깝게도, 많은 학생들이 몇 년간 공부를 하고 난 이후에서야 비로소 자신들이 원하는 것이 무언지 이해하거나 알게 된다는 점이에요.
학생: 네...
교수: 학생의 보고서를 읽어봤는데, 아주 뛰어났다고 생각했어요. 학생이 써넣은 자료들, 수업에서 배운 것을 어떻게 반영했는지... 그게 모두 보고서 안에 있더군요. 하지만 가장 내 주목을 끌었던 것은, 학생이 그 모든 주장들을 하나의 일관된 것으로 한데 연결한 방식이었어요. 믿기 어렵겠지만, 내 어떤 수업에서도 그렇게 할 수 있는 학생이 많지 않거든요. 학생은 작가로서의 잠재성이 많은 것 같다는 생각이 들어요. 글을 쓰는 직업에 대해 생각해본 적이 있나요? 전공을 바꿀 필요도 없을 텐데.
학생: 와, 칭찬 감사 드려요! 하지만... 저는 컴퓨터를 정말 좋아해요. 사실, 저는 프로그래밍에 무척 열정이 있거든요. 프로그래밍은 제 전공의 일부는 아니지만, 일반 필수과목으로 프로그래밍 수업을 들었는데, 너무 좋아하게 된 거예요. 하지만...
교수: 하지만... 제때 졸업하지 못할 것 같다고 생각하는 거지요? 인문학과 컴퓨터 공학은 완전히 다른 분야니까요.
학생: 바로 그거에요.
교수: 좋아요. 학생의 딜레마가 뭔지 알겠어요. 그럼 이건 어때요? 프로그래밍이나 엔지니어링과 관련이 있는 과목을 뭔가 듣고 있는 게 있나요?
학생: 이번 학기에 인공 지능 수업을 듣고 있어요.
교수: 그것에 관해 연구 보고서를 써보는 것에 대해 생각해봤나요? 그에 관한 보고서를 쓰는 것이 정말 좋다면, 적어도 어느 분야가 학생에게 가장 맞을지에 대해 알 수 있게 될 테니까요. 그 수업에 보고서가 필수가 아니라 하더라도, 교수님께 그것에 대해 이야기해볼 수 있다고 생각해요. 수업과 관련된 개인적 연구 프로젝트들에는 추가 학점을 주도록 하는 정책이 대개 있거든요. 그러니 그게 학생의 성적에도 도움이 될지도 몰라요. 보고서 작성이 어떻게 되어가는지 내게 말해주고요. 학생은 글 쓰기에 매우 재능이 있으니, 학생이 컴퓨터를 좋아한다면 보고서가 잘 나올 거예요. 컴퓨터가 학생의 전공은 아니지만, 컴퓨터에 관해 졸업논문을 쓸 선택권도 항상 있고 말이죠.
학생: 하지만 제 현재 전공은 어떻게 하고요? 그다지 많이 좋아하지도 않는 분야의 학위를 가지고 졸업하게 될지도 모르는데요.
교수: 음, 모두가 전공에 의해서만 채용이 되거나 대학원에 진학한다면... 그냥 세상은 무척 다른 곳일 거라고 해두죠. 우선 내가 제안한 걸 해보는 게 어때요? 언제든 컴퓨터 공학 분야로 대학원을 갈 수 있어요. 다른 배경 출신인 것이 실제로 학생의 가능성을 높여줄지도 모르고요. 그리고 대학원에 대비하기 위해 언제든 컴퓨터에 대한 연구 보고서를 쓸 수 있어요. 이제 거의 기말고사 시기이니, 시험 준비를 끝내는 것과 내가 말해준 그 보고서에 집중하는 게 어때요? 그 후에, 학생이 무엇을 할 수 있을지 목록을 작성해보고요. 모든 선택 가능한 사항들을 적고, 그리고 나서 그것에 대해 더 이야기해보도록 하죠.
학생: 감사합니다.

W humanity class 인문학 수업   reflect [riflékt] 반영하다   in the same boat 같은 상황에 있는   coherent [kouhíərənt] 일관성 있는

potential [pəténʃəl] (...이 될) 가능성이 있는   compliment [kɑ́:mpləmənt] 칭찬   requirement [rikwáiərmənt] 필요조건(필수 과목)   (someone) ended up loving ~ ...를 좋아하게 되다   dilemma [dilémə] 딜레마, 진퇴양난   artificial intelligence 인공 지능   extra credit 추가 점수 (추가 학점보다는 class 내의 추가적인 점수)   senior thesis 마지막 학년 학위 논문   based solely on ~ 단지 ...에만 근거하여

01 학생이 교수를 찾아간 이유는?
Ⓐ 인문학 전공을 하는 것에 대해 문의하려고
Ⓑ 자신의 전공에 대해 무엇을 해야 할지 조언을 구하려고
Ⓒ 보고서에서 받은 점수에 대해 이야기하려고
Ⓓ 졸업 논문을 쓰는 것에 대해 정보를 구하려고

02 학생의 딜레마에 대한 교수의 태도는?
Ⓐ 자신이 가르치는 수업과는 관련이 없다고 생각한다.
Ⓑ 학생이 아무것도 아닌 것으로 큰 문제를 삼는다고 생각한다.
Ⓒ 학생만 그런 고민을 하는 게 아니라고 생각한다.
Ⓓ 학생이 그것에 대해 더 많은 시간을 들여 생각해야 한다고 생각한다.

03 교수가 작가들에 대해 암시하는 것은?
Ⓐ 그들 중 많은 이가 주장들을 한데 연결하지 못한다.
Ⓑ 그들 중 많은 이가 알맞은 전공을 찾는 데 고군분투했다.
Ⓒ 그들은 컴퓨터에 대한 지식을 가져야 할 필요가 있다.
Ⓓ 그들은 일반적으로 그들이 원하는 어떤 것이든 전공을 할 수 있다.

04 학생이 컴퓨터 공학 수업에서 연구 보고서를 쓰도록 교수가 제안한 이유는?
Ⓐ 대학원은 졸업 논문을 요구한다.
Ⓑ 학생이 졸업하기 위해 추가 학점이 필요하다.
Ⓒ 학생은 자신이 무엇을 하고 싶은지를 확인할 필요가 있다.
Ⓓ 교수들은 좋은 보고서를 쓰는 학생들을 선호한다.

05 교수가 다음과 같이 말할 때 암시하는 것은? 🔊 **MP3 88_1**

> Well, if everyone got hired or went to graduate school based solely on their majors... Let's just say the world would be a very different place.

Ⓐ 더 많은 학생들이 자신들의 공부 분야와 일치하는 일자리를 얻어야 한다.
Ⓑ 대학들은 학생들이 직업에서 성공할 수 있도록 더 잘 훈련을 시켜야 한다.
Ⓒ 많은 졸업생들이 그들의 전공과 다른 일자리를 구할 때 그들의 잠재능력을 낭비한다.
Ⓓ 많은 직업인들이 전공한 것과는 다른 분야의 일을 선택한다.

[06 ~ 11] Listen to part of a lecture in an English literature class. 🔊 **MP3 89**
Professor(male): All right, continuing with our series of lectures on English writers, I'd like to spend some time talking about Mary Shelley and her best known novel, *Frankenstein – The Modern Prometheus*. Well, I'm assuming you know how the story goes. Shelley and her husband were on vacation with a few friends who were also incredible writers, and they made a challenge to write a horror novel. Shelley took up the challenge and wrote arguably one of the most famous horror stories ever written. So can anyone tell me what the story was about?
Student(female): Well, it's a story about a mad scientist that creates a monster, Frankenstein.
P: 🎧 **Q11** No, no, the monster's name isn't Frankenstein. That's what most kids think because of horror movies. The creator, the scientist you were talking about, his name was Victor Frankenstein. You don't want to forget that.
S: Oops. Yeah, I always get that mixed up.
P: Okay, so go on.
S: So the scientist leaves the monster after creating it, and the monster starts murdering everyone close to his

creator for revenge. Frankenstein becomes angry, because he's lost everything, so he goes after his creation but dies in the end.

P: That's right, that's basically it. So, **Q6** what was her inspiration? What do you think made her write the novel she did?

S: I know that she wrote during the early 1800s, during the age of the Industrial Revolution. I remember hearing somewhere that she wrote *Frankenstein* in response to the rapid development of science. Something about… people were afraid of technology developing too quickly, they were afraid that they were playing God. So I think Shelley was thinking about these anxieties when she wrote her book.

P: Good. That's how most critics analyze her work. **Q7** Even the subtitle, "the Modern Prometheus", seems to reflect this theme. Prometheus was the titan who stole fire from Zeus and gave it to humans. He was given an eternal punishment for giving people something that only the gods should have. There's definitely a connection there between Prometheus and Frankenstein. Frankenstein tried to do something that only gods should do, create life. And as a result, he was punished greatly for it. **Q6** But there's another reason why Shelley wrote the story, something that is very different from what most people think – the weather. That's right, the weather during the time when Shelley was on vacation could have been the impetus behind this great novel. You see, in 1816, which was the year Shelley started writing, **Q8** a volcano named Mount Tambora erupted in Southeast Asia, sending plumes of ash into the atmosphere. Even though this happened far away from Europe, it still changed the weather drastically for a few years. The volcanic ash in the atmosphere made it dark and cold. So cold, in fact, that harvests failed for three years and people were dying from starvation. The weather obviously impacted the trip. They were originally supposed to hike the Swiss Alps, but the horrible weather made it impossible to go out. So, just like a lot of children do on dark and scary nights, they started telling scary stories to one another until one of them decided they should all write a scary story themselves. **Q9** This particular motivation is not… well, not as complex as most people suggest.

S: But what does that have to do with the content of the novel?

P: Other than revenge, what was a reoccurring theme in the novel?

S: Um… Frankenstein was sick a lot.

P: And…

S: Oh, the weather! Yeah, come to think of it, there was horrible weather every time something bad happened. Like, it was raining when Frankenstein made his monster, and it was a foggy night when Frankenstein disposed of his monster's wife.

P: Good. That's what makes people think Shelley wrote *Frankenstein* as a response to the horrible weather she was experiencing. **Q10-C** In one of her letters to her sister, Shelley writes about the thunderstorms and cold weather she had to deal with. Well, **Q10-D** almost every time Frankenstein's monster goes outside, it's either cold or there's a thunderstorm. And in the end, Frankenstein dies in the cold Arctic while chasing his monster. Some people are now saying it's not just coincidence that they went to the coldest part of the world. So, in a way, *Frankenstein* can be considered a novel about the weather.

해석 영문학 수업의 다음 강의 일부를 들으시오.

교수(남자): 좋아요. 영국 작가들에 대한 강의 시리즈를 계속하며, Mary Shelley와 그녀의 가장 잘 알려진 소설인 〈프랑켄슈타인: 현대의 프로메테우스〉에 대해 이야기하는 시간을 좀 가져볼까 합니다. 음, 그 이야기가 어떻게 되는지 알고 있을 거라 생각해요. Shelley와 그녀의 남편은 뛰어난 작가들인 몇몇 친구들과 휴가를 보내고 있었는데, 공포 소설을 써보자는 도전을 하게 됩니다. Shelley는 도전을 받아들였고, 틀림없이 지금까지 쓰여진 가장 유명한 공포 소설들 중 하나를 쓰게 되지요. 그 이야기가 무엇에 대한 건지 말해줄 사람 있나요?

학생(여자): 음, 괴물 프랑켄슈타인을 만들어낸 한 미친 과학자에 대한 이야기에요.

교수: 아니, 아니. 괴물의 이름은 프랑켄슈타인이 아니에요. 그건 공포 영화 때문에 대부분의 아이들이 생각하는 것이죠. 그 창조자, 학생이 말했던 그 과학자, 그 사람의 이름이 Victor Frankenstein이었어요. 잊지 말도록 하세요.

학생: 이런. 네, 항상 그게 혼동돼요.

교수: 좋아요. 계속 하세요.

학생: 그래서 그 과학자는 괴물을 만든 뒤 떠나고, 그 괴물은 복수를 위해 자신의 창조자와 가까운 모든 사람들을 죽이기 시작하죠. 프랑켄슈타

인은 모든 것을 잃어 분노했고, 그래서 자신의 창조물을 뒤쫓지만 결국 죽어요.

교수: 맞아요, 기본적으로 그렇죠. 자, 작가의 영감은 무엇이었을까요? 무엇이 그녀에게 그 소설을 쓰도록 했을까요?

학생: 그녀가 1800년대 초에 글을 썼다는 걸 알고 있어요. 산업 혁명의 시기 동안이요. 그녀가 급속한 과학 발달에 대응하여 〈프랑켄슈타인〉을 썼다고 어디선가 들었던 기억이 나네요. 어떤 거였냐면요… 사람들이 기술이 너무 빨리 발달하는 것을 두려워했다는 거예요. 자신들이 신처럼 행동하고 있는 것을 두려워해서 말이죠. 그래서 저는 Shelley가 책을 썼을 때 이런 불안들에 대해 생각하고 있었던 것 같아요.

교수: 좋아요. 그게 대부분의 비평가들이 그녀의 작품을 분석하는 방식이죠. 심지어 부제인 '현대의 프로메테우스'도 이 주제를 반영하는 것 같아 보입니다. 프로메테우스는 제우스로부터 불을 훔쳐 인간에게 준 타이탄이었죠. 그는 신들만이 가져야 하는 무언가를 사람들에게 준 죄로 영원한 형벌을 받았습니다. 거기에 프로메테우스와 프랑켄슈타인 간의 연관성이 분명히 있습니다. 프랑켄슈타인은 신들만이 해야 하는 무언가를 하려 애썼죠, 생명을 창조하는 것 말입니다. 그리고 그 결과로, 그것에 대해 크나큰 형벌을 받았습니다. 하지만 Shelley가 그 소설을 쓴 것에는 또 다른 이유가 있습니다. 대부분의 사람들이 생각하는 것과는 매우 다른 것인데, 바로 날씨입니다. 맞아요, Shelley가 휴가를 즐기고 있던 때의 날씨가 이 위대한 소설 뒤에 숨은 원동력이 되었을 수도 있습니다. 그러니까, Shelley가 집필을 하기 시작했던 해인 1816년에, Tambora 산이라는 이름의 화산이 동남아시아에서 분출하여 재가 가득한 연기들을 대기로 뿜어냈습니다. 비록 이것이 유럽에서 멀리 떨어져 발생했지만, 그것은 몇 년간 날씨를 급격히 변화시키긴 했습니다. 대기의 화산 재는 날씨를 어둡고 춥게 만들었죠. 사실 너무 추워서, 삼 년간 흉작이 이어졌고 사람들은 기아로 죽어갔습니다. 그 날씨가 그 여행에 분명히 영향을 미쳤지요. 그들은 원래는 스위스 알프스 산에 하이킹을 가려고 했었지만 끔찍한 날씨 때문에 밖에 나가는 것이 불가능해졌어요. 그래서 많은 아이들이 어둡고 무서운 밤에 하는 것처럼, 그들도 서로서로 무서운 이야기를 하기 시작했습니다. 그들 중 하나가 그들 모두 무서운 이야기를 직접 쓰자고 결정할 때까지 말이죠. 이 특정한 동기는… 음, 대부분의 사람들이 생각하는 것처럼 복잡한 것은 아니죠.

학생: 하지만 그것이 그 소설의 내용과 무슨 관련이 있지요?

교수: 복수 외에, 이 소설에서 반복되는 주제가 무엇이었나요?

학생: 음… 프랑켄슈타인은 많이 아팠어요.

교수: 그리고…

학생: 아, 날씨요! 그래요. 생각해보니 무언가 나쁜 일이 일어났을 때마다 날씨가 끔찍했어요. 그러니까, 프랑켄슈타인이 괴물을 만들었을 때는 비가 오고 있었고, 프랑켄슈타인이 괴물의 아내를 없앨 때는 안개가 낀 밤이었어요.

교수: 좋아요. 그것이 사람들로 하여금 Shelley가 자신이 겪고 있던 끔찍한 날씨에 대한 응답으로 〈프랑켄슈타인〉을 썼다고 생각하게 한 것이죠. 여동생에게 보낸 그녀의 편지 중 하나에서 Shelley는 자신이 겪어야 했던 뇌우와 추운 날씨에 대해 쓰고 있어요. 음, 프랑켄슈타인의 괴물이 밖에 나갈 때마다 거의 날씨가 춥거나 뇌우가 있었죠. 그리고 끝에, 프랑켄슈타인은 괴물을 쫓다가 추운 북극에서 죽게 되어요. 몇몇 사람들은 그들이 세상에서 가장 추운 곳에 간 것은 단순히 우연이 아니라고 이제 말하고 있습니다. 그러니, 어떤 면에서는, 〈프랑켄슈타인〉은 날씨에 대한 소설로 간주되어도 되는 거죠.

Ⓦ novel [návəl] 소설　horror novel 공포 소설　arguably [ɑ́ːrgjuəbli] 주장하건대　murder [mə́ːrdər] 살인　revenge [rivéndʒ] 복수　inspiration [inspəréiʃən] 영감　Industrial Revolution 산업 혁명　in response to ~ ...에 응하여　anxiety [æŋzáiəti] 불안(감)　critic [krítik] 비평가　subtitle [sʌ́btaitl] 부제　eternal punishment 크나큰 형벌 영원한 형벌　impetus [ímpətəs] 자극, 원동력　volcano [valkéinou] 화산　erupt [irʌ́pt] (화산이) 분출하다　plume [pluːm] 연기 기둥　ash [æʃ] 재　drastically [drǽstikəli] 과감하게　starvation [staːrvéiʃən] 굶주림　reoccur [riːəkə́ːr] 재발생하다　foggy [fɔ́ːgi] 안개가낀　thunderstorm [θʌ́ndərstɔ̀ːrm] 뇌우　coincidence [kouínsidəns] 우연의 일치

06 강의의 주된 내용은?
Ⓐ 현대 과학 발전이 문학에 어떤 영향을 미치는지
Ⓑ 한 소설의 제목과 관련된 흔한 오해
Ⓒ 작가들이 다른 작가들로부터 가끔씩 어떻게 영감을 얻는지
Ⓓ 어떤 소설의 뒤에 얽힌 동기에 대한 대안이 되는 설명

07 교수가 '현대의 프로메테우스'라는 부제를 언급한 이유는?
Ⓐ Shelley가 공포 소설을 쓰기로 한 이유를 설명하려고
Ⓑ 소설의 줄거리에 대한 배경 지식을 제공하려고
Ⓒ 사람들이 Shelley의 영감을 어떤 특정한 방식으로 바라보는 이유를 지적하려고
Ⓓ 그리스 신화와 〈프랑켄슈타인〉 간의 유사성을 알려주려고

08 교수에 의하면, 무엇이 Shelley의 휴가 동안의 날씨를 더 나쁘게 만들었는가?
Ⓐ 북극의 얼음이 녹기 시작했다.

Ⓑ 화산 폭발이 대기에 영향을 미쳤다.
Ⓒ 큰 기후 변화가 발생했다.
Ⓓ 산업 혁명이 대기 오염을 일으켰다.

09 〈프랑켄슈타인〉에 얽힌 동기에 대해 교수가 생각하는 것은?
Ⓐ 대부분의 사람들이 생각하는 것보다 더 단순할 수도 있다.
Ⓑ 결코 풀리지 않을지도 모르는 미스터리이다.
Ⓒ 여러 다른 많은 것들의 조합이었다.
Ⓓ 한때 생각되었던 것과 정반대였다.

10 교수에 의하면, 날씨가 Shelley의 동기가 되었을 수도 있다고 사람들이 생각하는 이유는? (두 가지 선택)
Ⓐ 그 당시의 많은 작가들이 날씨에 관심이 있었다.
Ⓑ 소설의 부제에서 그리스 신화가 언급된다.
Ⓒ Shelley가 나쁜 날씨에 대해 그녀의 여동생에게 편지를 썼다.
Ⓓ 괴물이 밖에 나갈 때마다 날씨가 더 나빠진다.

11 교수가 다음과 같이 말할 때 암시하는 것은? 🔊 **MP3 89_1**

> No, no, the monster's name isn't Frankenstein. That's what most kids think because of horror movies.

Ⓐ 아이들은 공포 영화를 보는 것을 좋아한다.
Ⓑ 대부분의 사람들은 프랑켄슈타인이 누구인지 안다.
Ⓒ 학생들은 과제를 해야 한다.
Ⓓ 영화들이 소설의 등장인물들을 잘못 나타냈다.

[12 ~ 17] Listen to part of a lecture in a music history class. 🔊 **MP3 90**

Professor(female): Okay, moving on from our last lecture about popular instruments in the Baroque period, ▶Q12◀ **let's focus on the history of a very common instrument – the guitar.** So, I'm assuming you know how an acoustic guitar looks… you know, the double curve with a narrow waist in the middle. There are also six strings attached to a bridge on one end, as well as a sound hole and a neck that extends out. At the end of the neck are the tuning keys, to which the strings are attached, and all along the neck there are metal bars called frets. These are used by the musician to obtain specific notes. You may think that this is how the guitar always looked, but it actually went through many different phases before reaching its modern form.

The modern guitar is a direct descendant of an earlier guitar that originated in Spain about 500 years ago. Um, let's go a little further than that… The Spanish guitar was actually influenced by two closely related instruments, the oud and the lute.

First, ▶Q13◀ **let's take a look at the oud. The name comes from Arabic and refers to the fact that it was made from wood. This was different from most Middle Eastern stringed instruments, which were mostly made with animal hides.** This instrument has been prominent in the music of Islamic cultures for centuries and still is today. Historians believe ▶Q14◀ **it was first brought to Europe in the eighth century, when the Muslim people of North Africa came to Spain.** Although the oud somewhat resembles a guitar, it is actually a lot smaller and doesn't have any frets on its neck. This makes playing an oud a little different from playing a modern guitar, as the musician's finger positions don't need to be as accurate, but the notes and the overall sound the instrument makes are actually very similar.

Um, about the same time that the oud was being developed, its cousin the lute was becoming a widely used instrument. The lute was different from the oud in that it had a longer neck and frets. This instrument has a closer resemblance to the modern guitar, and the notes that the instrument makes when open strings are played are very similar to those of the guitar.

▶Q15◀ **This similarity is due to the tuning of the two instruments.** You see, most stringed instruments have a set interval between strings. So, you would say a harp is tuned in "ones" because, well, the strings represent all the notes that can be played, excluding the sharps and flats… um, you know, the slight variations in pitch.

The modern guitar has a tuning of what we call "fourths". That's different from classical stringed instruments, which are tuned in fifths… well except the bass. **So, the lute, although it had many tunings, its standard tuning was in fourths, just like the modern guitar.**

Although both instruments vary a bit from the modern guitar, together they became the basis for the **Q16 Spanish vihuela** in the 15th and 16th centuries. **This instrument most closely resembles the modern guitar in both shape and tuning.** The curves weren't as pronounced as the guitar's, but it did have a double-curved shape like most modern guitars. The tuning was almost identical to that of modern guitars, other than the fact that the third string was tuned a half step lower. The rest were tuned in fourths and had six intervals like the six strings we see on the guitar today. The main difference was that, instead of six strings, the vehuela had 12. So there were two sets of six strings, and the two sets' strings were tuned to the same notes. So, today's guitars represent a kind of evolution of this instrument.

Okay, finally, a quick word about the name "guitar." It comes from the Latin word "cithara". There is a Roman instrument with the exact same name, but it is not actually an ancestor of the modern guitar. The Roman version looked more like a miniature harp. **Q17 You know when you see Valentine's Day cartoons and Cupid is holding a little harp? That's what it looks like.** However, since the only thing it has in common with the guitar is that it has strings, it's safe to say that the two are not related.

해석 음악사 수업의 다음 강의 일부분을 들으시오.

교수(여자): 좋아요, 바로크 시대의 인기 있는 악기들에 대한 지난 강의에 이어, 매우 흔한 악기의 역사에 초점을 맞춰봅시다. 바로 기타입니다. 자, 어쿠스틱 기타가 어떻게 생겼는지 여러분이 알고 있을 거라 생각합니다… 가운데에 좁게 들어간 허리 부분이 있는 두 개의 커브죠. 또 한쪽 끝에 있는 다리 부분에는 여섯 개의 줄이 부착되어 있지요. 소리가 나는 구멍과 바깥쪽으로 이어진 목 부분도 있고요. 목 부분 끝에는 줄들이 부착되어 있는 조율용 키들이 있고, 목 부분에 죽 걸쳐서 프렛(fret)이라고 불리는 금속 선들이 있습니다. 프렛은 음악가들이 특정한 음을 얻기 위해 사용하는 것이죠. 여러분은 기타의 모양이 언제나 이랬을 거라고 생각할지도 모르지만, 기타는 사실, 현대의 형태에 도달하기 전에 여러 많은 단계들을 거쳤습니다.

현대의 기타는 약 5백 년 전에 스페인에서 유래한 초기 기타의 직접적인 후손입니다. 음, 그보다 좀 더 이전으로 가보도록 하지요… 스페인 기타는 사실 두 가지의 서로 긴밀한 관련이 있는 악기인 우드(oud)와 류트(lute)에서 영향을 받았습니다.

우선, 우드를 살펴보도록 하죠. 이 이름은 아랍어에서 왔고 나무로 만들어졌다는 사실을 지칭합니다. 우드는 대부분의 중동지방의 현악기들과는 달랐는데, 중동지방의 현악기들은 대부분 동물 가죽으로 만들어졌습니다. 우드는 수 세기 동안 이슬람 문화권 음악에 있어 중요한 위치를 차지했으며 지금도 여전히 그렇습니다. 역사가들은 우드가 북부 아프리카의 이슬람 교도들이 스페인에 온 8세기에 처음 유럽으로 건너왔다고 생각합니다. 우드가 어느 정도 기타와 닮긴 했지만, 우드는 사실 그보다 훨씬 더 작고 목 부분에 프렛이 없습니다. 이 때문에 우드를 연주하는 것은 현대 기타를 연주하는 것과 조금 다른데, 음악가의 손가락 위치가 기타만큼 정확할 필요가 없기 때문입니다. 하지만 우드가 만드는 음과 전체적인 소리는 사실 (기타와) 매우 유사합니다.

음, 우드가 발전되고 있던 같은 시기쯤에, 그 사촌격인 류트가 널리 사용되는 악기가 되었죠. 류트는 목 부분이 더 길고 프렛이 있었다는 점에서 우드와 달랐습니다. 류트는 현대 기타와 좀 더 닮아 있고, 개방현들이 연주될 때 만들어내는 류트의 음은 기타의 음과 매우 유사합니다.

이러한 유사성은 그 두 악기의 조율 때문입니다. 대부분의 현악기는 현들 사이에 정해진 음정이 있습니다. 그래서, 하프의 경우라면 '1도'씩 조율된다고 할 수 있지요, 왜냐하면, 음, 그 현들이 연주될 수 있는 모든 음정을 나타내기 때문입니다. 샵이나 플랫 같은… 음, 음의 높이에 있어 약간의 변화를 제외하고 말이죠. 현대 기타는 '4도' 간격으로 조율됩니다. 그 점이 5도 간격으로 조율되는 클래식 현악기들과는 다르죠… 음, 베이스를 제외하고요. 그래서, 류트는 많은 조율법이 있기는 했지만, 류트의 표준 조율은 4도 간격이었습니다. 현대 기타처럼 말이죠.

이 두 악기들이 현대의 기타와는 조금 다르긴 하지만, 그 둘이 합쳐져 15세기와 16세기의 스페인 비우엘라(vihuela)의 기초가 되었습니다. 비우엘라는 형태와 조율 양쪽 면에서 현대 기타와 가장 가깝게 닮아 있습니다. (비우엘라 몸체의) 커브는 기타만큼 분명하지는 않지만, 대부분의 현대 기타들처럼 비우엘라는 두 개의 커브를 가진 형태를 하고 있었습니다. 조율 역시 세 번째 현이 반 음 낮게 조율되었다는 사실을 제외하고는 현대 기타의 조율과 거의 똑같았고요. 나머지들은 4도 간격으로 조율되었고, 우리가 오늘날 기타에서 보는 여섯 개의 줄들처럼 여섯 개의 음정들을 가지고 있었습니다. 주된 차이점은, 여섯 개의 줄 대신, 비우엘라는 12개의 줄이 있었다는 것이죠. 그래서, 여섯 개의 줄로 된 두 개의 세트가 있었던 것입니다. 그리고 그 두 세트의 줄들은 같은 음정으로 조율되었지요. 그러니, 오늘날의 기타들은 이 악기가 일종의 진화를 한 것이라 할 수 있지요.

좋아요, 마지막으로, '기타'라는 이름에 대해 짧게 말해보도록 하죠. 기타라는 이름은 라틴어 '키타라(cithara)'에서 유래했습니다. 완전히 똑같은 이름을 가진 로마의 악기가 있는데, 그것은 사실 현대 기타의 조상은 아닙니다. 로마 버전의 악기는 미니 하프 쪽에 가까워 보였지요. 발렌타인 데이 만화들을 보면 큐피드가 작은 하프를 들고 있는 것이 보이지요? 그것이 키타라의 모습입니다. 하지만, 키타라가 기타와 공유하고 있는 유일한 공통점은 줄이 있다는 것뿐이기 때문에, 그 둘은 서로 관련이 없다고 말할 수 있죠.

instrument [ínstrəmənt] 기구, 악기　Baroque [bəróuk] 바로크 양식의　descendant [diséndənt] 후손　originated in ~ ...에서 비롯하다　stringed instrument 현악기　hide [haid] 가죽　resemble [rizémbl] 닮다, 유사하다　interval [íntərvəl] 음정　excluding [iksklú:diŋ] ...을 제외하고　pitch [pitʃ] 음의 높이　identical to ~ ...와 동일한　evolution [èvəlú:ʃən] 진화　ancestor [ǽnsestər] 조상, 선조　miniature [míniətʃər] 미니어처[조그마한]

12 교수가 주로 논의하는 것은?
Ⓐ 기타 음악의 인기
Ⓑ 기타의 기술적 측면들
Ⓒ 현대 기타의 진화
Ⓓ 스페인 악기들의 여러 다른 종류들

13 교수에 의하면, 무엇이 우드를 다른 중동 악기들과 구별 지었는가?
Ⓐ 나무로 만들어졌다.
Ⓑ 동물 가죽으로 덮여 있었다.
Ⓒ 목 부분에 프렛이 없었다.
Ⓓ 다른 지역에서 기원했다.

14 북부 아프리카의 이슬람 교도들에 대해 교수가 이야기한 것은?
Ⓐ 그들은 다른 방식으로 기타를 연주했다.
Ⓑ 그들은 우드를 스페인에 전했다.
Ⓒ 그들은 우드를 변형시킨 최초의 사람들 중 하나였다.
Ⓓ 그들은 스페인 기타가 아프리카에서 대중화되는 것을 도왔다.

15 교수가 류트의 조율에 대해 언급한 이유는?
Ⓐ 류트가 시간이 지나면서 어떻게 발전했는지를 보여주려고
Ⓑ 고대 악기들의 다재다능함을 강조하려고
Ⓒ 무엇이 류트를 기타와 유사하게 만드는지를 지적하려고
Ⓓ 연주되는 음악의 종류를 구분하는 방법을 설명하려고

16 교수가 스페인 비우엘라에 대해 말한 것은?
Ⓐ 우드나 류트와는 매우 다르게 생겼다.
Ⓑ 여러 많은 다른 나라들에서 널리 사용되었다.
Ⓒ 현대 기타보다 더 연주하기 어려웠다.
Ⓓ 현대 기타와 비슷하게 생기고 소리도 비슷했다.

17 교수가 큐피드를 언급한 이유는?
Ⓐ 악기들이 신화에서 어떻게 사용되었는지를 알려주려고
Ⓑ 또 다른 악기의 모양을 묘사하려고
Ⓒ 학생들에게 기타의 일반적인 사용에 대해 알려주려고
Ⓓ 줄로 연주되는 다른 악기들이 거의 없다는 것을 지적하려고

Part 2

01 B	02 B	03 D	04 B	05 D	06 D	07 B	08 A	09 C	10 B	11 D	12 B	13 C	14 D
15 A	16 B	17 C											

본문 p. 474 ~ 479

[01 ~ 05] Listen to a conversation between a student and her English professor. ◁ MP3 91

Student(female): Hello, Professor Stevens?
Professor(male): Hey, Jenna. I was expecting you. Come, have a seat.
S: So... uh... did you want to talk to me about the literacy program that I have going on? I remember you saying that you wanted to talk about it a little more. I think it'd be great if you can get involved. I'm more than happy to go over the details with you.
P: Oh, actually, **Q1** I asked you to stop by because, well... you know the volunteer award you received? The city newspaper wants to do an interview with you about it.
S: Wow! I never thought... really? I mean, I've been in the campus newspaper a few times, but the city newspaper... Wow, that's great! I'm so excited.
P: So let's talk about the award a little bit so I can give some information to the reporter, and then we can talk about your literacy program afterward.
S: Oh, okay, but they're connected anyway.
P: **Q5** I'm sorry?
S: Oh, I meant to say that the award and my literacy program are related. **Q2** I started volunteering as a storybook reader at the local elementary school. You know, reading books to kids out loud. Anyway, as I was teaching the children about the words that were in the book, I noticed that a lot of parents had a hard time reading books to their children.
P: Really?
S: Uh-huh. I mean, I would ask the children to take books home and ask their parents to read it to them, but some students never did it. **Q3** I did some research and found that a lot of parents actually didn't know how to read properly. I figured I'd change the class and open the doors to everyone by starting a program that involved reading and vocabulary. We even have 12 volunteers in the program!
P: That's great. I had no idea you did so much work!
S: Oh, no, it's really nothing.
P: No, it isn't. Anyway, that's a great story for the newspaper to write about. I'm sure the reporter is going to love to hear it from you. **Q4** Having an article will definitely help raise awareness of your program.
S: Yeah, it's great, isn't it? I was thinking I'd use the reward money to hire a professional instructor or put an ad in the newspaper, but I guess that's going to be taken care of by the article.
P: It's great seeing a student apply what she learned in class. A lot of students don't even think about using the English skills they acquire in class. If you need my help with anything, I'll be more than happy to lend a hand.
S: Great! I'll definitely take you up on that offer. We always need people to speak and listening to a college professor would be a great experience for everyone!
P: I'll even do it for free, so you can use the money to invite another speaker.
S: Great! Even better! Thank you so much!
P: No, thank you. Oh, and the interview will be on this Friday. I know it's short notice, but since finals week starts three weeks from now, I figured you'd like to get done with it as soon as possible.
S: Hmm... I'll make time if I have to! What time is it going to be at?
P: Does 3 p.m. sound good?
S: Sure!

해석 학생과 영어 교수간의 다음 대화를 들으시오.

학생(여자): 안녕하세요, Stevens 교수님?

교수(남자): 아, Jenna, 기다리고 있었어요. 와서 앉아요.

학생: 그러니까... 어... 제가 진행하는 글읽기 프로그램에 대해 말씀하시고 싶어 하셨지요? 그것에 대해 좀 더 이야기하시고 싶으시다고 하셨던 게 기억이 나서요. 교수님이 참여하실 수 있다면 정말 좋을 거라 생각했어요. 교수님과 세부사항에 대해 기꺼이 이야기하고 싶고요.

교수: 아, 사실, 내가 학생에게 들르라 한 건... 음... 학생이 받은 자원봉사자 상 있죠? 시(市) 신문사에서 그 상에 관해 학생과 인터뷰를 하고 싶어 해요.

학생: 와! 그런 건 생각도 못했는데... 정말이에요? 학교 신문에는 몇 번 실린 적이 있지만, 시 신문이라, 와, 그거 멋진데요! 신나네요.

교수: 그러니, 기자한테 정보를 좀 줄 수 있도록 그 상에 대해 조금 이야기를 해보죠. 그 다음에 글읽기 프로그램에 대해 이야기해보고요.

학생: 아, 알겠습니다. 하지만 그 둘은 어쨌든 연결되어 있어요.

교수: 무슨 말이죠?

학생: 아, 상과 제 글읽기 프로그램이 관련이 있다는 말씀이었어요. 제가 동네 초등학교에서 이야기책 읽어주는 사람으로 자원봉사를 시작했거든요. 아이들에게 책을 크게 읽어주는 일 말이에요. 어쨌든, 아이들에게 책에 있는 단어들을 가르치면서, 저는 많은 부모들이 아이들에게 책을 읽어주는 데 어려움을 겪는다는 것을 알게 되었어요.

교수: 정말이요?

학생: 네, 그러니까, 아이들에게 책을 집으로 가져가서 부모님께 읽어달라고 하라고 말하곤 했었는데, 일부 학생들은 절대 그렇게 하지 않는 거예요. 조사를 좀 해봤더니, 많은 부모들이 실제로 제대로 읽는 법을 모른다는 것을 알게 되었죠 뭐에요. 저는 수업을 바꿔서, 읽기와 단어를 포함하는 프로그램을 시작함으로써 모두에게 수업을 들을 기회를 주자고 판단했어요. 그 프로그램의 자원봉사자가 12명이나 되었어요!

교수: 그거 멋지네요. 그렇게 많은 일을 했는지 몰랐어요!

학생: 아, 아녜요. 정말 아무것도 아니에요.

교수: 아니, 그렇지 않아요. 어쨌든, 신문에 싣기에 아주 좋은 이야기네요. 분명 기자가 학생에게서 그 이야기를 듣고 싶어할 거예요. 기사가 나면 학생의 프로그램에 대한 인식을 높이는 데 분명 도움을 줄 거고요.

학생: 맞아요. 멋지네요, 그렇죠? 상금을 전문 강사를 고용하거나 신문에 광고를 내는 데 사용하려고 생각 중이었는데, 기사가 그 일을 대신해줄 것 같아요.

교수: 학생이 수업시간에 배운 것을 적용하는 걸 보니 정말 멋지군요. 많은 학생들이 수업시간에 습득한 영어 기술을 이용하는 것에 대해 생각조차 하지 않거든요. 어떤 것이든 내 도움이 필요하다면, 기꺼이 도울게요.

학생: 좋아요! 교수님 제안을 꼭 받아들일게요. 저희는 강연을 해주실 분들이 항상 필요하거든요. 게다가 대학 교수님께 강연을 듣는 건 모두에게 멋진 경험이 될 거예요!

교수: 심지어 무료로 해줄게요. 학생이 상금을 다른 연사를 초빙하는 데 쓸 수 있도록 말이죠.

학생: 멋지네요! 더욱 더 좋고요! 정말 감사합니다!

교수: 아니, 내가 고맙죠. 아, 그리고 인터뷰는 이번 주 금요일이에요. 너무 촉박한 통보지만, 기말고사가 지금부터 3주 후에 시작하니까, 학생이 가능한 한 빨리 이 일을 끝내기를 바랄 거라고 생각했어요.

학생: 음... 필요하다면 제가 시간을 낼게요! 몇 시 정도가 될까요?

교수: 오후 3시 괜찮나요?

학생: 물론이죠!

Ⓦ literacy program 글읽기 프로그램   elementary school 초등학교   raise awareness 의식을 높이다   reward [riwɔ́:rd] 상   put an ad in ~ ...에 광고를 내보내다   acquire [əkwáiər] 습득하다   lend a hand 도움을 주다   short notice 촉박한 통보   final [fáinl] 기말고사   to get done with ~ ...를 끝내다   as soon as possible 가능한 한 빨리

01 교수가 학생에게 자신의 사무실에 들르라고 한 이유는?
Ⓐ 초청 연사가 될 가능성이 있는지 이야기하려고
Ⓑ 학생에게 곧 있을 인터뷰에 대해 알려주려고
Ⓒ 글읽기 프로그램에 자리가 나는지 문의하려고
Ⓓ 학생에게 영어 교육에 대한 기사를 쓰는 걸 도와달라고 요청하려고

02 학생이 한 자원봉사의 종류는?
Ⓐ 유아기 글읽기 프로그램에 대한 강연하기
Ⓑ 초등학교 아이들에게 책 읽어주기

Ⓒ 교내 신문에 기사 쓰기
Ⓓ 성인들에게 어휘 확장법을 가르치기

03 학생이 글읽기 프로그램을 시작한 이유는?
Ⓐ 수업 프로젝트의 일부로 해야 했다.
Ⓑ 교사가 되기 전에 경험이 필요했다.
Ⓒ 아이들에게 글쓰기를 가르치고 싶어했다.
Ⓓ 글을 잘 읽을 수 없는 부모들이 있다는 것을 알게 되었다.

04 인터뷰에 대한 학생의 태도는?
Ⓐ 인정을 받게 되어 신이 나있다.
Ⓑ 글읽기 프로그램에 도움이 될 것이라 여겨 기뻐한다.
Ⓒ 인터뷰가 중요한 것이 아니라고 확신한다.
Ⓓ 인터뷰를 할 수 없을지도 몰라 염려한다.

대화의 일부분을 다시 듣고 질문에 답하시오. ◁》 MP3 91_1

> S: Oh, okay, but they're connected anyway.
> P: I'm sorry?
> S: Oh, I meant to say that the award and my literacy program are related.

05 교수가 다음과 같이 말한 이유는?

> I'm sorry?

Ⓐ 글읽기 프로그램을 도울 수 없어 학생에게 사과해야 한다.
Ⓑ 상에 대해 자신이 이미 알고 있는 것을 확인하고 싶어한다.
Ⓒ 인터뷰에 대한 학생의 견해에 동의하지 않는다.
Ⓓ 상이 그 프로그램과 관련이 있는지 알지 못했다.

[06 ~ 11] Listen to part of a lecture in a US history class. ◁》 MP3 92

Professor(male): Okay, **Q6** today I'm going to give you a brief history of our capital, Washington, D.C. As you know, Washington, D.C. is not actually part of a state. Instead, it's a special district. Hence, the name District of Columbia. **Let's talk about how our nation's capital came to be.**

So, first, believe or not, the nation's capital wasn't Washington, D.C. when the nation was first established. It wasn't until Thomas Jefferson, the third president of the United States, took office that the current nation's capital came to be. When the nation's first president, George Washington, was elected, the capital city was actually New York. However, this was just for a very short period. By the time he was reelected, the capital had moved to Philadelphia. In fact, the capital moved several times in a span of just 20 years.

Philadelphia was actually a great location for the nation's capital. **Q7** **The Congress of the Confederation, where the representatives of each state would meet on a regular basis, was held in Philadelphia, so it was only natural that the nation's capital was initially located there.** So, why did Congress decide it was best to move to a new location? One factor you have to consider is that **Q8** the federal government was quite different back then… **It just wasn't as strong as it is today. Most laws were actually passed and enforced by the states, not the federal government.** I mean, when Thomas Jefferson took office, he lived in a boardinghouse. That's how weak the federal government was back then.

So, what happened? An event which would later be called the Pennsylvania Mutiny of 1783 took place. When Congress asked the governor of Pennsylvania to protect them from the protestors, who were demanding payment for their services during the Revolutionary War, he refused to do so. The governor, um… he sympathized with the protestors and refused to remove them. The representatives had to flee to Princeton, New Jersey.

This would be unheard of now, but back then the states had a lot of power individually. I guess in a sense, the country really wasn't united. The failure to defend the national government was discussed, and the delegates present agreed to give congress the power to move the nation's capital. Some representatives argued that the capital needed to be distinct from the states, so they wouldn't have to rely on them for their protection. Many agreed that this is what should be done, but agreeing on a specific site for the location of the district was another complicated matter altogether.

Now, the Northern states wanted the capital to be located in one of the nation's prominent cities, which unsurprisingly, were all in the north. ▶Q9◀ **The Northern state representatives were predominantly bankers, financiers, and merchants that wanted more economic power. They could obtain this by having the capital located close by. However, the Southern state representatives preferred the capital to be located near their agricultural and slave-holding interests. This was a very sensitive matter for everyone involved.**

An agreement was finally reached to create the district along the Potomac River, which is located between Virginia and Maryland. It might seem like this location was chosen because it's right between the north and the south, but in reality ▶Q10◀ **it was considered to be located among the Southern states.** Well, when I say Southern states, I mean the states where slavery was legal. **This was because the Southern states had repaid all their war debts from the Revolutionary War, but the Northerners couldn't. So, in the agreement, the South paid a big portion of the Northerners' debt. In exchange, the capital was established in its current location,** between two states where slavery was legal and agriculture was a big part of the economy.

In July 6, 1790, delegates signed the Residence Act, which mandated a site for permanent government use. They originally had a different site in mind, but President Washington wanted to include some more land in the district. So the Residence Act was amended and the location was finally settled.

So, how did Washington, D.C. get its name? ▶Q11◀ **Its original name was the Territory of Columbia, in honor of Christopher Columbus, the man who discovered the Americas.** Since, it technically wasn't a state, it was named a territory. Within the territory, the federal city became the city of Washington, named after the first U.S. President. It was not until 1878, more than 80 years after its inception, that the city was given the name that we know today.

해석 미국사 수업의 다음 강의 일부를 들으시오.

교수(남자): 좋아요, 오늘은 우리의 수도인 워싱턴 D.C.의 간단한 역사에 대해 알려주겠습니다. 여러분도 알다시피, 워싱턴 D.C.는 사실상 어떤 주의 일부가 아닙니다. 대신, 워싱턴 D.C.는 특별 구역이죠. 따라서 District of Columbia(컬럼비아 특별구)라는 이름이 붙었죠. 우리 나라의 수도가 어떻게 생기게 되었는지에 대해 이야기해보죠.

자, 우선, 믿을 수 없을지도 모르지만, 우리 나라가 처음 설립되었을 때, 수도는 워싱턴 D.C.가 아니었습니다. 현재의 수도가 된 것은 미국의 제3대 대통령이었던 Thomas Jefferson이 취임하고 난 뒤였지요. 초대 대통령이었던 George Washington이 선출되었을 때는, 수도가 사실 뉴욕이었습니다. 하지만, 이것은 매우 짧은 기간 동안만이었습니다. 그가 재선되었을 즈음에는 수도가 필라델피아로 옮겨졌었죠. 사실, 수도는 고작 20년 정도 되는 기간 동안 여러 번 이동했습니다.

필라델피아는 사실 수도로서 아주 좋은 위치였습니다. 각 주의 대표자들이 정기적으로 회담을 가졌던 연합의회가 필라델피아에서 열렸으므로, 수도가 처음에 그곳에 위치하는 것이 당연했습니다. 그럼, 의회는 어째서 새로운 지역으로 옮기는 것이 좋다고 결정했을까요? 고려해야 할 한 가지 요인은, 연방정부가 그 당시는 굉장히 달랐다는 점입니다... 오늘날만큼 강력하지 않았습니다. 대부분의 법률들은 연방정부가 아닌, 사실상 주(州)들에 의해 통과되고 시행되었습니다. Thomas Jefferson이 취임했을 때, 그는 기숙사에 살았습니다. 그것이 그 당시 연방정부가 얼마나 약했는지를 보여주지요.

그래서, 무슨 일이 생겼을까요? 후에 1783년 펜실베이니아 폭동으로 불리게 된 한 사건이 발생했습니다. 독립전쟁 동안 복무를 한 것에 대해 급여를 요구하는 시위자들로부터 보호를 해달라고 연합의회가 펜실베이니아 주지사에게 부탁을 했을 때, 그는 그렇게 하기를 거부했습니다. 주지사는, 음... 시위자들에 공감을 했고 그들을 몰아내는 것을 거부했던 것이죠. 주 대표자들은 뉴저지의 프린스턴으로 도망을 가야 했습니다. 이것은 오늘날에는 들어볼 수도 없는 일이겠지만, 그 당시에는 주들이 각자 많은 힘을 가지고 있었습니다. 어떤 의미에서는, 나라가 실제로 통일되지 않았던 셈입니다. 중앙 정부를 방어하지 못한 점이 논의되었고, 참석한 대표자들은 연합의회에게 나라의 수도를 옮길 수 있는 힘을 주기로 동의했습니다. 보호를 받기 위해 주(州)들에 의존해야 할 필요가 없도록, 몇몇 대표자들은 수도가 주들과는 완전히 별개의 것이 되어야 한다고 주장했습니다. 많은 이들이 이렇게 되어야 한다는 것에 동의했지만, (수도의) 지역 위치를 위한 특정한 장소에 동의하는 것은 완전히 또 다른 복잡한 문제가 되었습니다.

자, 북부 주들은 수도가 미국의 중요한 도시들 중 하나에 있기를 바랬는데, 그 도시들은 당연히 모두 북부에 있었습니다. 북부 주의 대표들은 대부분 더 많은 경제적 힘을 원했던 은행가, 자본가, 상인들이었습니다. 그들은 수도를 가까이 둠으로써 이런 경제적 힘을 얻을 수 있었습니다. 하지만, 남부 주의 대표들은 그들의 농업적, 그리고 노예 소유와 관련된 이해에 가까운 곳에 수도가 위치하기를 더 선호했습니다. 이것은 연관된 모든 이들에게 매우 민감한 문제였지요.

버지니아주와 메릴랜드주 사이에 위치한 포토맥 강을 따라 수도 지구를 만드는 것에 최종적으로 합의에 도달했습니다. 이 장소가 북부와 남부 사이에 위치하기 때문에 이곳으로 정해진 것처럼 보일 수도 있지만, 사실상은 그곳은 남부 주들 사이에 위치한 것으로 간주되었습니다. 음, 남부 주들이라고 말하는 것은, 노예제도가 합법이었던 주들을 말하는 것입니다. 이는 남부 주들이 독립전쟁에서 생긴 그들의 전쟁 부채를 모두 상환했기 때문이었습니다. 하지만 북부 주들은 그렇지 못했죠. 그래서, 협정서에서, 남부 주들은 북부인들의 부채의 큰 부분을 지불해주었죠. 그 대가로, 수도는 현재의 위치, 즉 노예제도가 합법이었고 농업이 경제의 큰 부분이었던 두 주(州) 사이에 설립되게 된 것이죠.

1790년 7월 6일에, 대표들은 거주 법안에 서명했는데, 그것은 한 지역을 영구적인 정부 사용을 위한 곳으로 지정하는 법안이었죠. 그들은 원래는 다른 지역을 마음에 두고 있었지만, **Washington** 대통령은 그 지구에 부지를 좀 더 포함시키기를 원했습니다. 그래서 거주 법안은 수정되었고, 그 지역이 최종적으로 결정되었죠.

자, 워싱턴 D.C.는 어떻게 그 이름을 갖게 되었을까요? 그곳의 원래 이름은 미국대륙을 발견했던 사람인 **Christopher Columbus**를 기리는 의미에서 '**Columbia**의 영토'였습니다. 그곳은 엄밀하게 말해 주(州)가 아니었기 때문에, 영토라는 이름이 붙었지요. 그 영토 내에서, 연방 도시는 미국의 첫 번째 대통령의 이름을 따서 워싱턴시가 되었습니다. 그 지역이 시작되고 나서 80년 이상이 흐른 뒤인 1878년이 되어서야, 그 시는 우리가 현재 알고 있는 이름이 붙여지게 되었습니다.

Ⓦ special district 특별구   elect [ilékt] 선출[당선]   capital city 수도   in a span of ~ …의 기간에   Congress of the Confederation 연합의회   representative [rèprizéntətiv] 대표자   federal government 연방 정부   enforce [infɔ́ːrs] (법이) 시행되다   boarding-house 기숙사   governor [gʌ́vərnər] 주지사   protester [proutéstər] 항의자[시위자]   refuse [rifjúːz] 거절하다   Revolutionary War 독립 전쟁   sympathize with ~ …에 공감하다   flee [fliː] 도망가다   delegate [déligət] 대표   congress [káŋgris] 의회   predominantly [pridámənəntli] 대부분   financier [finənsír] 금융업자   merchant [mə́ːrtʃənt] 상인   slave-holding [sleiv-hóuldiŋ] 노예 소유의   slavery [sléivəri] 노예제도   debt [det] 부채   mandate [mǽndeit] 권한을 주다   amend [əménd] 개정하다   territory [térətɔ̀ːri] 지역, 영토

06 강의의 주요 목적은?
Ⓐ 북미의 수도 도시들의 차이점에 대해 논의하려고
Ⓑ 지리와 정치의 관계에 대해 설명하려고
Ⓒ 미국이 특별 자치구를 만들 수 없었던 이유를 보여주려고
Ⓓ 미국의 수도 설립을 이끌었던 사건들을 설명하려고

07 교수에 의하면, 수도가 필라델피아로 옮겨진 이유는?
Ⓐ 첫 대통령이 그 지역 출신이었다.
Ⓑ 주의 대표들이 그곳에서 정기적으로 만났다.
Ⓒ 은행가들과 상인들이 수도가 더 북쪽으로 있기를 바랐다.
Ⓓ 그곳이 미국의 중심부에 위치해 있었다.

08 초기의 연방 정부에 대해 교수가 암시하는 것은?
Ⓐ 일부 주 정부들만큼 힘이 강하지 않았다.
Ⓑ 몇몇 주의 주지사들로부터 공격을 받고 있었다.
Ⓒ 영국의 정치 체계를 닮도록 구성되었다.
Ⓓ 대표들을 정기적으로 만나게 할 수 있는 힘을 가지고 있지 못했다.

09 수도의 새로운 위치에 동의하는 것이 어려웠던 이유를 설명하기 위해 교수가 제시한 이유는?
Ⓐ 한 지역을 구체적으로 명시하기 위해서는 헌법이 수정되어야 했다.
Ⓑ 수도는 적의 공격에 방어하기 쉬워야 했다.
Ⓒ 북부 주들과 남부 주들이 상충하는 이해관계에 있었다.
Ⓓ 미국은 급속하게 그 물리적 크기가 증가하고 있었다.

10 수도 지구가 남부 주들 사이에 위치했던 이유는?
Ⓐ 은행가들이 더 많은 경제적 힘을 원했다.
Ⓑ 남부 주들이 일부 부채를 감당하기로 동의했다.

Ⓒ 수도를 유지하기 위해 노예들이 필요했다.
Ⓓ 수도의 건설이 농업에 의해 자금 지원을 받았다.

11 교수가 미국대륙을 발견했던 사람에 대해 언급한 이유는?
Ⓐ 애국적인 이름의 예를 들려고
Ⓑ 주(州)들 간의 의견 불일치를 설명하려고
Ⓒ 수도의 이름을 정하는 데 시간이 걸린 이유를 알려주려고
Ⓓ 수도 시의 원래 이름의 기원을 설명하려고

[12 ~ 17] Listen to part of a lecture in a theater class. 🔊 MP3 93

Professor(male): Most of you are all probably aware that actors must change depending on the characters they play. It's a pretty obvious fact. But sometimes ▶Q12 **the medium you're acting in has an even bigger impact than the character you're playing. Let's take a look at the two main acting styles.**

So, the most basic and oldest type of acting is acting in front of an audience. It's what we call stage acting. The actors perform up on a stage, while people sit in the audience and enjoy the show. This environment actually has had a profound impact on how we approach acting. When I was a young actor just starting my career, ▶Q13 **one of the biggest critiques I ever got was that my acting was too normal. The critic said that there really wasn't that much of a difference between my stage performance and what would be expected of me in an everyday situation.** I just didn't understand it then. I mean, I thought acting was all about being natural and forgetting that you're even acting. If the audience could see how natural my acting was, I thought they'd be drawn deeper into my character. But I was wrong.

You see, in stage acting, the audience can be quite large, and the people sitting in the back rows are sometimes very far away from the stage. So, if an actor's performance is similar to a person's normal behavior, they just won't be able to catch all of the emotion. When we're, um, angry at someone… I mean, in real life… we might just yell at the person. We wouldn't move our arms around and exaggerate our emotions through our body language. But in stage acting, doing this is often necessary to make sure everyone gets what you're trying to express.

That's very ▶Q12 **different from how you would perform in film or screen acting.** That negative aspect of my stage acting actually turned out to be one of my greatest assets when I acted in front of a camera. Being extremely natural didn't cause any problems in front of the camera. The camera was really close to me and could capture every single expression that I made. Even the smallest twitches of my eyebrows were caught on camera. Film can capture the smallest gestures and magnify them 20 or 30 times, so ▶Q15 **cinema demands less stylized body language than theater does. Being natural actually helped viewers relate to me on film,** just like I had originally thought it would.

Actors in the early 20th century struggled with a similar problem, although… well, it was the total opposite of what I went through. You see, cinema had just started developing at the start of the 20th century, so most actors and actresses came from a theater background. They were used to making exaggerated, flamboyant movements when they acted, and many of them acted the same way in front of the camera. Remember what I said about how cameras magnify even the smallest of gestures? Well, in this case, large gestures were magnified even more! Stage acting really seemed out of place on the screen. The filmmaking pioneer ▶Q14 **D.W. Griffith realized this problem and became one of the first directors to experiment on a large scale with a mode of acting that would better suit cinema. Realizing that theatrical acting looked ridiculous, he started training his actors to equip them with the appropriate skills.**

Expressing emotion is probably the most difficult aspect of screen acting to master. Actors have to be natural. They can't use exaggerated gestures, but they still need to express their emotions. Therefore, they have to rely on subtle facial expressions to create believable characters. That's why so many stage actors fail to make it in Hollywood. ▶Q17 **You might be surprised to hear some of the names, but let's save that for another time.** Because the medium is different, the acting must be adapted to suit it. But that's not the only difficult part of screen acting.

Unlike theater performances, which have to be continuous, film can be cut into pieces and put together in a totally different order. You might think that makes acting easier because you can have multiple takes, but it can actually make things quite difficult. This is because film actors sometimes have to reflect several different stages of character development in a single day of shooting. In a stage production, the character develops as the story goes on, but **Q16** **film actors don't always have the luxury of acting out a story in chronological order.**

해석 영화 수업의 다음 강의 일부분을 들으시오.

교수(남자): 여러분 모두는 아마도, 배우들은 그들이 연기하는 인물에 따라 변화해야 한다는 것을 잘 알고 있을 겁니다. 그것은 무척이나 분명한 사실이지요. 하지만 가끔은, 연기를 펼치는 장이 되는 매체가, 배우가 연기하는 인물보다 훨씬 더 큰 영향을 가지고 있기도 합니다. 두 가지 주요한 연기 스타일에 대해 살펴보도록 하죠.

자, 가장 기본적이고 오래된 연기 유형은 관객 앞에서 연기하는 것입니다. 그것은 무대 연기라고 불리는 것이죠. 배우들은 무대에서 연기를 하고, 사람들은 관객석에 앉아 쇼를 즐기죠. 이런 환경은 사실 우리가 연기에 어떻게 접근하는가에 심대한 영향을 끼쳐 왔습니다. 내가 경력을 막 시작하던 풋내기 배우였을 때, 내가 받았던 가장 큰 비평들 중 하나는 내 연기가 너무 평범하다는 것이었습니다. 그 비평가는, 내 무대 연기와 일상 상황에서 내게 기대하는 모습 사이에 실제로 그다지 차이가 많지 않다고 말했지요. 그때는 그 말을 이해하지 못했습니다. 그러니까, 나는 연기는 자연스러워야 하고 심지어 연기를 하고 있다는 것조차 잊어 버려야 한다고 생각했었죠. 내 연기가 얼마나 자연스러운지 관객이 알 수 있다면, 나는 그들이 내가 연기하는 인물에 더 깊이 빠져들 것이라 생각했습니다. 하지만 내가 틀렸었죠.

무대 연기에서는 관객의 수가 매우 많을 수 있습니다. 그리고 뒷줄에 앉은 사람들은 때때로 무대로부터 매우 멀리 떨어져 있기도 하지요. 그래서, 배우의 연기가 어떤 사람의 보통 행동과 유사하다면, 관객들은 모든 감정을 잡아낼 수 없을 것입니다. 우리가, 음, 누군가에게 화가 날 때… 그러니까, 실제 생활에서 말이죠… 우리는 그냥 그 사람에게 소리를 지를지도 모릅니다. 우리는 팔을 움직이거나 신체 언어를 통해 감정을 과장하지 않을 것입니다. 하지만 무대 연기에서는, 모든 사람들이 배우가 표현하려고 하는 것을 알아차리도록 하기 위해 이렇게 하는 것이 종종 필요합니다. 그것은 영화나 영상 연기에서 연기하는 것과는 매우 다릅니다. 내 무대 연기의 부정적인 측면이, 내가 카메라 앞에서 연기했을 때는 실제로 나의 가장 큰 자산들 중 하나가 되었습니다. 엄청나게 자연스러운 것은, 카메라 앞에서는 아무 문제가 되지 않았지요. 카메라는 나를 매우 가까이 잡았고, 내가 하는 하나 하나의 표현을 모조리 잡아냈습니다. 심지어 눈썹을 실룩거리는 아주 작은 움직임도 카메라에 잡혔지요. 영화는 가장 작은 몸짓들을 잡아내 그것들을 20배 또는 30배로 확대시키죠. 그래서 영화는 연극보다 덜 양식화된 몸짓 언어를 필요로 합니다. 자연스러운 것이 실제로 시청자들이 영화에서 나와 동일시하는 것을 도왔습니다. 내가 처음에 그럴 것이라 생각했던 것처럼 말이죠.

20세기 초의 배우들은 비슷한 문제로 고군분투했습니다. 비록… 음, 내가 겪었던 것과는 완전히 반대되는 것이긴 했지만요. 영화는 20세기 초에 막 발달하기 시작했고, 그래서 배우들은 연극에 바탕을 둔 사람들이었습니다. 그들은 연기를 할 때 과장되고 현란한 움직임을 하는 데 익숙했고, 그들 중 많은 이들이 카메라 앞에서 같은 식으로 연기를 했습니다. 카메라가 아주 작은 몸짓조차 확대한다고 말했던 것을 기억하나요? 음, 이 경우에는, 큰 몸짓들이 그보다도 더 많이 확대된 거지요! 무대 연기는 화면에는 맞지 않아 보였습니다. 영화 제작의 선구자인 D.W. Griffith는 이 문제점을 깨닫고, 영화에 더 잘 어울릴 연기 유형을 대규모로 실험했던 최초의 감독 중 하나가 되었습니다. 연극조의 연기가 우스꽝스러워 보인다는 것을 깨닫고, 그는 자신의 배우들로 하여금 적절한 기술을 갖출 수 있도록 그들을 훈련하기 시작했습니다.

감정을 표현하는 것이 아마도, 숙달하기에 가장 어려운 영상 연기의 측면일 겁니다. 배우들은 자연스러워야 합니다. 그들은 과장된 몸짓을 사용하면 안 되지만, 그래도 감정을 나타내기는 해야 합니다. 따라서, 그들은 있음직한 인물들을 만들어 내기 위해 미묘한 얼굴 표정에 의존해야 합니다. 그것이 그렇게 많은 무대 연기자들이 할리우드에서 성공하지 못하는 이유입니다. 여러분이 들으면 놀랄 이름들이지만, 그건 또 다른 때를 위해 남겨두도록 하지요. 매체가 다르기 때문에, 그것에 맞추기 위해 연기가 조정되어야 합니다. 하지만 그것이 영상 연기의 유일한 애로점은 아닙니다.

계속 이어져야 하는 연극 연기와는 달리, (영화) 필름은 여러 조각들로 나뉘어 완전히 다른 순서로 합쳐질 수 있습니다. 여러 번 찍을 수 있기 때문에 그것이 연기를 더 쉽게 만들어준다고 생각할지 모르지만, 사실 그것은 일을 굉장히 어렵게 만들 수도 있습니다. 이는 영화 배우들은 가끔씩 단 하루의 촬영에 인물 전개의 여러 다른 단계들을 나타내야 하기 때문입니다. 연극에서는, 인물이 이야기가 진행됨에 따라 발전되게 되는데, 영화 배우들은 시간 순으로 이야기를 연기해 나가는 사치를 항상 누릴 수가 없거든요.

W character [kǽriktər] (극중의) 캐릭터, 연기하는 역[인물] play [plei] 연기하다 medium [míːdiəm] 매체 audience [ɔ́ːdiəns] 관객 stage acting 무대 연기 critique [kritíːk] 비평 exaggerate [igzǽdʒərèit] 과장하다 asset [ǽset] 자산 struggle [strʌ́gl] 고군분투, 몸부림치다 flamboyant [flæmbɔ́iənt] 현란한, 화려한 ridiculous [ridíkjuləs] 우스꽝스러운 equip with ~ …을 갖추다, 갖추게 하다 subtle [sʌ́tl] 미묘한 in chronological order 연대순으로

12 교수가 주로 논의하는 것은?
Ⓐ 영화 편집 방식을 바꾼 한 감독
Ⓑ 영상 연기와 무대 연기간의 차이점들

- Ⓒ 효과적으로 감정을 묘사하는 여러 다른 방법들
- Ⓓ 연극 작품들에 대한 관객의 반응

13 교수가 자신의 경력 초기에 받았던 비평에 대해 언급한 이유는?
- Ⓐ 우호적이지 않은 관객들에 의해 생긴 문제들의 예를 들려고
- Ⓑ 영화 경력을 시작할 때 배우들이 겪는 어려움들을 증명하려고
- **Ⓒ 연극과 영화에 필요한 서로 다른 연기 방법들을 예를 들어 설명하려고**
- Ⓓ 자신이 연극과 영화 연기에 둘 다 경험이 있다는 것을 알려주려고

14 교수에 의하면, D.W. Griffith가 연기에 기여한 것은 무엇인가?
- Ⓐ 그는 작은 몸짓들을 포착하기 위해 클로즈업 장면들을 사용했다.
- Ⓑ 그는 항상 장면들을 시간 순서대로 찍었다.
- Ⓒ 그는 그의 모든 영화에 무대 배우들만을 사용했다.
- **Ⓓ 그는 영화에 알맞은 기법들을 배우들에게 가르쳤다.**

15 영상 배우들에 대해 교수가 말한 것은?
- **Ⓐ 자연스러워 보일 때 훨씬 더 효과적이다.**
- Ⓑ 자신의 말이 분명히 들리도록 하기 위해 크게 말한다.
- Ⓒ 감정을 카메라로부터 숨기는 것을 더 선호한다.
- Ⓓ 실제 삶과는 매우 다른 몸짓을 한다.

16 영화 배우들이 가끔씩 겪는 문제점으로 교수가 말한 것은?
- Ⓐ 장면들을 한 번만 찍을 수 있다.
- **Ⓑ 장면들을 순서에 벗어나서 찍어야 한다.**
- Ⓒ 연극 비평가들에 의해 받아들여지지 않는다.
- Ⓓ 여러 다른 많은 등장인물들을 연기해야 한다.

강의의 일부분을 다시 듣고 질문에 답하시오. 🔊 MP3 93_1

> Therefore, they have to rely on subtle facial expressions to create believable characters. That's why so many stage actors fail to make it in Hollywood. You might be surprised to hear some of the names, but let's save that for another time. Because the medium is different, the acting must be adapted to suit it.

17 교수가 다음과 같이 말할 때 의미하는 것은?

> You might be surprised to hear some of the names, but let's save that for another time.

- Ⓐ 교수는 배우들의 중요성을 강조하고 싶어 한다.
- Ⓑ 교수는 연극 배우들이 영화 배우들처럼 재능이 있다고 생각하지 않는다.
- **Ⓒ 교수는 배우들의 이름들을 거론하는 데 시간을 쓰고 싶어 하지 않는다.**
- Ⓓ 교수는 학생들이 몇몇 실패한 배우들의 예를 들어주기를 바란다.

MEMO

MEMO

MEMO

전략이 있는 영단기 토플

영단기가 하면 토플도 다르다!
- 토플도 단기에 끝낼 수 있는 체계적 학습법과 적중률 높은 실전 전략 소개
- 국내 최고 토플 강사진이 선사하는 실전 감각이 있는 토플 강의

영단기 TOEFL Listening의 전략
- 실전 난이도와 실전 길이의 지문을 90개 이상 수록하여 완벽한 실전 대비가 가능하다.
- 각 대화와 강의 지문의 내용 전개 및 문제와 연결되는 상황별/주제별 출제포인트를 미리 학습하여 지문과 질문을 예측하여 들을 수 있다.
- 상황별/주제별 출제포인트와 단서 표현을 이용해 정답 찾기에 필요한 부분만 note-taking할 수 있다.
- 시각적인 flow chart를 통해 주제별 강의 전개와 관련 출제포인트를 한 눈에 정리할 수 있다.
- 대화와 강의의 문제 유형을 10가지 이상 세분화하여 각 유형별 맞춤형 풀이 방법을 제시하였다.

영단기 토플 대표 강사 온라인 강의 제공(유료)

eng.conects.com